ANOTHER RECORD-BREAKING YEAR AT GUINNESS!
THE 1994 EDITION OF
THE GUINNESS BOOK OF RECORDS
IS CRAMMED FULL OF FASCINATING, AMAZING
REAL-LIFE RECORDS SUCH AS . . .

* CAST-IRON STOMACH! . . . The man who ate 10 bicycles,
7 televisions, a computer, and a Cessna aircraft [p. 181]

* REAL-LIFE RAPUNZEL! . . . The woman whose hair measures
nearly 13 feet long [p. 163]

* WRITER'S CRAMP! . . . The bestselling author who received
743 rejection slips before publishing his first book [p. 402]

* LONG-WINDED! . . . The college debate on homelessness that
lasted 517 hours and 45 minutes [p. 389]
PLUS!!!

* THE 86,535-FOOT-LONG SAND SCULPTURE [p. 384]

* THE 50-FOOT-LONG SOAP BUBBLE [p. 525]

* THE 1,650-GALLON COCKTAIL [p. 533]
AND
THE HEAVIEST JELLY DONUT, THE LONGEST
SHISH-KEBOB, AND THE LARGEST LASAGNE! [p. 538]

Bantam Books in the Guinness Series

GUINNESS BOOK OF OLYMPIC RECORDS
THE GUINNESS BOOK OF RECORDS 1994

THE GUINNESS BOOK OF RECORDS 1994

Editor
Peter Matthews

Executive Editor, U.S. Edition
Michelle Dunkley McCarthy

Editor, U.S. Edition (New York)
Mark Young

Founding Editor
Norris McWhirter

BANTAM BOOKS
NEW YORK • TORONTO • LONDON • SYDNEY • AUCKLAND

This edition contains the complete text of the original hardcover edition.
NOT ONE WORD HAS BEEN OMITTED.

THE GUINNESS BOOK OF RECORDS 1994
*A Bantam Book / Published by arrangement with
Guinness Publishing, Ltd.*

Bantam edition / April 1994

ISBN 0-553-56561-3

Published simultaneously in the United States and Canada

PRINTED IN THE UNITED STATES OF AMERICA

OPM   0 9 8 7 6 5 4 3 2 1

CONTENTS

EARTH AND SPACE............1

The Universe........................2
The Earth........................17
Structure and Dimensions..18
  Featuring: Highs and
  Lows........................20
Natural Phenomena............39
  Featuring: Violent
  Volcanoes........................44
Weather........................46
  Featuring: Temperature
  ranges........................47
Gems, Jewels and Precious
  Stones........................53

LIVING WORLD................58

Records for 17 major animal
orders, from mammals to
sponges, extinct animals, plus
a new section on rare and
endangered flora and fauna.
The Plant Kingdom features
giant fruits, vegetables and
flowers. Also included are
the Kingdoms Protista, Fungi
and Pro-caryota, as well as
Parks, Zoos, Oceanaria and
Aquaria.

Animal Kingdom................59
  Featuring: One-Mile
  Challenge........................62
  Featuring: Migration......84
Extinct Animals.................114
  Featuring: Most Primitive
  Dinosaur........................115
Plant Kingdom.................121

HUMAN BEINGS............143

Origins........................144
Dimensions........................146
Reproductivity...................152
Longevity........................158

Anatomy and Physiology..162
  Featuring: Sound
  Effects........................172

**SCIENCE AND
TECHNOLOGY...............186**

Elements........................187
Chemical Extremes...........191
Physical Extremes.............192
Mathematics........................197
Computing........................199
  Featuring: Computer
  Data........................202
Power........................204
Engineering........................207
Borings and Mines...........212
  Featuring: Waves of
  Destruction.....................216
Timepieces........................220
Telephones and
  Facsimiles........................222
Telescopes........................224
Rocketry........................228
Space Flight........................230
  Featuring: Race for
  Space........................234

**BUILDINGS AND
STRUCTURES.................239**

Origins........................240
Buildings for Living..........241
Buildings for Working......245
Buildings for
  Entertainment.................248
  Featuring: House of
  Cards........................250
Towers and Masts............256
Bridges........................257
Canals........................261
Dams........................263
Tunnels........................265
Specialized Structures.......267
  Featuring: Abominable
  Snowman........................278

TRANSPORT **282**

Ships 283
   Featuring: Bathtub
   Kings 288
Bicycles 296
Motorcycles 298
Automobiles 301
Specialized Vehicles 310
Services 317
Roads 318
Railroading 320
Aircraft and Flight 326
   Featuring: Paper
   aircraft 344

BUSINESS WORLD **346**

Commerce 347
Economics 354
   Featuring: Greatest
   Miser 356
Agriculture 369

**ARTS AND
ENTERTAINMENT** **382**

Art 383
Paintings 383
Antiques 387
Language 389
Literature 396
Music 410
Recorded Sound 421
Dancing 425
Theater 426
   Featuring: Lowest Theater
   Attendance 429
Circus 430
Photography 433
Cinema 435
Radio 442
Television 444

HUMAN WORLD **448**

Political and Social 449
Heads of State and
   Royalty 463

Legislatures—United
   States 465
Legislatures—World 473
Judicial 478
Honors, Decorations and
   Awards 489
   Featuring: Operation
   Welcome Home 493
Military and Defense 494
   Featuring: Shortest War .495
Education 503
Religions 505

**HUMAN
ACHIEVEMENTS** **512**

Endurance and Endeavor ..513
   Featuring: Survival on a
   Raft 518
Miscellaneous Endeavors .523
Juggling 531
Food 532
   Featuring: Cookie
   Caper 534
   Featuring: Strawberries
   Galore 540
Drink 542
   Featuring: The Oldest
   Wine 543
Manufactured Articles 545

SPORTS AND GAMES **555**

Records for over 90 Sports,
Games and Pastimes, from
Aerobatics to Yachting, including all the major sports
such as Baseball, Basketball,
Football, Tennis and Track
and Field, and lesser known
ones like Croquet, Rugby,
Orienteering and Pelota.

   Featuring: Ups and Downs
   of Record Breaking 656
   Featuring: Leapfrogging ..659
   Featuring:
   Skateboarding 702

EXTRA! EXTRA! **784**
INDEX **793**

INTRODUCTION

Welcome to the 33rd edition of *The Guinness Book of Records*. Once again the book has been completely revised and re-illustrated. We are continually updating the text, and this means that we are always looking for new items to include in the book. Many existing categories are permanent, but others we like to change to provide fresh information for our readers. For logistic reasons, we tend to concentrate on categories that are the subject of widespread, and preferably international, competitiveness.

We would like to help people achieve their record breaking ambitions. If you wish to set a new record category for *The Guinness Book of Records*, then contact us and submit a brief proposal at least two months in advance of your attempt. This gives us a chance to say whether we think that your activity might have a chance of being included in future editions. We are a very small editorial team, and receive hundreds of letters every week, so provide us with enough time to give your inquiry the attention it deserves.

To start the hunt for meaningful new categories, we have listed several areas of interest to us:

Oldest human beings—if your parent, grandparent, or even yourself(!) is over 105, we would like to hear about it.

Tallest human beings—somewhere in the world there may be a man or woman who is taller than our current candidates as the tallest human being.

The most accomplished linguist—who can speak the most languages fluently?

Environmental records—We suggest a challenge for the most trees planted by a team in a week. Also, collecting (and recycling) cans and building the largest can pyramid in a set period of time.

Longest golf ball carry—from drive to pitch mark on a level surface.

Step climbing—the most in a set period of time.

Smallest house in the United States

Highest house number in the United States

Longest escalator in the United States

Oldest American motorcyclist

Most economical car in the United States

Most efficient battery-powered vehicle in the United States

Longest-serving chairman in the United States

Largest ice cream cone—the longest on record is 16 ft high.

Our hope remains that, like the first edition, this new edition can assist in resolving inquiries on facts and may turn the heat of argument into the light of knowledge.

THE GUINNESS BOOK
STORY

The Guinness Book of Records was first produced to assist in resolving arguments that might take place on matters of fact. In 1951 the then managing director of Guinness, Sir Hugh Beaver (1890–1967), was out shooting on the North Slob, by the river Slaney in County Wexford in the southeast of Ireland. Some golden plover were missed by the party, and later he discovered that reference books in the library of his host at Castlebridge House could not confirm whether that bird was Europe's fastest game bird. Sir Hugh thought that there must be many other such questions debated nightly, but there was no book with which to settle the arguments about records.

On 12 Sep 1954, Sir Hugh challenged Norris and Ross McWhirter, who ran a fact and figure agency in London, Great Britain, to compile a book of records. An office was set up in Fleet Street, London and work began on the initial 198-page edition. The first copy was bound by the printers on 27 August 1955. Well before Christmas, *The Guinness Book of Records* was No. 1 on the British bestseller's list, and every edition since has been similarly represented.

The book began its worldwide expansion in 1956, when the first United States edition was published in New York City, followed by editions in French (1962) and German (1963). In 1967 there were first editions in Danish, Japanese, Norwegian and Spanish, while the following year editions were published in Finnish, Italian and Swedish. In the 1970s there followed Czech, Dutch, Hebrew, Icelandic, Portuguese and Serbo-Croatian editions; in the 1980s translations into Arabic, Chinese, Greek, Hindi, Hungarian, Indonesian, Malay and Turkish followed. Most recently, in the 1990s, editions have been published in Bulgarian, Korean, Macedonian, Polish, Romanian and Russian.

EARTH
AND SPACE

- **THE UNIVERSE**
- **THE EARTH**
- **STRUCTURE AND DIMENSIONS**
- **NATURAL PHENOMENA**
- **WEATHER**
- **GEMS, JEWELS, AND PRECIOUS STONES**

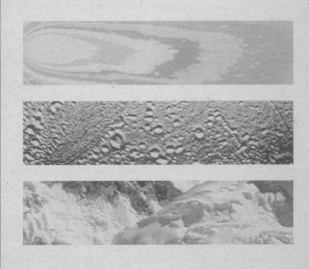

THE UNIVERSE

Large structures in the Universe Our own Milky Way galaxy is only one of 10 billion galaxies. It is part of the so-called Local Group of galaxies moving at a speed of 370 miles/sec with respect to the cosmological frame in the general direction of a dense concentration of galaxy clusters known as the "Great Attractor."

In November 1989 Margaret Geller and John Huchra (USA) announced the discovery of a "Great Wall" in space, a concentration of galaxies in the form of a "crumpled membrane" with a minimum extent of 280×800 million light years (1.6×10^{21} miles $\times 4.7 \times 10^{21}$ miles) and a depth of up to 20 million light years (9.6×10^{19} miles).

Based on the effect of line of sight on the spectra of distant quasars, Josef Hoell and Wolfgang Priester (Germany) suggested in July 1991 that the large-scale structure of the Universe consists of "bubbles," each up to 100 million light years (5.8×10^{20}) in diameter, with galaxies being formed on the "surfaces" of the "bubbles" and with the interiors being virtually devoid of matter.

Galaxies Largest The largest galaxy is the central galaxy of the Abell 2029 galaxy cluster, 1,070 million light years (6.3×10^{21} miles) distant in Virgo. Its discovery was announced in July 1990 by Juan M. Uson, Stephen P. Boughn and Jeffrey R. Kuhn (USA). It has a major diameter of 5.6 million light years (3.3×10^{19} miles), which is eighty times the diameter of our own galaxy, and has a light output equivalent to 2 trillion times that of the Sun.

Brightest The brightest galaxy (or galaxy in the process of forming) is IRAS F10214+4724, which was detected as a faint source by IRAS (Infra Red Astronomy Satellite) in 1983 but was shown in February 1991 to have a far-infrared luminosity 3×10^{14} times greater than that of the Sun. It has a red shift of 2.286, equivalent to a distance of 11.6 billion light years (6.8×10^{22} miles), but the remotest galaxy is the radio source 4C41.17, determined by K. Chambers, G. Miley and W. Van Bruegel in January 1990 to have a red shift of 3.800, equivalent to a distance of 12.8 billion light years (7.5×10^{22} miles).

Age of the Universe It is impossible to be definite about the origin of the Universe. However, a consensus value of 14 ± 3 eons or gigayears (an eon or gigayear being 1 billion years) is obtained from various cosmological techniques. The equivalent value of the Hubble constant based on a Friedman model of the Universe without cosmological constant is 70 ± 15 km/s/Mpc.

Farthest visible object The remotest heavenly body visible to the naked eye is the Great Galaxy in *Andromeda* (mag. 3.47), known as Messier 31. It was first noted from Germany by Simon Marius (1570–1624). It is a rotating nebula in spiral form at a distance from the Earth of about 2,309,000 light years, or 1.36×10^{19} miles (13 million trillion miles), and our galaxy is moving towards it. It is just possible that under good conditions for observations, Messier 33, the Spiral in Triangulum (mag. 5.79), can be glimpsed by the naked eye at a distance of 2,509,000 light years.

Remotest object   The interpretation of the red shifts of quasars in terms of distance is limited by a lack of knowledge of the Universal constants. The record red shift is 4.897 for the quasar PC 1247+3406 as determined by Donald P. Schneider, Maarten Schmidt (Netherlands) and James E. Gunn and announced in May 1991, following spectroscopic and photometric observations made in February and April of the same year using the Hale Telescope at Palomar Observatory, CA. If it is assumed that there is an

---

Age of the Universe   It was announced on 23 Apr 1992 that the COBE (Cosmic Background Explorer) satellite, launched by NASA on 18 Nov 1989, had detected minute fluctuations from the cosmic microwave background temperature of –454.745° F. This has been interpreted as evidence for the initial formation of galaxies within the Universe only a million years after the Big Bang. (See also Age of the Universe, page 2.)

Zodiac   The term "Zodiac" comes from the Greek *zodiakos* —"of living things"— originally formalized by the Greek astronomer Hipparchus in 150 B.C., who divided the sky extending 8 degrees either side of the ecliptic (the path of the Sun in the sky) into twelve equal zones of 30 degrees. With the redefinition of the constellation boundaries in 1928, the zodiacal constellations are no longer of equal size, with the largest being Virgo with an area of 1,294.428 square degrees and the smallest being Capricornus (Capricorn) with an area of 413.947 square degrees. Taurus is the zodiacal constellation with the most bright stars, with 125 down to magnitude 6, while Aries, Capricornus and Libra have only 50 each.

Largest scale model   The largest scale model of the solar system was developed by the Lakeview Museum of Arts and Sciences in Peoria, IL and inaugurated in April 1992. The Sun, with a diameter of 36 ft, was painted on the exterior of the museum's planetarium, and the planets (spheres ranging in diameter from 1 in in the case of Pluto up to 3 ft 9 in for Jupiter) were situated in appropriate locations in accordance with their distance from the Sun. This meant that the Earth was 3/4 mile away, with Pluto being in the town of Kewanee, some 40 miles from the museum.

A smaller model of the solar system was created by Lars Broman and inaugurated by the Futures' Museum, Borlänge, Sweden on 29 Nov 1986. Its Sun had a diameter of 5 ft and the planets ranged from 1/8 in to 5 1/2 in in diameter., with the closest to the Sun being 200 ft away and the farthest 3 3/4 miles away. Unlike the American model, it also included the nearest star to the Sun, Proxima Centauri, which was sited to scale in the Museum of Victoria, Melbourne, Australia. (See Stars, Nearest.)

"observable horizon," where the speed of recession is equal to the speed of light, i.e., at 14 billion light years or 82.3 million trillion miles, then a simple interpretation would place this quasar at 94.4 percent of this value or 13,200 million light years distant (7.8×10^{22} miles).

Quasars   An occultation of 3C 273, observed from Australia on 5 Aug 1962, enabled the existence of quasi-stellar radio sources (now called Quasi-Stellar Objects [QSOs] by many astronomers) to be announced by Maarten Schmidt (Netherlands).

Quasars have immensely high luminosity for bodies so distant and of such small diameter. The discovery of the most luminous object in the sky, the quasar HS 1946+7658, which is at least 1.5×10^{15} times more luminous than the Sun, was announced in July 1991 following the Hamburg Survey of northern quasars. This quasar has a red shift of 3.02 and is therefore at a distance of 12,400 million light years (7.3×10^{22} miles).

The first double quasar (0957 + 561) among over 4,300 known quasars was announced in May 1980.

The most violent outburst observed in a quasar was recorded on 13 Nov 1989 by a joint US–Japanese team which noted that the energy output of the quasar PKS 0558-504 (which is about 2 billion light years distant) increased by two-thirds in three minutes, equivalent to the total energy released by the Sun in 340,000 years.

STARS

Nearest   Except for the special case of our own Sun, the nearest star is the very faint *Proxima Centauri*, discovered in 1915, which is 4.225 light years (25 trillion miles) away.

The nearest star visible to the naked eye is the southern hemisphere binary *Alpha Centauri*, or *Rigel Kentaurus* (4.35 light years distant), with an apparent magnitude of –0.29. By A.D. 29,700 this binary will reach a minimum distance from the Earth of 2.84 light years and should then be the second brightest star, with an apparent magnitude of –1.20.

Largest   The largest star is the M-class supergiant *Betelgeux* (Alpha Orionis—the top left star of Orion), which is 310 light years distant. It has a diameter of 400 million miles, which is about 500 times greater than that of the Sun. It is surrounded by a dust "shell" and also by an outer tenuous gas halo up to 5.3×10^{11} miles in diameter.

Heaviest   The heaviest star is the variable *Eta Carinae*, 9,100 light years distant in the Carinae Nebula, with a mass 200 times greater than that of our own Sun.

Most luminous   If all the stars could be viewed at the same distance, *Eta Carinae* would also be the most luminous star, with a total luminosity 6,500,000 times that of the Sun. However, the *visually* brightest star viewed through a telescope is the hypergiant Cygnus OB2 No. 12, which is 5,900 light years distant. It has an absolute visual magnitude of –9.9 and is therefore visually 810,000 times brighter than the Sun. This brightness may be matched by the supergiant IV b 59 in the nearby galaxy Messier 101. During the year 1843 the absolute luminosity and absolute visual brightness of *Eta Carinae* temporarily increased to values 60 and 70 million times the corresponding values for the Sun.

Longest name *Torcularis Septentrionalis* is the name applied to the star *Omicron Piscium* in the constellation *Pisces*.

Smallest The smallest star appears to be the white dwarf L362-81 with an estimated diameter of 3,500 miles or only 0.0040 that of the Sun.

Lightest A mass 0.014 that of the Sun is estimated for RG 0058.8-2807, which was discovered by I. Neill Reid and Gerard Gilmore using the UK Schmidt telescope (announced in April 1983).

Faintest RG 0058.8-2807 is also the faintest star detected, with a total luminosity only 0.0021 that of the Sun and an absolute visual magnitude of 20.2, so the visual brightness is less than one millionth that of the Sun.

Brightest (as seen from Earth) The brightest of the 5,776 stars visible to the naked eye is *Sirius A* (Alpha Canis Majoris), also known as the Dog Star. It has an apparent magnitude of –1.46 but because of the relative motions of this star and the Sun this should rise to a maximum value of -1.67 in about 61,000 years. *Sirius A* is 8.64 light years distant and has a luminosity 26 times greater than that of the Sun. It has a diameter of 1.45 million miles and a mass 2.14 times that of the Sun. The faint white dwarf companion *Sirius B* has a diameter of only 6,000 miles, which is less than that of the Earth, but its mass is slightly greater than that of the Sun. *Sirius A* is in the constellation *Canis Major* and is visible in the winter months of the northern hemisphere, being due south at midnight on the last day of the year.

Youngest The youngest stars appear to be two protostars known collectively as IRAS – 4 buried deep in dust clouds in the nebula NGC 1333, which is 1,100 light years (6.5×10^{15} miles) distant. Announced in May 1991 by a combined British, German and American team, these protostars will not blaze forth as fully fledged stars for at least another 100,000 years.

Oldest The oldest stars in the galaxy have been detected in the halo, high above the disc of the Milky Way, by a group led by Timothy Beers (USA) that discovered 70 such stars by January 1991 but eventually expects to detect 500. These stars are characterized by having the lowest abundances of heavy elements, whereas later-generation stars (such as our own Sun) have higher heavy element abundances because of a buildup of such elements in galaxies from the successive explosions of supernova stars.

Pulsars The earliest observation of a pulsating radio source, or "pulsar," CP 1919 (now PSR 1919+21), by Dr Jocelyn Burnell (nee Bell; Great Britain) was announced from the Mullard Radio Astronomy Observatory, Cambridgeshire, Great Britain on 24 Feb 1968. It had been detected on 28 Nov 1967.

For pulsars whose spin rates have been accurately measured, the fastest-spinning is PSR 1937+214, which was discovered by a group led by Donald C. Backer in November 1982. It is in the minor constellation *Vulpecula* (the Little Fox), 16,000 light years (9.4×10^{16} miles) distant, and has a pulse period of 1.5578064850 millisec, which is equivalent to a spin rate of 641.9282560 revolutions per sec. However, the pulsar that has the

BRIGHTEST SUPERNOVA   A supernova is an exploding star whose luminosity suddenly increases greatly on eruption. The nearest and brightest in modern times was in 1987 in a galaxy known as the Large Magellanic Cloud. The resulting effect was visible with the naked eye—on average this will happen only four times in a thousand years. (Photo: Science Photo Library)

slowest spin-down rate, and is therefore the most accurate stellar clock, is PSR 1855+09 (discovered in December 1985) at only 2.1×10^{-20} sec per sec.

Brightest and latest supernova   The brightest supernova ever seen in historic times is believed to be SN 1006, noted in April 1006 near *Beta Lupi*. It flared for two years and attained a magnitude of –9 to –10. The remnant is believed to be the radio source G.327.6 + 14.5, nearly 3,000 light years distant. Others have occurred in 1054, 1604, 1885, and most recently on 23 Feb 1987, when Ian Shelton sighted the one designated –69°202 in the Large Magellanic Cloud 170,000 light years distant. This supernova was visible to the naked eye when at its brightest in May 1987.

Black holes   The concept of super-dense bodies was first proposed by the Marquis de LaPlace (1749–1827). This term for a star that has undergone complete gravitational collapse was first used by John Archibald Wheeler at an Institute for Space Studies meeting in New York City on 29 Dec 1967.

The first tentative identification of a black hole was announced in December 1972 in the binary-star X-ray source Cygnus X–1.

The best black hole candidate is the central star of the binary (or triple) star system V404, which is 5,000 light years (2.9×10^{16} miles) distant in the constellation Cygnus and which first showed a possible black hole signature as the transient X-ray source GS 2023+338, discovered by the Ginga satellite in May 1989. In September 1991 J. Casares, P.A. Charles and T.

Naylor firmly established the mass as being greater than six times that of the Sun (and more likely eight to fifteen times) and for the first time obtained a black hole candidate mass unequivocally above the maximum value of five solar masses for a neutron star. For a black hole weighing ten times the mass of our Sun, light cannot escape (i.e., the point at which the black hole becomes "black") if it is within 18.3 miles of the center (the Schwarzschild or gravitational radius, named after the German astronomer Karl Schwarzschild).

Evidence continues to accumulate to suggest that galaxies are powered by super-massive black holes at their centers. In the case of our own galaxy there is increasing evidence of a 2-million-solar-mass black hole in the region of the radio point source Sagittarius A*.

Constellations   The largest of the 88 constellations is Hydra (the Sea Serpent), which covers 1,302.844 deg^2 or 3.16 percent of the whole sky and contains at least 68 stars visible to the naked eye (to 5.5 mag). The constellation Centaurus (Centaur), ranking ninth in area, however, embraces at least 94 such stars.

The smallest constellation is Crux Australis (Southern Cross), with an area of only 0.16 percent of the sky, or 68.477 deg^2 compared with the 41,252.96 deg^2 of the whole sky.

THE SUN

Distance extremes   The true distance of the Earth from the Sun is 1.00000102 astronomical units—the distance from the center of the Earth to the center of the Sun as defined in 1938, equivalent to 92,955,807 miles—or 93 million miles. Our orbit being elliptical, the distance of the Sun varies between a minimum (perihelion) of 91.5 million miles and a maximum (aphelion) of 94.5 million miles. Based on an orbital circumference of 58.4 million miles and an orbital period (sidereal year) of 365.256366 days, the average orbital velocity is 66,620 mph, but this varies between a minimum of 65,520 mph at aphelion and a maximum of 67,750 mph at perihelion.

Temperature and dimensions   The Sun has a stellar classification of a yellow dwarf type G2, although its mass at 2 octillion tons is 332,946.04 times that of the Earth and represents over 99 percent of the total mass of the Solar System. The solar diameter at 865,040 miles leads to a density of 1.408 times that of water or a quarter that of the Earth.

The Sun has a central temperature of about 15,400,000 K (Kelvins) and a core pressure of 1.65 million tons/in^2. It uses up about 4.4 million tons of hydrogen per sec, equal to an energy output of 3.85×10^{26} watts, although it will have taken 10 billion years to exhaust its energy supply (about 5 billion years from the present). The luminous intensity of the Sun is 2.7 octillion candela, which is equal to a luminance of 290,000 candela/in^2.

Sunspots   To be visible to the *protected* naked eye, a sunspot must cover about 1/2,000th part of the Sun's disc and thus have an area of about 0.5 billion miles^2. The largest sunspot ever noted was in the Sun's southern hemisphere on 8 Apr 1947. Its area was about 7 billion miles^2 with an extreme longitude of 187,000 miles and an extreme latitude of 90,000 miles.

Sunspots appear darker because they are more than 2,700° F cooler than the rest of the Sun's surface temperature of 9,945° F.

In October 1957 a smoothed sunspot count showed 263, the highest recorded index since records started in 1755. In 1943 one sunspot lasted for 200 days, from June to December.

PLANETS

Largest   The nine major planets (including the Earth) are bodies within the Solar System and revolve round the Sun in definite orbits.

Jupiter, with an equatorial diameter of 88,846 miles and a polar diameter of 83,082 miles, is the largest of the nine major planets, with a mass 317.828 times, and a volume 1,323.3 times, that of the Earth. It also has the shortest period of rotation, resulting in a Jovian day of only 9 hr 50 min 30.003 sec in the equatorial zone.

Smallest and coldest   Pluto, with a mass 0.0023 that of the Earth, has a diameter of 1,430 miles, while its moon, Charon, has a diameter of 737 miles and a mass about one eleventh that of Pluto. The lowest observed surface temperature of any natural body in the Solar System is –391° F in the case of Neptune's large moon *Triton*, but the discovery in 1992 of solid nitrogen, methane and carbon monoxide on Pluto's surface indicates that its surface temperature must be very similar to that of *Triton*.

LARGEST PLANET   Jupiter is the largest of the nine major planets. This photograph, taken from a distance of 17.6 million miles by the *Voyager I* spacecraft, also shows two of its satellites—volcanic *Io*, which can be seen towards the right of the planet's disc, and billiard-ball smooth *Europa*, at the far right of the picture. (Photo: Science Photo Library)

Outermost The outermost planet is Pluto, with the Pluto–Charon system orbiting at a mean distance of 3,674,488,000 miles in a period of 248.54 years. Because of their orbital eccentricity they are closer to the Sun than Neptune in the period from 23 Jan 1979 to 15 Mar 1999. However, Pluto–Charon lost their status as the outermost bodies in the Solar System with the annoucement on 14 Sep 1992 of the discovery of a 124-mile diameter asteroid or comet by David Jewitt (Great Britain) of the University of Hawaii and Jane Luu (USA) of the University of California, Berkeley from observations between 30 August and 1 September. The object, given the temporary designation 1992 QB_1, orbits at a mean distance of 4,126 million miles in a period of 295.72 years.

Surface features By far the highest and most spectacular surface feature of any planet is *Olympus Mons* (formerly *Nix Olympica*) in the Tharsis region of Mars, with a diameter of 310–370 miles and a height of 75,450–95,150 ft above the surrounding plain.

Brightest and faintest Viewed from the Earth, by far the brightest of the five planets visible to the naked eye is Venus, with a maximum magnitude of −4.4. Uranus, the first planet to be discovered by telescope when it was sighted by Sir William Herschel (Great Britain) from his garden at 19 New King St, Bath, Great Britain on 13 Mar 1781, is only marginally visible, with a magnitude of 5.5.

The faintest planet is Pluto, with a magnitude of 15.0.

Conjunctions The most dramatic recorded conjunction (coming together) of the other seven principal members of the Solar System (Sun, Moon, Mercury, Venus, Mars, Jupiter and Saturn) occurred on 5 Feb 1962, when 16° covered all seven during an eclipse in the Pacific area. It is possible that the sevenfold conjunction that occurred in September 1186 spanned only 12°. The next notable conjunction will take place on 5 May 2000.

Fastest Mercury, which orbits the Sun at an average distance of 35,983,100 miles, has a period of revolution of 87.9686 days, thus giving the highest average speed in orbit of 107,030 mph.

Hottest For Venus a surface temperature of 864° F has been estimated from measurements made from the Russian *Venera* and US *Pioneer* surface probes.

Nearest planet The fellow planet closest to the Earth is Venus, which is, at times, only 26 million miles inside the Earth's orbit, compared with Mars' closest approach of 35 million miles outside the Earth's orbit.

Densest and least dense planet Earth is the densest planet, with an average density 5.515 times that of water, while Saturn has an average density only about one-eighth of this value or 0.685 times that of water.

MOST SATELLITES

The Solar System has a total of 61 satellites or moons.

Saturn has 18

Jupiter 16

Uranus 15

Neptune 8

Mars 2

Earth 1

Pluto 1

Mercury 0

Venus 0

Satellites can come in various sizes, and even different shapes. Three of Saturn's 18 moons are shown here. Its largest is Titan (top left), which is larger than both Mercury and Pluto, and is the only satellite with an extensive atmosphere.

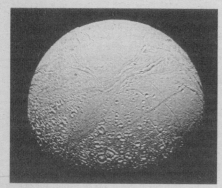

Enceladus (middle left) reflects back all of the light which it receives, making it the most reflective body in the Solar System.

Hyperion (bottom left) is potato-shaped and is the only satellite not to have a fixed rotation period. It is possibly the remnant of a larger satellite destroyed by an impact with a comet. (Photos: NASA/Image Select)

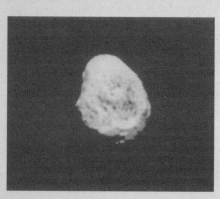

SATELLITES

Distance extremes   The distance of satellites from their parent planets varies from the 5,827 miles of *Phobos* from the center of Mars to the 14,700,000 miles of Jupiter's outer satellite *Sinope* (Jupiter IX).

Largest and smallest   The largest and heaviest satellite is *Ganymede* (Jupiter III), which is 2.017 times heavier than the Earth's Moon and has a diameter of 3,273 miles. Of satellites whose diameters have been measured the smallest is *Deimos*, the outermost moon of Mars. Although irregularly shaped, it has an average diameter of 7.8 miles.

Most recent   The most recently discovered satellite, announced on 16 Jul 1990 by Mark R. Showalter (USA), is the Saturnian satellite *Pan* (Saturn XVII), temporarily designated 1981 S13, which was found on 11 *Voyager 2* photographs taken during the close approach in August 1981. It has a diameter of only about 12 miles and orbits within the 200-mile Encke gap in the A ring.

ASTEROIDS

Number and distance extremes   There are estimated to be about 45,000 asteroids, but the orbits of only about 5,700 have been accurately computed. While most orbit between Mars and Jupiter, average distances from the Sun vary between 72,200,000 miles (just outside of Venus's orbit) for the Aten asteroid 1954XA (discovered 5 Dec 1954 but currently lost), and for objects which appear to be of an asteroidal nature, 1,902 million miles (just outside of Uranus' orbit) for 5145 *Pholus* (discovered 9 Jan 1992). (See Planets, Outermost.)

Because of the asteroids' large orbital eccentricities the closest approach to the Sun is by the Apollo asteroid 3200 *Phaethon* (discovered 11 Oct 1983) to within 12,980,000 miles at perihelion, while the farthest distance is achieved by 5145 *Pholus* (see above), which reaches to 2,997 million miles from the Sun at aphelion (beyond the orbit of Neptune). The closest known approach to the Earth by an asteroid was to within 105,600 miles on 18 Jan 1991 by 1991BA (the day after its discovery).

Largest and smallest _ The largest and first discovered (by G. Piazzi in Palermo, Sicily on 1 Jan 1801) is 1 *Ceres*, with a equatorial diameter of 596 miles and a polar diameter of 563 miles. The smallest asteroid is 1991BA (see above) with a diameter of 30 ft.

The only asteroid visible to the naked eye is 4 *Vesta* (discovered 29 Mar 1807), which is 323 miles in diameter and has a maximum apparent magnitude as viewed from the Earth of 5.0.

THE MOON

The Earth's closest neighbor in space and its only natural satellite is the Moon, which has an average diameter of 2,159.3 miles and a mass of 8.1×10^{19} tons, or 0.0123 that of the Earth, so its density is 3.344 times that of water.

The Moon orbits at a mean distance from the Earth of 238,854.5 miles center-to-center. In the present century the closest approach (smallest perigee) was 221,441 miles center-to-center on 4 Jan 1912 and the farthest distance (largest apogee) was 252,718 miles on 2 Mar 1984. The orbital period (sidereal month) is 27.321661 days, giving an average orbital velocity of 2,289 mph.

Craters Only 59 percent of the Moon's surface is directly visible from the Earth because it is in "captured rotation," i.e., the period of rotation is equal to the period of orbit. The largest wholly visible crater is the walled plain Bailly, towards the Moon's South Pole, which is 183 miles across, with walls rising to 14,000 ft. The Orientale Basin, partly on the averted side, measures more than 600 miles in diameter.

The deepest crater is the Newton Crater, with a floor estimated to be between 23,000 and 29,000 ft below its rim and 14,000 ft below the level of the plain outside. The brightest (most reflective) directly visible spot on the Moon is Aristarchus.

Highest mountains In the absence of a sea level, lunar altitudes are measured relative to an adopted reference sphere with a radius of 1,080 miles. The greatest elevation attained on this basis by any of the 12 US astronauts who have landed on the moon has been 25,688 ft on the Descartes Highlands by Capt. John Watts Young (USN) and Major Charles M. Duke, Jr. (USAF) on 27 Apr 1972.

Temperature extremes When the Sun is overhead the temperature on the lunar equator reaches 243° F (31° F above the boiling point of water). By sunset the temperature is 58° F, but after nightfall it sinks to –261° F.

ECLIPSES

Earliest recorded Although computer programs can predict eclipses far back in history, there now appears to be no real evidence for ancient descriptions of eclipses prior to the partial eclipse observed in Nenevah in Assyria on 15 Jun 763 B.C. The first definite evidence for a total eclipse stems from Chu-fu in China, observed on 17 Jul 709 B.C.

Longest duration The maximum *possible* duration of an eclipse of the Sun is 7 min 31 sec. The longest of recent date was on 20 Jun 1955 (7 min 8 sec), west of the Philippines, although it was clouded out along most of its track. An eclipse of 7 min 29 sec should occur in the mid-Atlantic Ocean on 16 Jul 2186.

Most and least frequent The highest number of eclipses possible in a year is seven, as in 1935, when there were five solar and two lunar eclipses. In 1982 there were four solar and three lunar eclipses.

The lowest possible number in a year is two, both of which must be solar, as in 1944 and 1969.

The only recent example of three total solar eclipses occuring at a single location was at a point 44° N, 67° E in Kazakhstan, east of the Aral Sea. These took place on 21 Sep 1941, 9 Jul 1945 and 25 Feb 1952.

AURORAE

Lowest latitudes   Extreme cases of displays in very low latitudes were recorded at Cuzco, Peru (2 Aug 1744), Honolulu, HI (1 Sep 1859), and possibly Singapore (25 Sep 1909).

Noctilucent clouds   These remain sunlit long after sunset because of their great altitude, and are thought to consist of ice crystals or meteoric dust. Regular observations (at heights of *c.* 52 miles) in Western Europe date only from 1964; since that year the record high and low number of nights on which these phenomena have been observed have been 43 (1979) and 15 (1970).

COMETS

Earliest recorded   Records date from the 7th century B.C. The speeds of the estimated 2 million comets vary from 700 mph in outer space to 1.25 million mph when near the Sun. The successive appearances of Halley's Comet have been traced back to 467 B.C. It was first depicted in the Nuremberg Chronicle of A.D 684.

The first prediction of its return by Edmund Halley (1656–1742) proved true on Christmas Day 1758, 16 years after his death. On 13–14 Mar 1986, the European satellite *Giotto* (launched 2 Jul 1985) penetrated to within 335 miles of the nucleus of Halley's Comet. It was established that the core was 9 miles in length and velvet black in color.

Eclipses   Although normally the maximum possible duration of an eclipse of the Sun is 7 min 31 sec, durations can be "extended" when observers are airborne. The totality of the Sun was "extended" to 74 min for observers aboard a Concorde that took off from Toulouse, France and stayed in the Moon's shadow from 10:51 to 12:05 GMT on 30 Jun 1973 over the Atlantic before landing in Chad.

Most frequent aurorae   Polar lights, known since 1560 as aurora borealis or northern lights in the northern hemisphere, and since 1773 as aurora australis in the southern, are caused by electrical solar discharges in the upper atmosphere and occur most frequently in high latitudes. Aurorae are visible at some time on *every* clear dark night in the polar areas within 20 degrees of the magnetic poles. The extreme height of aurorae has been measured at 620 miles, while the lowest may descend to 45 miles.

Closest approach by a comet   On 1 Jul 1770, Lexell's Comet, traveling at a speed of 86,100 mph (relative to the Sun), came within 745,000 miles of the Earth. However, more recently the Earth is believed to have passed through the tail of Halley's Comet on 19 May 1910.

Brightest   The brightest comets are held to be either the Curls Comet of 1862 or the Ikeya-Seki Comet of 1965.

Largest   The tail of the brilliant Great Comet of 1843 trailed for 205 million miles. The bow shock wave of Holmes Comet of 1892 once measured 1.5 million miles in diameter.

Shortest period   Of all the recorded periodic comets (that are members of the Solar System), the one that returns most frequently is the increasingly faint Encke's Comet, first identified in 1786. Its period of 1,206 days (3.3 years) is the shortest established. Only 8 of its 63 returns have been missed by astronomers—most recently in 1944.

The most frequently observed comets are Schwassmann-Wachmann I, Kopff and Oterma, which can all be observed every year between Mars and Jupiter.

Longest period   The longest period determined for a comet is 958 years, in the case of Comet 1894 Gale.

BRIGHTEST PERIODICAL COMET   Halley's comet, with a period of 76 years, is believed to be the brightest periodical comet, its successive appearances having been traced back to 467 B.C. It was first depicted in the Nuremberg Chronicle of A.D. 684 (right) and attracts great interest with each appearance. The image (below) is computer-generated, with false shading representing the profile of brightness, and was created in March 1986 at the time of the most recent return. (Photos: Ann Ronan Picture Library and Science Photo Library)

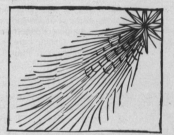

Meteor "shower"   The greatest shower on record occurred on the night of 16–17 Nov 1966, when the Leonid meteors (which recur every 33¼ years) were visible between western North America and eastern Russia. It was calculated that meteors passed over Arizona at a rate of 2,300 per min for a period of 20 min from 5 A.M. on 17 Nov 1966.

Meteorites   The most anxious time of day for meteorophobes should be 3 P.M. In historic times, the only recorded person injured by a meteorite was Mrs Ann Hodges of Sylacauga, AL. On 30 Nov 1954 a 9-lb stone, some 7 in in length, crashed through the roof of her home, hitting Mrs Hodges on the arm and bruising her hip. The physician who examined her, Dr Moody D. Jacobs, declared her fit but she was subsequently hospitalized as a result of the publicity.

METEORITES

Meteorites   When a *meteoroid* (consisting of broken fragments of cometary or asteroidal origin and ranging in size from fine dust to bodies several miles in diameter) penetrates to the Earth's surface, the remnant, which may be either aerolite (stony) or siderite (metallic), is described as a *meteorite*. Such events occur about 150 times per year over the whole land surface of the Earth.

Oldest   A revision by T. Kirsten in 1981 of the age estimates of meteorites that have remained essentially undisturbed after their formation suggests that the oldest accurately dated is the Krähenberg meteorite at 4,600 ± 20 million years, which is just within the initial period of Solar System formation.

Largest   There was a mysterious explosion of 10–15 megatons (high explosive equivalent) at Lat. 60° 55′ N, Long. 101° 57′ E, in the basin of the Podkamennaya Tunguska River, 40 miles north of Vanavar, in Siberia, Russia, at 00 hrs 17 min 11 sec UT (Universal Time) on 30 Jun 1908. The explosion devastated an area of 1,500 miles² and the shock was felt as far away as 625 miles. The cause was variously attributed to a meteorite (1927), a comet (1930), a nuclear explosion (1961), antimatter (1965), a small black hole (1973) and an exploding flying saucer (1976). Although the meteorite theory was initially rejected, a new assessment in 1992 suggests that the explosion can be accounted for by the energy released following a total disintegration at an altitude of 33,000 ft of a 98-ft-diameter common type stony asteroid traveling at hypersonic velocity at an incoming angle of 45 degrees.

The largest known meteorite was found in 1920 at Hoba West, near Grootfontein in Namibia, and is a block 9 ft long by 8 ft wide, estimated to weigh 65 tons. The largest meteorite exhibited by any museum is the "Tent" meteorite, weighing 68,085 lb, found in 1897 near Cape York, on the west coast of Greenland, by the expedition of Commander Robert Edwin Peary (USA; 1856–1920). It was known to the Inuits as the Abnighito

THE WORLD'S LARGEST CRATER   Coon Butte or Barringer Crater near Winslow, AZ. (Photo: Spectrum Colour Library)

and is now exhibited in the Hayden Planetarium in New York City. The largest piece of stony meteorite recovered is a piece weighing 3,902 lb, part of a 4.4-ton shower that struck Jilin (formerly Kirin), China on 8 Mar 1976.

Lunar Twelve known meteorites are believed to be of lunar origin as distinguished by characteristic element and isotopic ratios. The first 11 were found in Antarctica but the most recently discovered, which has only a 1 in diameter and weighs 0.67 oz, was found at Calcalong Creek on the Nullarbor Plain to the north of the Great Australian Bight by D.H. Hill, W.V. Boynton and R.A. Haag (USA), with the discovery being announced in January 1991. The name "Calcalong" is a corruption of the Aboriginal word meaning "seven sisters went up to the sky, chased by the Moon."

Craters It has been estimated that some 2,000 asteroid–Earth collisions have occurred in the last 600 million years. One hundred and two collision sites or astroblemes have been identified.

In 1962, a crater 150 miles in diameter and ½ mile deep in Wilkes Land, Antarctica was attributed to a meteorite. Such a crater could have been caused by a meteorite weighing 14,329,900,000 tons striking at 44,000 mph.

Soviet scientists reported in December 1970 an astrobleme with a diameter of 60 miles and a maximum depth of 1,300 ft in the basin of the River Popigai.

There is a crater-like formation or astrobleme 275 miles in diameter on the eastern shore of Hudson Bay, Canada, where the Nastapoka Islands are just off the coast.

The largest and best-preserved crater which was definitely formed by an asteroid is the Coon Butte or Barringer Crater, discovered in 1891 near Canyon Diablo, Winslow, AZ. It is 4,150 ft in diameter and now about 575 ft deep, with a parapet rising 130–155 ft above the surrounding plain. It has been estimated that an iron-nickel mass of some 2.2 million tons and a diameter of 200–260 ft gouged this crater in *c.* 25,000 B.C.

Tektites The largest tektite (a class of small natural glassy objects of uncertain origin found only in certain areas of the Earth's surface) of which details have been published weighed 7 lb and was found in 1932 at Muong Nong, Saravane Province, Laos. It is now in the Louvre Museum, Paris, France. Eight SNC meteorites (named after their find sites at Shergotty in India, Nakla in Egypt and Chassigny in France) are believed to have emanated from Mars.

Fireball The brightest fireball ever photographically recorded was by Dr Zdenek Ceplecha over Sumava, Czechoslovakia (now Czech Republic) on 4 Dec 1974; it had a momentary magnitude of –22 or 10,000 times brighter than a full Moon.

THE EARTH

The Earth is approximately 4,540 million years old. It is not a true sphere, but is flattened at the poles and hence an oblate spheroid. The area of the surface is estimated to be 196,937,400 miles^2 and the volume about 259,875,300,000 miles^2.

The mass of the Earth is 6.6 sextillion tons and the density is 5.515 times that of water. The Earth picks up cosmic dust, but estimates of the amount vary widely, with 33,000 tons a year being the upper limit. The period of axial rotation, i.e., the true sidereal day, is 23 hr 56 min 4.0989 sec, mean time.

Largest diameter The equatorial diameter (7,926.3803 miles) is 26.5757 miles larger than the polar diameter of 7,899.8046 miles. The Earth has a pear-shaped asymmetry, with the north polar radius being 148 ft longer than the south polar radius. There is also a slight ellipticity of the equator, since its major diameter at longitude 14.96° W is 456 ft longer than its minor axis. The greatest departures from the reference ellipsoid are a protuberance of 240 ft in the area of Papua New Guinea and a depression of 344 ft south of Sri Lanka, in the Indian Ocean.

Greatest circumference The greatest circumference of the Earth, at the equator, is 24,901.458 miles, compared with 24,859.731 miles at the meridian.

Most abundant element At the center of the Earth is the iron-rich core of radius 2,164 miles, and this consists of an outer liquid core 1,404 miles thick and a solid inner core of radius 759 miles. If the iron-rich theory of the core is correct, iron would be the most abundant element in the Earth at 34 percent. At the center of the core the estimated density is 13.09 g/cm^2, the temperature is 8,816° F and the pressure is 23,600 tons f/in^2.

STRUCTURE AND DIMENSIONS

OCEANS

The area of the Earth covered by oceans and seas (the hydrosphere) is estimated to be 139,782,000 miles^2 or 70.98 percent of the total surface. The mean depth of the hydrosphere is 12,234 ft and the volume 323,870,000 miles^3, compared to 8.4 million miles^3 of fresh water. The total weight of the water is estimated to be 1.45 quintillion tons, or 0.024 percent of the Earth's total weight.

Largest   The largest ocean in the world is the Pacific. Excluding adjacent seas, it represents 45.9 percent of the world's oceans and covers 64.2 million miles^2 in area. The average depth is 13,740 ft.

The shortest navigable transpacific distance, from Guayaquil, Ecuador to Bangkok, Thailand, is 10,905 miles.

Deepest oceans   A metal object—for example, a kilogram (2.2 lb) ball of steel—dropped into water above the Mariana Trench, would take nearly 64 min to fall to the seabed, where hydrostatic pressure is over 18,000 lb/in^2.

Deepest   The deepest part of the ocean was first pinpointed in 1951 by the British Survey Ship *Challenger* in the Mariana Trench in the Pacific Ocean. On 23 Jan 1960 the US Navy bathyscaphe *Trieste* descended to the bottom at 35,813 ft. A more recent visit produced a figure of 35,839 ft ± 33 ft, from data obtained by the survey vessel *Takuyo* of the Hydrographic Department, Japan Maritime Safety Agency in 1984, using a narrow multi-beam echo sounder.

United States   Defining US waters as within 200 nautical miles of any US territory (Economic Exclusive Zone [EEZ]), the deepest point in American waters is Challenger D in the Mariana Trench in the Pacific Ocean. Challenger D is 5,973 fathoms (35,838 ft) deep, 170 nautical miles SW of Guam at 11° 22.4 N, 142° 35.5 E.

The deepest point from an American state is the Vega Basin in the Aleutian Trench, which is 4,198 fathoms (25,188 ft) deep at 50° 51 N, 177° 11 E, 60 nautical miles south of the Aleutian Islands, AK.

Largest sea   The largest of the world's seas is the South China Sea, with an area of 1.1 million miles^2.

Largest bay   The largest bay in the world measured by shoreline length is Hudson Bay, northern Canada, with a shoreline of 7,623 miles and an area of 476,000 miles^2. The area of the Bay of Bengal, in the Indian Ocean, is larger, at 839,000 miles^2.

Largest gulf   The largest gulf in the world is the Gulf of Mexico, with an area of 596,000 miles^2 and a shoreline of 3,100 miles from Cape Sable, FL, to Cabo Catoche, Mexico.

Highest seamount   The highest known submarine mountain, or seamount, is one discovered in 1953 near the Tonga Trench, between Samoa and New Zealand in the South Pacific. It rises 28,500 ft from the seabed, with its summit 1,200 ft below the surface.

Longest fjord   The world's longest fjord is the Nordvest Fjord arm of the Scoresby Sound in eastern Greenland, which extends inland 195 miles from the sea.

Most southerly   The most southerly part of the oceans is located at 85° 34′ S, 154° W, at the snout of the Robert Scott Glacier, 305 miles from the South Pole.

Sea temperature   The temperature of water at the surface of the Earth's seas varies greatly. It is as low as 28° F in the White Sea and as high as 96° F in the shallow areas of the Persian Gulf in summer.

The highest temperature recorded in the ocean is 759° F, for a hot spring measured by an American research submarine some 300 miles off the west coast of the United States, in an expedition under the direction of Prof. Jack Diamond of Oregon State University in 1985. Remote probes measured the temperature of the spring, which was only kept from vaporizing by the weight of water above it.

Clearest   The Weddell Sea, 71° S, 15° W off Antarctica, has the clearest water of any sea. A Secchi disc was visible to a depth of 262 ft on 13 Oct 1986, as measured by Dutch researchers at the German Alfred Wegener Institute. Such clarity corresponds to what is attainable in distilled water.

STRAITS

Longest   The longest straits in the world are the Tatarskiy Proliv or Tartar Straits between Sakhalin Island and the Russian mainland, running from the Sea of Japan to Sakhalinsky Zaliv—500 miles, thus marginally longer than the Malacca Straits, between Malaysia and Sumatra.

Broadest   The broadest *named* straits in the world are the Davis Straits between Greenland and Baffin Island, Canada, with a minimum width of 210 miles. The Drake Passage, a deep waterway between the Diego Ramirez Islands, Chile and the South Shetland Islands, is 710 miles across.

Narrowest   The narrowest navigable straits are those between the Aegean island of Euboea and the mainland of Greece. The gap is only 131 ft wide at Khalkis.

Highs & Lows

This artist's impression brings together the world's superlative highs and lows—from the highest mountain to the deepest point of the ocean, and from the tallest man-made structure to the deepest penetration into the earth.

More information on the particular records can be found in the appropriate chapter of the book.

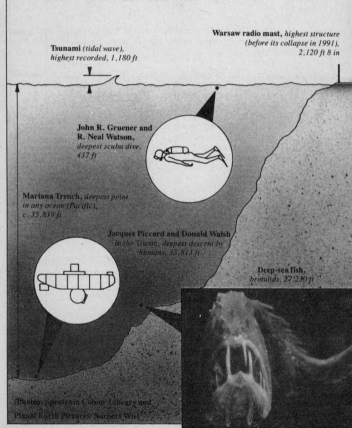

Tsunami *(tidal wave),
highest recorded, 1,180 ft*

Warsaw radio mast, *highest structure
(before its collapse in 1991),
2,120 ft 8 in*

**John R. Gruener and
R. Neal Watson,**
*deepest scuba dive,
437 ft*

Mariana Trench, *deepest point
in any ocean (Pacific),
c. 35,839 ft*

Jacques Piccard and Donald Walsh
*in the Trieste, deepest descent by
humans, 35,813 ft*

Deep-sea fish,
brotulids, 27,230 ft

(Photos: Spectrum Colour Library and
Planet Earth Pictures/Norbert Wu)

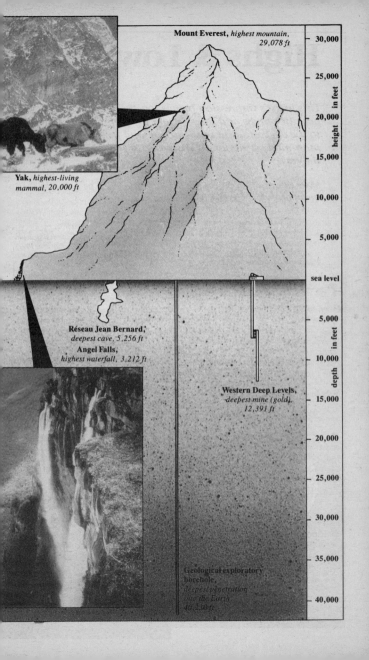

Mount Everest, *highest mountain,* *29,078 ft*

Yak, *highest-living mammal, 20,000 ft*

Réseau Jean Bernard, *deepest cave, 5,256 ft*
Angel Falls, *highest waterfall, 3,212 ft*

Western Deep Levels, *deepest mine (gold), 12,391 ft*

Geological exploratory borehole, *deepest penetration into the Earth, 40,230 ft*

height in feet

30,000
25,000
20,000
15,000
10,000
5,000
sea level
5,000
10,000
15,000
20,000
25,000
30,000
35,000
40,000

depth in feet

WAVES

Highest The highest officially recorded sea wave was calculated at 112 ft from trough to crest; it was measured by Lt Frederic Margraff (USN) from the USS *Ramapo* proceeding from Manila, Philippines to San Diego, CA on the night of 6–7 Feb 1933, during a 68-knot hurricane. The highest instrumentally measured wave was one 86 ft high, recorded by the British ship *Weather Reporter*, in the North Atlantic on 30 Dec 1972 at Lat. 59° N, Long. 19° W.

It has been calculated on the statistics of the Stationary Random Theory that one wave in more than 300,000 may exceed the average by a factor of four. On 9 Jul 1958 a landslip caused a 100 mph wave to wash 1,720 ft high along the fjord-like Lituya Bay in Alaska.

Highest seismic The highest estimated height of a *tsunami* (often wrongly called a tidal wave) was one of 1,180 ft, which struck the northern Shetland Isles *c.* 4950 B.C. at 110 mph. It was generated by a massive undersea landslip from the Storegga area of the South Norwegian Sea involving 430 miles² of mud and rock. The highest known in modern times appeared off Ishigaki Island, Ryukyu Chain on 24 Apr 1771. It tossed a 826.7-ton block of coral more than 1.3 miles. Tsunami (a Japanese word: *nami*, a wave; *tsu*, overflowing) have been observed to travel at 490 mph, and are usually caused by a submarine earthquake.

CURRENTS

Greatest The greatest current in the oceans is the Antarctic Circumpolar Current or West Wind Drift Current. On the basis of four measurements taken in 1982 in the Drake Passage, between South America and Antarctica, it was found to be flowing at a rate of 4.3 billion ft³ per sec. Results from computer modeling in 1990 estimate a higher figure of 6.9 billion ft³ per sec. Its width ranges from 185–1,240 miles and it has a proven surface flow rate of ⁴⁄₁₀ of a knot.

Strongest The world's strongest currents are the Nakwakto Rapids, Slingsby Channel, British Columbia, Canada (Lat. 51° 05′ N, Long. 127° 30′ W), where the flow rate may reach 16 knots.

United States The strongest current in the United States occurs on the coast of Alaska in Chatam Strait, Pt. Kootzhahoo at Pt. Bridge. The current ebbs at 7 knots. The strongest current on the east coast of the United States is at St Johns River in Pablo Creek, FL. The current ebbs at 5.2 knots.

TIDES

Extreme tides are due to lunar and solar gravitational forces affected by their perigee, perihelion and syzygies. Barometric and wind effects can superimpose an added "surge" element. Coastal and sea-floor configurations can accentuate these forces. The normal interval between tides is 12 hr 25 min.

Greatest The greatest tides occur in the Bay of Fundy, which divides the peninsula of Nova Scotia, Canada from Maine and the Canadian province of New Brunswick. Burncoat Head in the Minas Basin, Nova Scotia, has the greatest mean spring range, with 47 ft 6 in. A range of 54 ft 6 in was recorded at springs in Leaf Basin, in Ungava Bay, Quebec, Canada in 1953.

Least   Tahiti, in the mid-Pacific Ocean, experiences virtually no tide.

Highest and lowest   The highest and lowest tide in the United States is at Sunrise, AK on Turnagain Arm islet. Its range is 33.3 ft.

Remotest spot from land   The world's most distant point from land is a spot in the South Pacific, approximately 48° 30′ S, 125° 30′ W, which is about 1,660 miles from the nearest points of land, namely Pitcairn Island, Ducie Island and Cape Dart, Antarctica. Centered on this spot is a circle of water with an area of about 8,657,000 miles^2—about 2 million miles^2 larger than Russia, the world's largest country.

Most southerly arctic iceberg   The most southerly arctic iceberg was sighted in the Atlantic by a USN weather patrol at Lat. 28° 44′ N, Long. 48° 42′ W, in April 1935.

Most northerly antarctic iceberg   The most northerly antarctic iceberg was a remnant sighted in the Atlantic by the ship *Dochra* at Lat. 26° 30′ S, Long. 25° 40′ W, on 30 Apr 1894.

ICEBERGS

Largest   The largest iceberg on record was an antarctic tabular iceberg of over 12,000 miles^2, 208 miles long and 60 miles wide, sighted 150 miles west of Scott Island, in the South Pacific Ocean, by the USS *Glacier* on 12 Nov 1956. The 200 ft thick arctic ice island T.1 (140 miles^2), discovered in 1946, was tracked for 17 years.

Tallest   The tallest iceberg measured was one of 550 ft reported off western Greenland by the US icebreaker *East Wind* in 1958.

LAND

There is strong evidence that about 300 million years ago the Earth's land surface comprised a single primeval continent of 60 million miles^2, now termed Pangaea, and even before its existence it is possible that there had been other supercontinents. Pangaea is believed to have split about 190 million years ago, during the Jurassic period, into two supercontinents, which are called Laurasia (Eurasia, Greenland and North America) and Gondwana (Africa, Arabia, India, South America, Oceania and Antarctica), named after Gondwana, India, which itself split 120 million years ago. The South Pole was apparently in the area of the Sahara as recently as the Ordovician period of *c.* 450 million years ago. Consequently the Sa-

Dr. Samuel Bowring with some of the world's oldest rocks (Photo: Washington University/Joe Angeles)

hara, now one of the hottest areas of the world, was at one time the coldest.

United States On 18 Dec 1991 the Census Bureau reported that the total land area of the United States is 3,787,425 miles².

Coastline According to the measurements of the National Oceanic and Atmospheric Administration (NOAA), the entire coastline of the United States, including Hawaii, Alaska and the Great Lakes states, is 94,112 miles. Excluding Hawaii and Alaska, the coastline equals 59,156 miles. The state with the longest coastline is Alaska; it measures ±3,904 miles.

ROCKS

The age of the Earth is generally considered to be within the range of 4,540 ± 40 million years, based on the lead isotope systematics. However, no rocks of this great age have yet been found on the Earth, since geological processes have presumably destroyed them.

Oldest The greatest reported age for any scientifically dated rock is 3,962 million years in the case of the Acasta Gneisses, found in May 1984. The rocks were discovered approximately 200 miles north of Yellowknife, Northwest Territories, Canada by Dr Samuel Bowring as part of an ongoing Canadian geology survey mapping project. When the samples were analyzed in June 1989, Dr Bowring and scientists from the Australian National University in Canberra established their age, using a machine called SHRIMP (Sensitive High-mass Resolution Ion MicroProbe).

Older minerals that are not rocks have also been identified. Some zircon crystals discovered by Bob Pidgeon and Simon Wilde in the Jack Hills, 430 miles north of Perth, Western Australia in August 1984 were found to be 4,276 million years old, again using SHRIMP. These are the oldest fragments of the Earth's crust discovered so far.

United States The oldest rocks in the United States are the Morton Gneisses, found in 1935 by G.A. Phiel and C.E. Dutton scattered over an area of 50 miles from New Ulm, Brown Co. to Renville Co. in Minnesota. In 1980 these rocks were dated at 3.6 billion years by Sam Goldrich of the US Geological Survey in Denver, CO, using the uranium-lead dating method.

Largest The largest exposed monolith in the world is Ayers Rock, which rises 1,143 ft above the surrounding desert plain in Northern Territory, Australia. It is 1.5 miles long and 1 mile wide. The nearest major town is Alice Springs, which is 250 miles to the northeast.

It was estimated in 1940 that La Gran Piedra, a volcanic plug located in the Sierra Maestra, Cuba, weighs 67,632 tons.

Land remotest from the sea The point of land remotest from the sea is at Lat. 46° 16.8′ N, Long. 86° 40.2′ E in the Dzungarian Basin, which is in the Xinjiang Uighur Autonomous Region (Xinjiang Uygur Zu zhi ju), China's most northwesterly province. It is at a straight-line distance of 1,645 miles from the nearest open sea—Baydaratskaya Guba to the north (Arctic Ocean), Feni Point to the south (Indian Ocean) and Bo Haiwan to the east (Yellow Sea).

Largest state The largest state in land area is Alaska, with 591,004 miles². The largest in the 48 coterminous states is Texas, with 267,017 miles² of land.

Smallest state The smallest state is Rhode Island, with 1,212 miles².

CONTINENTS

Largest Of the Earth's surface, 41.25 percent, or 81.2 million miles², is covered by continental masses, of which only about 57,151,000 miles² (about two-thirds, or 29.02 percent of the Earth's surface) is land above water, with a mean height of 2,480 ft above sea level. The Eurasian landmass is the largest, with an area (including islands) of 20.7 million miles². The Afro-Eurasian landmass, separated artificially only by the Suez Canal, covers an area of 32.7 million miles² or 57.2 percent of the Earth's landmass.

Smallest The smallest continent is the Australian mainland, with an area of 2,941,526 miles², which, together with Tasmania, New Zealand, Papua New Guinea and the Pacific Islands, is sometimes described as Oceania.

ISLANDS

Largest   Discounting Australia, which is usually regarded as a continental landmass, the largest island in the world is Greenland, with an area of about 840,000 miles². There is evidence that Greenland is in fact several islands overlaid by an ice cap, without which it would have an area of 650,000 miles².

The largest sand island in the world is Fraser Island, Queensland, Australia with a sand dune 75 miles long.

The largest island in North America is Newfoundland, Canada, with an area of 42,030 miles².

Freshwater   The largest island surrounded mostly by fresh water (18,500 miles²) is the Ilha de Marajó in the mouth of the River Amazon, Brazil.

The world's largest inland island (i.e., land surrounded by rivers) is Ilha do Bananal, Brazil (7,000 miles²), which is the habitat of Carajá. The largest island in a lake is Manitoulin Island (1,068 miles²) in the Canadian section of Lake Huron.

Remotest   The remotest island in the world is Bouvet Island (Bouvetøya), discovered in the South Atlantic by J.B.C. Bouvet de Lozier on 1 Jan 1739, and first landed on by Capt. George Norris on 16 Dec 1825. Its position is 54° 26′ S, 3° 24′ E. This uninhabited Norwegian dependency is about 1,050 miles from the nearest land—the uninhabited Queen Maud Land coast of eastern Antarctica.

The remotest inhabited island in the world is Tristan da Cunha, discovered in the South Atlantic by Tristão da Cunha, a Portuguese admiral, in March 1506. It has an area of 38 miles². The first permanent inhabitant was Thomas Currie, who landed in 1810. The island was annexed by Great Britain on 14 Aug 1816. After evacuation in 1961 (due to volcanic activity), 198 islanders returned in November 1963. The nearest inhabited land to the group is the island of St Helena, 1,315 nautical miles to the northeast. The nearest continent, Africa, is 1,700 miles away.

Greatest archipelago   The world's greatest archipelago is the crescent of more than 13,000 islands, 3,500 miles long, that forms Indonesia.

Highest rock pinnacle   The world's highest rock pinnacle is Ball's Pyramid near Lord Howe Island in the Pacific, which is 1,843 ft high, but has a base axis of only 660 ft. It was first scaled in 1965.

Northernmost land   On 26 Jul 1978 Uffe Petersen of the Danish Geodetic Institute observed the islet of Odaaq Ø, 100 ft across, 0.8 miles north of Kaffeklubben Ø off Pearyland, Greenland at Lat. 83° 40′ 32.5″ N, Long. 30° 40′ 10.1″ W. It is 438.9 miles from the North Pole.

Southernmost land   The South Pole, unlike the North Pole, is on land. The Amundsen–Scott South Polar station was built there at an altitude of 9,370 ft in 1957. The station is drifting bodily with the ice cap 27–30 ft per year in the direction 43° W and was replaced by a new structure in 1975.

LARGEST ISLAND   This shot shows a typical landscape in the west of Greenland. (Photo: Robert Estall Photographs)

Newest   The world's newest island is Pulau Batu Hairan ("Surprise Rock Island"), some 40 miles to the northeast of Kudat, in Sabah, Malaysia. It was first sighted by three local fishermen on 14 Apr 1988. A week later it had doubled in height and now has an area of 1.9 acres and a maximum height of 10 ft.

Peninsula   The world's largest peninsula is Arabia, with an area of about 1.25 million miles².

Largest atoll   The largest atoll in the world is Kwajalein in the Marshall Islands, in the central Pacific Ocean. Its slender coral reef 176 miles long encloses a lagoon of 1,100 miles².

The atoll with the largest land area is Christmas Atoll, in the Line Islands in the central Pacific Ocean. It has an area of 251 miles², of which 124 miles² is land. Its principal settlement, London, is only 2½ miles distant from another settlement, Paris.

Longest reef   The Great Barrier Reef off Queensland, northeastern Australia is 1,260 miles in length. It is not actually a single reef, but consists of thousands of separate reefs. Between 1959 and 1971, and again between 1979 and 1991, corals on large areas of the central section of the reef—approximately between Cooktown and Proserpine—were devastated by the crown-of-thorns starfish (*Acanthaster planci*).

DEPRESSIONS

Deepest   The deepest depression so far discovered is the bedrock of the Bentley subglacial trench, Antarctica at 8,326 ft below sea level. The greatest submarine depression is an area of the northwest Pacific floor that has an average depth of 15,000 ft.

The deepest exposed depression on land is the shore surrounding the Dead Sea, now 1,310 ft below sea level. The deepest point on the bed of this saltiest of all lakes is 2,388 ft below sea level. The rate of fall in the lake surface since 1948 has been 13¾ in per year. The deepest part of the bed of Lake Baikal in Russia is 3,875 ft below sea level.

United States   The lowest-lying area in the United States is in Death Valley, CA at 282 ft below sea level.

Largest   The largest exposed depression in the world is the Caspian Sea basin in Azerbaijan, Russia, Kazakhstan, Turkmenistan and Iran. It is more than 200,000 miles², of which 143,550 miles² is lake area. The preponderant land area of the depression is the Prikaspiyskaya Nizmennost, lying around the northern third of the lake and stretching inland for a distance of up to 280 miles.

CAVES

Longest   The most extensive cave system in the world is that under the Mammoth Cave National Park, KY, first entered in 1799. Explorations by many groups of cavers have revealed the interconnected cave passages beneath the Flint, Mammoth Cave and Toohey Ridges to make a system with a total mapped length that is now 348 miles.

Largest   The world's largest cave chamber is the Sarawak Chamber, Lubang Nasib Bagus, in the Gunung Mulu National Park, Sarawak, Malaysia, discovered and surveyed by the 1980 British-Malaysian Mulu Expedition. Its length is 2,300 ft; its average width is 980 ft; and it is nowhere less than 230 ft high. It would be large enough to garage 7,500 buses.

Underwater The longest explored underwater cave is the Nohoch Na Chich cave system in Quintana Roo, Mexico, with 70,087 ft of mapped passages. Exploration of the system, which began in November 1987, has been carried out by the CEDAM Cave Diving Team under the leadership of Mike Madden.

The longest dive into a single flooded cave passage is 13,300 ft into the Doux de Coly, Dordogne, France by Olivier Issler (Switzerland) on 4 Apr 1991.

Greatest descent The world depth record was set by the Groupe Vulcain in the Gouffre Jean Bernard, France at 5,256 ft in 1989. However, this cave, explored via multiple entrances, has never been entirely descended, so the "sporting" record for the greatest descent into a cave is recognized as 4,947 ft in the Shakta Pantjukhina in the Caucasus Mountains of Georgia by a team of Ukrainian cavers in 1988.

Longest stalactite The longest known stalactite in the world is a wall-supported column extending 195 ft from roof to floor in the Cueva de Nerja, near Málaga, in Spain.

The longest freehanging stalactite in the world is one of 20 ft 4 in, in the Poll an Ionain cave in County Clare, Ireland.

Tallest stalagmite The tallest known stalagmite in the world is one in the Krásnohorská cave, near Rožňava in Slovakia, which is generally accepted as being about 105 ft tall.

The tallest cave column is considered to be the Flying Dragon Pillar, 128 ft high, in Daji Dong, Guizhou, China.

Deepest The deepest cave in the United States is Lechuguilla Cave in Carlsbad Caverns, Carlsbad, NM, which currently measures 1,565 ft.

MOUNTAINS

Highest An eastern Himalayan peak known as Peak XV on the Tibet–Nepal border was discovered to be the world's highest mountain in March 1856 by the Survey Department of the Government of India, from theodolite readings taken in 1849 and 1850. Its height was computed to be 29,002 ft. It was named Mt Everest after Col. Sir George Everest (1790–1866), formerly surveyor-general of India, who pronounced his name "Eve-rest."

The status of Everest as the world's highest mountain was challenged after 131 years by K2 (formerly Godwin Austen). The satellite transit surveyor of the US K2 expedition yielded altitudes of between 29,064 and 29,228 ft. However, Chinese authorities subsequently reaffirmed their own height measurements of 29,029 ft 3 in for Everest and 28,250 ft for K2, and the Research Council in Rome, Italy announced on 23 Oct 1987 that new satellite measurements restored Everest to primacy at 29,078 ft, and put K2 down to 28,238 ft. These are the latest accepted figures. (For details of ascents of Everest, see Mountaineering.)

The mountain whose summit is farthest from the Earth's center is the

US HIGHEST ALTITUDES

State	Highest point	Elevation (ft)
Alaska	Mt McKinley	20,320
California	Mt Whitney	14,494
Colorado	Mt Elbert	14,433
Washington	Mt Rainier	14,410
Wyoming	Gannett Peak	13,804
Hawaii	Mauna Kea	13,796
Utah	Kings Peak	13,528
New Mexico	Wheeler Park	13,161
Nevada	Boundary Peak	13,140
Montana	Granite Peak	12,799
Idaho	Borah Peak	12,662
Arizona	Humphrey's Peak	12,633
Oregon	Mt Hood	11,239
Texas	Guadalupe Peak	8,749
South Dakota	Harney Peak	7,242
North Carolina	Mt Mitchell	6,684
Tennessee	Clingmans Dome	6,643
New Hampshire	Mt Washington	6,288
Virginia	Mt Rogers	5,729
Nebraska	Johnson Township	5,426
New York	Mt Marcy	5,344
Maine	Mt Katahdin	5,267
Oklahoma	Black Mesa	4,973
West Virginia	Spruce Knob	4,861
Georgia	Brasstown Bald	4,784
Vermont	Mt Mansfield	4,393
Kentucky	Black Mountain	4,139
Kansas	Mt Sunflower	4,039
South Carolina	Sassafras Mountain	3,560
North Dakota	White Butte	3,506
Massachusetts	Mt Greylock	3,487
Maryland	Blackbone Mountain	3,360
Pennsylvania	Mt Davis	3,213
Arkansas	Magazine Mountain	2,753
Alabama	Cheaha Mountain	2,405
Connecticut	Mt Frissell	2,380
Minnesota	Eagle Mountain	2,301
Michigan	Mt Arvon	1,979
Wisconsin	Timms Hill	1,951
New Jersey	High Point	1,803
Missouri	Taum Sauk Mount	1,772
Iowa	Sec. 29, T 100N, R 41W	1,670
Ohio	Campbell Hill	1,549
Indiana	Franklin Township	1,257
Illinois	Charles Mound	1,235
Rhode Island	Jerimoth Hill	812
Mississippi	Woodall Mountain	806
Louisiana	Driskill Mountain	535
Delaware	Ebright Road	442
Florida	Sec. 30, T 6N, R 20W	345

Andean peak of Chimborazo (20,561 ft), 98 miles south of the equator in Ecuador, South America. Its summit is 7,057 ft further from the Earth's center than the summit of Mt Everest.

The highest insular mountain (of, relating to, or resembling an island) in the world is Puncak Jaya (formerly Puncak Sukarno, formerly Carstensz Pyramide) in Irian Jaya, Indonesia. A survey by the Australian Universities' Expedition in 1973 yielded a height of 16,023 ft. Ngga Pulu (also in Irian Jaya), which is now 15,950 ft, was in 1936 possibly 16,110 ft before the melting of its snow cap.

United States   The highest mountain in the United States is Mt McKinley in Alaska, with a highest point of 20,320 ft. McKinley, so named in 1896, was called Denali (Great One) in the Athabascan language of Native North Americans. The highest mountain in the 48 contiguous states is Mt Whitney in California, with a highest point of 14,494 ft.

Unclimbed   The highest unclimbed mountain is Kankar Punsum (24,741 ft), on the Bhutan/Tibet border. It is the 67th highest mountain in the world. The highest unclimbed summit is Lhotse Middle (27,605 ft), one of the peaks of Lhotse, in the Khumbu district of the Nepal Himalaya. It is the tenth highest individually recognized peak in the world, Lhotse being the fourth highest mountain.

Tallest   The world's tallest mountain measured from its submarine base (3,280 fathoms) in the Hawaiian Trough to its peak is Mauna Kea (White Mountain) on the island of Hawaii, with a combined height of 33,480 ft, of which 13,796 ft are above sea level.

Greatest ranges   The greatest of all mountain ranges is the submarine Mid-Ocean Ridge, extending 40,000 miles from the Arctic Ocean to the Atlantic Ocean, around Africa, Asia and Australia, and under the Pacific Ocean to the west coast of North America. It has a greatest height of 13,800 ft above the base ocean depth.

The world's greatest land mountain range is the Himalaya-Karakoram, which contains 96 of the world's 109 peaks of over 24,000 ft. *Himalaya* derives from the Sanskrit *him*, snow; *alaya*, home. The longest range is the Andes of South America, which is approximately 4,700 miles in length.

Greatest plateau   The most extensive high plateau in the world is the Tibetan Plateau in Central Asia. The average altitude is 16,000 ft and the area is 77,000 miles^2.

Longest lines of sight   Vatnajökull (6,952 ft), Iceland has been seen by refracted light from the Faeroe Islands 340 miles away.

United States   In Alaska, Mt McKinley (20,320 ft) has been sighted from Mt Sanford (16,237 ft), a distance of 230 miles. (See also Mountains, Highest.)

MOUNTAIN CLIMBING Pete Allard, Jim Grace, Shuan Lacher, David Sandway and Dennis Stewart reached each high point of the 48 contiguous states in a record time of 30 days 10 hours 51 minutes and 55 seconds 1–31 Jul 1991. They hiked a total of 253 miles and drove 17,284 miles during the entire trip. They are shown here at the summit of Mt Whitney (14,494 ft) in California on 4 Jul 1991. (Photo: Courtesy Dennis Stewart)

Mt. Everest, the world's highest mountain. (Photo: Bruce Herrod)

Sheerest wall   Mt Rakaposhi (25,550 ft) rises 3.72 miles from the Hunza Valley, Pakistan in 6.2 miles with an overall gradient of 31°.

The 3,200-ft-wide northwest face of Half Dome, Yosemite, CA is 2,200 ft high but nowhere departs more than 7° from the vertical. It was first climbed (Class VI) in 1957 by Royal Robbins, Jerry Gallwas and Mike Sherrick.

Highest halites   Along the northern shores of the Gulf of Mexico for 725 miles there exist 330 subterranean "mountains" of salt, some of which rise more than 60,000 ft from bedrock and appear as the low salt domes first discovered in 1862.

WATERFALLS

Highest   The highest waterfall (as opposed to vaporized "bridal-veil fall") in the world is the Salto Angel (Angel Falls) in Venezuela, on a branch of the Carrao River, an upper tributary of the Caroni, with a total drop of 3,212 ft—the longest single drop is 2,648 ft. The Angel Falls were named after the US pilot Jimmy Angel (d. 8 Dec 1956), who recorded them in his log book on 14 Nov 1933. The falls, known by the Indians as Churun-Meru, had been reported by Ernesto Sánchez la Cruz in 1910.

United States   The tallest continuous waterfall in the United States is Ribbon Falls in Yosemite National Park, California, with a drop of 1,612 ft. This is a seasonal waterfall and is generally dry from late July to early September.

Yosemite Falls, also in Yosemite National Park, has the greatest *total* drop at 2,425 ft, but actually consists of three distinct waterfalls. These are the Upper (1,430 ft), Middle (675 ft) and Lower falls (320 ft).

Greatest   On the basis of the average annual flow, the greatest waterfall in the world is the Boyoma (formerly Stanley) Falls in Zaïre with 600,000 cusec.

The flow of the Guaíra (Salto das Sete Quedas) on the Alto Paraná River between Brazil and Paraguay did on occasions in the past attain a peak rate of 1.75 million cusec. However, the closing of the Itaipú dam gates in 1982 ended this claim to fame.

It has been calculated that a waterfall 26 times greater than the Guaíra and perhaps 2,620 ft high was formed, when some 5.5 million years ago the Mediterranean basin began to be filled from the Atlantic through the Straits of Gibraltar.

Widest   The widest waterfall in the world is the Khône Falls (50–70 ft high) in Laos, with a width of 6.7 miles and a flood flow of 1.5 million cusec.

RIVERS

Longest   The two longest rivers in the world are the Nile (*Bahr el-Nil*), flowing into the Mediterranean, and the Amazon (*Amazonas*), flowing into the South Atlantic. Which is the longer is more a matter of definition than simple measurement.

Not until 1971 was the true source of the Amazon discovered, by Loren

McIntyre (USA) in the snow-covered Andes of southern Peru. The Amazon begins with snowbound lakes and brooks—the actual source has been named Laguna McIntyre—which converge to form the Apurimac. This joins other streams to become the Ene, the Tambo and then the Ucayali. From the confluence of the Ucayali and the Marañón the river is called the Amazon for the final 2,300 miles as it flows through Brazil into the Atlantic Ocean. The Amazon has several mouths that widen toward the sea, so that the exact point where the river ends is uncertain. If the Pará estuary (the most distant mouth) is counted, its length is approximately 4,195 miles.

The length of the Nile watercourse, as surveyed by M. Devroey (Belgium) before the loss of a few miles of meanders due to the formation of Lake Nasser, behind the Aswan High Dam, was 4,145 miles. This course is unitary from a hydrological standpoint and runs from the source in Burundi of the Luvironza branch of the Kagera feeder of the Victoria Nyanza via the White Nile (*Bahr el-Jebel*) to the delta in the Mediterranean.

United States   The longest river in the United States is the Mississippi, with a length of 2,348 miles. It flows from its source at Lake Itasca, MN through 10 states before reaching the Gulf of Mexico. The entire Mississippi River system, including the eastern and western tributaries, flows through 25 states in all.

Shortest   As with the longest river, two rivers could also be considered to be the shortest river with a name. The Roe River, near Great Falls, MT, has two forks fed by a large freshwater spring. These relatively constant forks measure 201 ft (East Fork Roe River) and 58 ft (North Fork Roe River) respectively. The Roe River flows into the larger Missouri River. The D River, located at Lincoln City, OR, connects Devil's Lake to the Pacific Ocean. Its length is officially quoted as 120 ± 5 ft.

Largest basin   The largest river basin in the world is that drained by the Amazon (4,007 miles), which covers about 2,720,000 miles². It has some 15,000 tributaries and sub-tributaries, including the Madeira, which at 2,100 miles is the longest tributary in the world.

Longest estuary   The world's longest estuary is that of the often frozen Ob, in the north of Russia, at 550 miles. It is up to 50 miles wide, and is also the widest river that freezes solid.

Submarine river   In 1952 a submarine river 190 miles wide, known as the Cromwell Current, was discovered flowing eastward below the surface of the Pacific for 4,000 miles along the equator. In places it flows at depths of up to 1,300 ft. Its volume is 1,000 times that of the Mississippi.

Subterranean river   In August 1958 a crypto-river, tracked by radio isotopes, was discovered flowing under the Nile with six times its mean annual flow, or 20 trillion ft³.

Largest delta The world's largest delta is that created by the Ganges (Ganga) and Brahmaputra in Bangladesh and West Bengal, India. It covers an area of 30,000 miles².

Greatest flow The greatest flow of any river in the world is that of the Amazon, which discharges an average of 4.2 million cusec into the Atlantic Ocean, increasing to more than 7 million cusec in full flood. The lower 900 miles of the Amazon average 55 ft in depth, but in some places the river reaches a depth of 300 ft. The flow of the Amazon is 60 times greater than that of the Nile.

Largest swamp The world's largest tract of swamp is the Gran Pantanal of Mato Grosso state in Brazil. It is about 42,000 miles² in area.

Largest marsh The Everglades is a vast plateau of subtropical saw-grass marsh in southern Florida, covering 2,185 miles². Fed by water from Lake Okeechobee, the third largest freshwater lake in the United States, the Everglades is the largest subtropical wilderness in the continental United States.

RIVER BORES

The bore (an abrupt rise of tidal water) on the Qiantong Jiang (Hangzhou He) in eastern China is the most remarkable of the 60 in the world. At spring tides the wave attains a height of up to 25 ft and a speed of 13–15 knots. It is heard advancing at a range of 14 miles.

The annual downstream flood wave on the Mekong, in southeast Asia, sometimes reaches a height of 46 ft.

The greatest volume of any tidal bore is that of the Furo do Guajarú, a shallow channel that splits Ilha Caviana in the mouth of the Amazon.

LAKES AND INLAND SEAS

Largest The largest inland sea or lake in the world is the Caspian Sea (in Azerbaijan, Russia, Kazakhstan, Turkmenistan and Iran). It is 760 miles long and its total area is 143,550 miles². Of the total area, some 55,280 miles² (38.5 percent) are in Iran, where it is named the Darya-ye-Khazar. Its maximum depth is 3,360 ft and the surface is 93 ft below sea level. Its estimated volume is 21,500 miles³ of saline water. Its surface has varied between 105 ft (11th century) and 72 ft (early 19th century) below sea level. (See also Depressions, largest.)

United States The largest lake in the United States is Lake Michigan, with a water surface area of 22,300 miles², a length of 307 miles, a breadth of 118 miles and a maximum depth of 923 ft. Both Lake Superior and Lake Huron have larger areas, but these straddle the Canadian/American border.

Excluding the Great Lakes, the largest natural lake wholly within the United States is the Great Salt Lake, UT, which has a water surface area of 1,361 miles².

Deepest The deepest lake in the world is Lake Baikal in southern part of eastern Siberia, Russia. It is 385 miles long and between 20–46 miles wide.

In 1974 the lake's Olkhon Crevice was measured by the Hydrographic Service of the Soviet Pacific Navy and found to be 5,371 ft deep, of which 3,875 ft is below sea level. (See also Depressions.)

United States The deepest lake in the United States is 6-mile-long Crater Lake, in Crater Lake National Park in the Cascade Mountains of Oregon. Its surface is 6,176 ft above sea level and its extreme depth is 1,932 ft, with an average depth of 1,500 ft. The lake has neither inlets nor outlets; instead it is filled and maintained solely by precipitation.

Highest The highest navigable lake in the world is Lake Titicaca (maximum depth 1,214 ft, with an area of about 3,200 miles^2) in South America (1,850 miles^2 in Peru and 1,350 miles^2 in Bolivia). It is 110 miles long and is 12,506 ft above sea level. There are higher lakes in the Himalayas, but most are glacial and of a temporary nature only. A survey of the area carried out in 1984 showed a lake at a height of 17,762 ft, named Panch Pokhri, which was 1 mile long.

Freshwater The freshwater lake with the greatest surface area is Lake Superior, one of the Great Lakes of North America. The total area is 31,800 miles^2, of which 20,700 miles^2 are in Minnesota, Wisconsin and Michigan and 11,100 miles^2 in Ontario, Canada. It is 600 ft above sea level. The freshwater lake with the greatest volume is Lake Baikal in Siberia, Russia, with an estimated volume of 5,500 miles^3.

Largest lagoon Lagoa dos Patos, located near the seashore in Rio Grande do Sul, southernmost Brazil, is 174 miles long and extends over 3,803 miles^2, separated from the Atlantic Ocean by long sand strips. It has a maximum width of 44 miles.

Underground lake The world's largest underground lake is believed to be that in the Drachenhauchloch cave near Grootfontein, Namibia, discovered in 1986. The surface of the lake is some 217 ft underground, and its depth is 276 ft.

Reputedly the United States' largest underground lake is the Lost Sea, 300 ft subterranean in the Craighead Caverns, Sweetwater, TN, measuring 4½ acres and discovered in 1905.

Lake in a lake The largest lake inside another lake is Manitou Lake (41.09 miles^2) on the world's largest lake island, Manitoulin Island (1,068 miles^2), in the Canadian part of Lake Huron. The lake itself contains a number of islands.

Thickest ice The greatest recorded thickness of ice is 2.97 miles, measured by radio echo soundings from a US Antarctic research aircraft at 69° 9′ 38″ S, 135° 20′ 25″ E, 250 miles from the coast of Wilkes Land on 4 Jan 1975.

OTHER FEATURES

Desert   Nearly an eighth of the world's land surface is arid, with a rainfall of less than 10 in per year. The Sahara in North Africa is the largest desert in the world. At its greatest length it is 3,200 miles from east to west. From north to south it is between 800 and 1,400 miles. The area covered by the desert is about 3,579,000 miles². The land level varies from 436 ft below sea level in the Qattâra Depression, Egypt to the mountain Emi Koussi (11,204 ft) in Chad. The daytime temperature range in the western Sahara may be more than 80 deg F. Desert surfaces have been known to heat up to 180° F.

United States   The largest desert in the United States is the Chihuahuan in Texas, New Mexico and Arizona, which extends into Mexico. It covers an area of approximately 140,000 miles².

Sand dunes   The world's highest measured sand dunes are those in the Saharan sand sea of Isaouane-N-Tifernine of east-central Algeria at Lat. 26° 42′ N, Long. 6° 43′ E. They have a wavelength of 3 miles and attain a height of 1,525 ft.

Largest gorge   The largest land gorge in the world is the Grand Canyon on the Colorado River in north-central Arizona. It extends from Marble Gorge to the Grand Wash Cliffs, over a distance of 277 miles. It varies in width from 4–13 miles and is 1 mile in depth. The submarine Labrador Basin canyon is c. 2,150 miles long.

Deepest canyon   A canyon or gorge is generally regarded as a valley with steep rock walls and a considerable depth in relation to its width. The Grand Canyon (see above) has the characteristic vertical sections of wall, but is much wider than its depth. The Vicos Gorge in the Pindus mountains of northwest Greece is 2,950 ft deep and only 3,600 ft between its rims. Gorges in many countries have a higher depth/width ratio, but none are as deep.

The often cited Colca canyon in Peru has the cross-profile of a valley, but is neither as deep nor as steep-sided as the Kali Gandaki valley (see below). The deepest submarine canyon yet discovered is one 25 miles south of Esperance, Western Australia; it is 6,000 ft deep and 20 miles wide.

United States   The deepest canyon in the United States is Kings Canyon, East Fresno, CA, which runs through Sierra and Sequoia National Forests. The deepest point, which measures 8,200 ft, is in the Sierra National Park Forest section of the canyon.

The deepest canyon in low relief territory is Hell's Canyon, dividing Oregon and Idaho. It plunges 7,900 ft from the Devil Mountain down to the Snake River.

Deepest valley   The Kali Gandaki valley lies 14,436 ft deep between the Dhaulagiri and Annapurna ranges of the Nepal Himalayas. The closest bastions of these ranges are Tukuche Peak (22,703 ft) and Nilgiri North Peak (23,166 ft), just 11.3 miles apart, with the Gandaki River in between, at an elevation of 8,464 ft.

LARGEST GORGE   The largest gorge in the world—the Grand Canyon
in Arizona. (Photo: James Clift for Guinness Publishing Ltd)

Cliffs The highest sea cliffs yet pinpointed anywhere in the world are those on the north coast of east Moloka'i, HI near Umilehi Point, which descend 3,300 ft to the sea at an average gradient of more than 55°.

United States The highest seacliffs are in Acadia National Park—Maine-at-Otter Cliff, at a height of 100 ft.

Natural arches The longest natural arch in the world is the Landscape Arch in the Arches National Park, 25 miles north of Moab in Utah. This natural sandstone arch spans 291 ft and is set about 100 ft above the canyon floor. In one place erosion has narrowed its section to 6 ft. Larger, however, is the Rainbow Bridge, UT, discovered on 14 Aug 1909, which although only 270 ft long, is more than 22 ft wide and rises 290 ft in elevation.

Longest glaciers It is estimated that 5,250,000 miles², or 9.7 percent of the Earth's land surface, is permanently glaciated. The Antarctic ice sheet accounts for 86.7 percent of this and the Greenland ice sheet for 10.9 percent. The world's longest glacier is the Lambert Glacier, discovered by an Australian aircraft crew in Australian Antarctic Territory in 1956–57. Draining about a fifth of the East Antarctic ice sheet, it is up to 40 miles wide and, with its seaward extension, the Amery Ice Shelf, it measures at least 440 miles in length.

The longest valley glaciers in the northern hemisphere are in Alaska, where the Hubbard Glacier flows for 91 miles from the St Elias Mountains into the sea at Yakutat Bay. The longest Himalayan glacier is the Siachen (47 miles) in the Karakoram range, though the Hispar and Biafo combine to form a continuous stream of ice 76 miles long.

The fastest-moving major glacier is the Jakobshavn Isbrae in Greenland, flowing an average of 62 ft per day.

Deepest permafrost The deepest recorded permafrost is more than 4,500 ft, reported from the upper reaches of the Viluy River, Siberia, Russia in February 1982.

Largest crater The world's largest caldera or volcano crater is that of Toba, north-central Sumatra, Indonesia, covering 685 miles²

NATURAL PHENOMENA

EARTHQUAKES

(Seismologists record all dates with the year *first*, based not on local time but on Universal Time/Greenwich Mean Time).

Greatest It is estimated that each year there are some 500,000 detectable seismic or microseismic disturbances, of which 100,000 can be felt and

WORST NATURAL DISASTERS IN THE WORLD

Type of Disaster	Number killed	Location	Date
Earthquake [1]	1,100,000	Near East and E. Mediterranean	c. July 1201
Circular Storm [2]	1,000,000	Ganges Delta Islands, Bangladesh	12–13 Nov 1970
Flood	900,000	Hwang-ho River, China	Oct 1887
Landslides	180,000	Kansu Province, China	16 Dec 1920
(triggered off by a single earthquake)			
Volcanic Eruption	92,000	Tambora, Sumbawa, Indonesia	5–7 Apr 1815
Avalanches [3]	c. 18,000	Yungay, Huascarán, Peru	31 May 1970
Tornado	c. 1,300	Shaturia, Bangladesh	26 Apr 1989
Hail	246	Moradabad, Uttar Pradesh, India	20 Apr 1888
Lightning	81	Boeing 707 jet airliner, struck by lightning near Elkton, MD	8 Dec 1963

[1] Has been quoted, but now considered to be a gross exaggeration—see Worst death toll, above.

[2] This figure published in 1972 for the Bangladeshi disaster was from Dr Afzal, Principal Scientific Officer of the Atomic Energy Authority Centre, Dacca. One report asserted that less than half of the population of the four islands of Bhola, Charjabbar, Hatia and Ramagati (1961 census 1.4 million) survived. The most damaging hurricane recorded was Hurricane Andrew from 23–26 Aug 1992, which was estimated to have done at least $15 billion worth of damage.

[3] A total of 18,000 Austrian and Italian troops were reported to have been lost in the Dolomite valleys of northern Italy on 13 Dec 1916 in more than 100 snow avalanches. Some of the avalanches were triggered by gunfire.

1,000 cause damage. The deepest recorded hypocenters are of 447 miles in Indonesia in 1933, 1934 and 1943.

The scale most commonly used to measure the size of earthquakes is Richter's magnitude scale (1954). It is named after Dr Charles Richter (USA; 1900–85), and the most commonly used form is M_S, based on amplitudes of surface waves, usually at a period of 20 sec. The largest reported magnitudes on this scale are about 8.9, but the scale does not properly represent the size of the very largest earthquakes, above M_S about 8, for which it is better to use the concept of seismic moment, M_O, devised by K. Aki in 1966.

Moment can be used to derive a "moment magnitude," M_W, first used by Hiroo Kanamori in 1977. The largest recorded earthquake on the M_W scale is the Chilean shock of 1960 22 May, which had $M_W = 9.5$, but measured only 8.3 on the M_S scale. For the largest events, such as the Chilean 1960 earthquake, the energy released is more than 10^{19} joules.

United States   The strongest earthquake in American history, measuring 8.4 on the Richter scale, was near Prince William Sound, AK (80 miles east of Anchorage) on 1964 27 Mar. It killed 131 people and caused an estimated $750 million in damage; it also caused a tsunami 50 feet high that traveled 8,445 miles at 450 mph. The town of Kodiak was destroyed, and tremors were felt in California, Hawaii and Japan.

Material damage   The greatest physical devastation was in the earthquake on the Kanto plain, Japan, of 1923 Sep 1 (Mag. M_S, epicenter in Lat. 35° 15' NN, Long. 139° 30' NE); in Sagami Bay the sea bottom in one area sank 1,310 ft. The official total of people killed and missing in this *Shinsai* (great 'quake) and the resultant fires was 142,807. In Tokyo and Yokohama 575,000 dwellings were destroyed. The costs of the damage was estimated at $3.4 billion.

Worst death toll   The greatest estimate for a death toll is the 830,000 fatalities in a prolonged earthquake (*dizhen*) in the Shaanxi, Shanxi and Henan provinces of China, of 1556 Feb 2 (new style; January 23 old style).

The highest death toll in modern times has been in the Tangshan earthquake (Mag. $M_S = 7.9$) in eastern China on 1976 Jul 27 (local time was 3 A.M. Jul 28). The first figure published on 4 Jan 1977 revealed 655,237 killed, later adjusted to 750,000. On 22 Nov 1979 the New China News Agency inexplicably reduced the death toll to 242,000. The figure of 1,100,000 sometimes attributed to the eastern Mediterranean earthquake of 1202 May 20 is a gross exaggeration, since it includes those who died in a famine the following year. A more plausible death toll is *c.* 30,000.

United States   The highest death toll for the United States is 503 in the Great San Francisco Earthquake of 1906 Apr 18, which measured an estimated 8.3 on the Richter Scale. Accurate records were not kept at that time, and some experts believe the 503 deaths to be a low calculation. There was also no Richter scale, and this measurement, although it is the consensus, is debated.

VOLCANOES

The total number of known active volcanoes in the world is 1,343, of which many are submarine. The word *volcano* derives from the now-dormant Vulcano Island (from the Roman god of fire *Vulcanus*) in the Mediterranean.

Greatest explosion   The greatest explosion in historic times (possibly since Santoriní in the Aegean Sea, 60 miles north of Crete, in 1628 B.C.) occurred at *c.* 10 A.M. (local time), or 3:00 A.M. GMT, on 27 Aug 1883, with an eruption of Krakatoa, an island (then 18 miles^2) in the Sunda Strait, between Sumatra and Java, in Indonesia. One hundred and sixty-three villages were wiped out and 36,380 people killed by the wave it caused. Pumice was thrown 34 miles high and dust fell 3,313 miles away 10 days later. The explosion was recorded four hours later on the island of Rodrigues, 2,968 miles away, as "the roar of heavy guns," and was heard over one-thirteenth of the surface of the globe. This explosion, estimated to have had about 26 times the power of the greatest H-bomb test (by the USSR; for details of thermonuclear explosions, see Human World, Bombs), was still only a third of the Santoriní cataclysm.

United States   The most deaths from a volcanic eruption in the United States was 60 people, on 18 May 1980 from the eruption of Mt St. Helens, WA.

Greatest eruption   The total volume of matter discharged in the eruption of Tambora, a volcano on the Indonesian island of Sumbawa, 5–10 Apr 1815, was 36–43 miles^3. This compares with a probable 14–16 miles^3 ejected by Santoriní (see above) and 5 miles^3 ejected by Krakatoa (see above). The energy of the Tambora eruption, which lowered the height of the island by 4,100 ft from 13,450 ft to 9,350 ft, was 8.4×10^{19} joules. A crater 5 miles in diameter was formed. More than 92,000 people were killed or died as a result of the subsequent famine.

The ejecta in the Taupo eruption in New Zealand *c.* A.D. 130 has been estimated at 33 billion tons of pumice moving at one time at 400 mph. It flattened 6,200 miles^2 (over 26 times the devastated area of Mt St. Helens, which erupted in Washington State on 18 May 1980). Less than 20 percent of the 15.4 billion tons of pumice carried up into the air in this most violent of all documented volcanic events fell within 125 miles of the vent.

Longest lava flow   The longest lava flow in historic times is a mixture of *pahoehoe*, ropey lava (twisted cordlike solidifications) and *aa*, blocky lava, resulting from the eruption of Laki in 1783 in southeast Iceland, which flowed 40 1/2–43 1/2 miles. The largest-known prehistoric flow is the Roza basalt flow in North America *c.* 15 million years ago, which had an unsurpassed length (190 miles), area (15,400 miles^2) and volume (300 miles^3).

Largest active   Mauna Loa in Hawaii has the shape of a broad gentle dome 75 miles long and 31 miles wide (above sea level), with lava flows that occupy more than 1,980 miles^2 of the island. It has a total volume of 10,200 miles^2, of which 84.2 percent is below sea level. Its caldera (Spanish *caldaria*, boiling pot) or volcano crater, Mokuaweoweo, measures 4 miles^2 and is 500–600 ft deep. Mauna Loa rises 13,680 ft and has averaged one eruption every 4$^{1}/_{2}$ years since 1843, although none have occurred since 1984.

United States   The most currently active volcano in the contiguous 48 states is Mt St. Helens, located near Seattle, WA. There have been 25 registered erruptions over the past decade, the last on 14 Feb 1991.

Highest active   The highest volcano regarded as active is Ojos del Salado (which has fumaroles), at a height of 22,595 ft, on the frontier between Chile and Argentina.

United States   The highest volcano and the only active one in the contiguous 48 states is Mt St. Helens (see above). It was 9,677 ft pre-eruption and now stands at 8,364 ft.

Northernmost and southernmost   The northernmost volcano is Beeren Berg (7,470 ft) on the island of Jan Mayen (71° 05′ N) in the Greenland Sea. It erupted on 20 Sep 1970, and the island's 39 inhabitants (all male) had to be evacuated. It was possibly discovered by Henry Hudson, the English navigator and explorer (d. 1611), in 1607 or 1608, but was definitely visited by Jan Jacobsz Mayen (Netherlands) in 1614. It was annexed by Norway on 8 May 1929. The Ostenso seamount (5,825 ft), 346 miles from the North Pole at Lat. 85° 10′ N, Long. 133° W, was volcanic. The most southerly known active volcano is Mt Erebus (12,447 ft), on Ross Island (77° 35′ S) in Antarctica. It was discovered on 28 Jan 1841 by the expedition of Capt. (later Rear-Admiral Sir) James Clark Ross of the British Navy (1800–62), and first climbed at 10 A.M. on 10 Mar 1908 by a British party of five, led by Prof. Tannatt William Edgeworth David (1858–1934).

AVALANCHES

Greatest   The greatest natural avalanches, though rarely observed, occur in the Himalayas, but no estimates of their volume have been published. It was estimated that 120 million ft^3 of snow fell in an avalanche in the Italian Alps in 1885.

The 250-mph avalanche triggered by the Mt St. Helens eruption in Washington State on 18 May 1980 was estimated to measure 96 billion ft^3 (see Worst Natural Disasters in the World table).

GEYSERS

Tallest   The Waimangu (Maori "black water") geyser, in New Zealand, erupted to a height in excess of 1,500 ft in 1903, when it was erupting every 30–36 hours, but has not been active since late 1904. In August 1903 four people were killed during one of its violent eruptions.

Currently the world's tallest active geyser is the National Park Service's Steamboat Geyser, in Yellowstone National Park, WY. During the 1980s it erupted at intervals ranging from 19 days to more than four years, although there were occasions in the 1960s when it erupted as frequently as every 4–10 days. The maximum height ranges from 195–380 ft.

The greatest measured water discharge was an estimated 740,000–1,000,000 gallons by the Giant Geyser, also in Yellowstone National Park. However, this estimate, made in the 1950s, was only a rough calculation.

Violent Volcanoes

When Mount Pinatubo in the Philippines erupted in 1991, the whole world saw the destruction which an erupting volcano can cause. The total volume of matter discharged was some 2 miles^3, but this was not even the greatest eruption this century. Novarupta, in Alaska, holds this honor, yet pales into insignificance compared to past eruptions, as the chart shows.

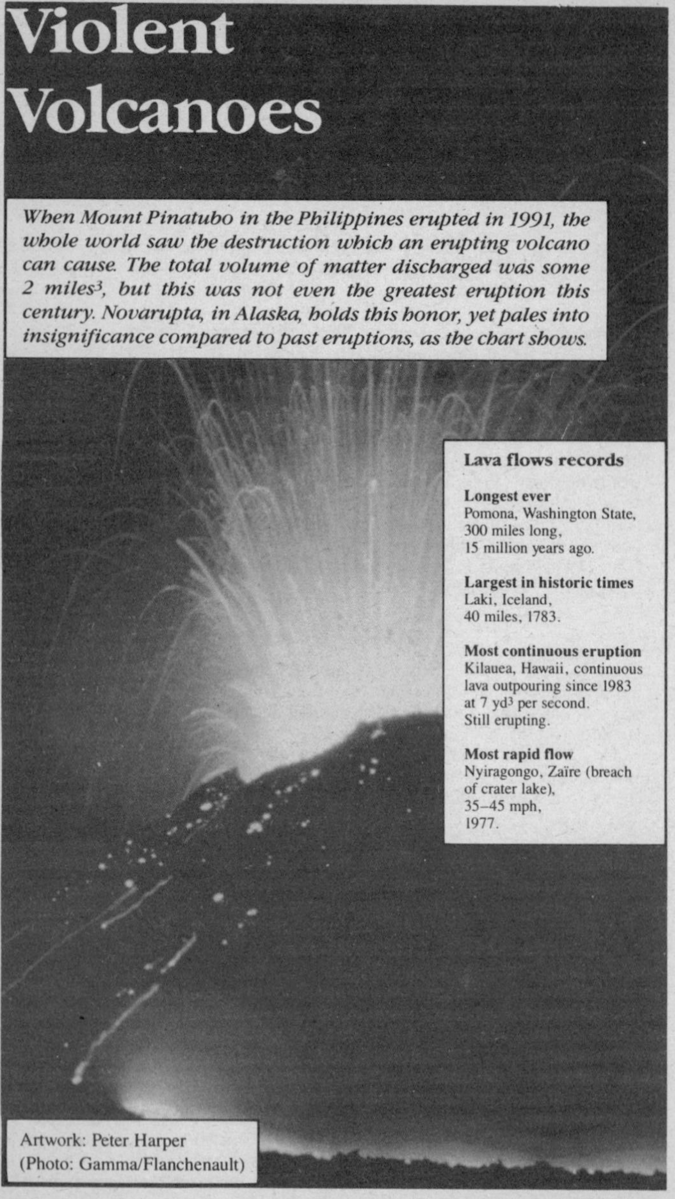

Lava flows records

Longest ever
Pomona, Washington State,
300 miles long,
15 million years ago.

Largest in historic times
Laki, Iceland,
40 miles, 1783.

Most continuous eruption
Kilauea, Hawaii, continuous
lava outpouring since 1983
at 7 yd^3 per second.
Still erupting.

Most rapid flow
Nyiragongo, Zaïre (breach
of crater lake),
35–45 mph,
1977.

Artwork: Peter Harper
(Photo: Gamma/Flanchenault)

In terms of lives lost, the most devastating volcanic eruption was that of Tambora, on the Indonesian island of Sumbawa in April 1815. Some 92,000 people lost their lives either directly, or as a result of the tsunamis—tidal waves—and the famine which followed. The eruption had far-reaching consequences, with an unusually cold summer in Europe and North America in 1816.

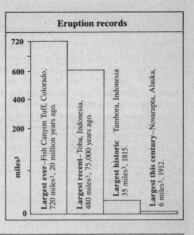

Eruption records

miles³

- **Largest ever**–Fish Canyon Tuff, Colorado, 720 miles³, 20 million years ago.
- **Largest recent**–Toba, Indonesia, 480 miles³, 75,000 years ago.
- **Largest historic** Tambora, Indonesia 35 miles³, 1815.
- **Largest this century**–Novarupta, Alaska, 6 miles³, 1912.

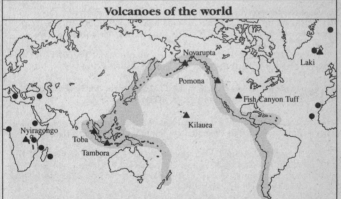

Volcanoes of the world

Novarupta
Laki
Pomona
Fish Canyon Tuff
Nyiragongo
Kilauea
Toba
Tambora

The name volcano derives from the now dormant Vulcano Island (from the god of fire, Vulcanus) in the Mediterranean. The total number of volcanoes in the world that might be described as active (believed to have erupted in the past 10,000 years) is 1,343, of which many are submarine. The greatest active concentration is in the so-called *Ring of Fire* (shown in shaded area on the map), which runs down the west coast of the Americas from Alaska to Chile and in a similar fashion down the east coast of Asia from Russia to New Zealand. It contains around 75 percent of the world's active volcanoes. Volcanic activity has also occurred in various other parts of the world, and some of the most notable of these are shown by •. Antarctica, although not shown on the map, also has volcanoes, including two that were discovered only in the 1980s.

WEATHER

The meteorological records given below necessarily relate largely to the last 150–170 years, since data before that time are both sparse and often unreliable. Reliable registering thermometers were introduced as recently as c. 1820. The longest continuous observations have been maintained at the Radcliffe Observatory, Oxford, Great Britain since 1814, and on a daily basis since 1874, though discontinuous records have enabled the Chinese to assert that 903 B.C. was a very bad winter.

Most equable temperature   The location with the most equable recorded temperature over a short period is Garapan, on Saipan in the Mariana Islands, Pacific Ocean. During the nine years from 1927–35, inclusive, the lowest temperature recorded was 67.3° F on 30 Jan 1934 and the highest was 88.5° F on 9 Sep 1931, giving an extreme range of 21.2° F.

Between 1911 and 1966 the Brazilian offshore island of Fernando de Noronha had a minimum temperature of 63.9° F on 17 Nov 1913 and a maximum of 90.0° F on 3 Mar 1968, 25 Dec 1972 and 17 Apr 1973, giving an extreme range of 26.1 deg F.

Annual mean temperature reading   The highest annual mean temperature in the United States is 78.2° F at Key West, FL, while the lowest mean temperature reading is 36.5° F at International Falls, MN.

Greatest temperature ranges   The greatest recorded temperature ranges in the world are around the Siberian "cold pole" in the east of Russia. Temperatures in Verkhoyansk (67° 33′ N, 133° 23′ E) have ranged 188° F, from –90° F to 98° F.

The greatest temperature variation recorded in a day is 100° F (a fall from 44° F to –56° F) at Browning, MT on 23–24 Jan 1916.

Highest shade temperature   The highest shade temperature ever recorded is 136° F at Al'Azīzīyah, Libya (alt. 367 ft) on 13 Sep 1922.

Hottest place   On an annual mean basis, with readings taken over a six-year period from 1960 to 1966, the temperature at Dallol, in Ethiopia, was 94° F.

The highest temperature ever recorded in the United States was 134° F at Greenland Ranch, Death Valley, CA on 10 Jul 1913. In Death Valley, maximum temperatures of over 120° F were recorded on 43 consecutive days, between 6 Jul and 17 Aug 1917.

At Marble Bar, Western Australia (maximum 121° F), 162 consecutive days with maximum temperatures of over 100° F were recorded between 30 Oct 1923 and 8 Apr 1924.

At Wyndham, also in Western Australia, the temperature reached 90° F or more on 333 days in 1946.

Driest place   The annual mean rainfall on the Pacific coast of Chile between Arica and Antofagasta is less than 0.004 in.

22 January 1943

Record temperature change

FORECASTERS GOT IT WRONG

An incredible weather record was set today, when the town of Spearfish, South Dakota, had one of the strangest mornings imaginable.

At 7:30, after a freezing night, and with the temperature rising, it was still - 4° F, but by 7:32 it was a comparatively mild 45° F. This represents an astounding rise of 49 degrees F in two minutes, or more than 1 degree F every 2 ½ seconds. Never before has such a freakish rise been recorded.

The weather forecasters may sometimes get criticized for inaccurate predictions, but not even the people of Spearfish could really blame them this time!

United States   In 1929 no precipitation was recorded for Death Valley, CA. Currently the driest state is Nevada, with an annual rainfall of only nine inches.

Longest drought   Desierto de Atacama, in Chile, experiences virtually no rain, although several times a century a squall may strike a small area of it.

United States   Commonly referred to as "Dust Bowl Days," the Great Plains suffered from drought conditions from the summer of 1930 to the fall of 1940. At its height, in the winter of 1935–36, the drought affected 50 million acres in parts of New Mexico, Texas, Oklahoma, Kansas and Colorado. During August 1934, in western Kansas, the Drought Severity Index reached –5.96. Below –4.0 on this index indicates extreme drought conditions.

The most intense drought in the United States lasted 57 months, from May 1952 to March 1957, in western Kansas. The Drought Severity Index reached a lowest point ever of –6.2, in September 1956.

Lowest screen temperature   A record low of –128.6° F was registered at Vostok, Antarctica (alt. 11,220 ft) on 21 Jul 1983.

The coldest permanently inhabited place is the Siberian village of Oymyakon (pop. 4,000), 63° 16′ N, 143° 15′ E (2,300 ft), in Russia, where the temperature reached –90° F in 1933, and an unofficial –98° F has been published more recently.

United States   The lowest temperature ever recorded in the United States was –79.8° F on 23 Jan 1971 in Prospect Creek, AK.

The lowest temperature in the continental United States was –69.7° F in Rogers Pass, MT on 20 Jan 1954.

Coldest place   Polus Nedostupnosti (Pole of Cold), Antarctica at 78° S, 96° E, is the coldest place in the world, with an extrapolated annual mean of –72° F.

The coldest measured mean is –70° F, at Plateau Station, Antarctica.

HOTTEST PLACE   Death Valley—the name dates from the mid-19th century, when a group of migrants endured great suffering while crossing it. One of its neighboring mountains is called Funeral Mountain.   (Photo: Spectrum Colour Library/G.R. Richardson)

United States   Langdon (Cavalier County), ND had 41 days below 0° F, from 11 Nov 1935–20 Feb 1936. Langdon also holds the record for most days below 32° F, with 92 days from 30 Nov 1935–29 Feb 1936.

Wettest place   By average annual rainfall, the wettest place in the world is Mawsynram, in Meghalaya State, India, with 467¹/₂ in per annum.

United States   The wettest state is Louisiana, with an annual rainfall of 56 inches.

Most rainy days   Mt Wai-'ale-'ale (5,148 ft), Kauai, HI has up to 350 rainy days per year.

Most intense rainfall   Difficulties attend rainfall readings for very short periods, but the figure of 1¹/₂ in in one min at Barst, Guadeloupe on 26 Nov 1970 is regarded as the most intense recorded in modern times.

Greatest rainfall   A record 73.62 in of rain fell in 24 hours in Cilaos (alt. 3,940 ft), La Réunion, Indian Ocean on 15 and 16 Mar 1952. This is equal to 8,327 tons of rain per acre.

For a calendar month, the record is 366 in, at Cherrapunji, Meghalaya, India in July 1861.

The 12-month record was also set at Cherrapunji, with 1,041.8 in between 1 Aug 1860 and 31 Jul 1861.

United States   In the United States, the 24-hr record is 19 in at Alvin, TX, on 25–26 Jul 1979. Over a 12-month period, 739 in fell at Kukui, Maui, HI from December 1981–December 1982. The greatest rainfall in the coterminous states is 184.56 in, at Wynoochee Oxbow, WA in 1931.

Deadliest floods   The most deaths from a flood in the United States was more than 2,000 people, at Johnstown, PA on 31 May 1889. First the Conemaugh River, just above Johnstown, overflowed its banks, reaching 20 ft above low water before the flood gauge swept away. Four hours later, a dam gave way at the South Fork Creek of the Little Conemaugh River 15 miles upstream from Johnstown. This combination of water formed a wall 20–30 ft high, rushing through the valley on the way to Johnstown at a rate of 15 mph.

The greatest property damage from a floodstorm in the United States is $2.1 billion, with 122 deaths, on 22 Jun 1972 when the remains of Hurricane Agnes brought heavy rains (12 inches) to Pennsylvania and New York. Wilkes Barre, PA on the Susquehanna River suffered most.

Windiest place   The Commonwealth Bay, George V Coast, Antarctica, where gales reach 200 mph, is the world's windiest place.

Highest surface wind speed   A surface wind speed of 231 mph was recorded at Mt Washington (6,288 ft), NH on 12 Apr 1934.

The fastest speed at a low altitude was registered on 8 Mar 1972 at the USAF base at Thule, Greenland (145 ft), when a peak speed of 207 mph was recorded.

The fastest speed measured to date in a tornado is 280 mph at Wichita Falls, TX on 2 Apr 1958.

Hurricanes   The most commonly used scale to measure the size of a hurricane is the Saffir-Simpson Scale, which rates hurricanes on a scale of one to five, five being the most severe.

The most damaging hurricane in the United States was Hurricane Hugo, which hit the mainland 21–22 Sep 1989 after devastating a number of islands in the Caribbean. The storm made landfall at Sullivan Island, northeast of Charleston, SC. On crossing the mainland, Hugo measured four on the Saffir-Simpson Scale. Winds measured 135 mph and 28 people were killed.

The greatest number of fatalities from an American hurricane is an estimated 6,000 deaths on 8 Sep 1900 in Galveston Island, TX.

The fastest sustained winds in a hurricane in the United States measured 200 mph, with 210 mph gusts, on 17–18 Aug 1969, when Hurricane Camille hit the Mississippi/Alabama coast at Pass Christian, MS. Hurricane Camille also had the greatest storm surge in the United States.

The greatest forward speed by a hurricane in the United States was in excess of 60 mph, with an average speed of 58 mph, for the Great New England Hurricane on 21 Sep 1938, when it struck central Long Island at Babylon, NY. The hurricane continued on to landfall at Milford, CT.

Tornadoes   The most deaths from one tornado in the United States is 695, on 18 Mar 1925 in Missouri, Illinois and Indiana. This tornado also ranks first as the tornado with the longest continuous track on the ground, 219 miles; first with a 3.5-hour continuous duration on the ground; first in total area of destruction, covering 164 miles^2; first in dimensions, with the funnel sometimes exceeding one mile wide; and third in forward speed, reaching a maximum of 73 mph, while averaging 62 mph over its duration.

The state with the most tornadoes recorded in a year is Texas, with 232 in 1967.

Highest waterspout   The highest waterspout of which there is a reliable record was one observed on 16 May 1898 off Eden, New South Wales, Australia. A theodolite reading from the shore gave its height as 5,014 ft. It was about 10 ft in diameter.

Heaviest hailstones   The heaviest hailstones on record, weighing up to 2¼ lb, are reported to have killed 92 people in the Gopalganj district of Bangladesh on 14 Apr 1986.

United States   The heaviest hailstone in the United States weighed 1.671 lb, had a circumference of 17.5 in and a diameter of 5.62 in in Coffeyville, KS on 3 Sep 1970.

Greatest snowfall   A total of 1,224½ in of snow fell over a 12-month period from 19 Feb 1971 to 18 Feb 1972 at Paradise, Mt Rainier, in Washington State.

The record for a single snowstorm is 189 in at Mt Shasta Ski Bowl, CA from 13–19 Feb 1959, and for a 24-hr period the record snowfall is 78 in, at Mile 47 Camp, Cooper River Division, AK on 7 Feb 1963.

The greatest depth of snow on the ground was 37 ft 7 in at Tamarac, CA in March 1911.

Cloud extremes   The highest standard cloud form is cirrus, averaging

Longest-lasting rainbow   A rainbow lasting over three hours was reported from the coastal border of Gwynedd and Clwyd, North Wales, Great Britain on 14 Aug 1979.

Lightning, most times struck   The only man in the world to be struck by lightning seven times is ex-park ranger Roy C. Sullivan (USA), the human lightning conductor of Virginia. His attraction for lightning began in 1942 (lost big toenail), and was resumed in July 1969 (lost eyebrows), in July 1970 (left shoulder seared), on 16 Apr 1972 (hair set on fire), on 7 Aug 1973 (hair set afire again and legs seared), on 5 Jun 1976 (ankle injured), and he was sent to Waynesboro Hospital with chest and stomach burns on 25 Jun 1977 after being struck while fishing. In September 1983 he died by his own hand, reportedly rejected in love.

Largest mirage   The largest mirage on record was that sighted in the Arctic at 83° N 103° W by Donald B. MacMillan in 1913. This type of mirage, known as the Fata Morgana, appeared as the same "hills, valleys, snow-capped peaks extending through at least 120 degrees of the horizon" that Peary had misidentified as Crocker Land six years earlier. On 17 Jul 1939 a mirage of the mountain Snaefells Jokull (4,715 ft) on Iceland was seen from the sea at a distance of 335–350 miles.

Most sunshine   The annual average at Yuma, AZ is 90 percent (over 4,000 hours of sunshine).
St Petersburg, FL recorded 768 consecutive sunny days from 9 Feb 1967 to 17 Mar 1969.

Least sunshine   At the South Pole there is zero sunshine for 182 days every year, and at the North Pole the same applies for 176 days.

Greatest flood   Scientists reported the discovery of the largest freshwater flood in history in January 1993. It occurred *c.* 18,000 years ago when an ancient ice dam lake in the Altay Mountains in Siberia, Russia, broke, allowing the water to pour out. The lake was estimated to be 75 miles long and 2,500 ft deep. The main flow of water was reported to be 1,600 ft deep and traveling at 100 mph.

27,000 ft and higher, but the rare nacreous or mother-of-pearl formation may reach nearly 80,000 ft (see also Noctilucent clouds). A cirrus cloud is composed almost entirely of ice crystals at temperatures of –40° F or below. The lowest is stratus, below 1,500 ft.

The cloud form with the greatest vertical range is cumulonimbus, which has been observed to reach a height of nearly 68,000 ft in the tropics.

Upper atmosphere   The lowest temperature ever recorded in the atmosphere is –225° F at an altitude of about 50–60 miles, during noctilucent cloud research above Kronogård, Sweden from 27 Jul to 7 Aug 1963.

Thunder-days   In Tororo, Uganda an average of 251 days of thunder per year was recorded for the 10-year period 1967–76.
Between Lat. 35° N and 35° S there are some 3,200 thunderstorms

every 12 nighttime hours, some of which can be heard at a range of 18 miles.

Lightning The visible length of lightning strokes varies greatly. In mountainous regions, when clouds are very low, the flash may be less than 300 ft long. In flat country with very high clouds, a cloud-to-Earth flash may measure 4 miles, though in the most extreme cases such flashes have been measured at 20 miles. The intensely bright central core of the lightning channel is extremely narrow. Some authorities suggest that its diameter is as little as 1/2 in. This core is surrounded by a "corona envelope" (glow discharge), which may measure 10–20 ft in diameter.

The speed of a discharge varies from 100–1,000 miles/sec for the downward leader track, and reaches up to 87,000 miles/sec (nearly half the speed of light) for the powerful return stroke.

Every few million strokes there is a giant discharge, in which the cloud-to-Earth and return strokes flash from and to the top of the thunderclouds. In these "positive giants" energy of up to 3 billion joules (3×10^{16} ergs) has been recorded. The temperature reaches about 54,032° F, which is higher than that of the surface of the Sun.

Most people killed Eighty-one people were killed when an airplane was struck by lightning and crashed near Elkton, MD on 8 Dec 1963. The state with the greatest number of deaths by lightning is Florida, with 313 since 1959, when records were first kept.

Fog The international definition of fog states that it exists when horizontal visibility is below 0.62 miles (1 km); while heavy fog takes place when there is less than 0.25 miles (0.4 km) of visibility.

Longest Sea-level fogs—with visibility less than 3,000 ft—persist for weeks on the Grand Banks, Newfoundland, Canada, with the average being more than 120 days per year.

Cape Disappointment, WA has the most fog days in the United States, with an average of 2,552 hours (or 106 complete days) of heavy fog per year.

Least Key West, FL averages less than one day a year of heavy fog.

Barometric pressure The highest barometric pressure ever recorded was 32 in at Agata, Siberia, Russia (alt. 862 ft) on 31 Dec 1968.

The lowest sea-level pressure was 425.69 in in Typhoon Tip, 300 miles west of Guam, Pacific Ocean, at Lat. 16° 44′ N, Long. 137° 46′ E, on 12 Oct 1979.

The highest barometric pressure recorded in the United States was 31.43 in at Barrow, AK on 3 Jan 1970. The highest in the coterminous states was 31.40 in, at Helena, MT on 9 Jan 1962.

The lowest barometric pressure recorded in the United States was 26.35 for the 1935 Labor Day Hurricane, which crossed the US coastline at Matecumbe Key, FL at 10:00 P.M. on 2 Sep 1935.

Humidity and discomfort Human comfort or discomfort depends not merely on temperature but on the combination of temperature, humidity, radiation and wind speed. The United States Weather Bureau uses a Temperature–Humidity Index (THI), which equals two-fifths of the sum of the dry and wet bulb thermometer readings plus 15.

Greatest temperature–humidity index A THI of 98.2 has been twice recorded in Death Valley, CA—on 27 Jul 1966 (119° F and 31 percent) and on 12 Aug 1970 (117° F and 37 percent).

GEMS, JEWELS AND PRECIOUS STONES

DIAMOND

Largest The largest diamond is 3,106 carats and was found on 25 Jan 1905 in the Premier Mine, Pretoria, South Africa. It was named *The Cullinan* after Sir Thomas Cullinan, who was chairman of the Syndicate that discovered the diamond pipe three years earlier. It was cut into 106 polished diamonds and produced the largest cut fine quality colorless diamond, weighing 530.2 carats. Several large pieces of low quality diamonds have been found, including a carbonado of 3,167 carats discovered in Brazil in 1905, but these stones are of very poor quality.

The largest-known single piece of rough diamond still in existence weighs 1,462 carats and is retained by De Beers Central Selling Organization in London, Great Britain for exhibition purposes.

Largest cut The largest cut diamond is the 545.67-carat gem known as the *Unnamed Brown*, which was fashioned from a 775.50-carat rough into a fire rose cushion cut. It acted as a forerunner to *Centenary Diamond*, the world's largest flawless top color modern fancy cut diamond at 273.85 carats. Both stones were found at the Premier Diamond Mine and were designed by master cutter Gabi Tolkowsky. The stones are owned by De Beers Consolidated Mines Ltd.

Largest natural intense fancy blue The largest diamond that is a natural intense fancy blue is the 45.52-carat *Hope Diamond*, named after a London banker, Henry Thomas Hope. The diamond has a long and complex history and is now on display in the Smithsonian Institute, Washington, D.C.

Smallest brilliant cut The smallest diamond is 0.0001022 carat, with a diameter of 0.009 in. The diamond was polished with all 57 facets by D. Drukker & Zn NV of Amsterdam, Netherlands.

Rarest color The rarest diamond color is blood red. The largest is a 5.05-carat flawless stone found in Lichtenburg, South Africa in 1927; it is now owned by a private collector of fancy colored diamonds.

Highest-priced Many polished diamond sales are considered private transactions, and the prices paid are not disclosed.

A superb 11-sided pear-shaped mixed-cut diamond of 101.84 carats was

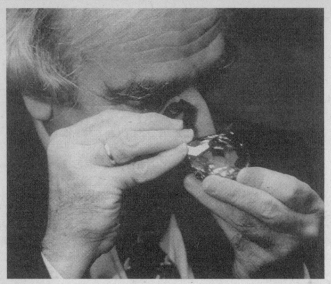

LARGEST CUT DIAMOND   Master cutter Gabi Tolkowsky examines the largest cut diamond, the Unnamed Brown. (Photo: De Beers)

bought at Sotheby's, Geneva, Switzerland on 14 Nov 1990 for $12,760,000. The stone is now known as the *Mouwad Splendour*.

The highest price known to be paid for a rough diamond was $10 million for a 255.10-carat stone from Guinea, by the William Goldberg Diamond Corporation in partnership with the Chow Tai Fook Jewelery Co. Ltd. of Hong Kong, in March 1989.

The record per carat is $926,315.79 for a 0.95-carat fancy purplish-red stone sold at Christie's, New York on 28 Apr 1987.

EMERALD

Largest cut   An 86,136-carat 37-lb 15.6 oz natural beryl was found in Carnaiba, Brazil in August 1974. It was carved by Richard Chan in Hong Kong and valued at £718,000 ($1,120,080) in 1982.

Largest single crystal   The largest single emerald crystal of gem quality was 7,025 carats. It was found in 1969 at the Cruces Mine, near Gachala, Colombia, and is owned by a private mining concern. Larger Brazilian and Russian stones do exist, but they are of low quality.

Highest-priced   The highest price paid for a single lot of emeralds was $3,080,000, for an emerald and diamond necklace made by Cartier, London, Great Britain in 1937 (a total of 12 stones weighing 108.74 carats), which was sold at Sotheby's, New York on 26 Oct 1989.

The highest price for a single emerald is $2,126,646, for a 19.77-carat emerald and diamond ring made by Cartier in 1958, which was sold at Sotheby's, Geneva, Switzerland on 2 Apr 1987. This also represented the record price per carat for an emerald, at $107,569.

GOLD

Largest nugget The 7,560-oz *Holtermann Nugget*, found on 19 Oct 1872 in the Beyers & Holtermann Star of Hope mine, Hill End, New South Wales, Australia, contained some 220 lb of gold in a 630-lb slab of slate.

Largest pure nugget The *Welcome Stranger*, found at Moliagul, Victoria, Australia in 1869, yielded 2,248 troy oz of pure gold from 2,280¼ oz.

OPAL

Largest The largest single piece of gem-quality white opal, *Jupiter-Five*, was 26,350 carats, found at the Jupiter Field at Coober Pedy in South Australia. It has been named *Jupiter-Five* and is in private ownership.

Largest polished The largest free-form cabochon cut precious opal, *Galaxy*, is 3,749 carats and measures $5^1/2 \times 4 \times 1^5/8$ in. It was excavated in Brazil in 1976.

Largest black A stone found on 4 Feb 1972 at Lightning Ridge, New South Wales, Australia produced a finished gem of 1,520 carats, called the *Empress of Glengarry*. It measures $4^3/4 \times 3^1/8 \times 5/8$ in, and is owned by Peter Gray.

Largest rough black The largest gem-quality uncut black opal was also found at Lightning Ridge, on 3 Nov 1986. After cleaning, it weighs 2,020 carats and measures $4 \times 2^5/8 \times 2^1/2$ in. It has been named *Halley's Comet* and is owned by a team of opal miners known as The Lunatic Hill Syndicate.

PEARL

Largest The 14 lb 1 oz *Pearl of Lao-tze* was found at Palawan, Philippines on 7 May 1934 in the shell of a giant clam. The property of Wilburn Dowell Cobb until his death, this $9^1/2$-in-long by $5^1/2$-in-diameter molluscan concretion was bought at auction on 15 May 1980 in San Francisco, CA by Peter Hoffman and Victor Barbish for $200,000. An appraisal by the San Francisco Gem Laboratory in May 1984 suggested a value of $40–42 million.

Largest abalone A baroque abalone pearl measuring $2^3/8 \times 2 \times 1^1/8$ in and 469.13 carats was found at Salt Point State Park, CA in May 1990. It is owned by Wesley Rankin and is called the *Big Pink*. It has been valued in the United States at $4.7 million.

Largest cultured A $1^1/2$-in round, 138.25-carat cultured pearl weighing 1 oz was found near Samui Island, off Thailand, in January 1988. The stone is owned by the Mikimoto Pearl Island Company, Japan.

Largest amber   The largest amber, *Burma Amber*, is 33 lb 10 oz and is located in the Natural History Museum, London, Great Britain. Amber is a fossil resin derived from extinct coniferous trees, and often contains trapped insects.

Crystal ball   The world's largest flawless rock crystal ball is 106.75 lb and 13 in in diameter, and was cut in China from Burmese rough material. It is now in the Smithsonian Institute in Washington, D.C.

Largest jade   A single lens of nephrite jade was found in the Yukon Territory of Canada in July 1992. It weighed 636 tons and is owned by Yukon Jade Ltd.

Highest-priced sapphire   A step-cut stone of 62.02 carats was sold as a sapphire and diamond ring at Sotheby's, St Moritz, Switzerland on 20 Feb 1988 for $2,791,723.

Largest topaz   The rectangular, cushion-cut 22,892.5-carat *American Golden Topaz*, with 172 facets and $5^7/8$ in in overall width, has been on display at the Smithsonian Institute, Washington, D.C. since 4 May 1988.

Highest-priced   *La Régente*, an egg-shaped pearl weighing 302.68 grains and formerly part of the French crown jewels, was sold at Christie's, Geneva, Switzerland on 12 May 1988 for $864,280.

PLATINUM

Largest   The largest platinum nugget ever found weighs 340 oz and was discovered in the Ural Mountains in Russia in 1843. It was melted down shortly after its discovery.

Largest existing   The largest surviving platinum nugget, the *Ural Giant*, weighs 277 oz and is currently in the custody of the Diamond Foundation in the Kremlin, Moscow, Russia.

RUBY

Largest star   The *Eminent Star* ruby, believed to be of Indian origin, is the largest ruby, at 6,465 carats. It is an oval cabochon with a six ray star, and measures $4^1/4 \times 3^5/8 \times 2^1/4$ in. It is owned by Eminent Gems Inc. of New York.

Largest   In July 1985 jeweler James Kazanjian of Beverly Hills, CA displayed an 8,500-carat $5^1/2$-in-tall red corundum carved to resemble the Liberty Bell.

Highest-priced   A ruby and diamond ring made by Chaumet, in Paris, France, weighs 32.08 carats and was sold at Sotheby's, New York on 26

Oct 1989 for $4,620,000. The record per carat is $227,300 for a ruby ring with a stone weighing 15.97 carats, which was sold at Sotheby's, New York on 18 Oct 1988.

SAPPHIRE

Largest carved The largest carved sapphire was 2,302 carats and was found at Anakie, Queensland, Australia in *c*. 1935. This corundum was carved into a 1,318-carat head of Abraham Lincoln and is now in the custody of the Kazanjian Foundation of Los Angeles, CA.

Largest star The largest double star Sapphire is the 9,719.50 carat gem *The Lone Star*. It was cut in London, Great Britain in November 1989 and is owned by Harold Roper.

LIVING WORLD

- **ANIMAL KINGDOM**
- **EXTINCT ANIMALS**
- **PLANT KINGDOM**
- **PROTISTA, FUNGI, PROCARYOTA**
- **PARKS, ZOOS, OCEANARIA, AQUARIA**

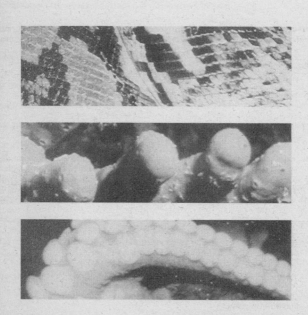

ANIMAL KINGDOM

GENERAL RECORDS

Noisiest The low-frequency pulses made by blue whales when communicating with each other have been measured up to 188 decibels, making them the loudest sounds emitted by any living source. They have been detected 530 miles away.

The noisiest land animals in the world are the howling monkeys (*Alouatta*) of Central and South America. The males have an enlarged bony structure at the top of the windpipe that enables the sound to reverberate, and their fearsome screams have been described as a cross between the bark of a dog and the bray of a donkey increased a thousandfold. Once they are in full voice they can be clearly heard for distances up to 10 miles.

Most fertile It has been calculated that a single cabbage aphid (*Brevicoryne brassica*) can give rise in a year to a mass of descendants weighing 906 million tons, more than three times the total weight of the world's human population. Fortunately the mortality rate is tremendous!

Strongest In proportion to their size, the strongest animals are the larger beetles of the family Scarabaeidae, which are found mainly in the tropics. In tests carried out on a rhinoceros beetle (*Dynastinae*) it was able to support 850 times its own weight on its back (compared with 25 percent of its body weight for an adult elephant).

Strongest bite Experiments carried out with a Snodgrass gnathodynamometer (shark-bite meter) at the Lerner Marine Laboratory in Bimini, Bahamas revealed that a 6-ft-6¾-in-long dusky shark (*Carcharhinus obscurus*) could exert a force of 132 lb between its jaws. This is equivalent to a pressure of 22 tons/in² at the tips of the teeth.

Suspended animation In 1846 two specimens of the desert snail *Eremina desertorum* were presented to the British Museum (Natural History) in London as dead exhibits. They were glued to a small tablet and placed on display. Four years later, in March 1850, the museum staff, suspecting that one of the snails was still alive, removed it from the tablet and placed it in tepid water. The

Largest structure The largest structure ever built by living creatures is the 1,260-mile-long Great Barrier Reef, off Queensland, Australia, covering an area of 80,000 miles². It consists of countless millions of dead and living stony corals (order Madreporaria or Scleractinia). Over 350 species of coral are currently found there, and its accretion is estimated to have taken 600 million years.

REGENERATION Sponges, which are made up of a mass of cells and fibers, can undergo complete regeneration from fragments or even individual cells. This fingerlike *Latrunculia corticata* of the Red Sea is just one of about 5,000 known species. (Photo: Planet Earth Pictures/Warren Williams)

snail moved and later began to feed. This hardy little creature lived for another two years before it fell into a torpor and then died.

Regeneration The sponge (*Porifera*) has the most remarkable powers of regeneration of lost parts of any animal, as it can regrow its entire body from a tiny fragment of itself. If a sponge is squeezed through a fine-meshed silk gauze, each piece of separated tissue will live as an individual.

Most dangerous The world's most dangerous animals (excluding human beings) are the malarial parasites of the genus *Plasmodium* carried by mosquitoes of the genus *Anopheles*, which, if we exclude wars and accidents, have probably been responsible directly or indirectly for 50 percent of all human deaths since the Stone Age. Even today, despite major campaigns to eradicate malaria, at least 200 million people are afflicted by the disease each year, and more than one million babies and children die annually from it in Africa alone.

Most poisonous The most active known poison found naturally among animals is the batrachotoxin derived from the skin secretions of the golden poison-dart frog (*Phyllobates terribilis*) of western Colombia, which are at least 20 times more toxic than those of any other known poison-dart frog (human handlers have to wear thick gloves); an average adult specimen contains enough poison (0.000067 oz) to kill nearly 1,500 people. This species is preyed upon by the frog-eating snake (*Leimadophis epinephelus*), which is thought to be immune to its poison.

Largest colonies The black-tailed prairie dog (*Cynomys ludovicianus*), a rodent of the family Sciuridae found in the western United States and northern

Mexico, builds the largest colonies. One single "town" discovered in 1901 contained about 400 million individuals and was estimated to cover 24,000 miles^2.

Greatest concentration   The greatest concentration of animals ever recorded was a huge swarm of Rocky Mountain locusts (*Melanoplus spretus*) that passed over Nebraska on 15–25 Aug 1875. According to one local scientist who watched their movements for five days, these locusts covered an area of 198,600 miles^2 as they flew over the state. If he overestimated the size of the swarm by 50 percent, it still covered 99,300 miles^2, which is approximately the area of Colorado or Oregon. It has been calculated that this swarm of locusts contained at least 12.5 trillion insects, with an aggregate weight of 27.5 million tons. For unexplained reasons, this pest mysteriously disappeared in 1902 and has not been seen since.

Most prodigious eater   The larva of the Polyphemus moth (*Antheraea polyphemus*) of North America consumes an amount equal to 86,000 times its own birth weight in the first 56 days of its life. In human terms, this would be equivalent to a 7-lb baby taking in 300 tons of nourishment!

Most valuable   The most valuable animals in cash terms are thoroughbred racehorses. The most ever paid for a yearling was $13.1 million on 23 Jul 1985 at Keeneland, KY by Robert Sangster and partners for Seattle Dancer. (See Horse Racing.)

Greatest size difference   Although many differences exist in the animal world between the males and females of species, the most striking difference in size can be seen in the marine worm *Bonellia viridis*. The females of this species are 4–40 in long compared with just 0.04–0.12 in for the male, making the females millions of times heavier than the males.

MAMMALS *Mammalia*

Largest   The longest and heaviest mammal in the world, and the largest animal ever recorded, is the blue or sulfur-bottom whale (*Balaenoptera musculus*), also called Sibbald's rorqual. Newborn calves measure 21 ft 3^1/$_2$ in–28^1/$_2$ ft in length and weigh up to 6,614 lbs. The barely visible ovum of the blue whale, weighing a fraction of a milligram, grows to a weight of *c.* 29 tons in 22^3/$_4$ months, made up of 10^3/$_4$ months' gestation and the first 12 months of life. This is equivalent to an increase of 30 billion.

Despite being protected by law since 1967 and the implementation of a global ban on commercial whaling, the population of the blue whale has declined to tens of thousands from peak estimates of about 220,000 at the turn of the century.

Heaviest   A female blue whale weighing 209 tons and measuring 90 ft 6 in was caught in the Southern Ocean on 20 Mar 1947.

1-Mile Challenge

The chart shows the times taken to cover one mile. Some figures are theoretical, based on extrapolations of available peak times.

Based on these calculations, in the time it takes the snail to walk one mile, the human in the rocket would travel some 4.6 million miles and the car about 124,000 miles. The tortoise, meanwhile, will have progressed 54 miles.

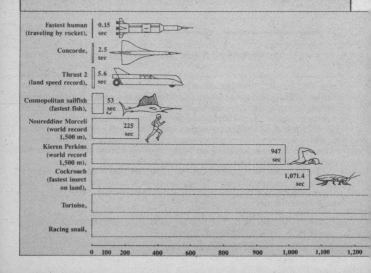

Fastest human (traveling by rocket),	0.15 sec	
Concorde,	2.5 sec	
Thrust 2 (land speed record),	5.6 sec	
Cosmopolitan sailfish (fastest fish),	53 sec	
Noureddine Morceli (world record 1,500 m),	225 sec	
Kieren Perkins (world record 1,500 m),	947 sec	
Cockroach (fastest insect on land),	1,071.4 sec	
Tortoise,		
Racing snail,		

0   100   200   400   600   800   900   1,000   1,100   1,200

Longest   The longest specimen ever recorded was a female blue whale landed in 1909 at Grytviken, South Georgia, Falkland Islands in the South Atlantic; it measured 110 ft 2¹/₂ in in length.

Deepest dive   In 1970 American scientists, by triangulating the location clicks of sperm whales, calculated that the maximum depth reached by this species was 8,202 ft. However, on 25 Aug 1969 a bull sperm whale was killed 100 miles south of Durban, South Africa after it had surfaced from a dive lasting 1 hr 5 min, and inside its stomach were found two small sharks that had been swallowed about an hour earlier. These were later identified as of the *Scymnodon* species, a type of dogfish found only on the sea floor. At this distance from land the depth of water exceeds 9,876 ft for a radius of 30–40 miles, which suggests that the sperm whale sometimes descends to a depth of over 9,840 ft when seeking food and is limited by pressure of time rather than by water pressure.

Slowest growth   The slowest growth in the animal kingdom is that of the deep-sea clam *Tindaria callistisormis* of the North Atlantic, which takes *c.* 100 years to reach a length of 0.31 in.

Largest eye   The Atlantic giant squid has the largest eye of any animal, living or extinct. It has been estimated that the one recorded at Thimble Tickle Bay had eyes 15³/₄ in in diameter—almost twice the width of this open book! (See Mollusks.)

Greatest weight loss   During a 7-month lactation period, a 132-ton female blue whale (*Balaenoptera musculus*) can lose up to 25 percent of her body weight nursing her calf.

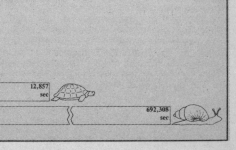

12,857
sec

692,308
sec

Largest on land   The largest living land animal is the African bush elephant (*Loxodonta africana*). The average adult bull stands 10 ft 6 in at the shoulder and weighs 6.3 tons. The largest specimen ever recorded was a bull shot in Mucusso, Angola on 7 Nov 1974. Lying on its side this elephant measured 13 ft 8 in a projected line from the highest point of the shoulder to the base of the forefoot, indicating that its standing height must have been about 13 ft. Other measurements included an overall length of 35 ft (tip of extended trunk to tip of extended tail) and a forefoot circumference of 5 ft 11 in. The weight was computed to be 13.5 tons.

Tallest   The endangered desert elephant of Damaraland in Namibia (reduced to 84 individuals in August 1981) is the tallest species of elephant in the world because it has proportionately longer legs than other elephants.

The tallest elephant ever recorded was a bull shot near Sesfontein in Damaraland, Namibia on 4 Apr 1978 after it had reportedly killed 11 people and caused widespread crop damage. Lying on its side, this mountain of flesh measured 14½ ft in a projected line from the shoulder to the base of the forefoot, indicating a standing height of about 13 ft 10 in. Other measurements included an overall length of 34 ft 1 in, and a forefoot circumference of 5 ft 2 in. This particular animal weighed an estimated 9 tons.

Largest marine   The largest toothed mammal ever recorded is the sperm whale (*Physeter catodon*), also called the cachalot. In the summer of 1950 a record-sized bull measuring 67 ft 11 in was captured off the Kurile Islands in the Pacific by a Soviet whaling fleet, but much larger bulls were reported in the early days of whaling. The 16-ft-4¾-in-long lower jaw of a sperm whale exhibited in the British Museum (Natural History) in London belonged to a bull measuring nearly 84 ft, and similar lengths have been reported for other outsized individuals killed.

Tallest on land   The giraffe (*Giraffa camelopardalis*), which is now found only in the dry savannah and semidesert areas of Africa south of the Sahara, is the tallest living animal. The tallest ever recorded was a Masai bull (*G. c. tippelskirchi*) named George, received at Chester Zoo, Great Britain on 8 Jan 1959 from Kenya. His "horns" *almost* grazed the roof of the 20-ft-high Giraffe House when he was nine years old. George died on 22 Jul 1969. Less-credible heights of up to 23 ft (measured between pegs) have been claimed for bulls shot in the field.

Smallest on land   Kitti's hog-nosed bat (*Craseonycteristhonglongyai*), also called the bumblebee bat, has a wing span of about 6.3 in and weighs 0.06–0.07 oz. It is confined to about 21 limestone caves on the Kwae Noi River, Kanchanaburi, Thailand. (See Bats.)

The smallest land mammal in terms of length is Savi's white-toothed pygmy shrew, also called the Etruscan shrew (*Suncus etruscus*), which has a head and body length of 1.32–2.04 in, a tail length of 0.94–1.14 in and weighs 0.05–0.09 oz. It is found along the Mediterranean coast and southwards to Cape Province, South Africa. (See Insectivores.)

Smallest marine   In terms of weight, the smallest totally marine mammal is probably Commerson's dolphin (*Cephalorhynchus commersonii*), also known

Fastest Marine Mammal, at Sea World, CA.
(Photo: Planet Earth Pictures/ James D. Watt)

as Le Jacobite, which is found off the tip of South America. The weights of a group of six adult specimens ranged from 51 lb to 77 lb. The sea otter (*Enhydra lutris*) of the North Pacific is of comparable size (55–81 lb), but this species sometimes comes ashore during storms.

Fastest on land Over a short distance (i.e., up to 1,800 ft) the cheetah or hunting leopard (*Acinonyx jubatus*) of the open plains of East Africa, Iran, Turkmenistan and Afghanistan has a probable maximum speed of 60–63 mph on level ground.

The fastest land animal over a sustained distance (i.e., 3,000 ft or more) is the pronghorn antelope (*Antilocapra americana*) of the western United States. Specimens have been observed to travel at 35 mph for 4 miles, at 42 mph for 1 mile, and at 55 mph for 1/2 mile.

Fastest marine On 12 Oct 1958 a bull killer whale (*Orcinus orca*), measuring an estimated 20–25 ft in length, was timed at 34.5 mph in the eastern Pacific. Similar speeds have also been reported for Dall's porpoise (*Phocoenoides dalli*) in short bursts.

Slowest The ai or three-toed sloth (*Bradypus tridactylus*) of tropical South America has an average ground speed of 6–8 ft per minute (0.07–0.1 mph), but in the trees it can "accelerate" to 15 ft per minute (0.17 mph).

Sleepiest Some armadillos (Dasypodidae), opossums (Didelphidae) and sloths (Bradypodidae) spend up to 80 percent of their lives sleeping or dozing, while it is claimed that Dall's porpoise (*Phocoenoides dalli*) never sleeps at all.

Oldest No other mammal can match the extreme proven age of 120 years attained by humans (*Homo sapiens*; see Human Beings). It is probable that the closest approach is made by the Asiatic elephant (*Elephas maximus*). Sri Lanka's famous bull elephant Rajah, which had led the annual Perahera procession through Kandi carrying the Sacred Tooth of the Buddha since 1931, died on 16 Jul 1988, reportedly at the age of 81 years. The greatest age that has been verified with certainty is 78 years in the case of a cow named Modoc, which died at Santa Clara, CA on 17 Jul 1975. She was imported into the United States from Germany in 1898 at the age of two.

Highest-living The yak (*Bos grunniens*), of Tibet and the Sichuanese Alps, China, occasionally climbs to an altitude of 20,000 ft when foraging.

Largest herds The largest herds on record were those of the springbok (*Antidorcas marsupialis*) during migration across the plains of the western parts of southern Africa in the 19th century. In 1849 John Fraser observed a herd that took three days to pass through the settlement of Beaufort West, Cape Province, South Africa. Another herd seen moving near Nels Poortje, Cape Province in 1888 was estimated to contain 100 million head, although 10 million is probably a more realistic figure. A herd estimated to be 15 miles wide and more than 100 miles long was reported from Karree Kloof, Orange River, South Africa in July 1896.

Largest litter The greatest number of young born to a *wild* mammal at a single birth is 31 (30 of which survived) in the case of the tailless tenrec (*Tenrec ecaudatus*) found in Madagascar and the Comoro Islands. The normal litter size is 12–15, although females can suckle up to 24.

Longest gestation period The Asiatic elephant (*Elephas maximus*) has an average gestation period of 609 days (over 20 months) and a maximum of 760 days—more than two and a half times that of a human.

Shortest gestation period The gestation periods of the American opossum (*Didelphis marsupialis*), also called the Virginian opossum, the rare water opossum or yapok (*Chironectes minimus*) of central and northern South America, and the eastern native cat (*Dasyurus viverrinus*) of Australia are all normally 12–13 days but can be as short as eight days.

CARNIVORES

Largest on land The average adult male Kodiak bear (*Ursus arctos middendorffi*), native to Kodiak Island and the adjacent Afognak and Shuyak islands in the Gulf of Alaska, has a nose-to-tail length of 8 ft, with the tail measuring about 4 in. It stands 52 in at the shoulder and weighs 1,050–1,175 lb. In 1894 a weight of 1,656 lb was recorded for a male shot at English Bay, Kodiak Island, whose*stretched* skin measured 13¹/₂ ft from nose to tail. This weight was exceeded by a "cage-fat" male in the Cheyenne Mountain Zoological Park, Colorado Springs, CO, which weighed 1,670 lb at the time of its death on 22 Sep 1955.

Heaviest In 1981 an unconfirmed weight of over 2,000 lb was reported for a peninsula giant bear (*Ursus a. gyas*) from Alaska on exhibition at the Space Farms Zoological Park in Beemerville, NJ.

Weights exceeding 2,000 lb have also been reported for the polar bear

(*Ursus maritimus*), but the average adult male weighs 850–900 lb and measures 8 ft from nose to tail. In 1960 a polar bear reportedly weighing 2,210 lb was shot at the polar entrance to Kotzebue Sound, AK. In April 1962 the 11-ft-1¼-in-tall mounted specimen was put on display at the Seattle World's Fair.

Youngest breeder   The streaked tenrec (*Hemicentetes semispinosus*) of Madagascar is weaned after only five days, and females can breed 3–4 weeks after their birth.

Largest litigon   An adult male litigon (a hybrid of an Indian lion and a tigon—itself the offspring of a tiger and a lioness) named Cubanacan at Alipore Zoological Gardens, Calcutta, India is believed to weigh at least 800 lb. This animal stands 52 in at the shoulder (compared with 44 in for the lion Simba) and measures a record 11½ ft in total length. Its death was reported on 12 Apr 1991.

Smallest   The smallest living member of the order Carnivora is the least weasel (*Mustela rixosa*), also called the dwarf weasel, which is circumpolar in distribution. Four races are recognized, the smallest of which is *Mustela r. pygmaea* of Siberia, Russia. Mature specimens have an overall length of 6.96–8.14 in and weigh 1¼–2½ oz.

Largest feline   The largest member of the cat family (*Felidae*) is the protected long-furred Siberian tiger (*Panthera tigris altaica*), also called the Amur or Manchurian tiger. Adult males average 10 ft 4 in in length from the nose to the tip of the extended tail, stand 39–42 in at the shoulder and weigh about 585 lb. In 1950 a male weighing 846½ lb was shot in the Sikhote Alin Mountains, Maritime Territory, Russia.

An outsized Indian tiger (*Panthera tigris tigris*) shot in northern Uttar Pradesh in November 1967 measured 10 ft 7 in between pegs (11 ft 1 in over the curves) and weighed 857 lb (compared with 9 ft 3 in and 420 lb for an average adult male). Its stuffed body is now on display in the Museum of Natural History at the Smithsonian Institution, Washington, D.C.

Captive   The largest tiger ever held in captivity, and the heaviest "big cat" on record, is a nine-year-old Siberian male named Jaipur, owned by animal trainer Joan Byron-Marasek of Clarksburg, NJ. This specimen measured 10 ft 11 in in total length and weighed 932 lb in October 1986.

Lions   The average adult African lion (*Panthera leo*) measures 9 ft overall, stands 36–38 in at the shoulder and weighs 400–410 lb. The heaviest wild specimen on record weighed 690 lb and was shot near Hectorspruit, Transvaal, South Africa in 1936.

Smallest feline   The smallest member of the cat family is the rusty-spotted cat

(*Felis rubiginosa*) of southern India and Sri Lanka. The average adult male has an overall length of 25–28 in (the tail measures 9–10 in) and weighs about 3 lb.

PRIMATES

Largest living   The average adult male eastern lowland gorilla (*Gorilla g. graueri*) of the lowland forests of eastern Zaïre and southwestern Uganda stands 5 ft 9 in tall and weighs 360 lb.

The mountain gorilla (*Gorilla g. beringei*) of the volcanic mountain ranges of western Rwanda, southwestern Uganda and eastern Zaïre is of comparable size, i.e., 5 ft 8 in tall and 343 lb, and most of the exceptionally large gorillas taken in the field have been of this race.

Tallest   The greatest height (top of crest to heel) recorded for a gorilla in the wild is 6 ft 2 in for a male of the mountain race shot in the eastern Congo (Zaïre) *c.* 1920. The tallest gorilla ever kept in captivity is reportedly an eastern lowland male named Colossus (b. 1966), who is currently on display at a zoo in Gulf Breeze, FL. He reportedly stands 6 ft 2 in tall and weighs 575 lb, but these figures have not yet been confirmed.

Heaviest   The heaviest gorilla ever kept in captivity was a male of the mountain race named N'gagi, who died in San Diego Zoo in California on 12 Jan 1944 at the age of 18. He weighed 683 lb at his heaviest in 1943. He was 5 ft 7$^3/4$ in tall and boasted a record chest measurement of 78 in.

Monkey   The only species of monkey reliably credited with weights of more than 100 lb is the mandrill (*Mandrillus sphinx*) of equatorial West Africa. The greatest reliable weight recorded is 119 lb for a captive male, but an unconfirmed weight of 130 lb has been reported. (Adult females are about half the size of males.)

Oldest   The greatest age recorded for a nonhuman primate is 59 years 5 months for a chimpanzee (*Pan troglodytes*) named Gamma, who died at the Yerkes Primate Research Center in Atlanta, GA on 19 Feb 1992. Gamma was born at the Florida branch of the Yerkes Center in September 1932. A similar age was reached by a male orangutan (*Pongo pygmaeus*) named Guas, who died in Philadelphia Zoological Garden, PA on 9 Feb 1977. He was at least 13 years old on his arrival at the zoo on 1 May 1931.

Monkey The world's oldest monkey, a male white-throated capuchin (*Cebus capucinus*) called Bobo, died on 10 Jul 1988 at the age of 53 following complications related to a stroke.

PINNIPEDS *Seals, Sea Lions, Walruses*

Largest The largest of the 34 known species of pinniped is the southern elephant seal (*Mirounga leonina*) of the sub-Antarctic islands. Adult bulls average 16¹/₂ ft in length from the tip of the inflated snout to the tips of the outstretched tail flippers, have a maximum girth of 12 ft and weigh about 5,000 lb. The largest accurately measured specimen was a bull that probably weighed at least 4.4 tons and measured 21 ft 4 in after flensing (stripping of the blubber or skin). Its original length was about 22¹/₂ ft. It was killed in the South Atlantic at Possession Bay, South Georgia on 28 Feb 1913.

Live The largest recorded live specimen is a bull nicknamed "Stalin" from South Georgia. It was tranquilized by members of the British Antarctic Survey on 14 Oct 1989 when it weighed 5,869 lb and measured 16¹/₂ ft.

Smallest The smallest pinnipeds are the ringed seal (*Phoca hispida*) of the Arctic and the closely related Baikal seal (*P. sibirica*) of Lake Baikal and the Caspian seal (*P. caspica*) of the Caspian Sea, Asia. Adult males measure up to 5¹/₂ ft in length and can weigh up to 280 lb.

Oldest A female gray seal (*Halichoerus grypus*) shot at Shunni Wick, Shetland, Great Britain on 23 Apr 1969 was believed to be "at least 46 years old" based on a count of dentine rings. The captive record is an estimated 41 years (1901–42) for a bull gray seal named "Jacob" held in Skansen Zoo, Stockholm, Sweden.

Most abundant The total population of the crabeater seal (*Lobodon carcinophagus*) of Antarctica was estimated in 1977 to be nearly 15 million.

Fastest The highest swimming speed recorded for a pinniped is a short spurt of 25 mph by a California sea lion (*Zalophus californianus*). The fastest-moving pinniped on land is the crabeater seal (*Lobodon carcinophagus*), which has been timed at speeds up to 12 mph.

Deepest dive In May 1988 a team of scientists from the University of California at Santa Cruz tested the diving abilities of the northern elephant seal (*Mirounga angustirostris*) off Ano Nuevo Point, CA. One female reached a record depth of 4,135 ft, and another remained submerged for 48 minutes. Similar experiments carried out by Australian scientists on southern elephant seals (*M. leonina*) in the Southern Ocean recorded a dive of 3,720 ft, with other dives lasting nearly two hours also observed. It was discovered that the seals regularly swam down to about 2,500 ft and when they resurfaced apparently had no "oxygen debt."

BATS

Largest The only flying mammals are bats (order Chiroptera), of which there are about 950 species. The largest in terms of wingspan is the Bismarck flying fox (*Pteropus neohibernicus*) of the Bismarck Archipelago and New Guinea.

One specimen preserved in the American Museum of Natural History in New York City has a wingspan of 5 ft 5 in, but some unmeasured bats probably reach 6 ft.

United States   Mature specimens of the large mastiff bat (*Eumops perotis*), found in southern Texas, California, Arizona and New Mexico, have a wingspan of 22.04 in.

Smallest   The smallest bat in the world is Kitti's hog-nosed bat at 6.3 in and 0.06–0.071 oz. (See Smallest land mammal.)

United States   The smallest native bat is the Western pipistrelle (*Pipistrellus hesperus*), found in the western United States. Mature specimens have a wingspan of 7.9 in.

Fastest   Because of great practical difficulties, little data on bat speeds has been published. The greatest velocity attributed to a bat is 32 mph in the case of a Mexican free-tailed bat (*Tadarida brasiliensis*), but this may have been wind-assisted. In one American experiment using an artificial mine tunnel and 17 different kinds of bat, only four of them managed to exceed 13 mph in level flight.

Oldest   The greatest age reliably reported for a bat is 32 years for a banded female little brown bat (*Myotis lucifugus*) in the United States in 1987.

Largest colonies   The largest concentration of bats found living anywhere in the world today is that of the Mexican free-tailed bat (*Tadarida brasiliensis*) in Bracken Cave, San Antonio, TX, where up to 20 million animals assemble after migration.

Deepest   The little brown bat (*Myotis lucifugus*) has been recorded at a depth of 3,805 ft in a zinc mine in New York State. The mine serves as winter quarters for 1,000 members of this species, which normally roost at a depth of 650 ft.

Bats' highest detectable pitch   Because of their ultrasonic echolocation, bats have the most acute hearing of any terrestrial animal. Vampire bats (family Desmodontidae) and fruit bats (Pteropodidae) can hear frequencies as high as 120–210 kHz, compared with 20 kHz for the adult human limit and 280 kHz for the common dolphin (*Delphinus delphis*).

Longest hibernation   The barrow ground squirrel (*Spermophilus parryi barrowensis*) of Point Barrow, AK hibernates for nine months of the year. During the remaining three months it feeds, breeds and collects food for storage in its burrow.

RODENTS

Largest   The capybara (*Hydrochoerus hydrochaeris*), also called the carpincho or water hog, of tropical South America, has a head and body length of 3¼–4½ ft and can weigh up to 250 lb (cage-fat specimen).

Smallest   The northern pygmy mouse (*Baiomys taylori*) of central Mexico and southern Arizona and Texas measures up to 4.3 in in total length and weighs 0.24–0.28 oz.

Oldest   The greatest reliable age reported for a rodent is 27 years 3 months for a Sumatran crested porcupine (*Hystrix brachyura*) that died in the National Zoological Park, Washington, D.C. on 12 Jan 1965.

Fastest breeder   The female meadow vole (*Microtus agrestis*), found in Great Britain, can reproduce from the age of 25 days and can have up to 17 litters of 6–8 young in a year.

INSECTIVORES

Largest   The moon rat (*Echinosorex gymnurus*), also known as Raffles' gymnure, which is found in Myanmar (Burma), Thailand, Malaysia, Sumatra and Borneo, has a head and body length of 10½–17½ in, a tail measuring 7.9–8.3 in and weighs up to 3.1 lb.

Heaviest   The European hedgehog (*Erinaceus europaeus*) is much shorter overall (7.7–11.7 in), but well-fed examples have been known to weigh as much as 4.2 lb.

Smallest   The smallest insectivore is Savi's white-toothed pygmy shrew (*Suncus etruscus*) at up to 3.2 in in total length and 0.09 oz in wieght. (See Smallest land mammals.)

Oldest   The greatest reliable age recorded for an insectivore is over 16 years for a lesser hedgehog-tenrec (*Echinops telfairi*), which was born in Amsterdam Zoo, Netherlands in 1966 and was later sent to Jersey Zoo, Channel Islands, Great Britain. It died on 27 Nov 1982.

ANTELOPES

Largest   The rare giant eland (*Taurotragus derbianus*) of western and central Africa may attain a height of 6 ft at the shoulder and weigh over 2,000 lb. The common eland (*Taurotragus oryx*) of eastern and southern Africa has the same shoulder height of up to 5 ft 10 in but is not quite so massive, although there is one record of a 5 ft 5 in bull shot in Malawi *c*. 1937 that weighed 2,078 lb.

Smallest   Mature specimens of the royal antelope (*Neotragus pygmaeus*) of western Africa measure 10–12 in at the shoulder and weigh only 7–8 lb, which is the size of a large brown hare (*Lepus europaeus*).

Lightest   Salt's dik-dik (*Madoqua saltina*) of northeastern Ethiopia and Somalia weighs only 5–6 lb when adult, but this species stands about 14 in at the withers (highest part of the back of an animal).

Oldest   The greatest reliable age recorded for an antelope is 25 years 4 months for an addax (*Addax nasomaculatus*) that died in Brookfield Zoo, Chicago, IL on 15 Oct 1960.

DEER

Largest   The largest deer is the Alaskan moose (*Alces alces gigas*). Adult bulls average 6 ft at the shoulder and weigh *c.* 1,100 lb. A bull standing 7 ft 8 in between pegs and weighing an estimated 1,800 lb was shot on the Yukon River in the Yukon Territory, Canada in September 1897.

Unconfirmed measurements of up to 8 ft 6 in at the shoulder and weights of up to 2,600 lb have been claimed.

Smallest   The smallest true deer (family Cervidae) is the northern pudu (*Pudu mephistopheles*) of Ecuador and Colombia. Mature specimens measure 13–14 in at the shoulder and weigh 16–18 lb.

The smallest ruminant is the lesser Malay chevrotain (*Tragulus javanicus*) of southeast Asia, Sumatra and Borneo. Adults measure 8–10 in at the shoulder and weigh 6–7 lb.

Oldest deer   The world's oldest recorded deer is a red deer (*Cervus elaphus scoticus*) named Bambi (b. 8 Jun 1963). Bambi is owned by the Fraser family of Kiltarlity, Great Britain.

United States   The greatest reliable age recorded for a deer is 26 years 8 months for a red deer (*Cervus elaphus scoticus*) that died in the Milwaukee Zoo, WI on 28 Jun 1954.

MARSUPIALS

Largest   The male red kangaroo (*Megaleia rufa* or *Macropus rufus*) of central, southern and eastern Australia stands up to 7 ft tall, measures up to 8 ft 1/2 in in total length and weighs up to 187 lb.

Smallest   The smallest-known marsupial is the rare long-tailed planigale (*Planigale ingrami*), a flat-skulled mouse of northeastern and northwestern Australia. Adult males have a head and body length of 2.16–2.48 in, a tail length of 2.24–2.36 in and weigh 0.13–0.19 oz.

Fastest speed   The fastest speed recorded for a marsupial is 40 mph for a mature female eastern gray kangaroo (*Macropus giganteus* or *M. canguru*). One large male red kangaroo died from his exertions after being paced for one mile at 35 mph.

TUSKS

Longest   The longest recorded elephant tusks (excluding prehistoric examples) are a pair from Zaïre preserved in the National Collection of Heads and Horns kept by the New York Zoological Society (Bronx Zoo), New York City. The right tusk measures 11 ft 5 1/2 in along the outside curve and the left tusk measures 11 ft. Their combined weight is 293 lb. A single tusk of 11 ft 6 in has been reported.

Largest antlers   The record antler spread or "rack" is 6 ft 6½ in (skull and antlers 91 lb) for a set taken from a moose killed near the headwaters of the Stewart River in the Yukon Territory, Canada in October 1897. The antlers are now on display in the Field Museum, Chicago, IL.

Oldest marsupial   The greatest reliable age recorded for a marsupial is 26 years 22 days for a common wombat (*Vombatus ursinus*) that died in London Zoo, Great Britain on 20 Apr 1906.

Highest jump   A captive eastern gray kangaroo once cleared an 8-ft fence when an automobile backfired, and there is also a record of a hunted red kangaroo clearing a stack of timber 10 ft high.

Longest jump   During the course of a chase in New South Wales, Australia in January 1951, a female red kangaroo made a series of bounds that included one of 42 ft. There is also an unconfirmed report of an eastern gray kangaroo jumping nearly 44 ft 8½ in on level ground.

The world's largest marsupial, a red kangaroo, at Sturt National Park, New South Wales, Australia. (Photo: Planet Earth Pictures/Ford Kristo)

Heaviest　A pair of tusks in the British Museum (Natural History), London collected from an aged bull shot in Kenya in 1897 originally weighed 240 lb (length 10 ft 2½ in) and 225 lb (length 10 ft 5½ in) respectively, giving a total weight of 465 lb, but their combined weight today is 440½ lb. A single elephant tusk collected in Benin, Africa and exhibited at the Paris Exposition, France in 1900 weighed 258 lb.

HORNS

Longest　The longest horns grown by any living animal are those of the water buffalo (*Bubalus arnee=B. bubalis*) of India. One bull shot in 1955 had horns measuring 13 ft 11 in from tip to tip along the outside curve across the forehead. The longest single horn on record measured 6 ft 9¼ in along the outside curve and was found on a specimen of domestic ankole cattle (*Bos taurus*) near Lake Ngami, Botswana.

Domestic animal　The largest spread on record is 10 ft 6 in, for a Texas longhorn steer. The horns are currently on exhibition at the Heritage Museum, Big Springs, TX.

HORSES AND PONIES

Earliest domestication　Evidence from the Ukraine indicates that horses may have been ridden by at least 4000 B.C. (See Agriculture.)

Largest　The tallest and heaviest documented horse was the shire gelding Sampson (later renamed Mammoth), bred by Thomas Cleaver of Toddington Mills, Bedfordshire, Great Britain. This horse (foaled 1846) measured 21.2½ hands (7 ft 2½ in) in 1850 and was later said to have weighed 3,360 lb.

　Boringdon Black King (foaled 1984), a shire gelding born and bred at the National Shire Horse Center in Plymouth, Great Britain, stands 19.2 hands (6½ ft), making him the world's tallest living horse.

Thoroughbred　The tallest recorded non-draft horse was a Canadian thoroughbred gelding named Tritonis, owned by Christopher Ewing of Southfield, MI. This show jumper, which died in September 1990 at the age of 7, stood 19.2 hands (6½ ft) and weighed 2,100 lb.

Smallest　The Falabela of Argentina was developed over a period of 70 years by inbreeding and crossing a small group of undersized horses originally discovered in the southern part of the country. Most adult specimens stand less than 30 in and average 80–100 lb in weight. The smallest mature horse bred by Julio Falabela of Recco de Roca before he died in 1981 was a mare that stood 15 in and weighed 26¼ lb.

> *Largest mules*　Apollo (foaled 1977) and Anak (foaled 1976), owned by Herbert L. Mueller of Chicago, IL, are the largest mules on record. Apollo measures 19.1 hands (6 ft 5 in) and weighs 2,200 lb, with Anak at 18.3 hands (6 ft 3 in) and 2,100 lb. Both are the hybrid offspring of Belgian mares and mammoth jacks.

The stallion Little Pumpkin (foaled 15 Apr 1973), owned by J.C. Williams Jr. of Della Terra Mini Horse Farm, Inman, SC, stood 14 in and weighed 20 lb on 30 Nov 1975.

Oldest   The greatest age reliably recorded for a horse is 62 years in the case of Old Billy (foaled 1760), believed to be a cross between a Cleveland and eastern blood, bred by Edward Robinson of Wild Grave Farm, Woolston, Great Britain. Old Billy later worked along the local canals until 1819 and died on 27 Nov 1822.

Thoroughbred   The greatest age recorded for a thoroughbred racehorse is 42 years, in the case of the chestnut gelding Tango Duke (foaled 1935), owned by Carmen J. Koper of Barongarook, Victoria, Australia. The horse died on 25 Jan 1978.

Pony   The greatest reliable age recorded for a pony is 54 years for a stallion owned by a farmer in central France (foaled 1919).

The oldest pony in the United States was Trigger, who lived for 47 years (1945–92). He was owned by Dorothy B. Crouse of Whiteside, MO.

DOGS

The canine population of the United States for 1992 was estimated by the Pet Food Institute at 52.3 million. There was at least one dog kept as a pet in 37.9 percent of the households in the United States.

Largest   The heaviest breeds of domestic dogs (*Canis familiaris*) are the Old English mastiff and the St Bernard, with adult males of both species regularly weighing 170–200 lb. The heaviest (and longest) dog ever recorded is Aicama Zorba of La-Susa (whelped 26 Sep 1981), an Old English mastiff owned by Chris Eraclides of London, Great Britain. Zorba stands 37 in at the shoulder and weighed 343 lb in November 1989. Other statistics include a chest girth of 58³/₄ in, a length of 8 ft 3¹/₂ in and a neck measurement of 37¹/₂ in.

Tallest   The Great Dane and the Irish wolfhound can exceed 39 in at the shoulder. The tallest dog ever recorded was Shamgret Danzas (whelped 1975), owned by Wendy and Keith Comley of Milton Keynes, Great Britain. He stood 41¹/₂ in, or 42 in when his hackles were raised, and weighed up to 238 lb. He died on 16 Oct 1984.

Smallest   Miniature versions of the Yorkshire terrier, the chihuahua and the toy poodle have been known to weigh less than 16 oz as adults.

The smallest mature dog on record was a matchbox-sized Yorkshire terrier owned by Arthur Marples of Blackburn, Great Britain, a former editor of *Our Dogs*. This tiny atom, which died in 1945 at the age of nearly two years, stood 2¹/₂ in at the shoulder and measured 3³/₄ in from the tip of its nose to the root of its tail. Its weight was just 4 oz.

The smallest living adult dog is a Yorkshire terrier named Summerann Thumberlina, 8 in long and weighing 20 oz. Born on 5 Jan 1992, she is owned by Maureen Howes of Stourport-on-Severn, Great Britain.

Oldest   Most dogs live between 8 and 15 years, and authentic records of dogs living over 20 years are rare. They are generally the smaller breeds. The greatest reliable age recorded for a dog is 29 years 5 months for an Australian cattle-dog named Bluey, owned by Les Hall of Rochester, Victoria, Australia. The dog was obtained as a puppy in 1910 and worked among cattle and sheep for nearly 20 years. He was put to sleep on 14 Nov 1939.

Most prolific The greatest sire ever was the champion greyhound Low Pressure, nicknamed Timmy (whelped Sep 1957), owned by Bruna Amhurst of London, Great Britain. From Dec 1961 until his death on 27 Nov 1969 he fathered 2,414 registered puppies, with at least 600 others unregistered.

Wealthiest The largest legacy willed to a dog was by Miss Ella Wendel of New York, who bequeathed her standard poodle Toby $75 million in 1931.

Highest jump The canine "high jump" record for a leap and a scramble over a smooth wooden wall (without ribs or other aids) is held by a German shepherd dog named Volse, who scaled 11 ft 9 in at a demonstration in Avignon, France in November 1989. The dog is owned by Phillipe Clement of Aix-en-Provence, France.

Duke, a three-year-old German shepherd dog, handled by Cpl Graham Urry of the Royal Air Force base at Newton, Great Britain, scaled a ribbed wall with regulation shallow slats to a height of 11 ft 9 in on the British Broadcasting Corporation *Record Breakers* TV program on 11 Nov 1986.

Tracking In 1925 a Doberman pinscher named Sauer, trained by Detective-Sergeant Herbert Kruger, tracked a stock thief 100 miles across the Great Karroo, South Africa by scent alone.

Top show dogs The greatest number of Challenge Certificates won by a dog is the 78 compiled by the famous chow chow Ch. U'Kwong King Solomon (whelped 21 Jun 1968). Owned and bred by Joan Egerton of Bramhall, Great Britain, Solly won his first CC at the Cheshire Agricultural Society Championship Show on 4 Jun 1969, and his 78th CC was awarded at the City of Birmingham Championship Show on 4 Sep 1976. He died on 3 Apr 1978.

The greatest number of Best-in-Show awards won by any dog in all-breed shows is 203, compiled by the Scottish terrier bitch Ch. Braeburn's Close Encounter (whelped 22 Oct 1978) by 10 Mar 1985. She is owned by Sonnie Novick of Plantation Acres, FL.

US TOP DOGS (1992)

Breed	Registrations
Labrador retriever	120,879
Rottweiler	95,445
Cocker spaniel	91,925
German shepherd	76,941
Poodle	73,449

American Kennel Club

Guide dog The longest period of *active service* reported for a guide dog is 14 years 8 months (August 1972–March 1987) in the case of a Labrador retriever bitch named Cindy-Cleo (whelped 20 Jan 1971), owned by Aron Barr of Tel Aviv, Israel. The dog died on 10 Apr 1987.

Largest dog show The centennial of the annual Crufts show, held at the National Exhibition Center, Birmingham, Great Britain on 9–12 Jan 1991, attracted a record 22,993 entries.

Longest jump A greyhound named Bang jumped 30 ft while chasing a hare at Brecon Lodge, Gloucestershire, Great Britain in 1849. He cleared a 4-ft-6-in gate and landed on a hard road, damaging his pastern bone.

Drug sniffing Snag, a US Customs Labrador retriever trained and partnered by Jeff Weitzmann, initiated the discovery of a 4.2 ton haul of cocaine hidden in a tanker in San Diego, CA in October 1990. Adopted as a stray in 1988 and trained at the US Customs Detector Dog Academy, to date Snag has made 118 drug seizures worth a canine record $810 million.

The greatest number of seizures by dogs is 969 (worth $182 million) in 1988 alone by Rocky and Barco, a pair of malinoises patrolling the Rio Grande Valley ("Cocaine Valley") along the Texas border, where the pair were so proficient that Mexican drug smugglers put a $30,000 price on their heads. The dogs hold the rank of honorary Sergeant Major and always wear their stripes on duty.

CATS

The feline population of the United States for 1992 was estimated by the Pet Food Institute to be 63 million. There was at least one cat in 32.3 percent of the households in the United States.

Largest The largest of the 330 breeds of domestic cat is the ragdoll, with males weighing 15–20 lb. In the majority of domestic cats (*Felis catus*) the average weight of the adult male (tom) is 8.6 lb, compared with 7.2 lb for female or queen. Neuters and spays are generally heavier.

In February 1988 an unconfirmed weight of 48 lb was reported for a cat named Edward Bear, owned by Jackie Fleming of Sydney, New South Wales, Australia.

The heaviest reliably recorded domestic cat was a neutered male tabby named Himmy, owned by Thomas Vyse of Redlynch, Queensland, Australia. At the time of his death (from respiratory failure) on 12 Mar 1986 at the age of 10 years 4 months he weighed 46 lb 15¹/₄ oz (neck 15 in, waist 33 in, length 38 in).

Smallest The smallest breed of domestic cat is the Singapura or drain cat of Singapore. Adult males average 6 lb in weight and adult females 4 lb.

A male blue point Himalayan-Persian cat named Tinker Toy, owned by Katrina and Scott Forbes of Taylorville, IL, is just 2¾ in tall and 7½ in long.

Oldest   Cats generally live longer than dogs. The average life expectancy of intact (unaltered) well-fed males raised under household conditions and receiving good medical attention is 13–15 years (15–17 years for intact females), but neutered males and females live on the average one to two years longer.

A tabby named Puss, owned by Mrs T. Holway of Clayhidon, Great Britain, reportedly celebrated his 36th birthday on 28 Nov 1939 and died the next day, but conclusive evidence is lacking. The oldest reliably recorded cat was the female tabby Ma, owned by Alice St George Moore of Drewsteignton, Great Britain. This cat was put to sleep on 5 Nov 1957 at the age of 34.

US TOP CATS (1992)

Breed	Registrations
Persian	50,133
Maine Coon	3,120
Siamese	3,047
Abyssinian	2,407
Exotic Shorthair	1,355

Cat Fanciers' Association, Inc.

Largest cat show   The largest cat show in the United States was the Purina Cat Chow/CFA Invitational held at the Cerrantes Convention Center, St. Louis, MO from 19–20 Nov 1988; it attracted a record 814 entries.

Best climber   On 6 Sep 1950 a four-month-old kitten belonging to Josephine Aufdenblatten of Geneva, Switzerland followed a group of climbers to the top of the 14,691 ft Matterhorn in the Alps.

Most prolific   A tabby named Dusty (b. 1935) of Bonham, TX produced 420 kittens during her breeding life. She gave birth to her last litter (a single kitten) on 12 Jun 1952.

In May 1987 Kitty, owned by George Johnstone of Croxton, Great Britain, produced two kittens at the age of 30 years, making her the oldest feline mother on record. She died in June 1989, just short of her 32nd birthday, having given birth to a known total of 218 kittens.

RABBITS AND HARES

According to the American Rabbit Breeders Association, as of 1 Jan 1992 there were at least 250,000 families in the United States with at least one pet rabbit.

Largest   The largest breed of domestic rabbit (*Oryctolagus cuniculus*) is the Flemish giant. Adults weigh 15 lb 7 oz–18 lb 12 oz (average toe-to-toe length when fully stretched is 36 in), but weights of up to 25 lb have been reliably reported for this breed. In April 1980 a five-month-old French lop doe weighing 26 lb 7 oz was exhibited at the Reus Fair in northeast Spain.

LARGEST PET LITTERS

Animal/Breed	No.	Owner	Date
Cat			
Burmese/Siamese	19[1]	V. Gane, Church Westcote, Great Britain	7 Aug 1970
Dog			
American foxhound	23	W. N. Ely, Ambler, PA	19 Jun 1944
St Bernard	23[2]	R. and A. Rodden, Lebanon, MO	6–7 Feb 1975
Great Dane	23[3]	M. Harris, Little Hall, Great Britain	June 1987
Ferret			
Domestic	15	J. Cliff, Denstone, Great Britain	1981
Gerbil			
Mongolian	14[4]	S. Kirkman, Bulwell, Great Britain	May 1983
Guinea pig	12	Laboratory specimen	1972
Hamster			
Golden	26[5]	L. and S. Miller, Baton Rouge, LA	28 Feb 1974
Mouse			
House	34[6]	M. Ogilvie, Blackpool, Great Britain	12 Feb 1982
Rabbit			
New Zealand white	24	J. Filek, Cape Breton, Nova Scotia, Canada	1978

[1]Four stillborn. [2]Fourteen survived. [3]Sixteen survived. [4]Litter of fifteen recorded in the 1960s by George Meares, geneticist-owner of gerbil-breeding farm in St Petersburg, FL, using special food formula. [5]Eighteen killed by mother. [6]Thirty-three survived.

The heaviest recorded wild rabbit (average weight 3½ lb) weighed 8 lb 4 oz and was killed on 20 Nov 1982.

Smallest The Netherland dwarf and the Polish dwarf both have a weight range of 2–2½ lb when fully grown. In 1975 Jacques Bouloc of Coulommière, France announced a new cross of the above breeds that weighed 14 oz.

Most prolific The most prolific domestic breeds are the New Zealand white and the Californian. Does produce 5–6 litters a year, each containing 8–12 kittens during their breeding life (compare with five litters and 3–7 young for the wild rabbit).

Longest ears The longest ears are found in the Lop family (four strains), and in particular the English Lop. The ears of a typical example measure about 24 in from tip to tip (taken across the skull), and 5½ in in width. In 1901 a specimen was exhibited in England that had 30½-in ears; it is not known, however, if this was a natural attainment or if weights had been used to stretch the ears, as the veins inside were badly varicosed.

"Sweet Majestic Star," a champion black English lop rabbit owned by Therese and Cheryl Seward of Exeter, Great Britain, had ears measuring 28½ in long and 7¼ in wide. He died on 6 Oct 1992. The ears of his grandson "Sweet Regal Magic" are the same length.

Largest hare In November 1956 a brown hare weighing 15 lb 1 oz was shot near Welford, Great Britain. The average adult weight is 8 lb.

CAGED PET LONGEVITY

Species	Name, Owner, etc.	Age
Bird *Parrot*	*Prudle*, captured 1958, I. Frost, East Sussex, Great Britain	35 yr
Budgerigar	*Charlie*, April 1948–20 Jun 1977, J. Dinsey, London, Great Britain	29 yr 2 mths
Rabbit *Wild*	*Flopsy*, caught 6 Aug 1964, d. 29 Jun 1983, L.B. Walker, Longford, Tasmania, Australia	18 yr 10¾ mths
Guinea *pig*	*Snowball*, d. 14 Feb 1979, M.A. Wall, Bingham, Great Britain	14 yr 10½ mths
Gerbil *Mongolian*	*Sahara*, May 1973–4 Oct 1981, A. Milstone, Lathrup Village, MI	8 yr 4½ mths
Mouse *House*	*Fritzy*, 11 Sep 1977–24 Apr 1985, B. Beard, West House School, Birmingham, Great Britain	7 yr 7 mths
Rat *Common*	*Rodney*, January 1983–25 May 1990, R. Mitchell, Tulsa, OK	7 yr 4 mths

BIRDS *Aves*

Largest   The largest living bird is the North African ostrich (*Struthio c. camelus*), which is found in reduced numbers south of the Atlas Mountains from Upper Senegal and Niger across to the Sudan and central Ethiopia. Male examples (adult hens are smaller) of this flightless (ratite) subspecies have been recorded up to 9 ft in height and 345 lb in weight. The heaviest subspecies is *S. c. australis*, which can weigh 330 lb, although there is an unsubstantiated record of 353 lb.

Largest flying   The world's heaviest flying (carinate) birds are the Kori bustard or paauw (*Ardeotis kori*) of northeast and southern Africa and the great bustard (*Otis tarda*) of Europe and Asia. Weights of 42 lb have been reported for the former, and there is an unconfirmed record of 46 lb 4 oz for a male great bustard shot in Manchuria that was too heavy to fly. The heaviest reliably recorded great bustard weighed 39 lb 11 oz.

The mute swan (*Cygnus olor*), which is resident in Britain, can reach 40 lb on very rare occasions, and there is a record from Poland of a male weighing 49 lb 10 oz that had temporarily lost the power of flight.

Bird of prey   The heaviest bird of prey is the Andean condor (*Vultur gryphus*), adult males averaging 20–25 lb. A weight of 31 lb has been claimed for an outsized male California condor (*Gymnogyps californianus*) now preserved in the California Academy of Sciences at San Francisco. This species is appreciably smaller than the Andean condor and rarely exceeds 23 lb.

Largest wingspan   The wandering albatross (*Diomedea exulans*) of the southern oceans has the largest wingspan of any living bird, adult males averaging 10 ft 4 in with wings at full stretch. The largest recorded specimen was a very old male with a wingspan of 11 ft 11 in, caught by members of the Antarctic research ship USGS *Eltanin* in the Tasman Sea on 18 Sep 1965. Unconfirmed measurements up to 13 ft 10 in have been claimed for this species.

The only other bird reliably credited with a wingspan exceeding 11 ft is the vulturelike marabou stork (*Leptoptilos crumeniferus*) of tropical Africa.

Smallest   The smallest bird in the world is the bee hummingbird (*Mellisuga helenae*) of Cuba and the Isle of Pines. Adult males (females are slightly larger) measure 2.24 in in total length, half of which is taken up by the bill and tail, and weigh 0.056 oz (females are slightly heavier).

The smallest American bird is the calliope hummingbird (*Stellula calliope*). Adult specimens measure 2³⁄₄–3¹⁄₂ in from bill to tail with a wingspan of 4¹⁄₂ in and an approximate weight of ¹⁄₁₀ oz. The calliope is found in the western United States.

Birds of Prey   The smallest bird of prey is the 1.23 oz, 5¹⁄₂–6 in long, white-fronted falconet (*Microhierax latifrons*) of northwestern Borneo, which is sparrow-sized.

Most talkative bird   A number of birds are renowned for their talking ability (i.e., the reproduction of words) but the African gray parrot (*Psittacus erythacus*) excels in this ability. A female named "Prudle," formerly owned by Lyn Logue (died January 1988) and now in the care of Iris Frost of Seaford, Great Britain, won the "Best talking parrot-like bird" title at the National Cage and Aviary Bird Show in London each December for 12 consecutive years (1965–76). "Prudle," who has a vocabulary of nearly 800 words, was taken from a nest at Jinja, Uganda in 1958. She retired undefeated. (See also Caged Pet Longevity table.)

Fastest wing-beat   The wing-beat of the horned sungem (*Heliactin cornuta*) of tropical South America is 90 beats/sec.

Most poisonous bird   The only poisonous bird found so far is the unsavory-sounding Pitohui of the *Pitohui* genus from New Guinea, identified in 1992. The skin, feathers and internal organs of this striking orange and black bird contain a homobatrachotoxin like that secreted by poison-dart frogs, which have similar warning colors. (See General records, Most poisonous.)

Most and least feathers   In a series of feather counts on various species of bird, a whistling swan (*Cygnus columbianus*) was found to have 25,216 feathers, 20,177 of which were on the head and neck. The ruby-throated hummingbird (*Archilochus colubris*) has only 940.

Fastest bird   The fastest bird on land is the ostrich, which despite its bulk can run at a speed of up to 40 mph when necessary.

Highest g force   Experiments have revealed that the beak of the red-headed woodpecker (*Melanerpes erythrocephalus*) hits the bark of a tree with an impact velocity of 13 mph. This means that when the head snaps back the brain is subject to a deceleration of about $10\,g$.

Longest feathers   The longest feathers grown by any bird are those of the phoenix fowl or onagadori (a strain of red jungle fowl *Gallus gallus*), which has been bred in southwestern Japan since the mid-17th century. In 1972 a tail covert measuring 34 ft 9^1/$_2$ in was reported for a rooster owned by Masasha Kubota of Kochi, Shikoku, Japan.
  Among flying birds the tail feathers of the male crested pheasant (*Rheinhartia ocellata*) of southeast Asia regularly reach 5 ft 8 in in length and 5 in in width, and the central tail feathers of the Reeves' pheasant (*Syrmaticus reevesi*) of central and northern China have reached 8 ft in exceptional cases.

Tallest bird   The tallest of the flying birds are cranes, tall waders of the family Gruidae, some of which can stand almost 6 ft 6 in high.

Most abundant   The red-billed quelea (*Quelea quelea*), a seed-eating weaver of the drier parts of Africa south of the Sahara, has an estimated adult breeding population of 1.5 billion, and at least 1 billion of these "feathered locusts" are slaughtered annually without having any impact on the population. One huge roost in the Sudan contained 32 million birds.

United States   The red-winged blackbird (*Agelaius phoeniceus*) had a population of 25.6 million birds as of January 1983. The US Fish and Wildlife Service estimates the current total is at least 30 million. The blackbird is found throughout the country, except for desert and mountainous regions.

Fastest-flying   The fastest creature on the wing is the peregrine falcon (*Falco peregrinus*) when swooping from great heights during territorial displays. In one series of German experiments, a velocity of 168 mph was recorded at a 30° angle of descent, rising to a maximum of 217 mph at an angle of 45°. The brown-throated spine-tail swift (*Hirundapus giganteus*) of Asia is also capable of 155–186 mph.

The fastest fliers in level flight are found among the ducks and geese (*Anatidae*); some powerful species such as the red-breasted merganser (*Mergus serrator*), the eider (*Somateria mollissima*), the canvasback (*Aythya valisineria*) and the spur-winged goose (*Plectropterus gambiensis*) can probably exceed an airspeed of 65 mph.

United States   America's fastest bird is the white-throated swift (*Aeronautes saxatilis*), which has been estimated to fly at speeds of 200 mph. The peregrine falcon (*Falco peregrinus*) has been credited with a speed of 175 mph while in a dive. The dunlin (*Calidris alpina*) has been clocked from a plane at 110 mph.

Slowest-flying   Probably at least 50 percent of the world's flying birds cannot exceed an air speed of 40 mph in level flight. The slowest-flying birds are the American woodcock (*Scolopax minor*) and the Eurasian woodcock (*S. rusticola*), which, during courtship flights, have been timed at 5 mph without stalling.

Oldest   An unconfirmed age of *c.* 82 years was reported for a male Siberian white crane (*Crus leucogeranus*) named Wolf at the International Crane Foundation, Baraboo, WI. The bird was said to have hatched in a zoo in Switzerland *c.* 1905. He died in late 1988 after breaking his bill while repelling a visitor near his pen.

The greatest irrefutable age reported for any bird is over 80 years for a male sulfur-crested cockatoo (*Cacatua galerita*) named Cocky, who died at London Zoo, Great Britain in 1982. He was presented to the zoo in 1925, and had been with his previous owner since 1902 when he was already fully mature.

Domestic   The longest-lived domesticated bird (excluding the ostrich, which has been known to live up to 68 years) is the domestic goose (*Anseranser domesticus*), which may live about 25 years. On 16 Dec 1976 a gander named George, owned by Florence Hull of Thornton, Great Britain, died at the age of 49 years 8 months. He was hatched in April 1927.

Polar Bear

Swarm of 12.5 trillion Rocky Mountain locusts

Photo: Gamma

Polar bear *(above)* Despite their great bulk, polar bears can cover distances of 975 miles walking across the ice from Alaska via the Bering Strait to set up winter dens in Russia.

Photo: Jacana

The gray whale holds the mammalian distance record of 6,000 miles.

Base artwork: Maltings Partnership, illustrations by Matthew Hillier.

Migration

Migratory patterns vary considerably throughout the animal world, and the diagram illustrates a small selection of diverse habits, showing aspects such as distances traveled and numbers of animals involved for different species. Further details can be found in the relevant sections of this chapter.

Monarch butterfly traveling from Canada to Mexico.

REPORT
NO. TO
ZOOLOGY
UNIVERSITY
TORONTO
CANADA

28009

Tagging butterflies *(above)* The photographs show a tagged monarch butterfly and an example of an actual alar tag used to monitor the movement of the insects. Distances traveled are then calculated from the known release and recapture sites.

Photos: Donald Davis

Migration

The all-time distance record is
14,000 miles by the
Arctic tern.

Green Turtle

Green turtle (above)
Reptiles only migrate
during the reproduction cycle,
and the green turtle *(Chelonia mydas)*,
in particular, swims vast distances (also showing
amazing navigational skills) to lay its eggs on the
specific beach of its own spawning. Distances of 1,400
miles have been recorded for green turtles swimming
between Ascension Island and the South American co

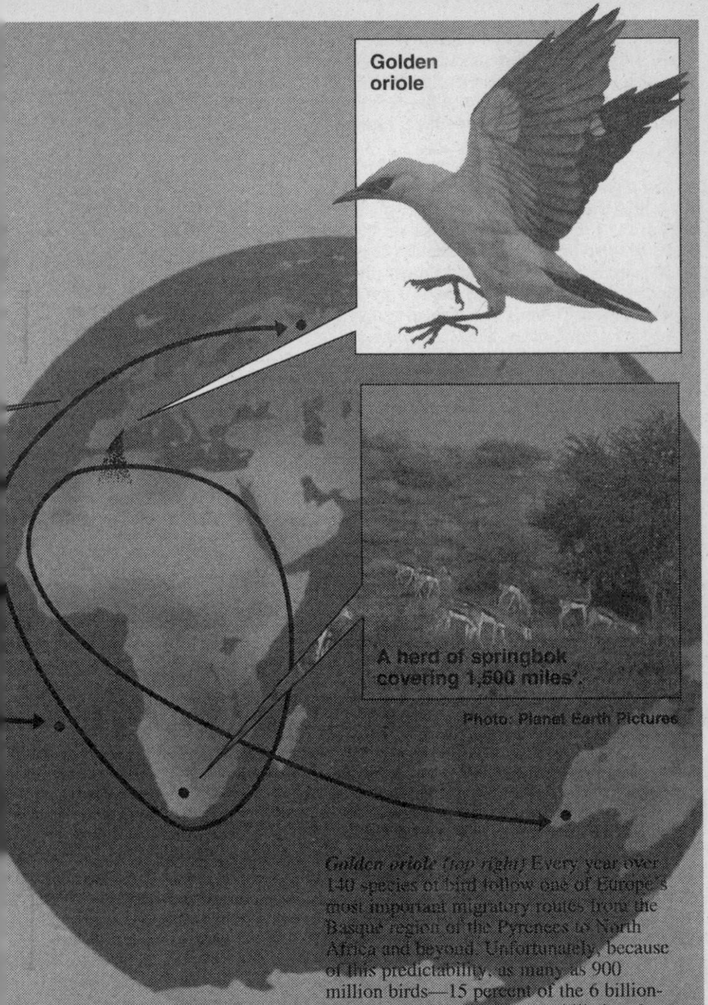

Golden oriole

A herd of springbok covering 1,500 miles?.

Photo: Planet Earth Pictures

Golden oriole (top right) Every year over 140 species of bird follow one of Europe's most important migratory routes from the Basque region of the Pyrenees to North Africa and beyond. Unfortunately, because of this predictability, as many as 900 million birds—15 percent of the 6 billion-strong migrating flocks—are killed each year by hunters. The golden oriole *(Oriolus oriolus)* is among the top ten species endangered through this practice.

Base artwork: Maltings Partnership, illustrations by Matthew Hillier.

Brooding   A female royal albatross (*Diomedea epomophora*) named Grandma
(Blue White), the oldest ringed seabird on record, laid an egg in November
1988 at the age of 60. She was first banded as a breeding adult in 1937 (such
birds do not start breeding until they are 9 years old). She has raised 10 chicks
of her own and fostered three others with her mate Green White Green, who
is 47.

Longest flights   The greatest distance covered by a ringed bird is 14,000 miles,
by an arctic tern (*Sterna paradisea*), which was banded as a nestling on 5 Jul
1955 in the Kandalaksha Sanctuary on the White Sea coast, Russia, and was
captured alive by a fisherman 8 miles south of Fremantle, Western Australia
on 16 May 1956. The bird had flown south via the Atlantic Ocean and then
circled Africa before crossing the Indian Ocean. It did not survive to make the
return journey. There is also a report of an Arctic tern flying from Greenland
to Australia, but further details are lacking.

In 1990 six foraging wandering albatrosses (*Diomedea exulans*) were
tracked across the Indian Ocean by satellite via radio transmitters fitted by
Pierre Jouventin and Henri Weimerskirch of the National Center for
Scientific Research at Beauvoir, France. Results showed that the birds
covered anywhere between 2,240 and 9,320 miles in a single feeding trip
and that they easily maintained a speed of 35 mph over a distance of more
than 500 miles, with the males going to sea for up to 33 days while their
partners remained ashore to incubate the eggs.

Highest-flying   Most migrating birds fly at relatively low altitudes (i.e., below
300 ft) and only a few dozen species fly higher than 3,000 ft.

The highest irrefutable altitude recorded for a bird is 37,000 ft for a
Ruppell's vulture (*Gyps rueppellii*), which collided with a commercial aircraft over Abidjan, Ivory Coast on 29 Nov 1973. The impact damaged one
of the aircraft's engines, causing it to shut down, but the plane landed
safely without further incident. Sufficient feather remains of the bird were
recovered to allow the Museum of Natural History in Washington, D.C. to

---

Largest nest   A nest measuring 9½ ft wide and 20 ft deep was built
by a pair of bald eagles (*Haliaeetus leucocephalus*), and possibly
their successors, near St Petersburg, FL. It was examined in 1963
and was estimated to weigh more than 2 tons. The golden eagle
(*Aquila chrysaetos*) also constructs huge nests, and one 15 ft deep
was reported from Scotland in 1954. It had been used for 45 years.

The incubation mounds built by the mallee fowl (*Leipoa
ocellata*) of Australia are much larger, measuring up to 15 ft in
height and 35 ft across, and it has been calculated that the nest site
may involve the mounding of 8,100 ft³ of material weighing
330 tons.

Smallest nest   The smallest nests are built by hummingbirds
(Trochilidae). That of the vervain hummingbird (*Mellisuga
minima*) is about half the size of a walnut, while the deeper one of
the bee hummingbird (*M. helenea*) is thimble-sized. (See Smallest
egg.)

make a positive identification of this high-flier, which is rarely seen above 20,000 ft.

United States The highest verified altitude record for a bird in the United States is 21,000 ft for a mallard (*Meleagris gallopavo*) that collided with a commercial jet on 9 Jul 1963 over Nevada. The jet crashed, killing all aboard.

Most airborne The most aerial of all birds is the sooty tern (*Sterna fuscata*), which, after leaving the nesting grounds, remains continuously aloft from 3–10 years as a sub-adult before returning to land to breed. The most aerial land bird is the common swift (*Apus apus*), which remains airborne for 2–3 years, during which time it sleeps, drinks, eats and even mates on the wing.

Fastest swimmer The gentoo penguin (*Pygoscelis papua*) has a maximum burst of speed of *c*. 17 mph.

Deepest dive In 1969 a depth of 870 ft was recorded for a small group of 10 emperor penguins (*Aptenodytes forsteri*) at Cape Crozier, Antarctica by a team of US scientists. One bird remained submerged for 18 minutes.

Keenest vision Birds of prey (Falconiformes) have the keenest eyesight in the avian world, and large species with eyes similar in size to those of humans have visual acuity at least twice that of human vision. It has also been calculated that a large eagle can detect a target object at a distance 3–8 times greater than that achieved by humans. Therefore a peregrine falcon (*Falco peregrinus*) can spot a pigeon at a range of over 5 miles under ideal conditions. In experiments carried out on the tawny owl (*Strix aluco*) at the University of Birmingham, Great Britain in 1977, it was revealed that the bird's eye on average was only $2\frac{1}{2}$ times more sensitive than the human eye. It was also discovered that the tawny owl sees perfectly adequately in daylight and that its visual acuity is only slightly inferior to that of humans.

The woodcock (family Scolopacidae) has eyes set so far back on its head that it has a 360° field of vision, enabling it to see all around and even over the top of its head.

Longest bills The bill of the Australian pelican (*Pelicanus conspicillatus*) is $13–18\frac{1}{2}$ in long. The longest bill in relation to overall body length is that of the sword-billed hummingbird (*Ensifera ensifera*) of the Andes from Venezuela to Bolivia. The bill measures 4 in in length and is longer than the bird's body excluding the tail.

Shortest bills The shortest bills in relation to body length are found among the smaller swifts (Apodidae) and in particular that of the glossy swiftlet (*Collocalia esculenta*), whose bill is almost nonexistent.

Largest egg The average ostrich (*Struthio camelus*) egg measures 6–8 in in length, 4–6 in in diameter and weighs 3.6–3.9 lb (about two dozen hens' eggs in volume). The egg requires about 40 min for boiling, and the shell, though only 0.06 in thick, can support the weight of a 280 lb man. On 28 Jun 1988 a 2-year-old cross between a northern and a southern ostrich (*Struthio c. camelus* and *Struthio c. australis*) laid an egg weighing a record 5.1 lb at the Kibbutz Ha'on collective farm, Israel.

United States The largest egg on the list of American birds is that of the trumpeter swan; it measures 4.3 in in length, 2.8 in in diameter. The average California condor egg measures 4.3 in in length and 2.6 in in diameter and weighs 9.5 oz.

Smallest egg Eggs emitted from the oviduct before maturity, known as "sports," are not considered to be of significance. The smallest egg laid by any bird is that of the vervain hummingbird (*Mellisuga minima*) of Jamaica. Two specimens measuring less than 0.39 in in length weighed 0.0128 oz and 0.0132 oz. (See Smallest nest.)

United States The smallest egg laid by a bird on the American list is that of

LONGEST BILL The bill of the Australian pelican can be up to 18^1/$_2$ in long, making it very useful for fishing and for reaching those awkward areas.
(Photo: Planet Earth Pictures/Pete Atkinson)

the Costa hummingbird (*Calypte coastae*); it measures 0.48 in in length and 0.33 in in diameter with a weight of 0.017 oz.

Longest incubation   The longest normal incubation period is that of the wandering albatross (*Diomedea exulans*), with a normal range of 75–82 days. There is an isolated case of an egg of the mallee fowl (*Leipoa ocellata*) of Australia taking 90 days to hatch, against its normal incubation of 62 days.

Shortest incubation   The shortest incubation period is 10 days in the case of the great spotted woodpecker (*Dendrocopus major*) and the black-billed cuckoo (*Coccyzus erythropthalmus*).

Bird-watchers   The world's leading bird-watcher or "twitcher" is Phoebe Snetsinger of Webster Groves, MO, who has logged 7,212 of the 9,672 known species, representing over 74 percent of the available total. (The exact number of species at a given time can vary because of changes in classifications.)

The greatest number of species spotted in a 24-hour period is 342, by Kenyans Terry Stevenson, John Fanshawe and Andy Roberts on day two of the Birdwatch Kenya '86 event held on 29–30 November. The 48-hour record is held by Don Turner and David Pearson of Kenya, who spotted 494 species at the same event.

Peter Kaestner of Washington, D.C. was the first person to see at least one species of each of the world's 159 bird families. He saw his final family on 1 Oct 1986. Since then Dr Ira Abramson of Miami, FL, Dr Martin Edwards of Kingston, Ontario, Canada and Harvey Gilston (last family seen in December 1988) have also succeeded in this achievement.

REPTILES *Reptilia*

CROCODILIANS

Largest   The largest reptile in the world is the estuarine or saltwater crocodile (*Crocodylus porosus*) of southeast Asia, the Malay Archipelago, Indonesia, northern Australia, Papua New Guinea, Vietnam and the Philippines. Adult males average 14–16 ft in length and weigh about 900–1,150 lb. There are four protected estuarine crocodiles at the Bhitarkanika Wildlife Sanctuary, Orissa State, eastern India that measure more than 19 ft 8 in in length. The largest individual is over 23 ft long.

Captive   The largest crocodile ever held in captivity is an estuarine/Siamese hybrid named Yai (b. 10 Jun 1972) at the Samutprakarn Crocodile Farm and Zoo, Thailand. He measures 19 ft 8 in in length and weighs 2,465 lb.

Smallest   Osborn's dwarf crocodile (*Osteolaemus osborni*), found in the upper region of the Congo River, West Africa, rarely exceeds 3 ft 11 in in length.

Oldest   The greatest age authenticated for a crocodile is 66 years for a female American alligator (*Alligator mississipiensis*) which arrived at Adelaide Zoo, South Australia on 5 Jun 1914 as a two-year-old, and died there on 26 Sep 1978.

LIZARDS

Largest   The largest of all lizards is the komodo monitor or ora (*Varanus komodoensis*), a dragonlike reptile found on the Indonesian islands of Komodo, Rintja, Padar and Flores. Adult males average 7 ft 5 in in length and weigh about 130 lb. Lengths up to 30 ft have been claimed for this species, but the largest specimen to be accurately measured was a male presented to an American zoologist in 1928 by the Sultan of Bima which was taped at 10 ft 1 in. In 1937 this animal was put on display in St Louis Zoological Gardens, MO for a short period. It then measured 10 ft 2 in in length and weighed 365 lb.

Smallest   *Sphaerodactylusparthenopion*, a tiny gecko indigenous to the island of Virgin Gorda, one of the British Virgin Islands, is believed to be the world's smallest lizard. It is known only from 15 specimens, including some pregnant females found between 10–16 Aug 1964. The three largest females measured 0.70 in from snout to vent, with a tail of approximately the same length.

It is possible that another type of gecko, *Sphaerodactylus elasmorhynchus*, may be even smaller. The only known specimen was an apparently mature female with a snout–vent measurement of 0.67 in and a tail of the same length. This specimen was found on 15 Mar 1966 among the roots of a tree in the western part of the Massif de la Hotte in Haiti.

Oldest   The greatest age recorded for a lizard is over 54 years for a male slow worm (*Anguis fragilis*) kept in the Zoological Museum in Copenhagen, Denmark from 1892 until 1946.

CHELONIANS

Largest   The largest living chelonian is the leatherback turtle (*Dermochelys coriacea*), which is circumglobal in distribution. The average adult measures 6–7 ft from the tip of the beak to the end of the tail (carapace 5–5½ ft), about 7 ft across the front flippers and weighs up to 1,000 lb.

The largest leatherback turtle ever recorded is a male found dead on the beach at Harlech, Great Britain on 23 Sep 1988. It measured 9 ft 5½ in in total length over the carapace (nose to tail), 9 ft across the front flippers and weighed an astonishing 2,120 lb. It is now in the possession of the National Museum of Wales, Great Britain and was put on public display on 16 Feb 1990.

The greatest weight reliably recorded in the United States is 1,908 lb for a male leatherback captured off Monterey, CA on 29 Aug 1961, which measured 8 ft 4 in.

Fastest reptile   The fastest speed measured for any reptile on land is 18 mph for a six-lined race runner (*Cnemidophorus sexlineatus*) near McCormick, SC in 1941.

Longest lizard   The slender Salvadori monitor (*Varanus salvadori*) of Papua New Guinea has been reliably measured up to 15 ft 7 in, but nearly 70 percent of the total length is taken up by the tail.

Tortoise   The largest living tortoise is the Aldabra giant tortoise (*Geochelone gigantea*) of the Indian Ocean islands of Aldabra, Mauritius and the Seychelles (introduced 1874). A male tortoise named Esmerelda, a longtime resident on Bird Island in the Seychelles, recorded a weight of 670 lb in November 1992.

Fastest   The fastest speed claimed for any reptile in water is 22 mph by a frightened Pacific leatherback turtle.

Deepest dive   In May 1987 it was reported by Dr Scott Eckert that a leatherback turtle (*Dermochelys coriacea*) fitted with a pressure-sensitive recording device had dived to a depth of 3,973 ft off the Virgin Islands in the West Indies.

LARGEST REPTILE   Feeding time at St. Augustine Alligator Farm, Florida for the estuarine crocodile Gomek, who, at 17 ft 8¼ in and about 1,800 lb, is the USA's largest captive specimen. However, this is still short of Yai from Thailand, the world record holder at 19 ft 8 in and 2,465 lb. (Photo: St Augustine Alligator Farm)

Smallest turtle   The smallest marine turtle in the world is the Atlantic ridley (*Lepidochelys kempii*), which has a shell length of 19.7–27.6 in and a maximum weight of 80 lb.

Oldest tortoise   The greatest authentic age recorded for a tortoise is over 152 years for a male Marion's tortoise (*Testudo sumeirii*), brought from the Seychelles to Mauritius in 1766 by the Chevalier de Fresne, who presented it to the Port Louis army garrison. This specimen, which went blind in 1908, was accidentally killed in 1918. The greatest proven age of a continuously observed tortoise is more than 116 years for a Mediterranean spur-thighed tortoise (*Testudo graeca*).

SNAKES, GENERAL

Longest The reticulated python (*Python reticulatus*) of southeast Asia, Indonesia and the Philippines regularly exceeds 20 ft 6 in. The record length is 32 ft 9½ in for a specimen shot in Celebes, Indonesia in 1912.

There are three species of snake in the United States with average measurements of 8 ft 6 in. These include the indigo snake (*Drymarchon corais*), the eastern coachwhip (*Masticophis flagellum*) and the black ratsnake (*Elaphe obsoleta*)—all found in the southeastern United States.

Captive The longest (and heaviest) snake ever held in captivity was a female reticulated python named Colossus who died in Highland Park Zoo, PA on 15 Apr 1963. She measured 28 ft 6 in in length, and weighed 320 lb at her heaviest.

Shortest The shortest snake in the world is the rare thread snake (*Leptotyphlops bilineata*), which is known only from the islands of Martinique, Barbados and St Lucia in the West Indies. In one series of eight specimens the two longest both measured 4¼ in.

Heaviest The anaconda (*Eunectes murinus*) of tropical South America and Trinidad is nearly twice as heavy as a reticulated python (*Python reticulatus*) of the same length. A female shot in Brazil *c.* 1960 was not weighed, but as it measured 27 ft 9 in in length with a girth of 44 in, it must have weighed nearly 500 lb. The average adult length is 18–20 ft.

Oldest The greatest reliable age recorded for a snake is 40 years 3 months 14 days for a male common boa (*Boa constrictor constrictor*) named Popeye, who died at the Philadelphia Zoo, PA on 15 Apr 1977.

VENOMOUS SNAKES

Longest The longest venomous snake in the world is the king cobra (*Ophiophagus hannah*), also called the hamadryad, of southeast Asia and the Philippines; it has an average adult length of 12–15 ft. A 18-ft-2-in specimen, captured alive near Fort Dickson in the state of Negri Sembilan, Malaya in April 1937, later grew to 18 ft 9 in in London Zoo, Great Britain. It was destroyed at the outbreak of war in 1939.

Shortest The namaqua dwarf adder (*Bitis schneideri*) of Namibia has an average adult length of 8 in.

Heaviest The heaviest venomous snake is probably the eastern diamondback rattlesnake (*Crotalus adamanteus*) of the southeastern United States. Adult examples average 5–6 ft in length and weigh 12–15 lb. One specimen, measuring 7 ft 9 in in length, weighed 34 lb.

The West African gaboon viper (*Bitis gabonica*) of the tropical rain forests is probably bulkier than the eastern diamond, but its average length is only 4–5 ft. A female 6 ft long was found to weigh 25 lb, and another female measuring 5 ft 8½ in weighed 18 lb with an empty stomach.

Most venomous All sea snakes are venomous, but the species *Hydrophis belcheri* has a myotoxic venom a hundred times as toxic as that of the Australian taipan (*Oxyuranus scutellatus*), whose bite can kill a man in minutes. The snake abounds in the Ashmore Reef in the Timor Sea, off the coast of northwest Australia.

The most venomous land snake is the 6-ft-6¾-in-long smooth-scaled snake (*Parademansia microlepidotus*) of the Diamantina River and Cooper's Creek drainage basins in Channel County, Queensland and western New South Wales, Australia, which has a venom nine times as toxic as that of the tiger snake (*Notechis scutatus*) of South Australia and Tasmania. One specimen yielded 0.00385 oz of venom after milking, enough to kill 125,000 mice, but so far no human fatalities have been reported.

More people die of snakebites in Sri Lanka than in any comparable area in the world. An average of 800 people are killed annually on the island by

Longest fangs The longest fangs of any snake are those of the highly venomous gaboon viper (*Bitis gabonica*) of tropical Africa. In a specimen of 6 ft length they measured 1.96 in. On 12 Feb 1963 a gaboon viper under severe stress sank its fangs into its own back at the Philadelphia Zoo, PA and died from traumatic injury to a vital organ. It did not, as has been widely reported, succumb to its own venom.

Fastest land snake The fastest-moving land snake is probably the slender black mamba (*Dendroaspis polylepis*) of the eastern part of tropical Africa. It is possible that this snake can achieve speeds of 10–12 mph in short bursts over level ground, and it is said to chase people aggressively.

LONGEST SNAKE   Uncoil this reticulated python and it could be over 20½ ft long. (Photo: Planet Earth Pictures/Ken Lucas)

snakes, and more than 95 percent of the fatalities are caused by the common krait (*Bungarus caeruleus*), the Sri Lankan cobra (*Naja n. naja*), and Russell's viper (*Vipera russelli pulchella*).

The saw-scaled or carpet viper (*Echis carinatus*) bites and kills more people in the world than any other species. Its geographical range extends from West Africa to India.

United States   The most venomous snake in the United States is the coral snake (*Micrurus fulvius*). In a standard LD99–100 test, which kills 99–100 percent of all mice injected with the venom, it takes 0.55 grain of venom per 2.2 lbs of mouse weight injected intravenously. In this test, the smaller the dosage, the more toxic the venom. However, the teeth of the coral snake point back into its mouth, and therefore it cannot inject the venom until it has a firm hold on the victim.

AMPHIBIANS *Amphibia*

Largest   The largest species of amphibian is the Chinese giant salamander (*Andrias davidianus*), which lives in northeastern, central and southern China. The average adult measures 3 ft 9 in in length and weighs 55–66 lb. One specimen collected in Hunan province weighed 143 lb and measured 5 ft 11 in in length.

Smallest   The smallest-known amphibian is the tiny Cuban frog (*Sminthillus limbatus*), which is less than 1/2 in long.

Oldest   The greatest authentic age recorded for an amphibian is 55 years for a Japanese giant salamander (*Andrias japonicus*) that died in Amsterdam Zoo in the Netherlands in 1881.

Highest and lowest   The greatest altitude at which an amphibian has been found is 26,246 ft for a common toad (*Bufo bufo*) collected in the Himalayas. This species has also been found at a depth of 1,115 ft in a coal mine.

FROGS

Largest   The largest-known frog is the rare African giant frog or goliath frog (*Conrana goliath*) of Cameroon and Equatorial Guinea. A specimen captured in April 1989 on the Sanaga River, Cameroon by Andy Koffman of Seattle, WA had a snout-to-vent length of 14 1/2 in (34 1/2 in overall with legs extended) and weighed 8 lb 1 oz on 30 Oct 1989.

Longest jump   (*Competition frog jumps are the aggregate of three consecutive leaps.*)

The greatest distance covered by a frog in a triple jump is 33 ft 5 1/2 in by a South African sharp-nosed frog (*Ptychadena oxyrhynchus*) named Santjie at a frog derby held at Lurula Natal Spa, Paulpietersburg, Natal, South Africa on 21 May 1977.

United States   At the annual Calaveras Jumping Jubilee held at Angels Camp, CA on 18 May 1986, an American bullfrog (*Rana catesbeiana*) called Rosie the Ribeter, owned and trained by Lee Giudicci of Santa Clara, CA, leapt 21 ft 5³/₄ in.

Longest amphibian gestation   The viviparous alpine black salamander (*Salamandra atra*) has a gestation period of up to 38 months at altitudes above 4,600 ft in the Swiss Alps, but this drops to 24–26 months at lower altitudes.

Smallest frog   The smallest frog in the world is *Sminthillus limbatus* of Cuba. (See Smallest amphibians.)

TOADS

Largest   The largest-known toad is the marine toad (*Bufo marinus*) of tropical South America and Queensland, Australia. An average adult specimen weighs 1 lb. The largest ever recorded was a male named Prinsen (The Prince), owned by Hakan Forsberg of Akers Styckebruk, Sweden. The toad weighed 5 lb 13¹/₂ oz and measured 15 in from snout to vent (21¹/₅ in when extended) in March 1991.

Smallest   The smallest toad in the world is the subspecies *Bufo taitanus beiranus*, originally of Mozambique, the largest specimen of which was 1 in long. (See Smallest amphibians.)

FISHES *Gnathostomata, Agnatha*

(See also Sports and Games—Fishing)

GENERAL RECORDS

Largest   The largest fish in the world is the rare plankton-feeding whale shark (*Rhincodon typus*), which is found in the warmer areas of the Atlantic, Pacific, and Indian Oceans. The longest scientifically measured one on record was a 41¹/₂-ft specimen captured off Baba Island near Karachi, Pakistan on 11 Nov 1949. It measured 23 ft around the thickest part of the body and weighed an estimated 16¹/₂ tons.

Bony   The longest of the bony or "true" fishes (Pisces) is the oarfish (*Regalecus glesne*), also called the "King of the Herrings," which has a world-wide distribution. In *c.* 1885 a specimen 25 ft long, weighing 600 lb, was caught by fishermen off Pemaquid Point, ME, but unconfirmed claims of 50 ft have been made.

**The world's largest carnivorous fish—the great white shark.
(Photo: Planet Earth Pictures/ Marty Snyderman)**

Heaviest The heaviest bony fish in the world is the ocean sunfish (*Mola mola*), which is found in all tropical, subtropical and temperate waters. On 18 Sep 1908 a specimen accidentally injured off Bird Island near Sydney, New South Wales, Australia weighed 4,927 lb and measured 14 ft between the anal and dorsal fins.

Carnivorous The largest carnivorous fish (excluding plankton-eaters) is the comparatively rare great white shark (*Carcharodon carcharias*), also called the "man-eater." Adult females (males are smaller) average 14–15 ft in length and generally weigh between 1,150–1,700 lb. The largest example accurately measured was 20 ft 4 in long and weighed 5,000 lb. It was harpooned and landed in the harbor of San Miguel, Azores in June 1978. (See Sports and Games, Fishing.)

Smallest The shortest recorded marine fish—and the shortest known vertebrate—is the dwarf goby (*Trimmatom nanus*) of the Chagos Archipelago, central Indian Ocean. In one series of 92 specimens collected by the 1978–79 Joint Services Chagos Research Expedition of the British Armed Forces, the adult males averaged 0.34 in in length and the adult females 0.35 in.

Oldest goldfish   Goldfish (*Carassius auratus*) have been reported to live for over 50 years in China.

A goldfish named Fred, owned by A.R. Wilson of Worthing, Great Britain, died on 1 Aug 1980 at 41 years of age.

Shortest-lived fish   The shortest-lived fish are probably certain species of the suborder Cyprinodontei (killifish), found in Africa and South America, which normally live about eight months.

Deepest fish   Brotulids of the genus *Bassogigas* are generally regarded as the deepest-living vertebrates. The greatest depth from which a fish has been recovered is 27,230 ft in the Puerto Rico Trench (27,488 ft) in the Atlantic by Dr Gilbert L. Voss of the US research vessel *John Elliott*, who took a 6$^{1}/_{2}$-in-long *Bassogigas profundissimus* in April 1970. It was only the fifth such brotulid ever caught.

Dr Jacques Piccard and Lt Don Walsh of the US Navy reported seeing a sole-like fish about 1 ft long (tentatively identified as *Chascanopsetta lugubris*) from the bathyscaphe *Trieste* at a depth of 35,820 ft in the Challenger Deep (Mariana Trench) in the western Pacific on 24 Jan 1960. This sighting, however, has been questioned by some authorities.

Most venomous   The most venomous fish in the world are the stonefish (Synanceidae) of the tropical waters of the Indo-Pacific, and in particular *Synanceja horrida*, which has the largest venom glands of any known fish. Direct contact with the spines of its fins, which contain a strong neurotoxic poison, often proves fatal.

Lightest   The lightest of all vertebrates and the smallest catch possible for any fisherman is the dwarf goby (*Schindleria praematurus*) from Samoa, which weighs only 2 mg (equivalent to 14,184 fish to the ounce) and is $^{1}/_{2}$–$^{3}/_{4}$ in long.

Shark   The spined pygmy shark (*Squaliolus laticaudus*) of the western Pacific matures at 6 in in length.

Fastest   The maximum swimming speed of a fish is dependent on the shape of its body and tail and its internal temperature. The cosmopolitan sailfish (*Istiophorus platypterus*) is considered to be the fastest species of fish over short distances, although the practical difficulties of measuring make data extremely difficult to secure. In a series of speed trials carried out at the Long Key Fishing Camp, FL, one sailfish took out 300 ft of line in 3 sec, which is equivalent to a velocity of 68 mph (compare with 60 mph for the cheetah).

Oldest   Aquaria are of too-recent origin to be able to establish with certainty which species of fish can be regarded as being the longest-lived. Early indications are, however, that it may be the lake sturgeon (*Acipenser fulvescens*) of North America. In one study of the growth rings (annuli) of 966 specimens caught in the Lake Winnebago region in Wisconsin between 1951 and 1954, the oldest sturgeon was found to be a male (length 6 ft 7 in) that gave a reading of 82 years and was still growing.

In 1948 the death was reported of an 88-year-old female European eel (*Anguilla anguilla*) named Putte in the aquarium at Hälsingborg Museum, southern Sweden. She was allegedly born in the Sargasso Sea, in the North Atlantic, in 1860, and was caught in a river as a 3-year-old elver.

In July 1974 a growth ring count of 228 years was reported for a female koi fish (a form of fancy carp) named Hanako living in a pond in Higashi Shirakawa, Gifu Prefecture, Japan, but the greatest authoritatively accepted age for this species is "more than 50 years."

The perchlike marine fish *Notothenia neglecta* of the Antarctic Ocean, whose blood contains a natural antifreeze, is reported to live up to 150 years, but this claim has not yet been verified.

Most eggs The ocean sunfish (*Mola mola*) produces up to 30 million eggs, each of them measuring about 0.05 in in diameter, at a single spawning.

Fewest eggs The mouth-brooding cichlid *Tropheus moorii* of Lake Tanganyika, East Africa, produces seven eggs or less during normal reproduction.

Most valuable The world's most valuable fish is the Russian sturgeon (*Huso huso*). One 2,706-lb female caught in the Tikhaya Sosna River in 1924 yielded 541 lb of best-quality caviar, which would be worth $300,000 on today's market.

The 30-in-long Ginrin Showa koi, which won the supreme championship in nationwide Japanese koi shows in 1976, 1977, 1979 and 1980, was sold two years later for 17 million yen. In March 1986 this ornamental carp was acquired by Derry Evans, owner of the Kent Koi Centre near Sevenoaks, Great Britain, for an undisclosed sum, but the 15-year-old fish died five months later. It has since been stuffed and mounted to preserve its beauty.

Most ferocious The razor-toothed piranhas of the genera *Serrasalmus*, *Pygocentrus* and *Pygopristis* are the most ferocious freshwater fish in the world. They live in the sluggish waters of the large rivers of South America, and will attack any creature, regardless of size, if it is injured or making a commotion in the water. On 19 Sep 1981 more than 300 people were reportedly killed and eaten when an overloaded passenger-cargo boat capsized and sank as it was docking at the Brazilian port of Obidos. According to one official, only 178 of the boat's passengers survived.

Most electric The most powerful electric fish is the electric eel (*Electrophorus electricus*), which is found in the rivers of Brazil, Colombia, Venezuela and Peru. An average-sized specimen can discharge 400 volts at 1 amp, but measurements up to 650 volts have been recorded.

MARINE

Largest The largest marine fish is the whale shark (*Rhincodon typus*), which can reach 30 ft in length. (See Fishes, General records.)

Smallest The shortest recorded marine fish is the dwarf goby (*Trimmatom nanus*) of the Chagos Archipelago in the Indian Ocean with average lengths of 0.34–0.35 in. (See Fishes, General records, Smallest.)

FRESHWATER

Largest   The largest fish that spends its whole life in fresh or brackish water is the rare pla beuk (*Pangasianodon gigas*). It is confined to the Mekong River and its major tributaries in China, Laos, Cambodia and Thailand. The largest specimen, captured in the River Ban Mee Noi, Thailand, was reportedly 9 ft 10¼ in long and weighed 533½ lb. This was exceeded by the European catfish or wels (*Silurus glanis*) in earlier times (in the 19th century lengths up to 15 ft and weights up to 720 lb were reported for Russian specimens), but today anything over 6 ft and 200 lb is considered large.

The arapaima (*Arapaima glanis*), also called the pirarucu, found in the Amazon and other South American rivers and often claimed to be the largest freshwater fish, averages 6½ ft and 150 lb. The largest authentically recorded specimen measured 8 ft 1½ in in length and weighed 325 lb. It was caught in the Rio Negro, Brazil in 1836.

Smallest   The shortest and lightest freshwater fish is the dwarf pygmy goby (*Pandaka pygmaea*), a colorless and nearly transparent species found in the streams and lakes of Luzon in the Philippines. Adult males measure only 0.28–0.38 in in length and weigh 0.00014–0.00018 oz.

The world's smallest commercial fish is the now-endangered sinarapan (*Mistichthys luzonensis*), a goby found only in Lake Buhi, Luzon, Philippines. Adult males measure 0.39–0.51 in in length, and a dried 1-lb fish cake contains about 70,000 of them!

STARFISHES *Asteroidea*

Largest   The largest of the 1,600 known species of starfish in terms of total arm span is the very fragile brisingid *Midgardia xandaros*. A specimen collected by the Texas A & M University research vessel *Alaminos* in the southern part of the Gulf of Mexico in the late summer of 1968 measured 4½ ft tip to tip, but the diameter of its disc was only 1.02 in. Its dry weight was 2.46 oz.

Heaviest   The heaviest species of starfish is the five-armed *Thromidia catalai* of the western Pacific. One specimen collected off Ilot Amédée, New Caledonia on 14 Sep 1969 and later deposited in Nouméa Aquarium weighed an estimated 13 lb 4 oz (total arm span 24.8 in).

> ***Most destructive starfish***   The crown of thorns (*Acanthaster planci*) of the Indo-Pacific region and the Red Sea has 12–19 arms and can measure up to 24 in in diameter. It feeds on coral polyps and can destroy 46½–62 in² of coral in one day. It has been responsible for the destruction of large parts of the Great Barrier Reef off Australia (See Jellyfishes and Corals; also Earth and Space, Longest reef).

Smallest   The smallest-known starfish is the asterinid sea star *Patiriella par-vivipara*, discovered by Wolfgang Zeidler on the west coast of the Eyre peninsula, South Australia in 1975. It has a maximum radius of only 0.18 in and a diameter of less than 0.35 in.

Deepest   The greatest depth from which a starfish has been recovered is 24,881 ft for a specimen of *Porcellanaster ivanovi* collected by the Soviet research ship *Vityaz* in the Mariana Trench, in the western Pacific, *c*. 1962.

CRUSTACEANS *Crustacea*

(Crabs, lobsters, shrimps, prawns, crawfish, barnacles, water fleas, fish lice, sandhoppers, krill, etc.)

Largest marine   The largest of all crustaceans (although not the heaviest) is the takashigani or giant spider crab (*Macrocheira kaempferi*), also called the stilt crab, which is found in deep waters off the southeastern coast of Japan. Mature specimens usually have a body measuring 10 x 12 in and a claw-span of 8–9 ft, but unconfirmed measurements up to 19 ft have been reported. A specimen with a claw-span of 12 ft 1½ in weighed 41 lb.

Heaviest   The heaviest of all crustaceans, and the largest species of lobster, is the American or North Atlantic lobster (*Homarus americanus*). On 11 Feb 1977 a specimen weighing 44 lb 6 oz and measuring 3 ft 6 in from the end of the tail fan to the tip of the largest claw was caught off Nova Scotia, Canada and later sold to a New York restaurant owner.

Largest freshwater   The largest freshwater crustacean is a species of crayfish, or crawfish (*Astacopsis gouldi*) found in the streams of Tasmania, Australia. It has been measured up to 2 ft in length and may weigh as much as 9 lb. In 1934 an unconfirmed weight of 14 lb (total length 29 in) was reported for an outsized specimen caught at Bridport, Tasmania, Australia.

Smallest   Water fleas of the genus *Alonella* may measure less than 0.01 in in length. They are found in British waters.

Deepest   The greatest depth from which a crustacean has been recovered is 34,450 ft for *live* amphipods from the Challenger Deep (Mariana Trench), western Pacific by the US research vessel *Thomas Washington* in November 1980.

Highest   Amphipods and isopods have also been collected in the Ecuadorean Andes at a height of 13,300 ft.

Largest concentration   The largest single concentration of crustaceans ever recorded was an enormous swarm of krill (*Euphausia superba*) estimated to weigh 11 million tons and tracked by US scientists off Antarctica in March 1981.

> **Oldest crustacean**   Very large specimens of the American lobster (*Homarus americanus*) may be as much as 50 years old.
>
> **Fastest spider**   The fastest-moving arachnids are the long-legged sun spiders of the order Solifugae, which live in the arid semidesert regions of Africa and the Middle East. They feed on geckos and other lizards and can reach speeds of over 10 mph.

ARACHNIDS *Arachnida*

SPIDERS (Araneae)

Largest   The world's largest-known spider is the goliath bird-eating spider (*Theraphosa leblondi*) of the coastal rain forests of Surinam, Guyana and French Guiana, northeastern South America; isolated specimens have also been reported from Venezuela and Brazil. A male example collected by members of the Pablo San Martin Expedition at Rio Cavro, Venezuela in April 1965 had a leg span of 11.02 in.

Heaviest   Female bird-eating spiders are more heavily built than males, and in February 1985 Charles J. Seiderman of New York City captured a female example near Paramaribo, Surinam which weighed a record peak 4.3 oz before its death from moulting problems in January 1986. Other measurements included a maximum leg span of 10½ in, a total body length of 4 in, and 1-in-long fangs.

United States   The *Aphonopelma chalcodes* of the family Theraphofidae, a type of tarantula found in Arizona and New Mexico, is the heaviest spider and has the longest body. The female weighs 2.8 oz with a body length of 10½ in.

Smallest   The smallest-known spider is *Patu marplesi* (family Symphytognathidae) of Western Samoa in the Pacific. The type specimen (male), found in moss at *c.* 2,000 ft in Madolelei, Western Samoa in January 1965, measured 0.017 in overall, which means that it was about the size of a period on this page.

United States   The *Troglonata paradoxum* of the family Mysmmenidae is the smallest spider in the United States.

Oldest   The longest-lived of all spiders are the primitive Mygalomorphae (tarantulas and allied species). One female therasophid collected in Mexico in 1935 lived for an estimated 26–28 years.

United States   The longest-lived species of American spider is the *Rhecosticta californica* of the family Theraphosidae, which has an average life span of 25 years.

LONGEST-LIVED SPIDER This orange-kneed tarantula (*Aphonopelma emiliae*) from Mexico is one example of the primitive Mygalomorphae spiders, which can live for up to 28 years. Although harmless to humans and often kept as pets, they can inflict a nasty bite when provoked. (Photo: Planet Earth Pictures/Mary Clay)

Most venomous The world's most venomous spiders are the Brazilian wandering spiders of the genus *Phoneutria*, and particularly *P. fera*, which has the most active neurotoxic venom of any living spider. These large and highly aggressive creatures frequently enter human dwellings and hide in clothing or shoes. When disturbed they bite furiously several times, and hundreds of accidents involving these species are reported annually. When deaths do occur, they are usually in children under the age of seven. Fortunately, an effective antivenin is available.

Webs Largest Aerial webs spun by the tropical orb weavers of the genus *Nephila* have been measured up to 18 ft 9¾ in in circumference.

Smallest The smallest webs are spun by spiders such as *Glyphesis cottonae* and cover about ¾ in².

SCORPIONS (Scorpiones)

Largest The largest of the 800 or so species of scorpion is the tropical "emperor" (*Pandinus imperator*) of Guinea, adult males of which can attain a body length of 7 in or more.

Smallest The smallest scorpion in the world is *Microbothus pusillus* from the Red Sea coast, which measures about ½ in in total length.

Most venomous The most venomous scorpion in the world is the Palestine yellow scorpion (*Leiurus quinquestriatus*), which ranges from the eastern part of North Africa through the Middle East to the shores of the Red Sea. Fortunately, the amount of venom it delivers is very small (0.000009 oz) and adult lives are seldom endangered; however, it has been responsible for a number of fatalities among children under the age of five.

INSECTS *Insecta*

It is estimated that there may be as many as 30 million species of insect—more than all other phyla and classes put together—but thousands are known only from a single type or specimen.

Heaviest The heaviest living insects are the Goliath beetles (family Scarabaeidae) of Equatorial Africa. The largest members of the group are *Goliathus regius*, *G. goliathus* (=*G. giganteus*) and *G. druryi*, and in one series of fully-grown males (females are smaller) the lengths from the tips of the small frontal horns to the end of the abdomen measured up to 4.33 in and the weights ranged from $2^{1}/2$–$3^{1}/2$ oz.

The elephant beetles (*Megasoma*) of Central America and the West Indies attain the greatest dimensions in terms of volume, but they lack the massive build-up of heavy chiton forming the thorax and anterior sternum of the goliaths, and this gives them a distinct weight advantage.

Longest The longest insects in the world are stick-insects (walking sticks), especially of the African species *Palophus*, which can attain lengths of $15^{3}/4$ in in the case of *Palophus leopoldi*.

Smallest The smallest insects recorded so far are the "feather-winged" beetles of the family Ptiliidae (=trichopterygidae) and the "battledore-wing fairy flies" (parasitic wasps) of the family Mymaridae; they are smaller than some species of protozoa (single-celled animals).

Lightest The male bloodsucking banded louse (*Enderleinellus zonatus*) and the parasitic wasp (*Caraphractus cinctus*) may each weigh as little as 5,670,000 to an oz. Eggs of the latter each weigh 141,750,000 to an oz.

Fastest-flying Acceptable modern experiments have now established that the highest maintainable air speed of any insect, including the deer botfly, hawkmoths (Sphingidae), horseflies (*Tabanus bovinus*) and some tropical butterflies (Hesperiidae) is 24 mph, rising to a maximum of 36 mph for the Australian dragonfly *Austrophlebia costalis* for short bursts. Experiments have proved that the widely publicized claim by an American scientist in 1926 that the deer botfly (*Cephenemyia pratti*) could attain a speed of 818 mph at an altitude of 12,000 ft was wildly exaggerated. If true, the fly would have had to develop the equivalent of 1.5 hp and consume $1^{1}/2$ times its own weight in food per second to acquire the energy that would be needed and, even if this were possible, it would still be crushed by the air pressure and incinerated by the friction.

Fastest-moving The fastest-moving insects are certain large tropical cockroaches, and the record is 3.36 mph, or 50 body lengths per second, registered by *Periplaneta americana* at the University of California at Berkeley in 1991.

Highest g force   The click beetle (*Athous haemorrhoidalis*) averages 400 g when "jack-knifing" into the air to escape predators. One example measuring 1/2 in in length and weighing 0.00014 oz that jumped to a height of 11¾ in was calculated to have "endured" a peak brain deceleration of 2,300 g by the end of the movement.

The cockroach—the world's fastest insect. (Photo: Planet Earth Pictures/John Lythgoe)

Loudest insect   The loudest of all insects is the male cicada (family Cicadidae). At 7,400 pulses/min its tymbal organs produce a noise (officially described by the US Department of Agriculture as "Tsh-ee-EEEE-e-ou") detectable more than a quarter of a mile distant.

Largest cockroach   The world's largest cockroach is *Megaloblatta longipennis* of Colombia. A preserved female in the collection of Akira Yokokura of Yamagata, Japan measures 3.81 in in length and 1.77 in across.

Largest termite mound   In 1968 W. Page photographed a specimen south of Horgesia, Somalia estimated to be 28½ ft tall.

Mantle of bees   Jed Shaner was covered by a mantle of an estimated 343,000 bees weighing an aggregate of 80 lb at Staunton, VA on 29 Jun 1991.

Fastest wing-beat   The fastest wing-beat of any insect under natural conditions is 62,760 per min by a tiny midge of the genus *Forcipomyia*. In experiments with truncated wings at a temperature of 98.6° F the rate increased to 133,080 beats/min. The muscular contraction-expansion cycle in 0.00045 sec represents the fastest muscle movement ever measured.

Oldest   The longest-lived insects are the splendor beetles (Buprestidae). On 27 May 1983 a *Buprestis aurulenta* appeared from the staircase timber in the the home of Mr W. Euston of Prittlewell, Great Britain, after 47 years as a larva.

Slowest wing-beat   The slowest wing-beat of any insect is 300 per min by the swallowtail butterfly (*Papilio machaon*). The average is 460–636 per min.

DRAGONFLIES (Odonata)

Largest   The species *Megaloprepus caeruleata* of Central and South America has been measured up to 4.72 in across the wings and 7.52 in in body length.

United States   The giant green darner (*Anax walsinghami*), found in the West, has a body length of up to $4^1/2$ in.

Smallest   The world's smallest dragonfly is *Agriocnemis naia* of Myanmar (Burma). A specimen in the British Museum (Natural History), London, Great Britain had a wing spread of 0.69 in and a body length of 0.71 in.

United States   The smallest dragonfly in the United States is the elfin skimmer (*Nannothaemis Bella*), which has a body length of $4/5$ in.

FLEAS (Siphonaptera)

Largest   Siphonapterologists recognize 1,830 varieties, of which the largest-known is *Hystrichopsylla schefferi*, which was described from a single specimen taken from the nest of a mountain beaver (*Aplodontia rufa*) at Puyallup, WA in 1913. Females are up to 0.3 in long.

BUTTERFIES AND MOTHS (Lepidoptera)

Largest   The largest-known butterfly is the protected Queen Alexandra's birdwing (*Ornithoptera alexandrae*), which is restricted to the Popondetta Plain in Papua New Guinea. Females may have a wingspan exceeding 11 in and weigh over 0.9 oz.

Longest jump   The champion jumper among fleas is the common flea (*Pulex irritans*). In one American experiment carried out in 1910 a specimen allowed to leap at will performed a long jump of 13 in and a high jump of $7^3/4$ in. In jumping 130 times its own height a flea subjects itself to a force of $200\,g$.

Most acute sense of smell   The most acute sense of smell exhibited in nature is that of the male emperor moth (*Eudia pavonia*), which, according to German experiments in 1961, can detect the sex attractant of the virgin female at the almost unbelievable range of 6.8 miles upwind. This scent has been identified as one of the higher alcohols ($C_{16}H_{29}OH$), of which the female carries less than 0.0001 mg.

The largest moth in the world (although not the heaviest) is the Hercules moth (*Cosdinoscera hercules*) of tropical Australia and New Guinea. A wing area of up to 41 in² and a wingspan of 11 in have been recorded. In 1948 an unconfirmed measurement of 14 in was reported for a female captured in Innisfail, Queensland, Australia.

The rare owlet moth (*Thysania agrippina*) of Brazil has been measured up to 12¹/₅ in wingspan in the case of a female taken in 1934.

United States The largest *native* butterfly in the United States is the giant swallowtail (*Papilio cresphontes*), found in the eastern states, with a wingspan of up to 6 in.

Smallest The smallest of the 140,000 known species of Lepidoptera is *Stigmella ridiculosa*, which has a wingspan of 0.079 in with a similar body length and is found in the Canary Islands.

United States The smallest butterfly in the United States is the pygmy blue (*Brephidium exilis*), found in the Southeast, with a wingspan of ³/₈–³/₄ in.

Migration A tagged female monarch butterfly (*Danaus plexippus*) released by Donald Davis at Presqu'ile Provincial Park near Brighton, Ontario, Canada on 6 Sep 1986 was recaptured 2,133 miles away, on a mountain near Angangueo, Mexico on 15 Jan 1987. This distance was obtained by measuring a line from the release site to the recapture site, but the actual distance traveled could be up to double this figure.

Largest butterfly farm The Stratford-upon-Avon Butterfly Farm, Warwickshire, Great Britain can accommodate 2,000 exotic butterflies in authentic rain forest conditions. The total capacity of all flight areas at the farm, which opened on 15 Jul 1985, is over 141,259 ft³. The complex also comprises insect and plant houses and educational facilities.

United States Butterfly World, in Coconut Creek, FL, accommodates 2,000 butterflies in authentic rain forest or North American conditions. About 80 species of butterfly can be seen at any one time, and in the course of a year up to 300 species are shown in the three large screened aviaries for display and 36 separate screen enclosures for breeding.

CENTIPEDES *Chilopoda*

Longest The longest-known species of centipede is a large variant of the widely distributed *Scolopendra morsitans* found on the Andaman Islands in the Bay of Bengal. Specimens measuring 13 in long and 1¹/₂ in wide have been recorded.

Shortest The shortest recorded centipede is an unidentified species which measures only 0.19 in.

United States *Nampabius georgianus*, found in Georgia, measures up to 0.19

in in length and 0.03 in in diameter. *Poaaphilis keywinus*, found in Iowa, is smaller in diameter at 0.007 in, but has a length of 0.25 in.

Most legs *Himantarum gabrielis*, found in southern Europe, has 171–177 pairs of legs.

Fastest The fastest centipede is probably *Scrutigera coleoptrata* of southern Europe, which can travel at 1.1 mph.

MILLIPEDES *Diplopoda*

Longest Both *Graphidostreptus gigas* of Africa and *Scaphistostreptus seychellarum* of the Seychelles have been measured up to 11 in in length and 0.8 in in diameter.

United States *Orthoporus ornatus*, found in Texas and Arizona, measures up to 7.28 in in length and 0.55 in in diameter.

Shortest The shortest millipede in the world is the British species *Polyxenus lagurus*, which measures 0.08–0.15 in.

United States *Polyxenus fasciculatus*, found in the Southeast, measures only 0.07 in in length and 0.03 in in diameter. The next-shortest millipede is *Buotus carolinus*, found in North Carolina and Virginia, which has been measured at 0.11 in in length and only 0.01 in in diameter.

Most legs The greatest number of legs reported for a millipede is 375 pairs (750 legs) for *Illacme plenipes* of California.

SEGMENTED WORMS *Annelida*

Longest The longest-known species of earthworm is *Microchaetus rappi* (=*M. microchaetus*) of South Africa. In *c.* 1937 a giant earthworm measur-

---

Worm-charming At the first World Worm Charming Championship held at Willaston, Great Britain on 5 Jul 1980, Tom Shufflebotham (b. 1960) charmed a record 511 worms out of the ground (a 9.84 ft ^{2} plot) in the allotted time of 30 min. Garden forks or other implements are vibrated in the soil by competitors to coax up the worms, but water is banned.

ing 22 ft in length when naturally extended and 0.8 in in diameter was collected in the Transvaal.

Shortest   *Chaetogaster annandalei* measures less than 0.02 in in length.

MOLLUSKS *Mollusca*

CEPHALOPODS

Largest invertebrate   The Atlantic giant squid, *Architeuthis dux*, is the world's largest-known invertebrate. The heaviest ever recorded was a 2.2-ton monster that ran aground in Thimble Tickle Bay, Newfoundland, Canada on 2 Nov 1878. Its body was 20 ft long and one tentacle measured 35 ft.

Longest   The longest mollusk ever recorded was a 57-ft giant *Architeuthis longimanus* that was washed up on Lyall Bay, Cook Strait, New Zealand in October 1887. Its two long slender tentacles each measured 49 ft 3 in.

Largest octopus   The largest-known octopus is the Pacific giant (*Octopus dofleini*), which ranges from California to Alaska and off eastern Asia south to Japan. It is not known exactly how large these creatures can grow but the average mature male weighs about 51 lb and has an arm span of about 8 ft. The largest recorded specimen, found off western Canada in 1957, had an estimated arm span of 31 1/2 ft and weighed about 600 lb.

The Pacific giant—the world's largest octopus.
(Photo: Planet Earth Pictures/Ken Lucas)

Smallest The smallest cephalopod is the squid *Idiosepius*, which rarely reaches 1 in in length.

Oldest The longest-lived mollusk is the ocean quahog (*Arctica islandica*), a thick-shelled clam found in the mid-Atlantic. A specimen with 220 annual growth rings was collected in 1982.

Most venomous The two closely related species of blue-ringed octopus *Hapalochlaena masculosa* and *H. lunulata*, found around the coasts of Australia, carry a neurotoxic venom so potent that scientists at the Commonwealth Serum Laboratories in Melbourne, Victoria, consider one bite sufficient to paralyze (or sometimes kill) seven people. The venom acts so quickly that an antivenin could only rarely, if ever, be used in time to save life. These molluscs have a radial spread of just 4-6 in.

Most tentacles Most cephalopods have eight or 10 tentacles, but some types of *Nautilus* use up to 94 suckerless tentacles for catching prey on the ocean floor.

BIVALVES

Largest The largest of all existing bivalve shells is that of the marine giant clam *Tridacna gigas,* found on the Indo-Pacific coral reefs. An outsized specimen measuring 45$^{1}/_{5}$ in in length and weighing 734 lb was collected off Ishigaki Island, Okinawa, Japan in 1956 but was not scientifically examined until August 1984. It probably weighed just over 750 lb when alive (the soft parts weigh up to 20 lb).

Longest Another giant clam collected at Tapanoeli (Tapanula) on the northwest coast of Sumatra, Indonesia before 1817 and now preserved at Arno's Vale measures 54 in in length and weighs 507 lb.

Smallest The smallest bivalve shell is the coinshell *Neolepton sykesi*, which is known only from a few examples collected off Guernsey, Channel Islands, Great Britain and western Ireland. It has an average diameter of 0.047 in.

Most venomous bivalve There are some 400–500 species of cone shell (*Conus*), all of which can deliver a poisonous neurotoxin. The geographer cone (*Conus geographus*) and the court cone (*C. aulicus*), marine mollusks found from Polynesia to East Africa, are considered to be the most deadly. The venom is injected by a unique, fleshy harpoon-like proboscis, and symptoms include impaired vision, dizziness, nausea, paralysis and death. Of the 25 people known to have been stung by these creatures, five have died, giving a mortality rate exceeding that for common cobras and rattlesnakes.

GASTROPODS

Largest   The largest-known gastropod is the trumpet or baler conch (*Syrinx aruanus*) of Australia. One specimen collected off Western Australia in 1979 and now owned by Don Pisor of San Diego, CA measures 30.4 in in length and has a maximum girth of 39³/₄ in. It weighed nearly 40 lb when alive.

The largest-known land gastropod is the African giant snail (*Achatina achatina*). A specimen named Gee Geronimo owned by Christopher Hudson of Hove, Great Britain, measured 15¹/₂ in from snout to tail when fully extended (shell length 10³/₄ in) in December 1978 and weighed exactly 2 lb. The snail was collected in Sierra Leone in June 1976.

Smallest   The smallest-known shellbearing species is the gastropod *Ammonicera rota*, which is found in British waters. It measures 0.02 in in diameter. A gastropod shell of the species *Bittium* measuring 0.015 in long and 0.012 in wide was found off the Nansha Islands by Zheng Genhai of Shanghai, China.

Fastest   The world's fastest gastropods are probably banana slugs of the species *Ariolimax*. The fastest recorded speed was 0.28 in/sec over 36 in set by a specimen of *A. columbianus* in a slug race at Northwest Trek, WA in July 1983.

Snails   The fastest land snails are probably the carnivorous (and Cannibalistic) species such as *Euglandina rosea* which outpace other snails in their hunt for prey. The snail-racing equivalent of a four-minute mile is 24 in in 3 min, or a 5¹/₂ day mile, by the common garden snail (*Helix aspersa*).

RIBBON WORMS *Nemertina*

Longest   The longest of the 550 recorded species of ribbon worm, also called nemertines (or nemerteans), is the "boot-lace" worm (*Lineus longissimus*), which is found in the shallow waters of the North Sea, Great Britain. A specimen that washed ashore at St Andrews, Fife, Great Britain in 1864 after a severe storm measured more than 180 ft in length.

JELLYFISHES AND CORALS *Cnidaria*

Largest jellyfish The largest jellyfish is the Arctic giant jellyfish (*Cyanea capillata arctica*) of the northwestern Atlantic. One that washed up in Massachusetts Bay had a bell diameter of 7 ft 6 in and tentacles stretching 120 ft.

Most venomous The beautiful but deadly Australian sea wasp (*Chironex fleckeri*) is the most venomous jellyfish in the world. Its cardiotoxic venom has caused the deaths of 66 people off the coast of Queensland since 1880, with victims dying within 1–3 minutes if medical aid is not available. One effective defense is women's pantyhose, outsize versions of which are now worn by Queensland lifesavers at surfing tournaments.

Coral The world's greatest stony coral structure is the Great Barrier Reef off Queensland, northeast Australia. It stretches 1,260 miles and covers 80,000 miles². (See Most destructive starfish.)

The world's largest reported example of discrete coral is a stony colony of *Galaxea fascicularis* found in Sakiyama Bay off Irimote Island, Okinawa on 7 Aug 1982 by Dr Shohei Shirai of the Institute for Development of Pacific Natural Resources. It has a long axis measurement of 23 ft 9 in, a height of 13 ft 1½ in and a maximum circumference of 59 ft 5 in.

SPONGES *Porifera*

Largest The largest-known sponge is the barrel-shaped loggerhead sponge (*Spheciospongia vesparium*) of the West Indies and the waters off Florida. Individuals measure up to 3 ft 6 in in height and 3 ft in diameter. Neptune's cup or goblet (*Poterion patera*) of Indonesia grows to 4 ft in height, but it is a less bulky animal.

Heaviest In 1909 a wool sponge (*Hippospongia canaliculatta*) measuring 6 ft in circumference was collected off the Bahamas. When taken from the water it weighed between 80–90 lb but after it had been dried and relieved of all excrescences it weighed 12 lb. (This sponge is now preserved in the National Museum of Natural History, Washington, D.C.)

Smallest The widely distributed *Leucosolenia blanca* measures 0.11 in in height when fully grown.

Deepest Sponges have been recovered from depths of up to 18,500 ft.

EXTINCT ANIMALS

DINOSAURS

Part of the reptile order, dinosaurs are undoubtably the best-known group of extinct animals. The first dinosaur to be scientifically described was *Megalosaurus bucklandi* ("great fossil lizard") in 1824. The remains of this bipedal flesh-eater were found by workmen before 1818 in a slate quarry near Woodstock, Great Britain and later placed in the University Museum, in Oxford, Great Britain. The first fossil bone of *Megalosaurus* was actually illustrated in 1677, but its true nature was not realized until much later. It was not until 1842 that the name Dinosauria ("terrible lizards") was given to these newly discovered giants.

Disappearance No wholly satisfactory theory has been offered for the dinosaurs' sudden extinction 65 million years ago. Evidence from the Hell Creek Formation of Montana suggests that dinosaurs dwindled in importance over a period of 5–10 million years and were replaced progressively by mammals, possibly because of long-term climatic changes.

Another theory is their sudden elimination by the impact of an asteroid, which would have had a diameter of some 5.6 miles, or by a shower of comets causing clouds of dust to block out the sun. The asteroid theory is supported strongly by the discovery of significant levels of the element iridium, a good indicator of extraterrestrial impact, at numerous locations around the world.

In 1991 the possible impact crater was found in the Yucatán region of Central America, called Chicxulub Crater. It dates to 65 million years ago and is associated with iridium, melt glasses and evidence of tsunamis (giant sea waves) around the proto-Caribbean.

A further hypothesis is that of a period of severe volcanic activity, which would also result in darkness caused by dust, acid rain and iridium.

Earliest-known The most primitive dinosaur is *Eoraptor lunensis* ("dawn stealer"), named in 1993 from a skeleton found in the foothills of the Andes in Argentina, in rocks dated as 230 million years old. This dinosaur was 39 in long and is classified as a theropod, a member of the group of meat-eating dinosaurs. It is the most primitive of the group since it lacks the dual-hinged jaw present in all other members.

Another dinosaur from the same area and rocks is *Herrerasaurus,* a carnivore known best from an almost complete skeleton discovered in 1989. *Herrerasaurus* was about 6½–8 ft long and weighed over 220 lb. Although of the same age as *Eoraptor*, it had a dual-hinged jaw.

Other dinosaurs of a similar age from the Late Triassic are known from incomplete remains found in Brazil, Morocco, India and Scotland.

United States The earliest dated remains of dinosaurs found in the United States are those of *Coelophysis*, found at Ghost Ranch, MI in 1947. They are slightly younger than the *Herrerasaurus* remains found in Argentina. The creatures ranged in size from smaller than a chicken to larger than a turkey. The

Most Primitive Dinosaur
Eoraptor Lunensis

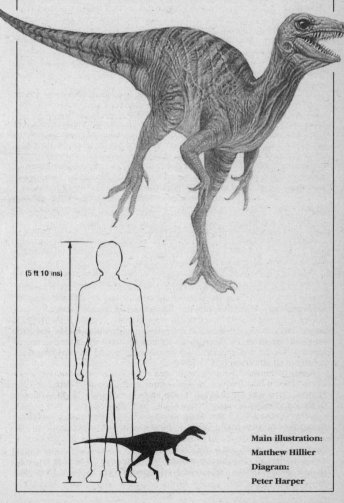

(5 ft 10 ins)

Main illustration:
Matthew Hillier
Diagram:
Peter Harper

find represents the largest concentration of skeletal remains, over 1,000, of meat-eating dinosaurs in the world.

Largest The largest-ever land animals were sauropod dinosaurs, a group of long-necked, long-tailed, four-legged plant-eaters that lumbered around most of the world during the Jurassic and Cretaceous periods 208–65 million years ago. However, it is difficult to determine precisely which of these sauropod dinosaurs was the largest (longest, tallest or heaviest). This is because many of the supposed giants are based only on incomplete fossil remains, and also because many discoverers have tended to exaggerate the sizes of their dinosaur finds. Estimating dinosaur lengths and heights is relatively straightforward when there is a complete skeleton. Sauropods are divided into five main groups: cetiosaurids, brachiosaurids, diplodocids, camarasaurids, and titanosaurids. The world's biggest dinosaur has been identified at different times as a brachiosaurid, a diplodocid or a titanosaurid.

Tallest The tallest and largest dinosaur is the *Brachiosaurus brancai* ("arm lizard") from the Tendaguru site in Tanzania, dated as Late Jurassic (150 million years ago). The site was excavated by German expeditions during the period 1909–11 and the bones prepared and assembled at the Humboldt Museum in Berlin. A complete skeleton was constructed from the remains of several individuals and put on display in 1937. It is also the world's largest and tallest mounted dinosaur skeleton, measuring 72 ft 9½ in overall length (height at shoulder 19 ft 8 in), and has a raised head height of 46 ft. A weight of 30–40 tons is likely. However, larger sizes are suggested by an isolated fibula from another *Brachiosaurus* in the same museum.

Heaviest The main contenders for the heaviest dinosaur are probably the titanosaurid *Antarctosaurus giganteus* ("Antarctic lizard") from Argentina and India, at 45–88 tons; the brachiosaurid *Brachiosaurus altithorax* (49–59 tons); and the diplodocids *Seismosaurus halli* and *Supersaurus vivianae* (both over 50 tons).

Such weights do not necessarily represent the ultimate weight limit for a land vertebrate. Theoretical calculations suggest that some dinosaurs approached the maximum body weight possible for a terrestrial animal, namely 120 tons. At weights greater than this, the legs would have to be so massive to support the bulk that the dinosaur could not have moved!

Longest Based on the evidence of footprints, the brachiosaurid *Breviparopus* attained a length of 157 ft, which would make it the longest vertebrate on record. However, a diplodocid from New Mexico named *Seismosaurus halli* was estimated in 1991 to be 128–170 ft long based on comparisons of individual bones.

Complete The longest dinosaur known from a complete skeleton is the diplodocid *Diplodocus carnegii* ("double beam"), assembled at the Carnegie Museum in Pittsburgh, PA from remains found in Wyoming in 1899. *Diplodocus* was 87½ ft long, with much of that length made up of an extremely long whiplike tail, and probably weighed 6.4–20.4 tons, the higher estimates being the more likely. The mounted skeleton was so spectacular that casts were requested by other museums, and copies may be seen in London, Great Britain; La Plata, Argentina; Washington, D.C.; Frankfurt, Germany; and Paris, France.

Most brainless *Stegosaurus* ("plated lizard"), which roamed across Colorado, Oklahoma, Utah and Wyoming about 150 million years ago, measured up to 30 ft in total length but had a walnut-sized brain weighing only 2½ oz. This represented 0.004 of 1 percent of its computed body weight of 1.9 tons (compare with 0.074 of 1 percent for an elephant and 1.88 percent for a human).

Earliest ancestor It was reported on 10 Jun 1992 that humankind's oldest ancestor may have been an eel-like fish that lived 515 million years ago, which was 40 million years earlier than previous estimates. The claim, made by scientists at Durham and Birmingham Universities, Great Britain, was based on studies of fossilized teeth from vertebrates known as conodonts found in Middle Ordovician and Late Cambrian deposits dating from 475–515 million years ago. The first complete fossilized conodont was discovered near Edinburgh, Scotland, in 1983.

Oldest land animals Animals moved from the sea to the land 414 million years ago, according to discoveries made in 1990 near Ludlow, Great Britain. The first land animals include two kinds of centipede and a tiny spider found among plant debris, suggesting that life moved onto land much earlier than previously thought.

Earliest reptile fossil The oldest reptile fossil, nicknamed "Lizzie the Lizard," was found on a site in Scotland by palaeontologist Stan Wood in March 1988. The 8-in-long reptile is estimated to be 340 million years old, 40 million years older than previously discovered reptiles. "Lizzie" was officially named *Westlothiana lizziae* in 1991.

Smallest dinosaur The chicken-sized *Compsognathus* ("pretty jaw") of southern Germany and southeast France, and an undescribed plant-eating fabrosaurid from Colorado, measured 29½ in from the snout to the tip of the tail and weighed about 15 lb.

Longest tracks In 1983 a series of four *Apatosaurus* (= *Brontosaurus*) tracks that ran parallel for a distance of over 705 ft were recorded from 145-million-year-old Morrison strata in southeast Colorado.

Largest footprints In 1932 the gigantic footprints of a large bipedal hadrosaurid ("duckbill") measuring 53½ in in length and 32 in wide were discovered in Salt Lake City, UT, and other reports from Colorado and Utah refer to footprints 37–40 in wide. Footprints attributed to the largest brachiosaurids also range up to 40 in wide for the hind feet.

Longest neck The sauropod *Mamenchisaurus* ("mamenchi lizard") of the Late Jurassic of Sichuan, China had the longest neck of any animal that has ever lived. It measured 36 ft—half the total length of the dinosaur.

Largest predatory dinosaur   The largest flesh-eating dinosaur recorded so far is *Tyrannosaurus rex* ("king tyrant lizard"), which seventy million years ago reigned over what are now the states of Montana, Wyoming and Texas and the provinces of Alberta and Saskatchewan, Canada. The largest and heaviest example, as suggested by a discovery in South Dakota in 1991, was 19¹/₂ ft tall, had a total length of 36¹/₂ ft and weighed an estimated 6–8 tons.

A composite skeleton of a slightly smaller specimen of this nightmarish beast can be seen in the American Museum of Natural History, New York City.

Longest   Specimens of the allosaur *Epanterias amplexus* from Masonville, CO has suggested that this theropod reached a length of 50 ft and a weight of 4.4 tons, but remains are incomplete. Similar lengths were also attained by *Spinosaurus aegyptiacus* ("thorn lizard") of Niger and Egypt.

Tallest   *Dynamosaurus imperiosus* ("dynamic lizard") of Shandong Province, China had a bipedal length of 20 ft and an overall length of 46 ft, but these tyrannosaurids were not as heavily built as those from North America.

Fastest   Tracks can be used to estimate dinosaur speeds, and one from the Late Morrison of Texas discovered in 1981 indicated that a carnivorous dinosaur had been moving at 25 mph. Some ornithomimids were even faster, and the large-brained, 220-lb *Dromiceiomimus* ("emu mimic lizard") of the Late Cretaceous of Alberta, Canada could probably outsprint an ostrich, which has a top speed of 40 mph.

Largest skull   The skulls of the long-frilled ceratopsids were the largest of all known land animals and culminated in the long-frilled *Torosaurus* sp. ("piercing lizard"). This herbivore, which measured about 25 ft in total length and weighed up to 8.8 tons, had a skull measuring up to 9 ft 10 in in length (including fringe) and weighing up to 2.2 tons. It ranged from Montana to Texas.

Largest claws   The therizinosaurids ("scythe lizards") from the Late Cretaceous of the Nemegt Basin, southern Mongolia, had the largest claws of any known animal, and in the case of *Therizinosaurus cheloniformis* the claws measured up to 36 in around the outer curve (compare with 8 in for *T. rex*). It has been suggested that these sickle claws were designed for grasping and tearing apart large victims, but this creature had a feeble skull partially or entirely lacking teeth, and probably lived on termites.

Largest eggs   The largest-known dinosaur eggs are those of *Hypselosaurus priscus* ("high ridge lizard"), a 40-ft-long titanosaurid that lived about 80 million years ago. Examples found in the Durance valley near Aix-en-Provence, France in October 1961 would have had, uncrushed, a length of 12 in and a diameter of 10 in (capacity 5.8 pt).

OTHER REPTILES

Largest predator   The largest-ever land predator may have been an alligator found on the banks of the Amazon in rocks dated as 8 million years old. Estimates from a 5-ft-long jaw (complete with 4-in-long teeth) indicate a length of 40 ft and a weight of about 20 tons, making it even larger than the fearsome *Tyrannosaurus rex*. It was subsequently identified as a giant example of *Purus-saurusbrasiliensis*, a species named in 1892 on the basis of smaller specimens.

Longest   Other fossil crocodiles suggest that the longest predator was probably the euschian *Deinocheirus mirificus* ("terrible crocodile") from the lakes and swamps of what is now Texas about 75 million years ago. Fragmentary remains discovered in Big Bend National Park, TX indicate a hypothetical length of 52 ft 6 in.

Largest chelonians   The largest prehistoric chelonian was *Stupendemys geographicus*, a pelomedusid turtle that lived about 5 million years ago. Fossil remains discovered by Harvard University palaeontologists in northern Venezuela in 1972 indicate that this turtle had a carapace (shell) measuring 7 ft 2 in–7 ft 6½ in in mid-line length, measured 9 ft 10 in in overall length and had a computed weight of 4,500 lb.

Tortoise   The largest prehistoric tortoise was probably *Geochelone* (= *Colossochelys*) *atlas*, which lived in what is now northern India, Myanmar (Burma), Java, the Celebes and Timor, about 2 million years ago. In 1923 the fossil remains of a specimen with a carapace 5 ft 11 in long (7 ft 4 in over the curve) and 2 ft 11 in high were discovered near Chandigarh in the Siwalik Hills, India. This animal had a total length of 8 ft and is computed to have weighed 2,100 lb.

Longest snake   The longest prehistoric snake was the pythonlike *Gigantophis garstini*, which inhabited what is now Egypt about 38 million years ago. Parts of a spinal column and a small piece of jaw discovered at Fayum in the Western Desert indicate a length of about 37 ft.

Largest marine reptile   *Kronosaurus queenslandicus*, a short-necked pliosaur from the Early Cretaceous period (135 million years ago) of Australia, measured up to 50 ft in length and had a 10-ft-long skull containing 80 massive teeth.

Largest flying creature   The largest-ever flying creature was the pterosaur *Quetzalcoatlus northropi* ("feathered serpent"). About 70 million years ago it soared over what is now Texas, Wyoming and New Jersey; Alberta, Canada; and Senegal and Jordan. Partial remains discovered in Big Bend National Park, TX in 1971 indicate that this reptile must have had a wingspan of 36–39 ft and weighed about 190–250 lb.

MAMMALS

Largest   The largest land mammal ever recorded was *Indricotherium* (=*Baluchitherium*), a long-necked, hornless rhinocerotid that roamed across western Asia and Europe about 35 million years ago and was first known from bones discovered in the Bugti Hills of Baluchistan, Pakistan in 1907–08. A restoration in the American Museum of Natural History, New York City measures 17 ft 9 in to the top of the shoulder hump and 37 ft in total length, and this gigantic browser weighed about 16–22 tons.

Mammoths   The largest prehistoric elephant was the steppe mammoth (*Mammuthus [Parelephas] trogontherii*), which, one million years ago, roamed

> **Earliest mammals** In 1991 a partial skull of a mammal named
> *Adelobasileus cromptoni* was reported from 225-million-year-old
> rocks in New Mexico. The first true mammals, as represented by
> odd teeth, appeared about 220 million years ago during the Late
> Triassic.
>
> Modern mammals (therians) arose in the Mid-Cretaceous
> period, and the earliest representatives of modern orders, such as
> *Purgatorius*, the first primate, by the end of the Cretaceous period,
> 65 million years ago. This creature was similar in appearance to
> modern tree shrews of the order Scandentia.

what is now central Europe. A fragmentary skeleton found in Mosbach,
Germany indicates a shoulder height of 14 ft 9 in.

Tusks The longest tusks of any prehistoric animal were those of the straight-
tusked elephant (*Paleoloxodom antiquus germanicus*), which lived in northern
Germany *c.* 300,000 years ago. The average length for tusks of adult bulls was
16 ft 5 in. A single tusk of a woolly mammoth (*Mammuthus primigenius*) preserved in the Franzens Museum at Brno, Slovakia measures 16 ft 5 1/2 in along
the outside curve.

Heaviest The heaviest single fossil tusk on record weighed 330 lb with a maximum circumference of 35 in and is now preserved in the Museo Civico di
Storia Naturale, Milan, Italy. The specimen, which is in two pieces, measures
11 ft 9 in in length.

Primates The largest-known primate was *Gigantopithecus* of the Middle
Pleistocene in what is now northern Vietnam and southern China. Males
would have stood an estimated 9 ft tall and weighed about 600 lb. It is risky,
however, to correlate tooth size and jaw depth of primates with their height
and body weight, and *Gigantopithecus* may have had a disproportionately large
head, jaws and teeth in relation to body size. The only remains discovered so
far are three partial lower jaws and more than 1,000 teeth.

Largest marine mammal The serpentine *Basilosaurus* (*Zeuglodon*) *cetoides*,
which swam in the seas that covered modern-day Arkansas and Alabama 50
million years ago, measured up to 70 ft in length.

Largest antlers The prehistoric giant deer (*Megaloceros giganteus*), which
lived in northern Europe and northern Asia as recently as 8000 B.C., had the
longest horns of any known animal. One specimen recovered from an Irish
bog had greatly palmated antlers measuring 14 ft across, which corresponds to
a shoulder height of 6 ft and a weight of 1,100 lb.

BIRDS

Earliest The earliest fossil bird is known from two partial skeletons found in
Texas in rocks dating from 220 million years ago. Named *Protoavis texensis* in
1991, this pheasant-sized creature has caused much controversy by pushing
the age of birds back 45 million years from the previous record, that of the
more familiar *Archeopteryx lithographica* from Germany.

120 ● Living World

Largest The largest prehistoric bird was the flightless *Dromornis stirtoni*, a huge emulike creature that lived in central Australia 11 million years ago. Fossil leg bones found near Alice Springs in 1974 indicate that the bird must have stood *c.* 10 ft tall and weighed about 1,100 lb.

The giant moa *Dinornis maximus* of New Zealand was even taller, attaining a maximum height of 12 ft, though 8 ft is the maximum accepted by most experts. It weighed only about 500 lb.

Flying bird The largest-known flying bird was the giant teratorn (*Argentavis magnificens*), which lived in Argentina about 6 million years ago. Fossil remains discovered at a site 100 miles west of Buenos Aires, Argentina in 1979 indicate that this gigantic vulture had a wingspan of over 19 ft 8 in, up to possibly 25 ft, and weighed 220–265 lb.

AMPHIBIANS

Largest The largest amphibian ever recorded was the gharial-like *Prionosuchus plummeri*, which lived 270 million years ago. Fragmented remains were discovered in northern Brazil in 1972. In 1991 the total body length was estimated at 30 ft based on a 5-ft-3-in-long skull.

FISH

Largest No prehistoric fish larger than living species has yet been discovered. Modern estimates suggest that the great shark *Carcharodon megalodon*, which abounded in Miocene seas some 15 million years ago, did not exceed 43 ft in length, far less than the 80 ft claimed in early, erroneous estimates based on ratios from fossil teeth.

INSECTS

Oldest A shrimp-like creature found in 1991 in rocks dated as 420 million years old may be the world's oldest insect. Found in Western Australia, this euthycarcinoid was a large (5 in long) freshwater predator.

Largest The largest prehistoric insect was the dragonfly *Meganeura monyi*, which lived about 300 million years ago. Fossil remains (impressions of wings) discovered at Commentry, France indicate a wing extending up to 27 1/2 in.

PLANT KINGDOM *Plantea*

GENERAL RECORDS

Oldest "King Clone," the oldest-known clone of the creosote plant (*Larrea tridentata*), found in southwest California, was estimated in February 1980 by Prof. Frank C. Vasek to be 11,700 years old. It is possible that crustose lichens in excess of 20 in in diameter may be as old, and in 1981 it was estimated that Antarctic lichens larger than 4 in in diameter are at least 10,000 years old.

Most massive   The most massive organism was reported in December 1992 to be a network of quaking aspen trees (*Populus tremuloides*) growing in the Wasatch Mountains, UT, from a single root system, covering 106 acres and weighing an estimated 6,600 tons. The clonal system is genetically uniform and acts as a single organism, with all the component trees, part of the willow family, changing color or shedding leaves in unison. This particular network was first described in 1975.

Northernmost   The yellow poppy (*Papaver radicatum*) and the Arctic willow (*Salix arctica*) survive, the latter in an extremely stunted form, on the northernmost land at Lat. 83° N .

Southernmost   Lichens resembling *Rhinodina frigida* have been found in Moraine Canyon at Lat. 86°09′S, Long. 157°30′W in 1971 and in the Horlick Mountain area, Antarctica at Lat. 86°09′S, Long. 131°14′W in 1965.

   The southernmost recorded flowering plant is the Antarctic hair grass (*Deschampsia antarctica*), which was found at Lat. 68° 21′S on Refuge Island, Antarctica on 11 Mar 1981.

Highest   The greatest certain altitude at which any flowering plants have been found is 21,000 ft on Kamet (25,447 ft) by N.D. Jayal in 1955. They were *Ermania himalayensis* and *Ranunculus lobatus*.

Deepest   The greatest depth at which plant life has been found is 884 ft, by Mark and Diane Littler off San Salvadore Island, Bahamas in October 1984. These maroon-colored algae survived although 99.9995 percent of sunlight was filtered out.

Fastest-growing   Some species of the 45 genera of bamboo have been found to grow up to 3 ft per day (0.00002 mph). (See Fastest-growing and Tallest grass.)

BLOOMS AND FLOWERS

Earliest flower   A flower believed to be 120 million years old was identified in 1989 by Dr Leo Hickey and Dr David Taylor of Yale University, New Haven, CT from a fossil discovered near Melbourne, Victoria, Australia. The flowering angiosperm, which resembles a modern black pepper plant, had two leaves and one flower and is known as the Koonwarra plant.

United States   The oldest fossil of a flowering plant with palmlike imprints in America was found in Colorado in 1953 and dated about 65 million years old.

Largest   The largest of all blooms are those of the parasitic stinking corpse lily (*Rafflesia arnoldii*), which measure up to 3 ft across and 3/4 in thick, and attain a weight of 15 lb. The plants attach themselves to the cissus vines in the jungles of southeast Asia. True to its name, the plant has an extremely offensive scent.

Inflorescence   The largest-known inflorescence (as distinct from the largest of all blooms) is that of *Puya raimondii*, a rare Bolivian monocarpic member of the Bromeliaceae family. Its erect panicle (diameter 8 ft) emerges to a height of 35 ft and each of these bears up to 8,000 white blooms. (See Slowest-

LARGEST BLOOM The 3 ft wide, 15 lb stinking corpse lily has only been seen in flower by a few people brave enough to approach it. (Photo: WWF Photolibrary/Alain Compost)

flowering plant.) The flower-spike of an agave measured in Berkeley, CA in 1974 was found to be 52 ft long.

Blossoming plant The giant Chinese wisteria (*Wisteria sinensis*) at Sierra Madre, CA was planted in 1892 and now has branches 500 ft long. It covers nearly 1 acre, weighs 25 tons and has an estimated 1.5 million blossoms during its blossoming period of five weeks, when up to 30,000 people pay admission to visit it.

Smallest flowering and fruiting The floating, flowering aquatic duckweed (*Wolffia angusta*) of Australia, described in 1980, is only 0.024 in long and 0.013 in wide. It weighs about $1/100{,}000$ oz and its fruit, which resembles a minuscule fig, weighs $1/400{,}000$ oz.

United States The smallest plant regularly flowering in the United States is *Wolffia globosa*, which is found in the San Joaquin Valley, central California, and rivers draining the Sierra Nevada Mountains. The plant weighs about 150 micrograms, and is listed as 0.015 in to 0.027 in length and 0.011 in width.

Fastest-growing It was reported from Tresco Abbey, Isles of Scilly, Great Britain in July 1978 that a *Hesperoyucca whipplei* of the family Liliaceae grew 12 ft in 14 days, a rate of about 10 in per day.

Slowest-flowering The slowest-flowering of all plants is the rare *Puya raimondii*, the largest of all herbs, discovered at 13,000 ft in Bolivia in 1870. The panicle emerges after about 80–150 years of the plant's life. It then dies. One planted near sea level at the University of California's Botanical Garden, Berkeley in 1958 grew to 25 ft and bloomed as early as August 1986 after only 28 years. (See Largest blooms.)

Oldest pot plant   The world's oldest and rarest pot plant is the cycad *Encephalartos altensteinii* brought from South Africa in 1775 and now housed at the Royal Botanic Gardens, Kew, Great Britain. It is the only example of the species.

Deepest roots   The greatest reported depth to which roots have penetrated is an estimated 400 ft for a wild fig tree at Echo Caves, near Ohrigstad, Transvaal, South Africa. A single winter rye plant (*Secale cereale*) has been shown to produce 387 miles of roots in 1.83 ft^3 of earth.

Longest daisy chain   The longest daisy chain measured 6,980 ft 7 in and was made in 7 hr by villagers of Good Easter, Great Britain on 27 May 1985. The team is limited to 16.

Hanging basket   A giant hanging basket measuring 20 ft in diameter and containing about 600 plants was created by Rogers of Exeter Garden Centre, Great Britain in 1987. Its volume was approximately 4,167 ft^3 and it weighed an estimated 4.4 tons. Another example from France with the same diameter but more conical in shape was smaller in terms of volume.

Biggest aspidistra   The biggest aspidistra in the world measures 56 in and belongs to Cliff Evans of Kiora, Moruya, New South Wales, Australia.

Orchids Tallest   The tallest of all orchids is *Grammatophyllum speciosum*, a native of Malaysia. Specimens have been recorded up to 25 ft in height.

A height of 49 ft has been recorded for *Galeola foliata*, a saprophyte of the vanilla family. It grows in the decaying rain forests of Queensland, Australia, but is not freestanding.

The tallest of all American orchids is the *Eulophia ecristata*, with a recorded height of 5.6 ft. There are five species of vanilla orchids that are vines and can spread to almost any length depending on the environment. These include *Phaeantha*, *Planifolia*, *Inodora*, *Dilliana*, and *Barbellata*. These orchids root in the ground and will grow in any direction over their surroundings.

Largest flower   The largest orchid flower is that of *Pathiopedilum sanderianum*, whose petals are reported to grow up to 3 ft long in the wild. It was discovered in 1886 in the Malay Archipelago. A plant of this variety grown in Somerset, Great Britain in 1991 had three flowers averaging 2 ft from the top of the dorsal sepal to the bottom of the ribbon petals, giving a record stretched length of 4 ft.

The largest flowering orchid in the United States is the yellow ladyslipper (Cypripedium calceolus) of the Pubsecens variety. Its petals grow up to 7 in long.

Smallest   The smallest orchid is *Platystele jungermannoides*, found in Central America. Its flowers are just 0.04 in in diameter.

The smallest orchid in the United States is *Lepanthopsis melanantha*, with a petal spread of 0.02 in and a maximum height of 1.6 in.

Largest cactus The largest of all cacti is the saguaro (*Cereus giganteus* or *Carnegiea gigantea*), found in Arizona, southeastern California and Sonora, Mexico. The green fluted column is surmounted by candelabra-like branches rising to a height of 57 ft 11¾ in in the case of a specimen discovered in the Maricopa Mountains, near Gila Bend, AZ on 17 Jan 1988.

An armless cactus 78 ft in height was measured in April 1978 by Hube Yates in Cave Creek, AZ. It was toppled in a windstorm in July 1986 at an estimated age of 150 years.

THE GUINNESS DAILY RECORD

16 November, 1992

Plenty of food for thought

The world's largest cornucopia was unveiled today on Daley Plaza in downtown Chicago.

The horn of plenty, 40 ft long, 12 ft 10 in high and 13 ft in diameter, was constructed of metal, covered with straw and trimmed with cord. It was then filled to overflowing with 24,000 lb of donated fresh fruit and vegetables.

The horn of plenty was created by the Produce for Better Health Foundation (PBH) in conjunction with the National Cancer Institute to increase public awareness of the link between diet and health and to encourage people to eat five servings of produce each day. At the end of the event the pallets of fruit and vegetables were donated to the Greater Chicago Food Depository, part of the national Second Harvest Network.

"The cornucopia event was another win-win for PBH. We were able to draw attention to our S-A-Day message, and contribute wholesome, nutritious produce to the less fortunate. "It's nice to see the media turn out for a positive story like ours," said Bob DiPiazza, a member of the board of directors.

FLOWERS, FRUITS AND VEGETABLES

In the interest of fairness and to minimize the risk of mistakes being made, all plants should, where possible, be entered in official international, national or local garden contests. Only produce grown primarily for human consumption will be considered for publication. The assistance of *Garden News* and the World Pumpkin Confederation is gratefully acknowledged.

Type	Size	Grower/Location	Year
Apple	3 lb 2 oz	Miklovic family, Caro, MI	1992
Cabbage	124 lb	B. Lavery, Llanharry, Great Britain	1989
Cantaloupe	62 lb	G. Draughtridge, Rocky Mount, NC	1991
Carrot[1]	15 lb 7 oz	I. Scott, Nelson, New Zealand	1978
Celery	46 lb 1 oz	B. Lavery, Llanharry, Great Britain	1990
Cucumber[2]	20 lb 1 oz	B. Lavery, Llanharry, Great Britain	1991
Chrysanthemum	8 ft 2½ in	F. Santini, Indre-et-Loire, France	1988
Dahlia	25 ft 7in	R. Blythe, Nannup, Western Australia	1990
Garlic	2 lb 10 oz	R. Kirkpatrick, Eureka, CA	1985
Grapefruit	6 lb 8½ oz	J. and A. Sosnow, Tucson, AZ	1984
Grapes	20 lb 11½ oz	Bozzolo y Perut Ltda, Santiago, Chile	1984
Leek (pot)	12 lb 2 oz	P. Harrigan, Linton, Great Britain	1987
Lemon	8 lb 8 oz	C. and D. Knutzen, Whittier, CA	1983
Marrow	108 lb 2 oz	B. Lavery, Llanharry, Great Britain	1990
Onion	11 lb 2 oz	R. Holland, Cumnock, Great Britain	1992
Parsnip	14 ft 3¾ in	B. Lavery, Llanharry, Great Britain	1990
Petunia	13 ft 8 in	B. Lawrence, Windham, NY	1985
Philodendron	1,114 ft	F. Francis, University of Massachusetts	1984
Pineapple[3]	17 lb 8 oz	Dole Philippines Inc, South Cotabato, Philippines	1984

Potato[1] ....7 lb 1 oz ....J. East, Spalding, Great Britain 1963
....7 lb 1 oz ....J. Busby, Atherstone, Great Britain 1982
Pumpkin ....827 lb ....J. Holland, Puyallup, WA 1992
Radish ....37 lb 15 oz ....Litterini family, Tanunda, South Australia 1992
Rhubarb ....5 lb 14 oz ....E. Stone, East Woodyates, Great Britain 1985
Runner bean ....39$^1/_2$ in ....J. Taylor, Shifnal, Great Britain 1986
Rutabaga ....48 lb 12 oz ....A. Foster, Alnwick, Great Britain 1980
Squash ....821 lb ....L. Stellpflug, Rush, NY 1990
Strawberry ....8.17 oz ....G. Anderson, Folkestone, Great Britain 1983
Sunflower[5] ....25 ft 5$^1/_2$ in ....M. Heijms, Oirschot, Netherlands 1986
Tomato ....7 lb 12 oz ....G. Graham, Edmond, OK 1986
Tomato plant[6] ....53 ft 6 in ....G. Graham, Edmond, OK 1985
Watermelon[7] ....262 lb ....B. Carson, Arrington, TN 1990
Zucchini ....64 lb 8 oz ....B. Lavery, Llanharry, Great Britain 1990

[1] *A 6 ft 10$^1/_2$ in long carrot was grown by Bernard Lavery of Llanharry, Great Britain in 1991.*

[2] *A Vietnamese variety 6 ft long was reported by L. Szabo of Debrecen, Hungary in September 1976. A.C. Rayment of Chelmsford, Great Britain grew one measuring 43$^1/_2$ in in 1984–86.*

[3] *Pineapples weighing up to 28 lb 11 oz were reported from Tarauaca, Brazil in 1978.*

[4] *One weighing 18 lb 4 oz reported dug up by Thomas Siddal in his garden in Chester on 17 Feb 1795. A yield of 515 lb was achieved from a 2$^1/_2$ lb parent seed by Bowcock planted in April 1977.*

[5] *A sunflower with a head measuring 32$^1/_4$ in in diameter was grown by Emily Martin of Maple Ridge, British Columbia, Canada in September 1983. A fully mature sunflower measuring just 2$^1/_2$ in was grown by Michael Lenke of Lake Oswego, OR in 1985 using a patented bonsai technique.*

[6] *It was reported at the Tsukuba Science Expo Center, Japan on 28 Feb 1988 that a single plant produced 16,897 tomatoes.*

[7] *Bill Rogerson of Robersonville, NC grew a watermelon which weighed 279 lb on 3 Oct 1988, but this was not measured under competition conditions...*

(continued)

US National Records

Type	Size	Grower/Location	Year
Beet	45¹/₂ lb	R. Meyer, Brawley, CA	1984
Collard[8]	35 ft tall	B. Rackley, Rocky Mount, NC	1980
Corn	31 ft high	D. Radda, Washington, IA	1946
Dahlia	16 ft 5 in	S. & P Barnes, Chattahoochee, FL	1982
Eggplant	5 lb 5¹/₄ oz	J. & J. Charles, Summerville, SC	1984
Gourd	93¹/₂ in long	B.W. Saylor, Licking, MT	1986
Gourd (weight)	78 lb	L. Childers, Stinesville, IN	1986
Kohlrabi	36 lb	E. Krejci, Mt Clemens, MI	1979
Lima bean	14 in	N. McCoy, Hubert, NC	1979
Okra stalk	17 ft 6¹/₄ in	C. H. Wilber, Crane Hill, AL	1983
	17 ft 6¹/₄ in	B. & E. Crosby, Brooksville, FL	1986
Onion	7¹/₂ lb	N. W. Hope, Tempe, AZ	1984
Peanut	4 in	E. Adkins, Enfield, NC	1990
Pepper	13¹/₂ in	J. Rutherford, Hatch, NM	1975
Pepper plant	12 ft 3 in	F. Melton, Jacksonville, FL	1992
Rutabaga[9]	39 lb	R. & J. Towns, Gresham, OR	1979
Sweet potato	40³/₄ lb	O. Harrison, Kite, GA	1982
Tomato (cherry)	28 ft 7 in	C. H. Wilber, Crane Hill, AL	1985
Zucchini	19.92 lb	W. C. Nicholas, Hatley, WI	1984

[8]This same collard holds the record for greatest width, measuring 62 in from leaf tip to leaf tip at its greatest point of width.
[9]A rutabaga weighing 51 lb was reported from Alaska in 1981, but this has not been substantiated.

Apple peeling   The longest single unbroken apple peel on record is one of 172 ft 4 in, peeled by Kathy Wafler of Wolcott, NY in 11 hr 30 min at Long Ridge Mall, Rochester, NY on 16 Oct 1976. The apple weighed 20 oz.

Apple picking   The greatest recorded performance is 15,830 lb picked in 8 hr by George Adrian of Indianapolis, IN on 23 Sep 1980.

Largest rhododendron   Examples of the scarlet *Rhododendron arboreum* reach a height of 65 ft on Mt Japfu, Nagaland, India. The cross-section of the trunk of a *Rhododendron giganteum*, reputedly 90 ft high, from Yunnan, China, is preserved at Inverewe Gardens, Highland, Great Britain.

Largest rose tree   A Lady Banks rose tree at Tombstone, AZ has a trunk 40 in thick, stands 9 ft high and covers an area of 5,380 ft². It is supported by 68 posts and several thousand feet of piping, which enables 150 people to be seated under the arbor. The cutting came from Scotland in 1884.

Longest lei   A 14,550-ft paper flower lei was made by local citizens at the Hyatt Regency Waikiki, Honolulu, HI on 19 Dec 1992.

Cucumber slicing   Norman Johnson of Blackpool College, Lancashire, Great Britain set a record of 13.4 sec for slicing a 12-in cucumber, 1¹/₂ in in diameter, at 22 slices to the inch (total 264 slices) at West Deutscher Rundfunk in Cologne, Germany on 3 Apr 1983.

Grape catching   The greatest distance at which a grape thrown from level ground has been caught in the mouth is 327 ft 6 in, by Paul J. Tavilla in East Boston, MA on 27 May 1991. The grape was thrown by James Deady.

Most jack-o'-lanterns   The United States record for most jack-o'-lanterns in one place at one time is 1,628, on 23 Oct 1992. The pumpkins were carved by the citizens of Keene, NH for their annual Harvest Festival.

Largest jack-o'-lantern   The largest jack-o'-lantern in the world was carved from a 827 lb pumpkin by Michael Green, Regina Johnson and Daniel Salcedo at Nut Tree, CA on 30 October 1992.

Potato peeling   The greatest quantity of potatoes peeled by five people to an institutional cookery standard with standard kitchen knives in 45 min is 1,064 lb 6 oz (net) by Marj Killian, Terry Anderson, Barbara Pearson, Marilyn Small and Janene Utkin at the 64th Annual Idaho Spud Day celebration, held in Shelley, ID on 19 Sep 1992.

FRUITS AND VEGETABLES

Most nutritive   An analysis of the 38 commonly eaten raw (as opposed to dried) fruits shows that the one with the highest caloric value is the avocado (*Persea americana*), with 741 kilocal/lb; it also contains vitamins A, C and E and 2.2 percent protein. Avocados probably originated in Central and South America.

Least nutritive   The fruit with the lowest caloric value is the cucumber (*Cucumis sativus*), with 73 kilocal/lb.

VINES AND VINEYARDS

Largest vine   This was planted in 1842 at Carpinteria, CA. By 1900 it was yielding more than 9.9 tons of grapes in some years, and averaged 7.7 tons per year until it died in 1920.

Largest vineyard   The world's largest vineyard extends over the Mediterranean slopes between the Pyrenees and the Rhône in the *départements* Gard, Hérault, Aude and Pyrénées-Orientales. It covers an area of 2,075,685 acres, 52.3 percent of which is *monoculture viticole*.

United States   The largest continuous vineyard in the United States is Minor Thornton Ranch in Fresno, CA. Owned by the Golden State Vintners Corp., the vineyard covers 5,200 acres and produces 6,500 tons of grapes each year.

Most northerly vineyard   There is a vineyard at Sabile, Latvia just north of Lat. 57° N.

Most southerly vineyard   The most southerly commercial vineyards are to be found in central Otago, South Island, New Zealand, south of Lat. 45° S.

This monster 827 lb pumpkin was grown by Joel Holland of Puyallup, WA in 1992. (Photo: Nut Tree, California, USA/Dudley Owens)

LEAVES

Largest The largest leaves of any plant belong to the raffia palm (*Raphia farinifera* = *R. raffia*) of the Mascarene Islands in the Indian Ocean, and the Amazonian bamboo palm (*R. taedigera*) of South America, whose leaf blades may measure up to 65½ ft in length with petioles up to 13 ft.

The largest leaves to be found in outdoor plants in America are those of the climbing fern (*Lygodium japonicum*) of the Gulf coast, with leaves of 23 ft.

Undivided The largest undivided leaf is that of *Alocasia macrorrhiza*, found in Sabah, Malaysia. A specimen found in 1966 was 9 ft 11 in long and 6 ft 3½ in wide, with a surface area of 34.12 ft². A specimen of the water lily *Victoria amazonica* (Longwood hybrid) on the grounds of the Stratford-upon-Avon Butterfly Farm, Warwickshire, Great Britain measured 8 ft in diameter on 2 Oct 1989.

Clovers A fourteen-leafed white clover (*Trifolium repens*) was found by Randy Farland near Sioux Falls, SD on 16 Jun 1975. A fourteen-leafed red clover (*T. pratense*) was reported by Paul Haizlip at Bellevue, WA on 22 Jun 1987. Clovers are not invariably three-leafed, and their collection is not considered to be botanically significant.

SEEDS

Largest The largest seed in the world is that of the giant fan palm *Lodoicea maldivica* (= *L. callipyge, L. seychellarum*), commonly known as the double coconut or coco de mer, found wild only in the Seychelles in the Indian Ocean. The single-seeded fruit weighs up to 44 lb and may take 10 years to develop.

Smallest The smallest are those of epiphytic (nonparasitic plants growing on others) orchids, at 35 million seeds/oz (compare with grass pollens at up to 6 billion grains/oz).

Most durable The most conclusive claim for the longevity of seeds is that made for the Arctic lupine (*Lupinus arcticus*) found in frozen silt at Miller Creek, Yukon, Canada in July 1954 by Harold Schmidt. The seeds were germinated in 1966 and were radiocarbon dated to at least 8000 B.C. and more probably to 13,000 B.C.

FERNS

Largest The largest of the more than 6,000 species of fern is the tree fern (*Alsophila excelsa*), the truck of which can reach heights of 60–80 ft. It is found on Norfolk Island in the South Pacific.

United States The highest in America is the giant fern (*Acrostichum danaeaefolium*) of the Gulf coast, which measures up to 16.4 ft. However, the bracken fern (*Pteridium aquilinum*) is the largest fern plant. It grows to a height of 4.9 ft above ground, but also grows giant clones or stem systems underground that can reach up to a quarter of a mile. This fern is found throughout the United States.

Smallest The world's smallest ferns are *Hecistopteris pumila*, found in Central

America, and *Azolla caroliniana*, which is native to the United States and has fronds as small as ¹/₂ in.

MOSSES

Tallest   The tallest variety of moss is the Australian species *Dawsonia superba*, which can reach a height of 24 in.

Smallest   The smallest variety of moss is the microscopic pygmy moss (*Ephemerum*), which appears to the naked eye as a mere greenish stain until closer examination. Its leaves are notable, however, for their large cells, which can measure up to 120 μm long and 25 μm wide.

Tallest grass   A thorny bamboo culm (*Bambusa arundinacea*) felled at Pattazhi, Travancore, India in November 1904 was 121¹/₂ ft tall.

Fastest-growing grass   Some species of bamboo have a growth rate of 3 ft per day. (See also Plant Kingdom, General records.)

Commonest grasses   The world's commonest grass is Bermuda grass (*Cynodon dactylon*), which is native to tropical Africa and the Indo-Malaysian region, but which extends from Lat. 45°N to 45°S. It is possibly the most troublesome weed of the grass family, affecting 40 crops in over 80 countries. The Callie hybrid, selected in 1966, grows as much as 6 in a day and stolons reach 18 ft in length.

Christmas tree   The world's tallest cut Christmas tree was a 221 ft Douglas fir (Pseudotsuga menziesii) erected at Northgate Shopping Center, Seattle, WA in December 1950.

Tree topping   Guy German climbed a 100-ft spar and sawed off the top (circumference 40 in) in a record time of 53.35 sec at Albany, OR on 3 Jul 1989.

Tree climbing   The fastest time up a 100-ft fir spar pole and back down to the ground is 24.82 sec, by Guy German of Sitka, AK on 3 Jul 1988 at the World Championship Timber Carnival in Albany, OR.
   The fastest time up a 29 ft 6 in coconut tree barefoot is 4.88 sec, by Fuatai Solo, 17, in Sukuna Park, Fiji on 22 Aug 1980.

Tree sitting   The duration record for staying in a tree is more than 22 years, by Bungkas, who went up a palm tree in the Indonesian village of Bengkes in 1970 and has been there ever since. He lives in a nest which he made from branches and leaves. Repeated efforts have been made to persuade him to come down, but without success.

Longest The longest is the mainly aquatic species (*Fontinalis*), especially *F. Antipyretica*, which forms streamers over 3 ft long in flowing water.

WEEDS

Largest The largest weed is the giant hogweed (*Heracleum mantegazzianum*), originally from the Caucasus. It reaches 12 ft and has leaves 3 ft long.

Most damaging The virulence of weeds tends to be measured by the number of crops they affect and the number of countries in which they occur. On this basis, the worst would appear to be the purple nutsedge, nutgrass or nutsedge (*Cyperus rotundus*), a land weed which is native to India but which attacks 52 crops in 92 countries.

United States The most damaging and widespread weed in America is the purple nutsedge (*Cyperus rotundus*), primarily found in the southern states. Its seeds can germinate at 95°F and will withstand temperatures of -68°F for two hours and remain viable. The purple nutsedge will grow to 39 in in height and spreads underground through its system of rhizomes and tubers. It remains dormant underground in extreme weather conditions.

Tallest The tallest weed in the United States is the Melaleuca tree (*Melaleuca quinquenervia*), introduced to the Florida and Gulf coasts from Australia in 1900. Growing to an average of 39 ft, the weed has infested 3.7 million of the 4.7 million acres of Florida wetlands. Very dense and resistant to fire, the crowns are destroyed by burning but the stem survives. It is a fire hazard in that it contains "essential" petroleums that spread fire quickly.

Most spreading The greatest area covered by a single clonal growth is that of the wild box huckleberry (*Gaylussacia brachycera*), a mat-forming evergreen shrub first reported in 1796. A colony covering about 100 acres was found on 18 Jul 1920 near the Juniata River, PA. It has been estimated that this colony began 13,000 years ago.

Aquatic weeds The worst aquatic weed of the tropics and subtropics is the water hyacinth (*Eichhornia crassipes*), which is a native of the Amazon basin but extends from Lat. 40° N to 45° S.

The intransigence of aquatic plants in man-made lakes is illustrated by the mat-forming water weed *Salvinia auriculata*, found in Africa. It was detected when Lake Kariba, which straddles the border of Zimbabwe and Zambia, was filled in May 1959, and within 13 months had choked an area of 200 miles^2, rising to 387 miles^2 in 1963.

SEAWEED

Longest The longest species of seaweed is the Pacific giant kelp (*Macrocystis pyrifera*), which, although it does not exceed 196 ft in length, can grow 18 in in a day.

TREES AND WOOD

Earliest The earliest species of tree still surviving is the maiden-hair tree (*Ginkgo biloba*), of Zhejiang, China, which first appeared about 160 million years ago, during the Jurassic era. It has been grown since *c*. 1100 in Japan, where it was known as *ginkyō* ("silver apricot") and is now known as *icho*.

United States The oldest species is the bristlecone pine, which grows in the desert regions of southern California and Nevada. The exact date of the oldest tree is not known; however, some living species are believed to be at least 4,000 years old.

Oldest Dendrochronologists estimate the *potential* life span of a bristlecone pine at nearly 5,500 years, and that of a giant sequoia (*Sequoiadendron giganteum*) at perhaps 6,000 years. No single cell lives more than 30 years. The oldest recorded tree was a bristlecone pine (*Pinus longaeva*) designated WPN-114, which grew at 10,750 ft above sea level on the northeast face of Mt Wheeler, NV. It was found to be 5,100 years old.

Living The oldest known *living* tree is the bristlecone pine named Methuselah, growing at 10,000 ft on the California side of the White Mountains, confirmed as 4,700 years old. In March 1974 it was reported that this tree had produced 48 live seedlings.

Most massive The most massive tree on earth is the biggest-known giant sequoia (*Sequoiadendron giganteum*), a tree named the General Sherman, standing 275 ft tall, in the Sequoia National Park, CA. In 1991 it had a girth of 83 ft, measured $4^{1}/_{2}$ ft above the ground. The General Sherman has been estimated to contain the equivalent of 600,120 board feet of timber, sufficient to make 5 billion matches. The foliage is blue-green, and the red-brown bark may be up to 24 in thick in parts. Estimates place its weight, including its root system, at 2,756 tons, but the timber is light (18 lb/ft³).

The seed of a "big tree" weighs only $^{1}/_{6,000}$ of an oz. Its growth at maturity may therefore represent an increase in weight of 13×10^{11}.

Greatest spread The tree canopy covering the greatest area is that of the great banyan (*Ficus benghalensis*) in the Indian Botanical Garden, Calcutta, with 1,775 prop or supporting roots and a circumference of 1,350 ft. It covers some 3 acres and dates from before 1787. However, it is reported that a 550-year-old banyan tree known as "Thimmamma Marrimanu" in Gutibayalu village near Kadiri Taluk, Andrha Pradesh, India spreads over 5.2 acres.

Greatest girth A circumference of 190 ft was recorded for the pollarded (trimmed to encourage a more bushy growth) European chestnut (*Castanea sativa*) known as the "Tree of the Hundred Horses" (*Castagno di Cento Cavalli*) on Mt Etna, Sicily, Italy in 1770 and 1780. It is now in three parts, widely separated.

"El Arbol del Tule" in the state of Oaxaca, Mexico is a 135-ft-tall Montezuma cypress (*Taxodium mucronatum*) with a girth in 1982 of 117.6 ft, measured 5 ft above the ground. Generally speaking, however, the largest girths are attributed to African baobob trees (*Adansonia digitata*), trunks of which have measured 180 ft in circumference.

United States The giant sequoia in the Sequoia National Park, CA has a girth of 83 ft 2 in (See Trees and Wood, Most massive).

Tallest A *Eucalyptus regnans* at Mt Baw Baw, Victoria, Australia is believed to have measured 470 ft in 1885. According to the researches of Dr A.C.

Carder, the tallest tree ever measured was another Australian eucalyptus (*Eucalyptus regnans*) at Watts River, Victoria, Australia, reported in 1872 by forester William Ferguson. It was 435 ft tall and almost certainly measured over 500 ft originally.

Living The tallest tree currently standing is the "National Geographic Society" coast redwood (*Sequoia sempervirens*) in Humboldt Redwoods State Park, CA. Its revised height, following earlier miscalculations, was 365 ft in October 1991, according to Ron Hildebrant of California.

The tallest nonconiferous flowering tree is an Australian mountain ash, or giant gum (*Eucalyptus regnans*), which grows to over 315 ft. The tallest is currently one of 312 ft in the Styx Valley, Tasmania, Australia.

The oldest living tree—4,700-year-old ""Methuselah" in the White Mountains, CA. (Photo: Planet Earth Pictures/William Smithey Jr)

Fastest-growing Discounting bamboo, which is not classified as a tree but as a woody grass, the fastest rate of growth recorded is 35 ft 3 in in 13 months by an *Albizzia falcata* planted on 17 Jun 1974 in Sabah, Malaysia.

Slowest-growing Excluding *bonsai*, the 14th century Oriental art of cultivating miniature trees, the extreme in slow growth is represented by the *Dioon edule* (Cycadaceae), measured in Mexico between 1981 and 1986 by Dr Charles M. Peters, who found the average annual growth rate to be 0.03 in; a specimen 120 years old measured 4 in in height.

Most leaves Little work has been done on the laborious task of establishing which species has the most leaves. A large oak has perhaps 250,000 but a cypress may have some 45–50 million leaf scales.

Remotest The tree believed to be the remotest from any other is a sole Norwegian spruce on Campbell Island, Antarctica. Its nearest companion would be over 120 nautical miles away on the Auckland Islands.

Largest forest The largest forested areas in the world are the vast coniferous forests of northern Russia, lying between Lat. 55°N and the Arctic Circle. The total wooded area amounts to 2.7 billion acres (25 percent of the world's forests), of which 38 percent is Siberian larch. The former USSR is 34 percent forested. In comparison, the largest area of forest in the tropics remains the Amazon basin, amounting to some 815 million acres.

United States The largest forest in the United States is the Tongass National Forest (16.7 million acres), in Alaska. The United States is 32.25 percent forested.

Longest avenue The world's longest avenue of trees is the Nikko Cryptomeria Avenue, comprising three parts converging on Imaichi City in the Tochigi Prefecture of Japan and measuring a total of 22 miles. It was planted in the period 1628–48, and over 13,500 of its original 200,000 Japanese cedar (*Cryptomeria japonica*) trees survive, at an average height of 88½ ft.

Wood cutting The first recorded lumberjack sports competition was held in 1572 in the Basque region of Spain.

The following records were set at the Lumberjack World Championships at Hayward, WI (founded 1960):

Power saw (three slices of a 20-in diameter white-pine log with a single-engine saw from a dead start)—8.71 sec by Ron Johnson (USA) in 1986.

Bucking (one slice from a 20-in diameter white-pine log with a crosscut saw)—one-man, 18.96 sec by Rolin Eslinger (USA) in 1987; two-man, 7.27 sec by Jim Colbert and Mike Sullivan (both USA) in 1988.

Standing block chop (chopping through a vertical 14-in diameter white-pine log 30 in in length)—22.05 sec by Melvin Lentz (USA) in 1988.

Underhand block chop (chopping through a horizontal 14-in diameter white-pine log 30 in in length)—17.84 sec by Laurence O'Toole (Australia) in 1985.

Springboard chopping (scaling a 9 ft spar pole on springboards and chopping a 14-in diameter white-pine log)—1 min 18.45 sec by Bill Youd (Australia) in 1985.

KINGDOM PROTISTA

Discovered in 1676 by microscopist Antonie van Leeuwenhoek of Delft, Netherlands (1632–1723), protista are one-celled or acellular organisms with characteristics common to both plants and animals. The more plant-like are termed Protophyta (protophytes), including unicellular algae, and the more animal-like are placed in the phylum Protozoa (protozoans), including amoeba and flagellates.

Largest   The largest protozoans in terms of volume that are known to have existed were calcareous foraminifera (Foraminiferida) belonging to the genus *Nummulites*, a species of which, in the Middle Eocene rocks of Turkey, attained 8$\frac{1}{2}$ in in diameter.
   The largest existing protozoan, a species of the fan-shaped *Stannophyllum* (Xenophyophorida), can exceed this in length (9$\frac{3}{4}$ in has been recorded) but not in volume.

Smallest protophytes   The marine microflagellate alga *Micromonas pusilla* has a diameter of less than 0.00008 in.

Fastest   The protozoan *Monas stigmatica* has been found to move a distance equivalent to 40 times its own length in a second. No human can cover even seven times his own length in a second.

Fastest reproduction   The protozoan *Glaucoma*, which reproduces by binary fission, divides as frequently as every three hours. Thus in the course of a day it could become a great-great-great-great-great-great-grandparent and the progenitor of 512 descendants!

KINGDOM FUNGI

Largest   The world's largest fungus is a single living clonal growth of the underground fungus *Armillaria ostoyae*, reported in May 1992 as covering some 1,500 acres in the forests of Washington state. Estimates based on its size suggest that the fungus is 500–1,000 years old, but no attempts have been made to estimate its weight. Also known as the honey or shoestring fungus, it fruits above ground as edible gilled mushrooms.

Heaviest   Another similar clonal growth, but of the fungus *Armillaria bulbosa*, reported on 2 Apr 1992 to be covering about 37 acres of forest in Michigan,

> **Largest edible fungus**   A giant puffball (*Langermannia gigantea*) measuring 8 ft 8 in in circumference and weighing 48½ lb was found by Jean-Guy Richard of Montreal, Canada in 1987.
>
> **Heaviest edible fungus**   An example of the edible chicken of the woods mushroom (*Laetiporus sulphureus*) weighing 100 lb was found in the New Forest, Great Britain by Giovanni Paba of Broadstone, Dorset, Great Britain on 15 Oct 1990.
>
> **Largest tree fungus**   The largest recorded tree fungus is the bracket fungus Rigidoporus ulmarius growing from dead elm wood on the grounds of the International Mycological Institute at Kew, Great Britain. It measured 59 x 56¾ in with a circumference of 178¾ in. In 1992 it was growing at a rate of 9 in per year, but this has now slowed.
>
> *United States*   In April 1992 Freda Kaplan of San Ramon, CA found a puffball (*Langermannia gigantea*) measuring 7 ft 3 in in circumference on the Wiedemann ranch in San Ramon.

was calculated to weigh over 110 tons, which is comparable with blue whales. The organism is thought to have originated from a single fertilized spore at least 1,500 years ago.

Most poisonous   The yellowish-olive death cap (*Amanita phalloides*) is regarded as the world's most poisonous fungus and is responsible for 90 percent of all fatal cases of poisoning caused by fungi. The total toxin content is 7–9 mg dry weight. The estimated lethal amount of amatoxins for humans, depending on body weight, is only 5–7 mg—equivalent to less than 1¾ oz of a fresh fungus. From 6–15 hours after eating, the victim experiences vomiting, delirium, collapse and death. Among its victims was Cardinal Giulio de' Medici, Pope Clement VII (b. 1478) on 25 Sep 1534.

Aeroflora   The highest total fungal spore count was 5,686,861/ft³ near Cardiff, Great Britain on 21 Jul 1971. The lowest counts of airborne allergens are zero.

KINGDOM PROCARYOTA

BACTERIA

Oldest   Viable bacteria were reported in 1991 to have been recovered from sediments 3–4 million years old from the Sea of Japan.

Living   In 1991 it was reported that live bacteria were found in the flesh of a mastodon (an ancestor of the elephant) from Ohio, which died 12,000 years

Microscopist Antony Van Leeuwenhoek (1632–1723) was the first to observe bacteria, in 1675. (Photo: Ann Ronan Picture Library)

earlier and which, on the evidence of spear marks found in the ribs, represented the first proof of humans killing a prehistoric animal. The bacteria gave the flesh "a bad smell" even after such a long time.

Largest　The largest bacterium is *Epulopiscium fishelsoni*, described in 1993 as a symbiont inhabiting the intestinal tract of the brown surgeonfish (*Acanthurus nigrofuscus*) from the Red Sea and the Great Barrier Reef. Measuring 80 x 600 μm or more and therefore visible to the naked eye, this mega-microorganism, first discovered by Israeli researchers in 1985, is so big it was originally thought to be a protozoan. At 1 million times larger than the human food poisoner *Escherichia coli*, it is a reminder of the strange new lifeforms we have yet to discover.

Smallest free-living entity　The smallest of all free-living organisms are the pleuro-pneumonia-like organisms (PPLO) of the *Mycoplasma*. One of these, *Mycoplasma laidlawii*, first discovered in sewage in 1936, has a diameter during its early existence of only 10^{-7} m. Examples of the strain known as H.39 have a maximum diameter of 3×10^{-7} m and weigh an estimated 10^{-16} g.

Highest　In April 1967 the National Aeronautics and Space Administration (NASA) reported that bacteria had been discovered at an altitude of $25\frac{1}{2}$ miles.

Fastest　The rod-shaped bacillus *Bdellovibrio bacteriovorus*, using a polar flagellum rotating 100 times/sec, can move 50 times its own length of 2 micrometers per sec. This would be the equivalent of a human sprinter reaching 200 mph.

Oldest DNA Proteins, the building blocks of life, normally disappear rapidly from carcasses. Original proteins are only rarely found in fossils, but in 1992, DNA, the specialized genetic-coding protein, was recovered from a termite that had become trapped in amber 25–30 million years ago in the Dominican Republic.

Toughest The bacterium *Micrococcus radiodurans* can withstand atomic radiation of 6.5 million roentgens or 10,000 times the dose that would be fatal to the average person. In March 1983 John Barras (University of Oregon) reported bacteria from sulfurous seabed vents thriving at 583° F in the East Pacific Rise at Lat. 21°N.

VIRUSES

Dmitriy Ivanovsky (1864–1920) first reported filterable objects in 1892, but Martinus Willem Beijerink (1851–1931) first confirmed the nature of viruses in 1898. These are now defined as aggregates of two or more types of chemical (including either DNA or RNA) that are infectious and potentially pathogenic.

Largest The longest-known virus is the rod-shaped *Citrus tristeza* virus with particles measuring 2×10^{-5} m.

Smallest The smallest-known viruses are the nucleoprotein plant viruses, such as the satellite of tobacco necrosis virus with spherical particles 17×10^{-9} m in diameter.

First chemical description of a virus The first chemical description of a living entity was published in December 1991 by A. Molla, A.V. Paul and Eckard Wimmer of the State University of New York. The formula for poliovirus is $C_{332,652}H_{492,388}N_{98,245}O_{131,196}P_{7,501}S_{2,340}$ and it is believed to be the largest empirical formula ever reported.

VIROIDS

Viroids were discovered by Theodor O. Diener (USA) in February 1972. They are infectious agents of plants, are smaller than viruses, and consist only of nucleic acid (RNA) cores.

A putative new infectious submicroscopic organism without nucleic acid, named a "prion," was announced from the University of California in February 1982.

PARKS, ZOOS, OCEANARIA, AQUARIA

PARKS

Largest The world's largest national park is the National Park of North-Eastern Greenland, covering 375,289 miles² and stretching from Liverpool Land in the south to the northernmost island, Odaaq Ø, off Pearyland. Established in 1974 and enlarged in 1988, much of the park is covered by ice and is home to a variety of protected flora and fauna, including polar bears, musk ox and birds of prey.

United States The largest public park in the United States is Wrangell-St Elias National Park and Preserve in Alaska. Of the 13.2 million acres, the National Park section is 8.33 million acres and the Preserve comprises 4.88 million acres.

Largest game reserve The world's largest zoological reserve is the Etosha National Park, Namibia. Established in 1907, it now covers an area of 38,427 miles².

ZOOS

It has been estimated that throughout the world there are some 757 zoos, with an estimated annual attendance of 350 million.

Oldest The earliest-known collection of animals was the one set up by Shulgi, a third-dynasty ruler of Ur from 2097–2094 B.C., at Puzurish in southeast Iraq. The oldest-known zoo is the one at Schönbrunn, Vienna, Austria, built in 1752 by the Holy Roman Emperor Franz I for his wife Maria Theresa.

The oldest existing public zoological collection in the world is that of the Zoological Society of London, Great Britain, founded in 1826. In January 1989 the collection comprised 11,108 specimens, housed in Regent's Park, London, Great Britain (36 acres) and at Whipsnade Park, Bedfordshire, Great Britain (541 acres; opened 23 May 1931). The record annual attendances are 3,031,571 in 1950 for Regent's Park and 756,758 in 1961 for Whipsnade.

United States The Philadelphia Zoo received its charter from the state of Pennsylvania in 1859, but did not open to the public until 1874.

Lincoln Park Zoo, a 60-acre public park owned by the city of Chicago, received a gift of two swans from Central Park, New York City in 1868. By 1870 a "small barn and paddocks" had been built to house additional animals that had been donated by the public. The current facility covers 35 acres.

According to the American Association of Zoological Parks and Aquariums, the top zoo for attendance is Lincoln Park Zoo with 4 million visitors each year.

Without bars The earliest zoo without bars was that at Stellingen, near Hamburg, Germany. It was founded in 1907 by Carl Hagenbeck (1844–1913), who made use of deep pits and large pens instead of cages to separate the exhibits from visitors.

OCEANARIA

Earliest The world's first oceanarium is Marineland of Florida, opened in 1938 at a site 18 miles south of St Augustine, FL. Up to 5.8 million gal of seawater are pumped daily through two major tanks, one rectangular (100 ft long by 40 ft wide by 18 ft deep) containing 375,000 gal, and one circular (233 ft in circumference and 12 ft deep) containing 330,000 gal. The tanks are seascaped, including coral reefs and even a shipwreck.

AQUARIA

Largest In terms of the volume of water held, the Living Seas Aquarium, opened in 1986 at the EPCOT Center, FL is the world's largest, with a total capacity of 6.25 million gal. It contains over 3,000 fish representing 65 species.

The largest in terms of marine-life is the Monterey Bay Aquarium in California. The aquarium was opened on 20 Oct 1984 at a cost of $55 million. It contains over 6,500 (525 species) of fauna and flora in its 95 tanks. The volume of water held is 750,000 gallons. The average annual attendance is 1.7 million visitors; however, in 1985 there were 2.3 million visitors, the highest for any aquarium in the United States.

HUMAN BEINGS

- ORIGINS
- DIMENSIONS
- REPRODUCTIVITY
- LONGEVITY
- ANATOMY AND PHYSIOLOGY

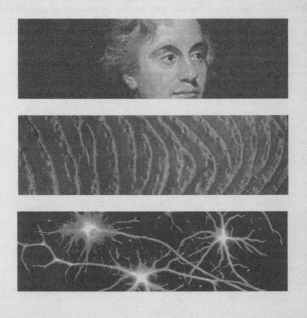

ORIGINS

EARLIEST HUMANS

If the age of the Earth–Moon system (latest estimate 4,540 ± 40 million years) is likened to a single year, hominids appeared on the scene at about 7:40 P.M. on 31 Dec, the Christian era began nearly 14 seconds before midnight, and the life span of a 120-year-old person would be about $^{84}/_{100}$ths of a second. Present calculations indicate that the Sun's increased heat as it becomes a "red giant" will make life on Earth untenable in about 5.5 billion years. Meanwhile there may well be colder epicycles.

Human beings (*Homo sapiens*) are a species in the subfamily Homininae of the family Hominidae of the superfamily Hominoidea of the suborder Simiae (or Anthropoidea) of the order Primates of the infraclass Eutheria of the subclass Theria of the class Mammalia of the subphylum Vertebrata (Craniata) of the phylum Chordata of the subkingdom Metazoa of the animal kingdom.

Earliest primates Primates appeared in the Paleocene epoch about 65 million years ago. The earliest members of the suborder Anthropoidea are known from both Africa and South America in the early Oligocene, 30–34 million years ago, when the two infra-orders, Platyrrhini and Catarrhini, from the New and Old Worlds respectively, were already distinct. New finds from the Fayum, in Egypt, are being studied and may represent primates from the Eocene period, as old as 37 million years.

Earliest hominoid The earliest hominoid fossil is a jawbone with three molars, discovered in the Otavi Hills, Namibia on 4 Jun 1991 by Martin Pickford (b. 1943) of the *Muséum Nationale d'Histoire Naturelle*, Paris,

---

Oldest human body The body of a Late Stone Age man, who is thought to have died *c.* 3300 B.C., was found almost perfectly preserved in an Austrian glacier in September 1991.

Oldest mummy Mummification (from the Persian word mūm, wax) dates from 2600 B.C. or the 4th dynasty of the Egyptian pharaohs. The oldest-known mummy is that of a high-ranking young woman who was buried *c.* 2600 B.C. on a plateau near the Great Pyramid of Cheops at Giza, or Al-Gizeh, Egypt. Her remains, which appear to represent an early attempt at mummification, were discovered in a 6-ft-deep excavation on 17 Mar 1989, but only her skull was intact. She is believed to have lived in the lost kingdom of Ankh Ptah.

The oldest complete mummy is of Wati, a court musician of *c.* 2400 B.C., from the tomb of Nefer in Saqqâra, Egypt, found in 1944.

France. It had been provisionally dated at 10–15 million years, but later refined to 12–13 million years and named *Otavi pithecus namibiensis*.

Earliest hominid The characteristics typical of the Hominidae include a large brain and bipedal locomotion (walking on two legs). The earliest hominid relic is an Australopithecine jawbone with two molars, each 2 in long, found by Kiptalam Chepboi near Lake Baringo, Kenya in February 1984 and dated to 4 million years ago by associated fossils and to 5.4–5.6 million years ago through rock correlation by potassium-argon dating.

Of early hominid material, one of the most complete is the skeleton of "Lucy" (40 percent complete), found by Dr Donald C. Johanson and T. Gray at Locality 162 near the Awash River, Hadar, in the Afar region of Ethiopia on 30 Nov 1974. She was estimated to be *c.* 40 years old when she died 3 million years ago, and she was 3 ft 6 in tall.

Parallel tracks of hominid footprints extending over 80 ft were discovered at Laetoli, Tanzania in 1978, by Paul Abell and Dr Mary Leakey, in volcanic ash dating to 3.6 million years ago. The height of the smallest of the seemingly three individuals was estimated to be 3 ft 11 in.

Earliest of the genus Homo The earliest species of this genus is *Homo habilis*, or "Handy Man," from Olduvai Gorge, Tanzania, named by Louis Leakey, Philip Tobias and John Napier in 1964 after a suggestion from Prof. Raymond Arthur Dart (1893–1988).

The greatest age attributed to fossils of this genus is about 2.4 million years for a piece of cranium found in western Kenya in 1965. At the time it could not be positively identified, but scientists in the USA were able to confirm the identification in 1991. The date was provided by Alan Deino of the Geochronology Center of the Institute of Human Origins, Berkeley, CA, who analyzed volcanic material in a layer just above the fossil site.

The earliest stone tools are abraded core-choppers dating from *c.* 2.7 million years ago. They were found at Hadar, Ethiopia in November–December 1976 by Hélène Roche (France). Finger-held (as opposed to fist-held) quartz slicers found by Roche and Dr John Wall (New Zealand) close to the Hadar site by the Gona River can also be dated to *c.* 2.7 million years ago.

Earliest Homo erectus The oldest example of this species (upright man), the direct ancestor of *Homo sapiens*, was discovered by Kamoya Kimeu on the surface at the site of Nariokotome III to the west of Lake Turkana, Kenya in August 1985. The skeleton of this 5 ft 5 in 12-year-old-boy is the most complete of this species yet found; only a few small pieces are missing. It is dated to 1.6 million years ago.

Earliest Homo sapiens Through the Pleistocene epoch (1.6 million to 10,000 years ago) the trend towards large brains continued. *Homo sapiens* ("wise man") appeared about 300,000 years ago as the successor to *Homo erectus*.

United States Over 500 artifacts 11,000 to 16,000 years old were found in Washington Co., PA in April 1973 after being brought to the attention of the University of Pittsburgh by Albert Miller, whose family owned the land. The dig, led by Dr James Adovasio, started in June 1973 and lasted until June 1983. The artifacts consist mainly of unfluted lanceolate projectile points (either spearheads or darts), an assortment of bifacial and unifacial tools (knives and scrapers), polyhedral blade cores (long thin flakes from which blades are made), and blades struck from this core. These items are all made from chert, a flintlike rock.

The site dates to the Pre-Clovis Paleo-Indian culture and it is believed that the *Homo sapiens* Paleo-Indians were the initial inhabitants of the site. The tools, dated by the mass accelerator spectrometer (MAS) technique, which measures the carbon content present in the amino acids at the time of death, resembled tools found in Manchuria. This supports theories that North America was first inhabited by peoples coming across a natural land bridge between Siberia and Alaska that is now deep beneath the Bering Sea.

In 1968 a burial site containing bones of two individuals believed to be an infant and an adolescent were uncovered by construction workers in Wilsall, MT. This site, called the Anzick burial site, also contained 120 artifacts with a red ocher covering believed to be grave offerings. These were mainly flint and stone bifacial (flaked by percussion along both sides of the chopping edge) tools and the remains of spear shafts.

The bones were dated by the MAS technique to not less than 10,600 years ago. The remains are believed to be of members of the Paleo-Indian culture, with the artifacts in the style of the Clovis Age. When taking into account the cultural material found in the next six levels below, the average range widely accepted for the existence of humans at the site is from 13,955 to 14,555 years ago.

DIMENSIONS

GIANTS

Growth of the body is determined by growth hormone. This is produced by the pituitary gland, set deep in the brain. Overproduction in childhood produces abnormal growth, and true gigantism is the result. The true height of human giants is frequently obscured by exaggeration and commercial dishonesty. The only admissible evidence on the actual height of giants is that collected since 1870 under impartial medical supervision. Unfortunately, even medical authors are not always blameless and can include fanciful, as opposed to measured, heights.

TALLEST MEN

Earliest opinion is that the tallest man in medical history of whom there is irrefutable evidence was Robert Pershing Wadlow, born at 6:30 A.M. on 22 Feb 1918 in Alton, IL. Weighing 8½ lb at birth, he began his abnormal growth at the age of two following a double hernia operation. On his 13th birthday he stood 7 ft 1¾ in tall and by 17 he had reached 8 ft ½ in.

On 27 Jun 1940 Dr C.M. Charles, associate professor of anatomy at Washington University's School of Medicine in St Louis, MO, and Dr Cyril MacBryde measured Robert Wadlow at 8 ft 11.1 in (arm span 9 ft 5¾ in) in St Louis. Wadlow died 18 days later at 1:30 A.M. on 15 Jul 1940 weighing 439 lb in a hotel in Manistee, MI as a result of a septic blister on

TALLEST MAN
Robert Wadlow
(b. 1918) seen
here with his two
brothers, Eugene
(b. 1922) (left) and
Harold Jr. (b.
1932). (Photo:
Alton Telegraph)

ROBERT WADLOW

Weighing 8½ lb at birth, Robert Wadlow started his abnormal growth at the age of two following a double hernia operation. His height progressed as follows:

Age	Height		Weight
	ft	in	lb
5	5	4	105
8	6	0	169
9	6	2 ¼	180
10	6	5	210
11	6	7	—
12	6	10 ½	—
13	7	1 ¾	255
14	7	5	301
15	7	8	355
16	7	10 ¼	374
17[1]	8	0 ½	315
18	8	3 ½	—
19	8	5 ½	480
20	8	6 ¾	—
21	8	8 ¼	491
22[2]	8	11 ¹⁄₁₀	439

[1]*Following severe influenza and infection of the foot.*
[2]*Still growing during his terminal illness.*

his right ankle caused by a poorly fitting brace. He was buried in Oakwood Cemetery, Alton, IL in a coffin measuring 10 ft 9 in.

His greatest recorded weight was 491 lb on his 21st birthday. His shoes were size 37AA (18½ in) and his hands measured 12¾ in from the wrist to the tip of the middle finger.

Living There are two claimants to the title of tallest person in the world: Haji Mohammad Alam Channa (b. 1956) of Bachal Channa, Sehulan Sharif, Pakistan, and the world's tallest living woman, Sandy Allen (see Tallest women), both of whom are around 7 ft 7¼ in tall.

Goliath of Gath The Bible states that Goliath of Gath (*c.* 1060 B.C.) stood 6 cubits (approximately 9 ft) with an arm span of 9 ft 6½ in, but this is open to doubt.

The Jewish historian Flavius Josephus (A.D. 37/38– *c.* 100) and some of the manuscripts of the Septuagint (the earliest Greek translation of the Old Testament) attribute to Goliath the wholly credible height of 4 Greek cubits (approximately 6 ft) and an arm span of 6 ft 10 in.

TALLEST WOMEN

The tallest woman in medical history was the giantess Zeng Jinlian (b. 26 Jun 1964) of Yujiang village in the Bright Moon Commune, Hunan Province, central China, who measured 8 ft 1¾ in when she died on 13 Feb 1982. This figure, however, represented her height with assumed normal spinal curvature, because she suffered from severe scoliosis (curvature of the spine) and could not stand up straight. She began to grow abnormally from the age of four months and stood 5 ft 1½ in before her fourth birthday and 7 ft 1½ in when she was 13. Her hands measured 10 in and her feet 14 in in length. Both her parents and her brother were of normal size.

The giantess Ella Ewing (1875–1913) of Gorin, MO was billed at 8 ft 2 in, but this height was exaggerated. She measured 7 ft 4½ in at the age of 23, and may have attained 7 ft 6 in at the time of her death.

Living The world's tallest woman is Sandy Allen, born 18 Jun 1955 in Chicago, IL. A 6½ lb baby, she began growing abnormally soon after birth. At 10 years of age she stood 6 ft 3 in, and she measured 7 ft 1 in when she was 16. On 14 Jul 1977 this giantess underwent a pituitary gland operation, which inhibited further growth at 7 ft 7¼ in. She now weighs 462 lb and takes a size 16 EEE shoe.

MARRIED COUPLE

Anna Hanen Swan (1846–88) of Nova Scotia, Canada was said to be 8 ft 1 in but actually measured 7 ft 5½ in. At the church of St Martin-in-the-Fields, London, Great Britain on 17 Jun 1871 she married Martin van Buren Bates (1845–1919) of Whitesburg, KY, who stood 7 ft 2½ in, making them the tallest married couple on record.

TALLEST TWINS

The world's tallest identical twins are Michael and James Lanier (b. 27 Nov 1969) from Troy, MI. They measured 7 ft 1 in at the age of 14 years and both now stand 7 ft 4 in. Their sister Jennifer is 5 ft 2 in tall.

The world's tallest female identical twins are Heather and Heidi Burge (b. 11 Nov 1971) from Palos Verdes, CA. They are both 6 ft 4¾ in tall.

Most variable stature Adam Rainer, born in Graz (Austria; 1899–1950), measured 3 ft 10½ in at the age of 21. He then suddenly started growing at a rapid rate, and by 1931 he had reached 7 ft 1¾ in. He became so weak as a result that he was bedridden for the rest of his life. At the time of his death on 4 Mar 1950, age 51, he measured 7 ft 8 in and was the only person in medical history to have been both a dwarf and a giant.

Tallest and shortet tribes The tallest major tribes in the world are the slender Tutsi (also known as the Watusi) of Rwanda and Burundi, Central Africa, and the Dinka of the Sudan. In some groups of the Tutsi, adult males average 6 ft 5 in and females 5 ft 10 in.

The smallest pygmies are the Mbuti of the Ituri forest, Zaire, Central Africa, with an average height of 4 ft 6 in for men and 4 ft 5 in for women.

DWARFS

The strictures that apply to giants apply equally to dwarfs, except that exaggeration gives way to understatement. In the same way as 9 ft may be regarded as the limit towards which the tallest giants tend, so 22 in must be regarded as the limit towards which the shortest adult dwarfs or midgets tend (compare with the average length of newborn babies, which is 18–20 in). In the case of child dwarfs, their *ages* are often exaggerated by their agents or managers.

There are many causes of short stature in humans. They include genetic abnormalities, lack of appropriate hormones, and malnutrition. Dwarfs of the past, whatever the cause of their condition, tended to be smaller because of lower nutritional standards.

Shortest person *Adult* The shortest mature human of whom there is independent evidence is the still-living Gul Mohammad (b. 15 Feb 1957) of Delhi, India. On 19 Jul 1990 he was examined at Ram Manohar Hospital, New Delhi, and found to measure 22^1/2 in in height and to weigh 37^1/2 lb. The other members of his immediate family are of normal height.

The shortest-ever female was Pauline Musters, a Dutch dwarf. She was born at Ossendrecht, Netherlands, on 26 Feb 1876 and measured 12 in at birth. At nine years of age she was 21.65 in tall and weighed only 3 lb 5 oz. She died on 1 Mar 1895 in New York City at the age of 19. Although she was billed at 19 in, a postmortem examination showed her to be exactly 24 in (there was some elongation after death). Her mature weight varied from 7^1/2–9 lb.

The shortest living female is Madge Bester (b. 26 Apr 1963) of Johannesburg, South Africa, at 25^1/2 in. She suffers from *Osteogenesis imperfecta* and is confined to a wheelchair. This disease means there is an inherited abnormality of collagen, which with calcium salts, produces a rigid structure within the bones. The disease is characterized by brittle bones and other deformities of the skeleton. Her mother, Winnie, is not much taller, measuring 27^1/2 in, and she too is confined to a wheelchair.

Child In 1979 a height of 19.7 in and a weight of 4 lb 6 oz were reported for Stamatoula, a nine-year-old Greek girl (1969–85). When she died on 22 Aug 1985 at the Lyrion Convent, Athens, Greece, she measured 26.4 in and weighed 11 lb. The child, believed to be the survivor of twins, suffered from Seckel's syndrome, also known as "bird-headed dwarfism."

Twins The shortest twins ever recorded were the dwarfs Matjus and Bela Matina (b. 1903–d. *c.* 1935) of Budapest, Hungary, who later became American citizens. They both measured 30 in.

Living The world's shortest living twins are John and Greg Rice (b. 3 Dec 1951) of West Palm Beach, FL, who both measure 34 in.

The shortest identical twin sisters are Dorene Williams of Oakdale and Darlene McGregor of Almeda, CA (b. 1949), who each stand 4 ft 1 in.

Oldest There are only two centenarian dwarfs on record. The older was Hungarian-born Susanna Bokoyni ("Princess Susanna") of Newton, NJ, who died at the age of 105 years on 24 Aug 1984. She was 3 ft 4 in tall.

The other was Miss Anne Clowes of Matlock, Derbyshire, Great

Britain, who died on 5 Aug 1784 at the age of 103 years. She was 3 ft 9 in tall.

WEIGHT

Heaviest male　The heaviest human in medical history was Jon Brower Minnoch (b. 29 Sep 1941) of Bainbridge Island, WA, who had suffered from obesity since childhood. The 6-ft-1-in-tall former taxi driver was 392 lb in 1963, 700 lb in 1966, and 975 lb in September 1976.

In March 1978, Minnoch was rushed to University Hospital, Seattle, saturated with fluid and suffering from heart and respiratory failure. It took a dozen firemen and an improvised stretcher to move him from his home to a ferryboat. When he arrived at the hospital he was put in two beds lashed together. It took 13 people just to roll him over. By extrapolating his intake and elimination rates, consultant endocrinologist Dr Robert Schwartz calculated that Minnoch must have weighed more than 1,387 lb when he was admitted. A great deal of this was water accumulation due to his congestive heart failure. After nearly 16 months on a 1,200-calorie-a-day diet, the choking fluid had gone, and he was discharged at 476 lb. In October 1981 he had to be readmitted, after having put on 197 lb. When he died on 10 Sep 1983 he weighed more than 798 lb.

Heaviest living male　The heaviest living man is T.J. Albert Jackson (b. 1941 Kent Nicholson), also known as "Fat Albert," of Canton, MS. He recently tipped the scales at 891 lb. He has a 120-in chest, a 116-in waist, 70-in thighs and a 29½-in neck.

Heaviest female　The heaviest woman ever recorded is Roselie Bradford (USA; b. 1944), who claimed to register a peak weight of 1,050 lb in January 1987. In August of that year she developed congestive heart failure and was rushed to a hospital. She was consequently put on a carefully controlled diet and by September 1992 weighed 314 lb. Her target weight is 150 lb. (See also Weight loss.)

Heaviest twins　Billy Leon (1946–79) and Benny Loyd (b. 7 Dec 1946) McCrary, alias McGuire, of Hendersonville, NC were normal in size until the age of six when they both contracted German measles. In November 1978 they weighed 743 lb (Billy) and 723 lb (Benny) and had 84-in waists. As professional tag-team wrestling performers they were billed at weights up to 770 lb. Billy died at Niagara Falls, Ontario, Canada on 13 Jul 1979.

Weight loss Dieting　The greatest recorded slimming feat by a male was that of Jon Brower Minnoch (see Heaviest male), who had reduced to 476 lb by July 1979, thus indicating a weight loss of at least 911 lb in 16 months.

Roselie Bradford (see Heaviest female) went from a weight of 1,050 lb in January 1987 to 314 lb in September 1992, a loss of a record 736 lb.

Sweating　Ron Allen (b. 1947) sweated off 21½ lb of his weight of 239 lb in Nashville, TN in 24 hours in August 1984.

Weight gain　The reported record for weight gain is held by Jon Brower Minnoch (see Heaviest male) at 196 lb in 7 days in October 1981 after readmittance to University Hospital, Seattle, WA. Arthur Knorr (USA; 1916–60) gained 294 lb in the last six months of his life.

Miss Doris James of San Francisco, CA is alleged to have gained 325 lb in the 12 months before her death in August 1965, age 38, at a weight of 675 lb. She was only 5 ft 2 in tall.

Greatest differential The greatest weight difference recorded for a married couple is *c.* 1,300 lb in the case of Jon Brower Minnoch (See Heaviest male) and his 110-lb wife Jeannette in March 1978.

Lightest The thinnest recorded adults of normal height are those suffering from anorexia nervosa. Losses of up to 65 percent of original body weight have been recorded in females, with a low of 45 lb in the case of Emma Shaller (1868–90) of St Louis, MO, who stood 5 ft 2 in.

The lightest adult was Lucia Zarate (Mexico, 1863–89), an emaciated Mexican dwarf of 26½ in, who weighed 4.7 lb at the age of 17. She "fattened up" to 13 lb by her 20th birthday. At birth she had weighed 2½ lb.

Edward C. Hagner (1892–1962), alias Eddie Masher (USA), is alleged to have weighed only 48 lb at a height of 5 ft 7 in.

In August 1825 an unsubstantiated claim was made for Claude-Ambroise Seurat (1797–1826) of Troyes, France giving his biceps measurement as 4 in and the distance between his back and his chest as less than 3 in. According to one report he stood 5 ft 7½ in and weighed 78 lb, but in another account he was described as being 5 ft 4 in and only 36 lb.

Most dissimilar couple Nigel Wilks (b. 1963), 6 ft 6 in tall, of Kingston-upon-Hull, Great Britain, on 30 Jun 1984 married Beverley Russell (b. 1963), 4 ft tall, who suffers from a skeletal disorder.

REPRODUCTIVITY

MOTHERHOOD

Most children The greatest officially recorded number of children born to one mother is 69, by the wife of Feodor Vassilyev (b. 1707–*fl.* 1782), a peasant from Shuya, 150 miles east of Moscow, Russia. In 27 confinements she gave birth to 16 pairs of twins, seven sets of triplets and four sets of quadruplets. The case was reported to Moscow by the Monastery of Nikolskiy on 27 Feb 1782. Only two of those who were born in the period *c.* 1725–65 failed to survive their infancy.

The world's most prolific mother is currently Leontina Albina (nee Espinosa; b. 1925) of San Antonio, Chile, who in 1981 produced her 55th and last child. Her husband Gerardo Secunda Albina (variously Alvina; b. 1921) states that they were married in Argentina in 1943 and had 5 sets of triplets (all boys) before coming to Chile. Only 40 (24 boys and 16 girls) survive.

Oldest mother Many apparently very late maternities may be cover-ups for illegitimate grandchildren. Post-menopausal women have been rendered fertile by recent hormonal techniques. Medical literature contains extreme but unauthenticated cases of septuagenarian mothers, such as Mrs Ellen Ellis, age 72, of Four Crosses, Clwyd, Great Britain, who allegedly produced a stillborn 13th child on 15 May 1776 in her 46th year of marriage.

In the *Gazette Médicale de Liège* (1 Oct 1891) Dr E. Derasse reported the case of one of his patients who gave birth to a healthy baby at the age of 59 years 5 months. The woman already had a married daughter age 40.

It was reported in the *British Medical Journal* (June 1991) that a mother gave birth at the age of 59 years.

BABIES

Heaviest single birth Big babies (i.e., over 10 lb) are usually born to mothers who are large, overweight or have some medical problem such as diabetes. The heaviest baby born to a healthy mother was a boy weighing 22 lb 8 oz who was born to Signora Carmelina Fedele of Aversa, Italy in September 1955.

Mrs Anna Bates (nee Swan; 1846–88), the 7-ft-5½-in Canadian giantess (see Dimensions, Married couple), gave birth to a boy weighing 23 lb 12 oz (length 30 in) at her home in Seville, OH on 19 Jan 1879, but the baby died 11 hours later.

Twins The world's heaviest twins were born to Mrs J.P. Haskin, Fort Smith, AR, collectively weighing 27 lb 12 oz on 20 Feb 1924.

Triplets The unconfirmed report of the world's heaviest triplets was a case from Iran (two male, one female) collectively weighing 26 lb 6 oz born on 18 Mar 1968.

Quadruplets The world's heaviest quadruplets (four girls) weighed 22 lb 13 oz collectively and were born to Mrs Ayako Takeda Tsuchihashi at the Maternity Hospital in Kagoshima, Japan on 4 Oct 1978.

Quintuplets Two cases have been recorded for heaviest quintuplets, both recording a total weight of 25 lb. The first set was born on 7 Jun 1953 to Mrs Lui Saulian of Zhejiang, China, and the second set to Mrs Kamalammal of Pondicherry, India on 30 Dec 1956.

Test-tube babies There are various methods by which babies can be conceived outside of the mother's body. These children are usually known as "test-tube" babies and the technique as IVF (in-vitro fertilization).

First   The world's first test-tube baby was born to Lesley Brown, age 31, who gave birth by cesarean section to Louise (5 lb 12 oz) in Oldham General Hospital, Great Britain at 11:47 P.M. on 25 Jul 1978. Louise was externally conceived on 10 Nov 1977.

The first test-tube baby in the United States was Elizabeth Jordan Carr (5 lb 12 oz), who was delivered by cesarean section from Judy Carr, age 28, in Norfolk General Hospital, VA on 28 Dec 1981. Elizabeth was externally conceived on 15 Apr 1981. Dr Howard Jones of Eastern Virginia Medical School performed the in-vitro procedure.

Twins   The world's first test-tube twins, Stephen and Amanda, were delivered by cesarean section to Mrs Radmila Mays, age 31, at the Queen Victoria Medical Centre, Melbourne, Australia on 5 Jun 1981. Amanda weighed in at 5 lb 6 oz and Stephen at 5 lb 3 oz.

Triplets   The world's first test-tube triplets (two girls and one boy) were born at Flinders Medical Centre, Adelaide, Australia on 8 Jun 1983. At the request of the parents, no names were released.

Quintuplets   Alan, Brett, Connor, Douglas and Edward were born to Linda and Bruce Jacobssen at University College Hospital, London, Great Britain on 26 Apr 1985.

First birth from frozen embryo   Zoe (last name withheld) was delivered by cesarean section weighing 5 lb 13 oz on 28 Mar 1984 in Melbourne, Australia. Scientists from Monash University announced the birth.

United States   A boy (9 lb 8 oz) was delivered by cesarean section on 4 Jun 1986 from Monique (last name withheld), age 36, in Cottage Hospital, Santa Barbara, CA. A second child (name withheld) was born on 23 Oct 1989 by the same procedure and it is believed that this is the only case of siblings from frozen embryos. Dr Richard Marrs was in charge of the procedure.

Most-premature babies   James Elgin Gill was born to Brenda and James Gill on 20 May 1987 in Ottawa, Ontario, Canada 128 days premature and weighing 1 lb 6 oz.

United States   In the United States the most premature baby is Ernestine Hudgins, who was born on 8 Feb 1983 in San Diego, CA about 18 weeks premature and weighing 17 oz.

Twins   Arron and Laura Gaskarth (non-identical twins) were born on 15 Jul 1991 in Bishop Auckland General Hospital, Durham, Great Britain, 107 days premature. Aaron weighed 1 lb 11 oz and Laura 1 lb 7½ oz.

Quadruplets   Tina Piper of St Leonards-on-Sea, Great Britain, had quadruplets on 10 Apr 1988, after exactly 26 weeks of pregnancy. Oliver, 2 lb 9 oz (d. Feb 1989), Francesca, 2 lb 2 oz, Charlotte, 2 lb 4½ oz, and Georgina, 2 lb 5 oz, were all born at The Royal Sussex County Hospital, Brighton, Great Britain.

MULTIPLE BIRTHS

Conjoined twins   Conjoined twins were formerly called "Siamese," from
the celebrated Chang and Eng Bunker ("Left" and "Right" in Thai), born
at Meklong, Siam (now Thailand) on 11 May 1811 of Chinese parents.
They were joined by a cartilaginous band at the chest. They married (in
1843) the Misses Sarah and Adalaide Yates of Wilkes County, NC, and fa-

**CONJOINED TWINS   The term "Siamese" for conjoined twins is
derived from the famous twins, Chang and Eng Bunker, born in
Meklong, Siam (now Thailand) in 1811. (Photo: Ann Ronan Picture
Library)**

thered 10 and 12 children respectively. They died within three hours of each other on 17 Jan 1874, age 62.

Rarest The most extreme form of conjoined twins is dicephales tetra-brachius dipus (two heads, four arms and two legs). The only fully reported example is Masha and Dasha Krivoshlyapovy, born in Russia on 4 Jan 1950.

Earliest successful separation The earliest successful separation of conjoined twins was performed on xiphopagus (joined at the sternum) girls at Mount Sinai Hospital, Cleveland, OH by Dr Jac S. Geller on 14 Dec 1952.

Lightest twins Mary, 16 oz, and Margaret, 19 oz, were born on 16 Aug 1931 to Mrs Florence Stimson of Old Fletton, Great Britain.

Longest interval between twins Mrs Danny Petrungaro (nee Berg; b. 1953) of Rome, Italy, who had been on hormone treatment after suffering four miscarriages, gave birth normally to a girl, Diana, on 22 Dec 1987, but the other twin, Monica, was delivered by cesarean on 27 Jan 1988, 36 days later.

Fastest triplet birth Bradley, Christopher and Carmon were born naturally to Mrs James E. Duck of Memphis, TN in two minutes on 21 Mar 1977.

Quindecaplets It was announced by Dr Gennaro Montanino of Rome that he had removed by hysterotomy after four months of pregnancy the fetuses of ten girls and five boys from the womb of a 35-year-old housewife on 22 Jul 1971. A fertility drug was responsible for this unique instance of quindecaplets.

Most sets of multiple births in a family
  Quintuplets There is no recorded case of more than a single set.
  Quadruplets Four sets to Mde Feodor Vassilyev, Shuya, Russia (b. 1707) (see Motherhood).
  Triplets 15 sets to Maddalena Granata, Italy (b. 1839–fl. 1886).
  Twins 16 sets to Mde Vassilyev (see p. 152). Mrs Barbara Zulu of Barbeton, South Africa bore three sets of girls and three mixed sets in seven years (1967–73). Mrs Anna Steynvaait of Johannesburg, South Africa produced two sets within 10 months in 1960.

Longest-parted twins Through the help of New Zealand's television program *Missing* on 27 Apr 1989, Iris (nee Haughie) Johns and Aro (nee Haughie) Campbell (b. 13 Jan 1914) were reunited after 75 years' separation.

United States Fraternal twins Lloyd Earl and Floyd Ellsworth Clark were born on 15 Feb 1917 in Nebraska. They were parted when only four months old and lived under their adopted names, Dewayne William Gramly (Lloyd) and Paul Edward Forbes (Floyd). Both men knew that they had been born twins but it wasn't until 16 Jun 1986 that they were reunited, after having been separated for over 69 years.

Highest number at a single birth   The highest number reported at a single birth were two males and eight females at Bacacay, Brazil on 22 Apr 1946. Reports were also received from Spain in 1924 and China on 12 May 1936.

The highest number medically recorded is nine (nonuplets) born to Mrs Geraldine Broderick at Royal Hospital for Women, Sydney, Australia on 13 Jun 1971. None of the five boys (two stillborn) and four girls lived for more than 6 days.

The birth of nine children has also been reported on at least two other occasions: Philadelphia, PA on 29 May 1971; and Bagerhat, Bangladesh *c.* 11 May 1977; in both cases none survived.

Septuplets were born on 21 May 1985 to Patti Jorgenson Frustaci of Orange, CA, a 30-year-old English teacher who had been taking a fertility drug. One baby was stillborn and the living infants weighed as little as 1 lb. In the weeks that followed, three more babies died, but three have survived.

The birth of six children (sextuplets) has occurred on a number of occasions, but very rarely do all children survive.

DESCENDANTS

In polygamous countries (countries that allow a man to have more than one wife at a time), the number of a person's descendants can become incalculable. The last Sharifian emperor of Morocco, Moulay Ismail (1672–1727), known as "The Bloodthirsty," was reputed to have fathered a total of 525 sons and 342 daughters by 1703 and to have achieved a 700th son in 1721.

At his death on 15 Oct 1992, Samuel S. Must, age 96, of Fryburg, PA, had 824 living descendants. The roll call comprised 11 children, 97 grandchildren, 634 great-grandchildren and 82 great-great-grandchildren.

Mrs Peter L. Schwartz (1902–88) of Missouri had 14 children, 13 of whom are still living; 175 grandchildren; 477 great-grandchildren; and 20 great-great-grandchildren.

Great-great-great-grandmother   Harriet Holmes of Newfoundland, Canada (b. 17 Jan 1899) became the youngest living great-great-great-grand-

---

Seven-generation family   Augusta Bunge (nee Pagel; b. 13 Oct 1879) of Wisconsin learned that she was a great-great-great-great-grandmother when she received news of her great-great-great-great-grandson, Christopher John Bollig (b. 21 Jan 1989).

Most living ascendants   Megan Sue Austin of Bar Harbor, ME had a full set of grandparents and great-grandparents and five great-great-grandparents, making 19 direct ascendants when born on 16 May 1982.

---

mother on 8 Mar 1987 at the age of 88 years 50 days. The families' average generation was only 17.6 years.

Family tree The lineage of K'ung Ch'iu or Confucius (551–479 B.C.) can be traced back further than that of any other family. His great-great-great-great-grandfather K'ung Chia is known from the 8th century B.C. This man's 85th lineal descendants, Wei-yi (b. 1939) and Wei-ning (b. 1947), live today in Taiwan.

LONGEVITY

No single subject is more obscured by vanity, deceit, falsehood and deliberate fraud than human longevity. Apart from the traces left by accidental markers (e.g. the residual effects of established dated events such as the Chernobyl incident), there is no known scientific method of checking the age of any part of the living body.

Centenarians surviving beyond their 113th year are in fact extremely rare and the present absolute proven limit of human longevity does not yet admit of anyone living to celebrate his or her 121st birthday.

From data on documented centenarians, actuaries have shown that only one 115-year life can be expected in 2.1 billion lives (note that the world population was estimated to be 5.48 billion by mid-1992).

With an estimated worldwide population of some 40,000 centenarians, only 22 percent are male. While husbands have a better chance than bachelors, it appears that spinsters have a better chance than wives of reaching 100 years.

The limits of credulity was reached on 5 May 1933, when a news agency filed a story from China with a Beijing source announcing that Li Zhongyun, the "oldest man on earth," born in 1680, had just died after 253 years (*sic*).

The latest census in China revealed only 3,800 centenarians, of whom two-thirds were women. According to a 1985 census carried out in the Chinese province of Xinjiang Uygur Zizhiqu, there were 850 centenarians in the area, one of whom was listed at a highly improbable 125 years of age. In the United States as of 1 Jul 1990 the figure was 37,306 centenarians.

In 1990 the United States population of people 65 and over was 31.2 million, representing 12.6 percent of the population. Since 1900 the American population 65 and over has increased tenfold from 3.1 million. It is projected that a child born in 1989 has a life expectancy of 75.6 years. In 1900 the figure was 46.9 years.

Oldest authentic centenarian The greatest authenticated age to which any human has ever lived is 120 years 237 days in the case of Shigechiyo Izumi of Asan on Tokunoshima, an island 820 miles southwest of Tokyo, Japan. He was born at Asan on 29 Jun 1865 and was recorded as a 6-year old in Japan's first census of 1871. He died in his ranch house at 12:15 GMT on 21 Feb 1986 after developing pneumonia. He worked until 105. His wife died when only 90 years of age. He drank *Sho-chu* (firewater) (distilled from sugar) and took up smoking when 70 years old. He attributed his long life to "God, Buddha and the Sun."

Oldest living   The oldest living person in the world whose date of birth can be reliably authenticated is Jeanne Louise Calment, who was born in France on 21 Feb 1875. She now lives in a nursing home in Arles, southern France, where she celebrated her 118th birthday with champagne. She met Vincent van Gogh (died 29 Jul 1890) in her father's shop.

Oldest twins   The chances of identical twins both reaching 100 are now probably about one in 50 million.

Eli Shadrack and John Meshak Phipps were born on 14 Feb 1803 at Affinghton, VA. Eli died at Hennessey, OK on 23 Feb 1911 at the age of 108 years 9 days, on which day John was still living in Shenandoah, IA.

Female   On 17 Jun 1984, identical twin sisters Mildred Widman Philippi and Mary Widman Franzini of St Louis, MO celebrated their 104th birthday. Mildred died on 4 May 1985, 44 days short of the twins' 105th birthday.

Oldest living triplets   Faith, Hope and Charity Cardwell were born in Sweetwater, TX on 18 May 1899, and live together in a Sweetwater retirement home.

Oldest quadruplets   The Ottman quads of Munich, Germany—Adolf, Anne-Marie, Emma and Elisabeth—were born on 5 May 1912. Adolf was the first to die, on 17 Mar 1992, at the age of 79 years 316 days.

United States   The Morlok quads of Lansing, MI—Edna, Wilma, Sarah and Helen—celebrated their 63rd birthday on 18 May 1993.

65+ POPULATION

State	Total (1,000's)
California	3,136
Florida	2,369
New York	2,364
Pennsylvania	1,829
Texas	1,717

Data AARP/AOA

AUTHENTIC LONGEVITY RECORDS

Country	Age	Name	Born	Died
Japan	120 yr 237 days	Shigechiyo Izumi	29 Jun 1865	21 Feb 1986
France	118 yr 40 days	Jeanne Louise Calment	21 Feb 1875	fl.* April 1993
United States[1]	116 yr 88 days	Carrie White (Mrs; nee Joyner)	18 Nov 1874	14 Feb 1991
Great Britain	115 yr 229 days	Charlotte Hughes (Mrs; nee Milburn)	1 Aug 1877	17 Mar 1993
Canada	113 yr 124 days	Pierre Joubert	15 Jul 1701	16 Nov 1814
Australia	112 yr 330 days	Caroline Maud Mockridge	11 Dec 1874	6 Nov 1987
Wales	112 yr 292 days	John Evans	19 Aug 1877	10 Jun 1990
Spain[2]	112 yr 228 days	Josefa Salas Mateo	14 Jul 1860	27 Feb 1973
Norway	112 yr 61 days	Maren Bolette Torp	21 Dec 1876	20 Feb 1989
Morocco	112 yr +	El Hadj Mohammed el Mokri (Grand Vizier)	1844	16 Sep 1957
Poland	112 yr +	Roswlia Mielczarak (Mrs)	1868	7 Jan 1981
Netherlands	111 yr 354 days	Thomas Peters	6 Apr 1745	26 Mar 1857
Ireland	111 yr 327 days	The Hon. Katherine Plunket	22 Nov 1820	14 Oct 1932
Scotland	111 yr 238 days	Kate Begbie (Mrs)	9 Jan 1877	5 Sep 1988
South Africa[3]	111 yr 151 days	Johanna Booyson	17 Jan 1857	16 Jun 1968
Sweden[4]	111 yr 90 days	Wilhelmine Sande (Mrs)	24 Oct 1874	21 Jan 1986
Czechoslovakia	111 yr +	Marie Bernatková	22 Oct 1857	fl. October 1968
Germany[5]	111 yr	Maria Corba	15 Aug 1878	fl. March 1990
Finland	111 yr +	Fanny Matilda Nystrom	30 Sep 1878	1989
Channel Islands	110 yr 321 days	Margaret Ann Neve (nee Harvey)	18 May 1792	4 Apr 1903
Northern Ireland	110 yr 234 days	Elizabeth Watkins (Mrs)	10 Mar 1863	31 Oct 1973
Yugoslavia	110 yr +	Demitrius Philipovitch	9 Mar 1818	fl. August 1928
Greece	110 yr +	Lambrini Tsiatoura (Mrs)	1870	19 Feb 1981
USSR	110 yr +	Khasako Dzugayev	7 Aug 1860	fl. August 1970
Italy	110 yr +	Damiana Sette (Sig)	1874	25 Feb 1985

OLDEST LIVING PERSON Madame Jeanne Calment on her 116th birthday outside the nursing home at Arles, France, where she lives. Madame Calment continues to thrive but had a narrow escape shortly after her 118th birthday, when the home was badly damaged by a fire that killed two—but she escaped unharmed. (Photo: Sipa Press)

Oldest living American The oldest living person in the United States is Mrs Margaret Skeete (nee Seward), who was born in Rockport, TX on 27 Oct 1878.

[1] Mrs Rena Glover Brailsford died in Summerton, SC on 6 Dec 1977 reputedly aged 118 years. The 1900 U.S. Federal Census for Crawfish Springs Militia District of Walker County, GA, records an age of 77 for a Mark Thrash. If the Mark Thrash (reputedly born in Georgia in December 1822) who died near Chattanooga, TN on 17 Dec 1943 was he, and the age attributed was accurate, then he would have survived for 121 years. According to Jackson Pollard's Social Security payments, he was born on 15 Dec 1869 in Georgia, but no birth certificate or family bible are available.

[2] Señor Benita Medrana of Avila died on 28 Jan 1979, allegedly aged 114 years 335 days.

[3] Mrs Susan Johanna Deporter of Port Elizabeth, South Africa was reputedly 114 years old when she died on 4 Aug 1954.

[4] Mrs Sande was born in present-day Norway.

[5] An unnamed female died in Germany in 1979 aged 112 years; and an unnamed male, aged also 112 years, died in 1969.

* Note: *fl.* is the abbreviation for the Latin *floruit*, meaning he or she was living at the relevant date.

ANATOMY AND PHYSIOLOGY

Hydrogen (63 percent) and oxygen (25.5 percent) constitute the most common of the 24 elements regarded as normally present in the human body. Potassium, carbon, sodium, calcium, sulfur, chlorine (as chlorides), phosphorus, iron and zinc are all present in significant quantities. Present in "trace" quantities, but generally regarded as normal in a healthy body (even if their "necessity" is a matter of controversy), are iodine, fluorine, copper, cobalt, chromium, manganese, selenium, molybdenum, and probably vanadium, nickel, silicon, tin and arsenic.

HANDS, FEET AND HAIR

Touch The extreme sensitivity of the fingers is such that a vibration with a movement of 0.02 microns can be detected.

Longest fingernails Fingernails grow at a rate of about 0.02 in a week—four times faster than toenails. The aggregate measurement of those of Shridhar Chillal (b. 1937) of Pune, Maharashtra, India, on 3 Mar 1993 was 205 in for the five nails on his left hand (thumb 48 in, index finger 36 in, second finger 39 in, third finger 42 in, and the pinkie 40 in). He last cut his nails in 1952.

Fewest toes The two-toed syndrome exhibited by some members of the Wadomo tribe of the Zambezi Valley, Zimbabwe and the Kalanga tribe of the eastern Kalahari Desert, Botswana is hereditary via a single mutated gene. They are not handicapped by their deformity, and can walk great distances without discomfort.

Shaving The fastest barbers on record are Denny Rowe, who shaved 1,994 men in 60 min with a retractor safety razor in Herne Bay, Great Britain on 19 Jun 1988, taking on average 1.8 sec per volunteer, and drawing blood four times; and Tom Rodden, of Chatham, Great Britain, who on 4 May 1993 shaved 262 even-braver volunteers in 60 min with a cut-throat razor, averaging 13.8 sec per face. He drew blood only once.

Balancing on one foot The longest recorded duration for balancing on one foot is 55 hr 35 min by Girish Sharma at Deori, India from 2–4 Oct 1992. The disengaged foot may not be rested on the standing foot, nor may any object be used for support or balance.

Hair splitting The greatest reported achievement in hair splitting by a human was that of the former champion cyclist and craftsman Alfred West (Great Britain; 1901–85), who succeeded in splitting a human hair 17 times into 18 parts on eight occasions.

Largest feet If cases of elephantiasis are excluded, then the biggest feet known currently are those of Matthew McGrory (b. 17 May 1973) of Pennsylvania, who wears size 23 shoes.

Longest hair Human hair grows at a rate of about 0.5 in a month. If left uncut it will usually grow to a maximum of 2–3 ft.

In 1780 a head of hair measuring 12 ft in length and dressed in a style known as the *plica candiforma* (hair forming matted spikes) was sent to Dresden after adorning the head of a Polish peasant woman for 52 years. The braid of hair had a circumference of 11.9 in.

The hair of Diane Witt of Worcester, MA measured over 12 ft 8 in in March 1993. This is the longest documented length of hair.

LONGEST HAIR Human hair usually stops growing at $2^{1}/_{2}$–3 ft long, but at 12 ft 8 in, Diane Witt's hair is over twice as long as she is tall. This extraordinary growth of hair is inexplicable: since 1981— when she last had it cut—it has more than doubled in length. Shampooing and combing her hair can take several hours at a time. To keep it out of her way, Diane normally wears it in a complicated braided arrangement piled on top of her head—held up by just two hairpins. (Photo: R.H.Witt)

Lord Nelson—owner of the most valuable hair (left). (Photo: Bridgeman Art Library)

LONGEST MUSTACHE (Below) The mustache that Kalyan Ramji Sain of Sundargarth, India has grown since 1976 reached a span of 128¾ in (right side 65¾ in and left side 63 in) in July 1992. (Photo: Dilip Mehta)

Most valuable hair   On 18 Feb 1988 a bookseller from Cirencester, Great Britain, paid £5,575 ($10,035) for a lock of hair that had belonged to British naval hero Lord Nelson (1758–1805) at an auction held at Crewkerne, Great Britain.

Longest beard   The beard of Hans N. Langseth (b. 1846 near Eidsvoll, Norway) measured 17½ ft at the time of his burial in Kensett, IA in 1927 after 15 years' residence in the United States. It was presented to the Smithsonian Institution, Washington, D.C., in 1967.

The beard of Janice Deveree, "the bearded lady" (b. Bracken Co., KY, 1842), was measured in 1884 at 14 in.

Longest mustache   The mustache of Kalyan Ramji Sain of Sundargarth, India, grown since 1976, reached a span of 128¾ in (right side 65¾ in and left side 63 in) in July 1992.

United States   Paul Miller of Alta Lorna, CA had grown a mustache measuring 8 ft long by March 1993.

DENTITION

Earliest   Tooth enamel is the only part of the human body that remains basically unchanged throughout life. It is also the hardest substance in the body. The first deciduous or milk teeth normally appear in infants at 5–8 months, these being the upper and lower jaw first incisors. There are many records of children born with teeth, the most distinguished example being Prince Louis Dieudonné, later Louis XIV of France, who was born with two teeth on 5 Sep 1638. Molars usually appear at 24 months, but in a case published in Denmark in 1970, a six-week premature baby was documented with eight teeth at birth, of which four were in the molar region.

Most   Cases of the growth in late life of a third set of teeth have been recorded several times. A reference to a case in France of a *fourth* dentition, known as Lison's case, was published in 1896.

Most dedicated dentist   Brother Giovanni Battista Orsenigo of the Ospedale Fatebenefratelli, Rome, Italy, a dentist, conserved all the teeth he extracted during the time he practiced his profession from 1868 to 1904. In 1903 the number was counted and found to be 2,000,744 teeth, indicating an average of 185 teeth, or nearly six total extractions, a day.

Lifting and pulling with teeth   Walter Arfeuille of Ieper-Vlamertinge, Belgium lifted weights totaling 621 lb a distance of 6¾ in off the ground with his teeth in Paris, France, on 31 Mar 1990.

Robert Galstyan of Masis, Armenia pulled two railroad cars coupled together, weighing a total of 483,197 lb, a distance of 23 ft along a railroad track with his teeth at Shcherbinka, Greater Moscow, Russia on 21 Jul 1992.

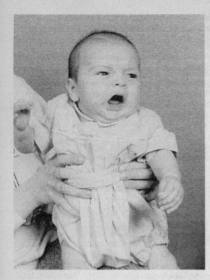

Most valuable tooth In 1816 a tooth belonging to British scientist Sir Isaac Newton (1643–1727) was sold in London, Great Britain for £730 ($3,650). It was purchased by a nobleman who had it set in a ring, which he wore constantly.

Earliest false teeth From discoveries made in Etruscan tombs, partial dentures of bridgework type were being worn in what is now the Tuscany region of Italy as early as 700 B.C. Some were permanently attached to existing teeth and others were removable.

OPTICS

Highest acuity The human eye is capable of judging relative position with remarkable accuracy, reaching limits of between 3 and 5 seconds of arc.

In April 1984 Dr Dennis M. Levi of the College of Optometry, University of Houston, TX, repeatedly identified the relative position of a thin bright green line within 0.85 sec of arc. This is equivalent to a displacement of some 1/4 in at a distance of one mile.

Color sensitivity The unaided human eye, under the best possible viewing conditions, comparing large areas of color, in good illumination, using both eyes, can distinguish 10 million different color surfaces. The most accurate photoelectric spectrophotometers possess a precision probably only 40 percent as good as this. About 7.5 percent of men and 0.1 percent of women are color-blind. The most extreme form, monochromatic vision, is very rare.

Light sensitivity Working in Chicago, IL in 1942, Maurice H. Pirenne detected a flash of blue light of 500 nm in total darkness, when as few as five quanta or photons of light were available to be absorbed by the rod photoreceptors of the retina.

BONES

Longest Excluding a variable number of sesamoids (small rounded bones), there are 206 bones in the adult human body, compared with 300 in children (as they grow, some bones fuse together). The thigh bone or femur is the longest. It constitutes usually 27.5 percent of a person's stature, and may be expected to be 19¾ in long in a 6-ft-tall man. The longest recorded bone was the 29.9-in femur of the German giant Constantine, who died in Mons, Belgium, on 30 Mar 1902, age 30. The femur of Robert Wadlow, the tallest man ever recorded, measured an estimated 29½ in. (See Tallest men.)

Smallest The stapes or stirrup bone, one of the three auditory ossicles in the middle ear, measures 0.10–0.13 in in length and weighs from 0.03–0.066 grains.

MUSCLES

Largest Muscles normally account for 40 percent of human body weight. The bulkiest of the 639 named muscles in the human body is usually the gluteus maximus or buttock muscle, which extends the thigh. However, in pregnant women the uterus or womb can increase its weight from about 1 oz to over 2.2 lb and becomes larger than even the most successful bodybuilder's buttock.

Smallest The stapedius, which controls the stapes (see above), is less than 0.05 in long.

Longest muscle name The muscle with the longest name is the *levator labii superioris alaeque nasi*, which runs inwards and downwards on the face, with one branch running to the upper lip and the other to the nostril. It is the muscle that everts or curls the upper lip, and its action was particularly well demonstrated in the performances of Elvis Presley (1935–77).

Largest chest measurements The largest are among endomorphs (those with a tendency towards a thick, chunky, well-rounded body). In the extreme case of Robert Earl Hughes (USA; 1926–58) the measurement was 124 in, and T.J. Albert Jackson, currently the heaviest living man, has a chest measurement of 120 in. (See Weight, Heaviest living.)

The largest muscular chest measurement recorded so far is 72½ in for American power-lifter Bruce Wayne Richardson (b. 23 Sep 1948) of Salt Lake City, UT, who has admitted using anabolic steroids. He is 5 ft 8 in tall and weighs 252 lb.

Longest　The longest muscle in the human body is the sartorius, which is a narrow, ribbonlike muscle running from the pelvis across the front of the thigh to the top of the tibia below the knee. Its function is to draw the lower limb into the cross-legged sitting position, proverbially associated with tailors (Latin = *sartor*).

Strongest　The strongest muscle in the human body is the masseter, of which there are two, one on each side of the mouth, which is responsible for the action of biting. In August 1986, Richard Hofmann (b. 1949) of Lake City, FL achieved a bite strength of 975 lb for approximately two seconds in a research test using a gnathodynamometer at the College of Dentistry, University of Florida. This figure is more than six times the normal biting strength.

Most active　It has been estimated that the eye muscles move 100,000 times a day or more. Many of these eye movements take place during the dreaming phase of sleep. (See Longest and shortest dreams.)

Largest and smallest biceps　Denis Sester (b. 18 Jul 1952) of Bloomington, MN has biceps 28¼ in cold (not pumped).

The biceps of Robert Thorn (Great Britain; b. 1842) measured 4¼ in when pumped up. A doctor who examined him said he had practically no muscle development, "although he could run along the road."

WAISTS

Largest　The largest waist ever recorded was that of Walter Hudson (1944–1991) of New York, which measured 119 in at his peak weight of 1,197 lb.

Smallest　The smallest waist in someone of normal stature was that of Mrs Ethel Granger (1905–82) of Peterborough, Great Britain, reduced from a natural 22 in to 13 in over the period 1929–39. A measurement of 13 in was also claimed for the French actress Mlle Polaire (real name Emile Marie Bouchand; 1881–1939).

Queen Catherine de Medici (1519–89) decreed a waist measurement of 13¾ in for ladies of the French court, but this was at a time when the human race was markedly more diminutive.

NECKS

Longest　The maximum measured extension of the neck by the successive fitting of copper coils, as practiced by the women of the Padaung or Kareni tribe of Myanmar (Burma), is 15¾ in. When the rings are removed, the muscles developed to support the head and neck shrink to their normal length.

BRAINS

Heaviest　In normal brains there is little correlation between intelligence and size.

The heaviest brain ever recorded was that of a 30-year-old male, which weighed 5 lb 1.1 oz and was reported by Dr T. Mandybur of the Department of Pathology and Laboratory Medicine at the University of Chicago, OH in December 1992.

Lightest The lightest "normal" or non-atrophied brain on record was one weighing 2 lb 6.7 oz reported by Dr P. Davis and Prof. E. Wright of King's College Hospital, London, Great Britain in 1977. It belonged to a 31-year-old woman.

Most expensive skull The skull of Emanuel Swedenborg (1688–1772), the Swedish natural philosopher and theologian, was bought in London, Great Britain by the Royal Swedish Academy of Sciences for £5,500 ($10,505) on 6 Mar 1978.

Computation Mrs Shakuntala Devi of India multiplied two 13-digit numbers (7,686,369,774,870 × 2,465,099,745,779) randomly selected by the Computer Department of Imperial College, London on 18 Jun 1980, in 28 sec. Her answer was 18,947,668,177,995,426,462,773,730 and was correct. Some experts on calculating prodigies refuse to give credence to Mrs Devi on the grounds that her achievements are so vastly superior to the calculating feats of any other judged prodigy that the judgment must have been defective.

Memory Bhandanta Vicittabi Vumsa (1911–93) recited 16,000 pages of Buddhist canonical texts in Yangon (Rangoon), Myanmar (Burma) in May 1974.

Gon Yangling, 26, has memorized more than 15,000 telephone numbers in Harbin, China according to the Xinhua News Agency. Rare instances of eidetic memory—the ability to re-project and hence "visually" recall material—are known to science.

Card memorizing Frost McKee of Georgetown, TX memorized on a single sighting a random sequence of 36 separate decks of cards (1,872 cards in all) that had been shuffled together, with only eight mistakes, at the Ramada Inn, Georgetown, TX on 17–18 Oct 1992.

Dominic O'Brien of Buntingford, Great Britain memorized a single deck of shuffled playing cards in a time of 55.62 seconds with no errors on 29 May 1992 at the *Guinness World of Records* Museum in London, Great Britain.

The greatest number of places of pi Hideaki Tomoyori (b. 30 Sep 1932) of Yokohama, Japan recited pi from memory to 40,000 places in 17 hr 21 min, including breaks totaling 4 hr 15 min, on 9–10 Mar 1987 at the Tsukuba University Club House.

VOICE

Greatest range The normal intelligible outdoor range of the male human voice in still air is 600 ft. The *silbo*, the whistled language of the Spanish-speaking Canary Island of La Gomera, is intelligible across the valleys, under ideal conditions, at five miles. There is a recorded case, under optimal acoustic conditions, of the human voice being detectable at a distance of 10½ miles across still water at night.

Screaming The highest scientifically measured emission has been one of

Sound

The intensity of noise or sound is measured in terms of pressure. The pressure of the quietest sound that can be detected by a person of normal hearing at the most sensitive frequency of c. 2,750 Hz is 2×10^{-5} Pa. One-tenth of the logarithm to this standard provides a unit termed a decibel (db). Since sound levels are measured using a logarithmic scale (to the base 10), a 10 decibel difference

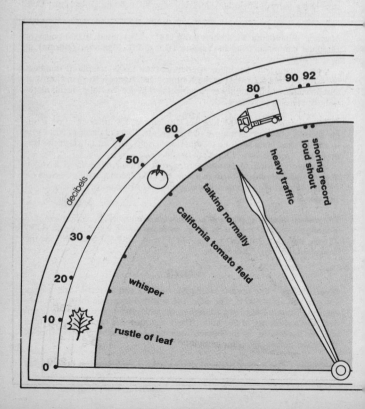

Effects

equates to one sound being 10 times louder than the other. For example, the ratio between 150 db and 10 db is 10 trillion to 1. The ear, therefore, can be seen to be a highly sensitive detector. This feature compares sources of noise from the rustle of a leaf to whales, and their effect if sustained for a prolonged period of time.

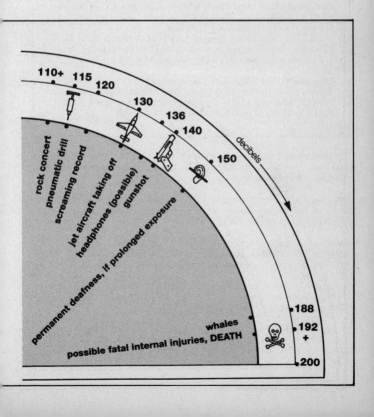

Hamlet's soliloquy   Sean Shannon, a Canadian residing in Oxford, Great Britain, recited Hamlet's soliloquy "To be or not to be" (259 words) in a time of 24 sec (equivalent to 647.5 words per min) on British Broadcasting Corporation's *Radio Oxford* on 26 Oct 1990.

Backwards talking   Steve Briers of Kilgetty, Great Britain recited the entire lyrics of Queen's album *A Night at the Opera* backwards at British Broadcasting Corporation North-West Radio 4's *Cat's Whiskers* on 6 Feb 1990 in a time of 9 min 58.44 sec.
    The American record is held by David Fuhrer of California, who recited the entire lyrics of Queen's album *A Night at the Opera* backwards at Trax Recording Studio, CA on 28 Jul 1989 in a time of 10 min 19 sec.

Fire-breather   Reg Morris blew a flame from his mouth to a distance of 31 ft at the Miner's Rest, Chasetown, Great Britain on 29 Oct 1986.

Fire extinguishers   Inge Widar Svingen, alias "Benifax" of Norway, on 10 Aug 1990 extinguished 25,270 torches of flame in his mouth in 2 hrs at Kolvereid in Nord-Trøndelag, Norway.
    On 26 Jul 1986 at Port Lonsdale, Victoria, Australia, Sipra Ellen Lloyd set a female record by extinguishing 8,357 torches.
    Fire-eating is potentially a highly dangerous activity.

Lung power   The inflation of a standardized 35 oz meteorological balloon to a diameter of 8 ft against time was achieved by Nicholas Berkeley Mason in 45 min 7 sec for the television program *Tarm Pai Du* in Thailand on 6 Nov 1992.

128 decibels at 8 ft 2 in produced by the screaming of Simon Robinson of McLaren Vale, South Australia at The Guinness Challenge at Adelaide, Australia on 11 Nov 1988.

Whistling   Roy Lomas achieved 122.5 decibels at 8 ft 2 in in the Dead-room at the British Broadcasting Corporation studios in Manchester, Great Britain on 19 Dec 1983.

Shouting   Annalisa Wray (b. 21 Apr 1974) of Comber, Northern Ireland, achieved 119.4 decibels in shouting at the 7th International Rally Arura held in Coleraine Academical Institution, Coleraine, Northern Ireland on 11 Aug 1992.
    Donald H. Burns of St George's, Bermuda achieved 119 decibels in shouting when he appeared on the Fuji TV film *Narvhodo the World* at Liberty State Park, NJ on 18 Jan 1989.

Yodeling   Yodeling has been defined as "repeated rapid changes from the chest-voice to falsetto and back again." The most rapid recorded yodel is 22 tones (15 falsetto) in 1 sec, by Peter Hinnen of Zürich, Switzerland on 9 Feb 1992.

Highest detectable pitch The upper limit is calculated to be 20,000 Hz (cycles per sec), although it has been alleged that children with asthma can detect sounds of 30,000 Hz. Bats emit pulses at up to 90,000 Hz. It was announced in February 1964 that experiments in the former USSR had conclusively proved that oscillations as high as 200,000 Hz can be detected if the oscillator is pressed against the skull.

Fastest talker Few people are able to speak *articulately* at a sustained speed above 300 words per minute. The fastest broadcaster is thought to have been Gerry Wilmot (b. Victoria, British Columbia, Canada, 6 Oct 1914), an ice hockey commentator of the late forties. In public life the fastest speed recorded was a burst in excess of 300 words per min in a speech made in December 1961 by President John Fitzgerald Kennedy (1917–63).

Steve Woodmore of Orpington, Great Britain spoke 595 words in a time of 56.01 sec, or 637.4 words per minute, on the ITV program *Motor Mouth* on 22 Sep 1990.

United States John Moschitta (USA) recited 545 words in 55.8 sec, or 586 words per minute, on 24 May 1988 in Los Angeles, CA.

BLOOD

Groups The preponderance of blood groups varies greatly from one locality to another. On a world basis Group O is the most common (46 percent), but in some areas, for example Norway, Group A predominates.

The most common subgroup in the United States is O+, which is found in 38.4 percent of the population. The rarest generic blood group is AB–, which occurs in only 0.7 percent of persons in the United States.

The rarest type in the world is a type of Bombay blood (subtype h-h) found so far only in a Czechoslovak nurse in 1961, and in a brother (Rh positive) and sister (Rh negative) named Jalbert in Massachusetts, reported in February 1968.

Recipient A 50-year-old hemophiliac, Warren C. Jyrich, required 2,400 donor units of blood, equivalent to 1,900 pints of blood, when undergoing open heart surgery at the Michael Reese Hospital, Chicago, IL in December 1970.

Largest vein The largest is the inferior vena cava, which returns the blood from the lower half of the body to the heart.

Largest artery The largest is the aorta, which is 1.18 in in diameter where it leaves the heart. By the time it ends at the level of the fourth lumbar vertebra it is about 0.68 in in diameter.

Most alcoholic The University of California Medical School, Los Angeles reported in December 1982 the case of a confused but conscious 24-year-old female, who was shown to have a blood alcohol level of 1.8 grains per 0.18 pt. After two days she discharged herself.

Tommy Johns of Brisbane, Queensland, Australia died in April 1988 from a brain tumor at the age of 66 years, after having been arrested nearly 3,000 times for being drunk and disorderly in a public place.

CELLS

Biggest The largest is the megakaryocyte, a blood cell, measuring 200 microns. It spends its life in the bone marrow, rarely venturing out in the main stream of the blood itself. In the marrow it produces the "stickiest" particles in the body—the platelets, which play an important role in stopping bleeding.

Smallest Some of the smallest cells are brain cells in the cerebellum that measure about 0.005 mm.

Longest The longest cells are neurons of the nervous system. Motor neurons 4.26 ft long have cell bodies (gray matter) in the lower spinal cord with axons (white matter) that carry nerve impulses from the spinal cord down to the big toe. Even longer are the cell systems that carry certain sensations (vibration and positional sense) back from the big toe to the brain. Their uninterrupted length, from the toe and up the posterior part of the spinal cord to the medulla of the brain, is about equal to the height of the body.

Fastest turnover of body cells The fastest turnover of body cells—i.e., the shortest life—is in the lining of the alimentary tract (gut), where the cells are shed every three days.

Longest life Those with the longest life are brain cells, which last for life. They may be three times as old as bone cells, which may live 25–30 years.

Longest memory The lymphocyte has the longest memory of any cell in the body. These white blood cells are part of the body's immune defense system. As successive generations of lymphocytes are produced during life, the cells never forget an enemy. So, for example, once a measles virus has introduced itself to the lymphocytes in the first years of life, these stalwarts of the immune system will still be ready to recognize and destroy the measles virus 70 years later. This is why you cannot get measles twice.

BODY TEMPERATURE

Highest Willie Jones, 52, was admitted to Grady Memorial Hospital, Atlanta, GA on 10 Jul 1980 with heatstroke on a day when the temperature reached 90° F with 44 percent humidity. His temperature was found to be 115.7° F. After 24 days he was discharged "at prior baseline status."

Lowest People may die of hypothermia with body temperatures of 95° F. The lowest authenticated body temperature is 64.4° F (rectal temperature) for a newborn baby born unexpectedly in an unheated house in Peterborough, Great Britain on 19 Apr 1992. After a delay the baby was taken to the hospital presumed dead; however, a pulse rate of around 10 beats per minute was found. The boy was then resuscitated, and over the next four hours his temperature rose to normal. The boy has made a full recovery and is perfectly healthy.

There are also three reported cases of individuals surviving body temperatures as low as 60.8° F.

ILLNESS AND DISEASE

Commonest Noncontagious The commonest noncontagious diseases are periodontal diseases such as gingivitis (inflammation of the gums). In their lifetime few people completely escape the effects of tooth decay.

Contagious The commonest contagious disease in the world is coryza (acute nasopharyngitis), or the common cold.

Rarest Medical literature periodically records hitherto undescribed diseases. A disease as yet undiagnosed but predicted by a Norwegian doctor is podocytoma of the kidney. This is a potential to develop tumors in the cells lining the part of the kidney (glomerus) that acts as a sieve or filter for the blood.

Highest mortality There are no reported recoveries from the disease AIDS (Acquired Immune Deficiency Syndrome), which was first reported in 1981. The virus that causes it, HIV, attacks the body's immune defense system, leaving the body wide open to attack from infections which in a healthy person would be fought off without any problems. Many people who are carriers of HIV may have none of the signs or symptoms of the disease AIDS, which may develop later. The World Health Organization (WHO) reported 611,589 HIV positive cases worldwide by 31 Jan 1993. WHO estimates that there are actually 2.5 million AIDS cases worldwide.

By 31 Mar 1993 the total number of HIV positive cases in the United States was 289,320. This total included 284,840 adults and 4,480 children under 13. The total number of deaths was 182,275. By the end of 1994, the United States can expect to reach 415,000 AIDS cases and 385,000 AIDS deaths.

AIDS STATISTICS

State	Cases
New York	55,154
California	53,851
Florida	28,376
Texas	20,662
New Jersey	16,171

Metropolitan Areas	Cases
New York	54,516
Los Angeles	18,900
San Francisco	15,329
Miami	8,295
Houston	8,261
Washington, D.C.	8,051
Chicago	8,023

Data: Centers for Disease Control (31 Mar 1993)

Most potent poison   The rickettsial disease Q-fever can be instituted by a *single* organism, though it is fatal in only 1 in 1,000 cases. About 10 organisms of *Francisella tularenesis* (formerly *Pasteurella tularenesis*) can initiate tularemia, variously called alkali disease, Francis disease or deerfly fever. This disease is fatal in upwards of 10 cases in 1,000.

Cardiopulmonary resuscitation   Brent Shelton and John Ash completed a CPR marathon (cardiopulmonary resuscitation—15 compressions alternating with two breaths) of 130 hr from 28 Oct–2 Nov 1991 at Regina, Saskatchewan, Canada.

In the United States, three teams of two, consisting of David Bailey and Les Williams, Angie Drinkard and Rich Martel, and Michelle Tyler and Sherri Johnson, all completed CPR marathons of 120 hr 6 min from 1–6 Sep 1988 at Melbourne, FL.

Most infectious and most often fatal   The pneumonic form of plague, as evidenced by the Black Death of 1347–51, killed everyone who caught it. A quarter of the population of Europe and some 75 million worldwide perished during the outbreak.

Leading cause of death   In industrialized countries, arteriosclerosis (thickening of the arterial wall) underlies much coronary and cerebrovascular disease.

In 1990, the top five causes of death in the United States were: heart disease, 725,010; cancer, 506,000; strokes, 145,340; accidents, including automobile, 93,550; and lung disease and related conditions, 88,980.

MEDICAL EXTREMES

Cardiac arrest   The longest is four hours in the case of a Norwegian fisherman, Jan Egil Refsdahl (b. 1936), who fell overboard in the icy waters off Bergen on 7 Dec 1987. He was rushed to nearby Haukeland Hospital after his body temperature fell to 77° F and his heart stopped beating, but he made a full recovery after he was connected to a heart–lung machine normally used for heart surgery.

United States   On 9 Oct 1986, Allen Smith, age 2, fell into the swollen waters of the Stanislaus River in Oakdale, CA. He was spotted 90 minutes later and rushed to Modesto Memorial Hospital, where two hours later his heart began beating again spontaneously.

Longest coma   Elaine Esposito (1934–78) of Tarpon Springs, FL, never stirred after an appendectomy on 6 Aug 1941, when she was 6 years old. She died on 25 Nov 1978 at the age of 43 years 357 days, having been in a coma for 37 years 111 days.

Longest and shortest dreams   Dreaming sleep is characterized by rapid eye movements known as REM, first described in 1953 by William Dement of the University of Chicago. The longest recorded period of REM is one of

2 hr 23 min on 15 Feb 1967 at the Department of Psychology, University of Illinois, Chicago by Bill Carskadon, who had had his previous sleep interrupted. In July 1984 the Sleep Research Center, Haifa, Israel recorded no REM in a 33-year-old male who had a shrapnel brain injury. (See Muscles, Most active.)

g forces   Racing driver David Purley (1945–85) survived a deceleration from 108 mph to zero in 26 in in a crash at Silverstone, Great Britain on 13 Jul 1977 that involved a force of 179.8 *g*. He suffered 29 fractures, three dislocations and six heart stoppages.

The highest *g* value voluntarily endured is 82.6 *g* for 0.04 sec by Eli L. Beeding, Jr. on a water-braked rocket sled at Holloman Air Force Base, NM on 16 May 1958. He was subsequently hospitalized for three days.

Heat endurance   The highest dry-air temperature endured by naked men in US Air Force experiments in 1960 was 400° F, and by heavily clothed men 500° F. (Steaks require only 325° F to cook.) Temperatures of 284° F have been found quite bearable in saunas.

Hiccupping   The longest recorded attack of hiccupping was that which afflicted Charles Osborne (1894–1991) of Anthon, IA, who had hiccupped continuously for 69 years 5 months, since 1922. He began hiccupping when he was slaughtering a hog and was unable to find a cure, but led a reasonably normal life in which he had two wives and fathered eight children. He hiccupped every 1½ seconds until a morning in February 1990. He died on 1 May 1991.

Hospital stay   The longest stay in a hospital was by Miss Martha Nelson, who was admitted to the Columbus State Institute for the Feeble-Minded in Ohio in 1875. She died in January 1975 at the age of 103 years 6 months in the Orient State Institution, OH after spending more than 99 years in hospitals.

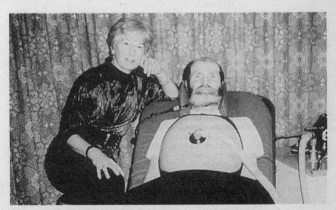

John Prestwich, the longest to survive in an "iron lung."

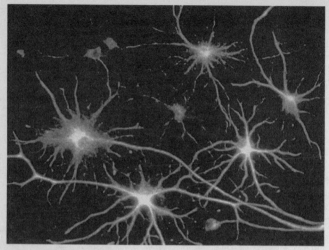

FASTEST NERVE IMPULSES Impulses within the human nervous system can be conducted at up to 223 mph. These impulses are carried on fibers known as processes which trail out in all directions from the nerve cell body, which contains the nucleus. The processes are of varying size, and it is the larger ones, which are insulated by a fatty substance known as myelin, that conduct at such high speeds. (Photo: Science Photo Library)

Opposite

The skin is medically considered to be an organ and it weighs around 5.9 lb in an average adult. It covers the body completely, acting as the first barrier against invading organisms. It also has sensory and excretory functions and plays an important part in regulating body temperature. Shown here (top) is a cross-section through the skin. The outer layer is the epidermis, which can roughly be divided into two parts: an outer protective layer of flattened, dead cells impregnated with keratin, and a lower layer of living dividing cells. Below this are the dermis and a subcutaneous layer of fat. Within the dermis are blood capillaries, sensory nerve endings, hair follicles (with associated sebaceous galnds and erector muscles), lymph vessels and sweat glands.

The photo (bottom) shows the distinctive, but unique, patterns of skin ridges on a finger (i.e., a fingerprint). The tiny depressions that can be seen on these ridges are sweat pores. (Photo: Science Photo Library)

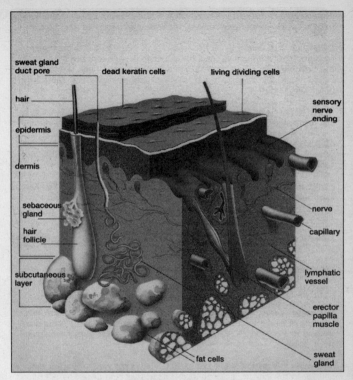

sweat gland duct pore
dead keratin cells
living dividing cells
hair
sensory nerve ending
epidermis
dermis
nerve
sebaceous gland
capillary
hair follicle
lymphatic vessel
subcutaneous layer
erector papilla muscle
sweat gland
fat cells

Illustration: Pat Gibbon

Most injections Samuel L. Davidson (b. 30 Jul 1912) of Glasgow, Scotland has had, at a conservative estimate, 76,500 insulin injections since 1923.

Longest in "iron lung" John Prestwich (b. 24 Nov 1938) of King Langley, Great Britain, has been dependent on a negative pressure respirator since his 17th birthday (24 Nov 1955) when he contracted polio. He has calculated that the respirator has mechanically operated his chest over 315,500,000 times.

United States Mrs. Laurel Nisbet (1912–85) of La Crescenta, CA was in an "iron lung" for 37 years 58 days continuously until her death.

Motionlessness António Gomes dos Santos of Zare, Portugal stood motionless for 15 hr 2 min 55 sec on 30 Jul 1988 at the Amoreiras Shopping Center, Lisbon.

Fastest nerve impulses The results of experiments published in 1966 have shown that messages transmitted by the human nervous system can travel at 223 mph. With advancing age, impulses are carried 15 percent more slowly.

Heaviest organ The heaviest internal organ is the liver at 3.3 lb. This is four times heavier than the heart.

Pill-taking The highest recorded total of pills swallowed by a patient is 565,939 between 9 Jun 1967 and 19 Jun 1988 by C.H.A. Kilner (1926–88) of Bindura, Zimbabwe.

Postmortem birth The longest gestation interval in a postmortem birth was one of 84 days in the case of a girl born on 5 Jul 1983 to a brain-dead woman in Roanoke, VA who had been kept on a life support machine since April.

Pulse rates A normal adult rate is 70–78 beats per min at rest for males and 75–85 for females. (The abnormal heart may beat as fast as 300 times per min, or the beat may be so slow as to be virtually undetectable.) The heart rate may increase to 200 or more during rigorous exercise.

Sleeplessness Victims of the very rare condition known as chronic colestites (total insomnia) have been known to go without definable sleep for many years.

Sneezing The longest-lasting sneezing fit ever recorded is that of Donna Griffiths (b. 1969) of Pershore, Great Britain. She started sneezing on 13 Jan 1981 and surpassed the previous duration record of 194 days on 27 Jul 1981. She sneezed an estimated one million times in the first 365 days. She achieved her first sneeze-free day on 16 Sep 1983—the 978th day.

The fastest speed at which particles expelled by sneezing have ever been measured to travel is 103.6 mph.

Snoring Melvyn Switzer of Dibden, Great Britain recorded peak levels of 91–92 dBA while sleeping at the South View Hotel, Lyndhurst, Great Britain on the evening of 29 Oct 1992. The microphone was placed 2 ft above his head.

Eating   Michel Lotito (b. 15 Jun 1950) of Grenoble, France, known as Monsieur Mangetout, has been eating metal and glass since 1959. Gastroenterologists have X-rayed his stomach and described his ability to consume 2 lb of metal per day as unique. His diet since 1966 has included 10 bicycles, a supermarket cart (in 4^1/$_2$ days), seven TV sets, six chandeliers, a low-calorie Cessna light aircraft and a computer. He is said to have provided the only example in history of a coffin (handles and all) ending up inside a man.

Underwater submergence   In 1986 two-year-old Michelle Funk of Salt Lake City, UT, made a full recovery after spending 66 minutes under water. The toddler fell into a swollen creek near her home while playing. When she was eventually discovered, rescue workers found she had no pulse or heartbeat. Her life was saved by the first successful bypass machine; it warmed her blood, which had dropped to 66° F. Doctors at the hospital described the time she had spent underwater as the "longest documented submergence with an intact neurological outcome."

Longest without food and water   The longest recorded case of survival without food *and* water is 18 days by Andreas Mihavecz, then 18, of Bregenz, Austria, who was put in a holding cell on 1 Apr 1979 in a local government building in Höscht, and then was totally forgotten by the police. On 18 Apr 1979 he was discovered close to death, having had neither food nor water. He had been a passenger in a car that crashed.

Swallowing   The worst reported case of compulsive swallowing of objects involved an insane female, Mrs H., who at the age of 42 complained of a "slight abdominal pain." She proved to have 2,533 objects, including 947 bent pins, in her stomach. These were removed by Drs Chalk and Foucar in June 1927 at the Ontario Hospital, Canada.

In a more recent case, 212 objects were removed from the stomach of a man admitted to Groote Schuur Hospital, Cape Town, South Africa in May 1985. They included 53 toothbrushes, two telescopic aerials, two razors and 150 handles of disposable razors.

A compulsive swallower in the United States, a 24-year-old psychoneurotic woman, gulped down a 5-in-long iron hinge bolt from a hospital door, which amazingly passed through the curve of the duodenum and the intestinal tract and broke the bedpan when the patient successfully passed the object.

The heaviest object extracted from a human stomach has been a 5 lb 3 oz ball of hair from a 20-year-old female compulsive swallower at the South Devon and East Cornwall Hospital, Great Britain, on 30 Mar 1895.

Most tattoos   The ultimate in being tattooed is represented by Tom Leppard of the Isle of Skye, Scotland. He has chosen a leopard-skin design, with all the skin between the dark spots tattooed saffron yellow. The area of his body covered is approximately 99.2 percent of totality.

Bernard Moeller of Pennsylvania has the most separate designs, with 14,000 individual tattoos up to January 1993.

The world's most decorated woman is strip artiste "Krystyne Kolorful" (b. 5 Dec 1952, Alberta, Canada). Her 95 percent bodysuit took 10 years to complete.

OPERATIONS

Longest   The most protracted reported operation was one of 96 hr performed from 4–8 Feb 1951 in Chicago, IL on Mrs Gertrude Levandowski for the removal of an ovarian cyst. During the operation her weight fell from 616 lb to 308 lb. The patient suffered from a weak heart and surgeons had to exercise the utmost caution during the operation.

Most performed   Dr M.C. Modi, a pioneer of mass eye surgery in India since 1943, has performed as many as 833 cataract operations in one day, visited 46,120 villages and 12,118,630 patients, performing a total of 610,564 operations to February 1993.

Dr Robert B. McClure (b. 1901) of Toronto, Ontario, Canada performed a career total of 20,423 major operations from 1924 to 1978.

Oldest patient   The greatest recorded age at which anyone has undergone an operation is 111 years 105 days in the case of James Henry Brett, Jr. (1849–1961) of Houston, TX. He had a hip operation on 7 Nov 1960.

Munchausen's syndrome   The most extreme recorded case of the rare and incurable condition known as Munchausen's syndrome (a continual desire to have medical treatment) was William McIloy (b. 1906), who cost Britain's National Health Service an estimated £2.5 million ($4 million) during his 50-year career as a hospital patient. During that time he had 400 major and minor operations, and stayed at 100 different hospitals using 22 aliases. The longest period he was ever out of the hospital was six months. In 1979 he hung up his bedpan for the last time, saying he was sick of hospitals, and retired to an old people's home in Birmingham, Great Britain, where he died in 1983.

Earliest general anesthesia   The earliest recorded operation under general anesthesia was for the removal of a cyst from the neck of James Venable by Dr Crawford Williamson Long (1815–78), using diethyl ether $(C_2H_5)_2O$, in Jefferson, GA on 30 Mar 1842.

Hemodialysis patient   Raymond Jones (1929–91) of Slough, Great Britain suffered from kidney failure from the age of 34, and received continuous hemodialysis for 28 years. He averaged three visits per week to the Royal Free Hospital, London, Great Britain.

Largest gallbladder   On 15 Mar 1989 at the National Naval Medical Center in Bethesda, MD, Prof. Bimal C. Ghosh removed a gallbladder that weighed 23 lb from a 69-year-old woman. The patient had been complaining of increasing swelling around the abdomen, and after removal of this enlarged gallbladder, which weighed more than three times as much as the average newborn baby, the patient felt perfectly well and left the hospital 10 days after the operation.

Fastest amputation The shortest time recorded for a leg amputation in the pre-anesthetic era was 13–15 seconds by Napoleon's chief surgeon, Dominique Larrey. There could have been no ligation of blood vessels.

Stretcher bearing The record for carrying a stretcher case with a 140-lb "body" is 158.2 miles in 46 hr 35 min from 27–29 May 1992. This was achieved by two four-man teams from the 85th Medical Batallion, Ft Meade, MD.

Most operations endured Since 22 Jul 1954 Charles Jensen of Chester, SD has had 925 operations (to February 1993) to remove the tumors associated with basal cell nevus syndrome. This is a rare genetically determined disorder characterized by multiple skin lesions which are usually first noticed in childhood and increase in size and number in late adolescence.

Gallstones The largest gallstone reported in medical literature was one of 13 lb 14 oz removed from an 80-year-old woman by Dr Humphrey Arthure at Charing Cross Hospital, London, Great Britain on 29 Dec 1952.

In August 1987 it was reported that 23,530 gallstones had been removed from an 85-year-old woman by Mr K. Whittle Martin at Worthing Hospital, Sussex, Great Britain, after she complained of severe abdominal pain.

Largest tumor The largest tumor ever reported was an ovarian cyst weighing an estimated 328 lb, removed from a woman in Texas in 1905 by Dr Arthur Spohn. The patient made a full recovery.

A better documented and more recently recorded tumor was a multicystic mass of the ovary weighing 303 lbs. This is as much as or more than the weight of the average defensive football player. The growth was removed intact in October 1991 from the abdomen of a 35-year-old woman by Prof. Katherine O'Hanlen of Stanford University Medical Center, CA.

The operation took over 6 hours and the patient, now weighing only 210 lb, left the operating theater on one stretcher while the cyst left on another. The patient made a full recovery.

Surgical instruments Largest The largest instruments are robot retractors used in abdominal surgery, introduced by Abbey Surgical Instruments of Chingford, Great Britain in 1968 and weighing 11 lb. Some bronchoscopic forceps measure 23$^{1}/_{2}$ in in length.

Smallest The smallest instrument is the Microcystotome, a microknife for cutting the lens in eye microsurgery. The working part is 0.004 in long and 0.0003 in wide. It contains the smallest blade—a natural diamond with a cutting edge of 200 Å. Both this and the robot retractor described above are licensed by the Microsurgery Research and Technology Complex, Moscow, Russia and patented by Svyatoslav Fyodorov, director of the Institute of Microsurgery.

> *Youngest heart transplant* Paul Holt of Vancouver, British Columbia, Canada underwent a heart transplant at Loma Linda Hospital in California on 16 Oct 1987 at the age of 2 hr 34 min. He was born six weeks premature weighing 6 lb 6 oz.

TRANSPLANTS

Heart The first heart transplant operation was performed on Louis Washkansky, age 55, at the Groote Schuur Hospital, Cape Town, South Africa between 1 A.M. and 6 A.M., on 3 Dec 1967, by a team of 30 headed by Prof. Christiaan Neethling Barnard. The donor was Miss Denise Ann Darvall, age 25. Washkansky lived for 18 days.

United States The first operation was performed on a 2½-week-old baby boy at Maimonides Hospital, Brooklyn, NY on 6 Dec 1967 by a team of 22 headed by Dr Adrian Kantrowitz. The donor was a newborn infant. The baby boy lived 6½ hours. The first adult transplant took place at the Stanford Medical Center in Palo Alto, CA on 6 Jan 1968 by Dr Norman E. Shumway and was performed on 54-year-old Mike Kasperak. Mr Kasperak, a retired steelworker, lived 14 days. From December 1967 until 31 Mar 1993 there have been 14,085 heart transplants. The greatest number of transplants in the United States in one year is 2,080, in 1990.

Longest surviving William George van Buuren of California (1929–91) received an unnamed person's heart at the Stanford Medical Center, Palo Alto, CA on 3 Jan 1970, and survived for 21 years 10 months 24 days. The surgeon who performed the operation was Dr Edward Stinson.

Currently living Arthur F. Gay (b. 3 Oct 1936) is the longest-surviving heart transplant patient currently alive. His operation was performed at the Medical College of Virginia on 11 Jan 1973 by Dr Richard Lower.

Double heart The first double heart transplant operation in the United States was performed on Darrell Hammarley, age 56, at the Stanford Medical Center in Palo Alto, CA on 20 Nov 1968 by Dr Norman E. Shumway. The first heart implanted failed to beat steadily and was replaced by a second transplant two hours later.

Animal-to-human The first operation in the United States was carried out on 23 Jan 1964 at the University of Mississippi Medical Center in Jackson, MS by a team of 12 headed by Dr James D. Hardy. The patient, age 64, received the heart of a chimpanzee, which beat for 90 minutes.

Heart–lung–liver The first triple transplant took place on 17 Dec 1986 at Papworth Hospital, Cambridge, Great Britain when Mrs Davina Thompson (b. 28 Feb 1951) of Rawmarsh, Great Britain underwent surgery for seven hours by a team of 15 headed by chest surgeon Dr John Wallwork and Prof. Sir Roy Calne.

Artificial heart On 1–2 Dec 1982 at the Utah Medical Center, Salt Lake City, UT, Dr Barney B. Clark, 61, of Des Moines, WA was the first recipient of an artificial heart. The surgeon was Dr William C. DeVries. The heart was a Jarvik-7 designed by Dr Robert K. Jarvik. Dr Clark died on 23 Mar 1983, 112 days later. William J. Schroeder survived 620 days with an artificial heart in Louisville, KY from 25 Nov 1984 to 7 Aug 1986. The Food and Drug Administration (FDA) recalled the Jarvik-7 on 11 Jan 1990. At the time of the recall it was the only artificial heart approved by the FDA and thus the only one allowed in the United States.

First synthetic heart implant   Haskell Karp, age 47, of Skokie, IL, received the first synthetic heart implant on 4 Apr 1969, at St Luke's Episcopal Hospital, Houston, TX. Dr Denton A. Cooley led the team of doctors, which included the developer of the heart, Dr Domingo Liotta. The artificial heart was replaced by a human transplant on 7 April.

Five-organ   Tabatha Foster (1984–1988) of Madisonville, KY, at 3 years 143 days of age, received a transplanted liver, pancreas, small intestine, portions of stomach and large intestine in a 15-hour operation at the Children's Hospital, Pittsburgh, PA on 31 Oct 1987. Before the operation, she had never eaten solid food.

Kidney   Dr Richard H. Lawler (USA; b. 1895) performed the first transplant of a kidney in a human at Little Company of Mary Hospital, Chicago, IL, on 17 Jun 1950.

The first successful kidney transplant operation was performed at Peter Bent Brigham Hospital (now Brigham and Women's Hospital) in Boston, MA on 23 Dec 1954 by a team of surgeons headed by Dr John P. Merrill. The patient, Richard Herrick, age 23, received a kidney from his identical twin, Ronald.

From 1977, when figures were first gathered, until 1992, there have been a total of 126,092 kidney transplants in the United States.

Longest surviving   The longest surviving kidney transplant patient is Johanna Leanora Rempel (nee Nightingale; b 24 Mar 1948) of Red Deer, Alberta, Canada who was given a kidney from her identical twin sister Lana Blatz on 28 Dec 1960. The operation was performed at the Peter Bent Brigham Hospital, Boston, MA. Both Johanna and her sister have continued to enjoy excellent health and both have borne healthy children. (See First transplantee to give birth.)

Lung   The first lung transplant operation in the United States took place on 11 Jun 1963 at the University of Mississippi Medical Center in Jackson, MS. The surgery, which was headed by Dr James D. Hardy, lasted three hours and involved the replacement of the patient's left lung. The patient, John Richard Russell, survived 18 days.

First transplantee to give birth   Johanna Rempel gave birth to a baby boy, Kerry Melvin Ross (7 lb 12 oz), at Winnipeg General Hospital, Manitoba, Canada on 7 Sep 1967. She had received a donor kidney in December 1960. (See Transplants, Kidney.)

United States   Betsy Sneith, 23, gave birth to a girl, Sierra (7 lb 10 oz), at the Stanford Medical Center, Palo Alto, CA on 17 Sep 1984. She had received a donor heart in Feb 1980.

SCIENCE AND TECHNOLOGY

- **ELEMENTS**
- **CHEMICAL EXTREMES**
- **PHYSICAL EXTREMES**
- **MATHEMATICS**
- **COMPUTING**
- **POWER**
- **ENGINEERING**
- **BORINGS AND MINES**
- **TIMEPIECES**
- **TELECOMMUNICATIONS**
- **TELESCOPES**
- **ROCKETRY**
- **SPACE FLIGHT**

ELEMENTS

Although ordinary matter can be described in terms of 94 naturally occurring elements, the dynamics of galaxies suggest that over 90 percent of all mass in the Universe is in an unknown form called "cold dark matter." This is thought to be an exotic form of matter unknown on Earth, but it is possible that it is ordinary matter which is too dim to be detected by present instruments. About 99 percent of all visible matter exists as ionized plasma in which negatively charged electrons and positively charged ions are in flux. Hydrogen (H) is the most common element, accounting for over 90 percent of all known matter in the Universe and 70.68 percent by mass in the Solar System.

SUBNUCLEAR PARTICLES

Quarks are a set of at least six (up, down, charmed, strange, top and bottom) elementary particles and their corresponding antiparticles postulated to be the basic constituents of all baryons and mesons. Evidence for all except the top quark is now available. The lightest is the up quark, with a short-range (current) mass of 6 MeV (eV—electron volt) and a long-range mass of 350 MeV, and the heaviest is the as-yet unobserved top quark, with a predicted mass of 140 GeV.

It is currently thought that there are only three "families" of quarks and leptons. The theoretical masses of the graviton (the as-yet unobserved gravitational gauge boson), the photon, and the three neutrino leptons should all be zero. Current experimental limits are less than 7.6×10^{-67} g for the graviton, less than 5.3×10^{-60} g for the photon, and less than 10 eV (less than 1.8×10^{-32} g) for the electron neutrino.

As of April 1990, physicists accepted the existence of three gauge bosons, six leptons and 136 hadron multiplets (77 meson multiplets and 59

Pharmaceutical company   The world's largest pharmaceutical company is Johnson & Johnson of New Brunswick, NJ. The company employed a workforce of 84,900, generating sales of $13.753 billion in 1992. Total assets for the year were $11.88 billion.

Longest index   The 11th collective index of *Chemical Abstracts*, completed in December 1987, contains 29,406,094 entries in 162,992 pages and 93 volumes and weighs 407 lb. It provides references to 2,812,413 published documents in the field of chemistry.

Chemicals   The largest manufacturer of chemicals in the United States is E. I. Du Pont de Nemours & Co. Inc. of Wilmington, DE. As of 31 December 1992, DuPont had sales of $37.8 billion.

baryon multiplets), representing the eventual discovery of 256 particles and an equal number of antiparticles.

Heaviest   The heaviest particle accepted is the neutral weak gauge boson, the $Z°$, of mass 91.17 GeV and lifetime 2.65×10^{-25} sec, which was discovered in May 1983 at CERN, Geneva, Switzerland.

Most stable   The "Grand Unified Theory" of the weak, electromagnetic, and strong forces predicts that the proton will not be stable, but experiments indicate that the lifetime of the most likely decay mode (to a positron and a neutral pion) has a lower limit of 3.1×10^{32} years, which is over 40 times longer than the maximum lifetime predicted by the theory.

Least stable   The shortest-lived sub-atomic particle is the boson $Z°$ particle, with a lifetime of 2.65×10^{-25} sec. (See Heaviest particle.)

ISOTOPES

Most   The highest number is 36, shared by the gas xenon (Xe), with nine stable and 27 radioactive isotopes, and cesium (Cs; one stable and 35 radioactive).

The greatest number of stable isotopes is 10, for the metallic element tin (Sn).

Least   Hydrogen (H) has only three confirmed isotopes, including two stable (protium and deuterium) and one radioactive (tritium). Twenty elements exist naturally only as single nuclides.

Most stable   The most stable radioactive isotope is the double-beta decaying tellurium 128 (Te-128), with a half-life of 1.5×10^{24} years, a property confirmed in 1968, 44 years after its identification.

The alpha-decay record is 8×10^{15} years for samarium 148 (Sm-148) and the beta-decay record is 9×10^{15} years for cadmium 113 (Cd-113).

Least stable   Lithium 5 (Li-5) has a lifetime of 4.4×10^{-22} sec, determined in 1950.

THE 109 ELEMENTS

There are 94 confirmed naturally occurring elements, while to date 15 transuranium elements (numbers 95 to 109) have been produced artificially. At room temperature they comprise 2 liquids, 11 gases and 96 solids (assuming that elements 101 to 109 would prove to be solid if obtained as more than a few atoms at a time). On this basis 88 elements are considered metallic.

Most common   The commonest element in the Earth's atmosphere is nitrogen (N), which is present at 78.08 percent by volume (75.52 percent by mass).

Rarest (natural)   The least abundant element in the Earth's atmosphere is the radioactive gas radon (Rn), with a volume of 6×10^{-18} parts by volume. This is only 5.3 lb overall, but concentrated amounts of this radioactive gas in certain granite areas have been blamed for a number of cancer deaths.

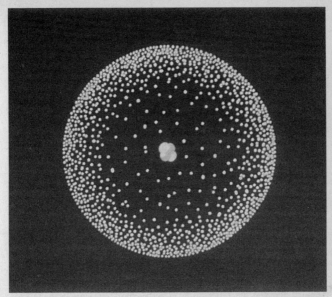

LOWEST BOILING POINT Computer image of an atom of helium (He) showing its nucleus of two protons and two neutrons surrounded by an electron cloud. Helium boils at –452.070° F, and, in addition to filling balloons, it is used for arc welding, as a coolant in nuclear reactors, for pressurizing liquid-fueled rockets and in gas lasers. (Photo: Science Photo Library/ Ken Eward)

Most dense Solid The densest solid at room temperature is osmium (Os) at 0.8161 lb/in³.

Gas The heaviest gas is radon (Rn) at 0.6274 lb/ft³.

Least dense Solid The least dense element at room temperature is the metal lithium (Li) at 0.01927 lb/in³, although the density of solid hydrogen at its melting point of –434.546° F is only 0.00315 lb/in³.

Gas The lightest gas at NTP (Normal Temperature and Pressure, 0° C and one atmosphere) is hydrogen (H) at 0.005612 lb/ft³.

Highest melting point The metallic element tungsten (or Wolfram) (W) melts at 6,188° F. On the assumption that graphite transforms to carbyne forms above 4,172° F, the nonmetal with the highest melting and boiling points would be carbon (C) at 6,386° F and 6,998° F respectively. However, this is disputed; an alternative suggestion is that graphite remains stable at high temperatures, sublimes directly to vapor at 6,728° F and can only be obtained in a liquid form above 8,546° F at a pressure of 100 atmospheres.

Lowest melting point Mercury (Hg) has the lowest melting (and boiling) point of the metals, at –37.892° F. Helium (He) cannot be obtained as a solid at atmospheric pressure. The minimum pressure necessary is 24.985 atm (2.532 MPa), for solidification at a temperature of –458.275° F.

Highest boiling point In addition to the highest melting point, tungsten has the highest boiling point at 10,580 ° F.

Lowest boiling point The lowest boiling point is –452.070° F for helium. The lowest for a metal is 673.92° F for mercury.

Purest In April 1978 P.V.E. McClintock of the University of Lancaster, Great Britain, reported success in obtaining the isotope helium 4 (He-4) with impurity levels at less than two parts in 10^{15}.

Hardest The carbon (C) allotrope diamond has a Knoop value of 8,400.

Thermal expansion The metal with the highest expansion is cesium (Cs), at 94×10^{-5} per deg C, while the diamond allotrope of carbon (C) has the lowest expansion at 10×10^{-6} per deg C.

Most ductile 1 oz of gold (Au) can be drawn to a length of 43 miles.

Highest tensile strength The element with the highest tensile strength is boron (B) at 5.7 GPa 8.3×10^5 lb/in^2.

Newest Element 108, provisionally named unniloctium (Uno) by the IUPAC (the International Union of Pure and Applied Chemistry), but with the name hassium (Hs) proposed, was announced in April 1984 based on the observation of only three atoms at the Gesellschaft für Schwerionenforschung (GSI), Darmstadt, Germany.

Liquid range Based on the differences between melting and boiling points, the element with the shortest liquid range (on the Celsius scale) is the inert gas neon (Ne) at only 2.542 degrees (from –248.594 to –246.052° C [–415.469° F to –410.894° F]). The radioactive transuranic element neptunium (Np) has the longest liquid range, at 3,453 degrees (from 637 to 4,090° C [1,179° F to 7,394° F]).

However, based on the true range of liquids from their melting points to their critical points, the shortest range is for helium (He) at 5.195 degrees C from absolute zero (i.e., –273.15° C to –267.955° C), and the largest range is for tungsten (W) at 10,200 degrees C (from 3,420 to 13,620° C [from 6,188° F to 24,548° F]).

Toxicity The most stringent restriction placed on a nonradioactive element is for beryllium (Be), with a threshold limit value in air of only 2 µg/m^3.

For radioactive isotopes occurring naturally or produced in nuclear installations having half-lives over six months, the severest restriction in air is placed on thorium 228 (Th-228) or radiothorium, at 2.4×10^{-16} grams/m^3 (equivalent radiation intensity 0.0074 becquerel/m^3).

The severest restriction in water is placed on radium 228 (Ra-228) or mesothorium I, at 1.1×10^{-13} grams/liter (equivalent radiation intensity 1.1 becquerel/liter).

CHEMICAL EXTREMES

Smelliest substance The most evil of the 17,000 smells so far classified may be a matter of opinion, but ethyl mercaptan (C_2H_5SH) and butyl seleno-mercaptan (C_4H_9SeH) are pungent claimants, each with a smell reminiscent of a combination of rotting cabbage, garlic, onions, burned toast and sewer gas.

Most powerful nerve gas Ethyl S-2-diisopropylaminoethylmethylphosphonoth-iolate or VX, developed at the Chemical Defense Experimental Establish-ment, Porton Down, Great Britain in 1952, is 300 times more powerful than the phosgene ($COCl_2$) used in World War I. The lethal dosage is 10 mg-minute/m^3 airborne or 0.3 mg orally.

Most lethal man-made chemical TCDD (2, 3, 7, 8-tetrachlorodibenzo-p-dioxin), the most deadly of the 75 known dioxins, is admitted to be 150,000 times more deadly than cyanide, at 3.1×10^{-9} moles/kg.

Strongest acid and alkaline solutions Normal solutions of strong acids such as perchloric acid ($HCLO_4$) and strong alkalis such as sodium hydroxide (NaOH), potassium hydroxide (KOH) and tetramethylammonium hydroxide ($N[CH_3]_4OH$) tend towards pH values of 0 and 14 respectively. However, this scale is inadequate for describing the "superacids," the strongest of which is estimated to be an 80 percent solution of antimony pentafluoride in hydroflu-oric acid (fluoroantimonic acid HF: SbF_5). The acidity function, H_o, of this so-lution has not been measured, but even a 50 percent solution has an acidity function of −30, so that this acid mixture is a quintillion (10^{18}) times stronger than concentrated sulfuric acid.

Bitterest substance The bitterest-tasting substances are based on the denato-nium cation N-(2-[2, 6-dimethyl phenyl amino]-2-oxoethyl)-N, N-diethyl-benzemethanaminium and have been produced commercially as benzoate and saccharide. Taste detection levels are as low as one part in 500 million, and a dilution of one part in 100 million will leave a lingering taste.

Sweetest substance Talin from arils (appendages found on certain seeds) of katemfe (*Thaumatococcus daniellii*), discovered in West Africa, is 6,150 times as sweet as a one percent sucrose solution.

Most absorbent substance The US Department of Agriculture Research Ser-vice announced on 18 Aug 1974 that "H-span" or Super slurper, composed of one-half starch derivative and one-fourth each of acrylamide and acrylic acid, can, when treated with iron, retain water 1,300 times its own weight.

Finest powder The ultimate is solid helium, which was first postulated to be a monatomic powder as early as 1964.

Most refractory substance The most refractory substance is tantalum carbide ($TaC_{0.88}$), which melts at 7,214° F.

Least dense solids These are the silica aerogels in which tiny spheres of bonded silicon and oxygen atoms are joined into long strands separated by pockets of air. In February 1990 the lightest of these aerogels, with a density of only 5 oz/ft3, was produced at Lawrence Livermore Laboratory, CA. The main use will be in space to collect micrometeoroids and the debris present in comets' tails.

Highest superconducting temperature In May 1991, bulk superconductivity with a transition to zero resistance at –231.3° F was obtained at the Superconducting Research Laboratory, International Superconducting Technology Center, Tokyo, Japan for a mixed oxide of thallium, barium, calcium and copper ($Tl_{1.7}Ba_2Ca_{2.3}Cu_3Ox$).

Most magnetic substance The most magnetic substance is neodymium iron boride ($Nd_2Fe_{14}B$) with a maximum energy product (the highest energy that a magnet can supply when operating at a particular operating point) of up to 280 kJ/m^3.

PHYSICAL EXTREMES

Highest temperature Temperatures produced in the center of a thermonuclear fusion bomb are of the order of 400,000,000° C. This temperature was attained in 1990 under controlled experimental conditions in the Tokamak Fusion Test Reactor at the Princeton Plasma Physics Laboratory, Princeton, NJ, by deuterium injection into a deuterium plasma.

Lowest temperature The absolute zero of temperature, 0 K on the Kelvin scale, corresponds to –459.67° F. The lowest temperature ever reached is 2 x 10^{-11} Kelvin, i.e., two billionths of a degree above absolute zero. This was achieved at the Low Temperature Laboratory, Helsinki University of Technology, Finland in a nuclear demagnetization device and announced in April 1993.

Highest pressures A sustained laboratory pressure of 1.70 megabars (11,000 tons force/in^2) was achieved in the giant hydraulic diamond-faced press at the Carnegie Institution's Geophysical Laboratory, Washington, D.C. and reported in June 1978.

   Using dynamic methods and impact speeds of up to 18,000 mph, momentary pressures of 75 million atmospheres (490,000 tons/in^2) were reported from the United States in 1958.

Lowest friction The lowest coefficient of static and dynamic friction of any solid is 0.04, in the case of polytetrafluoroethylene, or PTFE ($[-C_2F_4-]_n$), which is equivalent to wet ice on wet ice. It was first manufactured in quantity by E.I. du Pont de Nemours & Co. Inc. in 1943, and is marketed in the United States as Teflon.

   In the centrifuge at the University of Virginia a 30-lb rotor magnetically supported has been spun at 1,000 rev/sec in a vacuum of 10^{-6} mm of mercury pressure. It loses only one revolution per second per day, thus spinning for years.

Highest velocity   The highest velocity at which any solid visible object has been projected is 93 miles/sec (334,800 mph) in the case of a plastic disc at the Naval Research Laboratory, Washington, D.C., reported in August 1980.

Most powerful electric current   If fired simultaneously, the 4,032 capacitors comprising the Zeus capacitor at the Los Alamos Scientific Laboratory, NM would produce, for a few microseconds, twice as much current as that generated anywhere else on Earth.

Hottest flame   The hottest is carbon subnitride (C_4N_2), which, at one atmosphere pressure, can produce a flame calculated to reach 9,010° F.

Highest measured frequency   The highest *directly* measured frequency is a visible yellow-green light at 520.2068085 terahertz (a terahertz being a million million hertz or cycles per second) for the o-component of the 17–1 P (62) transition line of iodine-127.
  The highest measured frequency determined by precision metrology is a green light at 582.491703 terahertz for the b_{21} component of the R (15) 43–0 transition line of iodine-127.

Smallest hole   Holes corresponding to a diameter of 3.16 Å (3.16 x 10^{-10} m) were produced on the surface of molybdenum disulphide by Dr Wolfgang Henkl of the University of Munich, Germany, and Dr John Maddocks of the University of Sheffield, Great Britain, using a chemical method involving a mercury drill. The holes were drilled on 17 Jul 1992 at the University of Munich.

Brightest light   The brightest artificial sources are "laser" pulses generated at the Los Alamos National Laboratory, NM, announced in March 1987. An ultraviolet flash lasting one picosecond (1 x 10^{-12} sec) is intensified to a power of 5 x 10^{15} watts.
  The most powerful searchlight ever developed was one produced during World War II by the General Electric Company Ltd at the Hirst Research Center in London, Great Britain. It had a consumption of 600 kW and gave an arc luminance of 300,000 candles/in² and a maximum beam intensity of 2.7 billion candles from its parabolic mirror (diameter 10 ft).

Highest note   A laser beam striking a sapphire crystal at the Massachusetts Institute of Technology, Cambridge, MA in September 1964 generated a note of 60 gigahertz.

Longest echo   The longest echo in any building is one of 15 sec following the closing of the door of the Chapel of the Mausoleum, Hamilton, Scotland, built 1840–55.

Largest barometer   An oil-filled barometer, of overall height 42 ft, was constructed by Allan Mills and John Pritchard of the Department of Physics and Astronomy, University of Leicester, Great Britain in 1991. It attained a standard height of 40 ft (at which pressure mercury would stand at 2 ft 6 in).

Of continuously burning sources, the most powerful is a 313 kW high-pressure argon arc lamp of 1.2 million candlepower, completed by Vortek Industries Ltd of Vancouver, British Columbia, Canada in March 1984.

Shortest light pulse In April 1988 it was announced that Charles V. Shank and colleagues at the AT&T Laboratories in New Jersey generated light pulses lasting just 6 femtoseconds (6 x 10^{-15} sec). These pulses comprised three or four optical cycles (wavelengths of visible light).

Magnetic fields The strongest continuous field strength achieved was a total of 35.3 ± 0.3 teslas at the Francis Bitter National Magnet Laboratory, Massachusetts Institute of Technology in Cambridge, MA, on 26 May 1988, employing a hybrid magnet with holmium pole pieces. These had the effect of enhancing the central magnetic field of 31.8 teslas generated in the hybrid magnet.

The weakest magnetic field measured is one of 8 x 10^{-15} teslas in the heavily shielded room at the same laboratory. It is used by Dr David Cohen for research into the very weak magnetic field generated in the heart and brain.

Highest vacuum A vacuum of the order of 10^{-14} torr was obtained at the IBM Thomas J. Watson Research Center, Yorktown Heights, NY in October 1976 in a cryogenic system with temperatures down to –452° F. This is equivalent to depopulating baseball-sized molecules from 1 yard to 50 miles apart.

Lowest viscosity The California Institute of Technology first announced on 1 Dec 1957 that there was no measurable viscosity, i.e., perfect flow, in liquid helium II, which exists at temperatures close to absolute zero (–459.67° F).

Highest voltage The highest-ever potential difference obtained in a laboratory was 32 ± 1.5 million volts by the National Electrostatistics Corporation at Oak Ridge, TN on 17 May 1979.

SCIENTIFIC INSTRUMENTS

Largest The largest scientific instrument so far (and arguably the world's largest machine) is the electron–positron storage ring "LEP" at CERN, housed in a ring tunnel 16.8 mile in circumference. The tunnel, 12 1/2 ft in diameter, runs between 164 and 492 ft under the Earth's surface, and is accessible through 18 vertical shafts. Over 60,000 tons of technical equipment have been installed in the tunnel and its eight underground work zones. It is intended to be a "Z° factory" producing up to 10,000 of these neutral weak gauge bosons every day in order to obtain a deeper understanding of the subatomic nature of matter. (See Heaviest particle.)

Finest balance The Sartorius Model 4108 manufactured in Göttingen, Germany can weigh objects of up to 0.018 oz to an accuracy of 3.5 x 10^{-10} oz, equivalent to little more than one sixtieth of the weight of the ink on this period.

Largest bubble chamber The $7 million installation, completed in Oct 1973 at Weston, IL, is 15 ft in diameter. It contains 8,718 gallons of liquid hydrogen at a temperature of –413° F and has a superconducting magnet of 3 tesla (a unit of magnetic induction). The last trackway was recorded on 1 Feb 1988.

MOST POWERFUL LASER Ten laser beams generated by "Nova" bombarding a pellet containing deuterium and tritium in a vacuum chamber at the Lawrence Livermore National Laboratory produce temperatures found at the sun's core, triggering a fusion reaction. (Photo: Science Photo Library)

Fastest centrifuge The highest man-made rotary speed ever achieved, and the fastest speed of any earthbound object, is 4,500 mph by a swirling tapered 6-in carbon fiber rod in a vacuum at Birmingham University, Great Britain, reported on 24 Jan 1975.

Laser beams First The first laser (a term coined by Richard Gould) was constructed in 1960 by Theodore Maiman of the Hughes Research Laboratory in California, with similar devices developed independently by Soviet physicists N. Bassov and A. Prokhorov.

Most powerful The most powerful laser is the "Nova" at the Lawrence Livermore National Laboratory, CA. Its 10 arms produce laser pulses capable of generating 100×10^{12} W of power, much of which is delivered to a target the size of a grain of sand in 1×10^{-9} sec. For this brief instant, that power is 200 times greater than the combined output of all the electrical generating plants in the United States. Fitted with two target chambers, the laser itself is 300 ft long and about three stories high.

Heaviest magnet The heaviest magnet is in the Joint Institute for Nuclear Research at Dubna, near Moscow, Russia, for the 10 GeV synchrophasotron measuring 196 ft in diameter and weighing 42,000 tons.

Largest electromagnet The world's largest electromagnet is part of the L3 detector, an experiment on LEP (large electron–positron collider). The octagonal-shaped magnet consists of 6,400 tons of low carbon steel yoke and 1,100 tons of aluminum coil. The yoke elements are welded pieces of up to 30 tons each and the coil consists of 168 turns welded together to form an eight-sided frame. Thirty thousand amperes of current flow through the aluminum coil to create a uniform magnetic field of 5 kilogauss. The magnet is higher than a four-story building of about 59,320 ft³ volume. The total weight of the magnet, including the frame, coil and inner support tube, is 7,810 tons, and it is composed of more metal than the Eiffel Tower.

Smallest microphone   Prof. Ibrahim Kavrak of Bogazici University, Istanbul, Turkey developed a microphone for a new technique of pressure measurement in fluid flow in 1967. It has a frequency response of 10 Hz–10 kHz and measures 0.06 x 0.03 in.

Most powerful microscope   The scanning tunneling microscope (STM) invented at the IBM Zürich research laboratory, Switzerland, in 1981 has a magnifying ability of 100 million and is capable of resolving down to one-hundredth the diameter of an atom (3×10^{-10} m). The fourth generation of the STM, now being developed, is said to be "about the size of a fingertip."

By using field ion microscopy, the tips of probes of scanning tunneling microscopes have been shaped to end in a single atom—the last three layers constituting the world's smallest man-made pyramid, consisting of 7, 3 and 1 atoms. Since the announcement in January 1990 that D.M. Eigler and E.K. Schweizer of the IBM Almaden Research Center, San Jose, CA had used an STM to move and reposition single atoms of xenon on a nickel surface in order to spell out the initials "IBM," other laboratories around the world have used similar techniques on single atoms of other elements.

Most powerful particle accelerator   The world's highest energy "atom-smasher" is the 1.25 mile diameter proton synchroton "Tevatron" at the Fermi National Accelerator Laboratory (Fermilab) near Batavia, IL. On 3 Jan 1987 a center

---

Smallest thermometer   Dr Frederich Sachs, a biophysicist at the State University of New York at Buffalo, has developed an ultra-microthermometer for measuring the temperature of single living cells. The tip is one micron in diameter, about one-fiftieth the diameter of a human hair.

Finest cut   The $13 million large optics diamond turning machine at the Lawrence Livermore National Laboratory, CA was reported in June 1983 to be able to sever a human hair 3,000 times lengthwise.

Thinnest glass   The thinnest glass, type D263, has a minimum thickness of 0.00098 in and a maximum thickness of 0.00137 in. It is made by Deutsche Spezialglas AG, Grünenplan, Germany for use in electronic and medical equipment.

Largest blown glass vessel   A bottle standing 7 ft 8 in tall with a capacity of about 188 gal was blown at Wheaton Village, Millville, NJ on 26 Sep 1992 by a team led by glass artist Steve Tobin. The attempt was made during the "South Jersey Glass Blast," part of a celebration of the local glassmaking heritage.

of mass energy of 1.8 TeV (1.8 x 10^{12} eV) was achieved by colliding beams of protons and antiprotons.

The projected US Department of Energy superconducting supercollider (SSC) at Waxahachie, TX of 54.14 miles circumference and using two 20 TeV proton colliding beams is due to become fully operational in the late 1990s.

Smallest optical prism A glass prism with sides 0.001 in—barely visible to the naked eye—has been created at the National Institute of Standards and Technology laboratories in Boulder, CO in 1989.

Sharpest objects and smallest tubes The sharpest manufactured objects are glass micropipette tubes whose beveled tips achieved an outer diameter of $0.02\,\mu m$ and an $0.01\,\mu m$ inner diameter. The latter is 6,500 times thinner than a human hair. They are used in intracellular work on living cells in techniques developed in 1977.

MATHEMATICS

In dealing with large numbers, scientists use the notation of 10 raised to various powers to eliminate a profusion of zeros. For example, 19.16 trillion miles would be written 1.916 x 10^{13} miles. Similarly, a very small number, for example 0.0000154324 of a gram, would be written 1.54324 x 10^{-5}. Of the prefixes used before numbers the smallest is "yocto," symbol y, of power 10^{-24}, and the largest is "yotta," symbol Y, of power 10^{24}. Both are based on the Greek *octo*, eight (for the eighth power of 10^3).

Highest numbers The highest lexicographically accepted named number in the system of successive powers of ten is the centillion, first recorded in 1852. It is the hundredth power of a million, or 1 followed by 600 zeros.

The number 10^{100} is designated a googol. The term was suggested by the nine-year-old nephew of Dr Edward Kasner (USA). Ten raised to the power of a googol is described as a googolplex. Some conception of the magnitude of such numbers can be gained when it is considered that the number of electrons in some models of the observable universe is believed to be of the order of 10^{87}. The highest named number outside the decimal notation is the Buddhist *asankhyeya*, which is equal to 10^{140}, and is mentioned in Jain works of *c.* 100 B.C.

The highest number ever used in a mathematical proof is a bounding value published in 1977 and known as Graham's number. It concerns bichromatic hypercubes and is inexpressible without the special "arrow" notation, devised by Knuth in 1976, extended to 64 layers.

Prime numbers A prime number is any positive integer (excluding unity 1) having no integral factors other than itself and unity, e.g., 2, 3, 5, 7 or 11. The lowest prime number is thus 2.

The highest *known* prime number (known as a Mersenne prime) is $2^{756,839}-1$, discovered in February 1992 by analysts at AEA Technology's Harwell Laboratory, Great Britain. The number contains 227,832 digits and was found on a CRAY-2 supercomputer. (See Perfect numbers.)

The largest-known twin primes are $1,706,595 \times 2^{11,235} - 1$ and $1,706,595 \times 2^{11,235} + 1$, found on 6 Aug 1989 by a team in Santa Clara, CA using an Amdahl 1200 supercomputer.

Composite numbers   The lowest nonprime or composite number (excluding 1) is 4.

Perfect numbers   A number is said to be perfect if it is equal to the sum of its divisors other than itself, e.g., $1 + 2 + 4 + 7 + 14 = 28$. The lowest perfect number is 6 ($= 1 + 2 + 3$).

The highest known perfect number, and the 32nd so far discovered, is $(2^{756,838} - 1) \times 2^{756,838}$. It has a total of 455,663 digits, a consequence of the largest Mersenne prime (also the largest prime number known) being $2^{756,839} - 1$, discovered in February 1992. (See Prime numbers.)

Newest mathematical constant   The study of turbulent water, the weather and other chaotic phenomena has revealed the existence of a new universal constant, the Feigenbaum number. Named after its discoverer, Mitchell Feigenbaum (USA), it equals approximately 4.669201609102990.

Most-proved theorem   A book published in 1940 entitled *The Pythagorean Proposition* contained 370 different proofs of Pythagoras' theorem, including one by President James Garfield.

Longest proof   The proof of the classification of all finite simple groups is spread over more than 14,000 pages in nearly 500 papers in mathematical journals, contributed by more than 100 mathematicians over a period of more than 35 years.

Most innumerate   The Nambiquara of the northwest Mato Grosso of Brazil lack any system of numbers. They do, however, have a verb that means "they are alike."

Oldest mathematical puzzle   Apart from slight differences in wording, the following puzzle is identical to one found in the Rhind papyrus, an Egyptian scroll bearing mathematical tables and problems, copied by the scribe Ahmes *c.* 1650 B.C.:

As I was going to St Ives, I met a man with seven wives. Every wife had seven sacks, every sack had seven cats, every cat had seven kits. Kits, cats, sacks and wives, how many were going to St Ives?

Most accurate version of pi   On 19 Nov 1989 the greatest number of decimal places to which *pi* (π) had been calculated was 1,073,740,000 by Yasumasa Kanada and Yoshiaki Tamura of the University of Tokyo, Japan using a Hitac S-820/80E computer.

Most inaccurate version of pi   In 1897 the General Assembly of Indiana enacted Bill No. 246, stating that *pi* was *de jure* 4. In 1853 William Shanks published his calculation of π to 707 decimal places, all calculated by hand. Ninety-two years later, in 1945, it was discovered that the last 180 digits were in fact all incorrect.

Most prolific mathematician Leonard Euler (Switzerland; 1707–83) was so prolific that his papers were still being published for the first time more than 50 years after his death. His collected works have been printed bit by bit since 1910 and will eventually occupy more than 75 large quarto volumes.

Earliest measures The earliest known measure of weight is the *beqa* of the Amratian period of Egyptian civilization *c.* 3800 B.C., found at Naqada, Egypt. The weights are cylindrical, with rounded ends, and weigh 6.65–7.45 oz.

The unit of length used by the megalithic tomb-builders in northwestern Europe *c.* 3500 B.C. appears to have been 2.72 ± 0.003 ft. This was deduced by Prof. Alexander Thom (1894–1985) in 1966.

Time measure Because of variations in the length of a day, which is estimated to be increasing irregularly at an average rate of about a millisecond per century due to the moon's tidal drag, the second has been redefined. Instead of being $1/86,400$th part of a mean solar day, it has, since 1960, been reckoned as $1/315,569,259,747$th part of the solar (or tropical) year at A.D. 1900, January 0.12 hr, Ephemeris time. In 1958 the second of Ephemeris time was computed to be equivalent to 9,192,631,770 ± 20 cycles of the radiation corresponding to the transition of cesium-133 atoms when unperturbed by exterior fields. The greatest diurnal change recorded was 10 milliseconds on 8 Aug 1972, due to the most violent solar storm recorded in 370 years of observations.

The accuracy of the cesium beam frequency standard approaches eight parts in 10^{14}, compared to two parts in 10^{13} for the methane-stabilized helium-neon laser and six parts in 10^{13} for the hydrogen maser.

The longest measure of time is the *kalpa* in Hindu chronology. It is equivalent to 4,320 million years. In astronomy a cosmic year is the period of rotation of the sun around the center of the Milky Way galaxy, i.e., 225 million years. In the Late Cretaceous Period of *c.* 85 million years ago the Earth rotated faster, resulting in 370.3 days per year, while in Cambrian times, *c.* 600 million years ago, there is evidence that the year comprised 425 days.

COMPUTING

Earliest The earliest programmable electronic computer was the 1,500-valve Colossus formulated by Prof. Max H.A. Newman (1897–1985) and built by T.H. Flowers. It was run in December 1943 at Bletchley Park, Great Britain to break the German coding machine Enigma. It arose from a concept published in 1936 by Dr Alan Mathison Turing (Great Britain; 1912–54) in his paper *On Computable Numbers with an Application to the Entscheidungsproblem*. Colossus was declassified on 25 Oct 1975.

The world's first stored-program computer was the Manchester University (Great Britain) Mark I, which incorporated the Williams storage cathode ray tube (patented 11 Dec 1946). It ran its first program, by Prof. Tom Kilburn (b. 1921), for 52 min on 21 Jun 1948.

Computers were greatly advanced by the invention of the point-contact transistor by John Bardeen and Walter Brattain, announced in July 1948, and the junction transistor by R.L. Wallace, Morgan Sparks and Dr William Bradford Shockley (1910–89) in early 1951.

Computer company The world's largest computer firm is International Business Machines (IBM) Corporation of Armonk, NY. As of 31 Dec 1992, gross revenues were $64.523 billion, assets were $86.705 billion, but net losses were $4.965 billion—the third highest ever. The company has 301,542 employees worldwide (compared with a peak of 407,000 in 1986) and 764,630 stockholders.

Fastest transistor A transistor capable of switching 230 billion times per second was announced by the University of Illinois at Urbana-Champaign in October 1986. The devices were made of indium, gallium, arsenide and aluminum gallium arsenide and developed in collaboration with General Electric Company.

Highest transistor density Intel has the highest density of transistors per square millimeter in the semi-conductor industry. On the Intel486 CPU, in each mm^2 Intel has put 14,500 transistors. The Dec Alpha only has about 7,100 transistors per mm^2, and Motorola has about 5,900 per mm^2 for its chips.

The concept of the integrated circuit, which has made micro-miniaturization possible, was first published on 7 May 1952 by Geoffrey W.A. Dummer (Great Britain; b. 1909) in Washington, D.C.

The invention of the microcomputer was attributed to a team led by M.E. Hoff, Jr. of Intel Corporation with the production of the microprocessor chip "4004" in 1969–71. However, on 17 Jul 1990 priority was accorded to Gilbert Hyatt (b. 1938), who devised a single chip microcomputer at Micro Computer Inc. of Van Nuys, Los Angeles, CA in 1968–71 with the award of US Patent No. 4942516.

Most powerful The world's most powerful computer is the liquid-cooled CRAY-2, from Cray Research Inc., Minneapolis, MN. Its memory has a capacity of 256 million 64-bit words, resulting in a capacity of 2.12 gigabytes of central memory. (A "byte" is a unit of storage comprising eight "bits" that are collectively equivalent to one alphabetic symbol or two numericals; "giga" denotes 10^9.) It attains speeds of 250 million floating point operations per second (flops).

Fastest In 1992 it was reported that Cray Research had developed a parallel vector system, the Y-MP C90 supercomputer, with 2 gigabytes of central memory and with 16 CPUs (central processing units), giving a combined peak performance of 16 gigaflops.

Sandia National Laboratory, NM on 18 Mar 1988 announced a "massively parallel" hypercube computer with 1,024 parallel processors, which, by breaking down problems into parts for simultaneous solution, proved 1,019 times faster than any conventional mainframe computer.

Fastest chip In March 1992 it was reported that DEC of Maynard, MA had developed an all-purpose computer chip, a 64-bit processor known as Alpha, which could run at speeds of up to 150 MHz (compared with 25 MHz for many modern personal computers). One Alpha chip is claimed to have about the same processing power as a CRAY-1, which went on sale in 1976 as the Cray company's first supercomputer, at a cost of $7.5 million.

FASTEST COMPUTER CHIP
Digital Equipment Corporation's Alpha 21064 microprocessor can process 400 million instructions per second and contains 1.7 million transistors. Intel's Pentium Processor, launched in 1993, has more transistors, with 3.1 million, but it is not as fast as the Alpha 21064. (Photo: Digital Equipment Corporation)

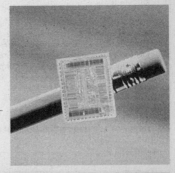

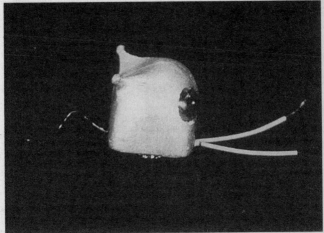

SMALLEST ROBOT The world's smallest robot is the "Monsieur" microbot, developed by the Seiko Epson Corporation of Japan in 1992. The light-sensitive robot measures less than 0.06 in³, weighs 0.05 oz and is made of 97 separate watch parts (equivalent to two ordinary watches). Capable of speeds of 0.4 in/sec for about 5 min when charged, the "Monsieur" earned a design award at the International Contest for Hill-Climbing Micromechanisms. (Photo: Seiko Epson Corporation)

Computer Data

The position of IBM as the world's top computer company is under increasing threat from leading software house Microsoft, developer of the Windows operating system running some 120 million PCs worldwide, and chip-maker Intel.

In 1992 IBM's market value fell by 63 percent from its peak in February 1991 and, while it has registered the third highest corporate loss ever, representing a 74 percent drop in profits, Intel has increased its performance by 30 percent and Microsoft by 53 percent.

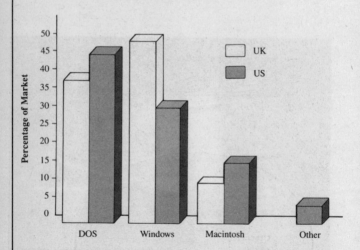

Comparative Software Use In UK and US

Although IBM still retains its lead in the PC market, the development of increasingly powerful microprocessors such as Intel's Pentium has resulted in a shift away from the mainframe computers on which IBM was built and toward fast, powerful and relatively inexpensive personal computers. As the largest semiconductor company, Intel's chips are fitted to some 70 percent of the world's PCs.

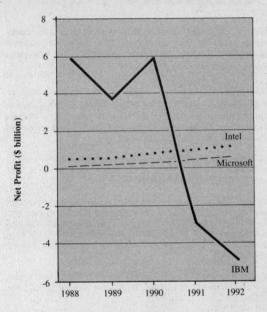

Comparative Performances of Leading Computer Companies

Net Profit ($ billion)

- Intel
- Microsoft
- IBM

1988 1989 1990 1991 1992

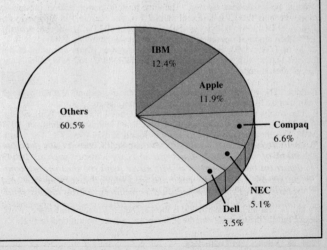

- **IBM** 12.4%
- **Apple** 11.9%
- **Others** 60.5%
- **Compaq** 6.6%
- **NEC** 5.1%
- **Dell** 3.5%

POWER

Steam engines Oldest   The oldest steam engine in working order is the Smethwick Engine dating from 1779. Designed by James Watt (1736–1819) and built by the Birmingham Canal Company, the pump—originally a 24-in bore with a stroke of 8 ft—worked on the canal locks at Smethwick, Great Britain until 1891. The engine was presented to the Birmingham Museum of Science and Industry in 1960 and is regularly steamed for the public.

Largest   The largest ever single-cylinder steam engine was designed by Matthew Loam of Cornwall and built by the Hayle Foundry Co. in 1849 for land draining at Haarlem, Netherlands. The cylinder was 12 ft in diameter and each stroke, also of 12 ft, lifted 16,140 gal of water.

Most efficient   The most efficient steam engine recorded was Taylor's engine built by Michael Loam for United Mines of Gwennap, Great Britain in 1840. It registered only 1.7 lb of coal per horsepower per hour.

Largest power plant   The most powerful installed power station is currently the Itaipu power station on the Paraná River near the Brazil–Paraguay border. Opened in 1984, the station's 18th turbine was put into operation in May 1991, giving a total capacity of 12,600 MW from a projected 13,320 MW. A 20,000 MW power station project on the Tunguska River, Russia was announced in February 1982.

Earliest atomic pile   The world's first atomic pile was built in a disused squash court at Stagg Field, University of Chicago, IL. It went "critical" at 3:25 P.M. local time on 2 Dec 1942.

Nuclear power stations Earliest   The first nuclear power station producing electricity was the EBR-1 (Experimental Breeder Reactor) in Shippingport, PA on 20 Dec 1951. The station had a capacity of 60 MW. It was shut down in 1974, then resumed operation in 1977 before it was retired in 1984.

As of 1 Mar 1993, there were 108 nuclear power plants operating in the United States, with a total net summer capability of 97.882 MW. Illinois has the greatest number of stations, at 13.

Largest   The world's largest nuclear power station, with 10 reactors and net output of 8,814 MW, is the station in Fukushima, Japan.

The largest nuclear power complex in the United States is at Wintersburg, AZ. The three Palo Verde, CA units have a net summer capability of 3,663 MW. The largest unit in the country is found in Bay City, TX. The South Texas 1 unit has a capability of 1,251 MW; the South Texas 2 unit's capability is 1,250 MW.

Nuclear reactors   The largest single nuclear reactor in the world is the Ignalina station, Lithuania, which came fully on line in January 1984 and has a net capacity of 1,380 MW.

The largest under construction is the CHOOZ-B1 reactor in France. Work began on site in July 1982 and the first reactor became operational in 1991.

Fusion power Tokamak-7, the experimental thermonuclear apparatus, was declared in January 1982 by the then Soviet academician Velikhov to be operating "reliably for months on end." An economically viable thermonuclear reactor is not anticipated anywhere in the world in this century.

The first significant controlled fusion power production was achieved on 9 Nov 1991 at the Joint European Torus (JET) at Culham, Great Britain by tritium injection into a deuterium plasma. Optimum fusion was sustained for about 2 sec and produced a power rating of 1.7 megawatts. Temperatures at the center of thermonuclear fusion explosions have been found to be about 400,000,000° C. (See Physical Extremes, Highest temperature.)

Solar power The largest solar furnace in the world is the LUZ plant, located in the Mojave Desert, 140 miles northeast of Los Angeles, CA. It is currently operating the world's nine largest solar electric generating systems (SEGS), which account for more than 92 percent of the the world's solar electricity. LUZ is now producing 354 MW. SEGS IX is the second phase in a six-plant, $1.5 billion solar development program due for completion in 1994 that will bring the total to 675 MW.

The $30 million thermal solar energy system at the Packerland Packing Co. Bellevue Plant, Green Bay, WI, completed in January 1984, comprises 9,750 4 x 8 ft collectors covering 7.16 acres. It can yield up to 8.44 MJ a month.

There were seven solar-powered and 16 wind-powered electric generating plants in the United States as of 1992, owned and operated by public utility companies. California had the most solar plants, with three, while Minnesota had the most wind-powered plants, also three.

Tidal power station The world's first major station is the *Usine marémotrice de la Rance*, officially opened on 26 Nov 1966 on the Rance estuary in Brittany, France. It has an installed power of 240 MW, and a net annual output of 544 million kW. The 2,640 ft barrage contains 24 turbo alternators.

Largest boilers The largest boilers ever designed were those ordered in the United States from Babcock & Wilcox, with a capacity of 1,330 MW, involving the evaporation of 9.33 million lb of steam per hour.

Largest generators The largest operational is a turbo generator of 1,450 MW (net) being installed at the Ignalina atomic power station in southern Lithuania. However, dynamos in the 2,000,000 kW (or 2,000 MW) range are now in the planning stages both in Great Britain and the United States.

Transformers The world's largest single-phase transformers are rated at 1,500,000 kVA. Eight of these are in service with the American Electric Power Service Corporation. Of these, five step down from 765 to 345 kV.

Transmission lines The longest span between pylons of any power line in the world is that across the Sogne Fjord, Norway, between Rabnaberg and Fatlaberg. Supplied in 1955 by Whitecross of Warrington, Great Britain, and projected and erected by A.S. Betonmast of Oslo as part of the high-tension power cable from Refsdal power station at Vik, it has a span of 16,040 ft and a weight of 13.3 tons. In 1967 two further high-tensile steel/aluminum lines 16,006 ft long, and weighing 36.4 tons, manufactured by Whitecross and BICC, were erected there.

Highest The world's highest transmission lines are those across the Straits of

Messina, Italy, with towers of 675 ft (Sicily side) and 735 ft (Calabria side) 11,900 ft apart.

Highest voltages The highest voltages now carried are 1,330 kV for 1,224 miles on the D.C. Pacific Inter-tie in the United States. The Ekibastuz D.C. transmission lines in Kazakhstan are planned to be 1,490 miles long with 1.5 MV capacity.

Turbines The largest hydraulic turbines are those rated at 815 MW (equivalent to 1.1 million hp), 32 ft in diameter with a 449 ton runner and a 350 ton shaft installed by Allis-Chalmers at the Grand Coulee Third Powerplant, WA.

Wind generators The $14.2 million GEC MOD-5A installation on the north shore of Oahu, HI produces 7,300 kW when the wind reaches 32 mph with 400 ft rotors. Installation was started in March 1984.

Tidal mill On 12 Nov 1989 the Eling Tide Mill, Great Britain attained 16 hr 7 min rotation of the waterwheel in one day. It is the only surviving mill in the world harnessing the power of the tide for regular production of whole-meal flour.

Oldest water mill The water mill with the oldest continuous commercial use is at Priston Mill near Bath, Great Britain, first mentioned in A.D. 931 in a charter to King Athelstan (924/5–939). It is driven by the Conygre Brook and is the only remaining working water mill of the 5,700 recorded in the Domesday Book of 1086.

Windmills Earliest The earliest recorded windmills were those used for grinding corn in Persia (now Iran) in the 7th century A.D.

Largest battery The 10 MW lead-acid battery at Chino, CA has a design capacity of 40 MW/h. It will be used at an electrical substation for leveling peak demand loads. This $13 million project is a cooperative effort by Southern California Edison Company Electric Power Research Institute and International Lead Zinc Research Organization Inc.

Most durable batteries The zinc foil and sulfur dry-pile batteries made by Watlin and Hill of London, Great Britain in 1840 have powered ceaseless tintinnabulation inside a bell jar at the Clarendon Laboratory, Oxford, Great Britain since that year.

Biggest blackout The greatest power failure in history struck seven northeastern US states and Ontario, Canada on 9–10 Nov 1965. About 30 million people in 80,000 miles² were plunged into darkness. Only two people died as a result of the blackout. In New York City the power failed at 5:27 P.M. and was not fully restored for 13½ hr.

The total losses in the 52-min New York City power failure of 13 Jul 1977, including looting, were put at $1 billion.

Tallest   The De Noord windmill in Schiedam, Netherlands at 109 ft 4 in is the tallest in Europe.

Largest   The largest windmill is the Dijkpolder in Maasland, built in 1718, with sails measuring 95 ft 9 in from tip to tip.

ENGINEERING

Oldest machinery   The earliest mechanism still in use is the *dâlu*—a water-raising instrument known to have been in use in the Sumerian civilization, which originated *c*. 3500 B.C. in what is now lower Iraq.

Blast furnace   The world's largest blast furnace, with a volume of 5,500 m³, is the no. 5 furnace at the Cherepovets works in Russia.

Catalytic cracker   The world's largest catalytic cracker is Exxon's Bayway Refinery plant at Linden, NJ, with a fresh feed rate of 5 million gals per day.

Conveyor belts   The world's longest single-flight conveyor belt is one of 18 miles in Western Australia installed by Cable Belt Ltd of Camberley, Great Britain.

The world's longest multiflight conveyor was one of 62 miles between the phosphate mine near Bucraa and the port of El Aiún, Morocco, built by Krupps and completed in 1972. It had 11 flights of 6–7 miles and was driven at 10.06 mph. It has since been closed down.

Most powerful cranes   The greatest single load lifted by cranes is over 10,750 metric tons during the positioning of an integrated module onto the Piper Bravo platform in the North Sea off Aberdeen, Scotland in December 1991. The record lift was carried out by twin AmClyde 6000 cranes, designed and built by AmClyde Engineered Products Inc. of St Paul, MN and installed onboard the vessel *Derrick Barge 102*. (See Greatest load raised.)

Gantry crane   The 92.3 ft wide Rahco (R.A. Hanson Disc Ltd) gantry crane at the Grand Coulee Dam Third Powerplant was tested to lift a load of 2,460 tons in 1975. It lowered a 1,972 ton generator rotor with an accuracy of 1.32 in.

Tallest mobile crane   The 890-ton Rosenkranz K10001, with a lifting capacity of 1,100 tons, and a combined boom and jib height of 663 ft, is carried on 10 trucks, each limited to a length of 75 ft 8 in and an axle weight of 130 tons. It can lift 33 tons to a height of 525 ft.

Greatest load raised   The heaviest lifting operation in engineering history was the raising of the entire 1-mile-long offshore Ekofisk complex in the North Sea, Great Britain, owing to subsidence of the seabed. The complex consists of eight platforms weighing some 44,090 tons. During 17–18 Aug 1987 it was raised 21 ft 4 in by 122 hydraulic jacks requiring a computer-controlled hydraulic system developed and supplied by Hydraudyne Systems & Engineering bv of Boxtel, Netherlands. (See also Most powerful cranes.)

Most powerful diesel engines Five 12RTA84 type diesel engines have been constructed by Sulzer Brothers of Winterthur, Switzerland, for containerships built for the American President Lines. Each 12-cylinder power unit gives a maximum continuous output of 57,000 bhp at 95 rev/min. The first of these ships, the *President Truman*, was handed over in April 1988.

Draglines The Ural Engineering Works in Yekaterinburg (formerly Sverdlovsk), Russia, completed in March 1962, has a dragline known as the ES-25 (100), with a boom of 328 ft, and a bucket with a capacity of 848 ft³.

The world's largest walking dragline is "Big Muskie," the Bucyrus-Erie 4250W with an all-up weight of 13,200 tons and a bucket capacity of 5,933 ft³ on a 310 ft boom. This is the largest mobile land machine and is now operating on the Central Ohio Coal Co. Muskingum site in Ohio.

Earthmover The giant wheeled loader developed for open-air coal mining in Australia by SMEC, a consortium of 11 manufacturers in Tokyo, Japan, is 55.1 ft in length, weighs 198 tons, and has rubber tires 11¹/₂ ft in diameter. The bucket has a capacity of 671 ft³.

Escalators The term "escalator" was registered in the United States on 28 May 1900, but the earliest "inclined escalator" was installed by Jesse W. Reno on the pier at Coney Island, NY in 1896.

The escalators at the station formerly named Lenin Square on the St Petersburg (Leningrad), Russia subway have 729 steps and a vertical rise of 195 ft 9¹/₂ in.

The world's longest *ride* is on the four-section outdoor escalator at Ocean Park, Hong Kong, which has an overall length of 745 ft and a total vertical rise of 377 ft.

Moving sidewalks The world's longest "moving sidewalks" are those installed in 1970 in the Neue Messe Center, Dusseldorf, Germany, which measure 738 ft between comb plates.

The ultimate in pampering for weary shoppers is the escalator at the shopping mall at Kawasaki-shi, Japan. It has a vertical height of 32.83 in and was installed by Hitachi Ltd.

Forging The largest forging on record is one of a 225-ton, 55-ft-long generator shaft for Japan, forged by the Bethlehem Steel Corporation of Pennsylvania in October 1973.

Forklift trucks Kalmar LMV of Sweden in 1991 manufactured ten counterbalanced forklift trucks capable of lifting loads up to 99 tons at a load center of 90¹/₂ in. They were built to handle the Libyan Great Man-made River Project, comprising two separate pipelines, one 620 miles long running from Sawir to the Gulf of Sirte and the other 575 miles from Tazirbu to Benghazi, Libya.

Lathe The largest is the 126-ft-long 460-ton giant lathe built by Waldrich Siegen of Germany in 1973 for the South African Electricity Supply Commission at Rosherville. It has a capacity for 330-ton workpieces and a swing-over bed of 16 ft 5 in in diameter.

Escalator riding   The record distance traveled on a pair of "up" and "down" escalators is 133.18 miles, by David Beattie and Adrian Simons at Top Shop in London, Great Britain, from 17 to 21 Jul 1989. They each completed 7,032 circuits.

Steel companies   The world's largest producer of steel is the Nippon Steel Corporation of Japan, which produced 30.52 million tons of crude steel in the year ending March 1992, compared with 31.959 million tons in 1991. It now has 37,388 employees, compared with 51,441 in 1988.

The Pohang works of the Pohang Iron & Steel Co. Ltd (POSCO) of South Korea produced 9.9 million tons of crude steel in 1988, the highest amount produced by a single integrated works.

The largest producer of steel in the United States in 1992 was USX Corporation, of Pittsburgh, PA, which produced 10.4 million tons of raw steel. The 1992 sales figure for the US Steel Group of USX was $4.95 billion and assets stood at $6.25 billion. The number of employees for the year was 18,000.

Top-spinning   The duration record for spinning a clock-balance wheel by unaided hand is 5 min 26.8 sec, by Philip Ashley, 16, of Leigh, Great Britain on 20 May 1968. The record using 36 in of string with a 7¼-oz top is 58 min 20 sec, by Peter Hodgson at Southend-on-Sea, Great Britain on 4 Feb 1985. A team of 25 from the Mizushima Plant of Kawasaki Steel Works in Okayama, Japan spun a giant top 6 ft 6¾ in tall and 8 ft 6¼ in in diameter, weighing 793.6 lb, for 1 hr 21 min 35 sec on 3 Nov 1986.

Largest nuts   The largest nuts ever made weigh 5 tons each with an outside diameter of 52 in and a 25 in thread. Known as "Pilgrim Nuts," they are manufactured by Pilgim Moorside Ltd of Oldham, Great Britain for use on the columns of a large forging press.

Passenger elevators   The fastest domestic passenger elevators in the world are the express elevators to the 60th floor of the 787 ft tall "Sunshine 60" building, Ikebukuro, in Tokyo, Japan, completed 5 Apr 1978. They were built by Mitsubishi Corporation and operate at a speed of 23 mph.

Much higher speeds are achieved in the winding cages of mine shafts. A hoisting shaft 6,800 ft deep, owned by Western Deep Levels Ltd in South Africa, winds at speeds of up to 41 mph. Otitis media (popping of the ears) presents problems above even 10 mph.

Pipelines Earliest   The world's earliest pipeline, of 2 in diameter cast iron, was laid at Oil Creek, PA in 1863, but was torn up by Luddites (opponents of industrial change or innovation).

Oil   The longest crude oil pipeline in the world is the Interprovincial Pipe Line Company installation from Edmonton, Alberta, Canada to Buffalo, NY, a distance of 1,775 miles. Along the length of the pipe, 13 pumping stations maintain a flow of 8.3 million gals of oil per day.

The ultimate length of the Trans-Siberian pipeline will be 2,319 miles, running from Tuimazy through Omsk and Novosibirsk to Irkutsk. The first 30-mile section was opened in July 1957.

Gas   The longest natural gas pipeline in the world is the Trans-Canada pipeline, which by 1974 had 5,654 miles of pipe up to 42 in in diameter. The world's longest submarine pipeline is 264 miles long and carries natural gas from the Union Oil platform to Rayong, Thailand. It opened on 12 Sep 1981.

Water   The world's longest water pipeline runs a distance of 350 miles to the Kalgoorlie goldfields from near Perth in Western Australia. Engineered in 1903, the system has since been extended fivefold by branches.

Most expensive   The world's most expensive pipeline is the Alaska oil pipeline running 800 miles from Prudhoe Bay to Valdez. On completion of the first phase in 1977, it had cost $8 billion. The pipe is 48 in in diameter and its capacity is now 2.1 million barrels per day.

Presses   The world's two most powerful production machines are forging presses in the United States. The Loewy closed-die forging press, in a plant leased from the US Air Force by the Wyman-Gordon Company at North Grafton, MA, weighs 10,438 tons and stands 114 ft 2 in high, of which 66 ft is sunk below the operating floor. It has a rated capacity of 49,160 tons and became operational in October 1955. A similar press is in operation at the plant of the Aluminum Company of America in Cleveland, OH.

The greatest press force of any sheet metal forming press is 116,840 tons for a QUINTUS fluid cell press delivered by ASEA to BMG AG in Munich, Germany in January 1986. The Bêché & Grohs counter-blow forging hammer, manufactured in Germany, is rated at 66,130 tons.

Printer   The world's fastest printer was the Radiation Inc. electro-sensitive system at the Lawrence Radiation Laboratory, Livermore, CA. It printed up to 36,000 lines per minute, each containing 120 alphanumeric characters per minute, attained by controlling electronic pulses through chemically impregnated recording paper that was moving rapidly under closely spaced fixed styli. It could thus print the entire wordage of the Bible (773,692 words) in 65 seconds—3,048 times as fast as the peak rate of the world's fastest typist. (See Miscellaneous Endeavors, Fastest typist.)

Radar installations   The largest of the three installations in the US Ballistic Missile Early Warning System (BMEWS) is that near Thule, in Greenland, 931 miles from the North Pole. It was completed in 1960 at a cost of $500 million. Its sister stations are one at Cape Clear, AK, which was completed in 1961, and the $115 million radar installation at Fylingdales Moor, Great Britain, which was completed in June 1963.

The largest scientific radar installation is the 21-acre ground array at Jicamarca, Peru.

Ropes   The largest rope ever made was a coir fiber launching rope with a circumference of 47 in made in 1858 for the British liner *Great Eastern* by John and Edwin Wright of Birmingham, Great Britain. It consisted of four strands, each of 3,780 yarns.

Wire ropes   The longest wire ropes in the world are the four made at British

Ropes Ltd, Wallsend, Great Britain, each measuring 15 miles. The ropes are 1.3 in in diameter, weigh 120 tons each, and were ordered by the CEGB for use in the construction of the 2,000 MW cross-Channel power cable.

The suspension cables on the Seto Grand Bridge, Japan, completed in 1988, are 41 in in diameter.

A 22 in diameter cable-laid rope with a calculated breaking strength of 11,120 tons was manufactured for demonstration purposes only by Franklin Offshore Supply & Engineering PTE LTD of Singapore in 1992. They also have the capacity to produce 25 in cable. The largest cable-laid sling made for practical use measures 16 in in diameter and has a minimum breaking load of 6,670 tons. It was made in 1992 by United Ropes of Ridderkerk, Netherlands for Heeremac of Leiden.

Ropeway or téléphérique   The longest ropeway in the world is the *Compagnie Minière de l'Ogoouè*, or COMILOG, installation built in 1959–62 for the Moanda manganese mine in Gabon, which extends 47 miles. It has 858 towers and 2,800 buckets, with 96 miles of wire rope running over 6,000 idler pulleys. The longest single-span ropeway is the 13,500 ft span from the Coachella Valley to Mt San Jacinto (10,821 ft), CA, inaugurated on 12 Sep 1963.

The highest and longest passenger-carrying aerial ropeway in the world is the *Teleférico Mérida* in Venezuela, from Mérida City (5,379 ft) to the summit of Pico Espejo (15,629 ft), a rise of 10,250 ft. The ropeway is in four sections, involving three car changes in the eight-mile ascent in one hour. The fourth span is 10,070 ft in length. The two cars have a maximum capacity of 45 persons and travel 3 mph.

Shovel   The Marion 6360 has a reach of 236 ft 9 in, a dumping height of 153 ft and a bucket capacity of 4,860 ft^3. Manufactured in 1964 by the Marion Power Shovel Co., Marion, OH, it weighs 24.3 million lb and uses 20 electric motors that generate 45,000 hp to operate its 220.5-ft-long boom arm. It is operated for open-cast coal mining near Percy, IL by the Arch Mineral Corporation.

Snow-plow blade   A blade measuring 50$\frac{1}{4}$ ft long and 4 ft high, with a clearing capacity of 1,095 ft^3 in one pass, was made by Aero Snow Removal Corporation of New York, NY in 1992 for operation at JFK International Airport.

Valve   The world's largest valve is the 32-ft diameter, 187-ton butterfly valve designed by Boving & Co. Ltd of London, Great Britain for use at the Arnold Air Force Base engine test facility in Tennessee.

Wind tunnel   The world's largest wind tunnel is that of the NASA Ames Research Center in Mountain View, Palo Alto, CA. The largest test section measures 118 x 79 m and is powered by six 17,000 kW motors, giving a top speed of 124 mph.

BORINGS AND MINES

Deepest The deepest penetration into the Earth's crust is a geological exploratory drilling near Zapolarny in the Kola Peninsula of Arctic Russia, begun on 24 May 1970 and reported in April 1992 to have surpassed a depth of 40,230 ft. The eventual target of 49,212 ft is expected in 1995. The drill bit is mounted on a turbine driven by a mud pump. The temperature at 39,400 ft (7.45 miles) was already 229° F.

The Germans announced the test drilling of the Erbendorf hole, Upper Bavaria on 9 Oct 1986. The planned depth of the $263 million project is 8.6 miles or 45,900 ft.

Ocean drilling The deepest recorded drilling into the seabed by the *Glomar Challenger* of the US Deep Sea Drilling Project is one of 5,709 ft off northwest Spain in 1976. The deepest site is now 23,077 ft below the surface on the western wall of the Mariana Trench, Pacific Ocean.

Fastest drilling The most footage drilled in one month is 34,574 ft, in June 1988 by Harkins & Company Rig Number 13 during the drilling of four wells in McMullen County, TX.

OIL

Production The world's largest oil producer is the former USSR, with a production in 1991 of 10.26 million barrels per day (b/d)—compared with a peak 12.5 million b/d in 1988, followed by Saudi Arabia with 8.2 million b/d. The United States was third with 7.4 million b/d.

US CRUDE OIL IMPORTS
(January–December 1992)

Country	Barrels 1,000 per day
Saudi Arabia	1,716
Venezuela	1,153
Canada	985
Mexico	703
Nigeria	608
Angola	336
United Kingdom	219
Virgin Islands*	161
Colombia	122
OPEC Countries	4,076
Persian Gulf Countries	1,800

* Supplier of products made from crude oil.
U.S. Department of Energy

Fields   The world's largest oil field is the Ghawar field, Saudi Arabia, developed by ARAMCO, which measures 150 x 22 miles.

United States   The largest oil field in the United States is the Permian Basin, which covers approximately 100,000 miles^2 in southeast New Mexico and western and northwestern Texas.

Refineries   The world's largest refinery is the Petroleos de Venezuela S.A. refinery in Judibana, Falcón, Venezuela. It is operated by the Lagoven subsidiary of Petroleos and in 1991 produced 530,000 barrels of crude oil per day.

United States   The largest refinery in the United States is Amoco Oil Co.'s Texas City, TX refinery, which has a capacity of 433,000 barrels per day.

Crude oil imports   During the period January–December 1992, the United States imported 7.8 million barrels of crude oil and its by-products per day. Saudi Arabia was the leading supplier at 1.7 million barrels per day, which represented 21.8 percent of US imports.
   OPEC countries supplied the US with 4.076 million barrels per day, or 51.9 percent of the total, while Persian Gulf countries supplied 1.8 million, or 26.3 percent.

Platforms Heaviest   The world's heaviest oil platform is the *Pampo* in the Campos Basin off Rio de Janeiro, Brazil, built and operated by the Petrobrás company. Opened in the 1970s, the platform weighs 26,560 tons, covering 32,292 ft^2, and processes 30,000 barrels per day. It operates at a height of 377 ft from the seabed (see below).

Tallest   The world's tallest production platform is the *Petrobrás 20* in the Marlim Field of Campos Basin, operating 2,051 ft from the seabed. The plat-

---

Coal shoveling   The record for filling a $1/2$ ton hopper with coal is 27.93 sec, by Wayne Miller at the Fingal Valley Festival in Fingal, Tasmania, Australia on 27 Feb 1993.
   The record by a team of two is 16.05 sec, by Wayne Miller of Fingal and Ian Austin of Megalong, Valley, New South Wales on the same occasion.

Ice-core drilling   The deepest borehole in ice was drilled at the Vostok station (Central Antarctica) by specialists of the Leningrad Mining Institute in September 1989, when a depth of 8,333 ft was achieved. The 18th Expedition drilled the deepest "dry" borehole (without antifreeze) in 1972; it reached 3,125 ft.

Oil tanks   The largest oil tanks ever constructed are the five ARAMCO $1^1/2$-million-barrel storage tanks at Ju'aymah, Saudi Arabia. They are 72 ft tall with a diameter of 386 ft and were completed in March 1980.

MINING RECORDS

Earliest
World   100,000 BC—CHERT(silica) Nazlet Sabaha Garb, Egypt.

Deepest
World[1]   12,391 ft—GOLD, Western Deep Levels, Carletonville, South Africa.

Coal
Largest (US)   27.9 million short tons per annum, ARCO Coal Co.'s Black Thunder Mine in Wright, WY.

Oldest   (US[2] c. 1750 at James River coalfield near Richmond, VA. This site is now abandoned.

Deepest   (exploratory shaft) 6,700 ft, Donbas field, Ukraine.

(open cast, lignite)   1,066 ft, near Bergheim, Germany.

Copper
Deepest (open pit)   2,625 ft, Bingham Canyon, near Salt Lake City, UT

Longest (underground)   994 miles, Division El Teniente, Codelco, Chile.

United States   356 miles of tunnels, San Manuel Mine, Magma Copper Co in Arizona.

Gold
Richest   49·4 million fine oz (all-time yield), Crown Mines, Transvaal, South Africa.

Largest (world)[3]   12,107 acres, East Rand Proprietary Mines Ltd, Boksburg, Transvaal, South Africa.

Iron
Largest   22.4 billion tons (45–65% ore), Lebedinsky, Kursk region, Russia.

United States[4]   13.708 million metric tons at Mountain Iron, MN.

Lead
Largest   >10 percent of world output, Viburnum Trend, MI.

Platinum
Earliest   2nd century B.C., La Tolita, Ecuador.

Largest   30.8 tons per year, Rustenburg Platinum Mines Group, Transvaal, South Africa.

Quarry
Largest (world)   2·81 miles[2], 3.698 billion tons (extracted), Bingham Canyon, UT

Spoil Dump
Largest (world)   7·4 billion ft[3], New Cornelia Tailings, Ten Mile Wash, AZ.

Tungsten
Largest   2,205 tons per day, Union Carbide Mount Morgan mine, near Bishop, CA.

Uranium[5]
Productivity   7,000 tons (ore) per day, Rio Algom Co. mine, Grant, NM.

---

[1] *Sinking began in June 1957 and 14,000 ft is regarded as the limit. Its No. 3 vertical ventilation shaft is the world's deepest shaft, at 9,675 ft. This mine requires 141,150 tons of air per day and enough refrigeration energy needed to make 41,440 short tons of ice. An underground shift comprises 11,150 men.*

[2] *The first recorded discovery of coal in the United States was in 1679 by French explorers, who reported a coal mine on the Illinois River.*

[3] *The world's most productive gold mine may be Muruntau, Kyzyl Kum, Uzbekistan, with an estimated 88 tons of gold per year. It has been estimated that South Africa has produced in 96 years (1886–1982) more than 31 percent of all gold mined since 3900 B.C. Over 51 percent of the world's output is produced at the 38 mines of the Witwatersrand fields, South Africa, first discovered in 1886. The largest gold mine currently in the United States is the Newmont Gold Company's Mine Complex in Eureka County and Elko County, NV.*

[4] *Minnesota produced the most iron in the U.S. in 1990, at 45.160 metric tons. The greatest year for iron production for the entire country was 1953, with 119.888 million metric tons.*

[5] *This has been shut down, but remains on standby. The Gas Hills mine in Wyoming, at 2,800 tons per day, is currently the most productive.*

form has been operational since July 1992 and processes 38,000 barrels per day (see p. 213).

The tallest production platform in the United States stands in water 1,760 ft deep about 100 miles off the Louisiana coast. It is operated by Conoco and co-owned by Conoco, Texas and Occidental Petroleum.

Rigs On 31 January 1990, the all-time lowest number of oil rigs in the United States was 653. This number includes all land rigs, those on inland barges and offshore rigs.

Oil gushers The greatest wildcat ever recorded blew at Alborz No. 5 well, near Qum, Iran on 26 Aug 1956. The uncontrolled oil gushed to a height of 170 ft at 120,000 barrels per day at a pressure of 9,000 lb/in^2. It was closed after 90 days' work by B. Mostofi and Myron Kinley of Texas.

The Lake View No. 1 gusher in California on 15 Mar 1910 may have yielded 125,000 barrels in its first 24 hours.

NATURAL GAS

Production The world's largest producer of natural gas is the former USSR, with 28.8 trillion ft^3 in 1992, followed by the United States with 18.4 trillion ft^3.

Deposits The largest gas deposit in the world is at Urengoi, Russia, with an eventual production of 261.6 billion yd^2 per year through six pipelines from proved reserves of 9.156 trillion yd^3. The trillionth cubic meter was produced on 23 Apr 1986.

Water wells The world's deepest water bore is the Stensvad Water Well 11-W1 of 7,320 ft, drilled by the Great Northern Drilling Co. Inc. in Rosebud County, MT in October–November 1961. The Thermal Power Co. geothermal steam well, begun in Sonoma County, CA in 1955, is down to 9,029 ft.

Greatest gas fire The greatest gas fire was the one that burned at Gassi Touil in the Algerian Sahara from noon on 13 Nov 1961 to 9:30 A.M. on 28 Apr 1962. The pillar of flame rose 450 ft and the smoke 600 ft. It was eventually extinguished by Paul Neal ("Red") Adair (b. 1916) of Houston, TX, using 550 lb of dynamite. His fee was reported to be about $1 million plus expenses.

Waves of Destruction

Oil slicks always leave devastating images and are a constant reminder of the vulnerability of our environment. Many factors can affect the eventual impact of any spill, including location, weather conditions and temperature.

An estimated average of 2.2 million tons of oil is spilled from a total of some 1.6 billion tons shipped each year, i.e., about 0.1 percent. The first major tanker spill, and the largest ever in British waters, was 132,000 tons from the grounding of the Torrey Canyon *off Cornwall in 1967.*

Despite our fears, the number of accidental tanker spills involving over 50 barrels (about 8 tons) has fallen from just over 120 in 1975 to under 40 in 1991.

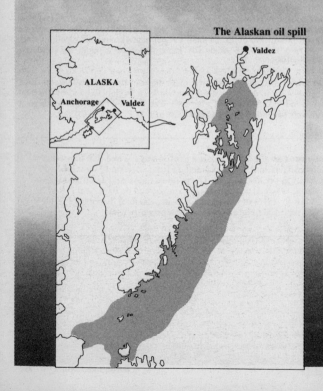

The Alaskan oil spill

Oil-covered bird, Shetland Islands (Photo: Gamma)

Largest slick
400 miles long (from 550,000 tons), *Ixtoc* (rig blowout, 1979–80), Gulf of Mexico

Oil from the *Exxon Valdez* spill (42,000 tons) in 1989 eventually affected 1,056 miles of the Alaskan coastline

Ecological damage
Although not ranking among even the top 20 largest spills, because of its environmentally sensitive location the *Exxon Valdez* spillage was an ecological disaster, with pollution eventually covering more than 1,000 miles^2 of land. An estimated 580,000 birds and 5,500 otters are thought to have died in this particular spill.

Generally speaking, in addition to already-endangered birds, marine mammals such as seals, porpoises and whales are also at risk, and crustaceans and mollusks are affected by oil sediment on the seabed. Long-term effects on the food chain and breeding patterns have yet to be evaluated fully.

The loss of some 92,400 tons from the tanker *Braer* off the Shetland Islands in January 1993, although relatively small, also seriously affected a number of species, and estimates suggest that losses of shags, great northern divers and black guillemots could reach over 1 percent of their total global populations.

(Artwork: Peter Harper)

IRAQ **IRAN** **KUWAIT** **SAUDI ARABIA** **UAE** **OMAN** PERSIAN GULF

Record spillage

An estimated total of 900,000 tons were deliberately released in January 1991 during the Gulf War. The oil, which was up to 17 in thick in places, spread over some 400 miles of coastline.

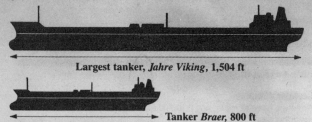

Largest tanker, *Jahre Viking*, 1,504 ft

Tanker *Braer*, 800 ft

Container truck, 20 ft

Kuwait's sea of oil
(Photo: Gamma)

The tanker _Braer_
(Photo: Gamma)

Largest tanker spills

330,000 tons, _Atlantic Empress/Aegean Captain_ (collision, 1979), Caribbean

275,000 tons, _Castillo de Bellver_ (fire, 1983), South Africa

242,500 tons, _Amoco Cadiz_ (grounded, 1978), France

The Gulf aflame
(Photo: Rex Features)

Extent of spillage from _Braer_

ORKNEY ISLANDS

SCOTLAND

SHETLAND ISLANDS

TIMEPIECES

Most accurate The most accurate timekeeping device is a commercially available atomic clock manufactured by Hewlett-Packard of Palo Alto, CA, unveiled in December 1991. Designated the HP 5071A primary frequency standard with cesium II technology, the device, costing $54,000 and about the size of a desktop computer, is accurate to one second in 1.6 million years.

Mechanical The Olsen clock, completed for the Copenhagen Town Hall, Denmark in December 1955, has more than 14,000 units, and took 10 years to make; the mechanism functions in 570,000 different ways. The celestial pole motion will take 25,753 years to complete a full circle and the clock is accurate to 0.5 sec in 300 years.

CLOCKS

Earliest The earliest mechanical clock—that is, one with an escapement—was completed in China in A.D. 725 by Yi Xing and Liang Lingzan.

Largest clock, at Cathedral of St-Pierre, Beauvais, France. (Photo: Rex Features)

Oldest   The oldest surviving working clock in the world is the faceless clock, dating from 1386, or possibly earlier, at Salisbury Cathedral, in Great Britain, which was restored in 1956, having struck the hours for 498 years and ticked more than 500 million times. Earlier dates, ranging back to *c*. 1335, have been attributed to the weight-driven clock in Wells Cathedral, Great Britain, but only the iron frame is original.

A model of Giovanni de Dondi's heptagonal astronomical clock of 1348–64 was completed in 1962.

Largest   The world's most massive clock is the astronomical clock in the Cathedral of St-Pierre, Beauvais, France, constructed between 1865 and 1868. It contains 90,000 parts and is 40 ft high, 20 ft wide and 9 ft deep.

The Su Song clock, built in China at Kaifeng in 1088–92, had a 23-ton bronze armillary sphere for 1.7 tons of water. It was removed to Beijing in 1126 and was last known to be working in its 40 ft high tower in 1136.

The largest by volume is "Timepiece," measuring 51 x 51 x 51 ft, and suspended over five stories in the atrium of the International Square building in Washington, D.C. Computer-driven and accurate to within $1/100$th of a second, it weighs 2.3 tons. It is lit by 400 ft of neon tube lighting and requires 1,500 ft of cable and wiring. Twelve tubes at its base light up to tell the hour and the minute. The clock, designed by the sculptor John Safer, also indicates when the sun is at its zenith in 12 international cities.

The largest digital clock has dimensions of 44 x 44 x 28 ft and revolves on top of the Texas Building in Fort Worth, TX.

Highest   The highest two-sided clock in the world is at the top of the Morton International Building, Chicago, IL. It is 580 ft above street level.

Largest sundials   The world's largest sundial has a base diameter of 122 ft and is 120 ft high, with a gnomon (projecting arm) of the same length. Designed by

---

Pendulum   The world's longest pendulum measures 73 ft $9^{3}/4$ in and is part of the water-mill clock installed by the Hattori Tokeiten Co. in the Shinjuku NS building in Tokyo, Japan in 1983.

The longest pendulum in the United States is a reconstruction of Foucault's experiment. It swings from a cable 90 ft long and 23 ft above the heads of visitors to the Convention Center in Portland, OR and weighs 900 lb.

Largest clock face   The world's largest is that of the floral clock constructed at Matsubara Park, Toi, Japan on 18 Jun 1991. The clock face is 101 ft in diameter.

Astronomical clockface   The entirely mechanical Planetarium Copernicus, made by Ulysse Nardin of Switzerland, is the only wristwatch that indicates the time of day, the date, the phases of the moon, and the astronomical position of the sun, Earth, moon and the planets known in Copernicus' day. It also represents the Ptolemaic universe showing the astrological "aspects" at any given time.

Arata Isozaki of Tokyo, Japan, as the centerpiece of the Walt Disney World Co. headquarters in Orlando, FL, it was unveiled on 1 Mar 1991.

Most expensive   The highest price paid for any clock is $1,540,000 for a rare "Egyptian Revival" clock made by Cartier in 1927. Designed as an ancient Egyptian temple gate, with figures and hieroglyphs, the exotic clock is made of mother-of-pearl, coral and lapis lazuli. It was sold at Christie's, New York on 24 Apr 1991 to a private bidder.

WATCHES

Oldest   The oldest portable clockwork timekeeper is one of iron made by Peter Henlein in Nürnberg (Nuremberg), Germany, *c.* 1504.

The earliest wristwatches were those of Jacquet-Droz and Leschot of Geneva, Switzerland, dating from 1790.

Largest   The largest "watch" was a "Swatch" 531 ft 6 in long and 65 ft 7½ in in diameter, made by D. Tomas Feliu, which was set up on the site of the Bank of Bilbao building, Madrid, Spain from 7–12 Dec 1985.

Heaviest   The Eta "watch" on the Swiss pavilion at Expo 86 in Vancouver, British Columbia, Canada from May–October weighed 38.5 tons and stood 80 ft high.

Smallest   The smallest watches are those produced by Jaeger le Coultre of Switzerland. Equipped with a 15-jeweled movement, they measure just over ½ in long and ³/₁₆ in in width. Movement and case weigh under 0.25 oz.

Most expensive   The record price paid for a watch is Swiss Francs 4.95 million ($3,315,000) at Habsburg Feldman, Geneva, Switzerland on 9 Apr 1989 for a Patek Philippe "Calibre '89" with 1,728 separate parts.

TELEPHONES AND FACSIMILES

Telephones   It has been estimated by the International Telecommunication Union that there were approximately 537 million telephone subscribers in the world by the end of 1991. The country with the greatest number was the United States, with 130,110,000. Monaco has the most telephones per head of population, with 810 per 1,000. The greatest number of calls made in any country is in the United States, with 436.22 billion per year.

Largest   The world's largest operational telephone was exhibited at a festival on 16 Sep 1988 to celebrate the 80th birthday of Centraal Beheer, an insurance company based in Apeldoorn, the Netherlands. It was 8 ft 1 in high and 19 ft 11 in long, and weighed 3.8 tons. The handset, being 23 ft 5 in long, had to be lifted by crane in order for a call to be made.

Smallest   The smallest operational telephone was created by Zbigniew Róza-

> **Morse code**   The highest recorded speed at which anyone has received Morse code is 75.2 words per minute—over 17 symbols per second. This was achieved by Ted R. McElroy of the United States in a tournament at Asheville, NC on 2 Jul 1939.
>
>   The fastest speed recorded for hand-key transmitting is 175 symbols a minute by Harry A. Turner of the US Army Signal Corps at Camp Crowder, MO on 9 Nov 1942.
>
> **Smallest modem**   Modems are devices that allow electron signals to be transmitted over large distances by MOdulating the signal at one end, and DEModulating the signal back to its original form at the destination, hence the name. The smallest is the SRM-3A, which is 2.4 in long, 1.2 in wide, and 0.8 in high, and weighs 1.1 oz. It is currently manufactured by RAD Data Communications Ltd of Tel Aviv, Israel.

nek of Pleszew, Poland in September 1992 and measured $2^5/8$ x $^3/4$ x $1^1/8$ in. The smallest operational telephone in the United States was created by Jeff Smith of GTE Northwest, Everett, WA in 1988 and measured $4^1/8$ x $^3/4$ x $1^1/2$ in.

Busiest routes   The busiest international telephone route is between the USA and Canada. In 1991 there were some 3.3 billion minutes of two-way traffic between the two countries.

Busiest telephone exchange   GPT (GEC Plessey Telecommunications Ltd) demonstrated the ability of the "System X" telephone exchange to handle 1,558,000 calls in an hour through one exchange at Beeston, Great Britain on 27 Jun 1989.

Largest switchboard   The world's biggest switchboard is the one in the Pentagon, Washington, D.C., with 34,500 lines handling over 1 million calls per day through 200,000 miles of telephone cable.

Longest telephone cable   The world's longest submarine telephone cable is ANZCAN, which runs for 9,415 miles (8,181 nautical miles) from Port Alberni, Canada to Auckland, New Zealand and Sydney, Australia via Fiji and Norfolk Island. It cost some \$379 million and was inaugurated by Queen Elizabeth II in November 1984.

Optical fiber   The longest distance at which signals have been transmitted without repeaters is 156.3 miles, at the British Telecom (BT) research laboratory at Martlesham Heath, Great Britain in 1985. The laser wavelength was 1,525 nm and the rate was 35 megabits per sec. The longest unspliced ducted optical fiber link, with a capacity of 8,000 telephone lines, was installed by BT in February 1991. The optical fibers, made by Optical Fibres of Deeside, Great Britain, are 8.45 miles long.

Largest telecommunications company   The largest telecommunications company in the United States is AT&T of New York, NY. As of 31 Dec 1992, gross revenues were $64.9 billion and net earnings were $3.8 billion. The company has 312,700 employees and 2.42 million stockholders.

Fax Largest The largest facsimile (fax) machine is manufactured by Wide-Com Group Inc of Ontario, Canada. "WIDE-fax 36" is able to scan, print and copy documents up to 36 in in width.

Smallest The world's smallest fax machine is the Real Time Strategies Inc. hand-held device Pagentry, which combines various functions including the transmission of messages to facsimile machines. It measures just 3 x 5 x 3/4 in and weighs 5 oz.

TELESCOPES

Earliest It is not known for certain when the first telescopes were made. Some of the refractive properties of lenses were certainly known in ancient times, and spectacles were in use in the 13th century. Roger Bacon (*c.* 1214–92) in England wrote about lenses, while Witelo (Poland; *c.* 1230–75) and John Pecham (England; *c.* 1230–92) covered both lenses and mirrors in detail.

Although claims for the telescope's invention have been made for Bacon, Leonardo da Vinci (1452–1519) and Girolamo Frascatoro (1473–1553), in October 1608 three Dutch spectacle-makers stated that they had each invented the instrument and produced refracting telescopes. Credit is usually given to one of these, Hans Lippershey (*c.* 1570–1619), but Galileo (1564–1642) brought the invention to the notice of the scientific world, first constructing and using telescopes in 1609.

However, recent examinations of evidence for the claims by Thomas Digges (*c.* 1547–95) that his father Leonard Digges (*c.* 1520–59) had invented both a refractor and, it seems, a reflector as well, strongly indicates that a refractor at least existed in Elizabethan times. Thomas Digges described in 1571 what seems to be a reflecting telescope, although the first detailed design known is that of Marin Mersenne (1588–1648). The first successful reflector to be made was that by Isaac Newton (1642–1727), constructed in 1668 or 1669. He presented it, or a copy of it, to the Royal Society in 1671.

Largest telescope The Keck telescope on Mauna Kea, HI, recently completed, has a 394 in mirror, made up of 36 segments fitted together to produce the correct curve. Each segment is 72 in in aperture. An active support system holds each segment in place, and ensures that the images produced are brought to the same focus. The first image of the spiral galaxy NGC 1232 was obtained on 24 Nov 1990, when nine of the segments were in place. A twin Keck telescope is to be set up close to the first. When completed, Keck I and Keck II will be able to work together as an interferometer. Theoretically they would be able to see a car's headlights separately from a distance of 15,500 miles.

Largest reflector The largest single-mirror telescope now in use is the 19 ft 8 in reflector sited on Mount Semirodriki, near Zelenchukskaya in the Caucasus Mountains, Russia, at an altitude of 6,830 ft, completed in 1976. It has never come up to expectations, partly because it is not set up on a really good observing site. The largest satisfactory single-mirror telescope is the 200 in Hale reflector at Mount Palomar, CA. Though the Hale was completed in 1948, it is now much more efficient than it was, as it is used with electronic devices that are more sensitive than photographic plates. The CCD (Charged-Coupled Device) increases the sensitivity by a factor of around 100.

Metal-mirror This 72 in reflector was made by the third Earl of Rosse, and set up at Birr Castle, Ireland in 1845. The mirror was of speculum metal (an alloy of copper and tin). With it, Lord Rosse discovered the spiral forms of the galaxies. It was last used in 1909.

Largest planned The largest telescope of the century should be the VLT (Very Large Telescope) being planned by the European Southern Observatory. It will consist of four 26 ft 3 in telescopes working together, providing a light-grasp equal to a single 52 ft 6 in mirror. The chosen site is Paranal in northern Chile, well to the north of the La Silla Observatory in the Atacama Desert of northern Chile (see First telescope to use active optics). It is hoped to have the first units working by 1995, and the complete telescope by 2000.

Multiple-mirror The MMT (Multiple-Mirror Telescope) at the Whipple Observatory at Mount Hopkins, AZ uses six 72 in mirrors together, giving a light-grasp equal to a single 176 in mirror. There are, however, considerable operational problems, and it is now planned to replace the six separate mirrors with a 256 in single circular mirror in July 1995. Its proposed name is Mono Mirror Telescope, thus retaining the MMT.

Infrared The largest infrared reflector in the world is the UKIRT (United Kingdom Infrared Telescope) on Mauna Kea, HI with a 147 in mirror. It is so good that it can be used for visual work as well as infrared.

Solar The McMath solar telescope at Kitt Peak, AZ has a 6 ft 11 in primary mirror; the light is sent to it via a 32° inclined tunnel from a coelostat (rotatable mirror) at the top end. Extensive modifications to it are now being planned.

Southern The largest southern hemisphere telescope is the 157⁷/₈ in reflector at Cerro Tololo in the Atacama Desert, northern Chile. The Anglo-Australian Telescope (AAT) at Siding Spring in New South Wales has a 153¹/₈ in mirror.

Submillimeter The James Clark Maxwell telescope on Mauna Kea, HI has a 49 ft 3 in paraboloid primary, and is used for studies of the submillimeter part of the electromagnetic spectrum (0.01–0.03 in). It does not produce a visual image.

Largest refractor A 62 ft long 40 in refractor completed in 1897 is situated at the Yerkes Observatory, Williams Bay, WI and belongs to the University of Chicago, IL. Although nearly 100 years old, it is still in full use on clear nights. A larger refractor measuring 59 in was built in France and shown at the Paris Exhibition in 1900. However, it was a failure and was never used for scientific work.

Largest radio dish   Radio waves from the Milky Way galaxy were first detected by Karl Jansky of Bell Telephone Laboratories, Holmdel, NJ in 1931 when he was investigating static with an improvised 100 ft aerial. The only radio telescope built for that purpose before the outbreak of the war in 1939 was made by an amateur, Grote Reber, who detected radio emissions from the sun. The diameter of the dish was 31 ft 2 in.

The pioneer large "dish" was the 250 ft telescope at Jodrell Bank, Great Britain, now known as the Lovell Telescope, completed in 1957. It is part of the MERLIN network, which includes other dishes in various parts of Britain.

The world's largest radio telescope is the partially-steerable ionospheric assembly built over the natural bowl at Arecibo, Puerto Rico, completed in November 1963 at a cost of $9.3 million. The reflector dish is 1,000 ft in diameter, 167 ft deep and covers 18 1/2 acres suspended 426 ft under a 600-ton triangular platform. Its sensitivity was raised by a factor of 1,000 and its range to the edge of the observable Universe at some 15 billion light years by the fitting of aluminum plates at a cost of $8.8 million. It was rededicated on 16 Nov 1974.

The world's largest fully steerable dish is the 328-ft-diameter, 3,360-ton assembly at the Max Planck Institute for Radio Astronomy of Bonn in the Effelsberger Valley, Germany; it was completed in 1971.

Largest radio installation   The largest radio installation is the Australia Telescope, which includes dishes at Parkes (210 ft in diameter), Siding Spring (72 ft) and Culgoora (also 72 ft). There are also links with tracking stations at Usuada and Kashima, Japan, and with the TDRS (Tracking and Data Relay Satellite), which is in a geosynchronous orbit. This is equivalent to a radio telescope with an effective diameter of 2.16 Earth diameters (17,102 miles).

The VLA (Very Large Array) of the US National Science Foundation is Y-shaped, with each arm 13 miles long and with 27 mobile antennae (each of 82 ft diameter) on rails. It is 50 miles west of Socorro in the Plains of San Augustin, NM. It was completed on 10 Oct 1980.

Planetaria   The ancestor of the modern planetarium is the rotatable Gottorp Globe, built by Andreas Busch in Denmark about 1660. It was 34 ft 7 in in circumference and is now preserved in St Petersburg, Russia. The stars were painted on the inside. The first modern planetarium was opened in 1923 in Jena, Germany; it was designed by Walther Bauersfelt of the Carl Zeiss company.

The world's largest planetarium is in Miyazaki, Japan, and was completed on 30 Jun 1987. The dome has a diameter of 88 ft 7 in.

United States   The Reuben H. Fleet Space Theater & Science Center in San Diego, CA and The Ethyl Universe Planetarium & Space Theater in Richmond, VA both have dome diameters of 75 1/2 ft.

The American Museum–Hayden Planetarium, New York City has a dome diameter of 75 ft 2 in, but has the largest seating capacity of any planetarium in the United States, with 650 seats.

The Adler Planetarium in Chicago, IL, which opened on 12 May 1930, is the oldest planetarium in the United States. Its dome is 68 ft in diameter and it seats 450 people.

**LARGEST RADIO
INSTALLATION**
Parkes radio telescope—
part of the largest radio
installation. (Photo:
Science Photo Library)

First telescope to use active optics Active optics involves automatic correction of the mirror curve as the telescope is moved around. It gives a great increase in resolution. The first major telescope to use active optics was the New Technology Telescope (NTT) at La Silla in the Atacama Desert of northern Chile, the observing site of the ESO (European Southern Observatory). The NTT, like all modern telescopes, has an altazimuth mount, and is probably the most effective ground-based telescope in use in the world today. It will shortly incorporate adaptive optics, which involves compensating the shape of the mirror for minor short-term variations in the atmosphere.

Observatory Oldest The oldest observatory building extant is the "Tower of the Winds" used by Andronichus of Cyrrhus in Athens, Greece *c.* 100 B.C., and equipped with sundials and clepsydra (water clock).

Highest The high-altitude observatory at Denver, CO is at 14,100 ft and was opened in 1973. The main instrument is a 24 in reflector. It is slightly higher than the observatory at the summit of Mauna Kea in Hawaii at 13,760 ft.

Lowest The lowest "observatory" is at Homestake Mine, SD, where the "telescope" is a tank of cleaning fluid (perchloroethylene), which contains chlorine, and can trap neutrinos from the sun. The installation is 1.1 miles below ground level, in the shaft of a gold mine; the detector has to be at this depth, as otherwise the experiments would be confused by cosmic rays. The Homestake Observatory has been operating since 1964 and has provided results of tremendous value.

Largest Schmidt telescope   A Schmidt telescope uses a spherical mirror with a correcting plate and can cover a very wide field with a single exposure. The largest is the 6 ft 6 in instrument at the Karl Schwarzschild Observatory at Tautenberg, Germany. It has a clear aperture of 52³/₄ in with a 78³/₄ in mirror, focal length 13 ft. It was brought into use in 1960.

Space telescope Largest   The largest is the $1.55 billion NASA Edwin P. Hubble Space Telescope of 12 tons and 43 ft in overall length with a 94¹/₂ in reflector. It was placed in orbit at 381 miles altitude aboard a US space shuttle on 24 Apr 1990. When it had been launched, it was found to have a defective mirror, because of a mistake in the original construction, leading to spherical aberration. A repair mission is to go up in December 1993 with the aim of putting in compensatory equipment to allow for the fault in the main mirror. However, despite the faulty optics, the telescope can still outperform any ground-based telescope in some areas of astronomy.

ROCKETRY

Earliest uses   War rockets, propelled by gunpowder (charcoal-saltpeter sulfur), were described by Zeng Gongliang of China in 1042. This early form of rocket became known in Europe by 1258.

The first launching of a liquid-fueled rocket (patented 14 Jul 1914) was by Dr Robert Hutchings Goddard (USA; 1882–1945), at Auburn, MA, on 16 Mar 1926, when his rocket reached an altitude of 41 ft and traveled a distance of 184 ft.

The earliest Soviet rocket was the semiliquid-fueled GIRD-R1 (referred to as object 09), begun in 1931 and tested on 17 Aug 1933. The first fully liquid-fueled rocket, GIRD-X, was launched on 25 Nov 1933.

Highest velocity   The first space vehicle to achieve the Third Cosmic

---

Most powerful rocket engine   The most powerful rocket engine was built in the former USSR by Scientific Industrial Corporation of Energetic Engineering in 1980. The engine has a thrust of 900 tons in open space and a thrust of 830 tons at the Earth's surface. The RD-170 has a turbopump of 190 MW and burns liquid oxygen and kerosene.

Lunar records   The first direct hit on the moon was achieved at 2 min 24 sec after midnight (Moscow time) on 14 Sep 1959, by the Soviet space probe *Lunar II*, near the *Mare Serenitatis*. The first photographic images of the hidden side of the moon were collected by the Soviet *Lunar III* from 6:30 A.M. on 7 Oct 1959 from a range of up to 43,750 miles, and transmitted to the Earth from a distance of 292,000 miles.

PROGRESSIVE ROCKET ALTITUDE RECORDS

Height (miles)	Rocket	Place	Launch Date
0.71	A 3 in rocket	London, Great Britain	April 1750
1.25	Reinhold Tiling[1] (Germany) solid fuel rocket	Osnabruck, Germany	April 1931
1.9	"07" with liquid fuel engine "02" (USSR)	Nakhabino, Moscow region, USSR (now Russia)	16 Jul 1935
52.46	A-4 rocket (Germany)[2]	Peenemünde, Germany	3 Oct 1942
c. 85	A-4 rocket (Germany)	Heidelager, Poland	early 1944
118	A-4 rocket (Germany)	Heidelager, Poland	mid 1944
244	V2/WAC Corporal (2-stage) Bumper No. 5 (USA)[3]	White Sands, NM	24 Feb 1949
682	Jupiter C (USA)	Cape Canaveral, FL	20 Sep 1956
>800	ICBM test flight R-7 (USSR)	Tyuratam, USSR (now Kazakhstan)	21 Aug 1957
>2,700	Farside No. 5 (4-stage; USA)	Eniwetok Atoll	20 Oct 1957
70,700	Pioneer 1-B Lunar Probe (USA)	Cape Canaveral, FL	11 Oct 1958
215,300,000*	Luna 1 or Mechtá (USSR)	Tyuratam, USSR (now Kazakhstan)	2 Jan 1959
242,000,000*	Mars 1 (USSR)	Tyuratam, USSR (now Kazakhstan)	1 Nov 1962
3,666,000,000[4]	Pioneer 10 (USA)	Kennedy Space Center, Cape Canaveral, FL	2 Mar 1972

* Apogee in solar orbit.

[1] There is some evidence that Tiling may shortly after have reached 5.9 miles with a solid fuel rocket at Wangerooge, East Friesian Islands, Germany.

[2] The A4 was later referred to as the V2 rocket, an acronym for second revenge weapon (vergeltungswaffe) following upon the V1 "flying bomb."

[3] The V2/WAC height may have been exceeded during the period 1950–56 before the Jupiter C flight, as the Soviets reported in 1954 that a rocket had reached 240 miles at an unspecified date.

[4] Distance on crossing Pluto's orbit on 17 Oct 1986. Pioneer II, Voyager I and Voyager 2 are also leaving the solar system.

velocity—sufficient to break out of the solar system—was *Pioneer 10*. The Atlas SLV-3C launcher with a modified Centaur D second stage and a Thiokol TE-364-4 third stage left the Earth at an unprecedented 32,114 mph on 2 Mar 1972. However, the fastest escape velocity from Earth was 34,134 mph, achieved by the ESA *Ulysses* spacecraft, powered by an IUS–PAM upper stage after deployment from the Space Shuttle *Discovery* on 7 Oct 1990, en route to a solar polar orbit via Jupiter.

Mariner 10 reached a recorded solar system speed of 131,954 mph as it passed Mercury in September 1974, but the fastest speed of approximately 158,000 mph is recorded by the NASA-German *Helios B* solar probe each time it reaches the perihelion of its solar orbit. Sister spaceship *Helios A* will also exceed *Mariner 10*'s velocity. (See Closest approach to the sun by a rocket.)

Most powerful rocket   The NI booster of the former USSR, first launched from the Baikonur Cosmodrome at Tyuratam, Kazakhstan on 21 Feb 1969, had a thrust of 5,200 tons but exploded at takeoff + 70 secs. Three other launch attempts also failed. Its current booster, *Energya*, first launched on 15 May 1987 from the Baikonur Cosmodrome, when fully loaded weighed 2,800 tons and had a thrust of 3,900 tons. It was capable of placing 116 tons into low Earth orbit and measured 192 ft 7 in tall with a maximum diameter of 52 ft 6 in. It comprised a core stage powered by four liquid oxygen and hydrogen engines—the first cryogenic units flown by the Russians. Four strap-on boosters powered by single RD-170 engines burning liquid oxygen and kerosene were used.

Closest approach to the sun by a rocket   The research spacecraft *Helios B* approached within 27 million miles of the sun, carrying both US and German instrumentation, on 16 Apr 1976. (See Highest velocity.)

Remotest man-made object   *Pioneer 10*, launched from Cape Canaveral, FL, crossed the mean orbit of Pluto on 17 Oct 1986, being then at a distance of 3.67 billion miles from Earth. In A.D. 34,593 it will make its nearest approach to the star *Ross 248*, 10.3 light years distant. *Voyager 1*, traveling faster, will have surpassed *Pioneer 10* in remoteness from the Earth by the end of the century. *Pioneer 11* and *Voyager 2* are also leaving the solar system.

SPACE FLIGHT

The physical laws controlling the flight of artificial satellites were first postulated by Sir Isaac Newton (1642–1727) in his *Philosophiae Naturalis Principia Mathematica* ("Mathematical Principles of Natural Philosophy"), begun in March 1686 and first published in July 1687.

The first artificial satellite was successfully put into orbit by an intercontinental ballistic missile from the Baikonur Cosmodrome at Tyuratam, Kazakhstan 170 miles east of the Aral Sea and 155 miles south of the town of Baikonur on the night of 4 Oct 1957. It reached an altitude of between 142 miles (perigee or nearest point to Earth) and 588 miles (apogee or furthest point from Earth) and a velocity of more than 17,750 mph. This spherical satellite, called *Sputnik 1* ("Fellow Traveler"), was officially designated "Satellite 1957 Alpha 2." It weighed 184.3 lb, with a diameter of 22³/4 in; its lifetime is believed to have been 92 days, ending on 4 Jan 1958. The 95 ft 8 in SL–1 launcher was designed under the direction of former Gulag prisoner Dr Sergey Pavlovich Korolyov (1907–66).

Earliest manned satellite The earliest manned spaceflight ratified by the world governing body, the *Fédération Aéronautique Internationale* (FAI, founded 1905), was by Cosmonaut Flight Major (later Col.) Yuri Alekseyevich Gagarin (1934–68) in *Vostok 1* on 12 Apr 1961. Details filed showed takeoff to be from the Baikonur Cosmodrome, Kazakhstan at 6:07 A.M. GMT and the landing near Smelovka, near Engels, in the Saratov region of Russia, 108 minutes later. Col. Gagarin landed separately from his spacecraft, by parachute, after ejecting as planned, as did all the *Vostok* pilots.

The maximum altitude during *Vostok 1*'s 25,394¹/2 mile flight was listed at 203 miles, with a maximum speed of 17,560 mph. Col. Gagarin, invested a Hero of the Soviet Union and awarded the Order of Lenin and the Gold Star Medal, was killed in a jet plane crash near Moscow on 27 Mar 1968.

There were 158 manned spaceflights to 6 Apr 1993, of which 83 were American and 75 Soviet or former Soviet Union, including three Russian. If the *Challenger 51L* spaceflight is included, then the US has had 84 manned spaceflights.

United States On 5 May 1961, aboard *Mercury 3*, Cdr. Alan B. Shepard, Jr. (USN) became the first American to pilot a spaceflight. The suborbital flight, which lasted 15 min 28 sec, covered 302 miles and reached an altitude of 116.5 miles.

John H. Glenn was the first American to orbit the Earth. His flight aboard *Mercury 6* (*Friendship 7*) was launched at 9:47 A.M. EST on 20 Feb 1962 and splashed down into the Atlantic Ocean at 2:43 P.M. EST that same day. Glenn completed three orbits of the Earth and traveled approximately 81,000 miles.

First woman in space The first woman to orbit the Earth was Junior Lt (now Lt-Col. Eng) Valentina Vladimirovna Tereshkova (b. 6 Mar 1937), who was launched in *Vostok 6* from the Baikonur Cosmodrome, Kazakhstan at 9:30 A.M. GMT on 16 Jun 1963, and landed at 8:16 A.M. on 19 June, after a flight of 2 days 22 hr 50 min, during which she completed over 48 orbits (1,225,000 miles) and passed momentarily within three miles of *Vostok 5*. As of 6 Apr 1993 a total of 21 women had flown in space—17 Americans, two Soviets, one from Great Britain and one Canadian—out of the total of 286 people who have been into space.

United States The first American woman in space was Sally Ride, who was launched in the US space shuttle *Challenger STS–7* on 18 Jun 1983, and returned to Earth on 24 June.

Astronauts *Oldest* The oldest astronaut of the 286 people in space (to 6 Apr 1993) was Vance DeVoe Brand (USA; b. 9 May 1931), age 59, while on the space shuttle mission aboard the *Columbia STS 35*, 2–10 Dec 1990. The oldest woman was Shannon Lucid (USA), age 48 years, on space shuttle mission *Discovery STS 43* in July 1991. Lucid is also the first woman to make three spaceflights and was scheduled to make a fourth flight in July 1993.

Youngest The youngest was Major (later Lt-Gen.) Gherman Stepanovich

Titov (b. 11 Sep 1935), who was 25 years 329 days when launched in *Vostok 2* on 6 Aug 1961. The youngest woman in space was Valentina Tereshkova, 26. (See First woman in space.)

The youngest American astronaut was astrophysicist Tamara Jernigan, who on 5 Jun 1991, aged 32 years, was launched aboard *STS 40 Columbia*.

Longest and shortest manned spaceflight The longest manned flight was by Col. Vladimir Georgeyevich Titov (b. 1 Jan 1947) and Flight Engineer Musa Khiramanovich Manarov (b. 22 Mar 1951), who were launched to the *Mir* space station aboard *Soyuz TM4* on 21 Dec 1987, and landed, in *Soyuz TM6* (with French spationaut Jean-Loup Chretien), at a secondary recovery site near Dzhezkazgan, Kazakhstan, on 21 Dec 1988, after a spaceflight lasting 365 days 22 hr 39 min 47 sec. The shortest manned flight was made by Cdr Alan B. Shepard, Jr. (USN; b. 18 Nov 1923) aboard *Mercury Redstone 3* on 5 May 1961. His suborbital mission lasted 15 min 28 sec.

Although not spaceflights, the space shuttle *Challenger* flew for 73 sec before being destroyed on 28 Jan 1986, while the launch escape system of *Soyuz* T10A took Vladimir Titov and Gennady Strekalov on an 18 *g* ride lasting about 20 sec after the *Soyuz* booster caught fire and eventually exploded before lift-off on 27 Sep 1983.

The most experienced space traveler is the Soviet (now Azerbaijani) flight engineer Musa Manarov, who clocked 541 days 31 min 10 sec on two space flights in 1987–88 and 1990–91.

United States Gerald P. Carr, Edward G. Gibson and William R. Pogue manned the longest American flight, aboard *Skylab 4*, which was launched 16 Nov 1973 and splashed down 8 Feb 1974, after 84 day 1 hr 15 min 31 sec in space. They are the most experienced US astronauts. The most experienced space shuttle flier is Daniel Brandenstein, with 32 days 22 hr 10 min.

Most journeys Capt. John Watts Young (USN ret.; b. 24 Sep 1930) completed his sixth spaceflight on 8 Dec 1983, when he relinquished command of *Columbia STS 9*/*Spacelab* after a space career of 34 days 19 hr 41 min 53 sec. Young flew *Gemini 3, Gemini 10, Apollo 10, Apollo 16, STS 1* and *STS 9*. The greatest number of flights by a Soviet cosmonaut is five, by Vladimir Dzhanibekov (between 1978 and 1985).

The most by a woman is three, by Shannon Lucid (USA) (*STS 419, 31* and *45*), Kathryn Sullivan (USA) (*STS 419, 31* and *45*) and Bonnie Dunbar (USA) (*STS 61A, 32* and *50*). Dunbar is also the woman with the most space experience, with 31 days 17 hr 15 min. Lucid was scheduled to make a fourth flight in 1993.

Largest crew The largest crew on a single space mission was eight. This included one woman and was launched on space shuttle *Challenger 9 STS 61A*, the 22nd shuttle mission, on 30 Oct 1985, carrying the German *Spacelab D1* laboratory. The mission, commanded by Henry Warren "Hank" Hartsfield, lasted 7 days 44 min 51 sec. The greatest number of women in a space crew is three (of seven) on *Columbia STS 40* in June 1991.

Most in space The greatest number of people in space at any one time has been 12, on three occasions. Seven Americans were aboard the space shuttle *Columbia STS 35*; two Soviet cosmonauts were aboard the *Mir* space station; and two cosmonauts and one Japanese journalist were aboard *Soyuz TM11* on 2–10 Dec 1990.

On 23–24 Mar 1992, six Americans and one Belgian were on space shuttle *Atlantis*, two CIS cosmonauts were on *Mir*, and two CIS cosmonauts and a German were on *Soyuz TM14*. Most recently, on 31 Jul 1992, four CIS cosmonauts and one Frenchman were aboard *Mir* at the same time as five US astronauts, one Swiss and one Italian were on *STS46 Atlantis*.

Lunar conquest   Neil Alden Armstrong (b. 5 Aug 1930), command pilot of the *Apollo 11* mission, became the first human to set foot on the moon, on the Sea of Tranquility, at 02:56 and 15 sec GMT on 21 Jul 1969. He was followed out of the lunar module *Eagle* by Col. Edwin Eugene "Buzz" Aldrin, Jr. (USAF; b. 20 Jan 1930) while the command module *Columbia*, piloted by Lt Col. Michael Collins (USAF; b. 31 Oct 1930), orbited above.

Eagle landed at 20:17 and 42 sec GMT on 20 July and lifted off at 17:54 GMT on 21 July, after a stay of 21 hr 36 min. *Apollo 11* had blasted off from Cape Canaveral, FL at 13:32 GMT on 16 July and was a culmination of the US space program up to that point. At its peak, the program employed 376,600 people and attained in 1966–67 a record budget of $5.9 billion.

There were six lunar landings altogether, and 12 people made a total of 14 EVAs on the moon totaling 79 hr 35 min between July 1969 and December 1972.

Most isolated human being   The farthest any human has been removed from his nearest living fellow human is 2,233.2 miles, in the case of the command module pilot Alred M. Worden on the US *Apollo 15* lunar mission of 30 Jul–1 Aug 1971, while David Scott and James Irwin (1930–91) were at Hadley Base exploring the surface.

Suit   EVA suits for extravehicular activity, worn by space shuttle crews since 1982, have a unit cost of $3.4 million.

First reusable spacecraft   The US space shuttle *Columbia STS 1*, the world's first reusable spacecraft, lifted off from its launch pad at Cape Canaveral, FL, on 12 Apr 1981 at 7 A.M. EST. After 36 orbits and 54 hours in space, the craft glided to a perfect landing on a dry lake bed at Edwards Air Force Base in the Mojave Desert, CA on 14 April at 1:21 P.M. EST. The craft was manned by John W. Young (USN) and Robert L. Crippen. As of 9 Jun 1993 there have been 55 space shuttle flights using five shuttle craft: *Columbia*, *Challenger*, *Discovery*, *Atlantis* and *Endeavor*. *Discovery* has flown the most times, with 13 missions.

Lunar conquest   A total of 12 men have walked on the moon. They are:

   Neil Armstrong and Edwin Aldrin, *Apollo 11*, July 1969
   Charles Conrad and Alan Bean, *Apollo 12*, November 1969
   Alan Shepard and Edgar Mitchell, *Apollo 14*, February 1971
   David Scott and James Irwin, *Apollo 15*, July 1971
   John Young and Charles Duke, *Apollo 16*, April 1972
   Eugene Cernan and Harrison "Jack" Schmitt, *Apollo 17*, December 1972

Race for Space

How do the USSR and USA compare in the so-called space race? The USSR's manned missions have actually totaled more than five times longer in space than those of the USA. Russia, in spite of having been a separate sovereign country for only a couple of years, comes third. Most people know that astronauts and cosmonauts from other countries have sometimes accompanied Soviets or Americans on flights, but which country comes in fourth in the list? The answer is in fact France, closely followed by Germany (excluding the former German Democratic Republic). These positions are determined by the number of days spent in space on missions by the leading nations. If the number of days spent in space by the individual astronauts and cosmonauts were taken into consideration instead, the top five countries would still be in the same order. The information is correct as of 31 Mar 1993, when the Soyuz TM 16 mission was in flight.

Russian cosmonaut Sergy Krikalyov made worldwide news in early 1992 when budget cuts and political wrangling prevented him from landing on schedule. He had gone up as a Soviet cosmonaut, but while he was in space his country broke up and the Soviet space program effectively became the Russian space program. For the first 221 days of his mission he was in effect a Soviet and for the remaining 91 days a Russian—the totals in the illustrations include these two figures for the respective countries.

In addition to France and Germany many other countries have also had astronauts and cosmonauts on Soviet, American or Russian missions. In order of the time spent in space these are:

Countries	Days	Countries	Days
Canada	26	United Kingdom	7
Japan	15	German Democratic	
Bulgaria	11	Republic	7
Belgium	8	Hungary	7
Afghanistan	8	Cuba	7
Italy	7	Mongolia	7
Switzerland	7	Vietnam	7
Syria	7	Romania	7
Czechoslovakia	7	Saudi Arabia	7
Austria	7	Netherlands	7
Poland	7	Mexico	6
India	7		

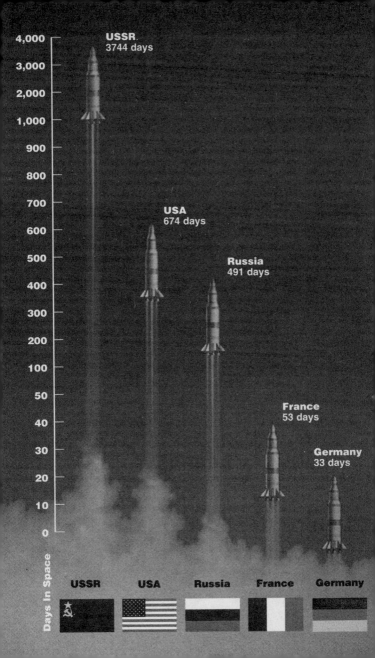

Laika, the first living creature to orbit around the earth. A number of animals had been launched into the atmosphere previously, although without going into orbit. Laika was sent up in the Soviet Sputnik 2 on 3 Nov 1957 but died during the trip.
(Photo: Science Photo Library)

Yuri Gagarin, who completed the first successful manned space mission in Vostok 1 on 12 April 1961, together with **Valentina Tereshkova**, the first woman in space, in Vostok 6 on 16 Jun 1963.
(Photo: Science Photo Library)

John Young, who holds the record for greatest number of space flights. He has been on six missions, the first in 1965 and the last in 1983. In 1972 he was on the Apollo 16 mission and became the ninth man to walk on the moon.
(Photo: Rex Features)

Longest spacewalk The longest spacewalk ever made was 8 hr 29 min, by Pierre Thuot, Rick Hieb and Tom Akers of *STS 49 Endeavor* on 13 May 1992.

The longest recorded spacewalk in Earth orbit was made outside space shuttle *Discovery STS 511* in September 1985, lasting 7 hr 20 min, by James van Hoften and Bill Fisher. *Soyuz TM9's* Anatoly Solovyov and Aleksandr Balandin made a 7 hr 16 min EVA outside the *Mir* space station on 1 Jul 1990, which was the longest by Soviet cosmonauts.

Lt-Col. (now Maj. Gen.) Aleksey Arkhipovich Leonov (b. 20 May 1934), from *Voskhod 2*, was the first person to engage in EVA ("extravehicular activity"), on 18 Mar 1965.

Capt. Bruce McCandless II (USN; b. 8 Jun 1937), from the space shuttle *Challenger*, was the first to engage in untethered EVA, at an altitude of 164 miles above Hawaii, on 7 Feb 1984. His MMU (Manned Maneuvering Unit) back-pack cost $15 million to develop.

The first woman to perform an EVA was Svetlana Savitskaya (b. 8 Aug 1948) from *Soyuz T12/Salyut 7* on 25 Jul 1984. The greatest number of spacewalks is eight, by Soviet cosmonauts Leonid Kizim and Vladimir Solovyov during two missions in 1984 and 1986.

The first American to "walk" in space was Edward H. White II (1930–67), from the spacecraft *Gemini 4* on 3 Jun 1965. Between 3–7 June, White and James McDivitt completed 62 circuits in orbit around the Earth, and it was during the third orbit that White left the capsule and, using a 25-ft lifeline, maneuvered for 20 minutes in space. The greatest number of spacewalks by an American is five, by Dave Scott during *Apollo* missions 9 and 15 in 1969 and 1971.

The first American woman to "walk" in space was Kathryn D. Sullivan, on 11 Oct 1984, as part of the space shuttle *Challenger* mission 5–13 Oct 1984. The longest spacewalk by a woman lasted 7 hr 49 min, by Kathryn Thornton (USA) of *STS 49 Endeavor* on 14 May 1992.

Space fatalities The greatest published number to perish in any of the 159 attempted spaceflights to 6 Apr 1993 is seven (five men and two women) aboard the *Challenger 51L* on 28 Jan 1986, when an explosion occurred 73 sec after liftoff, at a height of 47,000 ft. *Challenger* broke apart under extreme aerodynamic overpressure.

Four people, all Soviet, have been killed during actual spaceflight—Vladimir Komarov on 24 Apr 1967 on *Soyuz 1*, which crashed on landing; and the un-spacesuited Georgi Dobrovolsky, Viktor Patsayev and Vladislav Volkov, who died when their *Soyuz 11* spacecraft depressurized during reentry on 29 Jun 1971.

Altitude The greatest altitude attained by humans was when the crew of the *Apollo 13* were at apocynthion (i.e., their furthest point) 158 miles above the lunar surface, and 248,655 miles above the Earth's surface, at 1:21 A.M. EST on 14 Apr 1970. The crew were Capt. James Arthur Lovell, Jr. (USN; b. 25 Mar 1928), Fred Wallace Haise, Jr. (b. 14 Nov 1933) and John L. Swigert (1931–82).

The greatest altitude attained by an American woman is 330 miles, by astronaut Kathryn D. Sullivan (b. 3 Oct 1951) during her flight in space shuttle *Discovery* on 24 Apr 1990.

Speed The fastest speed at which humans have traveled is 24,791 mph when the command module of *Apollo 10*, carrying Col. (now Brig. Gen.) Thomas Patten Stafford (USAF; b. 17 Sep 1930), Cdr Eugene Andrew Cernan (USN;

b. 14 Mar 1934) and Cdr (now Capt.) John Watts Young (USN; b. 24 Sep 1930), reached this maximum value at the 75.7 mile altitude interface on its trans-Earth round-trip flight on 26 May 1969.

The fastest speed recorded by a woman is 17,864 mph, by Kathryn Sullivan at the start of reentry at the end of the *Discovery STS 31* shuttle mission on 29 Apr 1990.

The highest recorded by a Soviet space traveler was 17,470 mph, by Valentina Tereshkova of the USSR (see First woman in space) in *Vostok 6* on 16 Jun 1963, although because orbital injection of Soyuz spacecraft occurs at a marginally lower altitude, it is probable that Tereshkova's speed was exceeded twice by Svetlana Savitskaya aboard *Soyuz T7* and *T12* on 27 Aug 1982 and 28 Jul 1984, and also by Helen Sharman (Great Britain; b. 30 May 1963) aboard *Soyuz T12* on 18 May 1991.

First extraterrestrial vehicle   The first wheeled vehicle to land on the moon was the unmanned *Lunokhod I*, which began its Earth-controlled travels on 17 Nov 1970. It moved a total of 6.54 miles on gradients up to 30° in the Mare Imbrium and did not break down until 4 Oct 1971.

The lunar speed and distance record was set by the manned *Apollo 16* Rover, driven by John Young, at 11.2 mph downhill and 22.4 miles.

Heaviest and largest space objects   The heaviest object orbited is the Saturn V third stage of the Apollo 15 spacecraft, which, prior to translunar injection into parking orbit, weighed 310,000 lb. The 440 lb US RAE (Radio Astronomy Explorer) B, or *Explorer 49*, launched on 10 Jun 1973, was, however, larger, with antennae 1,500 ft from tip to tip.

Most expensive projects   The total cost of the US manned space program to the spring of 1993 has been estimated to be $80.8 billion. The first 15 years of the Soviet space program, from 1958 to September 1973, are estimated to have cost $45 billion. The aggregate cost of the NASA Shuttle program is $45.3 billion.

Duration record on the moon   The crew of *Apollo 17* collected a record 253 lb of rock and soil during their three EVAs of 22 hr 5 min. They were Capt. Eugene Cernan (see Speed) and Dr Harrison Hagen "Jack" Schmidt, who became the 12th man on the Moon. The crew were on the lunar surface for 74 hr 59 min during this longest of lunar missions, which took 12 days 13 hr 51 min on 7–19 Dec 1972.

BUILDINGS AND STRUCTURES

- **ORIGINS**
- **BUILDINGS FOR LIVING**
- **BUILDINGS FOR WORKING**
- **BUILDINGS FOR ENTERTAINMENT**
- **TOWERS AND MASTS**
- **BRIDGES**
- **CANALS**
- **DAMS**
- **TUNNELS**
- **SPECIALIZED STRUCTURES**

ORIGINS

The earliest-known human structure may be the footings of a windbreak. It is a rough circle of loosely piled lava blocks found on the lowest cultural level at the Lower Paleolithic site at Olduvai Gorge in Tanzania, revealed by Dr Mary Leakey in January 1960. The structure was associated with artifacts and bones on a work-floor, dating from *c.* 1,750,000 B.C.

The oldest freestanding structures in the world are now believed to be the megalithic temples at Mgarr and Skorba in Malta. With those at Ggantija in Gozo, they date from *c.* 3250 B.C., some 3½ centuries earlier than the earliest Egyptian pyramid. (See Specialized structures.)

United States   It was reported in March 1992 that archeologists have discovered the remains of a circular structure believed to be the oldest man-made structure in North America. Samples taken from the site confirmed it to be a Native American hunting camp in Medina County, near Akron, OH; it has been dated to 11,000 years old.

WOODEN STRUCTURES

Oldest   The oldest extant wooden buildings in the world are those comprising the Pagoda, Chumanar Gate and Temple of Horyu (Horyu-ji) at Nara, Japan, dating from *c.* A.D. 670 and completed in 715.

TALLEST SAND CASTLE The tallest sand castle, built only with hands, buckets and shovels, was made in 1991 at Harrison Hot Springs in Canada, and beat the record set at the same venue the previous year. (Photo: The Harrison Hot Springs and Sculpture Society)

BUILDINGS FOR LIVING

HABITATIONS

Earliest   The earliest evidence of a habitational structure yet discovered is that of 21 huts with hearths or pebble-lined pits and delimited by stake-holes found in October 1965 at the Terra Amata site in Nice, France, and thought to belong to the Acheulian culture of *c.* 400,000 years ago. Excavation in 1966 revealed one hut with palisaded walls with axes of 49 ft and 20 ft.

Northernmost   The Danish scientific station set up in 1952 in Pearyland, northern Greenland is over 900 miles north of the Arctic Circle and is manned every summer. The former USSR's drifting research station "North Pole 15" passed within 1¼ miles of the North Pole in December 1967.

Southernmost   The most southerly permanent human habitation is the United States' Amundsen–Scott South Polar Station, completed in 1957 and replaced in 1975.

CASTLES

Earliest   The castle at Gomdan in Yemen originally had 20 stories and dates from before A.D. 100.

Largest   The largest ancient castle in the world is Hradčany Castle, Prague, Czech Republic, originating in the 9th century. It is an oblong irregular polygon with an axis of 1,870 ft and an average transverse diameter of 420 ft for a surface area of 18 acres.
   The largest inhabited castle in the world is the royal residence of Windsor Castle at Windsor, Great Britain. It is primarily of 12th-century construction and is in the form of a waisted parallelogram measuring 1,890 × 540 ft.
   The total area of Dover Castle, Kent, Great Britain, however, covers 34 acres, with a width of 1,100 ft and a curtain wall of 1,800 ft, or if underground works are included, 2,300 ft.

Sand castles   The tallest sand castle on record, constructed only with hands, buckets and shovels, was 19 ft 6 in high and was made by Team Totally in Sand and Freddie and the Sandblasters at Harrison Hot Springs, British Columbia, Canada on 15 Oct 1991.
   The longest sand castle was 5.2 miles long, and was made by staff and pupils of Ellon Academy, near Aberdeen, Great Britain on 24 Mar 1988.

Largest Palace

LARGEST PALACE   The Forbidden City, Beijing, China across
the 98-acre expanse of Tiananmen Square (top), the Temple
of Heaven (bottom left); and a golden lion from within the City
(bottom right).   (Photos: Images Colour Library/Mike Langford)

PALACES

Largest   The Imperial Palace (Gugong) in the center of Beijing, China,
covers a rectangle 3,150 × 2,460 ft, an area of 178 acres. The outline survives from the construction of the third Ming emperor, Yongle (1402–24),
but due to constant reconstruction work most of the intramural buildings
are from the 18th century. These consist of five halls and 17 palaces.

The Palace of Versailles, 14 miles southwest of Paris, France, has a
façade 1,902 ft in length, with 375 windows. The building, completed in
1682 for Louis XIV (1643–1715), occupied over 30,000 workmen under
Jules Hardouin-Mansert (1646–1708).

Residential   The palace (Istana Nurul Iman) of HM the Sultan of Brunei
in the capital Bandar Seri Begawan, completed in January 1984 at a reported cost of $350 million, is the largest residence in the world, with

1,788 rooms and 257 lavatories. The underground garage accommodates the sultan's 110 cars.

Largest moat   From plans drawn by French sources it appears that those that surround the Imperial Palace in Beijing (see Largest palaces) measure 162 ft wide and have a total length of 10,800 ft. In all, the city's moats total 23½ miles.

HOUSING

According to the National Association of Realtors, as of 31 Dec 1992, the median price of existing homes sold in the 83 largest metropolitan areas in the United States is $104,200 and for new homes $125,000. The metropolitan area with the highest median price is Honolulu, HI, at $352,000.

Largest   The 250-room Biltmore House in Asheville, NC is owned by George and William Cecil, grandsons of George Washington Vanderbilt II (1862–1914). The house was built between 1890 and 1895 in an estate of 119,000 acres, at a cost of $4.4 million; it is now valued at $5.5 million, with 12,000 acres.

Most expensive   The most expensive private house ever built is the Hearst Ranch at San Simeon, CA. It was built from 1922–39 for William Randolph Hearst (1863–1951), at a total cost of more than $30 million. It has more than 100 rooms, a 104-ft-long heated swimming pool, an 83-ft-long assembly hall and a garage for 25 limousines. The house was maintained by 60 servants.

The highest price for any house on the global residential property market is £50 million ($87.5 million) asked in 1992 for the Casa Batlló in central Barcelona, Spain. It was built by José Batlló in 1887 and extensively remodeled by Antonio Gaudí (1852–1926).

Longest continuous home construction   Winchester House in San Jose, CA was under construction for 38 years. The original house was an eight-room farmhouse with separate barn on the 161-acre estate of Oliver Winchester, who did not invent the Winchester rifle, but owned its patent. Sarah Winchester, widowed in 1886, consulted a psychic in Boston, who told her that she alone could balance the ledger for those killed by Winchester firearms by never stopping construction of the estate.

Mrs. Winchester moved to California, where she transformed the farmhouse into a mansion, which now has 13 bathrooms, 52 skylights, 47 fireplaces, 10,000 windows, 40 staircases, 2,000 doorways and closets opening into blank walls, secret passageways, trapdoors, three $10,000 elevators and more. The constant remodeling of the house was intended to confuse the resident ghosts.

Largest nonpalatial residence   St Emmeram Castle, Regensburg, Germany, valued at more than $177 million, contains 517 rooms with a floor space of 231,000 ft². Only 95 rooms are personally used by the family of the late Prince Johannes von Thurn und Taxis.

Tallest apartment house   The 716-ft Metropolitan Tower on West 57th Street, New York City is 78 stories high; the upper 48 are residential.

The tallest purely residential apartment house is Lake Point Tower, Chicago, IL, which has 879 units consisting of 70 stories, standing 639 ft high.

HOTELS

Largest   The $290-million Excalibur Hotel/Casino, Las Vegas, NV, opened in April 1990, is built on a 117 acre site. It has 4,032 deluxe rooms and employs a staff of 4,000. Its facilities include seven theme restaurants and a total of 11 food outlets throughout the hotel and casino.

Most capacious   The Hotel Rossiya in Moscow, Russia opened in 1967 with 3,200 rooms and 5,300 beds, but because of its high proportion of dormitory accommodations, it is not on the international list of the largest hotels. The Izmailovo Hotel complex, consisting of five 32-story blocks, opened in July 1980 for the 22nd Olympic Games in Moscow. It was designed to accommodate 9,500 people in 5,000 rooms.

Hoteliers   With its acquisition of Holiday Inns North America in February 1991, Bass plc, Great Britain's largest brewing company, took ownership of the world's largest hotel chain. The company now owns, manages and franchises 1,645 hotels totaling 327,059 rooms in 52 countries. (See Business, World Brewers.)

United States   The largest hotel operator in the United States as of 31 Dec 1992, based on number of properties, was Best Western International of Phoenix, AZ, with 3,351. The largest hotel operator based on number of rooms was Holiday Inn Worldwide, which operates 328,244.

Largest lobby   The lobby at the Hyatt Regency, San Francisco, CA is 350 ft long and 160 ft wide, and at 170 ft is the height of a 17-story building.

Tallest   Measured from the street level of its main entrance to the top, the 73-story Westin Stamford in Raffles City, Singapore "topped out" in March

---

Camping out   The silent Indian *fakir* Mastram Bapu ("contented father") remained on the same spot by the roadside in the village of Chitra for 22 years from 1960–82.

Pole sitting   Modern records do not come close to that of St Simeon the Younger (*c.* A.D. 521–97), called Stylites, a monk who spent his last 45 years atop a stone pillar on the Hill of Wonders, near Antioch, Syria.

Living standards at the tops of poles can vary widely. Mellissa Sanders lived in a shack measuring 6 ft × 7 ft at the top of a pole in Indianapolis, IN from 26 Oct 1986–24 Mar 1988, a total of 516 days.

Rob Colley stayed in a barrel (maximum capacity 180 gal) at the top of a pole 43 ft high in Dartmoor Wildlife Park, near Plymouth, Great Britain for 42 days 35 min from 13 Aug–24 Sep 1992.

Largest teepee   The largest teepee in the United States measures 43 ft in height, 42 ft in diameter and utilizes 42 teepee poles. The teepee, owned by M.P. Doss of Washington, D.C., was exhibited near the Little Big Horn National Cemetery in 1992.

1985 at 741.9 ft tall. The $235 million hotel is operated by Westin Hotel Co. and jointly owned by the DBS Banking Corporation and the Overseas Chinese Banking Corporation. However, the Westin at the Renaissance Center in Detroit, MI, is 748 ft tall when measured from the rear entrance.

Most expensive The Galactic Fantasy Suite in the Crystal Palace Resort & Casino in the Bahamas can be rented for $25,000 per night. The price includes a female robot named Ursula who explains all the suite's high-tech toys. These include a lucite piano that produces images as well as music, a rotating sofa and bed and a thunder and lightning storm sound and light show. A sensoring device the guest carries opens doors in the two-bedroom, bi-level suite.

Most mobile The three-story brick Hotel Fairmount (built 1906) in San Antonio, TX, which weighed 1,600 tons, was moved on 36 dollies with pneumatic tires over city streets approximately five blocks and over a bridge, which had to be reinforced. The move by Emmert International of Portland, OR took six days, 30 Mar–4 Apr 1985, and cost $650,000.

BUILDINGS FOR WORKING

LARGEST

Construction project The Madinat Al-Jubail Al-Sinaiyah project in Saudi Arabia is the largest public works project in modern times. Construction started in 1976 for an industrial city covering 250,705 acres. At the peak of construction nearly 52,000 workers were employed, representing 62 nationalities. The total earth dredging and moving volume has reached 953.5 billion ft^3, enough to construct a 3-ft-3-in-high belt around the Earth at the equator seven times.

Urban development The largest urban regeneration project in the world is that of the London Docklands, which covers $8\frac{1}{2}$ miles^2. By 1992 £8 billion ($14 billion) had been invested by the private sector together with a further £1.1 billion injected by the London Docklands Development Corporation. Over 27 million ft^2 of commercial development space and over 17,000 new homes have been completed or are under construction, and £3.5 billion ($6.25 billion) is being invested in new public transport. More than 40,000 jobs have been created since 1981. The Canary Wharf development in the London Docklands is also the world's largest commercial development.

Industrial The largest multilevel industrial building that is one discrete structure is the container freight station of Asia Terminals Ltd at Hong Kong's Kwai Chung container port. The gross floor area completed by March 1993 was 7,110,719 ft^2, and the total area on completion of the 15-story building, scheduled for the end of 1994, will be 9,320,867 ft^2. The building plan area is 906×958 ft and 359.25 ft high. The building's volume will be 206,699,993 ft^3. The entire area in each floor is directly accessible by 46 ft container trucks, and the building includes 16.67 miles of roadway and 2,609 container truck parking bays.

LARGEST ADMINISTRATIVE BUILDING The Pentagon in Arlington, VA (left) and a small section of the building's 17 miles of corridors (below). (Photos: Department of Defense/ Helene Stikkel)

Hod carrying   Russell Bradley of Worcester, Great Britain carried bricks weighing 361 lb 9 oz up a ladder of the minimum specified length of 12 ft on 28 Jan 1991 at Worcester City Football Club. The hod weighed 94 lb 13 oz and he was therefore carrying a total weight of 456 lb 6 oz.

He also carried bricks with a weight of 574 lb 1 oz in a 105 lb 6 oz hod (giving a total weight of 679 lb 7 oz) a distance of 16 ft 5 in on level ground before ascending a runged ramp to a height of 7 ft at Worcester Rugby Club on 17 Mar 1991.

Brick carrying   The greatest distance achieved for carrying a 9 lb brick in a nominated ungloved hand in an uncradled downward pincer grip is 61¾ miles, by Reg Morris of Walsall, Great Britain on 16 Jul 1985.

The women's record for a 9 lb 12 oz brick is 22½ miles, by Wendy Morris of Walsall, Great Britain on 28 Apr 1986.

Largest brickworks   The largest brickworks in the world is the London Brick Co. Ltd plant at Stewartby, Great Britain. Established in 1898, the site now covers 221 acres and has a weekly production capacity of 10.5 million bricks and brick equivalent.

Commercial   In terms of floor area, the greatest ground area covered by any commercial building in the world under one roof is the flower auction building of the Co-operative VBA (Verenigde Bloemenveilingen Aalsmeer), Aalsmeer, Netherlands, with dimensions of 2,546 × 2,070 ft. The original floor surface of 3.7 million ft² has now been extended to 5.27 million ft².

The world's most capacious building is the Boeing Company's main assembly plant in Everett, WA, at 196,476,000 ft³ on completion in 1968. Subsequent expansion programs have increased the volume to 472 million ft³, with a further increase in volume of 50 percent due for completion in 1993 in preparation for production of the new 777 airliner. The site covers some 1,025 acres.

Administrative   The largest ground area covered by any office building is that of the Pentagon, in Arlington, VA. Built to house the US Defense Department's offices, it was completed on 15 Jan 1943 and cost an estimated $83 million. Each of the outermost sides is 921 ft long and the perimeter of the building is about 4,610 ft. Its five stories enclose a floor area of 149.2 acres. The corridors total 17 miles in length and there are 7,748 windows to be cleaned. There are 29,000 people working in the building. (See Science and Technology, Telephones and Facsimiles.)

OFFICES

Largest   The complex with the largest rentable space is the World Trade Center in New York City with a total of 12 million ft² of rentable space available in seven buildings, including 4.37 million ft² in each of the twin towers.

There are 99 elevators in each tower building and 43,600 windows comprising 600,000 ft² of glass. There are 50,000 people working in the complex and 90,000 visitors daily.

Most expensive The highest rentals in the world for prime offices, according to *World Rental Levels* by Richard Ellis of London, Great Britain, are in Tokyo, Japan at $186.90 per ft² per year (December 1992), compared with a peak of $206.68 in June 1991. With added service charges and rates this is increased to $205.72 per ft² (December 1992), as compared to $225.34 in June 1991.

Tallest The tallest office building in the world is the Sears Tower, national headquarters of Sears, Roebuck & Co. on Wacker Drive, Chicago, IL, with 110 stories, rising to 1,454 ft. The addition of two TV antennae brought the total height to 1,707 ft. Construction was started in August 1970 and it was "topped out" on 4 May 1973, having surpassed the World Trade Center in New York City in height at 2:35 P.M. on 6 Mar 1973 with the first steel column reaching to the 104th story. The building has a gross area of 4.5 million ft², is served by 18 elevators and has 16,100 windows.

Embassies The embassy of the former USSR, now the Russian embassy, on Bei Xiao Jie, Beijing, China, in the northeastern corner of the northern walled city, occupies the whole 45 acre area of the old Orthodox Church Mission (established 1728), now known as the *Beiguan*. It was handed over to the USSR in 1949.

The largest American embassy is in Bonn, Germany, at 6.6 acres.

BUILDINGS FOR ENTERTAINMENT

STADIUMS

Largest The open Strahov Stadium in Prague, Czech Republic, was completed in 1934 and could accommodate 240,000 spectators for mass displays of up to 40,000 Sokol gymnasts.

Soccer The Maracaña Municipal Stadium in Rio de Janeiro, Brazil, has a normal capacity of 205,000, of whom 155,000 can be seated. A crowd of 199,854 was accommodated for the World Cup final between Brazil and Uruguay on 16 Jul 1950. A dry moat, 10 ft wide and more than 5 ft deep, protects players from spectators and vice versa.

The largest stadium in the United States is Michigan Football Stadium, Ann Arbor, MI, which has a seating capacity of 102,501. The largest crowd ever to attend an event there was 106,255 for the Michigan *v.* Ohio State game on 17 Nov 1979. Ohio State won 18-15.

Covered The Aztec Stadium, Mexico City, opened in 1968, has a capacity of 107,000 for soccer, although a record attendance of 132,274 was achieved for boxing on 20 Feb 1993. Nearly all seats are under cover. (See Sports and Games, Boxing.)

Indoor   The $173-million 273-ft-tall Louisiana Superdome in New Orleans, LA, covering 13 acres, was completed in May 1975. Its maximum seating capacity for conventions is 97,365, or 76,791 for football. A gondola with six 312-in TV screens produces instant replay.

Largest roof   The transparent acrylic glass "marquee" roof over the Munich Olympic Stadium, Germany measures 914,940 ft^2 in area, resting on a steel net supported by masts.

The longest roof span in the world is 787 ft 4 in for the major axis of the elliptical Texas Stadium, completed in 1971 at Irving, TX.

Retractable roof   The world's largest covers the SkyDome, Toronto, Ontario, Canada, completed in June 1989 near the CN tower. The roof covers 8 acres, spans 674 ft at its widest point and rises to 282 ft. The stadium itself has a capacity of 67,000 for concerts, 53,000 for football and 50,600 for baseball. (See Sports and Games, Baseball.)

Largest air-supported building   The 80,638-capacity octagonal Pontiac Silverdome Stadium, Pontiac, MI is 522 ft wide and 722 ft long. The air pressure is 5 lb/ft^2 supporting the 10 acre translucent "Fiberglas" roofing. The main floor is 402 ft × 240 ft and the roof is 202 ft high. Geiger-Berger Associates of New York City were the structural engineers.

The largest standard size air hall (air-supported structure) is one 860 ft long, 140 ft wide and 65 ft high. One was first sited at Lima, OH, made by Irvin Industries of Stamford, CT.

LARGEST RETRACTABLE ROOF   The Toronto SkyDome showing part of the world's first and largest fully retractable roof. Operating on a system of steel tracks and 54 drive mechanisms, the 8-acre, 674-ft-wide roof moves at a rate of 71 ft per minute and takes 20 minutes to open or close. It is next to the CN Tower, the world's tallest self-supporting tower. (Photo: Allsport/Rick Stewart)

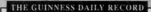
House of cards record toppled

—— 75 STORYS AND 208 DECKS ——

Bryan Berg, a high school student in Spirit Lake, IA, has just spent 30 hours creating the world's highest house of cards.

Berg, who achieved his record as part of a math project, actually became interested in card houses some years ago, and has spent many hours practicing and working on different construction methods.

Scaffolding and an adjustable platform enabled him to get higher and higher, but although he was aiming for 100 storys, he stopped at 75, simply because he got scared.

If it's hard work building a 14-foot 6-inch house, watching it come crashing down is easy, even if potentially dangerous.

RESORTS

Amusement resort Largest   Disney World is set in 28,000 acres of Orange and Osceola counties, 20 miles southwest of Orlando in central Florida. It was opened on 1 Oct 1971 after a $400 million investment.

Most attended   Disneyland, Anaheim, CA (opened 1955) received its 250-millionth visitor on 24 Aug 1985 at 9:52 A.M. Disneyland welcomed its 300-millionth visitor in 1989.

Largest pleasure beach   Virginia Beach, VA has 28 miles of beachfront on the Atlantic and 10 miles of estuary frontage. The area embraces 310 miles² with 157 hotels, motels and condos containing 11,189 rooms. There are also 2,230 campsites.

Piers Longest The longest pleasure pier in the world is Southend Pier at Southend-on-Sea, Great Britain. The original wooden pier was opened in 1830 and extended in 1846. The present iron pier is 1.34 miles in length and was first opened on 8 Jul 1889. In 1949–50 the pier had a peak 5.75 million visitors. The pier has been breached by 14 vessels since 1830 and there have been 3 major fires.

Most piers The resort with the most piers was Atlantic City, NJ with seven, though currently only five remain: the Garden Pier (1912), Million Dollar (1906; now called Shops on Ocean One), Auditorium (1900; now the Steeplechase), Steel (1898), and Apple-gates (1883), now known as Central.

Naturist resorts Oldest The oldest naturist resort is Der Freilichtpark, Klingberg, Germany, established in 1903. The oldest recorded naturist club was the Fellowship of Naked Trust in British India, in 1891.

Largest The largest naturist site is Domaine de Lambeyran, near Lodève in southern France, at 840 acres. The center Helio-Marin at Cap d'Agde, also in southern France, is visited by around 250,000 people per annum.

United States The largest naturist colony in the United States in terms of total acreage is Oaklake Trails, Tulsa, OK. The resort covers 418 acres. The most popular naturist resort is Club Paradise, Land O'Lakes, FL, which had 70,000 visitors in 1992.

Spas Spas are named after the town of Spa, a watering place in the Liège province of Belgium, where hydropathy was developed from 1626.

The largest spa, measured by number of available hotel rooms, is Vichy, Allier, France, with 14,000 rooms. The highest French spa is Barèges, Hautes-Pyrénées, at 4,068 ft above sea level.

FAIRS

Earliest The earliest major international fair was the Great Exhibition of 1851 in the Crystal Palace, London, Great Britain, which in 141 days attracted 6,039,195 admissions.

Largest The site of the Louisiana Purchase Exposition at St Louis, MO in 1904 covered 1,271.76 acres and there was an attendance of 19,694,855. Events of the 1904 Olympic Games were staged in conjunction with the fair.

Big wheels The original Ferris Wheel, named after its constructor, George W. Ferris (1859–96), was erected in 1893 at the Midway at the Chicago World's Fair for $385,000. It was 250 ft in diameter, 790 ft in circumference, weighed 1,283.8 tons and carried 36 cars, each seating 60 people, making a total of 2,160 passengers. The structure was removed in 1904 to St Louis, MO for the Louisiana Purchase Exposition (see above) and was eventually sold as scrap for $1,800.

In 1897 a Ferris wheel with a diameter of 248 ft was erected for the Earl's Court Exhibition, London, Great Britain. It had ten first-class and 30 second-class cars.

The largest-diameter wheel now operating is the Cosmoclock 21 at Yokohama City, Japan. It is 344 1/2 ft high and 328 ft in diameter, with 60 gondolas, each with eight seats. There are such features as illumination by laser beams and acoustic effects by sound synthesizers. The 60 arms holding the gondolas each serve as a second hand for the 42½-ft-long electric clock mounted at the hub.

United States The tallest Ferris wheel in the United States is the Texas Star at Fair Park in Dallas, TX. It is 212 ft 6 in high, with 44 gondolas and a passenger capacity of 244 riders. The wheel was built in 1985 and is operated during the annual State Fair of Texas.

ROLLER COASTERS

The maximum speeds claimed for switchbacks, scenic railroads or roller coasters have long been exaggerated for commercial reasons.

Oldest operating The *Rutschbahnen* (Scenic Railway) Mk.2 was constructed at the Tivoli Gardens, Copenhagen, Denmark, in 1913. This coaster opened to the public in 1914, and has remained open ever since.

United States The oldest operating roller coaster in the United States is the *Zippin Pippin*, constructed at Libertyland Amusement Park, Memphis, TN in 1915.

Longest The longest roller coaster in the world is *The Ultimate* at Lightwater Valley Theme Park in Ripon, Great Britain. The run is 1.42 miles.

United States The longest roller coaster in the United States is *The Beast* at Kings Island near Cincinnati, OH. The run of 1.40 miles incorporates 800 ft of tunnels and a 540-degree banked helix.

Tallest The tallest above ground is the *Moonsault Scramble* at the Fujikyu Highland Park, near Kawaguchi Lake, Japan, opened on 24 Jun 1983. It is 207 ft tall.
This is due to be overtaken by a non-looping coaster under construction at Blackpool Pleasure Beach, Great Britain, that will rise to a design height of 235 ft when it opens in 1994. It is designed by Arrow Dynamics Inc. of Clearfield, UT.

Greatest number The most roller coasters at any amusement park is 10, at Cedar Point Amusement Park in Sandusky, OH. There is a choice of two wood and eight steel track coasters.

Greatest and fastest drop The *Steel Phantom*, opened in April 1991 at Kennywood Amusement Park, West Mifflin, PA, has a vertical drop of 225 ft into a natural ravine, with a design speed of 80 mph.

Looping The first loop of the *Viper* at Six Flags Magic Mountain, Valencia, CA is 140 ft above ground. Riders are turned upside-down seven times over a 3,830 ft track.

The world's earliest restaurant—the Casa Botin restaurant in Madrid. (Photo: ALER)

BIG WHEEL The arms holding the 60 gondolas serve as second hands on the 328-ft-diameter Cosmoclock 21 big wheel in Yokohama City, Japan. (Photo: Rex Features/Roy)

NIGHT CLUBS AND RESTAURANTS

Night clubs   The earliest night club (*boîte de nuit*) was "Le Bal des Anglais" at 6 rue des Anglais, Paris, France. Established in 1843, it closed *c.* 1960.

Largest   Gilley's Club (formerly Shelly's), built in 1955, was extended in 1971 on Spencer Highway, Houston, TX, with a seating capacity of 6,000 under one roof covering 4 acres.

The largest night club in the world in the more classic sense of the term is The Mikado in the Akasaka district of Tokyo, Japan, with a seating capacity of 2,000. Binoculars can be essential to an appreciation of the floor show.

Lowest   The Minus 206 in Tiberias, Israel, on the shores of the Sea of Galilee, is 676 ft below sea level. An alternative candidate has been the oft-raided "Outer Limits," opposite the Cow Palace, San Francisco, CA. It has been called "The Most Busted Joint" and "The Slowest to Get the Message."

Restaurants Earliest   The Casa Botin was opened in 1725 in Calle de Cuchilleros 17, Madrid, Spain.

Largest   The Royal Dragon (Mang Gorn Luang) restaurant in Bangkok, Thailand, opened in October 1991, can seat 5,000 potential customers served by a staff of 1,200. In order to cover the large service area—8.35 acres—the employees wear roller skates, which helps to improve their service speed.

Highest   The highest restaurant in the world is in the Chacaltaya ski resort, Bolivia, at 17,519 ft.

Restaurateurs   The world's largest restaurant chain is operated by McDonald's Corporation of Oak Brook, IL, founded in 1955 by Ray A. Kroc (1902–84) after buying out the brothers Dick and "Mac" McDonald,

---

Largest exhibition center   The International Exposition Center in Cleveland, OH, the world's largest, is situated on a 188-acre site adjacent to Cleveland's Hopkins International Airport in a building that measures 2.5 million ft². An indoor terminal provides direct rail access and parking for 10,000 cars.

Largest casino   The Trump Taj Mahal, Atlantic City, NJ, which opened in April 1990, has a casino area of 2.75 acres.

Largest harem   The Winter Harem of the Grand Seraglio at Topkapi, Istanbul, Turkey was completed in 1589 and has 400 rooms. By the time Abdul Hamid II was deposed in 1909 the number of *carge* ("those who serve") had dwindled from 1,200 to 370 odalisques, wth 127 eunuchs.

Slot machines   The biggest beating handed to a "one-armed bandit" was $6,814,823.48 by Cammie Brewer, 61, at the Club Cal-Neva, Reno, NV on 14 Feb 1988.

---

pioneers of the fast-food drive-in. By December 1992 McDonald's licensed and owned 13,093 restaurants in 60 countries. Worldwide sales in 1992 were $21.9 billion.

Its most capacious outlet opened in Beijing, China on 23 Apr 1992, with almost 1,000 specially trained local staff at the 28,000 ft², 700-seater restaurant.

The largest McDonald's outlet in the United States is on the Will Rogers Turnpike in Vinita, OK. It has a seating capacity of 400, and is manned by a staff of 145. The restaurant includes two gift shops, two meeting rooms, a post office, a tourism room, 19 telephones and a big-screen (27 in) television.

Fish and chip restaurant   The world's largest fish and chip eatery is Harry Ramsden's at White Cross, Guiseley, Great Britain, with 140 employees serving 1 million customers per year, who consume 235 tons of fish and 392 tons of potatoes. Their Glasgow Branch sold and served 11,964 portions of fish and chips on 17 May 1992.

SHOPPING CENTERS

The world's first shopping center was built in 1896 at Roland Park, Baltimore, MD.

The world's largest center is the $1.1 billion West Edmonton Mall in Alberta, Canada, which was opened on 15 Sep 1981 and completed four years later. It covers 5.2 million ft² on a 121 acre site and encompasses over 800 stores and services as well as 11 major department stores. Parking is provided for 20,000 vehicles for more than 500,000 shoppers per week.

The world's largest wholesale merchandise mart is the Dallas Market Center on Stemmons Freeway, Dallas, TX, with nearly 9.3 million ft² in six buildings. Together with two further buildings under separate management, the whole complex covers 175 acres and houses some 2,580 permanent showrooms displaying merchandise of more than 30,000 manufacturers. The center attracts 760,000 buyers each year to its 107 annual markets and trade shows.

United States   The largest shopping center and entertainment complex in the United States is the Mall of America, located in Bloomington, MN. The mall was opened on 11 Aug 1992 and covers 4.2 million ft². It contains 350 stores and eight night clubs, and a 7-acre amusement park. Parking is provided for 12,750 vehicles for approximately 750,000 weekly shoppers.

Longest mall   The longest mall in the world is part of the £40 million ($68 million) shopping center at Milton Keynes, Great Britain. It measures 2,133 ft.

BARS

Largest   The largest beer-selling establishment in the world is the "Mathäser," Bayerstrasse 5, Munich, Germany, where daily sales reach 84,470 pints. It was established in 1829, demolished in World War II and rebuilt by 1955. It now seats 5,500 people.

Tallest   Humperdink's Seafood and Steakhouse Bar in Dallas, TX is 25 ft 3 in high with two levels of shelving containing over 1,000 bottles. The lower level has four rows of shelves approximately 40 ft across and can be reached from floor level. If an order has to be filled from the upper level, which has five rows of shelves, it is reached by climbing a ladder.

Longest The world's longest permanent bar is the 405-ft-10-in-long counter in the "Beer Barrel Saloon" at Put-in-Bay, South Bass Island, OH, opened in 1989. The "Bar at Erickson's," on Burnside Street, Portland, OR, in its heyday (1883–1920) possessed a bar measuring 684 ft that ran continuously around and across the main saloon. The chief bouncer, Edward "Spider" Johnson, had an assistant named "Jumbo" Reilly, who weighed 322 lb and was said to resemble "an ill-natured orangutan." Beer was five cents for 16 fluid ounces. Temporary bars of greater length have been erected, notably at beer festivals.

TOWERS AND MASTS

TALLEST STRUCTURES

World The tallest-ever structure in the world was the guyed Warszawa Radio mast at Konstantynow, 60 miles northwest of the capital of Poland. Prior to its fall during renovation work on 10 Aug 1991 it was 2,120²/₃ ft tall or more than four-tenths of a mile. It was completed on 18 Jul 1974 and put into operation on 22 Jul 1974. It was designed by Jan Polak and weighed 606 tons. The mast was so high that anyone falling off the top would reach terminal velocity and hence cease to be accelerating before hitting the ground. Work was begun in July 1970 on this tubular steel construction, with its 15 steel guy ropes. It recaptured for Europe, after 45 years, a record held in the United States since the Chrysler Building surpassed the Eiffel Tower in 1929. After 1991 it was described by the Poles as the "world's longest tower."

As a result of its fall, the tallest structure is now a stayed television transmitting tower 2,063 ft tall, between Fargo and Blanchard, ND. It was built at a cost of about $500,000 for Channel 11 of KTHI-TV, owned by the Pembina Broadcasting Company of North Dakota, a subsidiary of the Polaris Corporation of Milwaukee, WI. The tower was erected in 30 days (2 Oct to 1 Nov 1963) by 11 men of the Kline Iron and Steel Company of Columbia, SC, who designed and fabricated the tower. From then until the completion of the mast at Konstantynow it was the tallest structure in the world, and remained the second tallest between 1974 and 1991.

TALLEST TOWERS

The tallest self-supporting tower (as opposed to a guyed mast) in the world is the $63 million CN Tower in Metro Center, Toronto, Ontario, Canada, which rises to 1,815 ft 5 in. Excavation began on 12 Feb 1973 for

---

Lego tower The world's tallest lego tower was 65 ft 2 in high, consisted of 284,756 bricks, and was built by the people of Auckland, New Zealand on 22–23 Feb 1992.

---

the erection of the 143,300-ton reinforced, post-tensioned concrete structure, which was "topped out" on 2 Apr 1975. The 416-seat restaurant revolves in the Sky Pod at 1,150 ft, from which the visibility extends to hills 74½ miles distant. Lightning strikes the top about 75 times per year.

BRIDGES

Oldest Arch construction was understood by the Sumerians as early as 3200 B.C., and a reference exists to the bridging of the Nile in 2650 B.C.

The oldest surviving datable bridge in the world is the slab stone single-arch bridge over the River Meles in Izmir (formerly Smyrna) Turkey, which dates from *c*. 850 B.C.

Busiest The world's busiest bridge is the Howrah Bridge across the river Hooghly in Calcutta, India. In addition to 57,000 vehicles per day it carries an incalculable number of pedestrians across its 1,500-ft-long 72-ft-wide span.

LONGEST

Cable suspension The world's longest bridge span is the main span of the Humber Estuary Bridge, Humberside, Great Britain, at 4,626 ft. Work began on 27 Jul 1972, after a decision announced on 22 Jan 1966. The towers are 533 ft 1⅝ in tall and are 1⅜ in out of parallel to allow for the curvature of the Earth. Including the Hessle and the Barton side spans, the bridge stretches 1.37 miles. It was structurally completed on 18 Jul 1980 at a cost of £96 million ($192 million) and was opened by Queen Elizabeth II on 17 Jul 1981.

The Akashi-Kaikyo road bridge linking Honshū and Shikoku, Japan was started in 1988 and completion is planned for 1998. The main span will be 6,528 ft in length with an overall suspended length, with side spans, totaling 12,828 ft. Two towers will rise 974 ft 5 in above water level, and the two main supporting cables will be 43¼ in in diameter, making both tower heights at span world records.

The Seto-Ohashi double-deck road and rail bridge linking Kojima, Honshū with Sakaide, Shikoku, Japan opened on 10 Apr 1988 at a cost of $8.33 billion and 17 lives. The overall length of the bridge is 43,374 ft, making it the longest combined road–railway bridge in the world. The tolls for cars are $51 each way. The Minami Bisan-seto Bridge on this link has the world's longest suspension bridge span—3,609 ft for combined road–railroad traffic.

Cable-stayed The longest cable-stayed bridge span in the world is the 1,739 ft Skarnsundet Bridge over the Trondheim Fjord in Norway, completed in 1991.

The Pont de Normandie in Le Havre, France, planned for completion in 1994, will have a cable-stayed main span of 2,808 ft.

The Mackinac Straits Bridge between Mackinac City and St Ignace, MI is the longest suspension bridge between anchorages (1.58 miles), and has an overall length, including approaches, of 5 miles.

United States The longest suspension bridge in the United States is the Ver-

The world's longest bicycle bridge. (Photo:Woodward Staton Croft)

The longest covered bridge, at Hartland, New Brunswick, Canada. (Photo: Images Colour Library/Robert Estall)

razano–Narrows Bridge, which measures 4,260 ft. The bridge spans Lower New York Bay and connects Staten Island to Brooklyn. Construction was completed in 1964.

Cantilever   The Quebec Bridge over the St Lawrence River in Canada has the longest cantilever truss span of any in the world—1,800 ft between the piers and 3,239 ft overall. It carries a railroad track and two carriageways. Begun in 1899, it was finally opened to traffic on 3 Dec 1917 at a cost of Can $22.5 million and 87 lives.

United States   The longest cantilever bridge in the United States is the John Barry Bridge, in Chester, PA. It spans the Delaware River and measures 1,644 ft. Work was completed in 1974.

Covered   The longest is that at Hartland, New Brunswick, Canada, measuring 1,282 ft overall, completed in 1899.

Railway   The world's longest railway bridge is the 43,374-ft-long Seto-Ohashi double-deck road and rail bridge (see Cable suspension, p. 257).

United States   The longest is the Huey P. Long Bridge, Metairie, LA, with a railroad section 23,235 ft long (4.4 miles), including approach roads. It has a 3-span trestle: 529 ft, 790 ft and 531 ft, followed by a single span of 531.5 ft. It was completed on 16 Dec 1935.

Longest bridging   The Second Lake Pontchartrain Causeway was completed on 23 Mar 1969, joining Lewisburg and Metairie, LA. It has a length of 126,055 ft. It cost $29.9 million and is 228 ft longer than the adjoining First Causeway, completed in 1956.

Concrete arch   The longest concrete arch is the Jesse H. Jones Memorial Bridge, which spans the Houston Ship Canal in Texas. Completed in 1982, the bridge measures 1,500 ft.

Steel arch   The longest is the New River Gorge Bridge, near Fayetteville, WV, completed in 1977, with a span of 1,700 ft.

Stone arch   The longest stone arch bridge is the 3,810 ft-long Rockville Bridge north of Harrisburg, PA, with 48 spans containing 216,050 tons of stone. It was completed in 1901.
   The longest stone arch span is the Planen Bridge in Germany at 295 ft.

Widest   The widest long-span bridge is the 1,650 ft Sydney Harbor Bridge, Australia (160 ft wide). It carries two electric overhead railroad tracks, eight lanes of roadway, and bicycle and pedestrian lanes. It was officially opened on 19 Mar 1932.
   The Crawford Street Bridge in Providence, RI has a width of 1,148 ft.

HIGHEST

Railway   The highest railroad bridge in the world is the Mala Rijeka viaduct of Yugoslav Railways at Kolasin on the Belgrade–Bar line. It is 650 ft high and was opened on 1 Jun 1976. It consists of steel spans mounted on concrete piers.

Road   The road bridge at the highest altitude in the world, 18,380 ft, is the 98.4-ft-long Bailey Bridge, designed and constructed by Lt Col. S.G. Vombatkere and an Indian Army team in August 1982 near Khardung-La, in Ladakh, India.

TALLEST

The tallest bridge towers in the world are those of the Golden Gate Bridge, which connects San Francisco and Marin Co., CA. The towers of this suspension bridge extend 745 ft above the water. Completed in 1937, the bridge has an overall length of 8,966 ft.

Bridge building   A team of British soldiers from the 21st Engineer Regiment based at Nienburg, Germany constructed a bridge across a 26 ft gap using a five-bay single-story MGB (medium girder bridge) in 7 min 12 sec at Hamein, Germany on 3 Nov 1992.

Bridge sale   The largest antique ever sold was London Bridge, in Great Britain in March 1968. Ivan F. Luckin (d. 1992) of the Court of Common Council of the Corporation of London sold it to the McCulloch Oil Corporation of Los Angeles, CA for £1,029,000 ($2,469,600). The 11,800 tons of façade stonework were reassembled at a cost of $7.2 million at Lake Havasu City, AZ and rededicated on 10 Oct 1971.

Bicycle bridge   The longest bicycle bridge is over the 17 railroad tracks of Cambridge Station, Great Britain. It has a tower 115 ft high and two 164-ft-long approach ramps, and is 779 ft 6 in in length.

Floating bridge   The longest is the Second Lake Washington Bridge, Evergreen, Seattle, WA. Its total length is 12,596 ft and its floating section measures 7,518 ft. It was built at a total cost of $15 million and completed in August 1963.

Highest bridge   The highest bridge in the world is over the Royal Gorge of the Arkansas River in Colorado, at 1,053 ft above the water level. It is a suspension bridge with a main span of 880 ft and was constructed in six months, ending on 6 Dec 1929.

Longest viaduct   The longest railway viaduct is the rock-filled Great Salt Lake Railroad Trestle, carrying the Southern Pacific Railroad 11.85 miles across the Great Salt Lake, UT. It was opened as a pile and trestle bridge on 8 Mar 1904, but converted to rock fill in 1955–60.

AQUEDUCTS

Longest ancient The greatest of ancient aqueducts was the aqueduct of Carthage in Tunisia, which ran 87.6 miles from the springs of Zaghouan to Djebel Djougar. It was built by the Romans during the reign of Publius Aelius Hadrianus (A.D. 117–138). In 1895, 344 arches still survived. Its original capacity has been calculated at 7 million gal per day.

The triple-tiered aqueduct Pont du Gard, built in A.D. 19 near Nimes, France, is 157 ft high.

The tallest of the 14 arches of the Aguas Livres aqueduct, built in Lisbon, Portugal, in 1784 is 213 ft.

Longest modern The world's longest aqueduct, in the nonclassical sense of water conduit, excluding irrigation canals, is the California State Water Project aqueduct, completed in 1974, with a length of 826 miles, of which 385 miles is canalized.

CANALS

Earliest Relics of the oldest canals in the world, dated by archaeologists *c.* 4000 B.C., were discovered near Mandali, Iraq early in 1968.

Longest The longest canal in the ancient world was the Grand Canal of China from Beijing to Hangzhou. It was begun in 540 B.C. and not completed until A.D. 1327, by which time it extended (including canalized river sections) for 1,107 miles. The estimated work force *c.* A.D. 600 reached 5 million on the Bian section. By 1950 the canal had been allowed to silt up to the point that it was nowhere more than 6 ft deep; however, it is now plied by vessels of up to 2,200 tons.

The Beloye More (White Sea) Baltic Canal from Belomorsk to Povenets, Russia is 141 miles long and has 19 locks. It was completed with the use of forced labor in 1933 but cannot accommodate ships of more than 16 ft in draft.

The world's longest big-ship canal is the Suez Canal linking the Red Sea with the Mediterranean, opened on 16 Nov 1869. It is 100.6 miles in length from Port Said lighthouse to Suez Roads, and 197 ft wide. The canal was planned by the French diplomat Comte Ferdinand de Lesseps (1805–94) and

---

Longest artificial seaway The St Lawrence Seaway is 189 miles in length along the New York State–Ontario border from Montreal to Lake Ontario. It enables ships up to 728 ft long and 26.2 ft draft (some of which weigh 29,100 tons) to sail 2,342 miles from the North Atlantic up the St Lawrence estuary and across the Great Lakes to Duluth, MN. The project, begun in 1954, cost $470 million and was opened on 25 Apr 1959.

work began on 25 Apr 1859. The work force consisted of 8,213 men and 368 camels.

The largest vessel to transit the Suez Canal has been SS *Settebello*, of 355,400 tons (length 1,110 ft 4 in; beam 188 ft 2 in) at a maximum draft of 73 ft 4 in). This was southbound in ballast on 6 Aug 1986. The USS *Shreveport* transited southbound on 15–16 Aug 1984 in a record 7 hr 45 min. There are over 15,000 transits annually, or some 41 per day.

United States   The longest canal in the United States is the Erie Barge Canal, connecting the Hudson River at Troy, NY, with Lake Erie at Buffalo, NY. It is 365 miles long, 150 ft wide and 12 ft in depth. The Erie Barge is part of the main waterway of the New York State Barge Canal System, which covers a distance of 525 miles.

Busiest   The busiest ship canal is the Kiel Canal linking the North Sea with the Baltic Sea in Germany. Over 40,000 transits are recorded annually. The busiest in terms of tonnage of shipping is the Suez Canal, with nearly 338 million gross registered tons in 1992.

Longest irrigation   The Karakumsky Kanal stretches 745 miles from Haun-Khan to Ashkhabad, Turkmenistan. The "navigable" length in 1993 was 500 miles.

Longest canal system   The seawater cooling system associated with the Madnat Al-Jubail Al-Sinaiyah construction project in Saudi Arabia is believed to be the world's largest canal system, bringing 353 million ft^3 of seawater per day to cool the industrial establishment. (See Buildings for Working, Construction projects.)

BUSIEST CANAL   A ship passes through the Suez Canal, the longest big-ship canal and also the busiest in terms of tonnage carried. (Photo: Spectrum Colour Library/D & J Heaton)

LOCKS

Largest The Berendrecht lock, which links the River Scheldt with docks at Antwerp, Belgium, is the largest sea lock in the world. First used in April 1989, it has a length of 1,640 ft, a width of 223 ft and a sill level of 44 ft. Each of its four sliding lock gates weighs 1,770 tons. The cost of construction was approximately BFr 12,000 million ($305 million).

Deepest The deepest lock, although currently not operational, is the Zaporozhe on the Dnieperbug Canal, Ukraine, which can raise or lower barges at 128 ft.

United States The deepest lock in the United States is the John Day dam lock on the River Columbia, in Oregon and Washington State, completed in 1963. It can raise or lower barges 113 ft and is served by a 1,100-ton gate.

Highest rise and longest flight The world's highest lock elevator overcomes a head of 225 ft at Ronquières on the Charleroi–Brussels Canal, Belgium. Two 236-wheeled caissons are each able to carry 1,500 tons, and take 22 minutes to cover the 4,698-ft-long inclined plane.

Largest cut The Corinth Canal, Greece, opened in 1893, is 3.94 miles long, 26 ft deep, with an average depth of cutting of 1,003 ft over some 2.6 miles, and an extreme depth of 1,505 ft.

The Gaillard Cut (known as "the Ditch") on the Panama Canal is 270 ft deep between Gold Hill and Contractor's Hill with a bottom width of 500 ft. In one day in 1911 as many as 333 trains, each carrying 400 tons of earth, left this site—a total of more than 133,000 tons of spoil.

DAMS

Earliest The earliest-known dams were those uncovered by the British School of Archaeology in Jerusalem in 1974 and at Jawa in Jordan in 1975. These stone-faced earthen dams are dated to c. 3200 b.c.

Most massive Measured by volume, the Itaipú dam on the Paraná river, on the boundary between Brazil and Paraguay, is the most massive, with a volume of 1,024 billion ft³. Its barrage is 4.8 miles in length and 643 ft high at its high-est point. The dam is estimated to have cost $18 billion to construct.

Largest concrete The Grand Coulee Dam on the Columbia River, WA was begun in 1933 and became operational on 22 Mar 1941. It was finally com-pleted in 1942 at a cost of $56 million. It has a crest length of 4,173 ft and is 550 ft high. The volume of concrete poured was 285 million ft³ to a weight of 21.5 million tons.

Highest The highest will be the 1,098-ft-high Rogunskaya earth-filled dam across the river Vakhsh, Tajikistan, with a crest length of only 1,975 ft and a volume of 2.5 billion ft³. Preparations for building started in 1976, and con-struction began in March 1981. The completion date was set for 1992, but owing to the financial situation caused by the breakup of the Soviet Union, it has not been met. Meanwhile the tallest dam ever completed is the 984-ft-high Nurek, on the river Vakhsh, Tajikistan, of 2.05 billion ft³ volume.

United States The embankment–earthfill Oroville Dam is the United States' highest dam, reaching 754 ft and spanning the Feather River in California. It was completed in 1968.

Longest The 134½-ft-high Yacyreta–Apipe Dam across the Paraná on the Paraguay–Argentina border will extend for 43.2 miles. It was due for completion in 1992.

The Kiev Dam across the Dnieper, Ukraine, completed in 1964, has a crest length of 256 miles.

In the early 17th century an impounding dam of moderate height was built in Lake Hongze, Jiangsu province, China, of a reputed length of 62 miles.

The longest sea dam in the world is the Afsluitdijk, stretching 20.2 miles across the mouth of the Zuider Zee in two sections of 1.6 miles (mainland of North Holland to the Isle of Wieringen) and 18.6 miles from Wieringen to Friesland. It has a sea-level width of 293 ft and a height of 24 ft 7 in.

Strongest Completed, but not operational, the strongest is the 803-ft-high Sayano-Shushenskaya Dam on the River Yenisey, Russia, which is designed to bear a load of 20 million tons from a fully filled reservoir of 41 billion yd³ capacity.

Largest polder Of the five great polders (lands reclaimed from the sea) in the old Zuider Zee, Netherlands, the largest will be the Markerwaard, if it is completed, at 148,250 acres (231 miles²). However, for the time being the project has been abandoned. Work on the 65-mile-long surrounding dike began in 1957. The water area remaining after the erection of the dam (20 miles in length), built between 1927–32, is called IJsselmeer, which is due to have a final area of 487½ miles².

Largest levees The most massive ever built are the Mississippi levees, begun in 1717 but vastly augmented by the federal government after the disastrous floods of 1927. They extend for 1,732 miles along the main river from Cape Girardeau, MO to the Gulf of Mexico and comprise more than 1 billion yd³ of earthworks. Levees on the tributaries comprise an additional 2,000 miles.

Concrete pumping The world record distance for pumping ready mixed concrete without a relay pump is 4,986 ft, set on the Lake Chiemsee, Bavaria, Germany sewage tunnels project in 1989.

RESERVOIRS

Largest The most voluminous man-made reservoir is the Bratskoye reservoir, on the Angara River in Siberia, Russia, with a volume of 40.6 miles^3 and an area of 2,111 miles^2. It extends for 372 miles with a width of 21 miles. It was filled in 1961–67.

The world's largest artificial lake measured by surface area is Lake Volta, Ghana, formed by the Akosombo Dam, completed in 1965. By 1969 the lake had filled to an area of 3,275 miles^2, with a shoreline 4,500 miles in length.

The completion in 1954 of the Owen Falls Dam near Jinja, Uganda, across the northern exit of the White Nile from the Victoria Nyanza, marginally raised the level of that natural lake by adding 218.9 million acre-feet, and technically turned it into a reservoir with a surface area of 26,828 miles^2.

The $4-billion Tucuruí Dam in Brazil had, by 1984, converted the Tocantins River into a 1,180-mile-long chain of lakes.

United States The largest wholly artificial reservoir in the United States is Lake Mead in Nevada. It was formed by the Hoover Dam, which was completed in 1936. The lake has a capacity of 1,241,445 million ft^3 and a surface area of 28,255,000 acre–ft.

TUNNELS

LONGEST

Water-supply tunnel The longest tunnel of any kind is the New York City West Delaware water-supply tunnel, begun in 1937 and completed in 1944. It has a diameter of 13^1/$_2$ ft and runs for 105 miles from the Rondout Reservoir into the Hillview Reservoir, on the border of Yonkers, NY and New York City.

Rail tunnels The 33.46-mile-long Seikan Rail Tunnel was bored to 787 ft beneath sea level and 328 ft below the seabed of the Tsugaru Strait between Tappi Saki, Honshū, and Fukushima, Hokkaidō, Japan. Tests started on the subaqueous section (14^1/$_2$ miles) in 1964 and construction began in June 1972. It was holed through on 27 Jan 1983 after a loss of 34 lives. The first test run took place on 13 Mar 1988.

Proposals for a Brenner Pass Tunnel between Innsbruck, Austria and Italy envisage a rail tunnel 36–39 miles long.

Construction of the $13.5 billion Channel Tunnel, an electric railroad under the English Channel, began on 1 Dec 1987 and was completed in the spring of 1993. Road traffic is due to begin in the winter of 1993–94, with through passenger trains starting in mid-1994. A land link was created between Great Britain and France when the service tunnel drives met under the Channel on 1 Dec 1990. The length of the twin rail tunnels of 24 ft 11 in in diameter will be 31.03 miles.

United States The longest main-line tunnel railroad in the United States is the Moffat Tunnel, which cuts through a 6.2 mile section of the Rocky Mountains in Colorado. Tunnel construction was completed in 1928.

Continuous subway The Moscow Metro Kaluzhskaya underground railroad line from Medvedkovo to Bittsevsky Park is 23½ miles long and was completed in early 1990.

Road tunnels Longest The 10.14-mile-long two-lane St Gotthard road tunnel from Göschenen to Airolo, Switzerland opened to traffic on 5 Sep 1980. Nineteen lives were lost during its construction, begun in fall 1969, at a cost of SFr686 million (then $414 million).

The longest road tunnel in the United States is the 2.5-mile Lincoln Tunnel, linking New York City and New Jersey. The tunnel was dug beneath the Hudson River and was completed in 1937.

Largest The largest-diameter road tunnel in the world is the one blasted through Yerba Buena Island, San Francisco, CA. It is 77 ft 10 in wide, 56 ft high and 540 ft long. More than 250,000 vehicles pass through on its two decks every day.

Hydroelectric irrigation The 51½-mile-long Orange–Fish Rivers tunnel, South Africa, was bored between 1967 and 1973 at an estimated cost of $144 million. The lining to a minimum thickness of 9 in gave a completed diameter of 17 ft 6 in.

The Majes dam project in Peru involves 60.9 miles of tunnels for hydroelectric and water-supply purposes. The dam is at 13,780 ft altitude.

Sewerage The Chicago Water Reclamation District Tunnel and Reservoir Project (TARP) in Illinois, when complete, will involve 131 miles of sewerage tunneling. Also known as the "Deep Tunnel," it is divided into two segments. Phase I is the pollution control portion and Phase II the flood control portion, which includes three reservoirs. As of July 1993, 50.5 miles were in operation, 34.5 miles were under construction, and the remaining 24 miles were not yet funded. The system serves an area of 375 miles² with a population of 3.9 million residing in Cook County and 52 adjacent communities. The estimated cost of the total project, including the three 41 billion-gallon total capacity reservoirs is $3.6 billion. ($2.4 billion for Phase I and $1.2 billion for Phase II).

The Henriksdal plant in Stockholm, Sweden was the world's first major waste-water plant to be built underground. It was built between 1941 and 1971, and involved the excavation of nearly 35,300,000 ft³ of rock. It is now being enlarged, with the extension due for completion in 1997.

Bridge-tunnel The Chesapeake Bay Bridge-Tunnel extends 17.65 miles from the Eastern Shore peninsula to Virginia Beach, VA. It cost $200 million and was completed in 42 months. It opened to traffic on 15 Apr 1964. The longest bridged section is Trestle C (4.56 miles long) and the longest tunnel section is the Thimble Shoal Channel Tunnel (1.09 miles).

Longest and largest canal-tunnel The Rove Tunnel on the Canal de Marseille au Rhône in the south of France was completed in 1927 and is 23,359 ft long, 72 ft wide and 37 ft high. Built to be navigated by seagoing ships, it was closed in 1963 following a collapse and has not been reopened.

Oldest navigable The Malpas tunnel on the Canal du Midi in southwest France was completed in 1681 and is 528 ft long. Its completion enabled vessels to navigate from the Atlantic Ocean to the Mediterranean Sea via the river Garonne to Toulouse and the Canal du Midi to Sète.

Tunneling   The longest unsupported example of a machine-bored tunnel is the Three Rivers water tunnel, 5.82 miles long with a 10 ft 6 in diameter, constructed for the city of Atlanta, GA, from April 1980 to February 1982.

SPECIALIZED STRUCTURES

Advertising signs Highest   The highest is the logo "I" at the top of the 73-story 1,017-ft-tall First Interstate World Center building, Los Angeles, CA.

Most conspicuous   The most conspicuous sign ever erected was the electric Citroën sign on the Eiffel Tower, Paris, France. It was switched on on 4 Jul 1925, and could be seen 24 miles away. It was in six colors with 250,000 lamps and 56 miles of electric cables. The letter "N" that terminated the name "Citroën" between the second and third levels measured 68 ft 5 in in height. The whole apparatus was dismantled in 1936.

Largest   The largest advertisement on a building measured 41,756 ft^2 and was erected to promote Emirates, the international airline of the United Arab Emirates. It was located along the M4 motorway, near Chiswick, Great Britain, and was displayed from November 1992 to January 1993.

Airborne   Reebok International Ltd of Massachusetts flew a banner from a single-seater plane that read "Reebok Totally Beachin." The banner mea-

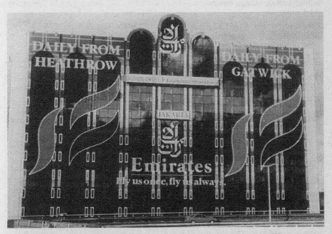

LARGEST ADVERTISEMENT ON A BUILDING   The huge advertisement for Emirates, which was located next to the main highway between central London and Heathrow Airport, Great Britain in late 1992 and early 1993. (Photo: Emirates Airline)

sured 50 ft in height and 100 ft in length, and was flown from 13–16 and 20–23 Mar 1990 for four hours each day at Daytona Beach, FL.

Animated The world's most massive is the one outside the Circus Circus Hotel, Reno, NV, which is named Topsy the Clown. It is 127 ft tall and weighs over 45 tons, with 1.4 miles of neon tubing. Topsy's smile measures 14 ft across.

Billboards The world's largest billboard is that of the Bassat Ogilvy Promotional Campaign for Ford España, measuring 475 ft 9 in in length and 49 ft 3 in in width. It is sited at Plaza de Toros Monumental de Barcelona, Barcelona, Spain, and was installed on 27 Apr 1989.

Illuminated The world's longest illuminated sign measures 197 ft × 66 ft. It is lit by 62,400 W metal-halide projectors and was erected by Abudi Signs Industry Ltd of Israel.

Neon The longest neon sign is the letter "M" installed on the Great Mississippi River Bridge, Old Man River at Memphis, TN. It is 1,800 ft long and comprises 200 high-intensity lamps.

The largest measures 210 × 55 ft and was built for Marlboro cigarettes at Hung Hom, Kowloon, Hong Kong in May 1986. It contains 35,000 ft of neon tubing and weighs approximately 126 tons.

An interior-lit fascia advertising sign in Clearwater, FL completed by the Adco Sign Corp in April 1983 measured 1,168 ft 6 1/2 in in length.

Bonfire The largest was constructed in Espel, in the Noordoost Polder, Netherlands. It stood 91 ft 5 in high with a base circumference of 276 ft 11 in and was lit on 19 Apr 1987.

Breakwater The world's longest breakwater is the one that protects the Port of Galveston, TX. The granite South Breakwater is 6.74 miles in length.

Buildings demolished by explosives The largest was the 21-story Traymore Hotel, Atlantic City, NJ on 26 May 1972 by Controlled Demolition Inc. of Towson, MD. This 600-room hotel had a cubic capacity of 6.5 million ft³.

The tallest chimney ever demolished by explosives was the Matla Power Station chimney, Kriel, South Africa, on 19 Jul 1981. It stood 902 ft and was brought down by the Santon (Steeplejack) Co. Ltd of Greater Manchester, Great Britain.

Grave digging It is recorded that Johann Heinrich Karl Thieme, sexton of Aldenburg, Germany, dug 23,311 graves during a 50-year career. In 1826 his understudy dug *his* grave.

Largest funeral casket The coffin of Walter Hudson (1944–92) of New York, one of the world's heaviest men, weighed 800 lb and measured 7 ft 4 in × 4 ft 6 in × 3 ft 4 in. It took 300 man-hours to complete.

LARGEST COOLING TOWERS The cooling towers at Uentrop, Germany. (Photo: Sgt G.E.M. Coffin)

Cemeteries Largest Ohlsdorf Cemetery in Hamburg, Germany is the largest cemetery, covering an area of 990 acres, with 965,000 burials and 393,000 cremations as of 31 Dec 1992. It has been in continuous use since 1877.

The United States' largest cemetery is Arlington National Cemetery, which is situated on the Potomac River in Virginia, directly opposite from Washington, D.C. It is 612 acres in extent and more than 200,000 members of the armed forces are buried there. Presidents William Howard Taft and John Fitzgerald Kennedy are also buried there.

Tallest The permanently illuminated Memorial Necropole Ecuméncio, located in Santos, near São Paulo, Brazil, is 10 stories high, occupying an area of 4.4 acres. Its construction started in March 1983 and the first burial was on 28 Jul 1984.

Chimneys Tallest The Ekibastuz, Kazakhstan coal power plant No. 2 stack is 1,377 ft tall and was built at a cost of 7.89 million rubles. It was started on 15 Nov 1983 and completed on 15 Oct 1987 by the Soviet Building Division of the Ministry of Energy. The diameter tapers from 144 ft at the base to 46 ft 7 in at the top. It weighs 53,600 tons and became operational in 1991.

Most massive The world's most massive chimney is one of 1,148 ft at Puentes de Garcia Rodriguez, northwest Spain, built by M.W. Kellogg Co. for Empresa Nacional de Electricidad S.A. It contains 556,247 ft³ of concrete and 2.9 million lb of steel and has an internal volume of 6.7 million ft³.

Columns The tallest are the thirty-six 90-ft-tall fluted pillars of Vermont marble in the colonnade of the Education Building, Albany, NY. Their base diameter is 6 ft 6 in.

The tallest load-bearing stone columns in the world are those measuring 69 ft in the Hall of Columns of the Temple of Amun at Karnak, opposite Thebes on the Nile, the ancient capital of Upper Egypt. They were built in the 19th dynasty in the reign of Rameses II *c.* 1270 B.C.

Cooling towers The largest is that adjacent to the nuclear power plant at Uentrop, Germany, which is 590 ft tall, completed in 1976.

Crematorium The largest crematorium in the world is at the Nikolo-

Arkhangelskiy Crematorium, east Moscow, Russia with seven twin cremators of British design, completed in March 1972. It covers an area of 519 acres and has six Halls of Farewell for atheists.

Domes The largest is the Louisiana Superdome, New Orleans, which has a diameter of 680 ft.

The largest dome of ancient architecture is that of the Pantheon, built in Rome in A.D. 112, with a diameter of 142 ft.

Doors Largest The four doors in the Vehicle Assembly Building near Cape Canaveral, FL have a height of 460 ft.

Heaviest The heaviest is that of the laser target room at Lawrence Livermore National Laboratory, CA. It weighs 360 tons, is up to 8 ft thick and was installed by Overly Manufacturing Company.

Earthworks The largest prior to the mechanical era were the linear earth boundaries of the Benin Empire (c. 1300) in the Edo state of Nigeria. Their existence was first reported in 1900 and they were partially surveyed in 1967. In March 1993 it was estimated by Dr Patrick Darling that the total length of the earthworks was probably around 10,000 miles, with the amount of earth moved estimated at 100 million yd^3.

Largest grain elevator The single-unit elevator operated by the C-G-F Grain Co. at Wichita, KS consists of a triple row of storage tanks, 123 on each side of the central loading tower or "head house." The unit is 2,717 ft long and 100 ft wide. Each tank is 120 ft high, with an inside diameter of 30 ft, giving a total storage capacity of 20 million bushels of wheat.

The world's largest collection of grain elevators are the 23 at Thunder Bay, Ontario, Canada, on Lake Superior, with a total capacity of 103.9 million bushels.

Fences Longest The dingo-proof wire fence enclosing the main sheep areas of Australia is 6 ft high, 1 ft underground and stretches for 3,437 miles. The Queensland state government discontinued full maintenance in 1982.

Tallest The world's tallest fences are security screens 65 ft high erected by Harrop-Allin of Pretoria, South Africa in November 1981 to protect fuel depots and refineries at Sasolburg from rocket attack.

Tallest flagpoles The tallest flagpole was erected outside the Oregon Building at the 1915 Panama-Pacific International Exposition in San Francisco, CA. It stood 299 ft 7 in in height, weighed 52 tons, and was trimmed from a Douglas fir.

The tallest unsupported flagpole in the world is the 282-ft-tall steel pole, weighing 120,000 lb, that was erected on 22 Aug 1985 at the Canadian Expo 86 exhibition in Vancouver, British Columbia and supports a gigantic ice hockey stick 205 ft in length.

Tallest fountain The tallest is the fountain at Fountain Hills, AZ, built at a cost of $1.5 million for McCulloch Properties Inc. At full pressure of 375 lb/in^2 and at a rate of 7,000 gal/min, the 562-ft-tall column of water weighs more than 8 tons. When all three pumps are on, the water column can reach 625 ft, if weather conditions are favorable. The nozzle speed achieved by the three 600 hp pumps is 146.7 mph.

Garbage dump   Reclamation Plant No. 1, Fresh Kills, Staten Island, NY, opened in March 1974, is the world's largest sanitary landfill. In its first four months of operation 503,750 tons of refuse from New York City carried by 700 barges was dumped on the site.

Largest gas tanks   The largest gas tanks are at Fontaine L'Evêque, Belgium, where disused mines have been adapted to store up to 17.6 billion ft^3 of gas at ordinary pressure.

The largest known remaining conventional gas tank is that at Simmering, Vienna, Austria, completed in 1968, with a height of 275 ft and a capacity of 10.6 million ft^3.

Longest deep-water jetty   The Quai Hermann du Pasquier at Le Havre, France, with a length of 5,000 ft, is part of an enclosed basin and has a constant depth of water of 32 ft on both sides.

TALLEST FOUNTAIN
The world's tallest fountain, located in the town which takes its name from its centerpiece—Fountain Hills, AZ. (Photo: MCO Properties Inc.)

Demolition work   Fifteen members of the Black Leopard Karate Club demolished a seven-room wooden farmhouse west of Elnora, Alberta, Canada in 3 hr 18 min by foot and unaided hand on 13 Jun 1982.

Largest revolving globe   The largest revolving globe is a 33-ton 33-ft-diameter sphere called "Globe of Peace," which was built in five years, from 1982 to 1987, by Orfeo Bartolucci from Apecchio, Pesaro, Italy.

Largest fumigation   Carried out during the restoration of the Mission Inn complex in Riverside, CA on 28 Jun–1 Jul 1987 to rid the buildings of termites, the fumigation was performed by Fume Masters Inc. of Riverside. Over 350 tarpaulins were used, each weighing up to 350 lb, and the operation involved completely covering the 70,000 ft² site and buildings—domes, minarets, chimneys and balconies, some of which exceeded 100 ft in height.

Kitchen   An Indian government field kitchen set up in April 1973 at Ahmadnagar, Maharashtra, then a famine area, daily provided 1.2 million subsistence meals.

Lampposts   The tallest lighting columns are the four made by Petitjean & Cie of Troyes, France and installed by Taylor Woodrow at Sultan Qaboos Sports Complex, Muscat, Oman. They stand 208 ft 4 in high.

Lighthouses *Tallest*   The 348 ft steel tower near Yamashita Park in Yokohama, Japan has a power of 600,000 candelas and a visibility range of 20 miles.

Greatest range   The lights with the greatest range are those 1,089 ft above the ground on the Empire State Building, New York City. Each of the four-arc mercury bulbs has a rated candlepower of 450 million, visible 80 miles away on the ground and 300 miles away from aircraft.

Marquee *Largest*   A marquee covering an area of 188,350 ft² (4.32 acres) was erected by the firm of Deuter of Augsburg, Germany for the 1958 "Welcome Expo" in Brussels, Belgium.

Mazes   The oldest datable representation of a labyrinth is that on a clay tablet from Pylos, Greece *c.* 1200 B.C.

The world's largest hedge maze is the one at Longleat, near Warminster, Great Britain, designed for Lord Weymouth by Greg Bright, which has 1.69 miles of paths flanked by 16,180 yew trees. It was opened on 6 Jun 1978 and measures 381 × 187 ft. "Il Labirinto" at Villa Pisani, Stra, Italy, in which Napoleon was "lost" in 1807, had 4 miles of pathways.

Menhir (prehistoric upright monolith)   The tallest known is the 420 ton Grand Menhir Brisé, now in four pieces, which originally stood 72 ft high at Locmariaquer, Brittany, France. Recent research suggests a possible 75 ft for the height of a menhir, in three pieces, weighing 280 tons, also at Locmariaquer.

Monuments Tallest The stainless-steel Gateway to the West arch in St Louis, MO, completed on 28 Oct 1965 to commemorate the westward expansion after the Louisiana Purchase of 1803, is a sweeping arch spanning 630 ft and rising to the same height of 630 ft. It cost $29 million and was designed in 1947 by the Finnish-American architect Eero Saarinen (1910–61).

Tallest column Constructed from 1936–39, at a cost of $1.5 million, the tapering column that commemorates the Battle of San Jacinto (21 Apr 1836), on the bank of the San Jacinto River near Houston, TX, is 570 ft tall, 47 ft square at the base, and 30 ft square at the observation tower, which is surmounted by a star weighing 220 tons. It is built of concrete with buff limestone, and weighs 35,000 tons.

Largest trilithons The largest trilithons exist at Stonehenge, to the south of Salisbury Plain, Wiltshire, Great Britain, with single sarsen blocks weighing over 50 tons and requiring over 550 men to drag them up a 9 degree gradient. The earliest stage of the construction of the ditch has been dated to 2800 B.C. Whether Stonehenge, which required some 30 million man-years, was built as a place of worship, as a lunar calendar, or as an eclipse predictor is still debated.

Largest artificial mound The largest artificial mound is the gravel mound built as a memorial to the Seleucid King Antiochus I (r. 69–34 B.C.), that stands on the summit of Nemrud Dagi (8,182 ft), southeast of Malatya, eastern Turkey. It measures 197 ft tall and covers 7.5 acres.

Obelisks Largest The "skewer" or "spit" (from the Greek *obeliskos*) of Tuthmosis III brought from Aswan, Egypt, by Emperor Constantius in the spring of A.D. 357 was repositioned in the Piazza San Giovanni in Laterane, Rome on 3 Aug 1588. Once 118 ft 1 in tall, it now stands 107 ft 7 in and weighs 500 tons.

The unfinished obelisk, probably commissioned by Queen Hatshepsut *c.* 1490 B.C., and *in situ* at Aswan, Egypt is 136 ft 10 in in length and weighs 1,300 tons.

The obelisk that has remained upright *in situ* for the longest time is the one still standing at Heliopolis, near Cairo, erected by Senwosret I *c.* 1750 B.C.

Tallest The world's tallest obelisk is the Washington Monument in Washington, D.C. Situated in a 106 acre site and standing 555 ft 5 1/8 in high, it was built to honor George Washington (1732–99), the first President.

Longest piers The Dammam Pier, Saudi Arabia, on the Persian Gulf, with an overall length of 6.79 miles, was begun in July 1948 and completed on 15 Mar 1950. The area was subsequently developed by 1980 into the King Abdul Aziz Port, with 39 deep-water berths. The original causeway, greatly widened, now extends to 7.95 miles including other port structures.

Longest covered promenade The Long Corridor in the Summer Palace in Beijing, China is a covered promenade running for 2,388 ft. It is built entirely of wood and divided by crossbeams into 273 sections. These crossbeams, as well as the ceiling and side pillars, have over 10,000 paintings of famous Chinese landscapes, episodes from folk tales, and flowers and birds.

Pyramids Largest The largest pyramid, and the largest monument ever constructed, is the Quetzalcóatl at Cholula de Rivadabia, 63 miles southeast of

Mexico City. It is 177 ft tall and its base covers an area of nearly 45 acres. Its total volume has been estimated at 4.3 million yd³ compared with 3.1 million yd³ for the Pyramid of Khufu or Cheops (a fourth-dynasty Egyptian pharaoh).

The largest-known single block in pyramid-building is from the Third Pyramid (Pyramid of Mycerinus) at El Gizeh, Egypt and weighs 320 tons.

Oldest The Djoser step pyramid at Saqqâra, Egypt dates from *c.* 2900 B.C. It was constructed by Imhotep to a height of 204 ft, and originally had a Tura limestone casing.

The oldest New World pyramid is that on the island of La Venta in southeastern Mexico, built by the Olmec people *c.* 800 B.C. It stands 100 ft tall with a base dimension of 420 ft.

Refuse electrical generation plants As of 1991 there were 13 refuse electrical generation utility plants in the United States, with an aggregate capacity of 276 Mw. The biggest plant in the country is the South Meadow, Hartford County, CT plant, and the Refuse and Coal Plant in Franklin County, OH, both with a capacity of 90 Mw.

Scaffolding The tallest scaffolding was 174 ft 8 in high, erected around the statue of the Albert Memorial in London, Great Britain in 1990 and to remain until restoration work has been completed. It was freestanding and clad with plastic sheeting and could resist wind forces of up to 90 mph.

United States The largest freestanding scaffolding in the United States is believed to be the one erected for the restoration of the Goldstone antenna in California. It was 170 ft high, 70 ft deep and went 180 ft around the circumference of the structure.

Scarecrow The tallest scarecrow ever built was "Stretch II," constructed by the Speers family of Paris, Ontario, Canada and a crew of 15 at the Paris, Ontario Fall Fair on 2 Sep 1989. It measured 103 ft 6¾ in in height.

Largest sewage works The Stickney Water Reclamation Plant (formerly the West-Southwest Sewage Treatment Works), in Stickney, IL began operation in 1930 on a 570-acre site and serves a 259.8 miles² area containing 2,380,000 people. It treated an average of 813 million gal of waste per day (MGD) in 1992. The Stickney Plant has a maximum treatment capacity of 1,440 MGD of wastewater. The plant has 651 employees.

Snow and ice constructions A snow palace 87 ft high, one of four structures which together spanned 702 ft 8 in, was unveiled on 7 Feb 1987 at Asahikawa City, Hokkaidō, Japan.

The world's largest ice construction was the ice palace built in January 1986, using 9,000 blocks of ice, at St Paul, MN during the Winter Carnival. Designed by Ellerbe Associates Inc., it was 120 × 90 ft and stood 128 ft 9 in high—the equivalent of a 13-story building.

Snowman The tallest stood 76 ft 2 in high and was named Prince William. It was built by Philip and Colleen Price, coordinators, with 10 others at Prince William Sound Community College, Valdez, AK on 2 Apr 1992.

Stairways Longest The service staircase for the Niesenbahn funicular near Spiez, Switzerland rises to 7,759 ft. It has 11,674 steps and a banister.

The stone-cut Tai Shan temple stairs of 6,600 steps in the Shandong Mountains, China ascend 4,700 ft.

Spiral The tallest spiral staircase is on the outside of the chimney Bobila Almirall, located in Angel Sallent in Tarrasa, Barcelona, Spain. Built by Mariano Masana i Ribas in 1956, it is 207 ft high and has 217 steps.

The longest spiral staircase is one 1,103 ft deep with 1,520 steps installed in the Mapco-White County Coal Mine, Carmi, IL by Systems Control Inc. in May 1981.

Statues *Longest* Near Bamiyan, Afghanistan there are the remains of the recumbent Sakya Buddha, built of plastered rubble, which was "about 1,000 ft" long and is believed to date from the 3rd or 4th century A.D.

Tallest A bronze statue of Buddha 394 ft high was completed in Tokyo, Japan in January 1993. It is 115 ft wide and weighs 110 tons. The statue took seven years to make, and was a joint Japanese–Taiwanese project.

The statue of Maitreya, which stands 85 ft high, is carved out of a single piece of wood from a white sandalwood tree at the Lama Temple (Yonghegong), built in 1649. It is located in the northwest of Beijing, China. The Imperial Court allowed two years for the carving of the statue in the Pavilion House of Ten Thousand Fortunes and finished the project in 1750.

The Statue of Liberty, originally named Liberty Enlightening the World, is the tallest statue in the United States. Designed and built in France to commemorate the friendship of the two countries, the 152 ft statue was shipped to

LARGEST SEWAGE WORKS The Stickney Water Reclamation Plant in Chicago. There are 166 tanks of different sizes serving specific purposes on the 570-acre site, which also has its own railway with 30 miles of track. (Photo: Stickney Water Reclamation Plant)

Stair climbing The 100-story record for stair climbing was set by Dennis W. Martz in the Detroit Plaza Hotel, Detroit, MI on 26 Jun 1978 at 11 min 23.8 sec.

Brain McCauliff ran a vertical mile (ascending and descending eight times) on the stairs of the Westin Hotel, Detroit, MI in 1 hr 38 min 5 sec on 2 Feb 1992.

Steve Silva climbed the 1,172 steps of the Westin Peachtree Plaza Hotel, Atlanta, GA (a total of 45,708 steps and a vertical height of 26,676 ft (in 9 hr 50 min 43 sec on 27–28 Jan 1992. He descended by elevator each time.

The record for the 1,760 steps (vertical height 1,122 ft) in the world's tallest freestanding structure, Toronto's CN Tower, Canada, is 7 min 52 sec by Brendan Keenoy on 29 Oct 1989.

The record for the 1,336 stairs of the world's tallest hotel, the Westin Stamford Hotel, Singapore, is 6 min 55 sec by Balvinder Singh, in its third annual Vertical Marathon on 4 Jun 1989.

Stair climbing Geoff Case raced up the 1,575 steps of the Empire State Building, New York City, on 16 Feb 1993 in 10 min 18 sec.

New York City, where its copper sheets were assembled. President Grover Cleveland accepted the statue for the USA on 28 Oct 1886.

The statue, which became a national monument in 1924, stands on Liberty Island in Upper New York Bay. The base of the statue is an eleven-pointed star; a 150 ft pedestal is made of concrete faced with granite. The statue was closed to the public on 23 Jun 1985 in order to complete restoration work, at a cost of $698 million. The statue was officially reopened by President Ronald Reagan on 4 Jul 1986 during a weekend-long celebration of the statue's 100th birthday.

Largest swing A glider swing 30 ft high was constructed by Kenneth R. Mack, Langenburg, Saskatchewan, Canada for Uncle Herb's Amusements in 1986. The swing is capable of taking its four riders 25 ft off the ground.

Tidal river barrier The largest tidal river barrier is the Oosterscheldedam, a storm-surge barrier in the southwestern corner of the Netherlands. It has 65 concrete piers and 62 steel gates, and covers a total length of 5 1/2 miles. It was opened by Her Majesty Queen Beatrix on 4 Oct 1986.

Largest tombs The Mount Li tomb, the burial place of Qin Shi Huangdi, the 1st Emperor of Qin, dates to 221 B.C. and is situated 25 miles east of Xianyang, China. The two walls surrounding the grave measure 7,129 × 3,195 ft and 2,247 × 1,896 ft. Several pits in the tomb contained a vast army of an estimated 8,000 life-sized terracotta soldiers. A tomb housing 180,000 World War II dead on Okinawa, Japan was enlarged in 1985 to accommodate another 9,000 bodies thought to be buried on the island.

Totem pole A 173-ft-tall pole was raised on 6 Jun 1973 at Alert Bay, British Columbia, Canada. It tells the story of the Kwakiutl tribe and took 36 man-weeks to carve.

**The Great Wall of China—the world's longest wall.
(Photo: Images Colour Library)**

SKI VALDEZ

VALDEZ
EXTREME SNOWMAN
WESC

Coca-Cola

Pepsi

Dartmouth,
New Hampshire;
February 1987;
47 ft 6 in

Anchorage, Alaska
March 1988;
63 ft 7 in

(Photo: Pat Lynn)

Abominable Snowmen

Whenever winter comes around and the snow falls, one of the traditional sights is that of children (and often adults) making a snowman. Usually it is about the same height as the people constructing it, but most winters bring attempts to build the tallest snowman. Since 1986, when the record was under 40 ft, there have been new records set on five occasions, the record height now being almost double that of seven years ago.

The current record for the tallest snowman was set in 1992, when a team of 12 under the leadership of Philip and Colleen Price made Prince William, who stood 76 ft 2 in high. He was completed on 2 Apr 1992 after nearly three weeks of painstaking work, and was named after the Prince William Sound Community College in Valdez, Alaska, where he was built.

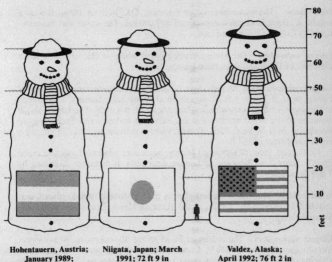

Hohentauern, Austria; January 1989; 69 ft 2 in

Niigata, Japan; March 1991; 72 ft 9 in

Valdez, Alaska; April 1992; 76 ft 2 in

Vats Largest   The largest wooden winecask in the world is the Heidelberg Tun, completed in 1751, in the cellar of the Friedrichsbau, Heidelberg, Germany. Its capacity is 58,570 gal. "Strongbow," used by H. P. Bulmer Ltd, the English cider-makers of Hereford, Great Britain, measures 64½ ft in height and 75½ ft in diameter, with a capacity of 1.95 million gal.

Oldest   The world's oldest-known vat still in use is at Hugel et Fils (founded 1639), Riqueweihr, Haut-Rhin, France. Twelve generations of the family have used it since 1715.

Walls Longest   The Great Wall of China has a main-line length of 2,150 miles. Completed during the reign of Qin Shi Huangdi (221–210 B.C.), it has a further 1,780 miles of branches and spurs. Its height varies from 15–39 ft and it is up to 32 ft thick. It runs from Shanhaiguan, on the Gulf of Bohai, to Yumenguan and Yanguan. Some 32 miles of the wall have been destroyed since 1966 and part of the wall was blown up to make way for a dam in July 1979. On 6 Mar 1985 a report from China stated that a five-year survey proved that its total length was once 6,200 miles. In October 1990 it was reported that after two years of exertion Lin Youdian had become the first person to walk its entire length.

Thickest   Urnammu's city walls at Ur (now Muqayyar, Iraq), destroyed by the Elamites in 2006 B.C., were 88 ft thick and made of mud brick.

Indoor waterfall   The tallest indoor waterfall measures 114 ft in height and is backed by 9,000 ft² of marble. It is situated in the lobby of Greektown's International Center Building, Detroit, MI.

Water tower   The waterspheroid at Edmond, OK, built in 1986, rises to a height of 218 ft, and has a capacity of 500,000 gal. The tower was manufactured by Chicago Bridge and Iron.

Largest waterwheel   The Mohammadieh Noria wheel at Hamah, Syria has a diameter of 131 ft and dates from Roman times.

Largest windows   The largest sheet of glass ever manufactured was one of 540 ft², or 65 ft 7 in by 8 ft 2¼ in, exhibited by the Saint Gobin Co. in France at the *Journées Internationales de Miroiterie* in March 1958. The largest single windows in the world are those in the Palace of Industry and Technology at *Rondpoint de la Défense*, Paris, France, with an extreme width of 715 ft and a maximum height of 164 ft.

The largest sheet of tempered (safety) glass ever processed was one made by P.T. Sinar Rasa Kencana of Jakarta, Indonesia. It measures 23 ft long by 7 ft wide and is ½ in thick.

Stained glass   The tallest stained glass is the 135-ft-high back-lit glass mural installed in 1979 in the atrium of the Ramada Hotel, Dubai (see Religions, Stained glass).

Largest wine cellars   The cellars at Paarl of the Ko-operative Wijnbouwers Vereeniging, known as KWV, Cape Province, in the center of the wine-growing district of South Africa, cover an area of 25 acres and have a capacity of 36 million gal.

United States   The Cienega Winery of the Almaden Vineyards in Hollister, CA covers 4 acres and can house 37,300 oak barrels containing 1.83 million gallons of wine.

Ziggurat   The largest ziggurat (from the Assyrian *ziqqurati*, meaning summit, height) ever built was that of the Elamite King Untas, *c.* 1250 B.C., known as the Ziggurat of Choga Zambil, 18.6 miles from Haft Tepe, Iran. The outer base was 344×344 ft and the fifth "box" 92×92 ft, nearly 164 ft above.

The largest partially surviving ziggurat is the Ziggurat of Ur (now Muqayyar, Iraq) with a base 200×150 ft, built to three stories and surmounted by a summit temple. The first and part of the second stories now survive to a height of 60 ft. It was built in the reign of Ur-nammu (*c.* 2113–2096 B.C.).

Largest Lego statue   The sculpture of the Indian chief Sitting Bull, at the Legoland Park, Billund, Denmark, measures 25 ft to the top of the feather. The largest statue ever constructed from Lego, it required 1.5 million bricks, individually glued together to withstand the weather.

Largest surveyors   The world's largest firm of surveyors and real estate consultants is Jones, Lang Wootton of London, Great Britain, with more than 60 offices in 23 countries and a staff of 3,500. Valuations completed in 1991 amounted to $153 billion, resulting in a worldwide fee income of $316 million.

Window cleaning   Keith Witt of Amarillo, TX cleaned three standard $42\frac{1}{2} \times 47$ in office windows with an 11.8-in-long squeegee and 2 gal of water in 10.13 sec on 31 Jan 1992 at the International Window Cleaning Association convention in San Antonio, TX. Smears are not tolerated and are penalized.

TRANSPORT

- **SHIPS**
- **ROAD VEHICLES**
- **ROADS**
- **RAILROADING**
- **AIRCRAFT AND FLIGHT**

SHIPS

EARLIEST SEAGOING BOATS

Aborigines are thought to have been able to cross the Torres Strait from New Guinea to Australia, then at least 43½ miles across, as early as 55,000 B.C. It is believed that they used double canoes.

The earliest surviving "vessel" is a pinewood dugout found in Pesse, Netherlands and dated to *c.* 6315 B.C. ± 275, now in the Provincial Museum, Assen.

An 18-in-long paddle was found at the Star Carr site in Great Britain in 1948. It has been dated to *c.* 7600 B.C. and is now in the Cambridge Museum of Archaeology, Great Britain.

The oldest surviving boat is a 27-ft-long 2½-ft-wide wooden eel-catching canoe discovered at Tybrind Vig on the Baltic island of Fünen, which is dated to *c.* 4490 B.C.

A fleet of 12 funerary boats discovered in 1991 at Abydos, Egypt have been tentatively dated to about 3000 B.C.; they measure up to 60 ft in length.

The oldest shipwreck ever found is one of a Cycladic trading vessel located off the islet of Dhókós, near the Greek island of Hydra, reported in May 1975 and dated to 2450 B.C. ± 250.

Earliest powered vessels Marine propulsion by steam engine was first achieved when in 1783 the Marquis Claude-François-Dorothée Jouffroy d'Abbans (1751–1832) ascended a reach of the river Saône near Lyons, France, in the 198-ton paddle wheeler *Pyroscaphe*.

The tug *Charlotte Dundas* was the first successful power-driven vessel. She was a stern paddle wheel steamer built for the Firth of Clyde Canal, Great Britain in 1801–02 by William Symington (1763–1831), using a double-acting condensing engine constructed by James Watt (1736–1819).

Message in a bottle The longest recorded interval between drop and pickup is 73 years in the case of a message thrown from the SS *Arawatta* out of Cairns, Queensland, Australia on 9 Jun 1910 in a lotion bottle and reported as found on Moreton Island, Queensland on 6 Jun 1983.

Most aircraft landings The greatest number of landings on an aircraft carrier in one day was 602, achieved by Marine Air Group 6 of the United States Pacific Fleet Air Force aboard the USS *Matanikau* on 25 May 1945 between 8 A.M. and 5 P.M.

Longest submarine patrol The longest submarine patrol that ever dove unsupported (of those that have been made public) is 111 days by HM Submarine *Warspite* in the South Atlantic from 25 Nov 1982 to 15 Mar 1983. She sailed 30,804 nautical miles.

Oldest active   The world's oldest active paddle wheeler continuously operated as such is *Skibladner*, which has plied Lake Mjøsa, Norway since 1856. She was built in Motala, Sweden and has had two major refits.

The world's oldest active oceangoing ship is the *MV Doulos* (Greek for "servant"), built in 1914 in the USA and first named *Medina*. She is currently operating as an international educational and evangelical Christian service vessel with approximately 300 crew members, personnel and passengers on board from 30 different nations.

Earliest turbine   The *Turbinia*, built in 1894 at Wallsend-on-Tyne, Great Britain to the design of Sir Charles Parson (1854–1931), was 100 ft long and of 46 tons displacement, with machinery consisting of three steam turbines totaling about 2,000 shp. At her first public demonstration in 1897 she reached a speed of 34.5 knots. She is now preserved at Newcastle-upon-Tyne, Great Britain.

WARSHIPS

Largest battleships   The Japanese battleships *Yamato* (completed on 16 Dec 1941 and sunk southwest of Kyūshū, Japan by US planes on 7 Apr 1945) and *Musashi* (sunk in the Philippine Sea by 11 bombs and 16 torpedoes on 24 Oct 1944) were the largest battleships ever commissioned, each with a full-load displacement of 81,545 tons. With an overall length of 863 ft, a beam of 127 ft and a full-load draft of 35¹/₂ ft, they mounted nine 18.1-in guns in three triple turrets. Each gun weighed 181.5 tons and was 75 ft in length, firing a 3,200 lb projectile.

United States   The largest battleships in active service were the USS *Missouri*, an Iowa class battleship, and the USS *Wisconsin*, 887 ft long and with a full load displacement of 64,960 tons. Both were first commissioned in 1944 and later recommissioned in 1986 and 1988, respectively following major refits. Armaments include nine 16-inch guns used in the Gulf War in 1991 and capable of firing 2,700 lb projectiles a distance of 23 miles. Both ships, together with two others of the same class, USS *New Jersey* and USS *Iowa*, are now in reserve. *New Jersey* last saw action off Lebanon in 1983–84.

Fastest warship   A US Navy hovercraft, the 78-ft-long 110-ton test vehicle SES-100B, achieved a speed of 91.9 knots (105.8 mph), on 25 Jan 1980. (See Hovercraft, fastest.)

Fastest destroyer   The fastest speed attained by a destroyer was 45.25 knots (51.84 mph) by the 3,120 ton French destroyer *Le Terrible* in 1935. She was built in Blainville, France and was powered by four Yarrow small-tube boilers and two Rateau geared turbines, giving 100,000 shp. She was removed from the active list at the end of 1957.

The fastest destroyers in the US Navy arsenal are the Spruance class and Kidd class ships, which attain a maximum speed of 38 mph (33 knots).

Largest aircraft carriers   The warships with the largest full-load displacement in the world are the Nimitz class US Navy aircraft carriers USS *Nimitz, Dwight D. Eisenhower, Carl Vinson, Theodore Roosevelt, George Washington,* and *Abraham Lincoln,* the last two of which displace

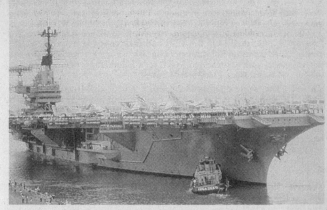

LARGEST AIRCRAFT CARRIER   The USS *Nimitz* is one of a fleet of six US Navy Nimitz class nuclear-powered aircraft carriers. (Photo: Sygma)

FASTEST HUMAN-POWERED SUBMARINE   *Subhuman II*, the two-man propeller submarine, is lowered into the Arctec Deepwater Tow Basin at Escondido, CA in preparation for its record attempt on 24 Oct 1992. (Photo: Subhuman Group)

100,846 tons. They are 1,092 ft in length overall, with 4½ acres of flight deck, and have a speed well in excess of 30 knots from their four nuclear-powered 260,000 shp geared steam turbines. They have to be refueled after about 900,000 miles of steaming. Their full complement of personnel is 5,986.

SUBMARINES

Largest   The world's largest submarines are of the Russian Typhoon class. The launch of the first at the covered shipyard at Severodvinsk in the White Sea was announced by NATO on 23 Sep 1980. They are believed to have a dive displacement of 27,557 tons, to measure 558 ft overall and to be armed with 20 SS-NX-20 missiles with a 4,800-nautical-mile range, each with seven warheads. By late 1987 two others built in St Petersburg, Russia (formerly Leningrad, USSR) were operational, each deploying 140 warheads.

The largest submarines in the US Navy are of the Ohio class. Each of the nine ships in active service has a displacement of 18,700 tons. At 560 ft, they are the longest submarines in the fleet by 42 ft, and also have the largest crew, at 165.

Fastest   The Russian Alpha class nuclear-powered submarines have a reported maximum speed of 45 knots plus (51.8 mph). With the use of titanium alloy in the hull, they are believed to be able to dive to 2,500 ft. A US spy satellite over Leningrad's naval yard on 8 Jun 1983 showed they were being lengthened and are now 260.1 ft long.

Deepest   The US Navy deep submergence vessel *Sea Cliff* (DSV 4), 30 tons, commissioned in 1973, reached a depth of 20,000 ft in March 1985.

Fastest underwater human-powered vehicle Propeller   The fastest speed attained by a human-powered propeller submarine is 4.72 ± 0.06 knots (2.43 m/sec), by *Subhuman II*, designed and built by the Mare Island Naval Shipyard, San Francisco, CA, using a counter-rotating propeller propulsion system, on 24 Oct 1992. The crew consisted of Dennis Hamilton, pilot; Christopher Reno, athlete; and team leader Jim Richardson.

Non-propeller   The fastest speed attained by a human-powered non-propeller submarine is 2.9 ± 0.1 knots (1.49 m/sec), by *SubDUDE*, designed by the Scripps Institution of Oceanography, University of California, San Diego, using a horizontal oscillating foil propulsion system, on 21 Aug 1992. The crew consisted of Kimball Millikan, pilot; Ed Trevino, athlete; and team leader Kevin Hardy.

Riveting   The world record for riveting is 11,209 rivets in 9 hr, by John Moir at the Workman Clark Ltd shipyard, Belfast, Northern Ireland in June 1918. His peak hour was his seventh, with 1,409 rivets, an average of nearly 23½ per min.

TANKERS

Largest The *Jahre Viking*, formerly the *Happy Giant*, is 622,420 tons deadweight. She is the world's largest oil tanker, and the world's largest ship of any kind, at 1,471 ft long overall, with a beam of 225 ft 11 in, and a draft of 80 ft 9 in. She was lengthened by Nippon Kokan in 1980 by adding a 265 ft 8 in midship section. She was attacked by Iraqi Mirage jets off Larak Island in the Persian Gulf on 22 Dec 1987 and was severely damaged in another attack on 14 May 1988. Despite this damage, she has been bought by an owner in Norway, and has been returned to service after refitting in Singapore.

The *Hellas Fos*, a steam turbine tanker built in 1979, is 611,839 ton deadweight, with 254,582 gross registered tonnage and 227,801 net registered tonnage. She is managed by the Bilinder Marine Corporation of Athens, Greece but has been laid up in Piraeus, Greece since April 1991.

Most massive collision The closest an irresistible force has come to striking an immovable object occurred on 16 Dec 1977, 22 miles off the coast of southern Africa, when the tanker *Venoil* (330,954 deadweight) struck her sister ship *Venpet* (330,869 deadweight).

CARGO VESSELS

Largest The largest ship carrying dry cargo is the Norwegian ore carrier *Berge Stahl*, 402,082.6 tons deadweight, built in South Korea for the Norwegian owner Signora Bergesen. She has a length of 1,125 ft, a beam measuring 208 ft and was launched on 5 Nov 1986.

Containership Earliest Shipborne containerization began in 1955 when the tanker *Ideal X* was converted by Malcolm McLean (USA). She carried containers only on deck.

Largest American President Lines has built five ships in Germany—*President Adams*, *President Jackson*, *President Kennedy*, *President Polk* and *President Truman*—that are termed post-Panamax, being the first container vessels too large for transit of the Panama Canal. They are 902.69 ft in length and 129.29 ft abeam; the maximum beam for the Panama transit is 105.97 ft. These vessels have a quoted capacity of 4,300 TEU (Standard length Twenty-foot Equivalent Unit Containers); they have in fact carried in excess of this in normal service.

Oil tanks The largest oil tanks ever constructed are the five ARAMCO 1½-million-barrel storage tanks at Ju'aymah, Saudi Arabia. They are 72 ft tall with a diameter of 386 ft and were completed in March 1980.

Largest whale factory The former USSR's *Sovietskaya Ukraina* (35,878 tons), with a summer deadweight of 51,519 tons, was completed in October 1959. She is 714½ ft in length and 84 ft 7 in abeam.

Barges The world's largest RoRo (roll-on, roll-off) ships are four *El Rey* class barges, weighing 18,408 tons and measuring 580 ft in length. They were built by the FMC Corp of Portland, OR and are operated by Crowley Maritime Corp of San Francisco between Florida and Puerto Rico with tri-level lodging for up to 376 truck-trailers.

Bathtub Kings

For many years motorized bathtub racing has been a popular activity. A 34-mile race using motorized bathtubs was first held in 1967 in Canada, and before long similar events also began to take place in Australia.

Before long, 36 miles had become the standard distance for championships. Two races that took place on a regular basis were across the Strait of Georgia, British Columbia, Canada, and on a river at Grafton, New South Wales, Australia.

Regardless of location, however, it was Australians who set records. Phil Holt did so in 1976 with a time of 1 hr 36 min 4 sec, which he achieved at Nanaimo, Australia. At the same venue in 1978, Gary Deathbridge cut the record to 1 hr 29 min 40 sec. This record stood for eight years until Greg Mutton recorded a time of 1 hr 27 min 38 sec. Since then he has remained the king of the bathtubs.

Illustration: Dick Millington

Most powerful tugs The largest and most powerful tugs are the *Nikolay Chiker* (SB–135) and *Fotiy Krylov* (SB–134), commissioned in 1989, and built by Hollming Ltd of Finland for V/O Sudoimport, in the former USSR, have 24,480 hp and are capable of 250 tons bollard pull at full power. At 324.8 ft long and 63.8 ft wide, they are now owned and operated under the names *Tsavliris Titan* and *Tsavliris Giant* by the Tsavliris Group of Companies of Piraeus, Greece.

Car ferries Largest The world's largest car and passenger ferry is the 58,376 gross registered tonnage *Silja Serenade*, which entered service between Stockholm, Sweden and Helsinki, Finland in 1990 and is operated by the Silja Line. She is 666 ft long and 103.34 ft abeam, and can carry 2,500 passengers and 450 cars.

Fastest The fastest is the 24,065 gross registered tonnage gas-turbine powered *Finnjet*, built in 1977, which operates in the Baltic Sea between Helsinki, Finland and Travemunde, Germany and is capable of exceeding 30 knots (34.47 mph).

Rail ferries The operating route of the biggest international rail ferries, *Klaipeda*, *Vilnius*, *Mukran* and *Greifswald*, is in the Baltic Sea, between the ports of Klaipeda, Lithuania and Mukran, Germany. Consisting of two decks 625 ft in length, 301.4 ft in breadth and 13,104 tons deadweight, these ferries were built in Wismar, Germany. Each of them can lift 103 railcars of standard 48.65 ft length and weighing up to 84 tons. The ferries can cover a distance of 273 nautical miles (314.2 miles) in 17 hours.

Largest hydrofoil The 212-ft-long *Plainview* (347 tons full-load) naval hydrofoil was launched by the Lockheed Shipbuilding and Construction Co. at Seattle, WA on 28 Jun 1965. She has a service speed of 57.2 mph.

Most powerful icebreakers The most powerful icebreakers built for that purpose are the *Rossiya* and her sister ships *Sovetskiy Soyuz* and *Oktyabryskaya Revolutsiya*. The 28,000-ton 460-ft-long *Rossiya*, powered by 75,000 hp nuclear engines, was built in Leningrad (now St Petersburg, Russia) and completed in 1985.

The largest *converted* icebreaker was the 1,007-ft-long SS *Manhattan* (43,000 shp), which was converted by the Humble Oil Co. into a 168,000 ton icebreaker. She made a double voyage through the Northwest Passage in Arctic Canada from 24 Aug to 12 Nov 1969.

The Northwest Passage was first navigated by Roald Engebereth Gravning Amundsen (Norway; 1872–1928) in the sealing sloop *Gjøa* in 1906.

Most powerful dredger The 468.4-ft-long *Prins der Nederlanden* of 10,586 gross tons can dredge up 22,400 tons of sand from a depth of 115 ft via two suction tubes in less than an hour.

Wooden ship Heaviest The *Richelieu*, 333²/₃ ft long and weighing 8,534 tons, was launched in Toulon, France on 3 Dec 1873.

HM Battleship *Lord Warden*, completed in 1869, displaced 7,940 tons.

Longest The longest ever built was the New York-built *Rochambeau* (1867–72), formerly the *Dunderberg*, which measured 377 ft 4 in overall.

It should be noted that the biblical length of Noah's ark was 300 cubits, or, at 18 in to a cubit, 450 ft.

PASSENGER VESSELS

Largest passenger liner The largest in current use, and the longest ever, is the *Norway*, 76,049 tons and 1,035 ft 7¹/₂ in in overall length, with a capacity of 2,022 passengers and 900 crew. She was built as the SS *France* in 1960 and renamed after purchase in June 1979 by Norwegian Knut Kloster. She normally cruises in the Caribbean and is based at Miami, FL. Work undertaken during an extensive refit, including two new decks, during the fall of 1990 increased the number of passenger decks to 11. Her draft is 34¹/₂ ft and her speed is 18 knots.

Largest yacht *Royal* The largest royal yacht in the world is the Saudi Arabian royal yacht *Abdul Aziz*, which is 482 ft long. Built in Denmark and completed in 1984 at Vospers Yard, Southampton, Great Britain, it was estimated in September 1987 to be worth more than $100 million.

Nonroyal The largest private (nonroyal) yacht is the *Alexander*, a former ferry converted to a private yacht in 1986, at 400 ft overall.

Largest passenger hydrofoil Three 185-ton Supramar PTS 150 Mk III hydrofoils carry 250 passengers at 40 knots across the Öre Sound between Malmö, Sweden and Copenhagen, Denmark. They were built by Westermoen Hydrofoil Ltd of Mandal, Norway.

SAILING SHIPS

Oldest active The oldest active square-rigged sailing vessel in the world is the restored SV *Maria Asumpta* (formerly the *Ciudad de Inca*), built near Barcelona, Spain in 1858. She is 98 ft overall and weighs 142.3 tons. She was restored in 1981–82 and is used for film work, promotional appearances at regattas, and sail training. She is operated by The Friends of *Maria Asumpta* of Lenham, Great Britain.

Largest The largest vessel ever built in the era of sail was the *France II* (5,806 gross tons), launched at Bordeaux, France in 1911. This was a steel-hulled, five-masted barque (square-rigged on four masts and fore-and-aft rigged on the aftermost mast). Her hull measured 418 ft overall. Although principally designed as a sailing vessel with a stump topgallant rig, she was also fitted with two auxiliary engines; however, these were removed in 1919 and she became a pure sailing vessel. She was wrecked off New Caledonia on 12 Jul 1922.

The only seven-masted sailing schooner ever built was the 375.6-ft-long *Thomas W. Lawson* (5,218 gross tons), built at Quincy, MA in 1902 and wrecked off the Isles of Scilly, Great Britain on 15 Dec 1907. (See Largest junks.)

Largest in service The largest now in service is the 357-ft-long *Sedov*, built in 1921 in Kiel, Germany and used for training by the Russians. She is 48 ft wide, with a displacement of 6,300 gross registered tons (4,267.2 tons) and a sail area of 45,123 ft².

The world's only surviving first rate ship-of-the-line is the British Royal Navy's 104-gun battleship HMS *Victory*, laid down at Chatham, Great Britain on 23 Jul 1759 and constructed from the wood of some 2,200 oak trees. She bore the body of Admiral Nelson from Gibraltar to Portsmouth, Great Britain, arriving 44 days after serving as his victorious flagship at the Battle of Trafalgar on 21 Oct 1805. In 1922 she was moved to No. 2 dock, Portsmouth—site of the world's oldest graving dock. The length of her cordage (both standing and running rigging) is 19.12 miles.

Longest The longest is the 613-ft-long French-built *Club Med I* with five aluminum masts. The 3,013 ft^2 polyester sails are computer-controlled. She is operated as a Caribbean cruise vessel for 425 passengers bound for Club Med. With her small sail area and powerful engines she is really a motor-sailer. A sister ship, *Club Med II*, is now being commissioned.

Largest junks A river junk 361 ft long, with treadmill-operated paddle wheels, was recorded in A.D. 1161.

The largest on record was the seagoing *Zheng He*, flagship of Admiral Zheng He's 62 treasure ships, *c.* 1420, with a displacement of 3,472 tons and a length variously estimated up to 538 ft. She is believed to have had nine masts.

In *c.* A.D. 280 a floating fortress 600 ft square, built by Wang Jun on the Yangzi River, took part in the Jin-Wu river war. Present-day junks do not, even in the case of the Jiangsu traders, exceed 170 ft in length.

Largest sails Sails are known to have been used for marine propulsion since 3500 B.C. The largest spars ever carried were those in HM Battleship *Temeraire*, completed at Chatham, Great Britain, on 31 Aug 1877. She was broken up in 1921. The fore and main yards measured 115 ft in length. The foresail contained 5,100 ft of canvas weighing 2.23 tons, and the total sail area was 25,000 ft^2.

Tallest mast The *Velsheda*, a J-class sailing vessel, is the tallest known single-masted yacht in the world. Measured from heel fitting to the mast truck, she is 169^1/$_4$ ft in height. Built in 1933, the second of the four British J-class yachts, she is unusual in that she was the only one ever built that was not intended to race for the America's Cup. With a displacement of 160 tons, she supports a sail area of 7,500 ft^2.

OCEAN CROSSINGS

Earliest Atlantic The earliest crossing of the Atlantic by a power vessel, as opposed to an auxiliary-engined sailing ship, was a 22-day voyage begun in April 1827, from Rotterdam, Netherlands, to the West Indies, by the *Curaçao*. She was a 127-ft wooden paddle boat of 490.5 tons, built as the *Calpe* in Dover, Great Britain in 1826 and purchased by the Dutch government for a West Indian mail service.

The earliest Atlantic crossing entirely under steam (with intervals for desalting the boilers) was by HMS *Rhadamanthus*, from Plymouth, Great Britain to Barbados in 1832.

The earliest crossing under continuous steam power was by the condenser-fitted packet ship *Sirius* (787 tons) from Queenstown (now Cóbh), Ireland to Sandy Hook, NJ, in 18 days 10 hr, from 4–22 Apr 1838.

Around the World in 79 Days   On 20 Apr 1993 skipper Bruno Peyron of France and his four-man crew arrived back in France to a hero's welcome after circling the globe nonstop in 79 days 6 hr 16 min in the catamaran *Commodore Explorer*, beating Philéas Fogg's fictional voyage of 1873. Their prize was the new Jules Verne Trophy put up by the French Government.

Peyron, 37-year-old veteran of some 27 Atlantic crossings, set out on 31 Jan 1993 from the departure line between Ushant, France and Lizard Point, Great Britain with crewmen Olivier Despaignes, Marc Vallin, Jack Vincent (all France) and Cameron Lewis (USA).

In winning this challenge, *Commodore Explorer*, the lengthened former *Jet Services 5*, also breaks the records for the fastest multihull, the fastest W-E and the fastest crewed circumnavigation.

Largest wreck   The 312,186 deadweight very large crude carrier (VLCC) *Energy Determination* blew up and broke in two in the Straits of Hormuz on 12 Dec 1979. Her full value was $58 million.

The largest wreck removal was carried out in 1979 by Smit Tak International, which removed the remains of the French tanker *Betelgeuse*, 120,000 tons, from Bantry Bay, Republic of Ireland, within 20 months.

Riverboat   The world's largest inland boat is the 382-ft *Mississippi Queen*, designed by James Gardner of London, Great Britain. The vessel was commissioned on 25 Jul 1976 in Cincinnati, OH and is now in service on the Mississippi River.

Longest canoe   The 117-ft-long Kauri wood Maori war canoe *Nga Toki Matawhaorua* was shaped with adzes at Kerikeri Inlet, New Zealand in 1940. The crew numbered 70 or more.

The "Snake Boat" *Nadubhagóm*, 135 ft long, from Kerala, southern India, has a crew of 109 rowers and nine "encouragers."

Fastest Atlantic   Under the rules of the Hales Trophy or "Blue Riband," which recognizes the highest average speed rather than the shortest duration, the record is held by the 222-ft Italian powerboat *Destriero* with an average speed of 53.09 knots between the Nantucket Light Buoy and Bishop Rock Lighthouse, Isles of Scilly on 6–9 Aug 1992, in a time of 58 hr 34 min 4 sec. *Destriero* is classed as a yacht by the trophy's trustees, and traditionalists still feel that the "Blue Riband" should be held by the vessel making the best passage in regular liner service.

That distinction goes to the *United States* (then 51,988, now 38,216 gross registered tonnage), former flagship of the United States Lines. On her maiden voyage between 3–7 Jul 1952 from New York to Le Havre, France and Southampton, Great Britain, she averaged 35.39 knots (40.75 mph) for three days 10 hr 40 min (6:36 P.M. GMT, 3 July to 5:16 A.M., 7 July) on a route of 2,949 nautical miles from the Ambrose Light Vessel to the Bishop Rock Lighthouse, Isles of Scilly, Great Britain. During this run, on 6–7

July, she steamed the greatest distance ever covered by any ship in a day's run (24 hr)—868 nautical miles (998.9 miles), thus averaging 36.17 knots (41.65 mph). The maximum speed attained from her 240,000 shp engines was 44.13 mph in trials on 9–10 Jun 1952.

Fastest Pacific The fastest crossing from Yokohama, Japan to Long Beach, CA—4,840 nautical miles (5,567.64 miles)—took 6 days 1 hr 27 min (30 Jun–6 Jul 1973) by the containership *Sea-Land Commerce* (56,353 tons), at an average speed of 33.27 knots (38.31 mph).

Water speed The fastest speed ever achieved on water is an estimated 300 knots (345.48 mph) by Kenneth Peter Warby (b. 9 May 1939) on the Blowering Dam Lake, New South Wales, Australia on 20 Nov 1977 in his unlimited hydroplane *Spirit of Australia*.

The official world water speed record is 277.57 knots (319.63 mph) set on 8 Oct 1978 by Warby on Blowering Dam Lake.

Fiona, Countess of Arran (b. 1918) drove her 15-ft three-point hydroplane *Stradag* (Gaelic "The Spark") to the first world water speed record for electrically propelled powerboats at a speed of 45.13 knots (51.97 mph), at the National Water Sports Center, Nottingham, Great Britain, on 22 Nov 1989.

Largest human powered ship The giant ship *Tessarakonteres*, a three-banked catamaran galley with 4,000 rowers, built for Ptolemy IV *c.* 210 B.C. in Alexandria, Egypt, measured 420 ft with up to eight men to an oar of 38 cubits (57 ft) in length.

Model boats Members of the Lowestoft Model Boat Club crewed a radio-controlled scale model boat on 17–18 Aug 1991 at Dome Leisure Park, Doncaster, Great Britain and set a 24-hr distance record of 111.18 miles.

David and Peter Holland of Doncaster, Great Britain, of the Conisbrough and District Modelling Association, crewed a 28-in-long scale model boat of the Bridlington trawler *Margaret H* continuously on one battery for 24 hours, and recorded a distance of 33.45 miles, at the Dome Leisure Complex, Doncaster, Great Britain on 15–16 Aug 1992.

Fastest shipbuilding The fastest times in which complete ships of more than 10,000 tons were ever built were achieved at Kaiser's Yard, Portland, OR during the wartime program for building 2,742 Liberty ships in 18 shipyards from 27 Sep 1941. In 1942 No. 440, named *Robert E. Peary,* had her keel laid on 8 November, was launched on 12 November and was operational after 4 days 15½ hr on 15 November. She was broken up in 1963.

HIGHEST ALTITUDE HOVERCRAFT Squadron Leader Michael Cole, leader of a ten-strong expedition which, in 1990, reached the navigable source of the Yangzi River, China in the hovercraft *Neste Enterprise*. (Photo: Michael Cole)

MERCHANT SHIPPING

Total The world total of merchant shipping, excluding vessels of less than 100 gross tonnage, sailing vessels and barges, was 79,845 ships of 444,304,999 gross tonnage on 1 Jul 1992.

As of November 1992, there were 462 privately-owned deep draft merchant ships with a gross tonnage of 1,000 or more in the United States. These ships are either oceangoing or Great Lakes motor carriers. Their carrying capacity is 22 million deadweight tons.

Shipbuilding Worldwide production completed in 1992 was 18.6 million gross tonnage of ships, excluding sailing ships, non-propelled vessels and vessels of less than 100 gross tonnage. The figures for the Commonwealth of Independent States (formerly part of the USSR), Romania and the People's Republic of China are incomplete. Japan completed 7.3 million gross tonnage (45 percent of the world total) in 1992.

The world's leading shipbuilder in 1992 was Hyundai of South Korea, which completed 28 ships of 1.85 million gross tonnage.

Biggest owner The largest ship owners are the Japanese NYK Group, whose fleet of owned vessels totaled 1,279,022 gross tonnage on 1 Feb 1993.

United States The largest shipping owner and operator in the United States is Exxon Corporation, whose fleets of owned/managed and chartered tankers in 1987 totaled a daily average of 10.42 million deadweight tons.

Largest fleet The largest merchant fleet in the world in mid-1992 was that under the flag of Liberia, with a fleet totaling 55,166,948 gross tonnage.

PORTS

Largest The largest port in the world is the Port of New York and New Jersey. The port has a navigable waterfront of 755 miles (295 miles in New Jersey), stretching over 92 miles^2. A total of 261 general cargo berths and 130 other piers gives a total berthing capacity of 391 ships at any one time. The total warehousing floor space is 422.4 acres.

Busiest The world's busiest port and largest artificial harbor is Rotterdam-Europoort in the Netherlands, which covers 38 miles^2, with 76 miles of quays. It handled 317.1 million tons of seagoing cargo in 1991.

Although the port of Singapore handled less tonnage in total seaborne cargo (than Rotterdam), it handled the greatest number of containers, making it the No. 1 container port in the world, with a record of 6.35 million TEUs in 1991.

United States The busiest port in the United States is New Orleans, LA, which handled 1.775 million tons of cargo in 1989.

Dry dock With a maximum shipbuilding capacity of 1.2 million deadweight tons, the Daewoo Okpo No. 1 Dry Dock, Koje Island in South Korea measures 1,740 ft long by 430 ft wide and was completed in 1979. The dock gates, 46 ft high and 33 ft thick at the base, are the world's most massive.

HOVERCRAFT

Fastest The world's fastest warship is the 78-ft-long 110.2-ton US Navy test hovercraft SES-100B. She attained a world record 91.9 knots (105.8 mph) on 25 Jan 1980 on the Chesapeake Bay Test Range, MD. As a result of the success of this test craft, a 3,307 ton US Navy Large Surface Effect Ship (LSES) was built by Bell Aerospace under contract from the Department of Defense in 1977–81.

Longest journey The longest hovercraft journey was one of 5,000 miles, by the British Trans-African Hovercraft Expedition, under the leadership of David Smithers, through eight West African countries in a Winchester class SRN6, between 15 Oct 1969 and 3 Jan 1970.

Highest The highest altitude reached by a hovercraft was on 11 Jun 1990 when *Neste Enterprise* and her crew of ten reached the navigable source of the Yangzi River, China at 16,050 ft.

The greatest altitude at which a hovercraft is operating is on Lake Titicaca, Peru, where since 1975 an HM2 Hoverferry has been hovering 12,506 ft above sea level.

BICYCLES

ORIGINS

The earliest machine propelled by cranks and pedals with connecting rods and actually built, was in 1839–40 by Kirkpatrick Macmillan (1810–78) of Dumfries, Scotland. A copy of the machine is now in the Science Museum, London, Great Britain.

The first practical bicycle was the *vélocipède* built in March 1861 by Pierre Michaux and his son Ernest of Rue de Verneuil, Paris, France.

In 1870, James Starley of Coventry, Great Britain constructed the first "penny-farthing" or ordinary bicycle. It had wire-spoked wheels for lightness and was later available with an optional-speed gear.

PRODUCTION

Longest   The longest true tandem bicycle ever built (i.e., without a third stabilizing wheel) is one designed and built by Terry Thessman of Pahiatua, New Zealand. It measures 72.96 ft long and weighs 340 lb. It was ridden by four riders a distance of 807 ft on 27 Feb 1988. Turning corners proved to be a problem.

Smallest   The world's smallest wheeled rideable bicycle is one with wheels of 0.76 in diameter which was ridden by its constructor, Neville Patten of Gladstone, Queensland, Australia for a distance of 13 ft 5½ in on 25 Mar 1988.

Jacques Puyoou of Pau, Pyrénées-Atlantiques, France has built a tandem of 14.1 in wheel diameter, which has been ridden by him and Madame Puyoou.

Largest   The largest bicycle as measured by the front-wheel diameter is "Frankencycle," built by Dave Moore of Rosemead, CA and first ridden by Steve Gordon of Moorpark, CA, on 4 Jun 1989. The wheel diameter is 10 ft and it is 11 ft 2 in high.

RIDING

Wheelie   A duration record of 5 hr 12 min 33 sec was set by David Robilliard at the Beau Sejour Leisure Center, St Peter Port, Guernsey, Channel Islands on 28 May 1990.

HUMAN-POWERED VEHICLES

Fastest land   The world speed records for human-powered vehicles (HPVs) over a 200 m (656.2 ft) flying start (single rider), are 65.484 mph by Fred Markham at Mono Lake, CA on 11 May 1986 and 62.92 mph (multiple riders) by Dave Grylls and Leigh Barczewski at the Ontario Speedway, CA, on 4 May 1980. The one-hour standing start (single rider) record is held by Pat Kinch, riding *Kingcycle Bean*, averaging a speed of 46.96 mph on 8 Sep 1990 at Millbrook Proving Ground, Great Britain.

Water cycle   The men's 6,562 ft (single rider) record is 12.84 mph, by Steve Hegg in *Flying Fish* at Long Beach, CA on 20 Jul 1987.

UNICYCLES

Tallest   The tallest unicycle ever mastered is one 101 ft 9 in tall ridden by Steve McPeak (with a safety wire suspended by an overhead crane) for a distance of 376 ft in Las Vegas, NV in October 1980. The freestyle riding (i.e., without a safety harness) of ever-taller unicycles would inevitably lead to serious injury or fatality.

Smallest   Peter Rosendahl (Sweden) of Las Vegas, NV rode a unicycle with a wheel diameter of $1^5/8$ in with no attachments or extensions fitted, a distance of 9 ft $9^1/2$ in at the Tangier Theater, Busch Gardens, Tampa, FL on 20 Nov 1992. The event was broadcast live on the Jack Harris & Co television show.

One hundred miles   Takayuki Koike of Kanagawa, Japan set a unicycle record for 100 miles in 6 hr 44 min 21.84 sec on 9 Aug 1987 (average speed 14.83 mph).

SMALLEST UNICYCLE
Peter Rosendahl on his
8-in-high unicycle.
(Photo: Busch Gardens,
Tampa/Jim Tuten)

Underwater tricycling   A team of 32 divers pedaled a distance of 116.66 miles in 75 hr 20 min on a standard tricycle at Diver's Den, Santa Barbara, CA on 16–19 Jun 1988 to raise money for the Muscular Dystrophy Association.

Endurance   Deepak Lele of Maharashtra, India unicycled 3,963 miles from New York to Los Angeles from 6 Jun–25 Sep 1984.

Backwards   Peter Rosendahl rode his 24-in-wheel unicycle backwards for a distance of 46.7 miles in 9 hr 25 min on 19 May 1990.

Sprint   Peter Rosendahl set sprint records from a standing start over 100 m (328.1 ft) of 12.74 secs (17.55 mph), and from a flying start for the same distance of 12.43 secs (17.99 mph), at the Wet 'N Wild Show, Las Vegas, NV on 1 Jul 1990.

MOTORCYCLES

ORIGINS

The earliest internal combustion-engined motorized bicycle was a wooden-framed machine built at Bad Cannstatt, Germany in October–November 1885 by Gottlieb Daimler (1834–1900) and first ridden by Wilhelm Maybach (1846–1929). It had a top speed of 12 mph and developed one-half of one horsepower from its single-cylinder 264 cc four-cycle engine at 700 rpm. Known as the "Einspur," it was lost in a fire in 1903.

The earliest factory that made motorcycles in quantity was opened in 1894 by Heinrich and Wilhelm Hildebrand and Alois Wolfmüller in Munich, Germany. In its first two years this factory produced over 1,000 machines, each having a water-cooled 1,488 cc twin-cylinder four-cycle engine developing about 2.5 bhp at 600 rpm—the highest-capacity motorcycle engine ever put into production.

PRODUCTION

As of October 1992 it was estimated that there were 4,081 million registered motorcycles in the United States.

Longest   Gregg Reid of Atlanta, GA designed and built a Yamaha 250 cc motorcycle that measures 15 ft 6 in long and weighs 520 lb. It is street legal and has been insured.

Smallest   Simon Timperley and Clive Williams of Progressive Engineering Ltd, Ashton-under-Lyne, Lancashire, Great Britain designed and constructed a motorcycle with a wheelbase of 4^1/$_4$ in, a seat height of 3^3/$_4$ in and a wheel diameter of 0.75 in for the front and 0.95 in for the back. The bike was ridden a distance of 3.2 ft.

Magnor Mydland of Norway constructed a motorcycle which, although not quite as small, traveled a far greater distance. It had a wheelbase of 4.72 in, a seat height of 5.82 in and wheel diameters of 1.49 in for the front and 3.39 in for the back. Mydland rode a distance of 1,870 ft, reaching a speed of 7.2 mph.

> **Wall of death**   The greatest endurance feat on a "wall of death" was 7 hr 0 min 13 sec, by Martin Blume, Berlin, Germany on 16 Apr 1983. He rode over 12,000 laps on the 33-ft-diameter wall on a Yamaha XS400, averaging 30 mph for the 181½ miles.
>
> **Ramp jumping**   The longest distance ever achieved by a motorcycle long-jumping is 251 ft, by Doug Danger on a 1991 Honda CR500 at Loudon, NH on 22 Jun 1991.

SPEED

Fastest production road machine   The 151 hp 1-liter Tu Atara Yamaha Bimota 6th edition EI has a road-tested top speed of 186.4 mph.

Fastest racing machine   There is no satisfactory answer to the identity of the fastest track machine other than to say that the current Honda, Suzuki and Yamaha machines have all been geared to attain speeds marginally in excess of 186.4 mph under race conditions.

Fastest speeds   *Official world speed records must be set with two runs over a measured distance made in opposite directions within a time limit of 1 hr for FIM records and of 2 hr for AMA records.*

Donald A. Vesco (USA; b. 8 Apr 1939), riding his 6.4-m-long *Lightning Bolt* streamliner, powered by two 1,016 cc Kawasaki engines, on Bonneville Salt Flats, UT on 28 Aug 1978 set AMA and FIM absolute records with an overall average of 318.598 mph and had a fastest run at an average of 318.865 mph.

The fastest time for a single run over 1,320 ft (1 km) from a standing start is 7.08 sec by Bo O'Brechta (USA) riding a supercharged 1,200 cc Kawasaki-based machine in Ontario, CA in 1980.

The highest terminal velocity recorded at the end of a 1 km run from a standing start is 199.55 mph by Russ Collins (USA) in Ontario, CA on 7 Oct 1978.

RIDING

Duration   The longest time a motor scooter has been kept in nonstop motion is 1,001 hr. A Kinetic Honda DX 100 cc, ridden by Har Parkash Rishi, Amarjeet Singh and Navjot Chadha, covered a distance of 19,241 miles at Traffic Park, Pune, Maharashtra, India between 22 Apr and Jun 1990.

Longest ride   Jari Saarelainen (Finland; b. 4 Apr 1959) rode his Honda Gold Wing 1,500 cc motorcycle over 67,109 miles through 43 countries. He set off from Helsinki, Finland on 1 Dec 1989 and returned 742 days later on 12 Dec 1991.

The first woman to circumnavigate the world solo was Moniika Vega (b. 9 May 1962) of Rio de Janeiro, Brazil, riding her Honda 125 cc motorcycle. Her journey began in Milan, Italy on 7 Mar 1990 and she returned to Italy on 24 May 1991, having covered a distance of 51,885 miles and visited 53 countries.

Jim Rogers and Tabitha Estabrook traveled 57,022 miles on two motorcycles, covering six continents. They set off from New York in March 1990 and returned in November 1991.

Trans-Americas Kurt Nerlich and Hans Shirmer traveled 67,000 miles (55,400 by motorcycle) around the Americas (North, South and Central) in 27 months from July 1954 to September 1956. Travel to and through Central and South America was much more primitive then than it is today.

LONGEST RIDE Jari Saarelainen of Finland traveled a distance of 67,109 miles and visited 43 countries on his Honda Gold Wing. He set off from Helsinki, Finland on 1 Dec 1989 and returned, 742 days later, on 12 Dec 1991. He only had two minor mishaps along the way—a collision with a donkey and, as seen here, when his bike fell off a ferry and into the River Siak at Pekanbaru, Indonesia. (Photo: Jari Saarelainen)

Trans-America   Ken Hatton of Chicago, IL completed a solo motorcycle trek across the United States, in September 1988, in a record time of 43 hr 17 min.

Biggest pyramid   The White Helmets of the Royal Signals Display Teams established a world record with a pyramid of 54 men on eight motorcycles. The pyramid was held together by muscle and determination only, with no straps, harnesses or other aids. It traveled a distance of 328 ft on 24 Oct 1992 at Catterick Airfield, Great Britain.

Backwards riding   Steering a motorcycle facing backwards from the top of a 10 ft ladder, over a continuous period of 1 hr 30 min, Signalman Dewi Jones of the Royal Signals White Helmets covered a distance of 20½ miles at Catterick Airfield, Great Britain on 30 Nov 1988.

Wheelie Distance   Yasuyuki Kudoh at the Japan Automobile Research Institute, Tsukuba City, Ibaragi-prefecture, Japan covered 205.7 miles nonstop on the rear wheel of his Honda TLM 220 R 216 cc motorcycle on 5 May 1991.

The United States record was set by Doug Domokos (USA) on the Alabama International Speedway, Talladega on 27 Jun 1984. He covered 145 miles nonstop on the rear wheel of his Honda XR 500. He stopped only when the gasoline ran out.

Speed   The highest speed attained on a rear wheel of a motorcycle is 150 mph, by Steve Burns on 3 Jul 1989 at Bruntingthorpe Proving Ground, Great Britain on his Suzuki GXS 1100 engine Spondon 1425 turbo.

Two-wheel sidecar riding   Konstantin Matreyev (Russia) rode a distance of 210.5 miles on a Ural at Irbit Stadium, Sverdloskaya, Russia, on 7–8 Jun 1992.

Most on one machine   The record for the most people on a single machine is 46 members of the Illawarra Mini Bike Training Club, New South Wales, Australia. They rode on a 1,000 cc motorcycle and traveled a distance of one mile on 11 Oct 1987.

AUTOMOBILES

ORIGINS

Model   The earliest "automobile" of which there is a record was a two-foot-long steam-powered model constructed by Ferdinand Verbiest (d. 1687), a Belgian Jesuit priest, and described in his *Astronomia Europaea*. His model of 1668 was possibly inspired either by Giovanni Branca's description of a steam turbine, published in his *La Macchina* in 1629, or even by *Nan Huairen* (writings on "fire carts") in the Chu kingdom (*c.* 800 B.C.).

Passenger-carrying   The world's first passenger-carrying automobile was a steam-powered road vehicle carrying eight passengers and built by Richard Trevithick (1771–1833). It first ran on 24 Dec 1801 in Camborne, Great Britain.

The earliest full-scale automobile was the first of two military steam tractors completed at the Paris Arsenal in October 1769 by Nicolas-Joseph Cugnot (1725–1804). This reached 2¼ mph. Cugnot's second, larger tractor, completed in May 1771, today survives in the *Conservatoire Nationale des Arts et Métiers* in Paris, France.

Internal combustion   The Swiss Isaac de Rivaz (d. 1828) built a carriage powered by his "explosion engine" in 1805. The first practical internal combustion engined vehicle was that built by the Londoner Samuel Brown (British Patent Number 5350, 25 Apr 1826), whose 4-hp two-cylinder atmospheric gas 88-liter engined carriage climbed Shooters Hill, Kent, Great Britain in May 1826.

The first successful gasoline-driven car, the Motorwagen, built by Karl-Friedrich Benz (1844–1929) of Karlsruhe, Germany, ran at Mannheim, Germany in late 1885. It was a 5 cwt three-wheeler reaching 8–10 mph. Its single-cylinder engine (bore 3.6 in, stroke 6.3 in) delivered 0.85 hp at 400 rpm. It was patented on 29 Jan 1886. Its first 1.6 mile road test was re-

---

Carriage driving   The only man to drive 48 horses in a single hitch is Dick Sparrow of Zearing, IA, between 1972 and 1977. The lead horses were on reins 135 ft long.

Floyd Zopfi of Stratford, WI has driven 52 llamas in a hitch on several occasions since 1990, with the lead llamas (four abreast) on reins 150 ft long.

Coaching   The longest horse-drawn procession was a cavalcade of 68 carriages that measured 3,018 ft "nose to tail," organized by the Spies Traveling Company of Denmark on 7 May 1986. It carried 810 people through the woods around Copenhagen to celebrate the coming of spring.

Car registrations Earliest   The world's first license plates were introduced by the Paris police in France in 1893.

License plate No. 8 was sold at a Hong Kong government auction for HK$5 million (approximately $602,250) on 13 Feb 1988 to Law Ting pong, a textile manufacturer. The number 8 is considered a lucky number.

As of 31 Dec 1992, it was estimated that there were 143.823 million automobiles and 45.871 million trucks and buses registered in the United States.

Car collection   The unrivaled collector of Rolls-Royces was Bhagwan Shree Rajneesh (Osho; ne Chandra Mohan Jain [1931–90]), the Indian mystic of Rajneeshpuram, OR. His disciples bestowed 93 of these upon him before his deportation from the United States in November 1985.

---

ported in the local newspaper, the *Neue Badische Landeszeitung*, of 4 Jun 1886, under the heading "Miscellaneous."

PRODUCTION

The total number of vehicles constructed worldwide in 1991 was 46,420,410, of which 34,998,534 were automobiles. The peak year for production was 1989, when 47,697,698 vehicles (35,195,749 cars) were manufactured, although the peak for cars only was 1990, when 35,277,986 were produced.

In 1992 the number of automobiles constructed in the United States was 5,665,863. The leading manufacturer was General Motors Corporation, which produced 2,468,869. The number of trucks manufactured in 1992 was 4,038,218; Ford was the leading manufacturer with 1,496,412.

The world's largest manufacturer of motor vehicles and parts (and the largest manufacturing company) is General Motors Corporation of Detroit, MI. The company has on average 750,000 employees. A peak figure of 948,000 vehicles was produced in 1978. The company's highest annual income was $126 billion in 1989.

Largest plant   The largest single automobile plant in the world is the Volkswagenwerk at Wolfsburg, Germany, with 60,000 employees and a capacity for producing 4,000 vehicles every week (208,000 per year). The factory buildings cover an area of 371 acres and the whole plant covers 1,878 acres, with 46 miles of rail sidings.

United States   The largest automobile plant in the United States is the Nissan Motor Manufacturing Corp.'s Smyrna, TN plant. The plant has a capacity of 450,000 cars and compact pickup trucks at the end of 1992. The plant covers an area of 5.1 million ft².

Longest in production   Among mass-production models, the Volkswagen "Beetle" dates from 1938. The 21 millionth "Beetle" rolled off the last remaining production line, at Puebla, Mexico, in December 1991.

FASTEST PRODUCTION CAR   The highest speed ever attained by a standard production car is 217.1 mph for a Jaguar XJ220, driven by Martin Brundle at the Nardo test track, Italy on 21 Jun 1992.

The Morgan 4/4, built by the Morgan Motor Car Co. of Malvern, Great Britain (founded 1910), celebrated its 57th birthday on 27 Dec 1992. There is still a six- to eight-year waiting list to buy this model.

United States   The luxury model Cadillac Fleetwood has been in continuous production since 1936. The oldest mass-production model still being made is the Chrysler Imperial, which was in production from 1926–84 and 1990–present.

Largest cars   Of cars produced for private use, the largest was the Bugatti Royale type 41, of which only six were assembled at Molsheim, France by the Italian Ettore Bugatti. First built in 1927, this machine has an eight-cylinder engine of 12.7 liters capacity, and measures over 22 ft in length. The hood is over 7 ft long.

Longest car   A 100-ft-long 26-wheeled limo was designed by Jay Ohrberg of Burbank, CA. It has many special features, including a swimming pool, a diving board and a king-sized water bed. It is designed to be driven as one piece, or it can be changed to bend in the middle. Its main purpose is for use in films and exhibitions.

Largest engines   The largest engine capacity of a production car is 13.5 liters, for the US Pierce-Arrow 6–66 Raceabout of 1912–18, the US Peerless 6–60 of 1912–14, and the Fageol of 1918.

Most powerful   The most powerful current production car is the Bugatti EB110 Super Sports, which develops in excess of 610 bhp.

Heaviest   The heaviest car recently in production (up to 25 were made annually) appears to be the Soviet-built Zil–41047 limousine with a 12.72 ft wheelbase. It weighs 7,352 lb (3.3 tons). A "stretched" Zil (two to three made annually) was used by former USSR President Mikhail Gorbachev until December 1991. It weighed 6.6 tons and was made of three-inch armor-plated steel. The eight-cylinder, 7-liter engine guzzled fuel at a rate of 6 miles to the gallon.

Lightest   Louis Borsi of London, Great Britain has built and driven a 21 lb car with a 2.5-cc engine. It is capable of 15 mph.

Smallest street-legal car   The smallest registered street-legal car in the United States has an overall length of 88¾ in and a width of 40½ in. It was built by Arlis Sluder and is now owned by Jeff Gibson.

Most expensive   The most expensive car ever built was the US Presidential 1969 Lincoln Continental Executive delivered to the US Secret Service on 14 Oct 1968. It has an overall length of 21 ft 6¼ in with a 13 ft 4 in wheelbase, and with the addition of 2.2 tons of armor plate weighs 6 tons (12,000 lb). The estimated cost of research, development and manufacture was $500,000, but it is rented at $5,000 per year. Even if all four tires were shot out it could travel at 50 mph on inner rubber-edged steel discs.

Used   The greatest confirmed price paid is $15 million, including commission, for the Bugatti Type 41 Royale Sports Coupé by Kellner, sold to the Meitec Corporation of Japan, completed on 12 Apr 1990.

Most inexpensive   The cheapest car of all time was the 1922 Red Bug Buckboard, built by the Briggs & Stratton Co. of Milwaukee, WI, listed at $125–$150. It had a 62 in wheelbase and weighed 245 lb. Early models of the King Midget cars were sold in kit form for self-assembly for as little as $100 in 1948.

SPEED

Land speed   The *official* one-mile land-speed record is 633.468 mph, set by Richard Noble (b. 1946) on 4 Oct 1983 over the Black Rock Desert, NV in his 17,000 lb thrust Rolls-Royce Avon 302 jet-powered *Thrust 2*, designed by John Ackroyd.

Rocket-engined   The fastest speed attained by any wheeled land vehicle is 631.367 mph by *The Blue Flame*, a rocket-powered four-wheeled vehicle driven by Gary Gabelich (USA; b. 23 Aug 1940) on the Bonneville Salt Flats, UT on 23 Oct 1970. Momentarily Gabelich exceeded 650 mph. The car was powered by a liquid natural gas/hydrogen peroxide rocket engine developing a maximum thrust of 22,000 lb.

The fastest reputed land speed figure in one direction is 739.666 mph, or Mach 1.0106, by Stan Barrett (USA) in the *Budweiser Rocket*, a rocket-engined three-wheeled car, at Edwards Air Force Base, CA on 17 Dec 1979. *This published speed of Mach 1.0106 is not officially sanctioned by the USAF, as the Digital Instrument Radar was not calibrated or certified. The radar information was not generated by the vehicle directly but by an operator aiming a dish by means of a TV screen.*

The fastest land speed recorded by a woman is 524.016 mph by Mrs Kitty Hambleton (nee O'Neil; USA) in the 48,000 hp rocket-powered three-wheeled SM1 *Motivator* over the Alvord Desert, OR on 6 Dec 1976. Her official two-way record was 512.710 mph and she probably touched 600 mph momentarily.

Piston-engined   The fastest speed measured for a wheel-driven car is 432.692 mph by Al Teague in *Speed-O-Motive/Spirit of 76* at Bonneville Salt Flats, UT on 21 Aug 1991 over the final 132 ft of a mile run (av. 425.230 mph for the whole mile).

Diesel-engined   The prototype 3-liter Mercedes C 111/3 attained 203.3 mph in tests on the Nardo Circuit, southern Italy on 5–15 Oct 1978, and in April 1978 averaged 195.4 mph for 12 hours, thus covering a world record 2,344.7 miles.

Rocket-powered sleds   The fastest speed recorded on ice is 247.93 mph by *Oxygen*, driven by Sammy Miller (b. 15 Apr 1945) on Lake George, NY on 15 Feb 1981.

Steam car   On 19 Aug 1985 Robert E. Barber broke the 79-year-old record for a steam car driving No. 744, *Steamin' Demon*, built by the Barber-Nichols Engineering Co, which reached 145.607 mph at Bonneville Salt Flats, UT.

Road cars   Various revved up track cars have been licensed for road use but are not normal production models.

The fastest speed ever attained by a standard production car is

217.1 mph for a Jaguar XJ220, driven by Martin Brundle at the Nardo test track, Italy on 21 Jun 1992.

The highest road-tested acceleration reported for a standard production car is 0–60 mph in 3.275 sec for a Ford RS200 Evolution, driven by Graham Hathaway at the Boreham Proving Ground, Essex, Great Britain, on 28 Apr 1993.

Fastest street-legal car   The highest road-tested acceleration is 0–60 mph in 3.89 sec for a Jankel *Tempest* driven by Mark Hargreaves at Millbrook Proving Ground, Bedfordshire, Great Britain on 13 Apr 1992.

DRIVING

Highest mileage   The highest recorded mileage for a car was 1,442,044 authenticated miles up to 25 Jan 1993 for a 1963 Volkswagen "Beetle" owned by Albert Klein of Pasadena, CA.

The highest record mileage for an automobile with the original gasoline motor without an overhaul is 577,363 miles to 5 Jan 1993 by Don Champion's 1979 Cadillac Sedan DeVille.

Six continents   The fastest drive taking in the six continents, with a total distance driven of more than an equator's length of driving (24,901 miles), is one of 39 days 20 hr. Driving a Nissan Sunny 1.4 car, Saloo and Neena Choudhury of Calcutta, India left New Delhi on 7 Nov 1991, and returned to the same place on 17 Dec 1991. On their journey they traveled through 25 countries.

Amphibious circumnavigation   The only circumnavigation by an amphibious vehicle was by Ben Carlin (Australia; d. 7 Mar 1981) in the amphibious jeep *Half-Safe*. He completed the last leg of the Atlantic crossing (the English Channel) on 24 Aug 1951. He arrived back in Montreal, Canada on 8 May 1958, having completed a circumnavigation of 39,000 miles over land and 9,600 miles by sea and river. He was accompanied on the transatlantic stage by his ex-wife Elinore (USA) and on the long transpacific stage (Tokyo, Japan to Anchorage, AK) by Broye Lafayette De-Mente (USA; b. 1928).

One-year duration record   The greatest distance ever covered in one year is 354,257 miles, by two Opel Rekord 2-liter passenger sedans, both of which achieved this distance between 18 May 1988 and the same date in 1989 without any major mechanical breakdowns. The vehicles were manufactured by the Delta Motor Corporation, Port Elizabeth, South Africa, and were driven on tar and gravel roads in the Northern Cape by a team of company drivers from Delta. The entire undertaking was monitored by the Automobile Association of South Africa.

Trans-Americas   Garry Sowerby (Canada), with Tim Cahill (USA) as co-driver and navigator, drove a 1988 GMC Sierra K3500 four-wheel-drive pickup truck powered by a 6.2-liter V8 Detroit diesel engine from Ushuaia, Tierra del Fuego, Argentina to Prudhoe Bay, AK, a distance of 14,739 miles, in a total elapsed time of 23 days 22 hr 43 min from 29 Sep to 22 Oct 1987. The vehicle and team were surface-freighted from Cartagena, Colombia to Balboa, Panama so as to bypass the Darién Gap.

HIGHEST MILEAGE The highest recorded mileage for a car is 1,442,044 miles up to 25 Jan 1993 for a 1963 Volkswagen "Beetle" owned by Albert Klein of Pasadena, CA.

BATTERY-POWERED CAR The greatest distance covered by a battery-powered car on a single charge is 339.898 miles.

The Darién Gap was first traversed by the Land Rover *La Cucaracha Carinosa* (The Affectionate Cockroach) of the Trans-Darién Expedition 1959–60, crewed by Richard E. Bevir (Great Britain) and engineer Terence John Whitfield (Australia). They left Chepo, Panama on 3 Feb 1960 and reached Quibdó, Colombia on 17 June, averaging 660 ft per hour of indescribable difficulty.

Trans-America   Jeremiah L. Burr (driver/leader), Kurt E. Detlefsen (driver) and Thaddeus E. Burr (navigator) of Connecticut completed the first documented traverse of all the contiguous 48 states of the United States from 13 May to 19 May 1991, in a total elapsed time of 5 days, 7 hours and 15 minutes and a total distance of 7,217.8 miles. The team drove a 1990 Chevrolet Astro Van and stopped only for fuel. Dehydrated foods and nine gallons of water made the team self-sufficient.

Gasoline consumption   A team of students from Lycée St Joseph La Joliverie, Nantes, France achieved 7,591 mpg in the Shell Mileage Marathon at Silverstone, Great Britain on 17 Jul 1992.

Longest fuel range   The greatest distance driven without refueling on a single fuel fill in a standard vehicle (38.2 gal carried in factory-optional twin fuel tanks) is 1,691.6 miles, by a 1991 Toyota LandCruiser diesel station wagon. Driven by Ewan Kennedy with Ian Lee (observer) from Nyngan, New South Wales, Australia to Winton, Queensland and back between 18–21 May 1992, the car averaged 37.3 mph, giving 44.2 mpg.

The greatest distance traveled by an unmodified production car on the contents of a standard fuel tank is 1,338.1 miles, giving 75.94 mpg, between 26–28 Jul 1992. Stuart Bladon and Robert Procter drove the length of Great Britain, from John O'Groats to Land's End, and returned to Scotland driving an Audi 100 TD1 diesel car. The fuel of the 17.62-gallon fuel tank ran out after 35 hr 18 min.

Driving in reverse   Charles Creighton (1908–70) and James Hargis of Maplewood, MO drove their Model A Ford 1929 roadster in reverse from New York 3,340 miles to Los Angeles, CA, from 26 Jul–13 Aug 1930 without once stopping the engine. They arrived back in New York in reverse on 5 September, having completed 7,180 miles in 42 days.

Brian "Cub" Keene and James "Wilbur" Wright drove their Chevrolet Blazer 9,031 miles in reverse in 37 days (1 Aug–6 Sep 1984) through 15 American states and Canada. Though it was prominently named "Stuck in Reverse," law-enforcement officers in Oklahoma refused to believe it and insisted they drive in reverse reverse—i.e., forward—out of the state.

The highest average speed attained in any nonstop reverse drive exceeding 500 miles was achieved by Gerald Hoagland, who drove a 1969 Chevrolet Impala 501 miles in 17 hr 38 min at Chemung Speed Drome, NY on 9–10 Jul 1976, to average 28.41 mph.

Two-side-wheel driving Car   Bengt Norberg (b. 23 Oct 1951) of Äppelbo, Sweden drove a Mitsubishi Colt GTi-16V on two side wheels nonstop for a distance of 192.873 miles in a time of 7 hr 15 min 50 sec. He also achieved a distance of 27.842 miles in 1 hr at Rattvik Horse Track, Sweden on 24 May 1989.

Sven-Erik Söderman (Sweden; b. 26 Sep 1960) achieved a speed of 102.14 mph over a 100 m (328.1 ft) flying start on the two wheels of an

Car wrecking In a career lasting 25 years from 1968 to 1993, Dick Sheppard of Gloucester, Great Britain wrecked a total of 2,003 cars.

Worst driver It was reported that a 75-year-old male driver received 10 traffic tickets, drove on the wrong side of the road four times, committed four hit-and-run offenses and caused six accidents, all within 20 minutes, in McKinney, TX on 15 Oct 1966.

Parade of Rolls-Royces A parade of 114 Rolls-Royce motor cars assembled on the northbound carriageway of the Tolo Harbour Highway in the New Territories of Hong Kong on 8 Sep 1991. The average length of the cars participating was 17 ft 2 in and the total length of the parade was 1 mile 22 yd.

Battery-powered car The greatest distance covered by a battery-powered car on a single charge is 339.898 miles, by the Horlacher Na-S Sport, driven by Paul Schweizer. The car, designed by Horlacher AG of Möhlin, Switzerland, was driven on public roads from Zurich to Geneva, via Berne and Lausanne, on 4 Mar 1992.

Opel Kadett at Mora Siljan airport, Mora, Sweden on 2 Aug 1990. Söderman achieved a record speed for the flying kilometer at 152.96 km (95.04 mph) at the same venue on 24 Aug 1990.

Truck Sven-Erik Söderman drove a Daf 2800 7.5 ton truck on two wheels for a distance of 6.73 miles at Mora Siljan airport, Mora, Sweden on 19 May 1991.

Bus Bobby Ore (Great Britain; b. Jan 1949) drove a double-decker bus a distance of 810 ft on two wheels at North Weald Airfield, Great Britain on 21 May 1988.

Wheelie Steve Murty, driving a Pirelli High Performer, established the record for the longest wheelie in a truck, covering 1,794.9 ft at the National Power Sports Festival in Blackpool, Great Britain on 28 Jun 1991.

Most durable driver Goodyear Tire and Rubber Co. test driver Weldon C. Kocich drove 3,141,946 miles from 5 Feb 1953 to 28 Feb 1986, thus averaging 95,210 miles per year.

Oldest drivers Roy M. Rawlins (b. 10 Jul 1870) of Stockton, CA was given a warning for driving at 95 mph in a 55 mph zone in June 1974. On 25 Aug 1974 he was awarded a California State license valid until 1978, but he died on 9 Jul 1975, one day short of his 105th birthday.

Mrs Maude Tull of Inglewood, CA, who took to driving at the age of 91 after her husband died, was issued a renewal on 5 Feb 1976 when she was 104.

Driving tests The world's easiest tests are those in Egypt, in which the ability to drive 19.64 ft forward and the same in reverse has been deemed sufficient. In 1979 it was reported that accurate reversing between two rubber traffic cones had been added. "High cone attrition" soon led to the substitution of white lines.

Mrs Fannie Turner (b. 1903) of Little Rock, AR passed the *written* test for drivers on her 104th attempt in October 1978.

Drivers' licenses Regular drivers' licenses are issued to 15-year-olds without a driver-education course only in Hawaii and Mississippi. Thirteen states issue restricted juvenile licenses at 14.

SPECIALIZED VEHICLES

GENERAL

Largest The most massive automotive land vehicle is "Big Muskie," the 12,004 ton mechanical shovel built by Bucyrus Erie for the Musk mine. It is 487 ft long, 151 ft wide and 222 ft high, with a grab capacity of 364 tons.

Longest The Arctic Snow Train owned by the world-famous tightrope-walker Steve McPeak (USA) has 54 wheels and is 572 ft long. It was built by R.G. Le Tourneau Inc. of Longview, TX for the US Army. Its gross train weight is 441 tons, with a top speed of 20 mph, and it was driven by a crew of six when used as an "overland train" for the military. It generates 4,680 shp and has a fuel capacity of 7,832 gal. McPeak undertook all repairs, including every punctured wheel, single-handedly in often sub-zero temperatures in Alaska.

AMBULANCES

Largest The world's largest are the 59-ft-long articulated Alligator Jumbulances Marks VI, VII, VIII and IX, operated by the ACROSS Trust to convey the sick and handicapped on vacations and pilgrimages across Europe. They are built by Van Hool of Belgium with Fiat engines, cost $350,000 and carry 44 patients and staff.

BUSES

Earliest The first municipal bus service in the world was inaugurated on 12 Apr 1903 and ran between Eastbourne railroad station and Meads, Great Britain.

Longest The longest are the articulated DAF Super CityTrain buses of Zaire, with 110 passenger seats and room for 140 "strap-hangers" in the first trailer, and 60 seated and 40 "strap-hangers" in the second, for a total of 350. Designed by President Mobutu of Zaire, the buses are 105.64 ft long and weigh 32 tons empty.

Rigid The longest rigid single bus is 49 ft long and carries 69 passengers. It was built by Van Hool of Belgium.

Largest fleet   The 10,364 single-deck buses in São Paulo, Brazil, make up the world's largest bus fleet.

Longest route   The longest regularly scheduled bus route is 3,559 miles long, operated by Group Ormeño, which since August 1978 has run a regular scheduled service between Tumbes, Peru and Buenos Aires, Argentina. The route takes 116 hr, with two hours stopover in Lima and 12 hours in Santiago, Chile.

United States   The longest scheduled bus route currently in use in the United States is by Greyhound from Chicago to San Francisco. It runs once per day, is 2,287 miles long, and takes 49 hours 50 minutes to complete, employing seven drivers, with no change of bus.

Greatest passenger volume   The city with the greatest passenger volume in the United States as of December 1992 was New York City, with 636.7 million for buses and 1.32 billion for trains and unlinked passenger trips. In 1992 the city with the highest aggregate for passenger miles traveled was also New York City, where riders logged approximately 1.9 billion miles.

CAMPERS

Largest   The largest camper is a two-wheeled, five-story vehicle built in 1990 by H.E. Sheik Hamad Bin Hamdan Al Nahyan of Abu Dhabi, United Arab Emirates. It is 66 ft long, 39 ft wide and stands 39 ft high. Weighing 120 tons, it comprises eight bedrooms, eight bathrooms, four garages and water storage for 6,340 gal.

FASTEST CAMPER   The world speed record for a camper is 126.76 mph for a Roadstar camper towed by a 1990 Ford EA Falcon saloon and driven by "Charlie" Kovacs, at Mangalore Airfield, Seymour, Victoria, Australia on 18 Apr 1991. (Photo: Rex Features/Brendan Beirne)

Longest journey The continuous motor camper journey of 143,716 miles by Harry B. Coleman and Peggy Larson in a Volkswagen Camper from 20 Aug 1976 to 20 Apr 1978 took them through 113 countries.

Fastest The world speed record for a camper is 126.76 mph, by a Roadstar camper towed by a 1990 Ford EA Falcon, driven by Charlie Kovacs, at Mangalore Airfield, Seymour, Victoria, Australia on 18 Apr 1991.

FIRE ENGINES

Greatest pumping capacity The fire appliance with the greatest pumping capacity is the 860 hp eight-wheel Oshkosh firetruck, weighing 66 tons and used for aircraft and runway fires. It can discharge 50,200 gal of foam through two turrets in just 150 sec.

Fastest The fastest on record is the Jaguar XJ12 "Chubb Firefighter," which on 2 Nov 1982 attained a speed of 130.57 mph in tests when servicing the *Thrust 2* land-speed record trials. (See Automobiles, Land speed.)

GO KARTS

Highest mileage The highest mileage recorded in 24 hours on an outdoor circuit by a four-man team is 1,018 miles, on a one-mile track at the Erbsville Kartway, Waterloo, Ontario, Canada on 4–5 Sep 1983. The 5-hp 140 cc Honda engined kart was driven by Owen Nimmo, Gary Ruddock, Jim Timmins and Danny Upshaw.

The highest mileage recorded in 24 hours on an indoor track by a four-man team driving 160 cc karts is 844.25 miles, in 7,289 laps on a 203 yd track at the Welsh Karting Centre, Newport, Great Britain on 19–20 Nov

Largest crawler The most massive vehicle ever constructed is the Marion eight-caterpillar crawler used for conveying Saturn V rockets to their launch pads at Cape Canaveral, FL. It measures 131 ft 4 in × 114 ft, and the two built cost $12.3 million. The loaded train weight is 9,000 tons. The windshield wiper blades are 42 in long and are the world's largest.

Fire pumping The greatest gallonage stirrup-pumped by a team of eight in an 80 hr charity pump is 37,898 gal, by firefighters at the Knaresborough Fire Station, Great Britain from 25–28 Jun 1992.

Fire pump handling The longest unaided tow of a fire appliance in excess of 1,120 lb in 24 hr on a closed circuit is 223 miles, by a 32-man team of the Dublin Fire Brigade with a 1,144-lb fire pump on 20–21 Jun 1987.

Model cars A Scalextric Jaguar XJ8 ran nonstop for 866 hr 44 min 54 sec and covered a distance of 1,771.2 miles from 2 May to 7 Jun 1989. The event was organized by the Rev. Bryan G. Apps and church members of Southbourne, Great Britain.

1992. The drivers were Ken Denscombe, Gerry Austin, Kevin Blanch and Mark Bowden of the Costain Civil Engineering Team.

Six hours   The record distance achieved in six hours in the 100 cc non-gearbox category is 249.117 miles by Zack Dawson at the Mesa Marin Raceway in Bakersfield, CA, on 9 Apr 1993.

LAWNMOWERS

Widest   The widest gang mower in the world is the 5.6-ton 60-ft-wide 27-unit "Big Green Machine" used by the turf farmer Jay Edgar Frick of Monroe, OH. It mows an acre in 60 sec.

Longest distance   The longest drive on a power lawn mower was 3,034 miles, when Ian Ireland of Harlow, Great Britain drove an Iseki SG15 between Harlow and Southend Pier, Great Britain from 13 Aug to 7 Sep 1989. He was assisted by members of 158 Round Table, Luton, Great Britain and raised over £15,000 ($26,250) to aid the Leukemia Research Fund.

SLOT CARS

24-hour slot car racing   On 5–6 Jul 1986 the North London Society of Model Engineers team at the ARRA club in Southport, Great Britain achieved a distance record for a 1:32 scale car of 305.949 miles in 24 hours, 11,815 laps of the track, driving a Rondeau M482C Group C Sports car, built by Ian Fisher. This was under the rules of the BSCRA (British Slot Car Racing Association). A team of eight set a new distance record of 168.56 miles for the H:scale 24-hour Le Mans Slot Car Race driving a Mercedes at the Welfare Sports Centre, Derby on 20–21 Jun 1992.

The longest slot car track measures 958 ft and was built at Mallory Park Circuit, Great Britain on 22 Nov 1991 using pieces collected from enthusiasts. One lap was successfully completed by a car.

SOLAR-POWERED

Fastest speed   The fastest speed attained by a solely solar-powered land vehicle is 48.71 mph, by Molly Brennan driving the General Motors *Sunraycer* at Mesa, AZ on 24 Jun 1988. The fastest speed of 83.88 mph using solar/battery power was achieved by Star Micronics' solar car *Solar Star*, driven by Manfred Hermann on 5 Jan 1991 at Richmond RAAF Base, Richmond, New South Wales, Australia.

TANKS

Earliest   The first tank was *No. 1 Lincoln*, modified to become *Little Willie*, built by William Foster & Co. Ltd of Lincoln, Great Britain. It first ran on 6 Sep 1915. Tanks were first taken into action by the Heavy Section, Machine Gun Corps, British Army, which later became the Tank Corps, at the Battle of Flers-Courcelette in France on 15 Sep 1916. The Mark I Male tank, armed with a pair of six-pounder guns and four machine guns, weighed 31.3 tons and was driven by a motor developing 105 hp, which gave it a maximum road speed of 3–4 mph.

Heaviest The heaviest tank ever constructed was the German Panzer Kampfwagen Maus II, which weighed over 210 tons. By 1945 it had reached only the experimental stage and was not developed further.

The heaviest operational tank used by any army was the 83-ton 13-man French Char de Rupture 2C bis of 1922. It carried a 155-mm howitzer and had two 250 hp engines giving a maximum speed of 8 mph. The world's most heavily armed tank since 1972 has been the Soviet T-72, with a 4^7/$_8$ in high-velocity gun.

The heaviest tank in the United States Army is the M1A1 Abrams, which weighs 67 tons when combat loaded, is 32 ft 3 in long, and can reach a maximum speed of 41.5 mph.

Fastest The fastest armored reconnaissance vehicle is the British Scorpion, which can reach 50 mph with a 75 percent payload.

The American experimental tank M1936, built by J. Walter Christie, was clocked at 64.3 mph during official trials in Great Britain in 1938.

Most prolific The greatest production of any tank was that of the Soviet T-54/55 series, of which more than 50,000 were built between 1954 and 1980 in the USSR alone, with further production in the one-time Warsaw Pact countries and China.

TAXIS

Largest fleet The largest taxi fleet is that in Mexico City, with 60,000 "normal" taxis, pesaros (communal fixed-route taxis) and settas (airport taxis).

United States The city with the largest taxi fleet in the United States is New York City, which on 1 Jan 1993 had 11,787 registered yellow medallion cabs and 40,000 licensed drivers serving an estimated 200 million passengers yearly. In addition, there are approximately 30,000 rental service vehicles in New York City. Both figures for 1992 show a significant drop from previous years.

Taxi drivers Carmen Fasanella (b. 19 Feb 1903) was continuously licensed as a taxicab owner and driver in the Borough of Princeton, NJ for 68 years 243 days, from 1 Feb 1921 to 2 Nov 1989.

Longest taxicab ride The longest taxicab ride on record is one of 14,414 miles at a cost of 70,000 FIM (approximately $16,000). Mika Lehtonen and Juhani Saramies left Nokia, Finland on 2 May 1991, traveling through Scandinavia down to Spain, and arrived back in Nokia on 17 May 1991.

TRACTORS

Largest The world's largest tractor is a $459,000 US Department of Agriculture Wide Tractive Frame Vehicle completed by Ag West of Sacramento, CA in June 1982. It measures 33 ft between its wheels, which are designed to run on permanent paths, and weighs 24.5 tons.

Tractor-pulling The sport of tractor-pulling was put on a national US championship basis in 1967 at Bowling Green, OH, where the winner was

"The Purple Monster" built and driven by Roger E. Varns. Today there are 12 classes ranging up to "12,200 lb unlimited."

Longest journey   The longest journey on record by tractor is 14,500 miles. The Young Farmers Group of Devon, Great Britain left their native country on 18 Oct 1990 in one tractor and a supporting trailer, and drove overland to Zimbabwe, arriving on 4 Mar 1991.

TROLLEYS

Oldest   The oldest trolleys in continuous service in the world are motor cars 1 and 2 of the Manx Electric Railway, dating from 1893. These run regularly on the 17¾-mile railroad between Douglas and Ramsey, Isle of Man, Great Britain.

Most extensive system   By early 1991, St Petersburg, Russia had the most extensive tramway system, with 2,402 cars on 64 routes and 429.13 miles of track.

Longest journey   The longest trolley journey now possible is from Krefeld St Tönis to Witten Annen Nord, Germany. With luck at the eight interconnections, the 65.5-mile trip can be completed in 5½ hours.

TRUCKS

Largest   The world's largest is the Terex Titan 33–19 manufactured by General Motors Corporation and now in operation at Westar Mine, British Columbia, Canada. It has a loaded weight of 604.7 tons and a capacity of 350 tons. When tipped, its height is 56 ft. The 16-cylinder engine delivers 3,300 hp. The fuel tank holds 1,300 gal.

Pedal car   The record from Marble Arch, London, Great Britain to the Arc de Triomphe, Paris, France, including a Channel crossing by ferry, is 21 hr 24 min 0 sec, for a distance of 238 miles, by a team of six members of the national childcare charity in Great Britain on 30 Aug 1991.

Snowmobile   John W. Outzen of Derry, NH (expedition organizer and leader), Andre, Carl and Dennis Boucher, traveled 10,252.3 miles across North America, from Anchorage, AK to Dartmouth, Nova Scotia, Canada, in 62 days (56 riding days) from 2 Jan to 3 Mar 1992 on four Arctic Cat Panther Deluxe Snowmobiles.

Tony Lenzini of Duluth, MN, drove his 1986 Arctic Cat Cougar snowmobile a total of 7,211 miles in 60 riding days between 28 Dec 1985 and 20 Mar 1986.

Heaviest load   On 14–15 Jul 1984 John Brown Engineers & Contractors BV moved the Conoco Kotter Field production deck with a roll-out weight of 325 tons for the Continental Netherlands Oil Co. of Leidsenhage, Netherlands.

Most powerful Les Shockley of Galena, KS drove his Jet Truck *Shock-Wave*, powered by three Pratt & Whitney jet engines developing 36,000 hp, to a record speed of 256 mph in 6.36 sec over a quarter-mile from a standing start on 4 Jun 1989 at Autodrome de Monterrey, Mexico. He set a further record for the standing mile at 376 mph at Paine Field, Everett, WA on 18 Aug 1991.

WRECKERS

Most powerful The world's most powerful wrecker is the Twin City Garage and Body Shop's 22.7-ton, 36-ft-long International M6-23 "Hulk" 1969 stationed at Scott City, MO. It can lift in excess of 325 tons on its short boom.

LARGEST TIRES   The world's largest are manufactured by the Goodyear Tire & Rubber Co. for giant dump trucks. They measure 12 ft in diameter, weigh 12,500 lb and cost $74,000. A tire 17 ft in diameter is believed to be the upper limit of what is practical. (Photo: Rex Features/Sipa Press)

SERVICES

FILLING STATIONS

Largest   The largest concentration of pumps is 204—96 of them Tokheim Unistar (electronic) and 108 Tokheim Explorer (mechanical)—in Jeddah, Saudi Arabia.

Highest   The highest filling station in the world is at Leh, Ladakh, India, at 12,001 ft, operated by the Indian Oil Corporation.

GARAGES

Largest   The largest private garage is one of two stories built outside Bombay, India for the private collection of 176 cars owned by Pranlal Bhogilal (b. 1939).

The KMB Overhaul Center, operated by the Kowloon Motor Bus Co. (1933) Ltd, Hong Kong, is the world's largest multi-story service center. Built expressly for double-decker buses, it has four floors occupying more than 11.6 acres.

PARKING LOTS

Largest   The world's largest is the one in the West Edmonton Mall, Edmonton, Alberta, Canada, which can hold 20,000 vehicles. There are overflow facilities on an adjoining lot for 10,000 more cars.

Parking meters   The earliest ever installed, put in the business district of Oklahoma City, OK on 19 Jul 1935, were the invention of Carl C. Magee (USA).

TIRES

Largest   The largest ever manufactured are by Goodyear Tire & Rubber Co. for giant dump trucks. They measure 12 ft in diameter, weigh 12,500 lb and cost $74,000. A tire 17 ft in diameter is believed to be the limit of what is practical.

Skid marks   The skid marks made by the jet-powered *Spirit of America*, driven by Norman Craig Breedlove, after the car went out of control at Bonneville Salt Flats, UT, on 15 Oct 1964, were nearly six miles long.

TOWS

Longest   The longest on record was one of 4,759 miles from Halifax, Nova Scotia to Canada's Pacific coast, when Frank J. Elliott and George A. Scott of Amherst, Nova Scotia, Canada persuaded 168 passing motorists in 89 days to tow their Model T Ford (in fact engineless) to win a $1,000 bet on 15 Oct 1927.

After his 1969 MGB broke down in the vicinity of Moscow, Russia (formerly USSR), the late Eddie McGowan of Chipping Warden, Great Britain was towed by Mark Steven Morgan, driving his 1968 MGC, a distance of 975 miles of the 1,456-miles journey from Moscow to Berlin, Germany on a single 7-ft nylon tow rope from 12–17 Jul 1987.

ROADS

Road mileages   The country with the greatest length of road is the United States (all 50 states), with 3,880,151 miles of graded road. The state with the most miles of road is Texas (305,951), while Hawaii has the least, with 4,099 miles.

Longest driveable road   The Pan-American Highway, from northwest Alaska to Santiago, Chile, then eastward to Buenos Aires, Argentina and terminating in Brasilia, Brazil is over 15,000 miles in length. There is, however, a small incomplete section in Panama and Colombia known as the Darién Gap. The first all-land crossing was achieved by Loren Lee Uption and Patricia Mercier in a 1966 CJ 5 Jeep. Their journey began at Yavisa, Republic of Panama on 22 Feb 1985 and ended on 4 Mar 1987 at Riosuico, Colombia.

United States   The longest highway solely in the United States is US-20, which runs 3,370 miles from Boston, MA to Newport, OR. The longest highway in the interstate system is I-90, 3,107 miles from Boston, MA to Seattle, WA.

Highest roads   The highest trail in the world is an eight-mile stretch of the Gangdise between Khaleb and Xinji-fu, Tibet, which in two places exceeds 20,000 ft. The highest road in the world is in Khardung La Pass, at an altitude of 18,640 ft. This is one of three passes of the Leh-Manali road completed in 1976 by the Border Roads Organization, New Delhi, India; motor vehicles were able to use it from 1988 on.

Lowest roads   The lowest road is along the Israeli shores of the Dead Sea at 1,290 ft below sea level.

The world's lowest named "pass" is Rock Reef Pass, Everglades National Park, FL, which is 3 ft above sea level.

Widest roads   The widest road in the world is the Monumental Axis, running for 1½ miles from the Municipal Plaza to the Plaza of the Three Powers in Brasilia, the capital of Brazil. The six-lane boulevard, opened in April 1960, is 820.2 ft wide.

Traffic volume   The most heavily traveled stretch of road is Interstate 405 (San Diego Freeway), in Orange County, CA, which has a rush-hour volume of 25,500 vehicles. This volume occurs on a 0.9 mile stretch between Garden Grove Freeway and Seal Beach Boulevard.

Traffic density   The territory with the highest traffic density in the world is

Hong Kong. In 1992 there were 418 vehicles per mile of serviceable road, that is, a density of 4.21 yd per vehicle.

Longest traffic jams   The longest ever reported was that of 16 Feb 1980, which stretched northwards from Lyons 109.3 miles towards Paris, France.

A record traffic jam was reported for 1½ million cars crawling bumper-to-bumper over the East–West German border on 12 Apr 1990.

Streets Longest   The longest designated street in the world is Yonge Street, running north and west from Toronto, Ontario, Canada. The first stretch, completed on 16 Feb 1796, ran 34 miles. Its official length, now extended to Rainy River on the Ontario–Minnesota border, is 1,178.3 miles.

Narrowest   The world's narrowest street is in the village of Ripatransone in the Marche region of Italy. It is called *Vicolo della Virilita* ("Virility Alley") and is 16.9 in wide.

Shortest   The title for "The Shortest Street in the World" is claimed by the town of Bacup, Great Britain, where Elgin Street, situated by the old market ground, measures just 17 ft.

Steepest   The steepest street in the world is Baldwin Street, Dunedin, New Zealand, which has a maximum gradient of 1 in 1.266.

The crookedest and steepest street in the United States is Lombard Street, San Francisco, CA. It has eight consecutive 90-degree turns of 20-ft radius.

Parking tickets   Mrs Silvia Matos of New York City has set what must be a world record in unpaid parking tickets, totaling $150,000. She collected the 2,800 tickets between 1985 and 1988, but authorities have been unable to collect any money; she registered her car under 19 addresses and 36 license plates and cannot be found.

Tire supporting   The greatest number of tires supported in a free-standing lift is 96, by Gary Windebank of Romsey, Great Britain in February 1984. The total weight was 1,440 lb. The tires used were Michelin XZX 155 × 13.

Worst exit to miss   The longest distance between controlled access exits in the United States is 51.1 miles from Florida Turnpike exit 193 (Yeehaw Junction, FL) to exit 244 (Kissimee, FL). The worst exit to miss on any interstate highway is 37.7 miles from I-80 exit 41 (Knolls, UT) to exit 4 (Bonneville Speedway, UT).

RAILROADING

TRAINS

Origins Wagons running on wooden rails were used for mining as early as 1550 at Leberthal, Alsace.

Richard Trevithick built his first steam locomotive for the 3-ft-gauge iron plateway at Coalbrookdale, Great Britain in 1803, but there is no evidence that it ran. His second locomotive drew wagons in which men rode on a demonstration run at Penydarren, Great Britain on 22 Feb 1804, but it broke the plate rails.

The earliest commercially successful steam locomotive worked in 1812 on the Middleton Colliery Railway to Leeds, Great Britain, and was authorized by Britain's first Railway Act of 9 Jun 1758.

The first practical electric railroad was Werner von Siemens' oval meter-gauge demonstration track, about 984 ft long, at the Berlin Trades Exhibition in Germany on 31 May 1879.

Fastest The fastest speed attained by a railed vehicle is 6,121 mph, or Mach 8, by an unmanned rocket sled over the 9½-mile-long rail track at White Sands Missile Range, NM on 5 Oct 1982.

The fastest speed recorded on any national rail system is 320 mph by the French SNCF high-speed train TGV (*Train à Grande Vitesse*) between Courtalain and Tours on 18 May 1990. It was brought into service on 27 Sep 1981. By September 1983 it had reduced its scheduled time for the Paris–Lyons run in France of 264 miles to exactly 2 hours, thus averaging 132 mph.

United States The fastest train in the United States is the Amtrak X2000, which has a maximum speed of 155 mph. The train completed its demonstration run between Washington, D.C. and New York on 1 Feb 1993. The Swedish-built passenger train will travel the New York–Washington corridor and the New Haven–to–Boston route in 1997. The train features convenient seat-side phonejacks, fax machines, cocktail service and gourmet food, as well as a glass-walled conference area.

The highest speed ever ratified for a steam locomotive was 125 mph over 1,320 ft, by the LNER 4–6–2 No. 4468 *Mallard* (later numbered 60022), which hauled seven coaches weighing 267.9 tons down Stoke Bank, near Essendine, Great Britain on 3 Jul 1938. Driver Joseph Duddington was at the controls with Fireman Thomas Bray. The engine suffered some damage to the middle big-end bearing.

Largest steam locomotive The largest operating steam locomotive is the Union Pacific RR *Challenger* type 4–6–6–4 No. 3985, built by the American Locomotive Co. in 1943. In working order, with tender, it weighs 543.2 tons. It is used on special trips for train buffs in the United States.

Most powerful The world's most powerful steam locomotive, measured by tractive effort, was No. 700, a triple-articulated or triplex six-cylinder 2–8–8–8–4 engine built by the Baldwin Locomotive Works in 1916 for the

Virginian Railway. It had a tractive force of 166,300 lb when working compound and 199,560 lb when working simple.

Probably the heaviest train ever hauled by a single engine was one of 17,135 tons made up of 250 freight cars stretching 1.6 miles by the *Matt H. Shay* (No. 5014), a 2–8–8–8–2 engine, which ran on the Erie Railroad from May 1914 until 1929.

Greatest load The world's strongest rail carrier, with a capacity of 838 tons, is the 36-axle "Schnabel," 301 ft 10 in long, built for a US railroad by Krupp, Germany in March 1981.

The heaviest load ever moved on rails is the 11,971-ton Church of the Virgin Mary (built in 1548 in the village of Most, Czech Republic), in October–November 1975, moved because it was in the way of coal operations. It was moved 2,400 ft at 0.0013 mph over four weeks, at a cost of $17 million.

Freight trains The world's longest and heaviest freight train on record, with the largest number of cars ever recorded, made a run on the 3-ft-6-in-

---

Model trains—nonstop duration A standard Life-Like BL2 HO scale electric train pulled six eight-wheel coaches for 1,207.5 hr from 4 Aug to 23 Sep 1990 and covered a distance of 909.5 miles. The event was organized by Ike Cottingham and Mark Hamrick of Mainline Modelers of Akron, OH.

The longest recorded run by a model steam locomotive is 144 miles in 27 hr 18 min by the 7¹/₄ in gauge "Winifred," built in 1974 by Wilf Grove, at Thames Ditton, Great Britain, on 8–9 Sep 1979. "Winifred" works on 80 lb/in² pressure and is coal-fired, with cylinders 2¹/₈ in in diameter and 3¹/₈ in stroke.

The most miniature model railway ever built is one of 1:1,000 scale by Jean Damery (b. 1923) of Paris, France. The engine runs on a 4¹/₂ volt battery and measures ⁵/₁₆ in overall.

Spike driving In the World Championship Professional Spike Driving Competition, held at the Golden Spike National Historic Site in Utah, Dale C. Jones, 49, of Lehi, UT, drove six 7-in railroad spikes in a time of 26.4 sec on 11 Aug 1984. He incurred no penalty points under the official rules.

Suggestion boxes The most prolific example on record of the use of a suggestion box is that of John Drayton (1907–87) of Newport, Great Britain, who plied the British rail system with a total of 31,400 suggestions from 1924 to August 1987. More than one in seven were adopted, and 100 were accepted by London Transport. In 1983 he was presented with a chiming clock by British Rail to mark almost 60 years of suggestions.

Longest issued train ticket A train ticket measuring 111 ft 10¹/₂ in was issued to Ronald, Norma and Jonathan Carter for journeys traveled on British Rail between 15–23 Feb 1992.

gauge Sishen–Saldanha railroad in South Africa on 26–27 Aug 1989. The train consisted of 660 cars each loaded to 105 tons gross, a tank car and a caboose, moved by nine 50 kV electric and seven diesel-electric locomotives distributed along the train. The train was 4^1/$_2$ miles long and weighed 77,720 tons excluding locomotives. It traveled a distance of 535 miles in 22 hr 40 min.

United States   The longest and heaviest freight train on record was about 4 miles in length. It comprised 500 coal motor cars with three 3,600 hp diesels pulling· and three more in the middle, on the Iaeger, WV–to–Portsmouth, OH stretch of 157 miles on the Norfolk and Western Railway on 15 Nov 1967. The total weight was nearly 47,040 tons.

Passenger train   The longest passenger train was 1,894 yds, consisted of 70 coaches, and had a total weight of over 2,800 tons. The National Belgium Railway Company's train was powered by one electric locomotive and took 1 hr 11 min 5 sec to complete the 38.5-mile journey from Ghent to Ostend on 27 Apr 1991.

TRACKS

Longest   The world's longest run is one of 5,864^1/$_2$ miles on the Trans-Siberian line from Moscow to Nakhodka, Russia, on the Sea of Japan. There are 97 stops on the journey, which is scheduled to take 8 days 4 hr 25 min.

Longest straight   The Commonwealth Railways Trans-Australian line over the Nullarbor Plain, from Mile 496 between Nurina and Loongana, Western Australia to Mile 793 between Ooldea and Watson, South Australia, is 297 miles dead straight, although not level.

United States   The longest straight track in the United States is 78.86 miles on CSX Railroad, between Wilmington and Hamlet, NC.

Widest and narrowest gauge   The widest in standard use is 5 ft 6 in. This width is used in Spain, Portugal, India, Pakistan, Bangladesh, Sri Lanka, Argentina and Chile.
   The narrowest gauge on which public services are operated is 10^1/$_4$ in on the Wells Harbor (0.7 mile) and the Wells–Walsingham Railways (4 miles) in Norfolk, Great Britain.

Highest line   At 15,806 ft above sea level, the standard gauge (4 ft 8^1/$_2$ in) track on the Morococha branch of the Peruvian State Railways at La Cima is the highest in the world.

Lowest line   The world's lowest is in the Seikan Tunnel between Honshu and Hokkaido, Japan. The rails are 786 ft below the Tsugaro Straits. The tunnel was opened on 13 Mar 1988 and is 33.4 miles long.
   The lowest in Europe is in the Channel Tunnel, where the rails are 417 ft below mean sea level.

Steepest railway   The world's steepest railway is the Katoomba Scenic Railway in the Blue Mountains of New South Wales, Australia. It is 1,020 ft long with a gradient of 1 in 0.82. A 220 hp electric winding ma-

HIGHEST RAILROAD   The highest railroad line is the Central Railway of the Peruvian State Railways, which reaches an altitude of 15,806 ft. There are 67 tunnels and 59 bridges, some of which are engineering marvels in themselves. (Photo: Chris Kapolka)

LONGEST RAILROAD   A dramatic shot of the Trans-Siberian Railway, the world's longest railroad. The first section was opened at the end of the last century, and a link from Moscow to the Sea of Japan was established in 1901. Additional stretches have been added from time to time since then to make the journey faster, most recently in 1984. (Photo: Sygma/D. Kirkland)

chine hauls the car by twin steel cables of 22 mm diameter. The ride takes about 1 min 40 sec and carries about 420,000 passengers a year.

Greatest length of railroad   As of 1991, the country that has the greatest length of railroad is the United States, with 173,808 miles operated for all classes of track. There were 128,939 miles of class I track (freight only) and 43,969 miles of non-class I track operated. There were 196,081 miles of track owned in the United States.

Steepest gradient   The world's steepest standard-gauge gradient by adhesion is 1:11, between Chedde and Servoz on the meter-gauge SNCF Chamonix line, France.

Busiest system   The railroad carrying the largest number of passengers is the East Japan Railway Co., which in 1992 carried 16,306,000 passengers daily.

TRAIN TRAVEL

Most countries in 24 hours   The greatest number of countries traveled through entirely by train in 24 hours is 10, by Aaron Kitchen on 16–17 Feb 1987. His route started in Yugoslavia and continued through Austria, Italy, Liechtenstein, Switzerland, France, Luxembourg, Belgium and the Netherlands, ending in Germany 22 hr 42 min later.

Most miles in seven days   Andrew Kingsmell and Sean Andrews of Bromley, Great Britain, together with Graham Bardouleau of Crawley, Great Britain, traveled 13,105 miles on the French National Railway System in 6 days 22 hr 38 min from 28 Nov–5 Dec 1992.

Handpumped railcars   A speed of 20.58 mph for a 984 ft course was achieved by a five-man team (one pusher, four pumpers) at Rolvenden, Great Britain on 21 Aug 1989, recording a time of 32.61 sec.

STATIONS

Largest   The world's largest is Grand Central Terminal, Park Avenue and 42nd Street, New York City, built from 1903–13. It covers 48 acres on two levels with 41 tracks on the upper level and 26 on the lower. On average there are more than 550 trains and 200,000 commuters, in addition to 300,000 who pass through the terminal. The Main Room is 80,000 ft² and is 250 ft tall.

Busiest   The busiest railroad junction in the world is Clapham Junction, London, Great Britain, in the Southern Region of British Rail, with an average of 2,200 trains passing through each 24 hours.

Highest   The Condor station in Bolivia at 15,705 ft on the meter-gauge Rio Mulato–to–Potosi line is the highest in the world.

Waiting rooms   The world's largest waiting rooms are the four in Beijing Station, Chang'an Boulevard, Beijing, China, opened in September 1959, with a total standing capacity of 14,000.

Platforms The longest railroad platform in the world is the Kharagpur platform, West Bengal, India, which measures 2,733 ft in length.

The State Street Center subway platform on "The Loop" in Chicago, IL measures 3,500 ft in length.

The two platforms comprising the New Misato railroad station on the Musashino line, Saitama, Japan are 984 ft apart and are connected by a bridge.

SUBWAY SYSTEMS

Most extensive The most extensive underground or rapid transit railway system of the 94 in the world is the London Underground, Great Britain, with 254 miles of route, of which 85 miles is bored tunnel and 20 miles is "cut and cover." The whole system is operated by a staff of 21,200 serving 273 stations. The 4,176 cars, forming a fleet of 570 trains, carried 751 million passengers in 1991–92.

The subway with the most stations in the world is the New York City Metropolitan Transportation Authority subway (first section opened on 27 Oct 1904). The network covers 238 route miles, comprising 469 subway stations, and serves an estimated 5 million subway and bus riders per day. In 1992, there were an average 3.2 million commuters per day.

Traveling New York subway The record time for traveling the whole system is 26 hr 21 min 08 sec, set by Kevin Foster (USA) on 25–26 Oct 1989.

Moscow Metro The record transit on 9 Dec 1988 (all 123 named stations) was 9 hr 39 min 50 sec by Peter Altman and Miss Jackie Smith (both Great Britain).

Busiest The world's busiest metro system has been the Greater Moscow Metro (opened 1935) in Russia, with as many as 3.3 billion passenger journeys per year at its peak—although by 1991 the figure had declined to 2.5 billion. It has 3,500 railcars and a workforce of 25,000. There are 141 stations (18 of which have more than one name, being transfer stations) and 140 miles of track. A 5 kopek fare was maintained for the first 56 years from 1935 to 1991, but the fare is now 3 rubles.

Worst subway disaster The worst subway accident in the United States occurred on 1 Nov 1918, in Brooklyn, NY when a BRT Line train derailed on a curve on Malbone St. in the Brighton Beach section. There were 97 fatalities on the scene and five more people died later from injuries sustained in the crash. The BRT line went bankrupt on 31 Dec 1918 as a result of the tragedy.

AIRCRAFT AND FLIGHT

EARLIEST FLIGHTS

The first controlled and sustained power-driven flight occurred near Kill Devil Hill, Kitty Hawk, NC, at 10:35 A.M. on 17 Dec 1903, when Orville Wright (1871–1948) flew the 12-hp chain-driven *Flyer I* for a distance of 120 ft at an airspeed of 30 mph, a ground speed of 6.8 mph and an altitude of 8–12 ft for about 12 seconds, watched by his brother Wilbur (1867–1912), four men and a boy. The *Flyer* was first exhibited in the National Air and Space Museum at the Smithsonian Institution, Washington, D.C. on 17 Dec 1948.

The first hop by a passenger-carrying airplane entirely under its own power was made when Clément Ader (1841–1925) of France flew in his *éole* for about 164 ft at Armainvilliers, France on 9 Oct 1890. It was powered by a lightweight steam engine of his own design, which developed about 20 hp.

Jet-engined Proposals for jet propulsion date back to Capt. Marconnet (1909) of France, and Henri Coanda (1886–1972) of Romania, and to the turbojet proposals of Maxime Guillaume (France) in 1921.

The first flight by an airplane powered by a turbojet engine was made by the Heinkel He 178, piloted by Flugkapitän Erich Warsitz, at Marienehe, Germany on 27 Aug 1939. It was powered by a Heinkel He S3b engine weighing 834 lb (as installed with long tailpipe) designed by Dr Hans Pabst von Ohain. First bench tests were made in 1937.

United States The earliest flight of a jet aircraft built in the United States was that of the Bell XP59A, using Whittle-designed engines, at Muroc, CA on 1 October 1942. The first US-built operational jet aircraft was the Lockheed P-80. The P-80's maiden flight was on 8 January 1944. It was first used in combat during the Korean War.

Transatlantic The first crossing of the North Atlantic by air was made by Lt-Cdr (later Rear Admiral) Albert Cushion Read (1887–1967) and his crew (Stone, Hinton, Rodd, Rhoads and Breese) in the 84-knot US Navy/Curtiss flying boat NC-4 from Trepassey Harbor, Newfoundland, Canada, via the Azores, to Lisbon, Portugal from 16–27 May 1919. The whole flight of 4,717 miles, originating from Rockaway Air Station, Long Island, NY on 8 May, required 53 hr 58 min, terminating at Plymouth, Great Britain on 31 May. The Newfoundland–Azores leg of the flight, comprising 1,200 miles, took 15 hr 18 min at 81.7 knots (94.1 mph).

Nonstop The first nonstop transatlantic flight was achieved 18 days later. The pilot, Capt John Williams Alcock (1892–1919), and navigator, Lt Arthur Whitton Brown (1886–1948), left Lester's Field, St John's, Newfoundland, Canada at 4:13 P.M. GMT on 14 Jun 1919, and landed at Derrygimla Bog near Clifden, Republic of Ireland, at 8:40 A.M. GMT, 15 June, having covered a distance of 1,960 miles in their Vickers Vimy, powered by two 360-hp Rolls-Royce Eagle VIII engines.

Solo　The first solo transatlantic flight was achieved by Capt. Charles Augustus Lindbergh (USA; 1902–74), who took off in his 220-hp Ryan monoplane *Spirit of St Louis* at 12:52 P.M. GMT on 20 May 1927 from Roosevelt Field, Long Island, NY. He landed at 10:21 P.M. GMT on 21 May 1927 at Le Bourget Airfield, Paris, France. His flight of 3,610 miles lasted 33 hr 29½ min and he won a prize of $25,000. The *Spirit of St Louis* is now in the National Air and Space Museum at the Smithsonian Institution, Washington, D.C.

North Atlantic flight　The first solo, two-way staged crossing of the North Atlantic in an open-cockpit home-built biplane was achieved by 70-year-old former US Air Force pilot Burdon L. "Dave" Davidson. Flying his Marquart MA5 Charger (registration N13DD) eastbound from Goose Bay, Newfoundland on 6 Jul 1991, via Greenland and Iceland, he reached Stornaway, Scotland on 16 July. The westbound flight over the same route was recorded between 16–28 Aug 1991.

Transpacific　The first nonstop flight was by Major Clyde Pangborn and Hugh Herndon in the Bellanca cabin monoplane *Miss Veedol*. They took off from Sabishiro Beach, Japan and covered the distance of 4,558 miles to Wenatchee, WA in 41 hr 13 min from 3–5 Oct 1931. (For earliest crossing, see Circumnavigational flights.)

Circumnavigational flights　Strict circumnavigation of the globe requires the aircraft to pass through two antipodal points, thus covering a minimum distance of 24,859.73 miles.

Earliest　The earliest such flight, of 26,345 miles, was by two US Army Douglas DWC amphibians in 57 "hops" between 6 April and 28 Sep 1924, beginning and ending in Seattle, WA. The *Chicago* was piloted by Lt Lowell H. Smith and Lt Leslie P. Arnold, and the *New Orleans* by Lt Erik H. Nelson and Lt John Harding. Their flying time was 371 hr 11 min.

First without refueling　Richard G. "Dick" Rutan and Jeana Yeager, in their specially constructed aircraft *Voyager*, designed by Dick's brother Burt Rutan, flew from Edwards Air Force Base, CA from 14–23 Dec 1986. Their flight took 9 days 3 min 44 sec and they covered a distance of 24,987 miles, averaging 115.65 mph. The plane was capable of carrying 1,240 gal of fuel weighing 8,934 lb. The pilot flew from a cockpit measuring 5.6×1.8 ft and the off-duty crew member occupied a cabin 7.5×2 ft. *Voyager* is now in the National Air and Space Museum at the Smithsonian Institution, Washington, D.C.

First circumpolar　Capt. Elgen M. Long, 44, achieved the first circumpolar flight in a Piper PA-31 Navajo from 5 Nov–3 Dec 1971. He covered 38,896 miles in 215 flying hours. The cabin temperature sank to –40° F over Antarctica.

Earliest supersonic flight　The first was achieved on 14 Oct 1947 by Capt. (later Brig. Gen.) Charles "Chuck" Elwood Yeager (b. 13 Feb 1923), over Edwards Air Force Base, Muroc, CA, in a Bell XS-1 rocket plane (*Glamorous Glennis*—named for Yeager's wife) at Mach 1.015 (670 mph) at an altitude of 42,000 ft. The XS-1 is now in the National Air and Space Museum at the Smithsonian Institution, Washington, D.C.

The former Soviet Tupolev TU-144 was first flown on 31 Dec 1968 as the world's first supersonic airliner, although it entered service initially as a cargo plane.

AIRCRAFT

Origins   The earliest "rational design" for a flying machine, according to the Royal Aeronautical Society, London, Great Britain, was that published by Emanuel Swedenborg (1688–1772) in Sweden in 1717.

Largest wingspan   The aircraft with the largest wingspan ever constructed is the $40-million Hughes H.4 Hercules flying boat (*Spruce Goose*). It was raised 70 ft into the air in a test run of 3,000 ft, piloted by Howard Hughes (1905–76), off Long Beach Harbor, CA, on 2 Nov 1947, but after this it never flew again. The eight-engined 212-ton aircraft had a wingspan of 319 ft 11 in and a length of 218 ft 8 in. In a delicate engineering feat it was moved bodily by the Goldcoast Corporation, aided by the US Navy barge crane YD-171, on 22 Feb 1982, to a hall across the harbor. In the summer of 1992 it was put up for sale, and the plan now is to make it the centerpiece of a new museum in McMinnville, OR.

Among current aircraft, the Russian Antonov An-124 has a span of 240 ft 5¾ in. The USAF C-5B cargo plane has a wingspan of 222 ft 8½ in, which is the greatest for any United States military aircraft.

Largest propeller   The largest propeller ever made is the triple-bladed screw of 36 ft 1 in diameter made by Kawasaki Heavy Industries, Japan, and delivered on 17 Mar 1982 for the 233,787-ton bulk carrier *Hoei Maru* (now renamed *New Harvest*).

Longest runways   The longest runway in the world is at Edwards Air Force Base on the west side of Rogers dry lakebed at Muroc, CA. It measures 39,104 ft, or 7.4 miles. The *Voyager* aircraft, taking off on its around-the-world unrefueled flight (see Circumnavigational flights), used 14,200 ft of the 15,000-ft-long main base concrete runway.

The world's longest civil runway is one of 3.04 miles at Pierre van Ryneveld Airport, Upington, South Africa, constructed in five months from August 1975 to January 1976.

The most southerly major runway (1.6 miles) in the world is at Mount Pleasant, East Falkland (Lat. 51° 50′ S), built in 16 months and completed in May 1985.

Electric plane   The MB-E1 is the first electrically propelled aircraft. A Bosch 10.7 hp motor is powered by Varta FP25 nickel-cadmium 25 Ah batteries. The aircraft, with a wingspan of 39.4 ft, is 23 ft long and weighs 882 lb. It was designed by the model aircraft constructor Fred Militky (USA) and made its maiden flight on 21 Oct 1973.

LARGEST WINGSPAN The Hughes H.4 Hercules flying boat
Spruce Goose has the largest wingspan of any aircraft, at 319 ft 11 in.
It flew just once, in a test run in 1947. (Photo: Sygma)

SMALLEST JET AIRCRAFT The smallest jet is the *Silver Bullet*,
with a wingspan of just 17 ft. (Photo: Rex Features /Oxley)

Heaviest The aircraft with the highest standard maximum takeoff weight is the Russian Antonov An-225 *Mriya* ("Dream") at 660 tons (1,322,750 lb). The aircraft lifted a payload of 344,579 lb to a height of 40,715 ft on 22 Mar 1989. This flight was achieved by Capt. Aleksandr Galunenko and his crew of seven pilots, and was made along the route Kiev–St Petersburg–Kiev without landing at a range of 1,305 miles and lasted 3 hr 47 min. (See Most capacious.)

Most capacious The Aero Spacelines Super Guppy has a cargo hold with a usable volume of 49,790 ft³ and a maximum takeoff weight of 87.5 tons. Its wingspan is 156 ft 3 in and its length 141 ft 3 in. Its cargo compartment is 108 ft 10 in long with a cylindrical section 25 ft in diameter.

The Russian Antonov An-124 *Ruslan* has a cargo hold with a usable volume of 35,800 ft³ and a maximum takeoff weight of 446 tons. It is powered by four Lotarev D-18T turbofans giving a cruising speed of up to 528 mph at 39,370 ft and a range of 2,796 miles. A special-purpose heavy-lift version of the An-124, known as An-225 *Mriya* ("Dream"), has been developed with a stretched fuselage providing as much as 42,000 ft³ usable volume. A new wing center section carries an additional two engines, permiting an estimated total 310,000 lb thrust. Having flown first on 21 Dec 1988, the aircraft was used to carry the Soviet space shuttle *Buran* for the first time on 13 May 1989, when it was airborne for 13 hr 13 min. (See Heaviest aircraft.)

Heaviest commercial cargo movement Russian manufacturer Antonov and British charter company Air Foyle claim a record for the heaviest commercial air cargo movement, by taking three transformers weighing 53 tons each and other equipment from Barcelona, Spain to Nouméa, New Caledonia (Pacific) between 10–14 Jan 1991. The total weight carried in the An-124 *Ruslan* (See Most capacious) was 164.6 tons.

Air Foyle also holds the record for carrying the heaviest single piece of cargo, by flying a 134-ton crane measuring 62 × 10 ft from Krivoy Rog, Ukraine to Berlin, Germany on 8 Sep 1992. The aircraft used was the Russian An-124 *Ruslan*.

Smallest The smallest biplane ever flown is the *Bumble Bee Two*, designed and built by Robert H. Starr of Arizona. It was 8 ft 10 in long, with a wingspan of 5 ft 6 in, and weighed 396 lb empty. The fastest speed it attained was 190 mph. On 8 May 1988, after flying to a height of approximately 400 ft, it crashed, and was totally destroyed.

The smallest jet is the 280 mph *Silver Bullet*, weighing 432 lb, with a 17 ft wingspan, built by Bob Bishop (USA).

Ultralight On 3 Aug 1985 Anthony A. Cafaro (b. 30 Nov 1951) flew an ultralight aircraft (ULA; maximum weight 245 lb, maximum speed 65 mph, fuel capacity 4¼ gal) single-seater Gypsy Skycycle for 7 hr 31 min at Dart Field, Mayville, NY. Nine fuel "pickups" were completed during the flight.

Most flights by propeller-driven airliner A Convair CV-580 turboprop airliner was reported by the manufacturer in April 1991 to have achieved 139,368 flights. Its exact age was not announced, but if it were the first such airliner, the figure equates to more than nine flights a day since 1952.

Bombers Heaviest The eight-jet swept-wing Boeing B-52H Stratofortress has a maximum takeoff weight of over 244 tons (488,000 lb), a wingspan of 185 ft, and is 157 ft 6¾ in in length. It has a speed of over 650 mph. Of the two series in active service, the B-52G is the longest bomber in the USAF at 160 ft 11 in. The B-52H has the greatest thrust of a bomber in the US fleet at 136,000 lbs and the greatest unrefueled range of over 8,800 miles.

Fastest The world's fastest operational bombers include the French Dassault Mirage IV, which can fly at Mach 2.2 (1,450 mph) at 36,000 ft.

The American variable-geometry or "swing-wing" General Dynamics FB-111A has a maximum speed of Mach 2.5, and the Soviet swing-wing Tupolev Tu-22M, known to NATO as "Backfire," has an estimated over-target speed of Mach 2.0 but could be as fast as Mach 2.5.

JET AIRLINERS

Oldest According to the British-based aviation information and consultancy company Airclaims, a first-generation jet airliner built in 1958—a Boeing 707—was still in service in April 1993.

Largest The first 747-400 entered service with Northwest Airlines on 26 Jan 1989 with a wingspan of 211 ft 5 in, a range exceeding 8,000 miles and a capacity for up to 567 passengers. The highest-capacity jet airliner is the Boeing 747 "Jumbo Jet," first flown on 9 Feb 1969, which has a capacity of from 385 to more than 560 passengers and a maximum speed of 602 mph. Its wingspan is 195 ft 5 in and its length 231 ft 10 in. It entered service on 22 Jan 1970.

Fastest The supersonic BAC/Aérospatiale Concorde, first flown on 2 Mar 1969, with a designed capacity of 128 (and potentially 144) passengers, cruises at up to Mach 2.2 (1,450 mph). It has a maximum takeoff weight of 408,000 lb. It flew at Mach 1.05 on 10 Oct 1969, exceeded Mach 2 for the first time on 4 Nov 1970, and became the first supersonic airliner used in passenger service on 21 Jan 1976. In service with Air France and British Airways, Concorde has now been laid out to carry 100 passengers. The New York–London, Great Britain record is 2 hr 54 min 30 sec, set on 14 Apr 1990.

Greatest passenger load The greatest passenger load carried by any single commercial airliner was 1,087 during *Operation Solomon*, which began on 24 May 1991 when Ethiopian Jews were evacuated from Addis Ababa to Israel on a Boeing 747 belonging to El Al airline.

Most flights by a jet airliner A survey of aging airliners or so-called "geriatric jets" in *Flight International* magazine for May 1993 reported a McDonnell Douglas DC-9 still in service that had logged 95,396 flights in less than 27 years. This comes to more than nine flights a day, averaging 43 min 12 sec each, but after allowing for "downtime" for maintenance the real average is higher.

The most hours recorded by a jet airliner still in service is 94,431 hours, reported for a Boeing 747 in the same issue of *Flight International* (see above).

AIRLINES

Oldest The oldest airline, Koninklijke-Luchtvaart-Maatschappij NV (KLM), the national airline of the Netherlands, was established on 7 Oct 1919. It opened its first scheduled service (Amsterdam–London, Great Britain) on 17 May 1920, seven months after its establishment.

Chalk's International Airline has been flying amphibious planes from Miami, FL to the Bahamas since July 1919. Albert "Pappy" Chalk flew from 1911–75.

Largest The Russian state airline Aeroflot, so named since 1932, was instituted on 9 Feb 1923 and has been the largest airline of all time. In its last complete year of formal existence (1990) it employed 600,000 (more than the top 18 US airlines put together) and flew 139 million passengers, with 20,000 pilots, along 620,000 miles of domestic routes across 11 time zones. The peak size of its fleet remains unknown, with estimates ranging up to 14,700, if both aircraft and helicopters were included. By late 1991 the fleet was operated by at least 46 domestic operators.

United States The largest US airline in terms of number of aircraft as of 1 April 1993 is American Airlines, with 680. As of 31 Dec 1992, American also led in number of passenger enplanements, 86.01 million, and available seat miles, with 152.94 billion. United Airlines led in revenue passenger miles, with 92.48 billion versus American's 82.21 billion.

Busiest The country with the busiest airlines system is the United States, where the total number of passenger enplanements by large commercial air carriers in domestic operations in 1992 was 429.9 million. The overall total, including regional/commuter service, was 473.3 million.

Busiest international route The city-pair with the highest international scheduled passenger traffic is London/Paris. More than three million passengers fly between the two cities annually, or more than 4,100 each way each day (although London-bound traffic is higher than that bound for Paris.)

Aerospace company The world's largest aerospace company is Boeing of Seattle, WA, with 1992 sales of $30.2 billion and a workforce of 148,600 worldwide. Cessna Aircraft Company of Wichita, KS had a total workforce of 5,700 in 1992. The company has produced over 177,800 aircraft since Clyde Cessna's first was built in 1911.

SCHEDULED FLIGHTS

Longest The longest nonstop flight currently operating is one of 7,983 miles by South African Airways for their flight from Johannesburg, South Africa to New York. In terms of time taken, the longest is 15 hr 5 min, from London's Heathrow airport to Osaka, Japan with British Airways and also from Los Angeles, CA to Hong Kong with Delta Air Lines.

The longest nonstop delivery flight by a commercial jet is 11,250 miles, from London, Great Britain to Sydney, Australia by a Qantas Boeing 747-400 *Longreach*, using 176.6 tons of specially formulated Shell Jet A-1 high-density fuel, in 20 hr 9 min on 16–17 Aug 1989. It is the first time this route has been completed nonstop by an airliner.

Longest airplane ticket   A ticket 39 ft 4¹/₂ in long was issued for $4,500 to M. Bruno Leunen of Brussels, Belgium in December 1984 for a 53,203-mile trip on 80 airlines with 109 layovers.

Fastest time to refuel   The record time for refueling an airplane (with 85 gal of 100 octane avgas) is 3 min 24 sec, for a 1975 Cessna 310 (N92HH), by the Sky Harbor Air Service Line Crew. It had landed at Cheyenne airport, WY, on 5 Jul 1992 during an around the world air race.

London—New York   The record time from central London, Great Britain to downtown New York City by helicopter and Concorde is 3 hr 59 min 44 sec, and for the return, 3 hr 40 min 40 sec, both by David J. Springbett and David Boyce on 8–9 Feb 1982.

Around the world—antipodal points   Brother Michael Bartlett of London, Great Britain traveled around the world on scheduled flights, taking in exact antipodal points, in a time of 67 hr 4 min from 10–13 Jun 1993. Leaving from London, he flew via Tokyo, Japan and Auckland, New Zealand, continuing by car to Ti Tree Point. He later changed planes at Madrid airport, Spain (the point exactly opposite Ti Tree Point on the other side of the world). His journey took him a total distance of 25,841 miles.

Stowaway   The most rugged stowaway was Socarras Ramirez, who escaped from Cuba on 4 Jun 1969 by stowing away in an unpressurized wheel well in the starboard wing of a Douglas DC-8 from Havana, Cuba to Madrid, Spain in a 5,600-mile Iberia Airlines flight.

Time zones parties   On 31 Dec 1992 a group of 97 Atlantic "Time-Tunnellers" saw the New Year in twice by having a party at Shannon, Republic of Ireland and leaving at 00:10 on Concorde for Bermuda, where they arrived at 23:21 the previous day, in time for a second New Year's celebration. In so doing they achieved the fastest west–east Atlantic crossing for a passenger aircraft, with a time of 2 hr 51 min.

Fastest coast-to-coast flight   The record aircraft time from coast-to-coast (Los Angeles to Washington, D.C.) is 68 min 17 sec by Lt Col. Ed Yeilding, pilot, and Lt Col. J.T Vida, reconnaissance systems officer, aboard the SR–71 Blackbird spy plane during its Air Force retirement flight to the Smithsonian Institution on 6 Mar 1990. The Blackbird was refueled over the Pacific Ocean at 27,000 ft before starting a climb to above 80,000 ft, heading east from the California coastline and crossing the finish line near Salisbury, MD. The plane averaged 2,145 mph between Los Angeles and Washington, and 2,190 mph between St Louis and Cincinnati. This is the first (and only) time that a sonic boom has traveled uninterrupted from coast-to-coast across the continental United States.

A Boeing 767–200ER flight from Seattle, WA, to Nairobi, Kenya on 8–9 Jun 1990 set a new speed and endurance record for the longest delivery flight by a twin-engined commercial jet. The Royal Brunei Airlines Boeing 767 flew 8,040 nautical miles great-circle distance in 18 hr 29 min, consuming 74.2 tons of fuel.

Shortest The shortest scheduled flight is by Loganair between the Orkney Islands of Westray and Papa Westray, Great Britain, which has been flown with Britten-Norman Islander twin-engined 10-seat transports since September 1967. Though scheduled for two minutes, in favorable wind conditions it was once completed in 58 sec by Capt. Andrew D. Alsop. The check-in time for the 2 min flight is 20 min.

Alaska Airlines provides the shortest scheduled flight by jet, by McDonnell Douglas MD-80 between San Francisco and Oakland, CA. There is one daily return flight six days a week; the time averages 5 minutes for the 12 mile journey. Some 25 minutes are allowed in the airline timetable.

Around the world The fastest time for a circumnavigation on scheduled flights is 44 hr 6 min, by David J. Springbett (b. 2 May 1938) of Taplow, Great Britain. His route took him from Los Angeles, CA eastwards via London, Bahrain, Singapore, Bangkok, Manila, Tokyo and Honolulu from 8–10 Jan 1980 over a 23,069 mile course. A minimum distance of 22,858.8 miles (the length of the Tropic of Cancer or Capricorn) must be flown.

Most flights in 24 hours Brother Michael Bartlett of London, Great Britain made 42 scheduled passenger flights with Heli Transport of Nice, France between Nice, Sophia Antipolis, Monaco and Cannes in 13 hr 33 min on 13 Jun 1990.

SPEED

Official record The airspeed record is 2,193.2 mph, by Capt. Eldon W. Joersz and Major George T. Morgan, Jr., in a Lockheed SR-71A "Blackbird" near Beale Air Force Base, CA over a 15 1/2 mile course on 28 Jul 1976.

Air-launched record The fastest fixed-wing aircraft in the world was the US North American Aviation X-15A-2, which flew for the first time (after modification from the X-15A) on 25 Jun 1964, powered by a liquid oxygen and ammonia rocket-propulsion system. Ablative materials on the airframe enabled it to withstand a temperature of 1,650° C. The landing speed was momentarily 242 mph. The fastest speed attained was 4,520 mph (Mach 6.7) when piloted by Major William J. Knight, USAF (b. 1930), on 3 Oct 1967.

An earlier version piloted by Joseph A. Walker (USAF; 1920–66) reached 354,200 ft, also over Edwards Air Force Base, CA, on 22 Aug 1963. The final flight (the 199th) was on 24 Oct 1968, after which the program, which had begun on 8 Jun 1959, was suspended.

The space shuttle *Columbia*, commanded by Capt. John W. Young (USN) and piloted by Capt. Robert L. Crippen (USN), was launched from the Kennedy Space Center, Cape Canaveral, FL on 12 Apr 1981 after expenditure of $9.9 billion since 1972. *Columbia* broke all records in space by a fixed-wing craft, with 16,600 mph at main engine cutoff. After reentry from 75.8 miles, experiencing temperatures of 3,920° F, it glided home weighing 107 tons, and with a landing speed of 216 mph, on Rogers Dry Lake, CA on 14 Apr 1981.

Fastest jet   The USAF Lockheed SR-71, a reconnaissance aircraft, has been the world's fastest jet (see Fastest speed, Official record). First flown in its definitive form on 22 Dec 1964, it was reportedly capable of attaining an altitude ceiling of close to 100,000 ft. It has a wingspan of 55.6 ft and a length of 107.4 ft and weighs 85 tons at takeoff. Its reported range at Mach 3 was 2,982 miles at 78,750 ft. At least 30 are believed to have been built before the plane was retired by the US Air Force.

Fastest combat jets   The fastest combat jet is the Russian Mikoyan MiG-25 fighter (NATO code name "Foxbat"). The reconnaissance aircraft "Foxbat-B" has been tracked by radar at about Mach 3.2 (2,110 mph). When armed with four large underwing air-to-air missiles known to NATO as "Acrid," the fighter "Foxbat-A" is limited to Mach 2.8 (1,845 mph). The single-seat "Foxbat-A" has a wingspan of 45 ft 9 in, is 78 ft 2 in long and has an estimated maximum takeoff weight of 82,500 lb.

United States   The fastest combat jets in the United States' arsenal are the F-111 and the F-15, both of which fly at Mach 2.5, although the F-15 is listed in one official release as flying at Mach 2.5 plus. The F-15E is a two-seat craft that is 63 ft 9 in long, has a wingspan of 42 ft 9³/4 in, and has a gross takeoff weight of 81,000 lb.

Fastest biplane   The fastest is the Italian Fiat CR42B, with a 1,010 hp Daimler-Benz DB601A engine, which attained 323 mph in 1941. Only one was built.

Fastest piston-engined aircraft   On 21 Aug 1989, in Las Vegas, NV, the Rare Bear, a modified Grumman Bearcat F8F piloted by Lyle Shelton, set the FAI approved world record for a 3 km run of 528.3 mph.

Fastest propeller-driven aircraft   The fastest propeller-driven aircraft in use is the former Soviet Tu-95/142 "Bear" with four 14,795 hp engines driving eight blade counter-rotating propellers with a maximum level speed of Mach 0.82 (575 mph).

Fastest transatlantic flight   The flight record is 1 hr 54 min 56.4 sec by Major James V. Sullivan (USA), 37, and Major Noel F. Widdifield (USA), 33, flying a Lockheed SR-71A "Blackbird" eastwards on 1 Sep 1974. The average speed, slowed from refueling by a KC-135 tanker aircraft, for the New York–London stage of 3,461.53 miles was 1,806.96 mph.

The solo record (Gander to Gatwick) is 8 hr 47 min 32 sec, an average speed of 265.1 mph, by Capt. John J.A. Smith in a Rockwell Commander 685 twin-turboprop on 12 Mar 1978, achieving an average speed of 265.214 mph.

Fastest circumnavigational flight   The fastest flight under the FAI (*Fédération Aéronatique Internationale*) rules, which permit flights that exceed the length of the Tropic of Cancer or Capricorn (22,858.8 miles), was that of the eastbound flight of 32 hr 49 min by an Air France Concorde (Capts. Claude Delorme and Jean Boyé) from Lisbon, Portugal via Santo

FASTEST PROPELLER-DRIVEN AIRCRAFT The fastest propeller-driven aircraft is the Bear, which can fly at a speed of 575 mph. (Photo: Aviation Picture Library)

Domingo, Acapulco, Honolulu, Guam, Bangkok and Bahrain on 12–13 Oct 1992. The AF1492 flight was undertaken to celebrate the 500th anniversary of Christopher Columbus' discovery of the New World.

Fastest climb Heinz Frick of British Aerospace took a Harrier GR5 powered by a Rolls-Royce Pegasus 11-61 engine from a standing start to 39,370 ft in 2 min 6.63 sec above the Rolls-Royce flight test center, Filton, Bristol, Great Britain on 15 Aug 1989.

Aleksandr Fedotov (USSR) in a Mikoyan E 266M (MiG-25) aircraft established the fastest time-to-height record on 17 May 1975, reaching 114,830 ft in 4 min 11.7 sec after takeoff from Podmoscovnoe, Russia.

United States The fastest time-to-height record for a United States aircraft is to 62,000 ft in 2 min 2.94 sec, by Major Roger J. Smith (USAF), in an F-15 Eagle on 19 January 1975.

DURATION RECORDS

Longest flight The longest flight on record is 64 days 22 hr 19 min 5 sec, set by Robert Timm and John Cook in the Cessna 172 *Hacienda*. They took off from McCarran Airfield, Las Vegas, NV just before 3:53 P.M. local time on 4 Dec 1958 and landed at the same airfield just before 2:12 P.M. on 7 Feb 1959. They covered a distance equivalent to six times around the world, being refueled without any landings.

Aerospacecraft Under the FAI (*Fédération Aéronautique Internationale*) regulations for Category P for aerospacecraft, the *Columbia* is holder of the current absolute world record for duration—13 days 19 hr 30 min to main touchdown—when on its 12th mission, STS 50, with seven crewmen, on 9 Jul 1992.

Altitude Orbiter *Discovery* holds the shuttle altitude record of 332 miles, achieved on 24 Apr 1990 on its 10th flight.

PERSONAL AVIATION RECORDS

Oldest and youngest passengers Airborne births are reported every year. The oldest person to fly was Mrs Jessica S. Swift (b. Anna Stewart, 17 Sep 1871), age 110 years 3 months. She flew from Vermont to Florida in December 1981.

Pilots Youngest The youngest age at which anyone has ever qualified as a military pilot is 15 years 5 months, by Sgt Thomas Dobney (b. 6 May 1926) of the Royal Air Force (RAF). He had overstated his age (14 years) on entry.

Oldest The world's oldest pilot is Stanley Wood (b. 22 Sep 1896) of Shoreham-by-Sea, Great Britain, who flew a US-built Harvard trainer plane on 6 Apr 1993 at the age of 96. His first solo flight had been an unofficial one during World War I.

Most flying hours Pilot John Edward Long (USA; b. 10 Nov 1915) between 1 May 1933 and 17 Sep 1991 logged 56,400 hr 5 min of flight time as a pilot—cumulatively more than six years airborne.

Passenger The record for a supersonic passenger is held by Fred Finn, who made his 687th Concorde crossing in February 1991. He commutes regularly from New Jersey to London, Great Britain. In April 1991 he became the first passenger to achieve 10 million miles.

Most planes flown James B. Taylor, Jr. (1897–1942) flew 461 different types of powered aircraft during his 25 years as an active experimental test and demonstration pilot for the US Navy and a number of American aircraft manufacturing companies. During one dive in 1939, he may have become the first pilot in history to fly faster than 500 mph and live.

Most transatlantic flights Between March 1948 and his retirement on 1 Sep 1984, Flight Service Manager Charles M. Schimpf logged a total of 2,880 Atlantic crossings—a rate of 6.4 per month.

Most experienced passenger Edwin A. Shackleton of Bristol, Great Britain has flown as a passenger in 462 different categories of aircraft. His first flight was in March 1943 in D.H. Dominie R9548; other aircraft have included helicopters, gliders, microlights, gas and hot air balloons.

Human-powered flight The Daedalus Project, centered at the Massachusetts Institute of Technology, Cambridge, MA, achieved its goal of human-powered flight when Kanellos Kanellopoulos (b. 25 Apr 1957) averaged 18.5 mph in his 112 ft wingspan machine from Crete to the island of Santorini, Greece on 23 Apr 1988, flying 74 miles.

AIRPORTS

Largest The largest is the $3.6 billion King Khalid International Airport outside Riyadh, Saudi Arabia, which covers an area of 87 miles^2 (55,040 acres). It was opened on 14 Nov 1983. It also has the world's largest control tower, 266 ft in height. The Hajj Terminal at the $4.76 billion King Abdul-Aziz Airport near Jeddah, Saudi Arabia is the world's largest roofed structure, covering 370 acres.

The world's largest airport terminal is at Hartsfield Atlanta International Airport, GA, opened on 21 Sep 1980, with floor space covering 2.4 million ft^2 (50^1/$_2$ acres) and still expanding. In 1992 the terminal serviced 42,023,988 passengers using 145 gates, although it has a capacity for 75 million.

Busiest The busiest airport is Chicago International Airport, O'Hare Field, IL, with a total of 64,441,087 passengers, total enplanement of 27,827,000 and 808,759,000 operational movements in the year 1991. This represents an average of 2,300 daily takeoffs or landings, or 110 every hour around the clock.

Heathrow airport, London, Great Britain, handles more international traffic than any other, with 38,245,900 international passengers in 1992.

The busiest landing area ever was Bien Hoa Air Base, South Vietnam, which handled approximately 1,000,000 takeoffs and landings in 1970.

Helipad The heliport at Morgan City, LA, one of a string used by helicopters flying energy-related offshore operations into the Gulf of Mexico, has pads for 46 helicopters. The world's largest helipad was An Khe, South Vietnam, during the Vietnam War.

Farthest and nearest to city or capital The airport farthest from the city center it allegedly serves is Viracopos, Brazil, which is 75 miles from São

FASTEST HELICOPTER The world record speed for a helicopter was achieved by a Westland Lynx helicopter, which reached a speed of 249.09 mph in 1986. It had taken ten years to design and develop the helicopter in such a way as to reach this speed. (Photo: Westland)

Paulo, although there is another airport which is closer to the city. Gibraltar Airport is a mere 880 yd from the city center.

Landing fields *Highest*   The highest is La Sa (Lhasa) Airport, Tibet, People's Republic of China, at 14,315 ft.

Lowest   The lowest landing field is El Lisan on the east shore of the Dead Sea, 1,180 ft below sea level, but during World War II BOAC Short C-class flying boats operated from the surface of the Dead Sea at 1,292 ft below sea level.

The lowest international airport is Schiphol, Amsterdam, Netherlands, at 15 ft below sea level.

Largest hangars   Hangar 375 ("Big Texas") at Kelly Air Force Base, San Antonio, TX, completed on 15 Feb 1956, has four doors each 250 ft wide, 60 ft high, and weighing 681 tons. The high bay is $2,000 \times 300 \times 90$ ft in area and is surrounded by a 44 acre concrete apron. It is the largest free-standing hangar in the world.

Largest wooden hangars   Between 1942 and 1943, 16 Navy airship wooden blimp hangers were built at various locations throughout the United States. They measure 1,040 ft long, 150 ft 4 in high at the crown and 296 ft 6 in wide at the base. There are only nine remaining—two each at Tillamook, OR, Moffett Field and Santa Ana, CA and Lakehurst, NJ, and one at Elizabeth City, NC.

HELICOPTERS

Earliest   Leonardo da Vinci (1452–1519) proposed the idea of a helicopter-type craft, although it is known that the Chinese had built helicopter-like toys as early as the 4th century B.C.

A craft bearing a resemblance to a helicopter was built in France by Paul Cornu and flown on 13 Sep 1907, but it was not until 1936 that the Focke-Achgelis (designated the FA 61) was flown, making it the first practical helicopter.

Fastest   Under FAI rules, the world's speed record for helicopters was set by John Trevor Eggington with co-pilot Derek J. Clews, who averaged 249.09 mph over Somerset, Great Britain on 11 Aug 1986 in a Westland Lynx company demonstrator helicopter.

Largest   The former Soviet Mil Mi-12 (NATO code-name "Homer") is powered by four 6,500 hp turboshaft engines and has a span of 219 ft 10 in over its rotor tips, with a length of 121 ft 4½ in. It weighs 114 tons.

Highest altitude   The record for helicopters is 40,820 ft by an Aérospatiale AS315B Lama, over Istres, France on 21 Jun 1972 by Jean Boulet.

The highest recorded landing was at 23,000 ft, below the southeast face of Mt Everest in a rescue sortie in May 1971.

Longest hover   Doug Daigle, Brian Watts and Dave Meyer of Tridair Helicopters, together with Rod Anderson of Helistream, Inc. of California, maintained a continuous hovering flight in a 1947 Bell B model for 50 hr 50 sec during 13 and 15 Dec 1989.

Plane pulling   Dave Gauder single-handedly pulled a Concorde 40 ft across the tarmac at Heathrow Airport, London, Great Britain on 11 Jun 1987.

Wing walking   Roy Castle, the host of the British Broadcasting Corporation *Record Breakers* television program, flew on the wing of a Boeing Stearman airplane for 3 hr 23 min on 2 Aug 1990, taking off from Gatwick, Great Britain and landing at Le Bourget, near Paris, France.

Smallest helicopter   The Aerospace General Co. one-person rocket-assisted minicopter weighs about 160 lb and can cruise for 250 miles at 185 mph.

Greatest load lifted by a helicopter   On 3 Feb 1982 at Podmoscovnoe in the USSR, a Mil Mi-26 heavy-lift helicopter (NATO codename "Halo"), crewed by G.V. Alfeurov and L.A. Indeyev (co-pilot), lifted a total mass of 6,560 ft.

Circumnavigation   H. Ross Perot, Jr. and Jay Coburn made the first helicopter circumnavigation in *Spirit of Texas* in 29 days 3 hr 8 min 13 sec on 1–30 Sep 1982 from Dallas, TX.

The first solo around-the-world flight in a helicopter was completed by Dick Smith (Australia) on 22 Jul 1983. Taking off from and returning to the Bell Helicopter facility at Fort Worth, TX, in a Bell Model 206L, LongRanger III, his unhurried flight began on 5 Aug 1982 and covered a distance of 35,258 miles.

AUTOGYROS

Earliest   The autogyro, or gyroplane, a rotorcraft with an unpowered rotor turned by the airflow in flight, preceded any practical helicopter with its engine-driven rotor.

Juan de la Cierva (Spain) designed the first successful gyroplane with his model C.4 (commercially named Autogiro), which flew at Getafe, Spain on 9 Jan 1923.

Speed, altitude and distance records   Wing-Cdr Kenneth H. Wallis (Great Britain) holds the straight-line distance record of 543.27 miles, set in his WA-116F autogyro on 28 Sep 1975 with a nonstop flight from Lydd to Wick, Great Britain. On 20 Jul 1982, flying from Boscombe Down, Great Britain, he established a new autogyro altitude record of 18,516 ft in his WA-121/Mc. Wing-Cdr Wallis also flew his WA-116/F/S, with a 60-hp Franklin aero-engine, to a record speed of 120.3 mph over a 1.86 mile straight course at Norfolk, Great Britain, on 18 Sep 1986.

FLYING BOATS

Fastest   The fastest flying boat ever built was the Martin XP6M-1 Seamaster, the US Navy four-jet-engined minelayer flown in 1955–59, with a top speed of 646 mph. In September 1946 the Martin JRM-2 Mars flying boat set a payload record of 68,327 lb.

The official flying boat speed record is 566.69 mph, set by Nikolay Andreievski and crew of two in a Soviet Beriev M-10, powered by two AL-7 turbojets, over a 9.3–15.5 mile course at Joukovsky-Petrovskoye, Russia on 7 Aug 1961.

The M-10 holds all 12 records listed for jet-powered flying boats, including an altitude record of 49,088 ft set by Georgiy Buryanov and crew over the Sea of Azov in the former USSR on 9 Sep 1961.

AIRSHIPS

Earliest flight   The earliest flight in an airship was by Henri Giffard from Paris to Trappes, France in his steam-powered coal-gas airship 88,300 ft³ in volume and 144 ft long, on 24 Sep 1852.

Earliest airline   Delag (Deutsche Luftschiffahrt AG) was founded at Frankfurt am Main, Germany on 16 Oct 1909 and started a scheduled airship service on 17 Jun 1910.

Largest Rigid   The largest was the 235-ton German *Graf Zeppelin II* (LZ 130), with a length of 804 ft and a capacity of 7.06 million ft³. It flew its maiden flight on 14 Sep 1938 and in May and August 1939 made radar spying missions in British air space. It was dismantled in April 1940. Its sister ship, *Hindenburg*, was 5 ft 7 in longer.

Non-rigid   The largest ever constructed was the US Navy ZPG 3-W, which had a capacity of 1.5 million ft³, a length of 403 ft, a diameter of 85.1 ft and a crew of 21. It first flew on 21 Jul 1958 but crashed into the sea in June 1960.

Greatest passenger load   The most people ever carried in an airship was 207, in the US Navy *Akron* in 1931. The transatlantic record is 117, by the German *Hindenburg* in 1937. It exploded into a fireball at Lakehurst, NJ on 6 May 1937.

The largest airship currently certified for the public transport of passengers (13) is the 193.6 ft-long non-rigid Skyship 600 series of 235,400 ft³ capacity, built by Airship Industries. Its maiden flight was on 27 Mar 1984.

Distance records   The FAI accredited straight-line distance record for airships is 3,967.1 miles, set by the German *Graf Zeppelin LZ127*, captained by Dr Hugo Eckener, between 29 Oct and 1 Nov 1928.

From 21–25 Nov 1917 the German *Zeppelin* L59 flew from Yambol, Bulgaria to a point south of Khartoum, Sudan and returned, covering a minimum of 4,500 miles.

Duration record   The longest recorded flight by a non-rigid airship (without refueling) is 264 hr 12 min by a US Navy Goodyear-built ZPG-2 class ship (Cdr J.R. Hunt, USN) that flew 9,448 miles from South Weymouth Naval Air Station, MA to Key West, FL, on 4–15 Mar 1957.

BALLOONING

Earliest The earliest recorded ascent was by a model hot-air balloon invented by Father Bartolomeu de Gusmão (ne Lourenço; 1685–1724), which was flown indoors at the Casa da India, Terreiro do Paço, Portugal on 8 Aug 1709.

First transatlantic crossing Col. Joe Kittinger (USAF) (see Sports and Games, Parachuting) became the first person to complete a solo transatlantic crossing by balloon. In the 101,000 ft³ helium-filled balloon *Rosie O'Grady*, Kittinger lifted off from Caribou, ME on 14 Sep 1984 and completed a distance of 3,543 miles before landing at Montenotte, near Savóna, Italy 86 hours later on 18 Sep 1984.

Duration record Richard Abruzzo, 29, together with Troy Bradley, 28, set a duration record of 144 hr 16 min in *Team USA* in crossing the Atlantic Ocean from Bangor, ME to Ben Slimane, Morocco on 16–22 Sep 1992. The previous record had been set by Richard's father, Ben in *Double Eagle II* in 1958.

Highest Unmanned The highest altitude attained by an unmanned balloon was 170,000 ft, by a Winzen balloon with a 47.8 million ft³ capacity, launched at Chico, CA in October 1972.

Manned The highest altitude reached in a manned balloon is an unofficial 123,800 ft by Nicholas Piantanida (1933–66) of Bricktown, NJ, from Sioux Falls, SD on 1 Feb 1966. He landed in a cornfield in Iowa but did not survive.

The official record (closed gondola) is 113,740 ft by Cdr Malcolm D. Ross (USNR) and the late Lt Cdr Victor A. Prother (USN), in an ascent from the deck of the USS *Antietam* over the Gulf of Mexico on 4 May 1961 in a balloon of 12 million ft³ capacity.

Largest The largest balloons ever built have an inflatable volume of 70 million ft³ and stand 1,000 ft tall. They are unmanned. The manufacturer is Winzen Research Inc. of Minnesota.

Hot-air The modern revival of this form of ballooning began in the United States in 1961, and the first world championships were held in Albuquerque, NM on 10–17 Feb 1973.

Mass ascent The greatest mass ascent of hot-air balloons from a single site took place within one hour on 15 Aug 1987 when 128 participants at the Ninth Bristol International Balloon Festival in Bristol, Great Britain took off.

Atlantic crossing Richard Branson (Great Britain) and his pilot, Per Lindstrand (Great Britain), were the first to cross the Atlantic in a hot-air balloon, on 2–3 Jul 1987. They ascended from Sugarloaf, ME and covered the distance of 3,075 miles to Limavady, Northern Ireland in 31 hours 41 minutes.

Pacific crossing Richard Branson and Per Lindstrand crossed the Pacific in the *Virgin Otsuka Pacific Flyer* from the southern tip of Japan to Lac la

Matre, Yukon, northwestern Canada on 15–17 Jan 1991 in a 2.6 million ft³ capacity hot-air balloon (the largest ever flown) to set FAI records for duration (46 hr 15 min) and distance (great circle 4,768 miles).

Unofficial world best performances were also set for the fastest speed from takeoff to landing, 147 mph. A speed of 239 mph was sustained over one hour.

Altitude Per Lindstrand (Great Britain) achieved the altitude record of 65,000 ft in a Colt 600 hot-air balloon over Laredo, TX on 6 Jun 1988.

The Dutch balloonist Henk Brink made an untethered flight of 656 ft in the 850,000 ft³ capacity *Nashua Number One*, carrying a total of 50 passengers and crew. The flight, on 17 Aug 1988, began from Lelystad Airport, Netherlands, lasted 25 minutes, and reached an altitude of 228 ft.

Gas The FAI endurance and distance record for a gas and hot-air balloon is 144 hr 16 min and 3,318 miles by *Team USA*, crewed by Richard Abruzzo and Troy Bradley on 16–22 Sep 1922 (See Duration record, page 342.)

Most passengers The balloon *Miss Champagne*, of 2.6 million ft³ capacity, was built by Tom Handcock of Portland, ME. Tethered, it rose to a height of 50 ft with 61 passengers on board on 19 Feb 1988.

First flight over Mount Everest Two balloons—*Star Flyer 1*, piloted by Chris Dewhirst with cameraman Leo Dickinson, and *Star Flyer 2*, piloted by Andy Elson with cameraman Eric Jones (all British)—achieved the first overflight of the summit of Mt Everest on 21 Oct 1991. The two 240,000 ft³ balloons had the highest recorded launch of a hot-air balloon at 15,536 ft and the highest recorded touch-down of a hot-air balloon at 16,200 ft.

Largest number to jump from a balloon On 5 Apr 1990, 12 members of the Red Devils Free Fall Parachute Team together made a jump from a Cameron A210 hot-air balloon over Bath, Great Britain, at a height of 6,000 ft.

Distance record The record distance traveled by a balloon is 5,208.68 miles, by the Raven experimental helium-filled balloon *Double Eagle V* (capacity 399.053 ft³) from 9–12 Nov 1981. The journey started at Nagashima, Japan and ended at Covello, CA. The crew for this first manned balloon crossing of the Pacific Ocean was Ben L. Abruzzo, 51, Rocky Aoki (Japan), 43, Ron Clark, 41, and Larry M. Newman, 34.

The first balloon crossing of the United States was by the helium-filled balloon *Super Chicken III* (pilots Fred Gorell and John Shoecraft), flying 2,515 miles from Costa Mesa, CA to Blackbeard's Island, GA from 9–12 Oct 1981.

MODEL AIRCRAFT

Altitude, speed and duration Maynard L. Hill (USA), flying a radio-controlled model, established the world record for altitude of 26,922 ft on 6 Sep 1970.

Gianmaria Aghem (Italy) holds the closed-circuit distance record, with 769.9 miles, achieved on 26 Jul 1986.

The speed record is 242.95 mph, set by W. Sitar (Austria), on 10 Jun 1977.

The record duration flight is one of 33 hr 39 min 15 sec by Maynard Hill (see above), with a powered model on 1–2 Oct 1992.

An indoor model with a wound rubber motor, designed by J. Richmond (USA), set a duration record of 52 min 14 sec on 31 Aug 1979.

Jean-Pierre Schiltknecht flew a solar-driven model aircraft for a duration of 10 hr 43 min 51 sec at Wetzlar, Germany on 10 July 1991.

Largest model glider   In January 1990 *Eagle III*, a radio-controlled glider weighing 14.5 lb with a wingspan of 32 ft 6 in, was designed and constructed by Carlos René Tschen and Carlos René Tschen Jr. of Colonia San Lázaro, Guatemala.

Smallest model aircraft   The smallest to fly is one weighing 0.004 oz, powered by an attached horsefly and designed by insectonaut Don Emmick of Seattle, WA. On 24 Jul 1979 an Emmick flew for 5 minutes at Kirkland, WA.

Paper aircraft   The level flight duration record for a hand-launched paper aircraft is 16.89 sec, by Ken Blackburn in the Reynolds Coliseum, North Carolina State University, on 29 Nov 1983.

An indoor distance of 193 ft was recorded by Tony Felch at the La Crosse Center, WI on 21 May 1985.

A paper plane was reported by "Chick" C.O. Reinhart to have flown 1¼ miles from a tenth-story office window at 60 Beaver Street, New York City across the East River to Brooklyn in August 1933, helped by a thermal from a coffee-roasting plant.

Largest   The largest flying paper airplane, with a wingspan of 30 ft 6 in, was constructed by pupils of various schools in Hampton, VA and flown on 25 Mar 1992. It was launched indoors from a 10-ft-high platform and flown for a distance of 114 ft 9 in.

BUSINESS WORLD

- **COMMERCE**
- **ECONOMICS**
- **AGRICULTURE**

COMMERCE

Oldest industry   The oldest-known industry is flint knapping, involving the production of chopping tools and hand axes, dating from 2.5 million years ago in Ethiopia. The earliest evidence of trading in exotic stone and amber dates from *c.* 28,000 B.C. in Europe. Agriculture is often described as "the oldest industry in the world," but in fact there is no firm evidence yet that it was practiced before *c.* 11,000 B.C.

Oldest company   The Faversham Oyster Fishery Co. is referred to in the Faversham Oyster Fishing Act of 1930 as having existed "from time immemorial," i.e., in English law, from before 1189.

The oldest existing documented company is Stora Kopparbergs Bergslags of Falun, the Swedish industrial and forestry enterprise, which has been in continuous operation since the 11th century. It is first mentioned in historical records in the year 1288, when a Swedish bishop bartered an eighth share in the enterprise, and it was granted a charter in 1347. Originally concerned with the mining and processing of copper, it is now the largest privately-owned power producer in Sweden. In June 1991 it was reported, however, that the company was closing down its 1,000-year-old copper mine at Falun.

Largest company   The largest manufacturing company in the world is General Motors Corporation of Detroit, MI, with operations throughout the world and a workforce of 750,000. In addition to its core business of motor vehicles and components, the company produces defense and aerospace materials and provides computer and communication services. Its assets in 1992 were $191.012 billion, with sales totaling $132.4 billion. Despite these figures, however, the company announced a loss of $23.5 billion for the year, representing the worst annual trading loss in the world. (See Greatest loss.)

Largest employer   The world's largest employer is Indian Railways, with 1,654,066 employees on 31 Mar 1992.

Greatest sales   The first company to surpass the $1 billion mark in annual sales was the United States Steel (now USX) Corporation of Pittsburgh, PA in 1917.

The *Fortune 500* list of leading industrial corporations in April 1993 is headed by the General Motors Corporation of Detroit, MI, with sales of $132.4 billion for 1992.

Greatest profit   The greatest net profit ever made by a corporation in 12 months is $7.6 billion, by American Telephone and Telegraph Co. (AT&T) from 1 Oct 1981 to 30 Sep 1982.

Greatest loss   The world's worst annual net trading loss is $23.5 billion, reported by General Motors for 1992. The bulk of this figure was, however, due to a single charge of some $21 billion for employees' health costs and pensions and was disclosed because of new US accounting regulations. (See also Largest companies.)

The record private company deficit, and the greatest loss reported by an American company, was $23.5 billion, posted by General Motors Corporation for 1992. (See Largest company.)

Takeover The highest bid in a corporate takeover was $21 billion, for RJR Nabisco Inc., the tobacco, food and beverage company, by the Wall Street leveraged buyout firm Kohlberg Kravis Roberts (KKR), which offered $90 a share on 24 Oct 1988. By 1 Dec 1988 the bid, led by Henry Kravis, had reached $109 per share to then total $25 billion.

Bankruptcies On 3 Sep 1992 Kevin Maxwell, son of the former press magnate Robert Maxwell (1923–91), became the world's biggest bankrupt with debts of £406.8 million (*c.* $813.6 million). The announcement followed a private hearing in the British High Court on a presentation by the liquidators of the Bishopsgate Investment Management company, from which millions of pounds of employee's pension funds were misappropriated. Kevin Maxwell also faced charges of theft and conspiracy to defraud involving some £135 million (*c.* $270 million).

Greatest auction The world's largest-ever public auction took place in Dallas, TX on 1–2 Dec 1992, organized by the Federal Deposit Insurance Corporation (FDIC). Bidders in five other US cities were able to participate via satellite. The 4,000 participants in attendance purchased $418,836,100 in foreclosed, commercial and multifamily property consisting of hotels, residential and office buildings. Lots were put on the block every two minutes.

Greatest barter deal The biggest barter in trading history was 30 million barrels of oil, valued at $1,710 million, exchanged for ten Boeing 747s for the Royal Saudi Airline in July 1984.

Company names The longest company name on the Index registered under The British Companies Acts is "The Only Ordinary People Trying to Impress the Big Guys with Extra Ordinary Ideas, Sales, Management, Creative Thinking and Problem Solving Consultancy Company Ltd," Company number 2660603. This is the specially adopted name of The Planet Hollywood Restaurant Company Ltd run by Arnold Schwarzenegger, Sylvester Stallone and Bruce Willis.

The shortest names on the Index are D Ltd, E Ltd, Q Ltd, X Ltd and Y Ltd.

Largest piggy bank The largest piggy bank in the United States measures 6 ft 11 in high x 10 ft x 17 ft 2 in and answers to the name of Penny the Pig. Created by Mary Ann Spanagel and Coldwell Banker Real Estate of Pittsburgh, PA, Penny is used to raise money for the homeless in Pennsylvania.

Corporate   The biggest corporate bankruptcy in terms of assets was $35.9 billion filed by Texaco in 1987.

Accountants   The world's largest firm of accountants and management consultants is KPMG Peat Marwick McLintock, whose worldwide fee income totaled $6.15 billion on 30 Sep 1992. The company had over 73,000 employees in 834 cities in 124 countries. In the United States KPMG also had the most offices at 135. Arthur Andersen & Co., SC, had the most sales in the United States, at $2.68 billion, and had 27,037 employees.

Banks Largest   The world's largest multilateral development bank is the International Bank of Reconstruction and Development, founded on 27 Dec 1945 and known as the World Bank. Based in Washington, D.C., the bank had an authorized share capital of $152.2 billion on 30 Jun 1992. There were 159 members with a subscribed capital of $126.2 billion on 30 Jun 1992, at which time the World Bank also had unallocated reserves and accumulated net income of $11.2 billion.

Commercial   The world's biggest commercial bank is the Dai-Ichi Kangyo Bank Ltd of Japan, with assets on 31 Mar 1993 of $427.1 billion.
   The largest commercial bank in the United States is Citibank, N.A., located in New York City, with total assets of $163.8 billion and deposits of $118.3 billion as of 31 Dec 1992.

Most branches   The bank with most branches is the State Bank of India, which had 12,664 outlets on 1 Jan 1993 and assets of $36 billion.

Oldest   The oldest bank in the United States in continuous operation is The Bank of New York, founded in 1834 by Alexander Hamilton.

Confectioners   The largest chocolate and confectionary factory is the one built by Hershey Chocolate United States in Hershey, PA in 1903–05. It has 2³/₄ million ft² of floor space.

Department stores   Woolworth Corporation now operates more than 9,000 general stores worldwide. Frank Winfield Woolworth opened his first store, "The Great Five Cent Store," in Utica, NY on 22 Feb 1879. The net income as of 30 Jan 1993 was $280 million.
   The world's largest department store is R.H. Macy & Co. Inc. at Herald Square, New York City. It covers 50.5 acres. In 1990 the company's total sales were $7.3 billion. Macy's is, however, now undergoing bankruptcy proceedings. The department store with the highest sales volume for 1992 was Nordstrom, based in Seattle, WA, with total sales for the company's 70 stores of $3.4 billion, and net earnings of $136 million. Nordstrom employs 35,000.

Drug stores   The largest chain of drug stores in the world is Rite Aid Corporation of Shiremanstown, PA, which in 1992 had 2,341 branches throughout the United States. The Walgreen Co. of Deerfield, IL has fewer stores, but a larger volume of sales, totaling $7.474 billion in 1992.

Grocery stores   The largest grocery chain in the United States is Kroger Co. of Cincinnati, OH with 1992 sales of $21.35 billion. The company also has the most stores in the United States with 2,231.

Biggest Toy Store

Hamleys of Regent Street, London, Great Britain—founded in 1760—is the world's oldest, largest and best-stocked toy store. Its selling space covers 45,000 ft² across six floors. Shown here is a small selection of the 50,000 different items for sale, ranging from simple plastic dinosaurs to high-tech simulators. Guarding the stuffed toy department is the largest toy, a magnificent giant rhinoceros priced at £2,000 ($3,100). The smallest is a 0.4 in teacup for a doll's house, at £2.99 ($4.60) for a set of four. The comics department includes the most expensive item, an original 1939 copy of Detective Comics 27, *available for £106,000 ($164,300). Hamleys has 400 employees during the Christmas season.*

Sales per unit area   Stew Leonard's Supermarket in Norwalk, CT has the greatest sales per unit area in the United States, with sales of $4,732 per ft², for the calendar year 1992 (total sales $123,666,147).

Insurance   The company with the highest volume of insurance in force in the world is the Metropolitan Life Insurance Co. of New York City, with $1.14 billion at year end 1992. The company set a world record with $1.0271 trillion in 1991. The Prudential Insurance Company of America of Newark, NJ has the greatest volume of consolidated assets, totaling $200 billion in 1992.

The largest single insurance association in the world is the Blue Cross and Blue Shield Association, the American-based hospital insurance organization. It had a membership of 67.5 million in 1992, and benefits paid out totaled $63.1 billion.

Policies   The largest life insurance policy ever issued was for $100 million, bought by a major American entertainment corporation on the life of a leading American entertainment figure. The policy was sold in July 1990 by Peter Rosengard of London, Great Britain and was placed by Shel Bachrach of Albert G. Ruben & Co. Inc. of Beverly Hills, CA and Richard Feldman of the Feldman Agency, East Liverpool, OH with nine insurance companies to spread the risk.

The highest payout on a single life was reported on 14 Nov 1970 to be some $18 million to Linda Mullendore, widow of an Oklahoma rancher. Her murdered husband had paid $300,000 in premiums in 1969.

Marine insurance   The largest-ever marine insurance loss was approximately $836 million for the Piper Alpha Oil Field in the North Sea, Great Britain. On 6 Jul 1988 a leak from a gas compression chamber underneath the living quarters ignited and triggered a series of explosions that blew Piper Alpha apart. Of the 232 people on board, only 65 survived.

The largest sum claimed for consequential losses was approximately $1.7 trillion against owning, operating and building corporations and Claude Phillips, resulting from the 55-million-gallon oil spill from MT *Amoco Cadiz* on the Brittany coast, France on 16 Mar 1978.

Paper company   The world's largest producer of paper, fiber and wood products is International Paper of Purchase, NY, with sales in 1992 of $13.5 billion, a net income of $86 million and assets of $16,459 billion. The company employs 70,500 workers.

Real estate Landowners   The world's largest landowner is the United States government, with a holding of 728 million acres, which is bigger than the world's eighth largest country, Argentina, and 12 times larger than Indiana.

Price, most expensive   The most expensive piece of property ever recorded was the land around the central Tokyo retail food store Mediya Building in the Ginza district, which was quoted in October 1988 by the Japanese National Land Agency at 358.5 million yen per ft² (then equivalent to $248,000).

Retailer   The largest retailer in the United States was Wal-Mart, Inc. of Bentonville, AR with a sales volume of $55.5 billion and a net income of

$1.9 billion, as of 31 Jan 1993. Wal-Mart was founded by Samuel Moore "Sam" Walton (1918–92) in Rogers, AR in 1962, and as of January 1993 Wal-Mart had over 1,880 retail locations employing 460,000 workers.

The largest retailing firm in the United States based on current assets is Sears Roebuck and Co. (founded by Richard Warren Sears in North Redwood, MN in 1886) of Chicago, IL, with $83.5 billion. Sears Merchandise Group had 859 retail stores, including 1,136 specialty stores, and 356 independent catalog merchants in the United States as of 31 Dec 1992.

Savings and loan association   The world's biggest lender is the Japanese-government-controlled House Loan Corporation.

The largest savings and loan association (S&L) in the United States is Home Savings of America, FA in Irwindale, CA. As of 31 Dec 1992 the company had total assets of $48.1 billion and total deposits of $39.2 billion. Home Savings also has the most branch offices of any S&L, with 375. As of 31 March 1993 Great Western Bank Association in Beverly Hills, CA has the most deposit accounts, with 4.3 million.

Greatest faux pas   If measured by financial consequences, the greatest *faux pas* on record was that of the young multimillionaire James Gordon Bennett (1841–1918), committed on 1 Jan 1877 at the family mansion of his demure fiancée, one Caroline May, on Fifth Avenue in New York City. Bennett arrived in a two-horse carriage, late and obviously drunk. By dint of intricate footwork, he entered the drawing room, where he was the center of attention. He mistook the fireplace for a plumbing fixture more usually reserved for another purpose. The May family broke the engagement and Bennett was obliged to spend the rest of his footloose and fancy-free life based in Paris, France, with the resultant noncollection of millions of dollars in taxes by the US Treasury.

Menswear store   The world's largest store selling only men's suits and accessories is Slater Menswear of Glasgow, Scotland, which has a weekly turnover in excess of 2,000 suits. The store covers 40,250 ft² and stocks over 17,000 suits at any one time.

Rummage sale   The Cleveland Convention Center, OH White Elephant Sale (instituted 1933) on 18–19 Oct 1983 raised $427,935.21. The greatest amount of money raised at a one-day sale was $208,723.00 at the 61st one-day rummage sale organized by the Winnetka Congregational Church, IL on 13 May 1993.

Employment agency   The world's largest employment services group is Manpower, with 560,000 workers, and with worldwide sales of all their brand units of $3.5 billion at year end 31 Mar 1992.

ECONOMICS

MONETARY AND FINANCIAL

Largest budget   The greatest governmental expenditure ever made by any country was $1.382 trillion by the United States government for the fiscal year 1992. The highest-ever revenue figure was $1.092 trillion in the same fiscal year. An expenditure budget of $1.468 trillion was sent to Congress on 30 Jan 1993 for the fiscal year 1994, which starts on 1 Oct 1993.

The greatest fiscal surplus ever was $8,419,469,844 in the United States in 1947/48. The worst deficit was $290 billion in the US fiscal year 1992.

Foreign aid   The greatest donor of foreign aid has been the United States—the total net foreign aid given by its government between 1 Jul 1945 and 30 Sep 1992 was $406.8 billion.

The country receiving most US aid in 1991 was Israel, with $3.65 billion. Egypt was second with $2.25 billion. These totals are for both economic and military aid. US foreign aid began with $50,000 to Venezuela for earthquake relief in 1812.

Least taxed   The sovereign countries with the lowest income tax in the world are Bahrain and Qatar, where the rate is zero, regardless of income. No tax is levied on the Sarkese (inhabitants of Sark), in the Channel Islands, Great Britain. There is no taxation in Tristan da Cunha apart from a nominal 65p a year paid by all males between the ages of 18 and 65.

United States   The lowest income tax rate in United States history was 1 percent between 1913 and 1915.

Highest taxation rates   The country with the highest taxation is Norway, where the highest rate of income tax in 1992 was 65 percent, although additional personal taxes make it possible to be charged in excess of 100 percent. In January 1974 the 80 percent limit was abolished there, and some 2,000 citizens were then listed in the *Lignings Boka* as paying more than 100 percent of their taxable income. The shipping magnate Hilmar Reksten (1897–1980) was assessed at 491 percent.

In Denmark the highest rate of income tax is 68 percent, but a net wealth tax of 1 percent can result in tax of over 100 percent on income in extreme situations.

United States   The highest income tax rate in United States history was implemented in 1944 by the Individual Tax Act with a 91 percent bracket. The current highest income tax bracket is 36.9 percent.

Highest tax levy   The highest recorded personal tax levy is one for $336 million on 70 percent of the estate of Howard Hughes.

Balance of payments (current account)   The record balance of payments deficit for any country for a calendar year is $163.5 billion in 1987 by the United States. The record surplus was Japan's $117.62 billion in 1992.

National debt   The largest national debt of any country in the world is that of the United States, where the gross federal public debt of the federal government surpassed the trillion dollar mark on 30 Sep 1981. By the end of 1992, it reached $4.071 trillion, with net interest payments on the debt of a record $199.4 billion.

Most foreign debt   The country most heavily in overseas debt at the end of fiscal year 1992 was the United States, with $449 billion, although the size of its debt is small relative to its economic strength. Among developing countries, Brazil has the highest foreign debt, with $123.2 billion at the end of 1991.

Gross national product   The country with the largest gross national product is the United States. Having reached $3 trillion in 1981, the GNP was running at $5.96 trillion for the year ending 31 Dec 1992.

National wealth   The richest country as listed in the 1992 *World Bank Atlas* ranking is Switzerland, which in 1991 had an average gross national product (GNP) per capita of $33,510. The United States, which had held the lead from 1910 to 1973, was tenth. It has been estimated that the value of all physical assets in the United States totalled $26.7 trillion at the end of 1991, equivalent to $105,659 per capita. By 31 Dec 1992 the per capita income for the United States was $22,560.

According to figures released by the Commerce Department's Bureau of Economic Analysis, in 1992 Connecticut enjoyed the highest per capita income level of any state ($26,979), while Mississippi continued to have the lowest ($14,088). Personal income in the United States totaled $19,841 per person for 1992. Personal income set a record high of $5.06 trillion in 1992.

The median household income in the United States in 1991 was $30,126. Connecticut enjoyed the highest level at $42,154 and Mississippi was the lowest at $19,475.

Poorest country   Mozambique had the lowest GNP per capita in 1991, with $70, although there are several countries for which the *World Bank Atlas* is not able to include data.

Gold reserves   The country with the greatest monetary gold reserves is the United States, whose Treasury held 262 million fine troy oz as of 31 Dec 1992. At $300 per fine oz, their value was $86.39 billion.

The United States Bullion Depository at Fort Knox, 30 miles southwest of Louisville, KY, has been the principal federal depository of US gold since December 1936. Gold is stored in 446,000 standard mint bars of 400 troy ounces measuring $7 \times 3^5/8 \times 1^5/8$ in. Gold's peak price was $875 per fine oz on 21 Jan 1980.

Inflation   The United States Department of Labor measures changes in the Consumer Price Index (CPI) in 12-month periods ending in December. The Bureau of Labor Statistics first began keeping the CPI in 1913. Since that time the change of the greatest magnitude was a 20.4 percent increase for the 12-month period ending December 1918, and the largest decline was –10.8 percent in December 1921. The largest peacetime increase, recorded in December 1979, was 13.3 percent. Figures are based on the United States city average CPI for all urban consumers.

Worst   The world's worst inflation occurred in Hungary in June 1946, when the 1931 gold pengö was valued at 130 million trillion paper pengös. Notes were issued for "Egymillard billion" (one billion billion) pengös on 3 June and withdrawn on 11 Jul 1946. Vouchers for 1 billion trillion pengös were issued for taxation payment only. On 6 Nov 1923 Germany's Reichsbank marks circulation reached 400,338,326,350,700,000,000 and inflation was 755,700 millionfold at 1913 levels.

The country with the worst inflation in 1992 was Zaire, where consumer price increases rose to 7,058 percent. Inflation in the CIS (formerly USSR) totaled 1,181.8 percent in 1992 according to IMF data.

Least   The country with the least inflation in 1992 was Gabon, where prices fell by 4.2 percent.

THE GUINNESS DAILY RECORD

4 July, 1916

You can't take it with you

WORLD'S GREATEST MISER DIES LEAVING A FORTUNE

Hetty Green, reputedly America's wealthiest woman and arguably the world's most miserly, died yesterday leaving an estate worth $95 million.

Mrs Green, a New York financier who at the age of 30 inherited $10 million following the deaths of her father and aunt, increased this amount tenfold by careful management and avoiding unnecessary expenditure.

Despite keeping over $31.4 million in one bank alone, Mrs Green ate cold cereal because she was too thrifty to heat it up,

Photo: Library of Congress, Washington, D.C.

and her son's leg had to be amputated because of her delays in finding a clinic offering free medical treatment.

Henrietta Howland Green (nee Robinson), born 21 November 1835, New Bedford, Massachusetts; died 3 July 1916, New York City.

RICHEST MAN His Majesty the Sultan of Brunei, whose fortune is estimated at $37 billion. (Photo: Sygma/T. Matsumoto)

WEALTH AND POVERTY

Comparisons and estimates of extreme personal wealth are beset with intractable difficulties. Quite apart from reticence and the element of approximation in the valuation of assets, as Jean Paul Getty (1892–1976) once said: "If you can count your millions you are not a billionaire." The term millionaire was invented *c*. 1740 and billionaire in 1861. The earliest dollar centimillionaire was Cornelius Vanderbilt (1794–1877), who left $100 million in 1877. The first billionaires were John Davison Rockefeller (1839–1937) and Andrew William Mellon (1855–1937), with Rockefeller believed to be the first to have a billion dollars.

Richest men Much of the wealth of the world's monarchs represents national rather than personal assets. The least fettered and most monarchical is HM Sir Muda Hassanal Bolkiah Mu'izzaddin Waddaulah (b. 15 Jul 1946) of Brunei. He appointed himself Prime Minister, Finance Minister and Home Affairs Minister on 1 Jan 1984. *Fortune* Magazine reported in June 1993 that his fortune was $37 billion.

The same source estimates the richest private individual to be John Werner Kluge of Metromedia, with $8.8 billion. The only other estimated deca-billionaire is Taikichiro Mori of Japan (1904–93), with assets of $10 billion.

Richest women Her Majesty Queen Elizabeth II is asserted by some to be the wealthiest woman, and *The Sunday Times* of London, Great Britain estimated in April 1993 that she had assets of £6.75 billion ($11.7 billion). However, few of her assets under the perpetual succession of the Crown are either personal or disposable, and her personal wealth was estimated at £500 million ($900 million). An alternative estimate published by the British magazine *The Economist* in January 1992 placed her personal wealth at much closer to £150 million ($270 million).

The cosmetician Madame C.J. Walker (nee Sarah Breedlove [USA]; 1867–1919) is reputed to have been the first self-made millionairess. She was an uneducated black orphan whose fortune was founded on a hair re-laxer.

Richest families It has been tentatively estimated that the combined value of the assets nominally controlled by the Du Pont family, of some 1,600 members, may be on the order of $150 billion. The family arrived in the United States from France on 1 Jan 1800. Capital from Pierre Du Pont (1730–1817) enabled his son Eleuthère Irénée Du Pont to start his explosives company in the United States.

A more conclusive claimant is the Walton retailing family, worth an estimated $23.5 billion.

Longest pension Miss Millicent Barclay was born on 10 Jul 1872, three months after the death of her father, Col. William Barclay, and became eligible for a Madras Military Fund pension to continue until her marriage. She died unmarried on 26 Oct 1969, having drawn the pension every day of her life of 97 years 3 months.

Youngest millionaires The youngest person ever to accumulate a million dollars was the American child film actor Jackie Coogan (1914–84), who co-starred with Charlie Chaplin (1889–1977) in *The Kid*, made in 1921.

The youngest of the 101 billionaires reported in the United States in 1992 was William Gates, 36, cofounder of Microsoft of Seattle, WA, whose *MS/DOS* operating system enables an estimated 72 million of the United States' 90 million *PCs* (personal computers) to work. Gates was 20 when he set up his company in 1976 and was a billionaire by 31.

The youngest millionairess was Shirley Temple (b. 23 Apr 1928), now Mrs Charles Black, who accumulated wealth exceeding $1 million before she was 10. Her childhood acting career spanned the years 1934 to 1939.

Highest incomes The largest incomes derive from the collection of royalties per barrel by rulers of oil-rich sheikhdoms who have not formally revoked personal entitlement. Sheikh Zayid ibn Sultan an-Nuhayan (b. 1918), head of state of the United Arab Emirates, arguably has title to some $9 billion of the country's annual gross national product.

Largest dowry The largest recorded dowry was that of Elena Patiño, daughter of Don Simón Iturbi Patiño (1861–1947), the Bolivian tin millionaire, who in 1929 bestowed $39 million from a fortune at one time estimated to be worth $607.5 million.

Return of cash The largest amount of cash ever found and returned to its owners was $500,000, discovered by Lowell Elliott, 61, on his farm in Peru, IN. It had been dropped in June 1972 by a parachuting hijacker.

Jim Priceman, 44, assistant cashier at Doft & Co. Inc., returned an envelope containing $37.1 million in *negotiable* bearer certificates found outside 110 Wall Street to A.G. Becker Inc. of New York on 6 Apr 1982. In announcing a reward of $250, Becker was acclaimed as being "all heart."

Greatest bequests   The largest single bequest in the history of philanthropy was of the art collection belonging to the American publisher Walter Annenberg, which was worth $1 billion. He announced on 12 Mar 1991 that he would be leaving the collection to the Metropolitan Museum of Art in New York City.

The largest single cash bequest was the $500 million gift, announced on 12 Dec 1955, to 4,157 educational and other institutions by the Ford Foundation (established 1936) of New York.

Highest salary   It was reported by the US government that Michael Milken, the "junk bond king" at Drexel Burnham Lambert Inc., was paid $550 million in salary and bonuses in 1987. (See Judicial, Fines.)

United States   The highest-paid chief executive in the United States is Thomas F. Frist Jr., who heads the Hospital Corporation of America. His 1992 combined income was $127 million; of that $1.068 million was salary and bonus and $125.9 million was long-term compensation in the form of stock options. He paid $39 million to the Internal Revenue Service.

Highest fees   The highest-paid investment consultant in the world is Harry D. Schultz, who lives in Monte Carlo and Zurich, Switzerland. His standard consultation fee for 60 minutes is $2,400 on weekdays and $3,400 on weekends. Most popular are the five-minute phone consultations at $200 (i.e., $40 a minute). His "International Harry Schultz Letter," instituted in 1964, sells for $50 per copy. A life subscription costs $2,400.

Golden handshake   *Business Week* Magazine reported in May 1989 that the largest "golden handshake" ever given was one of $53.8 million, to F. Ross Johnson, who left RJR Nabisco as chairman in February 1989.

Biggest payday   On Thursday 31 Dec 1992, a reported $75 million was paid in salary and benefits, the biggest payday in United States history. Through an unusual combination of weekly, twice-weekly and monthly paydays falling on the same day, and benefit checks being paid early because of the New Year's holiday, more than 10 million workers and benefit recipients joined together, albeit unwittingly, to enjoy a record-breaking New Year's Eve.

PAPER MONEY

The Department of the Treasury reported that in fiscal year 1993, 3.5 billion $1 bills were printed, the most of any denomination. For other bills, the estimates were as follows: $5 (1.12 billion), $10 (0.64 billion), $20 (2.16 billion), $50 (0.25 billion) and $100 (0.32 billion).

Earliest   Paper money was an invention of the Chinese, first tried in A.D. 812 and prevalent by A.D. 970. The world's earliest bank notes (*banco-*

sedler) were issued in Stockholm, Sweden in July 1661, the oldest survivor being one of five dalers dated 6 Dec 1662.

Largest The largest paper money ever issued was the one-guan note of the Chinese Ming Dynasty issue of 1368–99, which measured 9 × 13 in.

Smallest The smallest national note ever issued was the 10-bani note of the Ministry of Finance of Romania, in 1917. It measured (printed area) $1/16 × 11/2$ in. Of German *Notgeld*, the smallest were the 1–3 pfg notes of Passau (1920–21), measuring $11/16$ x $3/4$ in.

Highest values The highest-value notes in circulation are US Federal Reserve $10,000 bank notes, bearing the head of Salmon P. Chase (1808–73). It was announced in 1969 that no further notes higher than $100 would be issued, and only 345 $10,000 bills remain in circulation or unretired. The highest value ever issued by the US Federal Reserve System is a note for $100,000, bearing the head of Woodrow Wilson (1856–1924), which is only used for transactions between the Federal Reserve and the Treasury Department.

Most expensive The record price paid for a single lot of bank notes was £240,350 ($478,900 including buyer's premium) by Richard Lobel, on behalf of a consortium, at Phillips, London, Great Britain on 14 Feb 1991. The lot consisted of a cache of British military notes which were found in a vault in Berlin, Germany, and contained more than 17 million notes.

Bank note collection Chris Boyd of New Malden, Great Britain has accumulated bank notes from 204 different countries, since he started collecting in 1990.

CHECKS AND COINS

Largest The greatest amount paid by a single check in the history of banking was £1.425 trillion ($2.494 trillion). Issued on 11 Jul 1989 and signed by three treasurers, the check represented a payment from the expiring Abbey National Building Society in favor of the newly created Abbey National plc. A larger one, for $4,176,969,623.57, was drawn on 30 Jun 1954, although this was an internal US Treasury check.

Collection—record price The highest price ever paid for a coin collection was $25,235,360 for the Garrett family collection of US and colonial coins, which had been donated to Johns Hopkins University, Baltimore, MD. The sales were made at a series of four auctions held on 28–29 Nov 1979 and 25–26 Mar 1981 at the Bowers & Ruddy Galleries in Wolfeboro, NH. The collection was put together by members of the Garrett family between 1860 and 1942.

Hoards The most valuable hoard of coins was one of about 80,000 aurei found in Brescello near Modena, Italy in 1714, and believed to have been deposited *c.* 37 B.C. The largest deliberately buried hoard ever found was the Brussels hoard of 1908 containing *c.* 150,000 coins.

The largest accidental hoard on record was the 1715 Spanish Plate Fleet, which sank off the coast of Florida. A reasonable estimate of its contents would be some 60 million coins, of which about half were recovered by Spanish authorities shortly after the event. Of the remaining 30 million pieces, perhaps 500,000 have been recovered by modern salvagers. The other 29½ million coins are, presumably, still on the bottom of the sea, awaiting recovery.

The record in terms of weight is 47 tons of gold, from the White Star Liner HMS *Laurentic*, which was mined in 132 ft of water off Fanad Head, Donegal, Ireland in 1917. The Royal Navy, Cossum Diving Syndicate and Consortium Recovery Ltd. has since recovered 3,191 of the 3,211 gold ingots.

Mints Largest The largest mint in the world is that of the US Treasury. It was built from 1965–69 on Independence Mall, Philadelphia and covers 11½ acres, with an annual production capacity on a three-shift seven-day week of 12 billion coins. A new high-speed stamping machine (called the

---

COINS

Oldest
Electrum staters of King Gyges of Lydia, Turkey, *c.* 670 B.C.[1]

Earliest Dated
Samian silver tetradrachm struck in Zankle (now Messina), Sicily, dated year 1, *viz.* 494 B.C.—shown as "A". *Christian Era:* MCCXXXIIII (1234) Bishop of Roskilde coins, Denmark (6 known).

Heaviest
Swedish 10-daler copper plate, 1644, 43 lb 7¼ oz[2].

Lightest
Nepalese silver ¼ jawa *c.* 1740, 14,000 to the oz.

Most expensive
Set: $3,190,000 for the King of Siam Proof Set, a set of 1804 and 1834 US coins which had once been given to the King of Siam, purchased by Iraj Sayah and Terry Brand at Superior Galleries, Beverly Hills, CA on 28 May 1990. Included in the set of nine coins was the 1804 silver dollar, which had an estimated value of about $2,000,000.

Individual: $1,500,000 for the US 1907 Double Eagle Ultra High Relief $20 gold coin, sold by MTB Banking Corporation of New York to a private investor on 9 Jul 1990.

[1] *Chinese uninscribed "spade" money of the Zhou dynasty has been dated to c. 770 B.C.*
[2] *The largest coinlike medallion was completed on 21 Mar 1986 for the World Exposition in Vancouver, British Columbia, Canada, Expo 86—a $1,000,000 gold piece. Its dimensions were 37.5 in diameter and ¾ in thick and it weighed 365 lb 15 oz, or 5,337 oz (troy) of gold.*

MOST VALUABLE LINE OF COINS Part of the continuous line of coins that had a total value of $431,000, set in July 1992. (Photo: Marquette Industries/Jerry Stahl)

Coin snatching The greatest number of new British 10p pieces clean-caught from being flipped from the back of a forearm into the same downward palm is 328, by Dean Gould of Felixstowe, Great Britain on 6 Apr 1993.

Column of coins The most valuable column of coins was worth £18,701 ($28,986) and was 6 ft 3 in high. It was built by Robert Young and a team of helpers at Notton, Great Britain on 18 Jun 1992.

Coin balancing Hiem Shda of Kiriat Mozkien, Israel stacked a pyramid of 847 coins on the edge of a coin free-standing vertically on the base of a coin that was on a table on 30 Jul 1989.

The tallest single column of coins ever stacked on the edge of a coin was made up of 253 Indian one-rupee pieces on top of a vertical five-rupee coin, by Dipak Syal of Yamuna Nagar, India on 3 May 1991. He also balanced 10 one-rupee coins and 10 ten-paise coins alternately horizontally and vertically in a single column on 1 May 1991.

"Graebner Press") can produce coins at a rate of 42,000 per hour. The record production for coins was in 1982, when 19.5 billion were produced between the Philadelphia and Denver mints.

Smallest The smallest issuing mint in the world belongs to the Sovereign Military Order of Malta, in the City of Rome. Its single-press mint is housed in one small room and has issued proof coins since 1961.

Most popular coin More than 250 billion pennies with Lincoln's head have been minted in the 80 years since the première issue of this coin in 1909 for the 100th anniversary of Lincoln's birth. If lined up, the 250 billion coins would stretch 2,808,586 miles, and if piled up (17 to an inch) they would tower 220,851 miles into space.

Charity fund-raising Profits from the single *Do They Know It's Christmas*, recorded by Band Aid in 1984, and other related projects in support of the Ethiopian Famine Relief Fund raised $170 million at the close of the account in 1992.

The greatest recorded amount raised by a charity walk or run is $Cdn24.7 million by Terry Fox (1958–81) of Canada who, with an artificial leg, ran from St John's, Newfoundland to Thunder Bay, Ontario in 143 days from 12 Apr–2 Sep 1980. He covered 3,339 miles.

Line of coins The most valuable line of coins was made up of 1,724,000 quarters with a value of $431,000. It was 25.9 miles long, and was laid at the Atlanta Marriott Marquis Hotel, GA by members of the National Exchange Club on 25 Jul 1992.

The longest line of coins on record had a total length of 30.38 miles and was made using 1,886,975 two-pence coins. It was laid by the Friends of the Samaritans at the Great Park, Windsor, Great Britain on 16 Aug 1992.

Pile of coins The most valuable pile of coins had a total value of $126,463.61 and consisted of 1,000,298 coins of various denominations. It was constructed by the YMCA of Seattle-King County, WA in Redmond, WA on 28 May 1992.

LABOR

First labor union The first officially recognized labor organization in the United States was formed by the Shoemakers and Coopers of Boston, MA. They were granted a three-year charter by King Charles II in 1648. The charter was not renewed.

Largest labor union The world's largest union is Professionalniy Soyuz Rabotnikov Agro-Promyshlennogo Kompleksa (Agro-Industrial Complex Workers' Union) in the former Soviet Union, with 15.2 million members in January 1993.

United States As of 31 Aug 1991 the largest union in the United States was the National Education Association (NEA), which has 2.11 million members.

Smallest labor union The ultimate in small unions was the Jewelcase and Jewelry Display Makers Union (JJDMU), founded in 1894. It was dissolved on 31 Dec 1986 by its general secretary, Charles Evans. The motion was seconded by Fergus McCormack, its only other surviving member.

Longest name The union with the longest name is the International Association of Marble, Slate and Stone Polishers, Rubbers and Sawyers, Tile and Marble Setters' Helpers and Marble, Mosaic and Terrazzo Workers' Helpers, or the IAMSSPRSTMSHMMTWH, of Washington, D.C.

Earliest labor dispute A labor dispute concerning monotony of diet and working conditions was recorded in 1153 B.C. in Thebes, Egypt. The earliest recorded strike was one by an orchestra leader named Aristos from Greece, in Rome *c.* 309 B.C. The dispute concerned meal breaks.

Longest strike The world's longest recorded strike ended on 4 Jan 1961, after 33 years. It concerned the employment of barbers' assistants in Copenhagen, Denmark.

The longest recorded major strike in the world was that at the plumbing fixtures factory of the Kohler Co. in Sheboygan, WI, between April 1954 and October 1962. The strike is alleged to have cost the United Automobile Workers' Union about $12 million to sustain.

United States According to the Bureau of Labor Statistics, the most work stoppages occurred in 1952, with 470 strikes. In this same year 2.75 million workers, the highest ever, were involved in work stoppages employing 1,000 or more. The peak year for most days idle was 1959, with 60.85 million.

Unemployment Lowest In December 1973 in Switzerland (population 6.6 million), the total number of unemployed was reported to be 81.

United States The highest annual unemployment average in United States history was 24.9 percent, or 12,830,000 people, in 1933 during the Great Depression, and the lowest average was 1.2 percent, or 670,000 people, in 1944 during World War II. These figures are based on a labor force aged 14 and older. Since 1948 the United States Department of Labor has kept statistics based on household members aged 16 and older. According to these figures, the highest annual unemployment average since 1948 was 9.7 percent, or 10,717,000 people, in 1982, and the lowest was 2.9 percent, or 1,834,000 people, in 1953.

Longest working career The longest working life was one of 98 years, by Mr Izumi (see Human Beings, Oldest authentic centenarian), who began

Longest working week A case of a working week of 142 hours (with an average each day of 3 hr 42 min 51 sec for sleep) was recorded in June 1980 by Dr Paul Ashton, 32, the anesthetics registrar at Birkenhead General Hospital, Merseyside, Great Britain. He described the week in question as "particularly bad but not untypical."

work goading draft animals at a sugar mill at Isen, Tokunoshima, Japan in 1872. He retired as a sugar cane farmer in 1970 at the age of 105.

ENERGY CONSUMPTION

To express the various forms of available energy (coal, liquid fuels, water power, etc., but omitting vegetable fuels and peat), it is the practice to convert them all into terms of a fuel equivalent.

According to *World Bank Atlas* data for 1990, the highest energy consumption was in Qatar, at 17.09 tons oil equivalent per capita.

The lowest consumption from the available figures was less than 18 oz per capita in Lesotho and Namibia.

United States The Energy Information Administration reports that in 1990, total consumption of energy in the United States was 81.508 quadrillion Btu (British thermal units—the amount of energy needed to raise the temperature of 1 lb of water one degree at 39.2° F). Total consumption of coal was 18.807 quadrillion Btu; natural gas, 20.156 quadrillion Btu; petroleum, 32.720 quadrillion Btu; hydroelectric power, 3.082 quadrillion Btu, and nuclear electric power, 6.543 quadrillion Btu.

STOCK EXCHANGES

The oldest stock exchange in the world is that of Amsterdam, Netherlands, founded in 1602 with dealings in printed shares of the United East India Company of the Netherlands in the Oude Zijds Kapel. The largest in trading volume in 1992 was the New York Stock Exchange, with $1,741.5 billion, ahead of London, Great Britain with $1,567.5 billion and the Federation of German Stock Exchanges with $1,336 billion.

New York Stock Exchange The market value of stocks listed on the New York Stock Exchange reached an all-time high of $3.2 trillion at the end of March 1991. The record day's trading was 608,148,710 shares on 20 Oct 1987, compared with 16,410,030 shares on 29 Oct 1929, the "Black Tuesday" of the famous "crash," a record unsurpassed until April 1968.

The largest stock trade in the history of the New York Stock Exchange was a 48,788,800-share block of Navistar International Corporation stock at $10 in a $487,888,000 transaction on 10 Apr 1986.

The highest price paid for a seat on the New York Stock Exchange was $1.15 million in 1987. The lowest 20th-century price was $17,000, in 1942.

Closing prices The highest index figure on the Dow Jones Industrial average (instituted 8 Oct 1896) of selected stocks at the close of a day's trading was 3,554.83 on 27 May 1993. The index closed above 3,000 points for the first time on 17 Apr 1991, at 3,004.46, although it had edged past the 3,000 barrier on Friday 13 Jul 1990 after a strong run.

The Dow Jones Industrial average, which reached 381.71 on 3 Sep 1929, plunged 30.57 points on 29 Oct 1929, on its way to the Depression's lowest point of 41.22 on 2 Jul 1932. The largest decline in a day, 508 points (22.6 percent), occurred on 19 Oct 1987.

The total lost in security values from 1 Sep 1929 to 30 Jun 1932 was $74 billion. The greatest paper loss in a year was $210 billion in 1974.

The record daily increase on 21 Oct 1987 was 186.84 points to 2,027.85.

> **Largest stock offering**   On 19 May 1992 General Motors Corp. offered the biggest common-stock issue in the United States, with 55 million shares at $39 per share for a total offering of $2.15 billion.
>
> **Longest-serving current member**   As of 31 December 1992 the longest-serving current member of the New York Stock Exchange is David Granger. He became a member on 4 Feb 1926.

Largest flotation   The largest-ever flotation in stock market history was the £5.2 billion ($9.9 billion) sale of the 12 British regional electricity companies to 5.7 million stockholders at the end of 1990.

The earlier flotation of British Gas plc in 1986 had an equity offer that produced the higher sum of £7.75 billion ($10.85 billion), but to only 4.5 million stockholders.

Longest-listed company   Consolidated Edison Company of New York (ConEd) is reported to be the longest continually listed company on the New York Stock Exchange. First traded under the name New York Gas Light Company in 1824, it formed a merger to create the Consolidated Gas Company of New York in 1884. ConEd took its current name in 1936.

The longest-listed company traded under the same name is the Brooklyn Union Gas Company. Originally listed as the Brooklyn Gas Light Company in the late 1830s, it has been traded under its current name since the mid-1860s.

Most valued company   The greatest aggregate market value of any corporation in April 1993 was $120 billion for Exxon of Irving, TX.

Stockholders attendance, greatest   A total of 20,109 stockholders attended the annual general meeting in April 1961 of the American Telephone and Telegraph Co. (AT&T), thereby setting a world record.

Largest rights issue   The largest recorded rights issue was one of £921 million ($1.57 billion) by Barclays Bank, Great Britain, announced on 7 Apr 1988.

Gold prices   The highest closing spot price for gold on the Commodities Exchange (COMEX) in New York City was $875 per fine oz on 21 Jan 1980.

Silver prices   The highest closing spot price for silver on the Commodities Exchange (COMEX) in New York City was $50.35 per fine oz on 18 Jan 1980.

Highest par value   The highest denomination of any share quoted in the world is a single share in Moeara Enim Petroleum Corporation, worth 165,000 Dutch florins ($75,500) on 22 Apr 1992.

Largest investment house   The largest securities company in the United

States, and formerly the world's largest partnership, with 124 partners before becoming a corporation in 1959, is Merrill Lynch, Pierce, Fenner & Smith Inc. (founded 6 Jan 1914) of New York. At the end of 1991, the company had a net revenue of $7.3 billion, together with a net income of $696.1 million.

POSTAL SERVICES

Largest mail   The country with the largest mail service in the world is the United States, whose population mailed 166.4 billion letters and packages during the fiscal year 1992, when the US Postal Service employed 725,290 people, with the world's largest civilian vehicle fleet of 178,925 cars and trucks. The average number of letters and packages per capita was 665.

ROCK & ROLL SINGER, 1935-1977

LARGEST COMMEMORATIVE ISSUE   On 8 Jan 1993 Elvis Presley was honored with a stamp featuring a design showing Elvis as he looked in the 1950s. The Postal Service printed 500 million of these 29-cent stamps. (Photo: US Postal Service)

Post offices   The country with the greatest number of post offices is India, with 144,829 in 1988. There are 39,595 post offices in the US.

Stamp licking   John Kenmuir of Hamilton, Great Britain licked and affixed 393 stamps in 4 min at the BBC TV studios on 26 Sep 1990. His feat was later shown on the BBC *Record Breakers* TV program.

POSTAGE STAMPS

Earliest
Put on sale at GPO 1 May 1840. 1 d Penny Black of Great Britain, Queen Victoria, 68,158,080 printed.

USA
Put on sale in New York City 1 Jul 1847. 5-cent red-brown Benjamin Franklin, 3,712,200 issued, and 10-cent black George Washington, 891,000 issued.

Earliest Adhesive Stamp
Earliest adhesive stamps were those used for local delivery by the City Dispatch Post established in New York City 15 Feb 1842.

Highest Price (Auction)
Sw.Fr. 3,400,000 ($2,400,000), including buyer's premium. Penny Black, 2 May 1840 cover, bought at Harmers, Lugano, Switzerland, on behalf of a Japanese buyer on 23 May 1991.

£203,500 ($350,000), including buyer's premium, for a philatelic item. Bermuda 1854 Perot Postmasters' Stamp affixed to a letter, 1d red on bluish wove paper, sold by Christie's Robson Lowe, London, Great Britain on 13 Jun 1991.

USA
$1.1 million (including buyer's premium). "Curtiss Jenny" plate block of four 24-cent stamps from 1918 with inverted image of an airplane, bought by an unnamed American executive at Christie's, New York on 12 Oct 1989.

Largest Purchase
$11 million. Marc Haas collection of 3,000 US postal and pre-postal covers to 1869 by Stanley Gibbons International Ltd of London, Great Britain in August 1979.

Largest (Special)
$9^{3}/_{4}$ x $2^{3}/_{4}$ in. Express Delivery of China, 1913.

USA
$3^{3}/_{4}$ x 2 in. 1865 newspaper stamps.

Largest (Standard)
6.3 x 4.33 in. Marshall Islands 75-cent issued 30 Oct 1979.

USA
$1^{1}/_{11}$ x $1^{5}/_{11}$ in. 5-cent blue and carmine Air Beacon issued 25 Jul 1928, and 2-cent black and carmine George Rogers Clark issued 25 Feb 1929.

Smallest
0.31 x 0.37 in. 10-cent and 1-peso Colombian State of Bolivar, 1863–66.

Highest Denomination
$10,000. Documentary and Stock Transfer stamps, 1952–58.

USA
$100. Indian Maiden, 1895–97.

Lowest Denomination
3,000 pengö of Hungary. Issued 1946 when 604.5 trillion pengö=1 cent.

USA
$1/2$ cent. Earliest sepia Nathan Hale, 1925; George Washington, 1932; Benjamin Franklin, 1938 and 1954.

Rarest
Unique examples include: British Guiana (now Guyana) 1-cent black on magenta of 1856; Swedish 3-skilling banco yellow color error of 1855. Gold Coast provisional of 1885 and US postmaster stamp from Boscowen, NH and Lockport, NY.

Oldest mailboxes The first organized system of roadside mailboxes was established in 1653 in Paris, France, to facilitate the interchange of correspondence in the city. The mailboxes were erected at the intersections of main thoroughfares and were emptied three times a day.

AGRICULTURE

Origins It has been estimated that about 21 percent of the world's land surface is cultivable and that only 7.6 percent is actually under cultivation.

Evidence adduced in 1971 from Nok Nok Tha and Spirit Cave, Thailand tends to confirm that plant cultivation was part of the Hoabinhian culture *c.* 11,000 B.C., but it is still likely that hominids (humans and their human-like ancestors) probably survived for 99.93 percent of their known history with cultivating plants or domesticating animals. Various species of plants were being domesticated in the Near East by 8000–7500 B.C., for example, in Iraq, Syria, Iran and Jordan. It is agreed that maize was grown around 5000 B.C. in the Tehuacan Valley of Mexico, with rice being grown at about the same date at Hemudu, near Shanghai, China.

Animal husbandry It has been suggested that reindeer (*Rangifer tarandus*) may have been domesticated as early as 18,000 B.C., but definite proof is still lacking. The earliest known domesticated animal was probably of the order Carnivora (dogs), used in hunting about 9,000–9,500 years ago at sites such as Coyönü, Turkey and Star Carr in Great Britain.

The earliest-known animals domesticated for food were probably descendants of the wild goats of Bezoar (*Capra aegagrus = hircus*), which were herded at Asiah, Iran *c.* 7700 B.C. Sheep (*Ovisaries*) have been dated to *c.* 7200 B.C. at Argissa Magula in Thessaly, Greece, and pigs (*Sus domestica*) and cattle (*Bos primigenius = taurus*) to *c.* 7000 B.C. at the same site. Chickens were domesticated before 6000 B.C. in Indochina, and by 5900–5400 B.C. had spread to North China, as shown by radiocarbon dating from a Neolithic site at Peiligang, near Zhengzhou, and also at Wu'an Cishan and Tengxian Beixin.

FISHERIES

United Nations Food and Agricultural Organization figures for 1990 (the last year for which comparable data is available) showed the world's leading fishing nation to be China, with a total catch of 13.44 million tons, followed by the former USSR (11.63 tons) and Japan (11.59 million tons). The United States was in fifth place with 6.57 million tons out of a worldwide total of 108.86 million tons, down from a record 112 million tons in 1989.

The record value for a catch by a single trawler is $473,957 from a 41,776-ton catch by the Icelandic vessel *Videy* at Hull, Great Britain on 11 Aug 1987. The greatest catch ever recorded from a single throw is 2,724 tons by the purse seine-net boat M/S *Flømann* from Hareide, Norway in the Barents Sea on 28 Aug 1986. It was estimated that more than 120 million fish were caught in this shoal.

FARMS

Largest   The largest farms in the world were *kolkhozy*—collective farms in the former USSR. These were reduced in number from 235,500 in 1940 to 26,900 in 1988 and represented a total cultivated area of 417.6 million acres. Units of over 60,000 acres were not uncommon.

The pioneer farm owned by Laucidio Coelho near Campo Grande, Mato Grosso, Brazil *c*. 1901 covered 3,358 miles^2 and supported 250,000 head of cattle at the time of the owner's death in 1975.

Baling   A rick of 40,400 bales of straw was built between 22 Jul and 3 Sep 1982 by Nick and Tom Parsons with a gang of eight at Cuckoo Pen Barn Farm, Birdlip, Great Britain. It measured 150 × 30 × 60 ft high and weighed some 784 tons. The team baled, hauled and ricked 24,200 bales in seven consecutive days from 22–29 July.

Cattle ranch   Until 1915 the Victoria River Downs Station in Northern Territory, Australia had an area of 35,000 miles^2. The world's largest cattle ranch is currently the 11,600 miles^2 Anna Creek ranch in South Australia, owned by the Kidman family. The biggest component is Strangway, at 5,500 miles^2.

Chicken farm   The Agrigeneral Company L.P. in Ohio has 4.8 million hens laying some 3.7 million eggs daily.

Community garden   The largest such project is the one operated by the City Beautiful Council and the Benjamin Wegerzyn Garden Center in Dayton, OH. It comprises 1,173 plots, each measuring 812 ft^2.

Hop farm   The world's leading hop growers are John I. Haas Inc., with farms in Idaho, Oregon and Washington; Tasmania, Australia; and Kent, Great Britain, covering a total net area of 6,146 acres. The largest field covers 1,715 acres near Toppenish, WA.

Mushroom farm   The world's largest mushroom farm is owned by Moonlight Mushrooms Inc. and was founded in 1937 in a disused limestone mine near Worthington, PA. The farm employs over 1,106 people who work in a maze of underground galleries 156 miles long, producing over 54,000,000 lbs of mushrooms per year. The French annual consumption is unrivaled at 7 lb per capita.

Pig farm   The world's largest pig farm is the Sljeme pig unit in Yugoslavia, which is able to process 300,000 pigs in a year.

Rice farm   The largest wild rice (*Zizania aquatica*) farm in the world is that of Clearwater Rice Inc. in Clearbrook, MN, covering 2,000 acres. In 1986 it yielded 577,000 lb, the largest amount to date.

Sheep ranch   The largest sheep ranch in the world is Commonwealth Hill, in the northwest of South Australia. It grazes between 50,000 and 70,000 sheep, along with 24,000 uninvited kangaroos, in an area of 4,080 miles^2 enclosed by 138 miles of dog-proof fencing. The head count on Sir William Stevenson's 40,970-acre Lochinver station in New Zealand was 127,406 on 1 Jan 1993.

The largest sheep move on record occurred when 27 horsemen moved a flock of 43,000 sheep 40 miles from Barcaldine to Beaconsfield station, Queensland, Australia in 1886.

Turkey farm   The farms of Bernard Matthews plc in Norfolk, Great Britain, produce 10 million turkeys per year and employ a staff of 2,500. The largest farm, at North Pickenham, Great Britain, produces 1 million turkeys per year.

Bale rolling   Michael Priestley and Marcus Stanley of Heckington Young Farmers Club rolled a 3-ft-11-in-wide cylindrical bale over a 164-ft course in 18.06 sec at the Lincolnshire Federation of Young Farmers' Clubs' annual sports day at Sleaford, Great Britain on 25 Jun 1989.

Svend Erik Klemmensen of Trustrup, Djursland, Denmark baled 220 tons of straw in 9 hr 54 min using a Hesston 4800 baling machine on 30 Aug 1989.

Combine harvesting   Philip Baker of West End Farm, Merton, Great Britain harvested 182.5 tons of wheat in eight hours using a Massey Ferguson MF 38 combine on 8 Aug 1989. On 9 Aug 1990 an international team from CWS Agriculture, led by estate manager Ian Hanglin, harvested 394.73 tons of wheat in eight hours from 108.72 acres at Cockayne Hatley Estate, Sandy, Great Britain. The equipment consisted of a Claas Commandor 228 combine fitted with a Shelbourne Reynolds SR 6000 stripper head.

Field to loaf   The fastest time for producing 13 loaves of bread (a baker's dozen) from growing wheat is 12 min 11 sec, by representatives from the villages of Clapham and Patching in Great Britain on 23 Aug 1992. They used 13 microwaves to bake the loaves. Using a traditional baker's oven to bake the bread, the record time is 19 min 45 sec, by a team organized by John Haynes of millers Read Woodrow at Alpheton, Great Britain on 19 Sep 1992.

The fastest time for producing 13 loaves in the United States is 21 min 22 sec, by Wheat Montana at Three Forks, MT on 29 Aug 1991.

Chicken and turkey plucking   Ernest Hausen (1877–1955) of Fort Atkinson, WI died undefeated after 33 years as champion chicken plucker. On 19 Jan 1939 he was timed at 4.4 sec. Vincent Pilkington of Cootehill, County Cavan, Republic of Ireland killed and plucked 100 turkeys in 7 hr 32 min on 15 Dec 1978. His record for a single turkey is 1 min 30 sec in Dublin on 17 Nov 1980.

Hand-milking of cows   Joseph Love of Kilifi Plantations Ltd, Kenya milked 117 gal from 30 cows on 25 Aug 1992. The American record for hand-milking is 88.2 gal, by Andy Faust at Collinsville, OK in 1937 in 12 hours.

Crop Production

Barley The total amount of land farmed for barley production in the 1991/92 season was estimated to be 78.4 million hectares, with total production of 169.0 million metric tons and an average yield of 2.2 metric tons per hectare.

United States In 1992 2.9 million hectares of barley were farmed in the United States, with an average yield of 3.36 metric tons per hectare and a total production of 9.93 million metric tons.

Corn The total amount of land used for growing corn in 1991/92 was estimated to be 130.6 million hectares, producing 520 metric tons, of which 97 million metric tons was produced by China from an estimated 21.5 million hectares.

United States In 1992 29.2 million hectares of corn were farmed in the United States, yielding 8.25 metric tons of corn per hectare, for a total of 240.7 million metric tons. Also in that year, the amounts of corn for silage was 2.43 million hectares, yielding 32.4 metric tons per hectare, for a total of 78.8 million metric tons.

Cotton The total area of land used for cotton production in 1991/92 was estimated to be 33 million hectares, giving a total production of 87 million bales, each weighing 480 lb. The leading cotton producer is China, with figures estimated at 20.7 million such bales from 5.6 million hectares.

United States In 1992 4.5 million hectares were planted for cotton production in the United States. The average yield per hectare was 0.78 metric tons, with a total production of 3.5 million metric tons.

Oats The worldwide production of oats in 1991/92 was an estimated 32.5 million metric tons harvested from about 20.4 million hectares.

United States In 1992 1.8 million hectares of oats were farmed in the United States, with an average yield of 2.35 metric tons per hectare and a total production of 4.2 million metric tons.

Potatoes In 1992 527 million acres of potatoes were farmed in the United States with an average yield of 35.43 metric tons per acre and a total production of 18.7 million metric tons.

Rice About half of the world's population, including virtually the whole of East Asia, is totally dependent on rice as the staple food. The estimated total amount of land used for rice production in 1991/92 was 147 million hectares, with India leading in the area farmed, at 42.6 million hectares. The world's leading producer, however, is China, with estimated yields of 189.3 million metric tons from 33.1 million hectares.

United States In 1992 1.3 million hectares of rice were planted in the United States, with an average yield of 6.4 metric tons per hectare and a total production of 8.1 million metric tons.

Sugar beets The highest recorded yield for sugar beets is 62.4 tons per acre by Andy Christensen and Jon Giannini in the Salinas Valley, CA.

Sugar cane In 1992 378.1 acres of sugar cane were planted in the United States, with an average yield per acre of 75.01 metric tons and a total production of 28 million metric tons.

Wheat An estimated 222.1 million hectares of land was used for wheat production worldwide in 1991/92, giving a yield of 541.6 million metric tons.

The largest single fenced field sown with wheat measured 35,000 acres and was sown in 1951 southwest of Lethbridge, Alberta, Canada.

United States In 1992 25.2 million hectares of wheat were farmed in the United States, with an average yield of 2.31 metric tons per hectare and a total production of 66.9 million metric tons.

Plowing The world championship (instituted 1953) has been staged in 18 countries and won by competitors from 12 nations. Great Britain has been most successful, winning ten championships. The only person to take the title three times is Hugh B. Barr of Northern Ireland, in 1954–56.

The fastest recorded time for plowing an acre by the Society of Ploughmen (Great Britain) rules is 9 min 49.88 sec, by Joe Langcake at Hornby Hall Farm, Brougham, Great Britain on 21 Oct 1989. He used a case IH 7140 Magnum tractor and a Kverneland four-furrow plow.

The greatest area plowed with a six-furrow plow to a depth of 9 in in 24 hours is 173 acres. This was achieved by Richard Gaisford and Peter Gooding of Wiltshire Young Farmers, using a Case IH tractor and a Lemken plow, at Manor Farm, Pewsey, Great Britain on 25–26 Sep 1990.

LEADING CROP PRODUCERS
Barley is just one of the cereal crops grown in record amounts in the republics of the former USSR, which together produce an estimated 62 million tons from an area of about 4.2 million acres. (Photo: Images Colour Library)

LIVESTOCK PRICES

Some exceptionally high livestock auction prices are believed to result from collusion between buyer and seller to raise the ostensible price levels of the breed concerned. Others are marketing and publicity exercises with little relation to true market prices.

Cattle   The highest price ever paid was $2.5 million for the beefalo (³/₈ bison, ³/₈ Charolais, ¹/₄ Hereford) Joe's Pride, sold by D.C. Basalo of Burlingame, CA to the Beefalo Cattle Co. of Calgary, Canada on 9 Sep 1974.

Cow   The highest price paid for a cow is $1.3 million for a Holstein at auction in East Montpelier, VT in 1985.

Goat   On 25 Jan 1985 an Angora buck bred by Waitangi Angoras of Waitangi, New Zealand was sold to Elliott Brown Ltd of Waipu, New Zealand for $NZ 140,000.

Horse   The highest price paid for a draft horse is $47,000 by C.G. Good of Ogden, IA for the seven-year-old Belgian stallion Farceur at Cedar Falls, IA on 16 Oct 1917.

Pig   The highest price ever paid for a pig is $56,000 for a cross-bred barrow named Bud, owned by Jeffrey Roemisch of Hermleigh, TX and bought by E.A. Bud Olson and Phil Bonzio on 5 Mar 1983.

Sheep   The highest price ever paid for a sheep is $A450,000 ($358,750) by Willogoleche Pty Ltd for the Collinsville stud "JC&S 43" at the 1989 Adelaide Ram Sales, South Australia.

Wool   The highest price ever paid for wool is $A3,008.5 per kg greasy wool for a bale of Tasmania superfine at the wool auction in Tasmania, Australia on 23 Feb 1989, by Fujii Keori Ltd of Osaka, Japan—top bidders since 1973.

Lowest price   The lowest price ever realized for livestock was at a sale at Kuruman, Cape Province, South Africa in 1934, where donkeys were sold for less than 2 p (less than 5 cents) each.

CATTLE

As of 1991 the world's leading producer of cattle was India, with 271.4 million head from a world total of 1 billion head. However, the leading producer of milk in 1992 was the United States, with 68.8 million metric tons.

In 1992 there were 99.5 million head of cattle farmed in the United States. The leading cattle producer was Texas, with 13.6 million head.

Largest   The heaviest breed of cattle is the Chianini, which was brought to the Chiana Valley in Italy from the Middle East in pre-Roman times. Four types of the breed exist, the largest of which is the Val di Chianini, found on the plains and low hills of Arezzo and Sienna. Bulls average 5 ft 8 in at the forequarters and weigh 2,865 lb (compare with 1,873 lb for cows), but Chianini oxen have been known to attain heights of 6 ft 2¾ in. The sheer expense of feeding such huge cattle has put the breed under threat of extinction in Italy, but farmers in North America, Mexico and Brazil are still enthusiastic buyers of the breed.

The heaviest cattle on record was a Holstein–Durham cross named Mount Katahdin, exhibited by A.S. Rand of Maine from 1906–10, which frequently weighed in at an even 5,000 lb. He was 6 ft 2 in at the shoulder with a 13-ft girth, and died in a barn fire *c.*1923.

Smallest   The smallest breed of domestic cattle is the Ovambo of Namibia. Bulls and cows average 496 lb and 353 lb respectively.

Oldest   Big Bertha, a Dremon owned by Jerome O'Leary of Blackwaters-bridge, County Kerry, Republic of Ireland celebrated her 49th birthday in 1993. (See also Reproductivity.)

Reproductivity   On 25 Apr 1964 it was reported that a cow named Lyubik had given birth to seven calves in Mogilev. A case of five live calves at one birth was reported in 1928 by T.G. Yarwood of Manchester, Great Britain. The lifetime breeding record is 39 in the case of Big Bertha. (See Oldest.)

Sires   Soender Jylland's Jens, a Danish black-and-white bull, left 220,000 surviving progeny by artificial insemination when he was put away at the age of 11 in Copenhagen in September 1978.

Bendalls Adema, a Friesian bull, died at the age of 14 in Clondalkin, Dublin, Republic of Ireland on 8 Nov 1978, having sired an estimated 212,000 progeny by artificial insemination.

Birth weights   The heaviest recorded live birth weight for a calf is 225 lb for a British Friesian cow at Rockhouse Farm, Bishopston, Great Britain in 1961. On 28 May 1986 a Holstein cow owned by Sherlene O'Brien of Simitar Farms, Henryetta, OK gave birth to a perfectly formed stillborn calf weighing 270 lb. The sire was an Aberdeen-Angus bull that had "jumped the fence."

Lightest   A healthy female calf weighing 14 lb 5 oz was born on 27 Oct 1991 on the farm of Ole Willumsgaard Lauridsen and Roos Verhoven in Hemmet, Denmark. It was a cross between a Danish SDM and a Belgian blue-white. A crossbred Angus calf owned by Leroy and Jo Steiner of Hu-mansville, MI weighed 16 lb 12 oz at two weeks old and an estimated 9 lb at birth on 12 Sep 1991.

Milk yields   As of 1992, the world's leading producer of cow's milk was the United States, with 68.8 million metric tons. Wisconsin led the country, producing 10.9 million tons. The highest recorded world lifetime yield of milk for a single cow is 465,224 lb, by the unglamorously named cow No. 289 owned by M.G. Maciel & Son of Hanford, CA, to 1 May 1984.

The greatest recorded yield for one lactation (maximum 365 days) is 55,661 lb in 1975 by the Holstein Beecher Arlinda Ellen, owned by Mr and Mrs Harold L. Beecher of Rochester, IN. The highest reported milk yield in a day is 241 lb, by a cow named Urbe Blanca in Cuba on or about 23 Jun 1982.

Butterfat yields The world record lifetime yield is 16,370 lb, by the US Holstein Breezewood Patsy Bar Pontiac in 3,979 days.

The world record for 365 days is 3,126 lb, by Roybrook High Ellen, a Holstein owned by Yashuhiro Tanaka of Tottori, Japan.

Cheese Today there are 450 named cheeses in 18 major varieties, but many are merely named after different towns and differ only in shape or the method of packing. France has 240 varieties. The world's biggest producer of cheese is the United States, with an estimated factory production of 2.9 million tons. The US cheese consumption for 1992 was 6,665.2 million lb. Also in 1992, the annual per-person cheese consumption in the United States was 26 pounds, or a half-pound of cheese per week. The most avid cheese-eaters are the people of France, with an annual average of 43.6 lb per person.

Oldest The oldest and most primitive cheeses are the Arabian kishk, made of the dried curd of goats' milk.

GOATS

Largest The largest goat ever recorded was a British Saanen named Mostyn Moorcock, owned by Pat Robinson of Ewyas Harold, Great Britain, which reached a weight of 400 lb (shoulder height 44 in and overall length 66 in). He died in 1977 at the age of four.

Smallest Some pygmy goats weigh only 33–44 lb.

Oldest The oldest goat on record is a Toggenburg feral cross named Hongi (b. August 1971), belonging to April Koch of Glenorchy, near Otago, New Zealand, which was still alive in mid-March 1989 at the age of 17 years 8 months.

Reproductivity According to the British Goat Society, at least one or two cases of quintuplets are recorded annually out of the 10,000 goats registered, but some breeders only record the females born.

On 14 Jan 1980 a nanny goat named Julie, owned by Galen Cowper of Nampah, ID, gave birth to septuplets, but they all died, including the mother.

Milk yields The highest recorded milk yield for any goat is 7,714 lb in 365 days by Osory Snow-Goose, owned by Mr and Mrs G. Jameson of Leppington, New South Wales, Australia, in 1977.

Cynthia-Jean (Baba), owned by Carolyn Freund-Nelson of Northport, NY, has lactated continuously since June 1980.

PIGS

The world's leading producer of hogs in 1991 was China, with 365 million head from a world total of 768.1 million. As of 1 Dec 1992 there were 59.8 million heads of hogs farmed in the United States. The leading state was Iowa with 16.4 million head.

Largest The heaviest pig ever recorded was a Poland–China hog named Big Bill, who was so obese that his belly dragged along the ground. Bill weighed an astonishing 2,552 lb just before he was put away after suffering a broken leg in an accident en route to the Chicago World's Fair for exhibition in 1933. Other statistics included a shoulder height of 5 ft and a length of 9 ft. At the request of his owner, W.J. Chappall, this prized possession was mounted and put on display in Weekly County, TN until 1946, when the exhibit was acquired by a traveling carnival. On the death of the carnival's proprietor his family reportedly donated Big Bill to a museum, but no trace has been found of him since.

Smallest   The smallest breed of pig is the Mini Maialino, developed by Stefano Morini of St Golo d'Enza, Italy, after 10 years of experimentation with Vietnamese pot-bellied pigs. The piglets weigh 14 oz at birth and 20 lb at maturity.

Reproductivity   A breeding sow will live 12 years or more before it is slaughtered, but the maximum potential lifespan is 20 years. The highest recorded number of piglets in one litter is 34, farrowed on 25–26 Jun 1961 by a sow owned by Aksel Egedee of Denmark. In February 1955 a Wessex sow belonging to E.C. Goodwin of Paul's Farm, Leigh, Great Britain also had a litter of 34, of which 30 were stillborn.

A Large White owned by H.S. Pedlingham farrowed 385 pigs in 22 litters from December 1923 to September 1934. A Newsham Large White × Landrace sow of Meeting House Farm, Staintondale, Great Britain had farrowed 189 piglets (seven stillborn) in nine litters up to 22 Mar 1988. Between 6 May 1987 and 9 Feb 1988 she gave birth to 70 piglets.

Birth weights   The average birth weight for a piglet is 3 lb. A Hampshire–Yorkshire sow belonging to Rev. John Schroeder of Mountain Grove, MO farrowed a litter of 18 on 26 Aug 1979. Five were stillborn, including one male that weighed 5 lb 4 oz.

The highest recorded weight for a piglet at weaning (eight weeks) is 81 lb for a boar, one of a litter of nine farrowed on 6 Jul 1962 by the Landrace gilt Manorport Ballerina 53rd, alias "Mary," and sired by a Large White named Johnny at Kettle Lane Farm, West Ashton, Great Britain.

In November 1957 a total weight of 1,134 lb was reported at weaning for a litter of 18 piglets farrowed by an Essex sow owned by Mrs B. Ravel of Seaton House, Thorugumbald, Great Britain.

POULTRY

Figures for 1992 showed the United States to be the largest producer of chicken meat, or broiler, with a total of 9.453 million tons. The most produced by a state was 1.42 million tons, by Arkansas. The leading egg producer, however, is China, where 159 billion were laid in 1991. United States egg production in 1992 was 70.52 billion. The greatest state production was in California, with 7 billion eggs.

Chicken Largest   The heaviest breed of chicken is the White Sully, developed by Grant Sullens of West Point, CA by crossing and recrossing large Rhode Island Reds with other varieties. One monstrous rooster named Weirdo reportedly weighed 22 lb in January 1973 and was so aggressive that he killed two cats and crippled a dog that ventured too close. The largest recorded chicken is Big Snow, a rooster weighing 23 lb 3 oz on 12

Jun 1992, with a chest girth of 2 ft 9 in and standing 1 ft 5 in at the shoulder. Owned and bred by Ronald Alldridge of Deuchar, Queensland, Australia, Big Snow died of natural causes on 6 Sep 1992.

Reproductivity   The highest authenticated rate of egg-laying is by a White Leghorn, No. 2988, which laid 371 eggs in 364 days in an official test conducted by Prof. Harold V. Biellier ending on 29 Aug 1979 at the College of Agriculture, University of Missouri.

The highest recorded annual average per bird for a flock is 315 eggs in 52 weeks (August 1991–August 1992) from 5,997 free-range ISA Brown layers, owned by Vernon Wride of Park Farm, Heol-y-Cyw, Pencoed, Wales.

Largest egg   The heaviest egg reported was one of 16 oz, with double yolk and double shell, laid by a White Leghorn at Vineland, NJ on 25 Feb 1956. The largest egg recorded was one of nearly 12 oz for a five-yolked egg measuring 12¹/₄ in around the long axis and 9 in around the short, laid by a Black Minorca at Mr Stafford's Damsteads Farm, Mellor, Great Britain in 1896.

Most yolks   The highest claim for the number of yolks in a hen's egg is nine, reported by Diane Hainsworth of Hainsworth Poultry Farms, Mount Morris, NY in July 1971, and also from a hen in Kyrgyzstan in August 1977.

Flying   Sheena, a barnyard bantam owned by Bill and Bob Knox, flew 630 ft 2 in at Parkesburg, PA on 31 May 1985.

Egg shelling   Two kitchen hands, Harold Witcomb and Gerald Harding, shelled 1,050 dozen eggs in a 7¹/₄-hr shift at Bowyers, Great Britain on 23 Apr 1971. Both men were blind.

Egg dropping   The greatest height from which fresh eggs have been dropped (to the ground) and remained intact is 650 ft, by David S. Donoghue from a helicopter on 2 Oct 1979 on a golf course in Tokyo, Japan.

Duck Reproductivity   An Aylesbury duck belonging to Annette and Angela Butler of Princes Risborough, Great Britain laid 457 eggs in 463 days, including an unbroken run of 375 in as many days. The duck died on 7 Feb 1986. Another duck of the same breed, owned by Edmond Walsh of Gormanstown, Republic of Ireland, laid eggs every year right up to her 25th birthday. She died on 3 Dec 1978 at the age of 28 yr 6 months.

Goose   The heaviest goose egg on record was one of 24 oz that measured 13¹/₂ in around the long axis and had a maximum circumference of 9¹/₂ in around the short axis. It was laid on 3 May 1977 by a white goose named Speckle, owned by Donny Brandenberg of Goshen, OH. The average weight is 10–12 oz.

Turkey The greatest dressed weight recorded for a turkey is 86 lb for a stag named Tyson reared by Philip Cook of Leacroft Turkeys Ltd, Peterborough, Great Britain. It won the annual "heaviest turkey" competition held in London, Great Britain on 12 Dec 1989 and was auctioned for charity for a record £4,400 ($7,480). Stags of this size have been so overdeveloped for meat production that they are unable to mate because of their shape and the hens have to be artificially inseminated.

SHEEP

The world's leading producer of sheep is Australia, with a total of 177.8 million head in 1990. As of 1 Jan 1993 there were 10.2 million head of sheep farmed in the United States. The leading state was Texas, with 2 million head.

Largest The largest sheep ever recorded was a Suffolk ram named Stratford Whisper 23H, which weighed 545 lb and stood 43 in tall in March 1991. It is owned by Joseph and Susan Schallberger of Boring, OR.

Smallest The smallest breed of sheep is the Soay, which is now confined to the island of Hirta in the St Kilda group, Outer Hebrides, Great Britain. Adults weigh 55–60 lb.

Oldest A crossbred sheep owned by Griffiths & Davies of Dolclettwr Hall, Taliesin, Great Britain gave birth to a healthy lamb in the spring of

---

Sheep to shoulder At the International Wool Secretariat Development Center, Ilkley, Great Britain, a team of eight using commercial machinery produced a sweater—from shearing sheep to the finished article—in 2 hr 28 min 32 sec on 3 Sep 1986.

Fine spinning The longest thread of wool, hand-spun and plied to weigh 0.35 oz, was one with a length of 1,815 ft 3 in, achieved by Julitha Barber of Bull Creek, Western Australia, at the International Highland Spin-In, Bothwell, Tasmania, on 1 Mar 1989.

Longest fleece A Merino wether found on K.P. & B.A. Reynolds Company's Willow Springs Station, South Australia in November 1990 produced 65 lb of wool from a fleece 25 in long, representing a 7-year growth.

Shearing The fastest speed for sheep shearing in a working day was that recorded by Alan McDonald, who machine-sheared 805 lambs in nine hours (an average of 40.2 seconds per lamb) at Waitnaguru, New Zealand on 20 Dec 1990. Peter Casserly of Christchurch, New Zealand achieved a solo blade (i.e., hand-shearing) record of 353 lambs in nine hours on 13 Feb 1976. The women's record is 390 Merino lambs in eight hours, set by Deanne Sarre of Pingrup, Western Australia, on 1 Oct 1989.

LARGEST SHEEP STATION Appropriate transportation is advised when patroling Australia's record-sized sheep stations, the largest of which, at Commonwealth Hill, South Australia, covers 4,080 miles². (Photo: Rex Features)

1988 at the grand old age of 28, after lambing successfully more than 40 times. She died on 24 Jan 1989 just one week before her 29th birthday.

Reproductivity The record for lambs at a single birth is eight (five rams and three ewes) on 4 Sep 1991 from a Finnish Landrace ewe owned by the D.M.C. Partnership of Feilding, Manawatu, New Zealand. The partnership is made up of Trevor and Diane Cooke, Stephen and Mary Moss and Ken and Carole Mihaere. On 2 Dec 1992 a Charolais ewe owned by Graham and Jo Partt of Wem, Great Britain also gave birth to eight lambs, seven of which survived.

Seven live lambs (four rams and three ewes) were reported for a Finn × Targhoe ewe owned by Elsward Meine of Crookston, MN on 24 Mar 1980.

Birth weights Heaviest The highest recorded birth weight for a lamb is 38 lb at Clearwater, Sedgwick County, KS in 1975, but neither lamb nor ewe survived. Another lamb of the same weight was born on 7 Apr 1975 on the Gerald Neises Farm, Howard, SD but died soon after.

Combined weight A four-year-old Suffolk ewe owned by Gerry H. Watson of Augusta, KS gave birth to two live sets of triplets on 30–31 Jan 1982. The total weight of the lambs was 49½ lb.

Lowest The lowest live birthweight recorded for a lamb is 1 lb 15¾ oz for a female Texel (one of twins) born on 28 Mar 1991 at the farm owned by Verner and Esther Jensen in Rodekro, Denmark. This record was equalled on 8 Jun 1991 by a badger-faced Welsh mountain lamb named Lyle (also a twin), at Thorpe Park, Great Britain.

Sheep's survival On 24 Mar 1978 Alex Maclennan found one ewe still alive after he had dug out 16 sheep buried in a snowdrift for 50 days near the river Skinsdale on Mrs Tyser's Gordonbush Estate in Sutherland, Great Britain after the great January blizzard. The sheep's hot breath creates airholes in the snow, and the animals gnaw their own wool for protein, enabling them to survive in a snowdrift for a considerable length of time.

ARTS AND ENTERTAINMENT

- **PAINTINGS**
- **ANTIQUES**
- **LANGUAGE**
- **LITERATURE**
- **MUSIC**
- **RECORDED SOUND**
- **DANCING**
- **THEATER**
- **CIRCUS**
- **PHOTOGRAPHY**
- **CINEMA**
- **RADIO**
- **TELEVISION**

ART

Origins   Engravings showing circles, dots, lines and arcs have been dated by thermoluminescence (TL) and other techniques to 60,000–50,000 years old at the Malunkunanja II site in northern Australia. The oldest-known extant and dated examples of representational art are from layers dated to *c.* 25,000 B.C. from La Ferrassie, near Les Eyzies in the Périgord, France, where blocks of stone engraved with animals and female symbols have been found.

PAINTINGS

Earliest   Ochre and hematite pieces found in Australia from *c.* 60,000–50,000 years ago and later from Swaziland suggest that some form of painting was practiced, but none has survived to indicate what form it took.

LARGEST PAINTING   "Smily" face on canvas, designed by Australian artist Ken Done and painted with the help of students of Robb College, local schoolchildren and other college students from Armidale, New South Wales, Australia in aid of UNICEF. (Photo: Robb College, U.N.E.)

Largest The largest-ever painting measures 72,437 ft² after allowing for shrinkage of the canvas. It is made up of brightly colored squares with a "Smily" face superimposed, and was painted by students of Robb College at Armidale, New South Wales, Australia, aided by local schoolchildren and students from neighboring colleges. The canvas was completed by its designer, Australian artist Ken Done, and unveiled at the University of New England at Armidale on 10 May 1990.

Most valuable The "Mona Lisa" (*La Gioconda*) by Leonardo da Vinci (1452–1519) in the Louvre, Paris, France, was assessed for insurance purposes at $100 million for its move to Washington, D.C. and New York City for exhibition from 14 Dec 1962 to 12 Mar 1963. However, insurance was not purchased because the cost of the closest security precautions was less than that of the premiums. It was painted *c.* 1503–07 and measures 30.5 × 20.9 in.

Most prolific painter Pablo Diego José Francisco de Paula Juan Nepomuceno Crispin Crispiano de la Santisima Trinidad Ruiz y Picasso (1881–1973) of Spain was the most prolific of all painters in a career that lasted 78 years. It has been estimated that Picasso produced about 13,500 paintings or designs, 100,000 prints or engravings, 34,000 book illustrations and 300 sculptures or ceramics. His lifetime *oeuvre* has been valued at over $800 million.

Finest standard paintbrush The finest standard brush sold is the 000 in Series 7 by Windsor and Newton, known as a "triple goose." It is made of 150–200 Kolinsky sable hairs weighing 0.000529 oz.

Largest poster A poster measuring 215,280 ft² was made by the Sendai Junior Chamber Inc. of Sendai City, Japan on 18 Aug 1991.

Sand sculpture The longest sand sculpture ever made was the 86,535-ft-6-in-long sculpture named "The GTE Directories Ultimate Sand Castle" built by more than 10,000 volunteers at Myrtle Beach, SC on 31 May 1991.
   The tallest was the "Invitation to Fairyland," which was 56 ft 2 in high, and was built by 2,000 local volunteers at Kaseda, Japan on 26 Jul 1989 under the supervision of Gerry Kirk of Sand Sculptors International of San Diego and Shogo Tashiro of Sand Sculptors International of Japan.

Living artist The highest price paid at auction for a work by a living artist is $20.68 million for *Interchange*, an abstract by the American painter Willem de Kooning (b. Rotterdam, Netherlands, 1904) at Sotheby's, New York on 8 Nov 1989. Painted in 1955, it was bought by Japanese dealer-cum-collector "Mountain Tortoise."

Poster The record price for a poster is £68,200 (*c.* $102,000) for an advertisment for the 1895 Glasgow exhibition by Charles Rennie Macintosh (1868–1928), sold at Christie's, London on 4 Feb 1993.

GALLERIES

Largest The world's largest art gallery is the Winter Palace and the neighboring Hermitage in St Petersburg, Russia. One has to walk 15 miles to cover all of its 322 galleries, which house nearly 3 million works of art and objects of archaeological interest.

Most heavily endowed The J. Paul Getty Museum at Malibu, CA was established with an initial $1.4 billion budget in January 1974 and now has an annual budget of $180 million for acquisitions to stock its 38 galleries.

MOSAICS

Largest The world's largest mosaic is on the walls of the central library of the Universidad Nacional Autónoma de Mexico in Mexico City. Of the four walls, the two largest measure 12,949 ft², and the scenes on each represent the pre-Hispanic past.

MURALS

Earliest The earliest-known murals on man-made walls are the clay relief leopards at Catal Hüyük in southern Anatolia, Turkey, discovered by James Malaart at level VII in 1961 and dating from *c.* 6200 B.C.

Largest A mural on the 23-story Vegas World Hotel, Las Vegas, NV covers an area of 95,442 ft².

SCULPTURE

Earliest The earliest-known examples of sculpture date from the Aurignacian culture of *c.* 28,000–22,000 B.C. and include the so-called "Venus" figurines from Austria and numerous figurines from northern Italy and central France.

Largest The mounted figures of Jefferson Davis (1808–89), Gen. Robert E. Lee (1807–70) and Gen. Thomas Jonathan "Stonewall" Jackson (1824–63) cover 1.33 acres on the face of Stone Mountain, near Atlanta, GA. They are 90 ft high. Roy Faulkner was on the mountain face for 8 years 174 days with a thermo-jet torch, working with the sculptor Walker Kirtland Hancock and other helpers, from 12 Sep 1963 to 3 Mar 1972.

The largest scrap-metal sculpture was built by Sudhir Deshpande of Nashik, India and unveiled in February 1990. Named *Powerful*, the colossus weighs 30.24 tons and stands 55³/₄ ft tall.

Largest ground figures In the Nazca Desert, 185 miles south of Lima, Peru, there are straight lines (one more than 7 miles long), geometric shapes, and outlines of plants and animals that were drawn on the ground some time between 100 B.C. and A.D. 600 for probably religious, astronomical or even economic purposes by an imprecisely identified civilization. They were first detected from the air *c.* 1928 and have been described as the world's longest works of art.

Largest hill figures A 330-ft-tall figure was found on a hill above Tarapacá, Chile in August 1968.

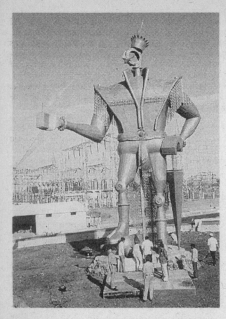

LARGEST METAL SCULPTURE
Powerful, a scrap metal statue created by Sudhir Deshpande of Nashik, India and unveiled in February 1990, stands 55¾ ft tall and weighs 30.24 tons. (Photo: Sudhir Deshpande)

HIGHEST PRICES

Painting   On 15 May 1990, *Portrait of Dr Gachet* by Vincent van Gogh (1853–90) was sold for $82.5 million at Christie's, New York. The painting depicts van Gogh's physician and was completed only weeks before the artist's suicide in 1890. The owner was subsequently identified as Ryoei Saito, Japan's second-largest paper manufacturer.

Miniature   The record price is the £352,000 ($621,632) paid by the Alexander Gallery of New York at Christie's, London on 7 Nov 1988 for a 2⅛-in-high miniature of George Washington. It was painted by the Irish-American miniaturist John Ramage (*c.* 1748–1802) in 1789.

Twentieth-century painting   The record bid at auction for a 20th-century painting is $47.8 million for a self-portrait by Pablo Picasso (1881–1973), *Yo Picasso* (1901), at Sotheby's, New York on 9 May 1989.

Print   The record price for a print at auction was £561,600 ($786,000) for a 1655 etching of *Christ Presented to the People* by Rembrandt (1606–69) at Christie's, London on 5 Dec 1985.

Drawing   The highest price ever paid for a drawing is $8.36 million for the pen-and-ink scene *Jardin de Fleurs*, drawn by Vincent van Gogh in Arles, France in 1888 and sold at Christie's, New York on 14 Nov 1990 to an anonymous buyer.

Sculpture The record price for a sculpture at auction is £6.82 million ($12 million) at Sotheby's, London on 7 Dec 1989 for a bronze garden ornament, *The Dancing Faun*, made by the Dutch-born sculptor Adrien de Vries (1545/6–1626). London dealer Cyril Humpris bought the figure from an un-named couple who had paid £100 ($240) in the 1950s and in whose garden it had stood undiscovered for 40 years.

The highest price paid for the work of a sculptor during his lifetime is the $1,265,000 at Sotheby's, New York on 21 May 1982 for the 75-in-long elm-wood *Reclining Figure* by Henry Moore (Great Britain; 1898–1986).

United States The highest price paid at auction for a sculpture by an American sculptor is $4.4 million for *Coming Through the Rye*, by Frederic Remington (1861–1909), at Christie's, New York on 25 May 1989.

ANTIQUES

All prices quoted are inclusive of the buyer's premium and all records were set at public auction unless otherwise stated.

Auctioneers The oldest firm of art auctioneers in the world is the Stockholms Auktionsverk of Sweden, which was established on 27 Feb 1647. The largest firm of art auctioneers in the world is the Sotheby Group of London, Great Britain and New York City, founded in 1744, which until 1778 traded primarily in books. Sotheby's turnover in 1989 was a record $2.9 billion. A single-session record of $360.4 million was set at Sotheby's, New York on 17 May 1990.

Art nouveau The highest auction price for any piece of art nouveau is $1.78 million for a standard lamp in the form of three lotus blossoms by the Daum Brothers and Louis Majorelle of France, sold at Sotheby's, New York on 2 Dec 1989.

Blanket The most expensive blanket was a Navajo Churro hand-spun serape of *c.* 1852 sold for $115,500 at Sotheby's, New York on 22 Oct 1983.

Bottle A cobalt-blue bottle made by the Isabella Glassworks of New Jersey *c.* 1855–65 was sold for $26,400 at the Robert W. Skinner Galleries in Bolton, MA on 7 Oct 1989.

Carpet In 1946 the Metropolitan Museum of Art in New York City privately paid $1 million for the 26.5 × 13.6 ft Anhalt Medallion carpet, made in Tabriz or Kashan, Persia (now Iran) *c.* 1590.

Ceramics The highest auction price for any ceramic is £3.74 million ($6.4 million) for a Chinese Tang dynasty (A.D. 618–906) horse sold by the British Rail Pension Fund and bought by a Japanese dealer at Sotheby's, London, on 12 Dec 1989. The horse was stolen from a warehouse in Hong Kong on 14 November, but was recovered on 2 December in time for the sale.

Furniture The highest price ever paid for a single piece of furniture is £8.58

million ($15 million) at Christie's, London on 5 Jul 1990 for the 18th-century Italian "Badminton Cabinet" owned by the Duke of Beaufort. It was bought by Barbara Piasecka Johnson of Princeton, NJ.

United States The highest price ever paid for a single piece of American furniture is $12.1 million at Christie's, New York on 3 Jun 1989 for a mahogany desk-cum-bookcase, made in the 1760s. It was bought by dealer Israel Sack.

Glass The auction record is £520,000 ($1,175,200) for a Roman glass cage-cup of *c.* A.D. 300, measuring 7 in in diameter and 4 in in height, sold at Sotheby's, London, on 4 Jun 1979 to Robin Symes.

Auctioneering The longest one-man auction on record was of 60 hr, conducted by Reg Coates at Gosport, Great Britain from 9–11 Sep 1988.

Most expensive carpet The most expensive carpet ever made was the Spring carpet of Khusraw, made for the audience hall of the Sassanian palace at Ctesiphon, Iraq. It was about 7,000 ft^2 of silk and gold thread, and was encrusted with emeralds. It was cut up as booty by looters in A.D. 635, and from known realization value of the pieces must have had an original value of some $170 million.

Music box The highest price paid for a music box is £20,900 ($22,990) for a Swiss example made for a Persian prince in 1901 and sold at Sotheby's, London on 23 Jan 1985.

Toy The most expensive antique toy was sold for $231,000, by the trustees in bankruptcy of London dealers Mint & Boxed, to an anonymous telephone bidder at Christie's, New York on 14 Dec 1991. The work is a hand-painted tinplate replica of the "Charles" hose reel, a piece of fire-fighting equipment pulled by two firemen, measuring 15 x 23 in and built c. 1870 by George Brown & Co. of Forestville, CT.

Guns A .45 caliber Colt single-action army revolver, Serial No. 1 from 1873 was sold for $242,000 at Christie's New York on 14 May 1987.

Helmet The highest price ever paid for an item of headwear is $66,000 by the Alaska State Museum at an auction in New York City in November 1981 for a native North American Tlingit Kiksadi ceremonial frog helmet dating from *c.* 1600.

Jewelry The world's largest jewelry auction, which included a Van Cleef and Arpels 1939 ruby and diamond necklace, realized over $50 million when the collection belonging to the Duchess of Windsor (1896–1986) was sold at Sotheby's, Geneva, Switzerland on 3 Apr 1987.
   The highest auction price for individual items of jewelry is $6.2 million

for two pear-shaped diamond drop earrings of 58.6 and 61 carats bought and sold anonymously at Sotheby's, Geneva on 14 Nov 1980.

Playing cards The highest price for a deck of playing cards is $143,352 paid by the Metropolitan Museum of Art, New York City at Sotheby's, London on 6 Dec 1983.

Silver The record for English silver is £1,485,000 ($2,578,700) for the "Maynard" sideboard dish made by the Huguenot silversmith Paul de Lamerie in 1736, which was sold at Christie's, London on 22 May 1991.

Tapestry The highest auction price for a tapestry is £638,000 ($1,124,794), paid by Swiss dealer Peter Kleiner at Christie's, London on 3 Jul 1990 for a fragment of a rare Swiss example woven near Basle in the 1430s. The tapestry was in the Benedictine Abbey at Muri until 1840 before descending through the Vischer family.

LANGUAGE

Earliest The ability to speak is believed to be dependent upon physiological changes in the height of the larynx between *Homo erectus* and *Homo sapiens sapiens* as developed *c.* 45,000 B.C. The discovery of a hyoid bone (from the base of the tongue) from a cave site on Mt Carmel, Israel shows that Neanderthal people may have been capable of speech 60,000 years ago, but the usual dating is 50,000–30,000 B.C.

Oldest English words It was first suggested in 1979 that languages ancestral to English (Indo-European) split *c.* 3,500 B.C. According to researches completed in 1989, about 40 words of a proto–Indo-European substratum survive in English, among them apple (apal), bad (bad), gold (gol) and tin (tin). The parent language is thought to have been spoken before 3,000 B.C. and to have split into different languages over the period 3,000–2,000 B.C.

Commonest language The language used by more people than any other is Chinese, spoken by an estimated 1 billion people. The so-called "common language" (*pǔtōnghuà*) is the standard form of Chinese, with a pronunciation

---

Debating Students at St Andrews Presbyterian College in Laurinburg, NC, together with staff and friends, debated the motion "There's no place like home" for 517 hr 45 min from 4–26 Apr 1992. The aim of the debate was to increase awareness of the problems of being homeless.

Commonest sound No language is known to be without the vowel "a" (as in the English "father").

---

based on that of Beijing. It is known in Taiwan as *guoyu* ("national speech") and in the West as Mandarin.

The most widespread language is English, with a conservative estimate of 800 million speakers, rising to a more generous estimate of 1.5 billion. Of these, some 350 million are native speakers, of whom 220 million are in the United States.

Most languages The former Australian territory of Papua New Guinea has, because of its many isolated valleys, the greatest concentration of separate languages in the world, with an estimated 869; each language has about 4,000 speakers.

Most complex The following extremes of complexity have been noted: the Ample language of Papua New Guinea has the most verb forms, with over 69,000 finite forms and 860 infinitive forms of the verb; Haida, a North American Indian language, has the most prefixes, with 70; Tabassaran, a language of Daghestan, Azerbaijan, uses the most noun cases, 48; and Inuit uses 63 forms of the present tense, and simple nouns have as many as 252 inflections.

Fewest irregular verbs The artificial language Esperanto, with no irregular verbs, was first published by its inventor, Dr Ludwig Zamenhof (1859–1917) of Warsaw, in 1887. It is now estimated (by textbook sales) to have a million speakers worldwide. The even earlier interlanguage Volapük, invented by Johann Martin Schleyer (1831–1912), also has absolutely regular configuration.

The Turkish language has a single irregular verb—*olmak*, meaning "to be."

Most irregular verbs According to *The Morphology and Syntax of Present-day English* by Prof. Olu Tomori, English has 283 irregular verbs, 30 of which are formed merely by adding prefixes.

Rarest sounds The rarest speech sound is probably that written "ř" in Czech and termed a "rolled post-alveolar fricative." It occurs in very few languages and is the last sound mastered by Czech children. In the southern Bushman language !xo there is a click articulated with both lips, which is written. This character is usually referred to as a "bull's eye" and the sound, essentially a kiss, is termed a "velaric ingressive bilabial stop." In some contexts the "l" sound in the Arabic word *Allah* is pronounced uniquely in that language.

Vocabulary The English language contains about 616,500 words plus another 400,000 technical terms, the most in any language, but it is doubtful if any individual speaker uses more than 60,000. The members of the International Society for Philosophical Enquiry (no admission for IQs below 148) have an average vocabulary of 36,250 words. Shakespeare employed a vocabulary of *c.* 33,000 words.

Greatest linguist The world's greatest linguist is believed to have been Dr Harold Williams of New Zealand (1876–1928), a journalist. Self-taught in Latin, Greek, Hebrew and many of the European and Pacific island languages as a boy, Dr Williams spoke 58 languages and many dialects fluently. He was the only person to attend the League of Nations (1920–46) in Geneva, Switzerland and converse with every delegate in their own language.

In terms of oral fluency, the most multilingual living person is Derick Herning of Lerwick, Shetland, whose command of 22 languages earned him victory

LANGUAGE VERSATILITY   The view from an interpreter's booth at an assembly of the United Nations in New York City, where many of the world's most versatile linguists have perfected their skills. (Photo: Gamma/J. Turpin)

in the inaugural "Polyglot of Europe" contest held in Brussels, Belgium in May 1990.

Alexander Schwartz of New York City *worked* with 31 languages as a translator for the United Nations between 1962 and 1986.

ALPHABET

Earliest   The earliest-known example of alphabetic writing was found at Ugarit (now Ras Sharma), Syria, dated to *c.* 1450 B.C. It comprised a clay tablet of 32 cuneiform letters.

Oldest letter   The letter "O" is unchanged in shape since its adoption in the Phoenician alphabet *c.* 1,300 B.C.

Newest letters   The newest letters to be added to the English alphabet are "j" and "v," which are of post-Shakespearean use (*c.* 1630). Formerly they were used only as variants of "i" and "u."

Longest   The language with the most letters in its alphabet is Cambodian, with 74 (including some without any current use).

Shortest   Rotokas of central Bougainville Island, Papua New Guinea has the fewest letters, with 11 (a, b, e, g, i, k, o, p, r, t and u).

Most and fewest consonants   The language with the greatest number of distinct consonantal sounds is Ubykhs in the Caucasus, with 80–85. Rotokas has the fewest, with six consonants.

Most and fewest vowels   The language with the most vowels is Sedang, a central Vietnamese language with 55 distinguishable vowel sounds, and the one with the fewest is the Caucasian language Abkhazian, with two.

WORDS

Longest   Lengthy concatenations and some compound or agglutinative words or nonce words are or have been written in the closed-up style of a single word. The longest known example is a compound "word" of 195 Sanskrit characters (which transliterates into 428 letters in the Roman alphabet) describing the region near Kanci, Tamil Nadu, India. The word appears in a 16th-century work by Tirumalāmbā, Queen of Vijayanagara.

English   The longest word in the *Oxford English Dictionary* is *pneumonoultra-microscopicsilicovolcanoconiosis (-koniosis)*, which has 45 letters and allegedly means "a lung disease caused by the inhalation of very fine silica dust." It is, however, described as "factitious" by the editors of the dictionary.

Longest scientific name   The systematic name for *deoxyribonucleic acid* (DNA) of the human mitochondria contains 16,569 nucleotide residues and is thus *c.* 207,000 letters long. It was published in key form in *Nature* on 9 Apr 1981.

Longest palindromes   The longest-known palindromic word (a word that reads the same backward or forward) is *saippuakivikauppias* (19 letters), which is Finnish for "a dealer in lye" (caustic soda). The longest in English is *tattarrat-tat*, with 12 letters, which appears in the *Oxford English Dictionary*.
   Some baptismal fonts in Greece and Turkey bear the circular 25-letter inscription NIψON ANOMHMATA MH MONAN OψIN, meaning "wash (my) sins not only (my) face."

Longest anagrams   The longest non-scientific English words that can form anagrams are the 17-letter transpositions *representationalism* and *misrepresen-*

Smallest letters   Scanning tunneling microscope (STM) techniques pioneered in April 1990 by physicists Donald Eigler and Erhard Schweizer at IBM's Almaden Research Center in San Jose, CA have enabled single atoms of various elements to be manipulated to form characters and pictures.

Most succinct word   The most challenging word for any lexicographer to define briefly is the Fuegian (southernmost Argentina and Chile) word *mamihlapinatapai,* meaning "looking at each other hoping that either will offer to do something which both parties desire but are unwilling to do."

Most synonyms   The condition of being inebriated has more synonyms than any other condition or object. *Dickson's Word Treasury*, published in 1992 and compiled by Paul Dickson of Garrett Park, MD, contains a list of 2,660 synonyms for that condition.

LONGEST WORDS

Japanese[1]	Chi-n-chi-ku-ri-n (12 letters) *a very short person (slang)*
Spanish	Superextraordinarisimo (22) *extraordinary*
French	Anticonstitutionnellement (25) *anticonstitutionally*
Italian	Precipitevolissimevolmente (26) *as fast as possible*
Portuguese	Inconstitucionalissimamente (27) *with the highest degree of unconstitutionality*
Icelandic	Haecstaréttarmálaflutningsmaôur (29 Icelandic letters, transliterating as 31) *supreme court barrister*
Russian	Ryentgyenoelyektrokardiografichyeskogo (33 Cyrillic letters, transliterating as 38) *of the X-ray electrocardiographic*
Hungarian	Megszentségtelenithetetlenségeskedéseitekért (44) *for your unprofanable actions*
Dutch[2]	Kindercarnavalsoptochtvoorbereidingswerkzaam- heden (49) *preparation activities for a children's carnival procession*
Mohawk[3]	Tkanuhstasrihsranuhwe'tsraaksahsrakaratattsrayeri' (50) *the praising of the evil of the liking of the finding of the house is right*
Turkish[2]	Cekoslovakyalılastırabilemediklerimizlerdenmisiniz (50) *"are you not of that group of persons that we were said to be unable to Czechoslovakianize?"*
German[2,4]	Donaudampfschiffahrtselektrizitaetenhauptbetrieb- swerkbauunterbeamtengesellschaft (80) *The club for subordinate officials of the head office management of the Danube steamboat electrical ser- vices (name of a prewar club in Vienna)*
Swedish[2]	Nordöstersjökustartilleriflygspaningssimulatoranlägg- ningsmaterielunderhållsuppföljningssystemdiskus- sionsinläggsförberedelsearbeten (130) *Preparatory work on the contribution to the discus- sion on the maintaining system of support of the ma- terial of the aviation survey simulator device within the northeast part of the coastartillery of the Baltic*

[1] *Patent applications sometimes harbor long compound "words." An extreme example is one of 13 kana (Japanese syllabary) which transliterates to the 40-letter* Kyūkitsūrohekimenfuchakunenryosekisanryo *meaning "the accumulated amount of fuel condensed on the wall face of the air intake passage."*

[2] *Agglutinative words are limited only by imagination and are not found in standard dictionaries. The first 100-letter such word was published in 1975 by the late Eric Rosenthal in Afrikaans.*

[3] *Lengthy concetenations are a feature of Mohawk.*

[4] *The longest dictionary word in everyday usage is* Rechtsschutzversicherungsgesellschaften *(39) meaning "insurance companies which provide legal protection."*

tation. The longest scientific transposals are *hydroxydesoxycorticosterone* and *hydroxydeoxycorticosterones*, with 27 letters.

Abbreviations Longest The initials S.K.O.M.K.H.P.K.J.C.D.P.W.B., which stand for the Syarikat Kerjasama Orang-orang Melayu Kerajaan Hilir Perak Kerana Jimat Cermat Dan Pinjam-meminjam Wang Berhad, are the Malay name for The Cooperative Company of the Lower State of Perak Government's Malay People for Money Savings and Loans Ltd, in Teluk Anson, Perak, West Malaysia (formerly Malaya). The abbreviation for this abbreviation is Skomk.

Shortest The 55-letter full name of Los Angeles (El Pueblo de Nuestra Señora la Reina de los Angeles de Porciuncula) is abbreviated to L.A., or 3.63 percent of its length.

Longest acronym The longest acronym is NIIOMTPLABOPARMBETZH-ELBETRABSBOMONIMONKONOTDTEKHSTROMONT with 56 letters (54 in Cyrillic) in the *Concise Dictionary of Soviet Terminology, Institutions and Abbreviations* (1969), meaning: the Laboratory for Shuttering, Reinforcement, Concrete and Ferroconcrete Operations for Composite-monolithic and Monolithic Constructions of the Department of the Technology of Building-Assembly Operations of the Scientific Research Institute of the Organization for Building Mechanization and Technical Aid of the Academy of Building and Architecture of the USSR.

Commonest words and letters The most frequently used words in written English are, in descending order of frequency: *the, of, and, to, a, in, that, is, I, it, for* and *as*. The most commonly used in conversation is "*I*." The commonest letter is "e." More words begin with the letter "s" than with any other, but the most commonly *used* initial letter is "t" as in "the," "to," "that" or "there."

Most meanings The most overworked word in English is "set," to which Dr Charles Onions (1873–1965) of Oxford University Press gave 58 uses as a noun, 126 uses as a verb and ten as a participial adjective.

PERSONAL NAMES

Earliest The earliest personal name that has survived seems to be that of a predynastic king of Upper Egypt *ante* 3,050 B.C., who is represented by the hieroglyphic sign for a scorpion. It has been suggested that the name should be read as Sekhen.

Longest personal name The longest name appearing on a birth certificate is that of Rhoshandiatellyneshiaunnevesehenk Koyaanfsquatsiuty Williams, born to Mr and Mrs James Williams in Beaumont, TX on 12 Sep 1984. On 5 Oct 1984 the father filed an amendment that expanded his daughter's first name to 1,019 letters and her middle name to 36 letters.

Most first names Laurence Watkins (b. 9 Jun 1965) of Auckland, New Zealand claims a total of 2,310 first names, added by deed poll in 1991 after official opposition by the registrar and a prolonged court battle. The great-great-grandson of Carlos III of Spain, Don Alfonso de Borbón y Borbón (1866–1934), had 94 first names, several of which were lengthened by hyphenation.

> *Most contrived name*   In the United States the determination to derive commercial or other benefit from being the last listing in the local telephone book has resulted in self-given names starting with up to nine "Z's" — an extreme example being Zachary *Zzzzzzzzzz*ra in the San Francisco book.

Shortest family names   The commonest single-letter surname is "O," prevalent in Korea but with 52 examples in US telephone books (1973–81) and 12 in Belgium. Every other letter, except "Q," has been traced as a surname in US telephone books by A. Ross Eckler.

Commonest family name   The Chinese name Zhang is borne, according to estimates, by between 9.7 and 12.1 percent of the Chinese population. Even at the lower estimate this means that there are at least some 113 million Zhangs—almost half the total population of the United States.

The commonest surname in the English-speaking world is Smith. There are an estimated 2,382,509 Smiths in the United States.

PLACE-NAMES

Earliest   The world's earliest-known place-names are pre-Sumerian, e.g., Kish, Ur and the now-lost Attara, and therefore earlier than *c.* 3,600 B.C.

Longest   The official name for Bangkok, the capital city of Thailand, is Krungthep Mahanakhon. However, the full name is Krungthep Mahanakhon Bovorn Ratanakosin Mahintharayutthaya Mahadilokpop Noparatratchathani Burirom Udomratchanivet mahasathan Amornpiman Avatarnsathit Sakkathattiyavisnukarmprasit (167 letters), which in its most scholarly transliteration emerges with 175 letters.

The longest place-name now in use in the world is Taumatawhakatangihangakoauauotamateaturipukakapikimaungahoro-nukupokaiwhenuakitanatahu, the unofficial 85-letter version of the name of a hill (1,002 ft above sea level) in the Southern Hawke's Bay district of North Island, New Zealand. The Maori translation means "The place where Tamatea, the man with the big knees, who slid, climbed and swallowed mountains, known as landeater, played his flute to his loved one."

United States   The longest place-name in the United States is Lake Chargoggugoggmonchauggagoggchaubunagungamaug near Webster, MA. The 44-letter name of this two-square-mile lake is derived from the Algonquin Indian "You fish on your side, we fish on our side; nobody fish in the middle." The standardized version has been reduced to Lake Chaubunagungamaug by the United States board on Geographic Names.

Shortest   The shortest place-names consist of just single letters, and examples can be found in various countries around the world.

There was once a town called "6" in West Virginia.

Most spellings   The spelling of the Dutch town of Leeuwarden has been recorded in 225 versions since A.D. 1046. Bromsberrow, Great Britain is recorded in 161 spellings since the 10th century as reported by local historian Lester Steynor.

LITERATURE

Earliest　Tokens or tallies from Tepe Asiab and Ganji-I-Dareh Tepe in Iran have been dated to 8,500 B.C. The earliest written language discovered is on Yangshao culture pottery from Paa-t'o in the Shaanxi province of China, found in 1962. This bears proto-characters for the numbers 5, 7 and 8 and has been dated to 5,000–4,000 B.C.

Paper dated to between 71 B.C. and A.D. 21, i.e., 100 years earlier than the previous presumed date for paper's invention, has been found in northwest China.

Oldest book　The oldest handwritten book, still intact, is a Coptic Psalter dated to about 1,600 years ago, found in 1984 at Beni Suef, Egypt.

Oldest mechanically printed　The oldest surviving printed work is the Dharani scroll or *sutra* from wooden printing blocks found in the foundations of the Pulguk Sa pagoda, Kyŏngju, South Korea on 14 Oct 1966. It has been dated to no later than A.D. 704.

It is widely accepted that the earliest mechanically printed full-length book was the 42-line-per-page Gutenberg Bible, printed in Mainz, Germany c. 1454 by Johann Henne zum Gensfleisch zur Laden, called "zu Gutenberg" (c. 1398–1468). The earliest exactly dated printed work is the Psalter completed on 14 Aug 1457 by Johann Fust (c. 1400–66) and Peter Schöffer (1425–1502), who had been Gutenberg's chief assistant.

Smallest book　The smallest marketed bound printed book is one printed on 22 gsm paper measuring $1/25 \times 1/25$ in, comprising the children's story *Old King Cole!* and published in 85 copies in March 1985 by The Gleniffer Press of Paisley, Great Britain. The pages can be turned (with care) only by the use of a needle.

Largest publications　The largest publication ever compiled was the *Yongle Dadien* (the great thesaurus of the Yongle reign) of 22,937 manuscript chapters (370 still survive) in 11,095 volumes. It was written by 2,000 Chinese scholars in 1403–08.

The entire Buddhist scriptures are inscribed on 729 marble slabs, each measuring $5 \times 3^{1}/_{2}$ ft, housed in 729 stupas in the Kuthodaw Pagoda, south of Mandalay, Myanmar (formerly Burma). They were incised in 1860–68.

Dictionaries　*Deutsches Wörterbuch*, started by Jacob and Wilhelm Grimm in 1854, was completed in 1971 and consists of 34,519 pages and 33 volumes.

The largest English-language dictionary is the 20-volume *Oxford English Dictionary*, with 21,728 pages. The first edition was published between 1884 and 1928. Work on the second edition began in 1984, and the work involved represented 500 person-years. Published in March 1989, it defines a total of 616,500 word-forms, with 2,412,400 illustrative quotations and approximately

350 million letters and figures. The longest entry in the second edition is that for the verb *set*, with over 75,000 words of text.

The largest English-language dictionary published in the United States is *Webster's Third New International Dictionary Unabridged*, published in 1986 by Merriam-Webster, Inc. It defines 470,000 word-forms, with 99,943 illustrative quotations and approximately 60 million letters and numerics. The longest entry is for the verb *turn*, with over 5,500 words of text.

Encyclopedias Largest The largest encyclopedia ever compiled was the Chinese *Yongle Dadian* (See Largest publications.)

Currently, the largest encyclopedia is *La Enciclopedia Universal Ilustrada Europeo-Americana* (J. Espasa & Sons, Madrid and Barcelona), totaling 105,000 pages, with an annual supplement since 1935. The encyclopedia comprises 165.2 million words. The number of volumes in the set in August 1983 was 104, and the price $2,325.

Fiction The novel *Tokuga-Wa Ieyasu* by Sohachi Yamaoka has been serialized in Japanese daily newspapers since 1951. Now completed, it will require nearly 40 volumes.

The longest novel of note ever published is *Les hommes de bonne volonté* by Louis-Henri-Jean Farigoule (1885–1972), alias Jules Romains, of France, pub-

---

MOST VALUABLE LITERATURE PRIZE

The Nobel Prize is the most valuable award for literature, and was worth SwKr6.5 million (about $1.12 million) in 1992. To date 32 different countries (counting Germany as two) have produced winners, the latest being St Lucia, birthplace of poet Derek Walcott, the 1992 literature prize winner.

The award has been declined twice, by Boris Pasternak (1890–1960) in 1958 and by Jean-Paul Sartre (1905–80) in 1964.

The table shows those countries with more than one winner (to 1992).

France	12
United States	10
Great Britain	8
Sweden	6
Germany*	5
Italy	5
Spain	5
Denmark	3
Netherlands	3
Poland	3
USSR (former)	3
Chile	2
Greece	2
Republic of Ireland	2
Switzerland	2

*Before 1948

lished in 27 volumes in 1932–46. The English version, *Men of Good Will*, was published in 14 volumes in 1933–46 as a "novel-cycle." The 4,959-page edition published by Peter Davies Ltd has an estimated 2,070,000 words, excluding the 100-page index.

MAPS

Oldest A clay tablet depicting the river Euphrates flowing through northern Mesopotamia (Iraq) dates to *c.* 2250 B.C. The earliest printed map in the world is one of western China dated to 1115.

Largest The largest permanent, two-dimensional atlas measures 49,000 ft^2 and was painted by students of O'Hara Park School, Oakley, CA in the summer of 1992.

The Challenger relief map of British Columbia, Canada, measuring 6,080 ft^2, was designed and built in the period 1945–52 by the late George Challenger and his son Robert. It is now on display at the Pacific National Exhibition in Vancouver, British Columbia.

Most expensive The highest price paid for an atlas is $1,925,000 for a copy of Ptolemy *Cosmographia*, which was sold at Sotheby's, New York City on 31 Jan 1990.

HIGHEST PRICES

Book The highest price paid for any book is £8.14 million ($12 million) for the 226-leaf manuscript *The Gospel Book of Henry the Lion, Duke of Saxony*, at Sotheby's, London on 6 Dec 1983. The book, which measures 13$^1/2$ × 10 in, was illuminated *c.* 1170 by the monk Herimann at Helmershansen Abbey, Germany with 41 full-page illustrations.

The highest price ever paid for a *printed* book is $5.39 million for an Old Testament (Genesis to the Psalms) Gutenberg Bible printed in 1455 in Mainz, Germany. It was bought by Tokyo booksellers Maruzen Co. Ltd at Christie's New York on 22 Oct 1987.

Broadsheet The highest price ever paid for a broadsheet was $2,420,000 for one of the 24 known copies of the Declaration of Independence, printed by John Dunlap in Philadelphia, PA in 1776, and sold to Donald J. Scheer of Atlanta, GA on 13 Jun 1991.

Manuscript The highest price ever paid for a complete manuscript is £2.97 million ($11.4 million) by London dealers Quaritch at Sotheby's, London on 29 Nov 1990 for the 13th-century *Northumberland Bestiary*, a colorful and heavily illustrated encyclopedia of real and imaginary animals.

On 16 Dec 1992, a Lincoln manuscript was sold for $1.54 million. The one-page script was written in preparation for a speech. It is the first surviving formulation of his "house divided" doctrine, written in the winter of 1857 or 1858. The manuscript was bought by Seth Kaller of Kaller Historical Documents.

Musical The auction record for a musical manuscript is $4,394,500 at Sotheby's, London on 22 May 1987 for a 508-page, 8$^1/2$ × 6$^1/2$ in bound volume of nine complete symphonies in Mozart's hand. The manuscript is owned by

MOST EXPENSIVE MANUSCRIPT The highest price ever paid for an American manuscript was $1,540,000 on 16 Dec 1992 for the earliest surviving formulation of Abraham Lincoln's "house divided" doctrine. The leaf came from a carpetbag containing Lincoln's papers, called his "literary bureau," which he left at his in-laws' house in Springfield, IL when he moved to Washington, D.C. in 1861. (Photo: Sotheby's New York)

Robert Owen Lehman and is on deposit at the Pierpont Morgan Library in New York City.

The record price paid for a single musical manuscript is £1.1 million (*c*. $2 million), paid at Sotheby's, London on 6 Dec 1991 for the autograph copy of the Piano Sonata in E minor, opus 90, by Ludwig van Beethoven (1770–1827).

Scientific The highest price paid for a scientific manuscript was $1.16 million for a 72-page document by Albert Einstein, which explained his theory of relativity, on 2 Dec 1987 at Sotheby's, New York.

DIARIES AND LETTERS

Longest-kept diary Col. Ernest Loftus of Harare, Zimbabwe began his daily diary on 4 May 1896 at the age of 12 and continued it until his death on 7 Jul 1987 at the age of 103 years 178 days. George C. Edler (1889–1987) of Bethesda, MD kept a handwritten diary continuously from 20 Sep 1909, a total of 78 years.

Longest and most letters Uichi Noda, from July 1961 until his bedridden wife Mitsu's death in March 1985, wrote her 1,307 letters amounting to 5 million characters during his overseas trips. These letters have been published in 25 volumes totaling 12,404 pages. Rev. Canon Bill Cook and his fiancée/wife Helen of Diss, Norfolk, Great Britain exchanged 6,000 love letters during their 4¼ year separation from March 1942–May 1946.

Shortest correspondence The shortest correspondence on record was that between Victor Marie Hugo (1802–85) and his publisher, Hurst and Blackett, in 1862. The author was on vacation and was anxious to know how his new novel *Les Misérables* was selling. He wrote "?" and received the reply "!"

Longest literary gestation The German dictionary *Deutsches Wörterbuch* was begun by the brothers Grimm in 1854 and finished in 1971. *Acta Sanctorum*, begun by Jean Bolland in 1643, arranged according to saints' days, reached the month of November in 1925; an introduction for December was published in 1940. Oxford University Press received back its proofs of *Constable's Presentments* from the Dugdale Society in December 1984. They had been sent out for correction in December 1949.

Pen pals The longest sustained correspondence on record is one of 75 years between Mrs Ida McDougall of Tasmania, Australia and Miss R. Norton of Sevenoaks, Kent, Great Britain from 11 Nov 1904 until Mrs McDougall's death on 24 Dec 1979.

Most personal mail The highest confirmed amount of mail received by any private citizen in a year is 900,000 letters by the baseball star Henry Louis "Hank" Aaron (b. 5 Feb 1934), reported by the US Postal Department in June 1974. About a third were letters of hate engendered by his bettering of George Herman "Babe" Ruth's career record for home runs. (See also Sports and Games, Baseball.)

AUTOGRAPHS AND SIGNATURES

Earliest The earliest surviving examples of autographs are those made by scribes on cuneiform clay tablets from Tell Abu Salābīkh period, Iraq dated to the early Dynastic III A *c.* 2,600 B.C. A scribe named "a-du" has added "dub-sar" after his name, translating to "Adu, scribe." The earliest surviving signature on a papyrus is that of the scribe Amen'aa, held in the St Petersburg Museum, Russia and dated to the Egyptian Middle Kingdom, which began *c.* 2,130 B.C.

Most expensive The highest price ever paid on the open market for a single signed autograph letter was $748,000 on 5 Dec 1991 at Christie's, New York for a letter written by Abraham Lincoln on 8 Jan 1863 defending criticism of the Emancipation Proclamation. It was sold to Profiles in History of Beverly Hills, CA.

Rarest and most valuable Only one example of the signature of Christopher Marlowe (1564–93) is known. It is in the County Archives in Kent, Great Britain on a will of 1583.

The only known document that bears ten US presidential signatures is a letter sent by President Franklin Delano Roosevelt to Richard C. Corbyn, then of Dallas (now of Amarillo), TX, dated 26 Oct 1932. It was subsequently signed by Herbert Hoover, Harry S Truman, Dwight D. Eisenhower, Gerald Ford, Lyndon Johnson, Jimmy Carter, Ronald Reagan and George Bush. Richard Nixon's first signature was signed with an auto-pen but he later resigned it.

AUTHORS

Most prolific A lifetime output of 72–75 million words has been calculated for Charles Harold St John Hamilton, alias Frank Richards (1876–1961), the creator of Billy Bunter. In his peak years (1915–26) he wrote up to 80,000 words a week for the boys' school weeklies *Gem* (1907–39), *Magnet* (1908–40) and *Boys' Friend*, published in Great Britain.

Novels The greatest number of novels published is 904, by Kathleen Lindsay (Mrs Mary Faulkner; 1903–73) of Somerset West, Cape Province, South Africa. She wrote under two other married names and eight pen names.

Baboorao Arnalkar (b. 9 Jun 1907) of Maharashtra State, India published 1,092 short mystery stories in book form and several nonfiction books between 1936 and 1984.

Top-selling The world's top-selling writer of fiction is Dame Agatha Christie (nee Miller, later Lady Mallowan, 1890–1976), whose 78 crime novels have sold an estimated 2 billion copies in 44 languages. Agatha Christie also wrote 19 plays and six romantic novels under the pseudonym Mary Westmacott. Royalty earnings from her works are estimated to be worth $4.25 million per year.

Highest-paid author per word In 1958 Mrs Deborah Schneider of Minneapolis, MN wrote 25 words to complete a sentence in a competition for the best slogan for Plymouth cars. She beat about 1.4 million other entrants to win a prize of $500 every month for life. Based on normal life expectancy, she should collect $12,000 per word. No known anthology includes Mrs Schneider's deathless prose, but it is in her safe deposit box at her bank, "Only to be opened after death."

Most rejections   The record for rejections before publication is 176 (plus nonacknowledgment from many other publishers) in the case of Bill Gordon's *How Many Books Do You Sell in Ohio?* from October 1983 to November 1985. The record was then spoiled by Mr Gordon's rejection of a written offer from Aames-Allen.

British novelist John Creasey (1908–73) received 743 rejection slips before becoming the best-selling author of 564 books.

Oldest   The oldest author in the world was Alice Pollock (nee Wykeham-Martin, 1868–1971) of Haslemere, Great Britain, whose first book, *Portrait of My Victorian Youth* (Johnson Publications), was published in March 1971 when she was aged 102 years 8 months. The oldest living author is Griffith R. Williams of Llithfaen, Great Britain, whose autobiography, *Cofio Canrif*, was published on his 102nd birthday on 5 Jun 1990.

Most pseudonyms   The writer with greatest number of pseudonyms is the minor Russian humorist Konstantin Arsenievich Mikhailov (b. 1868), whose 325 pen names are listed in the *Dictionary of Pseudonyms* by I.F. Masanov, published in Moscow in 1960. The names, ranging from Ab. to Z, were mostly abbreviations of his real name.

Longest poem   The longest poem ever published was the Kirghiz folk epic *Manas*, which appeared in printed form in 1958 but has never been translated into English. According to the *Dictionary of Oriental Literatures*, this three-part epic runs to about 500,000 lines.

The longest poem ever written in the English language is one on the life of King Alfred by John Fitchett (1766–1838) of Liverpool, Great Britain, which ran to 129,807 lines and took 40 years to write. His editor, Robert Riscoe, added the concluding 2,585 lines.

BEST-SELLING BOOKS

The world's best-selling and most widely distributed book is the Bible, which has been translated into 2,009 languages, and portions of it into a further 910 languages. This compares with 222 languages for Lenin's works. It has been estimated that between 1815 and 1992 some 6.1 billion copies of the Bible were printed, of which 36.97 percent were handled by bible societies. Since 1976, combined global sales of Today's English Version (*Good News*) New Testament and Bible (which is copyrighted by the bible societies) have exceeded 236.9 million copies. Apart from the King James version (averaging

Slowest seller   The prize for the world's slowest-selling book (a category known in publishing as slooow sellers) probably belongs to David Wilkins' translation of the New Testament from Coptic into Latin, published by Oxford University Press (OUP) in 1716 in a printing of 500 copies. Selling an average of one every 20 weeks, it remained in print for 191 years.

some 13 million copies printed annually), there are at least 14 other copyrights on other versions of the Bible. The oldest publisher of bibles is the Cambridge University Press, which began with the Geneva version in 1591.

Excluding versions of the Bible, the world's all-time best-selling book is *The Guinness Book of Records*, first published in October 1955 by the Guinness Brewery and edited by Norris Dewar McWhirter (b. 12 Aug 1925) and his twin brother Alan Ross McWhirter (1925–75). Global sales in 43 languages surpassed 74 million by May 1993.

Best-seller lists   The longest duration on the *New York Times* best-seller list (founded 1935) has been for *The Road Less Traveled* by M. Scott Peck, which had its 501st week on the list, as of 13 Jun 1993.

PUBLISHERS AND PRINTERS

Oldest publishers   Cambridge University Press has a continuous history of printing and publishing since 1584. The University received a Royal Letters Patent to print and sell all manner of books on 20 Jul 1534.

In 1978 the Oxford University Press (OUP) celebrated the 500th anniversary of the printing of the first book in the City of Oxford, Great Britain in 1478. This was before OUP itself was in existence.

United States   The firm of Lea Febiger of Malvern, PA (founded as Matthew Carey) has a continuous history of publishing since 1785.

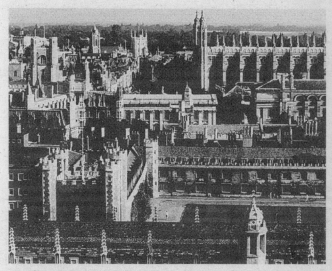

OLDEST PUBLISHER   The heart of the University of Cambridge in Great Britain. The building in the background with the square tower and flagpole is Cambridge University Press, the world's oldest publisher. (Photos: CUP/Tim Rawle)

Most prolific publisher   At its peak in 1989, Progress Publishers (founded in 1931 as the Publishing Association of Foreign Workers in the former USSR) of Moscow, Russia printed over 750 titles in 50 languages annually.

Largest publisher   The world's largest magazine and book publisher is Time Inc., a division of Time Warner of New York. Revenues in 1992 totaled $3.123 billion.

Fastest publishing   A thousand bound copies of *William and His Adventures*, published by the Royal Marsden Hospital Appeal and Scriptmate and printed by Booksprint, were produced from text on disk in 12 hr 18 min on 5 Jun 1992.

Largest printers   The largest printers in the world are believed to be R.R. Donnelley & Sons Co. of Chicago, IL. The company, founded in 1864, has nearly 100 manufacturing facilities, offices, service centers and subsidiaries worldwide, turning out $4.1 billion worth of work in 1992.

The largest printer under one roof is the United States Government Printing Office (founded 1861) in Washington, D.C. Encompassing 34.4 acres of floor space, the central office processes an average of 1,464 print orders daily, and uses 93.2 million lb of paper annually.

Highest printings   It is believed that in the United States, Van Antwerp Bragg and Co. printed some 60 million copies of the 1879 edition of *The McGuffey Reader*, compiled by Henry Vail in the pre-copyright era for distribution to public schools.

BOOKSTORES

The bookstore with the most titles and the longest shelving (30 miles) in the world is W. & G. Foyle Ltd of London, Great Britain. First established in 1904 in a small store, the company now has a site of 75,825 ft². The most capacious individual bookstore in the world measured by square footage is the Barnes & Noble Bookstore at 105 Fifth Ave at 18th Street, New York City. It covers 154,250 ft² and has 12.87 miles of shelving.

LIBRARIES

Earliest   One of the earliest-known collections of archival material was that of King Ashurbanipal at Nineveh (668–627 B.C.). He had clay tablets referring to events, personages and religious ideas as far back as the Dynasty of Agode *c.* 23rd century B.C.

United States   The first library in America was established at Harvard University in 1638. The first subscription library in the country was the Philadelphia Library Company in 1731. The first library in America that meets the definition of a modern public library was in Peterboro, NH, established on 9 Apr 1833. The original collection contained 700 books.

Largest   The United States Library of Congress (founded on 24 Apr 1800) in Washington, D.C. contains 101,395,257 items, including 15,700,905 books in the classified collections and 85,694,352 items in the nonclassified collections. The library occupies approximately 2.85 million ft² of space in its three Capitol Hill buildings. Additionally, the library has some seven different office and facility locations throughout the world, including one in Moscow. As of May 1992 there were 575 miles of shelving. The library employs 5,050 people.

The largest nonstatutory library in the world is the New York Public Library (founded 1895) on Fifth Avenue, New York City with a floor space of 525,276 ft^2 and 88 miles of shelving, plus an underground extension with the capacity for an additional 92 miles. Its collection, including 82 branch libraries, embraces 13,887,774 volumes, 18,349,585 manuscripts and 381,645 maps.

The largest public library in the United States is the Harold Washington Library Center, Chicago, IL, which opened on 7 Oct 1991. The ten-story, 750,000 ft^2 building contains 70.8 miles of bookshelves and cost $144 million.

Christmas cards The earliest-known Christmas card was sent out by Sir Henry Cole (1808–82) in 1843, but this practice did not become an annual ritual until 1862.

The greatest number of personal Christmas cards sent by an individual is believed to be 62,824, by Werner Erhard of San Francisco, CA in December 1975. Many must have been to unilateral acquaintances.

Christmas card exchange Frank Rose of Burnaby, British Columbia, Canada and Gordon Loutet of Lake Cowichan, British Columbia have exchanged the same Christmas card every year since 1929.

Warren Nord of Mesa, AZ and Thor (Tut) Andersen (d. 11 Sep 1988) of Ashtabula, OH exchanged the same Christmas card every year from 1930–87.

Public relations The world's largest public relations firm is Burson Marsteller. Based in New York, the company had a net fee income of $217.8 million in 1992. Burson Marsteller operates 64 offices worldwide with a staff of 2,071.

Most durable advertiser The Jos Neel Co., a clothing store in Macon, GA (founded 1880) has run an ad in the *Macon Telegraph* every day in the upper-left-hand corner of page 2 since 22 Feb 1889.

Most belated apology The *Hartford Courant* (See Newspapers, Oldest) issued an apology to Thomas Jefferson, 193 years late. In 1800 the newspaper ran a vehement editorial opposing his election as president, expounding on the ways in which the country would be irrevocably damaged as a result. At the 250th anniversary of his birth, in 1993, the *Courant* finally admitted the error of its judgment with a formal apology, and the words: "It's never too late to admit a mistake."

Most advertising pages The greatest number of pages of advertisements sold in a single issue of a periodical is 829.54 by the October 1989 issue of *Business Week*.

The collection includes 2 million books, 8,585 periodical titles, nearly 900,000 government documents, 100,000 pamphlets, 3.4 million microforms and 1.6 million recordings, audiovisual aids, picture files and sheet music.

Overdue books   The record for an unreturned and overdue library book was set when a book in German on the Archbishop of Bremen, published in 1609, was borrowed from Sidney Sussex College, Cambridge, Great Britain by Colonel Robert Walpole in 1667–68. It was found by Prof. Sir John Plumb in the library of the then-Marquess of Cholmondeley at Houghton Hall, Norfolk, Great Britain and returned 288 years later. No fine was exacted.

The most overdue book in the United States was a book on febrile diseases (London, 1805, by Dr J. Currie) checked out in 1823 from the University of Cincinnati Medical Library and returned 7 Dec 1968 by the borrower's great-grandson, Richard Dodd. The calculated fine of $2,264 was waived.

MUSEUMS

Oldest   The world's oldest extant museum is the Ashmolean in Oxford, Great Britain, built between 1679 and 1683 and named after the collector Elias Ashmole (1617–92).

Largest   The Smithsonian Institution comprises 16 museums containing over 140 million items and has over 6,000 employees.

The American Museum of Natural History in New York City was founded in 1869 and comprises 23 interconnected buildings in an 18-acre park. The buildings of the museum and the planetarium contain 1.2 million ft² of floor space, accommodating more than 30 million artifacts and specimens. Its exhibits are viewed by more than 3 million visitors each year.

Most popular   The highest attendance for any museum is over 118,437 on 14 April 1984 at the Smithsonian's National Air and Space Museum, Washington, D.C., opened in July 1976. The record-setting day required the doors to be temporarily closed.

NEWSPAPERS

Oldest   A copy has survived of a news pamphlet published in Cologne, Germany in 1470. The oldest existing newspaper in the world is the Swedish official journal *Post och Inrikes Tidningar*, founded in 1645 and published by the Royal Swedish Academy of Letters. The oldest existing commercial newspaper is the *Haarlems Dagblad/Oprechte Haarlemsche Courant*, published in Haarlem, Netherlands, first issued as the *Weeckelycke Courante van Europa* on 8 Jan 1656. A copy of issue No. 1 survives.

United States   The oldest continuously published newspaper in the United States is the *Hartford Courant*, established by Thomas Greene on 29 Oct 1764. Originally a weekly four-page newspaper, it became a daily newspaper in 1836. Its current circulation figures are 234,686 daily and 327,339 Sunday, as of 31 March 1993.

The oldest continuously published daily newspaper in the United States is the *New York Post*, established as the *New York Evening Post* by Alexander Hamilton on 16 Nov 1801.

OLDEST COMMERCIAL NEWSPAPER Pages from issue No. 1 of the Dutch newspaper *Weeckelycke Courante van Europa* of 8 Jan 1656, giving news from Spain, Germany, Prussia, France, England and Scotland, as well as the Netherlands.

Largest The most massive single issue of a newspaper was an edition of the Sunday *New York Times*, which weighed 12 lb and contained 1,612 pages, on 14 Sep 1987. The largest page size ever used was 51 × 35 in for *The Constellation*, printed in 1859 by George Roberts as part of the July 4th celebrations in New York City.

Smallest The smallest original page size was the 3 × 3¾ in of the *Daily Banner* (25 cents per month) of Roseberg, OR, issues of which, dated 1 and 2 Feb 1876, survive. The British Library Newspaper Library contains the *Watford News and Advertiser* of 1 Apr 1899, which measures 2.9 × 3.9 in.

Longest editorship Sir Etienne Dupuch (b. 16 Feb 1899) of Nassau, Bahamas was editor-in-chief of *The Tribune* from 1 Apr 1919 to 1972, and a contributing editor until his death on 23 Aug 1991—a total of 72 years.

Most Pulitzer prizes The *New York Times* has won 66 Pulitzer prizes, more than any other news organization. The Pulitzer is the highest award given annually in American journalism and for arts.

Most durable feature Mary MacArthur of Port Appin, Scotland has contributed a regular feature to *The Oban Times and West Highland Times* since 1926.

Most syndicated columnist Ann Landers (nee Eppie Lederer, b. 4 Jul 1918) appears in over 1,200 newspapers with an estimated readership of 90 million. Her only serious rival is "Dear Abby" (Mrs Pauline Phillips), her identical twin sister, based in Beverly Hills, CA.

CARTOON STRIPS

Earliest   "The Yellow Kid" first appeared in the *New York Journal* on 18 Oct 1896.

Most durable   The longest-lived newspaper comic strip is "The Katzenjammer Kids" (Hans and Fritz), created by Rudolph Dirks and first published in the *New York Journal* on 12 Dec 1897.

Most syndicated   "Peanuts" by Charles Schulz of Santa Rosa, CA, first published in October 1950, currently appears in 2,300 newspapers in 68 countries and 26 languages. In 1990 Schulz's income was estimated at $5 million per month.

Political cartoons   Ranan R. Lurie (USA; b. 26 May 1932) is the most widely syndicated political cartoonist in the world. As of March 1993 his work was published in 79 countries in 1,018 newspapers with a circulation of 85 million copies.

CIRCULATION

In 1992 the total number of morning and evening newspapers published in the United States was 1,570, with a total circulation of 60,083,265. There were 893 Sunday newspapers with a circulation of 62,542,031. The peak year for US newspapers was 1910, when there were 2,202.

The country with the leading number of newspaper readers in the world is Sweden, where 580 newspapers are sold for every 1,000 people.

Highest   The highest circulation for any newspaper in the world was that for *Komsomolskaya Pravda* (founded 1925), the youth paper of the former Soviet Communist Party, which reached a peak daily circulation of 21,975,000 copies in May 1990. The eight-page weekly newspaper *Argumenty i Fakty* (founded 1978) of Moscow, Russia attained a figure of 33,431,100 copies in May 1990, when it had an estimated readership of over 100 million.

United States   The highest-circulation daily newspaper in the United States is the *Wall Street Journal* (founded 1889), published by Dow Jones & Co. As of 31 March 1993, circulation was 1,852,967 copies.

PERIODICALS

Oldest   The oldest continuing periodical in the world is *Philosophical Transactions of the Royal Society*, published in London, Great Britain, which first appeared on 6 Mar 1665.

United States   The oldest continuously published periodical in the United States is *The Old Farmer's Almanac*, started in Massachusetts by Robert Thomas, a teacher and amateur astronomer, in 1792. *The Farmers Almanac*, as it was called originally, changed to its current title in 1848.

Largest circulations   The total dispersal through noncommercial channels by Jehovah's Witnesses of *The Truth that Leads to Eternal Life*, published by the Watchtower Bible and Tract Society of New York City on 8 May 1968, reached 107,562,995 in 117 languages by April 1991.

The peak circulation of any weekly periodical was achieved by *TV Guide*, which in 1974 became the first magazine to sell a billion copies in a year. As of December 1992 it had a circulation of 14.49 million. The world's highest-circulation magazine is currently *Modern Maturity*, with a figure as of December 1992 of 22.87 million.

In its 41 basic international editions, *Reader's Digest* (established February 1922) circulates 28.5 million copies monthly in 17 languages, including a US edition of more than 16.31 million copies. *Parade*, the syndicated color magazine, is distributed in a record 352 US newspapers every Sunday, giving a peak circulation since July 1993 of 36.73 million.

Largest   The bulkiest consumer magazine ever published was the January 1992 issue of *Hong Kong Toys*, running to 1,356 pages. Published by the Hong Kong Trade Development Council, it retails for HK$100 (about $12.50).

CROSSWORD PUZZLES

Earliest   Opinions differ on what constitutes a true crossword puzzle as distinct from other forms of word puzzle, but the earliest contender is considered to be a 25-letter acrostic of Roman provenance discovered on a wall in Cirencester, Great Britain in 1868. Another possible contender is an example of "blended squares," published in the women's magazine *The People's Home Journal* in September 1904. The modern crossword puzzle is believed to have evolved from Arthur Wynne's "Word Cross," published in the Sunday *New York World* on 21 Dec 1913.

Largest published   In July 1982 Robert Turcot of Québec, Canada compiled a crossword puzzle comprising 82,951 squares. It contained 12,489 clues across, 13,125 down, and covered 38.28 ft^2.

Compilers   The most prolific compiler is Roger F. Squires of Ironbridge, Great Britain, who compiles 39 published puzzles single-handedly each week. His total output to September 1991 was over 37,500 puzzles.

Fastest crossword puzzle solution   The fastest recorded time for completing *The Times* (London) crossword puzzle under test conditions is 3 min 45 sec, by Roy Dean of Bromley, Great Britain, in the British Broadcasting Corporation Today radio studio on 19 Dec 1970.

Dr John Sykes won *The Times*/Collins Dictionaries championship 10 times between 1972 and 1990, when he solved each of the four puzzles in an average time of 8 min and beat the field by a record margin of 9^1/$_2$ min on 8 Sep 1990 at the Hilton Hotel, London, Great Britain. He set a championship best time of 4 min 28 sec in 1989.

Slowest solution   In May 1966 *The Times* of London received an announcement from a Fijian woman that she had just succeeded in completing their crossword puzzle No. 673, published in the issue of 4 Apr 1932. As her husband, D.T. Lloyd, disclosed in a letter to *The Times* on 8 Feb 1990, he and his wife were stationed in Fiji by the British government. The problem wasn't that the puzzle was so fiendishly difficult—it was just that it was in an edition that had been used to wrap a package, and had subsequently lain uncompleted for 34 years.

MUSIC

Origins   Whistles and flutes made from perforated phalange bones (parts of fingers or toes) have been found at Upper Paleolithic sites of the Aurignacian period (*c.* 25,000–22,000 B.C.) at Istallóskö, Hungary and in Moldova.

The world's earliest surviving musical notation dates from *c.* 1800 B.C. A heptatonic scale deciphered from a clay tablet by Dr Duchesne-Guillemin in 1966–67 was found at a site in Nippur, Sumer, now Iraq. Musical history can, however, be traced back to the third millennium B.C., when the yellow bell (*huang zhong*) had a recognized standard musical tone in Chinese temple music.

The human voice   Before this century the extremes were a staccato E in *alt altissimo* (e^{iv}) by Ellen Beach Yaw (1869–1947) in Carnegie Hall, New York City on 19 Jan 1896, and an A_1 (55 Hz [cycles per sec]) by Kasper Foster (1617–73).

Madeleine Marie Robin (1918–60), the French operatic coloratura, could produce and sustain the B above high C in the Lucia mad scene in Donizetti's *Lucia di Lammermoor*. Ivan Rebroff, the German singer, has a voice that extends easily over four octaves, from a low F to a high F, one and a quarter octaves above C. Dan Britton of Branson, MI, can produce the note E-O (18.84 Hz).

The highest note put into song is G^{iv}, occurring in Mozart's *Popoli di Tessaglia*. The lowest vocal note in the classical repertoire is in Mozart's *Die Entführung aus dem Serail* in Osmin's aria, which calls for a low D (73.4 Hz).

SONGS

Oldest   The *shaduf* chant has been sung since time immemorial by irrigation workers on the human-powered, pivoted-rod bucket raisers of the Nile water mills (or *saqiyas*) in Egypt. The world's earliest surviving musical notation dates from *c.* 1800 B.C. An Assyrian love song, also *c.* 1800 B.C., to an Ugaritic god, from a tablet of notation and lyric, was reconstructed for an 11-string lyre at the University of California, Berkeley on 6 Mar 1974.

The oldest-known harmonized music performed today is the English song *Sumer is icumen in*, which dates from *c.* 1240.

National anthems   The oldest national anthem is the *Kimigayo* of Japan, the words of which date from the ninth century, although the music was written in 1881. The oldest music belongs to the anthem of the Netherlands, *Vilhelmus*, which was written *c.* 1570.

The shortest anthems are those of Japan, Jordan and San Marino, each with only four lines. Of the 11 wordless national anthems, the oldest is that of Spain, dating from 1770.

Top songs   The most frequently sung songs in English are *Happy Birthday to You* (based on the original *Good Morning to All*), by Kentucky Sunday school teachers Mildred Hill and Patty Smith Hill of New York (written in 1893 and under copyright from 1935 to 2010); *For He's a Jolly Good Fellow* (originally the French *Malbrouk*), known at least as early as 1781; and *Auld Lang Syne* (originally the Strathspey *I Fee'd a Lad at Michaelmass*), some words of which were written by Robert Burns (1759–1796). *Happy Birthday* was sung in space by the *Apollo IX* astronauts on 8 Mar 1969.

Songwriters   The most successful songwriters in terms of number-one singles are John Lennon (1940–80) and Paul McCartney (b. 18 Jun 1942). McCartney is credited as writer on 32 number-one hits in the United States to Lennon's 26 (with 23 co-written), whereas Lennon authored 29 Great Britain number-ones to McCartney's 28 (25 co-written).

Earliest hymns   The music and parts of the text of a hymn in the *Oxyrhynchus Papyri* from the second century are the earliest known hymnody. The earliest exactly datable hymn is the *Heyr Himna Smiður* (*Hear, the Maker of Heaven*) from 1208 by the Icelandic bard and chieftain Kolbeinn Tumason (1173–1208).

Longest hymns   The *Hora novissima tempora pessima sunt; vigilemus* by Bernard of Cluny (mid-12th century) runs to 2,966 lines. The longest in English is *The Sands of Time Are Sinking* by Anne Ross Cousin (nee Cundell, 1824–1906), which runs to 152 lines in full, though only 32 lines appear in the Methodist Hymn Book.

Worst singer   While no agreement exists as to the identity of history's greatest singer, there is unanimity on the worst. The excursions of the soprano Florence Foster Jenkins (1868–1944) into lieder and even high coloratura culminated on 25 Oct 1944 in her sellout concert at Carnegie Hall, New York City. The diva's high F was said to have been made still higher in 1943 by a crash in a taxi. It is one of the tragedies of musicology that Madame Jenkins's *Clavelitos*, accompanied by Cosme McMoon, was never recorded for posterity.

Longest rendering of a national anthem   "God Save the King" was played nonstop 16 or 17 times by a German military band on the platform of Rathenau railroad station, Brandenburg, Germany on the morning of 9 Feb 1909. The reason was that King Edward VII was struggling inside the train to put on a German field-marshal's uniform before he could emerge.

Most versions of the national anthem in 24 hours   Susan R. Jeske sang the *Star-Spangled Banner* live at 17 official events, attended by approximately 60,000 people, in California within a 24 hr period on 3–4 Jul 1992. She traveled to the functions by automobile, helicopter and boat.

Most prolific hymnist Frances (Fanny) Jane van Alstyne (nee Crosby, 1820–1915) of the United States wrote 8,500 hymns and is reputed to have knocked off one hymn in 15 minutes.

Oldest choral society The oldest active choral society in the United States is the Handel and Haydn Society of Boston, which gave its first concert performance on Christmas Day 1815 at Stone Chapel (now King's Chapel). The Handel and Haydn Society also gave the first complete performance of The Messiah in the United States on 25 Dec 1818 at Boylston Hall, Boston. It celebrated its 175th anniversary in 1990.

BELLS

Oldest The world's oldest bell is the tintinnabulum found in the Babylonian Palace of Nimrod in 1849 by Mr (later Sir) Austen Henry Layard (1817–94), dating from *c*. 1100 B.C. The oldest-known tower bell is one in St Benedict Church, Rome, Italy, that bears the date "anno domini millesimo sexagesimo IX" (1069).

United States The oldest bell in the United States is located at St Stephens Episcopal Church in East Haddam, CT. The bell was cast in Spain in 815 A.D. and shipped to the United States in 1834.

Heaviest The Tsar Kolokol, cast by Russian brothers I.F. and M.I. Motorin on 25 Nov 1735 in Moscow, weighs 222.6 tons, measures 22 ft in diameter and 20 ft high, and is 24 in at its thickest point. The bell was cracked in a fire in 1737 and a fragment, weighing about 12.91 tons, was broken from it. The bell has stood, unrung, on a platform in the Kremlin in Moscow since 1836 with the broken section alongside.

The heaviest bell still in use is the Mingun bell, weighing 101 tons, with a diameter of 16 ft 8½ in at the lip, in Mandalay, Myanmar (formerly Burma). The bell is struck by a teak boom from the outside. It was cast at Mingun late in the reign of King Bodawpaya (1782–1819). The heaviest swinging bell in the world is the Petersglocke in the southwest tower of Cologne Cathedral, Germany, cast in 1923, with a diameter of 11 ft 1¾ in, weighing 28 tons.

United States The largest bell in the United States weighs 17 tons and hangs at St Francis de Scelle church in Cincinnati, OH. It was cast *c*. 1895. The heaviest ring in the United States is that of 10 bells cast in 1963 for the Washington National Cathedral, Washington, D.C. The total bell weight is 13,682 lb—the heaviest bell weighs 3,588 lb.

Peals A ringing peal is defined as a diatonic "ring" of five or more bells hung for full-circle change ringing. Of 5,517 rings so hung, only 92 are outside the British Isles. The heaviest ring in the world is that of 13 bells cast in 1938–39 for the Anglican Cathedral in Liverpool, Great Britain. The total bell weight is 18.5 tons, of which Emmanuel, the tenor bell note *A*, weighs 9,195 lb.

Bell ringing Eight bells have been rung to their full "extent" (40,320 unrepeated changes) only once without relays. This took place in a bell foundry at Loughborough, Great Britain, beginning at 6:52 A.M. on 27 Jul 1963 and ending at 12:50 A.M. on 28 July, after 17 hr 58 min. The peal was composed by Kenneth Lewis of Altrincham, Great Britain, and the eight ringers were conducted by Robert B. Smith of Marple, Great Britain.

The greatest number of peals (minimum of 5,000 changes, all in tower bells) rung in a year is 303, by Colin Turner of Abingdon, Great Britain in 1989.

The late George E. Fearn rang 2,666 peals from 1928 to May 1974. Matthew Lakin (1801–1899) was a regular bell-ringer at Tetney Church near Grimsby, Great Britain for 84 years.

Largest carillon   The largest carillon (minimum of 23 bells) in the world is at Kirk in the Hills Presbyterian Church, Bloomfield, MI. The carillon is made up of 77 bells. *M*, the largest, weighs 8 tons.

INSTRUMENTS

Earliest piano   The earliest pianoforte in existence is one built in Florence, Italy in 1720 by Bartolommeo Cristofori (1655–1731) of Padua, and now preserved in the Metropolitan Museum of Art, New York City.

Grandest piano   The grandest grand piano was one of 1.4 tons and 11 ft 8 in in length made by Chas H. Challen & Son Ltd of London, Great Britain in 1935. Its longest bass string measured 9 ft 11 in, with a tensile strength of 33 tons.

Most expensive piano   The highest price ever paid for a piano was $390,000 at Sotheby Parke Bernet, New York City on 26 Mar 1980 for a Steinway grand of *c*. 1888 sold by the Martin Beck Theater. It was bought by a non-pianist.

Largest organ   The largest and loudest musical instrument ever constructed is the now only partially functional Auditorium Organ in Atlantic City, NJ. Completed in 1930, this instrument had two consoles (one with seven manuals and another movable one with five), 1,477 stop controls and 33,112 pipes, ranging in tone from $1/5$ in to the 64 ft tone. It had the volume of 25 brass bands, with a range of seven octaves.

The world's largest fully functional organ is the six manual 30,067 pipe Grand Court Organ installed in the Wanamaker Department Store, Philadelphia, PA in 1911 and enlarged between then and 1930. It has a 64 ft tone gravissima pipe.

The world's largest church organ is that in Passau Cathedral, Germany. It was completed in 1928 and has 16,000 pipes and five manuals. The chapel organ at the United States Military Academy at West Point, NY has, since 1911, been expanded from 2,406 to 18,200 pipes.

The world's most powerful electronic organ is Robert A. Nye's 7,000-watt "Golden Spirit" organ, designed by Henry N. Hunsicker. It has 700 speakers and made its public concert debut in Trump Castle, Atlantic City, NJ on 9 Dec 1988.

Largest brass instrument   The largest recorded brass instrument is a tuba standing $7^{1/2}$ ft tall, with 39 ft of tubing and a bell 3 ft 4 in across. This contrabass tuba was constructed for a world tour by the band of American composer John Philip Sousa (1854–1932), *c*. 1896–98.

Largest stringed instrument   The largest movable stringed instrument ever constructed was a pantaleon with 270 strings stretched over 50 ft^2 used by George Noel in 1767.

The greatest number of musicians required to operate a single instrument were the six required to play the gigantic orchestrion, known as the Apollonican, built in 1816 and played until 1840.

Largest double bass   A double bass measuring 14 ft tall was built in 1924 in Ironia, NJ by Arthur K. Ferris. It weighed 1,301 lb with a sound box 8 ft across, and had leather strings totaling 104 ft. Its low notes could be felt rather than heard.

Largest guitar   The largest playable guitar in the world is 38 ft 2 in tall, 16 ft wide and weighs 1,865 lb. It was made by students of Shakamak High School in Jasonville, IN, and was unveiled on 17 May 1991 when, powered by six amplifiers, it was played simultaneously by six members of the school.

Most expensive guitar   A Fender Stratocaster belonging to legendary rock guitarist Jimi Hendrix (1942–70) was sold by his former drummer Mitch Mitchell to an anonymous buyer for £198,000 ($338,580) at Sotheby's, London on 25 Apr 1990.

Most valuable violin   The highest price paid at auction for a violin is £902,000 ($1.7 million) for the 1720 "Mendelssohn" Stradivarius. It was sold to a mystery buyer at Christie's, London on 21 Nov 1990.

Most valuable cello   The highest auction price for a violoncello is £682,000 (approximately $1.2 million) at Sotheby's, London on 22 Jun 1988 for a Stradivarius known as "The Cholmondeley," which was made in Cremona, Italy *c.* 1698.

Double bass playing   Sixteen musicians from Blandford, Dorset, Great Britain played a double bass simultaneously (five fingering and eleven bowing) in a rendition of Strauss' *Perpetuum Mobile* at Blandford Town Hall on 6 Jun 1989.

Drumming   Four hundred separate drums were played in 20.50 sec by Carl Williams at the Alexander Stadium, Birmingham, Great Britain on 4 Oct 1992.

Loudest organ stop   The Ophicleide stop of the Grand Great in the Solo Organ in the Atlantic City Auditorium (see Instruments, Largest organ) is operated by a pressure of water $3^{1}/_{2}$ lb/in^2 and has a pure trumpet note of ear-splitting volume, more than six times the volume of the loudest locomotive whistles.

Largest pan pipes   The world's largest pan pipes, created by Simon Desorgher and Lawrence Casserley, consist of five contrabass pipes, each 4 in in diameter, with lengths of 19 in, 16 in, 14 in, 12 in and 10 in respectively, and five bass pipes of 2 in diameter with lengths of 9.5 in, 8 in, 7 in, 6 in and 5 in. Their first public appearance was at Jubilee Gardens, London, Great Britain on 9 Jul 1988.

Largest drum   A drum with a 13 ft diameter was built by the Supreme Drum Co., London, Great Britain and played at the Royal Festival Hall, London on 31 May 1987.

Largest drum kit   A drum kit consisting of 112 pieces—88 drums, 18 cymbals, 4 hi-hats, 1 gong, 1 cowbell and various other assorted accessories—was constructed by Jeffrey Carlo of Brentwood, NY, in 1990.

Longest alphorn   A 154 ft 8 in (excluding mouthpiece) long alphorn weighing 227 lb was completed by Swiss-born Peter Wutherich, of Boise, ID in December 1989. The diameter at the bell is $24\frac{1}{2}$ in and the sound takes 105.7 milliseconds to emerge from the bowl after entry into the mouthpiece.

Highest and lowest notes   The extremes of orchestral instruments (excluding the organ) range from a handbell tuned to g^v (6,272 cycles/sec) to the sub-contrabass clarinet, which can reach C_{11} or 16.4 cycles/sec. The highest note on a standard pianoforte is c^v (4,186 cycles/sec), which is also the violinist's limit. In 1873 a sub-double bassoon able to reach B_{111} ± or 14.6 cycles/sec was constructed, but no surviving specimen is known.

The extremes for the organ are g^{vi} (the sixth G above middle C) (12544 cycles/sec) and C_{111} (8.12 cycles/sec), obtainable from $\frac{3}{4}$ in and 64 ft pipes respectively.

ORCHESTRAS

Oldest   The first modern symphony orchestra—basically four sections consisting of woodwind, brass, percussion and bowed string instruments—was

---

Bottle orchestra   In an extraordinary display of oral campanology (bell ringing), the Brighton Bottle Orchestra—consisting of Terry Garoghan and Peter Miller—performed a musical medley on 444 Gordon's gin bottles at the Brighton International Festival, Great Britain on 21 May 1991. It took 18 hours to tune the bottles, and about 10 times the normal rate of puff (90 breaths/min) to play them. There was no risk of intoxication, as the bottles were filled with water.

Musical chairs   The largest game on record was one starting with 8,238 participants, ending with Xu Chong Wei on the last chair, which was held at the Anglo-Chinese School, Singapore on 5 Aug 1989.

Baton twirling   The greatest number of complete spins done between tossing a baton into the air and catching it is 10, by Donald Garcia, on the British Broadcasting Corporation *Record Breakers* TV program on 9 Dec 1986. The record for women is seven, shared by Lisa Fedick on the same program; Joanne Holloway, at Great Britain National Baton Twirling Association Championships in Paignton, Great Britain on 29 Oct 1987; and Rachel Hayes, on 18 Sep 1988.

founded at the court of Duke Karl Theodor at Mannheim, Germany in 1743. The oldest existing symphony orchestra, the Gewandhaus Orchestra of Leipzig, Germany, was also established in 1743. Originally known as the Grosses Concert and later as the Liebhaber-Concerte, its current name dates from 1781.

United States The oldest orchestra in the United States is the Philharmonic-Symphony Society of New York, which was founded by Ureli Corelli Hill in 1842.

Largest On 17 Jun 1872, Johann Strauss the younger (1825–99) conducted an orchestra of 987 pieces supported by a choir of 20,000, at the World Peace Jubilee in Boston, MA. The number of first violinists was 400.

On 14 Dec 1991 the 2,000-piece "Young People's Orchestra and Chorus of Mexico," consisting of 53 youth orchestras from Mexico plus musicians from Venezuela and the former USSR, gave a full classical concert conducted by Fernando Lozano and others at the Magdalena Mixhiuca Sports Center, Mexico City.

Largest band The most massive band ever assembled was one of 20,100 players at the Ullevaal Stadium, Oslo, Norway from Norges Musikkorps Forbund bands on 28 Jun 1964.

One-man band Rory Blackwell, of Starcross, Great Britain, aided by his double left-footed perpendicular percussion-pounder, plus his three-tier right-footed horizontal 22-pronged differential beater, and his 12-outlet bellow-powered horn-blower, played 108 different instruments (19 melody and 89 percussion) simultaneously in Dawlish, Great Britain on 29 May 1989. He also played 314 instruments in a single rendition in 1 min 23.07 sec, also at Dawlish, on 27 May 1985.

Marching band The largest marching band was one of 4,524, including 1,342 majorettes, under the direction of entertainer Danny Kaye (1913–87) at Dodger Stadium, Los Angeles, CA on 15 Apr 1985.

Musical march The longest recorded musical march was one of 46.7 miles, by members of showband Marum, a Dutch marching band, who walked from Assen to Marum, Netherlands on 9 May 1992. Of the 60 people who started, 52 managed to complete the march in 13 hr 50 min.

Conductors The Austrian conductor Herbert von Karajan (1908–89), principal conductor of the Berlin Philharmonic Orchestra for 35 years before his retirement from the position shortly before his death, was the most prolific conductor ever, having made over 800 recordings of all the major works.

The 1991–92 season was the 58th for the Cork Symphony Orchestra (Cork, Republic of Ireland) under the baton of Dr Aloys Fleischmann (1910–92).

Sir Georg Solti (b. 22 Oct 1912), the Hungarian-born principal conductor of the Chicago Symphony Orchestra, has won a record 31 Grammy awards for his recordings. (See also Most Grammy awards.)

United States The Chicago Symphony Orchestra was directed by Frederic Stock from 1905 until his death in 1942, a total of 37 seasons.

Largest choir Excluding "singalongs" by stadium crowds, the greatest choir is one of 60,000, which sang in unison as a finale of a choral contest among 160,000 participants in Breslau, Germany on 2 Aug 1937.

CONCERT ATTENDANCES

Classical An estimated record 800,000 attended a free open-air concert by the New York Philharmonic conducted by Zubin Mehta, on the Great Lawn of Central Park, New York City on 5 Jul 1986, as part of the Statue of Liberty Weekend.

Rock/pop festival The best claim is believed to be 725,000 for Steve Wozniak's 1983 US Festival in San Bernardino, CA. The Woodstock Music and Art Fair held on 15–17 Aug 1969 at Bethel, NY is thought to have attracted an audience of 300,000–500,000.

Solo performer The largest *paying* audience ever attracted by a solo performer was an estimated 180,000–184,000 in the Maracaña Stadium, Rio de Janeiro, Brazil to hear Paul McCartney (b. 1942) on 21 Apr 1990. Jean-Michel Jarre, the *son et lumière* specialist, entertained an estimated audience of two million in Paris, France at a free Bastille Day concert in 1990.

Most successful concert tour The Rolling Stones' 1989 "Steel Wheels" North American tour earned an estimated $310 million and was attended by 3.2 million people in 30 cities.

Most successful concert series Michael Jackson sold out for seven nights at Wembley, London, Great Britain in the summer of 1988. The stadium has a capacity of 72,000, so a total of 504,000 people saw Jackson perform 14–16, 22–23 Jul and 26–27 Aug 1988.

Singer's pulling power In 1850, up to $653 was paid for a single seat at the US concerts of Johanna ("Jenny") Maria Lind (1820–87), the "Swedish nightingale." She had a range from g to e[111], of which the middle register is still regarded as unrivaled.

Most durable musicians The Romanian pianist Cual Delavrancea (1887–1991) gave her last public recital, receiving six encores, at the age of 103. The longest international career in the history of Western music is held by Polish pianist Mieczyslaw Horszowski (1892–1993), who played for Emperor Franz-Joseph in Vienna, Austria in 1899 and was still playing in 1991.

The world's oldest active musician is Jennie Newhouse (b. 12 Jul 1889) of High Bentham, Great Britain, who has been the regular organist at the church of St Boniface in Bentham since 1920.

Clapping The duration record for continuous clapping (sustaining an average of 160 claps per min, audible at 120 yd) is 58 hr 9 min by V. Jeyaraman of Tamil Nadu, India from 12–15 Feb 1988.

SOLO PERFORMER (Above) The spectacular sight of an estimated 2 million people at La Defense, Paris, France for Jean-Michel Jarre's free *son et lumière* show on Bastille Day 1990. (Photo: Sygma/Jean Jean)

SINGER'S PULLING POWER (Left) "Jenny" Lind, the Swedish Nightingale, whose unrivaled singing voice could command ticket prices of $653 in 1850. (Photo: Bridgeman Art Library/Philip Mould, Historical Portraits Ltd)

Largest concert   On 21 Jul 1990, Potsdamer Platz, straddling East and West Berlin, was the site of the largest single rock concert in terms of participants and organization ever staged. Roger Waters' production of Pink Floyd's "The Wall" involved 600 people performing on a stage measuring 551 × 82 ft at its highest point. An estimated 200,000 people gathered for the symbolic building and demolition of a wall made of 2,500 Styrofoam blocks.

COMPOSERS

Most prolific   The most prolific composer of all time was probably Georg Philipp Telemann (1681–1767) of Germany. He composed 12 complete sets of services (one cantata every Sunday) for a year, 78 services for special occasions, 40 operas, 600 to 700 orchestral suites, 44 passions, plus concertos, sonatas and other chamber music. The most prolific symphonist was Johann Melchior Molter (*c.* 1695–1765) of Germany, who wrote over 170 symphonies. Franz Joseph Haydn (1732–1809) of Austria wrote 108 numbered symphonies, many of which are regularly played today.

Longest symphony   The longest single classical symphony is the orchestral Symphony No. 3 in D Minor by Gustav Mahler (1860–1911) of Austria. This work, composed in 1896, requires a contralto, a women's and a boys' choir in addition to a full orchestra. A full performance requires 1 hr 40 min, of which the first movement alone takes between 30 and 36 min.

The Symphony No. 2 (the Gothic), composed from 1919–22 by William Havergal Brian (Great Britain; 1876–1972), was played by over 800 performers (four brass bands) in the Victoria Hall, Hanley, Staffordshire, Great Britain on 21 May 1978 (conductor Trevor Stokes). A recent broadcast required 1 hr 45½ min. Brian wrote an even vaster work based on Shelley's "Prometheus Unbound" lasting 4 hr 11 min, but the full score has been missing since 1961.

The symphony *Victory at Sea*, written by US composer Richard Rodgers (1902–1979) and arranged by Robert Russell Bennett for NBC TV in 1952, lasted 13 hours.

Longest piano composition   The longest continuous nonrepetitious piano piece ever published is *The Well-Tuned Piano* by La Monte Young, first presented by the Dia Art Foundation at the Concert Hall, Harrison St, New York City on 28 Feb 1980. The piece lasted 4 hr 12 min 10 sec.

Symphonic Variations, composed in the 1930s for piano and orchestra by the British-born Kaikhosru Shapurji Sorabji (1892–1988) on 500 pages of close manuscript in three volumes, would last for six hours at the prescribed tempo.

OPERA

Longest   The longest of commonly performed operas is *Die Meistersinger von Nürnberg* by Wilhelm Richard Wagner (1813–83) of Germany. A normal uncut performance of this opera entails 5 hr 15 min of music. *The Heretics* by Gabriel von Wayditch (1888–1969), a Hungarian-American, is orchestrated for 110 pieces and lasts 8½ hr.

Shortest   The shortest opera published is *The Sounds of Time* by Simon Rees and Peter Reynolds, first performed by Rhian Owen and Dominic Burns on 27 Mar 1993 at Hayes, Wales; it lasted for 4 min 9 sec.

Most curtain calls   On 24 Feb 1988 Luciano Pavarotti (b. 12 Oct 1935) received 165 curtain calls and was applauded for 1 hr 7 min after singing the part of Nemorino in Gaetano Donizetti's *L'elisir d'Amore* at the Deutsche Oper in Berlin, Germany.

Longest silence   The longest interval between the known composition of a piece by a major composer and its performance in the manner intended is from 3 Mar 1791 until 9 Oct 1982 (over 191 years), in the case of Mozart's *Organ Piece for a Clock*, a fugue fantasy in F minor (K 608), arranged by the organ builders Wm Hill & Son and Norman & Beard Ltd at Glyndebourne, Great Britain.

Longest aria   The longest single aria, in the sense of an operatic solo, is Brünnhilde's immolation scene in Wagner's *Götterdämmerung*. A well-known recording of this has been precisely timed at 14 min 46 sec.

Youngest opera singer   Ginetta Gloria La Bianca, born in Buffalo, NY on 12 May 1934, sang Rosina in *The Barber of Seville* at the Teatro dell' Opera, Rome, Italy on 8 May 1950 at the age of 15 years 361 days, having appeared as Gilda in *Rigoletto* at Velletri 45 days earlier.

Oldest opera singers   The tenor Giovanni Martinelli sang Emperor Altoum in *Turandot* in Seattle, WA on 4 Feb 1967 when he was 81. Danshi Toyotake (b. Yoshie Yokota, 1891–1989) of Hyogo, Japan sang *Musume Gidayu* (traditional Japanese narrative) for 91 years from the age of seven. Her professional career spanned 81 years.

Largest opera houses   The Metropolitan Opera House, Lincoln Center, New York City, completed in September 1966 at a cost of $45.7 million, has a standing and seating capacity of 4,065 with 3,800 seats in an auditorium 451 ft deep. The stage is 230 ft wide and 148 ft deep.

The tallest opera house is in a 42-story building on Wacker Drive in Chicago, IL, which houses the Chicago Lyric Opera Company. The Teatro della Scala (La Scala) in Milan, Italy shares with the Bolshoi Theatre in Moscow, Russia the distinction of having the greatest number of tiers—six.

First opera company in US   The first opera company in the United States was The American Company, founded in 1752 by Lewis Hallam. The oldest continuously performing opera company in the United States is the Metropolitan Opera Company of New York City; its first season was in 1883.

Longest operatic encore   The longest operatic encore was of the entire opera *Il Matrimonio Segreto* by Cimarosa at its premiere in 1792. This was at the command of the Austro-Hungarian emperor Leopold II (r. 1790–92).

BALLET

Fastest "entrechat douze"   In the *entrechat*, the starting and finishing position each count as one, so that in an *entrechat douze* there are five crossings and uncrossings. This feat was performed by Wayne Sleep for the British Broadcasting Corporation *Record Breakers* TV program on 7 Jan 1973. He was in the air for 0.71 sec.

Grands jetés   On 28 Nov 1988, Wayne Sleep completed 158 grands jetés along the length of Dunston Staiths, Great Britain in 2 min.

Most turns   The greatest number of spins called for in classical ballet choreography is 32 *fouettés rond de jambe en tournant* in *Swan Lake* by Piotr Ilyich Tchaikovsky (1840–93). Delia Gray (Great Britain; b. 30 Oct 1975) achieved 166 such turns during the Harlow Ballet School's summer workshop at The Playhouse, Harlow, Great Britain on 2 Jun 1991.

Most curtain calls   The greatest recorded number of curtain calls ever received is 89, by Dame Margot Fonteyn de Arias (nee Margaret Evelyn Hookham; 1919–91) and Rudolf Hametovich Nureyev (1938–93) after a performance of *Swan Lake* at the Vienna Staatsoper, Austria in October 1964.

RECORDED SOUND

Origins   The phonograph was first conceived by Charles Cros (1842–88), a French poet and scientist, who described his idea in sealed papers deposited with the French Academy of Sciences on 30 Apr 1877. However, the realization of a practical device was first achieved by Thomas Alva Edison (1847–1931) of the United States.

The first successful wax cylinder machine was constructed by Edison's mechanic, John Kruesi, on 4–6 Dec 1877, demonstrated on 7 Dec and patented on 19 Feb 1878. The horizontal disc was introduced by Emile Berliner (1851–1929) and first demonstrated in Philadelphia on 18 May 1888.

Earliest recordings   The oldest existing recording was made in 1878 by Augustus Stroh, but it remains on the mandrel of his machine and has never been played. The oldest playable record is believed to be an engraved metal cylinder made by Frank Lambert in 1878 or 1879 and voicing the hours on the clock. The recording is owned by Aaron Cramer of New York City.

Tape recording   Magnetic recording was invented by Valdemar Poulsen (1869–1942) of Denmark with his steel wire Telegraphone in 1898 (US Pat. No. 661619). Fritz Pfleumer (German Patent 500900) introduced tape in 1928. Tapes were first used at the Blattner Studios, Elstree, Great Britain in 1929. Plastic tapes were devised by BASF of Germany in 1932–35, but were first marketed in 1950 by Recording Associates of New York.

Smallest cassette   The NT digital cassette made by the Sony Corporation of Japan for use in dictating machines measures just $1^{1}/_{5} \times {}^{4}/_{5} \times {}^{1}/_{5}$ in.

Smallest functional record   Six titles of $1^{5}/_{16}$ in diameter were recorded by HMV's studio at Hayes, Great Britain on 26 Jan 1923 for Queen Mary's Doll's

House. Some 92,000 of these miniature records were pressed, including 35,000 of *God Save the King*.

Most successful solo recording artist   Although no independently audited figures have ever been published for Elvis Aron Presley (1935–77), he has had over 170 major hit singles and over 80 top-selling albums since 1956.

Most successful group   The singers with the greatest sales of any group have been the Beatles. This group from Liverpool, Great Britain was comprised of George Harrison (b. 25 Feb 1943), John Lennon (1940–1980), James Paul McCartney (b. 18 Jun 1942) and Richard Starkey, alias Ringo Starr (b. 7 Jul 1940). The all-time Beatles sales up to May 1985 have been estimated by EMI at over one billion discs and tapes. All four ex-Beatles sold many million more records as solo artists.

Earliest golden discs   The first actual golden disc was one sprayed by RCA Victor for the US trombonist and bandleader Alton "Glenn" Miller (1904–44) for his *Chattanooga Choo Choo* on 10 Feb 1942.

Phonographic identification   Dr Arthur B. Lintgen (b. 1932) of Rydal, PA has an as-yet unique and proven ability to identify the music on phonograph records purely by visual inspection without hearing a note.

Smallest recorder   In April 1983 Olympic Optical Industry Co. of Japan marketed a micro-cassette recorder measuring $4^{1}/_{5}$ x 2 x $^{1}/_{2}$ in and weighing 4.4 oz.

Most Grammy awards   An all-time record 31 awards (including a special Trustees' award presented in 1967) have been won since 1958 by the British conductor Sir Georg Solti (b. Hungary; 21 Oct 1912), while the Chicago Symphony now has 46. The greatest number won in a year is eight, by Michael Jackson in 1984.

Best-selling classical album   *In Concert* is the best-selling classical album, with sales of five million to date. It was recorded by José Carreras, Placido Domingo and Luciano Pavarotti at the 1990 Soccer World Cup Finals in Rome, Italy.

Largest record store   HMV opened the world's largest record store at 150 Oxford Street, London, Great Britain on 24 Oct 1986.

Fastest rapper   Rebel X.C. of Chicago, IL rapped 674 syllables in 54.9 sec at the Hair Bear Recording Studio, Alsip, IL on 27 Aug 1992.

Number one in most countries   The most successful singer on records is Madonna (Madonna Louise Veronica Ciccone, b. 16 Aug 1958). Her album *True Blue*, with sales of over 17 million, was number one in 28 countries.

The first record eventually to aggregate a total sale of a million copies was of performances by Enrico Caruso (b. Naples, Italy, 1873, d. 2 Aug 1921) of the aria *"Vesti la giubba"* ("On with the Motley") from the opera *I Pagliacci* by Ruggiero Leoncavallo (1858–1919), the earliest version of which was recorded with piano on 12 Nov 1902. The first single recording to surpass the million mark was *Carry Me Back to Old Virginny*, sung by Alma Gluck, on the Red Seal Victor label on the 12-inch single-faced (later backed) record No. 74420.

Most golden discs   The only *audited* measure of gold, platinum and multiplatinum singles and albums within the United States is certification by the Recording Industry Association of America (RIAA), introduced on 14 Mar 1958.

The Rolling Stones, with 56 (34 gold, 16 platinum, 6 multiplatinum) have the most for any group. The group with the most multiplatinum albums is the Beatles, with 11.

In August 1992, following new audit figures, the estate of Elvis Presley was presented with 110 gold and platinum records, making him the most certified recording artist ever. The female solo artist to receive the most awards is Barbra Streisand, with 56 (7 gold singles, 30 gold albums and 20 platinum albums).

The first platinum album was awarded to the Eagles for *Greatest Hits, 1971–75* in 1976. The group Chicago holds the record for most platinum albums, with 17. Barbra Streisand holds the record for a solo artist, with 19, and the record for most multiplatinum, with seven. Paul McCartney holds the record for a male solo artist, with 12 platinum, while Billy Joel holds the record for the most multiplatinum albums for an individual, with eight.

Most recordings   One hundred and eighty compact discs containing the complete set of authenticated works by Mozart were produced by Philips Classics for release in 1990/91 to commemorate the bicentennial of the composer's death. The complete set comprises over 200 hours of music and would occupy $6^1/_2$ ft of shelving.

Biggest sellers (singles)   The greatest seller of any phonograph record to date is *White Christmas* by Irving Berlin (b. Israel Bailin, 1888–1989), recorded by Bing Crosby on 29 May 1942. North American sales alone reached 170,884,207 copies by 30 Jun 1987.

The highest claim for any "rock" record is an unaudited 25 million for *Rock Around the Clock*, copyrighted in 1953 by James E. Myers under the name Jimmy De Knight and the late Max C. Freedmann and recorded on 12 Apr 1954 by Bill Haley (1927–1981) and the Comets.

Biggest sellers (albums)   The best-selling album of all time is *Thriller* by Michael Jackson (b. 29 Aug 1958), with global sales of over 47 million copies to date. The best-selling album by a group is Fleetwood Mac's *Rumours* with over 21 million sales by May 1990.

Whitney Houston by Whitney Houston, released in 1985, is the best-selling debut album of all time. It has sold over 14 million copies, including over nine million in the United States, one million in Great Britain, and a further million in Canada.

Soundtrack   The best-selling movie soundtrack is *Saturday Night Fever*, with sales of over 26.5 million by May 1987.

LARGEST CONTRACTS

Michael Jackson ....$890 million* (Sony, March 1991)
Prince............................$100 million (Time Warner, September 1992)
Madonna...$60 million (Time Warner, 1992)
Paul McCartney..........$65 million (£100 million) (Capitol–EMI, 1993)
Barbra Streisand ....$40–60 million (Sony, December 1992)
Elton John/ ....$410 million (Time Warner, November 1992)
 Bernie Taupin
Rolling Stones ....$30–40 million (Virgin, November 1991)
Motley Crue ....+$35 million (Elektra Records)
Janet Jackson ....+$32–35 million (Virgin, March 1991)
Aerosmith..+$30 million (Columbia Records)

Prospective earnings of $1 billion were reported.

The charts (US singles)   Singles record charts were first published by *Billboard* on 20 Jul 1940, when the No. 1 single was *I'll Never Smile Again* by Tommy Dorsey (1905–56) with vocals by Frank Sinatra. *Near You* by Francis Craig stayed at the No. 1 spot for 17 weeks in 1947.

The Beatles have had the most No. 1's (20), Conway Twitty (1933–93) the most Country No. 1's (35) and Aretha Franklin the most Rhythm and Blues No. 1's (20). Aretha Franklin is also the female solo artist with the most million-selling singles, with 14 between 1967 and 1973. Elvis Presley has had the most hit singles on *Billboard*'s Hot 100—149 from 1956 to May 1990.

Bing Crosby's *White Christmas* spent a total of 72 weeks on the chart between 1942 and 1962, while *Tainted Love* by Soft Cell stayed on the chart for 43 *consecutive* weeks from January 1982.

The charts (US albums)   *Billboard* first published an album chart on 15 Mar 1945, when the No. 1 was *King Cole Trio* featuring Nat "King" Cole (1919–65). *South Pacific* was No. 1 for 69 weeks (nonconsecutive) from May 1949. *Dark Side of the Moon* by Pink Floyd enjoyed 730 weeks on the *Billboard* charts to April 1989.

The Beatles had the most No. 1's (15), Elvis Presley was the most successful male soloist (nine), and Simon and Garfunkel the top duo with three. Elvis Presley has had the most hit albums (94 from 1956 to April 1989).

The woman with the most No. 1 albums (six), and most hit albums in total (40 between 1963 and April 1992), is Barbra Streisand. (See Most golden discs.)

Fastest-selling   The fastest-selling non-pop record of all time is *John Fitzgerald Kennedy—A Memorial Album* (Premium Albums), recorded on 22 Nov 1963, the day of President Kennedy's assassination, which sold 4 million copies at 99 cents in six days (7–12 Dec 1963).

Advance sales   The greatest advance sale for a single worldwide is 2.1 million for *Can't Buy Me Love* by the Beatles, released on 21 Mar 1964.

Compact discs   Developed by Philips and Sony in 1978 and introduced in 1982, the compact disc (CD) increasingly challenges the LP and cassette as a recording medium. The first CD to sell a million copies worldwide was Dire Straits' *Brothers in Arms* in 1986. It subsequently topped a million sales in Europe alone.

DANCING

Marathon dancing must be distinguished from choreomania (dancing mania), or tarantism, which is a pathological condition. The worst outbreak of the latter was at Aachen, Germany in July 1374, when hordes of men and women broke into a frenzied and compulsive choreomania in the streets. It lasted for many hours until injury or complete exhaustion ensued.

Largest and longest dances An estimated 30,000 people took part in a Madison/Electric Slide line dance held during the 1991 Comin' Home African American Holiday Celebration in Columbus, OH on 12 Jul 1991.

The most taxing marathon dance staged as a public spectacle was one by Mike Ritof and Edith Boudreaux, who logged 5,148 hr 28½ min to win $2,000 at Chicago's Merry Garden Ballroom, Belmont and Sheffield, IL from 29 Aug 1930 to 1 Apr 1931. Rest periods were progressively cut from 20 to 10 to 5 to zero minutes per hour, with 10-inch steps and a maximum of 15 seconds for closure of eyes.

Cathy McConochie led an ensemble of 18 dancers through the streets of Sacramento, CA on 30 May 1992 during the Sacramento Children's Festival, in a choreographed routine, covering a distance of 8.8 miles.

Ballroom The world's most successful professional ballroom dancing champions have been Bill and Bobbie Irvine, who won 13 world titles between 1960 and 1968. The oldest competitive ballroom dancer was Albert J. Sylvester (1889–1989) of Corsham, Great Britain, who retired at the age of 94.

The oldest competitive ballroom dancer in the United States is Lorna S. Lengfeld, who is still competing at the age of 89.

Conga The longest recorded conga was the Miami Super Conga, held in conjunction with Calle Ocho—a party to which Cuban-Americans invite the rest of Miami for a celebration of life together. Held on 13 Mar 1988, the conga line consisted of 119,986 people.

Country dancing The largest genuine Scottish country dance ever held was a 512-person reel, held in Toronto, Ontario, Canada on 17 Aug 1991 and organized by the Toronto branch of the Royal Scottish Country Dance Society.

Flamenco The fastest flamenco dancer ever measured is Solero de Jerez, age 17, who in Brisbane, Australia in September 1967 attained 16 heel taps per second, in an electrifying routine.

Limbo The lowest height for a bar (flaming) under which a limbo dancer has passed is 6 in off the floor, by Dennis Walston, alias King Limbo, at Kent, WA on 2 Mar 1991.

The record for a performer on roller skates is 5⅛ in, achieved by Amitesh

Purohit at the national sub-junior school championships held at Indore, Madhya Pradesh, India on 19 Jul 1991.

Tap   The fastest *rate* ever measured for tap dancing is 32 taps per second, by Stephen Gare of Sutton Coldfield, Great Britain, at the Grand Hotel, Birmingham, Great Britain on 28 Mar 1990.

Roy Castle (b. 1933), host of the British Broadcasting Corporation *Record Breakers* TV program, achieved one million taps in 23 hr 44 min at the Guinness World of Records exhibition, London, Great Britain on 31 Oct–1 Nov 1985.

The greatest-ever assemblage of tap dancers in a single routine numbered 6,008 outside Macy's department store at 34th Street and Sixth Avenue, New York City on 23 Aug 1992.

Square dance calling   Alan Covacic called for 26 hr 2 min for the Wheelers and Dealers Square Dance Club at RAF Halton, Aylesbury, Great Britain from 18–19 Nov 1988.

Gladiatorial combat   Emperor Trajan of Rome (A.D. 98–117) staged a display involving 4,941 pairs of gladiators over 117 days. Publius Ostorius, a freedman, survived 51 combats in Pompeii.

Dancing dragon   The longest dancing dragon, created by South Yorkshire Cubscouts in Great Britain, measured 3,481 ft from the end of its tongue to the tip of its tail. A total of 1,118 people brought the dragon to life, making it dance for 5 minutes at the Don Valley Stadium, Sheffield, Great Britain, on 27 Jun 1992.

THEATER

Oldest   Theater in Europe has its origins in Greek drama performed in honor of a god, usually Dionysus. Small theaters had been built on several sites in Greece by the fifth century B.C.

Oldest indoor theater   The oldest indoor theater in the world is the Teatro Olimpico in Vicenza, Italy. Designed in the Roman style by Andrea di Pietro, alias Palladio (1508–80), it was begun three months before his death and finished by his pupil Vicenzo Scamozzi (1552–1616) in 1583. It is preserved today in its original form.

Largest   The world's largest building used for theater is the National People's Congress Building (*Ren min da hui tang*) on the west side of Tiananmen Square, Beijing, China. It was completed in 1959 and covers an area of 12.9 acres. The theater seats 10,000 and is occasionally used as such, as in 1964 for the play *The East Is Red*.

The theater with the largest capacity is the Perth Entertainment Center, Western Australia, opened on 26 Dec 1974, with 8,500 seats. The main stage measures 70 × 45 ft.

United States   The highest-capacity theater currently in use on Broadway is the Gershwin Theater (formerly the Uris Theater), with 1,933 seats. Designed by Ralph Alswang, the theater opened on 28 Nov 1972.

Smallest   The smallest regularly operated professional theater in the world is the Piccolo in Juliusstrasse, Hamburg, Germany. It was founded in 1970 and has a maximum capacity of 30 seats.

Largest amphitheater   The Flavian amphitheater or Colosseum of Rome, Italy, completed in A.D. 80, covers five acres and has a capacity of 87,000. It has a maximum length of 612 ft and a maximum width of 515 ft.

Largest stage   The largest stage in the world is in the Ziegfeld Room, Reno, NV, with 176 ft passerelle, three main elevators each capable of raising 1,200 show girls (72 tons), two $62\frac{1}{2}$-ft-circumference turntables and 800 spotlights.

Longest runs   The longest continuous run of any show in the world is *The Mousetrap* by Dame Agatha Christie (nee Miller; 1890–1976). This thriller opened on 25 Nov 1952 at the Ambassadors Theatre, London, Great Britain (capacity 453) and moved after 8,862 performances to the St Martin's Theatre next door on 25 Mar 1974. The 16,000th performance was on 6 May 1991, and the box office total was £20 million ($36 million) from more than nine million attenders.

The Vicksburg Theater Guild, MS has been playing the melodrama *Gold in the Hills* by J. Frank Davis discontinuously but every season since 1936.

Revue   The greatest number of performances of any theatrical presentation is 47,250 (to April 1986) in the case of *The Golden Horseshoe Revue*, a show staged at Disneyland, Anaheim, CA. It started on 16 Jul 1955 and closed on 12 Oct 1986 after being seen by 16 million people.

Broadway   *A Chorus Line* opened on 25 Jul 1975 and closed on 28 Apr 1990 after a record run of almost 15 years and 6,137 performances. It was created by Michael Bennett (1943–87).

Musical shows   The off-Broadway musical show *The Fantasticks* by Tom Jones and Harvey Schmidt opened on 3 May 1960, and the total number of performances to 5 May 1993 is 13,680 at the Sullivan Street Playhouse, Greenwich Village, New York City.

Shortest runs   The shortest theatrical run on record was that of *The Intimate Revue*, which took place on a single evening at the Duchess Theatre, London, Great Britain, on 11 Mar 1930. Anything that could go wrong did. With scene changes taking up to 20 min apiece, the management scrapped seven scenes to get the finale on before midnight. The run was described as "half a performance."

Most ardent theatergoer   Dr H. Howard Hughes (b. 1902), Prof. Emeritus of Texas Wesleyan College, Fort Worth, TX attended 6,136 shows in the period 1957–87.

Greatest loss   The greatest loss sustained by a theatrical show was by the American producers of the Royal Shakespeare Company's musical *Carrie*, which closed after five performances on Broadway on 17 May 1988 at a cost of $7 million. *King*, the musical about Martin Luther King, incurred a loss of £3 million ($5.04 million) in a six-week run in London, Great Britain ending on 2 Jun 1990, thus matching the record losses of *Ziegfeld* in 1988 in London.

Tony awards   Harold (Hal) S. Prince (b. 1928) has won 16 "Tonys"—the awards of the American Theater Wing, instituted on 6 Apr 1947—the most of any individual.

Prince has won eight awards as a producer, seven as a director and one special award. Three plays share the record for most Tonys, with five: *A Man for All Seasons* (1962), *Who's Afraid of Virginia Woolf?* (1963) and *Amadeus* (1981).

The only person to win five Tonys in a starring role is Julie Harris, in *I Am a Camera* (1952), *The Lark* (1956), *Forty Carats* (1969), *The Last of Mrs Lincoln* (1973) and *The Belle of Amherst* (1977).

The record number of awards for a starring role in a musical is four, by Angela Lansbury: *Mame* (1966), *Dear World* (1969), *Gypsy* (1975) and *Sweeney Todd* (1979). Gwen Verdon has also won four Tonys—three in leading roles: *Damn Yankees* (1956), *New Girl in Town* (1958), and *Redhead* (1959), and one in a supporting role, *Can-Can* (1954). The musical that has won the most awards is *Hello Dolly!* (1964), with 10.

One-man shows   The longest run of one-man shows is 849, by Victor Borge (b. Copenhagen, 3 Jan 1909) in his *Comedy in Music* from 2 Oct 1953 to 21 Jan 1956 at the Golden Theater, Broadway, New York City.

The world aggregate record for one-man shows is 1,700 performances of *Brief Lives* by Roy Dotrice (b. Guernsey, 26 May 1923), including 400 straight at the Mayfair Theatre, London, Great Britain ending on 20 Jul 1974. He was on stage for more than 2½ hr per performance of this 17th-century monologue and required 3 hr for makeup and 1 hr for removal of makeup, thus aggregating 40 weeks in the chair.

Most durable performer   Kanmi Fujiyama (b. 1929) played the lead role in 10,288 performances by the comedy company Sochiku Shikigeki from November 1966 to June 1983.

Advance sales   The musical *Miss Saigon*, produced by Cameron Mackintosh and starring Jonathan Pryce and Lea Salonga, opened on Broadway in April 1991 after generating record advance sales of $36 million.

Most roles   The greatest recorded number of theatrical, film and television roles portrayed is 3,385, from 1951 to March 1989, by Jan Leighton (USA).

Theatrical roles   Kanzaburo Nakamura (b. July 1909) performed in 806 Kabuki titles from November 1926 to January 1987. Since each title in this classical Japanese theatrical form lasts 25 days, he therefore played 20,150 performances.

Shakespeare   The longest of the 37 plays written by Shakespeare is *Hamlet* (1604), with 4,042 lines and 29,551 words. Of Shakespeare's 1,277 speaking parts, the longest is Hamlet with 11,610 words.

THE GUINNESS DAILY RECORD

24th November, 1983

Zero Attendance at First Night

It's a good thing nobody's turned up – I've forgotten my lines!

In these recessionary times, with shows facing early closing and large losses, we reflect on the unfortunate case of the play *Bag*, described as "an unusual comedy," which opened to a completely empty house at the Grantham Leisure Centre, Grantham, Great Britain, on 24 Nov 1983. Things did improve, however, for the second of its two performances, the following night, when a small audience was in attendance, presumably out of curiosity.

Ten years later the organizers, Grantham Live Productions, are still at a loss to explain the underwhelming enthusiasm, since, although the miserable weather was certainly a factor, it could not be totally to blame.

The production, written by Bryony Lavery and directed by Michele Frankel, included among its cast of five a youthful Josie Lawrence, who, unhindered by distractions such as audiences in her formative years, is now featured regularly on British television on Channel 4's comedy program *Whose Line Is It Anyway?*

Longest chorus lines The longest chorus line in performing history numbered up to 120 in some of the early *Ziegfeld Follies*. In the finale of *A Chorus Line* on the night of 29 Sep 1983, when it broke the record as the longest-running Broadway show ever, 332 top-hatted "strutters" performed on stage.

On 28 Mar 1992 at the Swan Center, Great Britain, 543 members of the cast of *Showtime News*, a major production by Hampshire West Girl Guides, performed a routine choreographed by professional dancer Sally Horsley.

Arts festival The world's largest arts festival is the annual Edinburgh Fringe Festival (instituted in 1947). In 1992, its record year, 540 groups gave 12,132 performances of 1,103 shows between 16 Aug and 5 Sep. Prof. Gerald Berkowitz of Northern Illinois University attended a record 145 separate performances at the 1979 Festival from 15 August–8 September.

Fashion shows   The greatest distance covered by a model on a catwalk is 83.1 miles, by Eddie Warke at Parke's Hotel, Dublin, Republic of Ireland from 19–21 Sep 1983. The record by female models is 71.1 miles, by Roberta Brown and Lorraine McCourt on the same occasion.

Fastest magician   Eldon D. Wigton, alias Dr Eldoonie, performed 225 different tricks in 2 min at Kilbourne, OH on 21 Apr 1991.

CIRCUS

The oldest permanent circus building is Cirque d'Hiver (originally Cirque Napoléon), which opened in Paris, France on 11 Dec 1852.

The largest traveling circus tent was that of Ringling Bros and Barnum & Bailey, which was used on tours in the United States from 1921 to 1924. It covered 91,415 ft², consisting of a round top 200 ft in diameter with five middle sections 60 ft wide.

The largest audience for a circus was 52,385 for Ringling Bros and Barnum & Bailey, at the Superdome, New Orleans, LA on 14 Sep 1975, and the largest in a tent was 16,702 (15,686 paid), also for Ringling Bros and Barnum & Bailey, at Concordia, KS on 13 Sep 1924.

Aerial acts   The highest trapeze act was performed by Ian Ashpole (Great Britain) at a height of 16,420 ft, suspended from a hot-air balloon between St. Neots and Newmarket, Great Britain, on 16 May 1986. Janet May Klemke (USA) performed a record 305 one-arm planges at Medina Shrine Circus, Chicago, IL on 21 Jan 1938. A single-heel hang on swinging bar was first performed by Angela Revelle in Australia in 1977.

Flying return trapeze   A flying return trapeze act was first performed by Jules Léotard (France) at Cirque Napoléon, Paris, France on 12 Nov 1859. A triple back somersault on the flying trapeze was first performed by Lena Jordan (Latvia) to Lewis Jordan (USA) in Sydney, Australia in April 1897. The back somersault record is a quadruple back, by Miguel Vasquez (Mexico) to Juan Vasquez at Ringling Bros and Barnum & Bailey Circus, Tucson, AZ on 10 Jul 1982. The greatest number of consecutive triple back somersaults successfully carried out is 135, by Jamie Ibarra (Mexico) to Alejandro Ibarra, between 23 July–12 Oct 1989, at various locations in the United States.

Flexible pole   The first and only publicly performed quadruple back somersault on the flexible pole was accomplished by Maxim Dobrovitsky (USSR) at the Egorov Troupe at the International Circus Festival of Monte Carlo in Monaco on 4 Feb 1989.

Corina Colonelu Mosoianu (Romania) is the only person to have performed a triple full twisting somersault, at Madison Square Garden, New York City, on 17 Apr 1984.

High wire   A seven-person pyramid (three layers) was achieved by the Great Wallendas (Germany) at Wallenda Circus in the United States in 1947. The highest high-wire act (ground supported) was at a height of 1,350 ft, by

OLDEST CIRCUS   The Cirque d'Hiver in Paris is the oldest permanent circus building and has brought in the crowds since it opened in 1852. (Photos: Ann Ronan Picture Library and James Clift for Guinness Publishing)

Philippe Petit (France) between the towers of the World Trade Center, New York City on 7 Aug 1974.

Horseback riding   The record for consecutive somersaults on horseback is 23, by James Robinson (USA) at Spalding & Rogers Circus, Pittsburgh, PA in 1856.

Willy, Beby and Rene Fredianis (Italy) performed a three-high column at Nouveau Cirque, Paris, France in 1908, a feat not since emulated. "Poodles" Hanneford (Ireland, b. England) holds the record for running leaps on and off, with 26 at Barnum & Bailey Circus, New York City in 1915.

Human pyramid   The weight record is 1,700 lbs, when Tahar Douis supported 12 members of the Hassani Troupe (three levels in height) at the BBC TV studios, Birmingham, Great Britain on 17 Dec 1979. The height record is 39 ft, when Josep-Joan Martinez Lozano of the Colla Vella dels Xiquets mounted a nine-high pyramid at Valls, Spain on 25 Oct 1981.

Plate spinning   The greatest number of plates spun simultaneously is 108, by Dave Spathaky of London, Great Britain for the *Tarm Pai Du* television program in Thailand on 23 Nov 1992.

High diving   Col. Harry A. Froboess (Switzerland) jumped 394 ft into the Bodensee from the airship *Graf Hindenburg* on 22 Jun 1936.

The greatest height reported for a dive into an air bag is 326 ft, by stuntman Dan Koko, who jumped from the top of Vegas World Hotel and Casino onto a 20 × 40 × 14 ft target on 13 Aug 1948.

Kitty O'Neil dove 180 ft from a helicopter over Devonshire Downs, CA on 9 Dec 1979 onto an air cushion measuring 30 x 60 ft for a TV film stunt.

Human cannonball   The first human cannonball was Eddie Rivers (USA), billed as "Lulu," from a Farini cannon at Royal Cremorne Music Hall, London, Great Britain in 1871. The record distance a human has been fired from a cannon is 175 ft in the case of Emanuel Zacchini (Italy) in the USA in 1940.

Traveling amusement park   The largest traveling amusement park or carnival in the United States is Amusements of America, which encompasses a route of over 18,000 miles, with a yearly attendance in excess of six million people.

Risley   A back somersault feet to feet was first performed by Richard Risley Carlisle and son (USA) at the Theater Royal, Edinburgh, Scotland, in February 1844.

Stilt-walking   The fastest stilt-walker on record is Roy Luiking, who covered 328 ft on 1-ft-high stilts in 13.01 sec at Didam, Netherlands on 28 May 1992. Over a long distance, the fastest is M. Garisoain of Bayonne, France, who in

1892 walked the 4.97 miles from Bayonne to Biarritz on stilts in 42 min, an average speed of 7.10 mph.

The greatest distance ever walked on stilts is 3,008 miles, from Los Angeles, CA to Bowen, KY by Joe Bowen from 20 Feb–26 Jul 1980.

Even with a safety or Kirby wire, very high stilts are *extremely* dangerous—25 steps are deemed to constitute "mastery." The tallest stilts ever mastered measured 40 ft 9½ in from ground to ankle. Eddy Wolf ("Steady Eddy") of Loyal, WI walked a distance of 25 steps without touching his safety handrail wires on 3 Aug 1988 using aluminum stilts of this length.

The heaviest stilts ever mastered weighed 57 lb each, and were the ones used by Eddy Wolf in his successful attempt on the height record (see above).

Teeter board   The Kehaiovi Troupe (Bulgaria) achieved a seven-person-high perch pole column at Blackpool Tower Circus, Blackpool, Great Britain on 16 Jul 1986.

Trampoline   Marco Canestrelli (USA) performed a septuple twisting back somersault to bed at Ringling Bros and Barnum & Bailey Circus, St Petersburg, FL on 5 Jan 1979. He also managed a quintuple twisting back somersault to a two-high column, to Belmonte Canestrelli at Ringling Bros and Barnum & Bailey Circus, New York City, on 28 Mar 1979. Richard Tison (France) achieved a triple twisting triple back somersault at Berchtesgaden, Germany on 30 Jun 1981.

Wild animal presentations   Willy Hagenbeck (Germany) worked with 70 polar bears in a presentation at the Paul Busch Circus, Berlin, Germany in 1904.

The greatest number of lions mastered and fed in a cage by an unaided lion-tamer was 40, by "Captain" Alfred Schneider in 1925.

Clyde Raymond Beatty (USA) handled 43 "cats" (lions and tigers) simultaneously in 1938. Beatty was the featured attraction at every show he appeared in for more than 40 years. He insisted upon being called a lion-trainer, not a lion-tamer.

PHOTOGRAPHY

Earliest photograph   The earliest-known surviving photograph, by Joseph Niépce (1765–1833), was taken in 1827 using a camera obscura and shows the view from the window of his home. Rediscovered by Helmut Gernsheim in 1952, it is now in the Gernsheim Collection at the University of Texas, Austin, TX.

Aerial photograph   The world's earliest aerial photograph was taken in 1858 by Gaspard Félix Tournachon (1820–1910), alias Nadar, from a balloon near Villacoublay, on the outskirts of Paris, France.

CAMERAS

Largest   The largest and most expensive industrial camera ever built is the 30 ton Rolls-Royce camera now owned by BPCC Graphics Ltd of Derby, commissioned in 1956. It measures 8 ft 10 in high, 8¼ ft wide and 46 ft in length. The lens is a 63 in f 16 Cooke Apochromatic and the bellows were made by Camera Bellows Ltd of Birmingham, Great Britain.

A pinhole camera was created from a Portakabin unit measuring 34 × 9½ × 9 ft by photographers John Kippen and Chris Wainwright at the National Museum of Photography, Film and Television at Bradford, Great Britain on 25 Mar 1990. The unit produced a direct positive measuring 33 × 4 ft 2 in.

Largest lens The National Museum of Photography, Film and Television, Bradford, Great Britain has the largest lens on display, made by Pilkington Special Glass Ltd, St Asaph, Clwyd, Great Britain. Its dimensions are: focal length 333 in, diameter 54 in, weight 474 lb. Its focal length allows writing on the museum's walls to be read from a distance of 40 ft.

Fastest A camera built for research into high-power lasers by The Blackett Laboratory of Imperial College of Science and Technology, London, Great Britain registers images at a rate of 33 billion per sec. The fastest production camera is currently the Imacon 675, made by Hadland Photonics Ltd of Bovington, Great Britain, at up to 600 million frames per sec.

Most expensive The most expensive complete range of camera equipment in the world is that of Nikon Corporation of Tokyo, Japan, which in May 1992 marketed its complete range of 29 cameras with 90 lenses and 659 accessories at a total cost of $250,000 excluding tax.

The highest auction price is £29,700 (*c.* $53,500) for a lady's patent watch camera of *c.* 1890 made by Lancaster and Son of Birmingham, Great Britain, sold at Christie's, London on 12 Mar 1992.

Longest negative On 6 May 1992 Thomas Bleich of Austin, TX produced a negative measuring 23 ft 4½ × 10½ in using a 10½ in focal length Turner-Reich lens and Kodak No. 10 Cirkut Camera. The photograph, a portrait of about 3,500 attendants at a concert in Austin, achieved a view of over 1,440 degrees in a single shot.

Most expensive photograph The black and white print of a woman's face dotted with glass tears, taken in 1930 by Man Ray, sold for £122,500 (*c.* $192,325) at Sotheby's, London, Great Britain, on 7 May 1993.

Smallest camera Apart from cameras built for intracardiac surgery and espionage, the smallest that has been marketed is the circular Japanese "Petal" camera, with a diameter of 1.14 in and a thickness of 0.65 in. It has a focal length of 0.47 in.

CINEMA

FILMS

Origins The earliest motion pictures were made by Louis Aimé Augustin Le Prince (1842–90), who was attested to have achieved dim moving outlines on a whitewashed wall at the Institute for the Deaf, Washington Heights, New York City as early as 1885–1887. The earliest surviving film (sensitized $2^1/8$ in wide paper roll) is from his camera, taken in early October 1888, of the garden of his father-in-law, Joseph Whitley, in Roundhay, Great Britain at 10 to 12 frames per second.

The first commercial presentation of motion pictures was at Holland Bros' Kinetoscope Parlor at 1155 Broadway, New York City on 14 Apr 1894. Viewers could see five films for 25 cents or 10 for 50 cents from a double row of Kinetoscopes developed by William Kennedy Laurie Dickson (1860–1935), assistant to Thomas Edison (1847–1931), in 1889–91.

The earliest publicly presented film on a *screen* was *La Sortie des Ouvriers de l'Usine Lumière*, probably shot in August or September 1894 in Lyons, France. It was exhibited at 44 rue de Rennes, Paris, France on 22 Mar 1895 by the Lumière brothers, Auguste-Marie-Louis-Nicholas (1862–1954) and Louis-Jean (1864–1948).

Earliest feature film The world's first full-length feature film was *The Story of the Kelly Gang*, made in Melbourne, Victoria, Australia in 1906. Produced on a budget of £450, this biography of the notorious armored bushranger Ned Kelly (1855–80) ran for 60–70 minutes and opened at the Melbourne Town Hall on 26 Dec 1906. It was produced by the local theatrical company J. and N. Tait.

Earliest "talkie" The earliest sound-on-film motion picture was achieved by Eugene-Augustin Lauste (1857–1935), who patented his process on 11 Aug 1906 and produced a workable system using a string galvanometer in 1910 at Benedict Road, London, Great Britain. The earliest public presentation of sound on film was by the Tri-ergon process at the Alhambra Theater, Berlin, Germany on 17 Sep 1922.

United States The earliest screening of a sound-on-picture motion picture in the United States before a paying audience was at the Rivoli Theater in New York City on 15 Apr 1923. The first all-talking motion picture was Warner Brothers' *Lights of New York*, shown at the Strand Theater, New York City on 6 Jul 1928.

Country with largest output India's production of feature-length films was a record 948 in 1990, and its annual output has exceeded 700 every year since 1979. In the United States, 330 films were produced in 1991; 479 were produced in 1988, the most in a year since 1968.

Most expensive film At the time of its release in July 1991, *Terminator 2: Judgment Day* was reported to have cost Carolco Pictures $95 million (revised from earlier reports of $104 million), plus print and advertising costs of about $20

MOST EXPENSIVE FILM Even at revised estimates of $95 million, *Terminator 2: Judgment Day* is still the world's costliest film. Nonstop action has title star Arnold Schwarzenegger risking more than an arm for his reported $15 million fee. (Photos: Sygma)

million. Its star, Arnold Schwarzenegger, was believed to have received a fee of $15 million for the film.

In terms of real costs adjusted for inflation, the most expensive film ever made was *Cleopatra* (USA, 1963), whose $44 million budget would be equivalent to over $200 million in 1993.

Least expensive full-length feature film The total cost of production for the 1927 film *The Shattered Illusion*, by Victorian Film Productions, was £300 ($1,458). It took 12 months to complete and included spectacular scenes of a ship being overwhelmed by a storm.

Most expensive film rights The highest price ever paid for film rights was $9.5 million announced on 20 Jan 1978 by Columbia for *Annie*, the Broadway musical by Charles Strouse starring Andrea McCardle, Dorothy Loudon and Reid Shelton.

Longest film The longest film commercially released in its entirety was Edgar Reitz's 25 hr 32 min *Die Zweite Heimat* (Germany, 1992), premièred in Munich on 5–9 Sep 1992.

Highest box office gross The box office gross champion is Steven Spielberg's *E.T.: The Extra-Terrestrial*, released on 11 Jun 1982, which had grossed over $700 million (including videos) by December 1989.

Batman Returns (Warner Brothers) set an opening-day record of $16.1 million on 19 Jun 1992 and also a single-day record of $16.8 million on 20 June during its US opening weekend at a record 2,644 theaters.

Largest loss The greatest loss incurred by a film is $57 million by Columbia Tri-Star's *Hudson Hawk* (USA, 1991), starring Bruce Willis (b. 19 Mar 1955) and directed by Michael Lehmann. Costing $65 million, this James Bond-type spoof returned $8 million in North America—and hardly anything elsewhere.

Highest earnings Jack Nicholson stood to receive up to $60 million for playing "The Joker" in Warner Brothers' $50 million *Batman*, through a percentage of the film's receipts in lieu of salary.

Most durable series The longest series of films is the 100 features made in Hong Kong about the 19th century martial arts hero Huang Fei-Hong, starting with *The True Story of Huang Fei-Hong* (1949) and continuing through *Once Upon a Time in China 2* (1992). The most durable continuing series with the same star is Shockiku Studios of Japan's 46 *Tora-San* comedy films, featuring Kiyoshi Atsumi (b. 1929) in a Chaplinesque role from August 1969 to December 1992.

Most profitable series The most successful movie series is the 18 James Bond films, from *Dr No* (1962) starring Sean Connery (b. 25 Aug 1930) to *License to Kill* (1989) with Timothy Dalton (b. 21 Mar 1944). The series has grossed over $1 billion worldwide to date.

Largest studios The largest complex of film studios in the world is the one at Universal City, Los Angeles, CA. The back lot contains 476 buildings and there are 34 sound stages on the 420-acre site.

Largest studio stage The world's largest studio stage is the 007 stage at

Pinewood Studios, Buckinghamshire, Great Britain. It was designed by Ken Adam and Michael Brown and built in 1976 for the James Bond film *The Spy Who Loved Me*. It measures 336 × 139 × 41 ft, and accommodates 1.2 million gallons of water, a full-scale 672,000 ton oil tanker and three nuclear scaled-down submarines.

Largest film set   The largest film set ever built was the 1,312 × 754 ft Roman Forum designed by Veniero Colosanti and John Moore for Samuel Bronston's production of *The Fall of the Roman Empire* (1964). It was built on a 55 acre site outside Madrid, Spain, where 1,100 workmen spent seven months laying the surface of the Forum with 170,000 cement blocks, erecting 22,000 ft of concrete stairways, 601 columns and 350 statues, and constructing 27 full-size buildings.

Largest film premiere   *A Few Good Men*, starring Tom Cruise, Demi Moore and Jack Nicholson, was released simultaneously in over 50 countries by Columbia Pictures in December 1992.

Largest number of extras   It is believed that over 300,000 extras appeared in the funeral scene of Sir Richard Attenborough's *Gandhi* (1982).

Highest paid stunt performer   Stuntman Dar Robinson was paid $100,000 for the 1,000 ft leap from the CN Tower, Toronto, Canada in November 1979 for *High Point*. His parachute opened just 300 ft above ground. He died on 21 Nov 1986 aged 39.

Most expensive prop   The highest price paid at auction for a film prop is $275,000 at Sotheby's, New York City on 28 Jun 1986 for James Bond's Aston Martin DB5 from *Goldfinger* (Great Britain, 1964).

Best-selling video   The world's best-selling video is Walt Disney's *Beauty and the Beast*. Released in North America in October 1992, it reached sales of $22 million by March 1993.

Most films seen   Gwilym Hughes of Dolgellau, Great Britain had seen 20,064 films by March 1991. He saw his first film in 1953 while in the hospital.

Albert E. van Schmus (b. 1921) saw 16,945 films in 32 years (1949–1982) as a rater for the Motion Picture Association of America Inc.

Fastest film production   The shortest time ever taken to make a feature-length film from scripting to screening was 13 days, for *The Fastest Forward*, produced by Russ Malkin and directed by John Gore. The all-star British cast, the crew, technicians and film suppliers accepted the charity challenge, and the 75-minute thriller was given a gala premiere in London, Great Britain on 27 May 1990 to raise money for the British Telethon '90.

Longest directorial career   The directorial career of King Vidor (1894–1982) lasted for 67 years, beginning with the two-reel comedy *Hurricane in Galveston* (1913) and culminating in another short, a documentary called *The Metaphor* (1980).

Oldest director   The Dutch director Joris Ivens (1898–1989) made the Franco-Italian co-production *Une Histoire de Vent* in 1988 at the age of 89. He made his directorial debut with the Dutch film *De Brug* in 1928. Hollywood's oldest director was George Cukor (1899–1983), who made his 50th and final film, MGM's *Rich and Famous*, in 1981 at the age of 81.

Oldest performer   The oldest screen performer in a speaking role was Jeanne Louise Calment (b. 1875–*fl.* March 1993), who portrayed herself in the 1990 Canadian film *Vincent and Me*. She is the last living person to have known Vincent van Gogh. (See Human Beings, Oldest living person.)

Most durable performers   The record for the longest screen career is 83 years, held by German actor Curt Bois (1900–91), who made his debut in *Der Fidele Bauer* at the age of eight and whose most recent films include *Wings of Desire* (1988). American actress Helen Hayes (1900–93) first appeared on screen at the age of 10 in *Jean and the Calico Doll*, with much of her later work being for television. Her last screen role was in *Divine Mercy, No Excape* (1988) in a career lasting 78 years. The most enduring star of the big screen was Lillian Gish (1893–1993 — although her birthdate is usually given as 1896). She made her debut in *An Unseen Enemy* (1912) and her last film in a career spanning 75 years was *The Whales of August* (1987).

Most portrayed character   The character most frequently recurring on the screen is Sherlock Holmes, created by Sir Arthur Conan Doyle (1859–1930). The Baker Street sleuth has been portrayed by some 75 actors in over 211 films since 1900.

In horror films the character most often portrayed is Count Dracula, created by the Irish writer Bram Stoker (1847–1912). Representations of the Count or his immediate descendants outnumber those of his closest rival, Frankenstein's monster, by 160 to 115.

Most generations of screen actors in a family   There are four generations of screen actors in the Redgrave family. Roy Redgrave (1872–1922) made his screen debut in 1911 and continued to appear in Australian films until 1920. His son, Sir Michael Redgrave, married actress Rachel Kempson, and their two daughters Vanessa and Lynn and son Corin are all actors. Vanessa's two daughters, Joely and Natasha, and Corin's daughter Jemma, are already successful actresses, with films such as *Wetherby*, *A Month in the Country* and *The Dream Demon* to their respective credit.

Costumes   The largest number of costumes used for any one film was 32,000 for the 1951 film *Quo Vadis*.

Most changes   Elizabeth Taylor changed costume 65 times in *Cleopatra* (1963). The costumes were designed by Irene Sharaff and cost $130,000.

Most expensive   Constance Bennett's sable coat in *Madame X* was valued at $50,000. The most expensive costume designed and made specially for a film was Edith Head's mink and sequins dance costume worn by Ginger Rogers in

Lady in the Dark. It cost Paramount $35,000. The ruby slippers, a personal prop worn by Judy Garland in the 1939 film *The Wizard of Oz*, were sold on 2 Jun 1988 to a mystery buyer at Christie's, New York for $165,000.

Oscar winners Walter (Walt) Elias Disney (1901–66) won more "Oscars"— the awards of the Academy of Motion Picture Arts and Sciences, instituted on 16 May 1929—than any other person. The physical count comprises 20 statuettes and 12 other plaques and certificates, including posthumous awards.

The only person to win four Oscars in a starring role is Katharine Hepburn (b. Hartford, CT, 8 Nov 1909), for *Morning Glory* (1932/33), *Guess Who's Coming to Dinner* (1967), *The Lion in Winter* (1968) and *On Golden Pond* (1981). She has been nominated 12 times. Edith Head (1907–81) won eight individual awards for costume design.

The film with the most awards is *Ben Hur* (1959) with 11. The film with the most nominations was *All About Eve* (1950) with 14. It won six (Best Supporting Actor: George Sanders; Best Picture; Best Costume Design: Edith Head, Charles Le Maire; Best Director: Joseph L. Mankiewicz; Best Sound Recording; Best Screenplay: Joseph L. Mankiewicz).

Youngest winners The youngest winner in competition was Tatum O'Neal (b. 5 Nov 1963), who was 10 when she received the award in 1974 for Best Supporting Actress in *Paper Moon* (1973). Shirley Temple (b. 23 Apr 1928) was awarded an honorary Oscar at the age of five in 1934.

Oldest winners The oldest recipients, George Burns (b. 20 Jan 1896) for *The Sunshine Boys* in 1976 and Jessica Tandy (b. 7 Jun 1909) for *Driving Miss Daisy* in 1990, were both 80 at the time of the presentation, although Miss Tandy was the elder by five months.

Most versatile personalities The only three people to have won Oscar, Emmy, Tony and Grammy awards have been actress Helen Hayes (1900–93) in 1932–76; composer Richard Rodgers (1902–79) and actress/singer/dancer Rita Moreno (b. 1931) in 1961–77. Barbra Streisand received Oscar, Grammy, and Emmy awards in addition to a special "Star of the Decade" Tony award.

Most honored entertainer The most honored entertainer in history is Bob Hope (ne Leslie Townes Hope; London, Great Britain, 29 May 1903). He has been uniquely awarded the USA's highest civilian honors—the Medal of Freedom (1969); Congressional Gold Medal (1963); Medal of Merit (1966); Distinguished Public Service Medal (1973); Distinguished Service Gold Medal (1971)—and is also an Hon CBE (1976), and was appointed Hon. Brigadier of the US Marine Corps. He also has 44 honorary degrees.

MOVIE THEATERS

Earliest The earliest structure designed and used exclusively for exhibiting projected films is believed to be one erected at the Atlanta Show, GA in October 1895 to exhibit C.F. Jenkins's phantoscope.

Largest The largest movie theater in the world is the Radio City Music Hall, New York City, opened on 27 Dec 1932, with 5,945 (now 5,874) seats. Kinepolis, the first eight screens of which opened in Brussels, Belgium in 1988, is the

world's largest theater complex. It has 24 screens and a total seating capacity of 7,000.

Highest movie theater attendance The largest cinema audience is that of China, with mainland attendance figures of 14 billion in 1991, compared with a peak of 21.8 billion in 1988.

Biggest screen The largest permanently installed theater screen, with an area of 96 × 70½ ft, is located at the Keong Emas Imax Theatre, Taman Mini Park, Jakarta, Indonesia, opened on 20 Apr 1984. The Six Flags Great America Pictorium, Gurnee, IL, opened in 1979, has a screen of equal size, but it is 3D. A temporary screen measuring 297 × 33 ft was used at the 1937 Paris Exposition in France.

Highest box office gross In 1992, domestic gross box office receipts (USA only) were $4.871 billion. In 1989 there was an all-time high of $5.033 billion.

RADIO

Earliest patent   The earliest patent for telegraphy without wires (wireless) was received by Dr Mahlon Loomis (USA; 1826–86). It was entitled "Improvement in Telegraphy" and was dated 20 Jul 1872 (US Pat. No. 129,971). He in fact demonstrated only potential differences on a galvanometer between two kites 14 miles apart in Loudoun County, VA in October 1866.

A public demonstration of wireless transmission of speech was, however, given in the town square of Murray, KY in 1892 by Nathan B. Stubblefield. The authentic first patent for a system of communication by means of electromagnetic waves, numbered No. 12039, was granted on 2 Jun 1896 to the Italian-Irish Marchese Guglielmo Marconi (1874–1937). The first permanent wireless installation was constructed at The Needles on the Isle of Wight, Great Britain, by Marconi's Wireless Telegraph Co. Ltd, in November 1897.

Earliest broadcast   The world's first advertised broadcast was made on 24 Dec 1906 by the Canadian-born Prof. Reginald Aubrey Fessenden (1868–1932) from the 420 ft mast of the National Electric Signalling Company at Brant Rock, MA. The transmission included Handel's *Largo*. Fessenden had achieved the broadcast of speech as early as November 1900 but it was highly distorted.

Transatlantic transmissions   The earliest claim to have received wireless signals (the letter S in Morse Code) across the Atlantic was made by Marconi, George Stephen Kemp and Percy Paget from a 10 kW station at Poldhu, Cornwall, Great Britain, to Signal Hill, St John's, Newfoundland, Canada, at 12:30 P.M. on 12 Dec 1901.

Human speech was first heard across the Atlantic in November 1915 when a transmission from the US Navy station at Arlington, VA was received by US radiotelephone engineers on the Eiffel Tower, Paris, France.

Earliest radio-microphones   The radio-microphone, which was in essence also the first "bug," was devised by Reg Moores (Great Britain) in 1947 and first used on 76 MHz in the ice show *Aladdin* at Brighton Sports Stadium, Great Britain in September 1949.

Most durable programs   *Rambling with Gambling*, the early morning program on WOR, New York City, was first broadcast in March 1925 and celebrated its 21,281st show as of 30 Apr 1993. The show has been hosted by three generations of the Gambling family: John B. Gambling (1925–59), John A. Gambling (1959–present) and John R. Gambling 1985–present). The show currently airs six days a week, year round.

The weekly sports report "The Tenpin Tattler" was first broadcast on WCFL, Chicago, IL on 24 Aug 1935. Fifty-eight years and more than 2,900 broadcasts later it still continues on WGN, Chicago with the original host, Sam Weinstein, who is probably the longest continuing host of a program.

Most hours broadcast per week   Larry King's radio and television programs are broadcast a combined 35 hours per week, the most of any broadcaster heard nationwide. He has been broadcasting 10 hours per week on CNN since 1985, and his program is aired in 131 countries. He has broadcast 36 hours per week on Mutual Broadcasting since 1978.

Most stations   The country with the greatest number of radio broadcasting stations is the United States, where there were 11,334 authorized broadcast stations as of 31 Dec 1992, made up of 4,961 AM (amplitude modulation) stations and 6,373 FM (frequency modulation) stations.

Largest audience   Surveys carried out in 90 countries showed that, in 1993, the global estimated audience for the British Broadcasting Corporation World Service, broadcast in 39 languages, was 124 million regular listeners—greater than the combined listenership of Voice of America, Radio Moscow and *Deutsche Welle*. This is, however, a conservative estimate because figures are unavailable for several countries, including China, Cuba, Myanmar (Burma), Iran, Afghanistan and Vietnam.

   The peak recorded listenership on British Broadcasting Corporation Radio was 30 million on 6 Jun 1950 for the boxing match between Lee Savold (USA) and Bruce Woodcock (Great Britain; b. 1921).

Largest response   The largest recorded response to a radio show occurred on 27 Nov 1974 when, on a 5-hr talk show on WCAU, Philadelphia, PA, astrologer Howard Sheldon registered a call count of 388,299 on the *Bill Corsair Show*.

Most durable radio program   The Grand Ole Opry has broadcast continuously from November 1925 to May 1992, a total of more than 66 years.

Longest continuous radio broadcast   Radio Telfis Éireann transmitted an unedited reading of *Ulysses* by James Joyce (1881–1941) for 29 hr 38 min 47 sec on 16–17 Jul 1982.

Most assiduous radio ham   The late Richard C. Spenceley of KV4AA at St Thomas, VI built his contacts (QSOs) to a record level of 48,100 in 365 days in 1978.

Biggest radio prize   Mary Buchanan, 15, on WKRQ Cincinnati won a prize of $25,000 for 40 years (or $1 million) on 21 Nov 1980.

TELEVISION

At the end of 1991 there were 1,132 commercial and educational licensed television stations in the United States.

Invention   The invention of television, the instantaneous viewing of distant objects by electrical transmission, was not a single event but a process of successive and interdependent discoveries.

The first commercial cathode ray tube was introduced in 1897 by Karl Ferdinand Braun (1850–1918), but was not linked to "electric vision" until 1907, by Prof. Boris Rosing (disappeared 1918) of Russia, in St Petersburg. A.A. Campbell Swinton (1863–1930) published the fundamentals of television transmission on 18 Jun 1908 in a brief letter to the publication *Nature* entitled "Distant Electric Vision."

The earliest public demonstration of television was given on 27 Jan 1926 by John Logie Baird (1888–1946) of Scotland, using a development of the mechanical scanning system patented by Paul Gottlieb Nipkow (1860–1940) on 6 Jan 1884. Baird had achieved the transmission of a Maltese Cross over 10 ft at 8 Queen's Arcade, Hastings, Great Britain, by February 1924, and the first facial image (of William Taynton, 15) at 22 Frith Street, London, Great Britain on 30 Oct 1925.

A patent application for the Iconoscope had been filed on 29 Dec 1923 by Dr Vladimir Kuzmich Zworykin (1889–1982) but was not issued until 20 Dec 1938.

Earliest service   Baird launched his first television "service" via a British Broadcasting Corporation transmitter on 30 Sep 1929 and marketed the first sets, Baird Televisors, in May 1930. The world's first high-definition (i.e., 405 lines) television broadcasting service was opened from Alexandra Palace, London, Great Britain on 2 Nov 1936, when there were about 100 sets in all of Great Britain.

First transatlantic transmissions   On 9 Feb 1928 the image of J.L. Baird and of a Mrs Howe was transmitted from Station 2 KZ at Coulsdon, Great Britain to Station 2 CVJ, Hartsdale, NY.

The earliest transatlantic transmission by satellite was achieved at 1 A.M. on 11 Jul 1962, via the active satellite *Telstar 1* from Andover, ME to Pleumeur Bodou, France. The picture was of Frederick R. Kappell, chairman of the American Telephone and Telegraph Company, which owned the satellite. The first "live" broadcast was made on 23 Jul 1962.

Longest telecast   The longest pre-scheduled telecast on record was a continuous transmission for 163 hr 18 min by GTV 9 of Melbourne, Australia, covering the *Apollo XI* moon mission from 19–26 Jul 1969.

Earliest videotape recording   Alexander M. Poniatoff first demonstrated videotape recording, known as Ampex (his initials plus "ex" for excellence), in 1956.

The earliest demonstration of a home video recorder was on 24 Jun 1963 at the British Broadcasting Corporation News Studio at Alexandra Palace, London, Great Britain, of the Telcan, developed by Norman Rutherford and Michael Turner of the Nottingham Electronic Valve Co.

Most durable shows The world's most durable TV show is NBC's *Meet the Press*, first transmitted on 6 Nov 1947 and broadcast weekly since 12 Sep 1948. As of 23 May 1993, 2,294 shows had been broadcast. The show was originated by Lawrence E. Spivak, who served as host and chief analyst through 1975. Tim Russert has succeeded as the show's new host since Garrick Utley left in December 1991.

On 1 Jun 1986 Joe Franklin presented the 26,815th version of his show, started in 1951. He has conducted 304,212 interviews since 1951.

Since 1949 over 150,000 individual episodes of the TV show *Bozo the Clown*, by Larry Harmon Pictures, have been aired daily on 150 stations in the United States and abroad.

The greatest number of hours on camera on US national television is 10,293 hr by the TV personality Hugh Downs in over 46 years up to 23 May 1993.

Most sets The United States had, by September 1991, 91,788,100 TV house-

---

TV's most frequent clapper It has been estimated that *Wheel of Fortune* hostess Vanna White claps 720 times per show, or 28,080 times in one year.

Longest-running commercial characters in TV history The longest-running characters in TV commercials in American television history are Dick Wilson, alias "Mr Whipple," from 1964 to 1989, and Jan Miner as "Madge the Manicurist" from 1965 to 1991.

Most expensive television rights In November 1991 it was reported that a group of US and European investors, led by CBS, had paid $8 million for the television rights to *Scarlett,* the sequel to Margaret Mitchell's *Gone With the Wind*, written by Alexandra Ripley. The proposed eight-hour miniseries is scheduled for screening in 1993.

Fastest video production Tapes of the Royal Wedding of HRH Prince Andrew and Miss Sarah Ferguson on 23 Jul 1986 were produced by Thames Video Collection. Live filming ended with the departure of the honeymoon couple from Chelsea Hospital by helicopter at 4:42 P.M. The first fully edited and packaged VHS tapes were purchased 5 hr 41 min later by Fenella Lee and Lucinda Burland of London at the Virgin Megastore in Oxford Street, London, Great Britain at 10:23 P.M.

Most takes The greatest number of takes for a TV commercial is 28, in 1973 by Pat Coombs, the British comedienne. Her explanation was "Every time we came to the punch line I just could not remember the name of the product."

holds, with 56,189,000, or 61.2 percent, receiving cable. A total 71,140,000 homes, 77.5 percent, owned a videocassette recorder as of April 1991. The global total of homes with television surpassed 500 million in 1987, led by the USA with 89,130,000. More than 60 percent of homes in the United States have two or more TV sets.

On 15 Feb 1988 the new China News Agency announced that China's number of TV viewers had risen to 600 million from 100 million sets.

TV watching   In June 1988 it was reported that the average US child sees at least 26,000 murders on TV by his or her 18th birthday. Between the ages of 2 and 11 the average viewing time is 31 hours 52 minutes per week. There are 8,250 TV transmitting stations worldwide, of which 1,241 are in the United States.

Greatest audience   The estimated global audience for the 1990 Soccer World Cup finals played in Italy from 8 June to 8 July was 26.5 billion.

An estimated 2.5 billion viewers tuned in to the live and recorded transmissions of the XXIIIrd Olympic Games in Los Angeles, CA from 27 Jul to 13 Aug 1984. The American Broadcasting Co. airing schedule comprised 187½ hours of coverage on 56 cameras.

The estimated viewership for the Live Aid concerts organized by Bob Geldof and Bill Graham (1931–91), via a record 12 satellites, was 1.6 billion, or nearly one-third of the world's population.

The highest-ever viewership was 133.4 million viewers watching the NBC transmission of Super Bowl XXVII on 31 Jun 1993.

The program that attracted the highest-ever viewership was the "Goodbye, Farewell and Amen" final episode of M*A*S*H (the acronym for Mobile Army Surgical Hospital 4077), transmitted by CBS on 28 Feb 1983 to 60.3 percent of all households in the United States. It was estimated that some 125 million people tuned in, taking a 77 percent share of all viewing.

The *Muppet Show* is the most widely viewed program in the world, with an estimated audience of 235 million in 106 countries as of August 1989.

Emmy Awards   *Instituted on 25 Jan 1949 by the Academy of Television Arts & Sciences, the Emmy is awarded for achievement in national nighttime television programming.*

Most   The most Emmys won by any individual is 16, by television producer Dwight Arlington Hemion (b. 14 Mar 1926). He also holds the record for most nominations, with 37. *The Mary Tyler Moore Show* (CBS) has won the most awards for a series, with 29. *Cheers* has received the most nominations, with 109. The most Emmys awarded to a miniseries was nine, to *Roots* (ABC) in 1977. In 1977 *Eleanor and Franklin: The White House Years* (ABC) received the most Emmys, 11, for a television movie. Columbia Broadcasting System (CBS) holds the record for most Emmys won by a network in a single season, with 44 in 1973–74.

Most expensive production   *The Winds of War*, a seven-part Paramount World War II saga aired by ABC, was the most-expensive-ever TV production, costing $42 million over 14 months' shooting. The final episode on 13 Feb 1983 attracted a rating of 41 percent of the total number of viewers, and a 56 percent share of total sets that were turned on.

Largest contract   John William "Johnny" Carson (b. 23 Oct 1925), the former host of *The Tonight Show*, had a contract with NBC reportedly calling for an annual payment of $5 million for his one-hour evening shows, aired four times weekly. He retired on 22 May 1992.

Most successful telethon   The world record for a telethon is $78,438,573 in pledges in 21 1/2 hours by the 1989 Jerry Lewis Labor Day Telethon on 4 September.

Biggest sale   The greatest number of episodes of any TV program ever sold was 1,144 episodes of *Coronation Street* by Granada Television to CBKST Saskatoon, Saskatchewan, Canada, on 31 May 1971. This constituted 20 days 15 hr 44 min of continuous viewing. A further 728 episodes (January 1974–January 1981) were sold to CBC in August 1982.

Most prolific scriptwriter   The most prolific television writer in the world was the Rt Hon Lord Willis (1918–92). Since 1949 he created 41 series, 37 stage plays and 39 feature films. He had 29 plays produced and his total output since 1942 is estimated to be 20 million words.

TV producers   The most prolific producer in television history is game show producer Mark Goodson (1915–92). Since 1948, Goodson produced 38,000 episodes totaling more than 20,800 hours of airtime. Since February 1950, a Mark Goodson-produced show has appeared on national television at least once every week.

Aaron Spelling (b. 1928) has produced more than 2,909.5 TV episodes totaling 2,490.5 hours of air time. The total 2,490.5 broadcast hours is equal to 14 million ft of film, and, projected 24 hours a day, it would take 108 days to screen it all. The average American TV is turned on six hours per day. At this rate, Spelling has produced enough film to last 432 days.

Highest TV advertising rates   The highest TV advertising rate was $800,000 per 30 sec for ABC network prime time during the transmission of Super Bowl XXV on 27 Jan 1991, watched by over 120 million viewers.

Highest-paid commercial spokesperson   It was reported in March 1988 that Pepsi Cola had paid Michael Jackson $12 million to do four TV commercials for them.

Largest sets   The Sony Jumbo Tron color TV screen at the Tsukuba International Exposition '85 near Tokyo, Japan in March 1985 measured 80 ft × 150 ft. The largest cathode ray tubes for color sets are 37 in models manufactured by Mitsubishi Electric of Japan.

Smallest sets   The Seiko TV-Wrist Watch, launched on 23 Dec 1982 in Japan, has a 1.2 in screen and weighs only 2.8 oz. Together with the receiver unit and headphones, the entire black and white system, costing 108,000 yen, weighs only 11.3 oz.

The smallest single-piece set is the Casio-Keisanki TV-10, weighing 11.9 oz with a 2.7 in screen, launched in Tokyo in July 1983.

The smallest and lightest color set is the Casio CV-1, launched by the Casio Computer Co. Ltd of Japan in 1992, with dimensions of 2.4 × 0.9 × 3.6 in, weighing, with batteries, only 6 oz. It has a screen size of 1.4 in and retails in Japan for 40,000 yen (about $350).

HUMAN WORLD

- **POLITICAL AND SOCIAL**
- **HEADS OF STATE AND ROYALTY**
- **LEGISLATURES—UNITED STATES**
- **LEGISLATURES—WORLD**
- **JUDICIAL**
- **HONORS, DECORATIONS, AND AWARDS**
- **MILITARY AND DEFENSE**
- **EDUCATION**
- **RELIGIONS**

POLITICAL AND SOCIAL

COUNTRIES

The world comprises 191 sovereign countries and 62 nonsovereign or other territories (dependencies of sovereign states, territories claimed in Antarctica and disputed territories), making a total of 253 as of May 1993.

Largest The country with the greatest area is Russia, with a total area of 6,592,800 miles^2, or 11.5 percent of the world's total land area. It is 1.8 times the size of the United States, but with a population in 1991 of 149.47 million has around 60 percent of the people in the United States.

The United States covers 3,787,425 miles^2, with a land area of 3,536,342 miles^2 and a water area of 251,083 miles^2. It ranks fourth in the world in area behind Russia, Canada, and China.

Smallest The smallest independent country in the world is the State of Vatican City or Holy See (Stato della Città del Vaticano), which was made an enclave within the city of Rome, Italy on 11 Feb 1929. The enclave has an area of 108.7 acres. The maritime sovereign country with the shortest coastline is Monaco, with 3^1/2 miles, excluding piers and breakwaters. The world's smallest republic is Nauru, less than 1 degree south of the equator in the western Pacific, which became independent on 31 Jan 1968. It has an area of 5,263 acres and a population of 9,600 (latest estimate 1992).

Colony The smallest colony in the world is Gibraltar (since 1969, the City of Gibraltar), with an area of 1,440 acres. However, Pitcairn Island, the only inhabited island (56 people in mid-1992) of a group of four (total area 18^1/2 miles^2), has an area of 960 acres. Until it was forcibly incorporated into Dahomey (now Benin) in 1961, the smallest colony was the Portuguese enclave of Ouidah, consisting of the Fort of St John the Baptist of Ajuda, with an area of just 5 acres.

The official residence, since 1834, of the Grand Master of the Sovereign Military Order of Malta, totaling 3 acres and including the Villa Malta on the Aventine and the Malta Palace at 68 Via Condotti maintains diplomatic relations with a number of foreign governments, through accredited representatives and its legal status is the same as other states, hence it is sometimes cited as the world's smallest "state."

Largest political division The Commonwealth, a free association of 50 independent states and their dependencies, covers an area of 11,323,906 miles^2

Flattest and most elevated The country with the lowest "high point" is Maldives, at 8 ft above sea level. The country with the highest "low point" is Lesotho, where the egress of the Senqu (Orange) riverbed is 4,530 ft above sea level.

SHORTEST COASTLINE Monaco has the shortest coastline of any sovereign country. (Photo: Images Colour Library)

with a population estimated to be 1,443,128,000. Almost all member countries once belonged to the former British Empire. They believe in democracy and equal rights for all men and women regardless of race, color, religion or politics. The Commonwealth promotes world peace, international understanding and an end to poverty and racism.

National boundaries There are 319 national land boundaries in the world. The continent with the greatest number is Africa, with 109. Of the estimated 420 maritime boundaries, only 140 have so far been ratified. The ratio of boundaries to area of land is greatest in Europe.

The frontier which is crossed most frequently is that between the United States and Mexico. In the fiscal year 1992 (to September 1992) there were 268,795,652 crossings.

Longest boundaries The longest *continuous* boundary in the world is that between Canada and the United States, which (including the Great Lakes boundaries) extends for 3,987 miles (excluding the frontier of 1,538 miles with Alaska). If the Great Lakes boundary is excluded, the longest land boundary is that between Chile and Argentina, which is 3,265 miles in length.

Shortest boundaries   The "frontier" of the Holy See in Rome measures 2.53 miles. The land frontier between Gibraltar and Spain at La Linea, closed between June 1969 and February 1985, measures 1 mile. Zambia, Zimbabwe, Botswana and Namibia, in Africa, almost meet at a single point on the Zambezi river.

Most boundaries   China has the most land frontiers, with 16—Mongolia, Russia, North Korea, Hong Kong, Macau, Vietnam, Laos, Myanmar (Burma), India, Bhutan, Nepal, Pakistan, Afghanistan, Tajikistan, Kyrgyzstan and Kazakhstan. These extend for 14,900 miles. The country with the largest number of maritime boundaries is Indonesia, with 19. The longest maritime boundary is that between Greenland and Canada at 1,676 miles.

POPULATIONS

World   The average daily increase in the world's population is rising towards 263,000 or an average of approximately 182 per minute. There are, however, seasonal variations in the numbers of births and deaths throughout the year. For past, present and future estimates, see World Population table.

United States   According to the Census Bureau, as of 1 Dec 1992 there were 256,682,000 million people in the United States. By 1 Jul 2000 the Census Bureau predicts that the country's population will be 268.3 million.

Most populous country   The most populated country is China, which in *pinyin* is written Zhongguo (meaning "central land"). It had an estimated population of 1,165,888,000 in mid-1992 and had a rate of natural increase of about 14.6 million per year or just over 40,000 per day. Its population is more than that of the whole world 200 years ago. India (mid-1992 population of 889,700,000) is expected to overtake China in size of population by A.D. 2050, with 1.591 billion against 1.555 billion for China.

Least populous country   The independent state with the smallest population is Vatican City or the Holy See (see Smallest country, above), with 750 inhabitants in 1992 and no births.

Most densely populated   The most densely populated territory in the world is the Portuguese province of Macau, on the southern coast of China. It has an estimated population of 367,000 (1992) in an area of 6.9 miles², giving a density of 53,188/mile².

Of countries over 1,000 miles² the most densely populated is Bangladesh, with a population of 110,602,000 (1992) living in 55,598 miles² at a density of 1,989/mile². The Indonesian island of Java (with an area of 51,073 miles²) had a population of 107,525,520 in 1990, giving a density of 2,107/mile².

Most sparsely populated   Antarctica became permanently occupied by relays of scientists from 1943 on. The population varies seasonally and reaches 2,000 at times.

The least populated territory, apart from Antarctica, is Greenland, with a population of 56,600 (1992) in an area of 840,000 miles², giving a density of one person to every 14.84 miles². Some 84.3 percent of the island is made up of an ice cap.

Emigration More people emigrate from Mexico than from any other country, mainly to the United States. The Soviet invasion of Afghanistan in December 1979 caused an influx of 2.9 million refugees into Pakistan and a further 2.2 million into Iran. By 1989 the number of Afghan refugees in Pakistan had increased to 3,622,000. In late 1992 there were some 27 million refugees worldwide.

Immigration The country that regularly receives the most legal immigrants is the United States. During fiscal year 1992 (October 1991–September 1992) 973,977 people legally entered the United States. Of these, 384,802 were from Mexico, by far the largest intake from a single country.

In fiscal year 1992 a total of 1,258,482 people were apprehended for immi-

WORLD POPULATION

Date	Millions	Date	Millions
8000 B.C.	c. 6	1970	3,698
A.D. 1	c. 255	1975	4,080
1000	c. 254	1980	4,450
1250	416	1985	4,854
1500	460	1986	4,936
1600	579	1987	5,023
1700	679	1988	5,111
1750	770	1989	5,201
1800	954	1990	5,292
1900	1,633	1991	5,385
1920	1,862	1992	5,480
1930	2,070	1993	5,576
1940	2,295	2000†	6,261
1950	2,515	2025†	8,504
1960	3,019	2050†	10,019

† *These projections are from the UN publication* World Population Prospects 1990.

Note: The all-time peak annual increase of 2.06 percent in the period 1965–70 had declined to 1.74 percent by 1985–90. By 2025 this should decline to 0.99 percent. In spite of the reduced percentage increase, world population is currently growing by 96 million people every year. Projections issued by the UN Population Fund on 29 Apr 1992 estimated that the population would stabilize at around 11.6 billion c. 2150.

Using estimates made by the French demographer J.N. Biraben and others, A.R. Thatcher, former Director of the Office of Population Censuses and Surveys, has calculated that the number of people who died between 40,000 B.C. and A.D. 1990 was nearly 60 billion. This estimate implies that the current world population is about one eleventh of all those who have ever lived before us.

gration violations. The largest group by nationality were 1,205,817 from Mexico.

Tourism The most popular tourist destination is France, which in 1991 received 55,731,000 foreign tourists. The country with the greatest receipts from tourism is the United States, with $45.6 billion in 1991. The biggest spenders on foreign tourism are Americans, who in the same year spent $39.4 billion abroad.

Birthrate *Highest and lowest* The crude birthrate—the number of births per 1,000 population—for the whole world was estimated to be 27.1 per 1,000 in the period 1985–90. The highest rate estimated by the United Nations for the period 1985–90 was 56.3 per 1,000 for Malawi. Excluding Vatican City, where the rate is zero, the lowest recorded rate was 9.5 per 1,000 for San Marino.

United States The National Center for Health Statistics (NCHS) estimates that 3.423 million babies were born in 1992. The estimated United States crude birthrate (the number of babies for every 1,000 people) is 16 percent. The most recent official statistics (1990) show that California led with 612,628 births, while Wyoming had the least, with 6,985. The most live births registered in the United States in any year were 4,300,000 in 1957. The highest birthrate recorded after 1909, the first year official records were recognized, was 30.1 percent in 1910.

World population Matej Gaspar, born 11 Jul 1987 in Yugoslavia, was symbolically named the world's 5-billionth inhabitant by the United Nations Secretary-General.

Housing crisis In 1959, at the peak of the housing crisis in Hong Kong, it was reported that in one house designed for 12 people the number of occupants was 459, including 104 in one room and four living on the roof.

Hospitals The country with the greatest number of hospitals is China, with 61,929 in 1989. Nauru has the most hospital beds per person (250 for every 10,000 people) and Bangladesh and Ethiopia the fewest (3 per 10,000).

Medical families The four sons and five daughters of Dr Antonio B. Vicencio of Los Angeles, CA all qualified as doctors during the period 1964–82. The Barcia family of Valencia, Spain have had the same medical practice for seven generations, since 1792. Eight sons of John Robertson of Strathclyde, Great Britain graduated as medical doctors between 1892 and 1914.

Mental health The country with the most psychiatrists is the United States. The registered membership of the American Psychiatric Association (instituted in 1844) was 38,000 as of 1 Jan 1993, and the membership of the American Psychological Association (instituted in 1892) was 118,000.

Death rate The crude death rate—the number of deaths per 1,000 population of all ages—for the whole world was an estimated 9.8 per 1,000 in the period 1985–90. East Timor had a rate of 45.0 per 1,000 from 1975–80, although this had subsided to 21.5 in 1985–90. The highest estimated rate for the same period was 23.4 for Sierra Leone. The lowest estimated rate for 1985–90 was 3.8 deaths per 1,000 for Bahrain and the United Arab Emirates.

United States The crude death rate for the United States in 1992 was 8.5 per 1,000 persons or 2,177,000 people.

Natural increase The rate of natural increase (crude birthrate minus crude death rate) for the whole world was estimated to be 17.3 (27.1 minus 9.8) per 1,000 in the period 1985–90 compared with a peak of 22 per 1,000 in 1965. The highest of the latest available recorded rates was 37.4 (51.1 less 13.7) for Zambia in 1985–90. The lowest rate of natural increase in any major independent country in recent times was in the former West Germany, which experienced a decline in the same period, with a figure of –1.5 per 1,000 (10.7 births and 12.2 deaths).

Suicide The estimated daily rate of suicide throughout the world surpassed 1,000 in 1965. The country with the highest suicide rate is Sri Lanka, with a rate of 47 per 100,000 population in 1991. The country with the lowest recorded rate is Jordan, with just a single case in 1970 and hence a rate of 0.04 per 100,000.

Marriage The marriage rate for the Northern Mariana Islands, in the Pacific Ocean, is 31.2 per 1,000 population.

United States In the United States the median age at first marriage in 1991 was 26.3 years for men and 24.1 years for women. In 1992, 3,362,000 couples were married.

Divorce The country with the most divorces is the United States, with a total of 1,215,000 in 1992—a rate of 4.7 per 1,000 population. The all-time high rate was 5.3 per 1,000 population in 1979 and 1981. The all-time low was 2.0 per 1,000 population in 1940.

Sex ratio There were estimated to be 1,014 males in the world for every 1,000 females in 1990. The country with the largest recorded shortage of males is the Ukraine, with an estimated 1,153 females to every 1,000 males. The country with the largest recorded shortage of women in 1990 was the United Arab Emirates, with an estimated 493 females to every 1,000 males.

Infant mortality The world infant mortality rate—the number of deaths at ages under one year per 1,000 live births—in 1985–90 was 71.0 per 1,000 live births. Based on deaths before one year of age, the lowest of the latest recorded rates is 5.0 in Japan in 1987.

In Ethiopia the infant mortality rate was unofficially estimated to be nearly 550 per 1,000 live births in 1969. The highest rate recently estimated is 172.1 per 1,000 in Afghanistan (1985–90).

United States The infant mortality rate for the United States in 1992 was estimated to be 8.5 per 1,000 live births, or 34,400. In 1990, California had most infant mortalities, with 4,722, while Vermont had the least, at 53.

LOWEST BIRTHRATE Apart from Vatican City, the country with the lowest birthrate is San Marino. (Photo: Sygma/Raymond Reuter)

TOURISM France is the most popular destination for tourists, with winter sports being just as much an attraction as summer vacations. (Photo: Sygma/B. Annebicque)

WORST DISASTERS IN THE WORLD

Type of Disaster	Number Killed	Location	Date
Pandemic	75,000,000	Eurasia: The Black Death (bubonic, pneumonic and septicemic plague)	1347–51
Genocide	c. 35,000,000	Mongol extermination of Chinese peasantry	1311–40
Famine[1]	c. 30,000,000	Northern China	1959–61
Influenza	21,640,000	Worldwide	1918–19
Atomic Bomb	155,200	Hiroshima, Japan (including radiation deaths within year)	6 Aug 1945
Convientional Bombing[2]	c. 140,000	Tokyo, Japan	10 Mar 1945
Marine (Single Ship)	c. 7,700	*Wilhelm Gustloff* (28,542.1 tons) German liner torpedoed off Danzig by USSR submarine S-13 (only 903 survivors)	30 Jan 1945
Dam Burst[3]	c. 5,000	Machhu River Dam, Morvi, Gujarat, India	11 Aug 1979
Panic	c. 4,000	Chongquig, China, air raid shelter	6 Jun 1941
Smog	3,500–4,000	London, Great Britain	4–9 Dec 1952
Industrial (Chemical)	3,350	Union Carbide methylisocyanate plant, Bhopal, India	2–3 Dec 1984
Tunneling (Silicosis)	c. 2,500	Hawk's Nest hydroelectric tunnel, West Virginia	1931–35
Fire (Single building)[4]	1,670	The Theatre, Canton, China	May 1845
Explosion[5]	1,635	Halifax, Nova Scotia, Canada	6 Dec 1917
Mining[6]	1,549	Honkeiko Colliery, (Benxihu) China (coal dust explosion)	26 Apr 1942
Tornado	c. 1,300	Shaturia, Bangladesh	26 Apr 1989
Riot	c. 1,200	New York draft riots	13–16 Jul 1863
Mass Suicide[7]	960	Jewish Zealots, Masada, Israel	A.D. 73
Railway	>800	Bagmati River, Bihar, India	6 Jun 1981
Fireworks	>800	Dauphin's wedding, Seine, Paris, France	16 May 1770
Aircraft (Civil)[8]	583	KLM-Pan Am Boeing 747 ground crash, Tenerife, Canary Islands, Spain	27 Mar 1977
Man-eating Animal	436	Champawat district, India, tigress shot by Col. Jim Corbet (died 1955)	1902–10
Terrorism	329	Bomb aboard Air-India Boeing 747, crashed into Atlantic southwest of Ireland. Sikh extremists suspected	23 Jun 1985
Road[9]	176	Gas tanker explosion inside Salang Tunnel, Afghanistan	3 Nov 1982
Offshore Oil Platform	167	Piper Alpha oil production platform, North Sea	6 Jul 1988

Submarine	130	Le Surcouf rammed by US merchantman Thomas Lykes in Caribbean	18 Feb 1942
Helicopter	61	Russian military helicopter carrying refugees shot down near Lata, Georgia	14 Dec 1992
Mountaineering	43	Lenin Peak, Tajikistan/Kyrgyzstan border (then USSR)	13 Jul 1990
Ski Lift (Cable car)	42	Cavalese resort, northern Italy	9 Mar 1976
Nuclear Reactor[10]	31	Chernobyl No. 4, Ukraine (then USSR)	26 Apr 1986
Elevator (Lift)	31	Gold mine lift at Vaal Reefs, South Africa fell 1.2 miles	27 Mar 1980
Yacht Racing	19	28th Fastnet Race—23 boats sank or abandoned in Force 11 gale	13–15 Aug 1979
Space Exploration[11]	7	US Challenger 51L Shuttle, Cape Canaveral, FL	28 Jan 1986
Nuclear Waste Accident[12]	high but undisclosed	Venting of plutonium extraction wastes, Kyshtym, Russia (then USSR)	c. Dec 1957

1 It has been estimated that more than 5 million died in the post–World War I famine of 1920–21 in the USSR. The USSR government in July 1923 informed Mr (later President) Herbert Hoover that the ARA (American Relief Administration) had since August 1921 saved 20 million lives from famine and famine-related diseases.

2 The number of civilians killed by the bombing of Germany has been put variously at 593,000 and "over 635,000," including some 35,000 deaths in the raids on Dresden, Germany from, 13–15 Feb 1945. Total Japanese fatalities were 600,000 (conventional) and 220,000 (nuclear).

3 The dynamiting of a Yangtze Kiang dam at Huayuan Kow by the Kuomintang during the Sino-Japanese war in 1938 is reputed to have resulted in 900,000 deaths.

4 >200,000 were killed in the sack of Moscow, as a result of fires started by the invading Tartars in May 1571. In the worst-ever hotel fire, 162 were killed in the Hotel Daeyungak, Seoul, South Korea, 25 Dec 1971. The worst circus fire killed 168 in Hartford, CT 6 Jul 1944.

5 Some sources maintain that the final death toll was over 3,000 on 6–7 December. Published estimates of the 11,000 killed at the BASF chemical plant explosion at Oppau, Germany on 21 Sep 1921 were exaggerated. The most reliable estimate is 561 killed.

6 The worst gold-mining disaster in South Africa was when 182 were killed in Kinross gold mine on 16 Sep 1986.

7 As reported by the historian Flavius Josephus (c. 37–100). In modern times, the greatest mass suicide was on 18 Nov 1978 when 913 members of the People's Temple cult died of mass cyanide poisoning near Port Kaituma, Guyana. In June 1943, 22,000 Japanese jumped off a cliff during the US Marines' assault on the island of Tarawa (now in Kiribati).

8 The crash of JAL's Boeing 747, flight 123, near Tokyo on 12 Aug 1985, in which 520 passengers and crew perished, was the worst crash involving a single plane in aviation history.

9 Western estimates gave the number of deaths at c. 1,100. Latvia has the highest fatality rate in road accidents, with 34.7 deaths per 100,000 population, and Malta the lowest, with 1.6 per 100,000. The worst year for road deaths in the United States was 1972 (56,278).

10 Explosion at 0123 hrs local time. Thirty-one was the official Soviet total of immediate deaths. It is not known how many of the c. 200,000 people involved in the cleanup died in the five-year period following the disaster since no systematic records were kept. The senior scientific officer, Vladimir Chernousen-ko, who gave himself two to four years to live due to his exposure to radiation, put the death toll at between 7,000 and 10,000 in a statement on 13 Apr 1991.

11 In the greatest space disaster on the ground, 91 people were killed when a R-16 rocket exploded during fueling at the Baikonur Space Center, Kazakhstan, on 24 Oct 1960.

12 More than 30 small communities in a 460 mile² area were eliminated from maps of the USSR in the years after the accident, with 17,000 people evacuated. It was possibly an ammonium nitrate-hexone explosion. A report released in 1992 indicated that 8,015 people had died over a 32-year period of observation as a direct result of discharges from the complex.

Life expectancy World life expectancy is rising from 47.5 years (1950–55) towards 63.9 years (1995–2000). In the decade 1890–1900, life expectancy among the population of India was 23.7 years.

The highest average life expectancy at birth is in Japan, with 82.1 years for women and 76.1 years for men in 1991. The lowest life expectancy at birth for the period 1985–90 is 39.4 years for males in Ethiopia and Sierra Leone, and 42.0 years for females in Afghanistan.

United States In the United States the average life expectancy is 75.4 years for men and 78.8 years for women.

Physicians The country with the greatest number of physicians is China, which had 1,763,000 physicians in 1990, including those practicing dentistry and those practicing traditional Chinese medicine. The United States had 653,062 physicians on 1 Jan 1992.

Chad has the highest number of people per physician, with 47,640, while at the other extreme, in Italy there is one physician for every 225 people.

Dentists The country with the most dentists is the United States, where there were 190,842, with 139,625 (72.3 percent) registered members of the American Dental Association on 31 Dec 1992.

POLITICAL UNREST

Biggest demonstration A figure of 2.7 million was reported from China for a demonstration against the USSR in Shanghai on 3–4 Mar 1969 following border clashes.

Saving of life The greatest number of people saved from extinction by one person is estimated to be nearly 100,000 Jews in Budapest, Hungary from July 1944 to January 1945 by the Swedish diplomat Raoul Wallenberg (b. 4 Aug 1912). After escaping an assassination attempt by the Nazis, he was imprisoned without trial in the Soviet Union. On 6 Feb 1957 Andrey Gromyko, Deputy Foreign Minister, said prisoner "Walenburg" had died in a cell in Lubyanka Jail, Moscow on 16 Jul 1947. Sighting reports within the Gulag system persisted for years after his disappearance. He was made an Honorary Citizen of the United States on 5 Oct 1981, and on 7 May 1987 a statue to him was unveiled in Budapest to replace an earlier one that had been removed.

Mass killings China The greatest massacre ever imputed by the government of one sovereign nation to the government of another is that of 26.3 million Chinese during the regime of Mao Zedong (Tse-tung) (1893–1976) between 1949 and May 1965. This accusation was made by an agency of the Soviet government in a radio broadcast on 7 Apr 1969. The broadcast broke down the figure into four periods: 2.8 million (1949–52); 3.5 million (1953–57); 6.7 million (1958–60); and 13.3 million (1961–May 1965).

The Walker Report, published by the US Senate Committee of the Judiciary in July 1971, placed the parameters of the total death toll within China since 1949 between 32.25 and 61.7 million. An estimate of 63.7 million was published by *Le Figaro* Magazine, 19–25 Nov 1978.

From the 13th through the 17th centuries there were three periods of wholesale massacre in China. The numbers of victims attributed to these events are assertions rather than reliable estimates. The figures given for the

Mongolian invasions of northern China from 1210–19 and from 1311–40 are both on the order of 35 million, while the number of victims of the bandit leader Zhang Xianzhong (*c.* 1605–47), known as the "Yellow Tiger," from 1643–47 in the Siechuan province has been put at 40 million.

SAVING OF LIFE   Mystery still surrounds the fate of Raoul Wallenberg, who is estimated to have saved the lives of nearly 100,000 people during World War II. This photograph shows him in Swedish military uniform. (Photo: Popperfoto)

USSR Scholarly estimates for the number of human casualties of Soviet communism hover around 40 million, excluding those killed in the "Great Patriotic War." Larger figures are claimed in Moscow today, but these are not necessarily more authoritative.

Nazi Germany Reliable estimates of the number of victims of the Holocaust, the genocidal "Final Solution" (*End-lösung*) ordered by Adolf Hitler, starting before or at the latest by the fall of 1941 and continuing into May 1945, range from 5.1 to 6 million Jews. At the SS death camp at Auschwitz-Birkenau (Oświecim-Brzezinka), near Oświecim (Auschwitz) in southern Poland (annexed by Germany), it is estimated that over a million Jews and up to 2 million others were murdered from 14 Jun 1940 to 18 Jan 1945. The greatest number killed in a day was 6,000.

Cambodia As a percentage of a nation's total population the worst genocide appears to have been that in Cambodia (or Kampuchea). According to the Khmer Rouge Foreign Minister, Ieng Sary, more than a third of the 8 million Khmers were killed between 17 Apr 1975, when the Khmer Rouge captured Phnom Penh, and January 1979, when they were overthrown. Under the rule of Saloth Sar, alias Pol Pot, a founding member of the CPK (Communist Party of Kampuchea, formed in September 1960), towns, money and property were abolished, and execution by bayonet and club (the most economical methods) introduced. Deaths at the Tuol Sleng interrogation center reached 582 in a day.

STATES

Most populous The most populous state in the United States as of 1 Jul 1992 was California, with an estimated 30,867,000 people.

Least populous The least populous state as of 1 Jul 1992 was Wyoming, with 466,000 people.

Thirteen original states The thirteen original states were Connecticut, Delaware, Georgia, Maryland, Massachusetts, New Hampshire, New Jersey, New York, North Carolina, Pennsylvania, Rhode Island, South Carolina and Virginia.

Confederate states Eleven states seceded from the union between December 1860 and June 1861. They were (in order of secession): South Carolina, Mississippi, Florida, Alabama, Georgia, Louisiana, Texas, Virginia, Arkansas, North Carolina and Tennessee.

COUNTIES

As of year end 1992 there were 3,142 counties in the United States (in Alaska, counties are known as divisions, and in Louisiana they are called parishes). The largest in the lower 48 states is San Bernardino County, CA, with an area of 20,062 miles². The biggest legally established county is the North Slope Borough of Alaska at 87,860 acres. The state with the most counties is Texas with 254, and the state with the fewest is Delaware with three (Kent, New Castle and Sussex).

TOWNS AND CITIES

Oldest The oldest-known walled town in the world is Arihā (Jericho). Radio-carbon dating on specimens from the lowest levels reached by archaeologists indicates habitation there by perhaps 2,700 people as early as 7800 B.C. The settlement of Dolní Věstonice, Czech Republic has been dated to the Gravettian culture *c.* 27,000 B.C. The oldest capital city in the world is Dimashq (Damascus), Syria. It has been continuously inhabited since *c.* 2500 B.C.

United States The oldest town of European origin in the United States is St Augustine, St John's County, FL (present population 12,000), founded on 8 Sep 1565, on the site of Seloy by Pedro Menendez de Aviles.

The oldest incorporated city is York, ME (present population 14,000), which received an English charter in March 1642, and was incorporated under the name Georgiana.

Most populous The most populous urban agglomeration in the world, as listed in the United Nations *Prospects of World Urbanization 1990*, is Mexico City, with a population of 20,200,000. By the year 2000 it is expected to have increased to 25,600,000.

Tokyo-Yokohama, Japan, which in the late 1980s had been the most populous, is expected to have declined to third in the list by the turn of the century, with São Paulo in Brazil second. Censuses from individual countries and other surveys may give slightly different figures.

United States The largest metropolitan area in the United States is that of New York City, with 18,087,251 residents.

MOST POPULOUS CITY Poverty is rife in Mexico City, the world's most populous city. (Photo: Sygma/D Goldberg)

Housing For comparison purposes, a dwelling unit is defined as a structurally separated room or rooms occupied by a private household of one or more people and having separate access or a common passageway to the street.

The country with the greatest number of dwelling units is China, with 276,947,962 in 1990.

At the end of the fiscal year 1992 there were 96,391,000 households in the United States. Of these, 61,823,000 were owner-occupied (65.2 percent) and 31,568,000 (34.1 percent) were rentals.

Smallest incorporated place The smallest incorporated place in the United States in 1990 was Valley Park, OK, with one resident.

Largest city in area The world's largest city (defined as a densely populated settlement), in area, is Mount Isa, Queensland, Australia. The area administered by the City Council is 15,822 miles^2.

Highest The new town of Wenzhuan, founded in 1955 on the Qinghai–Tibet road north of the Tangla range, is the highest city in the world at 16,730 ft above sea level.

The highest incorporated city in the United States is Leadville, CO, at an elevation of 10,152 ft. Founded in 1878, Leadville has a current population of 2,629.

Capital city The highest capital in the world, before the domination of Tibet by China, was Lhasa, at an elevation of 12,087 ft above sea level. La Paz, administrative and *de facto* capital of Bolivia, stands at an altitude of 11,916 ft above sea level. Its airport, El Alto, is at 13,385 ft. The city was founded in 1548 by Capt. Alonso de Mendoza on the site of an Indian village named Chuquiapu. Sucre, the legal capital of Bolivia, stands at 9,301 ft above sea level.

Most remote from the sea The large town most remote from the sea is Urumqi (Wu-lu-mu-ch'i) in Xinjiang, the capital of China's Xinjiang Uygur Autonomous Region, at a distance of about 1,500 miles from the nearest coastline. Its population was estimated to be 1,160,000 in late 1990.

Greatest altitude The settlement on the T'e-li-mo trail in southern Tibet is sited at an altitude of 19,800 ft.

The highest inhabited buildings in the world are those in the Indo-Tibetan border fort of Bāsisi by the Māna Pass (Lat. 31° 04′ N, Long. 79° 24′ E) at *c.* 19,700 ft.

In April 1961 a three-room dwelling was discovered at 21,650 ft on Cerro Llullaillaco (22,057 ft), on the Argentina–Chile border, believed to date from the late pre-Columbian period *c.* 1480.

Lowest The Israeli settlement of Ein Bokek, which has a synagogue, on the shores of the Dead Sea is the lowest in the world, at 1,291 ft below sea level.

United States   The lowest incorporated city in the United States is Calipatria, CA, founded on 28 Feb 1919, at 184 ft below sea level. The flagpole outside city hall is 184 ft tall, allowing "Old Glory" to fly at sea level.

Northernmost   The northernmost village is Ny Ålesund (78° 55′ N), a settlement on King's Bay, Vest Spitsbergen, in the Norwegian territory of Svalbard. Its population varies from around 25 in winter to approaching 100 in summer. The northernmost capital is Reykjavik, Iceland (64° 08′ N). Its population was 99,623 in 1991.

United States   The northernmost city in the United States is Barrow, AK (71° 17′ N).

Southernmost   The world's southernmost village is Puerto Williams (population about 1,000) on the north coast of Isla Navarino, Tierra del Fuego, Chile, 680 miles north of Antarctica. Wellington, North Island, New Zealand, with a 1989 population of 324,600, is the southernmost capital city (41° 17′ S). The world's southernmost administrative center is Port Stanley, Falkland (Malvinas) Islands (51° 43′ S), with a population of 1,643 in 1991.

United States   The southernmost city in the United States is Hilo, HI (19° 43′ N).

HEADS OF STATE AND ROYALTY

Forty-five of the world's 191 sovereign states are not republics. They are headed by 1 emperor, 13 kings, 3 queens, 2 sultans, 1 grand duke, 2 princes, 3 emirs, an elected monarch, the Pope, a president chosen from and by 7 hereditary sheiks, a head of state currently similar to a constitutional monarch, and 2 nominal nonhereditary "princes" in one country. Queen Elizabeth II is head of state of Great Britain and 15 other Commonwealth countries.

Oldest ruling house   The Emperor of Japan, Akihito (b. 23 Dec 1933), is the 125th in line from the first Emperor, Jimmu Tenno or Zinmu, whose reign was traditionally from 660 to 581 B.C., but more probably dates from *c.* 40 B.C. to *c.* 10 B.C.

Reigns *Longest all-time*   The longest recorded reign of any monarch is that of Phiops II (also known as Pepi II), or Neferkare, a Sixth Dynasty pharaoh of ancient Egypt. His reign began *c.* 2281 B.C., when he was 6 years of age, and is believed to have lasted *c.* 94 years. Musoma Kanijo, chief of the Nzega district of western Tanganyika (now part of Tanzania), reputedly reigned for more than 98 years, from 1864, when he was 8 years old, until his death on 2 Feb 1963.

Longest current   The King of Thailand, Bhumibol Adulyadej (Rama IX; b. 5 Dec 1927), is currently the world's longest-reigning monarch, having succeeded to the throne on 9 Jun 1946. The longest-reigning queen is Queen

OLDEST RULING HOUSE   The enthronement of Akihito, the Emperor of the oldest ruling house in the world, in Japan on 12 Nov 1990. (Photo: Sygma)

Elizabeth II of the United Kingdom, who succeeded to the throne on 6 Feb 1952 on the death of her father.

Shortest   Crown Prince Luis Filipe of Portugal was mortally wounded at the same time that his father was killed by a bullet that severed his carotid artery (one of the two great arteries carrying blood to the head), in the streets of Lisbon on 1 Feb 1908. He was thus technically King of Portugal (Dom Luis III) for about 20 minutes.

Longest-lived royal   The longest life among the European royal blood was that of the Princess Pauline Marie Madeleine of Croy (1887–1987), who celebrated her 100th birthday in her birthplace of Le Roeulx, Belgium on 11 Jan 1987.

Youngest king and queen   The country with the youngest king is Swaziland, where King Mswati III was crowned on 25 Apr 1986 at the age of 18 years 6 days. He was born Makhosetive, the 67th son of King Subhusa II. The country with the youngest queen is Denmark, with Queen Margrethe II (b. 16 Apr 1940).

Heaviest monarch   The world's heaviest monarch is the 6-ft-3-in-tall King Taufa'ahau of Tonga, who in September 1976 was weighed on the only adequate scales in the country, at the airport, recording 462 lb. By 1985 he was reported to have slimmed down to 308 lb, and in early 1993 he weighed 280 lb.

Heads of state Oldest and youngest   The oldest head of state in the world is Félix Houphouët-Boigny, president of Ivory Coast (b. 18 Oct 1905). The youngest is King Mswati III of Swaziland (b. 19 Apr 1968). (See Youngest King and Queen, previous page.)

First female presidents   Isabel Perón (b. 4 Feb 1931) of Argentina became the world's first female president when she succeeded her husband on his death on 1 Jul 1974. She held office until she was deposed in a bloodless coup on 24 Mar 1976. President Vigdis Finnbogadottir (b. 15 Apr 1930) of Iceland became the world's first democratically elected female head of state on 30 Jun 1980.

Largest meeting   The summit segment of the United Nations Conference on Environment and Development, on 12–13 Jun 1992, was attended by 92 heads of state and heads of government—the largest gathering of world leaders. The summit had 103 participants altogether and was one of the meetings at the "Earth Summit," which was held in Rio de Janeiro, Brazil from 3–14 Jun 1992.

LEGISLATURES *United States*

PRESIDENTS

Oldest   The oldest president was Ronald Wilson Reagan, who was 69 years 349 days old when he took the oath of office. He was reelected at age 73.

Youngest   The youngest president to assume office was Theodore Roosevelt. Vice-President Roosevelt became president at the age of 42 years, 10 months when President William McKinley was assassinated in 1901. The youngest president ever elected was John Fitzgerald Kennedy, who took the oath of office at age 43 years 236 days in 1961.

PRESIDENTIAL RECORDS

Article II of the Constitution provides for the office of the presidency. The President is head of all executive agencies, has full responsibility for the execution of the laws, is commander in chief of the armed forces, conducts foreign affairs, and with the advice and consent of Congress appoints cabinet members and any other executive officials. The Constitution sets the term of office at four years and requires that the position be filled by election through the Electoral College. The Twenty-second Amendment (1951) limits a president to two consecutive four-year terms. To be eligible for the presidency one must be a native-born citizen, over 35 years old, and at least 14 years resident in the United States.

Longest term in office	12 years 39 days	Franklin Delano Roosevelt	1933–45
Shortest term in office	32 days	William Henry Harrison	4 Mar–4 Apr 1841
Youngest to assume office	42 years 10 months	Theodore Roosevelt	1901–09
Youngest elected	43 years 236 days	John Fitzgerald Kennedy	1961–63
Oldest elected	69 years 349 days	Ronald Wilson Reagan	1981–89
Tallest	6 ft 4 in	Abraham Lincoln	1861–65
Shortest	5 ft 4 in	James Madison	1809–17
Longest-lived	90 years 258 days	John Adams	1797–1801
Shortest-lived	46 years 6 months	John Fitzgerald Kennedy	1961–63
Longest life after presidency	31 years 7 months	Herbert Clark Hoover	1929–33
Shortest life after presidency	105 days	James K. Polk	1845–49
Heaviest	354 lb	William Howard Taft	1909–13
Most children	15	John Tyler	1841–45
Most children (one spouse)	10	William Henry Harrison	1841
Bachelor		James Buchanan	1857–61
Resigned		Richard M. Nixon	1969–74
Assassinated	14 Apr 1865	Abraham Lincoln	1861–65
	2 Jul 1881	James A. Garfield	1881
	6 Sep 1901	William H. McKinley	1897–1901
	22 Nov 1963	John Fitzgerald Kennedy	1961–63

FIRST LADIES

Hillary Rodham Clinton is the 38th first lady. The term itself dates only from the time of Lucy Ware Webb Hayes, who was the 16th first lady in 1887–81.

First and earliest born ..21 Jun 1731 ....Martha Dandridge Custis (1731–1802) ....m George Washington

Longest tenure ....12 years 39 days; 1933–45 (Anna) Eleanor Roosevelt (1884–1962) ....m Franklin D. Roosevelt

Shortest tenure ....32 days in 1841 ....Anna Tuthill Symmes (1775–1864) ....m William H. Harrison

Most children ....6 sons, 4 daughters ....Anna Tuthill Symmes ....m William H. Harrison

Fewest children ....None ....Five first ladies were childless: Martha Dandridge Custis Washington
(1731–1802), Dorothea "Dolley" Payne Madison (1768–1849), Sarah
Childress Polk (1803–91), Edith Bolling Galt Wilson (1872–1961) and Florence
(Kling) De Wolfe Harding (1860–1924).

Largest gathering ....8 ....At inauguration of John F. Kennedy (1917–63) in Washington, D.C. on
20 Jan 1961—his wife, 4 past and 3 future first ladies.

Commonest home state ..New York (8) ....18 other states represented. Only foreign-born first lady has been Louisa
Catherine Johnson (1775–1852), in London, England on 12 Feb 1775. She mar-
ried John Quincy Adams there on 26 Jul 1797.

Commonest ancestry ......All 38 have British ancestry; 25 have purely English ancestry.

Rarest ancestry ....Only 1 has Native American ancestry—Edith Bolling Galt Wilson (see above) was a ninth-generation
descendant of Princess Pocahontas (c. 1595–1617).

HANDSHAKING While Theodore Roosevelt holds the handshaking record for a politician, Scott Killon shook hands with 25,289 different visitors in just eight hours at Expo 92 in Seville, Spain. He began at the pavilion of his own country, Canada, and visited a number of other areas of the exhibition in the course of the evening. (Photo: Canadian Government)

Term of office Franklin D. Roosevelt served the longest term—12 years 39 days (1933–45). The shortest term in office was 32 days (4 Mar–4 Apr 1841) by William Henry Harrison.

Largest gathering The largest gathering of men who had been or would become president was eight, on 30 Dec 1834 in the old House Chamber of the Capitol: ex-president John Quincy Adams; ex-president Andrew Jackson; Vice-President Martin Van Buren; Senator John Tyler; Senator James Buchanan; and Representatives James K. Polk, Millard Fillmore and Franklin Pierce.

ELECTIONS

Largest popular majority Since the introduction of the popular vote in presidential elections in 1872, the greatest majority won was 17,994,460 votes in 1972 when President Richard M. Nixon (Republican) defeated George S. McGovern (Democrat) with 47,165,234 votes to 29,170,774.

Smallest popular majority The smallest popular majority was 7,023 votes in 1880 when President James A. Garfield (Republican) defeated Winfield Scott Hancock (Democrat) with 4,449,053 votes to 4,442,030.

Largest electoral college majority Since 1872, the greatest electoral college majority was 515 votes in 1936 when President Franklin D. Roosevelt (Democrat) defeated Alfred M. Landon (Republican) with 523 votes to 8.

VICE-PRESIDENTS

Longest term of office   Only five vice-presidents have served two full four-year terms in office: John Adams (1789–97), Thomas R. Marshall (1913–1921), John Nance Garner (1933–41), Richard Nixon (1953–61) and George Bush (1981–89).

Youngest to hold office   The youngest man to become vice-president was John Cabell Breckinridge (Democrat; b. 21 Jan 1821), who took office on 4 Mar 1857 at the age of 36 years 1 month.

Handshaking   The record number of hands shaken by a public figure at an official function was 8,513, by President Theodore Roosevelt (1858–1919) at a New Year's Day White House presentation in Washington, D.C. in 1907.

Most roll calls   Senator William Proxmire (D-Wisconsin) did not miss a single one of the 9,695 roll calls from April 1966 to 27 Aug 1987. Rep. William H. Natcher (D- Kentucky) has cast 13,719 consecutive roll call votes and responded in person to 4,229 recorded quorum calls, for a total of 17,948 votes to 7 Jun 1993. He has not missed a roll call or quorum call since being sworn in as a House member on 6 Jan 1954, a total of 39 years.

Most patents   Thomas Alva Edison (1847–1931) has had the most patents, with 1,093 either on his own or jointly. They included the microphone, the motion-picture projector and the incandescent electric lamp.

Most expensive election   The Federal Election Commission reported on 30 Dec 1992 that the 1992 congressional campaign was the most expensive in history. Candidates spent a total of $504 million, Senate candidates spending $190 million and House candidates $314 million.

Most inexplicable legislation   Certain pieces of legislation have always defied interpretation, and the most inexplicable must be a matter of opinion. A judge of the Court of Session of Scotland once sent the Editor his candidate for most confusingly worded law, which reads: *"In the Nuts (unground), (other than ground nuts) Order, the expression nuts shall have reference to such nuts, other than ground nuts, as would but for this amending Order not qualify as nuts (unground) (other than ground nuts) by reason of their being nuts (unground)."*

Fastest amendment   The constitutional amendment that took the shortest time to ratify after congressional approval was the 26th Amendment, which gave 18-year-olds the right to vote. It was approved by Congress 23 Mar 1971, and ratified 1 Jul 1971.

GOVERNORS*

State	Youngest	Oldest
Alabama	Thomas Bibb (1820–21) ......36 yr	Hugh McVay (1837) ......71 yr
Alaska	Keith Miller (1969–70) ......44 yr 2 mo	Walter J. Hickell (1991–) ......71 yr 5 mo
Arizona	Bruce E. Babbitt (1978–87) ......39 yr 9 mo	George W.P. Hunt (1930–32) ......71 yr
Arkansas	Bill Clinton (1979–81, 1983–92) ......32 yr 5 mo	Thomas C. McRae (1921–25) ......69 yr 22 days
California	J. Neely Johnson (1856–58) ......30 yr 5 mo	Frank Merriam (1934–39) ......68 yr 5 mo
Colorado	James B. Grant (1883–85) ......35 yr 7 days	Edwin C. Johnson (1955–57) ......71 yr 10 days
Connecticut	Joseph R. Hawley (1866–67) ......39 yr 6 mo	Simeon E. Baldwin (1911–15) ......72 yr 10 mo
Delaware	William Temple (1846–47) ......31 or 32 yr	Caleb Prew Bennett (1833–36) ......74 yr
Florida	Park Trammell (1913–17) ......37 yr	Frederick P. Cone (1937–41) ......66 yr
Georgia	Herman E. Talmadge (1947–55) ......33 yr	Lamartine G. Hardman (1927–31) ......73 yr
Hawaii	William Quinn (1959–62) ......40 yr	John A. Burns (1962–73) ......61 yr
Idaho	Frank Steunenberg (1897–1900) ......35 yr 4 mo	James H. Hawley (1911–12) ......63 yr 11 mo
Illinois	John M. Hamilton (1883–84) ......35 yr 8 mo	Louis L. Emmerson (1929–33) ......65 yr 18 days
Indiana	James B. Ray (1825–31) ......30 yr	James D. Williams (1877–80) ......68 yr 11 mo
Iowa	Terry Branstad (1983–) ......36 yr 2 mo	Francis M. Drake (1896–98) ......65 yr 1 mo
Kansas	Samuel J.G. Crawford (1865–68) ......29 yr 8 mo	Joan Finney (1991–) ......65 yr 11 mo 2 days
Kentucky	J.C.W. Beckham (1900–07) ......30 yr 5 mo	James B. McCreary (1875–79,1911–15) ......73 yr 5 mo
Louisiana	Henry C. Warmouth (1868–72) ......26 yr 1 mo	Joshua Baker (1868) ......68 yr
Maine	William Tudor (1929–33) ......27 yr	S.S. Marble (1887–89) ......69 yr
Maryland	Edward Lloyd (1809–11) ......29 yr	Robert M. McLane (1884–85) ......68 yr
Massachusetts	William E. Russell (1891–94) ......33 yr	Samuel Adams (1793–97) ......71 yr
Michigan	Stevens T. Mason (1835–40) ......24 yr	Lauren D. Dickinson (1939–40) ......79 yr 11 mo
Minnesota	Harold E. Stassen (1939–43) ......31 yr 8 mo	Samuel Van Sant (1901–05) ......58 yr 7 mo
Mississippi	Albert G. Brown (1844–48) ......30 yr	Henry L. Whitfield (1924–27) ......65 yr

State	Youngest Governor	Age	Oldest Governor	Age
Missouri	Joseph W. Folk (1905–09)	35 yr 2 mo	Forrest Smith (1949–53)	62 yr 10 mo
Montana	Joseph K. Toole (1889–93, 1901–08)	38 yr 5 mo	John E. Erickson (1925–33)	69 yr 9 mo
Nebraska	Albinus Nance (1879–83)	30 yr 9 mo	John M. Thayer (1887–91, 1891–92)	67 yr
Nevada	Emet D. Boyle (1915–22)	35 yr 6 mo	Lewis R. Bradley (1871–78)	69 yr 2 mo
New Hampshire	Levi Woodbury (1823–24)	34 yr	Moody Currier (1885–87)	79 yr
New Jersey	Rodman M. Price (1854–57)	37 yr 7 mo	Charles S. Olden (1860–63)	61 yr
New Mexico	David E. Cargo (1967–71)	37 yr 11 mo	Bruce King (1971–75,1979–83, 1991–)	66 yr 8 mo
New York	Daniel D. Tompkins (1807–17)	33 yr	John Taylor (1817)	74 yr 7 mo
North Carolina	David L. Swain (1832–35)	31 yr	Samuel Ashe (1795–98)	70 yr
North Dakota	Joseph M. Devine (1898)	37 yr 5 mo	Walter Welford (1935–36)	66 yr 8 mo
Ohio	Thomas W. Barkley (1844)	32 yr	William Allen (1874–76)	71 yr
Oklahoma	J. Howard Edmondson (1959–63)	33 yr 3 mo	Henry Bellmon (1963–67, 1987–91)	65 yr 4 mo
Oregon	Jay Bowerman (1910–11)	33 yr 10 mo	Gen Charles H. Martin (1935–39)	71 yr 3 mo
Pennsylvania	Robert E. Pattison (1883–87, 1891–95)	32 yr	David L. Lawrence (1959–63)	69 yr
Rhode Island	William Sprague (1860–63)	29 yr	James Fenner (1807–11, 1824–31, 1843–45)	73 yr
South Carolina	John G. Evans (1894–97)	31 yr	James F. Byrnes (1951–55)	71 yr
South Dakota	Richard Kneip (1971–78)	37 yr 11 mo	Warren Green (1931–33)	60 yr 9 mo
Tennessee	James C. Jones (1841–45)	32 yr 4 mo	Alfred A. Taylor (1921–23)	72 yr 5 mo
Texas	Dan Moody (1927–31)	33 yr 7 mo	William Clements, Jr. (1979–83,1987–91)	69 yr 9 mo
Utah	Heber M. Wells (1896–1905)	36 yr	Simon Bamberger (1917–21)	70 yr
Vermont	F. Ray Keyser Jr (1961–63)	34 yr	Erastus Fairbanks (1852–53,1860–61)	78 yr
Virginia	William H. Cabel (1805–08)	32 yr 11 mo	William H. Mann (1910–14)	66 yr 6 mo
Washington	Daniel J. Evans (1965–77)	39 yr 2 mo	Elisha P. Ferry (1889–93)	64 yr 3 mo
West Virginia	Cecil H. Underwood (1957–61)	34 yr	Mathew M. Neeley (1941–45)	66 yr
Wisconsin	Edward Salomon (1862–64)	33 yr	Walter S. Goodland (1943–47)	84 yr
Wyoming	John E. Osborne (1893–95)	34 yr 11 mo	Joseph M. Carey (1911–15)	65 yr 11 mo

* Records are for the youngest and oldest governors per state at the time of election.

Oldest to hold office   Alben William Barkley (Democrat; b. 24 Nov 1877) took office on 20 Jan 1949 at the age of 71 years 40 days. He served a full four-year term.

Longest-lived   The longest-lived vice-president was John Nance Garner, who served under Franklin D. Roosevelt from 1933 to 1941. He was born in 1868 and died on 7 Nov 1967 at the age of 98.

CONGRESS

Speaker of the House of Representatives   In 1947 Congress enacted a law placing the Speaker of the House first in line to the presidency should both the president and vice-president die, become incapacitated or be disqualified from office. James K. Polk is the only person to hold the offices of speaker (1835–39) and president (1845–49).

Longest service   The longest time served by any speaker was 17 years, by Sam Rayburn (1882–1961; D-Texas). Rayburn served three terms: 1940–47, 1949–53, 1955–61.

Shortest term   The shortest term of any speaker was one day, 3 Mar 1869, served by Theodore Medad Pomeroy (1824–1905; R-New York).

Oldest speaker   The oldest speaker was Sam Rayburn (D-Texas), who was re-elected speaker for the 87th Congress on 3 Jan 1961 at age 78 years 11 months.

Youngest speaker   The youngest speaker was Robert Mercer Taliaferro Hunter (1809–87; D-Virginia), who was chosen speaker for the 26th Congress on 2 Dec 1839 at age 30 years 7 months.

House of Representatives   The longest any representative has ever served is 51 years 6 months (as of June 1993), by Rep. Jamie L. Whitten (D-Mississippi). He began his career on 4 Nov 1941.

Youngest elected   The youngest man ever to serve in the House was William Charles Cole Claiborne (1775–1817; Jeffersonian Democrat-Tennessee), who, in contravention of the 25-year age requirement of the Constitution, was elected in August 1797 at the age of 22.

Oldest elected   The oldest man ever elected representative was Claude Denson Pepper (1900–89; D-Florida), who was reelected on 8 Nov 1988 at age 88 years 2 months.

Senate   The longest any senator has ever served is 42 years, by Carl Trumbull Hayden (1877–1972; D-Arizona). Hayden served in the Senate from 1927–69. (See also Congressional service.) The current longest-serving member of the Senate is James Strom Thurmond (b. 5 Dec 1902; R-South Carolina). As of June 1993 Thurmond has served for 38 years. He was originally elected as a Democrat in December 1954, but changed to the Republican Party in 1964.

Oldest elected   The greatest age at which anyone has been returned as a senator is 87 years 11 months, the age at which Strom Thurmond (R-South Carolina) was reelected in November 1990.

Youngest elected   The youngest person ever elected senator was Brig. Gen. Armistead Thomson Mason (1787–1819; D-Virginia), who was elected on 3 Jan 1816 and was sworn in on 22 January at the age of 28 years 5 months 18 days. The youngest-ever senator was John Henry Eaton (1790–1856; D-Tennessee), who was appointed on 5 Sep 1818 and sworn in on 16 November at age 28 years 4 months 29 days.

Most expensive seats   In 1992 Rep. Barbara Boxer (D-California) spent a record $10,289,773 in her successful attempt to win the California senate seat vacated by the retirement of Sen. Alan Cranston (D). This election was the most expensive in congressional history, with Boxer's Republican opponent, Bruce Herschensohn, spending $7,408,101. Herschensohn also gained the dubious distinction of becoming the biggest-spending losing candidate in Senate history.

Highest-paid legislators   The most highly paid of all the world's legislators are members of the US Congress. The annual salary for members of the House of Representatives and members of the Senate is $133,600. The President of the United States has an annual salary of $200,000, a $50,000 per year expense account, and a lifetime pension of $138,900 per year.

Filibusters   The longest continuous speech in the history of the Senate was that of Senator Wayne Morse (1900–74; D-Oregon) on 24–25 Apr 1953, when he spoke on the Tidelands oil bill for 22 hr 26 min without resuming his seat. Interrupted only briefly by the swearing-in of a new senator, Senator Strom Thurmond (b. 5 Dec 1902) (R-South Carolina) spoke against a civil rights bill for 24 hr 19 min on 28–29 Aug 1957. The record on a state level is 43 hr, by Texas State Senator Bill Meier, who spoke against nondisclosure of industrial accidents, in May 1977.

POLITICAL OFFICE HOLDERS

Congressional service   Carl Hayden (1877–1972; D-Arizona) holds the record for the longest congressional service, a total of 57 consecutive years (1912–69), of which 42 years were spent as a senator and the remainder as a representative.

LEGISLATURES *World*

PARLIAMENTS

Earliest and oldest   The earliest-known legislative assembly or *ukkim* was a bicameral one in Erech, Iraq, *c.* 2800 B.C. The oldest recorded legislative body is the *Althing* of Iceland, founded in A.D. 930. This body was abolished in 1800, but restored by Denmark to a consultative status in 1843 and a legislative status in 1874. The legislative assembly with the oldest *continuous* history is the Isle of Man Tynwald, Great Britain, which may have its origins in the late ninth century and possibly predates the *Althing*.

Largest   The largest legislative assembly in the world is the National People's Congress of the People's Republic of China, which has 2,978 single-party members who are indirectly elected for a five-year term. The eighth congress convened in March 1993.

Smallest quorum   The House of Lords in Great Britain has the smallest quorum, expressed as a percentage of members eligible to vote, of any legislative body in the world—less than one-third of 1 percent. To transact business, there must be three peers present, including the lord chancellor or his deputy.

Greatest petitions   The largest petition on record was signed by 13,078,935 people in South Korea between 11 Nov–23 Dec 1991. They were protesting against efforts by advanced agricultural exporting countries to open their country's rice market to foreign imports.

Longest membership   The longest span as a legislator was 83 years, by József Madarász (1814–1915). He first attended the Hungarian Parliament from 1832–86 as *oblegatus absentium* (i.e., on behalf of an absent deputy). He was a full member from 1848–50 and from 1861 until his death on 31 Jan 1915.

Longest speeches   The longest speech made was one by Chief Mangosuthu Buthelezi, the Zulu leader, when he gave an address to the KwaZulu legislative assembly between 12 and 29 Mar 1993. He spoke on 11 of the 18 days, averaging nearly 2½ hours on each of the 11 days.

United Nations   The longest speech made in the United Nations was one of 4 hr 29 min on 26 Sep 1960 by President Fidel Castro Ruz (b. 13 Aug 1927) of Cuba.

Most crooked election   In the Liberian presidential election of 1927, President Charles D.B. King (1875–1961) was returned with an officially announced majority of 234,000 over his opponent, Thomas J.R. Faulkner of the People's Party. President King thus claimed a "majority" more than 15½ times greater than the entire electorate.

Largest political party   The largest political party is the Chinese Communist Party, formed in 1920, with a membership estimated to be 50,320,000 in 1991.

Largest field of candidates   There were 301 candidates running to represent one seat, that of Belgaum City, in the State Assembly (Vidhan Sabha) elections in Karnataka, India held on 5 Mar 1985.

Most coups   Statisticians contend that Bolivia, since it became a sovereign country in 1825, has had 191 coups, the latest on 30 Jun 1984, when President Hernan Siles Zuazo, age 70, was temporarily kidnapped from his official residence by more than 60 armed men masquerading as police officers.

Oldest treaty   The oldest treaty still in force is the Anglo-Portuguese Treaty, which was signed in London, Great Britain over 620 years ago on 16 Jun 1373. The text was confirmed "with my usual flourish" by John de Banketre, Clerk.

Constitutions   The world's oldest national constitution still in uninterrupted use is that of the United States of America, ratified by the necessary ninth state (New Hampshire) on 21 Jun 1788 and declared to be in effect on 4 Mar 1789.

Woman's suffrage   As far back as 1838 the Pitcairn Islands incorporated female suffrage in its constitution, although this was only *de facto* and not legally binding. The earliest legislature with female voters was that of the Territory of Wyoming in 1869, followed by that of the Isle of Man, Great Britain in 1881. The earliest country to have universal woman's suffrage was New Zealand in 1893.

United States   In 1920 the 19th Amendment to the Constitution granted nationwide suffrage to women.

ELECTIONS

Largest   The largest elections in the world were those beginning on 20 May 1991 for the Indian *Lok Sabha* (Lower House), which has 543 elective seats. A total of 315,439,908 people cast their votes out of an eligible electorate of 488,678,993. The elections were contested by 359 parties, and there were nearly 565,000 polling stations manned by 3 million people. As a result of the election a new government was formed under the leadership of P.V. Narasimha Rao of the Congress (I) Party.

Closest   The ultimate in close general elections occurred in Zanzibar (now part of Tanzania) on 18 Jan 1961, when the Afro-Shirazi Party won by a single seat, after the seat of Chake-Chake on Pemba Island had been gained by a single vote.
   The narrowest recorded percentage win in an election would seem to be for the office of Southern District Highway Commissioner in Mississippi on 7 Aug 1979. Robert E. Joiner was declared the winner over W.H. Pyron, with 133,587 votes to 133,582. The loser thus obtained more than 49.999 percent of the votes.

Most decisive   North Korea recorded a 100 percent turnout of electors and a 100 percent vote for the Workers' Party of Korea in the general election of 8 Oct 1962. An almost unanimous vote occurred in Albania on 14 Nov 1982, when a single voter spoiled national unanimity for the official (and only) candidates, who consequently obtained 99.99993 percent of the vote in a reported 100 percent turnout of 1,627,968.

Longest in power   In Mongolia the Communists (Mongolian People's Revolutionary Party) have been in power since 1924, although only in the last three years within a multiparty system. In February 1992 the term "People's Republic" was dropped from the name, and all Russian troops have now left the country.

Highest personal majority   The highest-ever personal majority for any politi-

POLITICAL PARTY—LONGEST IN POWER   The Mongolian People's Revolutionary Party has held power since 1924—until three years ago without any opposition, but since then in a multiparty system. The 1990 elections gave the people the opportunity to reject Communism, but they voted in favor of it. (Photo: Sygma/L Zilberman)

cian was 4,726,112 by Boris Yeltsin, in the parliamentary elections held in the former Soviet Union on 26 Mar 1989. Yeltsin received 5,118,745 votes out of the 5,722,937 that were cast in the Moscow constituency, his closest rival obtaining 392,633 votes. Benazir Bhutto achieved 96.71 percent of the vote in the Larkana-III constituency in the 1988 general election in Pakistan, with 82,229 votes. The next highest candidate obtained just 1,979 votes.

PRIME MINISTERS AND HEADS OF STATE

Oldest   The longest-lived prime minister of any country was Naruhiko Higashikuni (Japan), who was born on 3 Dec 1887 and died on 20 Jan 1990, at age 102 years 48 days. He was his country's first prime minister after World War II, but held office for less than two months, resigning in October 1945.

El Hadji Muhammad el Mokri, Grand Vizier of Morocco, died on 16 Sep 1957 at a reputed age of 116 Muslim (*Hijri*) years, equivalent to 112½ years.

The oldest age at first appointment was 81, in the case of Morarji Ranchhodji Desai of India (b. 29 Feb 1896) in March 1977.

Youngest   Currently the youngest head of government is HM Druk Gyalpo ("Dragon King") Jigme Singye Wangchuk of Bhutan (b. 11 Nov 1955), who has been head of government since March 1972 when he was 16 years of age.

Longest term of office   The longest-serving prime minister of a sovereign state is currently Khalifa bin Sulman al-Khalifa (b. 3 Jul 1933) of Bahrain, who has held office since Bahrain became independent in August 1971. By then he had already been in office for 1½ years.

Marshall Kim II Sung (ne Kim Sung Chu; b. 15 Apr 1912) has been head of government or head of state of the Democratic People's Republic of Korea since 25 Aug 1948.

Andrei Andreievich Gromyko (1909–89) had been Minister of Foreign Affairs of the USSR since 15 Feb 1957 (having been Deputy Foreign Minister since 1946), when he was elected President of the USSR on 2 Jul 1985, a position he held until 30 Sep 1988. Piotr Lomako (1904–90) served in the government of the former USSR as Minister for Non-Ferrous Metallurgy from 1940–86. He was relieved of his post on 1 Nov 1986 after 46 years at age 82, having served on the Central Committee of the Communist Party of the Soviet Union (CPSU) since 1952.

Woman Sirimavo Bandaranaike (b. 1916) of Ceylon (now Sri Lanka) became the first woman prime minister of any country when her party, the Sri Lanka ("Blessed Ceylon") Freedom Party, won the general election in July 1960. (See also Longest hearings.)

WOMEN PRESIDENTS AND PREMIERS

Sirimavo Bandaranaike PM of Sri Lanka 1960–65, 1970–77

Indira Gandhi PM of India 1966–77, 1980–84

Golda Meir PM of Israel 1969–74

Elisabeth Domitien PM of Central African Republic 1975–76

Isabel Perón president of Argentina 1975–76

Margaret Thatcher PM of the United Kingdom 1979–90

Maria de Lourdes Pintassilgo PM of Portugal 1979–80

Vigdis Finnbogadottir president of Iceland 1980–

Eugenia Charles PM of Dominica 1980–

Gro Harlem Bruntland PM of Norway 1981, 1986–89, 1990–

Agatha Barbara president of Malta 1982–87

Milka Planinc PM of Yugoslavia 1982–86

Corazon Aquino president of the Philippines 1986–92

Benazir Bhutto PM of Pakistan 1988–90

Violetta Chamorro president of Nicaragua 1990–

Ertha Pascal-Trouillot president of Haiti 1990–91

Kazimiera Prunskiene PM of Lithuania 1990–91
(before Lithuania's independence was internationally recognized)

Mary Robinson president of Ireland 1990–

Edith Cresson PM of France 1991–92

Khalida Zia PM of Bangladesh 1991–

Kim Campbell PM of Canada 1993–

JUDICIAL

LEGISLATION AND LITIGATION

Statutes *Oldest*   The earliest surviving judicial code was that of King Ur-Hammu during the third dynasty of Ur, Iraq, *c.* 2250 B.C.

Most protracted litigation   The dispute over the claim of the Prior and Convent (now the Dean and Chapter) of Durham Cathedral in Great Britain to administer the diocese during a vacancy in the See grew fierce in 1283. It flared up again in 1672 and 1890; an attempt in November 1975 to settle the issue, then 692 years old, was unsuccessful. Neither side admits the legitimacy of writs of appointment issued by the other, even though identical persons are named.

Gaddam Hanumantha Reddy, a civil servant, brought a series of legal actions against the Hyderabad state government and the Indian government covering a total period of 44 years 9 months and 8 days from April 1945 through to January 1990. The litigation outlasted the entire period of his employment in the Indian Administrative Service. He complained that his results in the entrance examination for the Hyderabad Civil Service entitled him to greater seniority and higher pay. After winning the legal battle he did indeed receive his promotion.

Longest hearings   The longest civil case heard before a jury is *Kemner* v. *Monsanto Co.*, which concerned an alleged toxic chemical spill in Sturgeon, MO in 1979. The trial started on 6 Feb 1984, at St Clair County Court House, Belleville, IL before Circuit Judge Richard P. Goldenhersh, and ended on 22 Oct 1987. The testimony lasted 657 days, following which the jury deliberated for two months. The residents of Sturgeon were awarded $1 million nominal compensatory damages and $16,280,000 punitive damages, but these awards were overturned by the Illinois Appellate Court on 11 Jun 1991 because the jury in the original trial had not found that any damage had resulted from the spill.

The Supreme Court of Sri Lanka spent a record 527 days hearing a challenge to the election of President Ranasinghe Premadasa as head of state in 1988. A total of 977 witnesses gave evidence over a three-year period from 19 Jun 1989 to 30 Jun 1992. The challenge, brought by the opposition leader, Sirimavo Bandaranaike (See Prime ministers and heads of state, Woman), was rejected by the court on 1 Sep 1992.

Greatest damages *Personal injury*   The greatest personal injury damages ever awarded were $78,183,000, to the model Marla Hanson, 26, on 29 Sep 1987. Her face was slashed with razors in Manhattan, New York City in June 1987. The award was uncontested and included $4 million in punitive damages. The three men convicted and now serving 5–15 years have no assets, but Miss Hanson is entitled to 10 percent of their post-prison earnings.

The greatest sum awarded in compensatory personal injury damages was $65,086,000, awarded on 18 Jul 1986 to Mrs Agnes Mae Whitaker against the New York City Health and Hospitals Corporation for medical malpractice. A misdiagnosis of food poisoning led to major surgery and severe disablement.

GREATEST DAMAGES The Union Carbide plant in Bhopal, India, where the gas leak disaster in 1984 resulted in compensation to the victims amounting to $470 million. (Photo: Sygma/Baldev)

The compensation for the disaster on 2–3 Dec 1984 at the Union Carbide Corporation plant in Bhopal, India was set at $470 million. The Supreme Court of India passed the order for payment on 14 Feb 1989 after a settlement between the corporation and the Indian government, which represented the interests of more than 500,000 claimants, including the families of 3,350 people who died. On 27 Mar 1992 the Bhopal Court put the death toll at more than 4,000, with 20,000 injured and the number of claimants rising to 600,000.

Civil damages The largest damages awarded in legal history were $11.12 billion to Pennzoil Company against Texaco Inc. concerning the latter's allegedly unethical tactics in January 1984 in attempting to break up a merger between Pennzoil and Getty Oil Company. The verdict was handed down by Judge Solomon Casseb, Jr. in Houston, TX on 10 Dec 1985. An out-of-court settlement of $5.5 billion was reached after a 48-hour negotiation on 19 Dec 1987.

The largest damages awarded against an individual were $2.1 billion. On 10 Jul 1992 Charles H. Keating, Jr., the former owner of Lincoln Savings and Loan of Los Angeles, CA, was ordered by a federal jury to pay this sum to 23,000 small investors who were defrauded by his company. The figure was subject to final approval by the judge.

Largest defamation award The largest amount awarded in a libel case is $58 million, to Vic Feazell, a former district attorney, on 20 Apr 1991 in Waco, TX. He claimed that he had been libeled by a Dallas-based television station and one of its reporters in 1985, and that this had ruined his reputation. The parties reached a settlement on 29 Jun 1991, but neither side would disclose the amount.

Greatest compensation for wrongful imprisonment Robert McLaughlin, 29, was awarded $1,935,000 in October 1989 for wrongful imprisonment as a result of a murder in New York City in 1979 which he did not commit. He had been sentenced to 15 years in prison and had actually served six years, from 1980 to

1986, when he was released after his foster father succeeded in showing the authorities that he had had nothing to do with the crime.

Largest alimony suit   Belgian-born Sheika Dena Al-Fassi, 23, filed the highest-ever alimony claim of $3 billion against her former husband, Sheik Mohammed Al-Fassi, 28, of the Saudi Arabian royal family, in Los Angeles, CA in February 1982. Attorney Marvin Mitchelson, explaining the size of the settlement claim, alluded to the Sheik's wealth, which included 14 homes in Florida alone and numerous private aircraft. On 14 Jun 1983 the claimant was awarded $81 million and declared she would be "very very happy" if she were able to collect.

Largest patent case   Polaroid Corporation was awarded $909.5 million in Boston, MA on 12 Oct 1990 in a suit involving Eastman Kodak Company for infringing patents on instant photography cameras and films. Polaroid had filed suit in 1976, claiming that Kodak had infringed patents used in Polaroid's 1972 SX-70 system. Both companies filed appeals, and eventually it was agreed that Kodak would pay $925 million.

Largest suit   The highest amount of damages ever sought to date is $675 trillion (then equivalent to 10 times the US national wealth) in a suit by Mr I. Walton Bader brought in the US District Court, New York City on 14 Apr 1971 against General Motors and others for polluting all 50 states.

Highest costs   The Blue Arrow trial, involving the illegal support of the company's shares during a rights issue in 1987, is estimated to have cost approximately £35 million (c. $60 million). The trial at the Old Bailey, London, Great

---

Best-attended trial   The greatest attendance at any trial was at that of Major Jesús Sosa Blanco, age 51, for an alleged 108 murders. At one point in the 12½-hr trial (5:30 P.M. to 6 A.M., 22–23 Jan 1959), 17,000 people were present in the Havana Sports Palace, Cuba. He was executed on 18 Feb 1959.

Longest lease   There is a lease concerning a plot for a sewage tank adjoining Columb Barracks, Mullingar, Ireland, which was signed on 3 Dec 1868 for 10 million years. It is to be assumed that a future civil servant will bring up the matter for review early in A.D. 10,001,868. Leases in Ireland lasting "forever" are quite common.

Largest divorce settlement   The largest publicly declared settlement, achieved in 1982 by the lawyers for Soraya Khashóggi, was £500 million ($950 million) plus property from her husband Adnan. Mrs Anne Bass, former wife of Sid Bass of Texas, was reported to have rejected $535 million as inadequate to live in the style to which she had become accustomed.

Oldest lawyer   The oldest lawyer in the United States is Corelius Van de Steeg, who as of 19 May 1993 was still practicing at 101 year 11 months of age.

Britain, lasted a year and ended on 14 Feb 1992 with four of the defendants being convicted. Although they received suspended prison sentences, they were later cleared on appeal.

United States The McMartin Pre-school case in Los Angeles, CA is estimated to have cost $15 million. The trial, concerning the alleged abuse of children at the school in Manhattan Beach, CA, had begun with jury selection on 20 Apr 1987 and resulted in the acquittal on 18 Jan 1990 of the two defendants on 52 counts of child molestation and conspiracy.

Wills Shortest The shortest valid will in the world consists of the words "Vše zene," the Czech for "All to wife," written and dated 19 Jan 1967 by Herr Karl Tausch of Langen, Germany. President Calvin Coolidge, who was known for his taciturn nature, left a will of 23 words: "Not unmindful of my son John, I give all my estate both real and personal to my wife, Grace Coolidge, in fee simple."

Longest The longest will on record was that of Mrs Frederica Evelyn Stilwell Cook (b. USA), proved in London, Great Britain on 2 Nov 1925. It consisted of four bound volumes containing 95,940 words, primarily concerning some $100,000 worth of property.

Oldest The oldest written will dates from 2061 B.C. and is that of Nek'ure, the son of the Egyptian pharaoh Khafre. The will was carved onto the walls of his tomb, and indicated that he would bequeath 14 towns, two estates and other property to his wife, another woman and three children.

Codicils The largest number of codicils (supplements modifying the details) to a will admitted to probate is 21, in the case of the will of J. Paul Getty. The will was dated 22 Sep 1958 and it had 21 codicils dating from 18 Jun 1960 through 11 Mar 1976. Getty died on 6 Jun 1976.

Most durable judge The oldest recorded active judge was Judge Albert R. Alexander (1859–1966) of Plattsburg, MO. He was enrolled as a member of the Clinton County Bar in 1926, and was later the magistrate and probate judge of Clinton County until his retirement at the age of 105 years 8 months on 9 Jul 1965.

Narrowest margin Judge Clarence Thomas was elected to the Supreme Court in 1991 by the narrowest margin ever recorded, 52 votes to 48.

Youngest judge No collated records on the ages of judicial appointments exist. However, David Elmer Ward had to await the legal age of 21 before taking office after nomination in 1932 as judge of the County Court in Fort Myers, FL.

Muhammad Ilyas passed the examination enabling him to become a civil judge in July 1952 at the age of 20 years 9 months, although formalities such as medicals meant that it was not until eight months later that he started work as a civil judge in Lahore, Pakistan.

Most judges Lord Balmerino was found guilty of treason by 137 of his peers on 28 Jul 1746. In the 20th century, 26 judges of the European Court of Human Rights in Strasbourg, France passed judgment in *Branigan and McBride* v. *the United Kingdom (no. 2)* and *United Kingdom* on 26 May 1993. The court rejected the applicants' challenge to their detention in Northern Ireland under the Prevention of Terrorism act.

Lawyers In the United States there were 826,130 resident and active lawyers in April 1992, or one lawyer for every 312 people.

Law firms The largest law firm in the world is Baker & McKenzie, employing 1,651 lawyers, 540 of whom are partners, in 28 countries as of 31 Mar 1993. The firm was founded in Chicago, IL in 1949.

CRIME

Largest criminal organizations In terms of profit, the largest syndicate in organized crime is the Mafia or La Cosa Nostra. The Mafia consists of some 3,000 to 5,000 individuals in 25 "families" federated under "The Commission," with an annual turnover in illegal activities that was estimated by *US News & World Report* in December 1982 at $200 billion, and a profit estimated in Mar 1986 by US District Attorney Rudolph Giuliani at $75 billion. Its origin in the United States dates from 1869 in New Orleans, LA.

In terms of numbers, the Yamaguchi-gumi gang of the *yakuza* in Japan is the largest, with 30,000 members. There are some 90,000 *yakuza* or gangsters altogether, in more than 3,000 groups. On 1 Mar 1992 Japan instituted new laws to combat their activities, which include drug trafficking, smuggling, prostitution and gambling.

Assassinations The most frequently assassinated heads of state in modern times have been the Tsars of Russia. In the two hundred years from 1718 to

ASSASSINATIONS Charles de Gaulle, who was the target of a record 31 assassination attempts. (Photo: Popperfoto)

1918, four Tsars and two heirs apparent were assassinated, and there were many other unsuccessful attempts.

The target of the highest number of *failed* assassination attempts on an individual head of state in modern times was Charles de Gaulle (1890–1970), President of France from 1958 to 1969. He was reputed to have survived no fewer than 31 plots against his life between 1944 and 1966 (although some plots were foiled before culminating in actual physical attacks).

Most successful murderers   It was established at the trial of Behram, the Indian Thug, that he had strangled at least 931 victims with his yellow and white cloth strip or *ruhmal* in the Oudh district between 1790 and 1840. It has been

---

Largest object stolen by a single person   On a moonless night at dead calm high water on 5 Jun 1966, at Wolfe's Cove, St Lawrence Seaway, Canada, N. William Kennedy, armed with only a sharp ax, slashed free the mooring lines of the 10,640-ton SS *Orient Trader*, owned by Steel Factors Ltd of Ontario. The vessel drifted to a waiting blacked-out tug, thus escaping the ban on any shipping movements during a violent wildcat waterfront strike. She then sailed for Spain.

Greatest bank note forgery   The greatest forgery was the German Third Reich's forging operation, code name "Operation Bernhard," engineered by Major Friedrich Krüger during World War II. It involved £150 million worth of British notes, nearly half of which were £5 notes, although various other denominations were also printed. They were produced by 140 Jewish prisoners at Sachsenhausen concentration camp.

Biggest bank fraud   The Banca Nazionale del Lavoro, Italy's leading bank, admitted on 6 Sep 1989 that it had been defrauded of an estimated $3 billion, with the disclosure that its branch in Atlanta, GA had made unauthorized loan commitments to Iraq. Both the bank's chairman, Nerio Nesi, and its director general, Giacomo Pedde, resigned following the revelation.

Computer fraud   Between 1964 and 1973, 64,000 fake insurance policies were created on the computer of the Equity Funding Corporation in the United States, involving $2 billion.

Stanley Mark Rifkin (b. 1946) was arrested in Carlsbad, CA by the FBI on 6 Nov 1978 and charged with defrauding a Los Angeles bank of $10.2 million by manipulation of a computer system. He was sentenced to eight years' imprisonment in June 1980.

Maritime fraud   A cargo of 198,414 tons of Kuwaiti crude oil on the supertanker *Salem* at Durban was sold without title to the South African government in December 1979. The ship mysteriously sank off Senegal on 17 Jan 1980, leaving the government to pay £148 million ($318.2 million) to Shell International, which owned the shipment.

ROBBERY   In April 1986 the new government of the Philippines found evidence that Ferdinand Marcos (above) and his wife Imelda had stolen more than $860 million while he had been president. (Photo: Sygma/A Hernandez)

MASS POISONING   The worst case of mass poisoning occurred in Spain in 1981 through the use of adulterated cooking oil, resulting in over 600 deaths. The photograph (left) shows samples of the oil being analyzed. (Photo: Sygma/Nova and Sygma/J Pavlovsky)

estimated that at least 2 million Indians were strangled by Thugs (*burtotes*) during the reign of the Thugee (pronounced tugee) cult from 1550 until its final suppression by the British raj in 1853.

The greatest number of victims ascribed to a murderess was 610, in the case of Countess Erzsébet Báthory (1560–1614) of Hungary. All her victims were alleged to be young girls from near her castle at Csejthe, where she died on 21 Aug 1614. She had been walled up in her room for 3½ years after being found guilty.

Twentieth century A total of 592 deaths was attributed to one Colombian bandit leader, Teófilo ("Sparks") Rojas, between 1948 and his death in an ambush near Armenia, Colombia on 22 Jan 1963. Some sources attribute 3,500 slayings to him during *La Violencia* of 1945–62.

United States The greatest mass murder committed in the United States was the Happy Land fire, which resulted in the deaths of 87 individuals. The fire was set by 36-year-old Julio Gonzalez, on 25 Mar 1990 at an illegal New York City social club, The Happy Land, in revenge for being thrown out of the club after an argument with a former girlfriend, Lydia Feliciano, who worked at the club. Ms Feliciano was one of six survivors.

In a drunken rampage lasting eight hours on 26–27 Apr 1982, policeman Wou Bom-Kon, 27, killed 57 people and wounded 35 with 176 rounds of rifle ammunition and hand grenades in the Kyong Sang-Namdo province of South Korea. He then blew himself up with a grenade.

Lynching The worst year in the 20th century for lynchings in the United States was 1901, with 130 lynchings, of which 125 were of blacks and five were of whites. The first year with no reported cases was 1952. The date on which lynchings were last reported was 21 Jun 1964, in Philadelphia, Mississippi. Three men, two white (Michael Schwerner and Andrew Goodman) and one black (James Chaney), were lynched in the Neshoba County town.

Mass poisoning On 1 May 1981 an eight-year-old boy became the first of more than 600 victims of the Spanish cooking oil scandal. On 12 June it was discovered that his cause of his death was the use of "denatured" industrial oil from rape-seed. The trial of 38 defendants, including the manufacturers, Ramón and Elías Ferrero, lasted from 30 Mar 1987 to 28 Jun 1988. The 586 counts on which the prosecution demanded jail sentences totaled 60,000 years.

Robbery The greatest robbery on record was that of the Reichsbank following Germany's collapse in April–May 1945. The Pentagon in Washington described the event as "an unverified allegation." The book *Nazi Gold* by Ian Sayer and Douglas Botting, published in 1984, however, finally revealed full details and estimated the total haul at what were then current values as £2.5 billion ($3.75 billion).

The government of the Philippines announced on 23 Apr 1986 that it had succeeded in identifying $860.8 million salted away by former President Ferdinand Edralin Marcos (1917–89) and his wife Imelda. The total since November 1965 was believed to be $5–$10 billion.

Art It is arguable that the *Mona Lisa*, though never appraised, is the most valuable object ever stolen. It disappeared from the Louvre, Paris, France on 21 Aug 1911. It was recovered in Italy in 1913, when Vincenzo Perugia was charged with its theft.

On 14 Apr 1991 20 paintings, estimated to be worth $500 million, were stolen from the van Gogh Museum in Amsterdam, Netherlands. However, only 35 min later they were found in an abandoned car not far from the museum. Just over a year earlier, on 18 Mar 1990, 11 paintings by Rembrandt, Vermeer, Degas, Manet and Flinck, plus a Chinese bronze beaker (also known as a *Ku*) of about 1200 B.C., worth in total an estimated $200 million, were stolen from the Isabella Stewart Gardner Museum in Boston, MA. Unlike the van Gogh paintings, these have not been recovered.

On 24 Dec 1985, 140 priceless gold, jade and obsidian artifacts were stolen from the National Museum of Anthropology, Mexico City. The majority of the stolen objects were recovered in June 1989 from the Mexico City home of a man described by officials as the mastermind of the theft.

Bank During the extreme civil disorder prior to 22 Jan 1976 in Beirut, Lebanon, a guerrilla force blasted the vaults of the British Bank of the Middle East in Bab Idriss and cleared out safe deposit boxes with contents valued by former Finance Minister Lucien Dahdah at $50 million and by another source at an "absolute minimum" of $20 million.

Jewels The greatest recorded theft of jewels was from the bedroom of the "well-guarded" villa of Prince Abdel Aziz bin Ahmed Al-Thani near Cannes, France on 24 Jul 1980. The jewels were valued at $16 million.

Greatest kidnapping ransom Historically the greatest ransom paid was that for Atahualpa by the Incas to Francisco Pizarro in 1532–33 at Cajamarca, Peru, which constituted a hall full of gold and silver, worth some $170 million on today's market.

The greatest ransom ever reported in modern times was 1,500 million pesos ($60 million) for the release of the brothers Jorge Born, 40, and Juan Born, 39, of the firm Bunge and Born, paid to the left-wing urban guerrilla group Montoneros in Buenos Aires, Argentina on 20 Jun 1975.

Greatest hijack ransom The highest amount ever paid to aircraft hijackers was $6 million, by the Japanese government, in the case of a JAL DC-8 at Dacca Airport, Bangladesh on 2 Oct 1977, with 38 hostages. Six convicted criminals were also exchanged. The Bangladesh government had refused to sanction any retaliatory action.

Largest narcotics haul The greatest haul in a drug seizure in terms of value was on 28 Sep 1989, when cocaine with an estimated street value of $6–7 billion was seized in a raid on a warehouse in Los Angeles, CA. The haul of 22 tons was prompted by a tip-off from a local resident who had complained about heavy truck traffic and people leaving the warehouse "at odd hours and in a suspicious manner."

The greatest haul in terms of weight was by the authorities in Bilo, Pakistan on 23 Oct 1991. The seizure comprised 85,846 lb of hashish and 7,128 lb of heroin.

Largest narcotics operation The bulkiest haul was 3,200 tons of Colombian marijuana in the 14-month-long "Operation Tiburon," carried out by the US Drug Enforcement Administration and Colombian authorities. The arrest of 495 people and the seizure of 95 vessels was announced on 5 Feb 1982.

CAPITAL PUNISHMENT

The discovery of Tollund man (found with a leather noose around his neck) in a bog near Silkeborg, Denmark in 1950 showed that capital punishment dates at least from the Iron Age. The countries in which capital punishment is still *prevalent* include China, Iran, Iraq, Saudi Arabia, Malaysia, the United States (36 states and U.S. government and military) and some independent countries that were formerly in the USSR. Capital punishment was first abolished *de facto* in 1798 in Liechtenstein.

To 7 Jun 1993, 203 people have been put to death in the United States since the Supreme Court permitted states to restore the death penalty. Executions have been permitted in 21 states; Texas has executed 59 men, the most of any state.

Earliest　The earliest recorded execution among white settlers in the United States was that of John Billington for murder at Plymouth, MA on 30 Sep 1630. The earliest judicial electrocution was of William Kemmler at Auburn Prison, NY, on 6 Aug 1890, for the murder of Matilda Zeigler 495 days before.

Largest hanging　The most people hanged from one gallows were 38 Sioux Indians by William J. Duly outside Mankato, MN on 26 Dec 1862 for the murder of unarmed citizens.

The Nazi Feldkommandant simultaneously hanged 50 Greek resistance fighters as a reprisal measure in Athens, Greece on 22 Jul 1944.

Last public hangings　The last public hanging in the United States occurred at Owensboro, KY on 14 August 1936, when Rainey Bethea was hung in a field by the banks of the Ohio River. He was executed in the presence of a crowd of between 10,000 and 15,000. The following year a "private" hanging was performed, which was actually witnessed by some 500 people although the number of official witnesses was limited to just 12—Roscoe "Red" Jackson was hung on 21 May 1937 at Galena, MO.

Witchcraft　The last legal execution of a witch occurred at Glarus, Switzerland in 1782. It is estimated that at least 200,000 people were executed during the European witch craze of the 16th and 17th centuries.

Last beheadings　The last person to be publicly guillotined in France was the murderer Eugen Weidmann, before a large crowd at Versailles, near Paris, France at 4:50 A.M. on 17 Jun 1939.

The last use before abolition on 9 Sep 1981 was on 10 Sep 1977 at Baumettes Prison, Marseilles, for torturer and murderer Hamida Djandoubi, age 28.

Death row　The longest sojourn on death row was the 39 years of Sadamichi Hirasawa (1893–1987) in Sendai Jail, Japan. He was convicted in 1948 of poisoning 12 bank employees with potassium cyanide to effect a theft of $403, and died in prison at the age of 94.

United States　Howard Virgil Lee Douglas spent 17½ years on death row, more than any other person in American penal history. On 15 May 1991 he was resentenced to life in prison.

PRISON SENTENCES

Longest sentences   Chamoy Thipyaso, a Thai woman known as the queen of underground investing, and seven of her associates were each sentenced to serve 141,078 years in jail by the Bangkok Criminal Court, Thailand on 27 Jul 1989 for swindling the public through a multimillion-dollar deposit-taking business.

The longest sentence imposed on a mass murderer was 21 consecutive life sentences and 12 death sentences in the case of John Wayne Gacy, Jr., who killed 33 boys and young men between 1972 and 1978 in Illinois. He was sentenced by a jury in Chicago, IL on 13 Mar 1980.

Longest time served   Paul Geidel (1894–1987) was convicted of second-degree murder on 5 Sep 1911 when he was a 17-year-old porter in a hotel in New York. He was released from the Fishkill Correctional Facility, Beacon, NY at the age of 85 on 7 May 1980, having served 68 years, 8 months and 2 days—the longest recorded term in US history. He first refused parole in 1974.

Oldest   Bill Wallace (1881–1989) was the oldest prisoner on record, spending the last 63 years of his life in Aradale Psychiatric Hospital, at Ararat, Victoria, Australia. He had shot and killed a man at a restaurant in Melbourne, Victoria in December 1925, and having been found unfit to plead, was transferred to the responsibility of the Mental Health Department in February 1926. He remained at Aradale until his death on 17 Jul 1989, shortly before his 108th birthday.

Most arrests   A record for arrests was set by Tommy Johns (1922–88) in Brisbane, Queensland, Australia on 9 Sep 1982 when he faced his 2,000th conviction for drunkenness since 1957. His total at the time of his last drink on 30 Apr 1988 was "nearly 3,000."

FINES

Heaviest   The largest fine ever was one of $650 million, which was imposed on the US securities firm of Drexel Burnham Lambert in December 1988 for insider trading. This figure represented $300 million in direct fines, with the balance to be put into an account to satisfy claims of parties who could prove they were defrauded by Drexel's actions.

The record for an individual is $200 million, which Michael Milken (see also Business World, Highest salary) agreed to pay on 24 Apr 1990. In addition, he agreed to settle civil charges filed by the Securities and Exchange Commission. The payments were in settlement of a criminal racketeering and securities fraud suit brought by the US government. On appeal Milken's sentence was reduced to 33 months and 26 days (5 Aug 1992). He was released from prison on 2 Mar 1993, but has to work 1,800 hrs community service.

PRISONS

Most secure prison   After it became a maximum security federal prison in 1934, no convict was known to have lived to tell of a successful escape from the prison on Alcatraz Island in San Francisco Bay, CA. A total of 23 men attempted it, but 12 were recaptured, five were shot dead, one drowned and five were presumed drowned. On 16 Dec 1962, just before the prison was closed

> **Greatest mass arrest** The greatest mass arrest reported in a democratic country was of 15,617 demonstrators on 11 Jul 1988, rounded up by South Korean police to ensure security in advance of the 1988 Olympic Games in Seoul.
>
> **Highest prison population** The country with the highest per capita prison population is the United States, with 455 prisoners per 100,000 population.

on 21 Mar 1963, one man reached the mainland alive, only to be recaptured on the spot. John Chase held the record for the longest time spent in Alcatraz, 26 years.

Most expensive prison Spandau Prison, Berlin, originally built in 1887 for 600 prisoners, was used solely for the Nazi war criminal Rudolf Hess (26 Apr 1894–17 Aug 1987) for the last 20 years of his life. The cost of maintenance of the staff of 105 was estimated in 1976 to be $415,000 per year. On 19 Aug 1987 it was announced that Hess had strangled himself with a piece of electrical cord and that he had left a note in old German script. Two months after his death, the prison was demolished.

Longest escape The longest recorded escape by a recaptured prisoner was that of Leonard T. Fristoe, 77, who escaped from Nevada State Prison on 15 Dec 1923 and was turned in by his son on 15 Nov 1969 at Compton, CA. He had had 46 years of freedom under the name of Claude R. Willis. He had killed two sheriff's deputies in 1920.

Greatest jail breaks In February 1979 a retired US Army colonel, Arthur "Bull" Simons, led a band of 14 to break into Gasre Prison, Tehran, Iran to rescue two fellow Americans. Some 11,000 other prisoners took advantage of this and the Islamic revolution in what became history's largest-ever jailbreak.

In September 1971, Raúl Sendic and 105 other Tupamaro guerrillas, plus five nonpolitical prisoners, escaped from a Uruguayan prison through a tunnel 298 ft long.

HONORS, DECORATIONS AND AWARDS

Oldest order The earliest honor known was the "Gold of Honor" for extraordinary valor awarded in the 18th Dynasty *c.* 1440–1400 B.C. A representative statuette was found at Qan-el-Kebri, Egypt. The oldest true order was the Order of St John of Jerusalem (the direct descendant of which is the Sovereign Military Order of Malta), legitimized in 1113.

Youngest awardee Kristina Stragauskaite of Skirmantiskes, Lithuania was awarded a medal "for courage in fire" when she was just 4 years 8 months old. She had saved the lives of her younger brother and sister when a fire had broken out on 7 April 1989 in the family's home while her parents were out. The award was decreed by the Presidium of the Lithuanian Soviet Socialist Republic.

MOST NOBEL PRIZES The International Committee of the Red Cross has won the most Nobel Prizes, with three peace awards. Its headquarters are in Geneva, where it has an independent council of 25 Swiss nationals. The statue in front of the building represents unknown prisoners of war. (Photo: James Clift for Guinness Publishing)

The youngest age at which an official gallantry award has ever been won is eight years, in the case of Anthony Farrer, who was given the Albert Medal on 23 Sep 1916 for fighting off a cougar at Cowichan Lake, Vancouver Island, Canada to save Doreen Ashburnham. She was also awarded the Albert medal, which she exchanged in 1974 for the George Cross.

Most valuable annual prize   The most valuable annual prize is the Louis Jeantet Prize for Medicine, which in 1993 was worth SFr 2 million (equivalent to approximately $1,342,000). It was first awarded in 1986 and is intended to "provide substantial funds for the support of biomedical research projects."

Most statues   The world record for raising statues to oneself was set by Joseph Vissarionovich Dzhugashvili, alias Stalin (1879–1953), the leader of the Soviet Union from 1924–53. It is estimated that at the time there were *c.* 6,000 statues to him throughout the USSR and in many cities in eastern Europe.

The man to whom the most statues have been raised is Buddha. The 20th-century champion is Vladimir Ilyich Ulyanov, alias Lenin (1870–1924), busts of whom have been mass-produced. This also has been the case with Mao Zedong (Mao Tse-tung) (1893–1976); and with Ho Chi Minh (1890–1969).

NOBEL PRIZES

Earliest 1901 for Physics, Chemistry, Physiology or Medicine, Literature and Peace.

Most Prizes The United States has won outright or shared 210 prizes, including most for Physiology or Medicine (71); Physics (55); Chemistry (37), Peace (18); Economics (19). France has most for Literature (12).

Oldest Laureate Professor Francis Peyton Rous (USA; 1879–1970) in 1966 shared in Physiology or Medicine prize at the age of 87.

Youngest Laureates *At time of award:* Professor Sir Lawrence Bragg (Great Britain; 1890–1971) 1915 Physics prize at 25. *At time of work:* Bragg, and Theodore W. Richards (USA; 1868–1928) 1914 Chemistry prize at 23. *Literature:* Rudyard Kipling (Great Britain; 1865–1936) 1907 prize at 41. *Peace:* Mrs Mairead Corrigan-Maguire (Republic of Ireland; b. 27 Jan 1944) 1976 prize (shared) at 32.

Most 3 Awards: International Committee of the Red Cross, Geneva (founded 1863) Peace 1917, 1944 and 1963 (shared); 2 Awards: Dr Linus Carl Pauling (USA; b. 28 Feb 1901) Chemistry 1954 and Peace 1962; Mme Marja Sklodowska Curie (Polish-French; 1867–1934) Physics 1903 (shared) and Chemistry 1911; Professor John Bardeen (USA; 1908–91) Physics 1956 (shared) and 1972 (shared); Professor Frederick Sanger (b. 13 Aug 1918) Chemistry 1958 and 1980 (shared); Office of the United Nations' High Commissioner for Refugees, Geneva (founded 1951) Peace 1954 and 1981.

Highest Prize Swedish Krona 6,700,000 (for 1993), equivalent to $911,000.

Lowest Prize Swedish Krona 115,000 (1923).

MILITARY

United States   The highest US military decoration is the Medal of Honor, usually referred to as the Congressional Medal of Honor. Five Marines received both the Army and Navy Medals of Honor for the same deeds in 1918, and 14 officers and men received the medal on two occasions between 1864 and 1915 for two distinct acts. The Defense Department refuses to recognize any military hero as having the most awards, but various heroes have been nominated by unofficial groups.

Since medals and decorations cannot be compared in value, the title of most decorated is a matter of subjective evaluation. General Douglas MacArthur (1880–1964), because of his high rank and his years of military service spanning three wars, would seem to hold the best claim to "Most Decorated American Soldier." In addition to the Congressional Medal of Honor, he received 58 separate awards and decorations with 16 Oak Leaf Clusters (for repeat awards), plus 18 campaign stars.

Germany   The Knight's Cross of the Iron Cross with swords, diamonds and golden oak-leaves was uniquely awarded to Col. Hans Ulrich Rudel (1916–82) for 2,530 operational flying missions on the Eastern Front in the period 1941–45. He destroyed 519 Soviet armored vehicles.

USSR   The USSR's highest award for valor is the Gold Star of a Hero of the Soviet Union, 11,040 of which were awarded in World War II.

The only wartime triple awards were to Marshal Georgi Konstantinovich Zhukov (1896–1974; subsequently awarded a fourth Gold Star), and to the leading air aces Guards Colonel (later Marshal of Aviation) Aleksandr Ivanovich Pokryshkin (1913–85) and Aviation Maj Gen Ivan Nikitovich Kozhedub (1920–91).

USSR AWARDS   **Military awards were a matter of great pride when the USSR was the leading superpower along with the USA, and Marshal Zhukov uniquely received the Gold Star of a Hero of the Soviet Union four times. He is seen here with Pandit Nehru, the Indian Prime Minister, in 1957. (Photo: Popperfoto)**

Most titles The most titled person in the world is the 18th Duchess of Alba (Alba de Tormes), Doña Maria del Rosario Cayetana Fitz-James Stuart y Silva (b. 28 Mar 1926). She is six times a duchess, once a viscountess, 18 times a marchioness, 19 times a countess and 17 times a Spanish grandee.

Most honorary degrees The greatest number of honorary degrees awarded to any individual is 127, given to Rev. Father Theodore M. Hesburgh (b. 25 May 1917), president of the University of Notre Dame, IN. These have been accumulated since 1954.

THE GUINNESS DAILY RECORD   10 June, 1991

"Operation Welcome Home"

MILES AND MILES OF YELLOW RIBBONS

New York City today was covered with the most yellow ribbon anywhere in the world, when 140 miles of ribbon were used for the massive "Operation Welcome Home" ticker-tape parade. The ribbon, worth $50,000, was donated to the city by Berwick Industries, Inc. to honor the troops returning from the Gulf.

The company's mill in Berwick, PA worked around the clock to produce the ribbon for the patriotic festivities. Thirteen reels of the ribbon were signed by thousands of people invited by Coca-Cola to the Amsterdam Festival, Yankee Stadium, and a celebration at the aircraft carrier *Intrepid* in New York harbor. One hundred reels of ribbon were signed at City Hall by Bronx schoolchildren, who presented the ribbon to Mayor Dinkins before the parade. Local radio stations also promoted locations for public ribbon signings.

The signed ribbon was strung festively along the parade route, rosettes made by the ribbon were given to parade watchers, and yellow streamers adorned each lamppost along the way. The ribbon was also shredded into one million small ribbons that were mixed with ticker-tape and showered on the 24,000 marchers during the four-hour extravaganza.

"Berwick has been doing business in New York for many years, and welcomes this opportunity to give something back to the city," said Henry Doherty, president of Berwick Industries, who was proud to contribute to "Operation Welcome Home."

MILITARY AND DEFENSE

WAR

Earliest conflict The oldest-known offensive weapon is a broken wooden spear found in April 1911 at Clacton-on-Sea, Great Britain by S. Hazzledine Warren. It is much beyond the limit of radiocarbon dating but is estimated to have been fashioned before 200,000 B.C.

Longest The longest war which could be described as continuous was the Thirty Years' War, between various European countries, from 1618 to 1648. The so-called Hundred Years' War between England and France, which lasted from 1338 to 1453 (115 years), was in fact a succession of wars rather than a single one. The *Reconquista*—the series of campaigns in the Iberian Peninsula to recover the region from the Islamic Moors—began in 718 and continued intermittently until 1492, when Granada, the last Moorish stronghold, was finally conquered.

Bloodiest By far the most costly war in terms of human life was World War II (1939–45), in which the total number of fatalities, including battle deaths and civilians of all countries, is estimated to have been 54.8 million, assuming 25 million Soviet fatalities and 7.8 million Chinese civilians killed. The country that suffered most was Poland, with 6,028,000 or 17.2 percent of its population of 35.1 million killed.

In the Paraguayan war of 1864–70 against Brazil, Argentina and Uruguay, Paraguay's population was reduced from 1.4 million to 220,000 survivors, of whom only 30,000 were adult males.

Dr William Brydon (1811–73) and two natives were the sole survivors of a seven-day retreat of 13,000 soldiers and camp-followers from Kabul, Afghanistan. Dr Brydon's horse died two days after his arrival at Jellalabad, some 70 miles to the east on the route to the Khyber Pass, on 13 Jan 1842.

Bloodiest civil The bloodiest civil war in history was the *Taiping* ("Great Peace") rebellion, which was a revolt against the Chinese Qing Dynasty between 1851 and 1864. According to the best estimates, the loss of life was some 20 million, including more than 100,000 killed by government forces in the sack of Nanjing on 19–21 Jul 1864.

Most costly The material cost of World War II far transcended that of all the rest of history's wars put together and has been estimated at $1.5 trillion. The total cost to the Soviet Union was estimated in May 1959 at 2.5 trillion rubles, while a figure of $530 billion has been estimated for the United States.

Bloodiest battles Modern It is difficult to compare the major battles of World Wars I and II because of the different time scales. The 142-day-long first battle of the Somme, France (1 Jul–19 Nov 1916) produced an estimated total number of casualties of over 1.22 million; of these, 623,907 were Allied and the rest German. The published German figure of *c.* 670,000 is no longer accepted. The greatest death toll in a battle has been estimated at *c.* 1,109,000 in the Battle of Stalingrad, USSR (now Volgograd, Russia), ending with the Ger-

BRITAIN & ZANZIBAR AT WAR

Conflict lasts 38 minutes

Britain went to war with Zanzibar yesterday, but only for 38 minutes. Following the death of the Sultan under somewhat suspicious circumstances three days ago, Sa'id Khalid and his supporters seized the palace and barricaded it, with Khalid proclaiming himself as the new Sultan.

British forces landed men at the custom house and an ultimatum was issued to Khalid that the palace would be bombarded if he did not surrender and take down his flag by 9 A.M. yesterday. At 7:30 Rear Admiral Harry Rawson repeated the ultimatum, and two minutes after the deadline had passed, with no response, Her Majesty's ships *Rangoon*,

Sparrow and *Thrush* opened fire on the palace. Fire was returned and there was a violent exchange, but less than 40 minutes later the palace was reduced to ruins and the occupants fled, with Khalid surrendering to the German consulate. Later in the day Hamud ibn Muhammad was appointed as the new Sultan.

The shortest war on record had finished almost as soon as it had begun.

---

man surrender on 31 Jan 1943 by Field Marshal Friedrich von Paulus (1890–1957). The Germans suffered 200,000 losses. The Soviet garrison commander was Gen. Vasiliy Chuikov; *c.* 650,800 soldiers from the Soviet army were injured but survived. Additionally, only 1,515 civilians from a prewar population of more than 500,000 were found alive after the battle. The final drive on Berlin, Germany by the Soviet Army and the battle for the city that followed, from 16 Apr–2 May 1945, involved 3.5 million men, 52,000 guns and mortars, 7,750 tanks and 11,000 aircraft on both sides.

Ancient Modern historians give no credence, on logistic grounds, to the casualty figures attached to ancient battles, such as the 250,000 reputedly killed at Plataea (Greeks *v.* Persians) in 479 B.C. or the 200,000 allegedly killed in a single day at Châlons-sur-Marne, France (Huns *v.* Romans) in A.D. 451.

United States   The American Civil War (1861–65) is the bloodiest war fought
on American soil. The bloodiest battles between the Northern (Union) and
the Southern (Confederate) forces were at Shiloh Church, near Pittsburg
Landing in Hardin County, TN on 6–7 Apr 1862, when each side reported casualties of over 10,000; at Fredericksburg, VA on 13 Dec 1862, when Union
losses were over 12,000, more than double those of the Confederacy; and at
Gettysburg, PA on 1–3 Jul 1863, when the Union reported losses of 23,000
and the Confederacy 25,000 (a disputed figure). The Civil War officially
ended when Confederate General Robert E. Lee surrendered to Union General Ulysses S. Grant at Appomattox Courthouse, VA on 9 Apr 1865.

Greatest naval battles Modern   The greatest number of ships and aircraft ever
involved in a sea–air action was 231 ships and 1,996 aircraft in the Battle of
Leyte Gulf, in the Philippines, during World War II. It raged from 22–27 Oct
1944, with 166 Allied and 65 Japanese warships engaged, of which 26 Japanese and six US ships were sunk. In addition, 1,280 US and 716 Japanese aircraft were engaged. The greatest purely naval battle of modern times was the
Battle of Jutland on 31 May 1916, during World War I, in which 151 British
Royal Navy warships were involved against 101 German warships. The Royal
Navy lost 14 ships and 6,097 men, and the German fleet lost 11 ships and
2,545 men.

Ancient   The greatest of ancient naval battles was the Battle of Salamis,
Greece in Sep 480 B.C. There were an estimated 800 vessels in the defeated
Persian fleet and 380 in the victorious fleet of the Athenians and their allies,
with a possible involvement of 200,000 men. The death toll at the Battle of
Lepanto on 7 Oct 1571 has been estimated at 33,000.

Greatest invasion Seaborne   The greatest invasion in military history was the
Allied land, air and sea operation against the Normandy coast of France on
D-Day, 6 Jun 1944. Thirty-eight convoys of 745 ships moved in during the first
three days, supported by 4,066 landing craft, carrying 185,000 men, 20,000 vehicles and 347 minesweepers. The air assault comprised 18,000 paratroopers
from 1,087 aircraft. The 42 available divisions had air support from 13,175 aircraft. Within a month 1.1 million troops, 200,000 vehicles and 840,000 tons of
stores were landed. The Allied invasion of Sicily from 10–12 Jul 1943 involved
the landing of 181,000 men in three days.

Airborne   The largest airborne invasion was the Anglo-American assault of three divisions (34,000 men), with 2,800 aircraft and 1,600 gliders, near Arnhem, in the Netherlands, on 17 Sep 1944.

Longest-range attacks The longest-range attacks in air history were those undertaken by seven B-52G bombers, which took off from Barksdale Air Force Base, LA on 16 Jan 1991 to deliver air-launched cruise missiles against targets in Iraq shortly after the start of the Gulf War. Each bomber flew a distance of 14,000 miles, refueling four times in flight, with the round-trip mission lasting some 35 hours.

Greatest evacuation The greatest evacuation in military history was that carried out by 1,200 Allied naval and civilian craft from the beachhead at Dunkerque (Dunkirk), France between 27 May and 4 Jun 1940. A total of 338,226 British and French troops were evacuated.

Longest march The longest march in military history was the famous Long March by the Chinese Communists in 1934–35. In 368 days, of which 268 were days of movement, from October to October, their force of some 100,000 covered 6,000 miles from Ruijin, in Jiangxi, to Yan'an, in Shaanxi. They crossed 18 mountain ranges and 24 rivers, and eventually reached Yan'an with only about 8,000 survivors, following continual rearguard actions against nationalist Guomindang (GMD) forces.

Worst sieges The worst siege in history was the 880-day siege of Leningrad, USSR (now St Petersburg, Russia) by the German Army from 30 Aug 1941 until 27 Jan 1944. The best estimate is that between 1.3 and 1.5 million defenders and citizens died. This included 641,000 people who died of hunger in the city and 17,000 civilians killed by shelling. More than 150,000 shells and 100,000 bombs were dropped on the city.
   The longest recorded siege was that of Azotus (now Ashdod), Israel, which according to Herodotus was besieged by Psamtik I of Egypt for 29 years, during the period 664–610 B.C.

Chemical warfare The greatest number of people killed through chemical warfare were the estimated 4,000 Kurds who died at Halabja, Iraq in March 1988 when President Saddam Hussein used chemical weapons against Iraq's Kurdish minority in revenge for the support it had given to Iran in the Iran–Iraq war.

DEFENSE SPENDING

In 1991 it was estimated that the world's spending on armaments was running at an annual rate of some $600 billion. In 1992 throughout the world there were 24,714,000 full-time armed forces regulars or conscripts plus 38,341,000 reservists, totaling 63,055,000. The budgeted expenditure on defense by the US government for the fiscal year 1992 was $270.9 billion. The defense expenditure of the former USSR is given as 411.3 billion rubles in 1992.

ARMED FORCES

Largest China's People's Liberation Army's strength in 1992 was estimated to be 3,030,000 (comprising land, sea and air forces), with reductions continuing. Her reserves number around 1.2 million. Prior to its breakup, the USSR

LARGEST ARMED FORCES   Including reserves, China has the largest armed forces in the world. A small proportion of them are seen here parading through Guangzhou. (Photo: Gamma/V. Clavieres)

had the largest regular armed force in the world, with 3,400,000 personnel in 1991. It is not possible to give the size of Russian armed forces; it is constantly changing as former republics convert Russian units into national forces, but plans are to maintain forces of about 1.5 million. The military forces of the United States for 1993 totaled 1,731,287. There were 586,401 active duty personnel in the United States Army as of 30 Mar 1993. The total number of reservist in the United States were 1,901,905 as of 30 Sep 1992.

Navies Largest   The largest navy in the world in terms of personnel is the United States Navy, with a total of 516,813 plus 181,925 Marines as of 30 Mar 1993. The active strength in 1992 included six nuclear-powered aircraft carriers, six conventionally powered aircraft carriers, 25 ballistic missile submarines, 48 nuclear attack submarines, one diesel attack submarine, 46 cruisers, 45 destroyers, 83 frigates and 65 amphibious warfare ships.

The navy of the former USSR had a larger submarine fleet, comprising 250 vessels (including 55 ballistic missiles). It also had four aircraft carriers, 33 cruisers, 26 destroyers, 129 frigates and 80 amphibious warfare ships. This excludes the Black Sea Fleet, which has 18 submarines (none with ballistic missiles), and 36 surface combatants. The Black Sea Fleet will be split among Ukraine, Russia and Georgia. The rest of the Navy is based at Russian ports.

Armies Oldest   The oldest army in the world is the 80–90 strong Pontifical Swiss Guard in Vatican City, founded 21 Jan 1506. Its origins, however, predate 1400.

Largest   Numerically, the world's largest army is that of the People's Republic of China, with a total strength of some 2.3 million in mid-1992. The total size of the former USSR's army in mid-1991 was estimated at 1,400,000, believed to be organized into 139 divisions (tank, motor rifle and airborne).

Oldest soldier   The oldest "old soldier" of all time was probably John B. Salling of the Army of the Confederate States of America and the last accepted survivor of the Civil War (1861–65). He died in Kingsport, TN on 16 Mar 1959, aged 113 years 1 day.

Youngest soldier   Luís Alves de Lima e Silva, Marshal Duke of Caxias (25 Aug 1803–7 May 1880), Brazilian military hero and statesman, entered his infantry regiment at the age of five in 1808. He was promoted to Captain in 1824 and made Duke in 1869.

Fernando Inchauste Montalvo (b. 18 Jun 1930), the son of a major in the Bolivian air force, went to the front with his father on his fifth birthday during the war between Bolivia and Paraguay (1932–35). He had received military training and was subject to military discipline.

Tallest soldier   The tallest soldier of all time was Väinö Myllyrinne (1909–63), who was conscripted into the Finnish Army when he was 7 ft 3 in and who later grew to 8 ft 3 in.

Greatest mutiny   In World War I, 56 French divisions, comprising some 650,000 men and their officers, refused orders on the Western front sector of General Robert Nivelle in April 1917 after the failure of his offensive.

Air forces Oldest   The earliest autonomous air force is the Royal Air Force, which can be traced back to 1878, when the War Office commissioned the building of a military balloon. Balloons had been used for military observation by both sides during the American Civil War (1861–1865). The Royal Engineers Balloon Section and Depot was formed in 1890 and the Air Battalion of the Royal Engineers followed on 1 Apr 1911. On 13 May 1912 the Royal Flying Corps (RFC) was formed, with both Military and Naval Wings, the latter being renamed the Royal Naval Air Service (RNAS). The Royal Air Force was formed on 1 Apr 1918 from the RFC and the RNAS, and took its place alongside the Royal Navy and the Army as a separate service with its own Ministry.

Speed march   A team of nine, representing II Squadron RAF Regiment from RAF Hullavington, Great Britain, each man carrying a pack weighing at least 40 lb, including a rifle, completed the London Marathon in 4 hr 33 min 58 sec on 21 Apr 1991.

Flt Sgt Chris Chandler set an individual record in the RAF Swinderby Marathon at Swinderby, Great Britain on 25 Sep 1992, with a pack weighing 40 lb. His time was 3 hr 56 min 10 sec.

Army drill   On 8–9 Jul 1987 a 90-man squad of the Queen's Color Squadron, Royal Air Force (RAF) performed a total of 2,722,662 drill movements (2,001,384 rifle and 721,278 foot) at RAF Uxbridge, Great Britain from memory and without a word of command in 23 hr 55 min.

Largest   The largest air force of all time was the United States Army Air Corps (now the US Air Force), which had 79,908 aircraft in July 1944 and 2,411,294 personnel in March 1944. The US Air Force, including strategic missile forces, had 446,148 personnel as of 30 Mar 1993. The Air Force of the former USSR had 11,370 aircraft and 895,000 personnel (including some 200,000 manning strategic air missiles) in mid-1991. In addition, the USSR's Offensive Strategic Rocket Forces had about 164,000 operational personnel in mid-1991. Eventually only Russia will have strategic rocket forces.

Anti-submarine successes   The highest number of U-boat kills attributed to one ship in World War II was 15, to HMS *Starling* (Capt. Frederic John Walker, RN). Captain Walker was in command at the sinking of a total of 25 U-boats between 1941 and the time of his death on 9 Jul 1944. The US destroyer escort *England* sank six Japanese submarines in the Pacific between 18 and 30 May 1944.

Most successful submarine captains   The most successful of all World War II submarine commanders was Lieutenant Otto Kretschmer, captain of the U.23 and U.99, who up to March 1941 sank one destroyer and 44 Allied merchantmen totaling 266,629 gross registered tons.

In World War I, Lieutenant (later Vice Admiral) Lothar von Arnauld de la Périère, in the U.35 and U.139, sank 195 Allied ships totaling 458,856 gross registered tons. The most successful boats were the U.35, which in World War I sank 54 ships of 90,350 gross registered tons in a single voyage and 224 ships of 539,711 gross registered tons all told, and the U.48, which sank 51 ships of 310,007 gross registered tons in World War II. The largest target ever sunk by a submarine was the Japanese aircraft carrier *Shinano* (66,131 tons) by USS *Archerfish* (Cdr Joseph F. Enright, USN) on 29 Nov 1944.

Top jet ace   The greatest number of kills in jet-to-jet battles is 16, by Capt. Joseph Christopher McConnell, Jr., of the United States Air Force, in the Korean War (1950–53). He was killed on 25 Aug 1954. Lt.-Col. Heinz Bär (Germany) also achieved 16 kills as a jet pilot, in 1945, although it was against propeller-driven airplanes. It is possible that an Israeli ace may have surpassed this total in the period 1967–70, but the identity of Israeli pilots is subject to strict security.

Top woman ace   The record score for any woman fighter pilot is 12, by Jnr-Lt Lydia Litvak (USSR; b. 1921) on the Eastern Front between 1941 and 1943. She was killed in action on 1 Aug 1943.

BOMBS

Heaviest   The heaviest conventional bomb ever used operationally was the Royal Air Force's *Grand Slam*, weighing 22,000 lb and measuring 25 ft 5 in long, dropped on Bielefeld railroad viaduct, Germany on 14 Mar 1945.

In 1949 the United States Air Force tested a bomb weighing 42,000 lb at Muroc Dry Lake, CA. The heaviest-known nuclear bomb was the MK 17, carried by US B-36 bombers in the mid-1950s. It weighed 42,000 lb and was 24 ft 6 in long.

Atomic   The first atom bomb dropped on Hiroshima, Japan by the United States at 8:16 A.M. on 6 Aug 1945 had an explosive power equivalent to that of

12.5 kilotons of trinitrotoluene ($C_7H_5O_6N_3$), called TNT. Code-named *Little Boy*, it was 10 ft long and weighed 9,000 lb. It burst 1,850 ft above the city center.

Thermonuclear The most powerful thermonuclear device so far tested is one with a power equivalent to that of 57 megatons of TNT, detonated by the former USSR in the Novaya Zemlya area at 8:33 A.M. GMT on 30 Oct 1961. The shock-wave circled the world three times, taking 36 hr 27 min for the first circuit. The largest US H-bomb tested was the 18–22 megaton *Bravo* at Bikini Atoll, Marshall Islands on 1 Mar 1954.

On 9 Aug 1961, Nikita Khrushchev, then the Chairman of the Council of Ministers of the USSR, declared that the Soviet Union was capable of constructing a 100-megaton bomb, and announced the possession of one during a visit to what was then East Berlin, East Germany on 16 Jan 1963. Such a device could make a crater in rock 355 ft deep and 1.8 miles wide, with a fireball 8.6 miles in diameter.

Largest nuclear weapons The most powerful ICBM (intercontinental ballistic missile) is the former USSR's SS–18 (Model 5), believed to be armed with ten 750-kiloton MIRVs (multiple independently targetable reentry vehicles). SS–18 ICBMs are located on both Russian and Kazakhstan territory—they are now controlled by the Commonwealth of Independent States. The US Titan II, carrying a W-53 warhead, was rated at 9 megatons but has now been withdrawn, leaving the 1.2 megaton W-56 as the most powerful US weapon.

Largest "conventional" explosion The largest use of conventional explosives was by a team of Chinese army engneers who blew up a mountain to allow for the expansion of an airport in Zhuhai, an economic development zone near Macao. A total of nearly 13,670 tons of TNT were detonated on 28 Dec 1992 after 1,000 technicians had spent several months preparing for the explosion.

GUNS

Earliest It is believed that the earliest guns were constructed in both China and North Africa in *c.* 1250. The earliest antiaircraft gun was an artillery piece on a high-angle mounting used in the Franco-Prussian War of 1870 by the Prussians against French balloons.

Most common The most commonly used gun in the US Army is the M16A2 rifle, of which 270,000 have been fielded.

Largest The largest gun ever constructed was used by the Germans in the siege of Sevastopol, USSR (now Russia) in Jul 1942. It was of a caliber of 31 in with a barrel 94 ft 8^1/$_2$ in long. It was built by Krupp, and its remains were discovered near Metzenhof, Bavaria in August 1945. The whole assembly of the gun was 141 ft long and weighed 1,481.5 tons, with a crew of 1,500. The range for an 8.9-ton projectile was 29 miles.

Lightest The lightest gun in the US Army is the M9 9mm pistol, which weighs 2.6 lbs, has the shortest range, 55 yd, and has the smallest magazine capacity of 15 rounds.

Heaviest The heaviest gun in the US Army is the MK19-3 40mm automatic grenade launcher, which weighs 72.5 lb and has both the greatest caliber and range of any US Army weapon: about 1,650 yd at point targets, over 2,400 yd at area targets. The bullets can penetrate 2 in into armor at 2,400 yd.

Greatest range   The greatest range ever attained by a gun was achieved by the HARP (High Altitude Research Project) gun, consisting of two 16½-in caliber barrels in tandem 119 ft 5 in long and weighing 165 tons, at Yuma, AZ. On 19 Nov 1966 an 185-lb projectile was fired to an altitude of 112 miles or 590,550 ft.

The static V3 underground firing tubes built in 50° shafts near Mimoyècques, near Calais, France by Germany during World War II, to bombard London, Great Britain, were never operative. This would have been a distance of some 95 miles.

The famous long-range gun that shelled Paris, France in World War I was the *Paris-Geschütz* (Paris Gun), with a caliber of 8¼ in, a designed range of 79½ miles and an achieved range of 76 miles from the Forest of Crépy in March 1918.

Field gun pull   Three teams of eight members from 72 Ordnance Company (Volunteers) Royal Army Ordnance Corps pulled a 25-pounder field gun over a distance of 110.6 miles in 24 hr at Donnington, Great Britain on 2–3 Apr 1993.

Armor   The highest auction price paid for a suit of armor was £1,925,000 ($3,657,000), by B.H. Trupin (USA) on 5 May 1983 at Sotheby's, London, Great Britain for a suit made in Milan by Giovanni Negroli in 1545 for Henri II of France. It came from the Hever Castle Collection in Kent, Great Britain.

Military engines   The largest military catapults, or onagers, could throw a missile weighing 60 lb a distance of 500 yd.

Mortars   The largest mortars ever constructed were Mallet's mortar (Woolwich Arsenal, London, Great Britain, 1857); and the *Little David* of World War II, made in the United States. Each had a caliber of 36 in, but neither was ever used in action.

The heaviest mortar ever employed was the tracked German 23½-in siege piece *Karl*; there were seven such mortars built. Only six of them were actually used in action, although never all at the same time—at Sevastopol, USSR in 1942; at Warsaw, Poland in 1944; and at Budapest, Hungary, also in 1944.

Largest cannon   The highest-caliber cannon ever constructed is the *Tsar Pushka* (*King of Cannons*), now housed in the Kremlin, Moscow, Russia. It was built in the 16th century with a bore of 35 in and a barrel 17 ft 6 in long. It weighs 44 tons.

The Turks fired up to seven shots per day from a bombard 26 ft long, with an internal caliber of 42 in, against the walls of Constantinople (now Istanbul) from 12 April–29 May 1453. The weapon was dragged by 60 oxen and 200 men and fired a 1,200-lb stone cannonball.

United States   The largest cannon in the US Army is the M185 155 mm (6.05 in) self-propelled howitzer. The M109A2/A3 unit has a range of 14.6 miles with a RAP (rocket assisted projectile), 11.2 miles unassisted. It is approximately 29 ft 11 in long, 10 ft 9½ in high, and 10 ft 3½ in wide. It weighs 28 tons, combat loaded, and carries a 50 caliber machine gun as well. This weapon is capable of firing nuclear munitions.

Nuclear delivery vehicles   As of September 1990 the USSR deployed 2,500 nuclear delivery launchers compared to the USA's 2,246, as counted under the START (Strategic Arms Reduction Talks) rules and compared to the START proposed limit of 1,600. Again under START counting rules, the former USSR could deliver a maximum of 10,271 warheads and the USA 10,563, but this is a theoretical total and not necessarily the number held. The START proposed limit for nuclear warheads is 6,000. There are four republics of the former USSR (Russia, Ukraine, Belarus and Kazakhstan) that hold strategic nuclear weapons, but the last three are commited to giving up their nuclear weapons. A second START treaty agreed to between the USA and Russia will reduce warhead numbers to between 3,000 and 3,500 each.

EDUCATION

Compulsory education was introduced for the first time in Prussia in 1819.

Universities Oldest   The Sumerians had scribal schools or *É-Dub-ba* soon after 3500 B.C. The oldest existing educational institution in the world is the University of Karueein, founded in A.D. 859 in Fez, Morocco. The University of Bologna, the oldest in Europe, was founded in 1088.

The oldest college in the United States is Harvard College in Cambridge, MA, founded in 1636 as Newtowne College and renamed in 1638 after its first benefactor, John Harvard. It was incorporated in 1650. The second oldest college in the US is the College of William and Mary, in Williamsburg, VA. It was chartered in 1693, opened in 1694, and acquired university status in 1779. However, its antecedents were in a university that was planned at Henrico, VA (1619–22) but was postponed because of the Indian massacre of 1622.

Largest   The largest existing university building in the world is the M.V. Lomonosov State University on the Lenin Hills, south of Moscow, Russia. It stands 787 ft 5 in tall, and has 32 stories and 40,000 rooms. It was constructed from 1949–53.

Greatest enrollment   The university with the greatest enrollment in the world is the State University of New York, which had 404,065 students at 64 campuses throughout the state in the fall of 1992. The greatest enrollment at a university centered in one city is at the University of Rome (*La Sapienza*), in Italy. It was built in the 1920s as a single-site campus, and still is mainly based there although some faculties are now outside the campus. Its record number of students was 180,000 in 1987, although the number has dropped slightly in the past few years.

Most graduates in family   Mr and Mrs Harold Erickson of Naples, FL saw all of their 14 children—11 sons and three daughters—obtain university or college degrees between 1962 and 1978.

Youngest university students   Michael Tan (b. 4 Apr 1984) of Christchurch, New Zealand took and passed his New Zealand bursary examination in mathematics (equivalent to high school graduation exams in the United States) in November 1991 at the age of 7 years 7 months. He started studying for a BSc degree in mathematics at Canterbury University, New Zealand in March 1992 at the age of 7 years 11 months.

United States   Adragon Eastwood De Mello (b. 5 Oct 1976) of Santa Cruz, CA obtained his BA in mathematics from the University of California in Santa Cruz on 11 Jun 1988 at the age of 11 years 8 months.

Youngest doctorate   On 13 Apr 1814 the mathematician Carl Witte of Lochau was made a Doctor of Philosophy of the University of Giessen, Germany at the age of 12.

Youngest college president   The youngest president of a major college was Ellen Futter, who was appointed to head Barnard College, New York City in May 1981 at the age of 31.

Schools Most expensive   The annual cost of keeping a pupil at the most expensive school in the United States for the academic year 1993/94 will be $29,900 at the Oxford Academy (founded 1906), in Westbrook, CT.

Most schools   The greatest documented number of schools attended by a pupil is 265, by Wilma Williams, now Mrs R.J. Horton, from 1933–43 when her parents were in show business traveling around the United States.

Schools   The country with the greatest number of primary schools is China, with 938,394 in 1990. San Marino has the lowest pupil-to-teacher ratio, with 5.5 children per teacher.

At general secondary level, India has the most schools, with 214,380 in 1990, while the Australian external territory of Cocos (Keeling) Islands has the best pupil-to-teacher ratio, with 6.0 pupils per teacher. Among sovereign countries, San Marino has the best ratio, with 6.5 pupils per teacher.

Higher education   India has the greatest number of institutions, with 6,600, while the USA has both the greatest number of students (13,711,000) and the highest ratio, at 5,596 tertiary level students per 100,000 population.

SAT scores   The maximum score possible for the Scholastic Aptitude Test (SAT) is 1,600. The highest number of students attaining perfect scores in one year is 13. This has occurred twice, in 1987 and 1992.

LONGEST TEACHING CAREER La Maestra Chucha still commands the attention of most of her pupils, more than 82 years after she set up a school with her sisters and began teaching children how to read and write.

Largest In 1988/89 Rizal High School, Pasig, Manila, Philippines had an enrollment of 16,458 regular students, although the numbers have slightly declined since then.

Most durable teacher Medarda de Jesús León de Uzcátegui, alias La Maestra Chucha, has been teaching in Caracas, Venezuela for a total of 82 years. In 1911, when she was 12, she and her two sisters set up a school there which they named *Modelo de Aplicación*. Since marrying in 1942, she has run her own school, which she calls the *Escuela Uzcátegui*, from her home in Caracas.

Highest endowment The greatest single gift in the history of higher education was $125 million, to Louisiana State University by C.B. Pennington in 1983.

Lecture fees Dr Ronald Dante was paid $3,080,000 for lecturing students on hypnotherapy at a two-day course held in Chicago on 1–2 Jun 1986. He taught for 8 hr each day, and thus earned $192,500 per hr.

RELIGIONS

Oldest Human burial, which has religious connotations, is known from c. 60,000 B.C. among *Homo sapiens neanderthalensis* in the Shanidar cave, northern Iraq.

Largest　Religious statistics are necessarily only tentative, since the test of adherence to a religion varies widely in rigor, while many individuals, particularly in the East, belong to two or more religions.

Christianity is the world's most widely practiced religion, with some 1,833 million adherents in 1992, or 33.4 percent of the world's population. There were 1,026 million Roman Catholics in the same year. The largest non-Christian religion is Islam (Muslim), with some 971 million followers in 1992.

The total of world Jewry is estimated to be 14.3 million. The highest concentration is in the United States, with 5,835,000. The total in Israel is 3,653,000. The total in Tokyo, Japan is only 750.

PLACES OF WORSHIP

Earliest　Many archaeologists are of the opinion that the decorated Upper Paleolithic caves of Europe (*c.* 30,000–10,000 B.C.) were used as places of worship or religious ritual. Claims have been made that the El Juyo cave in northern Spain contains an actual shrine, dated to *c.* 12,000 B.C. On the edge of an ancient lake near the northern Polish village of Tlokowo, carved wooden figurines were apparently thrown from the platform as ritual offerings. Small shrines preceded the building of larger temples in the Near East, for example at Tell Aswad, Syria *c.* 5200 B.C. The earliest complex temple in the Near East was the one in level XVII at Eridu, Iraq *c.* 3700 B.C.

The oldest surviving Christian church in the world is a converted house in Qal'at es Salihiye (formerly Douro-Europos) in eastern Syria, dating from A.D. 232.

Oldest Church　The oldest standing Protestant edifice in the United States is the Newport Parish Church, commonly known as St Luke's, in Isle of Wight County, VA, four miles south of Smithfield, VA. The church was built *c.* 1632 and was originally called Warrisquioke Parish Church. In 1637 it was renamed the Isle of Wight Parish Church and its present name was instituted in 1957.

Synagogue　The oldest synagogue in the United States is Touro Synagogue, Newport, RI. Construction was started in 1759 and completed in 1763. Originally called the Jewish Synagogue of Newport, the synagogue was closed in 1820, but reopened in 1883, renamed Touro Synagogue.

Largest temple　The largest religious structure ever built is Angkor Wat ("City Temple"), enclosing 402 acres in Cambodia (or Kampuchea), Southeast Asia. It was built to the Hindu god Vishnu by the Khmer King Suryavarman II in the period A.D. 1113–50. Its curtain wall measures 4,199 × 4,199 ft and its population, before it was abandoned in 1432, was 80,000. The whole complex of 72 major monuments, begun *c.* A.D. 900, extends over 15 × 5 miles.

The largest Buddhist temple in the world is Borobudur, near Jogjakarta, Indonesia, built in the eighth century. It is 103 ft tall and 403 ft square.

The largest Mormon temple is the Salt Lake Temple, UT, dedicated on 6 Apr 1893, with a floor area of 253,015 ft^2 or 5.8 acres.

Largest cathedral　The world's largest cathedral is the cathedral church of the Diocese of New York, St John the Divine, in New York City, with a floor area of 121,000 ft^2 and a volume of 16,822,000 ft^3. The cornerstone was laid on 27 Dec 1892, and work on the Gothic building was stopped in 1941. Work was restarted in earnest in July 1979, but is still not finished. The nave is the longest in the world at 601 ft, with a vaulting 124 ft in height.

The cathedral covering the largest area is that of Santa Mariá de la Sede in Sevilla (Seville), Spain. It was built in Spanish Gothic style between 1402 and 1519, and is 414 ft long, 271 ft wide and 100 ft high to the vault of the nave.

Smallest cathedral   The smallest church in the world designated as a cathedral (the seat of a diocesan bishop) is that of the Christ Catholic Church, Highlandville, MO. It was consecrated in July 1983. It measures 14 × 17 ft and has seating for 18 people.

Largest church   The largest church in the world is the Basilica of St Peter, built between 1506 and 1614 in Vatican City, Rome, Italy. Its length, including the walls of the apse and façade, is 717 ft 6 in. The area is 247,572 ft². The inner diameter of the famous dome is 139 ft 8 in and its center is 393 ft 4 in high. The external height is 448 ft 1 in. Taller, although not as tall as the cathedral

---

Largest clergies   The world's largest religious organization is the Roman Catholic Church—155 cardinals, 785 archbishops, 3,273 bishops, 403,173 priests and 882,111 nuns at the end of 1990.

Longest-serving chorister   John Love Vokins (1890–1989) was a chorister for 92 years. He joined the choir of Christ Church, Heeley, Great Britain in 1895 and that of St Michael's, Hathersage, Great Britain 35 years later, and was still singing in 1987.

Singing   Rev. Acharya Prem Bhikshuji (d. 18 Apr 1970) started chanting the Akhand Rama-Dhoon at Jamnagar, Gujarat, India on 1 Aug 1964, and devotees were still continuing the chant in May 1992.

Smallest church   The world's smallest church is the chapel of Santa Isabel de Hungría, in Colomares, a monument to Christopher Columbus at Benalmádena, Málaga, Spain. It is of irregular shape and has a total floor area of 21¹/₈ ft².

The smallest church in the United States is Cross Island Chapel, at Oneida, NY, with a floor area of 29.1 ft² (6 ft 9¹/₂ in × 4 ft 3¹/₂ in).

Brasses   The world's oldest monumental brass is that commemorating Bishop Yso von Wölpe in the Andreaskirche, Verden, near Hanover, Germany, dating from 1231. An engraved coffin plate of St Ulrich (d. 973), laid in 1187, was found buried in the Church of SS Ulrich and Afra, Augsburg, Germany in 1979.

Most rapidly canonized   The shortest interval that elapsed between the death of a saint and his or her canonization was in the case of St Peter of Verona, Italy, who died on 6 Apr 1252 and was canonized 337 days later on 9 Mar 1253. (For the other extreme of 857 years, see the table of Popes and Cardinals.)

POPES AND CARDINALS

Longest Papal Reign
Pius IX—Giovanni Maria Mastai-Ferretti (1846–78).
31 years 236 days

Shortest Papal Reign
Stephen II (*d*. 752). 2 days

Longest-lived Popes
St Agatho (*d*. 681; probably exaggerated), ?106 years
Leo XIII—Gioacchino Pecci (1810–1903). 93 years 140 days

Youngest elected
John XII—Ottaviano (*c*. 937–64) in 955. 18 years old

Last married
Adrian II (pre-celibacy rule). Elected 867

Last with children
Gregory XIII—Ugo Buoncompagni (1502–85). One son.
Elected 1572

Last non-Cardinal
Urban VI—Bartolomeo Prignano (1318–89), Archbishop of Bari.
Elected 8 Apr 1378

Last previous non-Italian
Adrian VI—Adrian Florensz Boeyens (Netherlands).
Elected 9 Jan 1522

Slowest election
Gregory X—Teobaldi Visconti. 31 months, Feb 1269–1 Sep 1271

Fastest election
Julius II—on first ballot, 21 Oct 1503

Slowest Canonization
St Leo III—over span of 857 years, 816–1673

Oldest Cardinal (all-time)
Georgio da Costa (*b*. Portugal 1406, d. Rome, Italy aged 102
years). Elected 18 Sep 1508
(*current*)
Henri De Lubac (*b*. Cambrai, France, 20 Feb 1896)

Youngest Cardinal (all-time)
Luis Antonio de Bourbon (*b*. 25 Jul 1727). 8 years 147 days.
Elected 19 Dec 1735
(*current*)
Alfonso Lopez Trujillo of Colombia (*b*. 18 Nov 1935).
47 years 76 days

Longest-serving Cardinal
Cardinal Duke of York, grandson of James VII of Scotland
and II of England. 60 years 10 days, 1747–1807

Longest-serving Bishop
Bishop Louis François de la Baume de Suze (1603–90).
76 years 273 days from 6 Dec 1613

in Ulm, Germany (see Tallest spire), is the Basilica of Our Lady of Peace (Notre Dame de la Paix) at Yamoussoukro, Ivory Coast, completed in 1989. Including its golden cross, it is 519 ft high.

The elliptical Basilica of St Pio X at Lourdes, France, completed in 1957 at a cost of $5.6 million, has a capacity of 20,000 under its giant span arches and a length of 660 ft.

Longest The crypt of the underground Civil War Memorial Church in the Guadarrama Mountains, 28 miles from Madrid, Spain, is 853 ft in length. It took 21 years (1937–58) to build, at a reported cost of $392 million, and is surmounted by a cross 492 ft tall.

Largest synagogue The largest synagogue in the world is Temple Emanu-El on Fifth Avenue at 65th Street, New York City. The temple, completed in September 1929, has a frontage of 150 ft on Fifth Avenue and 253 ft on 65th Street. The sanctuary proper can accommodate 2,500 people, and the adjoining Beth-El Chapel seats 350. When all the facilities are in use, more than 6,000 people can be accommodated.

Largest mosque The largest mosque is Shah Faisal Mosque, near Islamabad, Pakistan. The total area of the complex is 46.87 acres, with the covered area of the prayer hall being 1.19 acres. It can accommodate 100,000 worshippers in the prayer hall and the courtyard, and a further 200,000 people in the adjacent grounds.

Tallest minaret The tallest minaret in the world is that of the Great Hassan II Mosque, Casablanca, Morocco, measuring 576 ft. The cost of construction of the mosque was $381.5 million. Of ancient minarets, the tallest is the Qutb Minar, south of New Delhi, India, built in 1194 to a height of 238 ft.

Tallest and oldest stupa The now largely ruined Jetavanarama dagoba in the ancient city of Anuradhapura, Sri Lanka, measures 400 ft in height. The 326-ft-tall Shwedagon Pagoda, Yangon (Rangoon), Myanmar (Burma) is built on the site of a 27-ft-tall pagoda of 585 B.C.

Sacred object The sacred object with the highest intrinsic value is the 15th-century gold Buddha in Wat Trimitr Temple in Bangkok, Thailand. It is 10 ft tall and weighs an estimated 6.06 tons. At the April 1993 price of $340 per fine ounce, its intrinsic worth was $42.8 million. The gold under the plaster exterior was found only in 1954.

Tallest spire Cathedral The tallest cathedral spire in the world is that of the Protestant Cathedral of Ulm in Germany. The building is early Gothic and was begun in 1377. The tower, in the center of the west façade, was not finally completed until 1890 and is 528 ft high.

Church The world's tallest church spire is that of the Chicago Temple of the First Methodist Church on Clark Street, Chicago, IL. The building consists of a 22-story skyscraper (erected in 1924) surmounted by a parsonage at 330 ft, a "Sky Chapel" at 400 ft and a steeple cross at 568 ft above street level.

Stained glass Oldest Pieces of stained glass dated before A.D. 850, some possibly even to the seventh century, excavated by Prof. Rosemary Cramp, were set into a window of that date in the nearby St Paul's Church, Jarrow, Ireland.

TALLEST SPIRE The tallest cathedral spire is at Ulm in Germany, and can be seen particularly clearly from beyond the River Danube. (Photo: James Clift for Guinness Publishing)

The oldest complete stained-glass window in the world represents the Prophets in a window of the Cathedral of Augsburg, Germany, dating from the second half of the 11th century.

United States The oldest figured stained-glass window in the United States is in Christ Church, Pelham Manor, NY and was designed by William Jay Bolton and John Bolton in 1843.

Largest The largest stained-glass window is that of the Resurrection Mausoleum in Justice, IL, measuring 22,381 ft² in 2,448 panels, completed in 1971.

Although not one continuous window, the Basilica of Our Lady of Peace (Notre Dame de la Paix) at Yamoussoukro, Ivory Coast contains a number of stained-glass windows covering a total area of 80,000 ft².

CHURCH PERSONNEL

There are more than 2,000 "registered" saints, of whom around two-thirds are either Italian or French. The first Christian martyr was St Stephen, executed *c.* A.D. 36.

The first native-born American Roman Catholic saint was Mother Elizabeth Ann Bayley Seton (1774–1821), canonized 14 Sep 1975.

Bishops Oldest The oldest Roman Catholic bishop in recent years was Archbishop Edward Howard, formerly Archbishop of Portland, OR (b. 5 Nov 1877), who died at the age of 105 years 58 days on 2 Jan 1983. He had celebrated mass about 27,800 times.

Youngest   The youngest bishop of all time was HRH the Duke of York and Albany, the second son of George III, who was elected bishop of Osnabrück, through his father's influence as Elector of Hanover, at the age of 196 days on 27 Feb 1764. He resigned 39 years later.

United States   The first consecrated Roman Catholic bishop of the United States was John Carroll (1735–1815) of Baltimore, MD. In 1808, Carroll, a Jesuit, became the first Catholic archbishop of the United States, with suffragan sees at Boston, New York City, Philadelphia and Baidstown, KY. Carroll also founded Georgetown University in 1789.

Oldest parish priest   Father Alvaro Fernandez (8 Dec 1880–6 Jan 1988) served as a parish priest at Santiago de Abres, Spain from 1919 until he was 107 years old.

The oldest Anglican clergyman, Rev. Clement Williams (b. 30 Oct 1879), died at the age of 106 years 3 months on 3 Feb 1986. He stood on the route at Queen Victoria's funeral and was ordained in 1904.

Longest service   Rev. K.M. Jacob (b. 10 Jul 1880) was made a deacon in the Marthoma Syrian Church of Malabar in Kerala, southern India in 1897. He served his church until his death on 28 Mar 1984, 87 years later.

Sunday school   The pioneer of the Sunday school movement is generally accepted to be Robert Raikes (1736–1811). In 1780 he engaged a number of women in his home city of Gloucester, Great Britain to teach children on Sundays. Reading and religious instruction were the main activities from the outset, and by 1785 the Sunday School Society had been formed.

Perfect attendance   F. Otto Brechel (1890–1990) of Mars, PA completed 88 years (4,576 Sundays) of perfect attendance at church school at three different churches in Pennsylvania—the first from 1902 to 1931, the second from 1931 to 1954, and the third from 1954 onwards.

Bill Tom Adams (b. 30 Aug 1898) of Monroe, LA is the current record-holder; he has not missed Sunday school since June 1905, although there have been occasions when ill health has meant that someone from his class has come to his bedside and taught the lesson.

HUMAN ACHIEVEMENTS

- **ENDURANCE AND ENDEAVOR**
- **MISCELLANEOUS ENDEAVORS**
- **JUGGLING**
- **FOOD**
- **DRINK**
- **MANUFACTURED ARTICLES**

ENDURANCE AND ENDEAVOR

Most traveled The world's most traveled man is Parke G. Thompson, of Akron, OH, who has visited all of the sovereign countries and all but five of the nonsovereign or other territories that existed in the spring of 1993. (See Human World, Countries.)

The most traveled couple is Dr Robert and Carmen Becker of East Northport, NY, both of whom had visited all of the sovereign countries (the exception being Iraq) and all but six of the nonsovereign or other territories.

Allen F. Zondlak visited all 3,142 counties and county equivalents in the United States, completing his travels in 1991.

Most isolated The farthest any human has been removed from his nearest living fellow human is 2,233.2 miles in the case of the command module pilot Alfred M. Worden on the US *Apollo 15* lunar mission of 30 Jul–1 Aug 1971, while David Scott and James Irwin were at Hadley Base exploring the surface.

Longest walks The first person reputed to have "walked around the world" is George Matthew Schilling (USA) from 3 Aug 1897 to 1904, but the first *verified* achievement in this category was by David Kunst (USA; b. 1939) from 20 Jun 1970 to 5 Oct 1974. He wore out 21 pairs of shoes in the process.

Tomás Carlos Pereira (Argentina; b. 16 Nov 1942) spent 10 years, from 6 Apr 1968 to 8 Apr 1978, walking 29,800 miles around five continents. Steven Newman of Bethel, OH spent four years, from 1 Apr 1983 to 1 Apr 1987, walking 22,500 miles around the world, covering 20 countries and five continents.

Rick Hansen (Canada; b. 1957), who was paralyzed from the waist down in 1973 as a result of an auto accident, wheeled his wheelchair 24,901.55 miles through four continents and 34 countries. He started his journey from Vancouver, British Columbia on 21 Mar 1985 and arrived back there on 22 May 1987.

George Meegan (b. 2 Oct 1952) of Rainham, Great Britain walked 19,019 miles from Usuaia, in the southern tip of South America, to Prudhoe Bay in northern Alaska, taking 2,426 days from 26 Jan 1977 to 18 Sep 1983. He thus completed the first traverse of the Americas and the Western Hemisphere on foot.

Sean Eugene McGuire (USA; b. 15 Sep 1956) walked 7,327 miles from the Yukon River, north of Livengood, AK to Key West, FL in 307 days, from 6 Jun 1978 to 9 Apr 1979. The trans-Canada (Halifax to Vancouver) record

---

Most traveled man The most traveled man in the era before motor vehicles was believed to be the Methodist preacher Bishop Francis Asbury (b. Handsworth, Great Britain, 1745), who traveled 264,000 miles in North America between 1771 and 1815. During this time he preached some 16,000 sermons and ordained nearly 3,000 ministers.

Polar Conquest

Two major Antarctic expeditions took place in late 1992/early 1993, with records set by Erling Kagge (above) through his solo trek, and Sir Ranulph Fiennes (left) together with Dr Michael Stroud. (Photos: Rex Features and Sygma/Fiennes-Stroud-Howell)

walk of 3,764 miles is 96 days, by Clyde McRae, age 23, from 1 May to 4 Aug 1973. John Lees (b. 23 Feb 1945) of Brighton, Great Britain walked 2,876 miles across the United States from City Hall, Los Angeles to City Hall, New York City in 53 days 12 hr 15 min (averaging 53.75 miles a day) between 11 April and 3 Jun 1972.

North Pole conquest The claims of the two Arctic explorers Dr Frederick Albert Cook (1865–1940) and Cdr (later Rear-Ad.) Robert Edwin Peary (1856–1920), of the US Naval Civil Engineering branch, to have reached the North Pole are not subject to irrefutable proof, and several recent surveys have produced conflicting conclusions. On excellent pack ice and modern sleds, Wally Herbert's 1968–69 expedition (see Arctic crossing) attained a best day's route mileage of 23 miles in 15 hr. Cook claimed 26 miles twice, while Peary claimed an average of 38 miles per day over eight consecutive days, which many glaciologists regard as quite unsustainable.

The first people indisputably to have reached the North Pole at ground level—the exact point at Lat. 90° 00′ 00″ N (± 300 meters)—were Pavel Afanasyevich Geordiyenko, Pavel Kononovich Sen'ko, Mikhail Mikhaylovich Somov and Mikhail Yemel'yenovich Ostrekin (all of the former USSR), on 23 Apr 1948. They arrived and departed by air.

The earliest indisputable attainment of the North Pole by surface travel over the sea-ice took place at 3 P.M. CST on 19 Apr 1968, when expedition leader Ralph Plaisted (USA), accompanied by Walter Pederson, Gerald Pitzel and Jean Luc Bombardier, reached the Pole after a 42-day trek in four Ski-doos (snowmobiles). Their arrival was independently verified 18 hr later by a US Air Force weather aircraft. The party returned by aircraft.

Naomi Uemura (1941–84), the Japanese explorer and mountaineer, became the first person to reach the North Pole in a solo trek across the Arctic sea-ice at 4:45 A.M. GMT on 1 May 1978. He had traveled 450 miles, setting out on 7 March from Cape Edward, Ellesmere Island in northern Canada. He averaged nearly eight miles per day with his sled *Aurora* drawn by 17 huskies. He left by aircraft.

The first people to ski to the North Pole were the seven members of a Soviet expedition, led by Dmitry Shparo. They reached the Pole on 31 May 1979 after a trek of 900 miles that took them 77 days.

Dr Jean-Louis Etienne, age 39, was the first to reach the Pole solo and without dogs, on 11 May 1986 after 63 days. He left by aircraft.

On 20 Apr 1987 Shinji Kazama, age 36, of Tokyo, Japan reached the North Pole from Ward Hunt Island, northern Canada in 44 days, having started on his 200-cc motorcycle on 8 March. He also left by aircraft.

The first woman to set foot on the North Pole was Mrs Fran Phipps (Canada) on 5 Apr 1971. She traveled there by ski-plane with her husband, a bush pilot. Galina Aleksandrovna Lastovskaya (b. 1941) and Lilia Vladislavovna Minina (b. 1959) were crew members of the USSR atomic icebreaker *Arktika*, which reached the Pole on 17 Aug 1977.

Longest sled journeys Antarctic The longest polar sled journey was undertaken by the International Trans-Antarctica Expedition (six members), who traveled a distance of about 3,750 miles by sled in 220 days, from 27 Jul 1989 (Seal Nunataks) to 3 Mar 1990 (Mirnyy). The expedition was accompanied by a team of 40 dogs, but a number of the dogs were flown out from one of the staging posts for a period of rest before returning to the Antarctic. The expedition was supported by aircraft throughout its duration.

The longest *totally self-supporting* polar sled journey ever made was one of

1,350 miles from Gould Bay to the Ross ice shelf by Sir Ranulph Fiennes and Dr Michael Stroud. (See South Pole conquest.)

South Pole conquest The first men to cross the Antarctic Circle (Lat. 66° 33′ S) were the 193 crew members and Capt. James Cook, British Royal Navy (1728–79) of the *Resolution* (509 tons) and the *Adventure* (370 tons), captained by Lt. Tobias Furneaux, on 17 Jan 1773 at 39° E.

The first person known to have sighted the Antarctic ice shelf was Capt. Fabian Gottlieb Benjamin von Bellingshausen (Russia; 1778–1852) on 27 Jan 1820 from the vessel *Vostok* accompanied by the *Mirnyy*. The first people known to have sighted the mainland of the continent were Capt. William Smith (1790–1847) and Master Edward Bransfield, Royal Navy, in the brig *Williams*. They saw the peaks of Trinity Land three days later, on 30 Jan 1820.

The South Pole (alt. 9,186 ft on ice and 336 ft bedrock) was first reached at 11 A.M. on 14 Dec 1911 by a Norwegian party of five men led by Capt. Roald Engebereth Gravning Amundsen (1872–1928), after a 53-day march with dog sleds from the Bay of Whales, to which he had penetrated in the vessel *Fram*. Subsequent calculations showed that Olav Olavson Bjaaland and Helmer Hanssen of the Amundsen party probably passed within 1,300–2,000 ft of the exact location of the South Pole. The other two members of the party were Sverre H. Hassell (died 1928) and Oskar Wisting (died 1936).

The first person to reach the South Pole solo and unsupported was Erling Kagge (Norway) at the age of 29, on 7 Jan 1993 after a 50-day trek of 870 miles from Berkner Island.

The longest unsupported trek in Antarctica was by team-leader Sir Ranulph Fiennes, 48, with Dr Michael Stroud, 37, who set off from Gould Bay on 9 Nov 1992, reached the South Pole on 16 Jan 1993 and finally abandoned their walk on the Ross ice shelf on 11 February. They covered a distance of 1,350 miles during their 94-day trek. (See Longest sled journeys.)

The first woman to set foot on Antarctica was Mrs Karoline Mikkelsen, a whaling captain's wife, on 20 Feb 1935. It was not until 11 Nov 1969 that a woman stood at the South Pole. On that day Lois Jones, Eileen McSaveney, Jean Pearson, Terry Lee Tickhill (all USA), Kay Lindsay (Australia) and Pam Young (New Zealand) arrived by air at Amundsen-Scott station and walked to the exact point from there.

Pole to Pole circumnavigation The first Pole to Pole circumnavigation was achieved by Sir Ranulph Fiennes and Charles Burton of the British Trans-Globe Expedition, who traveled south from Greenwich, Great Britain (2 Sep

First to see both Poles The first people to see both Poles were Capt. Roald Engebereth Gravning Amundsen and Oskar Wisting, when they flew aboard the airship *Norge* over the North Pole on 12 May 1926, having previously been to the South Pole on 14 Dec 1911.

First to visit both Poles Dr Albert Paddock Crary (USA; 1911–87) reached the North Pole in a Dakota aircraft on 3 May 1952. On 12 Feb 1961 he arrived at the South Pole by Sno Cat on a scientific traverse party from the McMurdo Station.

1979), via the South Pole (15 Dec 1980) and the North Pole (10 Apr 1982), and back to Greenwich, arriving on 29 Aug 1982 after a 35,000 mile trek. (See Arctic crossing and Antarctic crossing.)

First to walk to both Poles   The first man to walk to both the North and the South Poles was Robert Swan (Great Britain; b. 28 Jul 1956). He led the three-man Footsteps of Scott expedition, which reached the South Pole on 11 Jan 1986, and three years later headed the eight-man Icewalk expedition, which arrived at the North Pole on 14 May 1989.

Arctic crossing   The first crossing of the Arctic sea-ice was achieved by the British Trans-Arctic Expedition, which left Point Barrow, AK on 21 Feb 1968 and arrived at the Seven Island archipelago northeast of Spitzbergen, Svalbard, Norway 464 days later, on 29 May 1969. This involved a haul of 2,920 statute miles with a drift of 700 miles, compared with the straight-line distance of 1,662 miles. The team was made up of Wally Herbert (leader), 34, Major Ken Hedges, RAMC, 34, Allan Gill, 38, Dr Roy Koerner (glaciologist), 36, and 40 huskies. The only crossing achieved in a single season was that by Fiennes and Burton (see Pole to Pole circumnavigation and Antarctic crossing) from Alert via the North Pole to the Greenland Sea in open snowmobiles. Both reached the North Pole and returned by land.

Antarctic crossing   The first surface crossing of the Antarctic continent was completed at 1:47 P.M. on 2 Mar 1958, after a trek of 2,158 miles lasting 99 days from 24 Nov 1957, from Shackleton Base to Scott Base via the Pole. The crossing party of 12 was led by Dr (now Sir) Vivian Ernest Fuchs (Great Britain; b. 11 Feb 1908).

The 2,600-mile trans-Antarctic leg from Sanae to Scott Base of the 1980–82 British Trans-Globe Expedition was achieved in 67 days and eight rest days, from 28 Oct 1980 to 11 Jan 1981, having reached the South Pole on 15 Dec 1980. The three-man party on snowmobiles comprised Sir Ranulph Fiennes (b. 1944), Oliver Shepard and Charles Burton. (See Pole to Pole circumnavigation and Arctic crossing.)

Greatest ocean descent   The record ocean descent was achieved in the Challenger Deep of the Mariana Trench, 250 miles southwest of Guam in the Pacific Ocean, when the Swiss-built US Navy bathyscaphe *Trieste*, manned by Dr Jacques Piccard (Switzerland; b. 28 Jul 1922) and Lt Donald Walsh (USN), reached a depth of 35,813 ft at 1:10 P.M. on 23 Jan 1960. (See Oceans, deepest.) The pressure of the water was 16,883 lbf/in^2 and the temperature 37° F. The descent took 4 hr 48 min and the ascent 3 hr 17 min.

Deep-diving records   The record depth for the *ill-advisedly* dangerous activity of breath-held diving is 351 ft, by Angela Bandini (Italy) on a marked cable off Elba, Italy on 3 Oct 1989. She was underwater for 2 min 46 sec.

The record dive with scuba (self-contained underwater breathing apparatus) is 437 ft, by John J. Gruener and R. Neal Watson (USA) off Freeport, Grand Bahama on 14 Oct 1968.

The record dive utilizing gas mixtures was a simulated dive to a depth of 2,300 ft of sea-water by Théo Mavrostomos as part of the HYDRA 10 operation at the Hyperbaric Center of Comex in Marseilles, France on 20 Nov 1992, during a 43-day dive. He was breathing "hydreliox" (hydrogen, oxygen and helium).

Record survival at sea

177 days adrift with the sharks

Tabwai Mikaie and Arenta Tebeitabu, two fisherman from the island of Nikunau in Kiribati, have been found alive after surviving for a record 177 days adrift at sea in their fishing boat, a 13-foot open dinghy.

They were apparently caught in a cyclone after setting out on a trip on 17 November last year, and although their boat overturned, they were able to set it upright and drift. They have survived on fish, caught by a spear and a fishing line, and the occasional floating coconut, with rainwater to drink. Twice they managed to catch turtles as they swam past. However, most of the time they had nothing at all to eat. A third man set out with them, but he died just a few days ago, although it is not known how. Barely conscious, the two men have now been washed ashore on the island of Upolu, in Western Samoa, some 1,100 miles away. It has been revealed that their families and friends even held a funeral for them. The local police commissioner has described the men as "just skin and bones."

Arnaud de Nechaud de Feral performed a saturation dive of 73 days from 9 Oct–21 Dec 1989 in a hyperbaric chamber simulating a depth of 985 ft, as part of the HYDRA 9 operation carried out by Comex at Marseilles, France. He was breathing "hydrox," a mixture of hydrogen and oxygen.

Richard Presley spent 69 days 19 min in a module underwater at a lagoon in Key Largo, FL from 6 May to 14 Jul 1992. The test was carried out as part of a mission entitled Project Atlantis which had as its aim to explore the human factors of living in an undersea environment.

Deepest underwater escapes   The deepest underwater rescue ever achieved was of the *Pisces III*, in which Roger R. Chapman (28) and Roger Mallinson (35) were trapped for 76 hours when their vessel sank to 1,575 ft, 150 miles southeast of Cork, Republic of Ireland on 29 Aug 1973. It was hauled to the surface

> **Submergence** The *continuous* duration record (i.e., no rest breaks) for scuba (i.e., self-contained underwater breathing apparatus, used without surface air hoses) is 212 hr 30 min, by Michael Stevens of Birmingham, Great Britain in a Royal Navy tank at the National Exhibition Center, Birmingham from 14–23 Feb 1986. There are numerous health risks in undertaking such endurance trials, and measures were taken to reduce them as far as possible.
>
> **High-altitude diving** The record for high-altitude diving is 16,509 ft, in a lake in the crater of Popocatépetl, a dormant volcano in Mexico. Roger Weihrauch (Germany) spent 20 minutes exploring the 16-ft-deep lake on 20 Nov 1983.
>
> **Longest on a raft** The longest recorded survival alone on a raft is 133 days (4 1/2 months) by Second Steward Poon Lim (b. Hong Kong) of Great Britain's Merchant Navy, whose ship, the SS *Ben Lomond*, was torpedoed in the Atlantic 565 miles west of St Paul's Rocks at Lat. 00° 30′ N, Long. 38° 45′ W at 11:45 A.M. on 23 Nov 1942. He was picked up by a Brazilian fishing boat off Salinópolis, Brazil on 5 Apr 1943 and was able to walk ashore.

on 1 September by the cable ship *John Cabot* after work by *Pisces V*, *Pisces II* and the remote-control recovery vessel US CURV.

The greatest depth from which an actual escape without any equipment has been made is 225 ft, by Richard A. Slater from the rammed submersible *Nekton Beta* off Catalina Island, CA on 28 Sep 1970.

The record for an escape with equipment was by Norman Cooke and Hamish Jones on 22 Jul 1987. During a naval exercise they escaped from a depth of 601 ft from the submarine HMS *Otus* in Bjornefjorden, off Bergen, Norway. They were wearing standard suits with a built-in life jacket, from which air expanding during the ascent passes into a hood over the escaper's head.

Deepest salvage The greatest depth at which salvage has been successfully carried out is 17,251 ft, in the case of a helicopter that had crashed into the Pacific Ocean in August 1991 with the loss of four lives. The crew of the USS *Salvor* and personnel from East Port International managed to raise the wreckage to the surface on 27 Feb 1992 so that the authorities could try to determine the cause of the accident.

The deepest salvage operation ever achieved with divers was on the wreck of HM cruiser *Edinburgh*, sunk on 2 May 1942 in the Barents Sea off northern Norway, inside the Arctic Circle, in 803 ft of water. Over 32 days (from 7 Sep–7 Oct 1981), 12 divers dove on the wreck in pairs, using a bell from the *Stephaniturm* (1,594 tons), under the direction of former British Royal Navy officer Michael Stewart. A total of 460 gold ingots (the only 100 percent salvage to date) was recovered, John Rossier being the first person to touch the gold.

Greatest penetration into the Earth The deepest penetration made into the

Deepest Salvage

When a US Navy UH-46 Sea Knight helicopter crashed at sea in August 1991, killing all its crew members, a major operation was begun to locate and recover it in order to determine the cause of the accident. Once the wreck was identified, the USS *Salvor* (ARS 52) was chosen to take responsibility for the salvage, and a painstaking operation ended in February 1992 with a record for the deepest salvage. Not surprisingly, handshakes and celebratory cigars were the order of the day afterwards.

ground by human beings is in the Western Deep Levels Mine at Carletonville, Transvaal, South Africa, where a record depth of 11,749 ft was attained on 12 Jul 1977. The virgin rock temperature at this depth is 131° F. (See also Science and Technology, Borings and Mines.)

Shaft-sinking record The one-month (31 days) world record is 1,251 ft for a standard shaft 26 ft in diameter at Buffelsfontein Mine, Transvaal, South Africa, in March 1962.

MARRIAGES

Most marriages The greatest number of marriages contracted by one person in the monogamous world is 27, by former Baptist minister Glynn "Scotty" Wolfe (b. 1908) of Blythe, CA, who first married in 1927. He believed that he had a total of 41 children.

The greatest number of monogamous marriages by a woman is 22, by Linda Lou Essex of Anderson, IN. She has been married to 15 different men since 1957, her most recent marriage being in October 1991. However, that also ended in divorce.

The record for bigamous marriages is 104, by Giovanni Vigliotto—one of many aliases used by either Fred Jipp (USA; b. 3 Apr 1936) or Nikolai Peruskov (Italy; b. 3 Apr 1929) during 1949–81 in 27 states and 14 foreign countries. Four victims were aboard one ship in 1968 and two were in London, Great Britain. On 28 Mar 1983 in Phoenix, AZ he received a sentence of 28 years for fraud and six for bigamy, and was fined $336,000. He died in February 1991.

Oldest bride and bridegroom The oldest recorded bridegroom was Harry Stevens, age 103, who married Thelma Lucas, 84, at the Caravilla Retirement Home, WI on 3 Dec 1984.

The oldest recorded bride is Minnie Munro, age 102, who married Dudley Reid, 83, at Point Clare, New South Wales, Australia on 31 May 1991.

Best man The world champion "best man" is Ting Ming Siong, from Sibu, Sarawak, in Malaysia, who in March 1993 officiated at a wedding for the 808th time since 1976.

Longest engagement The longest engagement on record was between Octavio Guillen and Adriana Martinez. They finally took the plunge after 67 years in June 1969 in Mexico City. Both were then 82 years old.

Most wedding ceremonies Richard and Carole Roble of South Hempstead, NY have married each other 52 times, with their first wedding being in 1969. They have chosen a different location each time, with ceremonies in all the states of the USA.

Youngest married It was reported in 1986 that an 11-month-old boy was married to a 3-month-old girl in Bangladesh to end a 20-year feud between two families over a disputed farm.

Longest marriage   The longest recorded marriages were both of 86 years. Sir Temulji Bhicaji Nariman and Lady Nariman, who were married from 1853 to 1940, were cousins, and the marriage took place when both were age five. Sir Temulji (b. 3 Sep 1848) died, at the age of 91 years 11 months, in August 1940 in Bombay, India. Lazarus Rowe (b. Greenland, NH in 1725) and Molly Webber were recorded as marrying in 1743. He died first, in 1829, also after 86 years of marriage.

Golden weddings   The greatest number of golden weddings in a family is 10, the six sons and four daughters of Joseph and Sophia Gresl of Manitowoc, WI all celebrating golden weddings between April 1962 and September 1988, and the six sons and four daughters of George and Eleonora Hopkins of Patrick County, VA all celebrating their golden weddings between November 1961 and October 1988.

Wedding ceremonies   The largest mass wedding ceremony was one of 20,825 couples officiated over by Sun Myung Moon (b. 1920) of the Holy Spirit Association for the Unification of World Christianity in the Olympic Stadium in Seoul, South Korea on 25 Aug 1992. An additional 9,800 couples around the world took part in the ceremony through a satellite link.

Most expensive   The wedding of Mohammed, son of Shaik Rashid Bin Saeed Al Maktoum, to Princess Salama in Dubai in May 1981 lasted seven days and cost an estimated $44 million. It was held in a stadium built especially for the occasion, accommodating 20,000 wedding guests.

Greatest attendance   At the wedding of cousins Menachem Teitelbaum and Brucha Sima Meisels in Uniondale, Long Island, NY on 4 Dec 1984, the attendance of the Satmar sect of Hasidic Jews was estimated to be 17,000–20,000.

Oldest divorced   The oldest aggregate age of a couple being divorced is 188. On 2 Feb 1984 a divorce was granted in Milwaukee, WI to Ida Stern, age 91, and her husband Simon, 97.

FEASTS AND CELEBRATIONS

Banquets Most lavish   The most lavish menu ever served was for the main banquet at the Imperial Iranian 2,500th Anniversary gathering at Persepolis in October 1971. The feast, which lasted 5¹/₂ hr, comprised quails' eggs stuffed with Iranian caviar, a mousse of crayfish tails in Nantua sauce, stuffed rack of roast lamb, a main course of roast peacock stuffed with *foie gras*, fig rings and

---

Dining out   The greatest altitude at which a formal meal has been held is 22,205 ft, at the top of Mt Huascaran, Peru, when nine members of the Ansett Social Climbers from Sydney, Australia scaled the mountain on 28 Jun 1989 with a dining table, chairs, wine and a three-course meal. At the summit they put on top hats and thermal evening attire for their dinner party, which was marred only by the fact that the wine turned to ice.

raspberry sweet champagne sherbet. The wines included *Château Lafite-Rothschild* 1945 at $160 (now $400) per bottle from Maxime's, Paris, France.

Largest   The largest feast was attended by 150,000 guests on the occasion of the renunciation ceremony of Atul Dalpatlal Shah, when he became a monk, at Ahmedabad, India on 2 Jun 1991.

Indoors   The greatest number of people served indoors at a single sitting was 18,000 municipal leaders at the Palais de l'Industrie, Paris, France on 18 Aug 1889.

Military   It was estimated that some 30,000 guests attended a military feast given at Radewitz, Poland on 25 Jun 1730 by King August II (1709–33).

Dining out   The world champion for eating out was Fred E. Magel of Chicago, IL, who over a period of 50 years dined out 46,000 times in 60 countries as a restaurant grader. He claimed that the restaurant that served the largest helpings was Zehnder's Hotel, Frankenmuth, MI. Mr Magel's favorite dishes were South African rock lobster and mousse of fresh English strawberries.

Party-giving   The International Year of the Child children's party in Hyde Park, London, Great Britain on 30–31 May 1979 was attended by the British royal family and 160,000 children.

The world's biggest birthday party was attended by 75,000 people at Buffalo, NY on 4 Jul 1991 as part of the 1991 Friendship Festival, an annual event held every July to celebrate the national birthdays of the United States and Canada.

The largest Christmas party ever staged was the one thrown by the Boeing Co. in the 65,000-seat Kingdome, Seattle, WA. The party was held in two parts on 15 Dec 1979, and a total of 103,152 people attended.

During St Patrick's week of 11–17 Mar 1985, Houlihan's Old Place hosted St Pat's Parties at the 48 Kansas City, MO-based Gilbert/Robinson restaurants, for a total of 206,854 documented guests.

The largest teddy bears' picnic ever staged was attended by 9,750 bears together with their owners in Auckland, New Zealand, on 14 Feb 1993.

MISCELLANEOUS ENDEAVORS

We are phasing out those record categories in the "Human Achievements" chapter in which the duration of the event is the only criterion for inclusion, and will not be adding any new marathon records or reintroducing ones which have been in the book in the past but are no longer included. If you are planning an attempt at an endurance marathon you should contact us at a very early stage to check whether that category is likely to be retained in future editions of the book.

Barrel rolling   The record for rolling a full 36-gallon metal beer barrel over a measured mile is 8 min 7.2 sec, by Phillip Randle, Steve Hewitt, John Round, Trevor Bradley, Colin Barnes and Ray Glover of Haunchwood Collieries Institute and Social Club, Nuneaton, Great Britain on 15 Aug 1982.

A team of 10 rolled a 140-lb barrel 150 miles in 30 hr 31 min in Chlumčany, Czech Republic, on 27–28 Oct 1982.

Barrow pushing   The heaviest loaded one-wheeled barrow pushed for a minimum 200 level feet was one loaded with bricks weighing a gross 8,275 lb. It was pushed a distance of 243 ft by John Sarich at London, Ontario, Canada on 19 Feb 1987.

Barrow racing   The fastest time attained in a 1-mile wheelbarrow race is 4 min 48.51 sec, by Piet Pitzer and Jaco Erasmus at the Transvalia High School, Vanderbijlpark, South Africa on 3 Oct 1987.

Bathtub racing   The record for a 36-mile bathtub race is 1 hr 22 min 27 sec, by Greg Mutton at the Grafton Jacaranda Festival, New South Wales, Australia on 8 Nov 1987. Tubs are limited to 75 in and 6 hp motors. The greatest distance for paddling a hand-propelled bathtub in still water in 24 hr is $90^{1}/_{2}$ miles, by 13 members of Aldington Prison Officers Social Club, near Ashford, Great Britain on 28–29 May 1983.

Bed making   The pair record for making a bed with one blanket, two sheets, an undersheet, an uncased pillow, one bedspread and "hospital" corners is 17.3 sec, by Sister Sharon Stringer and Nurse Michelle Benkel of the Royal Masonic Hospital, London, Great Britain on 19 Sep 1990, shown on the British Broadcasting Corporation's *Record Breakers* TV program.

The record time for one person to make a bed is 28.2 sec, by Wendy Wall, 34, of Hebersham, Sydney, Australia on 30 Nov 1978.

Bed pushing   The longest recorded push of a normally stationary object is of 3,233 miles, in the case of a wheeled hospital bed by a team of nine employees of Bruntsfield Bedding Center, Edinburgh, Scotland from 21 Jun–26 Jul 1979.

Bed race   The course record for a 10-mile bed race is 50 min, as established by the Westbury Harriers' three-man bed team at Chew Valley, Avon, Great Britain.

Beer coaster flipping   Dean Gould of Felixstowe, Great Britain flipped and caught a pile of 111 coasters (0.047 in wood pulp board) through 180 degrees and caught them all on 13 Jan 1993.

Beer keg lifting   George Olesen raised a keg of beer weighing 137 lb 13 oz above his head 670 times in the space of six hours at Horsens, Denmark on 25 Jun 1992.

Beer stein carrying   Barmaid Rosie Schedelbauer covered a distance of 49 ft $2^{1}/_{2}$ in in 4 sec with five full steins in each hand in a televised contest at Königssee, Germany on 29 Jun 1981.

Brick lifting   Russell Bradley of Worcester, Great Britain lifted 31 bricks laid side by side off a table, raising them to chest height and holding them there for two seconds on 14 Jun 1992. The greatest weight of bricks lifted was also by Russell Bradley, on 17 Nov 1990, when he succeeded in lifting 26 far-heavier bricks weighing a total of 189 lb 9 oz, again holding them for two seconds.

Catapulting   The greatest recorded distance for a catapult shot is 1,362 ft, by James M. Pfotenhauer, using a patented 17 ft 1½ in Monarch IV Supershot and a 53-caliber lead musket ball on Ski Hill Road, Escanaba, MI on 10 Sep 1977.

Cigar box balancing   Terry Cole of London, Great Britain balanced 220 unmodified cigar boxes on his chin for 9 sec on 24 Apr 1992.

Crocheting   Barbara Jean Sonntag (b. 1938) of Craig, CO crocheted 330 shells plus five stitches (equivalent to 4,412 stitches) in 30 min at a rate of 147 stitches per min on 13 Jan 1981.

Ria van der Honing of Wormerveer, Netherlands completed a crochet chain 38.83 miles long on 14 Jul 1986.

Crawling   The longest continuous voluntary crawl (progression with one or the other knee in unbroken contact with the ground) on record is 31½ miles, by Peter McKinlay and John Murrie, who covered 115 laps of an athletic track at Falkirk, Great Britain on 28–29 Mar 1992. Over a space of 15 months ending on 9 Mar 1985, Jagdish Chander, 32, crawled 870 miles from Aligarh to Jamma, India to propitiate his revered Hindu goddess, Mata.

Egg and spoon racing   Dale Lyons of Meriden, Great Britain ran 26 miles

---

Bubble   David Stein of New York City created a 50-ft-long bubble on 6 Jun 1988. He made the bubble using a bubble wand, dishwashing liquid and water.

Bubble-gum blowing   The greatest reported diameter for a bubble-gum bubble under the strict rules of this highly competitive activity is 22 in, by Susan Montgomery Williams of Fresno, CA in June 1985.

Fire bucket brigade   The longest fire company bucket brigade stretched over 11,471 ft, with 2,271 people passing 50 buckets along the complete course at the Centennial Parade and Muster held at Hudson, NY on 11 Jul 1992.

Largest garbage can   The world's largest garbage can was made by Natsales of Durban, South Africa for "Keep Durban Beautiful Association Week" from 16–22 Sep 1991. The 19-ft-9-in-tall fiberglass can is a replica of Natsales' standard model and has a capacity of 11,493 gal.

Grape catching   The greatest distance at which a grape thrown from level ground has been caught in the mouth is 327 ft 6 in, by Paul J. Tavilla at East Boston, MA on 27 May 1991. The grape was thrown by James Deady.

385 yd (the classic marathon distance) while carrying a dessert spoon with a fresh egg on it in 3 hr 47 min on 23 Apr 1990.

United States   Chris Riggio of San Francisco, CA took 4 hr 9 min 45 sec to run 26 miles 385 yd in a fresh-egg-and-dessert-spoon marathon on 7 Oct 1979.

Egg hunt   The greatest egg hunt on record in the United States involved 120,000 plastic and candy eggs at a community Easter egg hunt at Coquina Beach in Manatee, FL on 23 Mar 1991. The event, hosted by Meals on Wheels PLUS of Manatee, Inc., involved more than 40,000 children.

French knitting   Ted Hannaford of Sittingbourne, Great Britain has produced a piece of French knitting 4 miles 890 yds long since he started work in April 1989.

Garbage collection   The greatest number of volunteers involved in collecting garbage in one location in one day is 19,924, who cleaned up the city of Wellington, New Zealand in the "Keep Wellington Beautiful" campaign on 6 Oct 1991.

United States   The greatest number of volunteers involved in collecting garbage in one location in the United States in one day is 18,143, along the coastline of Florida on 22 Sep 1990 as part of the Center for Marine Conservation's National Beach Cleanup program.

Gold panning   The fastest time for "panning" eight planted gold nuggets in a 10-in diameter pan is 7.55 sec, by Don Roberts of Diamond Bar, CA in the 27th World Gold Panning Championship on 16 Apr 1989 at Dahlonega, GA.
   The women's record is 10.03 sec, by Susan Bryeans of Fullerton, CA at the 23rd World Gold Panning Championship on 6 Mar 1983 at Knott's Berry Farm, Buena Park, CA.

Gum wrapper chain   The longest gum wrapper chain on record was 7,400 ft in length, and was made by Cathy Ushler of Redmond, WA between 1969 and 1992.

Hopscotch   The greatest number of games of hopscotch successfully completed in 24 hr is 307, by Ashrita Furman of Jamaica, NY in Zürich, Switzerland on 5–6 Apr 1991.

Hula-hooping, simultaneous   The record for simultaneous hula-hooping is 2,010 participants, at the St John Labatt's Lite 24-Hour Relay in St John, New Brunswick, Canada on 21 Sep 1990.

Human centipede   The largest "human centipede" to move 98 ft 5 in (with ankles firmly tied together) consisted of 1,189 people at York, Great Britain on 16 Oct 1991. Nobody fell over in the course of the walk.

Kissing   Alfred A.E. Wolfram of New Brighton, MN kissed 8,001 people in 8 hr at the Minnesota Renaissance Festival on 15 Sep 1990—one every 3.6 seconds.

Kite flying   The following records are all recognized by *Kite Lines* Magazine.

Longest   The longest kite flown was 3,394 ft in length. It was made and flown by Michel Trouillet and a team of helpers at Nîmes, France on 18 Nov 1990.

Largest   The largest kite flown was 5,952 ft^2. It was first flown by a Dutch team on the beach at Scheveningen, Netherlands on 8 Aug 1991.

Highest   A record height of 31,955 ft was reached by a train of eight kites over Lindenberg, Germany on 1 Aug 1919.
   The altitude record for a single kite is 12,471 ft, in the case of a kite flown by Henry Helm Clayton and A.E. Sweetland at the Blue Hill Weather Station, Milton, MA on 28 Feb 1898.

Fastest   The fastest speed attained by a kite was 120 mph for a kite flown by Pete DiGiacomo at Ocean City, MD on 22 Sep 1989.

Greatest number of figure-eights   The greatest number of figure-eights achieved with a kite in an hour is 2,911, by Stu Cohen at Ocean City, MD on 25 Sep 1988.

Most on a single line   The greatest number of kites flown on a single line is 11,284, by Sadao Harada and a team of helpers at Sakurajima, Kagoshima, Japan on 18 Oct 1990.

Longest duration   The longest recorded flight is one of 180 hr 17 min by the Edmonds Community College team at Long Beach, WA from 21–29 Aug 1982. Managing the flight of this J-25 parafoil was Harry N. Osborne.

Knitting   The world's most prolific hand-knitter has been Mrs Gwen Matthewman of Featherstone, Great Britain. She attained a speed of 111 stitches per min in a test at Phildar's Wool Shop, Leeds, Great Britain on 29 Sep 1980.
   The Exeter Spinners—Audrey Felton, Christine Heap, Eileen Lancaster, Marjorie Mellis, Ann Sandercock and Maria Scott—produced a sweater by hand from raw fleece in 1 hr 55 min 50.2 sec on 25 Sep 1983 at British Broadcasting Corporation Television Centre, London, Great Britain.

Knot-tying   The fastest recorded time for tying the six Boy Scout Handbook knots (square knot, sheet bend, sheepshank, clove hitch, round turn and two half hitches, and bowline) on individual ropes is 8.1 sec, by Clinton R. Bailey, Sr., 52, of Pacific City, OR on 13 Apr 1977.

Land rowing   The greatest distance covered by someone on a land rowing machine is 3,280 miles, by Rob Bryant of Fort Worth, TX, who "rowed" across the United States. He left Los Angeles, CA on 2 Apr 1990, reaching Washington, D.C. on 30 July.

Log rolling   The record number of International Championships won is 10, by Jubiel Wickheim of Shawnigan Lake, British Columbia, Canada, between 1956 and 1969. At Albany, OR on 4 Jul 1956 Wickheim rolled on a 14-in log against Chuck Harris of Kelso, WA for 2 hr 40 min before losing.

Milk bottle balancing   The greatest distance walked by a person continuously balancing a milk bottle on the head is 64^3/$_4$ miles by Milind Deshmukh at

Pune, India on 14–15 May 1993. It took him 20 hr 43 min to complete the walk.

United States Ashrita Furman walked and jogged for 61 miles balancing a milk bottle on his head on 23 May 1992, at Jamaica High School Track in Jamaica, NY. It took him 15 hr 1 min 55 sec.

Milk crate balancing Terry Cole managed to balance 25 crates on his chin for 10.3 sec on the Isle of Dogs, London, Great Britain on 28 Jul 1991. John Evans of Marlpool, Great Britain balanced 84 crates (weighing a total of 275 lb) on his head for 10 seconds on 8 Dec 1992.

Needle threading The record number of times that a strand of cotton has been threaded through a number 13 needle (eye $1/2$ x $1/16$ in) in 2 hr is 11,796, set by Sujay Kumar Mallick of Bhopal, India on 5 Apr 1992.

United States The record number of times that a strand of cotton has been threaded through a number 13 needle in 2 hr is 5,370, set by Diane Sharp on 1 Aug 1987 at the Charitable Union's centennial event, Battle Creek, MI.

Oyster opening The record for opening oysters is 100 in 2 min 20.07 sec, by Mike Racz in Invercargill, New Zealand on 16 Jul 1990.

Paper chain A paper chain 36.69 miles long was made by 60 students from University College Dublin, Republic of Ireland, as part of UCD Science Day in Dublin on 11–12 Feb 1993. The chain consisted of nearly 400,000 links and was made over a period of 24 hours.

Pass the parcel The largest game of pass the parcel involved 3,464 people who removed 2,000 wrappers in two hours from a parcel measuring 5 x 3 x 3 ft at Alton Towers, Great Britain on 8 Nov 1992. The event was organized by Parcelforce International, and the final prize was an electronic keyboard, won by Sylvia Wilshaw.

Pogo stick jumping The greatest number of jumps achieved is 177,737, by Gary Stewart at Huntington Beach, Los Angeles, CA on 25–26 May 1992. Ashrita Furman of Jamaica, NY set a distance record of 14.99 miles in 5 hr 33 min on 25 May 1991 in Seoul, South Korea.

Rope slide The greatest distance recorded in a rope slide is from near the top of Blackpool Tower, Lancashire, Great Britain—at a height of 416 ft—to a fixed point 1,128 ft from the base of the tower. Set up by the Royal Marines, the rope was descended on 8 Sep 1989 by Sgt. Alan Heward and Cpl. Mick Heap of the Royal Marines, John Herbert of Blackpool Tower, and Cheryl Baker and Roy Castle of the British Broadcasting Corporation's *Record Breakers* TV program. The total length descended was 1,202 ft.

Scarf The longest scarf ever knitted measured an amazing 20 miles 13 ft long. It was knitted by residents of Abbeyfield Houses for the Abbeyfield Society in Potters Bar, Great Britain and was completed on 29 May 1988.

Shorthand The highest recorded speeds ever attained under championship conditions are 300 words per min (99.64 percent accuracy) for five minutes and 350 wpm (99.72 percent accuracy—that is, two insignificant errors) for two minutes, by Nathan Behrin (USA) in tests in New York in December 1922. Behrin (b. 1887) used the Pitman system, invented in 1837.

Morris I. Kligman, official court reporter of the US Court House, New York City, has taken 50,000 words in 5 hr (a sustained rate of 166.6 wpm). Rates are much dependent upon the nature, complexity and syllabic density of the material. Mr G.W. Bunbury of Dublin, Ireland held the unique distinction of writing at 250 wpm for 10 minutes on 23 Jan 1894. Mr Arnold Bradley achieved a speed of 309 wpm without error using the Sloan-Duployan system, with 1,545 words in 5 minutes, in a test in Walsall, Great Britain on 9 Nov 1920.

Spitting The greatest recorded distance for a cherry stone is 88 ft 5¹/₂ in, by Horst Ortmann at Langenthal, Germany on 29 Aug 1992. The record for projecting a watermelon seed is 68 ft 9¹/₈ in by Lee Wheelis at Luling, TX on 24 Jun 1989. Randy Ober of Bentonville, AR spat a tobacco wad 47 ft 7 in at the Calico 5th Annual Tobacco Chewing and Spitting Championships, held north of Barstow, CA on 4 Apr 1982.

United States Rick Krause of Flint, MI spat a cherry stone 72 ft 7¹/₂ in on 2 Jul 1988, at the International Cherry Pit Spitting Championship in Eau Claire, MI.

Stone skipping   The video-verified stone skipping record is 38 skips, achieved by Jerdone at Wimberley, TX on 20 Oct 1992.

Stroller pushing   The greatest distance covered in pushing a stroller in 24 hr is 350.23 miles, by 60 members of the Oost-Vlanderen branch of Amnesty International at Lede, Belgium on 15 Oct 1988. A 10-man team from the Royal Marines School of Music, Deal, Great Britain, with an adult "baby," covered a distance of 271.7 miles in 24 hr from 22–23 Nov 1990.

Tailoring   The fastest speed in which the manufacture of a three-piece suit has been executed from sheep to finished article is 1 hr 34 min 33.42 sec, by 65 members of the Melbourne College of Textiles, Pascoe Vale, Victoria, Australia on 24 Jun 1982. Catching and fleecing took 2 min 21 sec, and carding, spinning, weaving and tailoring occupied the remaining time.

Tightrope walking   The oldest tightrope walker was "Professor" William Ivy

Standing   The longest period on record that anyone has continuously stood is more than 17 years in the case of Swami Maujgiri Maharaj when performing the *Tapasya* or penance from 1955 to November 1973 in Shahjahanpur, Uttar Pradesh, India. When sleeping he would lean against a plank. He died at the age of 85 in September 1980.

Unsupported circle   The highest recorded number of people who have demonstrated the physical paradox of all being seated without a chair is an unsupported circle of 10,323 employees of the Nissan Motor Co. at Komazawa Stadium, Tokyo, Japan on 23 Oct 1982.

Quizzes   The greatest number of participants was 80,799 in the All-Japan High School Quiz Championship, televised by NTV on 31 Dec 1983.

Whip cracking   The longest whip ever "cracked" is one of 184 ft 6 in (excluding the handle), wielded by Krist King of Pettisville, OH on 17 Sep 1991.

Yo-yo   Yo-yos are said to have originated in the Philippines, and the word means "come-come." Donald F. Duncan of Chicago, IL initiated the craze in 1926. "Fast" Eddy McDonald of Toronto, Canada completed 21,663 loops in 3 hr on 14 Oct 1990 in Boston, MA, having previously set a 1-hr speed record of 8,437 loops in Cavendish, Prince Edward Island, Canada on 14 Jul 1990. Dr Allen Bussey in Waco, TX on 23 Apr 1977 completed 20,302 loops in 3 hr.

The largest yo-yo ever constructed was one measuring 6 ft in diameter made by the woodworking class of Shakamak High School in Jasonville, IN. It weighed 820 lb and was launched from a 160-ft crane on 29 Mar 1990, when it "yo-yoed" 12 times.

Baldwin (1866–1953), who crossed the South Boulder Canyon, CO on a 320-ft wire with a 125-ft drop on his 82nd birthday on 31 Jul 1948.

The world tightrope endurance record is 185 days, by Henri Rochatain (b. 1926) of France, on a wire 394 ft long, 82 ft above a supermarket in Saint Etienne, France from 28 Mar–29 Sep 1973. Doctors were puzzled by his ability to sleep on a wire.

Ashley Brophy of Neilborough, Victoria, Australia walked 7.18 miles on a wire 147.64 ft long and 32.81 ft above the ground at the Adelaide Grand Prix, Australia on 1 Nov 1985 in 3½ hr.

The greatest drop over which anyone has walked on a tightrope is 10,335 ft, above the French countryside, by Michel Menin of Lons-le-Saunier, France, on 4 Aug 1989.

Typewriting   The highest recorded speeds attained with a 10-word penalty per error on a manual machine are—five minutes: 176 wpm by Mrs Carole Forristall Waldschlager Bechen at Dixon, IL on 2 Apr 1959; one hour: 147 wpm by Albert Tangora (USA) on an Underwood Standard, 22 Oct 1923.

The official hour record on an electric typewriter is 9,316 words (40 errors) on an IBM machine, giving a net rate of 149 words per min, by Margaret Hamma, now Mrs Dilmore (USA), in Brooklyn, NY on 20 Jun 1941. In an official test in 1946, Stella Pajunas, now Mrs Garnand, attained a rate of 216 words in a minute on an IBM machine.

Gregory Arakelian of Herndon, VA set a speed record of 158 wpm, with two errors, on a personal computer in the Key Tronic World Invitational Type-off, which attracted some 10,000 entrants worldwide. He recorded this speed in the semifinal, in a three-minute test, on 24 Sep 1991.

Mihail Shestov set a numerical record by typing spaced numbers from 1 to 785 in 5 min in Fredriksberg, Denmark on 17 Oct 1991.

Les Stewart of Mudjimba Beach, Queensland, Australia has typed the numbers 1 to 775,000 in *words* on 15,390 quarto sheets as of 20 Mar 1992. His target is to become a "millionaire."

Writing, minuscule   In 1926 an account was published of Alfred McEwen's pantograph record, in which the 56-word version of the Lord's Prayer was written in diamond point on glass in the space of 0.0016 x 0.0008 in.

Surendra Apharya of Jaipur, India wrote 10,056 characters (speeches by Nehru) within the size of a definitive Indian postage stamp, measuring 0.78 x 0.70 in, in December 1990, and also wrote 1,749 characters (names of various countries, towns and regions) on a single grain of rice on 19 May 1991. Chang Shi-Qi of Wuhan, China wrote 308 characters ("God bless you" 28 times) on a human hair 0.8 in long at the Guinness World of Records Exhibition, Singapore on 2 Jun 1992.

JUGGLING

12 rings (flashed)   Albert Lucas (USA), 1985.

11 rings (juggled)   Albert Petrovski (USSR), 1963–66; Eugene Belaur (USSR), 1968; Sergey Ignatov (USSR), 1973.

11 bean bags (flashed)   Bruce Serafian (USA), 1992.

10 balls   Enrico Rastelli (Italy), 1920s; Albert Lucas (USA), 1984.

8 plates   Enrico Rastelli (Italy), 1920s; Albert Lucas (USA), 1984.

8 clubs (flashed)   Anthony Gatto (USA), 1989.

7 clubs (juggled)   Albert Petrovski (USSR), 1963; Sorin Munteanu (Romania), 1975; Jack Bremlov (Czechoslovakia), 1985; Albert Lucas (USA), 1985; Anthony Gatto (USA), 1988.

7 flaming torches   Anthony Gatto (USA), 1989.

7 ping-pong balls with mouth   Tony Ferko (Czechoslovakia), 1987.

5 balls inverted   Bobby May (USA), 1953.

Ball spinning (on one hand)   François Chotard (France), 9 balls, 1990.

Bounce juggling   Tim Nolan (USA), 10 balls, 1988.

Duration: 5 clubs without a drop   45 min 2 sec, Anthony Gatto (USA), 1989.

Duration: 3 objects without a drop   Jas Angelo (Great Britain), 8 hr 57 min 31 sec, 1989.

See also Sports and Games, Joggling.

Most objects aloft   Eight hundred and twenty-one jugglers kept 2,463 objects in the air simultaneously, each person juggling at least three objects, in Seattle, WA in 1990.

Pirouettes with 3 cigar boxes   Kris Kremo (Switzerland) performed a quadruple turn with 3 boxes in mid-air in 1977.

FOOD

Apple pie   The largest apple pie ever baked was made by chef Glynn Christian in a 40 x 23 ft dish at Hewitts Farm, Chelsfield, Great Britain from 25–27 Aug 1982. Over 600 bushels of apples were included in the pie, which weighed 30,115 lb. It was cut by Rear-Admiral Sir John Woodward.

Banana split   The longest banana split ever created measured 4.55 miles in length, and was made by residents of Selinsgrove, PA on 30 Apr 1988.

Barbecue The record attendance at a one-day barbecue was 35,072, at the Iowa State Fairgrounds, Des Moines, IA on 21 Jun 1988. The greatest meat consumption ever recorded at a one-day barbecue was at the same event— 20,130 lb of pork consumed in 5 hr. The greatest quantity of meat consumed at any barbecue was 21,112 lb of beef at the Sertoma Club Barbecue, New Port Richey, FL, from 7–9 Mar 1986.

Cakes Largest The largest cake ever created weighed 128,238 lb 8 oz, including 16,209 lb of icing. It was made to celebrate the 100th birthday of Fort Payne, AL, and was in the shape of Alabama. The cake was prepared by a local bakery, EarthGrains, and the first cut was made by 100-year-old resident Ed Henderson on 18 Oct 1989.

Tallest The tallest cake was 101 ft 2½ in high, created by Beth Cornell Trevorrow and her team of helpers at the Shiawassee County Fairgrounds, MI. It consisted of 100 tiers, and work was completed on 5 Aug 1990.

Oldest The Alimentarium, a museum of food in Vevey, Switzerland, has on display the world's oldest cake, which was sealed and "vacuum-packed" in the grave of Pepionkh, who lived in ancient Egypt around 2200 B.C. The 4.3-in-wide cake has sesame on it and honey inside, and was possibly made with milk.

Candy The largest candy was a marzipan chocolate weighing 4,078 lb 8 oz, made at the Ven International Fresh Market, Diemen, Netherlands on 11–13 May 1990.

Cheese The largest cheese ever created was a cheddar weighing 40,060 lb, made on 13–14 Mar 1988 at Simon's Specialty Cheese, Little Chute, WI. It was subsequently taken on tour in a specially designed, refrigerated "Cheese-mobile."

Cherry pie The largest cherry pie on record weighed 37,740 lb 10 oz and contained 36,800 lb of cherry filling. It measured 20 ft in diameter, and was baked by members of the Oliver Rotary Club in Oliver, British Columbia, Canada on 14 Jul 1990.

Chocolate model The largest chocolate model was one weighing 8,818 lb 6 oz in the shape of a traditional Spanish sailing ship. It was made by Gremi Provincial de Pastissería, Confitería i Bollería school, Barcelona in February 1991 and measured 42 ft 8 in x 27 ft 10½ in x 8 ft 2½ in.

Cocktail The largest cocktail on record was a "Hurricane" of 1,650 gal made at the annual Bartenders' Ball held on Long Island, New York, on 15 Mar 1993. It was named after Hurricane Gloria, which had battered the island in 1985, and consisted of rum, triple sec, sour mix, orange juice and grenadine.

Crepe The largest crepe was 41 ft 2 in in diameter and 1¼ in deep, and weighed 5,908 lb. It was baked by Jos van Achter and flipped at Bloemfontein, South Africa on 7 Mar 1992.

Doughnut The largest ever made was a jelly doughnut weighing 3,739 lb. It was 16 ft in diameter and 16 in high in the center. It was made by representatives from Hemstrought's Bakeries, Donato's Bakery and the radio station WKLL-FM at Utica, NY on 21 Jan 1993.

Cookie Caper

The largest cookie ever made was a chocolate chip cookie with an area of 907.9 ft², made at the annual Riponfest in Ripon, WI, on 11 Jul 1992. It was 34 ft in diameter and contained nearly 4 million chocolate chips.

Baking the biscuit

Serves 8,163

1,270 lb flour

600 lb granulated sugar

760 lb margarine

25½ lb table salt

12¾ lb vanilla extract

20½ lb powdered eggs

9 lb baking powder

27 gallons water

663 lb chocolate chips (3,839,207 chocolate chips)

Preheat oven to 220°F

Mix all ingredients in a large bowl

Add the chocolate chips and beat thoroughly.

Transfer dough mixture to cookie tray via semitrailer truck carrying 70 containers, each filled with 50 lbs of the dough mixture.

Bake on a rotating tray for approx 2½ hours.

Remove oven top and allow to cool. Slice using 10 pizza cutters soldered together at 4-inch intervals

Cutting the pieces

I TRIED TO EAT THE WORLD'S LARGEST COOKIE
WISCONSIN
RIPON

The idea was first discussed by the organizing committee eight months before the festival. Samples of different types of chocolate chip cookie were tasted and a recipe selected for the attempt.

At the next meeting the team discussed how the dough would be prepared and transported and the cookie safely baked and distributed.

A test run with a small oven and a comparatively small cookie revealed some problems, notably that the cookie was not evenly baked as the heat source was stationary. This was resolved by rotating the tray over the heat source.

Measuring the depth

Next a direct-fired burner was constructed, and a gas line was run to the location of the attempt. Before the big day a full trial run was attempted but not successfully concluded, as it was a cool, windy day and it was not possible to generate any heat buildup in the oven.

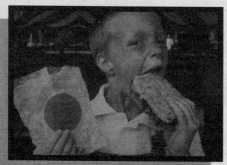

Even on baking day there were difficulties—the cookie tray became very hard to turn and one section of the outside frame gave way. The organizers were almost ready to announce to the crowd that the event could not continue, but just in time the cause of the prolem was solved, and the event could be resumed.

The best bit !!!

The biscuit actually took 2½ hours to bake, but the end result was a success and then it was just a case of distributing, eating and enjoying. The day can best be summed up by the organizers. "The project was a lot of fun, but I don't think that we will bake a bigger one next year."

Burrito   The Wilmington Chamber of Commerce and the Wilmington Coordinating Council constructed the world's longest burrito, 2,012.9 ft long, on 11 Apr 1992 in Wilmington, CA. The burrito was constructed with 738.5 lb of tortillas, 761.3 lb of refried beans and 156.4 lb of cheese. La Caseta Restaurant of Fallbrook, CA constructed the world's largest burrito, weighing 2,237 lb.

Dish   The largest item on any menu in the world is roasted camel, prepared occasionally for Bedouin wedding feasts. Cooked eggs are stuffed into fish, the fish stuffed into cooked chickens, the chickens stuffed into a roasted sheep's carcass and the sheep stuffed into a whole camel.

Most expensive food   The most expensive food is saffron from Spain, which comes from the stamen or stigma of a crocus. It is sold at Harrods, London, Great Britain, for £305 ($473) per 3.5 oz.

Rarest condiment   The world's most prized condiment is Cà Cuong, a secretion recovered in minute amounts from beetles in North Vietnam. Because of war conditions, the price had risen to $100 per oz before supplies virtually dried up in 1975.

Crepe tossing   The greatest number of times a crepe has been tossed in 2 min is 307, by Philip Artingstall in Durban, South Africa on 23 Feb 1993.

Noodle making   Happy Kuk made 4,096 noodle strings from a single piece of noodle dough in 45.14 sec at the launch of the Chinatown and Asian Food Festival in Melbourne, Australia on 19 Jan 1993. This is more than 90 noodles per second.

United States   Mark Pi made 4,096 noodle strings from a single piece of noodle dough in 54.8 sec at the Thomas/SYSCO Food Show held at Columbus, OH on 25 Mar 1992. This represented a speed of more than 74 noodles per second.

Omelet making   The greatest number of two-egg omelets made in 30 min is 427, by Howard Helmer at the International Poultry Trade Show held at Atlanta, GA on 2 Feb 1990.

Easter eggs   The heaviest Easter egg on record, and also the tallest, was one weighing 10,482 lb 14 oz, 23 ft 3 in high, made by the staff of Cadbury Red Tulip at their factory at Ringwood, Victoria, Australia, and completed on 9 Apr 1992.

Hamburger   The largest hamburger on record was one of 5,520 lb, made at the Outgamie County Fairgrounds, Seymour, WI on 5 Aug 1989. It was 21 ft in diameter.

Ice-cream sundae   The largest ice-cream sundae was one weighing 54,914 lb

13 oz, made by Palm Dairies Ltd under the supervision of Mike Rogiani in Edmonton, Alberta, Canada on 24 Jul 1988. It consisted of 44,689 lb 8 oz of ice cream, 9,688 lb 2 oz of syrup and 537 lb 3 oz of topping.

Ice pop The world's largest ice pop was one of 12,346 lb, made by Eric Rotte, owner of a local cafe and bar, together with a team of helpers at Oostkapelle, Netherlands on 1 Aug 1992.

United States The largest ice pop in the United States was 7,080 lb, constructed by students and staff at Lawrence University, Appleton, WI on 17 Feb 1990.

Jell-O The world's largest Jell-O, a 9,246 gal watermelon-flavored pink Jell-O made by Paul Squires and Geoff Ross, worth $14,000, was set at Roma Street Forum, Brisbane, Queensland, Australia on 5 Feb 1981 in a tank supplied by Pool Fab.

Kebab The longest kebab ever was one 2,066 ft 11 in long, made by the Namibian Children's Home at Windhoek, Namibia on 21 Sep 1991.

Lasagne The largest lasagne was one weighing 3,609 lb 10 oz and measuring 50 x 5 ft. It was made by Andreano Rossi and Ciro Geroso, along with a team of helpers, at the Royal Dublin Society Spring Show in Dublin, Republic of Ireland on 11 May 1990.

United States The largest lasagne in the United States weighed 3,477 lb and measured 63 ft x 7 ft. It was made by Shade Pasta Inc. and Cornell University's Panhellenic and Interfraternity Councils in Ithaca, NY on 26 Oct 1991.

Loaf The longest loaf on record was a Rosca de Reyes 3,491 ft 9 in long, baked at the Hyatt Regency Hotel in Guadalajara, Mexico on 6 Jan 1991. If a consumer of the "Rosca," or twisted loaf, finds the embedded doll, that person has to host the Rosca party (held annually at Epiphany) the following year.

The largest pan loaf ever baked weighed 3,163 lb 10 oz and measured 9 ft 10 in x 4 ft 1 in x 3 ft 7 in, by the staff of Sasko in Johannesburg, South Africa on 18 Mar 1988.

United States The longest loaf on record in the United States was one 2,357 ft 10 in long, baked by the Northlands Job Corps, Vergennes, VT on 3 Nov 1987. Some 35,840 lb of dough were required in the preparation of the loaf, and over 4,480 lb of charcoal and 4,700 ft of aluminum foil were used to bake it.

Lollipop The largest lollipop weighed 2,220.5 lb and was made by Lolly Pops/Johnson's Confectionary in Sydney, Australia on 18–19 Aug 1990.

Meat pie The largest meat pie on record weighed 19,908 lb and was the ninth in the series of pies baked in Denby Dale, Great Britain. It was baked on 3 Sep 1988 to mark the bicentennial of Denby Dale pie-making, the first one having been made in 1788 to celebrate King George III's return to sanity. The fourth pie (baked for Queen Victoria's Jubilee, 1887) went a bit "off" and had to be buried in quicklime.

LARGEST ICE POP The huge raspberry-flavored ice pop made at Oostkapelle, Netherlands in August 1992. (Photo: Ronald Vonk)

Milk shake The largest milk shake was a chocolate one of 1,891.69 gal, made by the Smith Dairy Products Co. at Orrville, OH on 20 Oct 1989.

Omelet The largest omelet in the world had an area of 1,324 ft² and was made in a skillet 41 ft 1 in in diameter. It was cooked by staff and pupils of the Municipal School for Special Education at Opwijk, Belgium on 10 Jun 1990.

United States The largest omelet in the United States was one with an area of 706 ft 8 in², made with 54,763 eggs and 531 lb cheese in a skillet 30 ft in diameter. It was cooked by Michael McGowan, assisted by his staff and the Sunrise Jaycees of Las Vegas, NV on 25 Oct 1986.

Paella The largest paella measured 65 ft 7 in in diameter and was made by Juan Carlos Galbis and a team of helpers in Valencia, Spain on 8 Mar 1992. It was eaten by 100,000 people.

Pastry The longest pastry in the world was a millefeuille (cream puff pastry) 3,403 ft in length, made by employees of Pidy, a company based in Ypres, Belgium, on 4–5 Sep 1992.

United States The longest pastry in the United States was a blueberry strudel of 2,040 ft, made by employees of the Hotel Fredonia and friends of the city of Nacogdoches, TX, on 5 Jun 1992.

Pizza The largest pizza ever baked was one measuring 122 ft 8 in in diameter with an area of 11,816 ft², made at Norwood Hypermarket, Norwood, South Africa on 8 Dec 1990.

United States   The largest pizza in the United States was one with an area of 10,057 ft², organized by L. Amato and L. Piancone and completed at Highway 27, Havana, FL on 13 Oct 1991.

Popcorn   The largest container full of popcorn was one with 5,979.33 ft³ of popped corn. It was just over 19 ft 6 in in diameter and 19 ft 1 in in height. It took the staff of United Cinemas International in Derby, Great Britain three days to achieve the record, beginning their attempt on 23 Aug 1991 and completing it on 26 August.

THE GUINNESS DAILY RECORD   30 June, 1990

Strawberries Galore !!!

If you like strawberries, then the Downtown Block Party in Alpena, MI was the place to be today—the world's largest strawberry shortcake was on display here.

The enormous shortcake, measuring 45 feet by 8 feet, was spread over a dozen conference tables and protected from the elements by two tents. After the cake was baked, the shortcake took 1½ hours to assemble, requiring 1,104 quarts of strawberries and 440 pounds of strawberry glaze. Whipped topping was available as an optional extra.

The berries were delivered three days before the event and moved by vanload to the First Congregational Church kitchen to be cleaned and mixed with the strawberry glaze. This mixture was then stored in commercial refrigerators until the day of the event. This morning, the tents and tables were raised and sections of styrofoam were affixed to the top of the tables. This styrofoam "pan" was covered with aluminum foil and topped with industrial plastic to form a safe eating environment. The tent poles were also covered with plastic so as not to touch the completed shortcake.

The shortcake was laid on the prepared tables and then covered with the berries-and-glaze mixture. The final task was to cut and enjoy the finished product.

United States The largest box of popcorn in the United States contained 5,438.16 ft³ of popped corn. It measured 52 ft 7¼ in x 10 ft 1½ in and was filled by Stanly Community College, Albermarle, NC from 6–8 Aug 1991. The average depth was 10 ft 2½ in.

Potato chips The Pringles plant in Jackson, TN produced a Pringle potato chip 23 in x 14½ in on 19 Apr 1990. Pringles potato chips are made from potato flour.

Salami The longest salami on record was one 68 ft 9 in long with a circumference of 25 in, weighing 1,492 lb 5 oz, made by employees of A/S Svindlands Pølsefabrikk at Flekkefjord, Norway from 6–16 Jul 1992.

United States The longest salami on record was one 61 ft 3½ in long with a circumference of 24 in, weighing 1,202 lb 8 oz, made by the Kutztown Bologna Co., PA and displayed at the Lebanon Bologna Fest in Kutztown on 11–13 Aug 1989.

Sausage The longest continuous sausage on record was one of 13⅛ miles, made at the premises of Keith Boxley at Wombourne, Great Britain in 15 hr 33 min on 18–19 Jun 1988.

Soda float The largest soda float ever made was one produced in a 2,000-gallon container, and consisted of 1,200 lbs skim milk and 936 gallons Coca-Cola. It was made by Coleman Quality Chekd Dairy, Inc., Cool 95 FM, and Coca-Cola of Arkansas at the Arkansas State Fairgrounds, Little Rock, AR on 14 Oct 1990.

Spice, "hottest" The hottest of all spices is believed to be habanero, belonging to the genus *capsicum*, found mainly in the Caribbean and the Yucatán area of Mexico. A single dried gram will produce detectable "heat" in 440 lb of bland sauce.

Spice, most expensive Prices for wild ginseng (root of *Panax quinquefolium*) from the Chan Pak Mountain area of China, thought to have aphrodisiac qualities, were reported in November 1979 to be as high as $23,000 per ounce in Hong Kong. Total annual shipments from Jilin Province do not exceed 140 oz a year. A leading medical journal in the United States has likened its effects to "corticosteroid poisoning."

Strawberry bowl The largest bowl of strawberries ever picked had a net weight of 4,832 lb. The strawberries were picked at Walt Furlong's farm at New Ross, Republic of Ireland during the Enniscorthy Strawberry Fair on 9 Jul 1989.

DRINK

Alcohol consumption   France has the greatest consumption of alcohol per person, with the equivalent of 22.3 pints of pure alcohol per annum.

Beer Oldest   Written references to beer have been found dating from as far back as *c.* 5000 B.C., as part of the daily wages of workers at the Temple of Erech in Mesopotamia. Physical evidence of beer dating from as far back as *c.* 3500 B.C. has been detected in remains of a jug found at Godin Tepe, Iran in 1973 during an expedition by the Royal Ontario Museum, Canada. It was only in 1991 that the remains were analyzed, which established that residues in deep grooves in the jug were calcium oxalate, also known as beerstone and still created in barley-based beers.

Strongest   Roger & Out, brewed at the Frog & Parrot in Sheffield, Great Britain, from a recipe devised by W.R. Nowill and G.B. Spencer, has an alcohol volume of 16.9 percent. It was first brewed in July 1985 and has been selling ever since. The strongest lager is Samichlaus Dark 1987, brewed by Brauerei Hürlimann of Zürich, Switzerland. It is 14.93 percent alcohol by volume at 68° F.

Brewers   The oldest brewery in the world is the Weihenstephan Brewery, Freising, near Munich, Germany, founded in A.D. 1040.

The largest single brewing organization in the world is Anheuser-Busch Inc. of St Louis, MO, with 12 breweries in the United States. In 1992 the company sold 2.7 billion gallons, the greatest annual volume ever produced by a brewing company in a year. One of its brands, Budweiser, is the top-selling beer in the world, with 1,488 million gal sold in 1991. The company's St Louis plant covers 100 acres, and has an annual capacity of 403 million gallons. The completion of current modernization projects in 1993 gave the plant an annual capacity of 416.6 million gallons.

The largest brewery on a single site is Coors Brewing Co. of Golden, CO, where 598 million gallons were produced in 1992. At the same location is the world's largest aluminum can manufacturing plant, with a capacity of more than 5 billion cans annually.

Bottles Largest   A bottle 8 ft 4 in tall and 7 ft 1½ in in circumference was unveiled at the Shepherd Neame Brewery at Faversham, Great Britain on 27 Jan 1993. It took 13 minutes to fill the bottle, with 165⅕ gal of Kingfisher beer, the leading Indian lager.

The largest bottles normally used in the wine and spirit trade are the Jeroboam (equal to 4 bottles of champagne or, rarely, of brandy, and from 5–6½ bottles of claret according to whether blown or molded) and the double magnum (equal, since *c.* 1934, to 4 bottles of claret or, more rarely, red Burgundy). A complete set of champagne bottles would consist of a quarter bottle, through a half bottle, bottle, magnum, Jeroboam, Rehoboam, Methuselah, Salmanazar and Balthazar, to the Nebuchadnezzar, which has a capacity of 28.14 pt, and is equivalent to 20 bottles.

A bottle containing 33.7 liters of Château Lalande Sourbet 1985, equal in volume to almost 45 standard wine bottles, was auctioned on 10 Oct 1989 in Copenhagen, Denmark.

Smallest The smallest bottles of liquor now sold are of White Horse Scotch Whiskey; they stand just over 2 in high and contain 22 minims. A mini case of 12 bottles costs about £8 ($14), and measures $2^1/_{16}$ x $1^7/_8$ x $1^5/_{16}$ in. The distributor is Cumbrae Supply Co., Linwood, Scotland.

Beer tankard The largest tankard was made by the Selangor Pewter Co. (now known as Royal Selangor International Sdn. BHD) of Kuala Lumpur, Malaysia and unveiled on 30 Nov 1985. It measures $6^1/_2$ ft in height and has a capacity of 615 gal.

THE GUINNESS DAILY RECORD   9 July, 1989

Oldest evidence of wine reported

New research reveals 5,500-year-old vintage

The earliest physical evidence of wine is now known to date from as far back as 3500 B.C., much earlier than was previously thought. The evidence has been detected in the remains of a Sumerian jar found at Godin Tepe, Iran in 1973 during an expedition organized by the Royal Ontario Museum of Toronto, Canada.

For many years the jar was simply stored in the museum, but recently Virginia Badler, a Ph.D. student at the University of Toronto, has been carrying out an analysis of the jar in connection with her thesis. She has now established that a large red stain shows the presence of tartaric acid, a chemical which in nature is found predominately in grapes. The jar also has a hole directly opposite the stain, in keeping with the normal procedure for winemaking in the past, so as to prevent the container from bursting after secondary fermentation.

A number of experts have said that they agree with the results of the analysis.

It is thought that Stone Age people may have been cultivating wine around 8000 B.C., but no firm proof of this has ever been found.

Distillers The world's largest distilling company is United Distillers, the spirits company of Guinness plc, which sells 56 million cases of "owned" distilled spirits brands per year. It is also the most profitable spirits company, having made £769 million ($1.2 billion) in 1992.

The largest blender and bottler of Scotch whiskey is also United Distillers, at their Shieldhall plant in Glasgow, Scotland, which has the capacity to fill an estimated 144 million bottles of Scotch a year. This is equivalent to approximately 28.82 million gal, most of which is exported. The world's best-selling brands of Scotch and gin, Johnnie Walker Red Label and Gordon's, are both products of United Distillers.

Most alcoholic drinks When Estonia was independent, between the two World Wars, the Estonian Liquor Monopoly marketed 98 percent alcohol distilled from potatoes (196 percent proof US). In 31 states, Everclear, 190 percent proof or 95 percent volume alcohol, is marketed by the American Distilling Co. "primarily as a base for home-made cordials."

Spirits Most expensive A bottle of 50-year-old Glenfiddich Scotch was sold for a record price of 99,999,999 lire (approximately $71,200) to an anonymous Italian businessman at a charity auction in Milan, Italy. The postal auction was held over a two-month period from October to December 1992. The most expensive spirit is Springbank 1919 Malt Whiskey, which is sold at Fortnum & Mason in London, Great Britain for £6,750 ($12,000, including tax) per bottle.

Vintners The world's oldest champagne firm is Ruinart Père et Fils, founded in 1729. The oldest cognac firm is Augier Frères & Cie, established in 1643.

Champagne cork flight The longest flight of a cork from an untreated and unheated bottle 4 ft from level ground is 177 ft 9 in, reached by Prof. Emeritus Heinrich Medicus, RPI, at the Woodbury Vineyards Winery, NY on 5 Jun 1988.

Champagne fountain The greatest number of stories achieved in a champagne fountain, successfully filled from the top and using traditional long-stem glasses, is 44 (height 24 ft 8 in), achieved by Pascal Leclerc with 10,404 glasses at the Biltmore Hotel, Los Angeles, CA on 18 Jun 1984.

Wine Oldest It is thought that New Stone Age people may have been cultivating wine as early as *c.* 8000 B.C. Physical evidence of wine dating from *c.* 3500 B.C. has been detected in remains of a Sumerian jar found at Godin Tepe, Iran in 1973 during an expedition by the Royal Ontario Museum, Canada. It was only in 1989 that the remains were analyzed, which established that a large red stain showed the presence of tartaric acid, a chemical naturally abundant in grapes.

The oldest bottle of wine sold at auction was a bottle of 1646 Imperial Tokay, which was bought by John A. Chunko of Princeton, NJ and Jay Walker of Ridgefield, CT for SFr1,250 at Sotheby's, Geneva, Switzerland on 16 Nov 1984. At the time the sum paid was equivalent to $510.

Most expensive £105,000 ($131,250) was paid for a bottle of 1787 Château Lafite claret, sold to Christopher Forbes (USA) at Christie's, London, Great Britain on 5 Dec 1985. The bottle was engraved with the initials of Thomas Jefferson (1743–1826), "Th J"—a factor that greatly affected the bidding. In November 1986 its cork, dried out by exhibition lights, slipped, making the wine undrinkable.

The record price for a half bottle of wine is Fr180,000 ($30,600), for a 1784 Château Margaux, also bearing the initials of Thomas Jefferson, which was sold by Christie's at Vinexpo in Bordeaux, France on 26 Jun 1987.

The record price for a glass of wine is Fr8,500 (*c.* $1,600), for the first glass of Beaujolais Nouveau 1992 released in Beaune (from Maison Jaffelin), in the wine region of Burgundy, France. It was bought by Patrick Thiébaut at Pickwick's, a British pub in Beaune, on 19 Nov 1992.

Auction The largest single sale of wine was conducted by Christie's of London, Great Britain on 10–11 Jul 1974 at Quaglino's Ballroom, London, when 2,325 lots comprising 432,000 bottles realized $2.4 million.

Wine tasting The largest ever reported was that staged by WQED on 22 Nov 1986 in San Francisco, CA. Some 4,000 tasters consumed 9,360 bottles of wine.

Soft drinks Pepsico of Purchase, NY topped the Fortune 500 list for beverage companies in April 1993, with total sales for 1992 of $22.1 billion, compared with $13.2 billion for the Coca-Cola Company of Atlanta, GA. Coca-Cola is, however, the world's most popular soft drink, with sales in 1991 of over 506 million drinks per day, representing an estimated 46 percent of the world market.

Mineral water The world's largest mineral water firm is Source Perrier, near Nîmes, France, with an annual production of more than 2.5 billion bottles, of which 1.1 billion now come from Perrier. The French drink about 136 pints of mineral water per person per year, although the highest average consumption is in Italy, with 185 pints per person per year.

MANUFACTURED ARTICLES

Because of the infinite number of objects it is possible to collect, we can include only a small number of claims that reflect proven widespread interest.

We are more likely to consider claims for items accumulated on a personal basis over a significant period of time, made through appropriate organizations, established and recognized, as these organizations are often in a better position to comment authoritatively in record terms.

Ax A steel ax measuring 60 ft long, 23 ft wide and weighing 7.7 tons was designed and built by BID Ltd of Woodstock, New Brunswick, Canada.

The ax was presented to the town of Nackawic, also in New Brunswick, on 11 May 1991 to commemorate the town's selection as Forestry Capital of Canada for 1991. Although calculations suggested it would take a 154-ton lumberjack to swing the ax, a crane was used to lift it into its concrete "stump."

United States   The largest ax in the United States was 36 ft long with a 10 ft 1 in x 5 ft 2 in blade. It was designed and built by Moran Iron Works in May 1992.

Balloon sculpture   The largest balloon sculpture was a reproduction of van Gogh's *Fishing Boats on the Beach of Les Saintes Maries*, made out of 25,344 colored balloons on 28 Jun 1992. Students from Haarlem Business School created the picture at a harbor in Ouddorp in the Netherlands.

Basket   The world's biggest basket measures 48 x 23 x 19 ft. It is a hand-woven maple example made by the Longaberger Company of Dresden, OH in 1990.

Beer cans   John F. Ahrens of Mount Laurel, NJ, has a collection of nearly 15,000 different cans.

A Rosalie Pilsner can sold for $6,000 in the United States in April 1981. A collection of 2,502 unopened bottles and cans of beer from 103 countries was bought for A$25,000 by the Downer Club ACT of Australia at the Australian Associated Press Financial Markets Annual Charity Golf Tournament on 23 Mar 1990.

Beer labels   Jan Solberg of Oslo, Norway has amassed 353,500 different labels from around the world as of May 1992.

Blanket   The world's largest hand-knitted blanket was made by the Friends of St Catherine's Hospice in Crawley, Great Btain. It measured 37,592 ft^2 and was completed in August 1991 at Gatwick Airport.

Bottle caps   Since 1950 Helge Friholm (b. 1909) of Søborg, Denmark has amassed 73,823 different bottle caps from 179 countries.

Pyramid   A pyramid consisting of 362,194 bottle caps was constructed by a team of 11 led by Yevgeniy Lepechov at Chernigov, Kiev, Ukraine from 17–22 Nov 1990.

Bottle collections   George E. Terren of Southboro, MA had a collection of 31,804 miniature and distilled spirit and liquor bottles on 31 May 1992.

The record for beer is 3,080 unduplicated full bottles from 102 countries collected by Ted Shuler of Germantown, TN. Ron Werner of Bothell, WA has a collection of 4,414 different bottles from 71 countries, but some 2,000 are empty.

David L. Maund of Upham, Great Britain has a collection of unduplicated miniature Scotch whiskey bottles amounting to 9,847 as of April 1993.

Bowl, wooden   The largest one-piece wooden bowl was made by Dan Cunningham, David Tarleton and Scott Hare in Kamuela, HI in September 1990. The bowl took 2,978 man-hours to complete, and was constructed of monkeypod wood. It stands 6 ft 7 in tall, and its widest diameter is 5 ft 9⅝ in with a circumference of 18 ft 1 in.

BALLOON SCULPTURE The scene at Ouddorp harbor in the Netherlands on 28 Jun 1992, when more than 25,000 balloons were used to recreate this van Gogh picture.

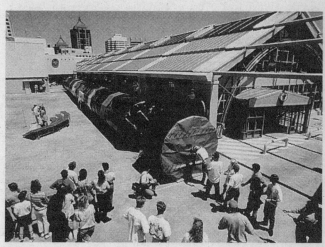

LARGEST CHRISTMAS SNAPPER Preparing to pull the 150-ft snapper at Westfield Shopping Town, New South Wales, Australia.

Candles   A candle 80 ft high and 8¹/₂ ft in diameter was exhibited at the 1897 Stockholm Exhibition by the firm of Lindahls. Including the candlestick, the overall height was 127 ft.

A candle constructed by Enham Industries at the Charlton Leisure Center, Andover, Great Britain on 2 Jul 1989 measured 101.7 ft high.

Carpets and rugs *Largest*   Of ancient carpets, the largest was a gold-enriched silk carpet of Hashim (dated A.D. 743) of the Abbasid caliphate in Baghdad, Iraq. It is reputed to have measured 180 x 300 ft (54,000 ft¹/₂). A 52,225 ft², 31.4-ton red carpet was laid on 13 Feb 1982, by the Allied Corporation, from Radio City Music Hall to the New York Hilton along the Avenue of the Americas, in New York City.

Most finely woven   The most finely woven carpet known is a silk hand-knotted example with 4,224 knots per in², measuring 14 x 22 in. It was made over a period of 22 months by the Kapoor Rug Corporation of Jaipur, India and completed in May 1993.

Chandeliers   The world's largest set of chandeliers was created by the Kookje Lighting Co. Ltd of Seoul, South Korea. It is 39 ft high, weighs 11.8 tons and has 700 bulbs. Completed in November 1988, it occupies three floors of the Lotte Chamshil Department Store in Seoul.

Check   The world's physically largest check measured 70 x 31 ft. It was presented by InterMortgage of Leeds, Great Britain to Yorkshire Television's 1992 Telephone Appeal on 4 Sep 1992, with a value of £10,000 (*c.* $19,000).

Christmas snapper   The largest functional snapper ever constructed was 150 ft long and 10 ft in diameter. It was made by Ray Price for Markson Sparks! of New South Wales, Australia and pulled at Westfield Shopping Town, Chatswood, Sydney, Australia on 9 Nov 1991.

Cigarettes   The world's largest collection of cigarettes was that of Robert E. Kaufman, of New York. It consisted of 8,390 different cigarettes made in 173 countries and territories. Upon his death in March 1992 his wife Naida took over the collection. The oldest brand represented is *Lone Jack*, made in the United States *c.* 1885.

Cigarette cards   The largest-known collection is that of Mr Edward Wharton-Tigar (b. 1913) of London, Great Britain, with more than 1 million cigarette and trade cards in about 45,000 sets. This collection has been accepted as a bequest by the British Museum, where it will eventually be available for public study.

Cigarette packs   The largest verified private collection consists of 111,870 packs accumulated by Claudio Rebecchi of Modena, Italy since 1962. A total of 260 countries and territories are represented.

Cigars   The largest cigar ever made measures 16 ft 8¹/₂ in in length and weighs 577 lb 9 oz. It took 243 hours to make and used 3,330 full tobacco leaves. It was made by Tinus Vinke and Jan Weijmer in February 1983 and is in the Tobacco Museum in Kampen, Netherlands.

The largest marketed cigar in the world is the 14-in Valdez Emperador, manufactured by Fábrica de Puros Santa Clara of San Andrés Tuxtla, Veracruz, Mexico and exclusively distributed by Tabacos San Andrés.

Coasters The world's largest collection of coasters is owned by Leo Pisker of Vienna, Austria, who has collected 140,100 different coasters from 159 countries to date.

Credit cards The largest collection of valid credit cards to date is one of 1,356 (all different) by Walter Cavanagh (b. 1943) of Santa Clara, CA. The cost of acquisition for "Mr Plastic Fantastic" was zero, and he keeps them in the world's longest wallet—250 ft long, weighing 37½ lb and worth more than $1.6 million in credit.

Doll, rag The largest rag doll in the United States is one 41 ft 11 in in total length, created by Apryl Scott at Autoworld in Flint, MI on 20 Nov 1990.

Catherine wheel A self-propelled horizontal firework wheel measuring 47 ft 4 in diameter, built by Florida Pyrotechnic Arts Guild, was displayed at the Pyrotechnics Guild International Convention in Idaho Falls, ID on 14 Aug 1992. It functioned for 3 min 45 sec. A vertical wheel at the same event, built by Essex Pyrotechnics of Saffron Waldon, Great Britain, was 45½ ft in diameter and functioned for 1 min 20 sec.

Greeting cards Craig Shergold of Carshalton, Great Britain was reported to have collected a record 33 million get-well cards by May 1991, when his mother pleaded for no more. Jarrod Booth of Salt Spring Island, British Columbia, Canada had a collection of 205,120 Christmas cards in February 1990.

Matchbox labels Teiichi Yoshizawa (b. 1904) of Chiba-Ken, Japan has amassed 730,113 different matchbox labels (including advertising labels) from 130 countries since 1925. Phillumenist Robert Jones of Indianapolis, IN has a collection of some 280,000 pieces (excluding any restaurant/bar or other advertising labels.)

Dress A wedding outfit created by Hélène Gainville with jewels by Alexander Reza is believed to be worth $7,301,587.20 precisely. The dress is embroidered with diamonds mounted on platinum and was unveiled in Paris, France on 23 Mar 1989.

Dress train The world's longest wedding dress train measured 515 ft and was made by the Hansel and Gretel bridal outfitters of Gunskirchen, Germany in 1992.

The longest wedding dress train in the United States measured 412 ft 11 in and was worn by Ann Margaret Boehlke on the occasion of her marriage to Mackinlay Polhemus on 14 Nov 1992 in Bolinas, CA.

Earrings Carol McFadden of Oil City, PA has collected 14,850 different pairs of earrings since 1951. She does not have pierced ears, but this is not a hindrance as special adaptors enable her to wear the earrings.

Egg   The largest and most elaborate jeweled egg stands 2 ft tall and was fashioned from 37 lb of gold, studded with 20,000 pink diamonds. Designed by British jeweler Paul Kutchinsky, the Argyle Library Egg took six British craftsmen 7,000 hours to create and has a price tag of £7 million ($12 million). It was unveiled on 30 Apr 1990 before going on display at the Victoria and Albert Museum, London, Great Britain.

Fabrics Oldest   The oldest surviving fabric, discovered at Çatal Hüyük, Turkey, has been radiocarbon dated to 5900 B.C.

Most expensive   The most expensive wool fabric is one manufactured by Fujii Keori Ltd of Osaka, Japan, which retailed at 3 million yen per meter in January 1989.

Fan   A handpainted Spanish fan made of fabric and wood, measuring 15.45 ft when unfolded and 8 ft high, was completed by D. Juan Reolid González of Torrent, Valencia, Spain in June 1991.

Fireworks Largest   The largest firework ever produced was *Universe I Part II*, exploded for the Lake Toya Festival, Hokkaido, Japan on 15 Jul 1988. The 1,543 lb shell was 54.7 in in diameter and burst to a diameter of 3,937 ft.

Display   The longest firecracker display was produced by the Johor Tourism Department, the United Malaysian Youth Movement and Mr Yap Seng Hock, and took place on 20 Feb 1988 at Pelangi Garden, Johor Bahru, Johor, Malaysia. The total length of the display was 18,777 ft and consisted of 3,338,777 firecrackers and 1,468 lb of gunpowder. It burned for 9 hr 27 min.

Flags Oldest   The oldest-known flag is one dated to *c*. 3000 B.C. found in 1972 at Khabis, Iran. It is of metal and measures 9 x 9 in and depicts an eagle, two lions and a goddess, three women and a bull.

The oldest Stars and Stripes in existence is that preserved in Bennington Historical Museum in Old Bennington, VT, dating from the 18th century.

Largest   The largest flag in the world, one of the Republic of China presented to the city of Kaohsiung, Taiwan by Unichamps Inpe'l Corp. on 9 Apr 1989, measured 413 x 275½ ft and weighed 1,807 lb. The largest flag *flown* from a flagpole is a Brazilian national flag measuring 229 ft 8 in x 328 ft 1 in in Brasilia.

Float   The largest float was the 155-ft-long, 24-ft-wide "Merry Christmas America" float bearing three double arches, a 17-ft Christmas tree, two 15-ft peppermint candy sticks and 5,380 ft^2 of wrapping paper, used at the 40th Annual Christmas Parade, Baton Rouge, LA on 5 Dec 1986.

Jigsaw puzzles Largest   The world's largest jigsaw puzzle measures 11,302.2 ft^2 but consists of only 2,250 pieces. Assembled on 19 Mar 1991, it was devised by J.N. Nichols (Vimto) plc of Manchester, Great Britain, and designed and built by students from Manchester Polytechnic.

A puzzle consisting of 204,484 pieces was made by BCF Holland b.v. of

Largest Matchstick Model

**Exterior and interior views of a matchstick scale
replica of St Publius Church, Floriana, Malta, made by
Joseph Sciberras. (Photos: Joseph Sciberras)**

Almelo, Netherlands and assembled by students of the local Gravenvoorde School on 25 May–1 Jun 1991. The completed puzzle measured 1,036 ft².

Most expensive Custom-made Stave puzzles made by Steve Richardson of Norwich, VT, consisting of 2,640 pieces, cost $8,680 in June 1992.

Kettle The largest antique copper kettle was one standing 3 ft high with a 6 ft girth and a 20 gal capacity, built in Taunton, Somerset, Great Britain, for the hardware merchants Fisher and Son *c.* 1800.

Knife The penknife with the greatest number of blades is the Year Knife, made by cutlers Joseph Rodgers & Sons, of Sheffield, Great Britain, whose trademark was granted in 1682. The knife was made in 1822 with 1,822 blades, and a blade was added every year until 1973, when there was no further space. It was acquired by Britain's largest hand tool manufacturers, Stanley Works (Great Britain) Ltd of Sheffield, Great Britain, in 1970.

Lego tower The world's tallest Lego tower, 65 ft 2 in, was built by the people of Auckland, New Zealand on 22–23 Feb 1992.

Matchstick model Joseph Sciberras of Malta constructed an exact replica, including the interior, of St Publius Parish Church, Floriana, Malta, consisting of over 3 million matchsticks. The model, made to scale, is 6½ ft² x 6½ x 5 ft.

Needles The longest needle is one 6 ft 1 in long made by George Davies of Thomas Somerfield, Bloxwich, Great Britain for stitching on mattress buttons lengthwise. One of these is preserved in the National Needle Museum at Forge Mill, Great Britain.

Pens The most expensive writing pen is the 5003.002 Caran D'Ache 18-carat solid gold Madison slimline ballpoint pen, incorporating white diamonds of 6.35 carats, exclusively distributed by Jakar International Ltd of London, Great Britain. Its recommended retail price, including tax, in 1993 is £25,995 ($40,000).

A Japanese collector paid 1.3 million French francs ($2,340,000) in February 1988 for the "Anémone" fountain pen made by Réden, France. It was encrusted with 600 precious stones, including emeralds, amethysts, rubies, sapphires and onyx, and took skilled craftsmen over a year to complete.

Best-selling pen The world's best-selling pen is the BiC Crystal, made by the BiC organization with daily global sales of over 15 million.

Piñata The biggest piñata made in the United States measured 27 ft high with a diameter of 30 ft, a circumference of 100 ft and a weight of 10,000 lb. It was built in March 1990 during the celebrations for Carnaval Miami in Miami, FL.

Pottery The largest thrown vase on record is one measuring 17 ft 6 in in height (including a 4 ft 3 in tall lid), weighing 1,322 lb 12 oz. It was completed on 1 Jun 1991 by Faiarte Ceramics of Rustenberg, South Africa. The Chinese ceramic authority Chingwah Lee of San Francisco, CA was reported in August 1978 to have appraised a unique 39-in Kangxi four-sided vase at $60 million.

Shoes Emperor Field Marshal Jean Fedor Bokassa of the Central African

Empire (now Republic) commissioned pearl-studded shoes at a cost of $85,000 from the House of Berluti, Paris, France for his self-coronation on 4 Dec 1977.

The most expensive manufactured shoes are mink-lined golf shoes with 18-carat gold embellishments and ruby-tipped spikes made by Stylo Matchmakers International of Northampton, Great Britain, which retail for $23,000 per pair.

Silver The largest single pieces of silver are a pair of water jugs of 10,408 troy oz (4.77 cwt) made in 1902 for the Maharaja of Jaipur (1861–1922). They are 5 ft 3 in tall, with a circumference of 8 ft 1 1/2 in, and have a capacity of 2,160 gal. They are now in the City Palace, Jaipur, India. The silversmith was Gorind Narain.

Sofa The longest standard sofa manufactured is the Augustus Rex Sofa, 12 ft 3 in in length, made by Dodge & Son of Sherborne, Great Britain.

In April 1990 a 21-ft-9-in-long jacquard fabric sofa was specially manufactured by Mountain View Interiors of Collingwood, Ontario, Canada, with an estimated value of $8,000.

Table The longest table was set up in Pesaro, Italy on 20 Jun 1988 by the US Libertas Scavolini Basketball team. It was 10,072 ft in length and was used to seat 12,000 people.

Tablecloth The world's largest tablecloth is 1,502 ft long and 4 1/2 ft wide, and was made by the Sportex division of Artex International in Highland, IL on 17 Oct 1990.

Tapestry and embroidery The largest tapestry ever woven is the *History of Iraq*, with an area of 13,370.7 ft². It was designed by the Yugoslavian artist Frane Delale and produced by the Zivtex Regeneracija Workshop in Zabok, Yugoslavia. The tapestry was completed in 1986 and it now adorns the wall of an amphitheater in Baghdad, Iraq.

Longest The famous Bayeux tapestry, *Telle du Conquest, dite tapisserie de la reine Mathilde*, a hanging tapestry 19 1/2 in x 23 ft, depicts events of 1064–66 in 72 scenes and was probably worked in Canterbury, Great Britain, *c.* 1086. It was "lost" for 2 1/2 centuries, from 1476 until 1724.

Quilt The world's largest quilt was made by 7,000 citizens of North Dakota for the 1989 centennial of North Dakota. It measured 85 x 134 ft.

String ball, largest The largest ball of string on record is one 13 ft 2 1/2 in in diameter, 41 ft 6 in in circumference, amassed by J.C. Payne of Valley View, TX between 1989 and 1991.

Stuffed toy, longest A "bookworm" measuring 675 ft was completed in December 1992 by students of Kendall Central School, New South Wales, Australia.

Embroidery   An 8-in-deep, 1,338-ft-long embroidery of scenes from C.S. Lewis's *Narnia* children's stories has been worked by Margaret S. Pollard of Truro, Great Britain to the order of Michael Maine. Its total area is about 937 ft².

Tartan   The earliest evidence of tartan is the so-called Falkirk tartan, found stuffed in a jar of coins in Bells Meadow, Scotland. It is of a dark and light brown pattern and dates from *c.* A.D. 245. The earliest reference to a specific named tartan is to a Murray tartan in 1618, although Mackay tartan was probably worn earlier. There are 2,179 tartans known to The Tartans Museum at the headquarters of the Scottish Tartans Society in Comrie, Great Britain. HRH Prince of Wales is eligible to wear 11, including the Balmoral, which has been exclusive to the British royal family since 1852.

Time capsule   The world's largest time capsule is the Tropico Time Tunnel of 10,000 ft³ in a cave in Rosamond, CA, sealed by the Kern Antelope Historical Society on 20 Nov 1966 and intended for opening in A.D. 2866.

Wallet   The most expensive wallet ever made is a platinum-cornered, diamond-studded crocodile creation made by Louis Quatorze of Paris, France and Mikimoto of Tokyo, selling in September 1984 for $84,000. (For Largest wallet, see Credit cards, p. 549.)

Wreath   The most expensive wreath on record was that presented to Sri Chinmoy in New York on 11 Jul 1983 by Ashrita Furman and Pahar Meltzer. It was handled by the Garland of Divinity's Love Florist, contained 10,000 flowers, and cost $3,500.

Zipper   The world's longest zipper was laid around the center of Sneek, Netherlands on 5 Sep 1989. The brass zipper, made by Yoshida (Netherlands) Ltd, is 9,353.56 ft long and consists of 2,565,900 teeth.

SPORTS
AND GAMES

- **INCLUDES OVER 90 SPORTS FROM THE MAJOR ONES OF BASEBALL, BASKETBALL, FOOTBALL AND TENNIS TO THE LESSER-KNOWN PURSUITS OF CRICKET, FOOTBAG, SLED DOG RACING AND TAEKWONDO**

GENERAL RECORDS

Fastest   The fastest projectile speed in any moving ball game is *c.* 188 mph, in jai alai. This compares with 170 mph (electronically timed) for a golf ball driven off a tee.

Slowest   In wrestling, before the rules were modified to favor "brighter wrestling," contestants could be locked in holds for so long that a single bout once lasted for 11 hr 40 min.

In the extreme case of the 2 hr 41 min pull in the regimental tug o' war in Jubbulpore, India, on 12 Aug 1889, the winning team moved a net distance of 12 ft at an average speed of 0.00084 mph.

World record breakers *Youngest*   The youngest age at which anybody has broken a nonmechanical world record is 12 yr 298 days for Gertrude Caroline

FASTEST SPORT   The fastest speed reached in a non-mechanical sport is in sky-diving, in which a speed of 185 mph is attained in a head-down free-falling position, even in the lower atmosphere. In delayed drops, speeds of 625 mph have been recorded at high, rarefied altitudes. (Photo: Allsport/Vandystadt/Didier Klein)

Ederle (USA; b. 23 Oct 1906), with 13 min 19.0 sec for women's 880 yd freestyle swimming, at Indianapolis, IN on 17 Aug 1919.

Oldest Gerhard Weidner (Germany; b. 15 Mar 1933) set a 20-mile walk record on 25 May 1974, at age 41 yr 71 days, the oldest to set an official world record recognized by an international governing body.

Most prolific Between 24 Jan 1970 and 1 Nov 1977, Vasiliy Alekseiev (USSR; b. 7 Jan 1942) broke 80 official world records in weightlifting.

Champions Youngest The youngest successful competitor in a world title event was a French boy, whose name is not recorded, who coxed the Netherlands' Olympic pair in the rowing competition at Paris, France on 26 Aug 1900. He was not more than ten and may have been as young as seven.

Fu Mingxia (China) won the women's world title for platform diving at Perth, Australia on 4 Jan 1991, at the age of 12.

The youngest individual Olympic winner was Marjorie Gestring (USA; b. 18 Nov 1922), who took the springboard diving title at the age of 13 yr 268 days at the Olympic Games in Berlin, Germany on 12 Aug 1936.

Oldest Fred Davis (Great Britain; b. 14 Feb 1913) won the world professional billiards title in 1980, at age 67.

World record The first world record by a woman at any sport for a category in direct and measurable competition with men was by Margaret Murdock, who set a world record for small-bore rifle (kneeling position) of 391 in 1967.

Largest contract In March 1990, the National Football League concluded a deal worth $3.64 billion for four years' coverage by the five major TV and ca-

---

Youngest national champion The youngest age at which any person has won international honors is eight, in the case of Joy Foster, the Jamaican singles and mixed doubles table tennis champion, in 1958.

Heaviest sportsman Professional wrestler William J. Cobb of Macon, GA, who in 1962 was billed as "Happy Humphrey," weighed 802 lb. The heaviest player of any ball game was Bob Pointer, the 487-lb football tackle formerly on the 1967 Santa Barbara High School team, CA.

Longest reign Jacques Edmond Barre (France; 1802–73) was a world champion for 33 years (1829–62) at court tennis.

Most participants On 15 May 1988 an estimated 110,000 (including unregistered athletes) ran in the *Examiner* Bay–to–Breakers 7.6-mile race in San Francisco, CA. The 1988 Women's International Bowling Congress (WIBC) Championship tournament attracted 77,735 bowlers for the 96-day event, held 31 March–4 July at Reno/Carson City, NV.

ble networks—ABC, CBS, NBC, ESPN and TBS. This represented $26.1 million for each league team in the first year, escalating to $39.1 million in the fourth.

Largest crowds The greatest number of live spectators for any one-day sporting spectacle is the estimated 2.5 million who have lined the route of the New York City Marathon. However, spread over three weeks, it is estimated that more than 10 million see the annual Tour de France cycling race.

Olympics The total attendance at the 1984 Summer Games, held at Los Angeles, CA, was 5,526,782 for all sports plus an estimated 275,000 spectators at road cycling and marathon events.

Stadium A crowd of 199,854 attended the Brazil *v* Uruguay World Cup Finals deciding soccer match, in the Maracaña Municipal Stadium, Rio de Janeiro, Brazil on 16 Jul 1950.

Worst disasters In recent history, the stands at the Hong Kong Jockey Club racetrack collapsed and caught fire on 26 Feb 1918, killing an estimated 604 people.

During the reign of Antoninus Pius (A.D. 138–161), 1,112 spectators were killed when the upper wooden tiers in the Circus Maximus, Rome collapsed during a gladiatorial combat.

AEROBATICS

World Championships This contest has been held biennially since 1960 (except 1974). Scoring is based on a system originally devised by Col. José Aresti of Spain. The competition consists of a known and unknown compulsory and a free program.

The USSR has won the men's team competition a record six times. Petr Jirmus (Czechoslovakia) is the only man to have become world champion twice, in 1984 and 1986. Betty Stewart (USA) won the women's competition in 1980 and 1982.

Lyubov Nemkova (USSR) won a record five medals: he was first in 1986, second in 1982 and 1984, and third in 1976 and 1978. The oldest-ever world champion has been Henry Haigh (USA; b. 12 Dec 1924), age 63 in 1988.

Inverted flight The duration record is 4 hr 38 min 10 sec by Joann Osterud (USA) from Vancouver to Vanderhoof, Canada on 24 Jul 1991.

Loops Joann Osterud achieved 208 outside loops in a "Supernova" Hyperbipe over North Bend, OR on 13 Jul 1989. On 9 Aug 1986, David Childs performed 2,368 inside loops in a Bellanca Decathlon over North Pole, AK.

AIR RACING

Air racing, or airplane racing, consists of piloted aircraft racing a specific number of laps over a closed circuit marked by pylons. As with auto racing, the first plane to cross the finish line is the winner. Air races are divided into several categories, depending on the type of plane and engine. The top level of the sport is the unlimited class.

The first international airplane racing competition, the Bennett Trophy, was held at Rheims, France from 22–28 Aug 1909. In 1964 the sport was revived in the United States by Bill Stead, who staged the first National Championship Air Races (NCAR) at Reno, NV; this is now the premier air racing event in the United States.

NATIONAL CHAMPIONSHIP AIR RACES

Staged annually in Reno, NV, since 1964, the NCAR has been held at its present site, the Reno/Stead Airport, since 1986. Races are staged in four categories: Unlimited class, AT-6 class, Formula One class and Biplane class.

Unlimited class   In this class the aircraft must use piston engines, be propeller-driven and be capable of pulling six G's. The planes race over a pylonmarked 9.128 mile course.

Most titles   Darryl Greenmyer has won seven unlimited NCAR titles: 1965–69, 1971 and 1977.

Fastest average speed (race)   Lyle Shelton won the 1991 NCAR title recording the fastest average speed at 481.618 mph, in his "Rare Bear."

Fastest qualifying speed   The one-lap NCAR qualifying record is 482.892 mph, by Lyle Shelton in 1992.

ARCHERY

Highest championship scores   The highest scores achieved in either a world or Olympic championship for Double FITA rounds are: men, 2,617 points (possible 2,880) by Darrell Owen Pace (USA; b. 23 Oct 1956) and Richard Lee McKinney (USA; b. 20 Oct 1963) at Long Beach, CA on 21–22 Oct 1983; and for women, 2,683 points by Kim Soo-nyung (South Korea; b. 5 Apr 1971) at Seoul, South Korea on 27–30 Sep 1988.

World Championships   The most titles won by a man is four, by Hans Deutgen (Sweden; 1917–89) in 1947–50, and the most by a woman is seven, by Janina

Spychajowa-Kurkowska (Poland; 1901–79) in 1931–34, 1936, 1939 and 1947. The USA has a record 14 men's and eight women's team titles.

Oscar Kessels (Belgium; 1904–68) participated in 21 world championships.

The most individual world titles by a US archer is three, by Richard McKinney: 1977, 1983 and 1985. Jean Lee, 1950 and 1952, is the only US woman to have won two individual world titles. Luann Ryon (b. 13 Jan 1953) was Olympic women's champion in 1976 and also world champion in 1977.

Olympic Games Hubert van Innis (Belgium; 1866–1961) won six gold and three silver medals at the 1900 and 1920 Olympic Games. The most successful US archer at the Olympic Games has been Darrell Pace, gold medalist in 1976 and 1984. He was also world champion in 1975 and 1979.

WORLD ARCHERY RECORDS

Men (Single FITA rounds)

Events	Points	Possible	Name & Country	Year
FITA	1,352	1,440	Vladimir Yesheyev (USSR)	1990
90 m	330	360	Vladimir Yesheyev (USSR)	1990
70 m	344	360	Hiroshi Yamamoto (Japan)	1990
50 m	345	360	Richard McKinney (USA)	1982
30 m	358	360	Antonio Vasquez Megido (Spain)	1992
Final	345	360	Vladimir Yesheyev (USSR)	1990
Team	3,963	4,320	USSR (Stanislav Zabrodskiy, Vadim Shikarev, Vladimir Yesheyev)	1989
Final	1,005	1,080	South Korea (Kim Sun-Bin, Yang Changhoon, Park Jae-pyo)	1990

Women (Single FITA rounds)

Events	Points	Possible	Name & Country	Year
FITA	1,375	1,440	Cho Youn-Jeong (South Korea)	1992
70 m	*341	360	Kim Soo-Nyung (South Korea)	1990
	338	360	Cho Youn-Jeong (South Korea)	1992
60 m	347	360	Kim Soo-Nyung (South Korea)	1989
50 m	338	360	Cho Youn-Jeong (South Korea)	1992
30 m	357	360	Joanne Edens (Great Britain)	1990
Final	346	360	Kim Soo-Nyung (South Korea)	1990
Team	4,025	4,320	South Korea (Kim Soo-nyung, Wang Hee-nyung, Kim Kyung-wook)	1989
Final	1,030	1,080	South Korea (Kim Soo-nyung, Lee Eun-Kyung, Lee Seon-hee)	1991

* unofficial

Indoor Double FITA rounds at 25 meters

Men	591	600	Erwin Verstegen (Netherlands)	1989
Women	592	600	Petra Ericsson (Sweden)	1991

Indoor FITA rounds at 18 meters

Men	591	600	Vladimir Yesheyev (USSR)	1989
Women	587	600	Denise Parker (USA)	1989

US Championships The US National Championships were first held in Chicago, IL from 12–14 Aug 1879, and are staged annually. The most US archery titles won is 17, by Lida Howell (nee Scott; 1859–1939), from 20 contested between 1883 and 1907. She won three Olympic gold medals in 1904, for Double National and Double Columbia rounds and for the US team. The most men's titles is nine (three individual, six pairs), by Richard McKinney, 1977, 1979–83, 1985–87. The greatest span of title winning is 29 years, by William Henry Thompson (1848–1918), who was the first US champion in 1879, and won his fifth and last men's title in 1908.

Twenty-four hours—target archery The highest recorded score over 24 hours by a pair of archers is 76,158, during 70 Portsmouth Rounds (60 arrows per round at 20 yd at 2-ft FITA targets) by Simon Tarplee and David Hathaway at Evesham, Great Britain on 1 Apr 1991. During this attempt Tarplee set an individual record of 38,500.

AUTO RACING

Oldest race The oldest auto race in the world still regularly run is the Royal Automobile Club (RAC) Tourist Trophy, first staged on 14 Sep 1905, in the Isle of Man, Great Britain.

Fastest circuits The highest average lap speed attained on any closed circuit is 250.958 mph, in a trial by Dr Hans Liebold (Germany; b. 12 Oct 1926), who lapped the 7.85 mile high-speed track at Nardo, Italy in 1 min 52.67 sec in a Mercedes-Benz C111-IV experimental coupé on 5 May 1979. It was powered by a V8 engine with two KKK turbochargers, with an output of 500 hp at 6,200 rpm. The fastest road circuit was the Francorchamps circuit near Spa, Belgium, then 8.76 miles in length, which was lapped in 3 min 13.4 sec (average speed 163.086 mph) on 6 May 1973, by Henri Pescarolo (France; b. 25 Sep 1942) driving a 2,993-cc V12 Matra-Simca MS670 Group 5 sports car.

Fastest race The fastest race is the Busch Clash at Daytona, FL over 50 miles on a 2½-mile 31-degree banked track. In 1987 Bill Elliott (USA; b. 8 Oct 1955) averaged 197.802 mph in a Ford Thunderbird. Al Unser, Jr. (USA; b. 19 Apr 1962) set the world record for a 500 mile race when he won the Michigan 500 on 9 Aug 1990 at an average speed of 189.727 mph.

INDIANAPOLIS 500

The Indianapolis 500 mile race (200 laps) was inaugurated in the United

States on 30 May 1911. Three drivers have four wins: Anthony Joseph "A.J." Foyt, Jr. (USA; b. 16 Jan 1935) in 1961, 1964, 1967 and 1977; Al Unser (USA; b. 29 May 1939) in 1970–71, 1978 and 1987; and Rick Ravon Mears (USA; b. 3 Dec 1951) in 1979, 1984, 1988 and 1991. The record time is 2 hr 41 min 18.404 sec (185.981 mph) by Arie Luyendyk (Netherlands) driving a Lola-Chevrolet on 27 May 1990. The record average speed for four laps qualifying is 232.482 mph by Roberto Guerrero (Colombia) in a Lola-Buick (including a one-lap record of 232.618 mph) on 9 May 1992. A.J. Foyt, Jr. has started a record 35 races, 1958–92, and Rick Mears has started from pole position a record six times, 1979, 1982, 1986, 1988–89, and 1991. The record prize fund is $7,681,300, awarded in 1993. The individual prize record is $1,244,184 by Al Unser, Jr., in 1992.

Closest finish The closest margin of victory was 0.043 sec in 1992 when Al Unser, Jr. edged Scott Goodyear.

INDY CAR CHAMPIONSHIPS

The first Indy Car Championship (CART) was held in 1909 under the auspices of the American Automobile Association (AAA). In 1959 the United States Automobile Club (USAC) took over the running of the Indy series. Since 1979 Championship Auto Racing Teams Inc. (CART) has organized the Indy Championship, which since 1979 has been called the PPG Indy Car World Series Championship.

Most wins National Championships The most successful driver in Indy car history is A.J. Foyt, Jr., who has won 67 races and seven championships (1960–61, 1963–64, 1967, 1975 and 1979). The record for the most victories in a season is 10, shared by two drivers: A.J. Foyt, Jr. (1964) and Al Unser (1970). Mario Andretti (USA; 28 Feb 1940) has the most laps (7,559) in Indy championships as of 16 Jun 1993; he also holds the record for most pole positions at 64.

Highest earnings Career Through 27 Jun 1993, Bobby Rahal holds the career earnings mark for Indy drivers with $11,468,328.

Season The single-season record is $2,461,734, set in 1991 by Michael Andretti.

NASCAR

NASCAR (National Association for Stock Car Auto Racing, Inc.) was founded by Bill France, Sr. in 1947. The first NASCAR championship was held in 1949. Since 1971 the championship series has been called the Winston Cup Championship. The championship has been won a record seven times by Richard Lee Petty (USA; b. 2 Jul 1937)—1964, 1967, 1971–72, 1974–75 and 1979.

Petty won 200 NASCAR Winston Cup races in 1,185 starts from 1958–1992, and his best season was 1967, with 27 wins. Petty, on 1 Aug 1971, was the first driver to pass $1 million in career earnings.

The NASCAR career money record is $17,082,772 to 13 Jun 1993, by Dale Earnhardt (USA; b. 29 Apr 1952). Earnhardt won a season record $3,083,056 in 1990.

Fastest pit stop   Robert William "Bobby" Unser (USA; b. 20 Feb 1934) took 4 seconds to take on fuel on lap 10 of the Indianapolis 500 on 30 May 1976.

Daytona 500   The Daytona 500 has been held at the 2½ mile oval Daytona International Speedway in Daytona, FL since 1959. The race is the major event of the NASCAR season. Richard Petty has a record seven wins—1964, 1966, 1971, 1973–74, 1979 and 1981. The record average speed for the race is 177.602 mph, by Buddy Baker in an Oldsmobile in 1980. The qualifying speed record is 210.364, by Bill Elliott in a Ford Thunderbird in 1987.

FORMULA ONE GRAND PRIX

Most successful drivers   The World Drivers' Championship, inaugurated in 1950, has been won a record five times by Juan-Manuel Fangio (Argentina; b. 24 Jun 1911), in 1951 and 1954–57. He retired in 1958, after having won 24 Grand Prix races (two shared) from 51 starts.

As of 13 Jun 1993, the following records stand for Formula One Grand Prix auto racing. Alain Prost (France; b. 24 Feb 1955) holds the records for both the most Grand Prix points in a career, 756.5, and the most Grand Prix victories, 49 from 192 races since 1980. The most Grand Prix victories in a year is nine, by Nigel Mansell (Great Britain; b. 8 Aug 1953) in 1992. The most Grand Prix starts is 247, by Ricardo Patrese (Italy; b. 17 Apr 1954) from 1977. The greatest number of pole positions is 61, by Ayrton Senna (Brazil) from 150 races (39 wins), since 1985.

Two Americans have won the World Drivers' Championship—Phil Hill in 1961, and Mario Andretti (USA; b. 28 Feb 1940) in 1978. Andretti has the most Grand Prix wins by a US driver: 12 in 128 races, 1968–82.

Oldest and youngest   The youngest world champion was Emerson Fittipaldi (Brazil; b. 12 Dec 1946), who won his first World Championship on 10 Sep 1972 at the age of 25 yr 273 days.

The oldest world champion was Juan-Manuel Fangio, who won his last World Championship on 4 Aug 1957 at the age of 46 yr 41 days.

The youngest Grand Prix winner was Bruce Leslie McLaren (New Zealand; 1937–70), who won the United States Grand Prix at Sebring, FL on 12 Dec 1959, age 22 yr 104 days. Troy Ruttman (USA) was 22 yr 80 days when he won the Indianapolis 500 on 30 May 1952; the Indianapolis 500 was part of the World Championships at the time. The oldest Grand Prix winner (in pre-World Championship days) was Tazio Giorgio Nuvolari (Italy; 1892–1953), who won the Albi Grand Prix at Albi, France on 14 Jul 1946, age 53 yr 240 days. The oldest Grand Prix driver was Louis Alexandre Chiron (Monaco; 1899–1979), who finished sixth in the Monaco Grand Prix on 22 May 1955, age 55 yr 292 days. The youngest driver to qualify for a Grand Prix was Michael Christopher Thackwell (New Zealand; b. 30 Mar 1961) at the Canadian Grand Prix on 28 Sep 1980, age 19 yr 182 days.

Manufacturers   Ferrari has won a record eight manufacturers' World Championships, 1961, 1964, 1975–77, 1979, 1982–83. Ferrari has 103 race wins in 492 Grands Prix, 1950–92.

The greatest dominance by one team since the Constructor's Championship was instituted in 1958 was by McLaren in 1988, when the team won 15 of the 16 Grands Prix. Ayrton Senna had eight wins and three seconds; Alain Prost had seven wins and seven seconds. The McLarens, powered by Honda engines, amassed over three times the points of their nearest rivals, Ferrari. Excluding the Indianapolis 500 race, then included in the World Drivers' Championship, Ferrari won all seven races in 1952 and the first eight (of nine) in 1953.

Fastest race   The fastest overall average speed for a Grand Prix race on a circuit in current use is 146.284 mph, by Nigel Mansell (Great Britain) in a Williams-Honda at Zeltweg in the Austrian Grand Prix on 16 Aug 1987. The qualifying lap record was set by Keijó "Keke" Rosberg (Finland) at 1 min 05.59 sec, an average speed of 160.817 mph, in a Williams-Honda at Silverstone in the British Grand Prix on 20 Jul 1985.

Closest finish   The closest finish to a World Championship race was when Ayrton Senna (Brazil) in a Lotus beat Nigel Mansell (Great Britain) in a Williams by 0.014 sec in the Spanish Grand Prix at Jerez de la Frontera on 13 Apr 1986. In the Italian Grand Prix at Monza on 5 Sep 1971, 0.61 sec separated winner Peter Gethin (Great Britain) from the fifth-placed driver.

MOST SUCCESSFUL   After a year's absence, Alain Prost returned to Formula 1 in 1993 and continued to add to his record-breaking achievements. Here he is seen winning the San Marino Grand Prix at Imola. (Photo: Allsport/Pascal Rondeau)

LE MANS

The greatest distance ever covered in the 24-hour *Grand Prix d'Endurance* (first held on 26–27 May 1923) on the old Sarthe circuit at Le Mans, France is 3,315.203 miles, by Dr Helmut Marko (Austria; b. 27 Apr 1943) and Gijs van Lennep (Netherlands; b. 16 Mar 1942) in a 4,907-cc flat-12 Porsche 917K Group 5 sports car, on 12–13 Jun 1971. The record for the greatest distance ever covered for the current circuit is 3,313.150 miles (average speed 137.047 mph) by Jan Lammers (Netherlands), Johnny Dumfries and Andy Wallace (both from Great Britain) in a Jaguar XJR9 on 11–12 Jun 1988.

The race lap record (now 8.411 mile lap) is 3 min 21.27 sec (average speed 150.429 mph) by Alain Ferté (France) in a Jaguar XRJ-9 on 10 Jun 1989. Hans Stück (West Germany) set the practice lap speed record of 156.377 mph, on 14 Jun 1985.

Most Le Mans wins The race has been won by Porsche cars 12 times, in 1970–71, 1976–77, 1979, 1981–87. The most wins by one man is six, by Jacques Bernard "Jacky" Ickx (Belgium; b. 1 Jan 1945), 1969, 1975–77 and 1981–82.

RALLYING

The earliest long rally, from Beijing, China to Paris, France, over about 7,500 miles from 10 Jun 1907, was promoted by the Parisian daily *Le Matin*. The winner, Prince Scipione Borghese (1872–1927) of Italy, arrived in Paris on 10 Aug 1907 in his 40-hp Itala accompanied by his chauffeur, Ettore, and Luigi Barzini.

Longest The longest-ever rally was the *Singapore Airlines* London–Sydney Rally over 19,329 miles from Covent Garden, London, Great Britain on 14 Aug 1977 to Sydney Opera House, Australia, won on 28 Sep 1977 by Andrew Cowan, Colin Malkin and Michael Broad in a Mercedes 280E.

The longest held annually is the Safari Rally (first run in 1953 as the Coronation Rally, through Kenya, Tanzania and Uganda, but now restricted to Kenya). The race has covered up to 3,874 miles, as in the 17th Safari held from 8–12 Apr 1971. It has been won a record five times by Shekhar Mehta (Kenya; b. 20 Jun 1945), in 1973, 1979–82.

Monte Carlo The Monte Carlo Rally (first run in 1911) has been won a record four times by Sandro Munari (Italy; b. 27 Mar 1940), in 1972, 1975, 1976 and 1977; and by Walter Röhrl (West Germany; b. 7 Mar 1947) (with co-driver Christian Geistdorfer) in 1980, 1982–84, each time in a different car. The smallest car to win was an 851-cc Saab driven by Erik Carlsson (Sweden; b. 5 Mar 1929) and Gunnar Häggbom (Sweden; b. 7 Dec 1935) on 25 Jan 1962, and by Carlsson and Gunnar Palm on 24 Jan 1963.

World Championship The World Drivers' Championships (instituted 1979) have been won by Juha Kankkunen (Finland; b. 2 Apr 1959), on a record three occasions, 1986–87 and 1991. The most wins in a season is six, by Didier Auriol (France; b. 1958) in 1992. The most wins in World Championship races

MOST WINS Björn Waldergård won a record 19 World Rallying Championship races in his career. Here he is seen driving a Toyota during the 1980 RAC rally. (Photo: Allsport/Don Morley)

MOST TITLES The most successful manufacturer in rallying's World Championships is Lancia, with 11 titles. Seen here is Didier Auriol (France), who won a record six races for Lancia in 1992. (Photo: Allsport/Anton Want)

is 19, by Hannu Mikkola (Finland; b. 24 May 1942), Markku Alen (Finland) and Björn Waldergård (Sweden; b. 12 Nov 1943).

Lancia has won a record 11 manufacturers' World Championships between 1972 and 1992.

DRAG RACING

Piston-engined   The lowest official elapsed time recorded by a piston-engined dragster from a standing start for 440 yd is 4.779 sec, by Eddie Hill (USA) at Pomona, CA on 29 Oct 1992. The highest terminal velocity at the end of a 440 yd run is 303.64 mph, by Pat Austin (USA) at Commerce, CA on 25 Apr 1993. In the Funny Car race, John Force (USA) has the quickest run at 5.019 on 22 Mar 1993 at Englishtown, NJ. A top speed of 295.37 was achieved by Freddie Neely (USA) at Gainesville, FL on 21 Mar 1993. For a gasoline-driven piston-engined car the lowest elapsed time is 7.027 sec and 195.05 mph respectively, by Warren Johnson (USA), driving an oldsmobile cutlass at Baytown, TX on 5 Mar 1993. The lowest elapsed time for a gasoline-driven piston-engined motorcycle is 7.615 sec, by John Myers (USA; b. 1958) at Dallas, TX on 11 Oct 1991, and the highest terminal velocity is 178.35 mph, by David Schultz (USA) at Pomona, CA.

Most wins   The greatest number of wins in National Hot Rod Association national events as of 18 Jun 1993 is 83, by Bob Glidden in Pro Stock, 1973–93.

BADMINTON

World Championships Individual   In this competition, instituted in 1977, a record five titles have been won by Park Joo-bong (South Korea; b. 5 Dec 1964)—men's doubles, 1985 and 1991, and mixed doubles, 1985, 1989 and 1991. Three Chinese players have won two individual world titles—men's singles: Yang Yang (b. 8 Dec 1963), 1987 and 1989; women's singles: Li Lingwei in 1983 and 1989; Han Aiping (b. 22 Apr 1962) in 1985 and 1987.

Team   The most wins at the men's International Team Badminton Championship for the Thomas Cup (instituted 1948) is eight, by Indonesia (1958, 1961, 1964, 1970, 1973, 1976, 1979 and 1984).

The most wins at the women's International Team Badminton Championship for the Uber Cup (instituted 1956) is five; by Japan (1966, 1969, 1972, 1978 and 1981), and China (1984, 1986, 1988, 1990 and 1992).

United States   The USA has never won the Thomas Cup, but won the Uber Cup on the first three occasions that it was contested, 1957, 1960 and 1963. Judy Hashman (nee Devlin; b. 22 Oct 1935) was the only player on all three teams.

United States Championships   The first competition was held in 1937.

Most titles   Judy Hashman won a record 31 US titles: 12 women's singles,

> **Longest badminton rallies** In the men's singles final of the 1987 All-England Championships between Morten Frost (Denmark) and Icuk Sugiarto (Indonesia), there were two successive rallies of over 90 strokes.
>
> **Shortest badminton game** In the 1992 Olympic Games at Barcelona, Spain, Christine Magnusson (Sweden) beat Martine de Souza (Mauritius) 11–1, 11–0 in 8 min 30 sec.

1954, 1956–63, 1965–67; 12 women's doubles, 1953–55, 1957–63, 1966–67 (11 with her sister Susan); and seven mixed doubles, 1956–59, 1961–62, 1967. David Freeman won seven singles titles: 1939–42, 1947–48, 1953.

Winning streak The longest continuous winning streak achieved by an American badminton team is 304 wins to 24 Jun 1992, by Miller Place High School, Miller Place, NY.

BASEBALL

MAJOR LEAGUE

Most games played Peter Edward "Pete" Rose (b. 14 Apr 1941) played in a record 3,562 games with a record 14,053 at-bats, for the Cincinnati Reds (NL), 1963–78 and 1984–86, the Philadelphia Phillies (NL), 1979–83, and the Montreal Expos (NL), 1984. Henry Louis "Lou" Gehrig (1903–41) played in 2,130 successive games for the New York Yankees (AL) from 1 Jun 1925 to 30 Apr 1939.

Most home runs Career Henry Louis "Hank" Aaron (b. 5 Feb 1934) holds the major league career record with 755 home runs—733 for the Milwaukee (1954–65) and Atlanta (1966–74) Braves (NL) and 22 for the Milwaukee Brewers (AL) 1975–76. On 8 Apr 1974 he bettered the previous record of 714 by George Herman "Babe" Ruth (1895–1948). Ruth hit his home runs from 8,399 times at bat, achieving the highest home run percentage of 8.5 percent. Joshua Gibson (1911–47) of the Homestead Grays and Pittsburgh Crawfords, Negro League clubs, hit an estimated 900 home runs in his career, including an unofficial season record of 84 in 1931. These totals are believed to include exhibition games.

Season The major league record for home runs in a season is 61, by Roger Eugene Maris (1934–85) for the New York Yankees (AL) in 162 games in 1961. The most official home runs in a minor league season is 72, by Joe Bauman of the Roswell Rockets of the Longhorn League in 1954. Bauman hit his record "dingers" in 138 games, while batting .400 and driving in 224 runs.

Game The most home runs in a major league game is four, first achieved by

Robert Lincoln "Bobby" Lowe (1868–1951) for Boston *v* Cincinnati on 30 May 1894. The feat has been achieved a further 10 times since then.

Consecutive games   The most home runs hit in consecutive games is eight, set by Richard Dale Long (b. 6 Feb 1926) for the Pittsburgh Pirates (NL), 19–28 May 1956, and tied by Donald Arthur "Don" Mattingly (b. 21 Apr 1961) for the New York Yankees (AL), on 18 Jul 1987.

Grand slams   Seven players have hit two grand slams in a single game. They are: Anthony Michael "Tony" Lazzeri (1903–46) for the New York Yankees (AL) on 24 May 1936, James Reubin "Jim" Tabor (1916–53) for the Boston Red Sox (AL) on 4 Jul 1939, Rudolph Preston "Rudy" York (1913–70) for the Boston Red Sox (AL) on 27 Jul 1946, James Edward "Diamond Jim" Gentile (b. 3 Jun 1934) for the Baltimore Orioles (AL) on 9 May 1961, Tony Lee Cloninger (b. 13 Aug 1940) for the Atlanta Braves (NL) on 3 Jul 1966, James "Jim" Thomas Northrup (b. 24 Nov 1939) for the Detroit Tigers (AL) on 24 Jun 1968, and Frank Robinson (b. 31 Aug 1935) for the Baltimore Orioles (AL) on 26 Jun 1970.

Don Mattingly of the New York Yankees (AL) hit six grand slams in 1987. Lou Gehrig hit 23 grand slams during his 16 seasons with the New York Yankees (AL), 1923–39.

Most career hits   The career record for most hits is 4,256, by Pete Rose. Rose's record hits total came from a record 14,053 at-bats, which gave him a career batting average of .303.

Longest throw of a baseball   Glen Edward Gorbous (Canada; b. 8 Jul 1930) threw a baseball 445 ft 10 in on 1 Aug 1957. Mildred Ella "Babe" Didrikson (USA [later Mrs Zaharias]; 1914–56) threw a baseball 296 ft at Jersey City, NJ on 25 Jul 1931.

Fastest base runner   The fastest time for circling bases is 13.3 sec, by Ernest Evar Swanson (1902–73) at Columbus, OH in 1932, at an average speed of 18.45 mph.

Largest baseball bat   The largest baseball bat in the United States measures 5 ft 8$\frac{1}{4}$ in high, 22$\frac{3}{4}$ in in width and weighs 57$\frac{1}{2}$ lb. The bat, owned by Stephen Koschal of Boynton Beach, FL, has genuine autographs of all living members of the Baseball Hall of Fame.

Longest home run   In a minor league game at Emeryville Ball Park, CA on 4 Jul 1929, Roy Edward "Dizzy" Carlyle (1900–56) hit a home run measured at 618 ft.

The longest measured home run in a regular-season major league game was 643 ft, by Mickey Mantle (b. 20 Oct 1931) for the New York Yankees *v* Detroit Tigers on 10 Sep 1960 at Briggs Stadium in Detroit.

MAJOR LEAGUE RECORDS
American League (AL), National League (NL)

Career Batting Records

Batting average ... .367 — Tyrus Raymond "Ty" Cobb (Detroit–AL, Philadelphia–AL) ... 1905–28
Runs scored ... 2,245 — Ty Cobb ... 1905–28
Runs batted in (RBI's) ... 2,297 — Henry Louis "Hank" Aaron (Milwaukee, Atlanta–NL, Milwaukee–AL) ... 1954–76
Base hits ... 4,256 — Peter Edward "Pete" Rose (Cincinnati–NL, Philadelphia–NL, Montreal–NL) ... 1963–86
Total bases ... 6,856 — Hank Aaron (Milwaukee, Atlanta–NL, Milwaukee–AL) ... 1954–76

Season Batting Records

Batting average ... .438 — Hugh Duffy (Boston–NL; 236 hits in 539 at-bats) ... 1894
  modern record (1900–present) ... .424 — Rogers Hornsby (St Louis–NL; 227 in 536 at-bats) ... 1924
Runs scored ... 196 — William Robert Hamilton (Philadelphia–NL; in 131 games) ... 1894
  modern record (1900–present) ... 177 — George Herman "Babe" Ruth (New York–AL; in 152 games) ... 1921
Runs batted in (RBI's) ... 190 — Lewis Robert "Hack" Wilson (Chicago–NL; in 155 games) ... 1930
Base hits ... 257 — George Harold Sisler (St Louis–AL; 631 times at bat, 143 games) ... 1920
Singles ... 202 — William H. "Wee Willie" Keeler (Baltimore–NL; in 128 games) ... 1898
  modern record (1900–present) ... 198 — Lloyd James Waner (Pittsburgh–NL; in 150 games) ... 1927
Doubles ... 67 — William Earl Webb (Boston–AL; in 151 games) ... 1931
Triples ... 36 — John Owen Wilson (Pittsburgh–NL; in 152 games) ... 1912
Total bases ... 457 — Babe Ruth (New York–AL); 85 singles, 44 doubles, 16 triples, 59 home runs ... 1921

Single-game Batting Records

Runs batted in (RBI's) ... 12 — James LeRoy Bottomley (St Louis–NL) v Brooklyn ... 16 Sep 1924
Base hits ... 9 — John Henderson Burnett (Cleveland–AL; in 18 innings) ... 10 Jul 1932
Total bases ... 18 — Joseph Wilbur "Joe" Adcock (Milwaukee–AL); 1 double, 4 home runs ... 31 Jul 1954

Career Pitching Records

Games won ... 511 — Denton T. "Cy(clone)" Young (in 906 games; Cleveland, St Louis, Boston–NL and Cleveland, Boston–AL) ... 1890–1911
Shutouts ... 110 — Walter Perry Johnson (Washington–AL; in 802 games) ... 1907–27

Strikeouts * ....5,678 Lynn Nolan Ryan (New York–NL, California–AL, Houston–NL, Texas–AL) 1968–93
*Through 7 Jun 1993

Season Pitching Records

Games won ....60 Charles Gardner "Old Hoss" Radbourn (Providence–NL; and 12 losses) 1884
  modern record (1900–present).......41 John Dwight "Jack" Chesbro (New York–AL) 1904
Shutouts ....16 George Washington Bradley (St Louis–NL; in 64 games) 1876
  modern record (1900–present) ....16 Grover Cleveland "Pete" Alexander (Philadelphia–NL; 48 games) 1916
Strikeouts ....513 Matthew Aloysius Kilroy (Baltimore–AL) 1886
  modern record (1900–present) ...383 Lynn Nolan Ryan (California–AL) 1973

Single-game Pitching Records

Strikeouts (9 innings) ....20 William Roger Clemens (Boston–AL) v Seattle ....29 Apr 1986
Strikeouts in extra innings ....21 Thomas Edgar Cheney (Washington–AL) v Baltimore (16 innings) ....12 Sep 1962

Holding 10 baseballs in one hand
James and Jason D'Amore of the Bronx, NY set a world record by holding 10 baseballs in one hand, 20 Oct 1991.

Father and son On 31 Aug 1990, Ken Griffey, Sr. and Ken Griffey, Jr., of the Seattle Mariners (AL), became the first father and son to play for the same major league team at the same time. Griffey Sr., an 18-year veteran, was signed by Seattle on 29 Aug. In 1989 the Griffeys had been the first father/son combination to play in the major leagues at the same time—Griffey Sr. played for the Cincinnati Reds (NL) during that season, while Griffey Jr. was in his first season with the Mariners.

Father, son and grandson On 19 Aug, 1992, Bret Boone made his major league debut for the Seattle Mariners (AL), making the Boone family the first three-generation family in major league history. Boone's father Bob Boone played 18 seasons in the majors, 1972–89, and his grandfather Ray Boone played from 1948–60.

MOST SAVES BY A PITCHER   Lee Smith holds the career record for most saves by a pitcher, with 379 through 22 Jun 1993. (Photo: Allsport/Stephen Dunn)

Most consecutive hits   Michael Franklin "Pinky" Higgins (1909–69) had 12 consecutive hits for the Boston Red Sox (AL) in a four-game span, 19–21 Jun 1938. This was equaled by Walter "Moose" Dropo (b. 30 Jan 1923) for the Detroit Tigers (AL), 14–15 Jul 1952. Joseph Paul "Joe" DiMaggio (b. 25 Nov 1914) hit in a record 56 consecutive games for the New York Yankees (AL) in 1941; he went to bat 223 times, with 91 hits, totaling 56 singles, 16 doubles, 4 triples and 15 home runs.

Home runs and stolen bases   The only player to have hit 40 or more home runs and have 40 stolen bases in a season was José Canseco (b. 2 Jul 1964) for the Oakland Athletics (AL) in 1988. His totals were 42 and 40 respectively.

Stolen bases   On 1 May 1991, Rickey Henley Henderson (b. 25 Dec 1958) of the Oakland Athletics (AL) broke baseball's all-time record for stolen bases when he stole his 939th base, surpassing Lou Brock's mark. As of 16 Jun 1993, Henderson had extended his record to 1,066 stolen bases. Henderson also holds the mark for most stolen bases in a season, which he set in 1982 when he stole 130 bases.

Walks   Babe Ruth holds the record for career walks, 2,056, and the single-season record, 170 in 1923.

Two players share a record six walks for a single game: James E. "Jimmie" Foxx (1907–67) of the Boston Red Sox (AL) set the mark on 16 Jun 1938, and Andre Thornton (b. 13 Aug 1949) of the Cleveland Indians (AL) tied the record on 2 May 1984 in a game that went 18 innings.

Strikeouts   The batter with the career strikeout record is Reginald Martinez "Reggie" Jackson (b. 18 May 1946), who struck out 2,597 times in 21 seasons with four teams. The season record is 189, by Bobby Lee Bonds (b. 15 Mar 1946), right fielder for the San Francisco Giants in 1970. The longest run of games without striking out is 115, by Joseph Wheeler "Joe" Sewell (b. 9 Oct 1898) while playing third base for the Cleveland Indians (AL) in 1929. He had a record seven seasons batting at least 500 times with less than 10 strikeouts, and struck out only 114 times in his 14-year career.

Most games won by a pitcher   Denton True "Cy" Young (1867–1955) had a record 511 wins and a record 750 complete games from a total of 906 games and 815 starts in his career for the Cleveland Spiders (NL) 1890–98, the St Louis Cardinals (NL) 1899–1900, the Boston Red Sox (AL) 1901–08, the Cleveland Indians (AL) 1909–11 and the Boston Braves (NL) 1911. He pitched a record total of 7,356 innings. The career record for most pitching appearances is 1,070, by James Hoyt Wilhelm (b. 26 Jul 1923) for a total of nine teams between 1952 and 1969; he set the career record with 143 wins by a relief pitcher. The season's record is 106 appearances, by Michael Grant Marshall (b. 15 Jan 1943) for the Los Angeles Dodgers (NL) in 1974.

Most consecutive games won by a pitcher   Carl Owen Hubell (1903–88) pitched for the New York Giants (NL) to win 24 consecutive games, 16 in 1936 and eight in 1937.

Shutouts   The record for the most shutouts in a career is 110, pitched by Walter Perry Johnson (1887–1946) in his 21-season career with the Washington Senators (AL), 1907–27. Donald Scott "Don" Drysdale (1936–93) pitched six consecutive shutouts for the Los Angeles Dodgers (NL) between 14 May and 4 Jun 1968. Orel Leonard Hershiser IV (b. 16 Sep 1958) pitched a record 59 consecutive shutout innings for the Los Angeles Dodgers (NL) from 30 Aug to 28 Sep 1988.

No-hitters   Nolan Ryan, playing for the Texas Rangers (AL) against the Toronto Blue Jays (AL), pitched his record seventh no-hitter on 1 May 1991. Ryan also holds the record for greatest number of walks, giving up 2,718 through 15 Jul 1992. John Samuel "Johnny" Vander Meer (b. 2 Nov 1914) of the Cincinnati Reds (NL) is the only player in baseball history to have pitched consecutive no-hitters, 11–15 Jun 1938.

Perfect game   A perfect nine-inning game, in which the pitcher allowed the opposition no hits, no runs and did not allow a man to reach first base, was first achieved by John Lee Richmond (1857–1929) for Worcester, MA against Cleveland in the NL on 12 Jun 1880. There have been 13 subsequent perfect games over nine innings, but no pitcher has achieved this feat more than once. On 26 May 1959 Harvey Haddix, Jr. (b. 18 Sep 1925) for Pittsburgh pitched a perfect game for 12 innings against Milwaukee in the National League, but lost in the 13th.

Saves   Robert Thomas "Bobby" Thigpen (b. 17 Jul 1963) saved a record 57 games for the Chicago White Sox (AL) in 1990. The career record for saves is 379 through 22 Jun 1993, by Lee Arthur Smith, Sr. (b. 4 Dec 1957) in his 14th season, playing for the Chicago Cubs (NL) 1980–87; the Boston Red Sox (NL) 1988–90; the St. Louis Cardinals (NL) 1990–93.

Youngest player   Frederick Joseph Chapman (1872–1957) pitched for Philadelphia in the American Association at 14 yr 239 days on 22 Jul 1887, but did not play again.

The youngest major league player of all time was the Cincinnati Reds (NL) pitcher Joseph Henry "Joe" Nuxhall (b. 30 Jul 1928), who played one game in Jun 1944, age 15 yr 314 days. He did not play again in the National League until 1952. The youngest player to play in a minor league game was Joe Louis Reliford (b. 29 Nov 1939), who played for the Fitzgerald Pioneers against the Statesboro Pilots in the Georgia State League, age 12 yr 234 days, on 19 Jul 1952.

Oldest player   Leroy Robert "Satchel" Paige (1906–82) pitched for the Kansas City A's (AL) at 59 yr 80 days on 25 Sep 1965.

Shortest and tallest players   The shortest major league player was Eddie Gaedel, a 3 ft 7 in, 65 lb midget, who pinch-hit for the St Louis Browns (AL) *v* the Detroit Tigers (AL) on 19 Aug 1951. Wearing number 1/8, the batter with the smallest-ever major league strike zone walked on four pitches. Following the game, major league rules were hastily rewritten to prevent the recurrence of such an affair. The tallest major leaguer of all time is Randy Johnson (b. 10 Sep 1963) of the Seattle Mariners (AL), a 6 ft 10 in pitcher, who played in his first game for the Montreal Expos on 15 Sep 1988.

Most Valuable Player Award   The most selections in the annual vote (instituted in 1931) of the Baseball Writers' Association for Most Valuable Player of the Year (MVP) in the major leagues is three, won by: *National League*: Stanley Frank "Stan" Musial (b. 21 Nov 1920; St Louis), 1943, 1946, 1948; Roy Campanella (1921–93), 1951, 1953, 1955; Mike Schmidt (b. 27 Sep 1949; Philadelphia), 1980–81, 1986; *American League*: James Emory "Jimmie" Foxx (1907–67; Philadelphia), 1932–33, 1938; Joe DiMaggio (New York), 1939, 1941, 1947; Yogi Berra (New York), 1951, 1954–55; Mickey Mantle (b. 20 Oct 1931; New York), 1956–57, 1962.

Cy Young Award   In the competition for this prize, awarded annually from 1956 on to the outstanding pitcher in the major leagues, the most wins is four, by Stephen Norman "Steve" Carlton (b. 22 Dec 1944; Philadelphia Phillies), 1972, 1977, 1980 and 1982.

Dwight Eugene Gooden (b. 16 Nov 1964) of the New York Mets became the youngest pitcher to win the Cy Young Award in 1985 by unanimous vote of the 24 sportswriters who make the selection.

Longest and shortest games   The Chicago White Sox (AL) played the longest major league ballgame in elapsed time—8 hours 6 min—beating the Milwaukee Brewers, 7–6, in the 25th inning on 9 May 1984 in Chicago. The game started on Tuesday night and was still tied at 3–3 when the 1 A.M. curfew caused suspension until Wednesday night. The most innings in a major league game were 26, when the Brooklyn Dodgers (NL) and the Boston Braves (NL) played to a 1–1 tie on 1 May 1920.

In the shortest major league game on record, the New York Giants (NL) beat the Philadelphia Phillies (NL), 6–1, in nine innings in 51 min on 28 Sep 1919. (A minor league game, Atlanta *v* Mobile in the Southern Association on 19 Sep 1910, took 33 min.)

Longest baseball game   The actual longest game was a minor league game in 1981 that lasted 33 innings. At the end of nine innings the score was tied, 1–1, with the Rochester (NY) Red Wings battling the home team Pawtucket (RI) Red Sox. At the end of 21 innings it was tied 2–2, and at the end of 32 innings, the score was still 2–2, at which point the game was suspended. Two months later, play was resumed, and 18 minutes later, Pawtucket scored one run and won. The winning pitcher was the Red Sox's Bob Ojeda.

Record attendances   The all-time season record for attendance for both leagues is 56,888,512 in 1991. The record for an individual league is 32,117,588, for the American League in 1991. The record for home-team attendance is held by the Toronto Blue Jays (AL) at 4,028,318 in 1992.

Managers   Connie Mack (b. Cornelius Alexander McGillicuddy; 1862–1956) managed in the major leagues for a record 53 seasons and achieved a record 3,731 regular-season victories (and a record 3,948 losses)—139 wins and 134 losses for the Pittsburgh Pirates (NL) 1894–96, and 3,592 wins and 3,814 losses for the Philadelphia Athletics (AL), a team he later owned, 1901–50. The most successful in the World Series was Charles Dillon "Casey" Stengel (1890–1975), who managed the New York Yankees (AL) to seven wins in 10 World Series, winning in 1949–53, 1956 and 1958, and losing in 1955, 1957 and 1960. Joseph Vincent "Joe" McCarthy (1887–1978) also coached the New York Yankees to seven wins, 1932, 1936–39, 1941, 1943, and his teams lost in 1929 (Chicago) and 1942 (New York). He had the highest win percentage of managers who achieved at least 1,500 regular-season wins, with .614—2,126 wins and 1,335 losses in his 24-year career with the Chicago Cubs (NL) 1926–30, the New York Yankees (AL) 1931–46, and the Boston Red Sox (AL) 1948–50, during which he never had an overall losing season.

WORLD SERIES

Most wins   The most wins for the World Series (first staged unofficially in 1903 and officially from 1905) is 22, by the New York Yankees between 1923 and 1978, during a record 33 Series appearances after winning the American League titles between 1921 and 1981. The most National League wins is 19, by the Dodgers—Brooklyn 1890–1957, Los Angeles 1958–88.

Most Valuable Player   The only players to have won the award twice are Sanford "Sandy" Koufax (b. 30 Dec 1935) (Los Angeles, NL, 1963, 1965), Robert "Bob" Gibson (b. 9 Nov 1935) (St Louis, NL, 1964, 1967) and Reggie Jackson (b. 18 May 1946) (Oakland, AL, 1973; New York, AL, 1977).

LEAGUE CHAMPIONSHIP SERIES

Most series played   Reggie Jackson has played in 11 series, with the Oakland Athletics (AL), 1971–75; New York Yankees (AL), 1977–78 and 1980–81; California Angels (AL), 1982, 1986.

Most games played   The record for most games played is 45, by Reggie Jackson. Jackson played for the Oakland Athletics (AL) from 1971–75; the New York Yankees (AL) from 1977–78 and 1980–81; and the California Angels (AL) during the 1982 and 1986 seasons.

WORLD SERIES RECORDS
American League (AL), National League (NL)

Most wins	New York Yankees–AL	22 1923–78
Most series played	Lawrence Peter "Yogi" Berra (New York Yankees–AL)	14 1947–63
Most series played by pitcher	Edward Charles "Whitey" Ford (New York Yankees–AL)	11 1950–64

World Series Career Records

Batting average (min. 75 at-bats)	Louis Clark "Lou" Brock (St Louis Cardinals–NL; 34 hits in 87 at-bats, 3 series)	.391 1964–68
Runs scored	Mickey Charles Mantle (New York Yankees–AL)	42 1951–64
Runs batted in (RBI's)	Mickey Mantle (New York Yankees–AL)	40 1951–64
Base hits	Yogi Berra (New York Yankees–AL)	71 1947–63
Home runs	Mickey Mantle (New York Yankees–AL)	18 1951–64
Victories pitching	Whitey Ford (New York Yankees–AL)	10 1950–64
Strikeouts	Whitey Ford (New York Yankees–AL)	94 1950–64

World Series Single Series Records

Batting average (4 or more games)	William Augustus "Billy" Hatcher (Cincinnati Reds–NL; 9 hits in 12 at-bats in four-game series)	.750 1990
Runs scored	Reginald Martinez "Reggie" Jackson (New York Yankees–AL)	10 1977
Runs batted in (RBI's)	Robert Clinton "Bobby" Richardson (New York Yankees–AL)	12 1960
Base hits (7-game series)	Bobby Richardson (New York Yankees–AL)	13 1960
	Lou Brock (St Louis Cardinals–NL)	13 1968
	Martin "Marty" Barrett (Boston Red Sox–AL)	13 1986
Home runs	Reggie Jackson (New York Yankees–AL; in 20 at-bats)	5 1977
Victories pitching	Christopher "Christy" Matthewson (New York Yankees–AL; in five-game series)	3 1905
	John Wesley "Jack" Coombs (Philadelphia A's–AL; in five-game series)	3 1910
	Ten other pitchers have won three games in more than five games.	
Strikeouts	Robert "Bob" Gibson (St Louis Cardinals–NL; in 7 games)	.35 1968
	Sanford "Sandy" Koufax (Los Angeles Dodgers–NL; in 4 games)	23 1963

World Series Game Records

Home runs	3	George Herman "Babe" Ruth (New York Yankees–AL) v St Louis Cardinals	6 Oct 1926
	3	Babe Ruth (New York Yankees–AL) v St Louis Cardinals	9 Oct 1928
	3	Reggie Jackson (New York Yankees–AL) v Los Angeles Dodgers	18 Oct 1977
Runs batted in (RBI's) in a game	6	Bobby Richardson (New York Yankees–AL) v Pittsburgh Pirates	8 Oct 1960
Strikeouts by pitcher in a game	17	Bob Gibson (St Louis Cardinals–NL) v Detroit Tigers	2 Oct 1968
Perfect game (9 innings)		Donald James "Don" Larsen (New York Yankees–AL)	8 Oct 1956
		v Brooklyn Dodgers	

1992 WORLD SERIES The 1992 World Series was the first won by a non–US team—the Toronto Blue Jays. Blue Jays catcher Pat Borders was named Series MVP. (Photo: Allsport [US]/Rick Stewart)

World series attendance The record attendance for a World Series is 420,784, for the six games when the Los Angeles Dodgers beat the Chicago White Sox 4–2 between 1 and 8 Oct 1959. The single-game record is 92,706, for the fifth game of this series at the Memorial Coliseum, Los Angeles on 6 Oct 1959.

Hits The record for most hits in a league championship series is 45, by Pete Rose, of the Cincinnati Reds (NL), 1970, 1972–73, 1975–76, and of the Philadelphia Phillies (NL) in 1980 and 1983.

Batting average (minimum 50 at-bats)   Mickey Rivers of the New York Yankees (AL) had a batting average of .386 in 1976–78. Rivers collected 22 hits in 57 at-bats in 14 games.

Most series pitched   Bob Welch has pitched in eight, with the Los Angeles Dodgers (NL), 1978, 1981, 1983, 1985; and the Oakland Athletics (AL), 1988–90 and 1992.

Most games pitched   The record for most games pitched is 15, held by two pitchers: Tug McGraw, New York Mets (NL), 1969, 1973, Philadelphia Phillies (NL), 1976–78, 1980; and Dennis Eckersley, Chicago Cubs (NL), 1984, Oakland Athletics (AL), 1988–90, 1992.

COLLEGE BASEBALL

Various forms of college baseball have been played throughout the 20th century; however, the National Collegiate Athletic Association (NCAA) did not organize a championship until 1947 and did not begin to keep statistical records until 1957.

NCAA Division I regular season Hitting records   The most career home runs was 100, by Pete Incaviglia for Oklahoma State in three seasons, 1983–85. The most career hits was 418, by Phil Stephenson for Wichita State in four seasons, 1979–82.

Pitching records   Don Heinkel won 51 games for Wichita State in four seasons, 1979–82. Derek Tatsumo struck out 541 batters for the University of Hawaii in three seasons, 1977–79.

College World Series   The first College World Series was played in 1947 in Kalamazoo, MI. The University of California at Berkeley defeated Yale University in a best-of-three-game series, 2–0. In 1949 the series format was changed to a championship game. Since 1950 the College World Series has been played annually at Rosenblatt Stadium, Omaha, NE.

Most championships   The most wins in Division I is 11, by the University of Southern California (USC) in 1948, 1958, 1961, 1963, 1968, 1970–74 and 1978.

Hitting records   The record for most home runs in a College World Series is four, shared by five players: Bud Hollowell (University of Southern California), 1963; Pete Incaviglia (Oklahoma State), 1983–85; Ed Sprague (Stanford University), 1987–88; Gary Hymel (Louisiana State University), 1990–1991; and Lyle Mewton (Louisiana State University), 1990–91.

Keith Moreland of the University of Texas holds the record for the most hits in a College World Series career, with 23 hits in three series, 1973–75.

Pitching records   The record for most wins in the College World Series is four games, shared by nine players: Bruce Gardner (University of Southern California), 1958, 1960; Steve Arlin (Ohio State), 1965–66; Bert Hooten (University of Texas at Austin), 1969–70; Steve Rogers (University of Tulsa), 1969, 1971; Russ McQueen (University of Southern California), 1972–73; Mark Bull (University of Southern California), 1973–74; Greg Swindell (University of

Texas), 1984–85; Kevin Sheary (University of Miami of Florida), 1984–85; Greg Brummett (Wichita State), 1988–89.

Carl Thomas of the University of Arizona struck out 64 batters in three College World Series, 1954–56.

World Amateur Championships In this contest, instituted in 1938, the most successful nation has been Cuba, with 19 wins between 1939 and 1988. Baseball has been a demonstration sport at six Olympic Games, and American teams have won the tournament four times, 1912, 1956, 1964 and 1988.

BASKETBALL

Highest score In a senior international match, Iraq scored 251 points against Yemen (33) at New Delhi, India, in November 1982 at the Asian Games.

Largest attendance The largest crowd for a basketball game was 80,000 for the final of the European Cup Winners' Cup between AEK Athens (89) and Slavia Prague (82) at the Olympic stadium, Athens, Greece on 4 Apr 1968.

NATIONAL BASKETBALL ASSOCIATION

Most championships The Boston Celtics have won a record 16 NBA titles— 1957, 1959–66, 1968–69, 1974, 1976, 1981, 1984 and 1986.

Individual scoring Wilton Norman "Wilt" Chamberlain (b. 21 Aug 1936) set an NBA record with 100 points for Philadelphia v New York at Hershey, PA on 2 Mar 1962. This included a record 36 field goals and 28 free throws (from 32 attempts) and a record 59 points in a half (the second). The free throws game record was equaled by Adrian Dantley (b. 28 Feb 1956) for Utah v Houston at Las Vegas on 5 Jan 1984. The most points scored in an NBA game in one quarter is 33, in the second quarter, by George Gervin for San Antonio v New Orleans on 9 Apr 1978.

Most games Kareem Abdul-Jabbar (formerly Ferdinand Lewis "Lew" Alcindor) (b. 16 Apr 1947) took part in a record 1,560 NBA regular season games over 20 seasons, totaling 57,446 minutes played, for the Milwaukee Bucks, 1969–75, and the Los Angeles Lakers, 1975–89. He also played a record 237 playoff games.

The most successive games is 906, by Randy Smith for the Buffalo Braves, the San Diego Clippers, the Cleveland Cavaliers and the New York Knicks from 18 Feb 1972 to 13 Mar 1983.

The record for most complete games played in one season is 79, by Wilt Chamberlain for Philadelphia in 1962, when he was on court for a record 3,882 minutes. Chamberlain went through his entire career of 1,045 games without fouling out. Moses Malone played his 1,140th consecutive game without fouling out to the end of the 1992/93 season. In his career, Malone has played 1,257 games, fouling out on only five occasions.

Most points Kareem Abdul-Jabbar set NBA career records with 38,387 points, including 15,837 field goals, in regular-season games, and 5,762 points, including 2,356 field goals, in playoff games. The previous record holder, Wilt Chamberlain, had an average of 30.1 points per game for his total of 31,419 for the Philadelphia Warriors 1959–62, the San Francisco 76ers 1962–65, the Philadelphia Warriors 1965–68 and the Los Angeles Lakers 1968–73.

Chamberlain holds the record for most games scoring 50 or more points—118, including 45 games in 1961/62 and 30 in 1962/63, to the next-best career total of 17. He set season records for points and scoring average with 4,029 at 50.4 per game, and also for field goals, 1,597, for Philadelphia in 1961/62.

The highest career average for players exceeding 10,000 points is 32.3 points per game, by Michael Jordan (b. 17 Feb 1963), 21,541 points in 667 games for the Chicago Bulls, 1984–93. Jordan also holds the career scoring average record for playoffs at 36.4, 4,040 points in 111 games 1984–93.

Kareem Abdul-Jabbar (Milwaukee, Los Angeles) had a record nine seasons scoring more than 2,000 points: 1970–74, 1976–77, 1980–81; and 19 scoring more than 1,000, 1970–88.

Steals   The most steals in an NBA game is 11, by Larry Kenon for San Antonio at Kansas City on 26 Dec 1976. Alvin Robertson (b. 22 Jul 1962) set season records for San Antonio in 1985/86 with 301 at a record average of 3.67 steals per game.

Blocked shots   The record for most blocked shots in an NBA game is 17, by Elmore Smith for Los Angeles *v* Portland at Los Angeles on 28 Oct 1973.

Most Valuable Player   Kareem Abdul-Jabbar was elected the NBA's most valuable player a record six times, 1971–72, 1974, 1976–77 and 1980.

MOST ASSISTS   In his career, 1979–91, for the Los Angeles Lakers, Magic Johnson had an NBA record 9,921 assists. (Photo: Allsport [USA]/Ken Levine)

Tallest basketball player   Tallest in NBA history has been Manute Bol (Sudan; b. 16 Oct 1962) of the Washington Bullets, Golden State Warriors and Philadelphia 76ers, at 7 ft 6¾ in. He made his pro debut in 1985.

Highest score   The highest aggregate score in an NBA match is 370, when the Detroit Pistons (186) beat the Denver Nuggets (184) at Denver, CO on 13 Dec 1983. Overtime was played after a 145–145 tie in regulation time. The record in regulation time is 320, when the Golden State Warriors beat Denver 162–158 at Denver on 2 Nov 1990. The most points in a half is 107, by the Phoenix Suns in the first half *v* the Denver Nuggets on 11 Nov 1990. The most points in a quarter is 58, in the fourth quarter, by Buffalo *v* Boston on 20 Oct 1972.

Winning streak   The Los Angeles Lakers won a record 33 NBA games in succession from 5 Nov 1971 to 7 Jan 1972, as during the 1971/72 season they won a record 69 games with 13 losses.

Highest points   Mats Wermelin, 13 years old (Sweden), scored all 272 points in a 272–0 win in a regional boys' basketball tournament in Stockholm, Sweden on 5 Feb 1974.

The record score by a woman is 156 points by Marie Boyd (now Eichler) of Central High School, Lonaconing, MD in a 163–3 defeat of Ursaline Academy, Cumbria on 25 Feb 1924.

Dribbling   Peter del Masto (USA) dribbled a basketball without "traveling" from near Lee to Provincetown, MA, a distance of 265.2 miles, from 12–25 Aug 1989.

Bob Nickerson of Gallitzin, PA, Dave Davlin of Garland, TX and Jeremy Kable of Highspire, PA have each successfully demonstrated the ability to dribble four basketballs simultaneously.

Longest goal   Christopher Eddy (b. 13 Jul 1971) scored a field goal measured at 90 ft 2¼ in for Fairview High School *v*. Iroquois High School at Erie, PA on 25 Feb 1989. The shot was made as time expired in overtime and it won the game for Fairview, 51–50.

Shooting speed   The greatest goal-shooting demonstration was by Ted St Martin of Jacksonville, FL who, on 25 Jun 1977, scored 2,036 consecutive free throws. On 11 Jun 1992 Jeff Liles scored 231 out of 240 free throws in 10 minutes at Southern Nazarene University, Bethany, OK. He repeated this total of 231 (241 attempts) on 16 June. This speed record is achieved using one ball and one rebounder.

In 24 hours Fred Newman scored 20,371 free throws from a total of 22,049 taken (92.39 percent) at Caltech, Pasadena, CA on 29–30 Sep 1990.

Steve Bontrager (USA; b. 1 Mar 1959) of the British team Polycell Kingston scored 21 points in one minute from seven positions in a demonstration for the British Broadcasting Corporation's *Record Breakers* TV program on 29 Oct 1986.

NBA RECORDS

Career Records

Points	38,387	Kareem Abdul-Jabbar: Milwaukee Bucks, Los Angeles Lakers	1970–89
Field-goal percentage	.599	Artis Gilmore: Chicago Bulls, San Antonio Spurs, Boston Celtics; min. 2,000 field goals	1977–88
Free throws made	8,395	Moses Eugene Malone: Buffalo Braves, Houston Rockets, Philadelphia 76ers, Washington Bullets, Atlanta Hawks, Milwaukee Bucks	1976–92
Free-throw percentage	900	Rick Barry: San Francisco / Golden State Warriors, Houston Rockets; 3,818 from 4,243 attempts (technically .89983)	1965–80
Field goals	15,837	Kareem Abdul-Jabbar	1970–89
Rebounds	23,924	Wilt Chamberlain: Philadelphia / San Francisco Warriors, Philadelphia 76ers, Los Angeles Lakers	1960–73
Assists	9,921	Earvin "Magic" Johnson: Los Angeles Lakers	1980–91
Steals	2,275	Maurice Cheeks: Philadelphia 76ers, San Antonio Spurs, New York Knicks, Atlanta Hawks	1979–92

Season Records

Points	4,029	Wilt Chamberlain: Philadelphia Warriors	1962
Field-goal percentage	.727	Wilt Chamberlain: Los Angeles Lakers; 426 of 586 attempts	1972
Free throws made	840	Jerry West: Los Angeles Lakers; from 977 attempts	1966
Free-throw percentage	.958	Calvin Murphy: Houston Rockets; 206 of 215 attempts	1981
Field goals	1,597	Wilt Chamberlain: Philadelphia Warriors	1962
Rebounds	2,149	Wilt Chamberlain: Philadelphia Warriors	1961
Assists	1,164	John Stockton: Utah Jazz	1991
Steals	301	Alvin Robertson: San Antonio Spurs	1986

Single-Game Records

Points	100	Wilt Chamberlain: Philadelphia Warriors v New York Knicks	2 Mar 1962
Field goals	36	Wilt Chamberlain	2 Mar 1962
Free throws made	28	Wilt Chamberlain	2 Mar 1962
	28	Adrian Dantley: Utah Jazz v Houston Rockets	5 Jan 1984
Rebounds	55	Wilt Chamberlain: Philadelphia Warriors v Boston Celtics	24 Nov 1960

| Assists | 30 | Scott Skiles: Orlando Magic v Denver Nuggets | 30 Dec 1990 |
| Steals | 11 | Larry Kenon: San Antonio Spurs v Kansas City Kings | 26 Dec 1976 |

NBA PLAYOFF RECORDS

Career Records

Most games played	237	Kareem Abdul-Jabbar: Milwaukee Bucks, Los Angeles Lakers	1970–89
Points	5,762	Kareem Abdul-Jabbar (in 237 playoff games)	1970–89
Field goals	2,356	Kareem Abdul-Jabbar	1970–89
Free throws made	1,213	Jerry West: Los Angeles Lakers; from 1,507 attempts	1961–74
Assists	2,142	Magic Johnson: Los Angeles Lakers	1980–91
Rebounds	4,104	Bill Russell: Boston Celtics	1957–69

Series Records

Points	284	Elgin Baylor: Los Angeles Lakers (v Boston Celtics); in 7 games	1962
Field goals	113	Wilt Chamberlain: San Francisco (v St Louis); in 6 games	1964
Free throws made	86	Jerry West: Los Angeles Lakers (v Baltimore); in 6 games	1965
Rebounds	220	Wilt Chamberlain: Philadelphia 76ers (v Boston Celtics); in 7 games	1965
Assists	115	John Stockton: Utah Jazz (v Los Angeles Lakers); in 7 games	1988

Single-Game records

Points	63	Michael Jordan: Chicago Bulls (v Boston Celtics); includes two overtime periods	20 Apr 1986
	61	Elgin Baylor: Los Angeles Lakers (v Boston Celtics)	14 Apr 1962
Field goals	24	Wilt Chamberlain: Philadelphia 76ers v Syracuse Nationals; in 42 attempts	14 Mar 1960
	24	John Havlicek: Boston Celtics (v Atlanta Hawks); in 36 attempts	1 Apr 1973
	24	Michael Jordan: Chicago Bulls (v Cleveland Cavaliers); in 45 attempts	1 May 1988
Free throws made	30	Bob Cousy: Boston Celtics (v Syracuse Nationals); includes four overtime periods and 32 attempts	21 Mar 1953
	23	Michael Jordan: Chicago Bulls (v New York Knicks); in 28 attempts	14 May 1989
Rebounds	41	Wilt Chamberlain: Philadelphia 76ers (v Boston Celtics)	5 Apr 1967
Assists	24	Magic Johnson: Los Angeles Lakers (v Phoenix Suns)	15 May 1984
	24	John Stockton: Utah Jazz (v Los Angeles Lakers)	17 May 1988

Vertical dunk height record Joey Johnson of San Pedro, CA successfully dunked a basketball at a rim height of 11 ft 7 in at the One-on-One Collegiate Challenge on 25 Jun 1990 at Trump Plaza Hotel and Casino in Atlantic City, NJ.

Youngest and oldest player The youngest NBA player has been Bill Willoughby (b. 20 May 1957), who made his debut for the Atlanta Hawks on 23 Oct 1975 at 18 yr 156 days. The oldest NBA regular player was Kareem Abdul-Jabbar, who made his last appearance for the Los Angeles Lakers at age 42 yr 59 days in 1989.

NBA record attendance The Minnesota Timberwolves set an NBA record for total attendance of 1,072,572 during the 1989/90 season, the Timberwolves' first in the league. The average crowd was 26,160 fans at the Metrodome in Minneapolis.

Winning margin The greatest winning margin in an NBA game is 68 points, by which the Cleveland Cavaliers, 148, beat the Miami Heat, 80, on 17 Dec 1991.

Coaches The most successful coach in NBA history has been Arnold "Red" Auerbach (b. 1917) with 938 wins (1,037 including playoffs), with the Washington Capitols 1946–49, the Tri-Cities Blackhawks 1949–50, and the Boston Celtics 1950–66. He led the Boston Celtics to a record nine NBA titles, including eight in succession in 1959–66.

Pat Riley has won a record 117 playoff games, 102 with the Los Angeles Lakers (1981–90) and 15 with the New York Knicks (1992–93), to set the NBA all-time mark.

The most games coached is 1,722, by Bill Fitch: Cleveland Cavaliers, 1970–79; Boston Celtics, 1979–83; Houston Rockets, 1983–88; New Jersey Nets, 1989–92. Fitch's career totals 845 wins and 877 losses.

NCAA RECORDS

Most wins In this competition, first held in 1939, the record for most Division I titles is 10, by the University of California at Los Angeles (UCLA), 1964–65, 1967–73, 1975.

Most valuable player The only player to have been voted the most valuable player in the NCAA final three times has been Lew Alcindor of UCLA in 1967–69. He subsequently changed his name to Kareem Abdul-Jabbar.

Most points The most points by an individual for an NCAA Division I team in a game is 100, by Frank Selvy for Furman *v* Newberry on 13 Feb 1954, including a record 41 field goals. Kevin Bradshaw scored 72 points for US International *v* Loyola-Marymount, two Division I teams, on 5 Jan 1991. In Division II, Clarence "Bevo" Francis scored 113 points for Rio Grande *v* Hillsdale on 2 Feb 1954.

NCAA MEN'S DIVISION I RECORDS
Through 1992/93 Season

Career Records

Points	3,667	Peter "Pistol Pete" Maravich: Louisiana State	1968–70
Field goals	1,387	Pistol Pete Maravich: Louisiana State	1968–70
Best percentage	.685	Stephen Sheffler: Purdue	1987–90
Rebounds	2,243	Tom Gola: La Salle	1952–55
Assists	1,076	Bobby Hurley:, Duke	1990–93

Season Records

Points	1,381	Pistol Pete Maravich: Louisiana State	1970
Field goals	522	Pistol Pete Maravich: Lousiana State (from 1,168 attempts)	1970
Best percentage	.749	Steve Johnson: Oregon State	1981
Three-point goals	.158	Darrin Fitzgerald: Butler (in 362 attempts)	1987
Free throws	355	Frank Selvy: Furman (in 444 attempts)	1954
Best percentage	.959	Craig Collins: Penn State	1985
Rebounds	734	Walt Dukes: Seton Hall (in 33 games)	1953
Assists	406	Mark Wade: Nevada–Las Vegas	1987
Blocked shots	207	David Robinson: Navy (in 35 games)	1986

Game Records

Points	100	Frank Selvy: Furman (v Newberry)	13 Feb 1954
Field goals	41	Frank Selvy: Furman	13 Feb 1954
Three-point goals	14	Dave Jamerson: Ohio (v Charleston)	21 Dec 1989
Free throws	30	Pistol Pete Maravich: Louisiana State (v Oregon State)	22 Dec 1969
Rebounds	51	Bill Chambers: William and Mary (v Virginia)	14 Feb 1953
Assists	22	Tony Fairly: Baptist (v Armstrong State)	9 Feb 1987
	22	Avery Johnson: Southern–B.R. (v Texas Southern)	25 Jan 1988
	22	Sherman Douglas: Syracuse (v Providence)	28 Jan 1989
Blocked shots	14	David Robinson: Navy (v North Carolina–Wilmington)	4 Jan 1986
	14	Shawn Bradley: BYU (v Eastern Kentucky)	7 Dec 1990

Career and season scoring Peter "Pistol Pete" Maravich (1947–88) set unmatched NCAA scoring records while at Louisiana State University: 1,138 points, an average 43.8 per game, in 1968; 1,148 at 44.2 per game in 1969; and the season record, 1,381 at 44.5 per game in 1970—the three highest season averages in NCAA history, for a total 3,667 points in 83 games. Maravich scored a career record 1,387 field goals. The career field goal percentage record (minimum 400 scored) is 67.8 percent by Steve Johnson, 828 of 1,222 attempts for Oregon State, 1976–81. In Division II competition, Travis Grant of Kentucky State scored a record 4,045 points in 121 games, 1969–72, and a

NCAA WOMEN'S DIVISION I
CHAMPIONSHIP GAME RECORDS
Through 1992/93 Season

Team Records

Most championships	3	Tennessee 1987, 1989, 1991
Most points	97	Texas (*v* USC) 1986
Most field goals	40	Texas (*v* USC) 1986
Highest field-goal percentage	.588	Texas (*v* USC; 40–68) 1986
Most 3-point field goals	11	Stanford (*v* Auburn) 1990
Rebounds	57	Old Dominion (*v* Georgia) 1985
Assists (since 1985)	22	Texas (*v* USC) 1986
Blocked shots (since 1988)	7	Tennessee (*v* Auburn) 1989
Steals (since 1988)	12	Louisiana Tech (*v* Auburn) 1988

Individual Records

Most points	47	Sheryl Swoopes, Texas Tech (*v* Ohio State) 1993
Most field goals	16	Sheryl Swoopes, Texas Tech (*v* Ohio State) 1993
Highest field-goal percentage	.889	Jennifer White, Louisiana Tech (*v* USC; 8–9) 1983
Most 3-point field goals (since 1988)	6	Katy Steding, Stanford (*v* Auburn) 1990
Rebounds	20	Tracy Claxton, Old Dominion (*v* Georgia) 1985
Assists (since 1985)	10	Kamie Ethridge, Texas (*v* USC) 1986
	10	Melissa McCray, Tennessee (*v* Auburn) .1989
Blocked shots (since 1988)	5	Sheila Frost, Tennessee (*v* Auburn) 1989
Steals (since 1988)	6	Erica Westbrooks, Louisiana Tech (*v* Auburn) 1988

season average record was set at 46.5 points by Clarence "Bevo" Francis, with 1,255 points in 27 games for Rio Grande in 1954. In all collegiate competition, Philip Hutcheson of David Lipscomb University scored a record 4,106 points in his career, 1987–90.

Coaches   The man to have coached most victories in NCAA Division I competition is Adolph Rupp (1901–77) at Kentucky, with 876 wins (and 190 losses), 1931–72. John Wooden (b. 1910) coached UCLA to all its 10 NCAA titles.

Henry Iba (1904–93) coached the most games, 1,105, with Northwest Missouri State 1930–33, Colorado 1934, and Oklahoma State 1935–70. Iba's career record was 767 wins and 338 losses.

Record attendances   The highest paid attendance for a college game is 66,144, for Louisiana State's 82–80 victory over Georgetown at the Louisiana Superdome, New Orleans, LA on 28 Jan 1989.

Women's   The record for a women's college game is 24,563, in Knoxville, TN for a game between the University of Tennessee and the University of Texas on 9 Dec 1987.

WOMEN'S BASKETBALL

Women's championships   In this competition, first held in 1982, the record for most Division I titles is three, by Tennessee, 1987, 1989 and 1991. The regular-season game aggregate record is 261, when St Joseph's (Indiana) beat North Kentucky 131–130 on 27 Feb 1988.

Coaches   Jody Conradt of the University of Texas has won the most games in Women's NCAA Division I competition, with 620 victories through the 1992/93 season.

Most points   The women's record for most points scored in a college career is 4,061, by Pearl Moore. She scored 177 points in eight games for Anderson Junior College, Anderson, SC, and 3,884 points for Francis Marion College, Florence, SC, 1975–79. Francis Marion was a member of the Association of Intercollegiate Athletics for Women (AIWA) during Moore's career. The career points leader in NCAA Division I competition is Patricia Hoskins of Mississippi Valley State, with 3,122 points (1985–89).

OTHER RECORDS

Olympic Games   Six men and two women have won two Olympic gold medals: Robert Albert "Bob" Kurland (b. 23 Dec 1924) in 1948 and 1952; William Marion "Bill" Houghland (b. 20 Jun 1930) in 1952 and 1956; Michael Jordan, Patrick Ewing, and Chris Mullin, all in 1984 and 1992; Burdette Eliele Haldorson (b. 12 Jan 1934) in 1956 and 1960; Anne Theresa Donovan (b. 1 Nov 1961) and Theresa Edwards, both in 1984 and 1988.

Most titles Olympic   The United States has won 10 men's Olympic titles. From the time the sport was introduced to the Games in 1936 until 1972, the USA won 63 consecutive matches in the Olympic Games, until it lost 51–50 to the

BASKETBALL SPINNING
(Above) Count them! One, two . . . fifteen, sixteen. Bruce Crevier sets a new basketball spinning record.

BASKETBALL
(Left) Michael Jordan in action for the US Dream Team against Croatia in the 1992 Olympics in Barcelona, Spain. (Photo: Allsport/ Mike Powell)

USSR in the disputed final match in Munich, Germany. Since then it has won a further 29 matches and has had another loss to the USSR (in 1988).

The women's title has been won a record three times by the USSR, in 1976, 1980 and 1992 (by the Unified team from the republics of the former USSR). The USA team won the title in 1984 and 1988.

World The USSR has won most titles at both the men's World Championships (instituted 1950) with three (1967, 1974 and 1982) and women's (instituted 1953), with six (1959, 1964, 1967, 1971, 1975 and 1983). Yugoslavia has also won three men's world titles: 1970, 1978 and 1990.

Most valuable basket Don Calhoun, a spectator at a Chicago Bulls home game on 14 Apr 1993, sank a basket from the opposite foul line—a distance of 75 feet—and won $1 million. He was randomly picked from the crowd to try his luck as part of a promotional stunt.

Basketball spinning The record for basketball spinning is held by Bruce Crevier (USA), who balanced 16 basketballs across his whole body in February 1992.

Highest score The NCAA aggregate record is 399, when Troy State (258) beat De Vry Institute, Atlanta (141) at Troy, AL on 12 Jan 1992. Troy's total was also the highest individual team score in a game.

BIATHLON

Most titles Olympic Two Olympic individual titles have been won: by Magnar Solberg (Norway; b. 4 Feb 1937), in 1968 and 1972; and by Franz-Peter Rötsch (East Germany; b. 19 Apr 1964) at both 10 km and 20 km in 1988. The USSR has won all six 4 × 7.5 km relay titles, from 1968 to 1988. Aleksandr Ivanovich Tikhonov (b. 2 Jan 1947), who was a member of the first four teams, also won a silver in the 1968 20 km.

World Championships Frank Ullrich (East Germany; b. 24 Jan 1958) has won a record six individual world titles—four at 10 km, 1978–81, including the 1980 Olympics, and two at 20 km, 1982–83. Aleksandr Tikhonov was on 10 winning Soviet relay teams, 1968–80, and won four individual titles. The Biathlon World Cup (instituted 1979) was won four times by Frank Ullrich, 1978 and 1980–82; and by Franz Peter Rötsch (East Germany), 1984–85 and 1987–88.

Women The first World Championships were held in 1984. The most individual titles is three, by Anne-Elinor Elvebakk (Norway), 10 km 1988, 7.5 km

1989–90. Kaya Parve (USSR) has won six titles, two individual and four relay, 1984–86, 1988. A women's World Cup began in 1988 and women's biathlon was included at the 1992 Olympics. Anfisa Restzova (Russia) is the only double World Cup winner 1992–93, and won the Olympic 7.5 km gold medal.

United States National Championships   In this competition, first held in 1965 in Rosendale, NY, men's events have been staged annually. Women's events were included in 1985.

Most titles   Lyle Nelson has won seven National Championships: five in the 10 km, 1976, 1979, 1981, 1985 and 1987; two in the 20 km, 1977 and 1985. Anna Sonnerup holds the women's record with five titles: two in the 10 km, 1986–87; two in the 15 km, 1989 and 1991; and one in the 7.5 km in 1989.

BILLIARDS

Most titles   The greatest number of World Championships (instituted 1870) won by one player is eight, by John Roberts, Jr. (Great Britain; 1847–1919), in 1870 (twice), 1871, 1875 (twice), 1877 and 1885 (twice). The record for world amateur titles is four, by Robert James Percival Marshall (Australia; b. 10 Apr 1910), in 1936, 1938, 1951 and 1962.

Youngest champion   The youngest winner of the world professional title is Mike Russell (b. 3 Jun 1969), age 20 yr 49 days, when he won at Leura, Australia on 23 Jul 1989.

Highest breaks   Tom Reece (1873–1953) made an unfinished break of 499,135, including 249,152 cradle cannons (two points each) in 85 hr 49 min against Joe Chapman at Burroughes' Hall, Soho Square, London, Great Britain between 3 Jun and 6 Jul 1907. This was not recognized, because press and public were not continuously present.

The highest certified break made by the anchor cannon is 42,746, by William Cook (England) from 29 May to 7 Jun 1907.

The official world record under the then balkline rule is 1,784, by Joe Davis in the United Kingdom Championship on 29 May 1936.

Walter Albert Lindrum (Australia; 1898–1960) made an official break of 4,137 in 2 hr 55 min against Joe Davis at Thurston's on 19–20 Jan 1932, before the balkline rule was in force.

Geet Sethi (India) made a break of 1,276 in the World Professional Championship in Bombay, India on 1 Oct 1992.

Fastest century in billiards   Walter Lindrum made an unofficial 100 break in 27.5 sec in Australia on 10 Oct 1952. His official record is 100 in 46.0 sec, set in Sydney, Australia in 1941.

The highest break recorded in amateur competition is 1,149, by Michael Ferreira (India) at Calcutta, India on 15 Dec 1978.

Under the more stringent "two pot" rule, restored on 1 Jan 1983, the highest break is Ferreira's 962 unfinished, in a tournament at Bombay, India on 29 Apr 1986.

THREE CUSHION

Most titles William F. "Willie" Hoppe (USA; 1887–1959) won 51 billiards championships in all forms, spanning the pre- and post-international era, from 1906 to 1952.

UMB The world governing body of three cushion billiards—the *Union Mondiale de Billiard* (UMB)—was formed in 1928. Raymond Ceulemans (Belgium; b. 12 Jul 1935) has won 20 world three-cushion championships (1963–73, 1975–80, 1983, 1985 and 1990).

BOARD GAMES

Largest The world's biggest board game was a version of the game "Goose," and was organized by "Jong Nederland." It stretched for 2,090 ft and was played by 1,631 participants at Someren, Netherlands on 16 Sep 1989.

BINGO

Bingo is a lottery game which, under the name of keno, was developed in the 1880s from lotto, whose origin is thought to be the 17th-century Italian game *tumbule*. The winner was the first to complete a random selection of numbers from 1 to 90. The US version called Bingo differs in that the selection is from 1 to 75.

Largest house The largest "house" in bingo sessions was 15,756, at the Canadian National Exhibition, Toronto on 19 Aug 1983. Staged by the Variety Club of Ontario Tent Number 28, there was total prize money of $Cdn250,000 with a record one-game payout of $Cdn100,000.

Earliest and latest full house A "full house" call occurred on the 15th number by Norman A. Wilson at Guide Post Working Men's Club, Bedlington, Great Britain on 22 Jun 1978; by Anne Wintle of Brynrethin, Great Britain, on a bus trip to Bath, Great Britain on 17 Aug 1982; and by Shirley Lord at Kahibah Bowling Club, New South Wales, Australia on 24 Oct 1983.

"House" was not called until the 86th number at the Hillsborough Working Men's Club, Sheffield, Great Britain on 11 Jan 1982. There were 32 winners.

CHECKERS

World champions Walter Hellman (USA; 1916–75) won a record eight world titles during his tenure as world champion, 1948–75.

Shortest backgammon game   Alan Malcolm Beckerson (b. 21 Feb 1938) devised a game of just 16 throws in 1982.

Domino toppling   The greatest number set up single-handedly and toppled is 281,581 out of 320,236, by Klaus Friedrich, 22, at Fürth, Germany on 27 Jan 1984. The dominoes fell within 12 min 57.3 sec, having taken 31 days (10 hr daily) to set up.
   Thirty students at Delft, Eindhoven and Twente Technical Universities in the Netherlands set up 1,500,000 dominoes representing all the European Community member countries. Of these, 1,382,101 were toppled by one push on 2 Jan 1988.

Domino stacking   David Coburn successfully stacked 291 dominoes on a single supporting domino on 19 Aug 1988 in Miami, FL.

Solitaire   The shortest time taken to complete the game of solitaire is 10.0 sec by Stephen Twigge at Scissett Baths (Great Britain) on 2 Aug 1991.

Youngest and oldest national champion   Asa A. Long (b. 20 Aug 1904) became the youngest US national champion, at age 18 yr 64 days, when he won in Boston, MA on 23 Oct 1922. He became the oldest, age 79 yr 334 days, when he won his sixth title in Tupelo, MS on 21 Jul 1984. He was also world champion from 1934 to 1938.

Most opponents   Charles Walker played a record 229 games simultaneously, winning 227, drawing 1 and losing 1, at the International Checkers Hall of Fame, Petal, MS on 25 Jan 1992.
   The largest number of opponents played without a defeat or draw is 172, by Nate Cohen of Portland, ME at Portland on 26 Jul 1981. This was not a simultaneous attempt, but consecutive play over a period of four hours.
   Newell W. Banks (1887–1977) played 140 games simultaneously, winning 133 and drawing 7, in Chicago, IL in 1933. His total playing time was 145 min, thus averaging about one move per sec. In 1947 he played blindfolded for 4 hr per day for 45 consecutive days, winning 1,331 games, drawing 54 and losing only 2, while playing six games at a time.

Longest game   In competition the prescribed rate of play is not less than 30 moves per hour, with the average game lasting about 90 min. In 1958 a game between Dr Marion Tinsley (USA) and Derek Oldbury (Great Britain) lasted 7 hr 30 min (played under the 5-minutes-a-move rule).

CHESS

World championships   World champions have been officially recognized since 1886. The longest undisputed tenure was 26 yr 337 days, by Dr Emanuel Lasker (1868–1941) of Germany, from 1894 to 1921.
   The women's world championship title was held by Vera Francevna Stevenson-Menchik (USSR, later Great Britain; 1906–44) from 1927 until her death, and was successfully defended a record seven times.

Highest Prize

**Gary Kasparov and Nigel Short will contest the chess World
Championship, beginning in September 1993. The prize money is a
record $2.5 million, with the winner receiving $1.5 million.
(Photos: Allsport/Howard Boylan & Shaun Botterill)**

The first American to be regarded as world champion was Paul Charles Morphy (1837–89) in 1858.

Team   The USSR has won the biennial men's team title (Olympiad) a record 18 times between 1952 and 1990. The women's title has been won 11 times by the USSR from its introduction in 1957 to 1986, with Georgia winning in 1992.

The USA has won the men's title five times: 1931, 1933, 1935, 1937 and 1976.

Youngest   Gary Kimovich Kasparov (USSR; b. 13 Apr 1963) won the title on 9 Nov 1985 at age 22 yr 210 days. Maya Grigoryevna Chiburdanidze (USSR; b. 17 Jan 1961) won the women's title in 1978 when only 17.

Oldest   Wilhelm Steinitz (Austria, later USA; 1836–1900) was 58 yr 10 days when he lost his title to Lasker on 26 May 1894.

Most active   Anatoly Yevgenyevich Karpov (USSR; b. 23 May 1951) in his tenure as champion, 1975–85, averaged 45.2 competitive games per year, played in 32 tournaments and finished first in 26.

Grand Masters   The youngest individual to qualify as an International Grand Master is Judit Polgar (Hungary; b. 23 Jul 1976), aged 15 yr 150 days on 20 Dec 1991.

United States   The youngest US Grand Master was Robert James "Bobby" Fischer (b. 9 Mar 1943) in 1958.

Masters   In August 1981, Stuart Rachels of Birmingham, AL became the

---

Most moves   The Master chess game with the most moves on record was one of 269 moves, when Ivan Nikolić drew with Goran Arsović in a Belgrade, Yugoslavia tournament, on 17 Feb 1989. The game took a total of 20 hr 15 min.

Slowest and longest chess games   The slowest reported moving (before time clocks were used) in an official event is reputed to have been by Louis Paulsen (Germany; 1833–91) against Paul Charles Morphy (USA; 1837–84) at the first American Chess Congress, NY on 29 Oct 1857. The game ended in a draw on move 56 after 15 hours of play, of which Paulsen used c. 11 hours.

Grand Master Friedrich Sämisch (Germany; 1896–1975) ran out of the allotted time (2 hr 30 min for 45 moves) after only 12 moves, in Prague, Czechoslovakia, in 1938.

The slowest move played, since time clocks were introduced, was at Vigo, Spain in 1980 when Francisco R. Torres Trois (b. 3 Sep 1946) took 2 hr 20 min for his seventh move *v* Luis M.C.P. Santos (b. 30 Jun 1955).

Oldest chess pieces   The oldest pieces identified as chess pieces were found at Nashipur, dated to c. A.D. 900.

---

youngest person in the history of the United States Chess Foundation to achieve a master rating, at the age of 11 yr 10 months.

Highest rating   The highest rating ever attained on the officially adopted Elo System (devised by Arpad E. Elo [1903–92]) is 2,805, by Gary Kasparov (USSR) at the end of 1992.

The highest-rated woman player is Judit Polgar, who achieved a peak rating of 2,595 at the end of 1992.

Fewest games lost by a world champion   José Raúl Capablanca (Cuba; 1888–1942) lost only 34 games (out of 571) in his adult career, 1909–39. He was unbeaten from 10 Feb 1916 to 21 Mar 1924 (63 games) and was world champion 1921–27.

US Championships   The most wins since the US Championships became determined by match play competition in 1888 is eight, by Bobby Fischer, 1958–66. Fischer, world champion 1972–75, reached a rating on the Elo system of 2,785, the highest ever until surpassed by Gary Kasparov in 1989.

Most opponents   The record for most consecutive games played is 663, by Vlastimil Hort (Czechoslovakia, later Germany; b. 12 Jan 1944) over $32\frac{1}{2}$ hours at Porz, Germany on 5–6 Oct 1984. He played 60–120 opponents at a time, scoring over 80 percent wins and averaging 30 moves per game. He also holds the record for most games played simultaneously, 201 during 550 consecutive games of which he lost only 10, in Seltjarnes, Iceland on 23–24 Apr 1977.

Eric G.J. Knoppert (Netherlands; b. 20 Sep 1959) played 500 games of 10-minute chess against opponents, averaging 2,002 on the Elo scale, on 13–16 Sep 1985. He scored 413 points (1 for win, $\frac{1}{2}$ for draw), a success rate of 82.6 percent.

MONOPOLY

Monopoly, a real-estate trading game, of which Parker Brothers has sold in excess of 85 million copies worldwide in 19 languages (the most recent in Russian), was devised by Charles Darrow (1889–1967) of Germantown, PA, in 1935. While unemployed as a heating engineer during the Depression, he created the game using the street names of Atlantic City, NJ, where he spent his vacations.

World Champions   The current holder of the World Monopoly Championship trophy and medal is Ikuo Hiyakuta of Japan. He won the eighth World Monopoly Tournament (held every three years under the auspices of Parker Brothers) at the Park Lane Hotel, London, Great Britain in 1988 after two days of grueling play. His prize was $15,140 and a personal computer.

SCRABBLE CROSSWORD GAME

Highest scores   The highest competitive game score is 1,049 by Phil Appleby (b. 9 Dec 1957) in June 1989. His opponent scored 253, and the margin of victory, 796 points, is also a record. His score included a single turn of 374 for the word "OXIDIZERS."

The highest competitive single-turn score recorded, however, is 392, by Dr

Saladin Karl Khoshnaw (of Kurdish origin) in Manchester, Great Britain in April 1982. He laid down "CAZIQUES," which means "native chiefs of West Indian aborigines."

Most tournaments   Chuck Armstrong, a hospital worker from Saline, MI, has won the most tournaments—65 to the end of 1989.

World Championships   The first world championship was held in London, Great Britain in 1991 and was played in English. The winner was Peter Morris (USA; b. 1962), who collected a first prize of $10,000.

BOBSLED AND LUGE

BOBSLEDDING

Most titles   The Olympic four-man bob title (instituted 1924) has been won five times by Switzerland (1924, 1936, 1956, 1972 and 1988).

The Olympic two-man bob title (instituted 1932) has been won three times by Switzerland (1948, 1980 and 1988).

The most gold medals won by an individual is three, by Meinhard Nehmer (East Germany; b. 13 Jun 1941) and by Bernhard Germeshausen (East Germany; b. 21 Aug 1951) in the 1976 two-man, 1976 and 1980 four-man events.

The most medals won is six (two gold, two silver, two bronze) by Eugenio Monti (Italy; b. 23 Jan 1928), 1956 to 1968.

World and Olympic   The world four-man bob title (instituted 1924) has been won 20 times by Switzerland (1924, 1936, 1939, 1947, 1954–57, 1971–73, 1975, 1982–83, 1986–90, 1993), including its five Olympic victories. Switzerland won the two-man title 16 times (1935, 1947–50, 1953, 1955, 1977–80 and 1982–83, 1987, 1990 and 1992), including its three Olympic successes.

Eugenio Monti was a member of 11 world championship crews, eight two-man and three four-man, in 1957–68.

United States   Two American bobsledders have won two gold medals: driver William Mead Lindsley "Billy" Fiske III (1911–40) and crewman Clifford Barton Grey (1887–1941) in 1928 and 1932. At age 16 yr 260 days in 1928, Fiske was America's youngest-ever Winter Games gold medalist.

LUGEING

Most titles   The most successful rider in the World Championships was Thomas Köhler (East Germany; b. 25 Jun 1940), who won the single-seater title in 1962, 1964 (Olympic) and 1967, and shared the two-seater title in 1965, 1967 and 1968 (Olympic). Margit Schumann (East Germany; b. 14 Sep 1952) has won five women's titles, 1973–75, 1976 (Olympic) and 1977.

Steffi Walter (nee Martin [East Germany]; b. 17 Sep 1962) became the first rider to win two Olympic single-seater luge titles, with victories at the women's event in 1984 and 1988.

United States National Championships   This competition was inaugurated in 1974.

Most titles   Frank Masley has won a record six men's championships, 1979, 1981–83 and 1987–88. Bonny Warner has won a record five women's titles, 1983–84, 1987–88 and 1990.

Fastest speed in lugeing   The fastest recorded photo-timed speed is 85.38 mph, by Asle Strand (Norway) at Tandådalens Linbana, Sälen, Sweden on 1 May 1982.

TOBOGGANING

Oldest club   The St Moritz Tobogganing Club, Switzerland, founded in 1887, is the oldest toboggan club in the world. It is notable for being the home of the Cresta Run, which dates from 1884.

Cresta Run   The course is 3,977 ft long with a drop of 514 ft, and the record is 50.41 sec (average. 53.79 mph) by Christian Bertschinger (Switzerland; b. 8 Feb 1964) on 23 Feb 1992. On 20 Jan 1991 he set a record from Junction (2,920 ft) of 41.45 sec.

The greatest number of wins in the Grand National (instituted in 1885) is eight, by the 1948 Olympic champion Nino Bibbia (Italy; b. 15 Mar 1922) in 1960–64, 1966, 1968 and 1973, and by Franco Gansser in 1981, 1983–86, 1988–89 and 1991. The greatest number of wins in the Curzon Cup (instituted 1910) is eight, by Bibbia in 1950, 1957–58, 1960, 1962–64 and 1969.

The only men to have won the four most important races (Curzon Cup, Brabazon Trophy, Morgan Cup and Grand National) in one season are Bruno Bischofberger (1972), Paul Felder (1974), Nico Baracchi (1982), Franco Gansser (1988) and Christian Bertschinger (1992), all from Switzerland.

The oldest person to have ridden the Cresta Run successfully is Robin Todhunter (Great Britain; b. 10 Mar 1903), aged 83 yr 329 days on 2 Feb 1987.

Oldest gold medalist   The oldest age at which a gold medal has been won at any sport at the Winter Olympics is 49 yr 7 days, for James Jay O'Brien (USA; 1883–1940) at four-man bob in 1932.

Longest slide   The Bromley Alpine Slide on Route 11 in Peru, VT has a length of 4,000 ft and a vertical drop of 700 ft.

BOWLING

World Championships The World (*Fédération Internationale des Quilleurs*) Championships were instituted for men in 1954 and for women in 1963.

The highest pinfall in the individual men's event is 5,963 (in 28 games) by Ed Luther (USA) at Milwaukee, WI on 28 Aug 1971.

For the current schedule of 24 games the men's record is 5,261, by Richard Clay "Rick" Steelsmith (b. 1 Jun 1964), and the women's record is 4,894, by Sandra Jo Shiery (USA), both at Helsinki, Finland in June 1987.

The World Cup (instituted 1965) is contested annually by the national champions of each member of FIQ. The most wins is three, by Paeng Neponuceno (Philippines; b. 30 Jan 1957), 1976, 1980 and 1992.

Highest scores The highest individual score for three sanctioned games (out of a possible 900) is 899, by Thomas Jordan (USA; b. 27 Oct 1966) at Union, NJ on 7 Mar 1989. He followed with a 299, setting a four-game series record of 1,198 pins.

The record by a woman is 864, by Jeanne Maiden (b. 10 Nov 1957) of Tacoma, WA at Sodon, OH on 23 Nov 1986. This series includes a record 40 consecutive strikes.

Youngest and oldest 300 shooters The youngest bowler to score 300 is said to be Richard Daff, Jr. of Crownsville, MD (b. 28 Aug 1978), who performed this feat at age 11, on 8 Apr 1990. The oldest bowler to score 300 is Leo Sites of Wichita, KS, who performed the feat on 10 Apr 1985 at age 80.

PROFESSIONAL BOWLERS ASSOCIATION

The Professional Bowlers Association (PBA) was founded in 1958 by Eddie Elias and is based in Akron, OH.

Most titles Earl Anthony (b. 27 Apr 1938) of Dublin, CA has won a lifetime total of 41 PBA titles. The record number of titles won in one PBA season is eight, by Mark Roth (b. 10 Apr 1951) of Lake Heights, NJ, in 1978.

Consecutive titles Only three bowlers have ever won three consecutive professional tournaments—Dick Weber (b. 23 Dec 1929) (three times), in 1959, 1960 and 1961; Johnny Petraglia (b. 3 Mar 1947) in 1971; and Mark Roth in 1977.

Perfect games A total of 141 perfect (300-pin) games were bowled in PBA tournaments in 1990, the most ever for one year.

Dick Weber rolled three perfect games in one tournament (Houston, TX) in 1965, as did Billy Hardwick (b. 25 Jul 1941) of Louisville, KY (in the Japan Gold Cup competition) in 1968, John Wilcox (at Detroit, MI), in 1979, Norm Meyers of St Louis (at Peoria, IL) in 1979, Ray Shackelford of Hartwood, VA (at St Louis, MO) in 1982, Shawn Christensen of Denver (at Denver, CO) in 1984, and Amleto Monacelli (b. 27 Aug 1961) of Venezuela (at Tucson, AZ) in 1989.

> **Highest bowling score—24 hours** A team of six scored 212,692 at Strykers Pleasure Bowl, Bushbury, Great Britain on 20–21 Jun 1992. The American record is held by a team of six called the Brunswick Thursday Nite Stars, who scored 209,072 at Brunswick Sharptown Lanes, Houston, TX on 20–21 Jun 1991.
>
> The highest individual total in 24 hours is 47,566, by Brian Larkins at Hollywood Bowl, Bolton, Great Britain on 9–10 Apr 1993.
>
> **Largest bowling center** The Fukuyama Bowl, Osaka, Japan has 144 lanes. The Tokyo World Lanes Center, Japan, now closed, had 252 lanes.

Amleto Monacelli rolled seven perfect games on the 1989 tour, and Guppy Troup (b. 18 Jan 1950) of Savannah, GA rolled six perfect games on the 1979 tour.

Triple Crown The United States Open, the PBA National Championship and the Firestone Tournament of Champions comprise the Triple Crown of men's professional bowling. No bowler has won each of the three titles in the same year, and only three have managed to win all three during a career.

The first bowler to accumulate the three legs of the triple crown was Billy Hardwick: National Championship (1963); Firestone Tournament of Champions (1965); US Open (1969). Hardwick's feat was matched by Johnny Petraglia: Firestone (1971); US Open (1977); National (1980); and by Pete Weber: Firestone (1987); US Open (1988); National (1989).

US Open Since its inauguration in 1942, the most wins in this tournament is four, by two bowlers: Don Carter in 1953–54 and 1957–58, and Dick Weber in 1962–63 and 1965–66.

PBA National Championship Since its inauguration in 1960, the most wins in this tournament is six, by Earl Anthony in 1973–75 and 1981–83.

Firestone Tournament of Champions Since its inauguration in 1965, the most wins in this tournament is three, by Mike Durbin in 1972, 1982 and 1984.

Highest earners Marshall Holman (b. 29 Sep 1954) won a record $1,692,000 in PBA competitions through 11 Jun 1993. Earl Roderick Anthony (b. 27 Apr 1938) was the first to win $1 million.

Mike Aulby (b. 25 Mar 1960) of Indianapolis, IN set a single-season earnings mark of $298,237 in 1989.

AMERICAN BOWLING CONGRESS

Highest score The highest individual score for three games is 899, by Thomas Jordan at Union, NJ on 7 Mar 1989 (see Bowling—Highest scores). Highest three-game team score is 3,858, by Budweisers of St Louis on 12 Mar 1958.

The highest season average attained in sanctioned competition is 245.63, by Doug Vergouven of Harrisonville, MO in the 1989/90 season.

The all-time ABC-sanctioned two-man single-game record is 600, held jointly by the teams of John Cotta (300) and Steve Larson (300) on 1 May 1981, at the Manteca, CA, Bowling Association Tournament; Jeff Mraz and Dave Roney of Canton, OH on 8 Nov 1987 in the Ann Doubles Classic in Canton, OH; William Gruner and Dave Conway of Oceanside, CA on 27 Feb 1990; and Scott Williams and Willie Hammar of Utica, MI on 7 Jan 1990.

Perfect scores   The highest number of sanctioned 300 games is 42, by Robert Learn, Jr. of Erie, PA.

Two perfect games were rolled back-to-back *twice* by two bowlers: Al Spotts of West Reading, PA, on 14 Mar 1982 and again on 1 Feb 1985; and Gerry Wright of Idaho Falls, ID, on 9 Jan 1992 and again on 26 Feb 1992.

ABC CHAMPIONSHIPS TOURNAMENT

Highest score   The highest three-game series in the ABC Championships tournament in singles is 826, by Ed Deines of Ft Collins, CO in 1991. The best three-game total in any ABC event is 857, by Norm Duke of Albuquerque, NM in 1989. George Hall of Mundelein, IL holds the record for a nine-game All-Events total with 2,227 (747–747–733), set in Wichita, KS in 1989.

ABC Hall of Famers Fred Bujack of Detroit, MI, Bill Lillard of Houston, TX and Nelson Burton, Jr. of St Louis, MO have won the most championships, with eight each.

Bujack shared in three team and four team All-Events titles between 1949 and 1955, and also won the individual All-Events title in 1955. Lillard bowled with regular and team All-Events champions in 1955 and 1956 and with the Classic team champions in 1962 and 1971, and won regular doubles and All-Events titles in 1956. Burton shared in three Classic team titles, two Classic doubles titles, and has won Classic singles twice and Classic All-Events.

Highest doubles   The ABC national tournament record of 561 was set in 1989 by Rick McCardy and Steve Mesmer of Redford, MI. The record score in a

---

Perfect scores   Les Schissler of Denver scored 300 in the Classic team event in 1967, and Ray Williams of Detroit scored 300 in regular team play in 1974, the first two perfect games bowled in team competition. In all, there have been only 160 perfect games in the regular ABC tournament through 1992.

Most tournament appearances   Bill Doehrman of Fort Wayne, IN competed in 71 consecutive ABC tournaments, beginning in 1908. (No tournaments were held 1943–45.)

Consecutive strikes, spares and splits   The record for most consecutive strikes is 40, by Jeanne Maiden (See WIBC, Perfect games.) Mabel Henry of Winchester, KY had 30 consecutive spares in the 1986/87 season. Shirley Tophigh of Las Vegas, NV holds the unenviable record of rolling 14 consecutive splits in 1968/69.

doubles series is 1,505, set in 1991 by Jimmy Johnson (784) of Columbus, OH and Dan Nadeau (721) of Las Vegas, NV.

Best finishes   Mike Newman of Buffalo, NY won the doubles, All-Events, and was on two winning teams in 1989 to tie Ed Lubanski of Detroit, MI and Bill Lillard of Houston, TX as the only men to win four ABC crowns in one year.

Youngest and oldest winners   The youngest champion was Ronnie Knapp of New London, OH, who was a member of the 1963 Booster team champions when he was 16 years old.

The oldest champion was Joe Detloff of Chicago, IL who, at the age of 72, was a winner in the 1965 Booster team event.

The oldest doubles team in ABC competition totaled 165 years in 1955: Jerry Ameling (83) and Joseph Lehnbeutter (82), both from St Louis, MO.

Strikes and spares in a row   In the greatest finish to win an ABC title, Ed Shay set a record of 12 strikes in a row in 1958, when he scored a perfect game for a total of 733 in singles. Most strikes in a row is 20, by Lou Veit of Milwaukee, WI in 1977. The most spares in a row is 23, by Lt Hazen Sweet of Battle Creek, MI in 1950.

WOMEN'S INTERNATIONAL
BOWLING CONGRESS (WIBC)

Highest scores   Patty Ann of Appleton, WI, had a record five-year composite average of 227 through the 1985/86 season. She also had the best one-season average, 232, in the 1983/84 season.

The highest five-woman team score for a three-game series is 3,493, by Lisa's Flowers and Gift Shop, Franklin, WI in the 1989/90 season.

The highest game score by a five-woman team is 3,437, by Goebel Beer of Detroit, MI in the 1988/89 season.

Championship Tournament   The highest score for a three-game series in the annual WIBC Championship Tournament is 773, by Debbie Kuhn of Baltimore, MD in the 1991 singles event. She also holds the record for highest All-Events score (nine games), with 2,036 in 1991.

The record for one game is 300, by Lori Gensch of Milwaukee, WI in the 1979 doubles event; by Rose Walsh of Pomona, CA in the 1986 singles event; and by Linda Kelly of Huber Heights, OH in the 1987 doubles event.

Dorothy Miller of Chicago, IL has won 10 WIBC Championship Tournament events, the most by an individual.

Oldest and youngest players   Mary Covell of Chicago, IL participated in her 61st WIBC tournament in 1992. The oldest participant was Ethel Brunnick (b. 30 Aug 1887) of Santa Monica, CA, at age 99 in 1987.

The youngest champion was Leila Wagner (b. 12 Jul 1960) of Annapolis, MD, who was 18 when she was a member of the championship five-woman team in 1979.

Perfect games   Jeanne Maiden of Tacoma, WA has rolled 20 perfect games to set the WIBC career record. She also set a record of 40 consecutive strikes in 1986 and rolled an 864 on games of 300–300–264.

The most 300 games rolled in a career is 20, by Jeanne Maiden. The oldest woman to bowl a perfect game (12 strikes in a row) is Evelyn Culbert of Austin, MN at age 66 in 1993. Of all the women who rolled a perfect game, the one with the lowest average was Diane Ponza of Santa Cruz, CA, who had a 112 average in the 1977/78 season.

BOXING

Longest fights   The longest recorded fight with gloves was between Andy Bowen of New Orleans (1867–94) and Jack Burke at New Orleans, LA on 6–7 Apr 1893. It lasted 110 rounds, 7 hr 19 min (9:15 P.M.–4:34 A.M.), and was declared a no-contest (later changed to a draw). Bowen won an 85-round bout on 31 May 1893.

The longest bare-knuckle fight was 6 hr 15 min, between James Kelly and Jack Smith at Fiery Creek, Dalesford, Victoria, Australia on 3 Dec 1855.

The greatest number of rounds was 276, in 4 hr 30 min, when Jack Jones beat Patsy Tunney in Cheshire, Great Britain in 1825.

Shortest fights   There is a distinction between the quickest knockout and the shortest fight. A knockout in $10^1/_2$ sec (including a 10 sec count) occurred on 23 Sep 1946, when Al Couture struck Ralph Walton while the latter was adjusting a gum shield in his corner at Lewiston, ME. If the time was accurately recorded it is clear that Couture must have been more than halfway across the ring from his own corner at the opening bell.

The shortest fight on record appears to have been one in a Golden Gloves tournament at Minneapolis, MN on 4 Nov 1947, when Mike Collins floored Pat Brownson with the first punch and the contest was stopped, without a count, 4 sec after the opening bell.

The shortest world title fight was 45 sec, when Lloyd Honeyghan (Great Britain; b. 22 Apr 1960) beat Gene Hatcher (USA) in an IBF welterweight bout at Marbella, Spain on 30 Aug 1987. Some sources also quote the Al McCoy (1894–1966) first-round knockout of George Chip in a middleweight contest on 7 Apr 1914 as being in 45 sec.

The shortest-ever heavyweight world title fight was the James J. Jeffries (1875–1953)–Jack Finnegan bout at Detroit, MI on 6 Apr 1900, won by Jeffries in 55 sec.

Eugene Brown, on his professional debut, knocked out Ian Bockes at Leicester, Great Britain, on 13 Mar 1989. The fight was officially stopped after 10 seconds of the first round. Bockes got up after a count of six, but the referee stopped the contest.

Tallest   The tallest boxer to fight professionally was Gogea Mitu (b. 1914) of Romania, in 1935. He was 7 ft 4 in and weighed 327 lb. John Rankin, who won a fight in New Orleans, LA in November 1967, was reputedly also 7 ft 4 in. Jim Culley, "The Tipperary Giant," who fought as a boxer and wrestled in the 1940s, is also reputed to have been 7 ft 4 in.

Most fights without loss   Edward Henry "Harry" Greb (USA; 1894–1926) was unbeaten in a sequence of 178 bouts, but these included 117 "no decision," of which five were unofficial losses, in 1916–23.

Of boxers with complete records, Packey McFarland (USA; 1888–1936) had 97 fights (five draws) in 1905–15 without a defeat.

Pedro Carrasco (Spain; b. 7 Nov 1943) won 83 consecutive fights from 22 April 1964 to 3 Sep 1970, drew once and had a further nine wins before his loss to Armando Ramos in a WBC lightweight contest on 18 Feb 1972.

Most knockouts The greatest number of finishes classed as "knockouts" in a career (1936–63) is 145 (129 in professional bouts), by Archie Moore (USA; b. Archibald Lee Wright, 13 Dec 1913 or 1916).

The record for consecutive KO's is 44, by Lamar Clark (USA; b. 1 Dec 1934) from 1958 to 11 Jan 1960. He knocked out six in one night (five in the first round) at Bingham, UT on 1 Dec 1958.

Attendances Highest The greatest paid attendance at any boxing match is 132,274 for four world title fights at the Aztec Stadium, Mexico City on 20 Feb 1993, headed by the successful WBC light-welterweight defense by Julio César Chavez (Mexico) over Greg Haugen (USA).

The indoor record is 63,350, at the Muhammad Ali *v* Leon Spinks (b. 11 Jul 1953) fight in the Superdome, New Orleans, LA on 15 Sep 1978.

The highest nonpaying attendance is 135,132, at the Tony Zale *v* Billy Pryor fight at Juneau Park, Milwaukee, WI on 16 Aug 1941.

Lowest The smallest attendance at a world heavyweight title fight was 2,434, at the Cassius Clay (Muhammad Ali) *v* Sonny Liston fight at Lewiston, ME on 25 May 1965.

MOST SUCCESSFUL Julio César Chavez is currently the most successful boxer, with 87 victories from 87 fights in his professional career. (Photo: Allsport/Holly Stein)

Lightest heavyweight Robert James "Bob" Fitzsimmons (1863–1917) from Great Britain weighed 165 lb when he won the title by knocking out James J. Corbett at Carson City, NV on 17 Mar 1897.

Heaviest Primo Carnera (Italy; 1906–67), the "Ambling Alp," who won the title from Jack Sharkey in New York City on 29 Jun 1933, scaled 260 lb for this fight, but his peak weight was 269 lb. He had an expanded chest measurement of 54 in and the longest reach at 85½ in (fingertip to fingertip).

Shortest boxer Tommy Burns, world heavyweight champion from 23 Feb 1906 to 26 Dec 1908, stood 5 ft 7 in and weighed between 168–180 lb.

Longest-lived boxer Jack Sharkey (b. Joseph Paul Zukauskas, 26 Oct 1902), champion from 21 Jun 1932 to 29 Jun 1933, surpassed the previous record of 87 yr 341 days held by Jack Dempsey (1895–1983) on 3 Oct 1990.

Most knockdowns in title fight Vic Toweel (South Africa; b. 12 Jan 1929) knocked down Danny O'Sullivan of London, Great Britain 14 times in 10 rounds in their world bantamweight fight at Johannesburg, South Africa on 2 Dec 1950, before the latter retired.

Oldest heavyweight "Jersey Joe" Walcott (USA; b. Arnold Raymond Cream, 31 Jan 1914) was 37 yr 168 days when he knocked out Ezzard Mack Charles (1921–75) on 18 Jul 1951 in Pittsburgh, PA. He was also the oldest holder, at 38 yr 236 days, losing his title to Rocky Marciano on 23 Sep 1952.

Youngest heavyweight Mike Tyson (USA) was 20 yr 144 days when he beat Trevor Berbick (USA) to win the WBC version at Las Vegas, NV on 22 Nov 1986. He added the WBA title when he beat James "Bone-crusher" Smith on 7 Mar 1987 at 20 yr 249 days. He became undisputed champion on 2 Aug 1987 when he beat Tony Tucker (USA) for the IBF title.

Greatest weight difference When Primo Carnera (Italy), 269 lb, fought Tommy Loughran (USA), 183 lb, for the world heavyweight title at Miami, FL on 1 Mar 1934, there was a weight difference of 86 lb between the two fighters. Carnera won the fight on points.

Oldest gold medalist Richard Kenneth Gunn (Great Britain; 1871–1961) won the Olympic featherweight gold medal on 27 Oct 1908 in London, Great Britain at the age of 37 yr 254 days.

WORLD HEAVYWEIGHT

Earliest title fight Long accepted as the first world heavyweight title fight, with gloves and 3-min rounds, was that between John Lawrence Sullivan (1858–1918) and James John "Gentleman Jim" Corbett (1866–1933) in New Orleans, LA on 7 Sep 1892. Corbett won in 21 rounds. However, the fight between Sullivan, then the world bare-knuckle champion, and Dominick F. McCaffery in Chester Park, Cincinnati, OH on 29 Aug 1885 was staged under Queensberry Rules with the boxers wearing gloves over six rounds. The referee, Billy Tait, left the ring without giving a verdict, but when asked two days later said that Sullivan had won.

Reign Longest Joe Louis (USA; b. Joseph Louis Barrow, 1914–81) was champion for 11 years 252 days, from 22 Jun 1937, when he knocked out James Joseph Braddock in the eighth round at Chicago, IL, until announcing his retirement on 1 Mar 1949. During his reign Louis made a record 25 defenses of his title.

Shortest Tony Tucker (USA; b. 28 Dec 1958) was IBF champion for 64 days, 30 May–2 Aug 1987, the shortest duration of a title won and lost in the ring.

Most recaptures Muhammad Ali is the only man to have regained the heavyweight championship twice. Ali first won the title on 25 Feb 1964, defeating Sonny Liston. He defeated George Foreman on 30 Oct 1974, after having been stripped of the title by the world boxing authorities on 28 Apr 1967. He won the WBA title from Leon Spinks on 15 Sep 1978, having previously lost to him on 15 Feb 1978.

Undefeated Rocky Marciano (USA; b. Rocco Francis Marchegiano, 1923–69) is the only world champion at any weight to have won every fight of his entire professional career from 17 Mar 1947 to 21 Sep 1955 (he announced his retirement on 27 Apr 1956); 43 of his 49 fights were by knockouts or stoppages.

Tallest There is uncertainty as to the tallest world champion. Ernest Terrell (USA; b. 4 Apr 1939), WBA champion 1965–67, was reported to be 6 ft 6 in. Slightly higher figures had been given for earlier champions, but, according to measurements by the physical education director of the Hemingway Gymnasium, Harvard University, Cambridge, MA, Primo Carnera was 6 ft 5.4 in, although widely reported and believed to be up to 6 ft 8 1/2 in. Jess Willard (1881–1968), who won the title in 1915, often stated to be 6 ft 6 1/4 in, was in fact 6 ft 5 1/4 in.

WORLD CHAMPIONS ANY WEIGHT

Reign Longest The Joe Louis heavyweight duration record of 11 yr 252 days stands for all divisions.

Shortest Tony Canzoneri (USA; 1908–59) was world light-welterweight champion for 33 days, 21 May to 23 Jun 1933, the shortest period for a boxer to have won and lost the world title in the ring.

Youngest Wilfred Benitez (b. New York, 12 Sep 1958) of Puerto Rico was 17 yr 176 days when he won the WBA light-welterweight title in San Juan, Puerto Rico on 6 Mar 1976.

Oldest   Archie Moore, who was recognized as a light-heavyweight champion up to 10 Feb 1962 when his title was removed, was then believed to be between 45 and 48 years old.

Longest career   Bob Fitzsimmons had a career of over 31 years, from 1883 to 1914. He had his last world title bout on 20 Dec 1905 at the age of 42 yr 208 days. Jack Johnson (USA; 1878–1946) also had a career of over 31 years, from 1897–1928.

Longest fight   The longest world title fight (under Queensberry Rules) was that between the lightweights Joe Gans (1874–1910), of the USA, and Oscar Matthew "Battling" Nelson (1882–1954), the "Durable Dane," at Goldfield, NV on 3 Sep 1906. It was terminated in the 42nd round when Gans was declared the winner on a foul.

Most different weights   The first to have won world titles at four weight categories was Thomas Hearns (USA; b. 18 Oct 1958), WBA welterweight in 1980, WBC super-welterweight in 1982, WBC light-heavyweight in 1987 and WBC middleweight in 1987. He added a fifth weight division when he won the super-middleweight title recognized by the newly created World Boxing Organization (WBO) on 4 Nov 1988, and he won the WBA light-heavyweight title on 3 Jun 1991.

Sugar Ray Leonard (USA; b. 17 May 1956) has also claimed world titles in five weight categories. Having previously won the WBC welterweight in 1979 and 1980, WBA junior-middleweight in 1981 and WBC middleweight in 1987, he beat Donny Lalonde (Canada) on 7 Nov 1988, for both the WBC light-heavyweight and super-middleweight titles. However, despite the fact that the WBC sanctioned the fight, it is against their rules to contest two divisions in one fight. Therefore, although Leonard won, he had to relinquish one of the titles.

The only man to hold world titles at three weights *simultaneously* was Henry "Homicide Hank" Armstrong (USA; 1912–88), at featherweight, lightweight and welterweight from August to December 1938. It is argued, however, that Barney Ross (b. Barney David Rosofsky [USA]; 1909–67) held the lightweight, junior-welterweight and welterweight titles simultaneously, from 28 May to 17 Sep 1934, although there is some dispute as to when he relinquished his lightweight title. In recent years there has been a proliferation of weight categories and governing bodies, but Armstrong was undisputed world champion at widely differing weights, which makes his achievement all the more remarkable.

Most recaptures   The only boxer to win a world title five times at one weight is "Sugar Ray" Robinson (USA; b. Walker Smith, Jr., 1921–89), who beat Carmen Basilio (USA) in Chicago Stadium, IL on 25 Mar 1958 to regain the world middleweight title for the fourth time.

Most title bouts   The record number of title bouts in a career is 37, of which 18 ended in "no decision," by three-time world welterweight champion Jack Britton (USA; 1885–1962) in 1915–22. The record for most contests without a "no decision" is 27 (all heavyweight), by Joe Louis between 1937–50.

Greatest "tonnage"   The highest aggregate weight recorded in any fight is 699 lb, when Claude "Humphrey" McBride (Oklahoma), 339½ lb, knocked out Jimmy Black (Houston, TX), 359½ lb, in the third round at Oklahoma City, OK on 1 Jun 1971.

The greatest "tonnage" in a world title fight was 488¼ lb, when Carnera, then 259 lb, fought Paolino Uzcudun (Spain), 229¼ lb, in Rome, Italy on 22 Oct 1933.

AMATEUR

Olympic titles   Only two boxers have won three Olympic gold medals: south-paw László Papp (Hungary; b. 25 Mar 1926), middleweight winner 1948, light-middleweight winner 1952 and 1956; and Teofilo Stevenson (Cuba; b. 23 Mar 1952), heavyweight winner 1972, 1976 and 1980.

The only man to win two titles in one Olympic celebration was Oliver L. Kirk (USA), who won both bantam and featherweight titles in St Louis, MO in 1904, but he needed only one bout in each class.

A record that will stand forever is that of the youngest Olympic boxing champion: Jackie Fields (ne Finkelstein [USA]; b. 9 Feb 1908), who won the 1924 featherweight title at age 16 yrs 162 days. The minimum age for Olympic boxing competitors is now 17.

World Championships   A record of four world titles (instituted 1974) have been won by Félix Savon (Cuba), heavyweight winner 1986, 1989, 1991, and 91 kg 1993.

Most US titles   US Amateur Championships were first staged in 1888. The most titles won is five, by middleweight W. Rodenbach, 1900–04.

CANOEING

Most titles Olympics   Gert Fredriksson (Sweden; b. 21 Nov 1919) won a record six Olympic gold medals, 1948–60. He added a silver and a bronze, for a record eight medals.

The most by a woman is four, by Birgit Schmidt (nee Fischer [Germany, formerly GDR]; b. 25 Feb 1962), 1980–92.

The most gold medals at one Games is three, by Vladimir Parfenovich (USSR; b. 2 Dec 1958) in 1980 and by Ian Ferguson (New Zealand; b. 20 Jul 1952) in 1984.

World   Including the Olympic Games, a women's record 23 titles have been won by Birgit Schmidt, 1978–92.

The men's record is 13, by Gert Fredriksson, 1948–60; Rüdiger Helm (East Germany; b. 6 Oct 1956), 1976–83; and Ivan Patzaichin (Romania; b. 26 Nov 1949), 1968–84.

United States   The only American canoeist to have won two Olympic gold medals is Gregory Mark Barton (b. 2 Dec 1959), who won at K1 and K2 1,000 m events in 1988. He also has a US record three medals, as he took bronze at K1 1,000 m in 1984.

MOST TITLES Birgit Schmidt (near lane) during the
500 meter K1 final at the 1992 Olympics, which she went on
to win by just 0.36 sec. It was her 23rd world or Olympic
title since 1978. (Photo: Allsport/Nathan Bilow)

HAND ROLLS Colin Hill holds three "hand rolling" canoe records.

Most US titles   Marcia Ingram Jones Smoke (b. 18 Jul 1941) won 35 US national titles between 1962 and 1981, as well as 24 North American Championships and three gold medals at the 1967 Pan-American Games. The men's record is 33 US titles, by Ernest Riedel (b. 13 Jul 1901) between 1930 and 1948, mostly at kayak events.

Fastest speed   The German four-man kayak Olympic champions in 1992 in Barcelona, Spain covered 1,000 m in 2 min 52.17 sec in a heat on 4 August. This represents an average speed of 12.98 mph.

At the 1988 Olympics in Seoul, South Korea the Norwegian four achieved a 250 m split of 42.08 sec between 500 m and 750 m for a speed of 13.29 mph.

Canoe raft   A raft of 568 kayaks and canoes, organized by the Nottinghamshire County Scout Council with the help of scouts from other counties, was held together by hands only, while free floating for 30 seconds on the River Trent, Nottingham, Great Britain on 30 Jun 1991.

Longest race   The Canadian Government Centennial Voyageur Canoe Pageant and Race from Rocky Mountain House, Alberta to the Expo 67 site at Montreal, Quebec was 3,283 miles. Ten canoes represented Canadian provinces and territories. The winner of the race, which took from 24 May to 4 Sep 1967, was the Province of Manitoba canoe *Radisson*.

Greatest lifetime distance in a canoe   Fritz Lindner of Berlin, Germany, totaled 64,278 miles of canoeing from 1928 to 1987.

Longest journey   Father and son Dana and Donald Starkell paddled from Winnipeg, Manitoba, Canada by ocean and river to Belem, Brazil, a distance of 12,181 miles, from 1 Jun 1980 to 1 May 1982. All portages were human-powered.

Without portages or aid of any kind, the longest is one of 6,102 miles, by Richard H. Grant and Ernest "Moose" Lassy, circumnavigating the eastern United States via Chicago, New Orleans, Miami, New York City and the Great Lakes from 22 Sep 1930 to 15 Aug 1931.

24 hours   Zdzislaw Szubski paddled 157.1 miles in a Jaguar K1 canoe on the Vistula River, Wockawek to Gdansk, Poland, on 11–12 Sep 1987.

Flat water   Marinda Hartzenberg (South Africa) paddled, without benefit of current, 137.13 miles on Loch Logan, Bloemfontein, South Africa on 31 Dec 1990–1 Jan 1991.

Open sea   Randy Fine (USA) paddled 120.6 miles along the Florida coast on 26–27 Jun 1986.

Eskimo rolls   Ray Hudspith (b. 18 Apr 1960) achieved 1,000 rolls in 34 min 43 sec at the Elswick Pool, Newcastle-upon-Tyne, Great Britain on 20 Mar

1987. He completed 100 rolls in 3 min 7.25 sec at Killingworth Leisure Center, Great Britain on 3 Mar 1991.

Randy Fine (USA) completed 1,796 continuous rolls at Biscayne Bay, Miami, FL on 8 Jun 1991.

"Hand rolls" Colin Brian Hill (b. 16 Aug 1970) achieved 1,000 rolls in 31 min 55.62 sec at Consett, County Durham, Great Britain on 12 Mar 1987. He also achieved 100 rolls in 2 min 39.2 sec in London, Great Britain on 22 Feb 1987. He completed 3,700 continuous rolls at Durham City Swimming Baths, Great Britain on 1 May 1989.

CARD GAMES

CONTRACT BRIDGE

Biggest tournament The Epson World Bridge Championship, held on 20–21 Jun 1992, was contested by more than 102,000 players playing the same hands, at over 2,000 centers worldwide.

Most world titles The World Championship (Bermuda Bowl) has been won a record 13 times by Italy's Blue Team (*Squadra Azzura*), 1957–59, 1961–63, 1965–67, 1969, 1973–75 and by the USA, 1950–51, 1953–54, 1970–71, 1976–77, 1979, 1981, 1983, 1985, 1987. Italy also won the team Olympiad in 1964, 1968 and 1972 and the USA won in 1988. Giorgio Belladonna (b. 7 Jun 1923) was on all the Italian winning teams.

The USA has a record six wins in the women's world championship for the

---

Card holding Ralf Laue held 310 standard playing cards in a fan in one hand, so that the value and color of each one was visible, at Zürich, Switzerland, on 6 Apr 1991.

Card throwing Kevin St Onge threw a standard playing card 185 ft 1 in at the Henry Ford Community College campus, Dearborn, MI on 12 Jun 1979.

Perfect deals in bridge The mathematical odds against dealing 13 cards of one suit are 158,753,389,899 to 1, while the odds against a named player receiving a "perfect hand" consisting of all 13 spades are 635,013,559,599 to 1. The odds against each of the four players' receiving a complete suit (a "perfect deal") are 2,235,197,406,895,-366,368,301,559,999 to 1.

Possible bridge auctions The number of possible auctions with North as dealer is 128,745,650,347,030,683,120,231,926,111,609,-371,363,122,697,557.

Venice Trophy, 1974, 1976, 1978, 1987, 1989 and 1991, and three women's wins at the World Team Olympiad, 1976, 1980 and 1984.

Most world championship hands In the 1989 Bermuda Bowl in Perth, Australia, Marcel Branco and Gabriel Chagas, both of Brazil, played a record 752 out of a possible 784 boards.

Most Master Points In the latest ranking list based on Master Points awarded by the World Bridge Federation, the leading players in the world are *(men)* Robert Hamman (b. 1938) of Dallas, TX, with 6,046 points, and *(women)* Sandra Landy (Great Britain; b. 1938), with 3,077.

CRIBBAGE

Rare hands Five maximum 29-point hands have been achieved by Sean Daniels of Astoria, OR, 1989–92. Paul Nault of Athol, MA had two such hands within eight games in a tournament on 19 Mar 1977.

Most points in 24 hours The most points scored by a team of four, playing singles in two pairs, is 126,414, by Mark Fitzwater, Eddie Pepper, Mark Perry and Gary Watson at The Green Man, Potton, Great Britain on 8–9 May 1993.

CRICKET

First-class records *Career* The most runs scored in a career is 61,237, by Sir John Berry "Jack" Hobbs (1882–1963) for Surrey and England, 1905–34. The most wickets taken by an individual is 4,187, by Wilfred Rhodes (1877–1973) for Yorkshire and England, 1898–1930. The most dismissals by a wicket-keeper is 1,649, by Robert William Taylor (b. 17 Jul 1941) for Derbyshire and England, 1960–88. The most catches by a fielder is 1,018, by Frank Edward Woolley (1887–1978) for Kent and England, 1906–38.

TEST CRICKET

Career records The most runs scored by an individual is 10,262, by Allan Robert Border (Australia; b. 27 Jul 1955) in 141 tests, 1978–93. The most wickets taken by a bowler is 431, by Sir Richard John Hadlee (New Zealand; b. 3 Jul 1951) in 86 Tests, 1973–90. The most dismissals by a wicket-keeper is 355, by Rodney William Marsh (Australia; b. 11 Nov 1947), in 96 Tests, 1970–84. The most catches by a fielder is 140, by Allan Border in 141 Tests, 1978–93.

The best all-around Test career record is that of Kapil Dev Nikhanj (India; b. 6 Jan 1959) with 5,069 runs, 420 wickets and 63 catches in 124 matches, 1978–93.

NATIONAL CRICKET CHAMPIONSHIPS

Australia The premier event in Australia is the Sheffield Shield, an interstate competition contested since 1891–92. New South Wales has won the title a record 41 times.

England The major championship in England is the County Championships, an intercounty competition officially recognized since 1890. Yorkshire has won the title a record 30 times.

India The Ranji Trophy is India's premier cricket competition. Established in 1934 in memory of K.S. Ranjitsinhji, it is contested on a zonal basis, culminating in a playoff competition. Bombay has won the tournament a record 30 times.

New Zealand Since 1975, the major championship in New Zealand has been the Shell Trophy. Otago, Wellington and Auckland have each won the competition four times.

Pakistan Pakistan's national championship is the Quaid-e-Azam Trophy, established in 1953. Karachi has won the trophy a record eight times.

South Africa The Currie Cup, donated by Sir Donald Currie, was first contested in 1889. Transvaal has won the competition a record 28 times.

MOST RUNS The leading run scorer in Test cricket is Allan Border of Australia, who surpassed Sunil Gavaskar's record against New Zealand on 26 Feb 1993. Border now has 10,262 runs. (Photo: Allsport/Joe Mann & Adrian Murrell)

West Indies The Red Stripe Cup, established in 1966, is the premier prize played for by the association of Caribbean islands (plus Guyana) that form the West Indies Cricket League. Barbados has won the competition a record 13 times.

CROQUET

International trophy The MacRobertson Shield (instituted 1925 and held every three years) has been won a record nine times by Great Britain, in 1925, 1937, 1956, 1963, 1969, 1974, 1982, 1990 and 1993. The United States competed for the first time in 1993 with Australia, New Zealand and the Great Britain/Ireland teams.

A record seven appearances have been made by John G. Prince (New Zealand; b. 23 Jul 1945), in 1963, 1969, 1975, 1979, 1982, 1986 and 1990; on his debut he was the youngest-ever international, at 17 yr 190 days.

World Championships The first World Championships were held at the Hurlingham Club, London, Great Britain in 1989 and have been held annually since. The only double winner is Robert Fulford (Great Britain; b. 1970), 1990 and 1992.

USCA National Championships The first United States Championships was played in 1977. J. Archie Peck has won the singles title a record four times, 1977, 1979–80 and 1982. Ted Prentis has won the doubles title four times with three different partners, 1978, 1980–81 and 1988. The teams of Ted Prentis and Ned Prentis (1980–81), Dana Dribben and Ray Bell (1985–86), and Reid Fleming and Debbie Cornelius (1990–91) have each won the doubles title twice. Fleming also won doubles in 1989 with Wayne Rodoni, so Fleming won three times, although with two different partners. The New York Croquet Club has won a record six National Club Championships, 1980–83, 1986 and 1988.

CROSS-COUNTRY RUNNING

World Championships The inaugural International Cross-Country Championships took place at the Hamilton Park Racecourse, Great Britain on 28 Mar 1903.

The greatest margin of victory is 56 sec or 390 yd by John "Jack" Thomas Holden (England; b. 13 Mar 1907) at Ayr Racecourse, Strathclyde, Great Britain on 24 Mar 1934.

Since 1973 the events have been official World Championships under the auspices of the International Amateur Athletic Federation.

United States The USA has never won the men's team race, but Craig Steven

Virgin (b. 2 Aug 1955) won the individual race twice, in 1980–81, and Lynn Jennings has won the women's title three times, 1990–92.

Most wins   The greatest number of team victories has been by England, with 45 for men, 11 for junior men and seven for women. The USA and the USSR each have a record eight women's team victories.

The greatest team domination was by Kenya at Auckland, New Zealand on 26 Mar 1988. Their senior men's team finished eight men in the first nine, with a low score of 23 (six to score), and their junior men's team set a record low score, 11 (four to score) with six in the first seven.

The greatest number of men's individual victories is five, by John Ngugi (Kenya; b. 10 May 1962), 1986–89 and 1992. The women's race has been won five times by Doris Brown-Heritage (USA; b. 17 Sep 1942), 1967–71; and by Grete Waitz (nee Andersen [Norway]; b. 1 Oct 1953), 1978–81 and 1983.

US championship   In this competition, first staged in 1890, the most wins in the men's race is eight, by Patrick Ralph Porter (b. 31 May 1959), 1982–89. The women's championship was first contested in 1972, and the most wins is six, by Lynn A. Jennings (b. 1 Jul 1960), 1985, 1987–90 and 1992.

Most appearances   Marcel van de Wattyne (Belgium; b. 7 Jul 1924) ran in a record 20 races, 1946–65. The women's record is 16, by Jean Lochhead (Wales; b. 24 Dec 1946), 1967–79, 1981, 1983–84.

Largest cross-country field   The largest recorded field in any cross-country race was 11,763 starters (10,810 finished), in the 18.6-mile Lidingöloppet, near Stockholm, Sweden on 3 Oct 1982.

CURLING

Most titles   Canada has won the men's World Championships (instituted 1959) 20 times, 1959–64, 1966, 1968–72, 1980, 1982–83, 1985–87, 1989–90.

The most Strathcona Cup (instituted 1903) wins is seven, by Canada (1903, 1909, 1912, 1923, 1938, 1957, 1965) against Scotland.

The most women's World Championships (instituted 1979) is six, by Canada (1980, 1984–87, 1989).

United States   The USA has won the men's world title four times, with Bud Somerville skip on the first two winning teams, 1965 and 1974.

United States National Championship Men   In this competition, first held in 1957, two curlers have been skips on five championship teams: Bud Somerville (Superior Curling Club, WI in 1965, 1968–69, 1974, 1981), and Bruce Roberts (Hibbing Curling Club, MN in 1966–67, 1976–77, 1984). Bill Strum of the Su-

> ***Longest curling throw***   The longest throw of a curling stone was a distance of 576 ft 4 in, by Eddie Kulbacki (Canada) at Park Lake, Neepawa, Manitoba, Canada on 29 Jan 1989. The attempt took place on a specially prepared sheet of curling ice on frozen Park Lake, a record 1,200 ft long.
>
> ***Fastest game in curling***   Eight curlers from the Burlington Golf and Country Club curled an eight-end game in 47 min 24 sec, with time penalties of 5 min 30 sec, at Burlington, Ontario, Canada on 4 Apr 1986, following rules agreed on with the Ontario Curling Association. The time is taken from when the first rock crosses the near hogline until the game's last rock comes to a complete stop.

perior Curling Club has been a member of five title teams, in 1965, 1967, 1969, 1974 and 1978.

Women   In this competition, first held in 1977, Nancy Langley, Seattle, WA has been the skip of a record four championship teams, 1979, 1981, 1983 and 1988.

The Labatt Brier (formerly the Macdonald Brier 1927–79)   The Brier is the Canadian Men's Curling championship. The competition was first held at the Granite Club, Toronto in 1927. Sponsored by Macdonald Tobacco Inc., it was known as the Macdonald Brier; since 1980 Labatt Brewery has sponsored the event. The most wins is 23, by Manitoba (1928–32, 1934, 1936, 1938, 1940, 1942, 1947, 1949, 1952–53, 1956, 1965, 1970–72, 1979, 1981, 1984 and 1992). Ernie Richardson (Saskatchewan) has been winning skip a record four times (1959–60, 1962–63). His brothers Arnold and Sam Richardson were also members of each championship team.

Largest bonspiel   The largest bonspiel (curling tournament) in the world is the Manitoba Curling Association Bonspiel, held annually in Winnipeg, Canada. In 1988 there were 1,424 teams of four men, a total of 5,696 curlers, using 187 sheets of curling ice.

Largest rink   The world's largest curling rink was the Big Four Curling Rink, Calgary, Alberta, Canada, opened in 1959 and closed in 1990. Ninety-six teams and 384 players are accommodated on two floors, each with 24 sheets of ice.

CYCLING

Fastest speed   The fastest speed ever achieved on a bicycle is 152.284 mph, by John Howard (USA) behind a windshield at Bonneville Salt Flats, UT on 20

Jul 1985. It should be noted that considerable help was provided by the slip-streaming effect of the lead vehicle.

The 24 hr record behind pace is 1,216.8 miles, by Michael Secrest at Phoenix International Raceway, AZ on 26–27 Apr 1990.

Most titles Olympic The most gold medals won is three, by Paul Masson (France; 1874–1945) in 1896; Francisco Verri (Italy; 1885–1945) in 1906; and Robert Charpentier (France; 1916–66) in 1936. Daniel Morelon (France) won two in 1968, and a third in 1972; he also won a silver in 1976 and a bronze in 1964. In the "unofficial" 1904 cycling program, Marcus Latimer Hurley (USA; 1885–1941) won four events.

Burton Cecil Down (USA; 1885–1929) won a record six medals at the 1904 Games, two gold, three silver and one bronze. The only American woman to win a cycling gold medal is Helen Constance "Connie" Carpenter-Phinney (b. 26 Feb 1957), who won the individual road race in 1984. She became the first woman to compete in the winter and summer Olympics, as she had competed as a speed skater in 1972.

World World Championships are contested annually. They were first staged for amateurs in 1893 and for professionals in 1895.

The most wins at a particular event is 10, by Koichi Nakano (Japan; b. 14 Nov 1955), professional sprint 1977–86.

The most wins at a men's amateur event is seven, by Daniel Morelon (France; b. 28 Jul 1944), sprint 1966–67, 1969–71, 1973, 1975; and by Leon Meredith (Great Britain; 1882–1930), 100 km motor paced 1904–05, 1907–09, 1911, 1913.

The most women's titles is eight, by Jeannie Longo (France; b. 31 Oct 1958), pursuit 1986 and 1988–89; road 1985–87 and 1989; and points 1989.

The most world titles won by a US cyclist is four, at women's 3 kilometers pursuit by Rebecca Twigg (b. 26 Mar 1963), 1982, 1984–85 and 1987. The most successful man has been Greg LeMond (b. 26 Jun 1960), winner of the individual road race in 1983 and 1989.

United States National cycling championships have been held annually since 1899. Women's events were first included in 1937.

Leonard Nitz has won the most titles, 16: five pursuit (1976 and 1980–83); eight team pursuit (1980–84, 1986 and 1988–89); two 1-km time-trial (1982 and 1984); and one criterium (1986). Connie Carpenter has won 11 titles in women's events: four road race (1976–77, 1979 and 1981); three pursuit (1976–77 and 1979); two criterium (1982–83); and two points (1981–82).

Highest altitude cycling Canadians Bruce Bell, Philip Whelan and Suzanne MacFadyen cycled at an altitude of 22,834 ft on the peak of Mt Aconcagua, Argentina on 25 Jan 1991.

Cycling the length of the Americas Daniel Buettner, Bret Anderson, Martin Engel and Anne Knabe cycled the length of the Americas, from Prudhoe Bay, AK to the Beagle Channel, Ushuaia, Argentina from 8 Aug 1986 to 13 Jun 1987. They cycled a total distance of 15,266 miles.

FASTEST CYCLIST Chris Boardman, winner of the 1992 Olympic individual pursuit title, on the revolutionary Lotus bike with which he set a 4 km world record. (Photo: Allsport/Davis Cannon)

FASTEST TOUR DE FRANCE Miguel Indurain (Spain), third from right in the photo, won the 1992 Tour de France with a record average speed of 24.547 mph. (Photo: Allsport/Vandystadt)

WORLD CYCLING RECORDS

These records are those recognized by the Union Cycliste Internationale (UCI). From 1 Jan 1993 their severely reduced list no longer distinguished between those set by professionals and amateurs, indoor and outdoor, or at altitude and sea level.

Men

Distance	min : sec	Name and Country	Venue	Date
Unpaced Standing Start				
1 km	1:02.091	Maic Malchow (East Germany)	Colorado Springs, CO	28 Aug 1986
4 km	4:24.496	Christopher Boardman (Great Britain)	Barcelona, Spain	28 Jul 1992
4 km team	4:08.06	Germany (Micheal Glöckner, Jens Lehmann,	Stuttgart, Germany	16 Aug 1991
		Stefan Steinway, Andreas Walzer)		
1 hour (km)	51.15135	Francesco Moser (Italy)	Mexico City, Mexico	23 Jan 1984
Unpaced Flying Start				
200 meters	10.099	Vladimir Adamashvili (USSR)	Moscow, USSR	6 Aug 1990
500 meters	26.649	Aleksandr Kirichenko (USSR)	Moscow, USSR	29 Oct 1988

Women

Distance	min : sec	Name and Country	Venue	Date
Unpaced Standing Start				
500 m	33.438	Galina Yenyukhina (Russia)	Moscow, Russia	29 Apr 1993
3 km	3:38.190	Jeannie Longo (France)	Mexico City, Mexico	5 Oct 1989
1 hour (km)	46.35270	Jeannie Longo (France)	Mexico City, Mexico	1 Oct 1989
Unpaced Flying Start				
200 meters	11.101	Galina Yenyukhina (Russia)	Moscow, Russia	2 Jul 1992
500 meters	29.655	Erika Salumäe (USSR)	Moscow, USSR	6 Aug 1987

Tour de France   The world's premiere stage race was first contested in 1903. Held over a three-week period, the longest race ever staged was over 3,570 miles in 1926. The greatest number of wins in the Tour de France is five, by Jacques Anquetil (France; 1934–1987), 1957, 1961–64; Eddy Merckx (Belgium; b. 17 Jun 1945), 1969–72 and 1974; and Bernard Hinault (France; b. 14 Nov 1954), 1978–79, 1981–82 and 1985. Greg LeMond (USA; b. 26 Jun 1960) became the first American winner in 1986, and returned from serious injury to win again in 1989 and 1990.

The closest race ever was in 1989, when after 2,030 miles over 23 days (1–23 July) Greg LeMond, who completed the Tour in 87 hr 38 min 35 sec, beat Laurent Fignon (France; b. 12 Aug 1960) in Paris, France by only 8 sec.

The fastest average speed was 24.547 mph, by Miguel Indurain (Spain; b. 16 Jul 1964) in 1992.

The longest-ever stage was the 486 km from Les Sables d'Olonne to Bayonne in 1919. The most participants was 210 starters in 1986.

Women   The inaugural women's Tour de France was staged in 1984. Jeannie Longo (France) has won the event a record four times, 1987–90.

Greatest distance in one hour   The greatest distance covered in one hour is 122.28 km, by Leon Vanderstuyft (Belgium; 1890–1964) on the Montlhéry Motor Circuit, France, on 30 Sep 1928, achieved from a standing start paced by a motorcycle.

Fastest rollercycling speed   James Baker (USA) achieved a record speed of 153.2 mph at El Con Mall, Tucson, AZ on 28 Jan 1989.

Cyclo-Cross   The greatest number of World Championships (instituted 1950) has been won by Eric de Vlaeminck (Belgium; b. 23 Aug 1945), with the Amateur and Open in 1966 and six Professional titles in 1968–73.

Six-day races   The most wins in six-day races is 88 out of 233 events, by Patrick Sercu (Belgium; b. 27 Jun 1944), 1964–83.

Longest one-day race   The longest single-day "massed start" road race is the 342–385 mile Bordeaux–Paris, France event. Paced over all or part of the route, the highest average speed was 29.32 mph, by Herman van Springel (Belgium; b. 14 Aug 1943) for 363.1 miles in 13 hr 35 min 18 sec, in 1981.

Cross-America   An annual transcontinental crossing of the United States from west to east, the Race Across AMerica was first staged in 1982. A women's division was introduced in 1984. The start and finish lines have varied, but currently the race starts in Irvine, CA and finishes in Savannah, GA. The racers must travel a minimum distance of 2,900 miles.

The trans-America solo record recognized by the Ultra-Marathon Cycling Association for men is 8 days 8 hr 45 min, by Paul Selon at age 35 from Costa, CA to New York, in the 1989 Race Across AMerica. Selon won the race while wearing a plastic neck brace. The women's record is 9 days 9 hr 9 min, by Susan Notorangelo at age 35, also in the 1989 Race Across AMerica. She clipped 16 hr 55 min off the previous women's record.

Most wins Three cyclists have won two men's titles: Lon Haldeman, 1982–83; Pete Penseyres, 1984, 1986; Bob Fourney, 1990–91. In the women's division Susan Notorangelo has won two titles, 1985 and 1989.

Cross-Canada The trans-Canada record is 13 days 9 hr 6 min, by William "Bill" Narasnek of Lively, Ontario, cycling 3,751 miles from Vancouver, British Columbia to Halifax, Nova Scotia on 5–18 Jul 1991.

Endurance Thomas Edward Godwin (Great Britain; 1912–75), cycling every day during the 365 days of 1939, covered 75,065 miles, or an average of 205.65 miles per day. Continuing his effort, he went on to complete 100,000 miles in 500 days to 14 May 1940.

Jay Aldous and Matt DeWaal cycled 14,290 miles on an around-the-world trip from Place Monument, Salt Lake City, UT in 106 days, from 2 Apr–16 Jul 1984.

Tal Burt (Israel) circumnavigated the world (13,523 road miles) from Place du Trocadero, Paris, France in 77 days 14 hr, from 1 Jun–17 Aug 1992.

Cycle touring The greatest mileage amassed in a cycle tour was more than 402,000 miles, by the itinerant lecturer Walter Stolle (b. Sudetenland, 1926) from 24 Jan 1959 to 12 Dec 1976. Starting from Romford, Great Britain, he visited 159 countries. From 1922 to 25 Dec 1973, Tommy Chambers (1903–84) of Glasgow, Great Britain rode a verified total of 799,405 miles.

Visiting every continent John W. Hathaway (b. Great Britain, 13 Jan 1925) of Vancouver, British Columbia, Canada covered 50,600 miles from 10 Nov 1974 to 6 Oct 1976.

Ronald and Sandra Slaughter hold the US record for tandem bicycling, having traveled 18,077.5 miles around the world from 30 Dec 1989 to 28 Jul 1991.

The most participants in a bicycle tour were 31,678, in the 56-mile London–to–Brighton Bike Ride (Great Britain) on 19 Jun 1988. However, it is estimated that 45,000 cyclists took part in the 44-mile Tour de l'Ile de Montréal, Canada on 7 Jun 1992. The most participants in a tour in excess of 1,000 km is 2,037 (from 2,157 starters) for the Australian Bicentennial Caltex Bike Ride from Melbourne to Sydney, from 26 Nov–10 Dec 1988.

DARTS

TOURNAMENT RECORDS

Most titles Eric Bristow (Great Britain; b. 25 Apr 1957) has the most wins in the World Masters Championship (instituted 1974) with five, 1977, 1979, 1981 and 1983–84; the most in the World Professional Championship (instituted 1978) with five, 1980–81 and 1984–86; and the most in the World Cup Singles (instituted 1977) with four, 1983, 1985, 1987 and 1989.

John Lowe (Great Britain; b. 21 Jul 1945) is the only man besides Eric Bristow to have won each of the four major titles: World Masters, 1976 and 1980; World Professional, 1979, 1987 and 1993; World Cup Singles, 1981; and *News of the World*, 1981.

SCORING RECORDS

First 180 score   The first recorded highest possible score of 180 was achieved by John Reader at the Highbury Tavern in Sussex, Great Britain, in 1902.

Fewest darts   Scores of 201 in four darts, 301 in six darts, 401 in seven darts and 501 in nine darts have been achieved on various occasions.

The lowest number of darts thrown for a score of 1,001 is 19, by Cliff Inglis (b. 27 May 1935) (160, 180, 140, 180, 121, 180, 40) at the Bromfield Men's Club, Devon, Great Britain on 11 Nov 1975; and by Jocky Wilson (Great Britain) (140, 140, 180, 180, 180, 131, Bull) at The London Pride, Bletchley, Great Britain on 23 Mar 1989.

A score of 2,001 in 52 darts was achieved by Alan Evans (Great Britain; b. 14 Jun 1949) at Ferndale, Great Britain on 3 Sep 1976.

A score of 3,001 in 73 darts was thrown by Tony Benson at the Plough Inn, Gorton, Great Britain on 12 Jul 1986.

Linda Batten (b. 26 Nov 1954) set a women's 3,001 record of 117 darts at

WORLD CHAMPION John Lowe, one of only two darts players to have won all the major tournaments, won the World Professional Championship for a third time in 1993. (Photo: Allsport/ Simon Bruty)

Record prize   John Lowe won £102,000 (*c.* $175,000) for achieving the first 501 scored with the minimum nine darts in a major event, on 13 Oct 1984 at Slough, Great Britain in the quarter-finals of the World Match-play Championships. His darts were six successive treble 20s, treble 17, treble 18 and double 18.

Million and One Up   *Men* (8 players): 36,583 darts by a team at the Buzzy's Pub and Grub, Lynn, MA on 19–20 Oct 1991.

Women (8 players): 70,019 darts by The Delinquents darts team at the Top George Pub, Combe Martin, Great Britain on 11–13 Sep 1987.

the Old Wheatsheaf, London, Great Britain on 2 Apr 1986. A score of 100,001 was achieved in 3,732 darts by Alan Downie of Stornoway, Great Britain on 21 Nov 1986.

Roy Edwin Blowes (Canada; b. 8 Oct 1930) was the first person to achieve a 501 in nine darts, "double-on, double-off," at the Widgeons Pub, Calgary, Canada on 9 Mar 1987. His scores were: bull, treble 20, treble 17, five treble 20s and a double 20 to finish.

Highest score Team   The highest score in 24 hr is 1,722,249, by the Broken Hill Darts Club (8 players) at Broken Hill, New South Wales, Australia on 28–29 Sep 1985. The women's record is 744,439 by a team of 8 players from the Lord Clyde, London, Great Britain on 13–14 Oct 1990.

Individual   The highest score in 24 hr by an individual is 518,060, by Davy Richardson-Page at Blucher Social Club, Newcastle, Great Britain on 6–7 Jul 1991.

SPEED RECORDS

The fastest time taken to complete three games of 301, finishing on doubles, is 1 min 47 sec, by Keith Deller on British Broadcasting Corporation's *Record Breakers* TV program on 22 Oct 1985.

The record time for going around the board clockwise in "doubles" at arm's length is 9.2 sec, by Dennis Gower at the Millers Arms, Hastings, Great Britain on 12 Oct 1975, and 14.5 sec in numerical order by Jim Pike (1903–60) at the Craven Club, Newmarket, Great Britain in March 1944.

The record for this feat at the 9-ft throwing distance, retrieving own darts, is 2 min 13 sec by Bill Duddy (b. 29 Sep 1932) at The Plough, London, Great Britain on 29 Oct 1972.

EQUESTRIAN SPORTS

SHOW JUMPING

Olympic Games   The most Olympic gold medals won by a rider is five, by Hans-Günter Winkler (West Germany; b. 24 Jul 1926)—four team wins in 1956, 1960, 1964 and 1972 and the individual Grand Prix in 1956. He also won team silver in 1976 and team bronze in 1968, for a record seven medals overall.

The most team wins in the Prix des Nations is six, by Germany in 1936, 1956, 1960, 1964 and as West Germany in 1972 and 1988.

The lowest score obtained by a winner is no faults, by Frantisek Ventura (Czechoslovakia; 1895–1969) on Eliot, 1928; Alwin Schockemöhle (West Germany; b. 29 May 1937) on Warwick Rex, 1976; and Ludger Beerbaum (Germany; b. 25 Aug 1963) on Classic Touch, 1992.

Pierre Jonquères d'Oriola (France; b. 1 Feb 1920) uniquely won the individual gold medal twice, in 1952 and 1964.

United States   Two US riders have won individual gold medals: William "Bill"

> **Carriage Driving** World Championships were first held in 1972. Three team titles have been won by Great Britain, 1972, 1974 and 1980; by Hungary, 1976, 1978 and 1984; and by the Netherlands, 1982, 1986 and 1988.
>
> Two individual titles have been won by György Bárdos (Hungary), 1978 and 1980; by Tjeerd Velstra (Netherlands), 1982 and 1986; and by Ijsbrand Chardon (Netherlands), 1988 and 1992.

Clark Steinkraus (b. 12 Oct 1925) won in 1968 and also won two silver and a bronze medal, 1952–68; and Joseph Halpin "Joe" Fargis (b. 4 Feb 1948) won both individual and team gold medals in 1984 as well as team silver in 1988.

World Championships The men's World Championships (instituted 1953) have been won twice by Hans-Günter Winkler (1954–55) and Raimondo d'Inzeo (Italy; b. 8 Feb 1925) (1956 and 1960).

The women's title (1965–74) was won twice by Jane "Janou" Tissot (nee Lefebvre [France]; b. Saigon, 14 May 1945) on Rocket (1970 and 1974).

A team competition was introduced in 1978, and the most wins is two, by France, 1982 and 1990.

President's Cup Instituted in 1965 for Nations Cup teams, it has been won a record 14 times by Great Britain, in 1965, 1967, 1970, 1972–74, 1977–79, 1983, 1985–86, 1989 and 1991.

World Cup In this competition, instituted in 1979, double winners have included Conrad Homfeld (USA; b. 25 Dec 1951), 1980 and 1985; Ian Millar (Canada; b. 6 Jan 1947), 1988 and 1989; and John Whitaker (Great Britain; b. 5 Aug 1955), 1990–91.

Jumping records The official *Fédération Equestre Internationale* records are: high jump, 8 ft 1¼ in, by Huasó, ridden by Capt. Alberto Larraguibel Morales (Chile) at Viña del Mar, Santiago, Chile on 5 Feb 1949; long jump over water, 27 ft 6¾ in, by Something, ridden by André Ferreira (South Africa) at Johannesburg, South Africa on 25 Apr 1975.

THREE-DAY EVENT

Olympic Games and World Championships Charles Ferdinand Pahud de Mortanges (Netherlands; 1896–1971) won a record four Olympic gold medals—team 1924 and 1928, individual (riding Marcroix) 1928 and 1932; he also won a team silver medal in 1932.

Bruce Oram Davidson (USA; b. 13 Dec 1949) is the only rider to have won two world titles (instituted 1966), on Irish Cap in 1974 and Might Tango in 1978.

United States The most medals won for the USA is six, by John Michael Plumb (b. 28 Mar 1940): team gold 1976 and 1984, and four silver medals, team 1964, 1968 and 1972, and individual 1976. Edmund Sloane "Tad" Coffin (b. 9 May 1955) is the only US rider to have won both team and individual gold medals in 1976.

OLYMPICS Nicole Uphoff and Rembrandt (above), winners of the Olympic individual dressage title for a record second time in 1992. (Photo: Allsport/Vandystadt/Frederic Chehu)

CLEAR ROUND On only three occasions has the winner of the individual Show Jumping Olympic title registered 0 faults, the latest being German Ludger Beerbaum (left) on Classic Touch in 1992. (Photo: Allsport/Chris Cole)

DRESSAGE

Olympic Games and World Championships Germany (West Germany 1968–90) has won a record eight team Olympic gold medals, 1928, 1936, 1964, 1968, 1976, 1984, 1988 and 1992, and has the most team wins, six, at the World Championships (instituted 1966). Dr Reiner Klimke (West Germany; b. 14 Jan 1936) has won a record six Olympic golds (team 1964–88, individual, 1984). He won individual bronze in 1976, for a record seven medals overall, and is the only rider to have won two world titles, on Mehmed in 1974 and on Ahlerich in 1982. Henri St Cyr (Sweden; 1904–79) won a record two individual Olympic gold medals, in 1952 and 1956. This was equaled by Nicole Uphoff (Germany) in 1992; she had previously won in 1988.

World Cup Instituted in 1986, this competition has had only one double winner: Christine Stückelberger (Switzerland; b. 22 May 1947) on Gauguin de Lully in 1987–88.

FENCING

Most titles World The greatest number of individual world titles won is five, by Aleksandr Romankov (USSR; b. 7 Nov 1953), at foil 1974, 1977, 1979, 1982 and 1983, but Christian d'Oriola (France) won four world foil titles, 1947, 1949, 1953–54, as well as two individual Olympic titles (1952 and 1956).

Four women foilists have won three world titles: Helene Mayer (Germany; 1910–53), 1929, 1931, 1937; Ilona Schacherer-Elek (Hungary; 1907–88), 1934–35, 1951; Ellen Müller-Preis (Austria; b. 6 May 1912), 1947, 1949–50; and Cornelia Hanisch (West Germany; b. 12 Jun 1952), 1979, 1981, 1985. Of these only Ilona Schacherer-Elek also won two individual Olympic titles (1936 and 1948).

The longest time span for winning an individual world or Olympic title is 20 years, by Aladár Gerevich (Hungary; b. 16 Mar 1910) at sabre, 1935–55.

Olympic The most individual Olympic gold medals won is three, by Ramón Fonst (Cuba; 1883–1959) in 1900 and 1904 (two); and by Nedo Nadi (Italy; 1894–1952) in 1912 and 1920 (two). Nadi also won three team gold medals in 1920, making five gold medals at one celebration, the record for fencing and a record for any sport at that time. Aladár Gerevich (Hungary) won seven golds—one individual and six team, 1932–60—a span of 28 years, an Olympic record.

Edoardo Mangiarotti (Italy; b. 7 Apr 1919), with six gold, five silver and two bronze, holds the record of 13 Olympic medals in fencing. He won them for foil and épée from 1936 to 1960.

The most gold medals won by a woman is four (one individual, three team) by Yelena Dmitryevna Novikova (nee Belova [USSR]; b. 28 Jul 1947) from 1968 to 1976, and the women's record for all medals is seven (two gold, three silver, two bronze) by Ildikó Sági (formerly Ujlaki, nee Retjö [Hungary]; b. 11 May 1937) from 1960 to 1976.

United States The only US Olympic champion was Albertson Van Zo Post

(1866–1938), who won the men's single sticks and team foil (with two Cubans) at the 1904 Games.

United States National Championships The most US titles won at one weapon is 12 at sabre, by Peter J. Westbrook, in 1974, 1975, 1979–86, 1988 and 1989. The women's record is 10 at foil, by Janice Lee York Romary in 1950–51, 1956–57, 1960–61, 1964–66 and 1968.

The most men's individual foil championships won is seven, by Michael Marx in 1977, 1979, 1982, 1985–87 and 1990. L.G. Nunes won the most épée championships, with six—1917, 1922, 1924, 1926, 1928 and 1932. Vincent Bradford won a record number of women's épée championships with four in 1982–84 and 1986.

NCAA Championship Division I (Men) Inaugurated in 1941, this event was discontinued in 1989. It was won a record 12 times by New York University (1947, 1954, 1957, 1960–61, 1966–67, 1970–71, 1973–74, 1976). Since 1989 it has been replaced by a combined team title.

Michael Lofton, New York University, has won the most titles in a career, with four victories in the sabre, 1984–87. Abraham Balk, New York University, is the only man to win two individual titles in one year, 1947 (foil and épée).

(Women) Inaugurated in 1982, this event was discontinued in 1989. Wayne State (MI) has won the most titles: three (1982, 1988–89).

Caitlin Bilodeaux (Columbia-Barnard) and Molly Sullivan (Notre Dame) have both won the individual title twice—Bilodeaux in 1985 and 1987; Sullivan in 1986 and 1988.

(Team) In 1990, the NCAA team competition was combined for the first time. Two teams have won two titles: Penn State (1990–91); and Columbia-Barnard (1992–93).

FIELD HOCKEY

Most Olympic medals India was Olympic champion from the reintroduction of Olympic hockey in 1928 until 1960, when Pakistan beat India 1–0 in Rome. India had its eighth win in 1980. Of the six Indians who have won three Olympic team gold medals, two have also won a silver medal—Leslie Walter Claudius (b. 25 Mar 1927), in 1948, 1952, 1956 and 1960 (silver), and Udham Singh (b. 4 Aug 1928), in 1952, 1956, 1964 and 1960 (silver).

A women's tournament was added in 1980, and there have been four separate winners.

United States US men won the bronze medal in 1932, but only three teams played that year; US women won the bronze in 1984.

Field hockey Champions' Trophy In this competition, first held in 1978 and contested annually since 1980 by the top six men's teams in the world, the most wins is five, by Australia, 1983–85, 1989–90. The first women's Champions' Trophy was won by the Netherlands in 1987. South Korea won in 1989 and Australia in 1991.

MEN

Highest international score   The highest score was achieved when India defeated the USA 24–1 at Los Angeles, CA in the 1932 Olympic Games.

Most international appearances   Heiner Dopp (b. 27 Jun 1956) represented West Germany 286 times between 1975 and 1990, indoors and out.

Greatest scoring feats   The greatest number of goals scored in international hockey is 267, by Paul Litjens (Netherlands; b. 9 Nov 1947) in 177 games.

Best goalkeeping   Richard James Allen (India; b. 4 Jun 1902) did not concede a goal during the 1928 Olympic tournament and gave up a total of only three in 1936.

WOMEN

Most international appearances   Valerie Robinson made a record 149 appearances for England, 1963–84.

United States   Sheryl Johnson has made a record 137 appearances for the USA from 1978 to 1990.
Highest scores   The highest score in an international match was when England beat France 23–0 at Merton, London, Great Britain on 3 Feb 1923.

NCAA Division I   In this competition, inaugurated in 1981, Old Dominion University, Norfolk, VA has won the most championships with seven titles: 1982–84, 1988 and 1990–92.

Field hockey World Cup   The World Cup for men was first held in 1971, and for women in 1974. The most wins are: (*men*) three by Pakistan, 1971, 1978 and 1982; (*women*) five by the Netherlands, 1974, 1978, 1983, 1986 and 1990.

Fastest goal in an international field hockey match   John French scored 7 sec after the bully-off for England *v* West Germany at Nottingham, Great Britain on 25 Apr 1971.

Highest field hockey attendance   The highest attendance was 65,165 for the match between England and the USA at Wembley, London, Great Britain on 11 Mar 1978.

WORLD RECORDS—FRESHWATER AND SALTWATER

A selection of All-Tackle records ratified by the International Game Fish Association as of 1 Jan 1993

Species	Weight lb	oz	Caught by	Location	Date
Arawana	10	2	Gilberto Fernandes	Puraquequara Lake, Amazon, Brazil	3 Feb 1990
Barracuda, Blackfin	15	0	Alejandron Caniz	Puerto Quetzal, Guatemala	29 Oct 1988
Barracuda, Great	85	0	John W. Helfriech	Christmas Island, Rep of Kiribati	11 Apr 1992
Barracuda, Mexican	21	0	E. Greg Kent	Phantom Isle, Costa Rica	27 Mar 1987
Bass, Giant Sea	536	8	James D. McAdam, Jr.	Anacapa Island, CA	20 Aug 1968
Bass, Largemouth	22	4	George W. Perry	Montgomery Lake, GA	2 Jun 1932
Bass, Smallmouth	11	15	David L. Hayes	Dale Hollow Lake, KY	9 Jul 1955
Bass, Striped	78	8	Albert R. McReynolds	Atlantic City, NJ	21 Sep 1982
Bass, Striped (landlocked)	67	8	Hank Ferguson	O'Neill Forebay, San Luis, CA	7 May 1992
Bass, Whiterock	24	3	David N. Lambert	Lessville Lake, VA	12 May 1989
Bluefish	31	12	James M. Hussey	Hatteras, NC	30 Jan 1972
Bonefish	19	0	Brian W. Batchelor	Zululand, South Africa	26 May 1962
Carp	75	1	Leo van der Gugten	Lac de St. Cassien, France	21 May 987
Catfish, Flathead	91	4	Mike Rogers	Lake Lewisville, TX	28 Mar 1982
Catfish, Blue	109	4	George A. Lijewski	Cooper River, Moncks Corner, SC	14 Mar 1991
Cod, Atlantic	98	12	Alphonse J. Bielevich	Isle of Shoals, NH	8 Jun 1969
Conger	110	8	Hans Christian Clausen	Plymouth, Great Britain	20 Aug 1991
Flounder, Summer	22	7	Charles Nappi	Montauk, NY	15 Sep 1975
Grouper, Black	113	6	Donald W. Bone	Dry Tortugas, FL	27 Jan 1990
Halibut (Pacific)	368	0	Celia H. Dueitt	Gustavus, AL	5 Jul 1991
Marlin, Black	1,560	0	Alfred C. Glassell, Jr.	Cabo Blanco, Peru	4 Aug 1953
Marlin, Blue (Atlantic)	1,402	2	Paulo Roberto A. Amorim	Vitoria, Brazil	29 Feb 1992

Species	lb	oz	Angler	Location	Date
Marlin, Blue (Pacific)	1,376	0	Jay Wm de Beaubien	Kaaiwi Point, Kona Coast, HI	31 May 1982
Marlin, Striped	494	0	Bill Boniface	Tutukaka, New Zealand	16 Jan 1986
Marlin, White	181	14	Evandro Luiz Coser	Vitoria, Brazil	8 Dec 1979
Muskellunge	69	15	Arthur Lawton	St Lawrence River, NY	22 Sep 1957
Perch, Nile	191	8	Andy Davison	Rusinga Island, Lake Victoria, Kenya	5 Sep 1991
Pike, Northern	55	1	Lothar Louis	Lake of Grefeern, Germany	16 Oct 1986
Sailfish (Atlantic)	135	5	Ron King	Lagos, Nigeria	10 Nov 1991
Sailfish (Pacific)	221	0	C. W. Stewart	Santa Cruz Island, Ecuador	12 Feb 1947
Salmon, Chinook	97	4	Les Anderson	Kenia River, AK	17 May 1985
Salmon, Coho	33	4	Jerry Lifton	Pulaski, NY	27 Sep 1989
Shark, Blue	437	0	Peter Hyde	Catherine Bay, NSW, Australia	2 Oct 1976
Shark, Hammerhead	991	0	Allen Ogle	Sarasota, FL	30 May 1982
Shark, Mako	1,115	0	Patrick Guillanton	Black River, Mauritius	16 Nov 1988
Shark, Tiger	1,780	0	Walter Maxwell	Cherry Grove, SC	14 Jun 1964
Shark, White	2,664	0	Alfred Dean	Ceduna, South Australia	21 Apr 1959
Snapper, Cubera	12	8	Mike Hebert	Cameron, LA	5 Jul 1982
Snapper, Red	46	8	E. Lane Nicholls	Destin, FL	1 Oct 1985
Stingray	294	0	Iain Foulger	River Gambia, The Gambia	4 Nov 1988
Sturgeon, White	468	0	Joey Pallotta III	Benicia, CA	9 Jul 1983
Swordfish	1,182	0	L. Marron	Iquique, Chile	17 May 1953
Tarpon	283	4	Yvon Viktor Sebag	Sherbo Islands, Sierra Leone	16 Apr 1991
Trout, Brown	40	4	Howard L. Collins	Little Red River, Heber Springs, AK	9 May 1992
Trout, Lake	66	8	Rodney Harback	Great Bear Lake, NWT, Canada	19 Jul 1991
Trout, Rainbow	42	2	David Robert White	Bell Island, AL	22 Jun 1970
Tuna, Bigeye (Atlantic)	375	8	Cecil Browne	Ocean City, MD	26 Apr 1977
Tuna, Bigeye (Pacific)	435	0	Dr Russel V. A. Lee	Cabo Blanco, Peru	17 Apr 1957
Tuna, Bluefin	1,496	0	Ken Fraser	Aulds Cove, Nova Scotia, Canada	26 Oct 1979
Wahoo	155	8	William Bourne	San Salvador, Bahamas	3 Apr 1990
Walleye	25	0	Mabry Harper	Old Hickory Lake, TN	1 Apr 1960

FISHING

Oldest existing club   The Ellem Fishing Club was formed by a number of Edinburgh and Berwickshire gentlemen in Scotland in 1829. Its first annual general meeting was held on 29 Apr 1830.

World Freshwater Championship   The *Confédération Internationale de la Pêche Sportive* (CIPS) championships were inaugurated as European championships in 1953 and recognized as world championships in 1957.

France won the European title in 1956 and 12 world titles between 1959 and 1990. Robert Tesse (France) took the individual title a record three times, 1959–60 and 1965.

The record weight (team) is 76.52 lb in 3 hr by West Germany on the Neckar at Mannheim, Germany on 21 Sep 1980. The individual record is 37.45 lb by Wolf-Rüdiger Kremkus (West Germany) at Mannheim on 20 Sep 1980. The most fish caught is 652, by Jacques Isenbaert (Belgium) at Danaújváros, Hungary on 27 Aug 1967.

IGFA world records   The International Game Fish Association (IGFA) recognizes world records for game fish—both freshwater and saltwater—for a large number of species of fish. Its thousands of categories include all-tackle, various line classes and tippet classes for fly fishing. New records recognized by the IGFA reached an annual peak of 1,074 in 1984.

Longest fight   The longest recorded individual fight with a fish is 37 hr, by Bob Ploeger (USA) with a King salmon on 12–13 Jul 1989.

Largest single catch   The largest officially ratified fish ever caught on a rod was a man-eating great white shark (*Carcharodon carcharias*) weighing 2,664 lb and measuring 16 ft 10 in long, caught on a 130 lb test line by Alf Dean at Denial Bay, near Ceduna, South Australia on 21 Apr 1959. A great white shark weighing 3,388 lb was caught by Clive Green off Albany, Western Australia on 26 Apr 1976 but will remain unratified, as whale meat was used as bait.

In June 1978 a great white shark measuring 20 ft 4 in in length and weighing over 5,000 lb was harpooned and landed by fishermen in the harbor of San Miguel, Azores.

The largest marine animal killed by *hand* harpoon was a blue whale 97 ft in length, by Archer Davidson in Twofold Bay, New South Wales, Australia in 1910. Its tail flukes measured 20 ft across and its jawbone 23 ft 4 in.

The largest fish ever taken underwater was an 804 lb giant black grouper or jewfish by Don Pinder of the Miami Triton Club, FL in 1955.

The heaviest freshwater category recognized by the IGFA is for the sturgeon; the record weight in this category is 468 lb, caught by Joey Pallotta III on 9 Jul 1983 off Benicia, CA.

Fly fishing   World fly fishing championships were inaugurated by the CIPS in 1981. The most team titles is five, by Italy, 1982–84, 1986, 1992. The most individual titles is two, by Brian Leadbetter (Great Britain), 1987 and 1991.

Casting   The longest freshwater cast ratified under ICF (International Casting Federation) rules is 574 ft 2 in, by Walter Kummerow (Germany), for the Bait Distance Double-Handed 30 g event held at Lenzerheide, Switzerland in the 1968 Championships.

At the currently contested weight of 17.7 g, known as 18 g Bait Distance, the longest Double-Handed cast is 457 ft 1/2 in, by Kevin Carriero (USA) at Toronto, Ontario, Canada on 24 Jul 1984.

The longest Fly Distance Double-Handed cast is 319 ft 1 in, by Wolfgang Feige (Germany) at Toronto, Ontario, Canada on 23 Jul 1984.

FOOTBAG

This sport originated in Oregon in 1972 and was invented by John Stalberger (USA). A footbag is a small, pliable, pellet-filled ball-like object with little or no bounce. The concept of the game is to keep the footbag in the air for the longest possible time. Both the time and the number of consecutive hacks (kicks) are recorded.

Men's singles   The world record for keeping a footbag airborne is 48,825 consecutive kicks or hacks, by Ted Martin (USA) in Memphis, TN on 4 Jun 1988.

Women's singles   The women's record is held by Francine Beaudry (Canada), with 15,458 on 28 Jul 1987 at Golden, CO.

Men's doubles   The record is 83,453 hacks, by Andy Linder and Ted Martin (both US) on 26 Sep 1992 in Mount Prospect, IL. The pair kept the footbag aloft for 12 hr 39 min 15 sec.

Women's doubles   The record is 21,025 hacks, by Constance Reed and Marie Elsner (both US) on 31 Jul 1986. The pair kept the footbag aloft for 3 hr 6 min 37 sec.

Five minutes   The greatest number of kicks in five minutes is 912, by Kenny Shults (USA) at Golden, CO on 30 Jul 1991, and for women the record is 705, by Sam Lundberg (USA) on 28 Jul 1992, again at Golden, CO.

Footbag circle   The largest continuous circle of people playing footbag was 862. This gathering of well-rounded people was staged at Colorado State University in Fort Collins on 24 Jun 1986.

FOOTBALL

NATIONAL FOOTBALL LEAGUE
(NFL) RECORDS

Most championships   The Green Bay Packers have won a record 11 NFL titles, 1929–31, 1936, 1939, 1944, 1961–62, 1965–67.

Most consecutive wins (regular season and playoffs)   The Chicago Bears have won 18 consecutive games twice, in 1933–34 and 1941–42. This was matched by the Miami Dolphins in 1972–73 and by the San Francisco 49ers in 1989–90. The most consecutive games without defeat is 25, by the Canton Bulldogs (22 wins and 3 ties) in 1921–23.

Most games played   George Frederick Blanda (b. 17 Sep 1927) played in a record 340 games in a record 26 seasons in the NFL, for the Chicago Bears (1948–58), the Baltimore Colts (1950), the Houston Oilers (1960–66), and the Oakland Raiders (1967–75).
   The most consecutive games played is 282, by Jim Marshall for the Cleveland Browns (1960) and the Minnesota Vikings (1961–79).

Longest run from scrimmage   Anthony Drew "Tony" Dorsett (b. 7 Apr 1954) completed a touchdown after a run of 99 yards for the Dallas Cowboys *v* the Minnesota Vikings on 3 Jan 1983.

Longest field goal   63 yards by Thomas John "Tom" Dempsey (b. 12 Jan 1947) for the New Orleans Saints *v* the Detroit Lions, 8 Nov 1970.

Longest pass completion   Pass completions for a touchdown of 99 yards were achieved by Frank Filchok (to Andy Farkas), Washington Redskins *v* Pittsburgh Steelers, 15 Oct 1939; George Izo (to Bobby Mitchell), Washington Redskins *v* Cleveland Browns, 15 Sep 1963; Karl Sweetan (to Pat Studstill), Detroit Lions *v* Baltimore Colts, 16 Oct 1966; Sonny Jurgensen (to Gerry Allen), Washington Redskins *v* Chicago Bears, 15 Sep 1968; Jim Plunkett (to

---

Largest deficit overcome   On 3 Jan 1993 the Buffalo Bills, playing at home in the AFC Wild Card game, trailed the Houston Oilers 35–3 with 28 minutes remaining. The Bills rallied to score 35 unanswered points and take the lead with 3:08 left. The Bills eventually won the game in overtime, overcoming a deficit of 32 points—the largest in NFL history.

Most valuable player   Joseph C. "Joe" Montana, Jr. (b. 11 Jun 1956), quarterback of the San Francisco 49ers, has been voted the Super Bowl MVP on a record three occasions: Super Bowl XVI, XIX, and XXIV.

NFL RECORDS

Most Points

Career 2,002, George Blanda (Chicago Bears, Baltimore Colts, Houston Oilers, Oakland Raiders), 1949–75. **Season** 176, Paul Hornung (Green Bay Packers), 1960. **Game** 40, Ernie Nevers (Chicago Cardinals), 28 Nov 1929.

Most Touchdowns

Career 126, Jim Brown (Cleveland Browns), 1957–65. **Season** 24, John Riggins (Washington Redskins), 1983. **Game** 6, Ernie Nevers (Chicago Cardinals), 28 Nov 1929; William "Dub" Jones (Cleveland Browns) 25 Nov 1951; Gale Sayers (Chicago Bears), 12 Dec 1965.

Most Yards Gained Rushing

Career 16,726, Walter Payton (Chicago Bears), 1975–87. **Season** 2,105, Eric Dickerson (Los Angeles Rams), 1984. **Game** 275, Walter Payton (Chicago Bears), 20 Nov 1977. **Highest career average** 5.22 yds per game (12,352 yds from 2,359 attempts), Jim Brown (Cleveland Browns), 1957–65.

Most Yards Gained Receiving

Career 13,821, James Lofton (Green Bay Packers, Los Angeles Raiders, Buffalo Bills), 1978–92. **Season** 1,746, Charley Hennigan (Houston Oilers), 1961. **Game** 336, Willie "Flipper" Anderson (Los Angeles Rams), 26 Nov 1989.

Most Yards Gained Passing

Career 47,003, Fran Tarkenton (Minnesota Vikings, New York Giants), 1961–78. **Season** 5,084, Dan Marino (Miami Dolphins), 1984. **Game** 554, Norm Van Brocklin (Los Angeles Rams), 28 Sep 1951.

Passing Attempts

Career 6,467, Fran Tarkenton (Minnesota Vikings, New York Giants), 1961–78. **Season** 655, Warren Moon (Houston Oilers), 1991. **Game** 68, George Blanda (Houston Oilers), 1 Nov 1964.

Most Passes Completed

Career 3,686, Fran Tarkenton (Minnesota Vikings, New York Giants), 1961–78. **Season** 404, Warren Moon (Houston Oilers), 1991. **Game** 42 (from 59 attempts), Richard Todd (New York Jets), 21 Sep 1980. **Consecutive** 22, Joe Montana (San Francisco 49ers), 29 Nov 1987 *v* Cleveland Browns (5); 6 Dec 1987 *v* Green Bay Packers (17).

Pass Receptions

Career 847, Art Monk (Washington Redskins), 1980–92. **Season** 108, Sterling Sharpe (Green Bay Packers), 1992. **Game** 18, Tom Fears (Los Angeles Rams), 3 Dec 1950.

Field Goals

Career 373, Jan Stenerud (Kansas City Chiefs, Green Bay Packers, Minnesota Vikings), 1967–85. **Season** 35, Ali Haji-Sheikh (New York Giants), 1983. **Game** 7, Jim Bakken (St Louis Cardinals), 24 Sep 1967; Rich Karlis (Minnesota Vikings), 5 Nov 1989.

Punting

Career 1,154, Dave Jennings (New York Giants, New York Jets), 1974–87. **Season** 114, Bob Parsons (Chicago Bears), 1981. **Game** 15, John Teltschik (Philadelphia Eagles *v* New York Giants), 6 Dec 1987.

Sacks

Career 126.5, Lawrence Taylor (New York Giants), 1982–92. **Season** 22, Mark Gastineau (New York Jets), 1984. **Game** 7, Derrick Thomas (Kansas City Chiefs *v* Seattle Seahawks), 11 Nov 1990.

Most Interceptions

Career 81, Paul Krause (Washington Redskins, Minnesota Vikings), 1964–79. **Season** 14, Dick "Night Train" Lane (Los Angeles Rams), 1952. **Game** 4; 16 players have achieved this feat.

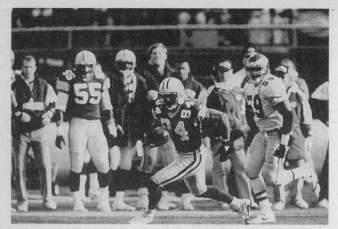

MOST PASS RECEPTIONS IN A SEASON   **Sterling Sharpe of the Green Bay Packers had a record 108 pass receptions during the 1992 season. (Photo: Allsport/Rick Stewart)**

MOST CAREER RECEPTIONS   **During the 1992 season Art Monk caught his NFL record 847th reception. (Photo: Allsport/Rick Stewart)**

Cliff Branch), Los Angeles Raiders *v* Washington Redskins, 2 Oct 1983; and Ron Jaworski (to Mike Quick), Philadelphia Eagles *v* Atlanta Falcons, 10 Nov 1985.

Longest punt 98 yards by Steve O'Neal for the New York Jets *v* the Denver Broncos, 21 Sep 1969.

Consecutive games Scoring 186, by Jim Breech for the Oakland Raiders, 1979, and the Cincinnati Bengals, 1980–92.

Scoring touchdowns 18, by Lenny Moore for the Baltimore Colts, 1963–65.

Pass receptions 177, by Steve Largent for the Seattle Seahawks, 1977–89.

Field goals 24, by Kevin Butler for the Chicago Bears, 1988–89.

Coaches The winningest coach in NFL history was George Stanley Halas (1895–1983), whose Chicago Bears teams won 325 games (and 7 NFL titles) to 151 losses and 31 ties while he was coach in 1920–29, 1933–42, 1946–55 and 1958–67. The highest winning percentage was .740, achieved by Vincent Thomas "Vince" Lombardi (1913–70): 105 wins, 35 losses and 6 ties with the Green Bay Packers, 1959–67, and the Washington Redskins, 1969.

Most seasons 40, George Halas, with the Decatur/Chicago Staleys/Chicago Bears (1920–29, 1933–42, 1946–55, 1958–67).

THE SUPER BOWL

The Super Bowl was first held in 1967 between the winners of the NFL and AFL championships. Since 1970 it has been contested by the winners of the National and American Conferences of the NFL. The most wins is four, by the Pittsburgh Steelers in 1974–75, 1978–79, coached by Chuck Noll on each occasion, and by the San Francisco 49ers in 1981, 1984, 1988 and 1989, coached by Bill Walsh (1981, 1984, 1988) and George Seifert (1989).

Most appearances The Dallas Cowboys have played in six Super Bowls: V, VI, X, XII, XIII, XXVII. The Cowboys have won three and lost three.

The most appearances by a player is five, shared by seven players: Marv Fleming (Green Bay Packers 1966–67, Miami Dolphins 1971–73); Larry Cole (Dallas Cowboys 1970–71, 1975, 1977–78); Cliff Harris (Dallas Cowboys 1970–71, 1975, 1977–78); D.D. Lewis (Dallas Cowboys 1970–71, 1975, 1977–1978); Preston Pearson (Baltimore Colts 1968, Pittsburgh Steelers 1974, Dallas Cowboys 1975, 1977–78); Charlie Waters (Dallas Cowboys 1970–71, 1975, 1977–1978); and Rayfield Wright (Dallas Cowboys 1970–71, 1975, 1977–78).

Don Shula has coached six Super Bowls to set the all-time mark: Baltimore Colts, 1968; Miami Dolphins, 1971–73, 1982, 1984. He won two games and lost four.

Highest scores The highest aggregate score was 69 points, when the Dallas Cowboys beat the Buffalo Bills 52–17 on 31 Jan 1993, in Super Bowl XXVII. The highest team score and record victory margin was when the San Francisco 49ers beat the Denver Broncos 55–10 in New Orleans, LA on 28 Jan 1990. In their 42–10 victory over the Denver Broncos on 31 Jan 1988, the Washington

Redskins scored a record 35 points in the second quarter. The narrowest margin of victory was one point, when the New York Giants defeated the Buffalo Bills 20–19 on 27 Jan 1991.

Individual records *Points* The most points scored is 18 by two players: Roger Craig, San Francisco 49ers (*v* Miami Dolphins, 1984) and Jerry Rice, San Francisco 49ers (*v* Denver Broncos, 1989).

Touchdowns The most touchdowns thrown is 5 by Joe Montana, San Francisco 49ers (*v* Denver Broncos, 1989). The most touchdowns scored is 3 by two players: Roger Craig, San Francisco 49ers (*v* Miami Dolphins, 1984) and Jerry Rice, San Francisco 49ers (*v* Denver Broncos, 1989).

Yards gained The most yards gained rushing is 204 by Timmy Smith, Washington Redskins (*v* Denver Broncos, 1987). The most yards gained passing is 357 by Joe Montana, San Francisco 49ers (*v* Cincinnati Bengals, 1988). The most yards gained receiving is 215 by Jerry Rice, San Francisco 49ers (*v* Cincinnati Bengals, 1988).

Completions The most completions thrown is 29 by Dan Marin, Miami Dolphins (*v* San Francisco 49ers, 1984). The highest pass completion mark is 88 percent (22–25) by Phil Simms, New York Giants (*v* Denver Broncos, 1986).

Receptions The most receptions is 11 by two players: Dan Ross, Cincinnati Bengals (*v* San Francisco 49ers, 1981) and Jerry Rice, San Francisco 49ers (*v* Cincinnati Bengals, 1988).

HIGHEST AGGREGATE SCORE **Action from Super Bowl XXVII, when the Dallas Cowboys beat the Buffalo Bills 52–17. (Photo: Allsport/Rick Stewart)**

COLLEGE FOOTBALL (NCAA)

Team records *Most wins*   Michigan has won 731 games out of 1,005 played, 1879–1992.

Highest winning percentage   The highest winning percentage in college football history is .761, by Notre Dame. The Fighting Irish have won 712, lost 210 and tied 41 out of 963 games played, 1887–1992.

Career records (Divisions 1-A, 1-AA, II and III) *Points scored*   474, Joe Dudek, Plymouth State (Div. III), 1982–85.

Rushing (yards)   6,320, Johnny Bailey, Texas A&I (Div. II), 1986–89.

Passing (yards)   15,031, Ty Detmer, Brigham Young (Div I-A), 1988–91.

Receptions (yards)   4,693, Jerry Rice, Mississippi Valley (Div. 1-AA), 1981–84.

Receptions (most)   301, Jerry Rice, Mississippi Valley (Div. 1-AA), 1981–84.

Field goals (game)   8, Goran Lingmerth, Northern Arizona (Div. 1-AA). Booting 8 out of 8 kicks, Lingmerth set the record on 25 Oct 1986 *v* Idaho.

Longest plays *Run from scrimmage*   99 yards by four players: Gale Sayers (Kansas *v* Nebraska), 1963; Max Anderson (Arizona State *v* Wyoming), 1967; Ralph Thompson (West Texas State *v* Wichita State), 1970; and Kelsey Finch (Tennessee *v* Flórida), 1977.

Field goal   67 yards by three players: Russell Erxleben (Texas *v* Rice), 1977; Steve Little (Arkansas *v* Texas), 1977; and Joe Williams (Wichita State *v* Southern Illinois), 1978. Ove Johansson kicked a 69-yard field goal for Abilene Christian University *v* East Texas State on 16 Oct 1976, but this was in an NAIA game.

Pass completion   99 yards on eight occasions by seven players: Fred Owens (to Jack Ford), Portland *v* St. Mary's, CA, 1947; Bo Burris (to Warren McVea), Houston *v* Washington State, 1966; Colin Clapton (to Eddie Jenkins), Holy Cross *v* Boston U, 1970; Terry Peel (to Robert Ford), Houston *v* Syracuse, 1970; Terry Peel (to Robert Ford), Houston *v* San Diego State, 1972; Chris Collingsworth (to Derrick Gaffney), Florida *v* Rice, 1977; Scott Ankrom (to James Maness), TCU *v* Rice, 1984; and Gino Torretta (to Horace Copeland), Miami *v* Arkansas, 1991.

Punt   99 yards by Pat Brady, Nevada-Reno *v* Loyola, CA in 1950.

Longest streak   The University of Oklahoma won 47 successive games from 1953 to 1957, when they were beaten 7–0 by Notre Dame. The longest unbeaten streak is 63 (59 won, 4 tied) by Washington from 1907 to 1917, ended by a 27–0 loss to California.

NCAA DIVISION 1-A INDIVIDUAL RECORDS

Points

Game	48	Howard Griffith (Illinois v Southern Illinois); 8 touchdowns	22 Sep 1990
Season	234	Barry Sanders (Oklahoma State; 39 touchdowns in 11 games)	1988
Career	423	Roman Anderson (Houston; 70 field goals, 213 point-after-touchdowns)	1988–91

Total yardage

Game	732	David Klingler (Houston v Arizona State; 716 passing, 16 rushing)	1 Dec 1990
Season	5,221	David Klingler (Houston; 5,140 passing, 81 rushing)	1990
Career	14,665	Ty Detmer (Brigham Young; 15,031 passing, −366 rushing)	1988–91

Yards gained rushing

Game	396	Tony Sands (Kansas v Missouri)	23 Nov 1991
Season	2,628	Barry Sanders (Oklahoma State; 344 rushes in 11 games, record av. 238.9)	1988
Career	6,082	Tony Dorsett (Pittsburgh)	1973–76

Yards gained passing

Game	716	David Klingler (Houston v Arizona State)	1 Dec 1990
Season	5,188	Ty Detmer (Brigham Young)	1990
Career	15,031	Ty Detmer (Brigham Young; completed 958 of 1,530)	1988–91

Pass completions

Game	48	David Klingler (Houston v SMU)	20 Oct 1990
Season	374	David Klingler (Houston)	1990
Career	958	Ty Detmer (Brigham Young; 1,530 attempts)	1988–91

Touchdown passes

Game	11	David Klingler (Houston v Eastern Washington)	17 Nov 1990
Season	54	David Klingler (Houston)	1990
Career	121	Ty Detmer (Brigham Young)	1988–91

Pass receptions

Game	22	Jay Miller (Brigham Young v New Mexico; 263 yards)	3 Nov 1973
Season	142	Emmanuel Hazard (Houston)	1989
Career	266	Aaron Turner (Pacific)	1989–92

Yards gained receiving

Game	349	Chuck Hughes (UTEP v North Texas; caught 10)	18 Sep 1965
Season	1,779	Howard Twilley (Tulsa; caught 134 in 10 games)	1965
Career	4,345	Aaron Turner (Pacific)	1989–92

Pass interceptions

Game	5	Dan Rebsch (Miami [Ohio] v Western Michigan; 88 yards; three others with less yards)	4 Nov 1972
Season	14	Al Worley (Washington; 130 yards, in 10 games)	1968
Career	29	Al Brosky (Illinois; 356 yards, 27 games)	1950–52

Touchdowns (receiving)

Game	6	Tim Delaney (San Diego State v New Mexico State)	15 Nov 1969
Season	22	Emmanuel Hazard (Houston)	1989
Career	43	Aaron Turner (Pacific)	1989–92

Field goals

Game	7	Mike Prindle (West Michigan v Marshall)	29 Sep 1984
	7	Dale Klein (Nebraska v Missouri)	19 Oct 1985
Season	29	John Lee (UCLA)	1984
Career	80	Jeff Jaeger (Washington)	1983–86
Consecutive	30	Chuck Nelson (Washington)	1981–82

Touchdowns

Game	8	Howard Griffith (Illinois v Southern Illinois)	22 Sep 1990
Season	39	Barry Sanders (Oklahoma State)	1988
Career	65	Anthony Thompson (Indiana)	1986–89

Highest score   The most points ever scored in a college game is 222, by Georgia Tech *v* Cumberland College (0) of Lebanon, TN on 7 Oct 1916. Tech set records for 63 points in a quarter, 32 touchdowns, and 30 points after touchdown in this game.

Coaches   In Division 1-A competition, Paul "Bear" Bryant (1913–83) won more games than any other coach, with 323 wins over 38 years: Maryland 1945, Kentucky 1946–53, Texas A&M 1954–57 and Alabama 1958–82. He led Alabama to five national titles and 15 bowl wins, including seven Sugar Bowls. The best win percentage in Division 1-A was 0.881, by Knute Rockne (1888–1931), with 105 wins, 12 losses and 5 ties, 12,847 points for and 667 against, at Notre Dame 1918–30. In overall NCAA competition, Eddie Robinson, Grambling (Division 1-AA) holds the mark for most victories, with 381 through 1992.

Record attendances   The highest attendances at college football games were estimated crowds of 120,000 at Soldier Field, Chicago, IL on 26 Nov 1927 when Notre Dame beat Southern California 7–6, and on 13 Oct 1928 when Notre Dame beat Navy 7–0. The highest average attendance for home games is 105,867 for the six games played by Michigan in 1992.

National College Football Champions   The most wins in the national journalists' poll, established in 1936, to determine the college team of the year is eight by Notre Dame, 1943, 1946–47, 1949, 1966, 1973, 1977 and 1988.

Bowl games   The oldest college bowl game is the Rose Bowl. It was first played on 1 Jan 1902 at Tournament Park, Pasadena, CA, when Michigan beat Stanford 49–0. The second game did not take place until 1916, and the game has been played continuously since. The University of Southern Califor-

RECORD BOWL APPEARANCES   Alabama has clinched a record 25 bowl wins in a record 45 bowl appearances. (Photo: Allsport (USA)/Tim Defrisco)

nia (USC) has a record 19 wins in the Rose Bowl. The University of Alabama has made a record 45 bowl appearances and had 25 wins. Most wins in the other "big four" bowl games: Orange Bowl: 11, Oklahoma; Sugar Bowl: 8, Alabama; Cotton Bowl: 9, Texas. Alabama, Georgia, Georgia Tech and Notre Dame are the only four teams to have won each of the "big four" bowl games.

Heisman Memorial Trophy This award has been given annually since 1935 by the Downtown Athletic Club of New York to the top college football player as determined by a poll of journalists. It was originally called the D.A.C. Trophy but the name was changed in 1936. Its full title is the John W. Heisman Memorial Trophy and it is named after the first athletic director of the Downtown Athletic Club. The only double winner has been Archie Griffin of Ohio State, 1974–75. The University of Notre Dame has had more Heisman Trophy winners than any other school, with seven selections.

GAELIC FOOTBALL

All-Ireland Championships The greatest number of All-Ireland Championships won by one team is 30, by Ciarraidhe (Kerry) between 1903 and 1986. The greatest number of successive wins is four, by Wexford (1915–18) and Kerry twice (1929–32, 1978–81).

The most finals contested by an individual is 10, including eight wins by the Kerry players Pat Spillane, Paudie O'Shea and Denis Moran, 1975–76, 1978–82, 1984–86.

The highest team score in a final was when Dublin, 27 (5 goals, 12 points), beat Armagh, 15 (3 goals, 6 points), on 25 Sep 1977. The highest combined score was 45 points, when Cork (26) beat Galway (19) in 1973. A goal equals three points.

The highest individual score in an All-Ireland final has been 2 goals, 6 points by Jimmy Keaveney (Dublin) *v* Armagh in 1977, and by Michael Sheehy (Kerry) *v* Dublin in 1979.

Largest Gaelic football crowd The record crowd was 90,556 for the Down *v* Offaly final at Croke Park, Dublin in 1961.

GOLF

Oldest club The oldest club of which there is written evidence is the Gentlemen Golfers (now the Honourable Company of Edinburgh Golfers) formed in March 1744—ten years prior to the institution of the Royal and Ancient Club of St Andrews, Fife, Scotland. However, the Royal Burgess Golfing Society of Edinburgh, Great Britain claims to have been founded in 1735.

United States   Two golf clubs claim to be the first established in the United States: the Foxberg Golf Club, Clarion Co., PA (1887) and St Andrews Golf Club of Yonkers, NY (1888).

Highest course   The Tuctu Golf Club in Morococha, Peru, is 14,335 ft above sea level at its lowest point. Golf has, however, been played in Tibet at an altitude of over 16,000 ft.

Lowest course   The Furnace Creek course in Death Valley, CA is 220 ft below sea level.

Longest course   The world's longest course is the par-77 8,325 yd International Golf Club in Bolton, MA from the "Tiger" tees, remodeled in 1969 by Robert Trent Jones.
   Floyd Satterlee Rood used the entire United States as a course, when he played from the Pacific surf to the Atlantic surf from 14 Sep 1963 to 3 Oct 1964 in 114,737 strokes. He lost 3,511 balls on the 3,397.7 mile trail.

Longest drives   The greatest recorded drive on a standard course is one of 515 yd, by Michael Hoke Austin (b. 17 Feb 1910) of Los Angeles, CA, in the US National Seniors Open Championship at Las Vegas, NV on 25 Sep 1974. Austin drove the ball to within a yard of the green on the par-4 450 yd fifth

---

Longest hole   The longest hole in the world is the sixth hole (par-7) of the Koolan Island Golf Course, Western Australia, which measures 948 yd.

Largest green   Probably the largest green in the world is that of the par-6 695 yd fifth hole at International Golf Club, Bolton, MA with an area greater than 28,000 ft^2.

Largest tournament   The Volkswagen Grand Prix Open Amateur Championship in Great Britain attracted a record 321,778 (206,820 men and 114,958 women) competitors in 1984.

Most shots for one hole   A woman player in the qualifying round of the Shawnee Invitational for Ladies at Shawnee-on-Delaware, PA, *c.* 1912, took 166 strokes for the short 130 yd 16th hole. Her tee shot went into the Binniekill River and the ball floated. She put out in a boat with her helpful but statistically minded husband at the oars. She eventually beached the ball 1$\frac{1}{2}$ miles downstream but was not yet out of the woods. She had to play through one on the home run.

World one-club record   Thad Daber (USA), with a six-iron, played the 6,037 yd Lochmore Golf Club course, Cary, NC in 70 to win the 1987 World One-Club Championship.

PGA TOUR ALL-TIME SCORING RECORDS*

Lowest score (9 holes)	27	Mike Souchak, Texas Open (back nine)	1955
	27	Andy North, B.C. Open (back nine)	1975
Lowest score (18 holes)	59	Al Geiberger, Danny Thomas Memphis Classic (2nd round)	1977
	59	Chip Beck, Las Vegas Invitational (3rd round)	1991
Lowest score (36 holes)	125	Ron Streck, Texas Open (3rd and 4th rounds)	1988
	125	Blaine McCallister, Hardee's Golf Classic (2nd and 3rd rounds)	1988
Lowest score (54 holes)	189	Chandler Harper, Texas Open (2nd, 3rd and 4th rounds)	1954
Lowest score (72 holes)	257	Mike Souchak, Texas Open	1955
Most shots under par	27	Ben Hogan, Portland Invitational	1945
	27	Mike Souchak, Texas Open	1955
Most birdies in a row	8	Bob Goalby, St Petersburg Open (4th round)	1961
	8	Fuzzy Zoeller, Quad Cities Open (1st round)	1976
	8	Dewey Arnette, Buick Open (1st round)	1987
Fewest putts (18 holes)	18	Sam Trahan, IVB-Philadelphia Golf Classic (4th round)	1979
	18	Mike McGee, Federal Express St Jude Classic (1st round)	1987
	18	Kenny Knox, MCI Heritage Classic (1st round)	1989
	18	Jim McGovern, Federal Express St Jude Classic (2nd round)	1992
Fewest putts (72 holes)	93	Kenny Knox, MCI Heritage Classic	1989

Source: PGA Tour
* All records listed are for 72-hole tournaments.

hole of the Winterwood course and it rolled 65 yd past the flagstick. He was aided by an estimated 35 mph tailwind.

A drive of 2,640 yd (1¹/₂ miles) across ice was achieved by an Australian meteorologist named Nils Lied at Mawson Base, Antarctica in 1962.

On the moon the energy expended on a mundane 300 yd drive would achieve, craters permitting, a distance of 1 mile.

Longest putt The longest recorded holed putt in a professional tournament is 110 ft, by Jack Nicklaus in the 1964 Tournament of Champions; and by Nick Price in the 1992 PGA Championship.

SCORES

Lowest 18 holes Men At least four players have played a long course (over 6,561 yd) in a score of 58—most recently Monte Carlo Money (USA; b. 3 Dec 1954), at the par-72, 6,607 yd Las Vegas Municipal Golf Club, NV on 11 Mar 1981.

The PGA tournament record for 18 holes is 59 (30 + 29), by Al Geiberger (b. 1 Sep 1937) in the second round of the Danny Thomas Classic, on the 72-par 7,249 yd Colonial Golf Club course, Memphis, TN on 10 Jun 1977; and by Chip Beck in the third round of the Las Vegas Invitational, on the 72-par 6,979 yd Sunrise Golf Club course, Las Vegas, NV on 11 Oct 1991.

Other golfers to have recorded 59 over 18 holes in major non-PGA tournaments include: Samuel Jackson "Sam" Snead (USA; b. 27 May 1912), at the Sam Snead Festival (third round) at White Sulphur Springs, WV on 16 May 1959; Gary Player (South Africa; b. 1 Nov 1935), in the second round of the Brazilian Open in Rio de Janeiro on 29 Nov 1974; David Jagger (Great Britain; b. 9 Jun 1949) in a Pro-Am tournament prior to the 1973 Nigerian Open at Ikoyi Golf Club, Lagos; and Miguel Martin (Spain) in the Argentine Southern Championship at Mar de Plata on 27 Feb 1987.

Women The lowest score on an 18-hole course over 5,000 yd is 60 (31 + 29) by Wanda Morgan (b. 22 Mar 1910), on the Westgate and Birchington Golf Club course, Kent, Great Britain, on 11 Jul 1929.

The lowest recorded score in an LPGA tour event on an 18-hole course (over 5,600 yd) is 62 (30 + 32) by Mary Kathryn "Mickey" Wright (USA; b. 14 Feb 1935) on the Hogan Park Course (par-71, 6,286 yd) at Midland, TX, in November 1964; Vicki Fergon at the 1984 San Jose Classic, San Jose, CA; Janice Arnold (New Zealand) (31 + 31) on the Coventry Golf Course, Great Britain (5,815 yd) on 24 Sep 1990; Laura Davies (Great Britain) (32 + 30) at the Rail Golf Club, Springfield, IL on 31 Aug 1991; and Hollis Stacy (USA) (30 +32) at the Meridian Valley CC, Seattle, WA on 18 Sep 1992.

Lowest 72 holes Men Horton Smith scored 245 (63, 58, 61 and 63) for 72 holes on the 4,700 yd course (par-64) at Catalina Country Club, CA to win the Catalina Open on 21–23 Dec 1928.

The lowest recorded score on a first class course is 255 (29 under par), by Leonard Peter Tupling (Great Britain; b. 6 Apr 1950) in the Nigerian Open at Ikoyi Golf Club, Lagos in February 1981, made up of 63, 66, 62 and 64 (average 63.75 per round).

The lowest 72 holes in a PGA tour event is 257 (60, 68, 64, 65), by Mike Souchak in the 1955 Texas Open at San Antonio.

Women Trish Johnson scored 242 (64, 60, 60, 58; 21 under par) in the Bloor

Biggest bunker   The world's biggest bunker is Hell's Half Acre on the 585 yd seventh hole of the Pine Valley course, Clementon, NJ, built in 1912 and generally regarded as the world's most trying course.

Most balls hit in one hour   The most balls driven in one hour, over 100 yds and into a target area, is 1,536, by Noel Hunt at Shrigley Hall, Pott Shrigley, Great Britain on 2 May 1990.

Most wins in a single event   Sam Snead won a record eight times at the Greater Greensboro Open—1938, 1946, 1949–50, 1955–56, 1960 and 1965.

Most times leading money winner   Jack Nicklaus has been the leading money winner eight times—1964–65, 1967, 1971–1973, 1975–76. Kathy Whitworth won eight times—1965–68, 1970–73.

Homes Eastleigh Classic at the Fleming Park Course (4,402 yd) at Eastleigh, Great Britain on 22–25 Jul 1987.

The lowest score in an LPGA tour event is 267 (68, 66, 67, 66), by Betsy King in the 1992 Mazda LPGA Championship.

Most shots under par   35, by Tom Kite at the 90 hole 1993 Bob Hope Chrysler Classic, 11–14 Feb 1993.

Fastest rounds Individual   With such variations in lengths of courses, speed records, even for rounds under par, are of little comparative value. The fastest round played with the golf ball coming to rest before each new stroke is 27 min 9 sec, by James Carvill (b. 13 Oct 1965) at Warrenpoint Golf Course, County Down, Northern Ireland (18 holes, 6,154 yd) on 18 Jun 1987.

Team   The 35 members of the Team Balls Out Diving completed the 18-hole 6,033 yd John E. Clark course at Point Micu, CA in 9 min 39 sec on 16 Nov 1992. They scored 71!

Slowest rounds   The slowest stroke-play tournament round was one of 6 hr 45 min, taken by South Africa in the first round of the 1972 World Cup at the Royal Melbourne Golf Club, Australia. This was a four-ball medal round; everything holed out.

Most holes in 24 hours On foot   Ian Colston, 35, played 22 rounds plus five holes (401 holes in all) at Bendigo Golf Club, Victoria, Australia (par-73, 6,061 yd) on 22–25 Jul 1987. (See Lowest 72 holes.)

Using golf carts   David Cavalier played 846 holes at Arrowhead Country Club, North Canton, OH (9 holes, 3,013 yd) on 6–7 Aug 1990.

Doug Wert played 440 holes in 12 hours on the 6,044-yd course at Tournament Players Club, Coral Springs, FL on 7 Jun 1993.

Most holes played in a week   Steve Hylton played 1,128 holes at the Mason

WORLD CUP (Above) Davis Love III (left in photo) and Fred Couples (both USA) celebrate their success in the 1992 World Cup. It was the USA's 18th win in the competition. (Photo: Allsport/David Cannon)

YOUNGEST MASTER (Left) Severiano Ballesteros won the 1980 Masters at age 23 years 2 days. (Photo: Allsport/Stephen Munday)

Rudolph Golf Club (6,060 yd), Clarksville, TN from 25–31 Aug 1980. Using a golf cart for transport, Colin Young completed 1,260 holes at Patshull Park Golf Club (6,412 yd), Pattingham, Great Britain from 2–9 Jul 1988.

MEN'S CHAMPIONSHIP RECORDS

Grand Slam   The four grand slam events are, in order of play, the Masters, the US Open, the British Open and the PGA Championship. No player has won all four events in one calendar year. Ben Hogan came closest to succeeding in 1951, when he won the first three legs, but he could not return to the United States from Britain in time for the PGA Championship.

The four grand slam events are also known as "the majors." Jack Nicklaus (b. 21 Jan 1940) has won the most major championships, with 18 professional titles (6 Masters, 4 US Opens, 3 British Opens and 5 PGA Championships). Additionally, Nicklaus has won two US Amateur titles, which are often included in calculating major championship victories.

The Masters   (played on the 6,980 yd Augusta National Golf Course, GA, first in 1934)

Most wins   Jack Nicklaus has won six green jackets (1963, 1965–66, 1972, 1975, 1986). Two players have won consecutive Masters: Jack Nicklaus (1965–66) and Nick Faldo (Great Britain; 1989–90).

Lowest total aggregate   271, by Jack Nicklaus (67, 71, 64, 69) in 1965, and by Raymond Loran Floyd (65, 66, 70, 70) in 1976.

Oldest and youngest winners   The oldest winner of the Masters was Jack Nicklaus, age 46 years 81 days in 1986. Severiano Ballesteros (Spain) was the youngest player to win the Masters, at 23 years 2 days in 1980.

US Open (inaugurated 1895) Most wins   Four players have won the title four times: Willie Anderson (1901, 1903–05), Bobby Jones (1923, 1926, 1929–30), Ben Hogan (1948, 1950–51, 1953) and Jack Nicklaus (1962, 1967, 1972, 1980). The only player to gain three successive titles was Willie Anderson, from 1903 to 1905.

Lowest total aggregate   The lowest 72-hole score is 272, achieved by two players: Jack Nicklaus, 272 (63, 71, 70, 68) on the lower course (7,015 yd) at Baltusrol Country Club, NJ, 12–15 Jun 1980; and Lee Janzen (67, 67, 69, 69), also at Baltusrol, 17–20 Jun 1993.

Oldest and youngest winners   The oldest US Open champion was Hale Irwin (b. 3 Jun 1945), at 45 yr 15 days on 18 Jun 1990. The youngest winner of the Open was John J. McDermott at 19 years 317 days in 1911; this is also the record for the youngest winner of any PGA event in the United States.

British Open   (inaugurated 1860, Prestwick, Strathclyde, Scotland)

Most wins   Harry Vardon won a record six titles, in 1896, 1898–99, 1903, 1911 and 1914. Tom Morris, Jr. is the only player to have won four successive British Opens, from 1868 to 1872 (the event was not held in 1871).

Fastest round of golf played on the PGA tour   At the 1977 Heritage Classic at Hilton Head, SC, Gary McCord and Bill Mallon played their fourth round of golf in 1 hr 27 min, still the fastest time ever played on the PGA tour.

Most club championships   Helen Gray has been ladies champion at Tormorden Golf Course, Great Britain 37 times between 1952 and 1991. The men's record is 36 (consecutive) by Richard John Fewster at Bandee Golf Club, Merredin, Australia, 1956–92.

At different clubs, Peter Toogood (Australia; b. 11 Apr 1930) has won 35 championships in Tasmania. At different clubs in the United States, Frances Miles-Maslon Hirsh (USA) was ladies champion 44 times between 1951–90.

Youngest LPGA winner   The youngest LPGA tour event winner was Marlene Hagge (b. 16 Feb 1934), who won the 1952 Sarasota Open at the age of 18 yr 14 days.

Lowest total aggregate   267 (66, 68, 69, 64) by Greg Norman (Australia; b. 10 Feb 1955) at Royal St. George's, in July 1993.

Oldest and youngest winners   The oldest British Open champion was "Old Tom" Morris (1821–1908), age 46 yr 99 days when he won at Prestwick in 1867. The oldest this century has been the 1967 champion, Roberto de Vicenzo (Argentina) at 44 yr 93 days. The youngest winner of the British Open was Tom Morris, Jr. (1851–75) at Prestwick, Strathclyde, Scotland, in 1868 at the age of 17 yr 249 days.

Professional Golfers Association (PGA) Championship Most wins   Two players have won the title five times: Walter Hagen (1921, 1924–27) and Jack Nicklaus (1963, 1971, 1973, 1975, 1980). Walter Hagen won a record four consecutive titles from 1924 to 1927.

Lowest total aggregate   271, by Bobby Nicholls (64, 71, 69, 67) at Columbus Country Club, OH in 1964.

Oldest and youngest winners   The oldest winner of the PGA was Julius Boros (USA; b. 3 Mar 1920) at the age of 48 years 110 days in 1968. Eugene "Gene" Sarazen (USA; b. 27 Feb 1902) was the youngest PGA winner in 1922 at the age of 20 years 170 days.

WOMEN'S CHAMPIONSHIP RECORDS

Grand Slam   The Grand Slam of women's golf has consisted of four tournaments since 1955. The format has changed many times. Since 1983, the US Open, LPGA Championship, du Maurier Classic and Nabisco Dinah Shore have been the major events. Patty Berg has won 15 professional Grand Slam events: US Open (1), Titleholders (7), Western Open (7); the latter two are now defunct. She also won one US Amateur title.

SOLHEIM CUP
(Above) The Solheim Cup (first held in 1990 and won by the USA) is the women's equivalent to the Ryder Cup, with the match format being very much the same. Here the European team celebrates its success over the USA in 1992. (Photo: Allsport/David Cannon)

GREATEST TOTAL PRIZE MONEY
(Right) Nick Faldo won the 1992 Johnnie Walker World Championship, which earned him a total prize of $2.7 million. (Photo: Allsport/David Cannon)

US Open This competition was first held in 1946 at Spokane, WA at match-play, but at 72 holes of stroke-play annually on different courses from 1947.

Most wins The most wins is four, by Elizabeth Earle "Betsy" Rawls (b. 4 May 1928), 1951, 1953, 1957 and 1960, and by Mickey Wright (b. 14 Feb 1935), in 1958–59, 1961 and 1964.

Lowest total aggregate The lowest 72 holes aggregate is 279, by Pat Bradley (b. 24 Mar 1951) in 1981.

Ladies' Professional Golfers Association (LPGA) Championship This competition was inaugurated in 1955 at Orchard Ridge Country Club, Fort Wayne, IN; since 1987 it has been officially called the Mazda LPGA Championship.

Most wins The most wins is four, by Mickey Wright in 1958, 1960–61 and 1963.

Lowest total aggregate The lowest score for 72 holes is 267, by Betsy King at the Bethesda Country Club, MD in 1992.

Du Maurier Classic (inaugurated 1973, Royal Montreal Golf Club, Montreal, Canada; formerly called La Canadienne [1973] and the Peter Jackson Classic [1974–83])

Most wins Pat Bradley holds the record for most wins, with three titles won in 1980, 1985–86.

Lowest total aggregate Pat Bradley and Ayako Okamoto share the record for the lowest score for 72 holes, 276, at the Board of Trade Country Club, Toronto, Ontario, Canada in 1986. Cathy Johnson matched Bradley and Okamoto in 1990 at Westmount Golf and Country Club, Kitchener, Ontario, Canada.

Nabisco Dinah Shore (inaugurated 1972, Mission Hills Country Club, Rancho Mirage, CA, the permanent site)

Most wins The most wins is three, by Amy Alcott (1983, 1988 and 1991).

Lowest total aggregate The lowest score for 72 holes is 273, by Amy Alcott in 1991.

INDIVIDUAL RECORDS

Richest prize The greatest first place prize money ever won is $1 million, awarded annually from 1987 to 1991 to the winners of the Sun City Challenge, Bophuthatswana, South Africa. Ian Woosnam (Wales) was the first winner. The greatest total prize money is $2.7 million (including a $550,000 first prize) for the Johnnie Walker World Championship at Tryall Golf Course, Montego Bay, Jamaica on 17–20 Dec 1992.

Highest earnings PGA and LPGA circuits The all-time top professional money-winner is Tom Kite (USA; b. 9 Dec 1949) with $8,299,794 to 21 Jun 1993. He also holds the earnings record for a year on the US PGA circuit,

$1,395,278 in 1989. The record career earnings for a woman is by Patricia Bradley (b. 24 Mar 1951), with $4,440,113 to 18 Jun 1993. The season's record is $863,578, by Elizabeth Ann "Beth" Daniel in 1990.

Greatest prize-money   On 1 Nov 1992, Jason Bohn (USA) won $1 million when he made a hole in one during a charity contest. He aced the 136 yard, second hole at the Harry S. Pritchett Gold Course in Tuscaloosa, AL using a nine-iron, having paid $10 to enter the event. The odds of making a hole in one are 1 in 12,000.

Most tournament wins   John Byron Nelson (USA; b. 4 Feb 1912) won a record 18 tournaments (plus one unofficial) in one year, including a record 11 consecutively from 8 Mar to 4 Aug 1945.

The LPGA record for one year is 13, by Mickey Wright (1963). She also holds the record for most wins in scheduled events, with four between August and September 1962 and between May and June 1963, a record matched by Kathrynne "Kathy" Ann Whitworth (b. 27 Sep 1939) between March and April 1969.

Successive wins   Between May and June 1978, Nancy Lopez won all five tournaments that she entered; however, these events did not follow each other and are therefore not considered consecutive tournament victories.

Career wins   Sam Snead, who turned professional in 1934, won 84 official PGA tour events, 1936–65. The ladies' PGA record is 88, by Kathy Whitworth from 1962 to 1985.

Oldest winner   Sam Snead won a PGA tournament at the age of 52 years 312 days at the 1965 Greater Greensboro Open.

Greatest winning margin   The greatest margin of victory in a professional tournament is 21 strokes, by Jerry Pate (USA; b. 16 Sep 1953), who won the Colombian Open with 262, from 10–13 Dec 1981.

Cecilia Leitch won the Canadian Ladies' Open Championship in 1921 by the biggest margin for a national title, 17 up and 15 to play.

Arthur D'Arcy "Bobby" Locke (South Africa; 1917–87) achieved the greatest winning margin in a PGA tour event by 16 strokes in the Chicago Victory National Championship in 1948.

NCAA Championships   Two golfers have won three NCAA titles: Ben Daniel Crenshaw (b. 11 Jan 1952) of the University of Texas in 1971–73, tying with Tom Kite in 1972; and Phil Mickelson of Arizona State University in 1989–90, 1992.

HOLES IN ONE

Longest   The longest straight hole ever holed in one shot was the tenth (447 yd) at, appropriately, the Miracle Hills Golf Course, Omaha, NE, by Robert Mitera (b. 1944) on 7 Oct 1965. Mitera stood 5 ft 6 in tall and weighed 165 lb. He was a two-handicap player who normally drove 245 yd. A 50 mph gust carried his shot over a 290 yd drop-off.

The longest "dog-leg" hole achieved in one shot is the 480 yd fifth at Hope Country Club, AR by L. Bruce on 15 Nov 1962.

The women's record is 393 yd, by Marie Robie on the first hole of the Furnace Brook Golf Club, Wollaston, MA on 4 Sep 1949.

Consecutive   There are at least 19 cases of "aces" being achieved in two consecutive holes, of which the greatest was Norman L. Manley's unique "double albatross" on the par-4 330 yd seventh and par-4 290 yd eighth holes on the Del Valle Country Club course, Saugus, CA on 2 Sep 1964.

The first woman to record consecutive "aces" was Sue Prell, on the 13th and 14th holes at Chatswood Golf Club, Sydney, Australia on 29 May 1977.

The closest to achieving three consecutive holes in one were Dr Joseph Boydstone on the third, fourth and ninth at Bakersfield Golf Club, CA, on 10 Oct 1962; and the Rev Harold Snider (b. 4 Jul 1900), who aced the 8th, 13th and 14th holes of the par-3 Ironwood course in Arizona on 9 Jun 1976.

Youngest and oldest   The youngest golfer recorded to have shot a hole-in-one is Coby Orr (5 years) of Littleton, CO on the 103 yd fifth at the Riverside Golf Course, San Antonio, TX in 1975.

The youngest American woman to score an ace was Kimberly C. Smith, at the Skaneateles Country Club, Skaneateles, NY on 14 Jun 1992, at age 12.

The oldest golfers to have performed this feat are: *(men)* 99 yr 244 days, Otto Bucher (Switzerland; b. 12 May 1885) on the 130 yd 12th at La Manga Golf Club, Spain on 13 Jan 1985; *(women)* 95 yr 257 days, Erna Ross (b. 9 Sep 1890) on the 112 yd 17th at The Everglades Club, Palm Beach, FL on 23 Apr 1986.

Youngest and oldest national champions   Thuashni Selvaratnam (b. 9 Jun 1976) won the 1989 Sri Lankan Ladies Amateur Open Golf Championship, aged 12 yr 324 days, at Nuwara Eliya GC on 29 Apr 1989. Maria Teresa "Isa" Goldschmid (nee Bevione; b. 15 Oct 1925) won the Italian Women's Championship, aged 50 yr 200 days, at Oligata, Rome on 2 May 1976.

Highest shot on Earth   Gerald Williams (USA) played a shot from the summit of Mt Aconcagua (22,834 ft), Argentina on 22 Jan 1989.

Oldest player to score his age   The oldest player to achieve a score equal to his age is C. Arthur Thompson (1869–1975) of Victoria, British Columbia, Canada, who scored 103, on the Uplands course of 6,215 yd in 1973.

Golf ball balancing   Lang Martin balanced seven golf balls vertically without adhesive at Charlotte, NC on 9 Feb 1980.

Throwing a golf ball   The lowest recorded score for throwing a golf ball around 18 holes (over 6,000 yd) is 82, by Joe Flynn (USA), 21, at the 6,228 yd Port Royal course, Bermuda on 27 Mar 1975.

TEAM COMPETITIONS

Ryder Cup   The biennial Ryder Cup professional match between the USA and Europe (British Isles or Great Britain prior to 1979) was instituted in 1927. The USA has won 22 to 5 (with 2 ties) to 1991.

Arnold Palmer has won the most Ryder Cup matches, with 22 out of 32 played, with 2 halved and 8 lost, in six contests from 1963 to 1973. Christy O'Connor, Sr. (Ireland; b. 21 Dec 1924) played in a record 10 contests, 1955–73. The most contests and matches for the USA is 8 and 37 (with 20 wins) by Billy Casper (b. 24 Jun 1931).

Walker Cup   The series was instituted in 1921 (for the Walker Cup since 1922 and now held biennially). The USA has won 29 matches, Great Britain and Ireland 3 (in 1938, 1971 and 1989), and the 1965 match was tied.

Jay Sigel (USA; b. 13 Nov 1943) has won a record 16 matches, with 5 halved and 9 lost, 1977–91. Joseph Boynton Carr (Great Britain & Ireland; b. 18 Feb 1922) played in 10 contests, 1947–67.

GREYHOUND RACING

Oldest club   St Petersburg Kennel Club, located in St Petersburg, FL, which opened on 3 Jan 1925, is the oldest greyhound track in the world still in operation on its original site.

Derby   Two greyhounds have won the American Derby twice, at Taunton, MA: Real Huntsman in 1950–51, and Dutch Bahama in 1984–85.

Longest odds   Apollo Prince won at odds of 250–1 at Sandown Greyhound Race Course, Springvale, Victoria, Australia on 14 Nov 1968.

Fastest greyhound   The fastest speed at which any greyhound has been timed is 41.72 mph (410 yd in 20.1 sec) by The Shoe on the then-straightaway track at Richmond, New South Wales, Australia on 25 Apr 1968. It is estimated that he covered the last 100 yd in 4.5 sec or at 45.45 mph.

United States   Tiki's Ace ran a distance of 5/16 mile in 29.61 sec in Naples, Ft Myers, FL in 1988. The fastest 3/8 mile time was 36.43 sec by P's Rambling in Hollywood, FL in 1987. Old Bill Drozd ran a 7/16 mile track in 42.83 sec in Tucson, AZ in 1973.

Most wins   The most career wins is 143, by the American greyhound JR's Ripper of Multnomah, Fairview, OR and Tucson, AZ in 1982–86. The most wins in a year is 61, by Indy Ann in Mexico and the United States in 1966.

The most consecutive victories is 32 in Great Britain, by Ballyregan Bob, owned by Cliff Kevern and trained by George Curtis, from 25 Aug 1984 to 9 Dec 1986, including 16 track record times. His race wins were by an average of more than nine lengths.

Joe Dump of Greenetrack, Eutaw, AL holds the US record, with 31 consecutive wins from 18 Nov 1978 to 1 Jun 1979.

Highest earnings The career earnings record is held by Homespun Rowdy with $297,000 in the United States, 1984–87.

The richest first prize for a greyhound race is $125,000, won by Ben G Speedboat in the Great Greyhound Race of Champions at Seabrook, NH on 23 Aug 1986.

Most stakes victories Real Huntsman achieved 10 wins in 1949–51, including the American Derby twice.

GYMNASTICS

World Championships Women The greatest number of titles won in the World Championships (including Olympic Games) is 12 individual wins and six team, by Larisa Semyonovna Latynina (nee Diriy [USSR]; b. 27 Dec 1934) between 1954 and 1964. Kim Zmeskal was the first American woman to win an all-around world championship, on 13 Sep 1991.

The USSR won the team title on 21 occasions (11 world and 10 Olympic).

Men Boris Anfiyanovich Shakhlin (USSR; b. 27 Jan 1932) won 10 individual titles between 1954 and 1964. He also had three team wins.

The USSR won the team title a record 13 times (eight World Championships, five Olympics) between 1952 and 1992.

The most successful US gymnast has been Kurt Bittereaux Thomas (b. 29 Mar 1952), who won three gold medals: floor exercises 1978 and 1979, horizontal bar 1979.

Youngest champions Aurelia Dobre (Romania; b. 6 Nov 1972) won the women's overall world title at age 14 yr 352 days on 23 Oct 1987. Daniela Silivas (Romania) revealed in 1990 that she was born on 9 May 1971, a year later than previously claimed, so that she was age 14 yr 185 days when she won the gold medal for balance beam on 10 Nov 1985.

The youngest male world champion was Dmitriy Bilozerchev (USSR; b. 17 Dec 1966), at 16 yr 315 days at Budapest, Hungary on 28 Oct 1983.

Olympics The men's title has been won a record five times, by Japan (in 1960, 1964, 1968, 1972 and 1976) and the USSR (1952, 1956, 1980, 1988 and 1992). The USSR won the women's title 10 times (1952–80, 1988 and 1992). The successes in 1992 were by the Unified Team from the republics of the former USSR.

The most men's individual gold medals is six, by Boris Shakhlin, one in 1956, four (two shared) in 1960 and one in 1964; and by Nikolay Yefimovich Andrianov (USSR; b. 14 Oct 1952), one in 1972, four in 1976 and one in 1980.

Vera Caslavska-Odlozil (Czechoslovakia; b. 3 May 1942) has won the most individual gold medals, with seven, three in 1964 and four (one shared) in 1968.

Larisa Latynina won six individual gold medals and was on three winning teams from 1956–64, earning nine gold medals. She also won five silver and four bronze, 18 in all—an Olympic record.

The most medals for a male gymnast is 15, by Nikolay Andrianov (USSR), seven gold, five silver and three bronze, from 1972–80. Aleksandr Nikolaivich Dityatin (USSR; b. 7 Aug 1957) is the only man to win a medal in all eight categories in the same Games, with three gold, four silver and one bronze at Moscow in 1980.

Vitaliy Scherbo (Belarus; b. 13 Jan 1972) won a record six golds at one Games in 1992, adding four individual titles to the all-around and team gold that he had won with the Unified Team.

EXERCISES
Speed and Stamina

Records are accepted for the most repetitions of the following activities within the given time span.

Chins (Consecutive)   370 Lee Chin-yong (South Korea; b. 15 Aug 1925) at Backyon Gymnasium, Seoul, South Korea on 14 May 1988.

Chins (one arm; from a ring)—Consecutive   22 Robert Chisnall (b. 9 Dec 1952) at Queen's University, Kingston, Ontario, Canada on 3 Dec 1982. (Also 18 two-finger chins, 12 one-finger chins).

Parallel bar dips—1 hour   3,726 Kim Yang-ki (South Korea) at the Rivera Hotel, Seoul, South Korea on 28 Nov 1991.

Sit-ups–24 hours   70,715 Lou Scripa, Jr. at Beale Airforce Base, Marysville, CA on 1–2 Dec 1992.

Leg lifts—12 hours   41,788 Lou Scripa, Jr. at Jack La Lanne's American Health & Fitness Spa, Sacramento, CA on 2 Dec 1988.

Squats—1 hour   4,289 Paul Wai Man Chung at the Yee Gin Kung Fu of Chung Sze Health (HK) Association, Kowloon, Hong Kong on 5 Apr 1993.

Squat thrusts—1 hour   3,552 Paul Wai Man Chung at the Yee Gin Kung Fu of Chung Sze Kung Fu (HK) Association, Kowloon, Hong Kong on 21 Apr 1992.

Burpees—1 hour   1822 Paddy Doyle at the Irish Centre, Digbeth, Birmingham on 6 Feb 1993.

Pummel horse double circles—consecutive   75 by Lee Thomas (Great Britain) on British Broadcasting Corporation on 12 Dec 1985.

For push-up records, see page 656

The Ups and Downs of Record-Breaking

The true degree of exertion required to perform push-ups correctly is often underestimated by the casual observer; nevertheless, the records are frequently challenged and frequently broken. Described below are some of the rules to be followed by athletes seeking to break records.

Demonstrated right are the correct positions for completing one push-up. The body must remain straight throughout, that is, no bending at knees or waist (fig a). The body must be lowered until at least a 90° angle is attained at the elbow (fig b). The body must then be raised until the arms are straight (fig c). This sequence completes one push-up. This basic principle applies to all our push-up entries with minor modifications.

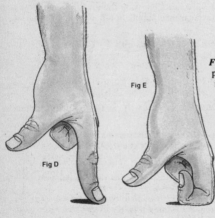

Fig E

Fig D

Fingertip: Instead of the palms of both hands touching the floor, ONLY the fingertips (including the tip of each thumb) may touch.

Onearm: ONLY one arm may be used and the same arm must be used throughout the attempt. In this attempt the hand is placed flat on the floor.

One Finger: Similar to the one arm, except that ONLY one finger of one hand may be used. The thumb may NOT be used. The record is for the number of repetitions; no rest breaks are permitted. The one finger position should be maintained throughout. Middle or index finger is recommended and how they can be used is illustrated above (figs d & e). The side of the index finger should NOT be used as this means other parts of the hand will come into contact with the ground and therefore invalidate the attempt.

Push-Ups

Fig A

Fig B

Fig C

Push-ups—24 hours 46,001 Charles Servizio (USA) at Fontana City Hall, Fontana, CA on 24–25 Apr 1993.

Push-ups (one arm)—5 hours 7,683 John Decker (Great Britain) at Congleton Cricket Club, Cheshire, Great Britain on 16 Jun 1991.

Push-ups (fingertip)—5 hours 7,011 Kim Yang-ki (South Korea) at the Swiss Guard Hotel, Seoul, South Korea on 30 Aug 1990.

Push-ups (one finger)—consecutive 124 Paul Lynch (Great Britain) at the Hippodrome, London, Great Britain on 21 Apr 1992.

Push-ups in a year Paddy Doyle, pictured below (Great Britain) achieved a documented 1,500,230 push-ups from October 1988 to October 1989.

Static wall "sit" Ramesh Khachi (India) stayed in an unsupported sitting position against a wall for 11 hr 2 min in Jawahar Navodaya Vidyalaya, Theog, India on 22 Sep 1992.

Club swinging Albert Rayner set a world record of 17,512 revolutions (4.9 per sec) in 60 min at Wakefield, Great Britain on 27 Jul 1981.

Gymnastics/aerobics display The largest number of participants is 15,017 for the 1993 Boots Aerobathon at the Earls Court Exhibition Centre, London, Great Britain on 9 May 1993.

Somersaults Ashrita Furman performed 8,341 forward rolls in 10 hr 30 min over 12 miles 390 yards from Lexington to Charleston, MA on 30 Apr 1986.

Shigeru Iwasaki (b. 1960) somersaulted backwards 54.68 yd in 10.8 sec at Tokyo, Japan on 30 Mar 1980.

United States The best US performances were in the 1904 Games, when there was only limited foreign participation. Anton Heida (b. 1878) won five gold medals and a silver, and George Eyser (b. 1871), who had a wooden leg, won three gold, two silver and a bronze medal. Mary Lou Retton (b. 24 Jan 1968) won a women's record five medals in 1984, gold at all-around, two silver and two bronze. The most medals won by a US male gymnast since 1904 is four, by Mitchell Jay "Mitch" Gaylord (b. 10 Mar 1961), a team gold and a silver and two bronze in individual events in 1984, when both Bart Conner (b. 28 Mar 1958) and Peter Glen Vidmar (b. 3 Jun 1961) won two gold medals.

Youngest international Pasakevi "Voula" Kouna (b. 6 Dec 1971) was age 9 yr 299 days at the start of the Balkan Games at Serres, Greece on 1 Oct 1981, when she represented Greece.

Highest score Hans Eugster (Switzerland; b. 27 Mar 1929) scored a perfect 10.00 in the compulsory parallel bars at the 1950 World Championships. Nadia Comaneci (Romania; b. 12 Nov 1961) was the first to achieve a perfect score (10.00) in the Olympics, and achieved seven perfect scores in all at Montreal, Canada in July 1976.

World Cup Gymnasts who have won two World Cup (instituted 1975) overall titles are three men: Nikolay Andrianov, 1975, 1977; Aleksandr Ditiatin, 1978, 1979; and Li Ning (China; b. 8 Sep 1963), 1982, 1986; and one woman: Maria Yevgenyevna Filatova, 1977, 1978 (USSR; b. 19 Jul 1961).

US Championships Alfred A. Jochim (1902–81) won a record seven men's all-around US titles, 1925–30 and 1933, and a total of 34 at all exercises, between 1923 and 1934. The women's record is six all-around, 1945–46 and 1949–52, and 39 at all exercises, including 11 in succession at balance beam, 1941–51, by Clara Marie Schroth Lomady (b. 5 Oct 1920).

NCAA Championships Men The men's competition was first held in 1932.

The most team championships won is nine, by two colleges: University of Illinois, 1939–42, 1950, 1955–56, 1958, 1989; and Pennsylvania State University, 1948, 1953–54, 1957, 1959–61, 1965, 1976.

The most individual titles in a career is seven, by two gymnasts: Joe Giallombardo, University of Illinois, tumbling, 1938–40, all-around title, 1938–40, and floor exercise, 1938; and Jim Hartung, University of Nebraska, all-around title, 1980–81, rings, 1980–82, and parallel bar, 1981–82.

Women The women's competition was first held in 1982. The most team championships is seven, by the University of Utah, 1982–86, 1990 and 1992.

The most individual titles in a career is five, by Missy Marlowe, University of Utah, all-around title, 1992, balance beam, 1991–92, uneven bars, 1992, floor exercise, 1992.

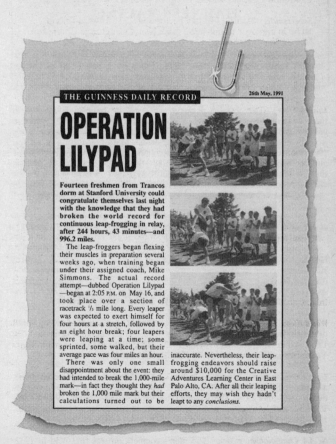

THE GUINNESS DAILY RECORD   26th May, 1991

OPERATION LILYPAD

Fourteen freshmen from Trancos dorm at Stanford University could congratulate themselves last night with the knowledge that they had broken the world record for continuous leap-frogging in relay, after 244 hours, 43 minutes—and 996.2 miles.

The leap-froggers began flexing their muscles in preparation several weeks ago, when training began under their assigned coach, Mike Simmons. The actual record attempt—dubbed Operation Lilypad—began at 2:05 P.M. on May 16, and took place over a section of racetrack ⅕ mile long. Every leaper was expected to exert himself for four hours at a stretch, followed by an eight hour break; four leapers were leaping at a time; some sprinted, some walked, but their average pace was four miles an hour.

There was only one small disappointment about the event: they had intended to break the 1,000-mile mark—in fact they thought they *had* broken the 1,000 mile mark but their calculations turned out to be inaccurate. Nevertheless, their leap-frogging endeavors should raise around $10,000 for the Creative Adventures Learning Center in East Palo Alto, CA. After all their leaping efforts, they may wish they hadn't leapt to any *conclusions*.

Modern rhythmic gymnastics   The most overall individual world titles in modern rhythmic gymnastics is three, by Maria Gigova (Bulgaria) in 1969, 1971 and 1973 (shared). Bulgaria has a record seven team titles, in 1969, 1971, 1981, 1983, 1985, 1987 and 1989 (shared). Bianka Panova (b. 27 May 1960) of Bulgaria won all four apparatus gold medals, all with maximum scores, and won a team gold in 1987.

Lilia Ignatova (Bulgaria) has won both of the individual World Cup titles that have been held, in 1983 and 1986. Marina Lobach (USSR; b. 26 Jun 1970) won the 1988 Olympic title with perfect scores for all six disciplines.

HARNESS RACING

Most successful driver   The most successful sulky driver in North American harness racing history has been Herve Filion (b. 1 Feb 1940) of Québec, Canada, who had achieved 13,876 wins and prize earnings of $79,116,785 through 21 Jun 1993, including a then-record 814 wins in a year, 1989. The most records in a year is 843, by Walter Case (USA) in 1992.

John D. Campbell (USA; b. 8 Apr 1955) has the highest career earnings, $111,731,928 through 21 Jun 1993. This includes a season record of $11,620,878 in 1990, when he won 543 races.

Hambletonian   The most famous trotting race in North America, the Hambletonian Stakes, run annually for three-year-olds, was first staged at Syracuse, NY in 1926. The race is named after the great sire Hambletonian, born in 1849, from whom almost all harness horses trace their pedigree. The race record time is 1 min 53³/₅ sec, by Mack Lobell, driven by John Campbell in 1987.

Little Brown Jug   Pacing's three-year-old classic has been held annually at Delaware, OH from 1946. The name honors a great 19th-century pacer. The race record time is 1 min 52¹/₅ sec by Nihilator, driven by Bill O'Donnell in 1985.

HARNESS RACING MILE RECORDS

Trotting	Horse (driver)	Place	Date
World 1:52 ¹/₅	*Mack Lobell*		
	(John Campbell)	....Springfield, IL	.........21 Aug 1987
Pacing			
World 1:48 ²/₅	*Matt's Scooter*		
	(Michel Lachance)	Lexington, KY	..........23 Sep 1988
Race 1:49 ²/₅	*Artsplace*		
	(Catello Manzi)	.....East Rutherford, NJ	20 Jun 1992

Highest prices The highest prices paid were $19.2 million for Nihilator (a pacer), who was syndicated by Wall Street Stable and Almahurst Stud Farm in 1984; and $6 million for Mack Lobell (a trotter) by John Erik Magnusson of Vislanda, Sweden in 1988.

Greatest winnings For any harness horse the record amount is $4,907,307, by the trotter Peace Corps, 1988–92. The greatest amount won by a pacer is $3,225,653, by Nihilator, who won 35 of 38 races in 1984–85.

The single-season records are $2,217,222 by the pacer Precious Bunny in 1991, and $1,878,798 by the trotter Mack Lobell in 1987.

The largest-ever purse was $2,161,000, for the Woodrow Wilson two-year-old race over one mile at The Meadowlands, East Rutherford, NJ on 16 Aug 1984. Of this sum a record $1,080,500 went to the winner, Nihilator, driven by William O'Donnell (b. 4 May 1948).

HOCKEY

NATIONAL HOCKEY LEAGUE

Team records The Montreal Canadiens won a record 60 games and 132 points (with 12 ties) in 80 games played in 1976/77; their eight losses were also a record, the least ever in a season of 70 or more games. The highest percentage of wins in a season was .875, achieved by the Boston Bruins, with 30 wins in 44 games in 1929/30.

The longest undefeated run during a season, 35 games (25 wins and 10 ties), was established by the Philadelphia Flyers from 14 Oct 1979 to 6 Jan 1980.

The Pittsburgh Penguins won 17 consecutive games from 9 Mar–10 Apr 1993.

The most goals scored in a season is 446, by the Edmonton Oilers in 1983/84, when they also achieved a record 1,182 points.

The most shutouts in a season is 22, in 1928/29 by the Montreal Canadiens, in just 44 games, all by George Hainsworth, who also achieved a record low for goals against percentage of .98 that season.

Most goals in a game The NHL record is 21 goals, when the Montreal Canadiens beat Toronto St Patrick's, 14–7, at Montreal on 10 Jan 1920, and the Edmonton Oilers beat the Chicago Blackhawks, 12–9, at Chicago on 11 Dec 1985. The NHL single-team record is 16, by the Montreal Canadiens *v* the Québec Bulldogs (3), at Québec City on 3 Nov 1920.

INDIVIDUAL RECORDS

Most games played Gordon "Gordie" Howe (Canada; b. 31 Mar 1928) played

in a record 1,767 NHL regular-season games (and 157 playoff games) over a record 26 seasons, from 1946 to 1971, for the Detroit Red Wings and in 1979/80 for the Hartford Whalers. He also played 419 games (and 78 playoff games) for the Houston Aeros and for the New England Whalers in the World Hockey Association from 1973 to 1979, for a grand total of 2,421 professional hockey games.

Fastest goals   The fastest goal was after 4 sec by Joseph Antoine Claude Provost (b. 17 Sep 1933; Montreal Canadiens) *v* Boston Bruins in the second period at Montreal on 9 Nov 1957, and by Denis Joseph Savard (b. 4 Feb 1961; Chicago Black Hawks) *v* Hartford Whalers in the third period at Chicago on 12 Jan 1986. From the opening whistle, the fastest is 5 sec, by Doug Smail (b. 2 Sep 1957; Winnipeg Jets) *v* St Louis Blues at Winnipeg on 20 Dec 1981, and by Bryan John Trottier (b. 17 Jul 1956; New York Islanders) *v* Boston Bruins at Boston on 22 Mar 1984. Bill Mosienko (b. 2 Nov 1921; Chicago Blackhawks) scored three goals in 21 sec *v* New York Rangers on 23 Mar 1952.

Most goals and points Career   The North American career record for goals is 1,071 (including a record 801 in the NHL) by Gordie Howe (Detroit Red Wings, Houston Aeros, New England Whalers and Hartford Whalers) from 16 Oct 1946 in 32 seasons ending in 1979/80. Howe took 2,204 games to achieve the 1,000th goal, but Robert Marvin "Bobby" Hull (Great Britain; b. 3 Jan 1939; Chicago Blackhawks and Winnipeg Jets) scored his 1,000th in 1,600 games on 12 Mar 1978.

Wayne Gretzky (Edmonton Oilers 1979–88, Los Angeles Kings 1988–93) holds the NHL record for assists, 1,563, and points, 2,328.

Season The most goals scored in a season in the NHL is 92, in the 1981/82 season by Wayne Gretzky (b. 26 Jan 1961) for the Edmonton Oilers. He scored a record 215 points, including a record 163 assists, in 1985/86.

Game The most goals in an NHL game is seven, by Michael Joseph "Joe" Malone (b. 28 Feb 1890) in Québec's 10–6 win over Toronto St Patricks at Québec City on 31 Jan 1920.

The most assists in an NHL game is seven, by William "Billy" Taylor (b. 3 May 1919) for Detroit, 10–6 *v* Chicago on 16 Mar 1947, and three by Wayne Gretzky for Edmonton, 8–2 *v* Washington on 15 Feb 1980, 12–9 *v* Chicago on 11 Dec 1985, and 8–2 *v* Québec on 14 Feb 1986.

The record number of assists in one period is five, by Dale Hawerchuk, for the Winnipeg Jets *v* the Los Angeles Kings on 6 Mar 1984.

Consecutive games Harry Broadbent scored in 16 consecutive games for Ottawa in the 1921/22 season.

Most hat tricks The most hat tricks (three or more goals in a game) in a career is 49, by Wayne Gretzky through the 1992/93 season for the Edmonton Oilers and the Los Angeles Kings. Gretzky also holds the record for most hat tricks in a season, 10, in both the 1982 and 1984 seasons for the Oilers.

Most points in one game The North American major league record for most points scored in one game is 10, by Jim Harrison (b. 9 Jul 1947)—three goals, seven assists for Alberta, later Edmonton Oilers, in a World Hockey Association game at Edmonton on 30 Jan 1973; and by Darryl Sittler (b. 18 Sep 1950)—six goals, four assists for the Toronto Maple Leafs *v* the Boston Bruins in an NHL game at Toronto on 7 Feb 1976.

Period The most points in one period is six, by Bryan Trottier—three goals and three assists in the second period, for the New York Islanders *v* the New York Rangers (9–4) on 23 Dec 1978. Nine players have a record four goals in one period.

Most successful goaltending The most shutouts played by a goaltender in an NHL career is 103, by Terry Sawchuck of Detroit, Boston, Toronto, Los Angeles and New York Rangers, between 1949 and 1970. Gerry Cheevers (b. 2 Dec 1940; Boston Bruins) went a record 32 successive games without a defeat in 1971/72. George Hainsworth completed 22 shutouts for the Montreal Canadiens in 1928/29. Alex Connell played 461 min 29 sec without conceding a goal for Ottawa in the 1928/29 season. Roy Worters saved 70 shots for the Pittsburgh Pirates *v* the New York Americans on 24 Dec 1925.

Defensemen Paul Coffey (Edmonton Oilers 1980–87, Pittsburgh Penguins 1988–92, Los Angeles Kings 1992–93, Detroit Red Wings 1993) holds the record for most goals (330), assists (871) and points (1,201) by a defenseman. He scored a record 48 goals in 1985/86. Bobby Orr (Boston Bruins) holds the single-season marks for assists (102) and points (139), both of which were set in 1970/71.

Player awards The Hart Trophy, awarded annually starting with the 1923/24 season by the Professional Hockey Writers Association as the Most Valuable Player award of the NHL, has been won a record nine times by Wayne Gretzky, 1980–87, 1989. Gretzky has also won the Art Ross Trophy a record nine times, 1981–87 and 1990–91; this has been awarded annually since 1947/48 to the NHL season's leading scorer. Bobby Orr of Boston won the James Norris Memorial Trophy, awarded annually starting with the 1953/54 season to the league's leading defenseman, a record eight times, 1968–75.

Coaches   Scotty Bowman holds the records for most victories, highest winning percentage and most games coached by an NHL coach. He won 834 games (110, St Louis Blues 1967–71; 419, Montreal Canadiens 1971–79; 210, Buffalo Sabres 1979–87; 95, Pittsburgh Penguins, 1991–93). His career record is 834 wins, 380 losses, 226 ties for a record .658 winning percentage from a record 1,440 games.

Longest hockey game   The longest game was 2 hr 56 min 30 sec (playing time) when the Detroit Red Wings beat the Montreal Maroons 1–0 in the sixth period of overtime at the Forum, Montreal, at 2:25 A.M. on 25 Mar 1936. Norm Smith, the Red Wings goaltender, turned aside 92 shots for the NHL's longest single shutout.

Fastest goals   Toronto scored eight goals in 4 min 52 sec *v* the New York Americans on 19 Mar 1938.

Most consecutive games played   A record of 962 consecutive games played was achieved by Doug Jarvis for the Montreal Canadiens, the Washington Capitals and the Hartford Whalers from 8 Oct 1975–5 Apr 1987.

Most consecutive 50-or-more-goal seasons   Mike Bossy (New York Islanders) scored at least 50 goals in nine consecutive seasons from 1977/78 through 1985/86. Wayne Gretzky (Edmonton Oilers, Los Angeles Kings) has also scored at least 50 goals in one season nine times, but his longest streak is eight seasons.

Most consecutive points   The most consecutive games scoring points was 51, by Wayne Gretzky from 5 Oct 1983–27 Jan 1984 for the Edmonton Oilers.

Goaltending Career   Terrance "Terry" Gordon Sawchuck (1929–70) played a record 971 games as a goaltender, for the Detroit Red Wings, the Boston Bruins, the Toronto Maple Leafs, the Los Angeles Kings and the New York Rangers, from 1949 to 1970. He achieved a record 435 wins (to 337 losses, and 188 ties). Jacques Joseph Ormar Plante (1929–86), with 434 NHL wins, surpassed Sawchuck's figure by adding 15 wins in his one season in the WHA, for a total of 449 in 868 games.

Season   Bernie Parent (b. 3 Apr 1945) achieved a record 47 wins in a season, with 13 losses and 12 ties, for Philadelphia in 1973/74.

STANLEY CUP

The top NHL teams compete annually for the Stanley Cup, which was first presented in 1893 by Lord Stanley of Preston, then Governor-General of Canada. From 1910 it became the award for the winners of the professional league playoffs. It has been won most often by the Montreal Canadiens with 24 wins in 1916, 1924, 1930–31, 1944, 1946, 1953, 1956–60, 1965–66, 1968–69, 1971, 1973, 1976–79, 1986, 1993 from a record 33 finals. The longest Stanley Cup final game was settled after 115 min 13 sec, in the third period of overtime, when the Edmonton Oilers beat the Boston Bruins 3–2 on 15 May 1990.

Most games played   Larry Robinson has played in 227 Stanley Cup playoff games, for the Montreal Canadiens (1973–89) and the Los Angeles Kings (1990–92).

Scoring records   Wayne Gretzky (Edmonton Oilers, Los Angeles Kings) has scored a record 346 points in Stanley Cup games, a record 110 goals and a record 236 assists. Gretzky scored a playoff record 47 points (16 goals, record 31 assists) in 1985. The most goals in a season is 19, by Reggie Leach for Philadelphia in 1976 and by Jari Kurri (Finland; b. 18 May 1960) for Edmonton in 1985.

Five goals in a Stanley Cup game were scored by Maurice Richard (b. 14 Aug 1924) in Montreal's 5–1 win over the Toronto Maple Leafs on 23 Mar 1944; by Darryl Glen Sittler (b. 18 Sep 1950) for Toronto's 8–5 victory over Philadelphia on 22 Apr 1976; by Reggie Leach for Philadelphia's 6–3 victory over the Boston Bruins on 6 May 1976; and by Mario Lemieux (b. 5 Oct 1965) for the Pittsburgh Penguins' 10–7 victory over Philadelphia on 25 Apr 1989. Reggie Leach (Philadelphia) scored at least one goal in nine consecutive playoff games in 1976. The streak started on 17 Apr *v* the Toronto Maple Leafs, and ended on 9 May when he was shut out by the Montreal Canadiens. Overall, Leach scored 14 goals during his record-setting run.

A record six assists in a game were achieved by Mikko Leinonen (Finland; b. 15 Jul 1955) for the New York Rangers in their 7–3 victory over Philadelphia on 8 Apr 1982, and by Wayne Gretzky for Edmonton's 13–3 victory over Los Angeles on 9 Apr 1987, when his team set a Stanley Cup game record of 13 goals. The most points in a game is eight, by Patrik Sundström (Sweden; b. 14 Dec 1961), three goals and five assists, for the New Jersey Devils (10) *v* the Washington Capitals (4) on 22 Apr 1988, and by Mario Lemieux, five goals and three assists, for the Pittsburgh Penguins (10) *v* the Philadelphia Flyers (7) on 25 Apr 1989.

Point-scoring streak   Bryan Trottier (New York Islanders) scored a point in 27 playoff games over three seasons (1980–82), scoring 16 goals and 26 assists for 42 points.

Defensemen   During his career with the Edmonton Oilers, 1980–87, Paul Coffey set marks for the most points in a playoff game (6) and in a season (37)—both set in 1985. Also in 1985, Coffey set the record for most goals by a defenseman in a playoff season, with 12 in 18 games. The record for most goals in a game by a defenseman is three, shared by seven players: Bobby Orr (Boston Bruins *v* Montreal Canadiens, 11 Apr 1971); Dick Redmond (Chicago Blackhawks *v* St Louis Blues, 4 Apr 1973); Denis Potvin (New York Islanders *v* Edmonton Oilers, 17 Apr 1981); Paul Reinhart twice (Calgary Flames *v* Edmonton Oilers, 14 Apr 1983; *v* Vancouver Canucks, 8 Apr 1984);

Doug Halward (Vancouver Canucks *v* Calgary Flames, 7 Apr 1984); Al Iafrate (Washington Capitals *v* New York Islanders, 26 Apr 1993); and Eric Desjardins (Montreal Canadiens *v* Los Angeles Kings, 3 Jun 1993).

Goaltending   Jacques Plante holds the record for most shutouts in a playoff career, with 14, with the Montreal Canadiens (1953–63) and the St Louis Blues (1969–1970). The record for most victories in a playoff career is 88, by Billy Smith for the New York Islanders (1975–88).

Most valuable player   The Conn Smythe Trophy for the most valuable player in the playoffs has been awarded annually since 1965. It has been won twice by five players: Bobby Orr (Boston), 1970 and 1972; Bernie Parent (Philadelphia), 1974 and 1975; Wayne Gretzky (Edmonton), 1985 and 1988; Mario Lemieux (Pittsburgh), 1991 and 1992; and Patrick Roy (Montreal), 1986 and 1993.

Henri Richard played on a record 11 winning teams for the Montreal Canadiens between 1956 and 1973.

Coaches   "Toe" Blake coached the Montreal Canadiens to eight championships (1956–60, 1965–66, 1968), the most of any coach. Scotty Bowman holds the record for most playoff wins at 137: 26, St Louis Blues, 1967–71; 70, Montreal Canadiens, 1971–79; 18, Buffalo Sabres, 1979–87; 23, Pittsburgh Penguins, 1991–93.

WORLD CHAMPIONSHIPS
AND OLYMPIC GAMES

World Championships were first held for amateurs in 1920 in conjunction with the Olympic Games, which were also considered world championships up to 1968. Since 1976, the World Championships have been open to professionals. The USSR won 22 world titles between 1954 and 1990, including the Olympic titles of 1956, 1964 and 1968. It has a record eight Olympic titles with a further five in 1972, 1976, 1984, 1988 and 1992 (as the CIS, with all players Russian). The longest Olympic career is that of Richard Torriani (Switzerland; 1911–88) from 1928 to 1948. The most gold medals won by any player is three, achieved by Soviet players Vitaliy Semyenovich Davydov, Anatoliy Vasilyevich Firsov, Viktor Grigoryevich Kuzkin and Aleksandr Pavlovich Ragulin in 1964, 1968 and 1972, and by Vladislav Aleksandrovich Tretyak in 1972, 1976 and 1984.

Women   The first two world championships were won by Canada, in 1990 and 1992.

Most goals   The greatest number of goals recorded in a world championship match was when Australia beat New Zealand 58–0 at Perth on 15 Mar 1987.

Fastest goals   In minor leagues, Per Olsen scored two seconds after the start of the match for Rungsted against Odense in the Danish First Division at Hørsholm, Denmark on 14 Jan 1990. Three goals in 10 seconds was achieved by Jørgen Palmgren Erichsen for Frisk *v*. Holmen in a junior league match in Norway on 17 Mar 1991. The Skara Ishockeyclubb, Sweden, scored three goals in 11 seconds against Örebro IK at Skara on 18 Oct 1981. The Vernon Cougars scored five goals in 56 seconds against the Salmon Arm Aces at Vernon, British Columbia, Canada on 6 Aug 1982. The Kamloops Knights of

Columbus scored seven goals in 2 min 22 sec *v* the Prince George Vikings on 25 Jan 1980.

HORSE RACING

Highest prizes   The highest prize money won for a day's racing is $10 million, for the Breeders' Cup series of seven races staged annually since 1984. Included each year is a record $3 million for the Breeders' Cup Classic.

Breeders' Cup   Three jockeys have won six Breeders' Cup races: Laffit Pincay, Jr.; Juvenile (1985, 1986, 1988), Classic (1986), Distaff (1989, 1990); Pat Day; Classic (1984, 1990), Distaff (1986, 1991), Juvenile Fillies (1987), and Turf (1987); Pat Valenzuela; Juvenile (1991), Juvenile Fillies (1986, 1992), Sprint (1987) and Turf (1991–92). The trainer with the most wins is D. Wayne Lukas, with 10.

HORSES

Most successful   The horse with the best win–loss record was Kincsem, a Hungarian mare foaled in 1874, who was unbeaten in 54 races (1876–79) throughout Europe, including the Goodwood Cup of 1878.

Longest winning sequence   Camarero, foaled in 1951, was undefeated in 56 races in Puerto Rico from 19 Apr 1953 to his first defeat on 17 Aug 1955 (in his career to 1956, he won 73 of 77 races).

Career   Chorisbar (foaled 1935) won 197 of his 325 races in Puerto Rico, 1937–47. Lenoxbar (foaled 1935) won 46 races in one year, 1940, in Puerto Rico from 56 starts.

The most career wins in the United States is 89, by Kingston in 138 starts, 1886–94. This included 33 in stakes races, but the horse with the most wins in stakes races in the USA is Exterminator (foaled 1915), with 34 between 1918 and 1923. John Henry (foaled 1975) won a record 25 graded stakes races, including 16 at Grade 1, 1978–84. On his retirement in 1984, his career prize money was $6,597,947, nearly twice as much as the next best. Of 83 races, he won 39, was second 15 times and third 9 times.

Same race   Doctor Syntax (foaled 1811) won the Preston Gold Cup on seven successive occasions, 1815–21.

Triple Crown winners   The Triple Crown (Kentucky Derby, Preakness Stakes, Belmont Stakes) has been achieved 11 times, most recently by Affirmed in 1978. Eddie Arcaro is the only jockey to board two Triple Crown winners, Whirlaway in 1941 and Citation in 1948. Two trainers have schooled two Triple Crown winners: James Fitzsimmons, Gallant Fox in 1930 and Omaha in 1935; Ben A. Jones, Whirlaway in 1941 and Citation in 1948.

Greatest winnings   The career earnings record is $6,679,242, by the 1987 Ken-

TRIPLE CROWN QUEEN Julie Krone is the first woman to win a Triple Crown race, the Belmont Stakes, riding Colonial Affair on 5 Jun 1993. (Photo: Allsport/Mike Hewitt)

Biggest weight The biggest weight ever carried is 420 lb, by both Mr Maynard's mare and Mr Baker's horse in a match won by the former over a mile at York, Great Britain on 21 May 1788.

Highest price The most paid for a yearling is $13.1 million on 23 Jul 1985 at Keeneland, KY by Robert Sangster and partners for Seattle Dancer.

Perfect card The only recorded instance of a racing correspondent forecasting 10 out of 10 winners on a race card was at Delaware Park, Wilmington, DE on 28 Jul 1974, by Charles Lamb of the *Baltimore News American.*

Biggest payout Anthony A. Speelman and Nicholas John Cowan (both Great Britain) won $1,627,084.40, after federal income tax of $406,768.00 was withheld, on a $64 nine-horse accumulator at Santa Anita Racetrack, CA on 19 Apr 1987. Their first seven selections won and the payout was for a jackpot, accumulated over 24 days.

Oldest winners The oldest horses to win on the flat have been the 18-year-olds Revenge, at Shrewsbury, Great Britain on 23 Sep 1790; Marksman, at Ashford, Great Britain, on 4 Sep 1826; and Jorrocks, at Bathurst, Australia on 28 Feb 1851. At the same age Wild Aster won three hurdle races in six days in March 1919 and Sonny Somers won two steeplechases in February 1980.

tucky Derby winner Alysheba (foaled 1984), from 1986–88. Alysheba's career record was 11 wins, 8 seconds and 2 thirds from 26 races. The most prize money earned in a year is $4,578,454, by Sunday Silence (foaled 1986) in the USA in 1989. His total included $1,350,000 from the Breeders' Cup Classic and a $1 million bonus for the best record in the Triple Crown races: he won the Kentucky Derby and Preakness Stakes and was second in the Belmont Stakes.

The leading money-winning mare is Dance Smartly (foaled 1988), with $3,118,346 in North America, 1990–92. The one-race record is $2.6 million, by Spend A Buck (foaled 1982), for the Jersey Derby, Garden State Park, NJ on 27 May 1985, of which $2 million was a bonus for having previously won the Kentucky Derby and two preparatory races at Garden State Park.

World speed records The fastest race speed recorded is 43.26 mph, by Big Racket, 20.8 sec for ¼ mile, at Mexico City, Mexico on 5 Feb 1945. The four-year-old carried 114 lb. The record for 1½ miles is 37.82 mph, by three-year-old Hawkster (carrying 121 lb) at Santa Anita Park, Arcadia, CA on 14 Oct 1989, with a time of 2 min 22.8 sec.

JOCKEYS

Most successful Billie Lee "Willie" Shoemaker (USA; b. weighing 2½ lb, 19 Aug 1931, whose racing weight was 97 lb at 4 ft 11 in) rode a record 8,833 winners out of 40,350 mounts from his first ride on 19 Mar 1949 and first winner on 20 Apr 1949 to his retirement on 3 Feb 1990. Laffit Pincay, Jr. (USA; b. 29 Dec 1946) has earned a career record $173,689,406 from 1964 to 23 Jul 1993.

The most races won by a jockey in a year is 598, in 2,312 rides, by Kent Jason Desormeaux (USA; b. 27 Feb 1970) in 1989. The greatest amount won in a year is 2,356,280,400 yen (c. $16,250,000) by Yutaka Take (Japan; b. 1969) in Japan in 1990. The greatest amount won in the United States in a year is $14,877,298, by José Adeon Santos (USA; b. 26 Apr 1961, Chile) in 1988. Pat Day (USA) rode a season record 60 stakes race winners in 1991.

Wins One day The most winners ridden in one day is nine, by Chris Wiley Antley (USA; b. 6 Jan 1966) on 31 Oct 1987. They consisted of four in the afternoon at Aqueduct, NY and five in the evening at The Meadowlands, NJ.

One card The most winners ridden on one card is eight, by six riders, most recently (and in fewest rides) by Pat Day, in only nine rides at Arlington, IL on 13 Sep 1989.

Consecutive The longest winning streak is 12, by Sir Gordon Richards (Great Britain; 1904–86)—one race at Nottingham, Great Britain on 3 October, six out of six at Chepstow on 4 October, and the first five races next day at Chepstow, in 1933; and by Pieter Stroebel at Bulawayo, Southern Rhodesia (now Zimbabwe), 7 Jun–7 Jul 1958.

The longest consecutive winning streak for an American jockey is nine races, by Albert Adams (USA) at Marlboro Racetrack, MD over three days, 10–12 Sep 1930. He won the last two races on 10 September, all six races on 11 September and the first race on 12 September.

Highest earnings Pat Day has won a record $8,875,000 in Breeders' Cup racing, 1984–92.

MAJOR RACING RECORDS

Triple Crown

Race (instituted)	Record Time	Most Wins Jockey	Trainer	Owner	Largest Field
Kentucky Derby (1875) 1¼ miles Churchill Downs, Louisville, KY	1 min 59.4 sec *Secretariat* 1973	5-Eddie Arcaro 1938, 41, 45, 48, 52 5-Bill Hartack 1957, 60, 62, 64, 69	6-Ben Jones 1938, 41, 44, 48, 49, 52	8-Calumet Farm 1941, 44, 48, 49, 52, 57, 58, 68	23 (1974)
Preakness Stakes (1873) 1 mile 1½ furlongs Pimlico, Baltimore, MD	1 min 53.2 sec *Tank's Prospect* 1985	6-Eddie Arcaro 1941, 48, 50, 51, 55, 57	7-Robert Wyndham Walden 1875, 78, 79, 80, 81, 82, 88	5-George Lorillard 1878, 79, 80, 81, 82	18 (1928)
Belmont Stakes (1867) 1½ miles Belmont Park, NY	2 min 24.0 sec *Secretariat* 1973 (By a record 31 lengths)	6-Jimmy McLaughlin 1882, 83, 84, 86, 87, 88 6-Eddie Arcaro 1941, 42, 45, 48, 52, 55	8-James Rowe Sr 1883, 84, 1901, 04, 07, 08, 10, 13	5-Dwyer Bros 1883, 84, 86, 87, 88 5-James R. Keene 1901, 04, 07, 08, 10 5-William Woodward Sr (Belair Stud) 1930, 32, 35, 36, 39	15 (1983)

Famous International Races

Race	Record time				
Derby (1780) 1½ miles Epsom Downs, Great Britain	2 min 33.8 sec *Mahmoud* 1936 2 min 33.84 sec *Kahyasi* 1988 (Electronically timed)	9-Lester Piggott 1954, 57, 60, 68, 70, 72, 76, 77, 83	7-Robert Robson 1793, 1802, 09, 10, 15, 17, 23 7-John Porter 1868, 82, 83, 86, 90, 91, 99 7-Fred Darling 1922, 25, 26, 31, 38, 40, 41	5-3rd Earl of Egremont 1782, 1804, 05, 07, 26 5-HH Aga Khan III 1930, 35, 36, 48, 52	34 (1862)
Prix de l'Arc de Triomphe (1920) 1 mile 864 yd Longchamp, France	2 min 26.3 sec *Trempolino* 1987	4-Jacques Doyasbère 1942, 44, 50, 51 4-Frédéric "Freddy" Head 1966, 72, 76, 79 4-Yves Saint-Martin 1970, 74, 82, 84 4-Pat Eddery 1980, 85, 86, 87	6-Charles Semblat 1942, 44, 46, 49 4-Alec Head 1952, 59, 76, 81 4-François Mathet 1950, 51, 70, 82	6-Marcel Boussac 1936, 37, 42, 44, 46, 49	30 (1967)
VRC Melbourne Cup (1861) 1 mile 1739 yd Flemington, Victoria, Australia	3 min 16.3 sec *Kingston Rule* 1990	4-Bobby Lewis 1902, 15, 19, 27 4-Harry White 1974, 75, 78, 79	9-Bart Cummings 1965, 66, 67, 74, 75, 77, 79, 90, 91	4-Etienne de Mestre 1861, 62, 67, 78	39 (1890)
Grand National (1839) 4¼ miles Aintree, Liverpool, Great Britain	8 min 47.8 sec *Mr Frisk* 1990	5-George Stevens 1856, 63, 64, 69, 70	4-Fred Rimell 1956, 61, 70, 76	3-James Machell 1873, 74, 76 3-Sir Charles Assheton-Smith 1893, 1912, 13	66 (1929)

TRAINERS

Jack Charles Van Berg (USA; b. 7 Jun 1936) has the greatest number of wins in a year, 496 in 1976. The career record is 6,000, by Dale Baird (USA; b. 17 Apr 1935) from 1962 to August 1992. The greatest amount won in a year is $17,842,358, by Darrell Wayne Lukas (USA; b. 2 Sep 1935) in 1988.

The only trainer to saddle the first five finishers in a classic race is Michael William Dickinson (Great Britain; b. 3 Feb 1950), in the Cheltenham Gold Cup on 17 Mar 1983; he won a record 12 races in one day, 27 Dec 1982.

OWNERS

The most lifetime wins by an owner is 4,775, by Marion H. Van Berg (1895–1971), in North America, in 35 years. The most wins in a year is 494, by Dan R. Lasater (USA) in 1974. The greatest amount won in a year is $6,881,902, by Sam-Son Farm in North America in 1991.

HORSESHOE PITCHING

World Championships　First staged in 1909, the tournament was staged intermittently until 1946; since then it has been an annual event.

Most titles (men)　Ted Allen (USA) has won 10 world titles: 1933–35, 1940, 1946, 1953, 1955–57 and 1959.

Most titles (women)　Vicki Winston (née Chapelle) has won a record 10 women's titles: 1956, 1958–59, 1961, 1963, 1966–67, 1969, 1975 and 1981.

HURLING

Most titles All-Ireland　The greatest number of All-Ireland Championships won by one team is 27, by Cork, between 1890 and 1990. The greatest number of successive wins is four, by Cork (1941–44).

Most appearances　The most appearances in All-Ireland finals is 10, shared by Christy Ring (Cork and Munster) and John Doyle (Tipperary). They also share the record of All-Ireland medals, won with eight each. Ring's appearances on the winning side were in 1941–44, 1946 and 1952–54, while Doyle's were in 1949–51, 1958, 1961–62 and 1964–65. Ring also played in a record 22 interprovincial finals (1942–63), and was on the winning side 18 times.

Highest and lowest scores　The highest score in an All-Ireland final (60 min) was in 1989, when Tipperary, 41 (4 goals, 29 points) beat Antrim, 18 (3 goals,

9 points). The record aggregate score was when Cork, 39 (6 goals, 21 points), defeated Wexford, 25 (5 goals, 10 points), in the 80-minute final of 1970. A goal equals three points.

The highest recorded individual score was by Nick Rackard (Wexford), who scored 7 goals and 7 points against Antrim in the 1954 All-Ireland semifinal. The lowest score in an All-Ireland final was when Tipperary (1 goal, 1 point) beat Galway (zero) in the first championship at Birr in 1887.

> **Largest hurling crowd**   The largest crowd was 84,865 for the All-Ireland final between Cork and Wexford at Croke Park, Dublin in 1954.

ICE AND SAND YACHTING

Fastest speeds Ice   The fastest speed officially recorded is 143 mph, by John D. Buckstaff in a Class A stern-steerer on Lake Winnebago, WI in 1938. Such a speed is possible in a wind of 72 mph.

Sand   The official world record for a sand yacht is 66.48 mph, set by Christian-Yves Nau (France; b. 1944) in *Mobil* at Le Touquet, France on 22 Mar 1981, when the wind speed reached 75 mph. A speed of 88.4 mph was attained by Nord Embroden (USA) in *Midnight at the Oasis* at Superior Dry Lake, CA on 15 Apr 1976.

> **Largest ice yacht**   The largest ice yacht was *Icicle*, built for Commodore John E. Roosevelt for racing on the Hudson River, NY in 1869. It was 68 ft 11 in long and carried 1,070 ft² of canvas.

ICE SKATING

FIGURE SKATING

Most titles Olympic   The most Olympic gold medals won by a figure skater is three: by Gillis Grafström (Sweden; 1893–1938) in 1920, 1924 and 1928 (also silver medal in 1932); by Sonja Henie (Norway; 1912–69) in 1928, 1932 and 1936; and by Irina Konstantinovna Rodnina (USSR; b. 12 Sep 1949) with two different partners in the pairs in 1972, 1976 and 1980.

World   The greatest number of men's individual world figure skating titles (instituted 1896) is 10, by Ulrich Salchow (Sweden; 1877–1949) in 1901–05 and 1907–11. The women's record (instituted 1906) is also 10 individual titles, by Sonja Henie between 1927 and 1936. Irina Rodnina won 10 pairs titles (instituted 1908), four with Aleksey Nikolayevich Ulanov (b. 4 Nov 1947), 1969–72, and six with her husband Aleksandr Gennadyevich Zaitsev (b. 16 Jun 1952), 1973–78.

The most ice dance titles (instituted 1952) won is six, by Lyudmila Alekseyevna Pakhomova (1946–86) and her husband Aleksandr Georgiyevich Gorshkov (USSR; b. 8 Oct 1946), 1970–74 and 1976. They also won the first-ever Olympic ice dance title in 1976.

Richard Totten "Dick" Button (b. 18 Jul 1929) set US records with two Olympic gold medals, 1948 and 1952, and five world titles, 1948–52. Five women's world titles were won by Carol Elizabeth Heise (b. 20 Jan 1940), 1956–60, as well as the 1960 Olympic gold.

United States   The US Championships were first held in 1914. The most titles won by an individual is nine, by Maribel Y. Vinson (1911–61), 1928–33 and 1935–37. She also won six pairs titles, and her aggregate of 15 titles is equaled by Therese Blanchard (nee Weld; 1893–1978), who won six individual and nine pairs titles between 1914 and 1927. The men's individual record is seven, by Roger Turner, 1928–34, and by Dick Button, 1946–52. At age 16 in 1946, Button was the youngest-ever winner.

Barrel jumping on ice skates   The official distance record is 29 ft 5 in over 18 barrels, by Yvon Jolin at Terrebonne, Quebec, Canada on 25 Jan 1981. The women's record is 20 ft 4^{1}/$_{4}$ in over 11 barrels, by Janet Hainstock in Wyandotte, MI on 15 Mar 1980.

Greatest distance on ice skates   Robin John Cousins (Great Britain; b. 17 Aug 1957) achieved 19 ft 1 in in an axel jump and 18 ft with a back flip at Richmond Ice Rink, Surrey, Great Britain on 16 Nov 1983.

Highest marks   The highest tally of maximum six marks awarded in an international championship was 29, to Jayne Torvill (Great Britain; b. 7 Oct 1957) and Christopher Dean (Great Britain; 27 Jul 1958) in the World Ice Dance Championships at Ottawa, Canada on 22–24 Mar 1984. This comprised seven in the compulsory dances, a perfect set of nine for presentation in the set pattern dance, and 13 in the free dance, including another perfect set from all nine judges for artistic presentation. They previously gained a perfect set of nine sixes for artistic presentation in the free dance at the 1983 World Championships in Helsinki, Finland and at the 1984 Winter Olympic Games in Sarajevo, Yugoslavia. In their career Torvill and Dean received a record total of 136 sixes.

The most by a soloist is seven: by Donald George Jackson (Canada; b. 2 Apr 1940) in the World Men's Championship at Prague, Czechoslovakia in 1962; and by Midori Ito (Japan; b. 13 Aug 1969) in the World Women's Championships at Paris, France in 1989.

SPEED SKATING

Most titles *Olympic*   The most Olympic gold medals won in speed skating is six, by Lidiya Pavlovna Skoblikova (USSR; b. 8 Mar 1939) in 1960 (two) and 1964 (four). The men's record is five, by Clas Thunberg (Finland; 1893–1973), in 1924 and 1928 (including one tied); and Eric Arthur Heiden (USA; b. 14 Jun 1958), uniquely at one Games at Lake Placid, NY in 1980. The most medals won is seven, by Clas Thunberg, who won a silver and a bronze in addition to his five gold medals, and Ivar Ballangrud (Norway; 1904–69), four gold, two silver and a bronze, 1928–36.

World   The greatest number of world overall titles (instituted 1893) won by any skater is five—by Oscar Mathisen (Norway; 1888–1954) in 1908–09 and 1912–14; and by Clas Thunberg in 1923, 1925, 1928–29 and 1931.

The most titles won in the women's events (instituted 1936) is five, by Karin Kania (nee Enke [East Germany], b. 20 Jun 1961) in 1982, 1984, 1986–88. Kania also won a record six overall titles at the World Sprint Championships, 1980–81, 1983–84, 1986–87. A record six men's sprint overall titles have been won by Igor Zhelezovskiy (USSR/Belarus), 1985–86, 1989 and 1991–93.

The record score achieved for the world overall title is 157.396 points, by Johann-Olav Koss (Norway) at Heerenveen, Netherlands on 9–10 Feb 1991. The record low women's score is 171.630 points, by Jacqueline Börner (East Germany) at Calgary, Canada on 10–11 Feb 1990.

United States   Eric Heiden won a US record three overall world titles, 1977–79. His sister Elizabeth Lee "Beth" Heiden (b. 27 Sep 1959) became the only US women's overall champion in 1979. She completed a unique double championship when in the following year she became the first American woman to win the cycling road race world title. Later, at the University of Vermont, she took up cross-country skiing, and won the NCCA title.

FASTEST   Dan Jansen (USA), current holder of the 500 meter speed skating world record. (Photo: Allsport/Pascal Rondeau)

SPEED SKATING
World Records

Men

Meters	min : sec	Name and Country	Place	Date
500	36.02	Dan Jansen (USA)	Calgary, Canada	21 Mar 1993
1,000	1:12.58†	Pavel Pegov (USSR)	Medeo, USSR	25 Nov 1983
	1:12.58	Igor Zhelozovskiy (USSR)	Heerenveen, Netherlands	25 Feb 1989
	1:12.05*†	Nick Thometz (USA)	Medeo, USSR	27 Mar 1987
1,500	1:52.06	André Hoffmann (East Germany)	Calgary, Canada	20 Feb 1988
3,000	3:56.16	Thomas Bos (Netherlands)	Calgary, Canada	3 Mar 1992
5,000	6:36.57	Johann-Olav Koss (Norway)	Heerenveen, Netherlands	14 Mar 1993
10,000	13:43.54	Johann-Olav Koss (Norway)	Heerenveen, Netherlands	10 Feb 1991

*Unofficial
† Set at high altitude.

Women

Meters	min : sec	Name and Country	Place	Date
500	39.10	Bonnie Blair (USA)	Calgary, Canada	22 Feb 1988
1,000	1:17.65	Christa Rothenburger (now Luding) (East Germany)	Calgary, Canada	26 Feb 1988
1,500	1:59.30†	Karin Kania (East Germany)	Medeo, USSR	22 Mar 1986
3,000	4:10.80	Gunda Kleeman (Germany)	Calgary, Canada	9 Dec 1990
5,000	7:14.13	Yvonne van Gennip (Netherlands)	Calgary, Canada	28 Feb 1988
10,000 *	15:25.25	Yvonne van Gennip (Netherlands)	Heerenveen, Netherlands	19 Mar 1988

* Record not officially recognized for this distance.
† Set at high altitude.

SHORT TRACK

Men

500	43.10	Mirko Vuillermin (Italy)	Beijing, China	27 Mar 1993
1,000	1:28.47	Mike McMillen (New Zealand)	Denver, CO	4 Apr 1992
1,500	2:22.77	Andrew Nicholson (New Zealand)	Nobeyama, Japan	7 Apr 1992
3,000	5:04.24	Tatsuyoshi Ishihara (Japan)	Amsterdam, Netherlands	17 Mar 1985
5,000 relay	7:10.95	New Zealand	Beijing, China	28 Mar 1993

Women

500	46.72	Sylvie Daigle (Canada)	Albertville, France	16 Nov 1991
1,000	1:38.93	Yulia Vlasova (CIS)	Denver, CO	4 Apr 1992
1,500	2:28.26	Eden Donatelli (Canada)	Seoul, South Korea	1 Mar 1991
3,000	5:18.33	Maria-Rosa Candido (Italy)	Budapest, Hungary	17 Jan 1988
3,000 relay	4:26.56	Canada	Beijing, China	28 Mar 1993

Grand Slam Karl Schäfer (Austria; 1909–76) and Sonja Henie achieved double "Grand Slams," both in the years 1932 and 1936. This feat was repeated by Katarina Witt (East Germany; b. 3 Dec 1965) in 1984 and 1988.

Most mid-air rotations Kurt Browning (Canada; b. 18 Jun 1966) was the first to achieve a quadruple jump in competition—a toe loop—in the World Championships at Budapest, Hungary on 25 Mar 1988. The first woman to do so was Suruya Bonaly (France; b. 15 Dec 1973) in the Women's World Championships at Munich, Germany on 16 Mar 1991.

Largest rink The world's largest indoor ice rink is in the Moscow Olympic arena, which has an ice area of 86,800 ft². The five rinks at Fujikyu Highland Skating Center in Japan total 285,243 ft².

World Short-track Championships   The most successful skater in these championships (instituted 1978) has been Sylvie Daigle (Canada; b. 1 Dec 1962), women's overall champion in 1979, 1983 and 1989–90.

Longest race   The "Elfstedentocht" ("Tour of the Eleven Towns"), which originated in the 17th century, was held in the Netherlands from 1909–63, and again in 1985 and 1986, covering 200 km (124 miles 483 yd). As the weather does not permit an annual race in the Netherlands, alternative "Elfstedentocht" take place at suitable venues. These venues have included Lake Vesijärvi, near Lahti, Finland; Ottawa River, Canada; and Lake Weissensee, Austria.

The record time for 200 km is: *(men)* 5 hr 40 min 37 sec, by Dries van Wijhe (Netherlands); and *(women)* 5 hr 48 min 8 sec, by Alida Pasveer (Netherlands), both at Lake Weissensee (altitude 3,609 ft), Austria on 11 Feb 1989. Jan-Roelof Kruithof (Netherlands) won the race nine times—1974, 1976–77, 1979–84. An estimated 16,000 skaters took part in 1986.

Twenty-four hours   Martinus Kuiper (Netherlands) skated 339.67 miles in 24 hr in Alkmaar, Netherlands on 12–13 Dec 1988.

JAI ALAI (PELOTA VASCA)

World Championships   The *Federacion Internacional de Pelota Vasca* stages World Championships every four years (the first in 1952). The most successful pair have been Roberto Elias and Juan Labat (Argentina), who won the *Trinquete Share* four times, 1952, 1958, 1962 and 1966. Labat won a record seven world titles in all between 1952 and 1966. Riccardo Bizzozero (Argentina) also won seven world titles in various *Trinquete* and *Frontón corto* events, 1970–82. The most wins in the long court game *Cesta Punta* is three, by José Hamuy (Mexico; 1934–83), with two different partners, 1958, 1962 and 1966.

Fastest speed   An electronically measured ball velocity of 188 mph was recorded by José Ramon Areitio (Spain; b. 6 Jul 1947) at the Newport Jai Alai, RI on 3 Aug 1979.

Longest domination   The longest domination as the world's No. 1 player was enjoyed by Chiquito de Cambo (ne Joseph Apesteguy [France]; 1881–1955) from the beginning of the century until succeeded in 1938 by Jean Urruty (France; b. 19 Oct 1913).

Largest frontón   The world's largest frontón (enclosed stadium) is the Palm Beach Jai Alai, West Palm Beach, which has a seating capacity of 6,000 and covers three acres. The record attendance for a jai alai contest was 15,052 people at the World Jai Alai at Miami, FL, on 27 Dec 1975. The frontón, which is the oldest in the United States (1926), has seating capacity for only 3,884.

JUDO

Most titles World and Olympic World Championships were inaugurated in Tokyo, Japan in 1956. Women's championships were first held in 1980 in New York. Yashiro Yamashita (b. 1 Jun 1957) won nine consecutive Japanese titles from 1977 to 1985: four world titles—Over 95 kg in 1979, 1981 and 1983; Open in 1981; and the Olympic Open category in 1984. He retired undefeated after 203 successive wins between 1977 and 1985. Two other men have won four world titles—Shozo Fujii (Japan; b. 12 May 1950), Under 80 kg 1971, 1973 and 1975, Under 78 kg 1979; and Naoya Ogawa (Japan), Open 1987, 1989, 1991 and Over 95 kg 1989.

The only men to have won two Olympic gold medals are Wilhelm Ruska, Over 93 kg and Open in 1972; Peter Seisenbacher (Austria; b. 25 Mar 1960), 86 kg 1984 and 1988; Hitoshi Saito (Japan; b. 2 Jan 1961), Over 95 kg 1984 and 1988; and Waldemar Legien (Poland), 78 kg 1988 and 86 kg 1992.

Ingrid Berghmans (Belgium; b. 24 Aug 1961) has won a record six women's world titles (first held 1980): Open 1980, 1982, 1984 and 1986 and Under 72 kg in 1984 and 1989. She has also won four silver medals and a bronze. She

MOST TITLES   Action from the 1992 men's up-to-86 kg Olympic judo final. Waldemar Legien (Poland) defeated Pascal Tayot (France) and won gold for a record second time. (Photo: Allsport/Vandystadt/Yann Guichaoua)

won the Olympic 72 kg title in 1988, when women's judo was introduced as a demonstration sport.

The only US judo players to win world titles have been Michael Swain (b. 21 Dec 1960), at men's 71 kg class in 1987, and Ann-Maria Bernadette Burns (b. 15 Aug 1958) at women's 56 kg in 1984.

Highest grades   The efficiency grades in judo are divided into pupil (*kyu*) and master (*dan*) grades. The highest awarded is the extremely rare red belt *judan* (10th dan), given to only 13 men so far. The Judo protocol provides for an 11th dan (*juichidan*) who also would wear a red belt, a 12th dan (*junidan*) who would wear a white belt twice as wide as an ordinary belt, and the highest of all, *shihan* (ductor), but these have never been bestowed, except for the 12th dan, to the founder of the sport, Dr Jigoro Kano.

KARATE

World Championships   Great Britain has won a record six world titles (instituted 1970) at the kumite team event, in 1975, 1982, 1984, 1986, 1988 and 1990. Two men's individual kumite titles have been won by Pat McKay (Great Britain) at Under 80 kg, 1982 and 1984; Emmanuel Pinda (France) at Open, 1984, and Over 80 kg, 1988; Theirry Masci (France) at Under 70 kg, in 1986 and 1988; and José Manuel Egea (Spain) at Under 80 kg, 1990 and 1992.

Four women's kumite titles have been won by Guus van Mourik (Netherlands) at Over 60 kg, in 1982, 1984, 1986 and 1988. Three individual kata titles have been won by: *(men)* Tsuguo Sakumoto (Japan) in 1984, 1986 and 1988; *(women)* Mie Nakayama (Japan) in 1982, 1984 and 1986.

Top exponents   The leading exponents among karateka are a number of 10th dans in Japan.

Judo throws   Gary Foster and Lee Finney completed 20,052 judo throwing techniques in a 10-hour period at the Forest Judo Club, Leicester, Great Britain on 22 Aug 1992.

Jiu-Jitsu   The World Council of Jiu-Jitsu Organization has staged World Championships biennially since 1984. The Canadian team has been the winner on each occasion.

LACROSSE

MEN

Most titles World   The USA has won five of the six World Championships, in 1967, 1974, 1982, 1986 and 1990. Canada won the other world title in 1978, beating the USA 17–16 after extra time; this was the first tied international match.

Most international appearances   The record number of international appearances is 42, by Peter Daniel Roden (Great Britain; b. 8 Nov 1954) from 1976–90.

NCAA   National champions were determined by committee from 1936, and received the Wilson Wingate Trophy; since 1971 they have been decided by NCAA playoffs. Johns Hopkins University has the most wins overall: seven NCAA titles between 1974 and 1987, and six wins and five ties between 1941 and 1970.

Most points   The record for most points in the NCAA lacrosse tournament is 25, by Eamon McEneaney (Cornell) in 1977 and Tim Goldstein (Cornell) in 1987. Both players played in three games. Ed Mullen scored the most points in an NCAA championship game, with 12, for Maryland *v* Navy in the 1976 championship game.

WOMEN

The first reported playing of lacrosse by women was in 1886. The women's game has evolved separately from the men's game, so the rules now differ considerably.

World Championships/World Cup   The first World Cup was held in 1982, replacing the world championships which had been held three times since 1969. The USA has won three times, in 1974, 1982 and 1989.

NCAA   The NCAA first staged a women's national championship in 1982.

Most titles   Four teams have won two titles: Temple, 1984 and 1988; Penn State, 1987 and 1989; Maryland, 1986 and 1992; and Virginia (1991, 1993).

Highest lacrosse score   The highest score in an international lacrosse match was the USA's 32–8 win over England at Toronto, Ontario, Canada in 1986.

The highest score by the women's team was by Great Britain and Ireland in their 40–0 defeat of Long Island during their 1967 tour of the United States.

MICROLIGHTING

The *Fédération Aéronautique Internationale* has established two classes of aircraft for which records are accepted, C1 a/o and R 1-2-3, and the following are the overall best of the two classes (all in the C1 a/o class).

World records   Distance in a straight line: 1,011.45 miles, Wilhelm Lischak (Austria), Volsau, Austria to Brest, France, 8 Jun 1988.

Distance in a closed circuit: 1,679.04 miles, Wilhelm Lischak (Austria), Wels, Austria, 18 Jun 1988.

Altitude: 30,147 ft, Eric S. Winton (Australia), Tyagarah Aerodrome, New South Wales, Australia, 8 Apr 1989.

Speed over a 500 km closed circuit: 182 mph, C.T. Andrews (USA), 3 Aug 1982.

Microlighting endurance   From 1 Dec 1987 to 29 Jan 1988, Brian Milton (Great Britain) flew from London, Great Britain to Sydney with a flying time of 241 hr 20 min and covered 13,650 miles.

Eve Jackson flew from Biggin Hill, Great Britain to Sydney, Australia from 26 Apr 1986 to 1 Aug 1987. Flying time was 279 hr 55 min and the flight covered 13,639 miles.

MODERN PENTATHLON

Most titles World   András Balczó (Hungary; b. 16 Aug 1938) won the record number of world titles (instituted 1949), six individual and seven team. He won the world individual title in 1963, 1965–67 and 1969 and the Olympic title in 1972. His seven team titles (1960–70) comprised five world and two Olympic. The USSR has won a record 14 world and four Olympic team titles. Hungary has also won a record four Olympic team titles and 10 world titles.

Women's World Championships were first held in 1981, replacing the World Cup, which began in 1978. Poland has won a record five women's world team titles: 1985, 1988–91; Great Britain won three world titles, 1981–83, and three World Cups, 1978–80. The only double individual champions have been Wendy Norman (Great Britain), 1980 and 1982; Irina Kiselyeva (USSR), 1986–87, and Eva Fjellerup (Denmark), 1990–91.

The only US modern pentathletes to win world titles have been Robert Nieman (b. 21 Oct 1947), 1979, when the men's team also won, and Lori Norwood (women's) in 1989.

Olympic   The greatest number of Olympic gold medals won is three, by András Balczó, a member of the winning team in 1960 and 1968 and the 1972 individual champion. Lars Hall (Sweden; b. 30 Apr 1927) has uniquely won two individual championships (1952 and 1956). Pavel Serafimovich Lednyev (USSR; b. 25 Mar 1943) won a record seven medals (two team gold, one team silver, one individual silver, three individual bronze), 1968–80.

The only US individual Olympic medalist has been Robert Lee Beck, who won the bronze in 1960.

Probably the greatest margin of victory was by William Oscar Guernsey Grut (Sweden; b. 17 Sep 1914) in the 1948 Games, when he won three events and placed fifth and eighth in the other two.

US National Championships   The men's championship was inaugurated in 1955. Mike Burley has won a record four titles (1977, 1979, 1981, 1985). The women's championship was first held in 1977; Kim Dunlop (nee Arata) has won a record nine titles (1979–80, 1984–89 and 1991).

MOTORCYCLE RACING

Oldest race   The oldest continuous motorcycle races in the world are the Auto-Cycle Union Tourist Trophy (TT) series, first held on the 15.81 mile "Peel" (St John's) course in the Isle of Man, Great Britain on 28 May 1907, and still run in the island on the "Mountain" circuit.

Earliest race   The first reported race in the United States was won by George Holden of Brooklyn, NY in 1903, recording 14 min 57.2 sec for 10 miles.

Fastest circuits   The highest average lap speed attained on any closed circuit is 160.288 mph, by Yvon du Hamel (Canada; b. 1941) on a modified 903 cc four-cylinder Kawasaki Z1 at the 31-degree banked 2.5 mile Daytona International Speedway, FL in Mar 1973. His lap time was 56.149 sec.

The fastest road circuit used to be Francorchamps circuit near Spa, Belgium, then 8.77 miles in length. It was lapped in 3 min 50.3 sec (average speed 137.150 mph) by Barry Stephen Frank Sheene (Great Britain; b. 11 Sep 1950) on a 495 cc 4-cylinder Suzuki during the Belgian Grand Prix on 3 Jul 1977. On that occasion he set a record time for this ten-lap (87.74 mile) race of 38 min 58.5 sec (average speed 135.068 mph).

Most successful riders   Angel Roldan Nieto (Spain; b. 25 Jan 1947) won a record seven 125 cc titles, 1971–72, 1979, 1981–84, and he also won a record six titles at 50 cc, 1969–70, 1972, 1975–77. Phil Read (Great Britain; b. 1 Jan

---

Longest circuit   The 37.73-mile "Mountain" circuit on the Isle of Man, Great Britain, over which the principal TT races have been run since 1911 (with minor amendments in 1920), has 264 curves and corners and is the longest used for any motorcycle race.

1939) won a record four 250 cc titles, 1964–65, 1968, 1971. Klaus Enders (Germany; b. 2 May 1937) won six world sidecar titles, 1967, 1969–70, 1972–74.

Giacomo Agostini (Italy; b. 16 Jun 1942) won 122 races (68 at 500 cc, 54 at 350 cc) in the World Championship series between 24 Apr 1965 and 25 Sep 1977, including a record 19 in 1970, a season's total also achieved by Mike Hailwood (Great Britain) in 1966.

World Championships   The most World Championship titles (instituted by the *Fédération Internationale Motocycliste* in 1949) won is 15, by Giacomo Agostini—seven at 350 cc, 1968–74, and eight at 500 cc in 1966–72, 1975. He is the only man to have won two World Championships in five consecutive years (350 cc and 500 cc titles, 1968–72).

The most world titles won by an American motorcyclist is four, by Eddie Lawson (b. 11 Mar 1958), at 500 cc in 1984, 1986, 1988–89.

Trials   A record four World Trials Championships have been won by Jordi Tarrés (Spain), 1987, 1989–91.

Most successful machines   Japanese Yamaha machines won 45 World Championships between 1964 and 1992.

Moto-cross   Joël Robert (Belgium; b. 11 Nov 1943) won six 250 cc Moto-cross World Championships (1964, 1968–72). Between 25 Apr 1964 and 18 Jun 1972 he won a record fifty 250 cc Grand Prix. The youngest moto-cross world champion was Dave Strijbos (Netherlands; b. 9 Nov 1968), who won the 125 cc title at the age of 18 yr 296 days on 31 Aug 1986. Eric Geboers (Belgium) has uniquely won all three categories of the Moto-cross World Championships, at 125 cc in 1982 and 1983, 250 cc in 1987 and 500 cc in 1988 and 1990.

MOTORCYCLING   Wayne Rainey (USA; b. 23 Oct 1960), winner of the 500 cc world championship for three successive years, 1990–92, all riding a Yamaha. (Photo: Allsport/Chris Cole)

Youngest and oldest world champions   Loris Capirossi (Italy; b. 4 Apr 1973) is the youngest to win a World Championship. He was 17 yr 165 days when he won the 125 cc title on 16 Sep 1990. The oldest was Hermann-Peter Müller (1909–76) of West Germany, who won the 250 cc title in 1955 at the age of 46.

MOUNTAINEERING

Mount Everest   Everest (29,078 ft) was first climbed at 11:30 A.M. on 29 May 1953, when the summit was reached by Edmund Percival Hillary (b. 20 Jul 1919), of New Zealand, and Sherpa Tenzing Norgay (1914–86, formerly called Tenzing Khumjung Bhutia). The successful expedition was led by Col. (later Hon. Brigadier) Henry Cecil John Hunt (b. 22 Jun 1910).

Most conquests   Ang Rita Sherpa (b. 1947), with ascents in 1983, 1984, 1985, 1987, 1988, 1990 and 1992, has scaled Everest seven times, and all without the use of bottled oxygen.

Solo   Reinhold Messner (Italy; b. 17 Sep 1944) was the first to make the entire climb solo, on 20 Aug 1980. Also, Messner, with Peter Habeler (Austria; b. 22 Jul 1942), made the first entirely oxygen-less ascent, on 8 May 1978.

First woman   Junko Tabei (Japan; b. 22 Sep 1939) reached the summit on 16 May 1975.

Oldest mountain climber   Teiichi Igarashi (Japan; b. 21 Sep 1886) climbed Mt Fuji (Fujiyama) (12,388 ft) at the age of 99 years 302 days on 20 Jul 1986.

Rappeling   Wilmer Pérez and Luis Aulestia set a rappeling record of 3,376 ft by descending from above the Angel Falls in Venezuela down to its base on 24 Aug 1989. The descent took 1/4 hr.

The longest descent down the side of a building is one of 1,122 ft by a team of eight men from the Code Four Rescue unit, who rappeled from the observation deck of the CN Tower in Toronto, Ontario, Canada to the ground on 26 Jun 1985.

The greatest distance rappeled by a team of 10 in an eight-hour period is 45 miles, by Royal Marines from the Commando Training Center at Lympstone, Great Britain. They achieved the record by rappeling 1,382 times down the side of the Civic Center at Plymouth, Great Britain, on 22 May 1993.

Human fly   The longest climb achieved on the vertical face of a building occurred on 25 May 1981 when Daniel Goodwin, 25, of California climbed a record 1,454 ft up the outside of the Sears Tower in Chicago, using suction cups and metal clips for support.

Oldest Richard Daniel Bass (USA; b. 21 Dec 1929) was age 55 yr 130 days when he reached the summit on 30 Apr 1985.

Most successful expedition The Mount Everest International Peace Climb, a team of American, Russian and Chinese climbers, led by James W. Whittaker (USA), in 1990 succeeded in putting the greatest number of people on the summit, 20, from 7–10 May 1990.

Most in a day On 12 May 1992, 32 climbers (30 men and 2 women) from the USA, Russia, New Zealand, India, the Netherlands, Belgium, Israel, Hong Kong and Nepal, from five separate expeditions, reached the summit.

Mountaineer Reinhold Messner was the first person to successfully scale all 14 of the world's mountains of over 26,250 ft, all without oxygen. With his ascent of Kanchenjunga in 1982, he became the first person to climb the world's three highest mountains, having earlier reached the summits of Everest and K2.

Greatest walls The highest final stage in any wall climb is the one on the south face of Annapurna I (26,545 ft). It was climbed by the British expedition led by Christian John Storey Bonington (b. 6 Aug 1934) when from 2 Apr to 27 May 1970, using 18,000 ft of rope, Donald Whillans (1933–85) and Dougal Haston scaled to the summit.

The longest wall climb is on the Rupal-Flank from the base camp, at 11,680 ft, to the South Point, at 26,384 ft, of Nanga Parbat—a vertical ascent of 14,704 ft. This was scaled by the Austro-German-Italian expedition led by Dr Karl Maria Herrligkoffer (b. 13 Jun 1916) in April 1970.

The most demanding free climbs in the world are those rated at 5.13, the premier location for these being in the Yosemite Valley, CA.

SEA LEVEL TO SUMMIT Timothy John Macartney-Snape (Australia; b. 1956) traversed Mount Everest's entire altitude from sea level to summit. He set off on foot from the Bay of Bengal near Calcutta, India on 5 Feb 1990 and reached the summit on 11 May, having walked approximately 745 miles. (Photo: Australian Geographic)

Highest bivouac   Four Nepalese summiters bivouacked at more than 28,870 ft in their descent from the summit of Everest on the night of 23 Apr 1990. They were Ang Rita Sherpa, on his record-breaking sixth ascent of Everest; Ang Kami Sherpa (b. 1952); Pasang Norbu Sherpa (b. 1963); and Top Bahadur Khatri (b. 1960).

MOUNTAIN RACING

Mount Cameroon   The Mt Cameroon races started in 1973 and have been held every other year since 1988. Reginald Esuke (Cameroon) descended from the summit at 13,435 ft to Buea at 3,002 ft in 1 hr 2 min 15 sec on 24 Jan 1988, achieving a vertical rate of 167.5 ft per min. Timothy Leku Lekunze (Cameroon) set the record for the race to the summit and back of 3 hr 46 min 34 sec on 25 Jan 1987, when the temperature varied from 35° C at the start to 0° C at the summit. The record time for the ascent is 2 hr 25 min 20 sec, by Jack Maitland (Great Britain) in 1988. The women's record for the race is 4 hr 42 min 31 sec, by Fabiola Rueda (Colombia; b. 26 Mar 1963) in 1989.

NETBALL

Most titles World   Australia has won the World Championships (instituted 1963) a record six times—1963, 1971, 1975, 1979, 1983 and 1991.

Highest scores   On 9 Jul 1991, during the World Championships in Sydney, Australia, the Cook Islands beat Vanuatu 120–30. The record number of goals in the World Tournament is 402, by Judith Heath (England; b. 1942) in 1971.

Most international appearances   The record number of appearances is 100, by Jillian Hipsey of England, 1978–87.

OLYMPICS

Best attendance   All Olympic records include the Intercalated Games of 1906. Five countries have been represented at each of the 22 celebrations of the Summer Games (1896–1992): Australia, France, Greece, Great Britain and Switzerland (which only contested the equestrian events, held in Stockholm, Sweden, in 1956, and did not attend the Games in Melbourne, Australia). Of these, only France, Great Britain and Switzerland have been present at all Winter celebrations (1924–1992) as well.

Largest crowd   The largest crowd at any Olympic site was 104,102 at the 1952 ski-jumping competition at the Holmenkøllen, outside Oslo, Norway. Estimates of the number of spectators of the marathon race through Tokyo, Japan on 21 Oct 1964 ranged from 500,000 to 1.5 million. The total spectator attendance at Los Angeles in 1984 was given as 5,797,923 (see General Records).

Olympic torch relay The longest journey of the torch within one country was for the XV Olympic Winter Games in Canada in 1988. The torch arrived from Greece at St John's, Newfoundland on 17 Nov 1987 and was transported 11,222 miles (5,088 miles on foot, 4,419 miles by aircraft/ferry, 1,712 miles by snowmobile and 3 miles by dogsled) until its arrival at Calgary on 13 Feb 1988.

Most medals In the ancient Olympic Games, victors were given a chaplet of wild olive leaves. Leonidas of Rhodos won 12 running titles 164–152 B.C. The most individual gold medals won by a male competitor in the modern Games is 10, by Raymond Clarence Ewry (USA; 1874–1937) (see Track and Field). The female record is seven, by Vera Cáslavská-Odlozil (Czechoslovakia) (see Gymnastics).

The most medals won by an American Olympian is 11, at shooting, by Carl Townsend Osburn (1884–1966) from 1912 to 1924—five gold, four silver, two bronze; by Mark Andrew Spitz (b. 10 Feb 1950), at swimming, from 1968 to 72—nine gold, one silver, one bronze; and by Matt Biondi, at swimming, 1984–92—eight gold, two silver, one bronze.

The most gold medals won by an American woman is four, by three athletes: Patricia Joan McCormick (nee Keller, b. 12 May 1930), diving, 1952–56; Evelyn Ashford, track and field, 1984–92; and Janet Evans, swimming, 1988–92. The most medals won by an American woman is eight, by swimmer Shirley Babashoff (b. 31 Jan 1957)—gold at 4 × 100 meters freestyle relay 1972 and 1976, and six silver medals 1972–76, a record for any competitor in Olympic history.

The only Olympian to win four consecutive individual titles in the same

PARALYMPICS One of the most successful participants in the 1992 Paralympics in Barcelona was Tanni Grey (Great Britain), who won four golds. The year 1992 was a very successful one for Tanni as she set world records for 100 m, 200 m, 400 m and 800 m. (Photo: Allsport/Gray Mortimore)

event has been Alfred Adolph Oerter (USA; b. 19 Sep 1936), who won the discus in 1956–68. However, Raymond Clarence Ewry (USA) won both the standing long jump and the standing high jump at four games in succession, 1900, 1904, 1906 (the Intercalated Games) and 1908. Also, Paul B. Elvström (Denmark; b. 25 Feb 1928) won four successive gold medals at monotype yachting events, 1948–60, but there was a class change (1948 Firefly class, 1952–60 Finn class).

Swimmer Mark Andrew Spitz (USA) won a record seven golds at one celebration, at Munich in 1972, including three in relays. The most won in individual events at one celebration is five, by speed skater Eric Arthur Heiden (USA; b. 14 Jun 1958) at Lake Placid, NY in 1980.

The only man to win a gold medal in both the Summer and Winter Games is Edward Patrick Francis Eagan (USA; 1898–1967), who won the 1920 light-heavyweight boxing title and was a member of the winning four-man bob in 1932.

Christa Luding (nee Rothenburger [East Germany]; b. 4 Dec 1959) became the first woman to win a medal at both the Summer and Winter Games when she won a silver in the cycling sprint event in 1988. She had previously won medals for speed skating—500 meter gold in 1984, and 1,000 meter gold and 500 meter silver in 1988.

Gymnast Larisa Latynina (USSR; b. 27 Dec 1934) won a record 18 medals, and the men's record is 15, by Nikolay Andrianov (see Gymnastics). The record at one celebration is eight, by gymnast Aleksandr Dityatin (USSR; b. 7 Aug 1957) in 1980.

Youngest and oldest gold medalist The youngest-ever winner was a French boy (whose name is not recorded) who coxed the Netherlands pair in rowing in 1900. He was 7–10 years old and he substituted for Dr Hermanus Brockmann, who coxed in the heats but proved too heavy.

The youngest-ever female champion was Marjorie Gestring (USA; b. 18 Nov 1922, now Mrs Bowman), age 13 yr 268 days, in the 1936 women's springboard diving event. Oscar Swahn (Sweden) was on the winning running deer shooting team in 1912 at the age of 64 yr 258 days, and in this event was the oldest medalist—silver—at 72 yr 280 days in 1920.

The youngest American medalist and participant was Dorothy Poynton (b. 17 Jul 1915), who won the springboard diving bronze medal at 13 yr 23 days in 1928. She went on to win the highboard gold in 1932 and 1936 (by then Mrs Hill). The youngest American male medalist was Donald Wills Douglas, Jr. (b.

Most participants The greatest number of competitors at a Summer Games celebration was 9,369 (6,659 men, 2,710 women), who represented a record 169 nations, at Barcelona, Spain in 1992.

The greatest number at the Winter Games was 1,729 (1,269 men, 460 women) representing 64 countries, at Albertville, France in 1992.

Most Olympic Games contested Equestrian J. Michael Plumb completed in his seventh Olympics, the most by an American athlete in the history of the games. He also holds the record for the longest span of competition, with 32 years.

3 Jul 1917) with silver at 6-meter yachting in 1932, at 15 yr 40 days. The youngest American gold medalist was Jackie Fields, who won the 1924 featherweight boxing title at 16 yrs 161 days (see Boxing).

The oldest American Olympic champion was retired minister Galen Carter Spencer (1840–1904), who assisted the Potomac Archers to an archery team medal two days after his 64th birthday in 1904.

The oldest American medalist and Olympic participant was Samuel Harding Duvall (1836–1908), who was 68 yrs 194 days when he was a member of the Cincinnati Archers silver medal team in 1904.

Longest span   The longest span of an Olympic competitor is 40 years, by Dr Ivan Osiier (Denmark; 1888–1965) in fencing, 1908–32 and 1948; Magnus Konow (Norway; 1887–1972) in yachting, 1908–20, 1928 and 1936–48; Paul Elvström (Denmark) in yachting, 1948–1960, 1968–72 and 1984–88; and Durward Randolph Knowles (Great Britain 1948, then Bahamas; b. 2 Nov 1917) in yachting, 1948–72 and 1988. Raimondo d'Inzeo (b. 8 Feb 1925) competed for Italy in equestrian events at a record eight celebrations from 1948–76, gaining one gold, two silver and three bronze medals. This was equaled by Paul Elvström and Durward Knowles in 1988.

The longest span by a woman is 28 years, by Anne Jessica Ransehousen (nee Newberry [USA]; b. 14 Oct 1938) in dressage, 1960, 1964 and 1988. Fencer Kerstin Palm (Sweden; b. 5 Feb 1946) competed in a women's record seven celebrations, 1964–88.

The US record for longest span of Olympic competition by a man is 28 years, by fencer Norman Cudworth Armitage (ne Cohn, 1907–72), who competed in the six Games held between 1928 and 1956; he won a team bronze at sabre in 1948. He was also selected for the Games of 1940, which were canceled. Four other Americans contested six games: Frank Davis Chapot (b. 24 Feb 1932), at show jumping 1956–76, winner of two team silver medals; Lt. Col. William Willard McMillan (b. 29 Jan 1929) at shooting, 1952–76, missing 1956, winning gold at rapid-fire pistol in 1960; Janice Lee York Romary (b. 6 Aug 1928), at fencing 1948–68; and John Michael Plumb (b. 28 Mar 1940) at three-day event, 1960–84, winner of a gold and four silver medals. Plumb was also named for the 1980 Games, which the US boycotted.

ORIENTEERING

Most titles   The men's relay has been won a record seven times by Norway—1970, 1978, 1981, 1983, 1985, 1987 and 1989. Sweden has won the women's relay nine times—1966, 1970, 1974, 1976, 1981, 1983, 1985, 1989 and 1991. Three women's individual titles have been won by Annichen Kringstad (Sweden; b. 15 Jul 1960), in 1981, 1983 and 1985.

The men's title has been won twice by Age Hadler (Norway; b. 14 Aug 1944), in 1966 and 1972; Egil Johansen (Norway; b. 18 Aug 1954), in 1976 and 1978; and Øyvin Thon (Norway; b. 25 Mar 1958), in 1979 and 1981.

US National Championships   This competition was first held on 17 Oct 1970. Sharon Crawford of the New England Orienteering Club, has won a record 11 overall women's titles, 1977–82, 1984–87, 1989. Mikell Platt, of the Blue Star

Komplex Orienteering Club, has won a record six overall men's titles, 1985 and 1988–92.

> **Most competitors**   The most competitors at a one-day orienteering event is 38,000, in the Ruf des Herbstes held in Sibiu, Romania in 1982. The largest event is the five-day Swedish O-Ringen at Småland, which attracted 120,000 competitors in July 1983.
>
> The most competitors in a one-day event in the United States is 1,090, at the US Orienteering Club in Baltimore, MD, held on 9 Nov 1991.
>
> **Ski orienteering**   The World Championships in ski orienteering were instituted in 1975. Sweden has won the men's relay five times (1977, 1980, 1982, 1984 and 1990) and Finland has won the women's relay five times (1975, 1977, 1980, 1988 and 1990). The most individual titles is four, by Ragnhild Bratberg (Norway), Classic 1986, 1990, Sprint 1988, 1990. The men's record is three, by Anssi Juutilainen (Finland), Classic 1984, 1988, Sprint 1992.

PARACHUTING

World championships *Team*   The USSR won the men's team title in 1954, 1958, 1960, 1966, 1972, 1976 and 1980, and the women's team title in 1956, 1958, 1966, 1968, 1972 and 1976.

Individual   Nikolay Ushamyev (USSR) has won the individual title twice, 1974 and 1980.

Greatest accuracy   At Yuma, AZ, in March 1978, Dwight Reynolds scored a record 105 daytime dead centers, and Bill Wenger and Phil Munden tied with 43 night-time dead centers, competing as members of the US Army Golden Knights.

With electronic measuring, the official *Fédération Aeronautique Internationale* (FAI) record is 50 dead centers, by Linger Abdurakhmanov (USSR) at Fergana in 1988, when the women's record was set at 41, by Natalya Filinkova (USSR) in 1988.

The Men's Night Accuracy Landing record on an electronic score pad is 31 consecutive dead centers, by Vladimir Buchenev (USSR) on 30 Oct 1986. The women's record is 21, by Inessa Stepanova (USSR) at Fergana on 18 Oct 1988.

Paragliding   The greatest distance flown is 174.9 miles by Alex Lowe (South Africa) from Kuruman, South Africa on 31 Dec 1992.

The women's distance record is 77 miles, by Judy Leden (Great Britain) on 9 Dec 1992. The height gain record is 14,665 ft by Robby Whittal (Great

PARACHUTE RECORDS

First *Tower*[1] • Louis-Sébastien Lenormand (1757–1839), quasi-parachute, Montpellier, France, 1783.

Balloon • André-Jacques Garnerin (1769–1823), 2,230 ft, Monceau Park, Paris, France, 22 Oct 1797.

Aircraft • *Man:* "Captain" Albert Berry, an aerial exhibitionist, St Louis, MO, 1 Mar 1912. *Woman:* Mrs Georgina "Tiny" Broadwick (b. 1893), Griffith Park, Los Angeles, CA, 21 Jun 1913.

Longest Duration Fall • Lt. Col. Wm H. Rankin, USMC, 40 min due to thermals, North Carolina, 26 Jul 1956.

Longest Delayed Drop *Man* • Capt Joseph W. Kittinger,[2] 84,700 ft (16.04 miles), from balloon at 102,800 ft, Tularosa, NM, 16 Aug 1960.

Woman • E. Fomitcheva (USSR), 48,556 ft over Odessa, USSR, 26 Oct 1977.

Mid Air Rescue *Earliest* • Miss Dolly Shepherd (1886-1983) brought down Miss Louie May on her single 'chute from balloon at 11,000 ft, Longton, Great Britain, 9 Jun 1908.

Lowest • Gregory Robertson saved Debbie Williams (unconscious), collision at 9,000 ft, pulled her ripcord at 3,500 ft—10 secs from impact, Coolidge, AZ, 18 Apr 1987.

Escape *Highest* • Flt. Lt. J. de Salis, RAF and Fg Off P. Lowe, RAF, 56,000 ft, Monyash, Derby, Great Britain, 9 Apr 1958.

Lowest • S/Ldr. Terence Spencer DFC, RAF, 30–40 ft, Wismar Bay, Baltic, 19 Apr 1945.

Landing *Highest* • Ten USSR parachutists[3], 23,405 ft, Lenina Peak, USSR, May 1969.

Most Southerly • T/Sgt. Richard J. Patton (USA; d. 1973), Operation Deep Freeze, South Pole, 25 Nov 1956.

Most Northerly • Six members of the Canadian Armed Forces were the first people to jump at Lat. 90° 00′ N, 27 Apr 1974.

Cross-Channel (Lateral Fall) • Sgt. Bob Walters with three soldiers and two British Royal Marines, 22 miles from 25,000 ft, Dover, Great Britain to Sangatte, France, 31 Aug 1980.

Total Sport Parachuting Descents *Man* • Don Kellner (USA), 18,000, various locations up to 31 Oct 1992.

Woman • Valentina Zakoretskaya (USSR), 8,000, over USSR, 1964–September 1980.

24-Hour Total • *Man* Dale Nelson (USA), 301 (in accordance with United States Parachute Association rules), PA, 26–27 May 1988.

Woman • Cheryl Stearns (USA), 255 at Lodi, CA, 26–27 Nov 1987.

Most Traveled • Kevin Seaman from a Cessna Skylane (pilot Charles E. Merritt), 12,186 miles, jumps in all 50 US states, 26 Jul–15 Oct 1972.

Heaviest Load • US Space Shuttle *Columbia*, external rocket retrieval, 80 ton capacity, triple array, each 120 ft diameter, Atlantic, off Cape Canaveral, FL, 12 Apr 1981.

Highest Canopy Formation • 37, a team of French parachutists at Brienne le Chateau, Troyes, France, held for 13 secs on 16 Aug 1992.

Largest Free-fall Duration *Men* • 150, from 21 countries, held for 5.47 sec from 19,192 ft, Koksijde military base, Belgium, 4 Jul 1992.

Women • 100, from 20 countries, held for 5.97 sec, from 17,000 ft, Aéreodrome du Cannet des Maures, France, 14 Aug 1992.

USA: 144, held for 8.8 sec, from 16,000 ft, Quincy, IL, 11 Jul 1988.

Oldest *Man* • Edwin C. Townsend (d. 7 Nov 1987), 89 years, Vermillion Bay, LA, 5 Feb 1986.

Woman • Mrs Sylvia Brett (Great Britain), 80 years 166 days, Cranfield, Great Britain, 23 Aug 1986.

Oldest Tandem *Man* • George Salyer (USA), 91 years, Snohomish, WA, 18 Jun 1992

Woman • Corena Leslie (USA) 89 years 326 days, Buckeye Airport, Sun Valley, AZ, 11 Jun 1992.

Longest Fall without Parachute • Vesna Vulovic (Yugoslavia), air hostess in DC–9 that blew up at 33,330 ft over Srbská Kamenice, Czechoslovakia (now Czech Republic), 26 Jan 1972.

[1] *The king of Ayutthaya, Siam in 1687 was reported to have been amused by an ingenious athlete parachuting with two large umbrellas. Faustus Verancsis is reputed to have descended in Hungary with a framed canopy in 1617.*
[2] *Maximum speed in rarefied air was 625.2 mph at 90,000 ft—marginally supersonic.*
[3] *Four were killed.*

MOST PARACHUTE JUMPS For the past 30 years Don Kellner has been parachuting; he achieved his 18,000th jump on 31 Oct 1992. (Photo: Darlene Kellner)

PARACHUTING—WOMEN'S 24-HOUR RECORD Cheryl Stearns made 255 parachute jumps in 24 hours in November 1987, which at the time was a joint overall record (shared with Russell Fish), and remains the most in a 24-hour period by a woman.

Britain), also at Kuruman, on 22 Jan 1993. All these records were tow launched.

Nigel Horder scored four successive dead centers at the Dutch Open, Flevhof, Netherlands on 22 May 1983.

PÉTANQUE

World Championships   Winner of the most World Championships (instituted 1959) has been France, with 12 titles to 1992. Two women's World Championships were held in 1988 and 1990, and Thailand won on both occasions.

Highest pétanque score in 24 hours   Chris Walker (b. 16 Jan 1942) and his son Richard (b. 26 Dec 1966), scored a record 2,109 points in 24 hours (172 games) at the Gin Trap, Ringstead, Great Britain on 24–25 Jun 1988.

POLO

Oldest   The oldest existing polo club in the United States is Meadow Brook Polo Club, Jericho, NY, founded in 1879.

The United States Open Championship was inaugurated in 1904 and has been played continuously since then, with the exception of 1905–09, 1911, 1915, 1917–18 and 1942–45. The most wins is 28, by the Meadow Brook Polo Club, in 1916, 1920, 1923–41, 1946–51 and 1953.

Most polo chukkas   The greatest number of chukkas played on one ground in a day is 43. This was achieved by the Pony Club on the Number 3 Ground at Kitlington Park, Great Britain on 31 Jul 1991.

Highest score in polo   The highest aggregate number of goals scored in an international polo match is 30, when Argentina beat the USA 21–9 at Meadowbrook, Long Island, NY in September 1936.

World Championships The first World Championships were held in Berlin, Germany in 1989. The USA won the title, defeating Great Britain 7–6 in the final.

Highest handicap The highest handicap based on six $7\frac{1}{2}$-min "chukkas" is 10 goals, introduced in the USA in 1891. A total of 55 players have received 10-goal handicaps.

A match of two 40-goal teams has been staged on three occasions—in Argentina in 1975, in the United States in 1990, and in Australia in 1991.

POOL

14.1 CONTINUOUS POOL
(AMERICAN STRAIGHT POOL)

World Championship The two most dominant 14.1 players have been Ralph Greenleaf (USA; 1899–1950), who won the "world" professional title six times and defended it 13 times (1919–37), and William "Willie" Mosconi (USA; b. 27 Jun 1913), who dominated the game from 1941 to 1956, and also won the title six times and defended it 13 times.

Longest consecutive run The longest consecutive run in 14.1 recognized by the Billiard Congress of America (BCA) is 526 balls, by Willie Mosconi in March 1954 during an exhibition in Springfield, OH. Michael Eufemia is reported to have pocketed 625 balls at Logan's Billiard Academy, Brooklyn, NY on 2 Feb 1960, but this run has never been ratified by the BCA.

Most balls pocketed The greatest number of balls pocketed in 24 hr is 16,125, by James Abel at White Plains, NY on 17–18 Dec 1991.

Pool pocketing speed The record times for pocketing all 15 balls in a speed competition are: (*men*) 37.9 sec, by Rob McKenna at Blackpool, Great Britain on 7 Nov 1987; (*women*) 44.5 sec, by Susan Thompson at Shrublands Community Centre, Gorleston, Great Britain on 20 Apr 1990.

Projectiles

The greatest distance that any object has been propelled by human power is 6,141 ft 2 in, in the case of an arrow shot by Harry Drake

(USA; b. 7 May 1915), using a crossbow at the Smith Creek Flight Range near Austin, NV on 30 Jul 1988.

The longest independently authenticated throw of any inert object heavier than air is 1,257 ft, for a flying ring, by Scott Zimmerman on 8 Jul 1986 at Fort Funston, CA.

SPEAR THROWING
Wayne Brian (left) with his spear and atlatl. He beat the old record on two occasions in 1992. (Photo: Richard Jamison.)

SLINGING The latest slinging record is held by David Engvall (left). The equipment used is pictured below. (Photos: Beverly Hargrove and David Engvall)

Records achieved with other miscellaneous objects:

Boomerang juggling (Consecutive catches with two boomerangs, keeping at least one boomerang aloft at all times) 207
Michael Girvin (USA) at Elkton, MD on 6 Jul 1991.

Boomerang throwing (Consecutive two-handed catches) 801
Stéphane Marguerite (France) on 26 Nov 1989 at Lyons, France.
(Longest out-and-return distance)..440 ft 3 in
Jim Youngblood (USA) on 12 Jun 1989 at Gaithersburg, MD
(Longest flight, [self-catch]) ....2 min 59.94 sec
Dennis Joyce at Bethlehem, PA on 25 Jun 1987

Brick (standard 5-lb building brick)......................................146 ft 1 in
Geoff Capes at Braybrook School, Orton, Great Britain on 19 Jul 1978.

Egg (fresh hen's; without breakage) ....317 ft 10 in
Risto Antikainen to Jyrki Korhonen at Siilinjärvi, Finland on 6 Sep 1981.

Rolling pin (2 lb)..175 ft 5 in
Lori La Deane Adams, 21, at Iowa State Fair, IA on 21 Aug 1979.

Slingshot (50-in-long sling and a 2∞ oz dart)....................1,565 ft 4 in
David P. Engvall at Baldwin Lake, CA on 13 Sep 1992.

Spear (With an atlatl/hand-held device that fits onto a short spear) ....638 ft 8 in
Wayne Brian at Fairplay, CO on 11 Jul 1992.

Flying disc throwing (formerly Frisbee) World Flying Disc Federation distance records are: (men) 623 ft 7 in, by Sam Ferrans (USA) on 2 Jul 1988 at La Habra, CA; (women) 426 ft 10 in, by Amy Bekken (USA) on 25 Jul 1990 at La Habra, CA

Throw, run and catch records: (men) 303 ft 11 in, by Hiroshi Oshima (Japan) on 20 Jun 1988 at San Francisco, CA; (women) 196 ft 11 in, by Judy Horowitz (USA) on 29 Jun 1985 at La Mirada, CA.

24-hour distance records for a pair are: (men) 362.40 miles, by Leonard Muise and Gabe Ontiveros (USA) on 21–22 Sep 1988 at Carson, CA; (women) 115.65 miles, by Jo Cahow and Amy Berard (USA) on 30–31 Dec 1979 at Pasadena, CA.

Records for maximum time aloft are: (men) 16.72 sec, by Don Cain (USA) on 26 May 1984 at Philadelphia, PA; (women) 11.81 sec, by Amy Bekken (USA) at Santa Cruz, CA on 1 Aug 1991.

Cow chip tossing The greatest distance achieved under the "non-sphericalization and 100 percent organic" rule (established in 1970) is 266 ft, by Steve Urner at the Mountain Festival, Tehachapi, CA on 14 Aug 1981.

POWERBOAT RACING

APBA Gold Cup The American Power Boat Association (APBA) held its first Gold Cup race at the Columbia Yacht Club on the Hudson River, NY in 1904, when the winner was *Standard*, piloted by C.C. Riotto at an average speed of 23.6 mph. The most wins by a pilot is nine, by Chip Hanauer (USA), 1982–88, 1992–93.

The most successful boat has been *Atlas Van Lines*, piloted by Bill Muncey to victory in 1972, 1977–79 and by Hanauer in 1982–84. Hanauer went on to complete a record seven successive victories to 1988. The highest average speed for the race is 143.176 mph by Tom D'Eath, piloting *Miss Budweiser* in 1990.

Longest races The longest offshore race has been the Port Richborough London, Great Britain to Monte Carlo Marathon Offshore international event. The race extended over 2,947 miles in 14 stages from 10–25 Jun 1972. It was won by *H.T.S.* (Great Britain), driven by Mike Bellamy, Eddie Chater and Jim Brooker, in 71 hr 35 min 56 sec, for an average of 41.15 mph. The longest circuit race is the 24-hour race held annually since 1962 on the River Seine at Rouen, France.

RACKETS

World Championships Of the 22 world champions since 1820, the longest reign is by Geoffrey Willoughby Thomas Atkins (Great Britain; b. 20 Jan 1927), who gained the title by beating the professional James Dear (Great Britain; 1910–81) in 1954, and held it until retiring, after defending it four times, in April 1972.

United States The first American to be world champion was Jock Souter, and he had the longest span as champion, 1913–28.

RACQUETBALL

World Championships First held in 1982, the IARF World Championships have been held biennially since 1984. The United States has won all six team titles, in 1981, 1984, 1986 (tie with Canada), 1988, 1990 and 1992. Egan Inoue (USA) has won the most men's singles titles with two, in 1986 and 1990. Two women have won the world singles championships twice: Cindy Baxter (USA) in 1981 and 1986; Heather Stupp (Canada) in 1988 and 1990.

US titles In 1968, championships were initiated by the AARA (the governing body for the sport in the United States). A record four men's open titles have been won by Ed Andrews of California, 1980–81 and 1985–86, and a record five women's open titles by Michelle Gilman-Gould, 1989–93.

REAL/ROYAL TENNIS

Oldest The oldest of the surviving active courts in Great Britain is the one at Falkland Palace, Fife, Scotland built by King James V of Scotland in 1539.

Most titles World The first recorded world tennis champion was Clergé (France), *c.* 1740. Jacques Edmond Barre (France; 1802–73) held the title for a record 33 years from 1829 to 1862. Pierre Etchebaster (1893–1980), a Basque, holds the record for the greatest number of successful defenses of the title, with eight between 1928 and 1952.

The Women's World Championships (instituted in 1985) has been won twice by Judith Anne Clarke (Australia; b. 28 Dec 1954), 1985 and 1987; and Penny Lumley (nee Fellows; Great Britain), 1989 and 1991.

United States Jay Gould, Jr. (1888–1935) won his first US singles title in 1906, and retained the title until he retired from singles play in 1926. During his career he lost only one singles match. He also won 19 US doubles titles between 1909 and 1932.

RODEO

The largest rodeo in the world is the National Finals Rodeo, organized by the Professional Rodeo Cowboys Association (PRCA) and the Women's Professional Rodeo Association (WPRA). The top 15 money-earning cowboys in each of the six PRCA events and the top 15 WPRA barrel racers compete at the Finals. The event was first held at Dallas, TX in 1959, and was held at Oklahoma City, OK for 20 years before moving to Las Vegas, NV in 1985. The 1991 Finals had a paid attendance of 171,414 for 10 performances. In 1992 a record $2.6 million in prize money was offered for the event.

Most world titles The record number of all-around titles (awarded to the leading money winner in a single season in two or more events) in the PRCA World Championships is six, by Larry Mahan (USA; b. 21 Nov 1943) in 1966–70 and 1973, and, consecutively, 1974–79 by Tom Ferguson (b. 20 Dec 1950). Jim Shoulders (b. 13 May 1928) of Henrietta, TX won a record 16 World Championships at four events between 1949 and 1959.

Earnings records Roy Cooper holds the career rodeo earnings mark at $1,406,423 through 19 Jul 1993. The single-season record is $258,750, by Ty

Murray (b. 11 Oct 1969) in 1991. Murray won a record $101,531 for one saddle bronc-riding rodeo in December 1992 at the National Finals Rodeo in Las Vegas, NV.

Time records Records for PRCA timed events, such as calf-roping and steer wrestling, are not always comparable, because of the widely varying conditions due to the sizes of arenas and amount of start given the stock. The fastest time recorded for calf-roping under the current PRCA rules is 6.7 sec, by Joe Beaver (b. 13 Oct 1965) at West Jordan, UT in 1986, and the fastest time for steer wrestling is 2.4 sec, by James Bynum at Marietta, OK in 1955; Carl Deaton at Tulsa, OK in 1976; and Gene Melton at Pecatonica, IL in 1976. The fastest team roping time is 3.7 sec, by Bob Harris and Tee Woolman at Spanish Fork, UT in 1986.

Women's barrel racing The greatest number of titles won in women's barrel racing is nine, by Charmayne Rodman, 1984–92.

Bull riding Jim Sharp (b. 6 Oct 1965) of Kermit, TX became the first rider to ride all 10 bulls at a National Finals Rodeo at Las Vegas in December 1988. This feat was matched by Norm Curry of Deberry, TX at the 1990 National Finals Rodeo.

The highest score in bull riding was 100 points out of a possible 100, by Wade Leslie on Wolfman Skoal at Central Point, OR in 1991.

Saddle bronc-riding The highest scored saddle bronc ride is 95 out of a possible 100, by Doug Vold on *Transport*, at Meadow Lake, Saskatchewan, Canada in 1979. Descent, a saddle bronc owned by Beutler Brothers and Cervi Rodeo Company, received a record six PRCA Saddle Bronc of the Year awards, 1966–69, 1971–72.

Bareback riding Joe Alexander of Cora, WY scored 93 out of a possible 100 on *Marlboro*, at Cheyenne, WY in 1974. Sippin' Velvet, owned by Bernis Johnson, has been awarded a record five PRCA Bareback Horse of the Year titles between 1978 and 1987.

Top bull The top bucking bull Red Rock dislodged 312 riders, 1980–88, and was finally ridden to the 8-sec bell by Lane Frost (1963–89; world champion bull rider 1987) on 20 May 1988. Red Rock was retired at the end of the 1987 season but still continued to make guest appearances.

Youngest rodeo champions The youngest winner of a world title in rodeo is Anne Lewis (b. 1 Sep 1958), who won the WPRA barrel racing title in 1968, at 10 years of age. Ty Murray (b. 11 Oct 1969) is the youngest cowboy to win the PRCA All-Around Champion title, at age 20, in 1989.

Texas Skips Vince Bruce (USA) performed 4,001 Texas Skips (jumps back and forth through a large, vertical spun loop) on 22 Jul 1991 at the Empire State Building, New York City.

ROLLER SKATING

Most titles *Speed*   The most world speed titles won is 18, by two women: Alberta Vianello (Italy), eight track and 10 road, 1953–65; and Annie Lambrechts (Belgium), one track and 17 road, 1964–81, at distances from 500 meters to 10,000 meters.

Figure   The records for figure titles are five by Karl Heinz Losch (West Germany) in 1958–59, 1961–62 and 1966; and four shared by Astrid Bader (West Germany) in 1965–68, and Rafaella del Vinaccio (Italy), 1988–91. The most world pair titles is six, by Tammy Jeru (USA) in 1983–86 (with John Arishita), and in 1990–91 (with Larry McGrew).

Speed skating   The fastest speed posted in an official world record is 26.85 mph, when Luca Antoniel (Italy; b. 12 Feb 1968) recorded 24.99 sec for 300 meters on a road at Gujan-Mestras, France on 31 Jul 1987. The women's record is 25.04 mph, by Marisa Canofogilia (Italy; b. 30 Sep 1965) for 300 meters on the road at Grenoble, France on 27 Aug 1987. The world records for 10,000 meters on a road or track are: *(men)* 14 min 55.64 sec, Giuseppe de Persio (Italy; b. 3 Jun 1959) at Gujan-Mestras, France on 1 Aug 1988; *(women)* 15 min 58.022 sec, Marisa Canofogilia (Italy) at Grenoble, France on 30 Aug 1987.

ROLLER HOCKEY   Portugal is the most successful nation in the history of roller hockey, winning a record number of World and European titles. Here is the team in action against Holland at the 1992 Olympic Games, where roller hockey was one of the demonstration sports. (Photo: Allsport/Bernard Asset)

Largest rink The largest indoor rink ever to operate was located in the Grand Hall, London, Great Britain. Opened in 1890 and closed in 1912, it had an actual skating area of 68,000 ft². The current largest is the main arena of 34,981 ft² at Guptill Roll-Arena, Boght Corner, NY. The total rink area is 41,380 ft².

ROLLER HOCKEY

First held in Stuttgart, Germany in 1936, the world championships have been held under several formats, both annual and biennial. Currently the tournament is an annual event. Portugal has won most world titles, with 13: 1947–50, 1952, 1956, 1958, 1960, 1962, 1968, 1974, 1982 and 1991.

THE GUINNESS DAILY RECORD   16th March, 1990

SKATEBOARD SPEED RECORD SMASHED

HICKEY EXCEEDS THE SPEED LIMIT

Skateboard fanatic Roger Hickey, of Westminster, CA, yesterday recorded the highest speed ever achieved on a skateboard, clocking 78.37 mph on a 3-mile course near Los Angeles.

He set the record lying in a prone position on his skateboard, and hopes to set a speed record in a stand-up position later this year. However, skateboarding at great speed does have its dangers — Hickey has suffered 44 fractures over the years. Fortunately, the attempt was not made when members of the driving public were using the road, as the police would surely not have liked the fact that Hickey ignored the regular speed limit in beating the record.

SKATEBOARDING

World championships have been staged intermittently since 1966. David Frank, 25, covered 270.5 miles in 36 hr 43 min 40 sec in Toronto, Ontario, Canada on 11–12 Aug 1985.

Fastest speed   The stand-up record is 55.43 mph, achieved by Roger Hickey, at San Demas, CA on 3 Jul 1990.

Jumps   The high-jump record is 5 ft 5¾ in, by Trevor Baxter (b. 1 Oct 1962) of Burgess Hill, Great Britain at Grenoble, France on 14 Sep 1982.

At the World Professional Championships, at Long Beach, CA on 25 Sep 1977, Tony Alva, 19, jumped 17 barrels (17 ft).

ROWING

Most Olympic medals   Seven oarsmen have won three gold medals: John Brendan Kelly (USA; 1889–1960), father of the late Princess Grace of Monaco, who won at Single Sculls (1920) and Double Sculls (1920 and 1924); his cousin, Paul Vincent Costello (USA; 1894–1986) Double Sculls (1920, 1924 and 1928); Jack Beresford, Jr. (Great Britain; 1899–1977), Single Sculls (1924), Coxless Fours (1932) and Double Sculls (1936); Vyacheslav Nikolayevich Ivanov (USSR; b. 30 Jul 1938), Single Sculls (1956, 1960 and 1964); Siegfried Brietzke (East Germany; b. 12 Jun 1952), Coxless Pairs (1972) and Coxless Fours (1976, 1980); Pertti Karppinen (Finland; b. 17 Feb 1953), Single Sculls (1976, 1980 and 1984); and Steven Redgrave (Great Britain; b. 23 Mar 1962), Coxed Fours (1984) and Coxless Pairs (1988 and 1992).

World Championships   World rowing championships distinct from the Olympic Games were first held in 1962, and were held four times a year at first, but from 1974 were held annually, except in Olympic years.

The most gold medals won at World Championships and Olympic Games is nine, at coxed pairs by the Italian brothers Giuseppe (b. 24 Jul 1959) and Carmine Abbagnale (b. 5 Jan 1962), World 1981–82, 1985, 1987, 1989–91, Olympics 1984 and 1988. At women's events Yelena Terekhina has won a record seven golds, all eights for the USSR, 1978–79, 1981–83 and 1985–86.

The most wins at Single Sculls is five, by Peter-Michael Kolbe (West Germany; b. 2 Aug 1953), 1975, 1978, 1981, 1983 and 1986; Pertti Karppinen, 1979 and 1985, and with his three Olympic wins (above); Thomas Lange (Germany; b. 27 Feb 1964), 1987, 1989 and 1991 and two Olympics 1988 and 1992; and in the women's events by Christine Hahn (nee Scheiblich [East Germany]; b. 31 Dec 1954), 1974–75, 1977–78 (and the 1976 Olympic title).

Collegiate Championships   The first intercollegiate boat race in the United States was between Harvard and Yale in 1852. The Intercollegiate Rowing Association (IRA) was formed in 1895, and in 1898 inaugurated the Varsity Challenge Cup, which was recognized as the national championship. In 1982, the United States Rowing Assocation introduced the National Collegiate Championships, and this race now decides the national champion. Overall,

> **Longest race**   The longest annual rowing race is the annual Tour du Lac Leman, Geneva, Switzerland for coxed fours (the five-man crew taking turns as cox) over 99 miles. The record winning time is 12 hr 52 min, by LAGA Delft, Netherlands on 3 Oct 1982.

Cornell University has won the most national championships, with 25 titles (all Varsity Cup wins). Since 1982, Harvard University has won five titles (1983, 1985, 1987–89). The women's national championship was inaugurated in 1979. The University of Washington has won a record seven times (1981–85, 1987–88).

Henley Royal Regatta   The annual regatta at Henley-on-Thames, Great Britain was inaugurated on 26 Mar 1839. Since then the course, except in 1923, has been about 1 mile 550 yd, varying slightly according to the length of the boat. In 1967 the shorter craft were "drawn up" so all bows start level.

The most wins in the Diamond Challenge Sculls (instituted 1844) is six, by Guy Nickalls (Great Britain; 1866–1935), 1888–91, 1893–94, and consecutively, by Stuart A. Mackenzie (Australia and Great Britain; b. 5 Apr 1937), 1957–62. The record time is 7 min 23 sec, by Vaclav Chalupa (Czechoslovakia; b. 7 Dec 1967) on 2 Jul 1989. The record time for the Grand Challenge Cup (instituted 1839) event is 5 min 58 sec, by Hansa Dortmund, West Germany on 2 Jul 1989.

Fastest speed   The fastest recorded speed on non-tidal water for 2,187 yd is by an American eight in 5 min 27.14 sec (13.68 mph) at Lucerne, Switzerland on 17 Jun 1984. A crew from Penn AC was timed in 5 min 18.8 sec (14.03 mph) in the FISA Championships on the River Meuse, Liège, Belgium on 17 Aug 1930.

Twenty-four hours   The greatest distance rowed in 24 hours (upstream and downstream) is 135.22 miles, by a coxed quad (Peter Halliday, Paul Turnbull, Mike Skerry, Belinda Goglia and Margaret Munneke) on the Yarra River, Melbourne, Australia on 26–27 Jan 1992.

International Dragon Boat Race   In this race, instituted in 1975 and held annually in Hong Kong, the fastest time achieved for the 700-yd course is 2 min 27.45 sec, by the Chinese Shun De team on 30 Jan 1985. Teams have 28 members—26 rowers, one steersman and one drummer.

RUGBY

Records are determined in terms of present-day scoring values, i.e., a try at 4 points; a dropped goal, penalty or goal from a mark at 3 points; and a conversion at 2 points. The actual score, in accordance with whichever of the eight earlier systems was in force at the time, is also given, in parentheses.

OLYMPIC GAMES

In competitions held from 1900 to 1924, the only double gold medalist was the United States, which won in 1920 and 1924, defeating France in the final on both occasions.

WORLD CUP

The World Cup has been held on two occasions, 1987 and 1991, with the winners being New Zealand and Australia respectively. The highest team score was New Zealand's 74-13 victory over Fiji at Christchurch, New Zealand on 27 May 1987. New Zealand scored 10 goals, 2 tries and 2 penalty goals. The individual match record was 30 (3 tries, 9 conversions), by Didier Camberabero (France; b. 9 Jan 1961) v Zimbabwe at Auckland on 2 Jun 1987. The leading scorer in the tournament was the New Zealand goal-kicker, Grant James Fox (b. 6 Jun 1962), with 170 points (including a record 126 in 1987).

INTERNATIONAL CHAMPIONSHIPS

The International Championship was first contested by England, Ireland, Scotland and Wales in 1884. France first played in 1910. Wales has won the championship a record 21 times outright and tied for first a further 11 times up to 1988. The most Grand Slams, winning all four matches, is 10, by England, 1913–14, 1921, 1923–24, 1928, 1957, 1980 and 1991–92.

Highest team score The highest score in a Championship match was set at Swansea, Wales on 1 Jan 1910 when Wales beat France 49-14 (8 goals, 1 penalty goal, 2 tries, to 1 goal, 2 penalty goals, 1 try).

MOST APPEARANCES The most appearances in rugby union's International Championship is 42, by Serge Blanco and Philippe Sella, both of France. Sella (b. 14 Feb 1962), the world's most capped center, is seen here in action against Scotland. (Photo: Allsport)

HIGHEST SCORES

Teams   The highest score in any full international was when New Zealand beat Japan by 106–4 at Tokyo, Japan on 1 Nov 1987. France beat Paraguay 106–12 at Asunción, Paraguay on 28 Jun 1988.

Individuals   Phil Bennett (Wales; b. 24 Oct 1948) scored 34 points (2 tries, 10 conversions, 2 penalty goals) for Wales *v* Japan at Tokyo on 24 Sep 1975, when Wales won 82–6. A record eight penalty goals were kicked by Mark Andrew Wyatt (b. 12 Apr 1961) when he scored all Canada's points in their 24–19 defeat of Scotland at St John, New Brunswick, Canada on 25 May 1991.

Career   In all internationals, Michael Patrick Lynagh (b. 25 Oct 1963) scored a record 762 points in 61 matches for Australia, 1984–93. The most tries is 54, by David Campese (b. 21 Oct 1962) in 73 internationals for Australia, 1982–93.

SEVEN-A-SIDES

Seven-a-side rugby dates from 28 Apr 1883, when Melrose RFC Borders (Scotland), in order to compensate for the poverty of a club in such a small town, staged a seven-a-side tournament. The idea was that of Ned Haig, the town's butcher.

Hong Kong Sevens   This, the world's most prestigious international tournament for seven-a-side teams, was first held in 1976. The record of seven wins is held by Fiji, 1977–78, 1980, 1984, 1990–92.

Rugby all-arounder   Canadian international Barrie Burnham scored all possible ways—try, conversion, penalty goal, drop goal, goal from mark—for Meralomas *v* Georgians (20–11) at Vancouver, British Columbia, Canada on 26 Feb 1966.

Highest rugby posts   The world's highest rubgy union goal posts are 110 ft 1/2 in high, at the Roan Antelope Rugby Union Club, Luanshya, Zambia.

Women's rugby   The first women's World Cup was contested by 12 teams in 1991, with the USA beating England 19–6 in the final at Cardiff, Great Britain on 14 Apr 1991.

SHOOTING

Most Olympic medals Carl Townsend Osburn (USA; 1884–1966) won 11 medals, in 1912, 1920 and 1924—five gold, four silver and two bronze. Six other marksmen have won five gold medals. Gudbrand Gudbrandsönn Skatteboe (Norway; 1875–1965) is the only marksman to win three individual gold medals, in 1906. Separate events for women were first held in 1984.

Six other marksmen have won five gold medals, including three Americans: Alfred P. Lane (b. 26 Sep 1891), 1912–20; Willis Augustus Lee, Jr. (1888–94), all in 1920; and Morris Fisher (1890–1968), 1920–24. In 1920 a record seven medals were won by both Willis Lee, who also won a silver and bronze, and Lloyd S. Spooner—four gold, a silver and two bronze.

The first US woman to win an Olympic medal in shooting was Margaret L. Murdock (nee Thompson; b. 25 Aug 1942), who took the silver at small-bore rifle (three positions) in mixed competition in 1976. The first to win an Olympic gold medal was Patricia Spurgin (b. 10 Aug 1965), at women's air rifle in 1984.

Clay pigeon The most world titles have been won by Susan Nattrass (Canada; b. 5 Nov 1950) with six, 1974–75, 1977–79, 1981. The record number of clay birds shot in an hour is 4,557, by John Cloherty (USA) in Seattle, WA on 31 Aug 1992.

The maximum 200/200 was achieved by Ricardo Ruiz Rumoroso at the Spanish Clay Pigeon Championships at Zaragossa on 12 Jun 1983.

Noel D. Townend achieved the maximum 200 consecutive down-the-line targets at Nottingham, Great Britain on 21 Aug 1983.

Highest shooting score in 24 hours The Easingwold Rifle and Pistol Club (Yorkshire, Great Britain) team of John Smith, Edward Kendall, Phillip Kendall and Paul Duffield scored 120,242 points (averaging 95.66 per card) on 6–7 Aug 1983.

Bench rest shooting The smallest area on record into which a group of shots have been fired at 1,000 yd is 4.375 in, by Earl Chronister with a .30–378 Weatherby Mag at Williamsport, PA on 12 Jul 1987.

The smallest at 500 m (546 yd) is 2.297 in, by Dennis Tobler (Australia) using a .30–06 rifle of his own design at Canberra, Australia on 28 Mar 1992.

SHOOTING—INDIVIDUAL WORLD RECORDS

In 1986, the International Shooting Union (UIT) introduced new regulations for determining major championships and world records. Now the leading competitors undertake an additional round with a target subdivided to tenths of a point for rifle and pistol shooting, and an extra 25 shots for trap and skeet. Harder targets have since been introduced, and the table below shows the world records, as recognized by the UIT on 1 Jan 1992, for the 13 Olympic shooting disciplines, giving in parentheses the score for the number of shots specified plus the score in the additional round.

MEN

	Score	Name and Country	Venue	Date
Free Rifle 50 m 3 × 40 shots	1,276.7 (1,179 + 97.7)	Rajmond Debevec (Yugoslavia)	Munich, Germany	2 Jun 1990
	1,276.7 (1,177 + 99.7)	Rajmond Debevec (Yugoslavia)	Zürich, Switzerland	7 Jun 1991
Free Rifle 50 m 60 shots prone	703.5 (599 + 104.5)	Jens Harskov (Denmark)	Zürich, Switzerland	6 Jun 1991
Air Rifle 10 m 60 shots	699.4 (596 + 103.4)	Rajmond Debevec (Yugoslavia)	Zürich, Switzerland	8 Jun 1990
Free Pistol 50 m 60 shots	671 (579 + 92)	Sergey Pyzhyanov (USSR)	Munich, Germany	31 May 1990
	671 (577 + 94)	Spas Koprinkov (Bulgaria)	Moscow, USSR	9 Aug 1990
Rapid-Free Pistol 25 m 60 shots	891 (594 + 297)	Ralf Schumann (West Germany)	Munich, Germany	3 Jun 1989
Air Pistol 10 m 60 shots	695.1 (593 + 102.1)	Sergey Pyzhyanov (USSR)	Munich, Germany	13 Oct 1989
Running Target 50 m 30 + 30 shots	679 (582 + 97)	Lubos Racansky (Czechoslovakia)	Munich, Germany	30 May 1991

WOMEN

	Score	Name and Country	Venue	Date
Standard Rifle 50 m 3 × 20 shots	684.9 (584 + 100.9)	Vessela Letcheva (Bulgaria)	Munich, Germany	29 Aug 1991
Air Rifle 10 m 40 shots	500.8 (399 + 101.8)	Valentina Cherkasova (USSR)	Los Angeles, CA	23 Mar 1991
Sport Pistol 25 m 60 shots	693 (593 + 100)	Nino Salukvadse (USSR)	Zagreb, Yugoslavia	13 Jul 1989
Air Pistol 10 m 40 shots	492.4 (392 + 100.4)	Lieslotte Breker (West Germany)	Zagreb, Yugoslavia	18 May 1989

OPEN

	Score	Name and Country	Venue	Date
Trap 200 targets	224 (200 + 24)	Jörg Damme (West Germany)	Moscow, USSR	18 Aug 1990
Skeet 200 targets	225 (200 + 25)	Axel Wegner (Germany)	Munich, Germany	31 Aug 1991
	225 (200 + 25)	Hennie Dompeling (Netherlands)	Munich, Germany	31 Aug 1991

SKIING

Most titles World/Olympic Championships—Alpine The World Alpine Championships were inaugurated at Mürren, Switzerland in 1931. The greatest number of titles won has been by Christel Cranz (b. 1 Jul 1914) of Germany, with seven individual—four slalom (1934, 1937–39) and three downhill (1935, 1937, 1939), and five combined (1934–35, 1937–39). She also won the gold medal for the combined in the 1936 Olympics. The most won by a man is seven, by Anton "Toni" Sailer (Austria; b. 17 Nov 1935), who won all four in 1956 (giant slalom, slalom, downhill and the non-Olympic Alpine combination) and the downhill, giant slalom and combined in 1958.

The only US skier to win two Olympic gold medals has been Andrea Mead-Lawrence (b. 19 Apr 1932), at slalom and giant slalom in 1952.

World/Olympic Championships—Nordic The first World Nordic Championships were those of the 1924 Winter Olympics in Chamonix, France. The greatest number of titles won is 11, by Gunde Svan (Sweden; b. 12 Jan 1962), seven individual—15 km 1989, 30 km 1985 and 1991, 50 km 1985 and 1989, and Olympics, 15 km 1984, 50 km 1988; and four relays—4 × 10 km, 1987 and 1989, and Olympics, 1984 and 1988. The most titles won by a woman is nine, by Galina Alekseyevna Kulakova (USSR; b. 29 Apr 1942), in 1970–78. The most medals is 23, by Raisa Petrovna Smetanina (USSR; b. 29 Feb 1952), including seven gold, 1974–92. Ulrich Wehling (East Germany; b. 8 July 1952) has also won four Nordic combined, winning the World Championship in 1974 and the Olympic title, 1972, 1976 and 1980—the only skier to have won the same event at three successive Olympics. The record for a jumper is five, by Birger Ruud (Norway; b. 23 Aug 1911), in 1931–32 and 1935–37. Ruud is the

---

Longest ski run The longest all-down-hill ski run in the world is the Weissfluhjoch-Küblis Parsenn course, near Davos, Switzerland, which measures 7.6 miles. The run from the Aiguille du Midi top of the Chamonix lift (vertical lift 9,052 ft) across the Vallée Blance is 13 miles.

Snowshoeing The IASSRF (International Amateur SnowShoe Racing Federation) record for covering one mile is 5 min 56.7 sec, by Nick Akers of Edmonton, Alberta, Canada on 3 Feb 1991. The 100 m record is 14.07 sec, by Jeremy Badeau at Canaseraga, NY on 31 May 1991.

Long-distance (Nordic) In 24 hours Seppo-Juhani Savolainen covered 258.2 miles at Saariselkä, Finland on 8–9 Apr 1988. The women's 24 hr record is 205.05 miles, by Sisko Kainulaisen at Jyväskylä, Finland on 23–24 Mar 1985.

In 48 hours Bjørn Løkken (Norway; b. 27 Nov 1937) covered 319 miles 205 yd on 11–13 Mar 1982.

MOST OLYMPIC SKIING TITLES

MEN

Alpine	3	Anton "Toni" Sailer (Austria; b. 17 Nov 1935) ....Downhill, slalom, giant slalom 1956
	3	Jean-Claude Killy (France; b. 30 Aug 1943) ....Downhill, slalom, giant slalom 1968
	3*	Alberto Tomba (Italy) ....Slalom, giant slalom 1988; giant slalom 1992
Nordic	4*	Sixten Jernberg (Sweden; b. 6 Feb 1929) ....50 km 1956; 30 km 1960; 50 km and 4 × 10 km 1964
	4	Gunde Svan (Sweden; b. 12 Mar 1962) ....15 km and 4 × 10 km 1984; 50 km and 4 × 10 km 1988
	4	Thomas Wassberg (Sweden; b. 27 Mar 1956) ....15 km 1980; 50 km 1984; 4 × 10 km 1984, 1988
Jumping	4	Matti Nykänen (Finland; b. 17 Jul 1963) ....70 m hill 1988; 90 m hill 1984, 1988; team 1988

WOMEN

Alpine	2	Andrea Mead-Lawrence (USA; b. 19 Apr 1932) ....Slalom, giant slalom 1952
	2	Marielle Goitschel (France; b. 28 Sep 1945) ....Giant slalom 1964; slalom 1968
	2	Marie-Thérèse Nadig (Switzerland; b. 8 Mar 1954) ....Downhill, giant slalom 1972
	2	Rosi Mittermaier (now Neureuther [West Germany]; b. 5 Aug 1950) ....Downhill, slalom 1976
	2*	Hanni Wenzel (Liechtenstein; b. 14 Dec 1956) ....Giant slalom, slalom 1980
	2	Vreni Schneider (Switzerland; b. 26 Nov 1964) ....Giant slalom, slalom 1988
	2	Petra Kronberger (Austria; b. 21 Feb 1969) ....Slalom, combined 1992
Nordic	4	Galina Kulakova (USSR; b. 29 Apr 1942) ....5 km, 10 km and 3 × 5 km relay 1972; 4 × 5 km relay 1976
	4*	Raisa Smetanina (USSR/CIS; b. 29 Feb 1952) ....10 km, 4 × 5 km 1976; 5 km 1980; 4 × 5 km 1992
(individual)	3	Marja-Liisa Hämäläinen (Finland; b. 10 Aug 1955) ....5 km, 10 km and 20 km 1984

* Most medals: *(women)* 10, Raisa Smetanina, four gold, five silver and one bronze.
(men) 9, Sixten Jernberg, four golds, three silver and two bronze.

In Alpine skiing, the record is four; Hanni Wenzel won a silver in the 1980 downhill and a bronze in the 1976 slalom, and Tomba won a silver in the 1992 slalom.

Most Titles

Yelena Välbe (left), winner of bronze in all four individual events at the 1992 Olympics, won the women's World Cup Nordic overall title for a record, equaling third time in 1993. (Photo: Allsport/Pascal Rondeau)

Marc Girardelli (below) won a record fifth World Cup overall title in 1993. (Photo: Allsport/ Vandystadt/ Zoom)

only person to win Olympic events in each of the dissimilar Alpine and Nordic disciplines. In 1936 he won the ski-jumping and the Alpine downhill (which was not then a separate event, but only a segment of the combined event).

World Cup   The World Cup was introduced for Alpine events in 1967 and for Nordic events in 1981. The most individual event wins is 86 (46 giant slalom, 40 slalom from a total of 287 races) by Ingemar Stenmark (Sweden; b. 18 Mar 1956) in 1974–89, including a men's record 13 in one season in 1978/79, of which 10 were part of a record 14 successive giant slalom wins from 18 Mar 1978, his 22nd birthday, to 21 Jan 1980. Franz Klammer (Austria; b. 3 Dec 1953) won a record 25 downhill races, 1974–84. Annemarie Moser (nee Pröll [Austria]; b. 27 Mar 1953) won a women's record 62 individual event wins, 1970–79. She had a record 11 consecutive downhill wins from December 1972 to January 1974. Vreni Schneider (Switzerland; b. 26 Nov 1964) won a record 13 events and a combined including all seven slalom events in 1988/89.

The Nation's Cup, awarded on the combined results of the men and women in the World Cup, has been won a record 14 times by Austria—1969, 1973–80, 1982, 1990–93.

United States   The most successful US skier has been Phillip Ferdinand Mahre (b. 10 May 1957), winner of the overall title three times, 1981–83, with two wins at giant slalom and one at slalom. The most successful US woman has been Tamara McKinney (b. 16 Oct 1962), overall winner 1983, giant slalom 1981 and 1983, and slalom 1984.

The only American to win a Nordic skiing World Cup title has been William Koch (b. 7 Jun 1955), at cross-country in 1982.

Ski-jumping   The longest ski-jump ever recorded is one of 636 ft, by Piotr Fijas (Poland) at Planica, Yugoslavia on 14 Mar 1987. The women's record is 361 ft, by Tiina Lehtola (Finland; b. 3 Aug 1962), at Ruka, Finland on 29 Mar 1981. The longest dry ski-jump is 302 ft, by Hubert Schwarz (West Germany) at Berchtesgarten, Germany on 30 Jun 1981.

Fastest speed   The official world record, as recognized by the International Ski Federation for a skier, is 145.161 mph by Philippe Goitschel (France) on 21 Apr 1993 and the fastest by a woman is 136.232 mph, by Tarja Mulari (Finland), both at Les Arcs, France on 22 Feb 1992. On 16 Apr 1988 Patrick Knaff (France) set a one-legged record of 115.306 mph.

The fastest average speed in the Olympic downhill race was 64.95 mph, by William D. Johnson (USA; b. 30 Mar 1960), at Sarajevo, Yugoslavia on 16 Feb 1984. The fastest in a World Cup downhill is 67.00 mph, by Harti Weirather (Austria; b. 25 Jan 1958), at Kitzbühel, Austria on 15 Jan 1982.

Fastest speed—cross-country   Bill Koch (USA; b. 13 Apr 1943), on 26 Mar 1981 skied 10 times around a 3.11 mile loop on Marlborough Pond, near Putney, VT. He completed the 50-km (31.07-mile) course in 1 hr 59 min 47 sec, an average speed of 15.57 mph. A race includes uphill and downhill sections; the record time for a race in World Championships or Olympic Games is 2 hr 3 min 31.6 sec, by Torgny Mogren (Sweden) in 1991, an average speed of 15.09 mph.

Longest races   The world's longest Nordic ski race is the Vasaloppet, which commemorates an event of 1521 when Gustav Vasa (1496–1560), later King

FASTEST Philippe Goitschel (France) failed to win gold in speed skiing at the 1992 Olympics by the narrow margin of $^1/_2$ km/h, but a year later set the official world speed record. (Photo: Allsport/Nathan Bilow)

Gustavus Eriksson, fled 53.3 miles from Mora to Sälen, Sweden. He was overtaken by loyal, speedy scouts on skis, who persuaded him to return eastwards to Mora to lead a rebellion and become the king of Sweden. The reenactment of this return journey is now an annual event at 55.3 miles. There were a record 10,934 starters on 6 Mar 1977 and a record 10,650 finishers on 4 Mar 1979. The fastest time is 3 hr 48 min 55 sec, by Bengt Hassis (Sweden) on 2 Mar 1986.

The Finlandia Ski Race, 46.6 miles from Hämeenlinna to Lahti, on 26 Feb 1984, had a record 13,226 starters and 12,909 finishers.

The longest downhill race is the Inferno in Switzerland, 9.8 miles from the top of the Schilthorn to Lauterbrunnen. The record number of entries was 1,401 in 1981, and the record time was 13 min 53.40 sec by Urs von Allmen (Switzerland) in 1991.

Freestyle skiing   The first World Championships were held at Tignes, France in 1986, titles being awarded in ballet, moguls, aerials and combined. A record two titles have been won by a number of skiers. Of these, Edgar Grospiron (France), who won moguls, 1989 and 1991, also won an Olympic title, 1992. The three separate disciplines were included in the 1988 Olympics but only as demonstration events. Moguls were contested with full status at the 1992 Olympics, when Grospiron won the men's gold medal. Donna Weinbrecht (USA) won the women's moguls title in 1991 and at the Olympics in 1992. The most Overall titles in the World Cup (instituted 1980) is 10, by Connie Kissling (Switzerland; b. 18 Jul 1961), 1983–92. The men's record is five, by Eric Laboureix (France; b. 12 Apr 1962), 1986–87, 1989–91.

Longest ski lift The longest gondola ski lift is 3.88 miles long, at Grindelwald-Männlichen, Switzerland (in two sections, but one gondola). The longest chair lift in the world was the Alpine Way-to-Kosciusko Chalet lift above Thredbo, near the Snowy Mountains, New South Wales, Australia. It took from 45 to 74 min to ascend the 3.5 miles, depending on the weather. The chair lift has now collapsed. The highest lift is at Chacaltaya, Bolivia, rising to 16,500 ft.

Ski-bob The *Fédération Internationale de Skibob* was founded on 14 Jan 1961 in Innsbruck, Austria, and the first World Championships were held at Bad Hofgastein, Austria in 1967.
  The fastest speed attained is 103.1 mph, by Erich Brenter (Austria; b. 1940), at Cervinia, Italy in 1964.

World Championships The only ski-bobbers to retain a world championship are: *(men)* Alois Fischbauer (Austria; b. 6 Oct 1951), 1973 and 1975; Robert Mühlberger (West Germany), 1979 and 1981; *(women)* Gerhilde Schiffkorn (Austria; b. 22 Mar 1950), 1967 and 1969; Gertrude Geberth (Austria; b. 18 Oct 1951), 1971 and 1973.

GRASS SKIING

World Championships (now awarded for Super G, giant slalom, slalom and combined) were first held in 1979. The most titles won is 10, by Ingrid Hirschhofer (Austria), 1979–89. The most by a man is seven, by Erwin Gansner (Switzerland), 1981–87.
  The speed record is 53.99 mph, by Erwin Gansner at Owen, Germany on 5 Sep 1982.

SKIPPING ROPE

Ten mile skip-run Vadivelu Karuna-karen (India) skipped rope 10 miles in 58 min at Madras, India, 1 Feb 1990.

Most turns of the rope One hour 14,628, by Park Bong Tae (South Korea) at Pusan, South Korea, 2 Jul 1989. Robert Commers holds the US record, with 13,783, at Woodbridge, NJ, 13 May 1989.

On a single rope, team of 90 160, by students from the Nishigoshi Higashi Elementary School, Kumamoto, Japan, 27 Feb 1987.

On a tightrope 358 (consecutive), by Julian Albulet (USA) at Las Vegas, NV, 2 Jul 1990.

Most on a rope (minimum 12 turns obligatory) 260, by students of the Yorkton Regional High School, Yorkton, Saskatchewan, Canada, on 28 May 1992.

SLED DOG RACING

Racing between harnessed dog teams (usually huskies) was practiced by the Inuits and the northern Indians of North America and in Scandinavia, but the first formal record of a race was in 1908, when the All-Alaskan Sweepstakes were contested on a run of 408 miles from Nome to Candle and back.

Iditarod trail   Now recognized as the world's most prestigious sled dog race, the Iditarod trail is also the oldest established trail. It has existed since 1910 and has been raced annually since 1967 by dog teams, 1,049 miles from Anchorage to Nome, AK. The inaugural winner, Dick Wilmarth, took 20 days 49 min 41 sec to complete the course, beating 33 other racers.

The fastest time was set by Jeff King (USA) in 1993 with 10 days 15 hr 38 min 15 sec. Rick Swenson (USA) has won the race a record five times (1977, 1979, 1981–82 and 1991).

Longest trail   The longest race is the 1,243-mile Benergia Trail from Esso to Markovo, Russia, which started as a 155-mile route in April 1990. Now established as an annual event, the 1991 race was won by Pavel Lazarev in 10 days 18 hr 17 min 56 sec.

Longest trail   On 8 Feb 1988 Rev. Donald Ewen McEwen, owner of Nekanesu Kennels, Eldorado, Ontario, Canada drove a 76-dog sled for 2 miles single-handedly on the ice and around the shore of Lingham Lake. The team, consisting of 25 Siberian huskies and 51 Alaskan huskies, was assembled for the filming of a British TV commercial.

SNOOKER

Most world titles   The world professional title was won a record 15 times by Joe Davis, on the first 15 occasions it was contested, 1927–40 and 1946. The most wins in the Amateur Championships have been two—by Gary Owen (England) in 1963 and 1966; Ray Edmonds (England) 1972 and 1974; and Paul Mifsud (Malta) 1985–86.

Maureen Baynton (nee Barrett) won a record eight Women's Amateur Championships between 1954 and 1968, as well as seven at billiards.

World Championships   The youngest man to win a world title is Stephen O'Connor (Ireland; b. 16 Oct 1972), who was 18 yr 40 days when he won the World Amateur Snooker Championship in Colombo, Sri Lanka on 25 Nov

1990. Stephen Hendry (Scotland; b. 13 Jan 1969) became the youngest World Professional champion, at 21 yr 106 days on 29 Apr 1990. He had been the youngest winner of a major professional title, at 18 yr 285 days, when he won the Rothman's Grand Prix on 25 Oct 1987.

Stacey Hillyard (Great Britain; b. 15 Sep 1969) won the Women's World Amateur Championship in October 1984 at the age of 15.

MOST CENTURIES (Left) Stephen Hendry celebrates winning the World Professional Snooker Championship. In this tournament he has compiled a record 35 breaks of 100 or more, while in all competitions his career total is 206, also a record. (Photo: Allsport/ Howard Boylan)

MOST SNOOKER TITLES (Below) Allison Fisher, who has won the women's World Snooker Championship six times, holds the women's record for the highest break, with 133. (Photo: Allsport/ Howard Boylan)

Highest breaks Over 200 players have achieved the maximum break of 147. The first to do so was E.J. "Murt" O'Donoghue (b. New Zealand 1901) at Griffiths, New South Wales, Australia on 26 Sep 1934. The first officially ratified 147 was by Joe Davis against Willie Smith in London, Great Britain on 22 Jan 1955. Cliff Thorburn (Canada; b. 16 Jan 1948) has scored two tournament 147 breaks (the World Professional Championship), on 23 Apr 1983 and 8 Mar 1989. Paul Ebdon (b. 27 Aug 1970) and James Wattana (Thailand; b. 17 Jan 1970) have also achieved this feat.

The first century break by a woman in competitive play was 114, by Stacey Hillyard in a league match at Bournemouth, Great Britain on 15 Jan 1985. The highest break by a woman in competition is 133, by Allison Fisher in the Dubai Duty Free Classic at Blackpool, Great Britain on 1 Sep 1992.

Longest unbroken run From 17 Mar 1990 to his defeat by Jimmy White (b. 2 May 1962) on 13 Jan 1991, Stephen Hendry won five successive titles and 36 consecutive matches in ranking tournaments. During the summer of 1992, Ronnie O'Sullivan won 38 consecutive matches, but these were in qualifying competitions.

SOARING

At least 3,000 years ago, the Chinese developed the flying of kites, some of which were large enough to support a person, although there is no evidence of actual flight.

Most titles The most World Individual championships (instituted 1937) won is four, by Ingo Renner (Australia) in 1976 (Standard class), 1983, 1985 and 1987 (Open).

The most titles won by a US pilot is two, by George Moffat, in the Open category, 1970 and 1974.

Women's altitude records The women's single-seater world record for absolute altitude is 41,460 ft, by Sabrina Jackintell (USA) in an Astir GS on 14 Feb 1979.

The height gain record is 33,506 ft, by Yvonne Loader (New Zealand) at Omarama, New Zealand on 12 Jan 1988.

HANG GLIDING

World Championships The World Team Championships (officially instituted in 1976) have been won most often by Great Britain (1981, 1985, 1989 and 1991).

World records The *Fédération Aéronautique Internationale* recognizes world records for rigid-wing, flex-wing and multiplace flex-wing. The following records are the greatest in each category—all by flex-wing gliders.

Men Greatest distance in straight line and declared goal distance:

303.35 miles, Larry Tudor (USA), Wills Wing Hobbs Airpark, NM to Elkhart, KS, 3 Jul 1990.

Height gain: 14,250 ft, Larry Tudor (USA), Owens Valley, CA, 4 Aug 1985.

Out and return distance: 192.818 miles, Larry Tudor (USA) and Geoffrey Loyns (Great Britain), Owens Valley, 26 Jun 1988.

Triangular course distance: 121.81 miles, James Lee (USA), San Pedro, Mesa, CA, 4 Jul 1991.

Women   Greatest distance: 208.63 miles, Kari Castle (USA), Horseshoe-Mid, NV, 22 Jul 1991.

Height gain: 11,998.62 ft, Tover Buas-Hansen (Norway) and Keven Klinefelder (USA), Owens Valley, 6 Jul 1989.

Out and return distance in a single turn: 181.47 miles, Kari Castle (USA), Hobbs Airpark, 3 Jul 1990.

Declared goal distance: 132.04 miles, Liavan Mallin (Ireland), Owens Valley, 13 Jul 1989.

Triangular course distance: Judy Leden, 70.904 miles, Konsen, Austria, 22 Jun 1991.

SOCCER

OLYMPIC GAMES

Soccer has been an official sport at the Olympics since 1908, except for 1932, when it was not staged in Los Angeles. The leading gold medal winner is Hungary, with three wins (1952, 1964, 1968). The highest Olympic score is 17, by Denmark *v* France in 1908. A record 126 nations took part in qualifying for the 1992 tournament.

THE FIFA WORLD CUP

FIFA, which was founded on 21 May 1904, instituted the first World Cup on 13 Jul 1930, in Montevideo, Uruguay. It is now held quadrennially. Three wins have been achieved by Brazil, in 1958, 1962 and 1970; Italy, in 1934, 1938 and 1982; and West Germany, in 1954, 1974 and 1990.

***Team records** Most appearances*   Brazil is the only country to qualify for all 14 World Cup tournaments.

Most goals   The highest score by one team in a game is 10, by Hungary in a 10–1 defeat of El Salvador at Elche, Spain on 15 Jun 1982. The most goals in tournament history is 148 (in 66 games) by Brazil.

Highest-scoring game   The highest-scoring game took place on 26 Jun 1954 when Austria defeated Switzerland 7–5.

***Individual records** Most wins*   Pelé (Brazil) is the only player to have played on three winning teams, 1958, 1962 and 1970. He played during the 1962 Finals, but was injured before the final match and was therefore unable to play in it.

Mario Zagalo (Brazil) was the first man to play (in 1958 and 1962) and be manager (1970) of a World Cup winning team. Franz Beckenbauer emulated Zagalo when he managed the West German team to victory in 1990. He had previously captained the 1974 winning team. Beckenbauer is the only man to have both captained and managed a winning side.

Most goals   The most goals scored in a final is three, by Geoff Hurst for England *v* West Germany on 30 Jul 1966.

Most games played   Two players have appeared in 21 games in the finals tournament: Uwe Seeler (West Germany; b. 5 Nov 1936) 1958–70; and Wladyslaw Zmuda (Poland; b. 6 Jun 1954) 1974–86.

Most goals scored   The most goals scored by a player in a game is four; this has occurred nine times. The most goals scored in one tournament is 13, by Just Fontaine (France) in 1958, in six games. The most goals scored in a career is 14, by Gerd Muller (West Germany), 10 goals in 1970 and four in 1974.

NCAA DIVISION I CHAMPIONSHIPS

Men   In this competition, first held in 1959, the University of St Louis has won the most Division I titles with 10 victories, including one tie: 1959–60, 1962–63, 1965, 1967, 1969–70, 1972–73.

Women   In this competition, first held in 1982, the University of North Carolina has won a record 10 Division I titles. Its victories came in 1982–84, 1986–92.

Largest soccer crowds   The top attendance for a soccer match in the USA was 101,799, for France's 2–0 Olympic final win over Brazil at the Rose Bowl, Pasadena, CA on 11 Aug 1984.

Ball control   Huh Nam Jin (South Korea) juggled a regulation soccer ball with feet, legs and head for 17 hr 10 min 57 sec nonstop, without the ball ever touching the ground, at Swiss Grand Hotel, Seoul, South Korea on 24 May 1991. Tomas Lundman (Sweden) "headed" a ball for 7 hr 5 min 5 sec at Nöjeskällan, Märsta, Sweden on 5 Sep 1992.

Most dismissive referee   It was reported on 1 Jun 1993 that in a league soccer match between Sportivo Ameliano and General Caballero in Paraguay, referee William Weiler ejected 20 players. Trouble flared after two Sportivo players were thrown out, a 10-minute fight ensued, and Weiler then dismissed a further 18 players, including the rest of the Sportivo team. Not surprisingly, the match was abandoned.

SOFTBALL

Most titles The USA has won the men's World Championship (instituted 1966) five times, 1966, 1968, 1976 (shared), 1980 and 1988, and the women's title (instituted 1965) four times, in 1974, 1978 and 1986 and 1990. The world's first slow pitch championships for men's teams were held in Oklahoma City in 1987, when the winner was the USA.

US National Championships The most wins in the fast pitch championships (first held in 1933) for men is 10, by the Clearwater (Florida) Bombers between 1950 and 1973, and for women is 23, by the Raybestos Brakettes of Stratford, CT, between 1958 and 1992.

Slow pitch championships have been staged annually since 1953 for men and since 1962 for women. Three wins for men have been achieved by Skip Hogan A.C. of Pittsburgh, 1962, 1964–65, and by Joe Gatliff Auto Sales of Newport, KY, 1956–57, 1963. At super slow pitch, four wins have been achieved by Steele's Silver Bullets, Grafton, OH, 1985–87 and 1990. The Dots of Miami, FL have a record five women's titles, playing as the Converse Dots, 1969; Marks Brothers; North Miami Dots, 1974–75; and Bob Hoffman Dots, 1978–79.

SPEEDWAY

World Championships The World Speedway Championship was inaugurated at Wembley, London, Great Britain on 10 Sep 1936. The most wins have been six, by Ivan Gerald Mauger (New Zealand; b. 4 Oct 1939) in 1968–70, 1972, 1977 and 1979. Barry Briggs (New Zealand; b. 30 Dec 1934) made a record 18 appearances in the finals (1954–70, 1972) and won the world title in 1957–58, 1964 and 1966. He also scored a record 201 points in world championship competition in 87 races.

Ivan Mauger also won four World Team Cups (three for Great Britain), two World Pairs (including one unofficial) and three world long track titles. Ove Fundin (Sweden; b. 23 May 1933) won 12 world titles: five individual, one pairs, and six World Team Cup medals in 1956–70. In 1985 Erik Gundersen (Denmark) became the first man to hold world titles at individual, pairs, team and long-track events simultaneously.

Maximum points The only speedway rider to have scored maximum points in every test series was Arthur "Bluey" Wilkinson (1911–40), in five matches for Australia *v* England in Sydney in 1937/38.

The World Pairs Championships (instituted unofficially 1968, officially 1970) have been won a record eight times by Denmark, 1979, 1985–91. The most successful individual in the World Pairs has been Hans Hollen Nielsen (b. 26 Dec 1959) with seven wins for Denmark. His partners were Ole Olsen, 1979, Erik Gundersen, 1986–89, and Jan O. Pederson, 1990–91. Maximum points (then 30) were scored in the World Pairs Championship by Jerzy Szczakiel (b. 28 Jan 1949) and Andrzej Wyglenda (Poland) at Rybnik, Poland in 1971; and by Arthur Dennis Sigalos (b. 16 Aug 1959) and Robert Benjamin ("Bobby") Schwartz (USA; b. 10 Aug 1956) at Liverpool, New South Wales, Australia on 11 Dec 1982.

The World Team Cup (instituted 1960) has been won a record nine times by England/Great Britain (Great Britain 1968, 1971–73; England 1974–75, 1977, 1980, 1989); and by Denmark 1978, 1981, 1983–88, 1991. Hans Nielsen (Denmark) has ridden in a record eight Team wins.

SQUASH

World Championships Jahangir Khan (Pakistan; b. 10 Dec 1963) won six World Open (instituted 1976) titles, 1981–85 and 1988, and the International Squash Federation (ISRF) world individual title (formerly World Amateur, instituted 1967) in 1979, 1983 and 1985. Geoffrey B. Hunt (Australia; b. 11 Mar 1947) won four World Open titles, 1976–77 and 1979–80, and three World Amateur, 1967, 1969 and 1971. The most women's World Open titles is five, by Susan Devoy (New Zealand; b. 4 Jan 1964), 1985, 1987 and 1990–92.

Australia (1967, 1969, 1971, 1973, 1989 and 1991) has won six men's world titles. England won the women's title in 1985, 1987, 1989 and 1990, following Great Britain's win in 1979.

Most titles Open Championship The most wins in the Open Championship held annually in Britain is 10, by Jahangir Khan, in successive years, 1982–91. Hashim Khan (Pakistan; b. 1915) won seven times, 1950–55 and 1957, and also won the Vintage title six times, in 1978–83.

The most British Open women's titles is 16, by Heather Pamela McKay (nee Blundell [Australia]; b. 31 Jul 1941) from 1961 to 1977. She also won the World Open title in 1976 and 1979.

Fastest squash ball speed In tests at Wimbledon Squash and Badminton Club, London, Great Britain in January 1988, Roy Buckland hit a squash ball by an overhead service at a measured speed of 144.6 mph over the distance to the front wall. This is equivalent to an initial speed off the racket of 150.8 mph.

Largest squash crowd The finals of the ICI World Team Championships at the Royal Albert Hall, London, Great Britain had a record attendance for squash of 3,526 on 30 Oct 1987.

United States   The US amateur squash championships were first held for men in 1907 and for women in 1928; the most singles wins is six, by Stanley W. Pearson, 1915–17 and 1921–23; G. Diehl Mateer won a record 11 men's doubles titles between 1949 and 1966 with five different partners. Sharif Khan (Pakistan) won a record 13 North American Open Championships (instituted 1953), 1969–74 and 1976–82. Alicia McConnell has won a record seven women's national championships (1982–88).

Unbeaten sequences   Heather McKay was unbeaten from 1962 to 1980. Jahangir Khan was unbeaten from his loss to Geoff Hunt at the British Open on 10 Apr 1981 until Ross Norman (New Zealand) ended his sequence in the World Open final on 11 Nov 1986.

Longest and shortest championship matches   The longest recorded competitive match was one of 2 hr 45 min when Jahangir Khan beat Gamal Awad (Egypt; b. 8 Sep 1955) 9–10, 9–5, 9–7, 9–2, the first game lasting a record 1 hr 11 min, in the final of the Patrick International Festival at Chichester, Great Britain on 30 Mar 1983. Philip Kenyon (England) beat Salah Nadi (Egypt) in just 6 min 37 sec (9–0, 9–0, 9–0) in the British Open at Lamb's Squash Club, London, Great Britain on 9 Apr 1992.

Most international appearances   The men's record is 122 by David Gotto (b. 25 Dec 1948) for Ireland. The women's record is 108 by Marjorie Croke (nee Burke; b. 31 May 1961) for Ireland, 1981–93.

SURFING

Most titles   World Amateur Championships were inaugurated in May 1964 at Sydney, Australia. The most titles is three, by Michael Novakov (Australia), who won the Kneeboard event in 1982, 1984 and 1986. A World Professional series was started in 1975. The men's title has been won five times, by Mark Richards (Australia), 1975 and from 1979 to 1982, and the women's title (instituted 1979) four times, by Freida Zamba (USA), 1984–86, 1988; and by Wendy Botha (Australia, formerly South Africa), 1987, 1989, 1991–92.

Longest ride   About four to six times each year, ridable surfing waves break in Matanchen Bay near San Blas, Nayarit, Mexico, which makes rides of *c.* 5,700 ft possible.

Highest waves ridden   Waimea Bay, HI reputedly provides the most consistently high waves, often reaching the ridable limit of 30–35 ft. The highest wave ever ridden was the *tsunami* of "perhaps 50 ft" that struck Minole, HI on 3 Apr 1868, and was ridden to save his life by a Hawaiian named Holua.

SWIMMING

FASTEST Tom Jager, the world's fastest swimmer. (Photo: Allsport/Simon Bruty)

Fastest swimmer In a 25-yd pool, Tom Jager (USA; b. 6 Oct 1964) achieved an average speed of 5.37 mph for 50 yards in 19.05 sec at Nashville, TN on 23 Mar 1990. The women's fastest is 4.48 mph, by Yang Wenyi (China) in her 50 m world record (see World Records table).

Most world records Men: 32, Arne Borg (Sweden; 1901–87), 1921–29. *Women:* 42, Ragnhild Hveger (Denmark; b. 10 Dec 1920), 1936–42. For currently recognized events (only metric distances in 50 m pools) the most is (*men*) 26, by Mark Andrew Spitz (USA; b. 10 Feb 1950), 1967–72, and (*women*) 23, by Kornelia Ender (East Germany; b. 25 Oct 1958), 1973–76. The most by a US woman is 15, by Deborah "Debbie" Meyer (b. 14 Aug 1952), 1967–70.

The most world records set in a single pool is 86, in the North Sydney pool, Australia between 1955 and 1978. This total includes 48 imperial distance records, which ceased to be recognized in 1969. The pool, which was built in 1936, was originally 55 yards long but was shortened to 50 meters in 1964.

Most world titles In the World Championships (instituted 1973) the most medals won is 13, by Michael Gross (West Germany; b. 17 Jun 1964)—five gold, five silver and three bronze, 1982–90. The most medals won by a woman is 10, by Kornelia Ender, with eight gold and two silver in 1973 and 1975. The most gold medals won is six (two individual and four relay) by James Paul Montgomery (USA; b. 24 Jan 1955) in 1973 and 1975. The most medals won at a single championship is seven, by Matthew Nicholas "Matt" Biondi (USA; b. 8 Oct 1965)—three gold, one silver, three bronze, in 1986.

SWIMMING WORLD RECORDS (set in 50 meter pools)

MEN

Event	min:sec	Name & Country	Place	Date
Freestyle				
50 meters	21.81	Thomas "Tom" Jager (USA; b. 6 Oct 1964)	Nashville, TN	24 Mar 1990
100 meters	48.42	Matthew Nicholas "Matt" Biondi (USA; b. 8 Oct 1965)	Austin, TX	10 Aug 1988
200 meters	1:46.69	Giorgio Lamberti (Italy; b. 28 Jan 1969)	Bonn, Germany	15 Aug 1989
400 meters	3:45.00	Evgueni Sadovyi (EUN)[1]	Barcelona, Spain	29 Jul 1992
800 meters	7:46.60	Kieren John Perkins (Australia)	Sydney, Australia	14 Feb 1992
1,500 meters	14:43.40	Kieren John Perkins (Australia)	Barcelona, Spain	31 Jul 1992
4 × 100 meter relay	3:16.53	United States (Christopher Jacobs, Troy Dalbey, Tom Jager, Matt Biondi)	Seoul, South Korea	25 Sep 1988
4 × 200 meter relay	7:11.95	EUN (Dimitri Lepikov, Vladimir Pychenko, Veniamin Taianovitch, Evgueni Sadovyi)	Barcelona, Spain	27 Jul 1992
Breaststroke				
100 meters	1:01.29	Norbert Rosza (Hungary; b. 9 Feb 1972)	Athens, Greece	20 Aug 1991
200 meters	2:10.60	Michael Ray Barrowman (USA; b. 4 Dec 1968)	Fort Lauderdale, FL	13 Aug 1991
Butterfly				
100 meters	52.84	Pedro Pablo Morales (USA; b. 5 Dec 1964)	Orlando, FL	23 Jun 1986
200 meters	1:55.69	Melvin Stewart (USA; b. 16 Nov 1968)	Perth, Australia	12 Jan 1991
Backstroke				
100 meters	53.86	Jeff Rouse (USA; b. 6 Feb 1970—relay leg)	Barcelona, Spain	31 Jul 1992
200 meters	1:56.57	Martin Lopez-Zubero (Spain; b. 23 Apr 1964)	Tuscaloosa, AL	23 Nov 1991
Medley				
200 meters	1:59.36	Tamás Darnyi (Hungary; b. 3 Jun 1967)	Perth, Australia	13 Jan 1991
400 meters	4:12.36	Tamás Darnyi (Hungary)	Perth, Australia	8 Jan 1991
4 × 100 meter relay	3:36.93	United States (David Berkoff, Richard Schroeder, Matt Biondi, Christopher Jacobs)	Seoul, South Korea	23 Sep 1988

WOMEN

Freestyle

Event	Time	Athlete	Location	Date
50 meters	24.79	Yang Wenyi (China; b. 11 Jan 1972)	Barcelona, Spain	31 Jul 1992
100 meters	54.48	Jenny Thompson (USA; b. 26 Feb 1973)	Indianapolis, IN	1 Mar 1992
200 meters	1:57.55	Heike Friedrich (East Germany; b. 18 Apr 1970)	Berlin, Germany	18 Jun 1986
400 meters	4:03.85	Janet B. Evans (USA; b. 28 Aug 1971)	Seoul, South Korea	22 Sep 1988
800 meters	8:16.22	Janet B. Evans (USA)	Tokyo, Japan	20 Aug 1989
1,500 meters	15:52.10	Janet B. Evans (USA)	Orlando, FL	26 Mar 1988
4 × 100 meter relay	3:39.46	United States (Nicole Haislett, Dara Torres, Angel Martino, Jenny Thompson)	Barcelona, Spain	28 Jul 1992
4 × 200 meter relay	7:55.47	East Germany (Manuela Stellmach, Astrid Strauss, Anke Möhring, Heike Friedrich)	Strasbourg, France	18 Aug 1987

Breaststroke

Event	Time	Athlete	Location	Date
100 meters	1:07.91	Silke Hörner (East Germany; b. 12 Sep 1965)	Strasbourg, France	21 Aug 1987
200 meters	2:25.35	Anita Nall (USA; b. 21 Jul 1976)	Indianapolis, IN	2 Mar 1992

Butterfly

Event	Time	Athlete	Location	Date
100 meters	57.93	Mary Terstegge Meagher (USA; b. 27 Oct 1964)	Milwaukee, WI	16 Aug 1981
200 meters	2:05.96	Mary Terstegge Meagher (USA)	Milwaukee, WI	13 Aug 1981

Backstroke

Event	Time	Athlete	Location	Date
100 meters	1:00.31	Krizstina Egerszegi (Hungary; b. 16 Aug 1974)	Athens, Greece	22 Aug 1991
200 meters	2:06.62	Krizstina Egerszegi (Hungary)	Athens, Greece	25 Aug 1991

Medley

Event	Time	Athlete	Location	Date
200 meters	2:11.65	Lin Li (China)	Barcelona, Spain	30 Jul 1992
400 meters	4:36.10	Petra Schneider (East Germany; b. 11 Jan 1963)	Guayaquil, Ecuador	1 Aug 1982
4 × 100 meter relay	4:02.54	United States (Lea Loveless, Anita Nall, Crissy Ahmann-Leighton, Jenny Thompson)	Barcelona, Spain	30 Jul 1992

¹EUN=Unified Team

SHORT-COURSE SWIMMING WORLD BESTS (set in 25 meter pools)

MEN

Event	min : sec	Name & Country	Place	Date
Freestyle				
50 meters	21.60	Mark Foster (GBR)	Sheffield, Great Britain	17 Feb 1993
100 meters*	48.20	Michael Gross (West Germany; b. 17 Jun 1964)	Offenbach, Germany	11 Feb 1988
200 meters	1:43.64	Giorgio Lamberti (Italy; b. 28 Jan 1969)	Bonn, Germany	11 Feb 1990
400 meters	3:40.81	Anders Holmertz (Sweden; b. 1 Dec 1968)	Paris, France	4 Feb 1990
800 meters	7:38.75	Michael Gross (West Germany)	Bonn, Germany	8 Feb 1985
1,500 meters	14:32.40	Kieren Perkins (Australia; b. 14 Aug 1973)	Canberra, Australia	2 Feb 1992
4 × 50 meters	1:27.94	Sweden	Espoo, Finland	21 Nov 1992
4 × 100 meters	3:14.00	Sweden	Malmö, Sweden	19 Mar 1989
4 × 200 meters	7:05.17	West Germany	Bonn, Germany	9 Feb 1986
Backstroke				
50 meters	25.06	Mark Tewksbury (Canada; b. 2 Jul 1968)	Saskatoon, Canada	2 Mar 1990
100 meters	51.43	Jeff Rouse (USA)	Sheffield, Great Britain	11 April 1993
200 meters	1:52.51	Martin Zubero (Spain)	Gainesville, FL	10 Apr 1991
Breaststroke				
50 meters	27.15	Dmitriy Volkov (USSR; b. 3 Mar 1966)	Saint-Paul de la Réunion	30 Dec 1989
100 meters	59.30	Dmitriy Volkov (USSR)	Bonn, Germany	11 Feb 1990
200 meters	2:07.93	Nicholas Gillingham (Great Britain; b. 22 Jan 1967)	Birmingham, Great Britain	20 Oct 1991
Butterfly				
50 meters	23.80	Jan Karlsson (Sweden)	Espoo, Finland	21 Nov 1992
100 meters	52.07	Marcel Gery (Canada; b. 15 Mar 1965)	Leicester, Great Britain	23 Feb 1990
200 meters	1:54.21	Danyon Loader (New Zealand)	Gelsenkirchen, Germany	13 Feb 1993
Medley				
100 meters	53.78	Jani Sievinen (Finland)	Espoo, Finland	21 Nov 1992
200 meters	1:55.59	Jani Sievinen (Finland)	Malmö, Sweden	10 Feb 1993
400 meters	4:07.10	Jani Sievinen (Finland)	Malmö, Sweden	9 Feb 1992
4 × 50 meters	1:38.10	Finland	Espoo, Finland	22 Nov 1992
4 × 100 meters	3:34.86	University of Calgary (Canada)	Winnipeg, Canada	23 Feb 1992

WOMEN

Freestyle

50 meters	24.75	Franziska van Almsick (Germany; b. 1978)	Schäbisch Gmünd, Germany .... 7 Nov 1992
100 meters	53.33	Franziska van Almsick (Germany)	Beijing, China .... 9 Jan 1993
200 meters	1:56.35	Birgit Meineke (East Germany; b. 4 Jul 1964)	Indianapolis, IN .... 7 Jan 1983
400 meters	4:02.05	Astrid Strauss (East Germany; b. 24 Dec 1968)	Bonn, Germany .... 8 Feb 1987
800 meters	8:15.34	Astrid Strauss (East Germany)	Bonn, Germany .... 6 Feb 1987
1,500 meters	15:43.31	Petra Schneider (East Germany; b. 11 Jan 1963)	Gainesville, FL .... 10 Jan 1982
4 X 50 meters	1:40.63	Germany	Espoo, Finland .... 22 Nov 1992
4 X 100 meters	3:38.77	East Germany	Monte Carlo, Monaco .... 12 Dec 1987

Backstroke

50 meters	28.57	Sandra Völker (Germany)	Espoo, Finland .... 22 Nov 1992
100 meters	59.89	Betsy Mitchell (USA; b. 15 Jan 1966)	Los Angeles, CA .... 26 Apr 1987
200 meters	2:06.78	Nicole Stevenson (Australia)	Melbourne, Australia .... 7 Mar 1992

Breaststroke

50 meters	31.19	Louise Karlsson (Sweden)	Espoo, Finland .... 21 Nov 1992
100 meters	1:07.05	Silke Hörner (East Germany; b. 12 Sep 1965)	Bonn, Germany .... 8 Feb 1986
200 meters	2:22.92	Susanne Börnicke (East Germany; b. 13 Aug 1968)	Bonn, Germany .... 11 Feb 1989

Butterfly

50 meters	27.30	Qian Hong (China; b. 1971)	Perth, Australia .... 6 Jan 1991
100 meters **	58.91	Mary Terstegge Meagher (USA; b. 27 Aug 1964)	Gainesville, FL .... 3 Jan 1981
200 meters	2:05.65	Mary Meagher (USA)	Gainesville, FL .... 2 Jan 1981

Medley

100 meters	1:01.03	Louise Karlsson (Sweden)	Espoo, Finland .... 22 Nov 1992
200 meters	2:10.60	Petra Schneider (East Germany)	Gainesville, FL .... 8 Jan 1982
400 meters	4:31.36	Noemi Lung (Romania; b. 16 May 1968)	Paris, France .... 31 Jan 1987
4 X 50 meters	1:52.44	Germany	Espoo, Finland .... 21 Nov 1992
4 X 100 meters	4:02.85	East Germany	Indianapolis, IN .... 8 Jan 1983

* Hand timed for first leg.   **Slower than long-course bests.*

The most gold medals by an American woman is five, by Tracy Caulkins, all in 1978, as well as a silver. The most medals overall is nine, by Mary Terstegge Meagher (b. 27 Oct 1964)—two gold, five silver, two bronze, 1978–82.

US Championships Tracy Caulkins (b. 11 Jan 1963) won a record 48 US swimming titles and set 60 US records in her career, 1977–84. The men's record is 36 titles, by Johnny Weissmuller (ne Janos Weiszmuller; 1904–84), between 1921 and 1928.

OLYMPIC RECORDS

Most medals Men The greatest number of Olympic gold medals won is nine, by Mark Spitz (USA): 100 m and 200 m freestyle, 1972; 100 m and 200 m butterfly, 1972; 4 × 100 m freestyle, 1968 and 1972; 4 × 200 m freestyle, 1968 and 1972; 4 × 100 m medley, 1972. All but one of these performances (the 4 × 200 m freestyle of 1968) were also new world records. He also won a silver (100 m butterfly) and a bronze (100 m freestyle) in 1968, for a record 11 medals. His record seven medals at one Games in 1972 was equaled by Matt Biondi (USA), who took five gold, a silver and a bronze in 1988. Biondi has also won a record 11 medals in total, winning a gold in 1984, and two golds and a silver in 1992.

Women The record number of gold medals won by a woman is six, by Kristin Otto (East Germany; b. 7 Feb 1966) at Seoul in 1988: 100 m freestyle, backstroke and butterfly, 50 m freestyle, 4 × 100 m freestyle and 4 × 100 m medley. Dawn Fraser (Australia; b. 4 Sep 1937) is the only swimmer to win the same event, the 100 m freestyle, on three successive occasions (1956, 1960 and 1964). The most gold medals won by a US woman is three, by 14 swimmers.

The most medals won by a woman is eight, by three swimmers: Dawn Fraser—four golds (100 m freestyle, 1956, 1960 and 1964, 4 × 100 m freestyle, 1956) and four silvers (400 m freestyle, 1956, 4 × 100 m freestyle, 1960 and 1964, 4 × 100 m medley, 1960); Kornelia Ender—four golds (100 m and 200 m freestyle, 100 m butterfly, and 4 × 100 m medley in 1976) and four silvers (200 m individual medley, 1972, 4 × 100 m medley, 1972, 4 × 100 m

FREESTYLE RECORD Matt Biondi equaled Mark Spitz's record of 11 Olympic medals, winning three at the 1992 Games at Barcelona. In the top photo, second from right, he can be seen with the other members of the successful US 4 × 100 m freestyle team. (Photos: Allsport/Simon Bruty)

US NATIONAL SWIMMING RECORDS (set in 50 meter pools)

MEN

Event	Time	Name	Place	Date
Freestyle				
50 meters	21.81	Thomas "Tom" Jager (b. 6 Oct 1964)	Nashville, TN	24 Mar 1990
100 meters	48.42	Matthew Nicholas "Matt" Biondi (b. 8 Oct 1965)	Austin, TX	10 Aug 1988
200 meters	1:47.72	Matt Biondi	Austin, TX	8 Aug 1988
400 meters	3:48.06	Matthew Cetlinski (b. 4 Oct 1964)	Austin, TX	11 Aug 1988
800 meters	7:52.45	Sean Killion (b. 24 Oct 1967)	Clovis, CA	27 Jul 1987
1,500 meters	15:01.51	George Thomas DiCarlo (b. 13 Jul 1963)	Indianapolis, IN	30 Jun 1984
4 × 100 meter relay	3:16.53	United States (Christopher Jacobs, Troy Dalbey, Tom Jager, Matt Biondi)	Seoul, South Korea	23 Sep 1988
4 × 200 meter relay	7:12.51	United States (Troy Dalbey, Matthew Cetlinski, Douglas Gjertsen, Matt Biondi)	Seoul, South Korea	21 Sep 1988
Breaststroke				
100 meters	1:01.40	Nelson Diebel (b. 9 Nov 1970)	Indianapolis, IN	1 Mar 1992
200 meters	2:10.60	Michael Ray Barrowman (b. 4 Dec 1968)	Ft Lauderdale, FL	13 Aug 1991
Butterfly				
100 meters	52.84	Pedro Pablo Morales (b. 5 Dec 1964)	Orlando, FL	23 Jun 1986
200 meters	1:55.69	Melvin Stewart (b. 16 Nov 1968)	Perth, Australia	12 Jan 1991
Backstroke				
100 meters	53.93	Jeff Rouse (b. 6 Feb 1970)	Edmonton, Canada	25 Aug 1991
200 meters	1:58.66	Royce Sharp (b. 25 May 1972)	Indianapolis, IN	2 Mar 1992
Medley				
200 meters	2:00.11	David Wharton (b. 16 May 1969)	Tokyo, Japan	20 Aug 1989
400 meters	4:15.21	Eric Namesnik (b. 7 Aug 1970)	Perth, Australia	8 Jan 1991
4 × 100 meter relay	3:36.93	United States (David Berkoff, Richard Schroeder, Matt Biondi, Christopher Jacobs)	Seoul, South Korea	25 Sep 1988

WOMEN

Freestyle

50 meters	25.20	Jenny Thompson (b. 26 Feb 1973)	Indianapolis, IN	6 Mar 1992
100 meters	54.48	Jenny Thompson	Indianapolis, IN	1 Mar 1992
200 meters	1:58.23	Cynthia Woodhead (b. 7 Feb 1964)	Tokyo, Japan	3 Sep 1979
400 meters	4:03.85	Janet B. Evans (b. 28 Aug 1971)	Seoul, South Korea	22 Sep 1988
800 meters	8:16.22	Janet B. Evans	Tokyo, Japan	20 Aug 1989
1,500 meters	15:52.10	Janet B. Evans	Orlando, FL	26 Mar 1988
4 × 100 meter relay	3:43.26	United States World Championship Team (Nicola Haislett, Julie Cooper, Whitney Hedgepeth, Jenny Thompson)	Perth, Australia	9 Jan 1991
4 × 200 meter relay	8:02.12	United States (Betsy Mitchell, Mary Terstegge Meagher, Kim Brown, Mary Alice Wayte)	Madrid, Spain	22 Aug 1986

Breaststroke

100 meters	1:08.91	Tracey McFarlane (b. 20 Jul 1966)	Austin, TX	11 Aug 1988
200 meters	2:25.35	Anita Nall (b. 21 Jul 1976)	Indianapolis, IN	2 Mar 1992

Butterfly

100 meters	57.93	Mary Terstegge Meagher (b. 27 Oct 1964)	Brown Deer, WI	16 Aug 1981
200 meters	2:05.96	Mary Terstegge Meagher	Brown Deer, WI	13 Aug 1981

Backstroke

100 meters	1:00.84	Janie Wagstaff (b. 22 Aug 1974)	Indianapolis, IN	3 Mar 1992
200 meters	2:08.60	Betsy Mitchell (b. 15 Jan 1966)	Orlando, FL	27 Jun 1986

Medley

200 meters	2:12.64	Tracy Anne Caulkins (b. 11 Jan 1963)	Los Angeles, CA	3 Aug 1984
400 meters	4:37.76	Janet B. Evans	Seoul, South Korea	19 Sep 1988
4 × 100 meter relay	4:05.98	United States (Janie Wagstaff, Keli King, Crissy Ahmann-Leighton, Nicole Haislett)	Edmonton, Canada	25 Aug 1991

Sponsored swim   The greatest amount of money collected in a charity swim was £122,983.19 (*c.* $350,000) in "Splash '92," organized by the Royal Bank of Scotland Swimming Club and held at the Royal Commonwealth Pool, Edinburgh, Scotland on 25–26 Jan 1992 with 3,218 participants. The record for an event staged at several pools was £548,006.14 (*c.* $986,400) by "Penguin Swimathon '88", when 5,482 swimmers participated at 43 pools throughout London, Great Britian, on 26–28 Feb 1988.

Largest pools   The largest swimming pool in the world is the seawater Orthlieb Pool in Casablanca, Morocco. It is 1,574 ft long and 246 ft wide, and has an area of 8.9 acres. The largest land-locked swimming pool with heated water was the Fleishhacker Pool on Sloat Boulevard, near Great Highway, San Francisco, CA. It measured 1,000 × 150 ft, was up to 14 ft deep and contained 7.5 million gal of heated water. It was opened on 2 May 1925 but has now been abandoned. The largest land-locked pool in current use is Willow Lake in Warren, OH. It measures 600 × 150 ft. The greatest spectator accommodation is 13,614 at Osaka, Japan.

Manhattan swim   The fastest swim around Manhattan Island in New York City was in 5 hr 53 min 57 sec, by Kris Rutford (USA) on 29 Aug 1992. Drury J. Gallagher set the men's record, 6 hr 41 min 35 sec, on 7 Sep 1983.

freestyle, 1972 and 1976); and Shirley Babashoff (USA; b. 3 Jan 1957), who won two golds (4 × 100 m freestyle, 1972 and 1976) and six silvers (100 m freestyle, 1972, 200 m freestyle, 1972 and 1976, 400 m and 800 m freestyle, 1976, 4 × 100 m medley 1976).

Most individual gold medals   The record number of individual gold medals won is four, by Charles Meldrum Daniels (USA [1884–1973]; 100 m freestyle, 1906 and 1908, 220 yd freestyle 1904, 440 yd freestyle, 1904); by Roland Matthes (East Germany; b. 17 Nov 1950) with 100 m and 200 m backstroke in 1968 and 1972; by Mark Spitz and Kristin Otto (see Most Medals); and by the divers Pat McCormick and Greg Louganis (see Diving).

DIVING

Most Olympic medals   The most medals won by a diver is five, by Klaus Dibiasi (Austria; b. 6 Oct 1947 [Italy]), three gold, two silver, 1964–76; and by Gregory Efthimios "Greg" Louganis (USA; b. 29 Jan 1960), four golds, one silver, 1976, 1984, 1988. Dibiasi is the only diver to win the same event (highboard) at three successive Games (1968, 1972 and 1976). Two divers have won the highboard and springboard doubles at two Games: Patricia Joan McCormick (nee Keller; b. 12 May 1930), 1952 and 1956, and Greg Louganis, 1984 and 1988.

Most world titles   Greg Louganis (USA) won a record five world titles—highboard in 1978, and both highboard and springboard in 1982 and 1986, as well as four Olympic gold medals, in 1984 and 1988. Three gold medals at one event have also been won by Philip George Boggs (USA; 1949–90)—springboard, 1973, 1975 and 1978.

United States Championships   The Amateur Athletic Union (AAU) organized the first national diving championships in 1909. Since 1981, United States Diving has been the governing body of the sport in this country, and thus responsible for the national championships.

Most titles   Greg Louganis has won a record 47 national titles: 17 at 1-meter springboard; 17 at 3-meter springboard; 13 at platform. In women's competition Cynthia Potter has won a record 28 titles.

Highest scores   Greg Louganis achieved record scores at the 1984 Olympic Games in Los Angeles, CA, with 754.41 points for the 11-dive springboard event and 710.91 for the highboard. At the world championships in Guayaquil, Ecuador in 1984 he was awarded a perfect score of 10.0 by all seven judges for his highboard inward 1 1/2 somersault in the pike position.

The first diver to be awarded a score of 10.0 by all seven judges was Michael Holman Finneran (b. 21 Sep 1948) in the 1972 US Olympic Trials, in Chicago, IL, for a backward 1 1/2 somersault, 2 1/2 twist, from the 10 m board.

High diving   The highest regularly performed head-first dives are those of professional divers from La Quebrada ("The Break in the Rocks") at Acapulco, Mexico, a height of 87 1/2 ft. The base rocks, 21 ft out from the takeoff, necessitate a leap of 27 ft out. The water is 12 ft deep.

The world record high dive from a diving board is 176 ft 10 in, by Olivier Favre (Switzerland) at Villers-le-Lac, France on 30 Aug 1987.

The women's record is 120 ft 9 in, by Lucy Wardle (USA) at Ocean Park, Hong Kong on 6 Apr 1985.

LONG-DISTANCE SWIMMING

Longest swims   The greatest recorded distance ever swum is 1,826 miles down the Mississippi River between Ford Dam near Minneapolis, MN and Carrollton Ave, New Orleans, LA, by Fred P. Newton (b. 1903) of Clinton, OK from 6 Jul to 29 Dec 1930. He was in the water for 742 hr.

In 1966 Mihir Sen of Calcutta, India uniquely swam the Palk Strait from Sri Lanka to India (in 25 hr 36 min on 5–6 Apr); the Straits of Gibraltar (in 8 hr 1 min on 24 Aug); the length of the Dardanelles (in 13 hr 55 min on 12 Sep); the Bosphorus (in 4 hr on 21 Sep); and the length of the Panama Canal (in 34 hr 15 min on 29–31 Oct).

Twenty-four hours   Anders Forvass (Sweden) swam 63.3 miles at the 25 meter Linköping public swimming pool, Sweden on 28–29 Oct 1989. In a 50 meter pool, Evan Barry (Australia) swam 60.08 miles, at the Valley Pool, Brisbane, Australia on 19–20 Dec 1987.

The women's record is 51.01 miles, by Irene van der Laan (Netherlands) at Amersfoort, Netherlands on 20–21 Sep 1985. The longest distance swum by an American woman is 45.45 miles, by Jill Oviatt at the University of Michigan pool in Ann Arbor, MI on 24–25 Nov 1988.

Long-distance relays   The New Zealand national relay team of 20 swimmers swam a record 113.59 miles in Lower Hutt, New Zealand in 24 hours, passing 100 miles in 20 hr 47 min 13 sec on 9–10 Dec 1983. The 24-hour club record by a team of five is 100.99 miles, by the Portsmouth Northsea SC at the Victoria Swimming Center, Portsmouth, Great Britain on 4–5 Mar 1993. The women's record is 88.93 miles by the British City of Newcastle ASC on 16–17 Dec 1986. The most participants in a one-day swim relay is 2,145, each swimming a length, organized by Ken Applebaum and Jeff D. Van Buren at Hamilton College in Clinton, NY on 8 Apr 1989.

Underwater swimming Paul Cryne (Great Britain) and Samir Sawan al Awami (Qatar) swam 49.04 miles in a 24-hr period from Doha, Qatar to Umm Said and back on 21–22 Feb 1985 using sub-aqua equipment. They were swimming under water for 95.5 percent of the time. A relay team of six swam 94.44 miles in a swimming pool at Olomouc, Czechoslovakia on 17–18 Oct 1987.

CHANNEL SWIMMING

The first to swim the English Channel from shore to shore (without a life jacket) was the Merchant Navy captain Matthew Webb (1848–83), who swam an estimated 38 miles to make the 21-mile crossing from Dover, Great Britain to Calais Sands, France, in 21 hr 45 min from 12:56 P.M. to 10:41 A.M., 24–25 Aug 1875.

Paul Boyton (USA) had swum from Cap Gris-Nez, France to the South Foreland, Great Britain in his life-saving suit in 23 hr 30 min on 28–29 May 1875.

It is reported that Jean-Marie Saletti, a French soldier, escaped from a British prison hulk off Dover by swimming to Boulogne in July or August 1815.

The first woman to succeed was Gertrude Caroline Ederle (USA; b. 23 Oct 1906), who swam from Cap Gris-Nez, France to Deal, Great Britain on 6 Aug 1926, in the then-overall record time of 14 hr 39 min.

Fastest The official Channel Swimming Association (founded 1927) record is 7 hr 40 min by Penny Dean (b. 21 Mar 1955) of California, from Shakespeare Beach, Dover, Great Britain to Cap Gris-Nez, France on 29 Jul 1978.

TABLE TENNIS

Most titles World (instituted 1926) G. Viktor Barna (1911–72; b. Hungary, Győző Braun) won a record five singles, 1930, 1932–35, and eight men's doubles, 1929–35, 1939, in the World Championships (first held in 1926).

Angelica Rozeanu (Romania; b. 15 Oct 1921) won a record six women's singles, 1950–55, and Maria Mednyánszky (Hungary; 1901–79) won seven women's doubles, 1928, 1930–35. With two more at mixed doubles and seven team, Viktor Barna won 22 world titles in all, while 18 have been won by Maria Mednyanszky.

With the staging of championships biennially, the breaking of the above records would now be very difficult.

Youngest table tennis player The youngest-ever international competitor was Joy Foster, who represented Jamaica in the West Indies Championships at Port of Spain, Trinidad in August 1958 at the age of eight.

Counter hitting in table tennis The record number of hits in 60 sec is 173, by Jackie Bellinger (b. 9 Sep 1964) and Lisa Lomas (nee Bellinger; b. 9 Mar 1967), at the Northgate Sports Center, Ipswich, Great Britain, on 7 Feb 1993.

With a paddle in each hand, Gary D. Fisher of Olympia, WA completed 5,000 consecutive volleys over the net in 44 min 28 sec on 25 Jun 1975.

The most men's team titles (Swaythling Cup) is 12, by Hungary, 1927–31, 1933–35, 1938, 1949, 1952 and 1979.

The women's record (Marcel Corbillon Cup) is 10, by China, 1965 and eight successive from 1975–89 (biennially) and 1993.

United States The US won the Swaythling Cup in 1937 and the Corbillon Cup in 1937 and 1949. Ruth Aarons was the women's world champion in 1936 and 1937, sharing the title in the latter year.

No American has won the men's world singles title, but James McClure won three men's doubles titles, with Robert Blattner in 1936–37 and with Sol Schiff in 1938.

English Open (instituted 1921) Richard Bergmann (Austria, then Great Britain; 1920–70) won a record six singles, 1939–40, 1948, 1950, 1952, 1954, and Viktor Barna won seven men's doubles titles, 1931, 1933–35, 1938–39, 1949.

The women's singles record is six, by Maria Alexandru (Romania; b. 1941), 1963–64, 1970–72, 1974, and Diane Rowe (now Scholer [Great Britain]; b. 14 Apr 1933) won 12 women's doubles titles, 1950–56, 1960, 1962–65. Viktor Barna won 20 titles in all, and Diane Rowe won 17. Her twin Rosalind (now Mrs Cornett) has won nine (two in singles).

US Championships US national championships were first held in 1931. Leah Neuberger (nee Thall) won a record 21 titles between 1941 and 1961: nine women's singles, 12 women's doubles. Richard Miles won a record 10 men's singles titles between 1945 and 1962.

TAEKWONDO

Most titles The most world titles won is four, by Chung Kook-hyun (South Korea), light-middleweight 1982–83, welterweight 1985, 1987. Taekwondo was included as a demonstration sport at the 1988 Olympic Games.

United States Three American women won gold medals at the 1988 Olympics; one of them, Lynette Love (b. 21 Sep 1957), at heavyweight (over 70 kg), was also world champion in 1987.

TEAM HANDBALL

Most championships Olympic The USSR won five titles—*(men)* 1976, 1988 and 1992 (by the Unified Team from the republics of the former USSR), *(women)* 1976 and 1980. South Korea has also won two women's titles, in 1988 and 1992.

World Championships (instituted 1938) For indoor handball (now the predominant version of the game), the most men's titles won is three, by Romania, 1961, 1964 and 1970; and by Sweden, 1954, 1958 and 1990. However, Germany/West Germany won the outdoor title five times, 1938–66, and has won the indoor title twice, 1938 and 1978. Three women's titles have been won by three teams: Romania, 1956, 1960 (both outdoor) and 1962 (indoor); the GDR, 1971, 1975 and 1978 (all indoor); and the USSR, 1982, 1986 and 1990 (all indoor).

Highest score The highest score in an international match was recorded when the USSR beat Afghanistan 86–2 in the "Friendly Army Tournament" at Miskolc, Hungary in August 1981.

MOST TITLES Oh Sung-ok of South Korea helped her team win the Olympic team handball title for a record second time in 1992. (Photo: Allsport/ Michael Hewitt)

TENNIS

Grand Slam The grand slam for a tennis player is to hold all four of the world's major championship singles titles at the same time: the Australian Open, French Open, Wimbledon and US Open. The traditional slam is winning the four events in one year. The first man to have won all four was Frederick John Perry (Great Britain; b. 18 May 1909) when he won the French title in 1935. The first man to hold all four championships simultaneously, and thus achieve a grand slam, was John Donald "Don" Budge (USA; b. 13 Jun 1915) in 1938, and with Wimbledon and US in 1937, he won six successive grand slam tournaments. The first man to achieve the grand slam twice was Rodney George "Rod" Laver (Australia; b. 9 Aug 1938), as an amateur in 1962 and again in 1969, when the titles were open to professionals.

Four women have achieved the grand slam, and the first three won six successive grand slam tournaments: Maureen Catherine Connolly (USA; 1934–69), in 1953; Margaret Jean Court (nee Smith [Australia]; b. 16 Jul 1942) in 1970; and Martina Navratilova (USA; b. 18 Oct 1956) in 1983–84. The fourth was Stefanie Maria "Steffi" Graf (Germany; b. 14 Jun 1969) in 1988, when she also won the women's singles Olympic gold medal. Pamela Howard "Pam" Shriver (USA; b. 4 Jul 1962) with Navratilova won a record eight successive grand slam tournament women's doubles titles and 109 successive matches in all events from April 1983 to July 1985.

The first doubles pair to win the grand slam were the Australians Frank Allan Sedgeman (b. 29 Oct 1927) and Kenneth Bruce McGregor (b. 2 Jun 1929) in 1951.

The most singles championships won in grand slam tournaments is 24, by Margaret Court (11 Australian, 5 US, 5 French, 3 Wimbledon), 1960–73. She also won the US Amateur in 1969 and 1970 when this was held, as well as the US Open. The men's record is 12, by Roy Stanley Emerson (Australia; b. 3 Nov 1936), 6 Australian, 2 each French, US, Wimbledon, 1961–67.

"Golden set" The only known example of a "golden set" (winning a set 6–0 without dropping a single point, i.e., winning 24 consecutive points) in professional tennis was achieved by Bill Scanlon (USA; b. 13 Nov 1956) against Marcos Hocevar (Brazil) in the first round of the WCT Gold Coast Classic at Del Ray, FL on 22 Feb 1983. Scanlon won the match, 6–2, 6–0.

Fastest tennis service The fastest service timed with modern equipment is 138 mph, by Steve Denton (USA; b. 5 Sep 1956) at Beaver Creek, CO on 29 Jul 1984.

Oldest champions The oldest champion was Margaret Evelyn du Pont at 44 yr 125 days when she won the mixed doubles in 1962 with Neale Fraser (Australia). The oldest singles champion was Arthur Gore (Great Britain) in 1909 at 41 yr 182 days.

The most grand slam tournament wins by a doubles partnership is 20, by Althea Louise Brough (USA; b. 11 Mar 1923) and Margaret Evelyn du Pont (nee Osborne [USA]; b. 4 Mar 1918)—12 US, 5 Wimbledon, 3 French, 1942–57; and by Martina Navratilova and Pam Shriver—7 Australian, 5 Wimbledon, 4 French, 4 US, 1981–89.

United States   The most singles wins in grand slam tournaments by a US player is 19, by Helen Wills Moody (b. 6 Oct 1905)—8 Wimbledon, 7 US and 4 French.

Martina Navratilova (formerly of Czechoslovakia) has won a total of 55 grand slam titles—18 singles, a world record 31 women's doubles and 6 mixed doubles. Billie-Jean King (nee Moffit; b. 22 Nov 1942) has the most of US-born players, with 39 titles—12 singles, 16 women's doubles and 11 mixed doubles.

WIMBLEDON
CHAMPIONSHIPS

Most wins Women   Billie-Jean King won a record 20 titles between 1961 and 1979—six singles, 10 women's doubles and four mixed doubles. Elizabeth Montague Ryan (USA; 1892–1979) won a record 19 doubles (12 women's, seven mixed) titles from 1914 to 1934.

Men   The greatest number of titles by a man has been 13, by Hugh Laurence Doherty (Great Britain; 1875–1919) with five singles titles (1902–06) and a record eight men's doubles (1897–1901, 1903–05) partnered by his brother Reginald Frank (Great Britain; 1872–1910).

The most titles won by a US man is eight, by John Patrick McEnroe (b. 16 Feb 1959)—singles 1981, 1983 and 1984; men's doubles (all with Peter Fleming) 1979, 1981, 1983–84, and 1992 (with Michael Stich).

Singles   Martina Navratilova won a record nine titles, 1978–79, 1982–87 and 1990. The most men's singles wins since the Challenge Round was abolished in 1922 is five consecutively, by Björn Rune Borg (Sweden) in 1976–80. William Charles Renshaw (Great Britain; 1861–1904) won seven singles, in 1881–86 and 1889.

Mixed doubles   The male record is four titles, shared by Elias Victor "Vic" Seixas (USA; b. 30 Aug 1923), in 1953–56; Kenneth Norman Fletcher (Australia; b. 15 Jun 1940), in 1963, 1965–66, 1968; and Owen Keir Davidson (Australia; b. 4 Oct 1943) in 1967, 1971, 1973–74. The women's record is seven, by Elizabeth Ryan (USA) between 1919 and 1932.

Most appearances   Arthur William Charles "Wentworth" Gore (Great Britain; 1868–1928) made a record 36 appearances at Wimbledon between 1888 and 1927. In 1964, Jean Borotra (France; b. 13 Aug 1898) made his 35th appearance since 1922. In 1977 he appeared in the Veterans' Doubles at the age of 78.

Youngest champions   The youngest champion was Charlotte "Lottie" Dod (Great Britain; 1871–1960), who was 15 yr 285 days when she won in 1887. The youngest male champion was Boris Becker (West Germany; b. 22 Nov 1967), who won the men's singles title in 1985 at 17 yr 227 days. The youngest-ever player at Wimbledon was reputedly Mita Klima (Austria), who was 13 yr in the 1907 singles competition. The youngest seed was Jennifer Capriati (USA; b. 29 Mar 1976) at 14 yr 89 days at the time of her first match on 26 Jun 1990. She won this match, making her the youngest-ever winner at Wimbledon.

US OPEN CHAMPIONSHIPS

Most wins Margaret Evelyn du Pont won a record 25 titles between 1941 and 1960. She won a record 13 women's doubles (12 with Althea Louise Brough), nine mixed doubles and three singles. The men's record is 16, by William Tatem "Bill" Tilden (1893–1953), including seven men's singles, 1920–25, 1929—a record for singles shared with: Richard Dudley Sears (1861–1943), 1881–87; William A. Larned (1872– 1926), 1901–02, 1907–11; and at women's singles by Molla Mallory (nee Bjurstedt; 1884–1959), 1915–16, 1918, 1920–22, 1926; and Helen Wills Moody, 1923–25, 1927–29, 1931.

Youngest and oldest The youngest champion was Vincent Richards (1903–59), who was 15 yr 139 days when he won the men's doubles with Bill Tilden in 1918. The youngest singles champion was Tracy Ann Austin (b. 12 Dec 1962), who was 16 yr 271 days when she won the women's singles in 1979. The youngest men's singles champion was Pete Sampras (USA; b. 12 Aug 1971), who was 19 yr 28 days when he won the 1990 title. The oldest champion was Margaret du Pont, who won the mixed doubles at age 42 yr 166 days in 1960. The oldest singles champion was William Larned at 38 yr 242 days in 1911.

FRENCH CHAMPIONSHIPS

Most wins (from international status 1925) Margaret Court won a record 13 titles—five singles, four women's doubles and four mixed doubles, 1962–73. The men's record is nine, by Henri Cochet (France; 1901–1987)—four singles, three men's doubles and two mixed doubles, 1926–30. The singles record is seven, by Christine Marie "Chris" Evert (USA; b. 21 Dec 1954), 1974–75, 1979–80, 1983, 1985–86. Björn Borg won a record six men's singles, 1974–75, 1978–81.

Youngest and oldest The youngest doubles champions were the 1981 mixed doubles winners Andrea Jaeger (b. 4 Jun 1965), at 15 yr 339 days, and Jimmy Arias (b. 16 Aug 1964), at 16 yr 296 days. The youngest singles winners have been Monica Seles (Yugoslavia; b. 2 Dec 1973), who won the 1990 women's title at 16 yr 169 days in 1990, and Michael Chang (USA; b. 22 Feb 1972), who won the men's title at 17 yr 109 days in 1989. The oldest champion was Elizabeth Ryan, who won the 1934 women's doubles with Simone Mathieu (France) at 42 yr 88 days. The oldest singles champion was Andrés Gimeno (Spain; b. 3 Aug 1937) in 1972 at 34 yr 301 days.

AUSTRALIAN OPEN CHAMPIONSHIPS

Most wins Margaret Jean Court won the women's singles 11 times (1960–66, 1969–71 and 1973) as well as eight women's doubles and two mixed doubles, for a record total of 21 titles. A record six men's singles were won by Roy Stanley Emerson, 1961 and 1963–67. Thelma Dorothy Long (nee Coyne; b. 30 May 1918) won a record 12 women's doubles and four mixed doubles for a

MOST WINS The USA won the Davis Cup for a record 30th time in 1992. Here in action against Switzerland in the 1992 final is John McEnroe, who has played for five winning teams, 1978–79, 1981–82 and 1992. In finals he has won nine of ten singles and three of four doubles matches. (Photo: Allsport/Mike Powell)

record total of 16 doubles titles. Adrian Karl Quist (b. 4 Aug 1913) won 10 consecutive men's doubles from 1936 to 1950 (the last eight with John Bromwich) and three men's singles.

Longest span, oldest and youngest Thelma Long won her first (1936) and last (1958) titles 22 years apart. Kenneth Robert "Ken" Rosewall (b. 2 Nov 1934) won the singles in 1953, and in 1972, 19 years later, at 37 yr 62 days, became the oldest singles winner. The oldest champion was (Sir) Norman Everard Brookes (1877–1968), who was 46 yr 2 months when he won the 1924 men's doubles. The youngest champions were Rodney W. Heath, age 17 when he won the men's singles in 1905, and Monica Seles (Yugoslavia), who won the women's singles at 17 yr 55 days in 1991.

ATP WORLD CHAMPIONSHIPS

The first Grand Prix Masters Championships were staged in Tokyo, Japan in 1970. They were held in New York City annually from 1977 to 1989, with qualification by relative success in the preceding year's Grand Prix tournaments. The event was replaced from 1990 by the ATP Tour Championship, held in Frankfurt, Germany. A record five titles have been won by Ivan Lendl (Czechoslovakia; b. 7 Mar 1960), 1982–83, two in 1986 (January and December) and 1987, and he appeared in nine successive finals, 1980–88. James Scott "Jimmy" Connors (USA; b. 2 Sep 1952) uniquely qualified for 14 consecutive years, 1972–85. He chose not to play in 1975, 1976 and 1985, and won in 1977. He qualified again in 1987 and 1988, but did not play in 1988.

A record seven doubles titles were won by John McEnroe and Peter Fleming (USA; b. 21 Jan 1955), 1978–84.

Virginia Slims Championships The women's tour finishes with the Virginia Slims Championship, first contested in 1971 (with Avon Products the sponsor, 1979–82). Since 1983 the Virginia Slims final has been the one women's match played over the best of five sets. Martina Navratilova has a record six singles wins, between 1978 and 1986. She also has a record nine doubles wins, one with Billie Jean King in 1980, and eight with Pam Shriver to 1991.

OLYMPIC GAMES

Tennis was reintroduced to the Olympic Games in 1988, having originally been included from 1896 to 1924. It was also a demonstration sport in 1968 and 1984.

A record four gold medals, as well as a silver and a bronze, were won by Max Decugis (France; 1882–1978), 1900–20. A women's record five medals (one gold, two silver, two bronze) were won by Kitty McKane (later Mrs Godfree [Great Britain]; 1897–1992) in 1920 and 1924.

United States Four US players have won two Olympic gold medals: Beals Coleman Wright (1879–1961) in 1904; Vincent Richards (1903–59) and Helen Wills Moody in 1924, all at both singles and doubles; and Hazel Virginia Hotchkiss Wightman (1886–1974), at ladies' and mixed doubles in 1924. Richards won a US record third medal, silver at mixed doubles (with Marion Jessup) in 1924.

INTERNATIONAL TEAM

Davis Cup (instituted 1900) The most wins in the Davis Cup, the men's international team championship, has been 30, by the USA between 1900 and 1992. The most appearances for Cup winners is eight, by Roy Emerson (Australia), 1959–62, 1964–67. Bill Tilden (USA) played in a record 28 matches in the final, winning a record 21—17 out of 22 singles and four out of six doubles. He was on seven winning sides, 1920–26, and then on four losing sides, 1927–30.

Nicola Pietrangeli (Italy; b. 11 Sep 1933) played a record 163 rubbers (66 ties), 1954 to 1972, winning 120. He played 109 singles (winning 78) and 54 doubles (winning 42).

John McEnroe has played for the US team on 31 occasions, 1978–92. He also has the most wins—60 matches in Davis Cup competition (41 singles and 19 doubles).

Wightman Cup (instituted 1923) The annual women's match was won 51 times by the United States and 10 times by Great Britain. The contest was suspended in 1990 after a series of wipeouts by the US team. Chris Evert won all 26 of her singles matches, from 1971 to 1985, and including doubles achieved a record 34 wins from 38 rubbers played. Virginia Wade (Great Britain; 10 Jul 1945) played in a record 21 ties and 56 rubbers, 1965–85. Jennifer Capriati became the youngest-ever Wightman Cup winner and player at 13 yr 168 days, when she beat Clare Wood (Great Britain) 6–0, 6–0 at Williamsburg, VA on 14 Sep 1989.

Federation Cup (instituted 1963) The most wins in the Federation Cup, the women's international team championship, is 14, by the USA between 1963 and 1990. Virginia Wade (Great Britain) played each year from 1967 to 1983, in a record 57 ties, playing 100 rubbers, including 56 singles (winning 36) and 44 doubles (winning 30). Chris Evert won her first 29 singles matches, 1977–86. Her overall record, 1977–89, is 40 wins in 42 singles and 16 wins in 18 doubles matches.

Highest earnings   Monica Seles (Yugoslavia) won a women's season's record $2,662,352 in 1992. Stefan Edberg (Sweden; b. 19 Jan 1966) won a men's season's record $2,363,575 in 1991. Ivan Lendl had career earnings of $19,471,453 in prize money from 1978 to August 1993. Martina Navratilova's holds the women's career lifetime earnings record, with $18,929,570 by 18 Jul 1993. Earnings from special restricted events and team tennis are not included.

The greatest first-place prize money ever won is $2 million, by Pete Sampras when he won the Grand Slam Cup in Munich, Germany on 16 Dec 1990. In the final he beat Brad Gilbert (USA; b. 9 Aug 1961) 6–3, 6–4, 6–2. Gilbert received $1 million, also well in excess of the previous record figure. The highest total prize money was $9,002,000 for the 1993 US Open Championships.

Largest crowd   A record 30,472 people were at the Astrodome, Houston, TX on 20 Sep 1973, when Billie Jean King beat Robert Larimore "Bobby" Riggs (USA; b. 25 Feb 1918). The record for a standard tennis match is 25,578 at Sydney, New South Wales, Australia on 27 Dec 1954, in the Davis Cup Challenge Round (first day), Australia *v* USA.

Longest game   The longest-known singles game was one of 37 deuces (80 points) between Anthony Fawcett (Rhodesia) and Keith Glass (Great Britain) in the first round of the Surrey Championships at Surbiton, Great Britain on 26 May 1975. It lasted 31 min. Noëlle van Lottum and Sandra Begijn played a game lasting 52 min in the semifinals of the Dutch Indoor Championships at Ede, Gelderland on 12 Feb 1984.

The longest tiebreak was 26–24 for the fourth and decisive set of a first round men's doubles at the Wimbledon Championships on 1 Jul 1985. Jan Gunnarsson (Sweden) and Michael Mortensen (Denmark) defeated John Frawley (Australia) and Victor Pecci (Paraguay) 6–3, 6–4, 3–6, 7–6.

TRACK AND FIELD

Fastest speed   An analysis of split times at each 10 meters in the 1988 Olympic Games 100 m final in Seoul, South Korea on 24 Sep 1988, won by Ben Johnson (Canada) in 9.79 (average speed 22.85 mph but later disallowed as a world record due to his positive drug test for steroids) from Carl Lewis (USA), 9.92, showed that both Johnson and Lewis reached a peak speed (40 m–50 m and 80 m–90 m respectively) of 0.83 sec for 10 m, i.e., 26.95 mph. In the women's final, Florence Griffith Joyner was timed at 0.91 sec for each 10 m from 60 m–90 m, i.e., 24.58 mph.

Highest jump above own head   The greatest height cleared above an athlete's own head is 23¼ in, by Franklin Jacobs (USA; b. 31 Dec 1957), 5 ft 8 in tall, who jumped 7 ft 7¼ in at New York City, on 27 Jan 1978. The greatest height cleared by a woman above her own head is 12¾ in, by Yolanda Henry (USA;

Most international appearances The greatest number of international matches contested for any nation is 89, by shot-putter Bjørn Bang Andersen (b. 14 Nov 1937) for Norway, 1960–81.

Most track records in a day Jesse Owens (USA; 1913–80) set six world records in 45 min at Ann Arbor, MI on 25 May 1935, with a 9.4 sec 100 yd at 3:15 P.M., a 26 ft 8¼ in long jump at 3:25 P.M., a 20.3 sec 220 yd (and 200 m) at 3:45 P.M., and a 22.6 sec 220 yd (and 200 m) low hurdles at 4 P.M.

Longest career span Duncan McLean (1884–1980) of Scotland set a world age (92) record of 100 m in 21.7 sec in Aug 1977, more than 73 years after his best-ever sprint of 100 yd in 9.9 sec in South Africa in February 1904.

Greatest annual mileage The greatest competitive distance run in a year is 5,502 miles, by Malcolm Campbell (Great Britain; b. 17 Nov 1934) in 1985.

b. 2 Dec 1964), 5 ft 6 in tall, who jumped 6 ft 6¾ in at Seville, Spain on 30 May 1990.

Most Olympic titles The most Olympic gold medals won is 10 (an absolute Olympic record), by Raymond Clarence Ewry (USA; 1873–1937) in the standing high, long and triple jumps in 1900, 1904, 1906 and 1908.

Women The most gold medals won by a woman is four, shared by Francina "Fanny" E. Blankers-Koen (Netherlands; b. 26 Apr 1918), with 100 m, 200 m, 80 m hurdles and 4 × 100 m relay, 1948; Betty Cuthbert (Australia; b. 20 Apr 1938), with 100 m, 200 m, 4 × 100 m relay, 1956 and 400 m, 1964; Bärbel Wöckel (nee Eckert [East Germany]; b. 21 Mar 1955), with 200 m and 4 × 100 m relay in 1976 and 1980; and Evelyn Ashford (USA; b. 15 Apr 1957), 100 m and 4 × 100 m relay in 1984, 4 × 100 m relay in 1988 and 1992.

Most wins at one Game The most gold medals at one celebration is five, by Paavo Johannes Nurmi (Finland; 1897–1973) in 1924: 1,500 m, 5,000 m, 10,000 m cross-country, 3,000 m team and cross-country team. The most at individual events is four, by Alvin Christian Kraenzlein (USA; 1876–1928) in 1900: 60 m, 110 m hurdles, 200 m hurdles and long jump.

Most Olympic medals The most medals won is 12 (nine gold and three silver), by Paavo Nurmi (Finland) in the Games of 1920, 1924 and 1928.

Women The most medals won by a woman athlete is seven, by Shirley Barbara de la Hunty (nee Strickland [Australia]; b. 18 Jul 1925) with three gold, one silver and three bronze in the 1948, 1952 and 1956 Games. A reappraisal of the photo-finish indicates that she finished third, not fourth, in the 1948 200-meter event, thus unofficially increasing her medal haul to eight. Irena Szewinska (nee Kirszenstein [Poland]; b. 24 May 1946) won three gold, two

WORLD RECORDS
Despite having set 34 pole vault world records (16 outdoor, 18 indoor) and dominated the discipline for over 10 years, Sergey Bubka failed to clear any height in the 1992 Olympic final. (Photo: Allsport/Mike Hewitt)

Jacqueline Joyner-Kersee has won three world championships, a record she shares with four other athletes. (Photo: Allsport [USA]/Billy Stickland)

silver and two bronze in 1964, 1968, 1972 and 1976, and is the only woman athlete to win a medal in four successive Games.

United States   The most Olympic medals won is 10, by Ray Ewry (see Most Olympic titles). The most by a woman is five, by Delorez Florence Griffith Joyner (b. 21 Dec 1959): silver at 200 m in 1984, gold at 100 m, 200 m and 4 × 100 m relay, silver at 4 × 400 m relay in 1988; and Evelyn Ashford: gold at 100 m and 4 × 100 m relay in 1984, gold at 4 × 100 m relay, silver at 100 m in 1988, and gold at 4 × 100 m relay in 1992. Ashford's four gold medals are the most by an American woman in track and field.

Four gold medals at one Game were won by Alvin Kraenzlein (see page 743). Jesse Owens (1913–80) in 1936 and Frederick Carleton "Carl" Lewis (b. 1 Jul 1961) in 1984 both won four gold medals at one Games, both at 100 m, 200 m, long jump and the 4 × 100 m relay.

Olympic champions Oldest and youngest   The oldest athlete to win an Olympic title was Irish-born Patrick Joseph "Babe" McDonald (ne McDonnell; 1878–1954), who was age 42 yr 26 days when he won the 56 lb weight throw at Antwerp, Belgium on 21 Aug 1920. The oldest female champion was Lia Manoliu (Romania; b. 25 Apr 1932), age 36 yr 176 days when she won the discus at Mexico City on 18 Oct 1968. The youngest gold medalist was Barbara Pearl Jones (USA; b. 26 Mar 1937), who at 15 yr 123 days was a member of the winning 4 × 100 m relay team, at Helsinki, Finland on 27 Jul 1952. The youngest male champion was Robert Bruce "Bob" Mathias (USA; b. 17 Nov 1930), age 17 yr 263 days when he won the decathlon at the London Games on 5–6 Aug 1948.

The oldest Olympic medalist was Tebbs Lloyd Johnson (Great Britain; 1900–84), age 48 yr 115 days when he was third in the 1948 50,000 m walk. The oldest woman medalist was Dana Zátopková (Czechoslovakia; b. 19 Sep 1922), age 37 yr 348 days when she was second in the javelin in 1960.

World Championships   Quadrennial World Championships, distinct from the Olympic Games, were inaugurated in 1983, when they were held in Helsinki, Finland. In 1991 the event became a biennial Championship. The most medals won is nine, by Frederick Carleton "Carl" Lewis (USA; b. 1 Jul 1961)—eight gold, at 100 m, long jump and 4 × 100 m relay in 1983; 100 m, long jump and 4 × 100 m relay in 1987; 100 m and 4 × 100 m relay, 1991; and silver at long jump in 1991. The most golds won by a woman is three, shared by Marita Koch (GDR; b. 18 Feb 1957), 200 m, 4 × 100 m and 4 × 400 m relay 1983; Silke Gladisch (GDR; b. 21 Nov 1964), 4 × 100 m relay 1983, 100 m and 200 m 1987; Sabine Busch (GDR; b. 21 Nov 1962), 4 × 400 m relay 1983, 1987, 400 m hurdles 1987; Tatyana Samolenko (now Dorovskikh) (USSR; b. 12 Aug 1961), 1,500 m 1987, 3,000 m 1987, 1991; and Jackie Joyner-Kersee (USA; b. 3 Mar 1962), long jump 1987, 1991, heptathlon, 1987. The most medals by a woman is seven, by Merlene Ottey (Jamaica; b. 10 May 1960), gold, 4 × 100 m, one silver, five bronze, 1983–91.

Indoor   First held as the World Indoor Games in 1985, they are now staged biennially. The most individual titles is four, shared by Stefka Kostadinova (Bulgaria; b. 25 Mar 1965), high jump 1985, 1987, 1989, 1993; and Mikhail Shchennikov (Russia; b. 24 Dec 1967), 5,000 m walk 1987, 1989, 1991, 1993.

Decathlon

Dan O'Brien is the current world record holder for the decathlon. Here and opposite he is seen in action in four of the ten disciplines during his world record at Talence, France on 4–5 Sep 1992. (Photo: Allsport/Vandystadt/Richard Martin)

WORLD RECORDS—Men

World records for the men's events scheduled by the International Amateur Athletic Federation.
Fully automatic electric timing is mandatory for events up to 400 meters.

Running	min : sec	Name & Country	Place	Date
100 meters	9.86*	Frederick Carleton "Carl" Lewis (USA; b. 1 Jul 1961)	Tokyo, Japan	25 Aug 1991
200 meters	19.72†	Pietro Mennea (Italy; b. 28 Jun 1952)	Mexico City, Mexico	12 Sep 1979
400 meters	43.29	Harry Lee "Butch" Reynolds, Jr. (USA; b. 8 Aug 1964)	Zürich, Switzerland	17 Aug 1988
800 meters	1:41.73	Sebastian Newbold Coe (Great Britain; b. 29 Sep 1956)	Florence, Italy	10 Jun 1981
1,000 meters	2:12.18	Sebastian Newbold Coe (Great Britain)	Oslo, Norway	11 Jul 1981
1,500 meters	3:28.86	Noureddine Morceli (Algeria; b. 20 Feb 1970)	Rieti, Italy	6 Sep 1992
1 mile	3:46.32	Steven Cram (Great Britain; b. 14 Oct 1960)	Oslo, Norway	27 Jul 1985
2,000 meters	4:50.81	Saïd Aouita (Morocco)	Paris, France	16 Jul 1987
3,000 meters	7:28.96	Moses Kiptanui (Kenya; b. 1 Sep 1971)	Cologne, Germany	16 Aug 1992
5,000 meters	12:58.39	Saïd Aouita (Morocco)	Rome, Italy	22 Jul 1987
10,000 meters	26:58.38	Yobes Ondieki (Kenya; b. 21 Feb 1961)	Oslo, Norway	10 Jul 1993
20,000 meters	56:55.6	Arturo Barrios (Mexico)	La Flèche, France	30 Mar 1991
25,000 meters	1 hr 13:55.8	Toshihiko Seko (Japan; b. 15 Jul 1956)	Christchurch, New Zealand	22 Mar 1981
30,000 meters	1 hr 29:18.8	Toshihiko Seko (Japan)	Christchurch, New Zealand	22 Mar 1981
1 hour	13.111 miles	Arturo Barrios (Mexico)	La Flèche, France	30 May 1991

* Ben Johnson (Canada; b. 30 Dec 1961) ran 100 m in 9.79 sec at Seoul, South Korea on 24 Sep 1988, but was subsequently disqualified when he tested positive for steroids. He later admitted to having taken drugs over many years, and this also invalidated his 9.83 sec at Rome, Italy on 30 Aug 1987.
† This record was set at high altitude—Mexico City 7,349 ft. Best mark at low altitude: 200 m: 19.75 sec, Carl Lewis, Indianapolis, IN, 19 Jun 1983, and Joseph Nathaniel De-Loach (USA; b. 5 Jun 1967) at Seoul, South Korea on 28 Sep 1988.

Hurdling

110 meters (3′ 6″)	12.92	Roger Kingdom (USA; b. 26 Aug 1962)	Zürich, Switzerland	16 Aug 1989
400 meters (3′ 0″)	46.78	Kevin Young (USA)	Barcelona, Spain	6 Aug 1992
3,000 meter steeplechase	8:02.08	Moses Kiptanui (Kenya)	Zürich, Switzerland	20 Aug 1992

Relays

4 × 100 meters	37.40	United States.	Barcelona, Spain	8 Aug 1992
		(Mike Marsh, Leroy Burrell, Dennis Mitchell, Carl Lewis)		
4 × 200 meters	1:19.11	Santa Monica Track Club (USA)	Barcelona, Spain	8 Aug 1992
		(Mike Marsh, Leroy Burrell, Floyd Wayne Heard, Carl Lewis)		
4 × 400 meters	2:55.74	United States	Barcelona, Spain	8 Aug 1992
		(Andrew Valmon, Quincy Watts, Michael Johnson, Steve Lewis)		
4 × 800 meters	7:03.89	Great Britain	London, Great Britain	30 Aug 1982
		(Peter Elliott, Garry Peter Cook, Steven Cram, Sebastian Coe)		
4 × 1,500 meters	14:38.8	West Germany	Cologne, Germany	17 Aug 1977
		(Thomas Wessinghage, Harald Hudak, Michael Lederer, Karl Fleschen)		

Field Events

	m	ft	in			
High jump	2.44	8	0	Javier Sotomayor (Cuba; b. 13 Oct 1967)	San Juan, Puerto Rico	29 Jul 1989
Pole vault	6.13	20	1/4	Sergey Nazarovich Bubka (Ukraine; b. 4 Dec 1963)	Tokyo, Japan	19 Sep 1992
Long jump	8.95	29	4 1/2	Michael Anthony "Mike" Powell (USA; b. 10 Nov 1963)	Tokyo, Japan	30 Aug 1991
Triple jump	17.97	58	11 1/2	William Augustus "Willie" Banks (USA; b. 11 Mar 1956)	Indianapolis, IN	16 Jun 1985
Shot 16 lb	23.12	75	10 1/4	Eric Randolph "Randy" Barnes (USA; b. 16 Jun 1966)	Los Angeles, CA	20 May 1990
Discus 4 lb 8 oz	74.08	243	0	Jürgen Schult (East Germany; b. 11 May 1960)	Neubrandenburg, Germany	6 Jun 1986
Hammer 16 lb	86.74	284	7	Yuriy Georgiyevich Sedykh (USSR; b. 11 Jun 1955)	Stuttgart, Germany	30 Aug 1986
Javelin	95.54	313	5	Jan Zelezny (TCH)	Pietersburg, South Africa	6 Apr 1993

Decathlon

8,891 points	Dan O'Brien (USA; b. 18 Jul 1966)	Talence, France	4–5 Sep 1992

(1st day: 100 m 10.43 sec, Long jump 26 ft 1/4 in, Shot put 54 ft 9 1/4 in, High jump 6 ft 9 1/2 in, 400 m 48.51 sec)

(2nd day: 110 m hurdles 13.98 sec, Discus 159 ft 4 in, Pole vault 16 ft 4 3/4 in, Javelin 205 ft 4 in, 1,500 m 4:42.10 sec)

WORLD RECORDS—Women

World records for the women's events scheduled by the International Amateur Athletic Federation.

Running	min : sec	Name & Country	Place	Date
100 meters	10.49	Delorez Florence Griffith Joyner (USA; b. 21 Dec 1959)	Indianapolis, IN	16 Jul 1988
200 meters	21.34	Delorez Florence Griffith Joyner (USA)	Seoul, South Korea	29 Sep 1988
400 meters	47.60	Marita Koch (East Germany; b. 18 Feb 1957)	Canberra, Australia	6 Oct 1985
800 meters	1:53.28	Jarmila Kratochvílová (Czechoslovakia; b. 26 Jan 1951)	Münich, Germany	26 Jul 1983
1,000 meters	2:30.6	Tatyana Providokhina (USSR; b. 26 Mar 1953)	Podolsk, USSR	20 Aug 1978
1,500 meters	3:52.47	Tatyana Kazankina (USSR; b. 17 Dec 1951)	Zürich, Switzerland	13 Aug 1980
1 mile	4:15.61	Paula Ivan (Romania; b. 20 Jul 1963)	Nice, France	10 Jul 1989
2,000 meters	5:28.69	Maricica Puică (Romania; b. 29 Jul 1950)	London, Great Britain	11 Jul 1986
3,000 meters	8:22.62	Tatyana Kazankina (USSR)	Leningrad, USSR	26 Aug 1984
5,000 meters	14:37.33	Ingrid Kristiansen (nee Christensen [Norway]; b. 21 Mar 1956)	Stockholm, Sweden	5 Aug 1986
10,000 meters	30:13.74	Ingrid Kristiansen (Norway)	Oslo, Norway	5 Jul 1986

Hurdling	min : sec	Name & Country	Place	Date
100 meters (2′ 9″)	12.21	Yordanka Donkova (Bulgaria; b. 28 Sep 1961)	Stara Zagora, Bulgaria	20 Aug 1988
400 meters (2′ 6″)	52.94	Marina Styepanova (nee Makeyeva [USSR]; b. 1 May 1950)	Tashkent, USSR	17 Sep 1986

Relays	min : sec	Name & Country	Place	Date
4 × 100 meters	41.37	East Germany (Silke Gladisch [now Möller], Sabine Rieger [now Günther], Ingrid Auerswald [nee Brestrich], Marlies Göhr [nee Oelsner])	Canberra, Australia	6 Oct 1985
4 × 200 meters	1:28.15	East Germany (Marlies Göhr [nee Oelsner], Romy Müller [nee Schneider], Bärbel Wöckel [nee Eckert], Marita Koch)	Jena, Germany	9 Aug 1980
4 × 400 meters	3:15.17	USSR (Tatyana Ledovskaya, Olga Nazarova [nee Grigoryeva], Maria Pinigina [nee Kulchunova], Olga Bryzgina [nee Vladykina])	Seoul, South Korea	1 Oct 1988
4 × 800 meters	7:50.17	USSR (Nadezhda Olizarenko [nee Mushta], Lyubov Gurina, Lyudmila Borisova, Irina Podyalovskaya)	Moscow, USSR	5 Aug 1984

Field Events

	m	ft	in			
High jump	2.09	6	10¼	Stefka Kostadinova (Bulgaria; b. 25 Mar 1965)	Rome, Italy	30 Aug 1987
Long jump	7.52	24	8¼	Galina Chistyakova (USSR; b. 26 Jul 1962)	Leningrad, USSR	11 Jun 1988
Triple jump	14.95	49	1	Inessa Kravets (USSR; b. 5 Oct 1966)	Moscow, USSR	10 Jun 1991
Shot 8 lb 13 oz	22.63	74	3	Natalya Lisovskaya (USSR; b. 16 Jul 1962)	Moscow, USSR	7 Jun 1987
Discus 2 lb 3 oz	76.80	251	8	Gabriele Reinsch (East Germany; b. 23 Sep 1963)	Neubrandenburg, Germany	9 Jul 1988
Javelin 24 lb 7 oz	80.00	262	5	Petra Felke (East Germany; b. 30 Jul 1959)	Potsdam, Germany	9 Sep 1988

Heptathlon

7,291 points	Jacqueline Joyner-Kersee (USA; b. 3 Mar 1962)	Seoul, South Korea	23–24 Sep 1988

(100 m hurdles 12.69 sec; High jump 6 ft 1¼ in; Shot 51 ft 10 in; 200 m 22.56 sec; Long jump 23 ft 10 in; Javelin 149 ft 9 in; 800 m 2 min 08.57 sec)

US NATIONAL RECORDS—Women

Running	min : sec	Name	Place	Date
100 meters	10.49	Delorez Florence Griffith Joyner (b. 21 Dec 1959)	Indianapolis, IN	16 Jul 1988
200 meters	21.34	Florence Griffith Joyner	Seoul, South Korea	29 Sep 1988
400 meters	48.83	Valerie Ann Brisco (b. 6 Jul 1960)	Los Angeles, CA	6 Aug 1984
800 meters	1:56.90	Mary Thereza Slaney (nee Decker; b. 4 Aug 1958)	Berne, Switzerland	16 Aug 1985
1,000 meters	2:34.8	Mary Slaney	Eugene, OR	4 Jul 1985
1,500 meters	3:57.12	Mary Slaney	Stockholm, Sweden	26 Jul 1983
1 mile	4:16.71	Mary Slaney	Zürich, Switzerland	21 Aug 1985
2,000 meters	5:32.7	Mary Slaney	Eugene, OR	3 Aug 1984
3,000 meters	8:25.83	Mary Slaney	Rome, Italy	7 Sep 1985
5,000 meters	15:00.00	Patricia Susan "Patti-Sue" Plumer (b. 27 Apr 1962)	Stockholm, Sweden	3 Jul 1989
10,000 meters	30:13.74	Ingrid Kristiansen (Norway)	Oslo, Norway	5 Jul 1986
Marathon	2 hr 21:21	Joan Samuelson (nee Benoit; b. 16 May 1957)	Chicago, IL	20 Oct 1985

Hurdling				
100 meters	12.48	Yolanda Gail Devers (now Roberts; b. 19 Nov 1966)	Berlin, Germany	10 Sep 1991
400 meters	53.37	Sandra Marie Farmer-Patrick (b. 18 Aug 1962)	New York, NY	22 Jul 1989

(continued)

Relays	min : sec	Name	Place	Date
4 × 100 meters	41.55	National Team (Alice Regina Brown, Diane Williams, Florence Griffith, Pam Marshall)	Berlin, Germany	21 Aug 1987
4 × 200 meters	1:32.57	Louisiana State University (Tananjalyn Stanley, Sylvia Brydson, Esther Jones, Dawn Sowell)	Des Moines, IA	28 Apr 1989
4 × 400 meters	3:15.51	National Team (Denean Howard, Diane Lynn Dixon, Valerie Brisco, Florence Griffith Joyner)	Seoul, South Korea	1 Oct 1988
4 × 800 meters	8:17.09	Athletics West	Walnut, CA	24 Apr 1983

Field Events	ft	in	Name	Place	Date
High jump	6	8	Dorothy Louise Ritter (b. 18 Feb 1958)	Austin, TX	8 Jul 1988
	6	8	Louise Ritter	Seoul, South Korea	30 Sep 1988
Long jump	24	5½	Jacqueline Joyner-Kersee	Indianapolis, IN	13 Aug 1987
Triple jump	46	8¼	Sheila Hudson (b. 30 Jun 1967)	New Orleans, LA	21 Jun 1992
Shot	66	2½	Ramona Lu Pagel (nee Ebert; b. 10 Nov 1961)	San Diego, CA	25 Jun 1988
Discus	216	10½	Carol Therese Cady (b. 6 Jun 1962)	San Jose, CA	31 May 1986
Javelin	227	5½	Kathryn Joan "Kate" Schmidt (b. 29 Dec 1963)	Fürth, Germany	11 Sep 1977

Heptathlon

7,291 points	Jacqueline Joyner-Kersee	Seoul, South Korea	23–24 Sep 1988

(100 m hurdles 12.69 sec; High jump 6 ft 1¼ in; Shot 51 ft 10 in; 200 m 22.56 sec; Long jump 23 ft 10 in; Javelin 149 ft 9 in; 800 m 2 min 08.51 sec)

World record breakers Oldest and youngest For the greatest age at which anyone has broken a world record under IAAF jurisdiction, see General Records. The female record is 36 yr 139 days for Marina Styepanova (nee Makeyeva [USSR]; b. 1 May 1950) with 52.94 sec for the 400 m hurdles at Tashkent, USSR on 17 Sep 1986. The youngest individual world record breaker is Wang Yan (China; b. 9 Apr 1971), who set a women's 5,000 m walk record at age 14 yr 334 days with 21 min 33.8 sec at Jian, China on 9 Mar 1986. The youngest male is Thomas Ray (Great Britain; 1862–1904) at 17 yrs 198 days when he pole-vaulted 11 ft 2¾ in on 19 Sep 1879 (prior to IAAF ratification).

US championships The most American national titles won at all events, indoors and out, is 65, by Ronald Owen Laird (b. 31 May 1938) at various walks events between 1958 and 1976. Excluding the walks, the record is 41, by Stella Walsh (nee Walasiewicz, 1911–80), who won women's events between 1930 and 1954—33 outdoors and 8 indoors.

The most wins outdoors at one event in AAU/TAC history is 11, by James Sarsfield Mitchel (1864–1921) at 56 lb weight in 1888, 1891–97, 1900, 1903, 1905; Stella Walsh, 220 y/200 m 1930–31, 1939–40, 1942–48, and long jump 1930, 1939–46, 1948 and 1951; Maren Seidler (b. 11 Jun 1951) in shot 1967–68, 1972–80; and Dorothy Dodson (b. 28 Mar 1919) in javelin 1939–49.

Longest winning sequence Iolanda Balas (Romania; b. 12 Dec 1936) won a record 150 consecutive competitions at high jump from 1956 to 1967. The record at a track event is 122, at 400 m hurdles, by Edwin Corley Moses (USA; b. 31 Jul 1955) between his loss to Harald Schmid (West Germany; b. 29 Sep 1957) at Berlin, Germany on 26 Aug 1977 and that to Danny Lee Harris (USA; b. 7 Sep 1965) at Madrid, Spain on 4 Jun 1987.

Longest running races The longest races ever staged were the 1928 (3,422 miles) and 1929 (3,665 miles) transcontinental races from New York City to Los Angeles, CA. The Finnish-born Johnny Salo (1893–1931) was the winner in 1929 in 79 days, from 31 Mar to 18 Jun. His elapsed time of 525 hr 57 min 20 sec (averaging 6.97 mph) left him only 2 min 47 sec ahead of Englishman Pietro "Peter" Gavuzzi (1905–81).

The longest race staged annually is the New York 1,300 Mile race, held since 1987, at Flushing Meadows-Corona Park, Queens, NY. The fastest time to complete the race is 16 days 19 hr 31 min 47 sec by Al Howie (Great Britain; b. 16 Sep 1945), from 16 Sep–3 Oct 1991.

Backwards running Timothy "Bud" Badyana (USA) ran the fastest backwards marathon in 4 hr 15 sec at Columbus, OH on 10 Nov 1991. He has also run 10 km backwards in 45 min 37 sec at Toledo, OH on 13 Jul 1991. Donald Davis (USA; b. 10 Feb 1960) ran 1 mile backwards in 6 min 7.1 sec at the University of Hawaii on 21 Feb 1983. Ferdie Ato Adoboe (Ghana) ran 100 yd backwards in 12.7 sec at Smith College, Northampton, MA on 25 Jul 1991.

Arvind Pandya of India ran backwards across America—Los Angeles to New York—in 107 days, on 18 Aug–3 Dec 1984.

US NATIONAL RECORDS—Men

Running	min : sec	Name	Place	Date
100 meters	9.86	Frederick Carleton "Carl" Lewis (b. 1 Jul 1961)	Tokyo, Japan	25 Aug 1991
200 meters	19.73	Mike Marsh	Barcelona, Spain	6 Aug 1992
400 meters	43.29	Harry Lee "Butch" Reynolds, Jr. (b. 8 Aug 1964)	Zürich, Switzerland	17 Aug 1988
800 meters	1:42.60	John Lee "Johnny" Gray (b. 19 Jun 1960)	Koblenz, Germany	28 Aug 1985
1,000 meters	2:13.9	Richard Charles "Rick" Wohlhuter (b. 23 Dec 1948)	Oslo, Norway	30 Jul 1974
1,500 meters	3:29.77	Sydney Maree (b. 9 Sep 1956)	Cologne, Germany	25 Aug 1985
1 mile	3:47.69	Steven Michael Scott (b. 5 May 1957)	Oslo, Norway	7 Jul 1982
2,000 meters	4:52.44	James C. "Jim" Spivey (b. 7 Mar 1960)	Lausanne, Switzerland	15 Sep 1987
3,000 meters	7:33.37	Sydney Maree*	London, Great Britain	17 Jul 1982
	7:35.84	Douglas Floyd Padilla (b. 4 Oct 1956)	Oslo, Norway	9 Jul 1983
5,000 meters	13:01.15	Sydney Maree	Oslo, Norway	27 Jul 1985
10,000 meters	27:20.56	Marcus James Nenow (b. 16 Nov 1957)	Brussels, Belgium	5 Sep 1986
15,000 meters	43:39.8	William Henry "Bill" Rodgers (b. 23 Dec 1947)	Boston, MA	9 Aug 1977
20,000 meters	58:25.0	Bill Rodgers	Boston, MA	9 Aug 1977
25,000 meters	1 hr 14:11.8	Bill Rodgers	Saratoga, NY	21 Feb 1979
30,000 meters	1 hr 31:49	Bill Rodgers	Saratoga, NY	21 Feb 1979
1 hour	12 miles 135 yd	Bill Rodgers	Boston, MA	9 Aug 1977
Marathon	2 hr 08:52	Alberto Bauduy Salazar (b. 7 Aug 1958)	Boston, MA	19 Apr 1982

Prior to obtaining US citizenship.

Hurdling

Hurdling	min : sec	Name	Place	Date
110 meters	12.92	Roger Kingdom (b. 26 Aug 1962)	Zürich, Switzerland	16 Aug 1989
400 meters	47.02	Edwin Corley Moses (b. 31 Aug 1955)	Koblenz, Germany	31 Aug 1983
3,000 meter steeplechase	8:09.17	Henry Dinwoodey Marsh (b. 15 Mar 1954)	Koblenz, Germany	28 Aug 1985

Relays

4 × 100 meters	............................National Team .... Tokyo, Japan ....1 Sep 1991
	(Andre Cason, Leroy Russell Burrell, Dennis Mitchell, Carl Lewis)
4 × 200 meters	................1:19.11....Santa Monica Track Club .... Koblenz, Germany ....23 Aug 1989
	(Daniel Joe Everett, Leroy Burrell, Floyd Heard, Carl Lewis)
4 × 400 meters	................2:55.74....National Team .... Barcelona, Spain ....8 Aug 1992
	(Andrew Valmon, Quincy Watts, Michael Johnson, Steve Lewis)
4 × 800 meters	................7:06.5.....Santa Monica Track Club .... Walnut, GA ....26 Apr 1986
	(James Robinson, David Mack, Earl Jones, Johnny Gray)
4 × 1,500 meters	............14:46.3....National Team .... Bourges, France ....24 Jun 1969

Field Events

	ft	in			
High jump		.7	10½....Charles Austin .... Zürich, Switzerland ....7 Aug 1991
Pole vault	.19	6½....Daniel Joe Dial (b. 26 Oct 1962) .... Norman, OK ....18 Jun 1987
Long jump	.29	4½....Mike Powell .... Tokyo, Japan ....30 Aug 1991
Triple jump	.58	11½....William Augustus "Willie" Banks (b. 11 Mar 1956) ... Indianapolis, IN ....16 Jun 1985
Shot	.75	10¼....Earl Randolph "Randy" Barnes (b.16 Jun 1966) ... Westwood, LA ....20 May 1990
Discus	.237	4*....Walter "Ben" Plunkett (b. 13 Apr 1953) .... Stockholm, Sweden ....7 Jul 1981
Hammer	.268	8....Judson Campbell Logan (b. 19 Jul 1959) ...... University Park, PA ....22 Apr 1988
Javelin	.281	2....Tom Pukstys (b. 28 May 1968) .... Kuortane, Finland ....26 Jun 1993

* Ratified despite the fact that it was achieved after a positive drug test.

Decathlon

8,812 points ....Dan O'Brien .... Talence, France ....4–5 Sep 1992
(1st day: 100 m 10.43 sec; Long jump 26 ft ¼ in;
Shot put 54 ft 9¼ in; 3 ft 3½ in; High jump 6 ft 9½ in; 400 m 48.51 sec)
(2nd day: 110 m hurdles 13.98 sec, Discus 159 ft 4 in,
Pole vault 16 ft 4¾ in; Javelin 205 ft 4 in; 1,500 m 4:42.10
sec)

WORLD INDOOR RECORDS

Track performances around a turn must be made on a track of circumference no longer than 200 meters.

MEN

Running

Running	min : sec	Name & Country	Place	Date
50 meters	5.61*	Manfred Kokot (East Germany; b. 3 Jan 1948)	East Berlin, Germany	4 Feb 1973
50 meters	5.61*	James Sanford (USA; b. 27 Dec 1957)	San Diego, CA	20 Feb 1981
60 meters	6.41*	Andre Cason (USA; b. 13 Jan 1969)	Madrid, Spain	14 Feb 1992
200 meters	20.36	Bruno Marie-Rose (France; b. 20 May 1965)	Liévin, France	22 Feb 1987
400 meters	45.02	Danny Everett (USA; b. 1 Nov 1966)	Stuttgart, Germany	2 Feb 1992
800 meters	1:44.84	Paul Ereng (Kenya; b. 22 Aug 1967)	Budapest, Hungary	4 Mar 1989
1,000 meters (2:16.4 officially)	2:16.62	Robert Druppers (Netherlands; b. 29 Apr 1962)	The Hague, Netherlands	20 Feb 1988
1,500 meters	3:34.16	Noureddine Morceli (Algeria; b. 20 Feb 1970)	Seville, Spain	28 Feb 1991
1 mile	3:49.78	Eamonn Coghlan (Ireland; b. 21 Nov 1952)	East Rutherford, NJ	27 Feb 1983
3,000 meters	7:37.31	Moses Kiptanui (Kenya; b. 1 Sep 1971)	Seville, Spain	20 Feb 1992
5,000 meters	13:20.4	Suleiman Nyambui (Tanzania; b. 13 Feb 1953)	New York, NY	6 Feb 1983
50 meter hurdles	6.25	Mark McKoy (Canada; b. 10 Dec 1961)	Kobe, Japan	5 Mar 1986
60 meter hurdles	7.36†	Gregory "Greg" Foster (USA; b. 4 Aug 1958)	Los Angeles, CA	16 Jan 1987
	7.37	Roger Kingdom (USA; b. 26 Aug 1962)	Piraeus, Greece	8 Mar 1989

* Ben Johnson (Canada; b. 30 Dec 1961) ran 50 m in 5.55 sec at Ottawa, Canada on 31 Jan 1987 and 60 m in 6.41 sec at Indianapolis, IN on 7 Mar 1987, but these were invalidated due to his admission, at the 1988 Olympics, of having taken drugs over many years.

† Adjudged by observers to have been with a rolling start, but officially ratified.

Relays

Relays	min : sec	Name & Country	Place	Date
4 × 200 meters	1:22.11	United Kingdom (Linford Christie, Darren Braithwaite, Ade Mafe, John Regis)	Glasgow, Great Britain	3 Mar 1991
4 × 400 meter	3:03.05	Germany (Rico Lieder, Jens Carlowitz, Karsten Just, Thomas Schönlebe)	Seville, Spain	10 Mar 1991

Walking

Walking	min : sec	Name & Country	Place	Date
5,000 meters	18:11.41*	Ronald Weigel (East Germany; b. 8 Aug 1959)	Vienna, Austria	13 Feb 1988
	18:15.25	Grigoriy Kornev (Russia; b. 14 Mar 1961)	Moscow, Russia	7 Feb 1992

* Not officially recognized.

Field Events

	m	ft	in			
High jump	2.43	7	11½	Javier Sotomayor (Cuba; b. 13 Oct 1967)	Budapest, Hungary	4 Mar 1989
Pole vault	6.15	20	2¼	Sergey Nazarovich Bubka (Ukraine; b. 4 Dec 1963)	Donetsk, Ukraine	21 Feb 1993
Long jump	8.79	28	10¼	Frederick Carleton "Carl" Lewis (USA; b. 1 Jul 1961)	New York, NY	27 Jan 1984
Triple jump	17.76	58	3¾	Michael Alexander Conley (USA; b. 5 Oct 1962)	New York, NY	27 Feb 1987
Shot	22.66	74	4¼	Eric Randolph "Randy" Barnes (USA; b. 16 Jun 1966)	Los Angeles, CA	20 Jan 1989

Heptathlon	6,476 points	Dan O'Brien (USA; b. 18 Jul 1966)	Toronto, Canada	13–14 Mar 1993

60 m 6.67 sec; Long jump 7.84 m; Shot 16.02 m; High jump 2.13 m;
60 m hurdles 7.85 sec; Pole vault 5.20 m; 1,000 m 2:57.96)

WOMEN

Running

	min : sec			
50 meters	6.05	Irina Privalova (Russia; b. 12 Nov 1968)	Moscow, Russia	2 Feb 1993
60 meters	6.92	Irina Privalova (Russia)	Madrid, Spain	11 Feb 1993
200 meters	22.24	Merlene Ottey (Jamaica; b. 10 May 1960)	Seville, Spain	10 Mar 1991
400 meters	49.59	Jarmila Kratochvílová (Czechoslovakia; b. 26 Jan 1951)	Milan, Italy	7 Mar 1982
800 meters	1:56.40	Christine Wachtel (East Germany; b. 6 Jan 1965)	Vienna, Austria	13 Feb 1988
1,000 meters	2:33.93	Inna Yevseyeva (Ukraine; b. 14 Aug 1964)	Moscow, Russia	7 Feb 1992
1,500 meters	4:00.27	Doina Melinte (Romania; b. 27 Dec 1956)	East Rutherford, NJ	9 Feb 1990
1 mile	4:17.14	Doina Melinte (Romania)	East Rutherford, NJ	9 Feb 1990
3,000 meters	8:33.82	Elly van Hulst (Netherlands; b. 9 Jun 1957)	Budapest, Hungary	4 Mar 1989
5,000 meters	15:03.17	Elizabeth McColgan (Great Britain; b. 24 May 1964)	Birmingham, Great Britain	22 Feb 1992
50 meter hurdles	6.58	Cornelia Oschkenat (East Germany; b. 29 Oct 1961)	Berlin, Germany	20 Feb 1988
60 meter hurdles	7.69	Lyudmila Narozhilenko (USSR; b. 21 Apr 1964)	Chelyabinsk, Russia	4 Feb 1993

Relays

	min : sec			
4 × 200 meters	1:32.55	S. C. Eintracht Hamm (West Germany)	Dortmund, Germany	19 Feb 1988
		(Helga Arendt, Silke-Beate Knoll, Mechthild Kluth, Gisela Kinzel)		
4 × 400 meters	3:27.22	Germany	Seville, Spain	10 Mar 1992
		(Sandra Seuser, Katrin Schreiter, Annet Hesselbarth, Grit Breuer)		

(continued)

Walking	min : sec			Name & Country	Place	Date
3,000 meters	11:44.00			Alina Ivanova (Ukraine; b. 25 Jun 1969)	Moscow, Russia	7 Feb 1992

Field Events	m	ft	in			
High jump	2.07	6	9½	Heike Henkel (Germany; b. 5 May 1964)	Karlsruhe, Germany	9 Feb 1992
Long jump	7.37	24	2¼	Heike Drechsler (East Germany; b. 16 Dec 1964)	Vienna, Austria	13 Feb 1988
Triple jump	14.47	47	5¾	Inessa Kravets (Ukraine; b. 5 Oct 1966)	Toronto, Canada	14 Mar 1993
Shot	22.50	73	10	Helena Fibingerová (Czechoslovakia; b. 13 Jul 1959)	Jablonec, Czechoslovakia	19 Feb 1977

Pentathlon	points					
	4,991 points			Irina Belova (Russia; b. 27 Mar 1968)	Berlin, Germany	14–15 Feb 1992

(60 m hurdles 8.22 sec; High jump 1.93 m; Shot 13.25 m; Long jump 6.67 m; 800 m 2:10.26)

WORLD RECORD Ukrainian Inessa Kravets "stepping" her way to a new indoor triple jump world record at the 1993 World Indoor Championships at Toronto. (Photo: Allsport/Gray Mortimore)

Longest runs The longest run by an individual is one of 11,134 miles around the United States, by Sarah Covington-Fulcher (USA; b. 14 Feb 1962), starting and finishing in Los Angeles, CA, 21 Jul 1987–2 Oct 1988. Al Howie (Great Britain) ran across Canada, from St Johns, Newfoundland to Victoria, British Columbia, a distance of 4,533.2 miles, in 72 days 10 hr 23 min, 21 Jun–1 Sep 1991. Robert J. Sweetgall (USA; b. 8 Dec 1947) ran 10,608 miles around the perimeter of the United States, starting and finishing in Washington, D.C., 9 Oct 1982–15 Jul 1983. Ron Grant (Australia; b. 15 Feb 1943) ran around Australia, 8,316 miles in 217 days 3 hr 45 min, 28 Mar–31 Oct 1983. Max Telford (New Zealand; b. Hawick, Scotland 2 Feb 1955) ran 5,110 miles from Anchorage, AK to Halifax, Nova Scotia, in 106 days 18 hr 45 min from 25 Jul to 9 Nov 1977.

The fastest time for the cross-America run is 46 days 8 hr 36 min, by Frank Giannino, Jr. (USA; b. 1952) for the 3,100 miles from San Francisco to New York from 1 Sep–17 Oct 1980. The women's trans-America record is 69 days 2 hr 40 min, by Mavis Hutchinson (South Africa; b. 25 Nov 1942) from 12 Mar–21 May 1978.

Mass relay records The record for 100 miles by 100 runners from one club is 7 hr 53 min 52.1 sec, by the Baltimore Road Runners Club, Towson, MD on 17 May 1981. The women's record is 10 hr 47 min 9.3 sec on 3 Apr 1977, by the San Francisco Dolphins Southend Running Club. The record for 100 × 100 m is 19 min 14.19 sec, by a team from Antwerp at Merksem, Belgium on 23 Sep 1989.

The longest relay ever run was 10,806 miles by 23 runners of the Melbourne Fire Brigade, around Australia on Highway No. 1, in 50 days 43 min, 6 Aug–25 Sep 1991. The most participants is 6,500—260 teams of 25—for the Batavierenrace from Nijmegen to Enschede, Netherlands on 25 Apr 1992. The greatest distance covered in 24 hr by a team of 10 is 280.232 miles, by Oxford Striders RC at East London, South Africa on 5–6 Oct 1990.

United States The greatest distance covered by an American team of 10 runners in 24 hr is 271.974 miles, by students of Marcus High School in Flower Mound, TX, 17–18 May 1991.

Greatest mileage Douglas Alistair Gordon Pirie (Great Britain; 1931–91), who set five world records in the 1950s, estimated that he had run a total distance of 216,000 miles in 40 years up to 1981.

Dr Ron Hill (Great Britain; b. 21 Sep 1938), the 1969 European and Commonwealth marathon champion, has not missed a day's training since 20 Dec 1964. His meticulously compiled training log shows a total of 126,202 miles from 3 Sep 1956 to 17 May 1993. He has finished 114 marathons, all in less than 2:52, and has raced in 54 nations.

Roof of the world run Ultra runner Hilary Walker ran the length of the Friendship Highway from Lhasa, Tibet to Kathmandu, Nepal, a distance of 590 miles, in 14 days 9 hrs 36 min from 18 Sep–2 Oct 1991. The run was made at an average altitude of 13,780 ft.

ULTRA LONG DISTANCE WORLD RECORDS

MEN

Track	hr : min : sec	Name & Country	Place	Date
50 km	2:48:06	Jeff Norman (Great Britain)	Manchester, Great Britain	7 Jun 1980
50 miles	4:51:49	Don Ritchie (Great Britain)	London, Great Britain	12 Mar 1983
100 km	6:10:20	Don Ritchie (Great Britain)	London, Great Britain	28 Oct 1978
100 miles	11:30:51	Don Ritchie (Great Britain)	London, Great Britain	15 Oct 1977
200 km	15:11:10*	Yiannis Kouros (Greece)	Montauban, France	15–16 Mar 1985
200 miles	27:48:35	Yiannis Kouros (Greece)	Montauban, France	15–16 Mar 1985
500 km	60:23:00	Yiannis Kouros (Greece)	Colac, Australia	26–29 Nov 1984
500 miles	105:42:09	Yiannis Kouros (Greece)	Colac, Australia	26–30 Nov 1984
1,000 km	136:17:00	Yiannis Kouros (Greece)	Colac, Australia	26 Nov–1 Dec 1984
	kilometers			
24 hours	283.600	Yiannis Kouros (Greece)	Montauban, France	15–16 Mar 1985
48 hours	452.270	Yiannis Kouros (Greece)	Montauban, France	15–17 Mar 1985
6 days	1,023.200	Yiannis Kouros (Greece)	Colac, Australia	26 Nov–1 Dec 1984

Road	hr : min : sec	Name & Country	Place	Date
50 km	2:43:38	Thompson Magawana (South Africa)	Claremont–Kirstenbosch, South Africa	12 Apr 1988
50 miles	4:50:21	Bruce Fordyce (South Africa)	London–Brighton, Great Britain	25 Sep 1983
1,000 miles	10d 10hr 30min 35sec	Yiannis Kouros (Greece)	New York City	21–30 May 1988
	kilometers			
24 hours	286.463	Yiannis Kouros (Greece)	New York City	28–29 Sep 1985
6 days	1,028.370	Yiannis Kouros (Greece)	New York City	21–26 May 1988

WOMEN

Track	hr : min : sec			
15 km	49:44.0	Silvana Cruciata (Italy)	Rome, Italy	4 May 1981
20 km	1:06:55.5	Rosa Mota (Portugal)	Lisbon, Portugal	14 May 1983
25 km	1:29:30	Karolina Szabo (Hungary)	Budapest, Hungary	23 Apr 1988
30 km	1:47:06	Karolina Szabo (Hungary)	Budapest, Hungary	23 Apr 1988
50 km	3:35:31	Ann Transon (USA)	Santa Rosa, CA	28 Mar 1992
50 miles	6:14:34†	Ann Transon (USA)	Hayward, CA	3-4 Aug 1991
100 km	7:48:15†	Ann Transon (USA)	Hayward, CA	3-4 Aug 1991
100 miles	14:29:44	Ann Transon (USA)	Santa Rosa, CA	18-19 Mar 1989
200 km	19:28:48	Eleanor Adams (Great Britain)	Melbourne, Australia	19-20 Aug 1989
200 miles	39:09:03	Hilary Walker (Great Britain)	Blackpool, Great Britain	5-6 Nov 1988
500 km	77:53:46	Eleanor Adams (Great Britain)	Colac, Australia	13-15 Nov 1989
500 miles	130:59:58	Sandra Barwick (New Zealand)	Campbelltown, Australia	18-23 Nov 1990

kilometers				
1 hour	18.084	Silvana Cruciata (Italy)	Rome, Italy	4 May 1981
24 hours	240.169	Eleanor Adams (Great Britain)	Melbourne, Australia	19-20 Aug 1989
48 hours	366.512	Hilary Walker (Great Britain)	Blackpool, Great Britain	5-7 Nov 1988
6 days	866.631	Sandra Barwick (New Zealand)	Campbelltown, Australia	18-24 Nov 1990

Road *	hr : min : sec			
30 km	1:38:27	Ingrid Kristiansen (Norway)	London, Great Britain	10 May 1987
50 km	3:08:13	Frith van der Merwe (South Africa)	Claremont-Kirstenbosch, South Africa	25 Mar 1989
50 miles	5:40:18	Ann Transon (USA)	Houston, TX	23 Feb 1991
100 km	7:18:57	Birgit Lennartz (West Germany)	Hanua, Germany	28 Sep 1989
100 miles	13:47:41	Ann Transon (USA)	Queens, NY	4 May 1991
200 km	19:22:05	Ann Transon (USA)	Queens, NY	16-17 Sep 1989
	(indoors) 19:00:31	Eleanor Adams (Great Britain)	Milton Keynes, Great Britain	3-4 Feb 1990
1,000 km	7d 1hr 11min 00sec	Sandra Barwick (New Zealand)	Queens, NY	16-23 Sep 1991
1,000 miles	12d 14hr 38min 40sec	Sandra Barwick (New Zealand)	Queens, NY	16-29 Sep 1991

* Where superior to track bests and run on properly measured road courses.

It should be noted that road times must be assessed with care as course conditions can vary considerably.

†Timed on one running watch only.

Joggling 3 objects   Owen Morse (USA), 100 m in 11.68 sec, 1989, and 400 m in 57.32 sec, 1990. Kirk Swenson (USA), 1 mile in 4 min 43 sec, 1986, and 5,000 m (3.1 miles) in 16 min 55 sec, 1986. Ashrita Furman (USA), marathon—26 miles 385 yd—in 3 hr 22 min 32.5 sec, 1988, and 50 miles in 8 hr 52 min 7 sec, 1989. Michael Hout (USA), 110 m hurdles in 20 sec, 1992. Albert Lucas (USA), 400 m hurdles in 1 min 10.37 sec, 1989. Owen Morse, Albert Lucas, Tuey Wilson and John Wee (all USA), 1 mile relay in 3 min 57.38 sec, 1990.

5 objects   Owen Morse (USA), 100 m in 13.8 sec, 1988. Bill Gillen (USA), 1 mile in 7 min 41.01 sec, 1989, and 3.1 miles in 28 min 11 sec, 1989. (See also Endurance and Endeavor, juggling.)

MARATHON

Fastest   There are as yet no official records for the marathon, and it should be noted that courses may vary in severity. The following are the best times recorded, all on courses whose distance has been verified:

Men: 2 hr 6 min 50 sec, by Belayneh Dinsamo (Ethiopia; b. 28 Jun 1965) at Rotterdam, Netherlands on 17 Apr 1988. *Women:* 2 hr 21 min 6 sec, by Ingrid Kristiansen (nee Christensen [Norway]; b. 21 Mar 1956) at London, Great Britain on 21 Apr 1985.

Boston Marathon   First run by 15 men on 19 Apr 1897 over a distance of 24 miles 1,232 yards, the Boston Marathon is the world's oldest annual race. The full marathon distance was first run in 1927. It is run every year from Hopkinton to Boston on or about 19 April, Patriot's Day, which honors the famed ride of Paul Revere through Boston.

The most wins is seven, by Clarence DeMar (1888–1958), in 1911, 1922–24, 1927–28 and 1930.

Kathy Switzer (USA) contested the race in 1967, although the race director tried to prevent her from running; but pioneering efforts helped force the acceptance of women runners, and they were admitted officially for the first

---

Highest altitude   The highest start for a marathon is the biennially held Everest Marathon, first run on 27 Nov 1987. It begins at Gorak Shep at 17,100 ft and ends at Namche Bazar, 11,300 ft. The fastest times to complete this race are (*men*) 3 hr 59 min 4 sec, by Jack Maitland; (*women*) 5 hr 44 min 32 sec, by Dawn Kenwright, both in 1989.

One thousand hours   Ron Grant (Australia) ran 1.86 miles within an hour, every hour, for 1,000 consecutive hours at New Farm Park, Brisbane, Queensland, Australia from 6 Feb–20 Mar 1991.

Pancake race record   Dominic M. Cuzzacrea (USA; b. 8 Jun 1960) of Lockport, NY ran the Buffalo, New York Nissan Marathon (26.2 miles) while flipping a pancake in a time of 3 hours 6 min and 22 sec on 6 May 1990.

time in 1972. Rosa Mota (Portugal; b. 29 Jun 1958) has a record three wins, 1987–88 and 1990, in the women's competition.

The course record for men is 2 hr 7 min 51 sec by Rob de Castella (Australia) in 1986. The women's record is 2 hr 22 min 43 sec, by Joan Benoit (USA; now Samuelson) in 1983.

John A. Kelley (USA; b. 6 Sep 1907) finished the Boston Marathon 61 times through 1992, winning twice, in 1933 and 1945.

New York City Marathon   The race was run in Central Park each year from 1970 to 1976, when, to celebrate the US Bicentennial, the course was changed to a route through all five boroughs of the city. Since that year, when there were 2,090 runners, the race has become one of the world's great sporting occasions, and in 1992 there were a record 27,797 finishers.

William Henry "Bill" Rodgers (USA; b. 23 Dec 1947) had a record four wins—1976–79; and Grete Waitz (nee Andersen [Norway]; b. 1 Oct 1953) was the women's winner nine times—1978–80, 1982–86 and 1988.

The course record for men is 2 hr 8 min 1 sec, by Juma Ikangaa (Tanzania; b. 19 Jul 1957), and for women it is 2 hr 25 min 30 sec, by Ingrid Kristiansen (Norway), both set in 1989. On a course subsequently remeasured as about 170 yd short, Allison Roe (New Zealand) was the 1981 women's winner in 2 hr 25 min 29 sec.

Most competitors   The record number of confirmed finishers in a marathon is 27,797 for 28,656 starters in the New York City Marathon on 1 Nov 1992. A record 105 men ran under 2 hr 20 min, and 46 ran under 2 hr 15 min, in the World Cup Marathon at London, Great Britain on 21 Apr 1991; and a record six men ran under 2 hr 10 min at Fukuoka, Japan on 4 Dec 1983 and at London on 23 Apr 1989. A record nine women ran under 2 hr 30 min in the first Olympic marathon for women at Los Angeles on 5 Aug 1984.

Most run by an individual   Thian K. "Sy" Mah (Canada; 1926–88) ran 524 marathons of 26 miles 385 yd or longer from 1967 to his death in 1988. He paced himself to take 3½ hr for each run.

Three in three days   The fastest combined time for three marathons in three days is 8 hr 22 min 31 sec, by Raymond Hubbard (Belfast, Northern Ireland: 2 hr 45 min 55 sec; London, Great Britain: 2 hr 48 min 45 sec; and Boston: 2 hr 47 min 51 sec) on 16–18 Apr 1988.

Oldest finishers   The oldest man to complete a marathon was Dimitrion Yordanidis (Greece), age 98, in Athens, Greece on 10 Oct 1976. He finished in 7 hr 33 min. Thelma Pitt-Turner (New Zealand) set the women's age record in August 1985, completing the Hastings, New Zealand Marathon in 7 hr 58 min at the age of 82.

Half marathon   The distance of half the full marathon has become established in recent years as one of the most popular for road races. In 1992 the IAAF held the first official world championships at this distance.

The world best time on a properly measured course is 59 min 47 sec by Moses Tanui (Kenya; b. 20 Aug 1965) at Milan, Italy on 3 Apr 1993.

Ingrid Kristiansen (Norway) ran 66 min 40 sec at Sandes, Norway on 5 Apr 1987, but the measurement of the course has not been confirmed. She holds the recognized best by a woman with 68 min 32 sec at New Bedford, MA on 19 Mar 1989. Liz McColgan ran 67 min 11 sec at Tokyo, Japan on 26 Jan 1992, but the course was 33 m downhill, a little more than the allowable 1 in 1,000 drop.

Pram-pushing Priscilla Margaret "Tabby" Puzey, 38, pushed a pram while running the Abingdon half marathon in Abingdon, Great Britain, on 13 Apr 1986 in 2 hr 4 min 9 sec.

WALKING

Most titles Four-time Olympian Ronald Owen Laird (b. 31 May 1938) of the New York AC won a total of 65 US national titles from 1958 to 1976, plus four Canadian Championships.

Most Olympic medals Walking races have been included in the Olympic events since 1906. The only walker to win three gold medals has been Ugo Frigerio (Italy; 1901–68) with the 3,000 m in 1920, and 10,000 m in 1920 and 1924. He also holds the record for most medals, with four (he won the bronze medal at 50,000 m in 1932), a total shared with Vladimir Stepanovich Golubnichiy (USSR; b. 2 Jun 1936), who won gold medals for the 20,000 m in 1960 and 1968, the silver in 1972 and the bronze in 1964.

Longest race The race from Paris to Colmar (until 1980 from Strasbourg to Paris) in France (instituted 1926 in the reverse direction), now about 325 miles, is the world's longest annual race walk.

WALKING Double world champion and world record holder Maurizio Damilano. (Photo: Allsport/Gray Mortimore)

ROAD WALKING

It should be noted that the severity of the road race courses and the accuracy of their measurement may vary, sometimes making comparisons of times unreliable.

WORLD BESTS

MEN
20 km: 1 hr 18 min 13 sec, Pavol Blazek (Czechoslovakia; b. 9 Jul 1958) at Hildesheim, Germany on 16 Sep 1990.
30 km: 2 hr 2 min 41 sec, Andrey Perlov (USSR; b. 12 Dec 1961) at Sochi, USSR on 19 Feb 1989.
50 km: 3 hr 37 min 41 sec, Andrey Perlov (USSR) at Leningrad, USSR on 5 Aug 1989.

WOMEN
10 km: 41 min 30 sec, Kerry Ann Saxby (Australia; b. 2 Jun 1961) at Canberra, Australia on 27 Aug 1988.
20 km: 1 hr 29 min 40 sec, Kerry Saxby at Varnamo, Sweden on 13 May 1988.
50 km: 4 hr 50 min 51 sec, Sandra Brown (Great Britain; b. 1 Apr 1949) at Basildon, Great Britain on 13 Jul 1991.

TRACK WALKING WORLD RECORDS

The International Amateur Athletic Federation recognizes men's records at 20 km, 30 km, 50 km and 2 hours, and women's at 5 km and 10 km.

MEN

Event	hr:min:sec	Name & Country	Place	Date
10 km	38:02.60	Jozef Pribilinec (Czechoslovakia; b. 6 Jul 1960)	Banská Bystrica, Czechoslovakia	30 Aug 1985
20 km	1:18:35.2	Stefan Johansson (Sweden; b. 11 Apr 1967	Fana, Norway	18 May 1992
30 km	2:01:44.1	Maurizio Damilano (Italy; b. 6 Apr 1957)	Cuneo, Italy	4 Oct 1992
50 km	3:41:38.4	Raul Gonzalez (Mexico; b. 29 Feb 1952)	Fana, Norway	25 May 1979
1 hour	15,447 m	Josef Pribilinec (Czechoslovakia)	Hildesheim, Germany	6 Sep 1986
2 hours	29,572 m	Maurizio Damilano (Italy)	Cuneo, Italy	4 Oct 1992

WOMEN

Event	hr:min:sec	Name & Country	Place	Date
3 km	11:51.26	Kerry Ann Saxby (Australia; b. 2 Jun 1961)	Melbourne, Australia	7 Feb 1991
5 km	20:07.52	Beate Anders (East Germany; b. 4 Feb 1968)	Rostock, Germany	23 Jun 1990
10 km	41:56.23	Nadezhda Ryashkina (USSR; b. 22 Jan 1967)	Seattle, WA	24 Jul 1990

Walking on hands The distance record for walking on hands is 870 miles, by Johann Hurlinger of Austria, who in 55 daily 10 hr stints averaged 1.58 mph from Vienna, Austria to Paris, France in 1900. The four-man relay team of David Lutterman, Brendan Price, Philip Savage and Danny Scannell covered 1 mile in 24 min 48 sec on 15 Mar 1987 at Knoxville, TN.

Shin Don-mok of South Korea completed a 50-m inverted sprint in 17.44 sec at the Toda Sports Center, Saitama, Japan on 14 Nov 1986.

The fastest performance is by Robert Pietquin (Belgium; b. 1938), who walked 315 miles in the 1980 race in 60 hr 1 min 10 sec (after deducting 4 hr compulsory stops). This represents an average speed of 5.25 mph. Roger Quémener (France) has won a record seven times, 1979, 1983, 1985–89. The first woman to complete the race was Annie van der Meer (Netherlands; b. 24 Feb 1947), who was tenth in 1983 in 82 hr 10 min.

Twenty-four hours The greatest distance walked in 24 hr is 140 miles 1,229 yd, by Paul Forthomme (Belgium) on a road course at Woluwe, Belgium on 13–14 Oct 1984. The best by a woman is 131.27 miles, by Annie van der Meer-Timmerman (Netherlands) at Rouen, France on 10–11 May 1986.

Backwards walking The greatest-ever distance was 8,000 miles, by Plennie L. Wingo (b. 24 Jan 1895), who walked backwards from Santa Monica, CA to Istanbul, Turkey from 15 Apr 1931 to 24 Oct 1932. The longest distance recorded for walking backwards in 24 hr is 95.40 miles, by Anthony Thornton (USA) in Minneapolis, MN on 31 Dec 1988–1 Jan 1989.

TRAMPOLINING

World Championships World Championships were instituted in 1964. The most titles won is nine, by Judy Wills (USA; b. 1948)—a record five individual 1964–68, two pairs 1966–67 and two tumbling 1965–66. The men's record is four, by Yevgeniy Yanes (USSR), two individual 1976 (shared), 1978 and two pairs 1976–78; and Vadim Krasnochapaka (USSR), three pairs 1984–88 and individual 1988. Brett Austine (Australia) won three individual titles at double mini, 1982–86.

United States Championships The American Trampoline & Tumbling Association staged the first national individual trampoline championships in 1947. The inaugural event was open only to men; a women's event was introduced in 1961.

Most titles Stuart Ransom has won a record 12 national titles: six, individual (1975–76, 1978–80, 1982); three, synchronized (1975, 1979–80); and three, double mini-tramp (1979–80, 1982). Leigh Hennessy has won a record 10 women's titles: one, individual (1978); eight, synchronized (1972–73, 1976–78, 1980–82); and one, double mini-tramp (1978).

Somersaults   Christopher Gibson performed 3,025 consecutive somersaults at Shipley Park, Derbyshire, Great Britain on 17 Nov 1989.

The most complete somersaults in one minute is 75, by Richard Cobbing of Lightwater, Great Britain, at British Broadcasting Corporation Television Centre, London, Great Britain on 8 Nov 1989. The most baranis in a minute is 78, by Zoe Finn of Chatham, Great Britain at British Broadcasting Corporation Television Centre, London, Great Britain on 25 Jan 1988.

TRIATHLON

The triathlon combines long-distance swimming, cycling and running. Distances for each of the phases can vary, but for the best established event—the Hawaii Ironman—competitors first swim 2.4 miles, then cycle 112 miles, and finally run a full marathon of 26 miles 385 yards.

Fastest   The fastest time recorded over the Ironman distances is 8 hr 1 min 32 sec, by Dave Scott at Lake Biwa, Japan on 30 Jul 1989. The fastest time record for a woman is 8 hr 55 min, by Paula Newby-Fraser at Roth, Germany on 12 Jul 1992.

World Championships   After earlier abortive efforts, a world governing body, *L'Union Internationale de Triathlon* (UIT), was founded at Avignon, France on 1 Apr 1989, staging the first official World Championships in August 1989.

A World Championship race has been held annually in Nice, France from 1982; the distances are 3,200 m, 120 km and 32 km respectively, with the swim increased to 4,000 m from 1988. Mark Allen (USA) has won ten times, 1982–86, 1989–93. Paula Newby-Fraser (Zimbabwe) has a record four women's wins, 1989–92. The fastest times are: *(men)* 5 hr 46 min 10 sec in 1988, by Mark Allen; *(women)* 6 hr 27 min 6 sec in 1988, by Erin Baker (New Zealand; b. 23 May 1961).

Hawaii Ironman   Instituted in 1978, this is the first, and best known, of the triathlons. The first race, held on 18 Feb 1978, was contested by 15 athletes. The Ironman grew rapidly in popularity, and 1,000 athletes entered the 1984 race. Dave Scott (USA) has won the Ironman a record six times—1980, 1982–84, 1986–87. Mark Allen (USA) holds the record for fastest time, at 8 hr 9 min 8 sec on 10 Oct 1992. The women's event has been won a record five times by Paula Newby-Fraser (Zimbabwe), in 1986, 1988–89, 1991–92. Newby-Fraser holds the course record for women at 8 hr 55 min 28 sec on 10 Oct 1992.

TUG OF WAR

Most titles   The most successful team at the World Championships has been England, which has won 15 titles in all categories, 1975–90. Sweden has won the 520 kg twice and the 560 kg category three times at the Womens' World Championships (held bienially since 1986).

The Wood Treatment team (formerly the Bosley Farmers) of Cheshire, Great Britain won 20 consecutive AAA Catchweight Championships 1959–78, two world titles (1975–76) and 10 European titles at 720 kg. Hilary Brown (b. 13 Apr 1934) was on every team. Trevor Brian Thomas (Great Britain; b. 1943) of British Aircraft Corporation Club is the only holder of three winners' medals in the European Open club competitions and added a world gold medal in 1988.

Longest pulls Duration   The longest recorded pull (prior to the introduction of AAA rules) is one of 2 hr 41 min when "H" Company beat "E" Company of the 2nd Battalion of the Sherwood Foresters (Derbyshire Regiment) at Jubbulpore, India on 12 Aug 1889. The longest recorded pull under AAA rules (in which lying on the ground or entrenching the feet is not permitted) is one of 24 min 45 sec for the first pull between the Republic of Ireland and England during the world championships (640 kg class) at Malmö, Sweden on 18 Sep 1988. The record time for "The Pull" (instituted 1898), across the Black River, between freshman and sophomore teams at Hope College, Holland, MI, is 3 hr 51 min on 23 Sep 1977, but the method of bracing the feet precludes this replacing the preceding records.

Greatest tug of war distance   The longest tug of war is the 1.616 mile Supertug across Little Traverse Bay, Lake Michigan. It has been contested annually since 1980 between two teams of 20 from Bay View Inn and Harbor Inn.

VOLLEYBALL

Most Olympic titles   The sport was introduced to the Olympic Games for both men and women in 1964. The USSR won a record three men's (1964, 1968 and 1980) and four women's (1968, 1972, 1980 and 1988) titles. The only player to win four medals is Inna Valeryevna Ryskal (USSR; b. 15 Jun 1944), who won women's silver medals in 1964 and 1976 and golds in 1968 and 1972. The record for men is held by Yuriy Mikhailovich Poyarkov (USSR; b. 10 Feb 1937), who won gold medals in 1964 and 1968 and a bronze in 1972; and by Katsutoshi Nekoda (Japan; b. 1 Feb 1944), who won gold in 1972, silver in 1968 and bronze in 1964.

United States　The USA won the men's championship in 1984 and 1988. Three men played on each of the winning teams and on the only US teams to win the World Cup (1985) and World Championships (1986): Craig Buck (b. 24 Aug 1958), Charles "Karch" Kiraly (b. 3 Nov 1960), and Stephen Timmons (b. 29 Nov 1958). David Saunders (b. 19 Oct 1960) was a reserve on the 1984 team and played on those of 1986 and 1988. Karch Kiraly is the only player to win an Olympic gold medal and the World Championship of Beach Volleyball.

Most world titles in volleyball　World Championships were instituted in 1949 for men and in 1952 for women. The USSR won six men's titles (1949, 1952, 1960, 1962, 1978 and 1982) and five women's (1952, 1956, 1960, 1970 and 1990).

BEACH VOLLEYBALL

US Championships　Instituted in 1976 as the World Championship of Beach Volleyball, the event became the US Championships in 1989. Staged annually it is the premier event on the AVP tour.

Most wins　Three players have won five titles: Sinjin Smith (USA), 1979 and 1981 (with Karch Kiraly), 1982, 1988 and 1990 (with Randy Stoklos); and Mike Dodd (USA) and Tim Hovland (USA) who teamed up to win the 1983, 1985–87, 1989 titles.

AVP Tour Most wins　Sinjin Smith (USA) has won a record 134 AVP tour events, 1977–93.

Highest earnings　Randy Stoklos has the highest career earnings, reaching $1,209,333 as of 20 Jun 1993.

WATER POLO

Most Olympic titles　Hungary has won the Olympic tournament most often, with six wins, in 1932, 1936, 1952, 1956, 1964 and 1976.

Five players share the record of three gold medals: Britons George Wilkinson (1879–1946), in 1900, 1908, 1912; Paulo "Paul" Radmilovic (1886–1968), and Charles Sidney Smith (1879–1951), in 1908, 1912, 1920; and Hungarians Deszö Gyarmati (b. 23 Oct 1927) and György Kárpáti (b. 23 Jun 1935), in 1952, 1956, and 1964. Paul Radmilovic also won a gold medal for 4 × 200 m freestyle swimming in 1908.

United States　US teams took all the medals in 1904, but there were no foreign contestants. Since then their best result has been silver in 1984 and 1988.

World Championships　This competition was first held at the World Swimming Championships in 1973. The most wins is two, by the USSR, 1975 and 1982, and Yugoslavia, 1986 and 1991. A women's competition was introduced in 1986, when it was won by Australia. The Netherlands won the second women's world title in 1991.

Most goals The greatest number of goals scored by an individual in an international match is 13, by Debbie Handley for Australia (16) *v* Canada (10) at the World Championship in Guayaquil, Ecuador in 1982.

Most international appearances The greatest number of international appearances is 412, by Aleksey Stepanovich Barkalov (USSR; b. 18 Feb 1946), 1965–80.

US National Championships In this competition, inaugurated in 1891, the New York Athletic Club has won a record 25 men's championships: 1892–96, 1903–04, 1906–08, 1922, 1929–31, 1933–35, 1937–39, 1954, 1956, 1960–61, 1971. The women's championship was first held in 1926; the Industry Hills Athletic Club (California) has won a record five titles: 1980–81, 1983–85.

WATERSKIING

Most titles World Overall Championships (instituted 1949) have been won four times by Sammy Duvall (USA; b. 9 Aug 1962), in 1981, 1983, 1985 and 1987, and three times by two women, Willa McGuire (nee Worthington [USA]; b. 1928), in 1949–50 and 1955, and Elizabeth "Liz" Allan-Shetter (USA; b.1951), in 1965, 1969 and 1975. Liz Allan-Shetter has won a record eight individual championship events and is the only person to win all four titles—slalom, jumping, tricks and overall in one year, at Copenhagen, Denmark in 1969. The USA has won the team championship on 17 successive occasions, 1957–89.

United States US national championships were first held at Marine Stadium, Jones Beach State Park, Long Island, NY on 22 Jul 1939. The most overall titles is nine, by Carl Roberge, 1980–83, 1985–88, and 1990. The women's record is eight titles, by Willa Worthington McGuire, 1946–51 and 1954–55, and by Liz Allan-Shetter, 1968–75.

Fastest speed The fastest waterskiing speed recorded is 143.08 mph, by Christopher Michael Massey (Australia) on the Hawkesbury River, Windsor, New South Wales, Australia on 6 Mar 1983. His drag boat driver was Stanley Charles Sainty. Donna Patterson Brice (b. 1953) set a women's record of 111.11 mph at Long Beach, CA on 21 Aug 1977.

Longest run The greatest distance traveled is 1,321.16 miles, by Steve Fontaine (USA) on 24–26 Oct 1988 at Jupiter Hills, FL.

Barefoot The first person to waterski barefoot is reported to be Dick Pope, Jr. at Lake Eloise, FL on 6 Mar 1947. The barefoot duration record is 2 hr 42 min 39 sec, by Billy Nichols (USA; b. 1964) on Lake Weir, FL on 19 Nov

1978. The backwards barefoot record is 1 hr 27 min 3.96 sec, by Steve Fontaine at Jupiter, FL, on 31 Aug 1989.

WATERSKIING RECORDS

Slalom
Men: 3.5 buoys on a 10.25 m line, Andrew Mapple (Great Britain; b. 3 Nov 1958) at Miami, FL on 6 Oct 1991.
Women: 1 buoy on a 10.75 m line, Susi Graham (Canada), and Deena Mapple (nee Brush; USA) at West Palm Beach, FL on 13 Oct 1990, and Kristi Overton (USA) at Shreveport, LA on 25 Jul 1992.

Tricks
Men: 11,150 points, Cory Pickos (USA) at Mulberry, FL on 27 Sep 1992.
Women: 8,580 points, Tawn Larsen (USA) at Groveland, FL on 4 Jul 1991.

Jumping
Men: 208 ft, Sammy Duvall (USA) at Shreveport, LA on 24 Jul 1992.
Women: 156 ft, Deena Mapple (nee Brush; USA) at Charlotte, NC on 9 Jul 1988.

Walking on water Wearing 11-ft water ski shoes, called Skijaks, and using a twin-bladed paddle, David Kiner walked 155 miles on the Hudson River from Albany, NY to Battery Park, New York City. His walk took him 57 hr, from 22–27 Jun 1987.

Rémy Bricka of Paris, France "walked" across the Atlantic Ocean on waterskis 13 ft 9 in long in 1988. Leaving Tenerife, Canary Islands on 2 Apr 1988, he covered 3,502 miles, arriving at Trinidad on 31 May 1988.

He also set a speed record of 7 min 7.41 sec for 1,094 yd in the Olympic pool in Montreal, Canada on 2 Aug 1989. He "walks on water" by having ski-floats attached to his feet and by moving in the same way as in cross-country skiing, using a double-headed paddle instead of ski poles.

Most skiers towed by one boat A record 100 water-skiers were towed on double skis over a nautical mile by the cruiser *Reef Cat* at Cairns, Queensland, Australia on 18 Oct 1986. This feat, organized by the Cairns and District Powerboat and Ski Club, was then replicated by 100 skiers on single skis.

World Championships (instituted 1978)   The most overall titles is four, by Kim Lampard (Australia), 1980, 1982, 1985, 1986; and the men's record is three, by Brett Wing (Australia), 1978, 1980, 1982. The team title has been won five times by Australia, 1978, 1980, 1982, 1985 and 1986.

The official barefoot speed record is 135.74 mph, by Scott Michael Pellaton (b. 8 Oct 1956) over a quarter-mile course at Chandler, CA, in November 1989. The fastest by a woman is 73.67 mph, by Karen Toms (Australia) on the Hawkesbury River, Windsor, New South Wales on 31 Mar 1984.

The fastest official speed backwards barefoot is 62 mph, by Robert Wing (Australia; b. 13 Aug 1957) on 3 Apr 1982.

The barefoot jump record is: *(men)* 86 ft 3 in, by John Kretchman (USA); and *(women)* 54 ft 5 in, by Sharon Stekelenberg (Australia), both in 1991.

WEIGHTLIFTING

Most titles *Olympic*   Norbert Schemansky (USA; b. 30 May 1924) won a record four Olympic medals: gold, middle heavyweight 1952; silver, heavyweight 1948; bronze, heavyweight 1960 and 1964. Three US lifters won two gold medals: John Henry Davis, Jr. (b. 12 Jan 1921), heavyweight 1948 and 1952; Tommy Tamio Kono (b. 27 Jun 1930), lightweight 1952, light heavyweight 1956; Charles Thomas "Chuck" Vinci, Jr. (b. 28 Feb 1933), bantamweight 1956 and 1960.

World   The most world title wins, including Olympic Games, is eight, shared by John Henry Davis (USA; 1921–84) in 1938, 1946–52; Tommy Kono (USA; b. 27 Jun 1930) in 1952–59; and Vasiliy Alekseiev (USSR; b. 7 Jan 1942), 1970–77.

The only American woman to win a world title has been Karyn Marshall, at 82 kg in 1987.

United States   The most US national titles won is 13, by Anthony Terlazzo (1911–66), at 137 lb, 1932 and 1936 and at 148 lb, 1933, 1935, 1937–45.

Youngest world record holder   Naim Suleimanov (later Neum Shalamanov [Bulgaria]; b. 23 Jan 1967) (now Naim Suleymanoğlü of Turkey) set 56 kg world records for clean and jerk (160 kg) and total (285 kg), at 16 yr 62 days, at Allentown, NJ on 26 Mar 1983.

Oldest world record holder   The oldest is Norbert Schemansky (USA), who snatched 164.2 kg in the then unlimited Heavyweight class, aged 37 yr 333 days, at Detroit, MI on 28 Apr 1962.

Heaviest lift to body weight   The first man to clean and jerk more than three times his body weight was Stefan Topurov (Bulgaria), who lifted 396¼ lb at Moscow, USSR on 24 Oct 1983. The first man to snatch two-and-a-half times his own body weight was Naim Suleymanoğlü (Turkey), who lifted 330½ lb at Cardiff, Great Britain, on 27 Apr 1988. The first woman to clean and jerk more than two times her own body weight was Cheng Jinling (China), who lifted 198 lb in the class of the World Championships at Jakarta, Indonesia in December 1988.

Women's World Championships   These are held annually; the first were held at Daytona Beach, FL in October 1987. Women's world records have been ratified for the best marks at these championships. Peng Liping (China) won a record 12 gold medals with snatch, jerk and total in the 52-kg class each year, 1988–89 and 1991–92.

POWERLIFTING

Most world titles World   The winner of the most world titles is Hideaki Inaba (Japan) with 16, at 52 kg, 1974–83, 1985–90. Lamar Gant (USA) holds the record for an American with 15 titles, at 56 kg, 1975–77, 1979, 1982–84; and at 60 kg, 1978, 1980–81 and 1986–90. The most by a woman is six, shared by Beverley Francis (Australia; b. 15 Feb 1955), at 75 kg 1980, 1982; 82.5 kg 1981, 1983–85; and Sisi Dolman (Netherlands) at 52 kg 1985–86, 1988–91.

Timed lifts 24 hours   A deadlifting record of 5,960,631 lb in 24 hr was set by a team of 10 from Her Majesty's Prison, Wayland, Thetford, Great Britain on 10–11 May 1993. The 24-hr deadlift record by an individual is 818,121 lb, by Anthony Wright at Her Majesty's Prison, Featherstone, Wolverhampton, Great Britain, on 31 Aug–1 Sep 1990.

A bench press record of 8,529,699 lb was set by a nine-man team from the Hogarth Barbell Club, Chiswick, London, Great Britain on 18–19 Jul 1987. A squat record of 4,780,994 lb was set by a 10-man team from St Albans Weightlifting Club and Ware Boys Club, Hertfordshire, Great Britain on 20–21 Jul 1986. A record 133,380 arm-curling repetitions using three 48¼-lb weightlifting bars and dumbbells was achieved by a team of nine from Intrim Health and Fitness Club at Gosport, Great Britain on 4–5 Aug 1989.

12 hours   An individual bench press record of 1,134,828 lb was set by John "Jack" Atherton at Her Majesty's Prison, Featherstone, Great Britain on 27 May 1990.

Powerlifting feats   Lamar Gant (USA) was the first man to deadlift five times his own body weight, lifting 661 lb when weighing 132 lb in 1985. The greatest powerlift by a woman is a squat of 628 lb by Lorraine Constanzo (USA) at Dayton, OH on 21 Nov 1987. Cammie Lynn Lusko (USA; b. 5 Apr 1958) became the first woman to lift more than her body weight with one arm, with 131 lb at a body weight of 128.5 lb, at Milwaukee, WI on 21 May 1983.

MEN'S WEIGHTLIFTING RECORDS

Bodyweight Class	Lift	kg	lb	Name & Country	Place	Date
52 kg 114 1/2 lb	Snatch	121	266 3/4	H. Zhuoqiang (China)	Cardiff, Great Britain	31 May 1992
	Jerk	155.5	342 3/4	Ivan Ivanov (Bulgaria)	Donaueschingen, Germany	27 Sep 1991
	Total	272.5	600 3/4	Ivan Ivanov (Bulgaria)	Athens, Greece	16 Sep 1989
56 kg 123 1/4 lb	Snatch	135	297 1/2	Liu Shoubin (China)	Donaueschingen, Germany	28 Sep 1991
	Jerk	171	377	Neno Terziiski (Bulgaria)	Ostrava, Czechoslovakia	6 Sep 1987
	Total	300	661 1/4	Naim Suleimanov (Bulgaria)	Varna, Bulgaria	11 May 1984
60 kg 132 1/4 lb	Snatch	152.5	336	Naim Suleymanoğlü (Turkey)*	Seoul, South Korea	20 Sep 1988
	Jerk	190	418 3/4	Naim Suleymanoğlü (Turkey)*	Seoul, South Korea	20 Sep 1988
	Total	342.5	755	Naim Suleymanoğlü (Turkey)*	Seoul, South Korea	20 Sep 1988
67.5 kg 148 3/4 lb†	Snatch	160	352 3/4	Israil Militosyan (USSR)	Athens, Greece	18 Sep 1989
	Jerk	200.5	442	Mikhail Petrov (Bulgaria)	Ostrava, Czechoslovakia	8 Sep 1987
	Total	355	782 1/2	Mikhail Petrov (Bulgaria)	Seoul, South Korea	5 Dec 1987
75 kg 165 1/4 lb	Snatch	170	374 3/4	Angel Guenchev (Bulgaria)†	Miskolc, Hungary	11 Dec 1987
	Jerk	215.5	475	Aleksandr Varbanov (Bulgaria)	Seoul, South Korea	5 Dec 1987
	Total	382.5	843 1/4	Aleksandr Varbanov (Bulgaria)	Plovdiv, Bulgaria	20 Feb 1988
82.5 kg 181 3/4 lb	Snatch	183	403 1/4	Asen Zlatev (Bulgaria)	Melbourne, Australia	7 Dec 1986
	Jerk	225	496	Asen Zlatev (Bulgaria)	Sofia, Bulgaria	12 Nov 1986
	Total	405	892 3/4	Yurik Vardanyan (USSR)	Varna, Bulgaria	14 Sep 1984
90 kg 198 1/4 lb	Snatch	195.5	431	Blagoi Blagoyev (Bulgaria)	Varna, Bulgaria	1 May 1983
	Jerk	235	518	Anatoliy Khrapatiy (USSR)	Cardiff, Great Britain	29 Apr 1988
	Total	422.5	931 1/4	Viktor Solodov (USSR)	Varna, Bulgaria	15 Sep 1984

100 kg 220¼ lb	Snatch	200.5	442	Nicu Vlad (Romania)	Sofia, Bulgaria	14 Nov 1986
	Jerk	242.5	534½	Aleksandr Popov (USSR)	Tallinn, USSR	5 Mar 1988
	Total	440	970	Yuriy Zakharevich (USSR)	Odessa, USSR	4 Mar 1983
110 kg 242½ lb	Snatch	210	462¾	Yuriy Zakharevich (USSR)	Seoul, South Korea	27 Sep 1988
	Jerk	250.5	552¼	Yuriy Zakharevich (USSR)	Cardiff, Great Britain	30 Apr 1988
	Total	455	003	Yuriy Zakharevich (USSR)	Seoul, South Korea	27 Sep 1988
Over 110 kg 242½ lb	Snatch	216	476	Antonio Krastev (Bulgaria)	Ostrava, Czechoslovakia	13 Sep 1987
	Jerk	266	586¼	Leonid Taranenko (USSR)	Canberra, Australia	26 Nov 1988
	Total	475	1,047	Leonid Taranenko (USSR)	Canberra, Australia	26 Nov 1988

** Formerly Naim Suleimanov or Neum Shalamanov of Bulgaria.*
† Angel Guenchev (Bulgaria) achieved 160 kg snatch, 202.5 kg jerk for a 362.5 kg total at Seoul, South Korea on 21 Sep 1988 but was subsequently disqualified on a positive drug test.

WOMEN'S WEIGHTLIFTING RECORDS

Bodyweight class	Lift	kg	lb	Name & Country	Place	Date
44 kg 97 lb	Snatch	175	165¼	Guan Hong (China)	Varna, Bulgaria	16 May 1992
	Jerk	100	220¼	Guan Hong (China)	Varna, Bulgaria	16 May 1992
	Total	175	385½	Guan Hong (China)	Varna, Bulgaria	16 May 1992
48 kg 105¾ lb	Snatch	182.5	181¼	Liu Xiuhua (China)	Varna, Bulgaria	17 May 1992
	Jerk	105	231¼	Liu Xiuhua (China)	Varna, Bulgaria	17 May 1992
	Total	187.5	413¼	Liu Xiuhia (China)	Varna, Bulgaria	17 May 1992
52 kg 114½ lb	Snatch	187.5	192¾	Peng Liping (China)	Varna, Bulgaria	18 May 1992
	Jerk	115	253½	Peng Liping (China)	Varna, Bulgaria	18 May 1992
	Total	202.5	446¼	Peng Liping (China)	Varna, Bulgaria	18 May 1992

(continued)

Bodyweight class	Lift	kg	lb	Name & Country	Place	Date
56 kg 123 1/4 lb	Snatch	192.5	203 3/4	Sun Caiyan (China)	Varna, Bulgaria	19 May 1992
	Jerk	117.5	259	Sun Caiyan (China)	Varna, Bulgaria	19 May 1992
	Total	210	462 3/4	Sun Caiyan (China)	Varna, Bulgaria	19 May 1992
60 kg 132 1/4 lb	Snatch	197.5	214 3/4	Li Hongyun (China)	Varna, Bulgaria	20 May 1992
	Jerk	125	275 1/2	Li Hongyun (China)	Varna, Bulgaria	20 May 1992
	Total	222.5	490 1/4	Li Hongyun (China)	Varna, Bulgaria	20 May 1992
67.5 kg 148 3/4 lb	Snatch	198	216	Milena Trendafilova (Bulgaria)	Varna, Bulgaria	21 May 1992
	Jerk	130	286 1/2	Gao Lijuan (China)	Varna, Bulgaria	21 May 1992
	Total	222.5	490 1/4	Gao Lijuan (China)	Varna, Bulgaria	21 May 1992
75 kg 165 1/4 lb	Snatch	107.5	236 3/4	Hua Ju (China)	Varna, Bulgaria	22 May 1992
	Jerk	137.5	303	Zhang Xiaoli (China)	Donaueschingen, Germany	3 Oct 1991
	Total	242.5	534 1/2	Zhang Xiaoli (China)	Donaueschingen, Germany	3 Oct 1991
82.5 kg 181 3/4 lb	Snatch	110	242 1/2	Zhang Xiaoli (China)	Varna, Bulgaria	23 May 1992
	Jerk	142.5	314	Zhang Xiaoli (China)	Varna, Bulgaria	23 May 1992
	Total	252.5	556 1/2	Zhang Xaioli (China)	Varna, Bulgaria	23 May 1992
+82.5 kg	Snatch	115	253 1/2	Li Yajuan (China)	Varna, Bulgaria	24 May 1992
	Jerk	150	330 1/2	Li Yajuan (China)	Varna, Bulgaria	24 May 1992
	Total	265	584	Li Yajuan (China)	Varna, Bulgaria	24 May 1992

WORLD POWERLIFTING RECORDS (All weights in kilograms)

MEN

Class	Squat		Bench Press		Deadlift		Total	
52 kg	243	Hideaki Inaba (Japan) 1986	155	Andrzej Stanashek (Poland) 1991	242.5	Dennis Thios (Indonesia) 1990	587.5	Hideaki Inaba 1987
56 kg	248	Magnus Karlsson (Sweden) 1991	166.5	Magnus Karlsson 1991	289.5	Lamar Gant 1982	625	Lamar Gant 1982
60 kg	295	Joe Bradley (USA) 1980	180	Joe Bradley 1980	310	Lamar Gant 1988	707.5	Joe Bradley 1982
67.5 kg	300	Jessie Jackson (USA) 1987	200	Kristoffer Hulecki (Sweden) 1985	316	Daniel Austin (USA) 1991	762.5	Daniel Austin 1989
75 kg	328	Ausby Alexander (USA) 1989	217.5	James Rouse (USA) 1980	333	Jarmo Virtanen (Finland) 1988	850	Rick Gaugler (USA) 1982
82.5 kg	379.5	Mike Bridges (USA) 1982	240	Mike Bridges 1981	357.5	Veli Kumpuniemi (Finland) 1980	952.5	Mike Bridges 1982
90 kg	375	Fred Hatfield (USA) 1980	255	Mike MacDonald (USA) 1980	372.5	Walter Thomas (USA) 1982	937.5	Mike Bridges 1980
100 kg	422.5	Ed Coan (USA) 1989	261.5	Mike MacDonald 1977	378	Ed Coan 1989	1,032.5	Ed Coan 1989
110 kg	393.5	Dan Wohleber (USA) 1981	270	Jeffrey Magruder (USA) 1982	395	John Kuc (USA) 1980	1,000	John Kuc 1980
125 kg	428.5	Kirk Karwoski (USA) 1991	278.5	Tom Hardman (USA) 1982	387.5	Lars Norén (Sweden) 1987	1,005	Ernie Hackett (USA) 1982
125+ kg	445	Dwayne Fely (USA) 1982	300	Bill Kazmaier (USA) 1981	406	Lars Norén 1988	1,100	Bill Kazmaier 1981

WOMEN

Class	Squat		Bench Press		Deadlift		Total	
44 kg	147.5	Raija Koskinen (Finland) 1992	81	Ann Leverett (USA) 1991	165	Nancy Belliveau (USA) 1985	352.5	Marie-France Vassart (Belgium) 1985
48 kg	150	Claudine Cognac (France) 1990	82.5	Michelle Evris (USA) 1981	182.5	Majik Jones (USA) 1984	390	Majik Jones 1984
52 kg	177.5	Mary Jeffrey (USA, nee Ryan) 1991	105	Mary Jeffrey 1991	197.5	Diana Rowell (USA) 1984	452.5	Mary Jeffrey 1991
56 kg	191	Mary Jeffrey 1989	115	Mary Jeffrey 1988	200.5	Joy Burt (Canada) 1989	485	Mary Jeffrey 1988
60 kg	200.5	Ruthi Shafer (USA) 1983	105.5	Judith Auerbach (USA) 1989	213	Ruthi Shafer 1983	502.5	Vicki Steenrod 1985
67.5 kg	230	Ruthi Shafer 1984	120	Vicki Steenrod (USA) 1990	244	Ruthi Shafer 1984	565	Ruthi Shafer 1984
75 kg	235	Cathy Millen (New Zealand) 1991	142.5	Liz Odendaal (Netherlands) 1989	240	Cathy Millen 1991	602.5	Cathy Millen 1991
82.5 kg	240	Cathy Millen 1991	150	Beverley Francis (Aus) 1981	247.5	Cathy Millen 1991	612.5	Cathy Millen 1991
90 kg	252.5	Lorraine Constanzo (USA) 1988	130	Lorraine Constanzo 1988	227.5	Lorraine Constanzo 1988	607.5	Lorraine Constanzo 1988
90 kg	262.5	Lorraine Constanzo 1987	137.5	Myrtle Augee (Great Britain) 1989	237.5	Lorraine Constanzo 1987	622.5	Lorraine Constanzo 1987

WRESTLING

Most titles Olympic Three Olympic titles have been won by Carl Westergren (Sweden; 1895–1958), in 1920, 1924 and 1932; Ivar Johansson (Sweden; 1903–79), in 1932 (two) and 1936; and Aleksandr Vasilyevich Medved (USSR; b. 16 Sep 1937), in 1964, 1968 and 1972. Four Olympic medals were won by Eino Leino (Finland; 1891–1986) at freestyle 1920–32; and by Imre Polyák (Hungary; b. 16 Apr 1932) at Greco-Roman in 1952–64.

Three US wrestlers have won two Olympic freestyle titles: George Nicholas Mehnert (1881–1948), flyweight in 1904 and bantamweight in 1908; John Smith, featherweight in 1988 and 1992; and Bruce Baumgartner, superheavyweight in 1984 and 1992. The only US men to win a Greco-Roman title are Steven Fraser (b. 23 Mar 1953) at light-heavyweight and Jeffrey Blatnick (b. 27 Jul 1957) at super-heavyweight in 1984.

World The freestyler Aleksandr Medved (USSR) won a record 10 World Championships, 1962–64, 1966–72 at three weight categories. The only wrestler to win the same title in seven successive years has been Valeriy Grigoryevich Rezantsev (USSR; b. 2 Feb 1947) in the Greco-Roman 90 kg class in 1970–76, including the Olympic Games of 1972 and 1976.

United States The most world titles won by a US wrestler is six (four world, two Olympic), by John Smith (b. 9 Aug 1965), featherweight 1987–92.

Most wins In international competition, Osamu Watanabe (Japan; b. 21 Oct 1940), the 1964 Olympic freestyle 63 kg champion, was unbeaten and did not concede and score in 189 consecutive matches. Outside of FILA sanctioned competition, Wade Schalles (USA) won 821 bouts from 1964 to 1984, with 530 of these victories by pin.

NCAA Division I Championship Oklahoma State University was the first unofficial national champion, in 1928. Including five unofficial titles, Oklahoma State has won a record 29 NCAA titles, in 1928–31, 1933–35, 1937–1942, 1946, 1948–49, 1954–56, 1958–59, 1961–62, 1964, 1966, 1968, 1971, 1989–90. The

---

Longest sumo bout The longest recorded wrestling bout was one of 11 hr 40 min when Martin Klein (Estonia representing Russia; 1885–1947) beat Alfred Asikáinen (Finland; 1888–1942) for the Greco-Roman 75 kg "A" event silver medal in the 1912 Olympic Games in Stockholm, Sweden.

Heaviest heavyweight The heaviest wrestler in Olympic history was Chris Taylor (1950–79), bronze medalist in the super-heavyweight class in 1972, who stood 6 ft 5 in tall and weighed over 420 lb.

FILA introduced an upper weight limit of 286 lb for international competition in 1985.

University of Iowa has won the most consecutive titles, with nine championships from 1978–86.

SUMO

The sport's origins in Japan date from *c.* 23 B.C. The heaviest-ever *rikishi* is Samoan-American Salevaa Fuali Atisanoe of Hawaii, alias Konishiki, who weighed in at 580 lb at Tokyo's Ryogaku Kokugikau on 4 Jan 1993. Weight is amassed by over-alimentation with a high-protein stew called *chankonabe.*

The most successful wrestlers have been *yokozuna* Sadaji Akiyoshi (b. 1912), alias Futabayama, winner of 69 consecutive bouts in the 1930s; *yokozuna* Koki Naya (b. 1940), alias Taiho ("Great Bird"), who won the Emperor's Cup 32 times up to his retirement in 1971; and the *ozeki* Tameemon Torokichi, alias Raiden (1767–1825), who in 21 years (1789–1810) won 254 bouts and lost only 10, for the highest-ever winning percentage of 96.2. Taiho and Futabayama share the record of eight perfect tournaments without a single loss.

The youngest of the 64 men to attain the rank of *yokozuna* (grand champion) was Toshimitsu Ogata (b. 16 May 1953), alias Kitanoumi, in July 1974 at the age of 21 years and two months. He set a record in 1978, winning 82 of the 90 bouts that top *rikishi* fight annually.

Yokozuna Mitsugu Akimoto (b. 1 Jun 1955), alias Chiyonofuji, set a record for domination of one of the six annual tournaments by winning the Kyushu Basho for eight successive years, 1981–88. He also holds the record for most career wins, 1,045, and *Makunoiuchi* (top division) wins, 807. He retired in May 1991 but remains in sumo as a training coach.

Hawaiian-born Jesse Kuhaulua (b. 16 Jun 1944), now a Japanese citizen named Daigoro Watanabe, alias Takamiyama, and a stablemaster in the Japan Sumo Association with the sumo elder (*toshiyori*) name of Azumazeki

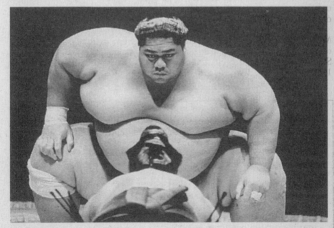

HEAVIEST   The heaviest-ever *rikishi*— Samoan-American Salevaa Fuali Atisanoe, alias Konishiki. (Photo: Allsport/Chris Cole)

Oyakaba, was the first non-Japanese to win an official top-division tournament, in July 1972, and in September 1981 he set a record of 1,231 consecutive top-division bouts.

Yukio Shoji (b. 14 Nov 1948), alias Aobajo, did not miss a single bout in his 22-year career, 1964–86, and contested a record 1,631 consecutive bouts. Kenji Hatano (b. 4 Jan 1948), alias Oshio, contested a record 1,891 nonconsecutive bouts in his 26-year career, 1962–88, the longest in modern sumo history.

Katsumi Yamanaka (b. 16 Mar 1967), alias Akinoshima, set a new *kinboshi* (gold star) record of 13 upsets over *yokozuna* by a *maegashira*.

Hawaiian-born Chad Rowan (b. 8 May 1969), alias Akebono, scored a majority of wins for a record 18 consecutive tournaments, March 1988–March 1991. He became the first foreign *rikishi* to be promoted to the top rank of *yokozuna* in January 1993. He is the tallest (6 ft 8 in) and heaviest (467 1/4 lb) *yokozuna* in Sumo history.

YACHTING

Modern ocean racing (in moderate or small sailing yachts, rather than professionally manned sailing ships) began with a race from Brooklyn, NY to Bermuda, 630 nautical miles, organized by Thomas Fleming Day, editor of the magazine *The Rudder*, in June 1906. The race is still held today in every even-numbered year, though the course is now Newport, RI to Bermuda.

The oldest race for any type of craft and either kind of water (fresh or salt) still regularly held is the Chicago-to-Mackinac race on Lakes Michigan and Huron, first sailed in 1898. It was held again in 1904, then annually until the present day, except for 1917–20. The record for the course (333 nautical miles) is 1 day 1 hr 50 min (average speed 12.89 knots), by the sloop *Pied Piper*, owned by Dick Jennings (USA) in 1987.

The current record holder of the elapsed-time records for both the premier American and British ocean races (the Newport, RI, to Bermuda race and the Fastnet race) is the sloop *Nirvana*, owned by Marvin Green (USA). The record for the Bermuda race, 635 nautical miles, is 2 days 14 hr 29 min, in 1982; and for the Fastnet race, 605 nautical miles, the record is 2 days 12 hr 41 min, in 1985—an average speed of 10.16 knots and 9.97 knots respectively.

Olympic titles   The first sportsman ever to win individual gold medals in four successive Olympic Games was Paul B. Elvström (Denmark; b. 25 Feb 1928), in the Firefly class in 1948 and the Finn class in 1952, 1956 and 1960. He also won eight other world titles in a total of six classes. The lowest number of penalty points by the winner of any class in an Olympic regatta is three points (five wins, one disqualified and one second in seven starts) by *Superdocious* of the Flying Dutchman class (Lt. Rodney Stuart Pattisson [b. 5 Aug 1943] and Iain Somerled Macdonald-Smith [b. 3 Jul 1945]), at Acapulco Bay, Mexico in Oct 1968.

United States   The only US yachtsman to have won two gold medals is Herman Frasch Whiton (1904–67), at six-meter class, in 1948 and 1952.

Admiral's Cup and ocean racing   The ocean racing series with the most partici-

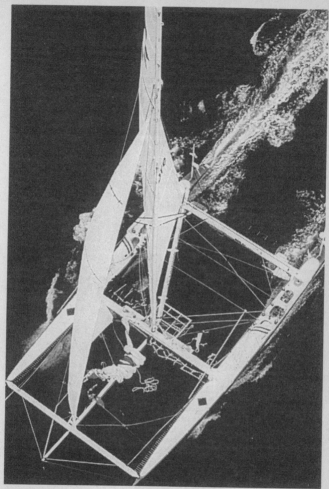

CIRCUMNAVIGATION   Jules Verne Trophy winner *Commodore Explorer* (See p. 292 for full details). (Photo: Allsport/Vandystadt/ Thierry Martinez)

pating nations (three boats allowed to each nation) is the Admiral's Cup, held by the Royal Ocean Racing Club. A record 19 nations competed in 1975, 1977 and 1979. Britain has a record nine wins.

Longest race The world's longest sailing race is the Vendée Globe Challenge, the first of which started from Les Sables d'Olonne, France on 26 Nov 1989. The distance circumnavigated without stopping was 22,500 nautical miles. The race is for boats between 50–60 ft, sailed single-handedly. The record time on the course is 109 days 8 hr 48 min 50 sec, by Titouan Lamazou (France; b. 1955) in the sloop *Ecureuil d'Aquitaine*, which finished at Les Sables on 19 Mar 1990.

The oldest regular sailing race around the world is the quadrennial Whitbread Round the World race (instituted August 1973) organized by the British Royal Naval Sailing Association. It starts in England, and the course around the world and the number of legs with stops at specified ports are varied from race to race. The distance for the 1993–94 race has been set at 32,000 nautical miles from Southampton, Great Britain and return, with stops and restarts at Punta del Este, Uruguay; Fremantle, Australia; Auckland, New Zealand; Punta del Este, Uruguay; and Fort Lauderdale, FL.

America's Cup The America's Cup was originally won as an outright prize (with no special name) by the schooner *America* on 22 Aug 1851 at Cowes,

REGATTAS The most consistently sailed regatta is that at Cowes, Great Britain, where the first race for a gold cup took place on 10 Aug 1826. Since then there has been a regatta with one or more races in early August every year except for 1915–18 and 1940–45. The greatest number of boats to take part in "Cowes Week" was in 1990, when there were 661 in 19 classes. (Photo: Allsport/Russell Cheyne)

Great Britain and was later offered by the New York Yacht Club as a challenge trophy. On 8 Aug 1870 J. Ashbury's *Cambria* (Great Britain) failed to capture the trophy from *Magic*, owned by F. Osgood (USA). The Cup has been challenged 28 times.

The United States was undefeated, winning 77 races and only losing eight, until 1983, when *Australia II*, skippered by John Bertrand and owned by a Perth syndicate headed by Alan Bond, beat *Liberty* 4–3, the narrowest series victory, at Newport, RI.

Dennis Walter Conner (USA; b. 16 Sep 1942) has been helmsman of American boats four times in succession: in 1980, when he successfully defended; in 1983, when he steered the defender, but lost; in 1987, when the American challenger regained the trophy; and in 1988, when he again successfully defended. He was also starting helmsman in 1974, with Ted Hood as skipper.

The largest yacht to have competed in the America's Cup was the 1903 defender, the gaff rigged cutter *Reliance*, with an overall length of 144 ft, a record sail area of 16,160 ft^2 and a rig 175 ft high.

Fastest speeds   The fastest speed reached under sail on water by any craft over a 500-meter timed run is by Thierry Bielak (France) on a boardsailer at 45.34 knots (51.39 mph) at Saintes Maries-de-la-Mer Canal, Camargue, France on 24 Apr 1993.

The women's record is held by boardsailer Babethe Coquelle (France), who achieved 39.70 knots at Tarifa, Spain in July 1991. The fastest speed ever by a true yacht is 36.22 knots (41.68 mph), by Jean Saucet (France) in Charante Maritime on the Bassin de Thau, near Sete, on 5 Oct 1992.

The record for a boat is 43.55 knots (80.65 km/h) by *Longshot*, steered by Russell Long (USA) at Tarifa, Spain in July 1992.

The American with the best time under sail over a 500 meter run is Jimmy Lewis, with 38.68 knots at Saintes Maries-de-la-Mer in February 1988.

Most competitors   The most boats ever to start in a single race was 2,072 in the Round Zeeland (Denmark) race on 21 Jun 1984, over a course of 235 nautical miles.

The largest transoceanic race was the ARC (Atlantic Rally for Cruisers), when 204 boats of the 209 starters from 24 nations completed the race from Las Palmas de Gran Canaria (Canary Islands) to Barbados in 1989.

Boardsailing (windsurfing)   World Championships were first held in 1973 and the sport was added to the Olympic Games in 1984, when the winner was Stephan van den Berg (Netherlands; b. 20 Feb 1962), who also won five world titles 1979–83.

Longest sailboard   The longest snake of sailboards was made by 70 windsurfers in a row at the Sailboard Show '89 event at Narrabeen Lakes, Manly, Australia on 21 Oct 1989.

The world's longest sailboard, 165 ft, was constructed at Fredrikstad, Norway, and first sailed on 28 Jun 1986.

EXTRA! EXTRA!

- **LAST-MINUTE ENTRIES FROM THE LARGEST BLANKET TO THE MOST CONSECUTIVE HOME RUNS**

EARTH & SPACE

Asteroids—number and distance extremes (p. 11)   The closest known approach to the Earth by an asteroid was to within 93,000 miles on 20 May 1993 by 1993KA$_2$, just a few hours before its discovery.

Asteroids—largest and smallest (p. 11)   The smallest asteroid is 1993KA$_2$ (see above), with a diameter of 20 ft.

Highest mountain (p. 29)   The height of Mt Everest announced on 20 Apr 1993 following measurements using the most advanced technology was 29,022 ft 8 in, although this may be revised further since the analysis of the findings is still continuing. The research was carried out by a team of Italian and Chinese scientists.

Worst flood damages   As of 10 Aug 1993 it was reported that an estimated $12 billion in property and agriculture damage had been caused by the great Midwest flood of 1993. The flood affected parts of nine states and covered an area estimated at twice the size of New Jersey.

Worst disasters in the world, table (p. 40)   Earthquake: 830,000, Shaanki, Shanxi and Henan provinces, China, 2 Feb 1556.

Visiting the national parks of the United States   Eloise and Charles Shields visited 331 of the national parks in the United States from 1991–1 Jul 1993. They have traveled over 55,000 miles in their van and have also flown to Hawaii to see seven national parks.

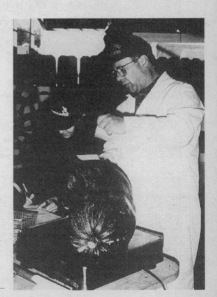

The largest zucchini in the United States, being weighed at the Alaska State Fair 1992.

LIVING WORLD

Tallest chrysanthemum (p. 126)   A chrysanthemum measuring 8 ft 10 in has been grown by Mary Comer of Desford, Great Britain.

Largest zucchini (page 126)   The largest zucchini in the United States weighed 35.6 lb and was grown by David Schroer of Homer, AK in 1992.

HUMAN BEING

Longest mustache (p. 165)   The mustache of Kalyan Ramji Sain had reached a span of 133$\frac{1}{2}$ in (right side 67$\frac{3}{4}$ in and left side 65$\frac{3}{4}$ in) by the end of June 1993.

Card memorizing (p. 169)   Mamoon Tariq (Pakistan) memorized a single pack of shuffled cards in 44.62 sec at the School of Business, Florida Institute of Technology, Melbourne, FL on 14 Jun 1993.

Stretcher bearing (p. 183)   The longest distance a stretcher with a 140 lb "body" has been carried is 167.86 miles, in 49 hr 2 min from 29 Apr–1 May 1993. This was achieved by two teams of four from CFB (Canadian Forces Base) Trenton in and around Trenton, Ontario, Canada.

Heart transplants, longest surviving, living (p. 184)   Arthur F. Gay died of an unrelated illness (cancer of the lesophagus) on 31 May 1993.

SCIENCE & TECHNOLOGY

Scientific instruments   The highest auction price paid for a scientific instrument is £385,000 ($654,500) for a 13$\frac{1}{2}$ in Dutch gilt-brass astrolabe of 1559 by Walter Arsenius, sold at Christie's, London on 29 Sep 1988. The sale of another instrument at auction for £7.7 million on 19 May 1993 has since fallen through.

Transmission lines (p. 205)   The longest power line betweeen pylons spans 17,638 ft across the Ameralik Fjord near Nuuk, Greenland and was constructed by A.S. Betonmast of Oslo, Norway in 1991–92.

Ice-core drilling (p. 213)   The deepest borehole in ice was reported in July 1993 to have reached the bottom of the Greenland ice sheet at a depth of 10,018 ft after five years' drilling by American researchers.

BUILDINGS & STRUCTURES

Brick carrying (p. 247)   The greatest distance achieved for carrying a 9-lb brick is 64 miles, by Ashrita Furman of Jamaica, New York on 13–14 Jun 1993.

Lego tower (p. 256)   The world's tallest Lego tower was 70 ft high and was built by Lego Belgium n.v./s.a. in Brussels on 26–27 Jun 1993.

Building demolished by explosives (p. 268)   The tallest chimney ever demolished by explosives was the Matla Power Station chimney, Kriel, South Africa, on 19 Jul 1981. It stood 902 ft and was brought down by a joint project between Dykon, Inc. of Tulsa, OK and the Santon (Steeplejack) Co. Ltd. of Greater Manchester, Great Britain.

Advertising signs—neon (p. 268)   The largest measures 365 ft 6 in × 62 ft 6 in and was built to promote 999, a traditional Chinese medicine from the Nanfang Pharmaceutical Factory in China. It was erected between November 1992 and April 1993 in Hong Kong and contains 8.16 miles of neon tubing.

Snow and ice constructions—snowman (p. 274)   The tallest stood 86 ft 2 in high and was named Thiro. It was built by Pierre Lacombe and a team of helpers at St Cyrille de Wendover, Quebec, Canada and was completed on 6 Mar 1993.

TRANSPORT

Highest mileage (p. 306)   Albert Klein's "Beetle" had traveled 1,483,938 miles by 5 Jul 1993.

Six continents (p. 306)   Navin Kapila, Man Bahadur and Vijay Raman completed the drive in 39 days 7 hr, driving a Contessa Classic. They left New Delhi, India on 22 Nov 1991 and returned to the same place on 31 Dec 1991.

Parade of Rolls-Royce cars (p. 309)   An uninterrupted parade of 147 Rolls-Royces, organized by the Rolls-Royce Owners' Club of Australia, drove around Lake Wendouree, Ballarat, Victoria on 19 Sep 1992.

Longest scheduled flights (p. 332)   The longest nonstop flight by a commercial airliner was 11,951 miles from Auckland, New Zealand to Le Bourget, Paris, France in 21 hr 46 min on 17–18 Jun 1993 by the Airbus Industrie A340-200. It was the return leg of a flight which had started at Le Bourget the previous day during the Paris Air Show.

Most flying hours—passenger (p. 337)   Fred Finn has now made 704 Concorde flights and his total distance flown has increased to 10,649,000 miles.

Most to jump from a balloon (p. 343)   On 12 Sep 1992 a record fifteen people parachuted from a hot-air balloon over the Somerset/Devon county boundary, Great Britain. The same group made a similar ascent on 1 Oct 1992 and this time a record ten people jumped simultaneously, from a height of 6,000 ft.

BUSINESS WORLD

Rummage sale (p. 353)   The greatest amount of money raised at a one-day sale is $203,247.12, at the 61st one-day rummage sale organized by the Winnetka Congregational Church, IL on 13 May 1993.

Largest lottery   On 7 Jul 1993 the largest lottery in United States' history was won by a couple from Fond du Lac, WI. The prize of $111 million was won by Leslie Robbins and his fiancee Colleen De Vries. The Powerball lottery was played in 14 states and the District of Columbia. The winners produced their winning ticket on 22 July.

Column of coins (p. 362)   The most valuable was worth Cdn$50,358

($39,793.70) and was 6 ft 6 in high. It was built by the Rotary Club for the Kidney Foundation of Canada at Brockville, Ontario, Canada on 8 May 1993.

New York Stock Exchange (p. 365) The highest closing figure on the Dow Jones Industrial index was 3,583.35 on 11 Aug 1993.

ARTS & ENTERTAINMENT

Most rejections (p. 402) Steve Canton of Port Richey, FL received a record 314 rejections (and several non-acknowledgments) of his manuscript "Dusty Roads" between December 1991 and its eventual publication in June 1993.

Oldest choral society (p. 412) The oldest choral society in the United States is the Old Stoughton Musical Society of Stoughton, MA, founded in 1786.

Largest marching band (p. 416) A record 5,034 players performed under the baton of Takeo Suzuki in Kobe, Japan on 20 Jun 1993.

Highest box-office gross (p. 437) Steven Spielberg's *Jurassic Park* (UIP) grossed a record $50,159,460 from 2,404 screens in North America, and a single day record of $18 million on 12 June, during its opening weekend on 11–13 Jun 1993.

HUMAN ACHIEVEMENTS

Wedding ceremonies—greatest attendance (p. 522) An estimated 30,000 guests from the Belz Hassidic community attended the wedding of Aharon Mordechai Rokeah and Sara Lea Lemberger in Jerusalem, Israel on 4 Aug 1993.

Beer stein carrying (p. 524) Duane Osborn covered a distance of 49 ft 2 1/2 in in 3.65 sec with five full steins in each hand in a contest at Cadillac, MI on 10 Jul 1992.

Tightrope walking (p. 530) The tightrope endurance record is 205 days, by Jorge Ojeda-Guzman of Orlando, FL on a wire 36 ft long and 35 ft above ground, from 1 Jan–25 Jul 1993.

Blanket (p. 546) A hand-knitted, machine-knitted and crocheted blanket measuring a world record 186,107.8 ft² was made by members of the Knitting and Crochet Guild worldwide, coordinated by Gloria Buckley of Bradford, Great Britain, and assembled at Dishforth Airfield, Thirsk, Great Britain on 30 May 1993.

Fabrics (p. 550) The oldest surviving fabric, radiocarbon dated to *c.* 7000 B.C. was reported in July 1993 to have been discovered in southeastern Turkey. The semi-fossilized cloth, measuring roughly $3 \times 1 1/2$ in, was believed to be linen.

Can construction A 1:4 scale-model of the Basilica di Sant'Antonio di Padova was built from 3,245,000 empty beverage cans in Padova (Padua), Italy by the charities AMNIUP, AIDO, AVIS and GPDS. The model, measuring $96 \times 75 \times 56$ ft, was completed on 20 Dec 1992 after 20,000 hours.

The world's largest blanket.

Flags (p. 550)   The world's largest flag, measuring 505 × 255 ft and weighing 1.36 tons, is the American "Superflag" owned by "Ski" Demski of Long Beach, CA. It was made by Humphrey's Flag Co. of Pottstown, PA and unfurled on Flag Day, 14 Jun 1992, in Washington, D.C.

Float (p. 550)   The world's largest float, 184 ft 8 in long, produced by the World of Dreams Foundation. It was used at the 169th St. Patrick's Day parade, Montreal, Quebec, Canada on 14 Mar 1993.

SPORTS & GAMES

Auto racing, Formula One Grand Prix (p. 563)   Alain Prost has won 51 Grand Prix races and scored 776.5 points. Riccardo Patrese has started 249 races.

Baseball, Consecutive home runs (p. 572)   On 28 Jul 1993 Ken Griffey Jr., Seattle Mariners (AL) hit a home run in his eighth consecutive game to tie the mark of Dale Long and Don Mattingly. The streak started on 20 July and ended on 29 July.

Baseball, Longest losing streak   On 27 Jun 1993 New York Mets (NL) pitcher Anthony Young achieved the dubious distinction of losing his 24th consecutive decision, a major league record. Young extended the streak to 27 games before gaining a win in the Mets' 5–4 defeat of the Florida Marlins on 28 Jul 1993.

Baseball   Wayne Zumwalt of Colorado Springs, CO attended a major league baseball game at all 28 major league baseball stadiums in 28 consecutive days, from 10 Jun–7 Jul 1993.

The world's largest flag.

Domino stacking (p. 592)   Ralf Laue successfully stacked 296 dominoes on a single supporting domino on 11 Jul 1993 in Leipzig, Germany.

Highest Scrabble scores (p. 595)   The highest score in a tournament Scrabble game (American-style competitive) is 770 points, by game inventor Mark Lansberg of Los Angeles, at the Scrabble tournament in Eagle Rock, CA on 13 Jun 1993. His opponent, Alan Stern, scored 338 points, and their combined total of 1,108 points is also a record for American-style competitive tournament play.

Boxing, Shortest fight (p. 602)   The shortest world title fight was 20 seconds, when Gerald McClellan (USA) beat Jay Bell (USA) in a WBC middle-weight bout at Bayamon, Puerto Rico on 7 Aug 1993.

Card throwing (p. 610)   Jim Karol of North Catasauqua, PA threw a standard playing card 201 ft at Mount Ida College, Newton Centre, MA on 18 Oct 1992.

Cricket, Test records (p. 611)   Allan Border (Australia) has played in 145 Tests, scoring 10,627 runs (average 51.59), and taken 146 catches.

Curling (p. 614)   At the 1993 World Championships, Canada won both the men's and women's title, for the twenty-first and seventh time respectively.

Cycling (table, p. 618)   World record: 1 hour, 52.27 km by Christopher Boardman (Great Britain) at Bordeaux, France on 23 Jul 1993.

Darts, 10-hr Bulls (individual)   1,200, by Johnny Mielcarek (USA) at the Pete Rose Ballpark Cafe, Boca Raton, FL on 27 May 1993.

Speed skating (table, p. 676)   Short track world records, men: 1,500 meters, 2 min 22.36 sec by Eric Flaim (USA) at Beijing, China on 21 Mar 1993. 3,000 meters, 5 min 00.83 sec by Ji-Hoon Chae (South Korea) at Lake Placid on 16 Jan 1993.
Women: 500 meters, 45.60 sec by Zhang Yanmei (China) at Beijing, China on 27 Mar 1993. 1,000 meters, 1 min 37.19 sec by Chun Lee-kyung (South Korea) at Beijing, China on 26 Mar 1993.

Judo, Most throws (p. 680)   Phil Crosby and Frank Lord completed 25,526 throws at The Leys Sports Centre, Redditch, Great Britain on 20 Jun 1993.

Projectiles (page 696)   Boomerang juggling—the number of consecutive catches with two boomerangs, keeping at least one boomerang aloft at all times—is 502, by Chet Snouffer (USA) at Geneva, Switzerland on 22 Aug 1992.
Boomerang throwing—The longest out-and-return distance is 489 ft 3 in by Michel Dufayard (France) on 5 Jul 1992 at Shrewsbury, Great Britain. Robert Parkins (USA) caught 75 boomerang throws in 5 min at Amherst, MA on 9 Aug 1992.
Flying disc throwing (formerly Frisbee)—The 24-hour distance record for a pair is 367.94 miles, by Conrad Damon and Pete Fust (USA) on 24–25 Apr 1993 at San Marino, CA.

Rodeo, Largest loop   Using a 100-ft rope, Ray Kozak spun the largest rodeo loop at 78 ft, on 18 Apr 1993 at the Aladdin Hotel in Las Vegas, NV.

Roller skating, Most titles (p. 701)   Sandro Guerra (Italy) won a record-equaling fifth men's world title in 1992, having previously won in 1987–89 and 1991. Also in 1992 Rafaella del Vinaccio (Italy) won a record fifth women's world title.

Rugby (p. 706)   The highest score in any full international match was 120–3, when Japan beat Singapore in the Asian Championships at Seoul, South Korea on 20 Sep 1992.

Swimming (table, p. 724)   World record: Men's 100 meters breaststroke, 1 min 0.95 sec by Karoly Guttler (Hungary) at Sheffield, Great Britain on 3 Aug 1993.

(table, p. 726)   Short-course world bests: Men's 800 meters freestyle, 7 min 34.90 sec by Kieren Perkins (Australia) at Sydney, Australia on 25 Jul 1993.
Men's 1,500 meters freestyle, 14 min 26.52 sec by Kieren Perkins at Auckland, New Zealand on 15 Jul 1993.

(p. 727)   Women's 24 hour distance record, 57.78 miles by Melissa Cunningham (Australia) at Chandler Aquatic Centre, Brisbane, Australia on 2–3 Jul 1993.
The most participants in a one-day swim relay is 2,305, each swimming a length, organized by the Auburn YMCA-WEIU at Auburn, NY on 5–6 Mar 1993.

Track and field (table, p. 748)   High jump, 8 ft ½ in by Javier Sotomayor (Cuba) at Salamanca, Spain on 27 Jul 1993.

(table, p. 761)   Walking, World best: 10 km, 41 min 30 sec by Ileana Salvador (Italy; b. 16 Jan 1962) at Livorno, Italy on 10 Jul 1993.

Waterskiing, Longest run (p. 770)   The greatest distance traveled is 1,327.65 miles, by Leonard Bonacci (USA) on 21–23 Jun 1993 at Ox Bow Lake, Tunkhannock, PA.

SUBJECT INDEX

How To Use: Major topics are in **boldface** type. Illustration locators are in *italics*. Asterisks* indicate an updated record in Extra! Extra!

A

abbreviations 394
absorbency 191
Academy Awards *See* Oscars
accidents *See* disasters
accountants 349
acids 191
acquired immune deficiency syndrome *See* AIDS
acronym 394
actors and actresses
　all genres
　　most honored entertainer 440
　　number of roles portrayed 428
　　versatility 440
　screen
　　durability 439
　　earnings 437
　　generations in family 439
　　oldest 439
　　Oscar winners 440, *441*
　stage
　　durability 428
　　number of roles 428
　　one-man shows 428
　　Tony winners 428
　television
　　in commercials 445
　　Emmy winners 446
Admiral's Cup 780, 782
advertising
　media
　　magazines 405
　　newspapers 405
　　television 445, 447
　signs *267*, 267–268, 787*
aerial acts 430
acrobatics 558
aerobics 658
aerospace company 332
agriculture 369–381
aid *See* foreign aid

AIDS (acquired immune deficiency syndrome) 175
　statistics (U.S.) 175
aircraft 326–345 *See also* balloons and ballooning; space flight
　disasters 456, 457
　flights 326–328, 330, 331, 332, 333, 334, 335–336, 787*
　microlighting *See* microlighting
　personal aviation records 337, 787*
　size 328–331, *329*
　　bombers 331
　　jets *329*, 331
　speed 333, 334–336, *336*
　　autogyros 340
　　bombers 331
　　helicopters *338*, 339
　　jet airliners 331
　types
　　electric 328
　　propeller-driven 330, 335, *336*
aircraft carriers 284, *285*, 286
　landings 283
air forces 499–500
　jet aces 500
　long-range attacks by 497
airlines 332
　airship fleets 341
　scheduled flights 332, 334
airports 337–339
　runways 328
air racing 559
airships 341
Alabama
　governors 470
　high point 30
　secession 460
Alaska
　city latitude 463
　coastline 24
　county size 460
　deep point offshore 18
　earthquake 41
　forest 136
　glaciers 39
　governors 470
　high point 30, 31
　land area 25
　oil pipeline 210
　oil spill *216–217*

park 141
　tidal range 23
　weather
　　barometric pressure 52
　　snowfall 50
　　temperature 48
albatrosses 81, 88, 91
albums *See* recordings
alcoholic drinks 542–545
　consumption of 255, 542
　blood alcohol level 173
　strength (proof) 544
algae 122, 137
alimony suit 480
alkalis 191
All About Eve (film) 440
alligator 91
　prehistoric 118–119
alphabet 391–392
Alpha Centauri (star) 4
alphorn 415
alpine slide 597
Amazon River 33–34, 35
amber 56
ambulances 310
America/Americas, crossings of *See* trans-America/ Americas crossings
American Museum of Natural History (New York City) 406
American Telephone & Telegraph Co. *See* AT&T
America's Cup 782–783
amphibians 96–97
　poisonous 60
　prehistoric 121
amphibious circumnavigation 306
amphitheater 427
amputation 183
amusement parks 250
　traveling 432
anaconda 94
anagrams 392, 394
anatomy and physiology (human) 162–185
anesthesia 182
Angel Falls (Venezuela) *21*, 33
　rappeling 685
Angkor Wat (Cambodia) 506

Anheuser-Busch Inc. 542
animal husbandry 369
animals 59–121
anorexia nervosa 152
Antarctic region *See also*
    South Pole
  expeditions *514,*
    515–517
    sled journeys 515–516
  habitation 241, 451
  plants 122
  remotest tree 136
antelopes 65, 71–72 *See*
    also springbok
anthems, national 410, 411
antiques 387–389
  London Bridge sale 260
antlers 73
  prehistoric 120
aorta 173
apartment houses 243
aphid 59
apology, belated 405
applause *See* clapping
apple 126
  peeling and pickling 129
  pie 532
aquaria 142
aqueducts 261
arachnids 103–105
archery 559–561
  arrow flight 696
  longbow draw 561
  world records 560
arches
  manmade 259 *See also*
    bridges
  natural 39
archipelago 26
Arctic region *See also*
    North Pole
  habitation 241
  northernmost land 26
  plants 122, 131
  sea-ice crossing 517
aria, operatic 420
aridity and drought 46–48
Arizona
  cactus 125
  copper mine 214
  crater formed by
    asteroid *16,* 17
  fountain 270–271, *271*
  gorge 37
  governors 470
  high point 30
  nuclear power 204
  rose tree 129
  spoil dump 214
  sunshine 51
Arkansas
  chicken production 377
  governors 470
  high point 30
  secession 460
Arlington (Va.) National
    Cemetery 269
armadillos 65

armed forces 497–500,
    498
armies 498–499
armor 502
arrests (judicial)
  of individual 488
  mass 489
arrow flight 696
art
  origins of 383
  paintings *See* paintings
  sculpture *See* sculpture
arteriosclerosis 176
artery 173
artistic productivity *See*
    prolificacy
art nouveau 387
arts festival 429
ascendants, living 157
aspidistra 124
assassinations 482–483,
    482
asteroids 11, 785*
  craters formed by 16–17
  dinosaur extinction
    linked to 114
astronauts 231–232
  lunar elevation 12
  singing by 411
Atlantic Ocean
  crossings
    by balloon 342
    by plane 326–327,
      335, 337
    by ship 291, 292–293
  transmissions
    radio 442
    television 444
atlases 398
atoll 28
atomic bombs *See* nuclear
    weapons
atomic pile 204
AT&T (American
    Telephone &
    Telegraph Co.)
  223–224, 347, 366
attendance *See also*
    audiences
  amusement park 250
  barbecue 533
  sporting events
    baseball 575, 577,
      789*
    basketball 579, 584,
      587
    boxing 603
    field hockey 627
    football (college) 640
    Gaelic Football 641
    hurling 673
    jai alai 678
    Olympics 558, 687
    soccer 558, 719
    squash 721
    tennis 742
  stockholders meeting
    366

succession of schools
    504
Sunday school 511
trial 480
wedding 522, 788*
auctions *See also specific*
    categories of objects
    (e.g., antiques)
  duration 388
  magnitude 348
audiences
  circus 430
  concerts 417, *418,* 419
  movie theater 441
  radio 443
  television 446
Auld Lang Syne (song) 411
aurorae (borealis and
    australis) 13
authors 401–402
  pay-per-word 401–402
autographs 401
autogyros 340
automobiles 301–310
  battery-powered *307,*
    309
  engine capacity 304
  ferries for 289
  mileage
    one-year 306
    per gallon 308
    total 306, *307,* 787*
  origins 298
  price extremes 304–305
  production 303–305
  registrations 302
  services 317–318
  size 304
  speed 62, *303,* 305–306
  weight 304
  wrecking 309, 316
auto racing 561–567
  drag racing 567
  Formula One Grand
    Prix 563–564, *564,*
    789*
  Indianapolis 500
    561–562, 563
  Indy Car
    Championships
    (CART) 562
  Le Mans 565
  NASCAR 562, 563
  rallying 565, *566,* 567
avalanches 40, 43
aviation *See* aircraft
avocado 130
awards *See* honors; *specific*
    awards (e.g., Tony
    awards)
axes 545–546
Ayers Rock (Australia) 25

B

babies 153–154
  birth weights 153

dentition 165, *166*
premature 153, 154
test-tube 153–154
backgammon 592
backwards
motorcycle riding 301
running 753
somersaults 658
talking 172
unicycle riding 298
walking 766
bacteria 138–140, *139*
badminton 567–568
Baker & McKenzie 482
balance (scale) 194
balance of payments 354
balancing
of cigar boxes 525
of coins 362
of golf balls 652
of milk bottles 527–528
of milk crates 528
on one foot 162
bale rolling 371
baling 370
ball, string 553
ballet 420–421
balloon
inflation 172
sculpture 546, *547*
balloons (aircraft)
342–343
Everest overflight 343
team jump 343, 787*
ballroom dancing 425
bamboo 122, 132
banana split 532
Banca Nazionale del
Lavoro (Italy) 483
bands (musical ensembles)
416, 788*
bank notes 359–360
collections 360
forgeries 483
Bank of New York, The
349
bankruptcies 348–349
banks 349
fraud 483
robberies 485, 486
banquets 522–523
barbecue 533
barbers 162
bareback riding 700
barges 287
barley 372, *373*
barometer 193
barometric pressure 52
barracudas 628
barrel
jumping
on ice skates 674
on roller skates 703
racing (women's rodeo
event) 700
rolling 523–524
bars (taverns) 255–256
barter deal 348

baseball 568–579
college 578–579
major league 568–578,
572, 789*
league championship
series 575, 577, 578
personal mail 400
World Series 575,
576–577, *577*
world amateur
championships 579
baseball bat 569
baseballs
distance thrown 569
held in one hand 571
basin, river 34
basket 546
hanging 124
basketball 579–589
NBA 579–584, *580*
NCAA 584–587
Division I records
585, *586*, 587
Olympic games 587,
588, 589
women's 587
world titles 589
basketball spinning *588,*
589
bass (fish) 628
bat, baseball 569
bathtub racing *288*, 524
Batman (film) 437
Batman Returns (film) 437
baton twirling 415
bats (mammals) 64, 69–70
hearing acuity 70
batteries 206
car powered by *307,* 309
battles *See* wars and
warfare
battleships 284
bays 19
beach (resort) 250
beach volleyball 769
beans
lima 128
runner 127
beards 165
shaving 162
bears 66–67, *84*
circus 433
bed
making 524
pushing 524
racing 524
beer 542
brewers 542
cans 546
coaster flipping 524
consumption (in bars)
255
keg lifting 524
labels 546
stein carrying 524, 788*
tankard 543
bees, mantle of 106
beet 128

beetles 59, 105, 106, 107
beheadings 487
bells 412–413
Ben Hur (film) 440
bequests 359
to dog 76
best man 521
best-sellers
books 402–403
records 422–425
videos 438
beverages *See specific type
(e.g.,* water)
Bhopal (India) disaster
456, *479,* 479
biathlon 589–590
Bible (book)
distribution 402–403
mechanical printing 396
price for 398
biceps 168
bicycles 296–298
bridges 257, *258,* 259
Billboard (magazine)
charts 424
billboard 268
billiards 590–591
billionaires *See*
millionaires
bills (of birds) 89, *90*
bingo 591
biplane
size 330
speed 335
birds 81–91, *86–87*
longevity of caged 80
prehistoric 120–121
talking 82
bird-watching 91
birthday party 523
birthrate (human) 453,
455
births *See also* babies
multiple 152–157
postmortem 180
by transplantee 185
birth weights (human) *See
under* babies
birth weights (livestock)
cattle 375
pigs 377
sheep 380–381
bishops 508, 510–511
bite strength
animal 59
human 168
bitterness 191
bivalves 111–112
bivouacking 687
blackbird 83
black holes 6–7
blackouts 206
blankets 387, 546, 788*,
789* *See also* quilt
blast furnace 207
blimps *See* airships
blood 173
alcohol level 173

cells (size/memory) 174
hemodialysis 182
blooms and flowers
122–125, *123*
Blue Cross and Blue
Shield Association
352
bluefish 628
boa constrictor 94
board games 591–596,
791*
boardsailing (windsurfing)
783
boating *See also specific
sport (e.g., power-
boat racing)*
boats *See ships*
boats, model *See model
boats*
bobsledding 596, 597
Boeing Co. 247, 332
boilers 205
boiling point *189,* 190
bomber planes 331
bombs 500–501
disasters (conventional/
atomic/terrorist)
456, 457
bonefish 628
bones
dinosaur 116
human 167
cell longevity 174
bonfire 268
books *See also types of
books (e.g., novels)*
best-selling 402–403
mechanical printing of
396
miniature 396
overdue 406
prices 398
slow-selling 402
bookstores 404
boomerang
juggling/throwing
697, 791*
bores, river *See river bores*
borings and mines
212–215
disasters 456, 457
penetration *21,* 212,
519–521
Boston (Massachusetts)
art theft 486
choral society 412
marathon 762–763
orchestral performance
416
bottle caps
collection 546
pyramid 546
bottle orchestra 415
bottles
antiques 387
collections 546
messages in 283
wine and spirit 542–543

boundaries, geographical
450–451
bowl
strawberry 541
wooden 546
bowling 598–602
boxing 602–607, *603,* 791*
box-office grosses 437,
441, 788*
Bozo the Clown (TV show)
445
brain
dinosaur 117
human 168–169
cells (size/longevity)
174
brass, monumental 507
brasses (musical
instruments) 413
bread-baking (field to
loaf) 371
breakwater 268
breeding *See
reproductivity*
brewers 542
brick
carrying 247, 786*
lifting 524–525
throwing 697
brickworks 247
brides/bridegrooms *See
marriage*
bridge, contract (card
game) *See contract
bridge*
bridges 257–260
bicycle *258,* 260
bridge-tunnels 266
cable suspension 257,
259
cantilever 259
concrete arch 259
covered *258,* 259
floating 260
railway 259, 260
road 260
ropeways 211
steel arch 259
stone arch 259
broadcasting *See radio;
television*
broadsheet 398
Broadway shows *See
theater*
Brothers in Arms
(recording) 425
bubble 525
bubble chamber 194
bubble-gum blowing 525
budgerigar 80
budgets, governmental
354
buildings 241–256
air-supported 249
demolition of 268, 272,
786–787*
for entertainment
248–256

for living 241–245
wooden 240
for working 245–248
industrial 245
bull riding 700
burpees 655
burritos 537
Burson Marsteller (public
relations firm) 405
buses 310–311
two-side-wheel-driving
308–309
Business Week (magazine)
405
bustards 81
butterfat yields 376
butterflies 107–108
flight speed 105
migration *84–85,* 108
wing-beat 107
butterfly farms 108

C

cabbages 126
cables *See bridges; ropes;
telephones*
cacti 125
cakes 533
strawberry shortcake
540
calderas *See
birthweights—
cattle*
roping 700
California *See also Los
Angeles; San
Francisco*
AIDS cases 175
aquarium 142
aqueduct 261
canyon 37
city below sea level 463
county size 460
dam height 264
egg production 377
free-climb site 686
governors 470
high point 30, 31, *32*
low point 28
mountain wall 33
planetarium 226
plant age 121
population 460
65 and over 159
infant mortality 454
live births 453
power
battery 206
nuclear 204
solar 205
prison security 488–489
roller coaster 252
runway length 328
traffic volume 318
tree
age 134, *135*

height 135
size 134
tree fungus 138
trial cost 481
tungsten mine 214
vineyard 130
waterfalls 33
weather
  aridity 47
  snowfall/snow depth
    on ground 50
  temperature 46, *48*
  temperature-
    humidity index 53
  winery 281
caloric value (of fruits and
  vegetables) 130
Cambridge University
  Press (Great
  Britain) 403, *403*
camel, roasted 537
cameras 433–434
Cameroon, Mount 687
campers (vehicles)
  311–312, *311*
camping out 244
Canada, crossing of
  by bicycle 620
  on foot 513, 515
canals 261–263, *262*
  canal-tunnels 266
  cutting depth 263
candles 548
candy 533
cannons 502–503
canoeing 607, *608*,
  609–610
canoes
  antiquity 283
  length 292
  raft of 609
canonizations 507, 508,
  510
cans
  beer 546
  construction made from
    788*
cantaloupe 126
Can't Buy Me Love
  (recording) 424
canyons and gorges 37, *38*
capital cities
  altitude 462
  antiquity 461
  latitude (north/south)
    463
capital punishment 487
car, pedal *See* pedal car
card games 610–611
cardiac arrest 176
cardinals (churchmen) 508
cardiopulmonary
  resuscitation 176
cards
  Christmas 405
  cigarette 548
  credit 549
  greeting 549

playing
  games *See* card
    games
  holding 610
  house of *250*
  memorization 169,
    786*
  price for deck 289
  throwing 610, 791*
cargo, air *See* loads—
  aircraft
cargo vessels 287, 289–290
carillon 413
carnivores 66–68
carp
  catch 628
  longevity 100
  value 100
carpets 548
  antiques 387, 388
carrige driving 302, 623
Carrie (musical) 428
carrot 126
cars *See* automobiles
  model *See* model cars
  slot *See* slot cars
cartoons 408
cash, return of 358–359
casino 254
casket, funeral 268
cassette 421
cassette recorder 422
casting (fishing) 631
castles 241
  sand *240*, 241
catalytic cracker 207
catamaran
  circumnavigation 292,
    781
  size 293
catapults/catapulting 502,
  525
catfish 101, 628
cathedrals 506–507
  clocks *220*, 221
  spires 509, *510*
catherine wheels 549
cats
  domestic 77–78, 79
    popular breeds 78
  wild
    gestation period 66
    size 67–68
cattle 374–376
  horns 74
  prices 374
  ranches 370
caves *21*, 28–29
caviar 100
CDs *See* compact discs
celery 126
cello 414
cells 174
cemeteries 269
centenarians 158–159,
  160–161, *161*
centipedes 108–109
  human 526

prehistoric 117
centrifuge 195
cephalopods *110*, 110–111
ceramics 387 *See also*
  pottery
chain
  daisy 124
  gum wrapper 526
  paper 529
Challenger (U.S. space
  shuttle) 233, 237
champagne
  cork flight 544
  fountain 544
  maker 544
chandeliers 548
Channel Tunnel 265, 322
charity fund-raising 363
  sponsored swim 732
check
  amount 360
  physical dimensions
    548
checkers 591–592
cheese
  production/
    consumption 376
  size 533
cheetah 65
chelonians 92–93
  prehistoric 119
Chemical Abstracts (index)
  187
chemical elements *See*
  elements
chemical extremes
  191–192
chemical formula 140
chemicals
  industrial disasters 456,
    479, 479
  lethal 191
  manufacturing 187
chemical warfare 497
cherry pie 533
chess 592, *593*, 594–595
chest measurements 167
Chicago (Illinois)
  AIDS cases 175
  air traffic 338
  apartment house 243
  atomic pile 204
  church spire 509
  clock 221
  office building 248
  opera house 420
  planetarium 226
  public library 405–406
  sewerage tunneling 266
  subway platform 325
  zoo attendance 141
chickens 377–378
  farms 370
  plucking 371
chimneys 269
  demolition of 268, 786*
chimpanzee 68
chins (exercise) 655

chip, computer 200–201, 201
chocolate
    factory 349
    model 533
choir 417
choral societies 412, 788*
chorister 507
Chorus Line, A (musical) 427
chorus lines 429
Christmas
    cards 405
    parade float 550
    party 523
    snapper *547,* 548
    tree 132
Christ Presented to the People (Rembrandt print) 386
chrysanthemum 126, 786*
chukkas *See* polo
churches (and other places of worship) 506–507, 509–510, 511
    personnel 507, 510–511
cicada 106
cigar boxes
    balancing of 525
    pirouettes with 532
cigarette cards 548
cigarette packs 548
cigarettes 548
cigars 548–549
cinema *See* movies
circular storm 40
circumnavigation
    by air 327, 333, 334, 335–336
    on helicopter 340
    on scheduled flights 334
    by amphibious vehicle 306
    by catamaran 292, *781*
    on foot 513
    polar 516–517
circus 430–433
Cirque d'Hiver (Paris, France) 430, *431*
Citibank, N.A. 349
cities 461–463, *461*
civil damages 479
civil wars 494
    United States (1861–65) 496
clams 63, 111
clapping 417
    by TV personality 445
claws, dinosaur 118
clay pigeon 707
Cleopatra (film) 437, 439
clergy *See* churches—personnel
cliffs 39
climbing
    by aircraft 336
    by cat 78

by humans
    building face 685
    mountain *See* mountaineering
    stair 276
    tree 132
clocks *220,* 220–222
clouds 50–51
    noctilucent 13
clovers 131
club swinging 658
CN Tower (Toronto, Canada) 256–257
    leap from 438
    rappeling 685
coaching 302
coal
    mines 214
    disasters 456
    shoveling 213
coasters (for drinks) 549
coastline
    any country *450*
    United States 24
cobras 94, 96
Coca-Cola Co. 545
cockatoo 83
cockroaches 62, 105–106, *106*
cocktail 533
coconut 131
cod 628
code, judicial 478
codicils *See* wills—texts
coffin 268
cognac firm 544
coins 360–363
    balancing 362
    column of 362, 787–788*
    line of *362,* 363
    pile of 363
    set of 361
    snatching 362
cold
    planetary 8
    terrestrial (cold places) 48–49
collard 128
colleges *See* education
collision, marine 287
colonies (of countries) 449
colonies, animal
    bat 70
    prairie dog 60–61
Colorado
    bridge height 260
    city altitude 462
    governors 470
    high point 30
    observatory 227
    tunnel railroad 265
color sensitivity/color blindness 166
columnists, syndicated 407–408
columns
    architectural 269, 273

cave 29
    of coins 362, 787–788*
coma 176
combine harvesting 371
comets 13–14, *14*
comic strips *See* cartoons
Coming Through the Rye (Remington sculpture) 387
commerce 347–353
commercials *See* advertising
Commodities Exchange (COMEX) *See* gold—prices; silver—prices
compact discs (CDs) 424–425
compilations, literary 396
composers 419
    versatility 440
computers 199–203
    fraud 483
    human 169
concert attendance 417, *418,* 419
conch 112
Concorde (supersonic aircraft) *See* supersonic flight
concrete
    arch 259
    dam 263
    pumping 264
condiment 537
condors 81, 90
conductors, orchestral 416
confectioners 349
Confederate states 460
confinements *See* pregnancies, multiple
conga line 425
Congress (U.S.) 472–473
    campaign spending 473
    filibusters 473
    length of service 472, 473
    Library of Congress 404–405
    Medal of Honor 492
    roll calls 469
    salaries 473
conjunctions, planetary 9
Connecticut
    governors 470
    high point 30
    original statehood 460
    per capita income 355
    refuse electrical generation plant 274
conscripts 496

consonants 391
constellations 7
Constitution 475
  amendment ratification
    time 469
construction
  public works 245
  residential 243
containerships 287
  Pacific crossings by 293
continents 25–26
contract bridge (card
  game) 610–611
contracts
  recording artists 424
  sports coverage 557–558
  TV personality 446–447
conveyor belts 207
cookie *534–536*
cooling towers 269, *269*
Coors Brewing Co. 542
copper mines 214
coral 113 *See also* Great
    Barrier Reef
coral snake 96
cork, champagne (distance
  flown) 544
corn
  plant height 128
  production 372
cornucopia *125*
Coronation Street (TV
    show) 447
corporations *See*
    companies
correspondence (letters)
    See letters (mail)
costumes, film 439–440
cotton 372
counties 460
countries 449–451
  coastline *450*
  terrain 449
country dancing 425
coups d'etat 474
courts *See* litigation
cow chip tossing 697
cows
  milk yields 371, 375–376
  prices 374
crabs 102
cranes (birds) 82, 83
cranes (construction) 207
crawler (vehicle) 312
crawling 525
crayfish (crawfish) 102
credit cards 549
crematorium 269–270
crepe 533
  tossing 537
cribbage 611
cricket 611–613, *612*, 791*
crime *See specific crime
    (e.g., murder)*

crime, organized 482
crocheting 525
crocodiles 91, *93*
  prehistoric 119
crop production 372–373,
    373
croquet 613
cross-country running
  613–614
crossword puzzles
  409–410
crowds *See also*
    attendance
crustaceans 102–103
crystal ball 56
cuckoo 91
cucumber 126, 130
  slicing 129
cultural festivals *See* arts
    festivals
curling 614–615, 791*
currents
  electric 193
  ocean 22
curtain calls
  ballerina 421
  opera singer 420
cut (degree of fineness)
  196
cycling 615–616, *617*,
  618–620, 791*
  Tour de France 558,
    617, 619
Cy Young Award 574

D

dahlia 126, 128
daisy chain 124
damages, legal *479*, 479
dams 263–264
  disasters 456, 457
  flood deaths (U.S.) 49
  tidal river barriers 276
dancing 425–426
  ballet *See* ballet
  square dance calling
    426
dancing dragon 426
Dancing Faun, The (de
    Vries sculpture)
    387
Dark Side of the Moon
    (recording) 424
darts 620–622, *621*, 791*
Davis Cup *740*, 741
Daytona 500 (auto race)
    563
death
  leading cause of 176
  penalty (capital
    punishment) 487
  rate 454
death row 487
Death Valley (California)
  28, 47, *48*, 53
debating 389

debt
  foreign 355
  national 355
decathlon *746–747*, 749,
    755
Declaration of
    Independence 398
decorations *See* honors
deer 72
  prehistoric 120
defamation *See* libel
    damages
defense spending 497
degrees, honorary 493
Delaware
  counties 460
  governors 470
  high point 30
  original statehood 460
delta 35
demography *See*
    population
demolition
  by explosives 268,
    786–787*
  by foot and hand 272
demonstration, political
  458
density 189, 191–192
dentists and dentistry 165,
  458
dentition 165–166, *166*
department stores 349
depressions (terrestrial)
  28
descendants, living
  153–158
deserts 37
destroyers (ships) 284
diamonds 53–54, *54*
diaries 400
dictionaries 396–397
diesel engines 208
dieting, weight lost
  through 151
dimensions *See specific
    type (e.g., height)*
dining out
  altitude 522
  frequency 523
dinosaurs 114–118, *115*
dioxin 191
directors, movie 439
dirigibles *See* airships
disasters 40, 325, 456–457,
  558, 785* *See also
    specific types (e.g.,
    earthquakes)*
diseases 175–176
  mortality rates 175
  pandemics/flu
    epidemics 456
  potency of infectious
    agents 176
Disneyland (Anaheim,
    Calif.) 250
Disney World (Orlando,
    Fla.)

resort size 250
sundial 221–222
distillers 544
diving
  by birds 89
  by humans
    deep 20, 517–519
    high 432, 733
    high-altitude 519
    springboard/platform 732–733
    underwater cave 29
  by seals 69
  by turtles 93
  by whales 63
divorce 454, 521, 522
  alimony suit 480
  settlement 480
DNA (deoxyribonucleic acid) 140
doctorate 504
doctors See physicians
dogs 75–77
  greyhound racing 653–654
  guide dog period of service 77
  litter size 79
  popular breeds 76
  show 76
  tracking 76
doll, rag 549
dolphin 64–65
domes 270 See also stadiums
domino stacking/toppling 592, 791*
donkeys, price of 374
Donnelley & Sons Co., R.R. 404
doors 270
double bass (musical instrument) 414
doughnut 533
Dow Jones Industrial average 365, 788*
dowry 358
draglines 208
dragon, dancing 426
dragon boat racing 704
dragonflies 107
  prehistoric 121
drag racing 567
drawing (art work) 386
dreams 176–177
dredger 289
dressage 624, 625
Drexel Burnham Lambert Group 359, 488
dribbling (basketball) 581
drill, military 499
drilling
  Earth's crust 21, 212
  footage in a month 212
  ice-core 213, 786*
  ocean 212
  road (decibel level) 171

drinks See specific type (e.g., alcoholic drinks)
drivers See also driving
  car
    age 309
    durability 309
    incompetence 309
    licensing of 310
  taxi 314
driving 306–310
  fuel range 308
  on lawn mower 313
  in reverse 308
  tests 309–310
  trans-America/ Americas 306, 308
drought See aridity
drugs (illegal) See narcotics
drug stores 349
drums and drumming 414, 415
drunkenness, arrests for 173
dry dock 295
dry places See aridity
ducks
  domesticated 378
  wild 83, 89
ductility 190
dunes, sand 37
dunking (basketball) 584
dwarfs, human 150–151

E

eagles 88, 89
earrings 549–550
ears, rabbit 80
Earth (planet)
  age 24
  density 9
  land surface 23–24
  structure and dimensions 17–39
  water surface 18
earthmover 208
earthquakes 39, 40, 41, 785*
earthworks 270
earthworm 109–110
Easter egg 537
Eastman Kodak Co. 480
eating
  by any animal 61
  by humans
    of food See food; dieting
    of metal and glass 181
eating out See dining out
echo 193
eclipses 12, 13
economics 354–369
editorship, newspaper 407
education 503–505, 505

honorary degrees 493
number of schools attended 504
religious See Sunday school
eels 100
  conger catch 628
egg and spoon racing 525–526
egg dropping 378
egg hunt 526
eggplant 128
eggs
  bird 89–91
  poultry 377–379
  dinosaur 118
  Easter 537
  fish 100
  jeweled 550
egg shelling 378
egg throwing 697
elections
  United States
    congressional 472–473
    presidential 468
  world 475–476
    crooked 474
    hotly contested 474
electric eel 100
electricity See also currents—electric; power plants
  from garbage 274
electric plane 328
electrocution 487
electromagnets See magnets
elements, chemical 187–190
elephants 64, 66
  prehistoric 119–120
  tusks 72, 74
elevators
  disasters 457
  grain 270
  lock (canals) 263
  passenger 209
embassies 248
embroidery 553
embryos, frozen 154
emeralds 54–55
emigration 452
Emmy awards 440, 446
Empire State Building (New York City)
  exterior lighting 272
  stair climbing 276
employer 347
employment agency 353
Enceladus (Saturnian moon) 10
encyclopedias 397
endowment
  museum 385
  university 505
endurance 513–523
energy consumption 365

engagement (premarital)
521
engineering 207–211
engines
diesel 208
jet 326
military (catapults) 502
rocket 228, 230
English (language)
anagrams 392, 394
commonest words/
letters 394
irregular verbs 390
longest word 392
oldest words 389
palindrome 392
prevalence of 390
songs in 410, 411
synonyms 392
vocabulary 390
word with most
meanings 394
English Channel
swimming 734
entertainment *See specific
kinds (e.g., movies)*
epidemics *See diseases*
equestrian sports
622–623, *624,* 625
Equity Funding Corp. 483
escalators 208
riding 209
Eskimo rolls (canoe)
609–610
estuary 34
E.T.: The Extra-Terrestrial
(film) 437
evacuation
civilian 496
military 497
Everest, Mount *21,* 29–30,
32, 785*
balloon flight over 343
bivouacking 687
climbing 685–686, *686*
marathon running 762
Everglades 35
executions *See capital
punishment*
exercises (gymnastics) 655,
656–657, 658
exhibition center 254
explosions
conventional
bombings 500
demolitions 268, 501,
786–787*
disasters 456, 457
nuclear
bombings 456
tests 501
extinct animals 114–121
extras (in movies) 438
extraterrestrial vehicle 238
Exxon Corp. 294, 366
Alaska oil spill *216–217*
eyesight *See vision*
eye size 63

F

fabrics 550, 788*
facsimile (fax) machines
224
fairs 251–252
falcon 83, 89
falconet 81
false teeth 166
families
of actors 439
ascendants/descendants
157–158
college graduates in 504
of doctors 453
wealthy 358
family names 395
family tree 158
famines 456, 457
fan, Spanish 550
fangs (of snakes) 95
Fantasticks, The (musical)
427
Farmer's Almanac, The
(periodical) *See
Old Farmer's
Almanac*
farms 370–371
fashion shows 430
faux pas 353
fax machines *See facsimile
machines*
feasts *See banquets*
feathers 82
fees 359
lecture 505
feet, human 163
felines *See cats*
fences 270
fencing 625–626
NCAA Division I 626
ferns 131–132
ferret 79
ferries
car 289
rail 289
Ferris wheels 251–252, *253*
fertility (of any animal) 59
Few Good Men, A (film)
438
fiber, optical 223
fiction *See novels*
field gun pull *See gun
pulling*
field hockey 626–627
fig tree 124
figure skating *See ice
skating*
filibusters 473
filling stations 317
films *See movies*
fines (judicial) 488
fingernails 162
fingerprint *178–179*
fire
building 456, 457
gas 215

fireball 17
fire-breather 172
fire bucket brigade 525
fire engines 312
fire extinguishers (human)
172
fire pump handling 312
fire pumping 312
fireworks 550
catherine wheels 549
disasters 456
first ladies (wives of U.S.
presidents) 467
fish and chips 255
fisheries *See fishing—
commercial*
fishes 97–101
deep-sea *20,* 99
prehistoric 117, 121
fishing
commercial 369
recreational 630–631
all-tackle records
(freshwater/
saltwater) 628–
629
fjord 19
flagpoles 270
flags 550, 789*, *790**
flame 193
flamenco 425
fleas 107
fleece 379
flight
aircraft *See aircraft—
flights*
arrow 696
birds 83, 88–89
chicken 378
insects 105
floats
parade 550, 789*
soda 541
floods 40, 49, 51, 785*
Florida
AIDS cases 175
aquarium 142
butterfly farm 108
governors 470
high point 30
lightning deaths 52
marsh 35
nudist colony 251
oceanarium 142
population (65 and
over) 159
secession 460
town of European
origin 461
weather
absence of fog 52
mean temperature 46
sunshine 51
weed growth 133
flotation (stocks) 366
flounder 628
flowers *See blooms and
flowers*

flu epidemic *See* influenza epidemic
flying boats 340–341
  wingspan 328, *329*
flying disc (Frisbee) throwing 697, 791*
flying hours 337
flying ring 696
fog 52
food 532–541
  cost 537
  dining out 522, 523
  edible fungi 137, 138
  feasts 522–523, 537
  fruits and vegetables *See* fruits and vegetables
  survival without 181
footbag 631
football 632–641
  NCAA 637–641, *640*
    Division 1-A 638–639
  NFL 632–633, *634*, 635–636, *636*
    deficit overcome 632
    Super Bowl *See* Super Bowl
  TV contract 557–558
footprints
  dinosaur 117
  hominid 145
Forbidden Palace (Beijing, China) *242*, 242, 243
Ford Foundation 359
foreign aid 354
foreign debt 355
forests 136
forgery 483
forging (metal) 208
  presses 210
For He's a Jolly Good Fellow (song) 411
forklift trucks 208
formula, chemical 140
Formula One Grand Prix Motor Racing 563–564, *564*, 789*
fossils
  animal *See* extinct animals
  plant 122
fountain 270–271, *271*
fraud
  bank 483
  computer 483
  maritime 483
  securities 488
French knitting 526
frequency (of light) 193
friction 192
Frisbee *See* flying disc throwing
frogs 60, 96–97
frontiers *See* boundaries
frontón 678
fruits and vegetables 129, 130

world/U.S. biggest specimens 126–128
fuel range (vehicles) 308
fumigation 272
funerals 511
  caskets 268
fungi 137–138
furnace, blast 207
furniture 387–388
fusion power 205

G

Gaelic football 641
galaxies 2–3
gallbladder 182
galleries, art 385
gallstones 183
game reserve 141
gantry crane 207
garages 317
garbage
  can 525
  collection 526
  dump 271
  electricity from 274
garden, community 370
garlic 126
gas, natural
  deposits 215
  fire 215
  pipelines 210
  production 215
  tanks 271
gas, nerve 191
gasoline consumption 308
gas stations *See* filling stations
gastropods 112
gauges, railroad 322
geese
  domesticated 83, 378
  wild 83
gems, jewels and precious stones 53–57
  auctions 388–389
  theft of 486
General Motors Corp. 303, 347–348
generations *See* families
generators 205, 206
genocide 456, 460
geography 17–39 *See also* specific geographic features, (e.g., lakes)
Georgia
  airport terminal 338
  governors 470
  high point 30
  original statehood 460
  secession 460
  Stone Mountain sculpture 385
  tunneling 267
gerbil 79, 80
Germany, Nazi

forgery 483
genocide 460
hanging of Greek resistance fighters 487
Hess imprisonment 489
Reichsbank robbery 485
gestation period
  amphibian 97
  for literary work 400
  mammalian 66
Getty Museum, J. Paul (Malibu, California) 385
geysers 43
g force
  for birds 82
  for human beings 177
  for insects 106, 107
giants, human 146–149, *147*
ginseng 541
giraffe 64
glaciers 39
gladiatorial combat 426, 558
glass
  antiques 388
  blowing 196
  eating 181
  stained 280, 509–510
  thinness 196
  window size 280
globe, revolving 272
goats 376
  prices 374
go karts 312–313
gold
  antiques
    sacred objects 509
    theft of 486
  discs (record sales) 422, 423
  mines 214
    disasters 457
  nuggets 55
  panning 526
  physical properties 190
  prices (COMEX) 366
  reserves 355
Golden Gate Bridge 260
golden handshake 359
"golden set" (tennis) 737
goldfish 99
golf 641–645, *646*, 647–648, *649*, 650–653
  holes in one 651–652
  prize money 651
  PGA tour records 643
golf balls
  balancing 652
  number hit in one hour 645
  throwing 652
Goliath (Biblical giant) 148
gorges *See* canyons

gorillas 68
Gospel Book of Henry the Lion, Duke of Saxony, The (book) 398
gourd 128
governors, U.S. 470–471
grain elevators 270
Grammy awards 416, 422, 440
Grand Canyon (Arizona) 37, *38*
Grand Ole Opry 443
grape catching 129, 525
grapefruit 126
grapes 126 *See also* vines and vineyards
grasses 132
grass skiing 714
grave digging 268
Great Barrier Reef (Australia) 28, 59, 101, 113
Great Wall of China *277*, 280
Great Western Bank Association 353
greeting cards 549
greyhound racing 653–654
grocery stores 349, 352
gross national product (GNP) 355
ground figures (sculpture) 385
guide dog 77
guillotinings *See* beheadings
guinea pig 79, 80
Guinness Book of Records, The (book) 403
guitar 414
gulf 19
gum wrapper chain 526
gun pulling 502
guns 501–503
    antique 388
gymnastics 654–660
    exercises 655
    modern rhythmic 660
    NCAA records 658–659
    Olympic records 654-655, 658
gyroplanes *See* autogyros

H

habitations 241 *See also* housing
hailstones and hailstorms 40, 50
hair, human
    length 163, *163*
    monetary value *164*, 165
    splitting 162, 196
halibut 628

halites 33
Halley's Comet 13, *14*
hamburger 537
Hanleys (London toy store) *350–351*
ham radio operator 443
hamster 79
handball, team *See* team handball
handcar racing 324
"hand rolls" (canoe) *608*, 610
handshaking *468*, 469
hangars 339
hang gliding 717–718
hanging basket 124
hangings (capital punishment) 487
Happy Birthday to You (song) 411
harbors *See* ports
hardness (physical property) 190
hare 80
harem 254
harness racing 660–661
    mile records 660
harpooning 630
Hartford Courant (newspaper) 406
Hawaii
    city latitude 463
    cliffs 39
    governors 470
    high point 30, 31
    housing costs 243
    Ironman triathlon 767
    rainfall/rainy days 49
    road mileage 318
    volcano 42–43
    wind generator 206
heads of state 463–465, *464*
    meeting 465
hearing
    of bats 70
    of humans 173
hearing, judicial 478
heart
    artificial 184–185
    stoppage 176
    synthetic implant 185
    transplants 184–185, 786*
heat
    oceanic 19
    planetary 8, 9
    terrestrial (hot places) 46, *48*
heat endurance 177
hedgehog 71
height, human 146–149, *147*
    in baseball 574
    in basketball 581
    in boxing 602, 604
    of president (U.S.) 466
    of soldier 499

variability (in single individual)149
Heisman Memorial Trophy 641
helicopters 338, *338*, 339–340
    disasters 457
    salvage operation 519, *520*
helipad 338
Hello Dolly! (musical) 428
helmet 388
hemodialysis 182
Henley Royal Regatta 704
herds 66
Heretics, The (opera) 419
Hermitage (St. Petersburg, Russia) 385
hibernation 70
hiccupping 177
high diving 432, 733
highways *See* roads
high wire *See* tightrope
hijack ransom *See* ransom payments
hill figure (sculpture) 385
hoards (of coins) 360–361
hockey, ice 661–667
    minor leagues 666–667
    NHL 661–664, *662*
    Stanley Cup 665–666
    world championships/ Olympic games 666
hod carrying 247
hole (minuteness) 193
Holocaust 460
Home Savings of America, FA 353
hominids 145
hominoid 144–145
Homo (genus) 145
    Homo erectus 145
    Homo sapiens 145–146
honors 489–493
    to entertainer 440
    military 492
hop farms 370
hopscotch 526
horns 74 *See also* antlers
horse racing 667–672
    disaster 558
    jockeys 669
        Triple Crown event woman winner 668
    major event records 670–671
    trainers/owners 672
    weight carried 668
horses 74–75
    carriage
        driving/coaching 302, 623
    circus stunts on 432
    prices
        livestock 374
        pacer/trotter 661
        racehorse 668

saddle bronc/bareback riding 700
horseshoe pitching 672
hospitals
    length of stay 177
    number of 453
hotels 244–245
    demolition 268
hot places *See* heat terrestrial
house of cards 250
House of Representatives, U.S. *See* Congress, U.S.
housing 243, 462
    apartments 243
    overcrowding 453
hovercraft *294, 295*
HPVs *See* human-powered vehicles
Hudson Bay (Canada) 19
Hudson Hawk (film) 437
hula-hooping 526
human beings 144–185
    anatomy and physiology 162–185
    dimensions 146–152
    illnesses *See* diseases
    longevity 158–161
    origins 117, 144–146
    population 451–454, 458
    reproductivity 152–158
human cannonball 432
human centipede 526
human fly 685
human-powered flight 337
human-powered ships *See under* ships
human-powered vehicles (HPVs) 296–297
human pyramid 432
    on high wire 430
humidity 52–53
hummingbirds 81, 82, 88, 90–91
hurling 672–673
hurricanes 40, 49, 50
    barometric pressure 52
hydraulic jacks, load raised by 207–208
hydrofoils 290
hydroplanes 293
hymns and hymnists 411–412
Hyperion (Saturnian moon) *10*

I

IBM *See* International Business Machines Corp.
ice
    borehole in (ice-core drilling) 213, 786*
    constructions 274
glaciation 39
    thickness 36
ice and sand yachting 673
icebergs 23
icebreakers 289
ice-cream sundae 537–538
ice hockey *See* hockey
ice pops 538, *539*
ice skating 673–678
    axel jump/back flip 674
    barrel jumping 674
    figure skating 673–674
    speed skating 675, *675, 678*
        world records 676–677, 791*
Idaho
    canyon 37
    governors 470
    high point 30
Iditarod trail 715
Illinois *See also* Chicago
    governors 470
    high point 30
    nuclear power 204
    sewage works 274, *275*
illnesses *See* diseases
immigration 452–453
immobility *See* motionlessness
Imperial Palace (Beijing, China) *See* Forbidden Palace
imprisonment, wrongful 479–480
incomes 358
In Concert (recording) 422
incubation (of bird eggs) 91
index 187
Indiana
    governors 470
    high point 30
Indianapolis 500 (auto race) 561–562, *563*
Indian Railways 347
industry, prehistoric 347
infant mortality 454
inflation 355–356
influorescence 122–123
influenza epidemic 456
injections 180
inland seas *See* lakes
innumeracy 198
insectivores 71
insects 105–108
    prehistoric 121
insomnia *See* sleeplessness
instruments
    musical 413–415
    scientific 194–197, 786*
    surgical 183
insurance
    companies 352
    fraud 483
    marine 352
    policies 352
Intel Corp. 200, *201*, 203

Interchange (de Kooning painting) 384
International Bank for Reconstruction and Development *See* World Bank
International Business Machines Corp. (IBM) 200, 203
International Paper Corp. 352
invasions, military 496–497
invertebrate size 110
investment
    consultant 359
    house 366–367
in vitro fertilization (IVF) *See* babies—test-tube
Iowa
    governors 470
    high point 30
    hog farming 376
iron
    abundance of 17–18
    mines 214
iron lung *177, 180*
irrigation
    canal 262
    tunnels 266
islands 26–28, *27*
isolation (from fellow human beings) 233
isotopes 188

J

jack-o'lanterns 129
jade 56
    theft of 486
jai alai 556, 678
jail breaks 488–489
Jardin de Fleurs (van Gogh drawing) 386
Jeantet Prize for Medicine, Louis 491
Jehovah's Witnesses 409
Jell-O 538
jellyfish 113
jets
    aces 500
    flights 331
    longevity 331
    origins 326
    passenger load 331
    size *329*, 330, 331
    speed 331, 333, 335
    takeoff noise *171*
jetty, deep-water 271
jewels *See* gems
jigsaw puzzles 550, 552
jiu-jitsu 680
jockeys 669
    Triple Crown race woman winner 668

joggling *See* juggling
Johnson & Johnson 187
judges 481–482
judicial system 478–479
judo 679–680, *679*
throws 680, 791*
juggling 531–532
of boomerangs 697,
791*
joggling 762
of soccer balls 719
jumps
by dogs 76, 77
by fleas 107
by frogs 96–97
by horses *See* show
jumping
by humans *See* ice
skating; pogo stick
jumping, ramp
jumping, roller
skating; skiing;
track and field
by kangaroos 73
junks 291
Jupiter (planet) 8, *8*, 9, 10,
11
Jurassic Park (film) 788*

K

kangaroos 72, 73, *73*
Kansas
drought 47–48
governors 470
grain elevator 270
hailstone 50
high point 30
karate 680
karting *See* go karts
"Katzenjammer Kids,
The" (comic strip)
408
kayaking *See* canoeing
kebab 538
kelp 133
Kentucky
cave system 28
governors 470
high point 30
public hanging 487
kettle 552
kidnapping *See* ransom
payments
kidney
hemodialysis patient
182
transplants 185
killings *see* murder
kings *See* royalty
kissing 526
kitchen 272
kite flying 526–527
knife 552
knitting 527
French 526
scarf length 529

knot-tying 527
Kohlberg Kravis Roberts
(KKR) 348
kohlrabi 128
krill 102
Kroger Co. 349

L

labels
beer 546
matchbox 549
labor 363–365
disputes/strikes 364
unions 363–364
lacrosse 681
NCAA (men/women)
681
lagoon 36
lakes 35–36
artificial 265
lake in a lake 36
underground 36
lamp (art nouveau) 387
lampposts 272
landing fields *See under*
Earth
landowner 352
land rowing 527
landslides 40
land surface *See under*
Earth
language and languages
389–396
lasagne 538
lasers 193, *195*, 195
lathe 208
lava flow 42
law firm 482
lawn mowers 313
laws *See* legislation;
litigation
lawyers (U.S.) 480, 482
lead mine 214
leapfrogging *659*
lease 480
leaves
abundance 136
rustling *170*
size 131
lecture fees 505
leek 126
legislation, inexplicable
469
legislatures
world 473–477
leg lifts 655
Lego
statue 281
tower 256, 552, 786*
legs
centipede 109
millipede 109
lei 129
Le Mans (auto race) 565
lemon 126
lens, camera 434

letters (alphabet) 391–392
letters (mail) 400
amount received 400
pen pals 400
levees 264
libel damages 479
libraries 404–406
license plates 405
licenses, drivers' *See under*
drivers
lichens 122
life
expectancy 158, 458
saving of 458, *459*
lifting operation
(engineering)
207–208
light
brightness 193
pulsation 194
sensitivity 166–167
lighthouses 272
lightning 52
deaths caused by 40, 52
individual struck by 51
limbo (dancing) 425–426
limousine 304
liners, passenger *See*
passenger liners
lines of sight 31
linguistics *See* language
and languages
linguists 390–391, *391*
lions 67
lion-taming 433
lion-tiger hybrid (litogon)
67
liquid ranges 190
literature 396–410
litigation 478
trial attendance 480
litters
caged mammal 79
cat 78, 79
dog 79
rabbit 79, 80
wild mammal 66
liver 180
livestock 374–377,
379–381
prices 374
lizards 92
llamas (in as hitch) 302
loads lifted/moved
by airship 341
by cargo plane 330
by helicopter 340
by hydraulic jacks
207–208
by rail 321–322
by specialized vehicle
315
loaves
production time 371
size 538
lobby, hotel 244
lobsters 102, *103*
locks (of canals) 263

locomotives 320–321
locusts 61
log rolling 527
lollipop 538
London Bridge 260
longbow draw 561
longevity
  amphibians 96
  antelopes 72
  bacteria 138–139
  bats 70
  birds 83
  caged pets 80
  cats 78
  crocodilians 91
  deer 72
  dogs 75–76
  elephants 66
  fish 99–100
  horses 75
  humans 158–161
    boxers 604
    heads of state 476
    popes/cardinals 508
    presidents 466
    prisoners 488
    royalty 464
    vice-presidents (U.S.)
      472
  insectivores 71
  insects 107
  lizards 92
  lobsters 103
  marsupials 73
  mollusks 111
  pinnipeds 69
  primates (nonhuman)
    68–69
  rodents 71
  snakes 94
  spiders 103, *104*
  tortoises 93
  trees 134, *135*
Los Angeles (California)
  advertising sign 267
  AIDS cases 175
  film studio complex 437
  narcotics haul 486
loss, financial
  by corporation 347–348
  by movie 437
  by stage show 428
lottery 787*
loudness *170–171*
  of blue whale 59
  of howling monkey 59
  of insects 106
  of organ stop 413
  screaming/whistling/
    shouting 169–170
  snoring 180
Louisiana
  bridging/railway bridge
    259
  domed stadium 249,
    270
  governors 470
  high point 30

port activity 295
secession 460
university endowment
  505
wetness 49
louse 105
lugeing 596–597
lung
  iron *177*, 180
  power 172
  transplant 184, 185
lynching 485

M

machinery 207–211
Macy & Co., Inc., R.H.
  349
Mafia (La Cosa Nostra)
  482
magazines See periodicals
magician 430
magnets/magnetism 192,
  194, 195
mail
  amount received 400
  postal services 367, 369
  post offices 367
  mailboxes 369
Maine
  city incorporation 461
  cliffs 39
  governors 470
  high point 30
malaria 60
malls 255
mammals 61–80
  marine See marine
    mammals
  prehistoric 119–120
mammoths 119–120
Manhattan Island, swim
  around 732
Manpower Inc. 353
manufactured articles
  545–554
manuscripts
  prices 398, *399*, 400
  rejection slips 402, 788*
  size 396
maps 398
marathons
  dancing 425
  running 762–764
    backwards 753
    spectators 558
march, military
  duration 497
  speed 499
marching bands
  length of march 416
  size 416, 788*
Mariana Trench 18, *20*,
  99, 517
marine mammals
  diving depth 63
  size 61, 63, 64–65

of caught specimen
  630
of prehistoric species
  120
speed 65
weight loss 63
marlin 628–629
marquee 272
marriage See also
  weddings
  age at 521–522
    median (U.S.) 454
  engagement length 521
  frequency 521
  height differential
    152
  length of 522
  rate 454
  tallness of partners
    149
  weight differential
    152
marrow 126
Mars (planet) 9, 10, 11
  meteorites from 17
marsh 35
marsupials 72, 73, *73*
martial arts
  jiu-jitsu 680
  judo 679–680, *679*
  karate 680
  taekwondo 735–736
Maryland
  bishop consecration 511
  governors 470
  high point 30
  original statehood 460
*Mary Tyler Moore Show,
  The* (TV show) 446
*M*A*S*H* (TV show) 446
Massachusetts *see also*
  Boston
  college 503
  forging press 210
  governors 470
  high point 30
  original statehood 460
  place-name length 395
  mass murders See
    murder
  masts
    nautical 291
    structural *20*, 256
  matchbox labels 549
  matchstick model *551*, 552
  mathematical constants
    198
    pi 169, 198
  mathematician 199
    human calculator 169
  mathematics 197–199
  Mauna Loa (volcano)
    42–43
  mazes 272
  McDonald's Corp.
    254–255
  McGuffey Reader, The
    (book) 404

McKinley, Mount 30, 31
meanings (of a word) 394
measures 199
meat pie 538
mechanical shovel 310
medical extremes 176–182
medical families 453
Meet the Press (TV show) 445
Meistersinger von Nurnberg, Die (opera) 419
melting point 189–190
memory 169, 786*
  cellular 174
menhir (upright monolith) 272
menswear store 353
mental health 453
merchant shipping 294–295
Mercury (planet) 9, 10
Merrill Lynch & Co. Inc. 367
meteorites 15–17
meteor shower 15
Metro *See* subways
Metropolitan Life Insurance Co. 352
Metropolitan Museum of Art (New York City) 359
Mexico City 461, *461*
mice 71, 79, 80
  marsupial 72
Michigan
  cable-stayed bridge 257
  governors 470
  high point 30
  indoor waterfall 280
  lead mine 214
  stadiums 248, 249
microlighting 682
microphone 196
  radio 442
microscope, scanning tunneling 196, 392
Microsoft Corp. *203*, 358
midge 106
migration, animal *84–87*
  monarch butterfly *84–85*, 108
military and defense 494–503
  awards
    Germany 492
    Soviet Union (USSR) 492, *492*
    United States 492
milk
  cow yields 371, 375–376
  goat yields 376
milk bottle balancing 527–528
milk crate balancing *528*, 528
milk shake 539

millionaires/billionaires *356, 357*, 357–359
millipedes 109
mills *See* tidal mill; water mill; windmills
minaret 509
mineral water 545
mines *See* borings and mines
miniature painting 386
Minnesota
  governors 470
  high point 30
  iron mine 214
  mean temperature 46
  rocks 25
  shopping center 255
  wild rice farm 370
  wind power 205
mints (coinage) 361, 363
mirages 51
miser *356*
missiles *See* rockets
Mississippi
  high point 30
  lynching 485
  per capita income 355
  secession 460
Mississippi River
  length 34
  levee system 264
  riverboat service 292
Missouri
  cathedral size 507
  governors 471
  high point 30
Miss Saigon (musical) 428
moats 243
model aircraft 344–345
model boats 293
model cars 312
models (fashion) 430
model trains 321
modem 223
Modern Maturity (magazine) 409
modern pentathlon 682–685
modern rhythmic gymnastics 660
mollusks 110–112
  poisonous 111
Mona Lisa (da Vinci painting) 384, 485
monarchs and monarchy 463–465
money, paper 359–360
monkeys 59, 68, 69
monoliths
  artificial *See* menhir; obelisks
  natural 25
Monopoly (board game) 595
Montana
  barometric pressure 52
  governors 471
  high point 30

temperature 46, 48
Monte Carlo Rally 565
monuments 273
  obelisks 273
Moon 11–12
  eclipses of 12
  meteorites stemming from 16
  space flights 228, 233, 238
moose 72, 73
Morse code 223
mortality *See* death—rate of; infant mortality
mortars 502
mosaics 385
mosque 509
mosquitos 60
mosses 132–133
motherhood (human) 152–153 *See also* babies; births
moths 61, 107–108
motionlessness 180
motion pictures *See* movies
motorcycle racing 683–685
  circuit length 683
  Moto-cross 684
  speedway 720–721
motorcycles 298–301, *300*
mound
  artificial 273
  termite 106
mountaineering 685–687, *686*
  Cameroon races 687
  disaster 457
  rappeling *See* rapelling
  U.S. high points *32*
mountains 29–33, 785*
  on Mars 9
  on Moon 12
  submarine (seamount) 19
mountain walls 33, 686
Mousetrap, The (play) 427
movies 435, *436*, 437–441
  annual output 435
  box-office grosses 437, 441, 788*
  costumes 439–440
  directors 439
  durable series 437
  extras 438
  Oscar winners 440, *441*
  production speed for single feature 438
  recurring characters 439
  sets 438
  studios 437–438
  theaters 440–441
  viewing of 438
mules 74
mummies 144
Munchausen's syndrome 182

Muppet Show, The (TV show) 446
murals 385
murder
  government-sanctioned 458–460
    genocide *459*, 460
  by individuals 483, 485
  punishment for 487
muscles 167–168
museums 406
  art 385
    thefts from 485–486
mushroom farm 370
mushrooms 137–138
music 410–421
  durable artists 416, 417
  manuscript 398, 400
  rap speed 422
  time between completion and performance of classical piece 420
musical chairs 415
musical shows 427
  advances sales 428
  on Broadway 427
  Tony awards 428
music box 388
mustaches *164*, 165, 786*
mutiny 499

N

names/name length
  anatomical 167
  astronomical 5
  corporate 348
  geographical 395–396
  of labor union 364
  personal 394–395
    contrived 395
    pseudonyms 402
    scientific 392
narcotics
  hauls/operations 486
  sniffer-dogs 77
NASCAR (National Association for Stock Car Auto Racing) 562, 563
national anthems 410, 411
National Collegiate Athletic Association (NCAA) *See* baseball—college; basketball; fencing; football; gymnastics; lacrosse; soccer; wrestling
national debt 355
National Education Association (NEA) 363
national parks *See* parks

national wealth 355
natural disasters *See* disasters
natural phenomena 39–45
naturist resorts *See* nudist colonies
navies 498
  battles 496
Nazis *See* Germany, Nazi
Nebraska
  governors 471
  high point 30
  locust swarm 61
necks
  dinosaur 117
  human 168
needles 552
  threading of 528
negative (photography) 434
neon sign 268, 787*
Neptune (planet) 8, 9, 10
nerve gas 191
nerves
  cells 174
  impulse transmission *178*, 180
nests 88
netball 687
neurons 174
Nevada
  aridity 47
  artificial lake 265
  governors 471
  high point 30
  hotel 244
  mural size 385
  theater stage 427
  tree age 134
New Hampshire
  governors 471
  high point 30
  original statehood 460, 475
  public library 404
  wind speed 49
New Jersey
  AIDS cases 175
  building demolished by explosives 268
  governors 471
  high point 30
  original statehood 460
  port size 295
New Mexico
  cave 29
  governors 471
  high point 30
  oil fields 213
  uranium mine 214
newspapers 406–408, *407*
  circulation 408
New Year's Eve party 333
New York City
  AIDS cases 175
  apartment house 243
  blackouts 206

bookstore 404
bus ridership 311
cathedral 506–507
commercial bank 349
concert attendance 417
garbage dump 271
marathon 558, 762–764
mass murder 483, 485
medical malpractice award 478
movie screenings (historic) 435
movie theater 440
museum 406
office complex 247–248
opera house/company 420
orchestra 416
planetarium 226
population 461
public library 405
road tunnel 266
subway system 325
  disaster 325
suspension bridge 257, 259
swim around Manhattan 732
synagogue 509
taxi fleet 314
train station 324
travel between London and 333
water tunnel 265
New York Post (newspaper) 406
New York State *See also* New York City
  AIDS cases 175
  bat colony 70
  canal length 262
  church size 507
  columns (architectural) 269
  governors 471
  high point 30
  hurricane speed 50
  original statehood 460
  population (65 and over) 159
  port size 295
  university enrollment 503
New York Stock Exchange 365, 366, 788*
  length of service by member of 366
  listings 366
New York Times, The (newspaper) 407
  best-seller list 154
  Pulitzer Prizes 407
  single issue size 407
night clubs 254
Nikon Corp. 434
Nile River 33–34
Nippon Steel Corp. 209
Nobel Prizes *490* 491

literature (by country) 397
noctilucent clouds 13
noise *See* loudness
nonuplets 157
noodle making 537
North Carolina
  governors 471
  high point 30
  original statehood 460
  secession 460
North Dakota
  governors 471
  high point 30
  temperature 49
  tower height 256
northernmost features
  antarctic iceberg 23
  habitation 241
  land location 26
  plant life 122
  towns and cities 463
  vineyard 130
  volcano 43
North Pole 515, 516–517
  conquest 515
  sunshine 51
Northumberland Bestiary 398
notes (sounds)
  musical extremes
    instrumental 415
    vocal 410
  physical extreme 193
novels 397–398, 401
  best-selling 401
nuclear delivery vehicles 503
nuclear power 204–205
  disasters 457
nuclear weapons 500–501
  disasters 456
nudist colonies (naturist resorts) 251
numbers 197–198
  pi (mathematical constant) 169, 198
  post-nominal 465
nutritional value (of fruits and vegetables) 130
nuts (industrial) 209

O

oarfish 97
oats 372
obelisks 273
obesity 151–152
observatories 227
oceanaria 142
oceans 18–19
  crossings *See* Atlantic crossings; Pacific crossings
  descent/diving 517–518
  drillings 212

octopus 110, *110*, 111
odors *See* smells
Ohio
  bar size 256
  church bell 412
  community garden 370
  exhibition center 254
  forging press 210
  governors 471
  high point 30
  refuse electrical generation plant 274
roller coasters 252
oil (petroleum)
  fields 213
  fraudulent sale of 483
  gushers 215
  imports (U.S.) 212, 213
  pipelines 209–210
  platforms 213, 215
    disasters 456
  production 212
  refineries 213
  rigs 215
  spills *216–219*
  tanks 213
oil, cooking (adulteration of) *484*, 485
Oklahoma
  governors 471
  high point 30
  incorporated place 462
  McDonald's outlet 255
  nudist colony 251
  parking meters 317
  water tower 280
okra 128
Old Farmer's Almanac, The (periodical) 408
Old King Cole! (book) 396
Olympic games 597, 687–690
  attendance 558, 687
  events
    archery 560
    basketball 587, *588*, 589
    biathlon 598, 590
    bobsled/luge 596
    boxing 607
    canoeing 607, *608*, 609
    cycling 616
    diving 732–733
    equestrian sports 622–623, *624*, 625
    fencing 625–626
    field hockey 626, 627
    gymnastics 654–655, 658, 660
    ice hockey 666
    ice skating 673, 674, 675
    judo 679–680
    modern pentathlon 682–683

rowing 703
rugby 705
shooting 707
skiing 709–710, 712, 713
soccer 718, 719
swimming 728, *729*, 732–733
team handball 736
tennis 741
track and field 743, 745
volleyball 768–769
walking 764
water polo 769
weightlifting 772
wrestling 778
yachting 780, 783
  participation 689
  torch relay length 688
  TV viewership 446
omelet 539
  making 537
one-man band 416
one-man shows 428
onion 126, 128
opals 55
opera 419–420
  curtain calls 420
operations, medical *See* surgery
opossums 66
optical fiber 223
optics
  active (telescopes) 227
  visual 166–167
orangutan 68
orchestras 415–417
  concert attendance 417
orchids 124–125
  seeds 131
Oregon
  canyon 37
  governors 471
  high point 30
  lake 36
  pendulum 221
organism size 122
organist 417
organs (human body) *178–179*, 180
  transplants *See* transplants, organ
organs (musical instruments) 413
  high/low notes 415
  loudness (of stop) 414
organ transplants *See* transplants, organ
orienteering 690–691
  on skis 691
oriole *87*
Oscars (Academy Awards) 440, *441*
ostriches 81, 82, 89
otter, sea *See* sea otter
overdue books 406
owl 89

Oxford English Dictionary 396–397
Oxford University Press 403
oyster opening 528

P

Pacific crossings
  by balloon 342, 343
  by plane 327
  by ship 293
paella 539
paintbrush 384
paintings 383–386, *383*
  thefts 485–486
palaces *242*, 242–243
  snow constructions 274
palindromes 392
palm trees 131
Pan-American Highway 318
pancake race 762
pandemics *See* diseases
panic (stampede) 456
pan pipes 414
paper
  chain 529
  company 352
  money 359–360
  planes *344*, 345
parachuting 691–692, *693*, 694
  from balloon 343
Parade (magazine) 409
parades
  floats 550, 789*
  of horse-drawn carriages 302
  ribbons 493
  of Rolls royces 309, 787*
paragliding 691, 694
parallel bar dips 655
Paralympics (Barcelona, 1992) 688
parking
  lots 317
  meters 317
  tickets 319
parks 141
  U.S. tour 785*
parliaments 473–475
parrot 82
parsnip 126
particle accelerator 196–197
parties, political
  size 474
  time in power 475, 476
party-giving 523
  New Year's Eve 333
par value 366
passenger liner 290
  Atlantic crossing by 292–293
pass the parcel 529

pastry 539
patents 469
  litigation 480
payday 359
peals (bell-ringing) 412–413
peanut 128
"Peanuts" (comic strip) 408
pearls 55–56
pedal car 315
pelican 89, *90*
pelota vasca *See* jai alai
pendulums 221
penguins 89
peninsula 28
Pennsylvania
  cantilever bridge 259
  flood deaths/property damage 49
  Gettysburg casualties 471
  governors 471
  high point 30
  mint (Philadelphia) 361, 363
  mushroom farm 370
  nuclear power 204
  original statehood 460
  population (65 and over) 159
  prehistoric artifacts 145–146
  roller coaster 252
  stone arch 259
  weed growth 133
Pennzoil Co. 479
pen pals 400
pens (writing instruments) 552
pension 358
Pentagon (Arlington, Va.)
  ground area *246*, 247
  switchboard 223
pentathlon *See* modern pentathlon
pepper 128
pepper plant 128
Pepsico Inc. 545
perch (fish) 629
periodicals 408–409
permafrost 39
Perrier (mineral water) *See* Source Perrier
personal injury awards 478–479
petanque 694
petition, political 474
petroleum *See* oil
pets *See also* cats; dogs; rabbits
  litter size 79
  longevity of caged 80
petunia 126
pharmaceuticals 187
pharmacies *See* drug stores

pheasant 82
Philadelphia *See* Pennsylvania
philodendron 126
Philosophical Transactions of the Royal Society (British periodical) 408
phonograph 421
  records *See* recordings
phonographic identification 422
photography 433–434
  aerial 433
physical extremes 192–194
physicians 458
  families of 453
physiology (human) *See* anatomy and physiology
pi (mathematical constant) 169, 198
pianists 417
piano compositions 419
pianos 413
  high note 415
pie
  apple 532
  cherry 533
  meat 538
piers 273
  pleasure 251
piggy bank 348
pigs 376–377
  farms 370
  prices 374
pike (fish) 629
pill-taking 180
pilots (aviation) 337
  military aces 500
piñata 552
pineapple 126
pinnacle, rock *See* rock pinnacle
pinnipeds 69
pipelines 209–210
piranhas 100
pitch (sound) 173
pizza 539–540
place-names 395–396
plane pulling 340
planetaria 226
planets 3, 8–11, *8*
plants 121–137
plateau 31
plate spinning 432
platforms
  oil 213, 215
  railroad 325
platinum
  discs (record sales) 423
  mines 214
  nuggets 56
plowing 373
Pluto (planet) 8, 9, 10
poems 402
pogo stick jumping 529
poisoning, mass *484*, 485

poisonous animals and plants
  birds 82
  bivalves 111
  cephalopods 111
  fish 99
  frogs 60
  fungi 138
  jellyfish 113
  scorpions 104–105
  snakes 94–96
  spiders 104
polar bear 66–67
polar circumnavigation 516–517
Polaroid Corp. 480
polder (land reclaimed from sea) 264
poles
  flexible 430
  sitting on 244
  totem 276
political cartoons 408
political division 449–450
political unrest 458–460
polo 694–695
ponies 75
pool (sport) 695
pools, swimming 732
popcorn 540–541
popes 508
pop music *See* rock/pop music
population 451–458
  65 and over (5 U.S. states) 159
  density 451
  sex ratio 454
  urban 461
  world growth 451, 452, 454
porcupine 71
porpoise
  sleeplessness 65
  speed 65
Portrait of Dr. Gachet (van Gogh painting) 386
ports 295
postage stamps *See* stamps
postal services 367, 369
poster
  price for 384
  size 384
post-nominal numbers 465
post offices 367
potato chips 541
potatoes
  production 372
  size 127
potato peeling 129
pot plant 124
pottery 552
poultry 377–379
poverty (of country) 355
powder (degree of fineness) 191
power 204–207
powerboat racing 698

Powerful (Deshpande sculpture) 385, *386*
powerlifting 773, 777
power plants 204–205
  garbage-using 274
  nuclear 204–205
  solar 205
  tidal 205
prairie dog 60–61
precious stones *See* gems
precipitation *See* rainfall; snowfall
pregnancies, multiple 152, 153
premiers *See* prime ministers
president, college 504
presidents (heads of state)
  United States 465–466, 468
    earnings 473
    wives of 467
  world
    theft by *484*, 485
    women 465, 477
presses (industrial) 210
pressure 192
  barometric *See* barometric pressure
  priests 511
  primates 68–69
    prehistoric 120, 144
  prime ministers 476–477
    women 477
print (art work) 386
printing
  in antiquity 396
  electronic 210
  mechanical 396
  operations 404
  volume (single edition) 404
prism 197
prisons 488–489
  per capita population 489
  sentences 488
prizes *See specific prizes (e.g.,* Nobel prizes)
procaryota 138–140
processions *See* parades
producers (television) 447
productivity, artistic *See* prolificacy
profit 347
projectiles 696–697, 791*
prolificacy, artistic
  composers 419
  conductors 416
  painters 384
  scriptwriters 447
promenade, covered 273
proofs, mathematical 198
prop (film) 438
propeller (ship) 328
propeller-driven aircraft 330, 335, *336*

protista (protozoa and protophytes) 137
Prudential Insurance Co. of America 352
pseudonyms 402
psychiatrists 453
psychologists 453
public relations firm 405
publishers 403–404, *403*
Pulitzer Prizes 407
pulling
  guns 502
  planes 340
  with teeth 165
  tractors 314–315
pulsars 5–6
pulse rates 180
pumpkins 127, 129, *130*
push-ups *656–657*
puzzles
  crossword 409–410
  jigsaw 550, 552
  mathematical 198
pyramids 273–274
  bottle-cap 546
  human 432
    on high wire 430
    on motorcycles 301
python 94, *95*

Q

quadruplets 153, 154, 156
quarks 187
quarry 214
quasars 4
queens *See* royalty
quilt 553
quindecaplets 156
quintuplets 153, 154, 156
quiz participation 530
quorum 474
Quo Vadis (film) 439

R

rabbits 79–80
rackets (sport) 698
racquetball 698–699
radar 210
radio 442–443
  ham 443
  microphones 442
radio astronomy
  dishes 226
  installations 226, *227*
Radio City Music Hall (New York City) 440
radish 127
raft
  of kayaks and canoes 609
  survival on *518*, 519
rail ferries 289

railroads 320–325
  altitude 322, *323*
  bridges 257, 259, 260
  disasters 456
  employees 347
  tracks 322, *323,* 324
  travel on 324
  tunnels 265
rainbow 51
rainfall 49
rallying
  titles (for
    manufacturer) *566*
  wins *566*
Rambling with Gambling
  (radio show) 442
ramp jumping
  (motorcycle) 299
ranges, mountain 31
ransom payments
  hijacking 486
  kidnapping 486
rap music 422
rappeling 685
rats 71, 80
rattlesnake 94
Reader's Digest (magazine)
  409
real estate 352
  consultants 281
real/royal tennis 699
Reclining Figure (Moore
  sculpture) 387
recordings (sound)
  421–425
  classical
    best-selling album
      422
    project devoted to
      one composer 423
  popular
    best-sellers 423–424
    golden/platinum discs
      422, *423*
record store 422
Red Cross, International
  Committee of the
  490, 491
reef 28
refineries, oil 213
reflectors, telescopic
  224–225
refractor, telescopic 224,
  225
refractoriness 191
refueling time (airplane)
  333
refuse electrical
  generation plants
  274
regattas *782*
regeneration *60,* 60
registrations, auto 302
reigns
  champion athlete 557
  royalty 463–464
rejection slips 402, 788*
religions 505–511

remoteness *See also*
  isolation
  of airport from city
    center 338–339
  of islands (uninhabited
    and inhabited) 26
  of man-made object 230
  of object in universe 3–4
  of spot from land 23
  of spot from sea 25
  of town from sea 462
  of tree from any other
    136
rentals, commercial
  247–248
reproductivity *See also*
  litters
  of cattle 375
  of chickens 378
  of ducks 378
  of goats 376
  of human beings
    152–158
    royalty 465
  of pigs 377
  of protozoa 137
  of sheep 380
  of streaked tenrec
    (youngest
    mammalian
    breeder) 67
reptiles 91–96
  prehistoric *See also*
    dinosaurs 117,
    118–119
rescue effort *See* life,
  saving of
reservoirs 265
resorts 250–251
restaurants *253,* 254–255
retailers 352–353
retractable roof 249, *249*
Rhode Island
  bridge width 259
  governors 471
  high point 30
  land area 25
  original statehood 460
  synogogue 506
rhododendron 129
rhubarb 127
rhythmic gymnastics *See*
  modern rhythmic
  gymnastics
ribbons, parade 493
rice 372–373 *See also* wild
  rice
rights
  film 437
  television 445
rights issue 366
rinks
  curling 615
  ice skating 677
  roller skating 702
riot 456
Rite Aid Corp. 349
river basin 34

riverboat 292
river bores 35
rivers 33–35
  submarine 34
  subterranean 34
riveting 286
RJR Nabisco Inc. 348, 359
Road Less Traveled, The
  (book) 403
roads 318–319
  disasters 456, 457
  distance between exits
    319
  tunnels 266
robbery *484,* 485–486
robot *201*
Rock Around the Clock
  (song) 423
rockets 62, 228–230
  altitude 229
  engines 228
  time in space (by
    country) 234–235
rock pinnacle 26
rock/pop music
  concerts 417, 419
    decibel level *171*
  recordings 422–424
rocks *24,* 24–25
rodents 71
rodeo 699–700, 791*
roll calls (U.S. Congress)
  469
roller coasters 252
rollercycling 619
roller hockey *701,* 702
roller skating 701–703,
  792*
  barrel jumping 703
  by limbo dancer
    425–426
rolling pin throwing 697
Rolls-Royces
  collection 302
  parades 309, 787*
Roman Catholic Church
  adherents 506
  canonizations 507, 508,
    510
  churches/cathedrals
    506–507, *509*
  clergy, 507, 510, 511
    bishops 510–511
    popes/cardinals 508
roofs 249, *249*
roots 124
ropes 210–211
rope skipping *See* skipping
  rope
rope slide 529
ropeways (téléphériques)
  211
rose tree 129
rowing 703–704
  land 527
  race length 704
royalty 463–465, *464*
rubies 56–57

rugby 704–706, *705*, 792*
rugs *See* carpets
rummage sales 353, 787*
Rumours (recording) 423
running 62, 742–764
  backwards 753
  circling bases 569
  cross-country *See* cross-country running
  race participation 557
  ultra long distance 753, 759–761
runways 328
rutabaga 127, 128
rye, 124

S

saffron 537
Sahara Desert 37
sailboards 783
sailfish 62, 99, 629
sailing *See* yachting
sailing ships *See under* ships
sails 291
St. Lawrence Seaway 261
saints *See* canonizations
salamanders 96, 97
salamis 541
salaries 359
  of legislators 473
salmon 629, 630
salvages, marine 519, *520*
Sand
  castles *240*, 241
  dunes 37
  island 26
  sculpture 384
  yachting 673
San Francisco (California)
  AIDS cases 175
  bridge towers 260
  crooked street 319
  earthquake death toll 41
  flight between Oakland and 334
  road tunnel 266
sapphires 56, 57
satellites (Solar System) *10*, 11 *See also* Moon
satellites, manmade 230–231
SAT (Scholastic Aptitude Test) scores 504
Saturday Night Fever (recording) 423
Saturn (planet) 9, *10*, 11
sausage 541
savings and loan associations 353
scaffolding 274
scale models (of Solar System) 3
scales *See* balances

scarecrow 274
scarf 529
Scholastic Aptitude Test *See* SAT
schools *See* education
scientific instruments 194–197, 786*
scientific manuscript 400
scorpions 104–105
Scrabble (board game) 595–596, 791*
scrap-metal sculpture 385, *386*
screaming 169, *171*, 172
screens
  movie 441
  television 447
scriptwriter, television 447
scuba diving *20*, 517–518
sculpture 385, *386*
  balloon 546, *547*
  prices 387
  sand 384
sea lion 69
seals (mammals) 69
seamount (submarine mountain) 19
sea otter 65
seaports *See* ports
searchlight 193
Sears Roebuck & Co. 353
Sears Tower (Chicago, Illinois) 248
  human fly 685
seas *See* oceans
  inland *See* lakes
sea wasp 113
seaway 261
seaweed 133
securities company 366–367
seeds 131
seismic wave (tusunami) *20*, 22
Senate, U.S. *See* Congress, U.S.
septuplets 63
seven-a-sides (rugby) 706
sewage/sewerage
  tunnels 266
  works 274, *275*
sex ratio 454
sextuplets 157
shaft-sinking 521
sharks
  bite strength 59
  catches 629, 630
  size 97, *98*, 98, 99, 100
  of prehistoric species 121
sharpness 197
shaving 162
sheep 379–381
  fleece 379
  move 371
  prices 374
  ranch 370–371
  shearing 379

station *380*
shells and shellfish 111–112
shipbuilding 294
  production speed 293
shipping, merchant 294–295
  canal transits/tonnage 262, *262*
ships 283–295
  collision impact 287
  crimes 483
  ocean crossings 291–293
  propellers 328
  torpedoings 456
  types
    human-powered *285*, 286, 293
    sailing 290–291
    wooden 289–290
  wrecks 283, 292
shoes 552–553
shooting 707–708
  clay pigeon 707
  individual records 708
  Olympic medals 707
shopping centers 255
shorthand 529
shouting *170*, 172
shovel 211
  mechanical 310
shoveling, coal 213
shower, meteor 15
show jumping (horses) 622–623, *624*
shrews (mammals) 64, 68, 71
"Siamese" twins *See* twins—conjoined
sidewalks, moving 208
sieges 497
sight, lines of 31
signatures 401
signs (advertising) 267–268, *267*, 787*
silicosis 456
silver
  antiques 389
  pieces (size) 553
  prices (COMEX) 366
singers
  choristers 507
  discordance 411
  opera 420
  performances
    of national anthem 411
    of religious chant 507
  popularity 417, *418*, 419
    funeral attendance (for Visotsky) 511
  rappers 422
  recordings 422–425
    contracts 424
    Grammy awards 422, 440
sitting
  in tree 132

unsupported against
    wall 658
    in unsupported circle
        530
sit-ups 655
size differential
    between husband/wife
        152
    between male/female of
        any species 61
skateboarding 702, 703
skating See specific sport
    (e.g., ice skating)
skeletons See bones
ski-bob 714
skid marks 317
skiing 709–710, 711,
    712–714, 713
    jumps 712
    lifts 714
        disasters 457
    Olympic events 709,
        711, 712
        moguls (freestyle
            skiing) 713
        speed in downhill
            race 712
    Olympic titles 709, 710,
        711
    orienteering See
        orienteering
    runs 709
skin 178–179
skipping rope 714
skulls
    dinosaur 118
    human (monetary
        value) 169
skydiving 556
SkyDome (Toronto,
    Canada) 249, 249
sled dog racing 715
    Iditarod trail 715
sleds
    polar journeys using
        515–516
    rocket-powered 305
sleep (of mammals) 65
sleeplessness
    human being 180
    mammal 65
slide
    alpine 597
    rope 529
slingshot 696, 697
slot cars 313
sloths
    sleepiness 65
    slowness 65
slot machines (winnings),
    254
slugs (gastropods) 112
smell, sense of 107
smells, foul 122, 123, 191
Smithsonian Institution
    406
smog 456
snail racing 112

snails 59, 62–63, 112
snakes 94–96, 95
    prehistoric 119
snappers (fish) 629
sneezing 180
snooker 715–717, 716
snoring 170, 180
snowfall 50
snowmen 274, 278–279,
    787*
snowmobiles 315
snow palace 274
snow-plow blade 211
snowshoeing 709
soaring 717–718
soccer 718–719
    NCAA Division I 719
    stadiums 248, 558
    TV viewership 446
soda float 541
sofas 553
softball 720
soft drinks 545
software See computers
solar power 205
    for land vehicle 313
Solar System 7–17
    scale models of 3
soldiers 499
solitaire 592
somersaults 658
    on flexible pole 430
    on horseback 432
    risley 432
    on trampoline 433, 767
    on trapeze 430
songs 410–412
songwriters 411
sonic boom 333
Sotheby Group 387
sound (recorded) See
    recordings (sound)
sounds
    detectability 173
    loudness See loudness
        of speech 389, 390, 392
Sounds of Time, The
    (opera) 419
soundtrack, film 423
Source Perrier (France)
    545
South Carolina
    governors 471
    high point 30
    hurricane damage 50
    original statehood 460
    secession 460
South Dakota
    governors 471
    high point 30
    observatory 227
    temperature rise 47
southernmost features
    arctic iceberg 23
    habitation 241
    land location 26
    part of the oceans 19
    plant life 122

runway 328
towns and cities 463
vineyard 130
volcano 43
South Pacific (recording)
    424
South Pole 516–517
southernmost land 26
sunshine 51
space
    objects orbited 238
    telescope 228
space flight 230–238
    altitude 237, 336
    disasters 237, 457
    duration 232, 336
    moon exploration 12,
        228, 233, 238
    people at one time
        232–233
    reusable spacecraft 233
    rockets See rockets
    satellites 230–231
    spacewalks 237
    speed 237–238,
        334–335
    by women 231, 232, 237,
        238
spas 251
spear throwing 696, 697
specialized structures
    267–281
specialized vehicles
    310–316
speech See talking
speeches, political 474
speed skating See ice
    skating
speedway 720–721
spellings, variant (of
    place-name)
    395–396
spices 541
spiders 103–104, 104
    prehistoric 117
spike driving 321
spinning
    basketball 588, 589
    fine (wool) 379
    plate 432
    top 209
spiral staircases 275
spires 509, 510
spirits (alcohol) 544
spitting 529
spoil dump 214
sponges 113
    regeneration 60, 60
spore count, fungal 138
sports See specific sport; for
    general records, see
    p. 556–558
springbok 66, 87
square dance calling 426
squash (sport) 721–722
squash (vegetable) 127
squats/squat thrusts
    (exercises) 655

squid 63, 110–111
squirrel 70
stadiums 248–249, *249*
   attendance 558
stages
   film studio 437–438
   theater 427
stained glass 280, 509–510
stair climbing 276
stairways 274–275
stalactite 29
stalagmite 29
stampede *See* panic
stamps, postage 368
   commemorative issue
      367
   licking of 367
standing 530
Stanley Cup 665–666
starfishes 101–102
stars (astronomy) 4–7
states (U.S.) 460
stations
   filling 317
   radio 443
   railroad 324–325
   sheep *380*
Statue of Liberty 275–276
statues *See also* sculpture
   dimensions of 275–276
   honorary 491
   Lego 281
steam
   car 305
   engines 204
      marine propulsion
         283
      locomotives 320–321
steel companies 209
stilt-walking 432–433
stingray 629
stock
   exchanges 365–367
   offering 366
stockholders' meeting 366
Stockholms Auktionsverk
   (Sweden) 387
stonefish 99
Stonehenge (Salisbury
   Plain, Great
   Britain) 273
stone skipping 530
stork 81
storms *See* circular storm;
   hailstones and
   hailstorms;
   hurricanes;
   tornadoes
stowaway 333
straits 19
strawberry 127
   bowl 541
   shortcake *540*
streets 319
stretcher bearing 183,
   786*
strikes (labor) 364
string ball 553

stringed musical
   instruments
      413–414
stroller pushing 530
stunt (film) 438
stupas 509
sturgeon
   catch 629, 631
   longevity 99
   value 100
subatomic particles
      187–188
   accelerators 196–197
submarine canyon 37
submarine mountain
   (seamount) 19
submarine river 34
submarines 283, 286
   disasters 457
   human-powered *285,*
      286
   sinking of (both world
      wars) 500
submergence underwater
   181, 519
subnuclear particles *See*
   subatomic
   particles
subways 266, 325
   disasters 325
Suez Canal 261–262, *262*
suffrage, woman's 475
sugar beets 373
sugar cane 373
suggestion box use 321
suicide 454
   mass 456, 457
suits (clothing)
   space 233
   store specializing in 353
   tailoring speed 530
suits (litigation) 480
sumo wrestling 778,
   779–780, *779*
Sun 7–8
   closest approach to (by
      rocket) 230
   eclipses of 12, 13
Sunday school 511
sundial 221–222
sunfish 98, 100
sunflower 127
sunshine 51
sunspots 7–8
Super Bowl (football)
   635–636, *636*
   MVP 632
   TV advertising rates
      447
   TV viewership 446
superconductivity 192
Superdome (New Orleans,
   La.) 249, 270, 430
supermarkets *See* grocery
   stores
supernovas *6,* 6
supersonic flight 327–328,
   333, 334–336

   by bomber 331
   by Concorde 62, 331,
      333, 335–336, 787*
surfing 722
surgery 182–185
   conjoined ("Siamese")
      twin sepration 156
   transplants 184–185
surveyors 281
survival
   on raft *518,* 519
   without food/water 181
suspended animation
      59–60
swallowing, compulsive
      181
swamp 35
swans 81, 82, 90
sweater production (sheep
   to shoulder) 379
sweating, weight lost
   through 151
sweetness 191
sweet potato 128
swifts 83, 89
swimming
   by birds 89
   by fish 99
   by pinnipeds 69
swimming (sport) *723,*
      723–734
   for charity 732
   diving *See* diving
   long-distance 733–734,
      792*
      across English
         Channel 734
      around Manhattan
         Island 732
   Olympic records 728,
      729, 732–733
   U.S. records (50-meter
      pools) 730–731
   world records (25-meter
      pools) 726–727,
      728, 792*
   world records (50-meter
      pools) 724–725,
      792*
swimming pools 732
swing 276
switchboard, telephone
      223
swordfish 629
symphonies 419
synagogues 506, 509
syndicated columnists
      407–408
synonyms (English
      language) 392

T

table 553
tablecloth 553
table tennis 734–735
taekwondo 735–736

tailoring 530
Tainted Love (song) 424
takeover, corporate 348
talking
    by birds 82
    by humans
        backwards 172
        normal volume *170*
        rapid 172, 173
tankard (beer) 543
tankers 287
    oil spills *216–219*
    tanks
        gas 271
        oil 213
tanks (vehicles) 313–314
tap dancing 426
tape recording 421
tapestry 389, 553
tarantulas 103, *104*
tarpon 629
tartans 554
tattoos 181–182
taverns See bars
taxes 354
taxis 314
teaching career *505*, 505
team handball 736, *736*
teddy bears' picnic 523
teeter board 433
teeth 165–166
    false 166
    lifting and pulling with
        165
Teflon 192
tektites 17
telecast 444
telegraphic transmission
    223
téléphériques See
    ropeways
telephones 222–224
    cables 223
    exchanges 223
    routes 223
    switchboards 223
telescopes 224–228
telethon 447
television 444–447
    contracts 446–447,
        557–558
    producers 447
    production expense 446
    program sales 447
    sets
        ownership 445–446
        size 447
    viewership 446
temperature
    atmosphere 51
    Earth 46, *47*, 48–49
    human body 174
    Moon 12
    oceans 19
    physical extremes 192
    planets 8, 9
    Sun 7
    superconducting 192

Temperature-Humidity
    Index (THI)
    52–53
temples 506
Tennessee
    automobile plant 303
    governors 471
    high point 30
    lake (underground) 36
    neon sign 268
    roller coaster 252
    secession 460
    Shiloh casualties 496
tennis 737–742, *740*
tenrecs 66, 67, 71
tensile strength 190
tent, circus 430
tentacles
    cephalopods 110, 111
    jellyfish 113
*Terminator 2: Judgment
    Day* (film) 435,
    436, 437
termites
    DNA recovery 140
    fumigation 272
    mounds 106
terns 88, 89
terrorism 456
Texaco Inc. 349, 479
Texas
    AIDS cases 175
    bar size 255–256
    bat colony 70
    cattle farming 374
    clock 221
    concrete arch 259
    counties 460
    Ferris wheel 252
    governors 471
    high point 30
    land area 25
    night club 254
    nuclear power 204
    oil fields 213
    oil refinery 213
    population (65 and
        over) 159
    road mileage 318
    roof span 249
    secession 460
    sheep farming 379
    undertakers 511
    weather
        hurricane deaths 50
        rainfall 49
        tornado frequency
            50
        tornado speed 49
    wholesale merchandise
        mart 255
Texas Skips 700
TGV (Train a Grande
    Vitesse) (French
    high-speed train)
    320
theater 426–430
    advance sales 428

    attendance by
        individual 427
    financial disaster 428
    long-running shows 427
    nonattendance 429
theft See robbery
theorem, mathematical
    198
thermal expansion 190
thermometer 196
thermonuclear devices See
    nuclear weapons
THI See Temperature-
    Humidity Index
Thriller (recording) 423
thunder 51–52
tickets
    airline 333
    parking 319
    train 321
tidal bores See river bores
tidal mill 206
tidal power 205
tidal river barrier 276
tidal waves See tsunami
tides 22–23
tiger-lion hybrid (litigon)
    67
tigers 67
    circus 433
    man-eating 456
tightrope (high wire) 430,
    432, 530–531, 788*
    skipping rope on 714
time
    capsule 554
    measurement 199
timepieces 220–222
Time Warner Inc. 404
tires *316*, 317
    lifting of 319
Titan (Saturnian moon)
    10
Titacaca, Lake (Bolivia)
    36, 295
titles (nobility) 493
toads 97
    altitude/depth 96
tobogganing 597
toes 162
tomato 127, 128
tomato plant 127
tombs 276
Tony awards 428, 440
tools, prehistoric 145–146
topaz 56
top-spinning 209
tornadoes 40, 49, 50
tortoises 62–63, 93
    prehistoric 119
totem pole 276
touch, sense of 162
Tour de France (bicycle
    race) 558, *617*, 619
tourism 453, *455* See also
        travelers
towers 256–257
    bridge 260

cooling 269, 269
Lego 256, 552, 786*
water 280
towing (of cars) 317–318
towns 461–463
toxicity *See also*
poisonous animals
and plants
chemical elements 190
man-made chemical
191
nerve gas 191
toys
antiques 388
rag doll 549
stuffed 553
teddy bears' picnic 523
toy store 350–351
track and field 742–766,
744
Olympic records 743,
745
U.S. records (men)
754–755
U.S. records (women)
751–752
world indoor records
(men/women)
756–758, *758*
world records (men)
748–749, 792*
ultra long distance
760
world records (women)
744, 750–751
ultra long distance
761
tracks
dinosaur 117
railroad 322, 324
tractors 314–315
traffic
decibel level *170*
density 318–319
jams 319
volume 318
trains 320–322 *See also*
subways
dress 549
freight 321–322
model 321
passenger 322
travel on 321, 324
trampolining 766–767
circus 433
trams *See* trolleys
trans-America/Americas
crossings
by bicycle 616, 619–620
by car/truck 306, 308
on foot 513, 515
running backwards
753
by motorcycle 300–301
by plane 333
trans-Atlantic crossings
See under Atlantic
Ocean

trans-Atlantic
transmissions *See
under* Atlantic
Ocean
transformers 205
transfusions, blood 173
transistors 200
transmission lines
205–206, 786
trans-Pacific crossings *See*
Pacific crossings
transplants, organ
184–185, 786*
Trans-Siberian Railway
322, *323*
trapeze 430
travelers 513
to U.S. national parks
785*
treaty 475
tree climbing 132
trees 131, 132, 133–136,
135
avenue of 136
Christmas 132
fungi growing from 138
tree sitting 132
tree topping 132
trials *See* litigation
triathlon 767
tribes (average height) 149
tributary *See* river basin
tricycling, underwater 297
triplets 153, 154, 156, 159
Triton (Neptunian moon)
8
trolleys 315
trout 629
trucks 315–316
driving 306
forklift 208
wheelies 309
True Blue (recording) 422
*Truth that Leads to Eternal
Life, The*
(periodical) 409
tsunami (tidal wave)
20–21, 22
ridden by surfer 722
tubes 197
tug boats 289
tug of war 768
duration 556
tumors 183
tuna 629
tungsten mine 214
tunnels 265–267
disasters 456
wind 211
turbines 206
ships 284
turkey 379
farm 371
plucking 371
turtles 92, 93
migration *86–87*
prehistoric 119
tusks 72, 74, 120

TV *See* television
TV Guide (magazine) 409
twins
adult weight 151
birth weight 153, 154
conjoined ("Siamese")
155–156, *155*
interval between 156
length of separation
156–157
longevity 159
stature 149, 150
two-side-wheel driving
bus 309
car 308–309
motorcycle 301
truck 309
typing 531

U

ultralight aircraft 330
undertakers 511
underwater *See also*
diving; submarines
caves 29
escapes 518–519
submergence 181
swimming 734
tricycling 297
unemployment 364
unicycles 297–298, *297*
Union Carbide Corp. *479*,
479
United Distillers (of
Guinness PLC)
(Great Britain)
544
United Nations
Conference on
Environment and
Development 465
language versatility *391*
painting in aid of
UNICEF 383
speech length 474
United States of America
See specific states
(*e.g.,* Maine)
United States Steel Corp.
See USX Corp.
universe 2–17
universities *See* education
unsupported circle 530
uranium mine 214
Uranus (planet) 9, 10
urban population *See*
cities
urban renewal 245
USX Corp. 209, 347
Utah
arches (natural) 39
copper mine 214
governors 471
high point 30
lake 35
quarry 214

V

vacuum 194
valley 37
valve 211
vases *See* pottery
vats 280
vein 173
velocity (of solid visible object) 193
venomous animals and plants *See* poisonous animals and plants
Venus (planet) 9, 10
verbs, irregular 390
Vermont
  governors 471
  high point 30
  infant mortality 454
viaduct, railway 260
vice-presidents (U.S.) 469
Victory at Sea (symphony) 419
videos
  production speed 445
  sales 438
  technological advances 444–445
vines and vineyards 130
vintners 544
violin
  high note 415
  price 414
Virginia
  cemetery 269
  church 506
  college 503
  Fredericksburg casualties 496
  governors 471
  high point 30
  original statehood 460
  planetarium 226
  secession 460
viroids 140
viruses 140
  HIV (AIDS virus) *See* AIDS
viscosity 194
vision
  of birds 89
  of humans 166–167
vocabulary (English language) 390
voice 169, 172–173
  singing 410
volcanoes 42–43, *44–45*
  craters (calderas) 39
  disasters 40, 42
  plugs 25
volleyball 768–769
voltage 194
  transmission lines 205–206
vowels 389, 392

vulture 88–89
  prehistoric 121

W

waists 168
waiting rooms 324
Walgreen Co. 349
walking 764–766, *764*
  on hands 766
  mileage 513, 515
  to the poles 517
  road (world records) 765, 792*
  in space 237
  on stilts 432–433
  tightrope 530–531, 788*
  track (world records) 765
    indoors 756, 758
  on water 771
walkways, moving *See* sidewalks, moving
wallet 554
  for credit cards 549
wall of death 299
walls *277, 280*
walls, mountain 33, 686
wall "sit" (gymnastics) 658
Wall Street Journal, The (newspaper) 408
Wal-Mart Inc. 352–353
wars and warfare 494–497
  brevity *495*
warships 284–286
  hovercraft 295
Washington (state)
  dam (concrete) 263
  floating bridge 260
  governors 471
  high point 30
  hydraulic turbines 206
  volcano
    avalanche caused by 43
    deaths caused by 42
    eruption 43
  weather
    fog 52
    rainfall 49
    snowfall 50
Washington, D.C.
  AIDS cases 175
  clock 221
  library 404–405
  museum 406
Washington Monument (Washington, D.C.) 273
wasp 105
watches 221, 222
water
  buffalo 74
  canals *See* canals
  clarity (of sea) 19
  cycle (HPV) 297
  fleas 102

mill 206
mineral 545
pipeline 210
speed on 293
survival without 181
tower 280
tricycling under 297
tunnels 265, 266, 267
walking on 771
wells 215
waterfalls 33
  indoor 280
watermelon 127
water polo 769–770
waterskiing 770–772, 792*
waterspout 50
waterwheel 280
waves 22
  ridden by surfers 722
wealth
  national 355
  personal *357,* 357–359
weapons *See* military
weasel 67
weather 46–53
webs (of spiders) 104
weddings
  attendance 522, 788*
  best man 521
  cost 522
  dresses/dress trains 549
  golden 522
  mass ceremonies 522
  menu item 537
Weeckelycke Courante van Europa (Dutch newspaper) 406, *407*
weeds 133
weight
  human 151–152
    babies 153, 156
    boxers 604, 606–607
    president (U.S.) 466
    royalty 464
    sportsmen 557
    wrestlers 778, 779, *779,* 780
  mammalian 61, 64–65, 66–67
weightlifting 772–777
  men's/women's records 774–776
  powerlifting records (men/women) 777
weight loss
  by any animal 63
  by humans 151
wells, water 215
West Virginia
  governors 471
  high point 30
  steel arch 259
wet places 49
whale factory 287
whales
  diving depth 63
  migration *84*

size 61, 63, 64
    of catch 630
    sounds emitted by 59,
        171
    speed *65*, 65
    weight loss 63
wheat 373
wheelbarrow
    pushing 524
    racing 524
wheelchair mileage 513
wheelies
    bicycle 296
    motorcycle 301
    truck 309
whip cracking 530
whistling 172
White Christmas
        (recording) 424
Whitney Houston
        (recording) 423
wild rice 370
wills
    bequests 76, 359
    texts 481
Wimbledon 738–739
wind 49–50
    disasters 40
    generator 206
    power *See* solar power;
        windmills
    tunnel 211
windmills 206
window cleaning 281
windows 280
Winds of War, The (TV
        mini-series) 446
windsurfing (boardsailing)
        783
wine *543*, 544–545
    cellars 280–281
    tasting 545
    vat 280
wing-beat
    of birds 82
    of insects 106, 107
wingspan
    aircraft 328, *329*
    bats 70
    birds 81
        prehistoric 121
    reptiles (prehistoric)
        119
wing walking 340
Winter Palace (St.
        Petersburg,
        Russia) 385
wire ropes 210–211
Wisconsin
    governors 471
    high point 30
    solar power 205
wisteria 123
witchcraft, capital
        punishment for 487
women
    athletes *See specific
        sport*

land speed reached by
        305
    military aces 500
    presidents 465, 477
    prime ministers 477
    in space 231, 232, 237,
        238
    voting by 475
    wealthy 357–358
woodcocks 83, 89
wood cutting 136–137
wooden objects/structures
    bowls 546
    buildings 240
    hangars 339
    ships 289–290
woodpeckers 82, 91
wool
    blanket 546
    fabric price 550
    price for 374
    spinning 379
Woolworth Corp. 349
words 392–394
    length of (various
        languages) 393
    succinctness 392
working
    career 364–365
    week 364
World Bank 349
World Series (baseball)
        575, 576–577, *577*
World Trade Center (New
        York City)
        247–248, 432
World War I (1914–18)
    Jutland, Battle of 496
    mutiny by French forces
        499
    Somme, First Battle of
        the 494
    submarine kills 500
World War II (1939–45)
    See also Germany,
        Nazi
    Arnhem assault
        496–497
    bombings
        atomic 456, 500–501
        conventional 456,
        457
    Dunkirk evacuation 497
    human cost 494–495
    Leningrad, Siege of 497
    Leyte Gulf, Battle of
        496
    material cost 494
    Normandy invasion 496
    Stalingrad, Battle of
        494–495
    submarine kills 500
worm-charming 109
worms
    marine 61
    ribbon 112
    segmented 109–110
wreath 554

wreckers/wrecking (cars)
        309, 316
wrecks (ships) *See under*
        ships
wrestling 778–780
    bout length 556
    NCAA Division I
        778–779
    sumo 779–780, *779*
wristwatches *See* watches
writing, minuscule 531
Wyoming
    coal mine 214
    geysers 43
    governors 471
    high point 30
    population 460
    women's suffrage 475

Y

yachting 780–783
    circumnavigation *781*
    disaster 457
    ice and sand *See* ice and
        sand yachting
    regatta 782
yachts 290
yak *21*, 66
yakuza (Japanese
        gangsters) 482
Yellow Kid, The (comic
        strip) 408
Yellowstone National
        Park (Wyoming)
        43
yodeling 172
yolks, egg 378
Yo Picasso (Picasso
        painting) 386
yo-yos 530

Z

zeppelins *See* airships
ziggurats 281
zipper 554
zodiac 3
zoos 141–142
zucchini, 127, 128, *785,**
        786**

NOW YOU CAN

G GUINNESS
WORLD OF RECORDS
EXHIBITIONS

AT THE EMPIRE STATE BUILDING, NEW YORK

EXPERIENCE THE EXTRAORDINARY

Life-size models, videos, graphics and audio technology bring thousands of record-breaking facts from The Guinness Book of Records to life at these amazing exhibitions. See the world's tallest, smallest, heaviest, fattest, loudest, richest and rarest. Open daily throughout the year.

and at the Trocadero, Piccadilly Circus, London – Clifton Hill, Niagara Falls – Fisherman's Wharf, San Francisco – Hollywood Boulevard, Hollywood – Las Vegas Blvd, Las Vegas – Parkway, Gatlinburg, Tenn. – World Trade Center, Singapore.